TREASURE CAY, ABACO, BAHAMAS

"Fish The Marlin Coast!"

THE HOTTEST fishing spot in the Bahamas!

On May 20, 1996, history was made at Treasure Cay, when Rick Smith, on the 'Weekend Hooker', caught a 1030 pound blue marlin, the 2nd largest ever in the Bahamas and the first 'Grander' taken off the Abacos!

TREASURE CAY HOTEL RESORT & MARINA

Phone (USA): **800-327-1584** or **954-525-7711**
Phone (Bahamas): **242-365-8250** (Marina)
Fax: (USA): **954-525-1699**
E-Mail: **abaco@gate.net**
Internet: **http://treasurecay.com**

Treasure Cay Features:

- Well-protected 150 Slip Marina
- Magnificent Sandy 3½ Mile Beach
- 18-Hole Championship Golf Course
- 2 Bedroom, 2 Baths Beach Villas
- Boat Charters & Fishing Guides
- Marinaview Rooms & Suites
- Marina Bar & Restaurant
- Freshwater Pool
- Boat Rentals
- Diesel & Gas Fuel
- Dive Shop

**134 lb Wahoo
Sun Dancer**

**87 lb Dolphin
Redneck Princess**

DON'T
BE
SORRY.

Use America's Strongest

Big Marlin don't just break your line, they break your heart.
That's why more fishermen trust Trilene® Big Game® than any
other brand. It's America's strongest monofilament. Super tough
and shock resistant. Spool up with Trilene. You won't be sorry.

Berkley®

Catch more fish℠

Trilene
SUPER STRONG
BIG GAME
SHOCK RESISTANT · EXTRA TOUGH

Trilene
SUPER STRONG
BIG GAME
SHOCK RESISTANT
EXTRA TOUGH

©Copyright 1996, Berkley, Inc.

Tropic Star Lodge
Piñas Bay

Over 140 World Records Broken!

Black, Blue and Striped Marlin abound in numbers unheard of elsewhere. Pacific Sailfish are there year-round, and from April through July, multiple hook ups are the rule rather than the exception. Dolphin are also caught year long and average from 20 to 50 lbs. In-shore, there are Amberjack, Snapper, Grouper, Roosterfish, Pompano, Rainbow Runner, Mackerel, Jack - the list keeps on going.

TROPIC STAR LODGE

A paradise sliced from the side of a mountain and surrounded by a jungle rich with wildlife and tropical flora, the lodge is 150 miles south of Panama City. Guests fly into a remote village on the Jacque river via charter plane where the lodge staff meets them and transports them into what is truly "National Geographic Country".

TROPIC STAR LODGE

635 N. Rio Grande Ave. Orlando, FL 32805•1-800-682-3424 • Int'n: (407) 843-0125 • Fax: (407) 839-3637

1999
World Record Game Fishes

PUBLICATIONS STAFF
Director: Michael Leech
Editor and Advertising
  Manager: Ray Crawford
Editorial Assistant: Patricia Virdee
World Record Secretary: Doug Blodgett
Biologist and Research: Glenda Kelley
Contributing Writers: Tim Choate, Larry Dahlberg,
Bob Dunn, Peter Goadby, Jack Samson, Pat Ford

IGFA STAFF
President: Michael Leech
Assistant to the President: Jim Brown
Director of Special Events: Tara Dailey
Executive Secretary: Jeanne Renick
Director of Marketing
  & Public Relations: Cheryl Parker McDonald
Marketing/Operations: Richard T. O'Neill
Marketing/Advertising Coordinator: Pat Treat
Special Clubs Executive Administrator: Patricia Brown
Membership Secretaries: Patricia Droege,
Julie Schultz, Susan Guerdon
Director of Retail Operations: Joyce Yaffe
Accountant: Fran Dillon
Junior Angler Program Coordinator: Kathy Corser
Receptionist: Elizabeth Santiago
Secretary: Toby Hubell
Maintenance: Al Carme

MUSEUM STAFF
Executive Director: Scott A. Woodburn
Assistant to the Executive Director: Sudie L. Shipman
Director of Environmental Education: Rosemary Krussman
Youth Programs Coordinator: Heather Starck
Reservations/Group Sales: Mary Washington
Volunteer Coordinator: William Uscher
Librarian: Gail M. Morchower
Museum Store Manager: Kathleen Collins
Exhibits Director: Richard S. Medve
Exhibits Coordinator: Linda Irwin

Audio Visual Specialist: Dale Carls
Facility Rental Coordinator: Steven Pollock
Annual Pass Sales: Andrea Sylvester
Administrative Coordinator: Romy Tudela
Director of Operations: Gary Zabrycki
Operations Manager: Matthew Dickinson

THE COVER: This year's cover is a reproduction of an original oil painting by Artist Lynn Bogue Hunt

ISSN 0084-2214 ISBN 0-93521725-8   Price: $12.95

THE INTERNATIONAL GAME FISH ASSOCIATION

300 Gulf Stream Way, Dania Beach, Florida 33004 USA
Phone (954) 927-2628 Fax (954) 924-4299 E-Mail: IGFAHQ@aol.com

Find out what the world's best fishermen have known for over 40 years...

Nickelite SERIES

All rods are not created equal!

Handcrafted SERIES

By incorporating the finest fishing rod components available in the world today, as well as our exclusive Power★Butt (patented) and Power★Patch™ Star★Rods are the finest rods available at any price.

Star★Rods are all handcrafted in the U.S.A. and have broken over 60 IGFA world records.

Over 190 models from ultralight to unlimited.

So be sure and visit your local bait and tackle shop and get hooked on Star★Rods.

Here are some of our IGFA World Records:

ELIZABETH M. HOGAN'S WORLD RECORDS

Stripe Marlin, 114 lb., 10 oz. / 4# test - Blue Marlin, 211 lb., 10 oz. / 12# test
Jack Crevalle, 13 lb., 11 oz. / 2# test - Permit, 10 lb., 12 oz. / 2# test
Tarpon, 85 lb., 8 oz. / 4# test - Tarpon, 56 lb. / 2# test
Stripe Marlin, 136 lb., 10 oz. / 4# test - Stripe Marlin, 111 lb., 5 oz. / 2# test
Kingfish, 28 lb., 6 oz. / 2# test - Barracuda, 37 lb. / 8# test
Barracuda, 35 lb. / 2# test - Cobia, 36 lb., 2 oz. / 2# test
Big Eyed Tuna, 24 lb. / 8# test - • Black Marlin, 445 lb. / 16# test
• Yellowfin Tuna, 20 lb. / 4# test - • African Pompano, 28 lb. / 6# test
• Redfish, 34 lb. / 4# test - Red Drum, 36 lb., 12 oz. / 2# test
Red Drum, 35 lb. / 2# test - Red Drum, 43 lb., 8 oz. / 6# test
King Mackerel, 28 lb., 8 oz. / 2# test - African Pompano, 27 lb. / 6# test
Snook, 12 lb., 14 oz. / 2# test - Snook, 19 lb. / 2# test
Snook, 23 lb. / 6# test - Tarpon, 19 lb. / 2# test
Tarpon, 134 lb., 3 oz. / 4# test - Tarpon, 115 lb. / 6# test
Tarpon, 141 lb., 9 oz. / 8# test - Blue Fin Tuna, 350 lb. / 30# test

GEORGE E. HOGAN, JR.'S WORLD RECORDS

Bull Dolphin, 52 lb., 14 oz. / 4# test - Stripe Marlin, 132 lb. / 2# test
Blue Marlin, 141 lb., 1 oz. / 4# test - Blue Marlin, 202 lb., 13 oz. / 8# test
Tarpon, 54 lb., 12 oz. / 2# test - Jack Crevalle, 15 lb., 4 oz. / 2# test
Tarpon, 60 lb., 8 oz. / 2# test - Tarpon, 106 lb. / 2# test
Tarpon, 128 lb., 8 oz. / 4# test - Roosterfish, 11 lb. / 2# test
Mako, 81 lb., 9 oz. / 2# test - Roosterfish, 28 lb., 10 oz. / 2# test
Big Eyed Tuna, 22 lb. / 4# test - • Chinook Salmon, 40 lb., 9 oz. / 2# test
• Pacific Halibut, 72 lb., 3 oz. / 4# test - • Pacific Halibut, 77 lb., 3 oz. / 4# test
Cobia, 22 lb., 14 oz. / 2# tippet - Cobia, 37 lb., 3 oz. / 4# tippet
Cobia, 50 lb., 11 oz. / 4# test - Red Drum, 41 lb., 8 oz. / 2# test
Red Drum, 52 lb., 5 oz. / 4# test - Snook, 41 lb., 8 oz. / 6# test
Snook, 24 lb., 4 oz. / 2# test - Tarpon, 139 lb., 14 oz. / 6# test

CONNIE L. CORA

Tiger Shark, 360 lb. / 16# test - Hammerhead Shark, 750 lb. / 50# test

NEAL LAUE African Pompano, 43 lb. / 20# test

ROBERT GILBERT Jack Crevalle, 37 lb. / 16# test

ROY VENTURA ROIG • ★Pacific Jack Crevalle, 31 lb. / 50# test

• NEW WORLD RECORD   ★ ALL TACKLE RECORD

Send for a color catalog:
Star Fishing Tackle LLC, Dept. IGFA, P.O. Box 608
158 Little Nine Drive, Morehead City, NC 28557

With Star Rods new Nickelite® Series, each graphite fiber in the outer layers is impregnated with nickel and then wrapped around a high modulus graphite core. The result is a rod that is more sensitive, stronger and more impact resistant.

Never before did power and precision come in such a beautiful package. Each Nickelite® blank has a beautiful silver metallic appearance with accented windings. They are fitted with the best components available. Smooth power, crisp sensitivity and unequalled impact resistance are the benchmarks of Nickelite® Rods.

Dozens of actions and weights are made for everything from freshwater bass to coastal tarpon. Nickelite® rods have extremely sensitive tips and hook-setting backbone to spare.

When you're ready to call "Fish on!", the rod you want in the fighting chair is a Star Handcrafted rod. Each starts with a unique custom blank featuring a graphite core and E-glass armor outside. You get a responsive rod with the inner power of graphite inside and the toughness of E-glass outside.

From building the blank to the diamond wrap accent, Star Rods does it all by hand. Designed for all-around fishing, Handcrafted rods are available for bottom fishing, casting, trolling, spinning, standup and drifting tactics. Naturally, they feature top quality components. Some actions feature the patented Power★Butt, and virtually all feature Star Rods' exclusive Power★Patch.

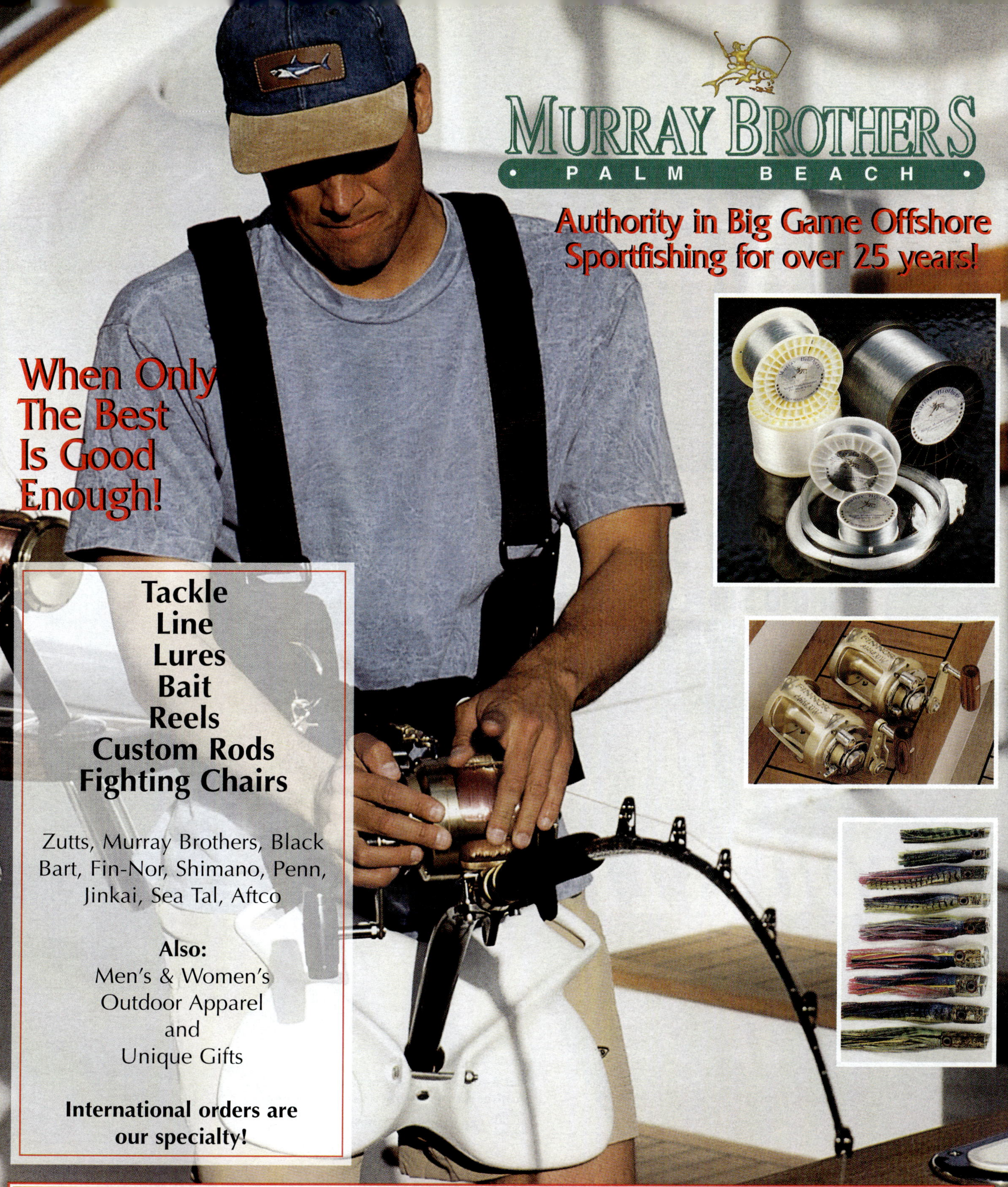
MURRAY BROTHERS
PALM BEACH

Authority in Big Game Offshore
Sportfishing for over 25 years!

When Only
The Best
Is Good
Enough!

Tackle
Line
Lures
Bait
Reels
Custom Rods
Fighting Chairs

Zutts, Murray Brothers, Black
Bart, Fin-Nor, Shimano, Penn,
Jinkai, Sea Tal, Aftco

Also:
Men's & Women's
Outdoor Apparel
and
Unique Gifts

International orders are
our specialty!

CALL FOR YOUR FREE CATALOGUE:
800-845-3474
Fax: 561-626-0131 • Call: 561-626-7840
North Palm Beach, FL
Internet: www.murraybros.com

INSIST ON CAPT. HARRY'S
NOT... EVERY NOW AND THEN
NOT... EVERY SO OFTEN
BUT... EVERY TIME!

Capt.
Harry's
FISHING SUPPLY™
MIAMI, FL

ORDER YOUR FREE CATALOG TODAY!!
1-800-327-4088
DEPT. T5310

Reel Repair Parts & Service
Authorized Warranty for
PENN REELS   SHIMANO   DAIWA

Photo Courtesy of Richard Gibson

VISIT OUR MIAMI STORE...LOCATED NEAR THE PORT OF MIAMI.
FREE PARKING, EASY ACCESS TO THE MIAMI INTERNATIONAL AIRPORT.
Dept. T5310-100 N.E. 11th Street • Miami, FL 33132 • Phone 305-374-4661 • Fax 305-374-3713
Internet – http://www.captharry.com   Email: sales@captharry.com
WORLDWIDE SERVICE

CONTENTS

FOREWORD — 10

PRESIDENT'S MESSAGE — 17

SECTION 1 — **International Game Fish Association** — 15
All about IGFA — its officers and representatives, philosophy and goals, library of fishes, and membership program for clubs and individuals.

SECTION 2 — **Articles** — 35
Contributing writers provide stories on, "Billfish Conservation Goes Full Circle", "The Most Dependable Knots I Know", "The Broadbill Swordfish: An Illustrated History", "Fly Rodders Make News, New Zealand a Hot Spot in 1998", "Mexico's Newest Bass Hotspot: Lake Huites", "Looking for Kanektok's Kings."

SECTION 3 — **Angling Rules** — 133
World Record, Contest and Club Requirements
(A) Equipment and angling regulations for fishing in fresh or salt water.
(B) Record categories, record catch regulations, instructions for preparing a record claim, and formulas for converting weights and measures.
(C) Requirements for entering the Annual Fishing Contest, 5, 10, 15 & 20 to 1 Clubs, Thousand Pound Club, the 10 Pound Bass Club, 25 Pound Snook Club, and Grand Slam Clubs.
(D) Application forms for entering a world record, contest, or special club claim and for entering the 10 Pound Bass Club.

SECTION 4 — **World Records** — 149
Line class, fly rod, all-tackle, and junior angler records for freshwater and saltwater.

SECTION 5 — **Guide To Fishes** — 245
Illustrations, charts and text to aid the angler in identifying major game fish species, including: a guide to over 150 freshwater and saltwater fishes.

SECTION 6 — **Special Club Members, Fishing Contest, and Discount Program** — 297

APPENDICES — 330
Worldwide Record-keeping Organizations, U.S.A. State Record-keeping Agencies, and Worldwide Tag-and-Release Programs.

INDEX TO ADVERTISERS — 352

Foreword

Are you ready for some fishing? Then, dive right into this 1999 edition of *World Record Game Fishes* for a compendium of information on your favorite sport. Variety is the theme ranging from articles by our contributing writers to the thousands of record holders, members of the prestigious special clubs, contest winners, and encyclopedic material in the species and index sections.

There's something for every angler--men, women and children-- including the biggest, best and most incredible catches of the year.

Consider that there are 96 pages of world records, and another 20 pages with the names of persons catching thousand-pounders, or chalking up grand slams, or qualifying for the 5-1, 10-1, 15-1, 20-1, 10-pound bass and 25-pound snook clubs. Just turn the pages and you'll see "who's who" in the fishing world. Maybe your name's in there.

The record section starts on page 149 and the special clubs on page 297. Information on IGFA's philosophy and background, trustees, international committee, and membership opportunities are in Section 1, page 15.

Entertaining and informative articles by well known writers are in Section 2. Long-time recreational fishing expert Tim Choate leads off with the provocative analysis of circle hooks and their advantages in "Conservation Goes Full Circle" on page 39.

If you've ever wondered which fishing knot is best for you, the answer probably can be found in the article by TV's traveling sportsman Larry Dahlberg in "The Most Dependable Knots I Know" on page 51.

The classic "The Broadbill Swordfish: An Illustrated History" by Bob Dunn and Peter Goadby explores the myths and reality of this wondrous fighting creature starting on page 61. Another TV personality Gary Laden talks about "Mexico's Newest Bass Hotspot: Lake Huites" on page 95, and Pat Ford, a globe-circling fisherman/lawyer has found the proverbial end of the world in "Looking for Kanektok's Kings" on page 101.

And, naturally, anglers will want to read about the best of 1998 compiled by IGFA President Mike Leech in "Flyrodders Make News, New Zealand a Hotspot".

The International Angling Rules, World Record Requirements, and Special Club Requirements are contained in Section 3, page 135. The updated list of world record holders for freshwater and saltwater catches in all-tackle, line class, and fly rod categories, and for juniors, is in Section 4, page 153. The Guide to Fishes on page 245 gives accurate biological information, plus how to identify your catch, and more.

Section 6, page 297, identifies members of the special clubs. Also in this section is the listing of IGFA's Discount Program participants. The advertising index is on page 352. Please consider these advertisers when shopping for your fishing needs.

Good fishing!

THE EDITOR

"I test rode everything that's out there. But, when I rode in the Cabo, I knew that was it."

Michael Friday, Owner Cabo 35 Express "Talisman"

"The Cabo hasn't stopped surprising us with its superior handling in all kinds of conditions. It's one of the best boats I've ever run." **Captain-Jimmy Sharpe Jr.**

He went looking for the perfect boat.

When retired surgeon Dr. Michael Friday decided to do serious tournament charters and world record fishing, he went looking for the perfect boat.

"I wanted a boat that was economical, had good value, and was well-constructed, a boat that rode well and had a good range. I test rode Blackfin, Tiara, Bertram, Hatteras—everything that's out there. But when I rode in the Cabo 35 Express, I knew that was it. The maneuverability of the Cabo is outstanding. She's quick and responsive, spins on a dime, and backs down extremely well, without cavitation."

"We either won overall grand champion, or placed 1st in various categories 9 out of 11 times"
Mike Friday-owner

"Next, I had to find the perfect crew. Jimmy Sharpe Jr. and Matt McLean had the expertise and enthusiasm that I was looking for. In the eleven tournaments that we've fished in the last year and a half, we either won overall grand champion or placed first in various categories nine times in eleven tournaments."

"We make and almost exclusively use Talisman offshore lures. We also named our Cabo *Talisman*, because of her magical ability to raise fish. The fish seem to like our lures, and they love my Cabo!"

"The Cabo 35 is an excellent, excellent boat."

"As the captain of Talisman, I am responsible for getting Mike to the fish. The handling and speed of the Cabo make that job a lot easier. We caught a 175-pound blue marlin, the other day, in about 15 minutes, on 30# test , in six-foot seas and 25 knot winds. The boat just sat right in the sea, perfectly. And, it's very responsive, very maneuverable, but it rides like a 40-footer. It's also easy to maintain. The excellent finish of the fiberglass and non-skid surfaces are

We can run 24 miles offshore, troll eight hours pulling lures, and run home on about 50 gallons. The Cabo 35 is one of the best boats I've ever run."
Captain-Jimmy Sharpe Jr.

easy to clean and the engine room design gives me total access all the way around both engines. It's the easiest boat to maintain that I have ever seen, and its economical to run. We can run 24 miles offshore, troll eight hours pulling lures, and run home on about 50 gallons. The Cabo 35 is one of the best boats I've ever run."

"We fish it hard and aggressive, and we take advantage of our shots."

"People just can't believe what this boat can do chasing a fish. We run and gun on plane and throw a bait on tailing fish. Then, it's all the boat, backing right down on that sailfish coming down seas. Run around, go backwards, turn circles, next thing you know, we

have a nice six or seven-foot fish on light spinning rods. In tournament fishing, you need to get as many points as you can in a hurry. The more quick releases, the better. That's the name of the game. The Cabo does everything we're looking for. It is far superior to everything else in its class."

The Cabo 35 is another reason that Cabo Sportfishers have become the #1 choice of dedicated anglers world wide. But don't take our word for it. You must see the Cabo 35 Express for yourself. For a complete literature package and the name of the Cabo dealer nearest you, call, write or fax:

"People just can't believe what this boat can do chasing a fish."
Matt McLean-Mate

CABO® Yachts, Inc.

9780 Rancho Road Adelanto CA 92301 FAX (760) 246-8970
Phone (760) 246-8917
www.caboyachts.com

CAT® Diesel Power

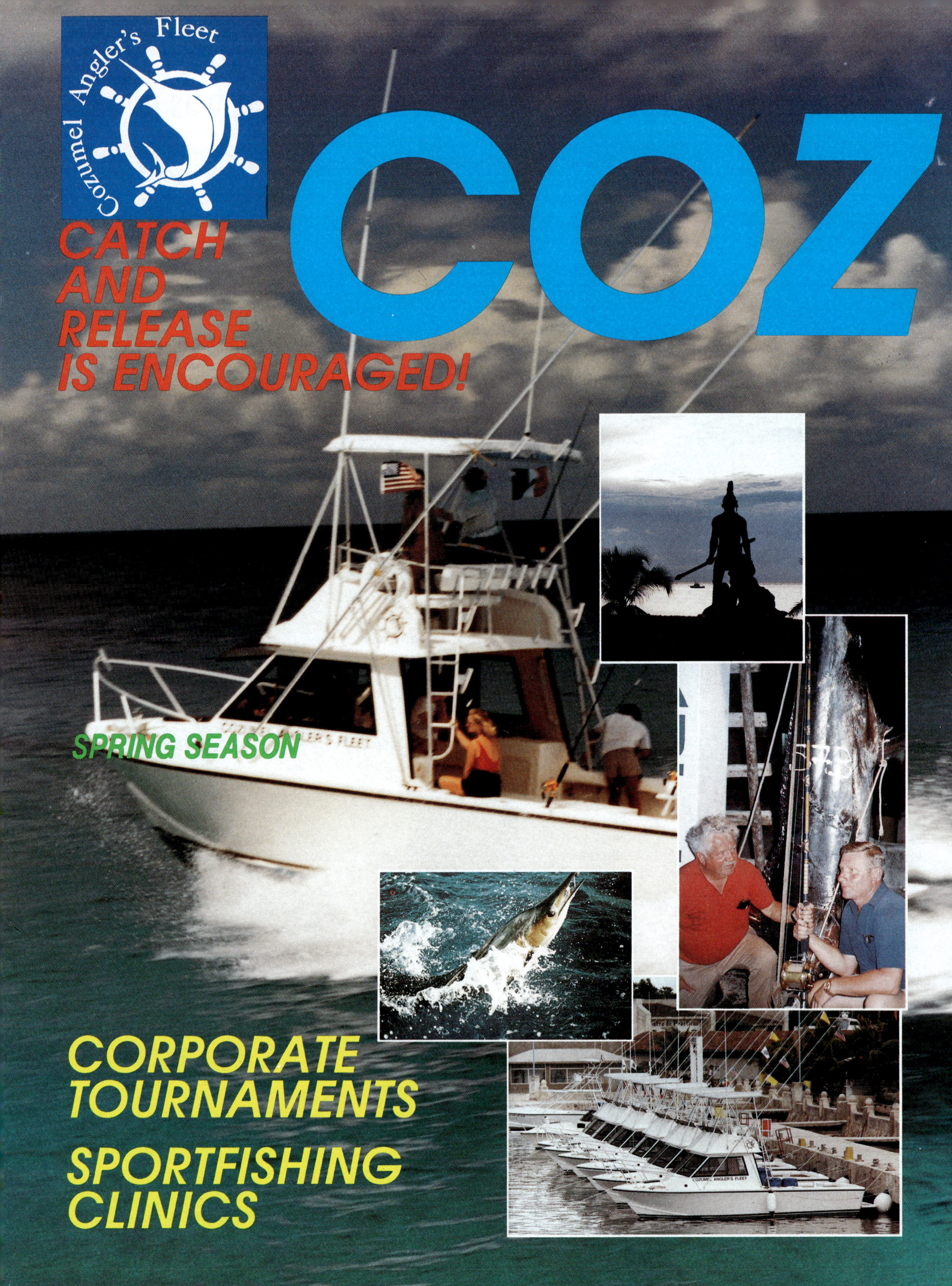

Cozumel Angler's Fleet
CATCH AND RELEASE IS ENCOURAGED!
COZ
SPRING SEASON
CORPORATE TOURNAMENTS
SPORTFISHING CLINICS

NEW "IT WON'T LET GO!"
Malin — the most complete line of wire and cable products...Since 1884.

"BOA is the first fishing product that I would label 'revolutionary'. It is the world's first metal shock leader. If you are targeting a species in pursuit of a NEW World Record, consider BOA as your first choice...It won't let go."

Dave Workman
President, C&H Lures

Malin

New BOA No-Kink is available in 10 lb. through 60 lb. test, 30 foot coils.

1. BOA No-Kink is a single strand metal shock leader. It is manufactured from high-tech stainless alloy wire.

2. BOA No-Kink, can be tied. Recommended knots are the standard Clinch or Perfection Loop. Connect to main line using Albright Knot. Tighten knot using pliers, pull until wire stretches.

3. The natural color and non-glare finish, make BOA No-Kink virtually invisible in most fishing applications.

4. BOA No-Kink is a corrosion proof metal shock leader with high flexibility and maximum abrasion resistance.

BOA
NO-KINK
Malin
SINGLE STRAND WIRE
TIE WITH KNOTS
STRETCHABLE
NO TWISTING
SEE BACK FOR INSTRUCTIONS
WORLD'S FIRST METAL SHOCK LEADER

Malin
Malin Company, Inc.
5400 Smith Road
Cleveland, Ohio 44142
© 1999 Malin Company, Inc.

Phone – 216-267-9080 Fax – 216-267-9077
Toll Free – 1-800-967-9697
email – malinco@sprynet.com
web – www.malinco.com

SECTION 1
INTERNATIONAL GAME FISH ASSOCIATION

OFFICERS AND TRUSTEES   16

PRESIDENT'S MESSAGE   17

PHILOSOPHY AND OBJECTIVES   18

E.K. HARRY LIBRARY OF FISHES   19

INTERNATIONAL COMMITTEE   23

MEMBERSHIP INFORMATION   30

MEMBERSHIP APPLICATION   31

Trustees

Dedicated to the World's Anglers

The IGFA Fishing Hall of Fame and Museum is open and has been visited by many thousands of visitors.

It not only gives IGFA a permanent home, but gives us a terrific base from which to pursue our mission of conservation, educating the public to the importance of ethical fishing, bringing new generations of anglers into the sport, and representing recreational anglers whenever the future of our sport is being discussed.

We have inducted the original 29 honorees into the World Fishing Hall of Fame and will be holding annual ceremonies to induct deserving leaders in the sport of fishing. Anyone can nominate prospective honorees, either living or deceased, and we welcome suggestions from our members.

Now that the hoopla of our grand opening is over, we have gotten down to the business of continuing our existing programs for the benefit of the world's recreational anglers. We have plans to expand some of these programs by adding new species for line and tippet class recognition, as well as expanding our popular junior angler program.

In the coming months we will be hosting thousands of students at the IGFA World Fishing Center with various education programs. Our living wetlands exhibit will help us stress the importance of preserving our environment.

Yes, the IGFA World Fishing Center truly is dedicated to the world's anglers. The facility has hosted several important gatherings in the spacious Events Hall and in the other public areas. A classroom and exhibit areas are available for special events as well. Our library with its video viewing rooms, reading room, displays, and vast collection of books and magazines is an international treasure. Much of the data that has been gathered here does not exist elsewhere.

The brand new state freshwater line class record program is already creating a lot of interest and we will be expanding this program. We are also considering going beyond the United States to other areas, where it may be appropriate for IGFA to create new record programs. We welcome your suggestions.

The Rolex/IGFA Invitational Tournament of Champions (ITOC) has exceeded our expectations in its initial year. Currently we have 51 tournaments as qualifying events for the championship tournament in Kona, Hawaii in 2000. These tournaments represent 18 countries, 9 states, and over 12,000 tournament anglers. Future plans call for an inshore/light tackle invitation tournament with qualifying events to take place in 2000, leading to the first championship event in 2001. We are seeking indications of interest from tournament directors.

IGFA is on a roll. We have many more plans for the future that will benefit both the recreational fishing industry and anglers worldwide. We will also be working hard to protect and restore our beleaguered fishery resources.

We can't do any of this without your continued help and support, so let's continue to work together to preserve and enhance the sport we all love.

MICHAEL LEECH
President

Philosophy and Objectives

IGFA's objectives are founded on the beliefs that game fish species, related food fish, and their habitat are economic, social, recreational, and aesthetic assets which must be maintained, wisely used, and perpetuated; and that the sport of game fish angling is an important recreational, economic, and social activity which the public must be educated to pursue in a manner consistent with sound sporting and conservation practices.

BACKGROUND

When founded in 1939, IGFA's primary responsibilities were to establish ethical international angling regulations and to serve as a central processing center for world record catch data.

In 1972, IGFA expanded its goals in view of the urgent need for a recognized agency to bring anglers into closer organization and better awareness of problems facing the species and the sport.

In March 1973, IGFA established various membership categories so that individuals and fishing clubs could help to support the expanded goals of the organization. Until that time, IGFA was privately funded. If the association is to grow and continue as an effective representative for anglers throughout the world, your support is needed.

MAJOR OBJECTIVES

1. To encourage and further the study of game fish angling, the related species, and the habitat requirements of such species.

2. To work at all levels of government and industry for the preservation of the species and the protection of their natural habitats.

3. To compile and distribute game fish information to all IGFA members, the general public, and scientific and legislative government bodies for the furtherance of education in the wise use and conservation of the species.

4. To ensure that the recreational angler is adequately represented at all meetings where the future of the game fish population and the angling sport is being determined.

5. To assist and participate in domestic and international game fish seminars and symposiums where the expertise, data and purposes of this organization may be helpful in assisting other organizations with similar objectives.

6. To develop and support game fish tagging programs and other scientific data collection efforts, and to aid scientific and educational institutions which provide vital instruction and research in ichthyology, the fishery sciences, and related studies.

7. To maintain and promote fair, uniform and ethical international angling regulations, and to compile and maintain world record data for game fish caught according to these regulations.

8. To develop and maintain an international museum and reference library on game fish, the sport of angling, and related subjects.

9. To accumulate and maintain a worldwide history of game fishing for the use and benefit of the public.

The International Library of Fishes and Museum was founded in 1973 by the International Game Fish Association, and is recognized as the most comprehensive reference library in the world on game fish, angling and related subjects. In 1992, IGFA Trustees voted to rename the library in honor of the late president, Elwood K. Harry.

The library and museum were established in response to the need for a permanent repository for angling literature, history, films, art, and photographs. Individuals who have spent a lifetime gathering such materials are assured that their collections will be preserved by an international fishing organization that will safeguard them for future generations of anglers.

Today, the E.K. Harry Library of Fishes, located in the IGFA World Fishing Center contains more data on recreational angling, fishing and related subjects than any other place in the world. This data and information has been collected during the past 60 years and is augmented on a daily basis from worldwide sources. Library materials are used for reference and research, and do not leave the premises.

Library Contents & Division

BOOKS

The library already boasts a collection of more than 12,000 books ranging from first editions of angling classics, donated by friends and trustees, to the latest books in print, received from publishers on a complimentary basis or purchased through donations. Subjects range from identity of species found in various areas of the world, to the how-to and where-to of angling, to biographies of famous anglers.   Books on related subjects, such as oceanography, boating, diving and underwater photography are also a part of the collection. IGFA initiates or assists in the publication of over 2,000 fishing articles each year in the United States publications alone. To continue providing this broadly based data and to improve efficiency, IGFA subjects in detail all significant publications in the library.   This information is stored in IGFA's computer system and updated on a daily basis.

PERIODICALS

Outdoor and fishing magazines from many countries in native languages are an important part of IGFA's library. Our goal is to receive every magazine related to fishing that is published in the world. Magazine subscriptions are usually obtained through reciprocal exchange agreements with publishers and organizations.

SCIENTIFIC PAPERS

Game fish research is well-documented in the library. IGFA receives important research publications from scientific institutions and government fishery agencies throughout the world in exchange for our assistance in providing sportfishing information and sport fishery data.

ANGLING CLUB DIVISION

IGFA Member Clubs participate in the growth of the library by sending us their yearbooks, releases, sportfishing data and other information on fishing in their areas. All of the material is indexed and maintained for data reference and historical purposes.

HISTORY OF ANGLING SECTION

One of the most important goals for the E.K. Harry Library of Fishes is the development of its section on the history of angling. Though this section is still in the embryo stage, many materials have been collected. IGFA has contributed all of its books, papers, and data accumulated since the inception of the organization in 1939. In addition, various "pioneer" anglers have donated their collections of books, documents, literature and news clippings. Many of IGFA's international representatives have compiled the early histories of angling in their areas of the world and will continue to add to these accounts as time progresses. History is being made every day in the angling world, and IGFA intends to document, compile and preserve this history.

ART, PHOTOGRAPHY, FILMS

Many valuable works of art and classic fishing films have been donated to this section of the library. Photographs range from historic record catches to underwater and action photos of fish and fishing retained for their excellence. All IGFA world records and other photographs dating back to the turn of the century are kept in the archives. IGFA has collection of photographs of famous anglers from the early pioneers to some of the present day greats.   The modern video library section has more than 1500 action-packed professionally produced films. Private collections of fishing photographs and fishing films or videos are solicited.

DONATIONS

The E.K. Harry Library of Fishes steadily growing through donations of materials, through publications exchange agreements, and through financial contributions from the angling community. Those who make donations can be assured that they will be given proper credit for their contribution. All gifts to the library are tax-deductible in the United States.

IGFA is the only organization of its kind in the world: it is an angler-oriented, and angler-financed nonprofit organization functioning entirely on behalf of the recreational fishing community. It has no other allegiance and depends on the anglers of the world for its support.

Museum

The one-of-a-kind, $32-million IGFA Fishing Hall of Fame and Museum provides the world's most comprehensive assemblage of sportfishing information, exhibits, educational classes, fishing demonstrations, interactive displays and virtual reality fishing.

Walk into the 60,000-square-foot museum's main entrance and you're seemingly immersed in an underwater world filled with fish. The ceiling was designed to look like a boat's bottom. There are 170 species of game fish that earned world record status from giant bluefin tuna to brown trout suspended overhead with informational plates on date of catch, angler, place, etc., displayed on the floor under each fish. The largest mount is Alfred Dean's 2,664 lb great white shark caught in Australia in 1959. It is the largest catch in the IGFA books.

Also part of the museum are seven educational and entertainment galleries, the hall of fame featuring great anglers of the past, antique tackle, descriptions of fishing hot spots throughout the world, a marina with fishing boats on display, a three-acre wetlands exhibit, and more.

The history of IGFA is traced from founder Michael Lerner through early officers Van Campen Heilner and Ernest Hemingway to the modern era Presidents Bill Carpenter, Elwood Harry, and Michael Leech, with special acknowledgement to the World Fishing Center's building project co-chairmen George Matthews and Don Tyson. Historic photos, movies, videos and sound tracks tell the story of IGFA.

OUR REPUTATION IS ON THE LINE.

World class fishermen around the globe are loyal to JINKAI® line for its unbeatable quality and superior performance. JINKAI offers consistent powerful strength and tough abrasion resistance yet remains soft and sensitive for the ultimate fishing experience. And JINKAI's micro-fine diameters allow greater reel-fill capacity, giving you the winning edge just when you need it!

Ask your favorite tackle dealer to supply you with the best! JINKAI is your assurance of quality.

International Committee

IGFA representatives act as a liaison between sportfishermen in their areas and IGFA headquarters. Chosen for their integrity, fishing knowledge, and concern for sportsmanship and conservation, they keep IGFA informed of local sportfishing activities, and help to oversee world record catch claims in their areas. All International Committee members contribute their services without remuneration of any kind.

ALGERIA
Michel de Caffarelli, Cheraga
American Samoa *(see U.S. TERRITORIES)*
ANGOLA
Dr. Iain J. Nicolson, Luanda
ANTIGUA & BARBUDA
Stephen R. Mendes, St. Johns, Antigua
ARGENTINA
Marcos J. Czerwinski, Tierra del Fuego
ARUBA
Michael F. Croes, Oranjestad
AUSTRALIA
James H. Allen, Melbourne, Victoria
Jason Caughlan, Cronulla, New South Wales
Rolf Czabayski, Burnside, South Australia
Glen Edwards, Bomaderry, New South Wales
Patrick V. Gay, Brisbane, Queensland
Peter Goadby, Sydney, New South Wales
Phillip Hall, Brinkin, Northern Territory
Tom Jenkins, Kingston, Tasmania
Robert H. Lowe, Sutherland, New South Wales
John O'Brien, Sydney, New South Wales
Kenneth Neil Patrick, Fremantle, Western Australia
Colin D. Roberts, Broome, Western Australia
Tom M. Roche, Point Piper, New South Wales
William Sawynok, North Rockhampton, Queensland
AUSTRIA
Richard F. Flasch, Vienna
Kurt Hölzl, Vienna
Azores *(see PORTUGAL)*
BAHAMAS
Walter B. Kitchen, Freeport, Grand Bahama Island
D. Neil McKinney, Nassau, New Providence Island
Raul V. Miranda, Bimini
BARBADOS
John David Marshall, Christ Church
BELGIUM
Dr. Michel Margoulies, Beaufays
Gerald Moonens, Dorinne
BELIZE
John Crump, Belize City
Bermuda *(see UNITED KINGDOM)*
BRAZIL
Hélio Barroso, Rio de Janeiro
Angelo Calmon de Sá, Salvador, Bahia
Dr. Gilberto Fernandes, Manaus, Amazonas
Otacilio José Coser-Filho, Vitória
Fernando A. Martins S., Rio de Janeiro
Ricardo Tosello, São Paulo
British West Indies *(see UNITED KINGDOM)*
CAMEROON
J. Jacques Arnopoulos
CANADA
Ken Fraser, Bridgetown, Nova Scotia
Russell M. Heslep, Yellowknife, NW Territories
A.E. Hillyard, Paradise, C.B., Newfoundland
Yves Laroche, Province of Quebec
Harry W. Robertson III, Labrador, Newfoundland
Allan J. Roschuk, Flin Flon, Manitoba
Canary Islands *(see SPAIN)*
CAPE VERDE ISLANDS
Dr. Jorge Luis da Fonseca, São Vicente
Cayman Islands *(see UNITED KINGDOM)*
COLOMBIA
Daniel J. Fernandez, Barranquilla
COSTA RICA
Carlos M. Barrantes R., San José
Alessandro Poma-Murialdo, San José
CROATIA
Georg Blänich
CUBA
José Miguel Díaz Escrich, Havana
Giuseppe Omegna, Havana
CYPRUS
Sophoclis Koutalis, Limassol
DENMARK
Hans Christian Clausen, Greve
DJIBOUTI, REPUBLIC OF
Alain Martinet, Djibouti
DOMINICAN REPUBLIC
Dr. Eduardo Read, Santo Domingo
Ernesto Vitienes C., Santo Domingo
ECUADOR
Victor E. Estrada, Guayaquil
Luis A. Flores, Guayaquil
EGYPT
Mohamed Safyadin "Safi" El- Sehrawy
EL SALVADOR
J. T. Bottoms
England *(see UNITED KINGDOM, Great Britain)*
FIJI ISLANDS
Albert A. W. Threadingham, Suva
FRANCE
Philippe Dolivet, La Feuillée
Constant Guigo, Antibes
Guy Real del Sarte, Paris
Sacha Tolstoi, Paris
French Guiana
Richard Dupont
French Polynesia
Alban Ellacott, Papeete, Tahiti
French West Indies
Jean-François Fedronic, Martinique
Jean Louis Le Dentu, St. Martin
GABON REPUBLIC
Guy Colombani, Libreville

NEW! PENN PRION.™
BUILT LIKE A PRECISION TIMEPIECE, YET RUGGED AS THEY COME.

Precision movement. Meticulous attention to detail. Gleaming precious metals. We're referring, of course, to Penn's new Prion™ series spinning reels. Reels with a look and feel so refined, they can only be described as… luxurious.

Diamond-hard Titanium Nitride coats the spool flange, bail assembly, line roller, and rear housing cover for superior performance, durability and good looks. Precision machined gears and five stainless steel ball bearings for ultra smooth retrieves. And when the big one strikes, there's infinite anti-reverse for rock-solid hookups.

Prion's exclusive Rotary Flat Oscillation winds line evenly on the spool, for longer, effortless casts, even with the lightest lures.

Four models. For ultralight freshwater to light-tackle saltwater fishing. Match a Prion™ with a quality Penn Sabre® or Power Graph™ rod for the ultimate spinning system. Look for the new Prion™ at your Penn tackle retailer. Or send $2 ($5 outside N. America) for a full-color catalog.

New! PR900

New! PR1200

New! PR1800

New! PR2400

Penn Performance… A Matter Of Record.

Visit our web site: www.pennreels.com

René Galissard, Libreville
GAMBIA, REPUBLIC OF THE
Graham Mavin, Banjul
GERMANY
Robert Rein, Munich
Michael Werner, Hamburg
GHANA
Johan Zietsman, Accra
Gibraltar *(see UNITED KINGDOM)*
Great Britain *(see UNITED KINGDOM)*
GUATEMALA
Julio Roberto Mansylla H., Guatemala City
Holland *(see NETHERLANDS)*
HONG KONG
Roy B. K. Laverty, Kowloon
Capt. Tim Richards, Chung Hom Kok
INDIA
Mohammed Abdul Ghani, Bombay
INDONESIA
Yahuda Tirtadihardja, Jakarta
IRELAND
Kevin Linnane, Dublin
ITALY
Alberto Banchetti, Rome
Fabrizio Bonanni, Florence
Luca Bonfanti, Milan
Massimo Ferri, Cattolica
Giacomo Di Gregorio, Bisceglie (Bari)
Paolo Sala, Sardinia & San Remo
IVORY COAST (CÔTE D'IVOIRE)
Franck Favarel, San Pedro
Nicolas Vivien, Abidjan
JAPAN
Yasumoto Innami, Tokyo
Hironao Ishii, Tokyo
Yoshihisa Murakami, Saitama
Eizo Maruhashi, Tokyo
Toshihiko Nagai, Osaka
Junzo Okada, Tokyo
Shizuo Saito, Naha, Okinawa
Tsutomu Wakabayashi, Tokyo
Kohei Yamamoto, Osaka
KENYA
Alec W. Dyer-Melville, Nairobi
Richard Moller, Malindi
KIRIBATI, REPUBLIC OF
Kim J. Andersen, Christmas Island
Peregrine Langston, Christmas Island
LIBERIA
Walter Blaser, Monrovia
LITHUANIA
Ricărdas Adamonis, Jonava, Lietuva
MADAGASCAR
Henri Duclos, Nosy Be
MALAYSIA
Aziz Daud, Kuala Lumpur
Mariana Islands *(see U.S. TERRITORIES)*
MAURITANIA
Christian Benazeth, Nouadhibou
MAURITIUS
Dr. J. Maurice de Speville, La Preneuse, Black River
MEXICO

Moray Applegate C., Puerto Vallarta
Luis Fernando Adachi K., Manzanillo
Luis Bulnes M., Los Cabos, Baja California Sur
Enrique Caraza G., Monterrey, Nuevo Leon
Geronimo Cevallos de Cima, Mazatlán, Sinaloa
Mario Alberto Cruz-Ayala, Tampico
Joaquin de Iturbide, Cozumel
Armando Ferrat T., Cancún
Curtis Fitzgerald, Acapulco
Gary C. Graham, Baja California
Alberto Madaria H., Tampico
Monty Padilla, Mexico City
Minerva Saenz-Smith, Cabo San Lucas
Felipe Jesus Valdez, East Cape, Baja California Sur
MONACO
Guy de Levis Mirepoix, Monte Carlo
MOROCCO
Fouad Sahiaoui, Casablanca
Dr. Jean-Pierre Cochain, Casablanca
Natal *(see SOUTH AFRICA)*
NETHERLANDS
Holland
Jan Eggers, Bovenkarspel
Jaap Tuit, Den Haag
Hans van Loenen, Loosdrecht
Netherlands Antilles
Dirk van Vliet, Curacao
NEW CALEDONIA
Didier De Stoppeleire, Nouméa Cédex
NEW ZEALAND
Grant Bradford, Greenlane, Auckland, North Island
Clive Chapman, Christchurch, South Island
John R. Chibnall, Paihia, North Island
Robert C. Dinsdale, Whangarei, North Island
John Hough, Gisborne, North Island
Norman C. Hudspith, Whangarei, North Island
A. N. "Tony" Hill, Whakatane, North Island
Pete Saunders, New Plymouth, North Island
NIGERIA
Ailsa P. Schwarzkopf, Apapa
NORWAY
Olaf Hjelmeland, Tiller
OMAN
Isma'il Abdullah
PACIFIC ISLANDS
Rick Gaffney, central Pacific Islands (at large)
PAKISTAN
Capt. Imran Qureshi, Karachi
PANAMA
Frank de la Guardia, Panama
Robert L. Novey, Jr., Balboa, Ancón
Marcos D. Ostrander-Mulford, Balboa, Ancón
PAPUA NEW GUINEA
John Lau, Boroko
Robert O'Dea, Boroko
PARAGUAY
Jorge E. Xifra, Asunción
PERU
Juan F. Helguero, Lima
PHILIPPINES
Victor V. Villavicencio, Metro Manila
Polynesia, French *(see FRANCE)*

PORTUGAL
Azores
    Joseph Gerrit Franck, Faial Island
Puerto Rico *(see U.S. TERRITORIES)*
Samoa *(see U.S. TERRITORIES)*
SÃO TOMÉ & PRINCIPE
    C. R. G. Hellinger
SCOTLAND
    Stan Massey, Glasgow
SENEGAL
    Cyril Calendini, Dakar
SEYCHELLES
    Maurice Loustau-Lalanne, Mahe
SIERRA LEONE
    Patrick Bermanne, Sherbro Island
SINGAPORE REPUBLIC
    Grant W. Pereira, Singapore
SOUTH AFRICA, REPUBLIC OF
    Eugene C. Kruger, Pretoria
    David Susman, Cape Town
Natal
    M. M. Brokensha, Howick, KwaZulu-Natal
    Erwin Bursik, Durban
Eastern Cape Province
    Peter Matthews, Port Elizabeth
    Geoffrey A. O. Wanvig, Port Elizabeth
    Graham V. Winch, Gonubie
Western Cape Province
    Nic de Kock, Hout Bay
SPAIN
    Esteban Graupera Monar, Balearic Islands
    Dr. Alberto Iriarte, Costa del Sol
Canary Islands
    Luis Pereda Otero, Las Palmas
    Albert R. Pond, Tenerife
    Federico Ravarino, Graciosa Island
SRI LANKA
    Mervyn Anderiesz, Colombo
ST. LUCIA
    Bernard Johnson, Castries
SWEDEN
    Jan Olsson, Göteborg
SWITZERLAND
    Hans-Jörg Dietiker, Wangen-Zürich
    Dr. Hans H. Pfenninger, Herrliberg
    Marc Richard, Opfikon-Zürich
TAIWAN
    William Y. P. Huang, Taipei
TANZANIA
    Frank J. W. Jansen, Dar es Salaam
    Carlo Vernocchi, Zanzibar
TONGA, KINGDOM OF
    Heinz Koester, Neiafu, Vava'u
TRINIDAD
    Malcolm A. Boyack, Diego Martin
TURKEY
    Ali G. Pasiner, Istanbul
Turks & Caicos *(see UNITED KINGDOM)*
UGANDA
    Arthur de Mello, Kampala
UNITED ARAB EMIRATES
    Barry Panzer, Dubai

UNITED KINGDOM
Bermuda
    John A. Barnes, Hamilton
    Thomas W. Smith, Hamilton
British West Indies
    Capt. Roddy S. Hays, Anguilla, Leeward Is.
Cayman Islands
    J. William Rewalt, Grand Cayman
Gibraltar
    Ernest Borrell
Great Britain
    Edward Entwistle, Southampton, Hampshire, England
    John F. Reece, Hastings, Sussex, England
    Ted Tuckerman, Torquay, Devon, England
Turks & Caicos Islands
    Ralph G. Wilcke, Providenciales
UNITED STATES
Alabama
    Stephen C. Boykin, Dog River
Alaska
    Christopher M. Batin, Fairbanks
    Mike Bethers, Auke Bay
    Gregory S. McIntosh, Halibut Cove
    Robert "Radar" Orth, Bethel
    Eric Stirrup, Kodiak Island
    Michael Tuhy, Kenai Peninsula
Arizona
    Terry Gunn, Marble Canyon
    Matt Vincent, Mesa
Arkansas
    A. H. "Pug" Jones, Hot Springs
    Ron Shuffield, Bismarck
California
    Donald L. Blackman, San Diego
    John S. Griffith, Jr., Newport Beach
    Bill Hoey, San Rafael
    John M. Jackson, Sacramento
    T. Neal McNamara, Napa
    Harold E. Neibling, Long Beach
    Darrell Ticehurst, San Mateo
Connecticut
    Edward C. Migdalski, New Haven
Florida
    Dr. Crawford W. Adams, Duck Key
    Art Barton, Key West
    Dr. Grant L. Beardsley, Placida
    Marsha Bierman, Plantation
    John Brownlee, Upper Keys
    William M. Camp, Tequesta
    Carl E. Cole, Tallahassee
    Joy H. Dunlap, Destin
    Capt. Lance Glaser, Royal Palm Beach
    Capt. Roger Greene, Key West
    Jim Hardie, Miami
    George Hommell, Jr., Florida Keys
    Walter P. Jennings, Venice
    Capt. Doug Kelly, Orlando
    Michael C. Kelley, Palm Harbor
    Paul F. Leader, Miami
    Capt. Dave Lear, northern Florida
    W.T.S. Montgomery, Jacksonville
    Douglas Olander, Winter Park

Frank Smith, Lighthouse Point
Georgia
    Robert L. Lynn, Atlanta
Hawaiian Islands
    Albert C. Bento, Jr., Honolulu, Oahu
    Ralph R. Conner, Kailua-Kona, Hawaii
    Winfred Ho, Sr., Honolulu, Oahu
    A. J. Huddleston, Maui County at large
    David G. Nottage, Holualoa-Kona, Hawaii
    Philip D. Parker, Kailua-Kona, Hawaii
    Jim Rizzuto, Kawaihae, Hawaii
    Michael R. Sakamoto, Hilo, Hawaii
    David T. Welker; Maalaea, Kahului, Kaliko, Maui
Idaho
    Charles E. Powell, Moscow
Illinois
    Jim C. Chapralis, Chicago
Indiana
    David A. Bishop, Schererville
    Larry Carr, Elkhart
Kansas
    Steve Cook, Lee's Summit, MO
Louisiana
    Richard K. Husser, Metairie
Maine
    Capt. Peter B. Ripley
Maryland
    John W. S. Foster III, Annapolis
Massachusetts
    Edward F. Andresen, Cape Cod
    Colin M. Cunningham, Jr., Boston
    Michael J. Syslo, Chilmark
Michigan
    Capt. William Muirhead, Fenton
Minnesota
    Larry Dahlberg, Brainerd
Mississippi
    Capt. Les D. Osborne III, Pascagoula
Missouri
    Steve Cook, Lee's Summit
Montana
    Rod Zullo, Bozeman
Nevada
    Thomas G. McMillan, Reno
New Jersey
    Pete Barrett, Brick
    William M. Feinberg, Bayonne
    Jerome J. McDonnell, Great Meadows
    Jeff Merrill, South Plainfield
New Mexico
    Jack Samson, Santa Fe
New York
    Hilton B. Bicknell, Henderson Harbor
    John Boesenberg, Massapequa
    William R. Hilts, Sr., Sanborn
    Dr. Gary Sherman, Brooklyn
North Carolina
    Richard C. Bailey, Wilmington
    Frederick C. Bonner, Sr., Garner
    Edward C. Davis, Fayetteville
    Robert A. Eakes, Buxton
    Michael E. Hayes, Kitty Hawk

    Raiford Trask, Wrightsville Beach
Ohio
    Richard J. Kotis, Kent
Oklahoma
    Paul B. Southerland, Oklahoma City
Oregon
    Ronald L. Chatham, Monmouth
Pennsylvania
    Michael Barcaskey, Oakdale
    Richard E. Faler, Greenville
    Stephen R. Murphy, Philadelphia
Rhode Island
    Capt. Al Anderson, Narragansett
South Carolina
    Charles J. Moore, Charleston
Tennessee
    Jack Tapscott, Knoxville
Texas
    Bruce Link Cartwright, Houston
    Frank W. Duncan, Freeport
    John R. Price, Port Aransas
Vermont
    Jim Lepage, Manchester
Virginia
    B. W. Beauchamp, Weems
    Dr. James C. Wright, Virginia Beach
Washington
    Richard K. Stoll, Poulsbo
West Virginia
    Robert M. Nutting, Wheeling
    Jean Ward, Fairmont
Wisconsin
    Cooke Bausmann III, Lake Tomahawk
Wyoming
    Merritt Benson, Casper
U. S. TERRITORIES
American Samoa
    James McGuire, Pago Pago
Guam
    LCDR Brandt G. Rousseaux
Northern Mariana Islands, Commonwealth of
    Norman T. Tenorio, Saipan
Puerto Rico
    Luis A. Battistini, Mayaguez
    Jaime Fullana, Jr., Santurce
    Ralph "Agie" Vicente, San Juan
Virgin Islands
    James H. Edmiston, St. Thomas
    Joseph Herbert, St. Thomas
VENEZUELA
    Federico Gonzales D., Caracas
    Felix Lairet S., Caracas
    Reinaldo Perdomo G., Caracas
Virgin Islands *(see U.S. TERRITORIES)*
West Indies *(see UNITED KINGDOM)*
ZAMBIA
    Reginald Hughes, Luanshya
ZIMBABWE
    Doug C. Dryden, Harare
    John L. Minshull, Bulawayo
    Dr. John M. Stubbs, Harare

Subscribe to the Fishing Authority.

Salt Water Sportsman has been America's #1 sportfishing magazine for 60 years. A leader in editorial excellence and marine conservation, *Salt Water Sportsman* delivers the latest in accurate how-to, where-to information on salt water fishing.

Low introductory prices. Subscribe Today!

☑ **Yes!** Send me *Salt Water Sportsman*

- ❑ 12 issues for $16.95 **SAVE 64%**
- ❑ 24 issues for $29.95 **SAVE 68%**
- ❑ 36 issues for $39.95 **SAVE 72%**

NAME

ADDRESS

CITY   STATE   ZIP

❑ payment enclosed   ❑ bill me later

Salt Water S P O R T S M A N

For faster service call:
1-800-759-2127
online address
www.saltwatersportsman.com
or clip coupon and send to:

**Salt Water Sportsman
P.O. Box 51496
Boulder, CO 80323-1496**

Please allow 6-8 weeks for delivery of first issue. *State sales tax, where applicable, will be added to your invoice. For Canada, add $10.00 per year for postage and G.S.T. Foreign subscriptions, add $30.00 per year for airmail delivery. Savings based on cover price of $3.99.

5BSC3

Go Fish!

Come on Downunder

and experience a diversity of locations and fishing options the rest of the world can only dream of. Whether you want to chase the legendary Black Marlin

across the Great Barrier Reef or test your light tackle skills against our spectacular

fighting Barramundi, Cairns Reef Charter Services can handle all of the arrangements for you!

1999 TOURNAMENTS

31 AUGUST - 3 SEPTEMBER
THE AUSTRALIAN
BLACK MARLIN
FLY FISHING MASTERS

✳

4-9 SEPTEMBER
TOWNSVILLE BILLFISH
CHALLENGE 99

✳

29 SEPT - 2 OCT
GREAT BARRIER REEF
BIG GAME MASTERS

✳

17-23 OCTOBER
LIZARD ISLAND
TOURNAMENT

With more than 15 years in the business and thousands of successful charters behind us we know that we can put together an individual fishing package tailored to fit any request... no matter how unusual. Our boats are world class, the crews friendly and expert and the fishing environment... unbeatable! Come on Downunder and fish for a fantastic variety of species on the fishing trip of a lifetime. Whatever you do, don't let this one get away. Fill in the coupon and return it by mail or fax, or if you just can't wait drop us an email, visit our web site or get on the phone. Guess we'll be seeing you then, eh?

I want to find out more about Australia's Fishing Hotspots and the amazing packages available from Australia's leading fishing charter service... Cairns Reef Charter Services - http://www.ausfish.com/crcs/

Mail this coupon to:
Cairns Reef
Charter Services
PO Box 5788 Cairns QLD 4870
or Fax to:
61 70 4031 4610
or phone Carol North on:
61 70 4031 4742
or email to crcs@ausfish.com

Name ....

Address ....
....
State .... Zip ....

Phone .... Fax: ....

WOOF1001/98

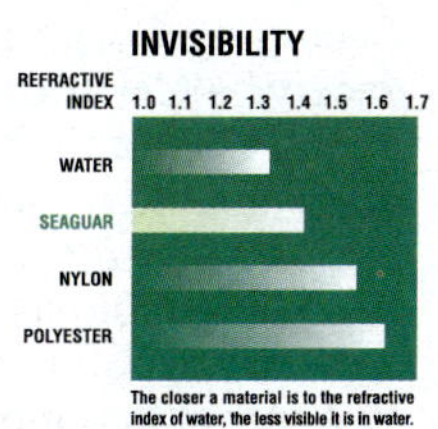

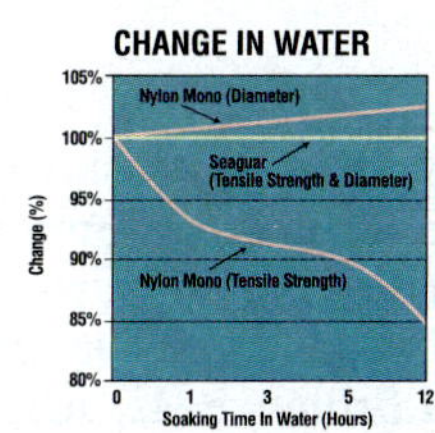

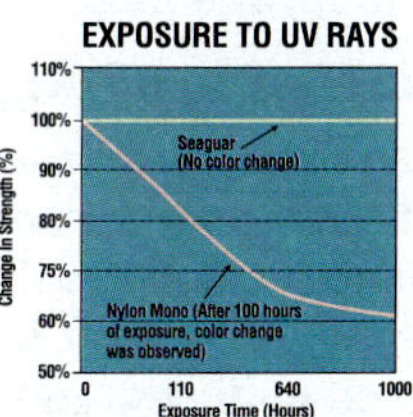

NEW *SEAGUAR® CARBON PRO*™ 100% FLUOROCARBON FISHING LINE

Introducing the first truly castable 100% Fluorocarbon fishing line. Now every fisherman can discover the benefit that ultra-low visibility 100% fluorocarbon has to offer. New Carbon Pro boasts the easy handling, low memory, smooth casting qualities of the finest premium monofilaments but the comparison with mono stops there. Carbon Pro is virtually invisible in the water, it is far more abrasion resistant than ordinary mono, it is unaffected by the sun's UV rays and the tensile strength of Carbon Pro is clearly superior. But perhaps the biggest reason to fish Seaguar Carbon Pro is that anglers claim it has increased their bites *up to 10 times!*

Visit our website
www.seaguar.com

The Inventor and World Leader in Fluorocarbon Fishing Lines

GBS Distribution, 513 N. W. Enterprise Drive, Port St. Lucie, FL 34986 • Toll Free: (888) 336-9775, In Florida: (561) 336-2280, Fax: (561) 336-9775

Membership Information

Individual Membership

Anglers can help to support the work of IGFA, and be kept abreast of worldwide events and activities related to their sport. An annual contribution of $35 (USA or International) entitles the donor to a Regular Membership in IGFA. For those who wish to further support IGFA's work and contribute to the objectives of the association, other membership categories have been established, including five levels of corporate membership.

MEMBERSHIP CATEGORIES

Junior Member - $15
Regular Member - $35
Associate Member - $15*
Family Member - $45
Fellow Member - $60 (annual)
Sustaining Member - $150 (annual)
Sponsor Member - $500 (annual)
Lifetime Member - $1,000
Benefactor - $5,000
*Associate members receive all membership privileges except *World Record Game Fishes* book and jacket patch.

MEMBERS RECEIVE

World Record Game Fishes

This annual book—the only official guide to world record catches and international angling rules—is sent to members each year at no additional cost. The book includes informative angling articles by renowned outdoor writers and fishery scientists, species identification information and illustrations, a knot-tying guide, tagging information, and more.

The International Angler

A bimonthly newsletter which reports angling activities throughout the world, updates world records, and presents information relating to the species and the sport. Also included are important research and tagging information, articles on both new and established fishing areas, and activities and decisions within IGFA.

Membership Card

Imprinted with member's name and type of membership.

Note: IGFA Junior members receive an IGFA Junior Angler Club hat, decal, embroidered patch, membership card, and subscription to the *International Junior Angler* newsletter.

Jacket Patch

A cloth, embroidered reproduction of IGFA's official logo, designed by artist Guy Harvey.

Membership Decals

The IGFA seal for display on windows, tackle boxes, etc.

News Releases

Late-breaking news that cannot be included in the official newsletter, or information requiring immediate distribution.

Club Membership

All established angling clubs are eligible for membership in IGFA.

CLUB MEMBERSHIP CATEGORIES

Small clubs (up to 150 members) USA & International — $50

*Large clubs (150 members or more) USA & International — $100

*Large clubs can request IGFA publications be sent to two club officers.

MEMBER CLUBS RECEIVE

A certificate of membership, suitable for framing, in addition to all publications and releases. Extra world record application forms and copies of the international angling rules are available to member clubs on request.

As a special service, IGFA maintains a permanent historical file on each member club that keeps the association informed of their membership, officers, tournaments, and activities at least once a year.

IGFA's E. K. Harry Library of Fishes includes an angling club division where yearbooks and releases are indexed and maintained for data reference and historical purposes.

Corporate Membership

Interested companies can show their support for IGFA's many programs that benefit recreational fishermen by becoming Corporate Members. All Corporate Members receive a Certificate of Membership, the right to use the IGFA Corporate Member logo in advertising, plus individual memberships and advertising space in the *World Record Game Fishes* book determined by the level of membership as follows:

Level 1 - $500 includes 1/6 page black & white ad plus two individual memberships.
Level 2 - $1,000 includes one-half page black & white ad plus 4 individual memberships.
Level 3 - $1,500 includes one-half page 4-color ad plus 5 individual memberships.
Level 4 - $2,000 includes full page black & white ad plus 6 individual memberships.
Level 5 - $2,500 includes full page 4-color ad plus 7 individual memberships.

Contributions to IGFA are tax deductible in the United States to the extent the law allows.

IGFA Membership Application

Enclosed is $_______________ for the IGFA Membership(s) indicated.

Remittance not enclosed. Please bill me for the amount of $_______________.

Please charge to my ☐ VISA   ☐ MASTERCARD   ☐ AMERICAN EXPRESS   ☐ DISCOVER

Account No. ☐☐☐☐☐☐☐☐☐☐☐☐☐☐☐☐☐☐☐

Expiration date _______________ Signature _______________________________

☐ $35 Regular Member USA (annual)
☐ $35 Regular Member International (annual)
☐ $15 Associate Member USA and International
☐ $15 Junior Member USA (annual)
☐ $15 Junior Member International (annual)

☐ $45 Family USA (annual)
☐ $45 Family International (annual)
☐ $60 Fellow (annual)
☐ $150 Sustaining Member (annual)
☐ $500 Sponsor (annual)

☐ $1,000 Life Member
☐ $5,000 Benefactor
☐ $50 Club Membership
☐ $100 Club Membership
Corporate membership begins at $500 annually.

NAME:_______________________________

ADDRESS: _______________________________

CITY/STATE: _________________________ ZIP: _______________

COUNTRY: ___________________________ PHONE: _______________

Make checks payable to INTERNATIONAL GAME FISH ASSOCIATION
(Donations are tax deductible in the U.S.A. to the extent the law allows.)
Mail to: IGFA, 300 Gulf Stream Way, Dania Beach, Florida 33004 USA
Phone: (954) 927-2628 Fax (954) 924-4299 E-Mail IGFAHQ@aol.com

---

IGFA Membership Application

Enclosed is $_______________ for the IGFA Membership(s) indicated.

Remittance not enclosed. Please bill me for the amount of $_______________.

Please charge to my ☐ VISA   ☐ MASTERCARD   ☐ AMERICAN EXPRESS   ☐ DISCOVER

Account No. ☐☐☐☐☐☐☐☐☐☐☐☐☐☐☐☐☐☐☐

Expiration date _______________ Signature _______________________________

☐ $35 Regular Member USA (annual)
☐ $35 Regular Member International (annual)
☐ $15 Associate Member USA and International
☐ $15 Junior Member USA (annual)
☐ $15 Junior Member International (annual)

☐ $45 Family USA (annual)
☐ $45 Family International (annual)
☐ $60 Fellow (annual)
☐ $150 Sustaining Member (annual)
☐ $500 Sponsor (annual)

☐ $1,000 Life Member
☐ $5,000 Benefactor
☐ $50 Club Membership
☐ $100 Club Membership
Corporate membership begins at $500 annually.

NAME: _______________________________

ADDRESS: _______________________________

CITY/STATE: _________________________ ZIP: _______________

COUNTRY: ___________________________ PHONE: _______________

Make checks payable to INTERNATIONAL GAME FISH ASSOCIATION
(Donations are tax deductible in the U.S.A. to the extent the law allows.)
Mail to: IGFA, 300 Gulf Stream Way, Dania Beach, Florida 33004 USA
Phone: (954) 927-2628 Fax (954) 924-4299 E-Mail IGFAHQ@aol.com

IGFA GIFT MEMBERSHIP
Please enter the following Gift Membership(s) in the categories indicated. (Membership categories are listed on reverse.)

GIFT TO: _______________________________

Address _______________________________

_______________________ Zip _______

Membership category: _______________________

GIFT TO: _______________________________

Address _______________________________

_______________________ Zip _______

Membership category: _______________________

DONOR _______________________________

Address _______________________________

_______________________ Zip _______

PLEASE SEND COMPLIMENTARY LITERATURE concerning IGFA to the following friends who might enjoy becoming members:

NAME _______________________________

Address _______________________________

_______________________ Zip _______

NAME _______________________________

Address _______________________________

_______________________ Zip _______

NAME _______________________________

Address _______________________________

_______________________ Zip _______

MEMBER'S NAME _______________________________

Address _______________________________

_______________________ Zip _______

IGFA GIFT MEMBERSHIP
Please enter the following Gift Membership(s) in the categories indicated. (Membership categories are listed on reverse.)

GIFT TO: _______________________________

Address _______________________________

_______________________ Zip _______

Membership category: _______________________

GIFT TO: _______________________________

Address _______________________________

_______________________ Zip _______

Membership category: _______________________

DONOR _______________________________

Address _______________________________

_______________________ Zip _______

PLEASE SEND COMPLIMENTARY LITERATURE concerning IGFA to the following friends who might enjoy becoming members:

NAME _______________________________

Address _______________________________

_______________________ Zip _______

NAME _______________________________

Address _______________________________

_______________________ Zip _______

NAME _______________________________

Address _______________________________

_______________________ Zip _______

MEMBER'S NAME _______________________________

Address _______________________________

_______________________ Zip _______

BIMINI

"HEMINGWAY'S ISLAND IN THE STREAM"

Never fished Bimini? Well, you're in for a Reel scorching experience. Bimini is the birth place of sportfishing as we know it today. Early fishermen like S.Kip Farrington and Michael Lerner discovered Bimini's fertile waters and Ernest Hemingway captured it in prose. Now hundreds each year set a spread of lures, deep drop a bait, or throw a fly to the elusive bonefish, all in pursuit of that record gamefish. Bimini is home to three world bonefish records and the largest Blue Marlin caught in the Bahamas, a 1060 1/2 pounder came from Bimini waters. The Famous Big Game Club is an all inclusive resort, including 50 deluxe rooms and cottages, 100

EASILY ACCESSIBLE BY BOAT
OR PLANE . . . . JUST 50 MILES
EAST OF THE SOUTH FLORIDA COAST

slip marina, superb restaurant and sports bar, freshwater pool, tennis courts, and more. Tournaments run throughout the year including the BACARDI® Rum Billfish Tournament and the world's largest wahoo tournament. If you love fishing, Bimini is a must do. Why not make your reservation now.

BIMINI BIG GAME
FISHING CLUB
BIMINI IN THE BAHAMAS

RESERVATIONS

1-800-737-1007

Web site: http://www.bimini-big-game-club.com

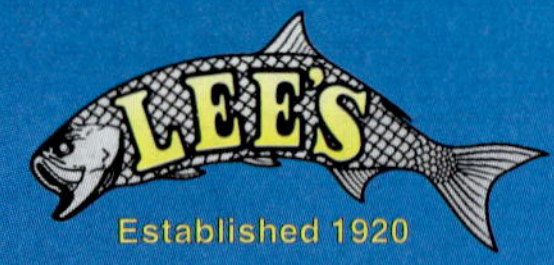

Lee's, the # 1 Family in Sportfishing Equipment

Helm Seats

Rocket Launchers & Tables

All Aluminum Clamp-on Rod Holders

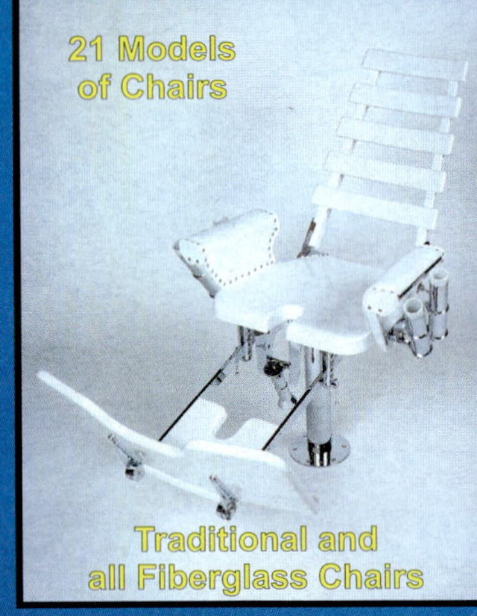

Traditional and
all Fiberglass Chairs

T- Top Rigger
OH-277T (holder)
& AP-3716XS (pole)

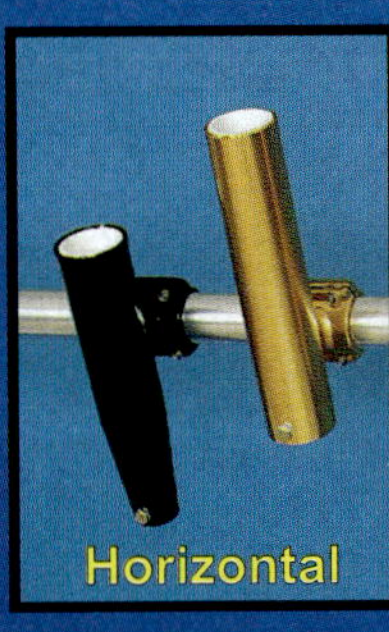
Horizontal

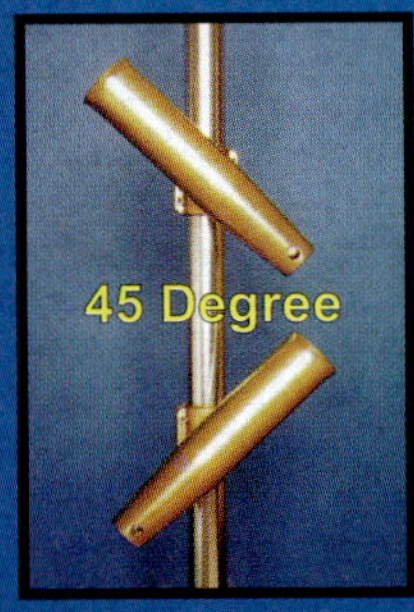
45 Degree

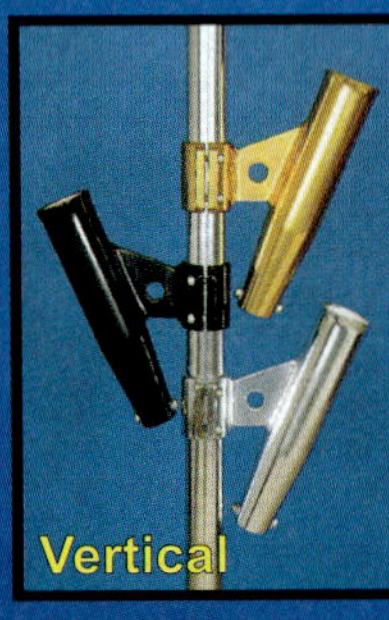
Vertical

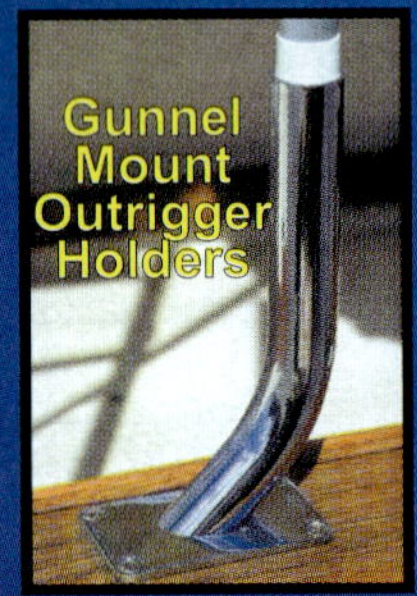
Gunnel
Mount
Outrigger
Holders

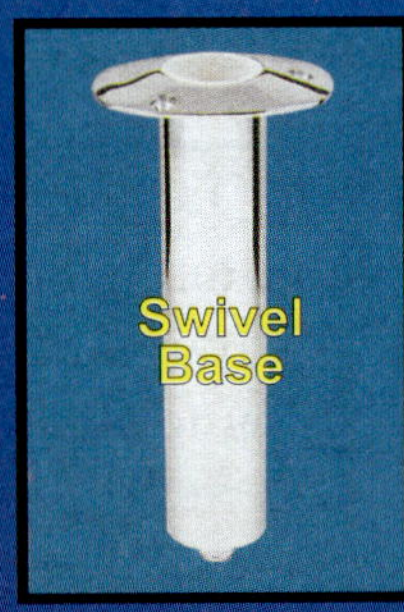
Swivel
Base

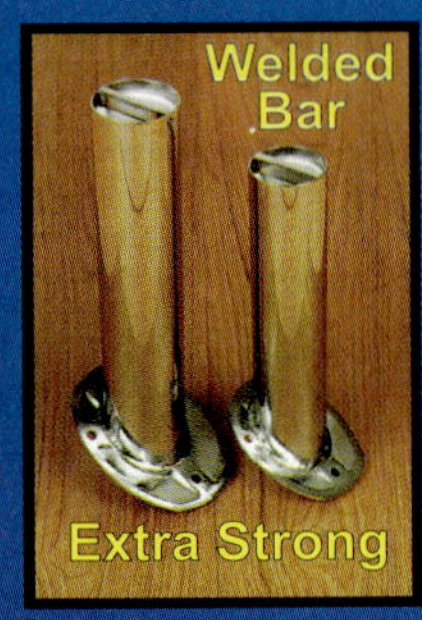

Extra Strong

Specialty Rod Holders

Sidewinders
New T-Top Outriggers
Quick Laydown Available

Outriggers from
11-1/2ft. to 41ft.

Clamp-on Outrigger
Systems

World Wide Web
www.leetackle.com
email: sales @ leetackle.com

LEE'S TACKLE INC
8227 NW 54th STREET MIAMI FL 33166
TEL (305) 599-9324 FAX (305) 599-0830

SECTION 2
ARTICLES

Billfish Conservation Goes Full Circle — 39
    by Tim Choate

The Most Dependable Knots I Know — 51
    By Larry Dahlberg

The Broadbill Swordfish: An Illustrated History — 61
    by Bob Dunn and Peter Goadby

The Best of '98 — 89
    by Mike Leech

Mexico's Newest Bass Hotspot: Lake Huites — 95
    By Gary Laden

Looking for Kanektok's Kings — 101
    By Pat Ford

Tired of "Surf" Fishing?... "Surf's Up" at FBN

Tired of "surfing the web" for quality fishing information? "Surf's up" at **FBN**. FBN, The Fishing Broadcast Network, is the only site dedicated to fishing available on BOTH America Online and the World Wide Web. FBN has one of the most loyal and active communities you'll find anywhere online. At FBN you can **chat** live with other FBN visitors (100,000+ monthly), play one of our 12 interactive online fishing **games**, enter to win **free trips** or fishing gear, or browse FBN's "Your Neck Of the Woods" for **regional fishing information** and conditions. FBN is your 24 hour-a-day fishing resource and interactive fun center. If you want to read about fishing then a book or a magazine will do you just fine. If you want to <u>participate</u> and <u>interact</u> with fishing enthusiasts around the world today, then join us at FBN.

FBN on AOL...

FBN on the Web...

AOL Keywords: "Angler", "Freshwater Fishing", "Saltwater Fishing", "Bass Fishing", "Flyfishing" and "FBN"

On the Web:
http://www.FBNonline.com

FBN Business Services

FBN's online publishing, production/design and consulting services offer businesses in the Fishing industry a way to maximize the return on their online investment. As we like to say, "Build it and they will come" is not an effective online marketing strategy. FBN services include:

- *FBN Advertising/Sponsorship*
- *Web Site Creation/Re-design*
- *Turnkey Web Site Management*
- *Web Site Hosting*
- *Online Marketing Consulting*
- *Cross-Promotional Programs*

FBN - Not Just Another Fish Story!

AOL Keyword: FBN • On the Web: www.FBNonline.com • Email: FBN4Value@aol.com

(301) 622-3090

BOONE ®
To order the following send:
$8.95   7" Cairns Plug
$11.86   12" Big Game Lure
$29.93   12" Bird
Boone Bait Company
440 Plumosa Ave. • Casselberry, FL 32707
Phone: (407) 830-7474 • FAX:(407) 830-9626
Either it's a Boone or it's an imitation

This sailfish caught off Guatemala during the Presidential Challenge of Central America offers graphic evidence that circle hooks are less stressful to the fish. The photo shows the circle hook placement in the corner of the sailfish's mouth which greatly reduces the mortality rate of released fish.The Presidential Challenge has a "circle hooks only" rule.

Billfish Conservation Goes Full Circle

Most anglers' first reaction to the circle hook is one of extreme skepticism. Having a point at 90 degrees to the shank, it is hard to imagine how it can possibly hook a fish.

Actually the design can be traced to bone hooks dating 2000 B.C. Over the past three decades commercial long line fishermen have found circle hooks increase their catch rate and also reduce mortality because nearly 100% of the fish are hooked in the corner of the mouth. Less gut hooking results in fresher fish and less predation than with fish caught on conventional "J" hooks.

It's ironic but certainly serendipitous that sport fishermen are finding circle hooks also increase their catch rates, but more importantly insure a much lower degree of mortality than fish caught and released with conventional hooks.

We've known for some time that circle hooks are a benefit to fishermen for a small handful of saltwater fish, but are now learning that many freshwater fish that suffer from high catch and release mortality can be caught just as successfully and with far less trauma with circle hooks. These include popular species like largemouth bass, smallmouth bass, catfish, and stripers!

IGFA is betting as manufacturers continue to offer smaller and finer circle hooks we'll see a circle hook for panfish that will all but eliminate the need for a disgorger.

With some species suffering mortality estimated in the 90% range when caught on live bait and conventional hooks, circle hooks may be a godsend to sportfishermen and to our declining fisheries. The only hitch about these remarkable hooks is that the sizes don't conform to those designated for conventional hooks, nor is there continuity between various manufacturers. However, try them and you'll be impressed. Use them for your favorite species and let us know the results.

Following is a report from Tim Choate, owner of Artmarina, plus a size chart of circle hooks from leading manufacturers to help you transpose your current hook preferences.

By Tim Choate

In most billfishing circles, no pun intended, it is a wonderful thing when a new fishing practice serves both an increased rate of effectiveness as well as the conservation of the quarry. The use of the circle hook to catch billfish is perhaps the greatest "wonderful thing" to happen to istiophorid fishing in a long time.

The crews of the Artmarina fishing fleet operating from the Fins `n Feathers Inn on Guatemala's southern Pacific coast have had extensive experience with the use of circle hooks.

As of October 1998, total catches of sailfish via use of the circle hook from these boats numbered 848 from the 1,370 bites recorded. This translates to a 62% success rate. With marlin, the release rate on circle hooks comes in at 29 for 43 or 67%. These numbers reflect a lot of experimentation and attempts at refinement that have obviously lessened

Smallmouth bass can suffer mortality rates in the 90 percent plus range when caught on conventional hooks and live bait. Implementation of circle hooks for smallmouth could save tens of thousands of fish annually. Try the Eagle Claw L787 in sizes 8-12. Owner's Mutu Light in size 2 also is effective. (Photo by Larry Dahlberg)

Try Eagle Claw's L787 or Owner's Mutu Light in sizes 3/0-5/0 when using shiners for largemouth bass. (Photo by Doug Hannon)

Catfish are easier to hook with circle hooks than with conventional styles. They work great on limb lines or with conventional gear. Size your hook to the size fish you're after. This bruiser was caught in the Amazon basin using a size 14/0 Mustad 39960. (Photo by Steve Yatomi)

these averages.

Using bait with the traditional "J" style hooks throughout 1997, the Artmarina boats recorded 5,111 sailfish catches out of 9,297 bites and 52 out of 96 marlin bites, a 55% and 54% rate respectively. In comparing these averages, there is no doubt that the hook up ratio has been improved by the use of the circle hook.

Conservation Served as Well

The concomitant benefit from the use of this hook is the vastly improved condition of the fish so caught. Borrowing by analogy from an ongoing study currently being conducted on bluefin tuna by Eric Prince (National Marine Fisheries Service), Greg Skomal, and Brad Chase the conclusion is that the survival rate is greatly increased by hooking a fish in the corner of the mouth rather than in its stomach, gills or other internal areas including eye sockets or throat latches.

The observations of all Artmarina crews conclusively support the view that the health of the average circle hook caught billfish is far better than the average one taken by a "J" hook. Bleeding is almost non-existent. Fish jump more often and more actively. Sounders, or fish swimming for the depths and sulking there, are far fewer.

Billfish photographers are well served by the lack of red water seen passing through the gill plates of a jumping fish and although not as completely reduced as the bleeding, the sight of an expelled stomach is much, much rarer. Yet another advantage of using the circle hook is the ability to use a much lighter leader as the leader is not subject to being chewed through or "pinched off". Lighter leaders generally attract more bites.

How it Happens

The first glance of a circle hook is likely to dissuade most billfishing enthusiasts. They look like they couldn't find a hole on the inside of a five-star restaurant's biggest sieve. So far, so good. Now try pulling it over the side!

The mechanics of how and why circle hooks actually work in a billfish's mouth is similar. Their shape essentially does what it looks like they should do - in the internal areas of a fish; prevent an exposed point from encountering or engaging any internal soft tissue or organs.

However, when the hook's shaft begins its departure from the side or corner of a billfish's mouth it is induced to rotate. The eye of the hook slides off more easily horizontally than vertically from the lateral opening of the billfish's mouth. As the shank no longer shields it, the point is exposed to one of the strongest yet least potentially harmful points of a fish's body; the corner of its mouth.

Because its point is angled in toward the shank at a 90-degree angle, it's difficult for a circle hook to catch soft flesh. This means a fish can swallow the hook, but when the pressure is put on the line, the hook slides cleanly out of the stomach, throat or gill areas, thus avoiding mortally wounding the quarry.

If you tie a line on a circle hook, put the point against your thumb and pull gently, you'll see the shank of the hook immediately tip downward so the point of the hook will be positioned to penetrate at an angle parallel to that at which you are pulling the line. This gives the hook amazingly efficient penetration. The points of ordinary hooks tilt as much as 45 degrees to the line vector, greatly increasing the amount of force it takes to make them sink in.

In circle hook fishing, the fish inhales the bait into his mouth or stomach and shuts his lips. He chomps down, shakes his head, turns, and starts swimming away. When the line gets tight, the hook slides cleanly out of the gut or throat, past the gills, and sticks inside the fish's jawbone.

It's important that 1) you have the right size circle hook, and 2) DON'T JERK. Let the fish take the bait with slack, then gradually tighten the line and start reeling.

Fully 95% of the billfish caught by the Artmarina fleet with circles are hooked in the upper or lower corner of the mouth.

Angling Suggestions

Logic correctly suggests that the angle of the hook up pull is critical. The more a fish is swimming away from the pull point, the more likely the hook will lodge in the rear corner of its mouth. It is critical that the fish be given the chance to change his angle from that of facing the boat. Billfish will usually do this as a matter of course.

One reason the success rate of circle hook pitch baiting is so high is that the fish is usually close enough to be seen and thus the appropriate time for tension can be more accurately determined. Without being able to watch a fish feeding on the far baits, it is generally suggested that "more is better than less" when it comes to the drop back. With

this hook, gone are the worries of "gut hooking" by dropping a bait back too much. Artmarina crews commonly witness successful hook ups with fish that have started to jump prior to tension being applied. Even when jumping toward the boat, the drag of the belly in the line will often be sufficient to get the point to set.

There are a few changes that the angler should make in the hook-up routine. The first is to omit the "wind fast" and "pull back hard" after the drop back. Suggested is a relatively slower increase in drag without the sudden striking motion. Billfish will tend to bite down harder on a bait trying to escape from their mouths thus narrowing the lateral opening between their jaws. It is believed that striking the fish prior to the point engaging will startle the fish and cause it to try to expel the bait. Slow and steady are the guides for getting circle hooks to find home in billfish mouths.

The Circle Hook Prophet

Capt. Ron Hamlin has fished around the world for 40 years. He had tagged well in excess of 1,000 billfish before 1997. In the fall of that year, when recognizing that he had received not a single return, he reasoned that his catch mortality may have been a more than incidental factor.

At this time, he rode with Captains Bud Gramer and Peter B. Wright, Skip Walton and this author on a sailfishing trip from Fins 'n Feathers. While these anglers experimented with the use of circle hooks, Ron quickly recognized the increased likelihood of the survival of the fish that were released using circle hooks. He took up their use and convinced a lot of his clients of the efficacy of this new billfishing hook.

After tagging 546 sailfish in 1997, the most ever tagged by any captain, Hamlin announced his decision to use nothing but circle hooks with bait in his pursuits of billfish. His policy of booking only those parties wishing to use

circle hooks was considered radically and economically unwise, but it has proved just the opposite for him as evidenced by his full reservation calendar.

Capt. Hamlin has continued to refine the rigging styles and has posted the best circle hook up ratio of any captain fishing from Guatemala's billfish hot spot at the Fins 'n Feathers Inn in Iztapa. His dedication to billfish conservation through the use of circle hooks should be applauded.

Other Believers

Among other notables who have taken up the use of circle hooks for billfishing include Captain Bobby Brown of the *Fonda Fishing*. Owner Fonda Huizenga, amongst hundreds of other releases, has captured a pair of daily grand slams with these hooks in the waters off Venezuela.

Capt. Peter B. Wright who brought the first circle hooks to Fins 'n Feathers for initial experimentation relies heavily on the circle hook in baits for marlin. Palm Beach's supreme sailfisherman, Nick Smith, has adopted their use. Dr. Eric Prince of the NMFS has totally endorsed the use of circle hooks for billfish from a conservationist point of view.

Capt. Hamlin has, of course, taken it to the fullest extent by using nothing but circles in his baits. He continues to explore even better ways to employ this style of hook. The entire Artmarina fleet is now committed to the exclusive use of circle hooks with bait.

The list of believers is growing fast. Certainly, circle hook users have suffered, and will continue to suffer their share of "sancochos" - a Spanish description of a bait whose body has been lost to the bite of a billfish without a hook-up. Artmarina's clients' shares are happily diminishing! What these fishermen have done, however, and will continue to do for the survival of an awful lot of sailfish and marlin is reason enough to go full circle for billfish.

Pictured here are six different styles for putting circle hooks in ballyhoo: Top, tied to eye socket; next, bridled to eye socket but hook back for finicky eaters; third from top, traditional style but without lead which "protects" hook with this style; next, bridled to lips; bottom, hook inserted up through lips and tied to lower jaw.

This photo shows a tightly bridled mullet.

Above is a loosely bridled mackerel.

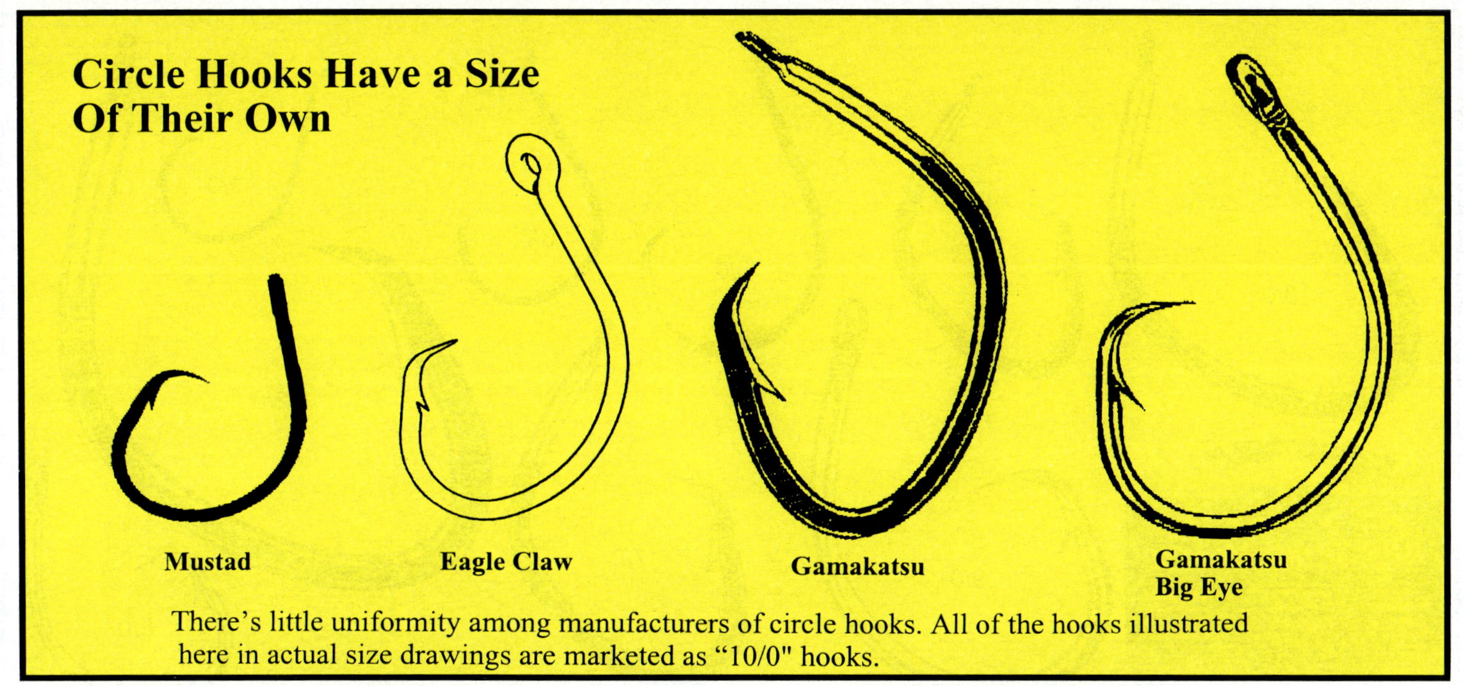

There's little uniformity among manufacturers of circle hooks. All of the hooks illustrated here in actual size drawings are marketed as "10/0" hooks.

Following are examples of some of the sizes offered by manufacturers:

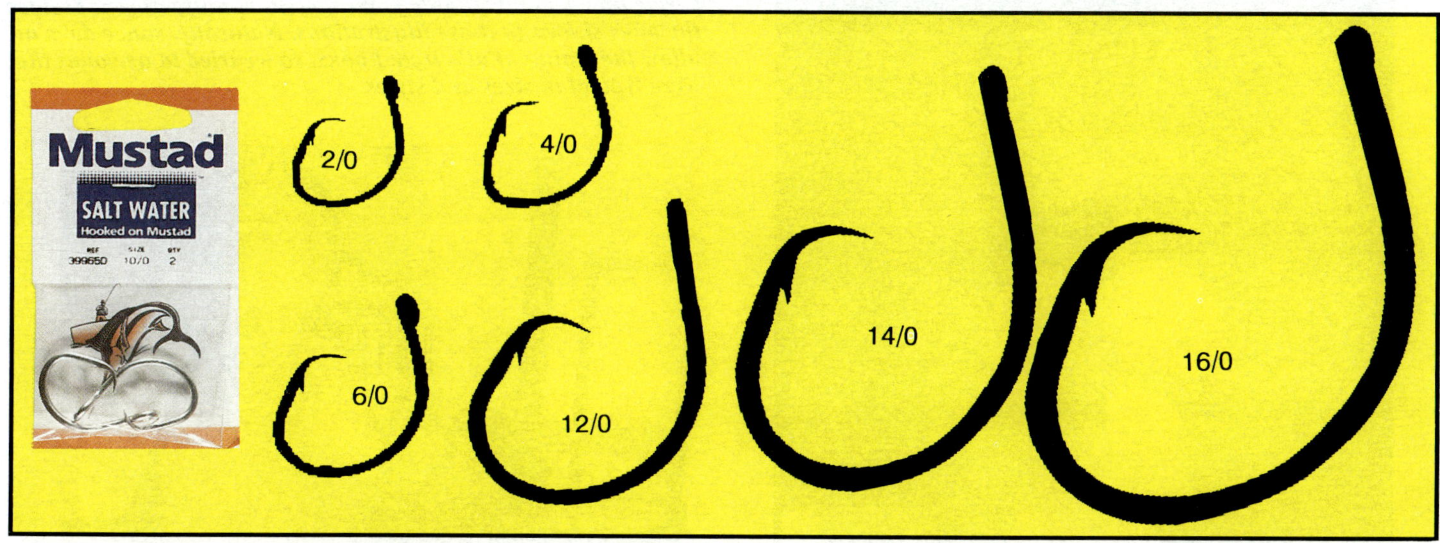

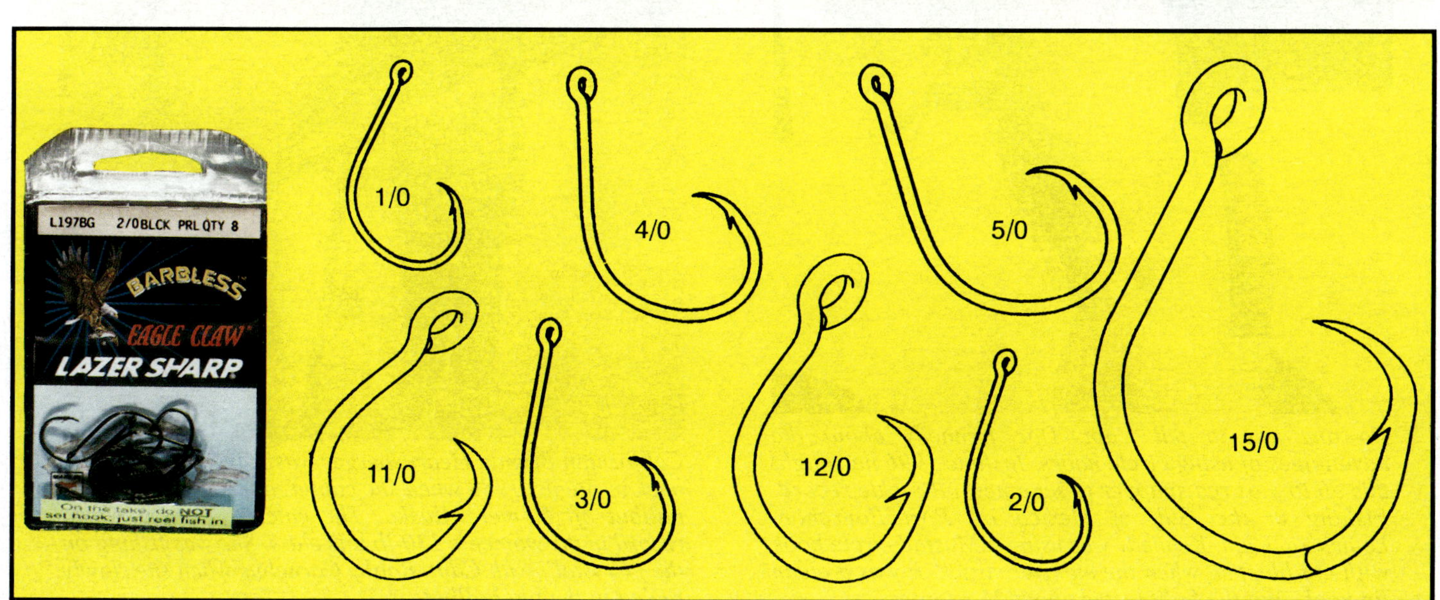

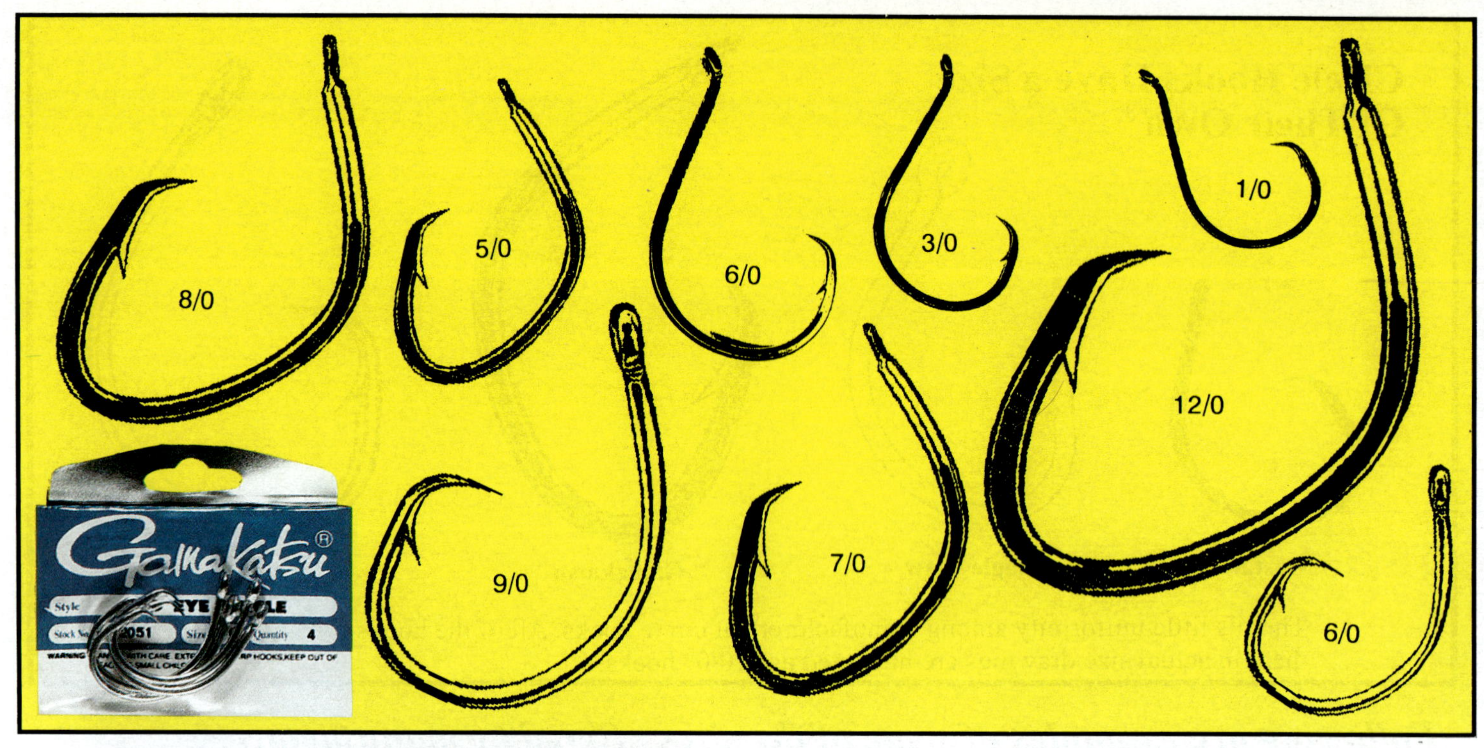

Circle hooks are available from several manufacturers besides the ones shown in these illustrations. Naturally, space does not allow the listing of all circle hooks, so we tried to use ones that were typical in sizes and styles.

No one has to tell Capt. Doc Kennedy about the advantages of using circle hooks. In June 1996 he caught this 50 lb 4 oz red snapper to set a new all-tackle record. Fishing in the Gulf of Mexico off Port Fourchon, Louisiana, Capt. Kennedy was using a Mustad circle hook with cut bluefish when the monster struck. It was a clean lip hook, and the fight lasted about 25 minutes.

Californian Brenda Hearnsberger was using a circle hook back in August 1988 when she captured this 237 lb Pacific halibut off Homer, Alaska. The catch earned a world record in the women's 130-lb line class. She was fishing on the "Crystal" with Capt. Bobby Cornelius when she slowly reeled in the big halibut.

Black Magic EQUALIZER™

the edge...

gimbal & harness

Outer Banks - North Carolina
David Gong tagged and
released eleven giant bluefin
tuna in a day, weights
estimated up to 500lb.
Fight times 10 - 20 minutes

The revolutionary Black Magic Equalizer gimbal and harness has become the stand-up system of choice with sport fishermen around the world...

Steve Sneddon - Sportangler Magazine
"A quantum leap for the comfort, safety and fish fighting power of the stand-up fisherman."

Dennis "Brazzaka" Wallace - "Born Free" - Cairns
"When fishing for granders we use only the best equipment available, these fish don't give you a second chance. This is the most advanced gimbal and harness in the world, it gives the angler the edge."

Bruce Smith - "Striker" - Bay of Islands NZ
"this system is a 'Winner' and is long overdue, we use it for both light and heavy tackle"

Rick Pollock - "Pursuit" - Whakatane NZ
"Ready for action, lightweight, sturdy and innovative."

"Bushy" - Queensland Fishing Monthly
"Definitely at the top of the game fishing tree as far as efficiency and comfort are concerned"

Carl Liederman - Capt. Harry's Fishing Supply- Miami FL
"The Black Magic Equalizer has become the system of choice for the bluefin fishery"

John Eichelsheim - Editor - NZ Fisherman Magazine
"Innovative, efficient and very effective"

the gimbal...

Wear the belt all day, the gimbal slips on in seconds.

more comfort... you will be amazed at the extra pressure you can apply, 30 pounds over the rod tip is as easy as pulling 20 pounds with other systems - dare we suggest it is up to 50% more efficient? Bad back? No strain, no pain!

more stability... the unique design features eliminate sideways movement of the gimbal when under load, especially in sloppy seas.

more leverage... your body weight is used to maximum advantage because the recessed gimbal pin is positioned low down and further back than other systems.

easy to use... wear the unique webbing belt all day, when the big strike comes the gimbal slips on in seconds with no hassles - even in a blind panic!

quality... designed and manufactured in New Zealand using the **best** materials available; high strength UV stabilised polyethylene, 316 stainless gimbal pin moulded in, and, polyester webbing belt and drop straps - far superior to commonly used nylon webbing.

the harness...

unique design... unlike conventional kidney harnesses the Black Magic Equalizer divides the strain between the upper thigh / buttocks area and the lower back using innovative twin element padded supports.

balance... the free running lug clips allow the load to be distributed evenly between the two elements of the harness regardless of the angle of the rod.

less effort... by having the angle of pull lower on the angler the pressure applied to the reel lugs is increased by up to 50% without any extra effort.

quality... New Zealand made using the best materials available; extra durable polyester webbing, top quality buckles and clips, closed cell foam padding and plastic coated fibreglass mesh.

We believe the Black Magic Equalizer stand-up system is the best in the world...

try it and experience the difference...

NEW ZEALAND PAT 264742, UNITED STATES PAT 081528985, AUSTRALIAN PAT PEN 30639/95, US DESIGN REGISTRATION 377563

COMPLETE SYSTEM
Gimbal, Harness, Drop Straps
One size fits all!

US $199

FREIGHT FREE
Delivered to your door by courier within 7 days <u>anywhere</u> in the world!

VISA Visa

MasterCard Master Card

AMERICAN EXPRESS American Express

Duty and import taxes (if applicable) are not prepaid.

HOW TO ORDER

NZ & Australia	• SEE YOUR NEAREST TACKLE RETAILER	
Web Site	• SIMPLE SECURE SYSTEM	• http://www.blackmagic.co.nz
USA & Canada	• 24hr TOLL FREE FAX	• 1-888-264-4843
Other Countries	• 24hr FAX	• 64-9-828-6009
Airmail to	• Black Magic Tackle, P.O. Box 15-170 New Lynn, Auckland 7, New Zealand.	

VISIT OUR WEB SITE OR FAX/WRITE FOR OUR FREE 1999 MAIL ORDER CATALOGUE
Includes a huge range of unique salt water and fresh water terminal tackle: Hooks, Swivels, Leaders, Monofilament, Sabiki Rigs & Game Lures

---

☐ Please send me your FREE 1999 mail order catalog

I WISH TO ORDER (write quantity in box):

☐ Black Magic Equalizer Systems (Gimbal, Harness and Drop Straps) at US$199 complete freight inclusive

☐ Gimbal at US$119 freight inclusive (including Drop Straps)

☐ Harness at US$119 freight inclusive

PLEASE CHARGE TO MY:

☐ Visa　☐ MasterCard　☐ American Express

Name: ______________________

Street Address: ______________________

____

City: ______________ State: ______________

Zip: ______________ Country: ______________

Phone: ______________ Fax: ______________
(include country code & area code)

Expiry Date: ____ / ____
　　　　　　month　year

Card No. ▢▢▢▢ ▢▢▢▢ ▢▢▢▢ ▢▢▢▢

Signature: ______________________

#15 - 129
$225
#14 - 107 $325
#14 - 37 $1160
#14 - 50 $495
Genuine Diamonds, Rubies, Sapphires
#40 - 24
$1250 18K.
#15 - 64
$1050
#0 - 32
$640
No Diam. $110
#14 - 28 SWIVEL 80   7" $340 · 18" $880
#0 - 87
$138
#13 - 76
$85
#13 - 75
$95
#13 - 62
$360
No Diam. $145
#15 - 86
$520
No Diam. $149
#15 - 66
$221
#0 - 94
$427
#11 - 70
$820
#15 - 68
$146
#14 - 40 All Diam. $787 · Half Diam. $562 · No Diam. $225
#1 - 14
$273
No Diam.
$80
#15 - 43
$449
No Diam.
$186
#1 - 91
$446
No Diam. $184
#17 - 02
$1158
No Diam. $880
Jewelry Solid 14K. Gold
SHOWN ACTUAL SIZE
#0 - 102
$281
#1 - 89
$971
#15 - 100
$206
#0 - 23
$195
#15 - 135
$295
No Diam. $195
#11 - 62
$498
No Big Diam. $333
No Diam. $108
#40 - 40
$2171 18K. - 2000 Yr. Old Coin
#0 - 36
$124
#0 - 25
$87
Ergs. $190

BASED $300 World Gold Spot

#14 - 06 SWIVEL 125 8" $521 - 22" $1480

#13 - 83
$640

#13 - 91
$820

#13 - 71
$371

#13 - 102
$446

#4 - 08
$160

#0 - 16½
$446

#0 - 70
$115

#4 - 02
$76

#2 - 06
$142

#16 - 09
$670
No Diam. $262

#0 - 07½
$93

#0 - 06½
$128

#0 - 08½
$224

#0 - 01½
$122

#0 - 02½
$123

#16 - 16
$290

#0 - 10½
$315

I.G.F.A. WORLD FISHING CENTER
Grand Opening!
CELEBRATE WITH SPECIAL PRICES!
Treasure Originals™
1-800-545-8135
8306 Mills Dr. #525
Miami, Florida 33183
SATISFACTION GUARANTEED

#16 - 28
$787

#16 - 17
$258

#4 - 57
$262

#0 - 48
$521

#8 - 09
$296

#0 - 50
$297

#16 - 34
$710

#14 - 05 SWIVEL 200
8½" $783 - 22" $2020

#14 - 04 SWIVEL 300
9" $1121 - 22" 2770

U.S. SHIP / INSURE $7.50

SOLID 14K. GOLD

SHOWN ACTUAL SIZE

VISA

MasterCard

AMERICAN EXPRESS

DISCOVER

MOTHER.

Stren High Impact.™ Strong. Abrasion and UV ray resistant. Built
to handle the nastiest saltwater conditions and better yet, the nastiest
saltwater fish. So no matter what kind of big game fish is calling you out, you'll
always be ready to fight. Find out more at www.stren.com

The Most Dependable Fishing Lines In The World.™

The Most Dependable KNOTS I Know

By Larry Dahlberg

Larry Dahlberg uses 50-lb Stren Hi Impact to catch giant beluga sturgeon in the Caspian Sea at Kazakhstan.

200 lb Nile perch brought in on 20-lb Magnathin in Lake Nassar, Egypt.

When I started the Hunt For Big Fish in 1992 one of the first things I did was spool up every reel with IGFA rated STREN. In the past six years I've released dozens of potential world records using Stren, and I can honestly tell you, in over a million miles of hunting for big fish with it, STREN has never let me down.

It's held up for me on: 1000 pound plus blue marlin caught in 24 minutes on 80-lb Hi Impact using stand-up gear at Bom Bom Island, West Africa; 200-lb plus Nile perch on 20-lb MagnaThin in Egypt; 400 lb porbeagle shark on 20-lb Hi Impact in Cordova, Alaska; 100 lb Atlantic sailfish at Bom Bom on 4 lb & 6 lb Hi Impact Gold; giant salmon, pike, muskies, walleyes, tarpon, cobia, bonefish, trout, largemouth and smallmouth bass, snook, tuna, pavon, payara, goldon dorado, all the tough customers.

I remember hooking a beluga sturgeon weighing nearly 300 lb fishing with 8-lb MagnaThin in the Caspian Sea out of Kazakhstan, in the former Soviet Union. I was using a

Atlantic sailfish falls to 4-lb Hi Impact off Bom Bom, West Africa.

walleye-sized spinning outfit and fishing out of a tiny aluminum boat with a Russian who didn't speak English and knew nothing about fishing. When the fish took off, I pulled up the anchor and let it tow us wherever it wanted to go.

The water was only four feet deep. There were dozens of other sturgeon in the school that frequently bumped into the line between me and the fish I was fighting. At times my fish ran right and the midpoint of the line ran left because it was lodged in the crack on the front side of the pectoral fin of a different beluga headed in the opposite direction!

I was certain the line would break but it didn't. After about an hour I jumped out of the boat, grabbed the thing by the tail, rolled it over and unhooked it. The water was only waist deep but as dirty and green as pea soup so I had to get

Big tigerfish taken on 20-lb Magnathin in Zambia River.

it up out of the water in order to be more visible to the camera.

Cradling it under my forearms and against my chest I arched back and struggled to get as much of it as I could out of the dirty water so its size would be clearly visible.

No one could believe how massive it was. It was as big around as a telephone pole, and nearly eight feet long. Its back was a ghostly blue grey that blended to an almost phosphorescent bone white on the flanks and belly.

As I lifted, it curled its tail around my left side and balanced. Somehow I got it up out of the water. But then it straightened its tail, shifting 3/4 of the weight on to my left arm and shoulder. I felt numbing pain and heard a soft pop as the AC in my left shoulder separated. I remember wondering how a line so thin could be so tough.

Now, I'll put my knots on the line!

Few things in fishing are as confusing or controversial as knots. If you've been confused by 100-page knot books, take heart. I've been a knot-nut for 40 years and have fished and tested them all both on the water and with machines. I'm here to tell you, if you use fresh, high quality line like Stren and choose the right product for your specific application you need less than a half dozen knots to be confident fishing in any situation in fresh or saltwater with any kind of gear.

Using the Uni-Knot for tying on a lure:

In the past dozen years or so, the Uni-Knot, (which is really a modified Nail Knot tied without a nail) has gained great popularity for good reason. It's easy to tie, super strong and can be used in one variation or another for 90% of your fishing needs. I've tested this knot with wraps varying from two times to seven and found that three wraps consistently test the strongest for a terminal knot. I feel this is the most important knot in angling.

TYING TO TERMINAL TACKLE

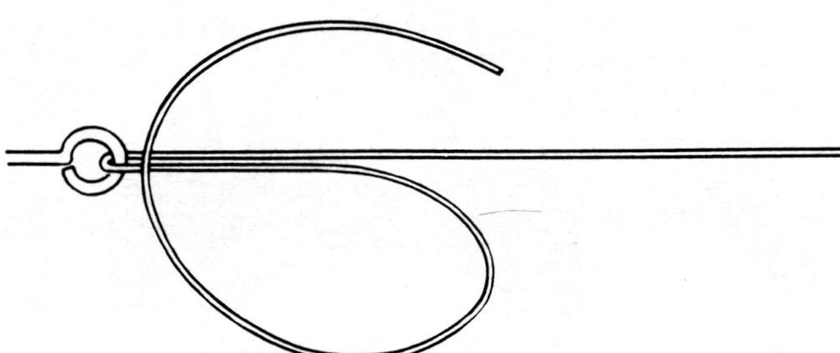

A. Run line through eye of hook, swivel or lure at least 6" and fold to make two parallel lines. Bring end of line back in a circle toward hook or lure.

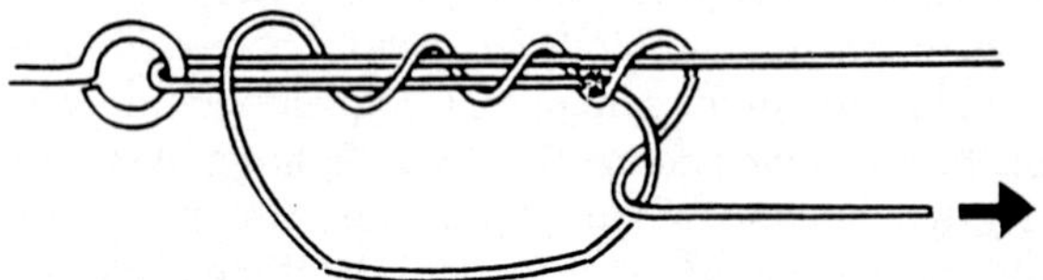

B. Make three turns with the tag around the double line and through the circle. Hold double line at point where it passes through eye and pull tag end to snug up turns

C. Now pull standing line to slide knot up against eye.

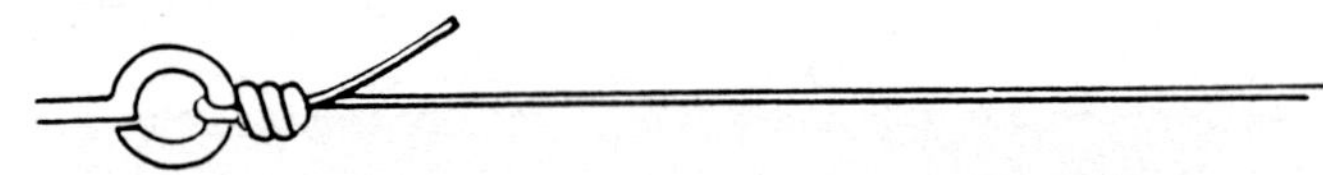

D. Continue pulling until knot is tight. Trim tag end flush with closest coil of knot. Uni-Knot will not slip.

LOOP CONNECTION

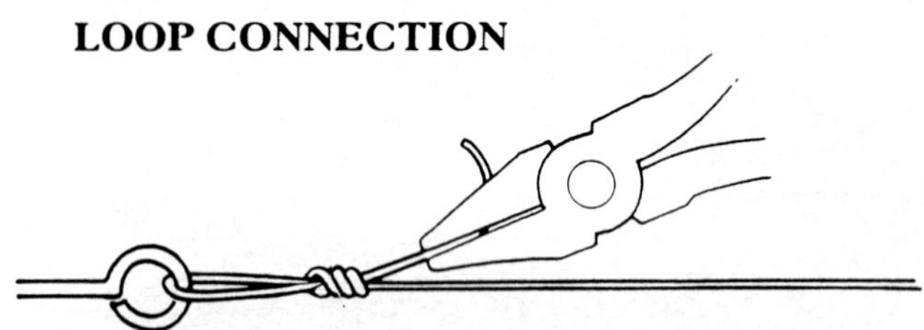

Tie same knot as above to point where turns are snugged up around standing line. Slide knot toward eye until loop size desired is reached. Pull tag end with pliers to maximum tightness. This gives lure a natural free movement in water. When fish is hooked, knot will slide tight against eye.

An even stronger way to use the Uni-Knot is to first double the line either with or without a Bimini twist. Treating the doubled line as a single strand, tie the knot as above. This method gives you a little more strength at the critical point where the line passes through the hook. This is a good variation to use when fishing with light or very small diameter lines and what I use most of the time.

Uses: Tying on lures, snaps, swivels, tying line to reel. Knot strength: 98%+

Using the Uni-Knot for joining two lines together.

This is by far the best way to splice mono, or in conjunction with a Bimini (Illustration # 3) to join your main line to a nylon coated wire or hard mono shock leader.

It's also good for attaching fly line backing to fly line. (be sure to peel 6" of coating off the fly line first to reduce its diameter). This method is almost 2X stronger than the commonly used Albright Knot.

DOUBLE UNI-KNOT

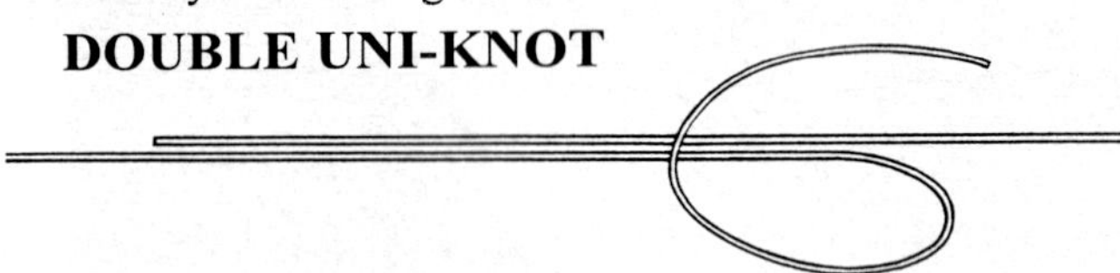

A. Overlap ends of two lines of about same diameter for about 6". With one end, form Uni-Knot circle, crossing the two lines about midway of overlapped distance.

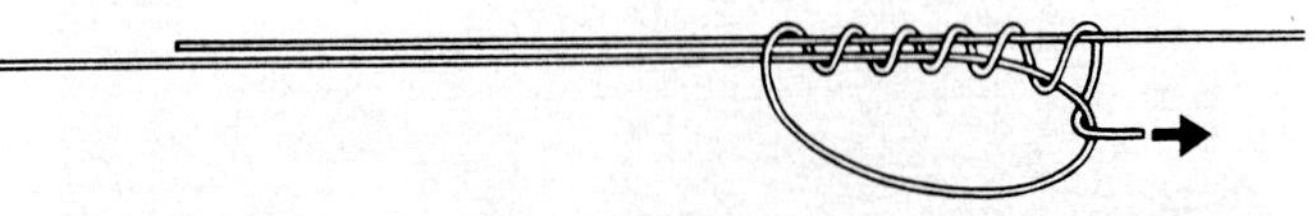

B. Tie basic Uni-Knot, making six turns around the two lines.

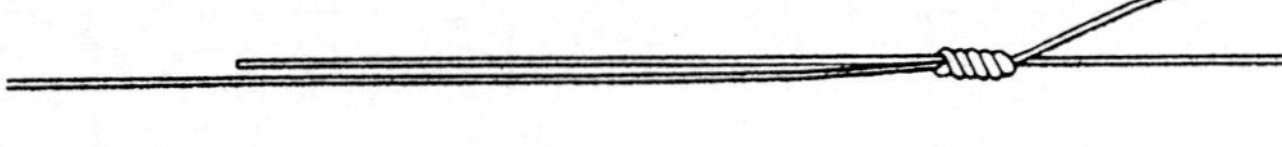

C. Pull tag end to snug knot tight around line.

D. Use loose end of overlapped line to tie another Uni-Knot and snug up.

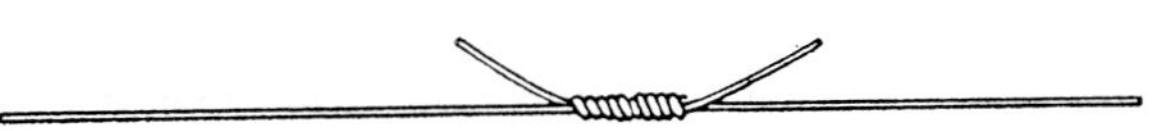

E. Pull the two standing lines in opposite directions to slide knots together. Pull as tight as possible and snip ends close to nearest coil.

Connecting double-line to shock leader.

A. As a replacement for Bimini Twist or Spider Hitch, first clip off amount of line needed for length of loop desired. Tie the two ends together with an overhand knot.

B. Double end of standing line and overlap 6" with knotted end of loop piece. Tie Uni-Knot with tied loop around doubled standing line, making four turns.

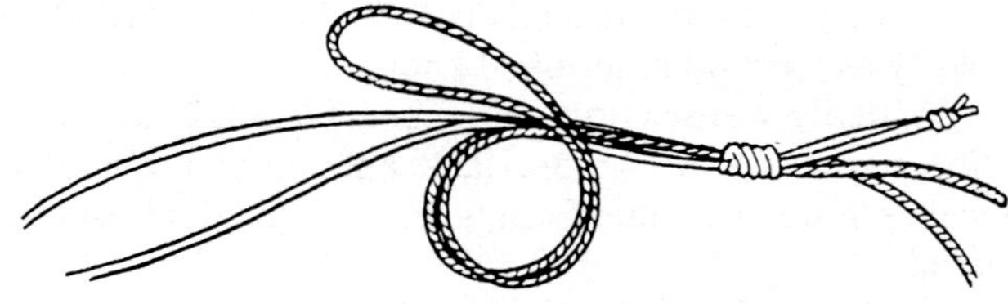

C. Now tie Uni-Knot with doubled standing line around loop piece. Again four turns.

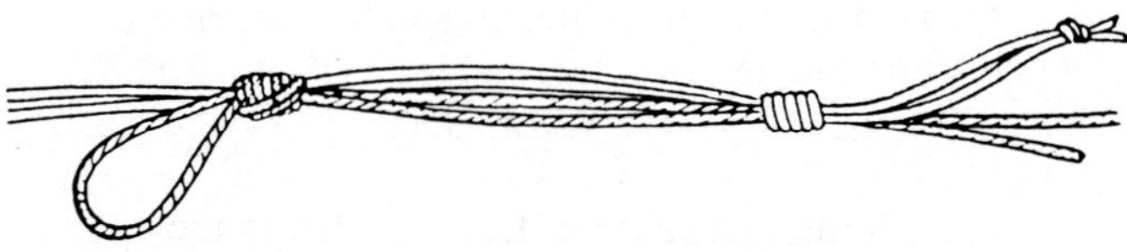

D. Hold both strands of doubled line in one hand, both strands of loop in other (see arrows). Pull knots together until they barely touch.

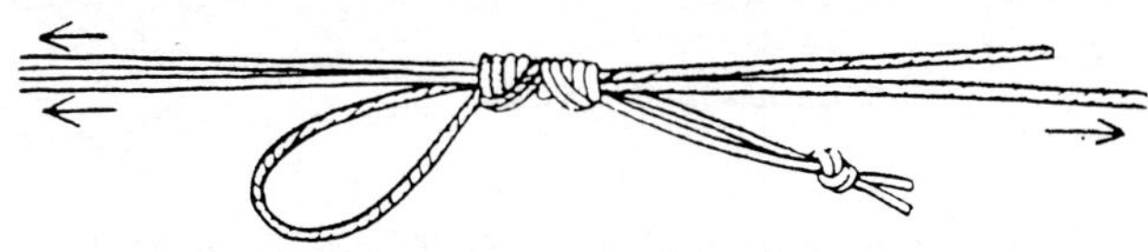

E. Tighten by pulling both strands of loop piece but only main strand of standing line. Trim off both loop tag ends, which eliminates overhand knot.

Uses:

Joining two single strands of line together of the same or differing diameters to add a "top shot" to a reel that's getting low on line, or for building tapered fly leaders.

Connecting heavy shock leader to mono when fishing for fish with abrasive mouths like snook, tarpon and billfish, or in conditions where rocks, logs or other cover may fray line ahead of terminal gear. Fabulous for all species of salmon, lake trout, Nile perch, peacock bass, largemouth in heavy cover or under docks.

Note: If you feel a heavier shock leader is spooking fish try using nearly invisible Hi Impact Fluorocarbon.

Connecting nylon coated wire direct to mono (best to use in conjunction with a Bimini (again treat the doubled line as a single strand as shown in illustration #3)

Great for fly fishing for fish with teeth like pike, muskies, tigerfish, payara and barracuda. Also great for conventional tackle if you want to avoid using snaps and swivels that may degrade lure action or spook finicky fish. Strength:

If tied with Bimini, which is what I strongly recommend, it tests 135% of your single main line with wire and over 190% tied mono to mono. Note: Be sure to use a shock leader at least 3X stronger than your main line.

If tied with two single strands it tests less than 100%, but usually over 90% and is always stronger than a barrel knot or any of the surgeon's knots.

Bimini Twist

A trick developed by saltwater anglers to further increase their knot efficiency is to double the line and treat it as a single strand. The best way to do this is to use a knot called the Bimini Twist Loop. When tied properly, this clever loop knot comes closer to 100% line strength than any other knot, and provides you with a doubled line to tie your terminal knot or to join to a leader. Because you're using a doubled line after the Bimini you can tie a knot with as little as 50% strength and still achieve nearly 100% line strength with it. It also gives you a little extra protection on the part of the line that takes the most abuse. You can make the loop several feet long or as short as a few inches. (For world record requirements, be sure to check the IGFA Angling Rules on page 134)

If you treat the doubled line you've created with the Bimini as a single strand and tie a Uni-Knot, you'll achieve nearly 200% line strength at the terminal connection where most of the wear and tear takes place!

Bimini Twist
These directions apply to tying double lines of around five feet or less. For longer double-line sections, two people may be required to hold the line and make initial twists.

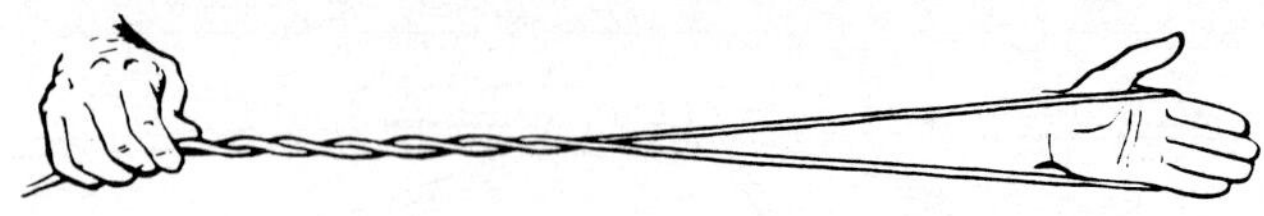

1. Measure a little more than twice the footage you'll want for the double line. Bring end back to standing line and hold together. Rotate end of loop 20 times, putting twists in it.

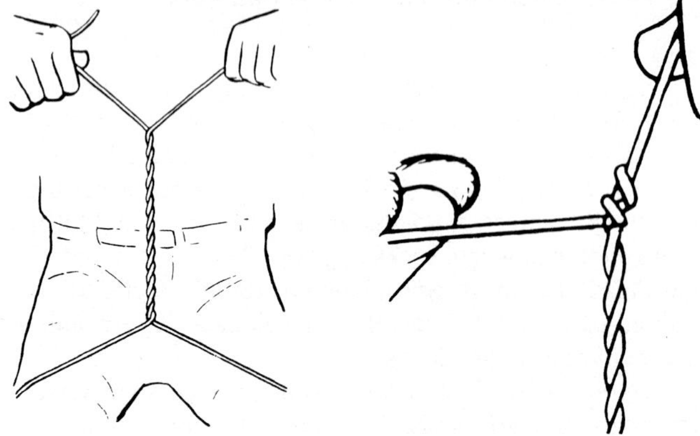

2. Spread loop to force twists together about 10" below tag end. Step both feet through loop and bring it up around knees so pressure can be placed on column of twists by spreading knees apart.

3. With twists forced tightly together, hold standing line in one hand with tension just slightly off the vertical position. With the other hand, move tag end to position at right angle to twists. Keeping tension on loop with knees, gradually ease tension of tag end so it will roll over the column of twists, beginning just below the upper twist.

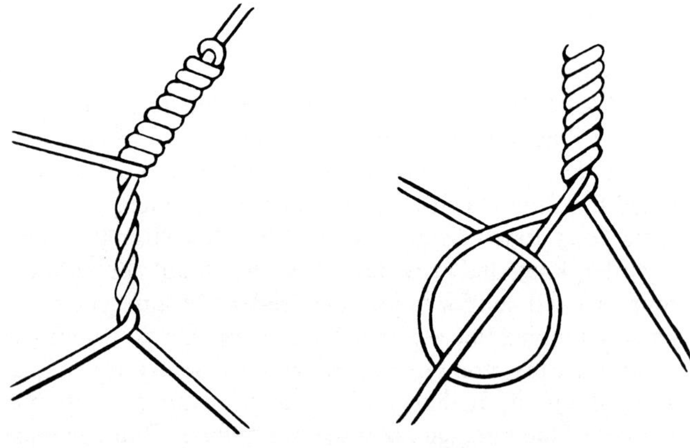

4. Spread legs apart slowly to maintain pressure on loop. Steer tag end into a tight spiral coil as it continues to roll over twisted line.

5. When spiral of tag end has rolled over column of twists, continue keeping knee pressure on loop and move hand which has held standing line down to grasp knot. Place finger in crotch of line where loop joins knot to prevent slippage of last turn. Take half-hitch with tag end around nearest leg of loop and pull up tight.

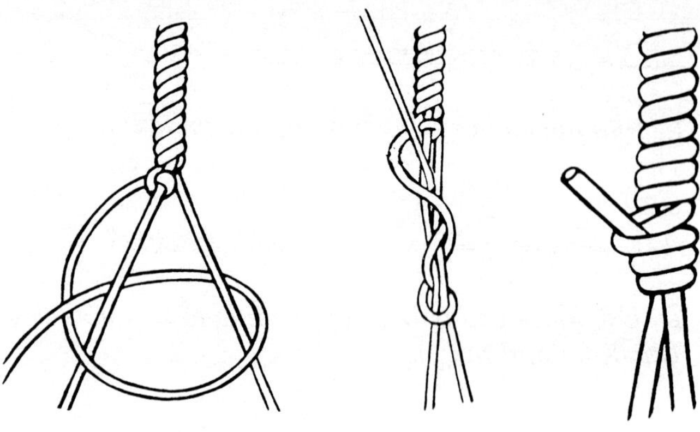

6. With half-hitch holding knot, release knee pressure but keep loop stretched out tight. Using remaining tag end, take half-hitch around both legs of loop, but do not pull tight.

7. Make two more turns with the tag end around both legs of the loop, winding inside the bend of line formed by the loose half-hitch and toward the main knot. Pull tag end slowly, forcing the three loops to gather in a spiral.

8. When loops are pulled up neatly against main knot, tighten to lock knot in place. Trim tag end about ¼" from knot.

Note: A variation I prefer is rather than finishing the knot with the tag sticking out the side of the triple half hitch, I like to put the tag back through between the two legs at the top of the loop. This allows it to pass though the guides more easily and also is more secure.

Knot Again

A great open loop knot for attaching and reattaching terminal gear to shock leaders.

I learned this knot from Costa Rican snook fishermen who didn't want to take the time and effort of tying on a new shock leader after changing lures several times. This is a cool knot you can tie, untie and re-tie for attaching a lure to hard mono shock leader. After you've tied it the first time, the shock leader "memorizes" and it's quick and simple to change lure and use the same knot over and over again! Plus, the tag end faces the lure so it doesn't gather weeds and moss as easily as most other terminal knots.

Actually you sea dogs will recognize this is like a boline, except you use an overhand knot instead of a loop. Since there was no name for this knot, I named it "Knot Again."

1) Tie overhand knot in main line ahead of lure or hook.

2) Pass line through lure and through overhand knot, back around main line and down through overhand knot. Adjust to form open loop of desired size.

3) Pinch knot between thumb and forefinger and tighten by pulling on main line and lure, DO NOT PULL ON TAG END OR KNOT WILL UNTIE! Leave tag of 1/4" to 1/2".

4) Push front and back of knot together to untie.

Uses: Can only be used with Hard Mono Shock Tippet or Nylon coated Stranded wire.

I use it on hooks and lures for snook, tarpon, lake trout, salmon, halibut, all billfish, almost all non-toothy saltwater fish. Also works great on tarpon and snook flies.

Prevents you from having to tie a separate fly leader section for each tarpon fly and eliminates the need for a huge, cumbersome fly box to keep shock tippets stretched. Since this knot can easily be tied, untied and retied it lets you change lures without having to cut your shock tippet. Because you don't have to cut the shock leader to remove the lure you don't have to redo the Double Uni or Bimini used to build your line and shock leader connection as often as you would with other knots. Strength: 65%

Note: since you're using shock leader at least 3X your line strength the Knot Again will test about 2 1/2 times the breaking strength of your single line.)

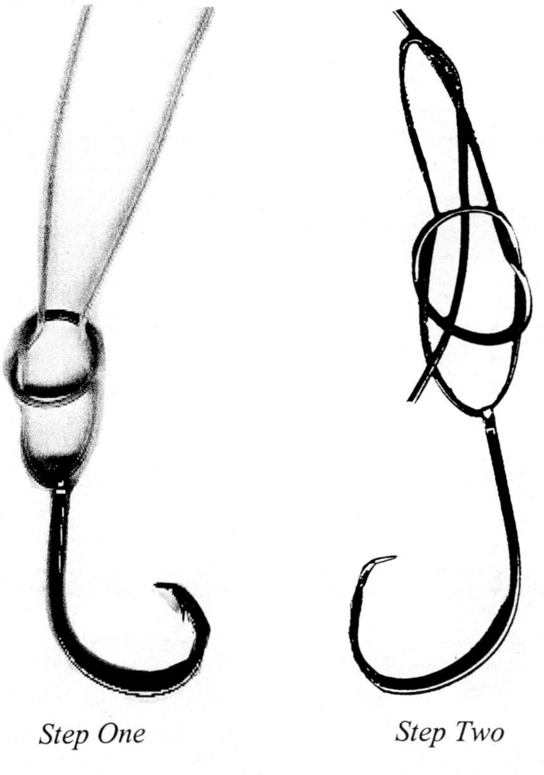

Step One   Step Two

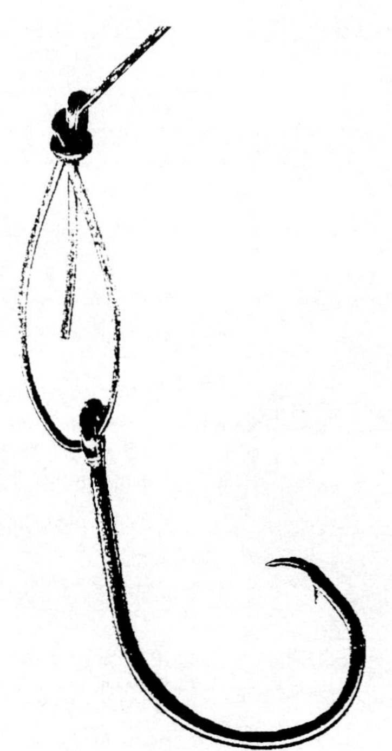

Finished Knot

SNELLING A HOOK

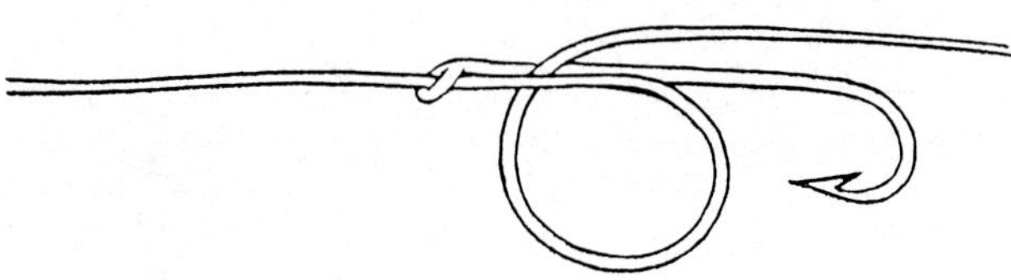

A. Thread line through hook eye about 6". Hold line against hook shank and form Uni-Knot circle.

B. Make as many turns through loop and around line and shank as desired. Close knot by pulling on tag end of line.

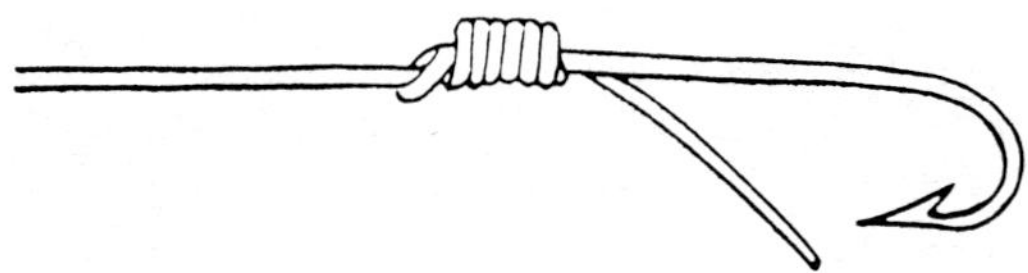

C. Tighten by pulling standing line in one direction and hook in the other.

LINE TO REEL SPOOL

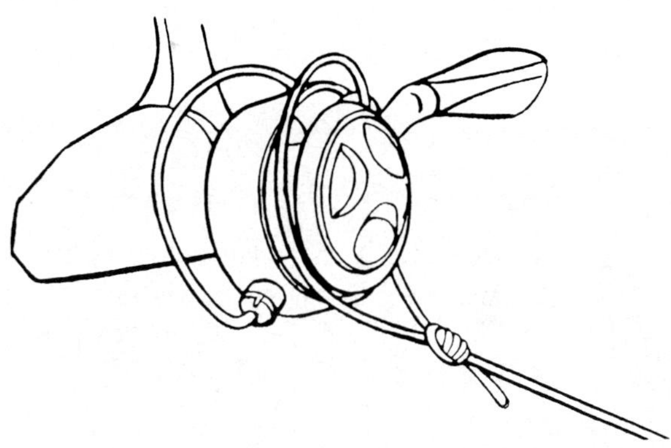

A. Tie loop in end of line with Uni-Knot; only three turns needed. With bail of spinning reel open, slip loop over spool. (With revolving spool, reel, line must be passed around reel hub before tying the Uni-Knot.)

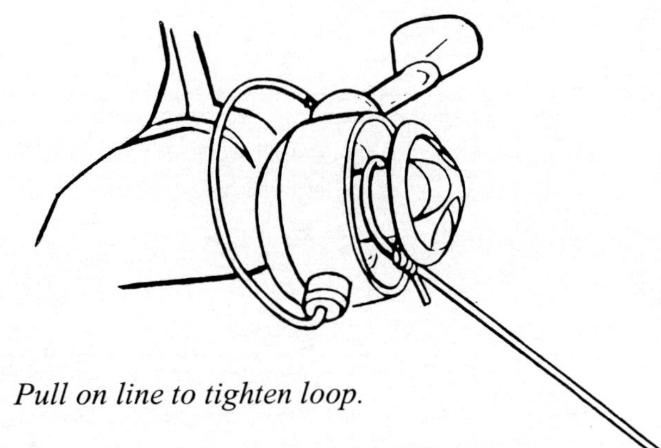

A. Pull on line to tighten loop.

This feature article presented by Stren.

Lb. Test	Stren Sensor	Original Stren	Stren Easy Cast	Magnathin	Super Tough	Powerbraid	High Impact Tournament	High Impact Monofilament	High Impact Mono Leader	High Impact Fluorocarbon Leader
2		.006		.004	.006		.006			.006
3										.006
4	.008	.008	.008	.006	.008		.008			.007
5				.007						
6	.010	.010	.010	.008	.010		.010			.008
8	.011	.011	.011	.010	.011		.012			.009
10	.012	.012	.012	.011	.012			.012		.011
12	.013	.013	.013	.012	.013		.014	.014		.013
14	.014	.014	.014		.014					
15						.011		.016		.015
16				.014			.016			
17	.016	.016	.016		.016					
20	.018	.018	.018	.016	.018		.018	.018	.018	.017
25		.020	.020		.020	.014		.020	.020	.019
30		.022	.022	.018	.022		.022	.022	.022	.020
35						.016				
40		.023		.022	.024			.026	.024	.024
50		.030		.024		.020	.028	.028	.026	.028
60									.031	.031
80		.039		.029			.035	.035	.035	.036
100									.039	.041
130				.038			.044	.044	.043	.047
150									.047	.055
200									.059	.063
250									.063	.072
300									.071	.080
400									.079	.093

Stren Fishing Lines
Remington Arms Company, Inc.
870 Remington Drive•Madison, NC 27025-0700•(336) 548-8700
www.stren.com

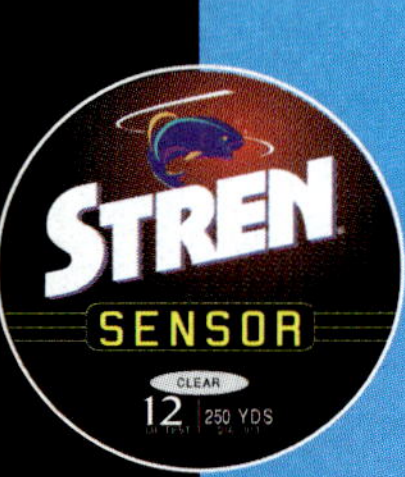

Stren Sensor™

This revolutionary low-stretch line has the handling, transparency, knot strength, and abrasion-resistant features of a monofilament plus the sensitivity and hook-setting advantages of "superlines."

Original Stren®

The line that makes it all balance out with the ideal combination of knot, shock and tensile strength, plus abrasion resistance, limpness, and controlled stretch.

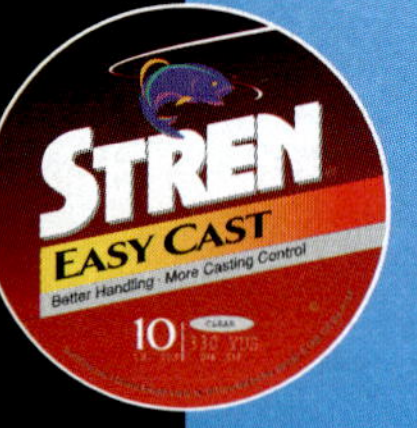

Stren Easy Cast™

Advanced Stren Easy Cast delivers the best of both worlds: superior strength and exceptional castability. It's the best casting, high-strength monofilament made.

Magnathin®

For all the advantages of thin line—handling, castability, and low-visibility—without compromising strength, Magnathin is the certain choice. Excellent for open water and light tackle fishing.

Super Tough™

When rugged conditions demand maximum abrasion resistance and incredible strength, this is the line that will pull that fish in. An extremely durable line with added insurance for heavy cover fishing.

Magnum 7/20™

This unique, oval-shaped line for bait-casting reels delivers the strength of 20 lb., yet it casts like 7-lb. test. It combines the aerodynamics of a light line with the abrasion resistance of a heavy line. It's an impressive combination that can't be ignored.

Powerbraid™

For hook-setting power, sensitivity, and pure muscle, this is one no-stretch line that rewrites the book. Its braided Kevlar® fibers make it stronger than nylon monofilament lines.

High Impact™

When the water is salty or the game is big, this is the family of monofilament, class line, braided Dacron,® and leader material that you want in your tackle box.

AMAZING
OUT-ROVER
MasterCard
VISA
Out-Rover Port
Out-Rover Starboard
Pat. #0337,6632
Pat. # 5,185,951
Replaces need for outriggers!!!
Eliminates Crossover on turns
Excellent surface fish teaser
Fish more lines with no fear of tangles
Pre-rigged
DIMENSIONS: 12" X 7"
1-888-OUTROVE Toll Free
7 days a week 24 hours a day.
Fax #. 1-954-975-0474
Office. 1-954-763-7271
Introductory Offer
$39.00 each or 2 for $70.00

Experience Brazil's World Record
Peacock Bass Fishing
Amazon Tours Inc.
For info & our agents:
www.peacockbassfishing.com
888-235-3874
Rio Negro Lodge
Luxury accommodations in the
heart of Brazil's World Redord
Peacock Bass Fishing
Amazon Queen
Our famous 82' floating hotel
offers the finest mobile fishing
accommodations in Brazil
Trout, tarpon, bonefish, tuna,
salmon, stripers, blues, billfish,
whatever.
QUALITY Abel PRODUCTS
The Super 6, Super 8, Super 10 and Super 12.
The Abel Reel • 165 Aviador Street • Camarillo, CA 93010 • Phone (805) 484-8789 • Fax (805) 482-0701
e-mail abelinc@gte.net • Visit our web site: http://www.Abelreels.com

SCOPINICH

This top of the line Tuna Chair represents the ultimate in strength and dependability. Only hand selected, highest grade teak is used throughout. All stainless steel hardware is used

NEW Scopinich's 316 mirror polished Stainless Steel Boat Package Includes 17" diameter, single spoke steering wheel, single level control and tuna door latch.

Scopinich custom table for your home, office or boat. We will customize your table with all types of wood veneers and hand painted inlays.

MODERATION

For the cigar smoker or just as a beautiful addition to your Boat, Home or office. These hand crafted Humidors come in Light or Dark wood finishes. Holds approximately 125 cigars. It measures 15"x10"x7.5".

SCOPINICH

SCOP BOAT WORKS, INC. AND
SCOPINICH FIGHTING CHAIRS, INC.
3716 S.E. Dixie HWY. Stuart, FL 34997
561-288-3111 • Fax· 561-288-1893
Website: www.scopinich.com • Email: scop@scopinich.com

BIG FISH. BIG POND.
THE ROLEX/IGFA INVITATIONAL
TOURNAMENT OF CHAMPIONS.

KONA, HAWAII. MARCH 2000.

For information on how your tournament can become a qualifying event for one of the world's great game fishing competitions, please call 1-800-442-HOOK.

ROLEX

Submariner Officially Certified Swiss Chronometer.
For the name and location of an Official Rolex Jeweler near you, please call 1-800-36ROLEX. Rolex, Oyster Perpetual and Submariner are trademarks.

The Broadbill Swordfish: An Illustrated History

By Bob Dunn and Peter Goadby

Few fish have captured the imagination of man like the broadbill swordfish.   This is equally true for the historian, seafarer, scientist or big game angler. For the nature historian some of the attraction lies in the direct lineage back to the very beginnings of natural science - a lineage documented in colourful detail by every important marine naturalist, from Aristotle to Nakamura.

Swordfish have a long and colorful history dating back at least to the ancient Greeks. After more than 2000 years, many of the fishes described by the ancient writers are virtually impossible to identify due to confusion caused by a diversity of popular names and the lack of any system of classification. Occasionally, however, the ancients described a fish whose physical characteristics were so distinctive that there can be no doubt as to its identity. Such a fish is the broadbill swordfish, *Xiphias gladius.*

The swordfish must have been sufficiently familiar to the early Greek fishermen for Aristotle (c.350 BC), the first of the great naturalists, to make no mention of the size or uniquely sword-shaped upper jaw, simply restricting his observations to its gill structure ("the swordfish has eight double ones") and its infestation with a parasite ("the gadfly which causes it such pain that the fish will leap out of the water, sometimes over the bulwarks of a vessel and falling back on its deck").

The first description of fishing for swordfish as it was practised in ancient times appears in the writings of the great geographer, Strabo, some 300 years or so after Aristotle. Here, as was often the case with the classical accounts, Strabo was reporting what had previously been observed by the Greek historian Polybius (204-c.125 BC). Unfortunately the first hand account of Polybius has not survived so it is necessary to rely upon Strabo's reporting of it. The fishing method described as employed in the

Broaching Broadbill, lithograph © 1940 W. Goadby Lawrence

Straits of Messina in Sicily is almost identical to that carried on two millennia later in the same area:

> "One look-out [on the rock Scylla?] directs the whole body of fishers, who are in a vast number of small boats, each furnished with two oars, and two men to each boat. One man rows, the other stands on the prow, spear in hand, while the look-out [on land] has to signal the appearance of a swordfish. This fish, when swimming, has about a third of its body above water. As it passes the boat, the fisher darts the spear from his hand, and when this [staff] is withdrawn, it leaves the sharp point with which it is furnished sticking in the flesh of the fish. This point is barbed, and loosely fixed to the spear for the purpose; it has a long end [of line] fastened to it; this they pay out to the wounded fish , till it is exhausted with its struggling and endeavors to escape. Afterwards they trail it to the shore, or unless it is too large or full-grown, haul it to the boat. If the spear [shaft?] should fall into the sea, it is not lost, for it is jointed of oak and pine, so that when the oak sinks on account of its weight, it causes the other end to rise , and thus is easily recovered. It sometimes happens that the rower is wounded, even through the boat, and such is the size of the sword with which the galeote [swordfish] is armed, such is the strength of the fish, and the method of capture, that it is not surpassed by the chase of the wild boar."

The fishing references are not the only intriguing aspects of Strabo's account. Given the source from which he is quoting, his reference to attacks by swordfish on vessels must represent the first in the recorded history of this fish. Over the next 2000 years there were to be many such accounts, yet eminent ichthyologists were to question their authenticity and, in at least one notable instance, refute them.

Pliny (c.50 AD) takes up the story of the swordfish, providing more evidence of its pugnacity. Citing an obscure source, Trebius Niger, he tells that "the swordfish has a pointed beak by which ships are pierced and sunk". That attacks by swordfish on vessels were far from

Fishing for Swordfish, Victor Meuniere
Les Grandes Peches, Paris 1871

uncommon is confirmed by Aelian (c.200 AD) when he describes, in an apparently unrelated incident, the fish and its use of this fearsome weapon:

> "No smith has forged this weapon which grows upon the fish, and Nature has made it sharp. And so, when these Sword-fish have attained a considerable size they even attack ships. And there are some who boast that they have seen a Bithynian vessel drawn up on shore in order that the keel which was suffering from age might receive the necessary attention, and fixed to the keel they saw the head of a swordfish. For the creature had planted the sword given it by Nature, in the vessel and when it attempted to withdraw, the whole of its body was rent from the neck owing to the force of the ship's onrush, while the sword remained fixed just as it entered originally."

Oppian (c.200AD), the last of our classical writers cited here, offers the most intriguing swordfish references of the period. Here the swordfish is recognized for the first time as a truly oceanic species, and apparently the recommended bait is the *Hippurus* or dolphin fish. Even the method of presenting the bait is described:

> "The Swordfish also men deceive by deadly hooks. But the doom of the swordfish is not like that of other fishes. For the fishermen do not put their bait upon the hooks, but the hook hangs from the line naked and without deceit, furnished with two recurved barbs, while some three palms above it they tie a soft white fish, fastening it skillfully by the tip of its mouth. When the

furious swordfish comes, straightway he rends the body of the fish with his fierce sword, and as the fish is wrent, its members slip down from the fastening and are entangled right about the barbs of the hook. But the fish perceives not the crooked guile but swallows the grievous bait and is caught and hauled up by the might of the man."

Unfortunately no illustration or further description of this unusual method of baiting for swordfish has survived. It is clear however, that, even at this early stage, the ancient fishermen understood the unique way in which the swordfish first stuns its prey by slashing with its sword before eating it. Oppian appears to be describing a deliberate ploy to ensure the swordfish is hooked, not when it first strikes the bait, but rather when it returns to swallow it.

Oppian goes on to describe a previously unreported strategem employed by the fishermen of the Tyrrhenian Sea and western Mediterranean:

> "Many are the devices which fishers contrive against the Swordfish, and those above all who fish the Tyrrhenian tract of sea and about the holy city of Massalia [Marseilles] and in the region of the Celts [Gauls]. For there, wondrous and not at all like fishes, range monster Swordfishes unapproachable. The fishermen fashion boats in the likeness of the Swordfishes themselves, with fishlike body and swords, and steer to meet the fish. The Swordfish shrinks not from the chase, believing that what he sees are not benched ships but other Swordfishes, the same race as himself, until the men encircle him on every side. Afterwards he perceives his folly when pierced by the three-pronged spear; and he has no strength to escape for all his desire but perforce is overcome. Many a time as he fights, the gallant fish with his sword pierces in his turn right through the belly of the ship; and the fishers with blows of brazen axe swiftly strike all his sword from his jaws, and it remains fast in the ship's wound like a rivet, while the fish, orphaned of his strength, is hauled in."

It appears that the Greek fishermen also used nets to trap the swordfish for Oppian goes on to describe:

> "Moreover when encircled in the crooked arms of the net, the greatly stupid swordfish perishes by his own folly. He leaps in his desire to escape but near at hand he is afraid of the plaited snare and shrinks back again.There is no weapon in his wits such as is set in his jaws, and like a coward remains aghast till they haul him forth upon the beach."

This apparent gullibility of the swordfish spawned the much quoted couplet from Oppian, "Nature her bounty to his mouth confined, gave him a sword but left unarm'd his mind" - which is found within this chapter in the first English translation in 1722 by John Jones. However, it is the reference to boats fashioned in the likeness of the swordfish which arouses the greater interest.

A 19th century writer, Victor Meunier, has discussed these Xiphias-shaped boats in his *Les Grandes Pêches* (Paris 1868 & 1871), at the same time providing illustrations. Another swordfish enthusiast of more recent times, E.W.Gudger, in *The Alleged Pugnacity of the*

Swordfish... (Calcutta 1940), has commented that while these intriguing illustrations are no doubt a product of the imagination of Meunier's artist [Riou], they offer a skilful and striking representation of what Oppian gives in his text.

Pêche de l'espadon.

Xiphias-shaped fishing boats, Victor Meuniere
Les Grandes Peches, Paris 1871

Pierre Belon (1551 & 1555) is credited with first pointing out the close resemblance of the swordfish to the tuna. He further supports his argument by relating how the people of Provence prepared these two fish in the same way for the table. The old writers had often grouped the swordfish with the whales simply because of their size. For them 'cetacean' simply meant large fish.

Guillaume Rondelet (1554) makes some important observations about the swordfish which can only have come from close personal examination of specimens. He notes that the sword lacks teeth, there are two pectoral fins ("at its gills"), one large anal fin ("in about the middle of its belly"), a large first dorsal fin ("in the middle of its back") and a second dorsal (" a smaller one closer to the tail"), the tuna-like caudal peduncle with a single median keel on each side ("the end of its body before the tail begins is broad and flat : in the middle of which a small swelling occurs") and of course the sword-shaped "pointed beak".

De Xiphia.

Rondelet's swordfish
Guillaume Rondelet, *Libri de Piscibus Marinis*, Lyons 1554

Despite the simplicity and brevity of Rondelet's description he has nonetheless identified all the major characteristics of the family of fishes later to be called *Xiphidae* (the only member of which is the swordfish) and its distinguishing features from the closely related *Istiophoridae* . Rondelet's detailed physical description and accompanying crude but recognisable figure are amongst the first in the literature.

His contemporary, Hippolyto Salviani (1554) provides an illustration which is more aesthetically pleasing - it is a copper engraving whereas Rondelet's was a simple woodcut - but both figures are inaccurate. Rondelet exaggerates the size of the rear dorsal fin.

Paradise on earth

Royalty, regents, poets and actors - Reid's Palace has been home from home for discerning travellers for more than 100 years. With its priveledged position on the cliff tops overlooking the beckoning Atlantic ocean, this luxury hotel offers all the style and comfort that ensures the perfect stay.

Peter Bristow, the renowned international skipper, is now resident on Madeira, and ready to guide you towards the best fishing around the island. The crew of the "Katherine B" are your best bet to land one of the giant Marlin or Tuna that hunt these famous waters

Team up with the people that know Madeira best!

For further information on Reid's Palace Sport Fishing package please contact:
Reid's Palace, Estrada Monumental,
P-9000 Funchal, Madeira, Portugal.
Tel: (351 91) 7007030 • Fax: (351 91) 7007177
Capt: Peter Bristow (351 91) 220334

65' MONTEREY '91/97. Tower. Fresh GM 16V96's. 33 Kts cruise. Luxurious interior. 4 Staterooms. Call Wayne Roman for complete details.

86' & 82' HATTERAS. Late Model. New to market. Long range. Ready for Islands.

72' DONZI 95. Tower. GM 16V92s. Only 650 Original hours. Luxurious interior.

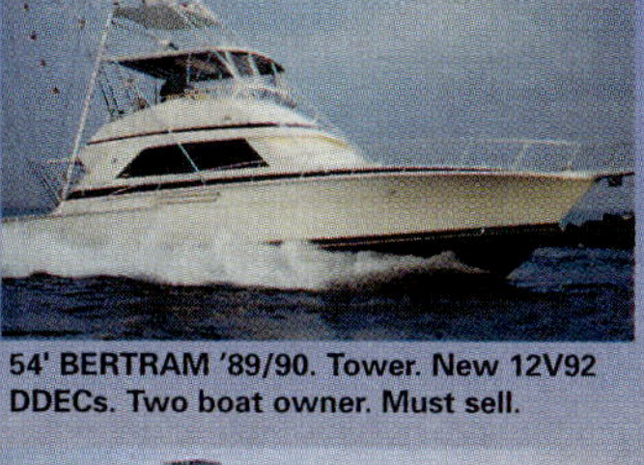
65' HATTERAS. Sistership. HT. Open FB. 65' HATTERAS '96/'97. Enclosed PH.

61' TRIBUTE '96. Tower 120183 MTU. Fast. 62' TRIBUTE '97. Tower 12 MANs. 35 kts. cruise.

Selected Listings

70' JIM SMITH '97 ..Fast. Long range capabilities.
65' DONZI '90................ Enclosed FB. 1692s. Mint.
63' GARLINGTON '90 .. 12 cyl MANs. 30 kt cruise.
61' JIM SMITH '90.....................12 cylinder MANs.
61' GARY DAVIS '98 ....New 2000 Series.
55' OCEAN YACHT '86 ....Tower. Captain maint.
55' OCEAN '84 ....Hard Top. GMs.
54' MONTEREY ....MANs. New Paint.
53' JARRETT BAY '93 ....6V92TA's. Low hours.
53' HATTERAS '78 .... Tower. Galley up.
53' OCEAN '97 ....Low hours. Sharp.
50' BERTRAM '90 ....12V71TI's. 29 knot cruise.
48' OCEAN '96 ....Fish equipped. Clean.
47' DAVIS '88 ....Left to be sold.
46' OCEAN..GMs. Tower.
46' MERRITT .... MANs. Fast. Mint.
45' RYBOVICH '94 ....6V92 DDECs.
44' SUNNY BRIGGS EXP. '97 Low hrs. 3176 CATS.
44' STRIKER '69/88 ....671TIs. Asking $235,000.
43' MERRITT '78 ..903s. Tower. New paint. Sharp.
43' EGG HARBOR '87 ....Price Reduced. Must sell.
40' GAMEFISHERMAN '91Tower. Volvos. Anxious.
40' NORSEMAN '98 ....Tower. Twin 3126 CATs.
40' MRD '98 ....Cold molded. 420 HP Cats.
37' RYBOVICH Tower. 3116 CATs. Open bulkhead.
37' CUBAVICH....Mint condition!. Owner anxious.
35' CABO '95/96 ....Low hours. Anxious seller.
34' PURSUIT '98 Twin Cummins. Extensive elecs.
31' BERTRAM '78 .... 504 Cummins. Must Sell.
30' PALM BEACH '86/95 ....CATS. Tower. Mint.

60' HATTERAS '98. Tower. 3412 Cats. Only 85 hours. Two 20 KW gens. Call Wayne Roman.

54' BERTRAM '89/90. Tower. New 12V92 DDECs. Two boat owner. Must sell.

54' HATTERAS '96. Hard top. 3412 CATs. 54' HATTERAS '97. MANs. Tower.

53' JARRETT BAY '92. Half tower. New paint. Fast. Economical. Priced to sell.

53' MONTEREY '79. Tower. 8V92's. Complete refit in '97. Price reduced.

44' GARLINGTON '96. CATs, 600 hp. Tower. Fast. Several Others.

48' GARLINGTON '87. Tower. Fast and beautiful. Great opportunity. Best mid-sized boat available. Call Wayne Roman.

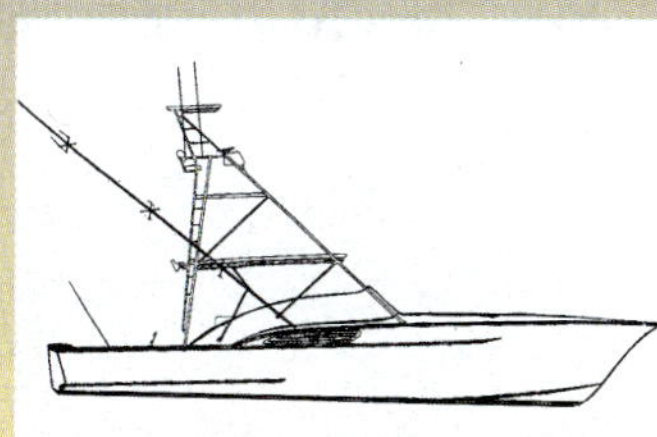
43' CAROLINA EXPRESS 1998. Full warranties. Powered by 3176 CATs, 660 hp. Fast & economical. Call for complete details.

WAYNE ROMAN YACHTS

We specialize in the world's finest _custom_ sport fisherman, and late model Hatteras, Viking, Bertram, Post, Ocean and many more.

Wayne Roman Yacht Sales, Inc.

155 E. Blue Heron Blvd.
Riviera Beach, FL 33404
Tel: 561-844-5000
Res: 561-743-4650
Fax: 561-844-0124

Brokers: Wayne Roman, Ben DeGutis, Noah V. Roman, Ross "Flash" Clark, Gary Pisano, Jim Hunter
http://www.justyachts.com/wayneroman

Your personal boat show, in your price range, any day of the week. 100's to choose from. Call for information.

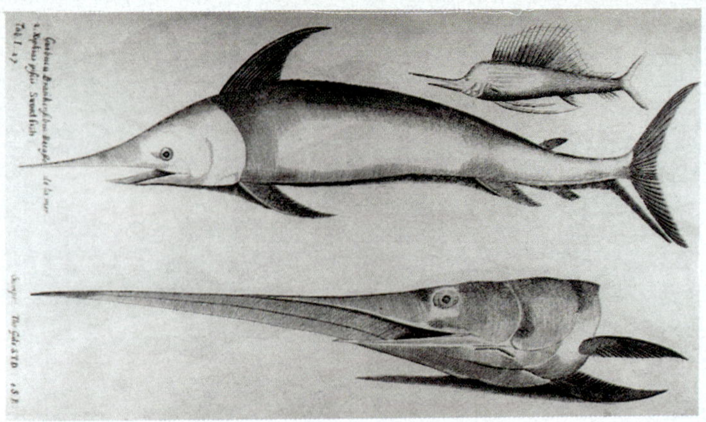

Salviani's swordfish reproduced by Francis Willughby
Willughby's Historia Piscium, Oxford 1686

Salviani commits the same error with the rear anal fin, which Rondelet omitted altogether.

Conrad Gesner (1558) added little to the sum of the swordfish scientific knowledge, offering instead a rambling compilation of Belon, Rondelet and the ancients. Indeed, he added to the confusion with the poor quality of his illustrations. The first of these was "drawn by a certain nobleman on the German ocean [which] although not particularly accurate I have placed here". Gesner's second illustration, with the exception of the snout, was not much better, despite having been depicted in part after direct observation of the remnant of a swordfish skeleton sent to him by Iovius Caius, an English doctor. In a later edition of Gesner's work, *Fischbuch* (1670) there was yet another figure of the swordfish which, while different again, was no more accurate and appears to have been copied from

his contemporary, Aldrovandi.

What Gesner's work lacked in scientific observation, was more than compensated by some intriguing gems he added to the growing swordfish lore. One of these was the claimed fear of swordfish for whales. Here he comments that:

> "The Xiphias having spotted a whale is overwhelmed by fear to such an extent that it drives its sword into the seabed or a rock or some other place of hiding under the water and thus remains with its head fixed. But the whale thinking that it is a log of wood or something similar, ignores it and swims past".

This bizarre account appears to be the origin for similar remarks by later writers, such as Jonston, who followed Gesner uncritically. Nearly 200 years later, two strange parallels to Gesner's story emerged on opposite sides of the Atlantic, both reported by eminent ichthyologists. In the first instance David Storer (1839) related how, when wounded with a harpoon, the North Atlantic swordfish had been known to dive with so much force towards the bottom of the sea, as to totally bury its sword in the sand or mud. Later, Francis Day (1880) reported an incident in 1862, involving a nine foot-long swordfish which was captured in Essex, England, after driving its sword into the mud and being captured alive.

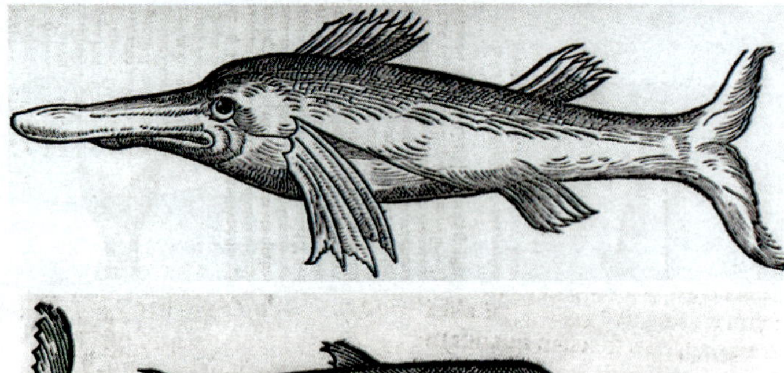

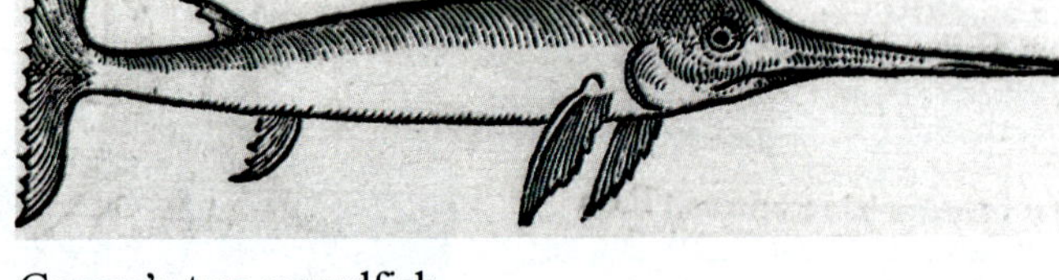

Gesner's two swordfish
Icones Animalium Aquatilium, Heidelberg 1605

The last of the great 16th century naturalists was Ulyssis Aldrovandi (1638), although his works were published posthumously in the first half of the 17th century. His illustration of the swordfish, a woodcut, does nothing to advance the state of the art. The fish is shown incorrectly with pelvic fins, a distorted first dorsal and grossly exaggerated rear dorsal fin. It is interesting to speculate on the origin of this particular figure, as it has clearly not been drawn from an actual specimen. Nor does it appear to have been borrowed from earlier writers. Yet Aldrovandi's fish appears to have been copied by Gesner (or his editor)for later editions of that writer's book on fishes, was certainly adopted by Jonston (1657) and, over 100 years later, by Duhamel (1769) and then indirectly by Bloch (1801).

Several 17th and early 18th century writers discussed the swordfish, three confirming Gesner's report of *Xiphias* being found in the seas off Germany. One source, Schelhammer (1707), provided an early analysis of the anatomy of the species working from specimens he had dissected at the German port of Kiel. Another, Schonevelde (1624), mentions a swordfish taken near Mecklenburg which was so large that it required two

WORLD-CLASS FISHING AT THE WORLD-FAMOUS HANNIBAL BANK

115' MOTHERSHIP. FLEET OF SPORTFISHING BOATS, COMPLETE ARRAY OF PENN INT'L EQUIPMENT, EXPERIENCED AND KNOWLEDGEABLE LOCAL CAPTAINS, AND THE BEST FISHING IN THE WORLD!

PANAMA'S ONLY LIVE-ABOARD MOTHERSHIP!

BOOKINGS ARE LIMITED, SO DON'T MISS THE BOAT!

CALL TODAY!

1-800-733-4742

VISIT OUR WEBSITE AT
WWW.COIBAEXPLORER.COM

strong horses to draw it from the water. The body without the sword was eleven feet long, the sword three feet and the tail two feet wide.

The compiler Jonston (1657) contents himself with summarising the views of the ancients and the 16th century naturalists. His figure of the swordfish, while elegantly formed, is an almost exact copy of that of Aldrovandi thus perpetuating that writer's errors.

Willoughby (1686) appears to have examined several specimens from both England and Italy and he described the dorsal fin as "one fin on its back starting from the upper corner of its gills and continuing almost to the tail". Yet, despite the obvious discrepancy, he was content to reproduce, without further comment, Salviani's illustration of the fish with its two, clearly distinct, dorsal fins.

With the exception of Artedi's improved description, for the greater part of the 18th century there was little advancement in the scientific knowledge of the swordfish. The lack of a suitable illustration continued. Indeed, the confusion was further compounded by yet another wildly inaccurate figure by Pennant (1770), who had, in turn, been provided with the illustration by the Polish naturalist, Jacob Klein.

It remained for Artedi and Linneaus to finally assign the swordfish its name in perpetuity, *Xiphias gladius* , thus incorporating the ancient Greek word *Xiphos* and the Latin equivalent *Gladius* both meaning sword. By the time of Linneaus' 13th edition of *Systema Naturae* , compiled by Gmelin in 1788, some appreciation had begun to emerge of the wide geographic distribution of the swordfish. Finally there was scientific acknowledgement of its inhabiting the waters of the Americas as well as the Southern ocean. Linneaus disclosed his sources for this knowledge as Catesby and Marcgrave. If he had simply been relying upon these two authorities he might well have been in error. Catesby's reference to the swordfish in his *Natural History of Carolina, Florida and the Bahama Islands* (London 1731), was probably based on anecdotal evidence, as the species was not described or figured. Equally, reliance on Marcgrave, based on his reference in *Historia Naturalis Brasiliae* (Amsterdam1648), would have proved unjustified as this naturalist was describing, albeit for the first time, a related species, the sailfish. In fact Linneaus was on stronger ground as he is known to have received from his American friend, Dr Garden, a portion of a *Xiphias* bill for examination. Dr Garden's swordfish had been found on the Florida coast.

The scientific acknowledgement in the 18th century of the swordfish's international status had been anticipated since the early 17th century by Cartenszoon, Josselyn, Dampier and other lay observers. These intrepid ocean voyagers had described sightings, and in some cases captures, of swordfish and like sea creatures in their widely read published accounts. In hindsight these accounts must be considered inconclusive as to species given the knowledge we now possess on the diverse habitat of the marlins and sailfishes.

The earliest allusion in the literature to the swordfish in the Western Atlantic occurred in Josselyn's *Account of Two Voyages to New England* (1674) where he decribed on the twentieth day at sea the capture of a great fish "having a long, strong and sharp finn like a sword-blade on the top of his head, with which he pierced our ship, and broke it off with striving to get loose, one of our sailors dived and brought it aboard." In his *History of the Sword Fishes* (New York1883) Goode gave details of an even earlier human contact with the swordfish which has special interest for Americans. Apparently Columbus returned from his voyage of discovery to the Americas with the sword of a *Xiphias*. This is now preserved in an old church (Goode did not say which one) in the ancient city of Siena in Northern Italy, the birthplace of Columbus.

In 1782, Bloch finally provided not only an artistically pleasing but also, reasonably accurate scientific figure of the swordfish. However, if the artist has correctly represented the extended first dorsal fin, the specimen must have been a juvenile.

Bloch's figure, the best known and most copied of all swordfish illustrations. M.E. Bloch, *Ichthyologie ou Histoire Naturelle Des Poissons*, Berlin 1796.

Bloch concluded by criticising all figures of the swordfish offered by earlier writers. Ironically Bloch himself later fell into much the same pitfall as had those he criticised. In the revised posthumous edition of his work edited by his friend Schneider (1801), there appeared a claimed new species of swordfish christened *Xiphias imperator* . The story of how Bloch was misled was later pieced together by Cuvier in the epic *Histoire Naturelle des Poissons* (1828-49).

"Bloch, in his posthumous *Systema Ichthyologie* introduced a species of Xiphias that he names *imperator* and which he bases solely on an illustration by Duhamel given as that of a fish, fished for at the mouth of the Loire in 1777, that used to be exhibited at Nantes for money. Duhamel actually recounts how this drawing was sent to him from Nantes, with this information, by a Mr Bonamy; but we can affirm that Bonamy did not do his drawing from nature, and that he was content to copy that of Aldrovandi, given as a representation of the ordinary Xiphias. What one has seen in several other circumstances, happened here. Aldrovandi gave, as for lots of other species, a false illustration."

Some later writers, influenced by Goode, were of the view that Bloch's *X. imperator* was in fact an intelligible, but unintentional, early description of the Mediterranean spearfish, *Tetrapturus belone.*. This view has not been sustained however, and Cuvier's explanation is now generally accepted.

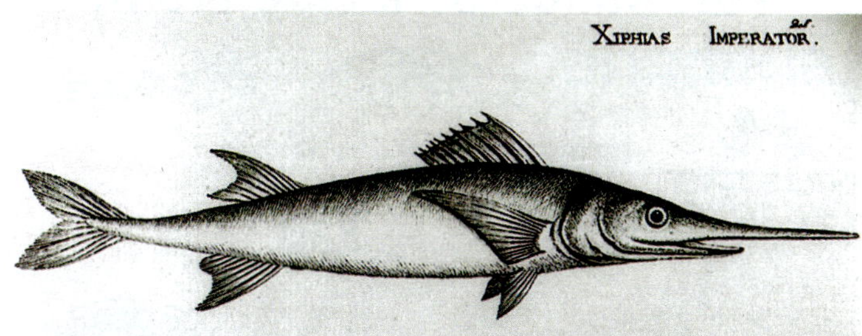

Bloch's fictitious Xiphias imperator. M.E. Bloch & J.O. Schneider, *Systema Ichthyologie*, Berlin 1801

Lacapede's *Histoire des Poissons* (Paris 1798) was prepared at the height of the French Revolution under difficult circumstances which imposed isolation from his contemporaries. His work was subject to much duplication of species, particularly with regard to foreign species. His writings on the common swordfish suffered less in this regard than for related species such as the sailfish. His illustration of *Xiphias*, with its extended dorsal fin, appears to be of a juvenile specimen.

The mystery of the changing dorsal was finally explained by Cuvier(1831) who had by then been able to examine a number of specimens at the markets of Nice, Toulon, Genoa and Naples. Supporting his claim with beautifully engraved figures of juvenile and adult specimens, he wrote:

> "It has but one dorsal which rises both from the front and back, and the middle of which wears out with age, so that it appears to have two."

Dealing with the pugnacity of the swordfish and its alleged predeliction for attacking boats, Cuvier pointed out:

> "So remarkable an animal in size and conformation as the swordfish could not have been unknown at any period. All the ancients speak of it in a manner which clearly proves their intimate acquaintance with it. They describe its weapon, the blows which it inflicts, the combats which it sustains, the attacks which are made upon it, the strategems by which it is lured to destruction. . . Pliny relates that vessels were pierced by the beak of the Xiphias and sprung a leak in consequence. This fact has been contested and yet one [attack] exactly similar is recorded by Cornide, of a Spanish vessel off the coast of Gallicia, which was on the point of perishing from having been pierced by one of these fish and he assures us that the plank and the beak which was implanted in it, are preserved in the Royal Cabinet of Madrid. We may well conceive that such accidents cannot happen except to slight and old vessels. But it frequently occurrs that the beaks of these fish are found broken in the keels of ships."

After only fleeting references to swordfish in American waters by Catesby and Garden and later, a brief comment by Mitchill in *American Monthly Magazine* (1818), the first extended account appeared in Jerome Smith's *Natural History of the Fishes of Massachusetts* (Boston 1833). In his discussion of the fish, Smith, like so many writers before him, was fascinated by its pugnacity and he provides the following colorful account:

> "This [fish] is evidently possessed of a highly irritable disposition and therefore appears to be constantly involved in perilous and fearful difficulties; it is voracious and yet without teeth; and though it seems to be the knight errant of the deep, by meddling with the affairs of others in which it has no personal interest, it also appears at other times to be at open war with whatever moves in the same liquid element. . .
>
> On a calm sunny day during last summer, as a pilot was leisurely rowing his little skiff over the glassy bosom of the gently swelling waves, he was suddenly roused from his seat by the plunge of a swordfish thrusting his long spear more than three feet up through the bottom of the slender bark; when the pilot with that presence of mind for which the whole fraternity are distinguished, broke it off on a level with the floor, by the butt of an oar, before the submarine assassin had time to withdraw his fearfully offensive weapon."

A few years later the swordfish was formally admitted to the American faunal list with its inclusion in Storer's *Fishes, Reptiles and Birds of Massachusetts* (Boston 1839). Storer's account is of particular interest as it includes one of the earliest descriptions of fishing for swordfish off Martha's Vineyard.

"It is generally discovered by the projection of its dorsal fin above the surface of the water as it is pursuing shoals of mackerel, upon which it feeds, about 15 or 20 miles from the shore of Martha's Vineyard. The fishermen capture it by means of an instrument called the "lily iron" from the form of its shafts or wings which resemble the leaves of a lily. This instrument is thrown like a harpoon with great force into the fish, the attempt always being made to wound the animal in front of the dorsal fin. . . When unmolested it not infrequently is observed to spring several times its length forwards, several feet above the surface of the water."

On the other side of the Atlantic, several British naturalists had written of the swordfish since Pennant in 1769. These included Shaw (1803) who was content to repeat what Bloch had said, including his figure. On the basis that the swordfish was an occasional visitor to British waters, it was admitted to British faunal lists with only brief comment by Turton (1807), Leach (1818) and Fleming (1828). Yarrell (1836) reminded the reader that Sibbald (c.1700) had first drawn attention to the presence of the swordfish in Scottish waters. Yarrell went on to offer a good summary of the contemporary knowledge of the fish, including the curious account of Daniel in his

Swordfish attacking a whale
Victor Meuniere, *Les Grandes Pechês*, Paris 1871

Supplement to the Rural Sports (London 1813) in which a man was fatally struck by a swordfish while bathing in the Severn river near Worcester, well above the tidal limit of the salt water. According to Daniel the fish was caught immediately afterwards so that its identity could be established beyond doubt. If this account is correct, and no authorities have subsequently challenged it, then it provides the first evidence since Aelian 1600 years previously, that the swordfish, albeit rarely, enters fresh water. An even choicer morsel of swordfish lore was offered by Yarrell when he related the second hand report of an encounter between a swordfish and a thresher shark with a whale. In light of the support it provided for similar stories by Gesner and others, the account is worth quoting in full.

The American swordfisherman
G.B. Goode, *Materials for a History
of Sword Fishes*, 1883

Harpooning swordfish
Harper's Magazine, date unknown

"Captain Crow, in a work lately published, relates the following as having occurred on a voyage to Memel:- 'One morning during a calm, when near the Hebrides, all hands were called up at 3am to witness a battle between several of the fish called Thrashers [sic] or Fox Sharks and some Swordfish on one side, and an enormous whale on the other. It was in the middle of summer, and the weather being clear and the fish close to the vessel, we had a fine opportunity of witnessing the contest. As soon as the whale's back appeared above the water, the thrashers springing several yards into the air, descended with great violence upon the object of their rancour, and inflicted upon him the most severe slaps with their long tails, the sound of which resembled the reports of muskets fired at a distance. The Swordfish, in their turn, attacked the distressed whale, stabbing from below; and thus beset on all sides and wounded, when the poor creature appeared, the water around him was dyed with blood. In this manner they continued tormenting and wounding him for many hours, until we lost sight of him; and, I have no doubt, they in the end completed his destruction."

Stories like these, together with those of Gesner and the ancients, contributed no doubt to the mythology of hostility between swordfish and whales Even that most eminent of 19th century British ichthyologists, Albert Günther, in his *Introduction to the Study of Fishes* (Edinburgh 1880) accepted, without apparent question, that swordfish frequently attack whales. Most modern authorities however, for example Goode (1883), Holder (1909) and Norman (1937), held the view that the so-called eye witness accounts had in fact observed attacks by killer whales. The last word on the swordfish/whale myth should be reserved for Gudger (1940) who, together with Goode, was responsible for accumulating a vast amount of swordfish lore from ancient through to modern times. He left no doubt of his views on the subject.

"By whom the time-honored story was first told - that the swordfish, either by himself or in league with the thresher shark, attacks the whale

Now You Can Tell The Tide As Easily As The Time. ^{SM}

This remarkable instrument is the *Professional Series* edition of our classic Tidal Chronometer, the first quartz sport watch to tell the tide. And it's going to change the lives of anyone with an interest in water-oriented activity. The Kriëger Tidal Chronometer display actually shows you the present state of the tides and also duplicates the shape of the moon. *You'll be able to tell how many hours until the next high tide and forecast Spring and Neap Tides.*

The Kriëger Tidal Chronometer is a rugged professional instrument able to withstand the severest conditions of the marine environment. This hand-crafted Swiss Chronometer features a sapphire crystal, and a screw-down crown for water resistance to 600ft (200M). A solid steel watch casing, machined from a solid block of stainless steel and hand polished to a matte finish. The matching bracelet with a locking safety clasp integrates beautifully. And each serial numbered quartz movement is independently tested and certified for shock resistance, accuracy and precision under extreme conditions by *Contrôle Officiel Suisse Chronomètres,* and has earned the distinction of being an Officially Certified Swiss Chronometer. A Chronometer certificate with individual test results accompanies each Kriëger. With its brilliant engraved dial and rotating bezel, 18kt gold tone accents, the Kriëger Tidal Chronometer commands attention everywhere it goes.

Shown: Professional Series, on the left, M929T.4.56 with blue and white dial, on the right M929T.4.4, black dial, both model are suggested retail price of $1,395. Other models available.

KRIËGER®
CHRONOMÈTRES SUISSES

Artist's impression of swordfish attacking a dory
Charles F. Holder, *Marvels of Animal Life*, New York 1885

- cannot be stated. Nor can it be foreseen by whom it will be last told, for like the brook 'it goes on forever'. That the thresher shark, despite its small mouth, sometimes attacks a whale is entirely possible but not probable. But that any of the swordfish tribe do so is preposterous. The adult swordfish is toothless, the adult spearfishes practically so. The swordfish could not take a bite out of the whale if it tried. Indeed the shark would surely make a meal of the swordfish, its alleged partner, rather than of the whale".

That the broadbill swordfish should become the target of sportsmen, was at the same time curious yet strangely predictable. Here was a fish whose pugnacity was legendary, whose attacks on vessels had been documented with almost monotonous regularity throughout many centuries of literature. Yet, as early as the 18th century, the first hints began to emerge, as when Brydone (1774) compared the slaughter of tunnies in the *tonnares* of the Sicilian fishermen with the "much more noble diversion" of taking the swordfish with the harpoon. He further commented that "as these fish are commonly of a great size and strength, they will sometimes run for hours after they are struck and afford excellent sport". One of the earliest allusions to 'sport fishing' for swordfish with the harpoon dates back to the American Civil War and appears in an obscure book by Charles Lanman *Recollections of Curious Characters and Pleasant Places* . Although published in Edinburgh in 1881, it referred to an episode which took place in 1864 about seventy miles from Block Island, off the coast of New England.

"As gamefish, the salmon and the striped bass must look to their laurels for in these warlike times the swordfish may chance to supercede them in gaining the affections of the more daring sportsmen. Possibly, it is only equalled by that wild and dangerous sport which was once practised in the waters of South Carolina by the late William Elliott while hunting the devil-fish. As is the case with every kind of fishing, the manifold charms associated with the capture of the swordfish are what gives the sport its chief zest. Not the least of the attractions is the appetite, born of hard exercise and bracing air, which makes the coarse fare of the sailor a real luxury. But when you recall the wayward wanderings of your little vessel out on the blue and lonely ocean, the wild and stormy nights, the heavy fogs forcing the sea to wear a placid aspect, the thousand and one wonders of the deep which constantly cross your pathway, the moan of the sea during the long leaden twilights, and the romantic stories of the mariners - all these things, in their reality, make a deep impression on the mind, and are ever remembered with pleasure."

In his *American Fishes* (Philadelphia 1888), Goode described the 'sport' of catching swordfish in more prosaic terms, likening it to the hunting of large land animals.

"The pursuit of the swordfish is much more exciting than ordinary fishing . . . and partakes more of the nature of the chase. There is no slow or careful baiting and patient waiting and no disappointment caused by the accidental capture of worthless "bait-stealers". The game is seen and followed, and outwitted by wary tactics and killed by strength of arm and skill. The Sword-fish is a powerful antagonist and sometimes sends his pursuer's vessel into harbour leaking and almost sinking from injuries which he has inflicted."

Despite the sense of anticipation in Lanman's account, anticipation of a grand new sport in the making, it was nearly 50 years before the first broadbill swordfish was captured by William Boschen employing the new technology of rod and reel. During this period there was to be a revolution culminating in the rebirth of the sport of sea fishing - a revolution not only in tackle and technique, but in angling attitude. A revolution which was to bring in its wake much progress in the scientific knowledge of the great oceanic fishes. It is indeed fitting that much of this knowledge was to be gained as a direct result of the experiments of the pioneering gamefish anglers and the many specimens they provided. How fitting also it was that a great fish, known by man as long as he had roamed the seas, should feature in the vanguard of this revolution.

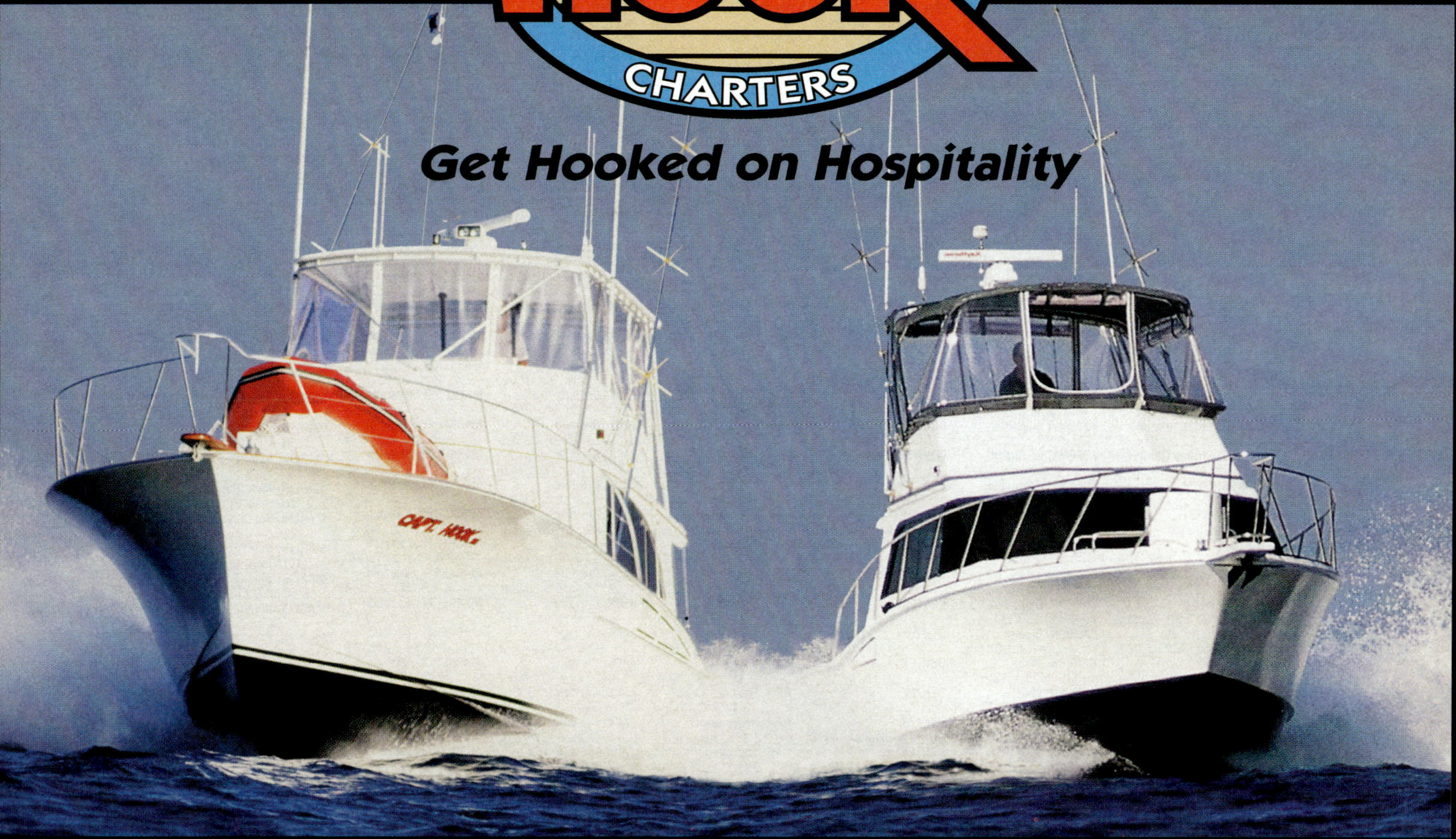

Over the years ANDE Monofilament has held 1,000's records as of 12-15-98. We thank all our anglers

*TIE

Line Class & Fly Rod

ALBACORE 50 lb., 0 oz., M-4
ALBACORE 68 lb., 12 oz., M-12
ALBACORE 71 lb., 12 oz., M-16
ALBACORE 83 lb., 12 oz., M-50
ALBACORE 26 lb., 0 oz., W-6
AMBERJACK, Greater 46 lb., 8 oz., M-4
AMBERJACK, Greater 90 lb., 0 oz., M-12
AMBERJACK, Greater 108 lb., 0 oz., M-16
AMBERJACK, Greater 2 lb., 4 oz., Tip.-2
AMBERJACK, Greater 36 lb., 8 oz., Tip.-8
AMBERJACK, Greater 22 lb., 4 oz., W-2
AMBERJACK, Greater 23 lb., 8 oz., W-4
AMBERJACK, Greater 56 lb., 12 oz., W-6
AMBERJACK, Greater 71 lb., 6 oz., W-8
AMBERJACK, Greater 99 lb., 8 oz., W-20
AMBERJACK, Greater 112 lb., 0 oz., W-30
AMBERJACK, Greater 87 lb., 0 oz., W-80
AMBERJACK, Greater 85 lb., 0 oz., W-130
BARRACUDA, Great 32 lb., 8 oz., M-4
BARRACUDA, Great 53 lb., 0 oz., M-6
BARRACUDA, Great 79 lb., 5 oz., M-30
BARRACUDA, Great 84 lb., 14 oz., M-80
BARRACUDA, Great 20 lb., 4 oz., Tip.-2
BARRACUDA, Great 25 lb., 8 oz., Tip.-4
BARRACUDA, Great 35 lb., 0 oz., W-2
BARRACUDA, Great 70 lb., 8 oz., W-20
BARRAMUNDI 28 lb., 15 oz., Tip.-16
BASS, Black Sea 6 lb., 13 oz., M-16
BASS, Black Sea 9 lb., 0 oz., M-20
BASS, Black Sea 9 lb., 8 oz., M-30
BASS, Black Sea 2 lb., 3 oz., Tip-4
BASS, Black Sea 1 lb., 10 oz., Tip.-8
BASS, Black Sea 2 lb., 3 oz., W-8
BASS, Black Sea 4 lb., 14 oz., W-16
BASS, Black Sea 5 lb., 2 oz., W-20
BASS, Giant Sea 91 lb., 8 oz., M-8
BASS, Giant Sea 77 lb., 11 oz., M-16
BASS, Giant Sea 343 lb., 0 oz., W-30
BASS, Kelp (Calico) 5 lb., 11 oz., M-2
BASS, Kelp (Calico) 7 lb., 2 oz., M-4
BASS, Kelp (Calico) 8 lb., 9 oz., M-6
BASS, Kelp (Calico) 10 lb., 10 oz., M-10
BASS, Kelp (Calico) 11 lb., 12 oz., M-16
BASS, Kelp (Calico) 10 lb., 4 oz., Tip.-2
BASS, Kelp (Calico) 1 lb., 1 oz., Tip.-2
BASS, Kelp (Calico) 5 lb., 4 oz., Tip.-12
BASS, Kelp (Calico) 3 lb., 14 oz., Tip.-20
BASS, Kelp (Calico) 3 lb., 2 oz., W-6
BASS, Kelp (Calico) 5 lb., 11 oz., W-8
BASS, Rock 2 lb., 0 oz., 2
BASS, Rock 2 lb., 0 oz., 4
BASS, Rock 2 lb., 8 oz., 6
BASS, Rock 3 lb., 0 oz., 8
BASS, Rock 1 lb., 8 oz., Tip.-2
BASS, Smallmouth 7 lb., 0 oz., 2
BASS, Smallmouth 6 lb., 8 oz., 6
BASS, Smallmouth 5 lb., 0 oz., Tip.-6
BASS, Smallmouth 5 lb., 8 oz., Tip.-12
BASS, Smallmouth 5 lb., 0 oz., Tip.-8
BASS, Spotted 7 lb., 5 oz., 4
BASS, Spotted 9 lb., 4 oz., 8
BASS, Striped 21 lb., 0 oz., M-2
BASS, Striped 41 lb., 8 oz., M-8
BASS, Striped 69 lb., 0 oz., M-16
BASS, Striped 78 lb., 8 oz., M-20
BASS, Striped 76 lb., 0 oz., M-50
BASS, Striped 70 lb., 0 oz., M-80
BASS, Striped 12 lb., 0 oz., Tip.-2
BASS, Striped 19 lb., 8 oz., Tip-4
BASS, Striped 46 lb., 12 oz., W-6
BASS, Striped 48 lb., 9 oz., W-12
BASS, Striped (landl.) 32 lb., 0 oz., 2
BASS, Striped (landl.) 44 lb., 0 oz., 4
BASS, Striped (landl.) 29 lb., 8 oz., Tip.-2
BASS, White 3 lb., 2 oz., Tip-12
BLUEFISH 17 lb., 4 oz., M-2
BLUEFISH 20 lb., 0 oz., M-4
BLUEFISH 20 lb., 1 oz., M-6
BLUEFISH 20 lb., 0 oz., M-8
BLUEFISH 19 lb., 12 oz., Tip.-16
BLUEFISH 12 lb., 0 oz., Tip.-12
BLUEFISH 18 lb., 11 oz., Tip.-20
BLUEFISH *14 lb., 9 oz., W-2
BLUEFISH 16 lb., 12 oz., W-4
BLUEFISH 20 lb., 0 oz., W-8
BLUEFISH 19 lb., 12 oz., W-12
BLUEFISH *21 lb., 11 oz., Tip.-20
BLUEFISH 23 lb., 15 oz., W-50
BLUEGILL 1 lb., 8 oz., 6
BLUEGILL *1 lb., 4 oz., 6
BLUEGILL 1 lb., 12 oz., Tip.-2
BLUEGILL 1 lb., 8 oz., Tip.-12
BLUEGILL 1 lb., 6 oz., Tip.-16
BONEFISH 11 lb., 12 oz., M-2
BONEFISH 13 lb., 8 oz., M-4
BONEFISH 13 lb., 15 oz., M-6
BONEFISH 15 lb., 12 oz., M-8
BONEFISH 10 lb., 0 oz., W-2
BONEFISH 12 lb., 6 oz., W-4
BONEFISH 14 lb., 4 oz., W-8
BONEFISH 12 lb., 14 oz., W-16
BONITO, Atlantic *10 lb., 7 oz., M-6
BONITO, Atlantic 17 lb., 15 oz., M-30
BONITO, Atlantic 10 lb., 9 oz., Tip.-8
BONITO, Atlantic 9 lb., 5 oz., W-8
BONITO, Atlantic 14 lb., 7 oz., W-16
BONITO, Pacific 12 lb., 10 oz., M-6
BONITO, Pacific 13 lb., 2 oz., M-8
BONITO, Pacific 14 lb., 12 oz., M-12
BONITO, Pacific 12 lb., 0 oz., Tip.-8
BONITO, Pacific 7 lb., 6 oz., Tip.16
BONITO, Pacific 10 lb., 3 oz., Tip.-20
BONITO, Pacific 9 lb., 8 oz., W-8
BOWFIN 9 lb., 10 oz., 2
BOWFIN 11 lb., 8 oz., Tip.-6
BOWFIN 6 lb., 4 oz., Tip.-8
BOWFIN 7 lb., 15 oz., Tip.-12
BOWFIN 6 lb., 8 oz., Tip.-16
BOWFIN 8 lb., 5 oz., Tip.-20
BUFFALO, Bigmouth 9 lb., 0 oz., Tip.-4
BUFFALO, Bigmouth 11 lb., 0 oz., Tip.-6
BUFFALO, Bigmouth 5 lb., 0 oz., Tip.-12
BUFFALO, Bigmouth 3 lb., 12 oz., Tip.-16
BURBOT 5 lb., 8 oz., 16
CARP, Common 29 lb., 8 oz., Tip.-20
CATFISH, Blue 25 lb., 0 oz., 2
CATFISH, Blue 47 lb., 0 oz., 4
CATFISH, Blue 111 lb., 0 oz., 30
CATFISH, Blue 8 lb., 5 oz., Tip.-2
CATFISH, Blue 28 lb., 11 oz., Tip.-6
CATFISH, Blue 14 lb., 9 oz., Tip.-8
CATFISH, Blue 16 lb., 7 oz., Tip.-12
CATFISH, Blue 42 lb., 0 oz., Tip.-16
CATFISH, Blue 18 lb., 11 oz., Tip.-20
CATFISH, Channel 10 lb., 12 oz., Tip.-2
CATFISH, Flathead 33 lb., 0 oz., 2
CATFISH, Flathead 69 lb., 0 oz., 80
CATFISH, White 7 lb., 4 oz., 6
CHAR, Arctic 17 lb., 4 oz., 2
CHAR, Arctic 21 lb., 0 oz., 4
CHAR, Arctic 16 lb., 0 oz., Tip.-20
COBIA 50 lb., 11 oz., M-4
COBIA 67 lb., 0 oz., M-6
COBIA 75 lb., 2 oz., M-8
COBIA 98 lb., 0 oz., M-12
COBIA 128 lb., 12 oz., M-16
COBIA 114 lb., 8 oz., M-20
COBIA 114 lb., 12 oz., M-50
COBIA 22 lb., 14 oz., Tip.-2
COBIA 37 lb., 3 oz., Tip.-4
COBIA 62 lb., 3 oz., Tip.-20
COBIA 36 lb., 2 oz., W-2
COBIA 66 lb., 0 oz., W-8
COBIA 75 lb., 4 oz., W-12
COBIA 70 lb., 6 oz., W-20
COBIA 103 lb., 8 oz., W-80
COD, Atlantic 85 lb., 0 oz., M-50
COD, Pacific 16 lb., 0 oz., M-4
COD, Pacific 17 lb., 0 oz., M-6
COD, Pacific 13 lb., 0 oz., M-8
COD, Pacific 17 lb., 0 oz., M-12
COD, Pacific 4 lb., 2 oz., Tip.-4
COD, Pacific 5 lb., 0 oz., Tip.-6
COD, Pacific 4 lb., 7 oz., Tip.-8
COD, Pacific 8 lb., 0 oz., Tip.-12
COD, Pacific 8 lb., 13 oz., Tip.-16
COD, Pacific 4 lb., 8 oz., Tip.-20
COD, Pacific 12 lb., 0 oz., W-4
COD, Pacific 15 lb., 0 oz., W-6
COD, Pacific 16 lb., 0 oz., W-12
COD, Pacific 19 lb., 0 oz., W-16
COD, Pacific 24 lb., 0 oz., W-20
COD, Pacific 10 lb., 12 oz., W-30
COD, Pacific 21 lb., 0 oz., W-50
CONGER 110 lb., 8 oz., M-50
CONGER 32 lb., 2 oz., W-8
CONGER 46 lb., 0 oz., W-12
CONGER 79 lb., 8 oz., W-50
CRAPPIE, Black 2 lb., 2 oz., Tip.-4
CRAPPIE, White 3 lb., 9 oz., 2
DENTEX 9 lb., 5 oz., M-2
DENTEX 14 lb., 5 oz., M-4
DENTEX 10 lb., 2 oz., M-6
DENTEX 17 lb., 10 oz., M-12
DENTEX 17 lb., 8 oz., M-16
DENTEX 14 lb., 1 oz., M-20
DENTEX 9 lb., 7 oz., W-16
DENTEX 10 lb., 14 oz., W-20
DOLLY VARDEN 5 lb., 8 oz., Tip.-4
DOLPHIN 52 lb., 14 oz., M-4
DOLPHIN 58 lb., 0 oz., M-6
DOLPHIN 77 lb., 2 oz., M-12
DOLPHIN 62 lb., 4 oz., M-16
DOLPHIN 76 lb., 8 oz., M-20
DOLPHIN 23 lb., 0 oz., Tip.-4
DOLPHIN 19 lb., 13 oz., Tip.-6
DOLPHIN 64 lb., 8 oz., W-8
DOLPHIN 82 lb., 2 oz., W-80
DORADO 37 lb., 0 oz., 20
DORADO 30 lb., 6 oz., 50
DRUM, Black 66 lb., 0 oz., M-6
DRUM, Black 12 lb., 4 oz., Tip.-2
DRUM, Black 28 lb., 14 oz., Tip.-6
DRUM, Black 33 lb., 0 oz., Tip.-16
DRUM, Black 49 lb., 0 oz., Tip.-20
DRUM, Black 12 lb., 0 oz., W-2
DRUM, Black 18 lb., 8 oz., W-8
DRUM, Black 80 lb., 8 oz., W-20
DRUM, Black 111 lb., 0 oz., W-80
DRUM, Freshwater 11 lb., 5 oz., 6
DRUM, Freshwater 10 lb., 4 oz., Tip.-20
DRUM, Red 41 lb., 8 oz., M-2
DRUM, Red 52 lb., 5 oz., M-4
DRUM, Red 46 lb., 0 oz., M-6
DRUM, Red 59 lb., 0 oz., M-16
DRUM, Red 90 lb., 0 oz., M-30
DRUM, Red 27 lb., 8 oz., Tip.-4
DRUM, Red 39 lb., 4 oz., Tip.-20
DRUM, Red 36 lb., 12 oz., W-2
DRUM, Red 40 lb., 0 oz., W-4
DRUM, Red 43 lb., 8 oz., W-6
DRUM, Red 65 lb., 0 oz., W-20
DRUM, Red 34 lb., 0 oz., W-80
FLOUNDER, Summer 4 lb., 2 oz., Tip.-2
FLOUNDER, Summer 3 lb., 8 oz., Tip.-12
FLOUNDER, Summer 18 lb., 15 oz., W-20
GAR, Florida 2 lb., 12 oz., 6
GAR, Florida 7 lb., 4 oz., 8
GAR, Florida 2 lb., 11 oz., Tip.-6
GAR, Florida 3 lb., 10 oz., Tip.-8
GAR, Florida 2 lb., 13 oz., Tip.-16
GAR, Florida 2 lb., 4 oz., Tip.-20
GAR, Alligator 34 lb., 8 oz., 2
GAR, Alligator 118 lb., 11 oz., 50
GAR, Alligator 24 lb., 13 oz., Tip.-16
GAR, Longnose 16 lb., 7 oz., 6
GAR, Shortnose 2 lb., 0 oz., Tip.-2
GAR, Shortnose 2 lb., 10 oz., Tip.-4
GAR, Shortnose 3 lb., 2 oz., Tip.-6
GAR, Shortnose 4 lb., 9 oz., Tip.-8
GAR, Shortnose 3 lb., 10 oz., Tip.-12
GAR, Shortnose 3 lb., 8 oz., Tip.-16
GAR, Shortnose 5 lb., 12 oz., Tip.-20
GAR, Spotted 5 lb., 0 oz., 6
GAR, Spotted 3 lb., 6 oz., Tip.-2
GAR, Spotted 4 lb., 10 oz., Tip.-4
GAR, Spotted 3 lb., 14 oz., Tip.-6
GAR, Spotted 5 lb., 14 oz., Tip.-8
GAR, Spotted 5 lb., 14 oz., Tip.-12
GAR, Spotted 5 lb., 10 oz., Tip.-16
GAR, Spotted 6 lb., 8 oz., Tip.-20
HALIBUT, California 20 lb., 14 oz., M-4
HALIBUT, California 40 lb., 12 oz., M-80
HALIBUT, California 13 lb., 2 oz., Tip.-20
HALIBUT, California 38 lb., 8 oz., W-6
HALIBUT, California 41 lb., 0 oz., W-16
HALIBUT, California 41 lb., 0 oz., W-30
HALIBUT, Pacific 72 lb., 3 oz., M-2
HALIBUT, Pacific 89 lb., 0 oz., M-4
HALIBUT, Pacific 124 lb., 0 oz., 6
HALIBUT, Pacific 244 lb., 8 oz., M-8
HALIBUT, Pacific 11 lb., 0 oz., Tip.-2
HALIBUT, Pacific 30 lb., 0 oz., Tip.-4
HALIBUT, Pacific 34 lb., 0 oz., Tip.-6
HALIBUT, Pacific 74 lb., 0 oz., Tip.-8
HALIBUT, Pacific 74 lb., 0 oz., Tip.-12
HALIBUT, Pacific 70 lb., 8 oz., Tip.-20
HALIBUT, Pacific 70 lb., 0 oz., W-4
HALIBUT, Pacific 123 lb., 0 oz., W-8
HALIBUT, Pacific 149 lb., 8 oz., W-12
HALIBUT, Pacific 27 lb., 12 oz., W-16
INCONNU 21 lb., 8 oz., Tip.-6
INCONNU 19 lb., 6 oz., Tip.-12
INCONNU 16 lb., 6 oz., Tip.-20
JACK, Pacific Crevalle 7 lb., 0 oz., M-2
JACK, Pacific Crevalle 18 lb., 7 oz., M-4
JACK, Pacific Crevalle 20 lb., 0 oz., M-8
JACK, Pacific Crevalle 22 lb., 8 oz., M-16
JACK, Pacific Crevalle 31 lb., 0 oz., M-50
JACK, Pacific Crevalle 11 lb., 2 oz., Tip.-8
JACK, Pacific Crevalle 14 lb., 5 oz., W-20
JACK, Pacific Crevalle 20 lb., 8 oz., W-30
JACK, Crevalle 27 lb., 2 oz., M-2
JACK, Crevalle 27 lb., 4 oz., M-4
JACK, Crevalle 31 lb., 4 oz., M-8
JACK, Crevalle 43 lb., 0 oz., M-12
JACK, Crevalle 44 lb., 8 oz., M-16
JACK, Crevalle 47 lb., 0 oz., M-20
JACK, Crevalle 57 lb., 5 oz., M-30
JACK, Crevalle 53 lb., 0 oz., M-50
JACK, Crevalle 11 lb., 0 oz., Tip.-2
JACK, Crevalle 29 lb., 8 oz., Tip.-4
JACK, Crevalle 30 lb., 8 oz., Tip.-6
JACK, Crevalle 31 lb., 0 oz., Tip.-8
JACK, Crevalle 34 lb., 0 oz., Tip.-20
JACK, Crevalle 24 lb., 4 oz., W-2
JACK, Crevalle 25 lb., 3 oz., W-4
JACK, Crevalle 30 lb., 4 oz., W-6
JACK, Crevalle 28 lb., 12 oz., W-8
JACK, Crevalle 39 lb., 13 oz., W-12
JACK, Crevalle 35 lb., 0 oz., W-16
JACK, Crevalle 36 lb., 8 oz., W-30
JACK, Crevalle 30 lb., 0 oz., W-50
JACK, Horse-eye 22 lb., 0 oz., M-8
JACK, Horse-eye 25 lb., 12 oz., M-12
JACK, Horse-eye 23 lb., 0 oz., M-16
JACK, Horse-eye 24 lb., 0 oz., M-20
JACK, Horse-eye 23 lb., 2 oz., M-2
JACK, Horse-eye 19 lb., 8 oz., Tip.-16
JACK, Horse-eye 18 lb., 0 oz., Tip.-20
JACK, Horse-eye 11 lb., 12 oz., W-6
JACK, Horse-eye 17 lb., 15 oz., W-8
JACK, Horse-eye 20 lb., 0 oz., W-50
JEWFISH 309 lb., 8 oz., M-6
JEWFISH 344 lb., 12 oz., M-20
JEWFISH 430 lb., 0 oz., M-30
JEWFISH 369 lb., 0 oz., M-50
JEWFISH 455 lb., 8 oz., M-130
JEWFISH 88 lb., 0 oz., W-20
KAWAKAWA 12 lb., 5 oz., W-4
KAWAKAWA 17 lb., 6 oz., W-16
LEERFISH (Garrick) 31 lb., 15 oz., M-16
LEERFISH (Garrick) 6 lb., 4 oz., W-6
LEERFISH (Garrick) 27 lb., 12 oz., M-16
LINGCOD 16 lb., 0 oz., M-2
LINGCOD 33 lb., 0 oz., M-4
LINGCOD 37 lb., 0 oz., M-6
LINGCOD 5 lb., 8 oz., Tip.-8
LINGCOD 26 lb., 13 oz., Tip.-16
LINGCOD 53 lb., 0 oz., W-6
LINGCOD 46 lb., 0 oz., W-16
MACKEREL, Spanish 6 lb., 1 oz., M-2
MACKEREL, Spanish 9 lb., 13 oz., M-6
MACKEREL, Spanish 7 lb., 15 oz., M-8
MACKEREL, Spanish 9 lb., 15 oz., M-12
MACKEREL, Spanish 12 lb., 0 oz., M-20
MACKEREL, Spanish 6 lb., 0 oz., Tip.-4
MACKEREL, Spanish 6 lb., 12 oz., Tip.-16
MACKEREL, Spanish 2 lb., 12 oz., Tip.-4
MACKEREL, Spanish 4 lb., 0 oz., Tip.-6
MACKEREL, Spanish 3 lb., 2 oz., Tip.-8
MACKEREL, Spanish 3 lb., 8 oz., Tip.-12
MACKEREL, Spanish 2 lb., 12 oz., Tip.-16
MACKEREL, Spanish 6 lb., 12 oz., W-4
MACKEREL, Spanish 7 lb., 0 oz., W-6
MACKEREL, Spanish 10 lb., 2 oz., W-8
MACKEREL, Spanish 10 lb., 15 oz., W-16
MACKEREL, Spanish 6 lb., 8 oz., W-20
MACKEREL, Cero 8 lb., 12 oz., M-2
MACKEREL, Cero 11 lb., 12 oz., M-4
MACKEREL, Cero 12 lb., 8 oz., M-6
MACKEREL, Cero 12 lb., 2 oz., M-8
MACKEREL, Cero 14 lb., 0 oz., M-16
MACKEREL, Cero 16 lb., 4 oz., M-20
MACKEREL, Cero 4 lb., 4 oz., Tip.-2
MACKEREL, Cero 6 lb., 4 oz., Tip.-6
MACKEREL, Cero 11 lb., 0 oz., Tip.-16
MACKEREL, Cero 5 lb., 6 oz., W-2
MACKEREL, Cero 9 lb., 4 oz., W-4
MACKEREL, Cero 9 lb., 8 oz., W-6
MACKEREL, Cero 11 lb., 8 oz., W-8
MACKEREL, Cero 13 lb., 0 oz., W-16
MACKEREL, King 43 lb., 4 oz., 6
MACKEREL, King 24 lb., 2 oz., M-2
MACKEREL, King 54 lb., 8 oz., M-4
MACKEREL, King 63 lb., 8 oz., M-8
MACKEREL, King 75 lb., 0 oz., M-12
MACKEREL, King 71 lb., 4 oz., M-16
MACKEREL, King 90 lb., 0 oz., M-80
MACKEREL, King 14 lb., 12 oz., Tip.-4
MACKEREL, King 51 lb., 4 oz., M-16
MACKEREL, King 6 lb., 0 oz., Tip.-20
MACKEREL, King 28 lb., 8 oz., W-2
MACKEREL, King 37 lb., 0 oz., W-4
MACKEREL, King 41 lb., 0 oz., W-8
MACKEREL, King 54 lb., 8 oz., W-12
MACKEREL, King 53 lb., 3 oz., W-16
MACKEREL, King 69 lb., 8 oz., W-20
MACKEREL, King 67 lb., 5 oz., W-30
MACKEREL, King 78 lb., 4 oz., W-80
MACKEREL, Nrwbrd. 16 lb., 0 oz., M-2
MADAI 11 lb., 7 oz., W-12
MARLIN, Black 46 lb., 15 oz., M-2
MARLIN, Black 24 lb., 4 oz., W-2
MARLIN, Black 445 lb., 0 oz., W-16
MARLIN, Blue (Atl.) 604 lb., 0 oz., M-12
MARLIN, Blue (Atl.) 1146 lb., 6 oz., M-50
MARLIN, Blue (Atl.) 1189 lb., 0 oz., M-80
MARLIN, Blue (Atl.) 1402 lb., 2 oz., M-130
MARLIN, Blue (Atl.) 112 lb., 0 oz., W-6
MARLIN, Blue (Atl.) 1059 lb., 0 oz., W-80
MARLIN, Blue (Atl.) 1073 lb., 0 oz., W-130
MARLIN, Blue (Pac.) 141 lb., 1 oz., M-4
MARLIN, Blue (Pac.) 142 lb., 0 oz., M-6
MARLIN, Blue (Pac.) 396 lb., 11 oz., M-12
MARLIN, Blue (Pac.) 450 lb., 0 oz., M-16
MARLIN, Blue (Pac.) 1103 lb., 8 oz., M-30
MARLIN, Blue (Pac.) 1166 lb., 0 oz., M-50
MARLIN, Blue (Pac.) 1014 lb., 0 oz., M-80
MARLIN, Blue (Pac.) 260 lb., 0 oz., Tip.-20
MARLIN, Blue (Pac.) *82 lb., 0 oz., W-8
MARLIN, Blue (Pac.) 639 lb., 0 oz., W-30
MARLIN, Striped 132 lb., 0 oz., M-2
MARLIN, Striped 276 lb., 7 oz., M-16
MARLIN, Striped 397 lb., 11 oz., M-30
MARLIN, Striped 494 lb., 0 oz., M-50
MARLIN, Striped 111 lb., 5 oz., M-2
MARLIN, Striped 262 lb., 5 oz., W-16
MARLIN, Striped 259 lb., 11 oz., W-130
MARLIN, White 132 lb., 11 oz., M-16
MARLIN, White 174 lb., 2 oz., M-20
MARLIN, White 181 lb., 14 oz., M-30
MARLIN, White 162 lb., 0 oz., M-80
MARLIN, White 106 lb., 8 oz., M-130
MARLIN, White 56 lb., 8 oz., W-2
MARLIN, White 74 lb., 1 oz., W-8
MARLIN, White 114 lb., 0 oz., W-16
MUSKELLUNGE 43 lb., 4 oz., 6
PEACOCK, Blackstr. 2 lb., 8 oz., 4
PEACOCK, Blackstr. 2 lb., 1 oz., 8
PEACOCK, Blackstr. 2 lb., 10 oz., 8
PEACOCK, Blackstr. 3 lb., 12 oz., 12
PEACOCK, Blackstr. 2 lb., 4 oz., 16
PEACOCK, Blackstr. 2 lb., 5 oz., 20
PEACOCK, Butterfly 5 lb., 8 oz., 2
PEACOCK, Butterfly 5 lb., 13 oz., 4
PEACOCK, Butterfly 5 lb., 8 oz., 6
PEACOCK, Butterfly 5 lb., 8 oz., 12
PEACOCK, Butterfly 6 lb., 0 oz., 20
PEACOCK, Butterfly 4 lb., 0 oz., Tip.-6
PEACOCK, Butterfly 4 lb., 0 oz., Tip.-12
PEACOCK, Butterfly 4 lb., 12 oz., Tip.-16
PEACOCK, Speckled 20 lb., 10 oz., 6
PEACOCK, Speckled 26 lb., 12 oz., 12
PERCH, Nile 18 lb., 9 oz., 4
PERCH, White 2 lb., 12 oz., 6
PERCH, White 1 lb., 7 oz., Tip.-2
PERCH, White 1 lb., 3 oz., Tip.-8
PERCH, Yellow *1 lb., 13 oz., 4
PERCH, Yellow 1 lb., 6 oz., Tip.-16
PERMIT 25 lb., 7 oz., M-2
PERMIT 44 lb., 12 oz., M-4
PERMIT 42 lb., 8 oz., M-8
PERMIT 46 lb., 4 oz., M-16
PERMIT 56 lb., 2 oz., M-20
PERMIT 51 lb., 8 oz., M-30
PERMIT 53 lb., 4 oz., M-50
PERMIT 9 lb., 12 oz., Tip.-2
PERMIT 36 lb., 0 oz., Tip.-16
PERMIT 20 lb., 0 oz., Tip.-20
PERMIT 19 lb., 4 oz., W-12
PERMIT 42 lb., 0 oz., W-12
PERMIT 46 lb., 0 oz., W-20
PERMIT 42 lb., 0 oz., W-30
PICKEREL, Chain 6 lb., 14 oz., 12
PICKEREL, Chain 4 lb., 5 oz., Tip.-4
PICKEREL, Chain 3 lb., 6 oz., Tip.-4
PIKE, Northern 25 lb., 8 oz., 4
POLLACK, European 22 lb., 14 oz., W-12
POLLOCK 29 lb., 0 oz., M-6
POLLOCK 45 lb., 15 oz., M-30
POLLOCK 46 lb., 10 oz., W-50
POMPANO, African 4 lb., 8 oz., 6
POMPANO, African 32 lb., 4 oz., M-4
POMPANO, African 40 lb., 8 oz., M-8
POMPANO, African 43 lb., 0 oz., M-20
POMPANO, African 46 lb., 8 oz., M-30
POMPANO, African 14 lb., 8 oz., Tip.-4
POMPANO, African 30 lb., 5 oz., Tip.-16
POMPANO, African 14 lb., 0 oz., W-2
POMPANO, African 21 lb., 8 oz., W-4
POMPANO, African 28 lb., 0 oz., W-6
POMPANO, African 38 lb., 0 oz., W-8
POMPANO, African 35 lb., 0 oz., W-16
POMPANO, African 44 lb., 0 oz., W-30
REDHORSE, Shorthd. 1 lb., 11 oz., 6
REDHORSE, Silver 3 lb., 12 oz., Tip.-8
ROOSTERFISH 28 lb., 10 oz., M-2
ROOSTERFISH 28 lb., 1 oz., M-4
ROOSTERFISH 68 lb., 12 oz., M-16

5409 Australian Ave.
West Palm Beach, Florida 33407

# of IGFA World Records...listed below are our current worldwide for fishing ANDE over the last 43 years...

ROOSTERFISH — 40 lb., 0 oz., Tip.-20
ROOSTERFISH — 26 lb., 0 oz., W-4
ROOSTERFISH — 60 lb., 0 oz., W-8
ROOSTERFISH — 55 lb., 0 oz., W-12
ROOSTERFISH — 63 lb., 0 oz., W-16
RUNNER, Rainbow — 13 lb., 0 oz., M-4
RUNNER, Rainbow — 24 lb., 0 oz., M-12
RUNNER, Rainbow — 22 lb., 0 oz., M-16
RUNNER, Rainbow — 14 lb., 4 oz., W-4
RUNNER, Rainbow — 17 lb., 0 oz., W-8
RUNNER, Rainbow — 14 lb., 7 oz., W-16
RUNNER, Rainbow — 19 lb., 5 oz., W-20
SAILFISH, Atlantic — 105 lb., 4 oz., M-8
SAILFISH, Atlantic — 105 lb., 0 oz., M-16
SAILFISH, Atlantic — 121 lb., 11 oz., M-30
SAILFISH, Atlantic — 133 lb., 9 oz., M-80
SAILFISH, Atlantic — 44 lb., 3 oz., Tip.-4
SAILFISH, Atlantic — 71 lb., 8 oz., Tip.-8
SAILFISH, Atlantic — 102 lb., 0 oz., Tip.-20
SAILFISH, Atlantic — 77 lb., 0 oz., Tip.-12
SAILFISH, Atlantic — 59 lb., 9 oz., Tip.-20
SAILFISH, Atlantic — 90 lb., 13 oz., W-6
SAILFISH, Atlantic — 97 lb., 0 oz., W-8
SAILFISH, Atlantic — 112 lb., 0 oz., W-12
SAILFISH, Atlantic — 99 lb., 13 oz., W-16
SAILFISH, Atlantic — *99 lb., 15 oz., W-16
SAILFISH, Atlantic — 128 lb., 1 oz., W-30
SAILFISH, Pacific — 140 lb., 0 oz., M-16
SAILFISH, Pacific — 103 lb., 0 oz., Tip.-6
SALMON, Chinook — 67 lb., 4 oz., 12
SALMON, Chinook — 29 lb., 0 oz., Tip.-4
SALMON, Chum — 23 lb., 4 oz., Tip.-8
SALMON, Chum — 19 lb., 2 oz., Tip.-20
SALMON, Coho — 19 lb., 8 oz., 8
SALMON, Coho — 26 lb., 10 oz., 16
SALMON, Coho — 19 lb., 9 oz., Tip.-8
SALMON, Coho — 19 lb., 4 oz., Tip.-20
SALMON, Pink — 5 lb., 0 oz., 8
SALMON, Pink — 10 lb., 0 oz., Tip.-2
SALMON, Pink — 11 lb., 8 oz., Tip.-4
SALMON, Pink — *6 lb., 8 oz., Tip.-6
SALMON, Sockeye — 9 lb., 8 oz., 2
SALMON, Sockeye — 13 lb., 0 oz., 20
SAUGER — 3 lb., 8 oz., 6
SAUGER — 3 lb., 8 oz., Tip.-2
SAUGER — 2 lb., 0 oz., Tip.-6
SAUGER — 2 lb., 8 oz., Tip.-6
SAUGER — 4 lb., 0 oz., Tip.-8
SAUGER — 4 lb., 0 oz., Tip.-12
SAUGER — 2 lb., 8 oz., Tip.-16
SAUGER — 3 lb., 0 oz., Tip.-20
SEABASS, Jap. (Suz.) — 15 lb., 13 oz., M-8
SEABASS, Jap. (Suz.) — 12 lb., 12 oz., Tip.-4
SEABASS, Jap. (Suz.) — 8 lb., 7 oz., W-6
SEABASS, White — 16 lb., 11 oz., M-2
SEABASS, White — 21 lb., 2 oz., M-4

SEABASS, White — 25 lb., 11 oz., M-6
SEABASS, White — 74 lb., 0 oz., M-20
SEABASS, White — 16 lb., 4 oz., W-4
SEABASS, White — 18 lb., 2 oz., W-6
SEABASS, White — 27 lb., 0 oz., W-8
SEABASS, White — 37 lb., 0 oz., W-16
SEATROUT, Spotted — 10 lb., 1 oz., M-2
SEATROUT, Spotted — 10 lb., 12 oz., M-4
SEATROUT, Spotted — *12 lb., 9 oz., M-16
SEATROUT, Spotted — 8 lb., 11 oz., Tip.-2
SEATROUT, Spotted — 8 lb., 6 oz., Tip.-4
SEATROUT, Spotted — 11 lb., 8 oz., Tip.-8
SEATROUT, Spotted — 8 lb., 6 oz., Tip.-20
SHAD, American — 5 lb., 12 oz., Tip.-6
SHAD, American — 5 lb., 10 oz., Tip.-20
SHARK, Blue — 114 lb., 12 oz., Tip.-6
SHARK, Blue — 68 lb., 12 oz., Tip.-16
SHARK, Hammerhead — 194 lb., 4 oz., M-8
SHARK, Hammerhead — 335 lb., 0 oz., M-12
SHARK, Hammerhead — 544 lb., 8 oz., M-50
SHARK, Hammerhead — 8 lb., 4 oz., Tip.-6
SHARK, Hammerhead — 6 lb., 4 oz., Tip.-8
SHARK, Hammerhead — 8 lb., 0 oz., Tip.-12
SHARK, Hammerhead — 106 lb., 8 oz., Tip.-16
SHARK, Hammerhead — 154 lb., 0 oz., Tip.-20
SHARK, Hammerhead — 15 lb., 8 oz., W-6
SHARK, Hammerhead — 750 lb., 0 oz., W-50
SHARK, Hammerhead — 463 lb., 0 oz., W-80
SHARK, Mako — 81 lb., 9 oz., M-2
SHARK, Mako — 41 lb., 14 oz., W-2
SHARK, Porbeagle — 138 lb., 10 oz., Tip.-20
SHARK, Porbeagle — 236 lb., 0 oz., W-80
SHARK, Thresher — 91 lb., 8 oz., M-6
SHARK, Thresher — 34 lb., 0 oz., M-8
SHARK, Thresher — 141 lb., 0 oz., W-16
SHARK, Thresher — 174 lb., 8 oz., W-20
SHARK, Thresher — 302 lb., 0 oz., W-30
SHARK, Tiger — 3 lb., 10 oz., M-2
SHARK, Tiger — 159 lb., 0 oz., M-6
SHARK, Tiger — 255 lb., 8 oz., M-6
SHARK, Tiger — 362 lb., 8 oz., M-12
SHARK, Tiger — 102 lb., 0 oz., Tip.-8
SHARK, Tiger — 74 lb., 0 oz., Tip.-12
SHARK, Tiger — 61 lb., 12 oz., Tip.-16
SHARK, Tiger — 220 lb., 0 oz., Tip.-20
SHARK, Tiger — 216 lb., 0 oz., W-12
SHARK, Tiger — 360 lb., 0 oz., W-16
SKIPJACK, Black — 14 lb., 3 oz., M-8
SKIPJACK, Black — 12 lb., 12 oz., M-16
SKIPJACK, Black — 18 lb., 6 oz., M-16
SKIPJACK, Black — 15 lb., 12 oz., M-20
SKIPJACK, Black — 26 lb., 0 oz., W-30
SKIPJACK, Black — 5 lb., 0 oz., W-4
SKIPJACK, Black — 15 lb., 12 oz., Tip.-20
SKIPJACK, Black — 4 lb., 0 oz., W-2
SKIPJACK, Black — 14 lb., 8 oz., W-6

SKIPJACK, Black — 5 lb., 8 oz., W-8
SKIPJACK, Black — 17 lb., 0 oz., W-12
SKIPJACK, Black — 17 lb., 0 oz., W-16
SKIPJACK, Black — 15 lb., 0 oz., W-30
SNAPPER, Squirefish — 20 lb., 8 oz., M-6
SNAPPER, Squirefish — 33 lb., 8 oz., M-8
SNAPPER, Squirefish — 33 lb., 1 oz., M-12
SNAPPER, Squirefish — 16 lb., 5 oz., W-6
SNAPPER, Squirefish — 24 lb., 4 oz., W-12
SNAPPER, Squirefish — 19 lb., 13 oz., W-16
SNAPPER, Pc. Cubera — 2 lb., 0 oz., M-2
SNAPPER, Pc. Cubera — 6 lb., 0 oz., M-6
SNAPPER, Pc. Cubera — 48 lb., 3 oz., M-8
SNAPPER, Pc. Cubera — 56 lb., 0 oz., M-16
SNAPPER, Pc. Cubera — 72 lb., 12 oz., M-20
SNAPPER, Pc. Cubera — 78 lb., 12 oz., M-30
SNAPPER, Pc. Cubera — 68 lb., 1 oz., M-50
SNAPPER, Pc. Cubera — 53 lb., 14 oz., M-130
SNAPPER, Pc. Cubera — 20 lb., 0 oz., Tip.-16
SNAPPER, Pc. Cubera — 31 lb., 12 oz., Tip.-20
SNAPPER, Pc. Cubera — 63 lb., 12 oz., W-20
SNAPPER, Pc. Cubera — 53 lb., 0 oz., W-30
SNAPPER, Pc. Cubera — 56 lb., 0 oz., W-80
SNAPPER, Cubera — 69 lb., 0 oz., M-12
SNAPPER, Cubera — 66 lb., 0 oz., M-16
SNAPPER, Cubera — 80 lb., 1 oz., M-20
SNAPPER, Cubera — 109 lb., 12 oz., M-50
SNAPPER, Cubera — 85 lb., 0 oz., M-130
SNAPPER, Cubera — 2 lb., 0 oz., Tip.-12
SNAPPER, Cubera — 68 lb., 5 oz., W-20
SNAPPER, Cubera — 45 lb., 0 oz., W-30
SNAPPER, Cubera — 32 lb., 12 oz., W-80
SNAPPER, Cubera — 38 lb., 9 oz., W-130
SNAPPER, Mutton — 12 lb., 12 oz., M-2
SNAPPER, Mutton — 19 lb., 0 oz., M-4
SNAPPER, Mutton — 17 lb., 0 oz., M-6
SNAPPER, Mutton — 18 lb., 4 oz., M-8
SNAPPER, Mutton — 21 lb., 0 oz., M-16
SNAPPER, Mutton — 26 lb., 4 oz., M-20
SNAPPER, Mutton — 14 lb., 12 oz., Tip.-16
SNAPPER, Mutton — 7 lb., 12 oz., Tip.-20
SNAPPER, Mutton — 9 lb., 0 oz., W-4
SNAPPER, Mutton — 16 lb., 0 oz., W-6
SNAPPER, Mutton — 16 lb., 8 oz., W-8
SNAPPER, Mutton — 18 lb., 0 oz., W-12
SNAPPER, Mutton — 22 lb., 0 oz., W-16
SNAPPER, Mutton — 18 lb., 12 oz., W-20
SNAPPER, Mutton — 17 lb., 8 oz., W-30
SNOOK — 24 lb., 8 oz., M-6
SNOOK — 41 lb., 8 oz., M-6
SNOOK — 34 lb., 0 oz., M-8
SNOOK — 55 lb., 8 oz., M-12
SNOOK — 49 lb., 13 oz., M-16
SNOOK — 57 lb., 12 oz., M-30
SNOOK — 44 lb., 0 oz., M-50
SNOOK — 11 lb., 0 oz., Tip.-2

SNOOK — 15 lb., 8 oz., Tip.-4
SNOOK — 30 lb., 4 oz., Tip.-20
SNOOK — 19 lb., 0 oz., W-2
SNOOK — 20 lb., 12 oz., W-4
SNOOK — 23 lb., 0 oz., W-6
SNOOK — 27 lb., 8 oz., W-8
SNOOK — 31 lb., 4 oz., W-16
SNOOK — 41 lb., 8 oz., W-20
SPEARFISH — 88 lb., 4 oz., M-30
SPEARFISH — 82 lb., 10 oz., M-80
SPEARFISH — 37 lb., 0 oz., Tip.-20
SPEARFISH — 28 lb., 0 oz., W-6
SPEARFISH — 31 lb., 8 oz., W-8
SPEARFISH — 39 lb., 0 oz., W-12
SPEARFISH — 40 lb., 0 oz., W-16
SPLAKE — 5 lb., 10 oz., 20
STURGEON — 58 lb., 3 oz., 6
STURGEON — 237 lb., 0 oz., 20
SUNFISH, Green — 1 lb., 4 oz., Tip.-8
SUNFISH, Redear — 2 lb., 5 oz., 2
SUNFISH, Redear — 1 lb., 2 oz., 6
SUNFISH, Redear — 1 lb., 2 oz., Tip.-16
SUNFISH, Redear — 1 lb., 0 oz., Tip.-20
SWORDFISH — 166 lb., 0 oz., M-12
SWORDFISH — 310 lb., 0 oz., M-20
SWORDFISH — 392 lb., 0 oz., M-30
SWORDFISH — 657 lb., 0 oz., M-80
SWORDFISH — 174 lb., 0 oz., W-16
SWORDFISH — 283 lb., 1 oz., W-20
TAIMEN — 8 lb., 6 oz., 4
TAIMEN — 35 lb., 14 oz., 8
TAIMEN — 21 lb., 4 oz., Tip.-16
TARPON — 106 lb., 0 oz., M-2
TARPON — 128 lb., 8 oz., M-4
TARPON — 139 lb., 14 oz., M-6
TARPON — 147 lb., 6 oz., M-8
TARPON — 202 lb., 13 oz., M-16
TARPON — *283 lb., 4 oz., M-30
TARPON — 265 lb., 0 oz., M-80
TARPON — 48 lb., 4 oz., Tip.-4
TARPON — 56 lb., 0 oz., W-2
TARPON — 134 lb., 3 oz., W-4
TARPON — 115 lb., 0 oz., W-6
TARPON — 141 lb., 9 oz., W-8
TARPON — 166 lb., 7 oz., W-16
TARPON — 230 lb., 0 oz., W-20
TARPON — 249 lb., 0 oz., W-30
TARPON — 225 lb., 0 oz., W-50
TARPON — *218 lb., 4 oz., W-80
TAUTOG — 9 lb., 15 oz., W-6
TAUTOG — 13 lb., 11 oz., W-16
TAUTOG — 14 lb., 2 oz., W-30
TIGERFISH — 15 lb., 6 oz., 6
TOPE — 98 lb., 8 oz., M-30
TREVALLY, Bigeye — 6 lb., 13 oz., M-2
TREVALLY, Bigeye — 13 lb., 14 oz., M-6

TREVALLY, Bigeye — 14 lb., 8 oz., M-12
TREVALLY, Bigeye — 8 lb., 1 oz., Tip.-6
TREVALLY, Bigeye — 12 lb., 0 oz., Tip.-16
TREVALLY, Bigeye — 4 lb., 13 oz., W-2
TREVALLY, Bigeye — 13 lb., 7 oz., W-16
TREVALLY, Bluefin — 16 lb., 0 oz., M-6
TREVALLY, Bluefin — 20 lb., 0 oz., M-12
TREVALLY, Bluefin — 3 lb., 5 oz., W-8
TREVALLY, Bluefin — 18 lb., 1 oz., W-16
TREVALLY, Bluefin — 19 lb., 13 oz., W-30
TREVALLY, Giant — 75 lb., 8 oz., Tip.-20
TREVALLY, Giant — 38 lb., 11 oz., W-6
TREVALLY, Giant — 59 lb., 8 oz., W-20
TRIPLETAIL — 17 lb., 12 oz., M-4
TRIPLETAIL — 23 lb., 6 oz., M-6
TRIPLETAIL — 26 lb., 0 oz., M-8
TRIPLETAIL — 34 lb., 0 oz., M-30
TRIPLETAIL — 23 lb., 0 oz., M-50
TRIPLETAIL — 8 lb., 0 oz., Tip.-2
TRIPLETAIL — 10 lb., 0 oz., Tip.-4
TRIPLETAIL — 6 lb., 0 oz., Tip.-4
TRIPLETAIL — 16 lb., 8 oz., W-2
TRIPLETAIL — *11 lb., 8 oz., W-4
TRIPLETAIL — 17 lb., 11 oz., W-6
TRIPLETAIL — 25 lb., 8 oz., W-8
TRIPLETAIL — 22 lb., 8 oz., W-12
TRIPLETAIL — 26 lb., 0 oz., W-20
TRIPLETAIL — 25 lb., 0 oz., W-50
TROUT, Brook — 8 lb., 8 oz., 8
TROUT, Brook — 8 lb., 8 oz., Tip.-2
TROUT, Brook — 9 lb., 7 oz., Tip.-12
TROUT, Brook — 9 lb., 2 oz., Tip.-16
TROUT, Brown — 12 lb., 4 oz., Tip.-2
TROUT, Brown — 19 lb., 0 oz., Tip.-4
TROUT, Cutthroat — 8 lb., 9 oz., Tip.-4
TROUT, Cutthroat — 10 lb., 0 oz., Tip.-12
TROUT, Cutthroat — 13 lb., 1 oz., Tip.-16
TROUT, Lake — 11 lb., 0 oz., 6
TROUT, Lake — 26 lb., 8 oz., Tip.-4
TROUT, Rainbow — 18 lb., 4 oz., 2
TROUT, Rainbow — 18 lb., 12 oz., 6
TUNA, Bigeye (Atl.) — 16 lb., 4 oz., M-8
TUNA, Bigeye (Atl.) — 329 lb., 0 oz., M-30
TUNA, Bigeye (Atl.) — 355 lb., 0 oz., M-80
TUNA, Bigeye (Atl.) — 117 lb., 8 oz., W-16
TUNA, Bigeye (Atl.) — 317 lb., 12 oz., W-80
TUNA, Bigeye (Pac.) — 83 lb., 0 oz., M-4
TUNA, Bigeye (Pac.) — 304 lb., 0 oz., M-16
TUNA, Bigeye (Pac.) — 341 lb., 0 oz., M-80
TUNA, Bigeye (Pac.) — 27 lb., 5 oz., Tip.-16
TUNA, Bigeye (Pac.) — 83 lb., 8 oz., W-16
TUNA, Bigeye (Pac.) — 157 lb., 0 oz., W-80
TUNA, Blackfin — 11 lb., 0 oz., M-2
TUNA, Blackfin — 28 lb., 0 oz., M-4
TUNA, Blackfin — 32 lb., 0 oz., M-8
TUNA, Blackfin — 36 lb., 8 oz., M-16

TUNA, Blackfin — 45 lb., 8 oz., M-20
TUNA, Blackfin — 29 lb., 0 oz., Tip.-8
TUNA, Blackfin — 30 lb., 4 oz., Tip.-12
TUNA, Blackfin — 21 lb., 8 oz., Tip.-16
TUNA, Blackfin — 22 lb., 8 oz., Tip.-20
TUNA, Blackfin — 3 lb., 3 oz., W-2
TUNA, Blackfin — 35 lb., 0 oz., W-8
TUNA, Blackfin — 30 lb., 0 oz., W-12
TUNA, Blackfin — 30 lb., 6 oz., W-16
TUNA, Blackfin — 33 lb., 0 oz., W-20
TUNA, Blackfin — 38 lb., 0 oz., W-30
TUNA, Blackfin — 37 lb., 11 oz., W-50
TUNA, Bluefin — 350 lb., 0 oz., W-30
TUNA, Bluefin — 16 lb., 11 oz., M-4
TUNA, Bluefin — 39 lb., 0 oz., M-6
TUNA, Bluefin — 188 lb., 0 oz., M-16
TUNA, Bluefin — 28 lb., 8 oz., Tip.-8
TUNA, Bluefin — 41 lb., 8 oz., W-6
TUNA, Bluefin — 45 lb., 0 oz., W-8
TUNA, Bluefin — 50 lb., 0 oz., W-12
TUNA, Bluefin — 65 lb., 0 oz., W-16
TUNA, Bluefin — 974 lb., 6 oz., W-80
TUNA, Dogtooth — 104 lb., 8 oz., W-80
TUNA, Skipjack — 21 lb., 9 oz., M-4
TUNA, Skipjack — 23 lb., 2 oz., M-6
TUNA, Skipjack — 33 lb., 1 oz., M-16
TUNA, Skipjack — 16 lb., 1 oz., Tip.-20
TUNA, Skipjack — 25 lb., 0 oz., W-8
TUNA, Skipjack — 26 lb., 0 oz., W-12
TUNA, Skipjack — 22 lb., 11 oz., W-16
TUNA, Yellowfin — 258 lb., 3 oz., M-30
TUNA, Yellowfin — 120 lb., 8 oz., W-16
TUNA, Yellowfin — 203 lb., 8 oz., W-20
TUNA, Yellowfin — 245 lb., 0 oz., W-30
TUNA, Yellowfin — 270 lb., 0 oz., W-80
TUNNY, Little — 16 lb., 8 oz., M-4
TUNNY, Little — 28 lb., 3 oz., M-12
TUNNY, Little — 35 lb., 2 oz., M-30
TUNNY, Little — 4 lb., 13 oz., Tip.-2
TUNNY, Little — 13 lb., 8 oz., Tip.-4
TUNNY, Little — 19 lb., 0 oz., Tip.-20
TUNNY, Little — 2 lb., 0 oz., Tip.-4
TUNNY, Little — 14 lb., 2 oz., Tip.-20
TUNNY, Little — 21 lb., 0 oz., W-6
TUNNY, Little — 17 lb., 0 oz., W-8
TUNNY, Little — 21 lb., 4 oz., W-20
WAHOO — 51 lb., 0 oz., M-6
WAHOO — 94 lb., 8 oz., M-16
WAHOO — 155 lb., 8 oz., M-80
WAHOO — 57 lb., 0 oz., Tip.-12
WAHOO — 21 lb., 9 oz., W-4
WAHOO — 52 lb., 0 oz., W-8
WAHOO — 82 lb., 0 oz., W-12
WAHOO — 74 lb., 0 oz., W-16
WAHOO — 83 lb., 0 oz., W-20
WAHOO — 153 lb., 8 oz., W-50

WALLEYE — 12 lb., 0 oz., 6
WALLEYE — 8 lb., 0 oz., Tip.-2
WALLEYE — 9 lb., 8 oz., Tip.-4
WALLEYE — 9 lb., 6 oz., Tip.-8
WALLEYE — 7 lb., 8 oz., Tip.-16
WEAKFISH — 16 lb., 9 oz., M-30
WEAKFISH — 3 lb., 13 oz., Tip.-8
WEAKFISH — 11 lb., 2 oz., Tip.-16
WEAKFISH — 16 lb., 1 oz., W-20
YELLOWTAIL, Calif. — 26 lb., 6 oz., M-4
YELLOWTAIL, Calif. — 37 lb., 14 oz., M-6
YELLOWTAIL, Calif. — 17 lb., 6 oz., M-8
YELLOWTAIL, Calif. — 43 lb., 4 oz., M-12
YELLOWTAIL, Calif. — 54 lb., 8 oz., M-30
YELLOWTAIL, Calif. — 17 lb., 8 oz., W-4
YELLOWTAIL, Calif. — 21 lb., 11 oz., W-6
YELLOWTAIL, Calif. — 13 lb., 1 oz., W-8
YELLOWTAIL, Calif. — 29 lb., 4 oz., W-12
YELLOWTAIL, Calif. — 37 lb., 8 oz., W-16
YELLOWTAIL, Calif. — 33 lb., 6 oz., W-20
YELLOWTAIL, Calif. — 48 lb., 0 oz., W-30
YELLOWTAIL, Calif. — 56 lb., 9 oz., W-50
YELLOWTAIL, Calif. — 37 lb., 0 oz., W-80
YELLOWTAIL, South. — 74 lb., 7 oz., M-12
YELLOWTAIL, South. — 18 lb., 0 oz., Tip.-8

All Tackle Records

BARRACUDA, Guinean — 66 lb., 12 oz.
BARRACUDA, Pacific — 7 lb., 11 oz.
BARRACUDA, Blackfin — 15 lb., 12 oz.
BASS, Barred Sand — 13 lb., 3 oz.
BASS, Black Sea — *9 lb., 8 oz.
BASS, Gldspttd. Rock — 6 lb., 0 oz.
BASS, Kelp (Cal.) — 14 lb., 7 oz.
BASS, Splittail — 1 lb., 8 oz.
BASS, Striped — 78 lb., 0 oz.
BIARA — 3 lb., 7 oz.
BICUDA (Pike-char.) — 5 lb., 11 oz.
BONITO, Pacific — 14 lb., 12 oz.
BREAM, Twoband — 2 lb., 13 oz.
CARP, Bighead — 20 lb., 0 oz.
CATFISH, Blue — 111 lb., 0 oz.
CATFISH, Flatwhisk. — 9 lb., 4 oz.
CATFISH, Hardhead — 3 lb., 5 oz.
CORVINA, Orangemth. — 54 lb., 3 oz.
CROAKER, Yellowfin — 2 lb., 1 oz.
CUTLASSFISH, Atl. — 8 lb., 1 oz.
EEL, American — 9 lb., 4 oz.
EMPEROR, Yellowlip — 12 lb., 0 oz.
FILEFISH, Unicorn — 5 lb., 15 oz.
FORKBEARD, Greater — 7 lb., 12 oz.
GAR, Shortnose — 5 lb., 12 oz.
GOLDFISH, Asian — 2 lb., 0 oz.
GROUPER, Nassau — 38 lb., 8 oz.
GROUPER, Black — *114 lb., 0 oz.
GROUPER, Broomtail — 89 lb., 0 oz.
GROUPER, Gag — 80 lb., 6 oz.

GROUPER, Graysby — 2 lb., 8 oz.
GROUPER, Leopard — 21 lb., 4 oz.
GROUPER, Mottled — 109 lb., 9 oz.
GROUPER, Red — 42 lb., 4 oz.
GROUPER, Snowy — 23 lb., 0 oz.
GROUPER, Spot.(Cab.) — 49 lb., 3 oz.
GROUPER, Tiger — 14 lb., 8 oz.
GROUPER, Warsaw — 436 lb., 12 oz.
GROUPER, Yellowedge — 25 lb., 2 oz.
GROUPER, Yellowfin — 40 lb., 12 oz.
GUITARFISH, Giant — 119 lb., 0 oz.
HERRING, Atlantic — 1 lb., 1 oz.
HIND, Red — 6 lb., 1 oz.
HIND, Rock — 9 lb., 0 oz.
HIND, Speckled — 52 lb., 8 oz.
HOGFISH — 19 lb., 8 oz.
HOTTENTOT — 3 lb., 0 oz.
HOUNDFISH — 7 lb., 6 oz.
JACK, Pacific Crevalle — 31 lb., 0 oz.
JACK, Almaco (Atl.) — 78 lb., 0 oz.
JACK, Horse-eye — 24 lb., 8 oz.
JACK, Yellow — 19 lb., 7 oz.
JANDIA — 8 lb., 14 oz.
KINGFISH, Southern — 1 lb., 14 oz.
LADYFISH — 6 lb., 0 oz.
LEATHERJACK, Longjaw — 3 lb., 8 oz.
LEERFISH, (Garrick) — 54 lb., 10 oz.
LIZARDFISH, Inshore — 18 lb., 0 oz.
MACKEREL, Pac. Si. — 17 lb., 2 oz.
MACKEREL, Cero — 4 lb., 12 oz.
MACKEREL, Chub — 90 lb., 0 oz.
MACKEREL, King — 18 lb., 5 oz.
MARGATE, Black — 12 lb., 12 oz.
MARGATE, White — 15 lb., 12 oz.
MARLIN, Blue (Atl.) — 1402 lb., 2 oz.
MARLIN, Striped — 494 lb., 0 oz.
MARLIN, White — 181 lb., 14 oz.
MATRINCHA — 7 lb., 5 oz.
MOONEYE — 1 lb., 3 oz.
MORAY, Blacktail — 2 lb., 6 oz.
MORAY, Green — 33 lb., 8 oz.
MORAY, Purplemouth — 1 lb., 10 oz.
MORAY, Viper — 2 lb., 14 oz.
NEEDLEFISH, Atlantic — 3 lb., 4 oz.
PACU, Black — 28 lb., 4 oz.
PALOMETA — 1 lb., 3 oz.
PANDORA — 7 lb., 2 oz.
PEACOCK, Blackstrip. — 3 lb., 4 oz.
PELLONA, Amazon — 13 lb., 8 oz.
PERMIT — 56 lb., 0 oz.
PIAU — 1 lb., 6 oz.
PICKEREL, Redfin — 2 lb., 4 oz.
PIRANHA, Black — 6 lb., 15 oz.
POMPANO, Florida — 8 lb., 1 oz.
PORGY, Jolthead — 23 lb., 4 oz.
PUFFER, Oceanic — 7 lb., 0 oz.

QUEENFISH, Dblespot. — 2 lb., 8 oz.
RAY, Southern Fiddler — 14 lb., 12 oz.
REDHORSE, Black — 2 lb., 4 oz.
REDHORSE, Golden — 4 lb., 1 oz.
SCAMP — 29 lb., 0 oz.
SCORPIONFISH, Sptd. — 3 lb., 7 oz.
SEAROBIN, Striped — 3 lb., 6 oz.
SEATROUT, Sand — 6 lb., 2 oz.
SENNET, Southern — 1 lb., 0 oz.
SHARK, Carib. Reef — 154 lb., 0 oz.
SHARK, Blacknose — 41 lb., 9 oz.
SHARK, Blacktip Reef — 29 lb., 13 oz.
SHARK, Bonnethead — 23 lb., 11 oz.
SHARK, Leopard — 40 lb., 10 oz.
SHARK, Nurse — 210 lb., 0 oz.
SHARK, Reef — 76 lb., 0 oz.
SHARK, Sand Tiger — 350 lb., 2 oz.
SHEEPSHEAD, Calif. — 21 lb., 8 oz.
SIERRA, Atlantic — 13 lb., 7 oz.
SKIPJACK, Black — 26 lb., 0 oz.
SMOOTHHOUND, Fla. — 30 lb., 6 oz.
SNAKEHEAD — 13 lb., 7 oz.
SNAPPER, Guinean — 89 lb., 15 oz.
SNAPPER, Pac. cubera — 78 lb., 12 oz.
SNAPPER, Colorado — 20 lb., 8 oz.
SNAPPER, Dog (Atl.) — 24 lb., 0 oz.
SNAPPER, Gray (Man.) — 17 lb., 0 oz.
SNAPPER, Greenbar — 21 lb., 2 oz.
SNAPPER, Lane — 7 lb., 0 oz.
SNAPPER, Mullet — 7 lb., 0 oz.
SNAPPER, Mutton — 28 lb., 5 oz.
SNAPPER, Silk — 18 lb., 5 oz.
SNAPPER, Vermillion — 7 lb., 3 oz.
SNAPPER, Yellow (amarillo) — 11 lb., 0 oz.
SNAPPER, Yellowtail — 8 lb., 8 oz.
SNAPPER, Yellowtail — *8 lb., 9 oz.
SNOOK, Pacific Black — 57 lb., 12 oz.
SNOOK, Fat — *8 lb., 0 oz.
STEED, Barbel (nigoi) — 4 lb., 11 oz.
STINGRAY, Atlantic — 10 lb., 12 oz.
STINGRAY, Diamond — 102 lb., 0 oz.
STINGRAY, Southern — 239 lb., 0 oz.
SUCKER, Spotted — 2 lb., 11 oz.
SURFPERCH, Barred — 4 lb., 2 oz.
TARPON — *283 lb., 4 oz.
TAUTOG — 25 lb., 0 oz.
THREADFIN, Moi — 6 lb., 0 oz.
TILAPIA, Mozambique — 2 lb., 8 oz.
TILAPIA, Redbreast — 3 lb., 9 oz.
TOADFISH, Oyster — 4 lb., 15 oz.
TRIGGERFISH, Ocean — 13 lb., 9 oz.
TROUT, Sand — 4 lb., 5 oz.
TUNA, Blackfin — 45 lb., 8 oz.
TUNNY, Little — 35 lb., 2 oz.
WRASSE, Purple (hou) — 2 lb., 9 oz.

GEOFFREY C. SMITH SCULPTURE

Busting Bait
Sailfish & Flying Fish
23"H, 17"L, 11W
Bronze, Ed. 48

Dolphin Duet
23"H, 13"L, 10"W
Bronze, Ed. 48

Geoffrey C. Smith Galleries, Inc.
47 W. Osceola St.
Stuart, Florida 34994

561-221-8031

FAX 561-221-2135

1-800-326-4877
www.geoffreysmith.com

DON'T MISS
THE
ACTION

Catch it online at Internet Waterway!

Fresh water, Salt water, Fly fishing and more, Internet Waterway gets you in the action for new products, boats, what to do, and where to go. Best of all, you can do it from the comfort of your home or office and spend more time fishing!

Catch us online at www.iwol.com

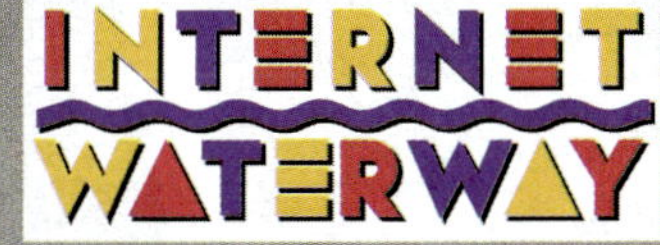

Internet Waterway is the web services provider for IGFA

South Fishing, Inc.

Your passport to the world's finest sportfishing destinations.

**7101 SW 99TH Ave.
Suite 107
Miami, FL 33173
(800) 333-3347
(305) 279-3252
Fax: (305) 279-3167
www.southfishing.com**

"The tarpon fishing in Belize was really hot! Thanks South Fishing." – Rob Burgess

"Alaska was the adventure I always dreamed of and more." – A. Suskin

Call us... we'll do the rest.

"Gigi Charters mates, Speedy & David, are the best in Venezuela!" – Pam Marmin

"South Fishing you were right, the peacock were huge!" – J. Dixon

"My biggest bonefish so far, thank you South Fishing." – Mrs. Carin Beaulieu

Fly Fishing for 'Dorado' Offers Fast Action

Not only are they beautiful, but pound-for-pound as tough as any

By Jack Samson

It was mid-day and not a sailfish had come up behind the 31-ft. Bertram beating southwest ahead of a moderate following sea.

Joe Hudson and I were a competing team in a four-day sailfish tournament off Flamingo Bay, Costa Rica and it was the third day. The fishing had been very slow--only a few fish up per team--and both Joe and I were bored as the hot May sun beat down on the cockpit.

I glanced up at the skipper, Raphael, leaning out of the tower to inspect something ahead. A strip bait skipped astern on the big teaser rod and a daisy chain of plastic squid danced in the wake from the starboard outrigger.

"Dorado!" Raphael shouted, pointing to the port side.

I got up from the fighting chair and looked where he was pointing. A big wooden hatch cover was tilting in the waves about 50 feet to port. It was festooned with seaweed and barnacles--a sure sign it had been in the sea a long time. I began to climb the tower ladder when the mate, Allejandro, let out a yell.

"Aiee," he shouted, pointing from beside Raphael, "Mucho dorado!"

I dropped back to the teak deck and grabbed the big 13-weight graphite fly rod from where it rested against the transom. I had been waiting for a sailfish to come up and the 12-weight forward sinking shooting head was ready to cast. Coils of 40-lb mono running line--50-ft of it--were curled up in the bottom of a plastic bucket in the port corner of the cockpit.

"What about the sailfish?" Joe asked as I moved to the casting corner.

"The hell with them," I said, beginning the cast, "They haven't come up all day. I'm going to have some fun. Ever catch a dorado on a fly?"

"Nope," Joe said, "But you're right. If we're not going to catch sailfish, we might as well catch whatever comes along."

"Mucho, mucho, y grande!" the mate shouted.

I had on one of my home-made popping bugs I make from # 10 bottle corks. The face is concave, a plume of

DAY OF THE DOLPHIN *On July 6, 1998, sisters Julie Pope Dantzler, left, and Annie Pope earned places in the saltwater fly rod world record listings with their catches of dolphin, or "dorado" in Spanish. Fly fishing off Islamorada in the Florida Keys, Julie landed a 23 lb 8 oz dolphin on 8-lb tippet, and Annie captured a 19 lb 13 oz dolphin on 6-lb tippet.*

feathers juts from the back of the white-painted body, and it is tied on a 5/0 stainless steel Mustad hook. Though I tie some double-hooked, this one was a single-hook bug.

Raphael spun the wheel to swing us to port as I dropped the white bug to the right of the wake and gave it several hard jerks to make it pop. Almost immediately the bug disappeared in a geyser of white water and the big rod doubled over. I glanced at where Joe was seated in a wood and canvas folding chair.

"Get your fly out," I shouted as Raphael put the boat into reverse. "The school will stay with the hooked fish. Just get it into the water and strip it fast...and hang on."

The fish I had on made a long, fast run to my right and I kept the rod tip high. Joe had his white, double-hooked sailfish streamer fly in the water and on the third strip was fast to a streaking dorado.

"Double-header!" he shouted as his big rod bent in an arc.

Those two dorado fought well and we finally boated both--after about a 10-minute fight. The mate swung both aboard with a gaff and dropped them into the big fish box against the transom--where they continued to beat against the sides. I looked up at Raphael. He raised his shoulders and shrugged.

"Go back," I yelled, "Dos mas--two more."

He grinned and spun the wheel to bring the boat about. Raphael is a fisherman first and a captain second. We were into two fish the moment we passed the floating hatch and I could see the colorful green and gold fish shoot out from the shelter of the hatch and fight for the lures.

We caught these two--about the same size as the first two, 10, 12 lb each-- and went back for more. On the third pass I hooked into a monster which took the sailfish popper bug with a terrific smash then headed for the horizon. While Joe brought his fish in and cast out and

Jack Samson with a nice dorado caught off Cabo San Lucas, Mexico, rated as excellent dorado grounds.

hooked another, I fought the big one. When I finally got it close to the transom, Raphael looked down from the bridge.

"Grande!" he shouted, "Tal vez, cincuenta!"

It was very big and I thought it might go around 50-60 lb. I had caught one off Florida years ago, when two of my sons and I were fishing off Fort Lauderdale in a 17-ft. Boston Whaler. Both John and Donald were afraid to gaff it and I had to hand the big spinning rod to John and gaff it myself. It had been caught on 20-lb mono and tore up that small boat. That fish had weighed 47 lb. This one looked a lot bigger. But Allejandro, trying to get the gaff hook into the belly, cut the 16-lb tippet instead and the fish was gone. The mate was distraught and Raphael looked disgustedly at him, but I waved it off. The sea around us was full of big dorado.

We took 12 good-sized dorado before both Joe and I quit because our arms were weary fighting those bruisers on fly rods. By that time, Raphael and the mate were grinning from ear-to-ear. They could sell the dorado at the docks

Here are typical dorado flies. Many anglers like to tie their own to suit the area where they're fly fishing.

for a good price that night. The catch, for them, more than made up for the slow day on sailfish.

My second popper bug was a battered mess and Joe's streamer fly was a tattered remnant of its former self. We both sank into chairs and opened cold beers. It had been a battle! We went back to fishing for sailfish, but were so elated with the dolphin battle we couldn't

have cared less whether we got sailfish up or not. It was probably not the proper attitude for a couple of supposedly serious tournament anglers, but then, dolphin always do that to me.

I have taken to calling them dorado in the last few years--as do the Spanish-speaking captains and mates. The word means "gold" and it could not be more appropriate, for it is truly a golden fish, in more ways than one. I also call them dorado because I grew tired of explaining to non-anglers that I was not catching a relative of "Flipper"---- the bottle-nosed dolphin mammal of TV fame.

The dolphin (fish) is a beautiful, green, black and gold fish that is found everywhere there are warm ocean currents. During the many years I fished with big-game tackle, I caught them all over the world--in the Pacific, Atlantic, Gulf of Mexico, the Indian Ocean and Caribbean. And even on 30 and 50-lb. line, they put up a spectacular battle though most big-game fishermen, when seriously fishing for billfish consider dorado a nuisance. They should try hooking them on saltwater fly tackle.

The average dolphin weighs between

SALINAS, ECUADOR'S OBLIGING MARLIN

by Allan J. Ristori

A while back the National Marine Fisheries Service, wondering just how hard it really is to catch marlin, conducted a survey of fishing conditions in the Atlantic, the Gulf, and the Caribbean. What they found, to the chagrin of fishermen in those waters, was that it took an average of ten days of trolling to hook a blue marlin and 17.8 days to hook the smaller white marlin. With offshore charters as much as $250 a day, you can figure it out for yourself. It's hardly a wonder that most anglers go after something else.

It's a pity, though. Catching one's first marlin is some sort of ultimate thrill. That's why it's nice to be able to report that there's a way to beat the odds at a reasonable price: spend a week in Salinas, Ecuador.

I first visited Salinas in 1970 and was instantly impressed. The small fleet of 28-to-34-foot cabin craft operated by Knud Holst was bringing in marlin practically every day.

✱ ✱ *This article has been reprinted with the author's permission.* ✱ ✱

There was a modest hotel, the Miramar, in Salinas itself and, ten miles to the south, the beautiful Punta Carnero. Best of all, Holst's charter rates were about half the cost of boats in more elegant areas. In short, conditions were—and, I'm happy to report, still are—ideal.

The best thing about marlin fishing in Ecuador is that your quarry is the obliging striped marlin, which signals its presence by moving along the surface, tail exposed. When you can see what you're after, it goes without saying, fishing is considerably more exciting than when you have to troll blind.

Both captain and mates keep a constant watch for marlin tails. When they see one, they immediately run the boat over, dragging the bait past the slowly moving fish. If the marlin is interested, you've got a fight on your hands. If not, the boat moves on to another prospect. On an average day you'll see as many as 20 tails. You'll be

lucky to hook two or three of them.

Striped marlin are spectacular fighters, and they're great fun on light tackle. Since most weigh between 100 and 200 pounds, 20- or 30-pound tackle is about right. Most striped marlin will jump a dozen or more times during a fight lasting up to 45 minutes.

For marlin fishermen, the prime season in Salinas is April to January, though billfish, including sailfish, are caught the year around. Winter is the rainy season, but that's no problem: annual rainfall in this desertlike area is only a couple of inches or so.

8 and 15 lb. The largest ever caught on rod and reel was an 87 lb whopper caught at Papagallo Gulf, Costa Rica in 1976, but they have been caught up to 100 lb in commercial nets and on long lines.

The first dolphin I caught on a fly was with IGFA Trustee Steve Sloan as we were returning from taking part in the first Hemingway billfish tournament in Havana, in the late 1970s. Sloan, Ed Zern and I fished as a team in that tournament, but did poorly. On the way back to Key West in Sloan's beautiful 31-ft. Rybovich, the mate spotted a school of dolphin attacking baitfish.

We broke out a spinning rod, equipped with a feather jig, and Sloan was soon fast to a dolphin that leaped beautifully. While fighting it, he remembered that he kept a fly rod rigged up and told me to go and get it from the cabin. It was rigged with a white streamer fly and when I cast to where Steve had his dolphin hooked I got an immediate strike. That dolphin put up such a battle on the 9-ft. 8-weight rod that I vowed to fish for dolphin only with a fly rod from then on.

It is very difficult to cast to a school of dolphin with a fly as the school is usually moving very fast. Unless one is lucky enough to find the fish under a floating object or along a weed bed there is little chance of getting a fly to the fish.

Fortunately, there is a way of solving this problem. Dolphin will readily strike a trolled lure on conventional and spinning gear. Once that hooked fish is brought near the boat, one needs only to keep the fish close to the hull. The school will continue to stay with the hooked fish almost indefinitely. A veteran charterboat skipper out of Islamorada told me that the reason the school stays close, is that the frantic fish begins to regurgitate food as soon as hooked and the other fish stick close to eat the bits of food.

When the school stays with the hooked fish, it is a simple task to throw flies over the circling fish with the boat in idle. IGFA rules state--when fishing for record fish the boat must be in neutral, or at rest, when the fly is cast. But if an angler just wants to catch dolphin on a fly rod for fun, or food, a fly may be trolled or cast to fish while a boat is in motion.

As a matter of fact, I have had a wonderful time catching dorado off Baja, California by trolling flies. After a

Veteran fly rod fisherman Cam Sigler with a big dorado taken on a fly off Panama.

day trying to catch marlin or sailfish with a fly, I have purposely set out to catch dorado for the evening meal and have used a fly rod. The technique is simple enough. Simply troll a big 3/0 or 5/0 streamer of any bright color behind the boat. I have found the farther back the fly is trolled, the better chance of a strike.

Catching dorado this way is a real thrill as one can see the fish coming. Occasionally a dorado will make a jump as much as 100 yards off to the side before hitting the fly. And when they do

hit, it is with a smashing strike. These marvelous game fish will jump like a billfish when hooked and are flat enough that when they turn that side to the angler, the battle is nothing less than spectacular.

I started out using 7-weight rods and matching line for dolphin, but after breaking several good rods and losing a lot of flies--I got smarter. Now I use a 9-weight 9 ft. graphite rod with a reel capable of carrying 200 yards of 20 lb Dacron backing, plus the 90-ft, fly line. Weight-forward floating lines are best for this type of fishing. Usually I make my own leaders of hard Mason nylon and, for dolphin, I use a 3-ft., 40-lb butt section. I fasten that to the fly line with a nail knot and loop the other end with a double surgeon's knot.

One doesn't need long leaders for most deep-water ocean fish as they seem to pay attention to the lure. I take a 5-ft. length of whatever tippet strength I plan to use, usually 12-lb or 16-lb, and form a big loop in one end. I tie a spider hitch to hold that loop.

I then tie a similar knot in the other end of the tippet section to form a class tippet in the center of those two knots. IGFA stipulates that class tippets be at least 15 inches long. There is no maximum limitation. I make double surgeon knot loops at the ends of the large tippet section. One end goes loop-to-loop with the butt section and the other end gets tied to the shock leader with an Albright knot. The shock leader

may be any pound test, but most deep water fly rodders use either 80 or 100 lb shock leader. It must be no longer than 12 inches by IGFA rules--a ruling with which I disagree. I have no objection to the 12-inch rule except where billfishing is concerned. The mouth and bill of sailfish and marlin is sandpaper rough and easily frays even 100-lb shock leader. I think at least an 18-inch section or longer, should be allowed in the case of billfish.

I know it will not be easy to convince the IGFA to change long-standing fly fishing angling rules. Those anglers who set world records under the old rules would, naturally, object to new fishermen getting a break with tackle.

The Albright knot, fastening the looped end of the tippet section to the shock leader, looks like an impossible knot to tie, but it is really not that complicated. Named for the legendary Keys guide, Jimmy Albright, who invented it, it can be tied easily once it is practiced. The shock leader is needed for dolphin as they have a formidable set of teeth and would cut right through a regular tippet.

One of the strange things about dorado is how quickly they lose their brilliant coloring. One minute they are a glistening gold and green and the next the colors have faded to dull black in death--which speaks volumes for releasing all of them unless they are sought for food. There is nothing more depressing to me than to see rows of black dolphin and billfish hung up on scales, drying in the sunlight.

It is especially disturbing when these fish are kept only to photograph and then are dragged off to a dump. There is no excuse for depleting such a marvelous natural resource just for an ego trip. A photograph of the fish, just before releasing it back to the sea, should serve better as a souvenir.

Dolphin can be caught just about anywhere in warm ocean currents. They are plentiful off the east coast of South Florida and around the Florida Keys. The Caribbean is filled with them and they are abundant off the west coasts of South and Central America and off Mexico and Baja. The Gulf of Mexico is prime habitat for the dorado.

JACK SAMSON, an IGFA representative, is a dedicated fly fisherman and author of several books, including *Line Down!* and *Saltwater Fly Fishing*. He holds several fly rod world records.

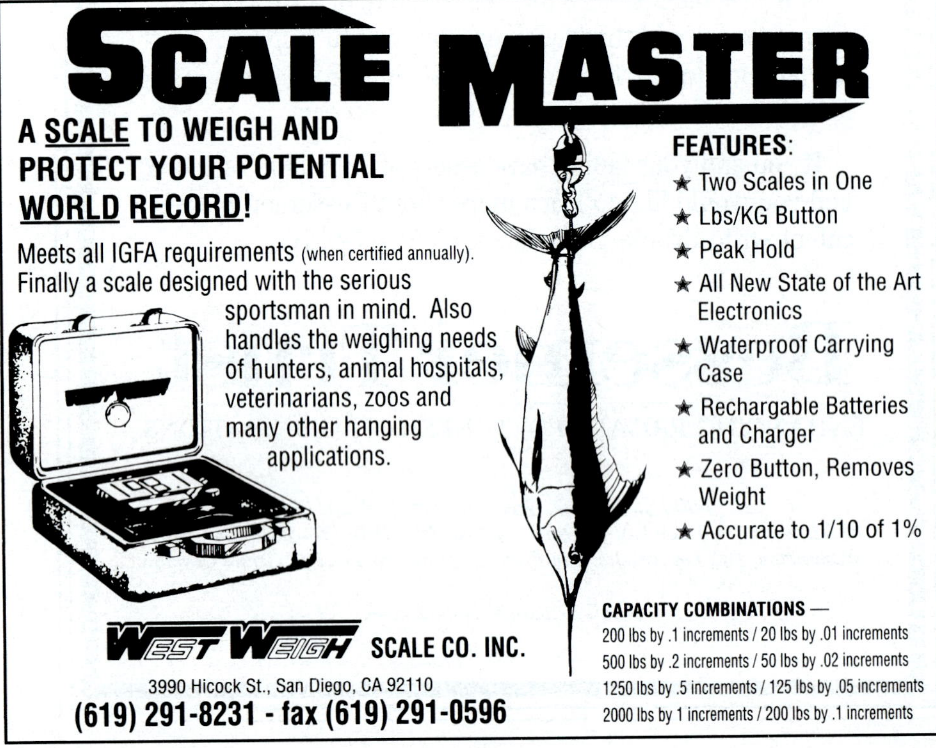

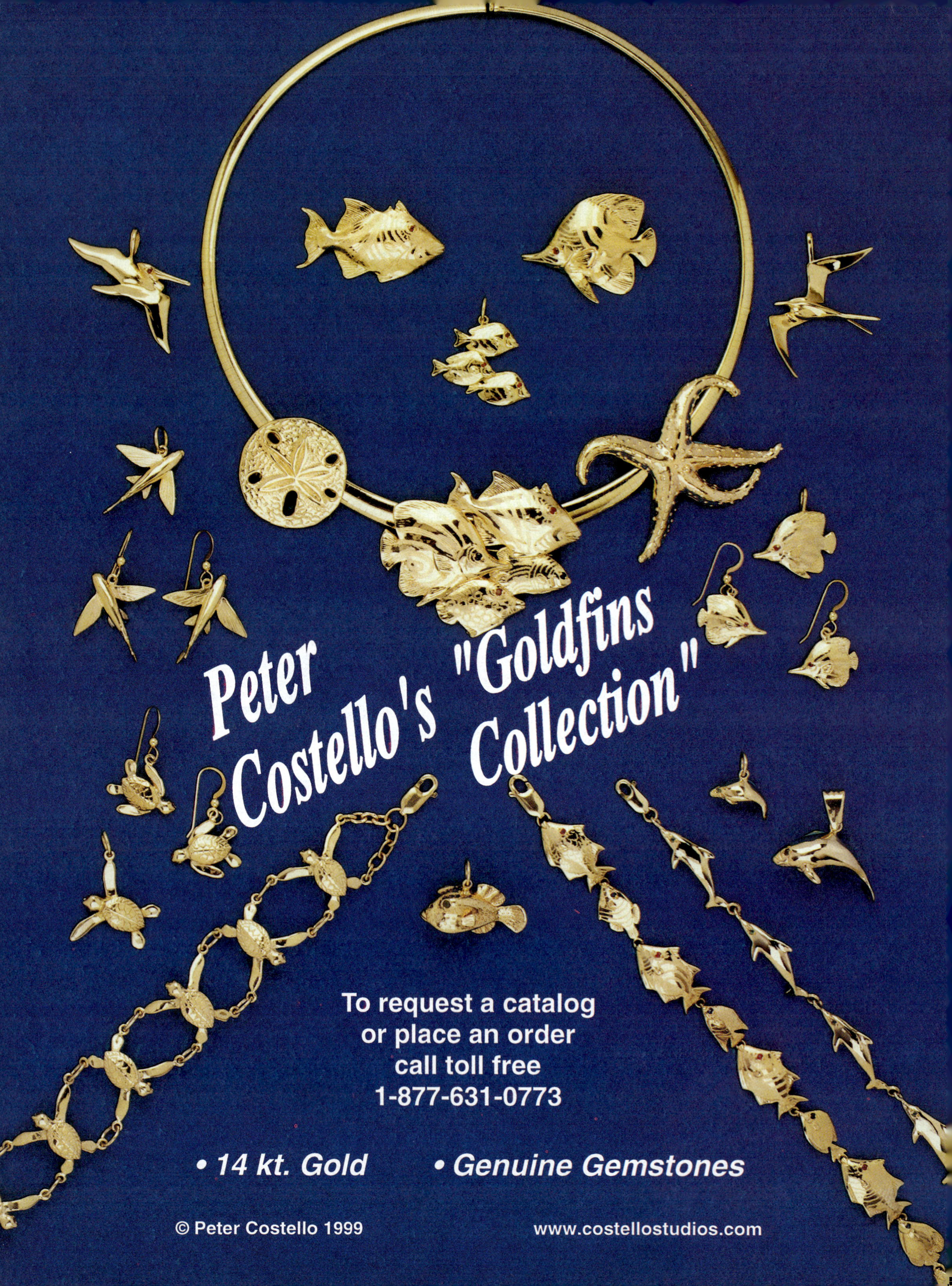

Peter Costello's "Goldfins Collection"

To request a catalog
or place an order
call toll free
1-877-631-0773

• 14 kt. Gold   • Genuine Gemstones

© Peter Costello 1999   www.costellostudios.com

Peter Costello's
"Goldfins Collection"

• 14 KT. Gold
• Genuine Gemstones

© Peter Costello 1999   www.costellostudios.com

Toll free
1-877-631-0773

W**e** support
the conservation
of fishes
according to
the IGFA ethics.

Japan Game Fish Association

Asahi Bldg., 2F
1-11-2 Ebisu, Shibuya-ku,
Tokyo, JAPAN
phone 81-3-5423-6022
fax 81-3-5423-6023
http://www.jgfa.or.jp/
E-mail:japan@jgfa.or.jp

EFSA 

A BRIEF HISTORY OF THE EFSA

The European Federation of Sea Anglers was formed in 1961 by a group of International anglers who were taking part in a fishing festival being held out of Looe in England.

Many of these anglers had fished together for a number of years and six nations were represented in this formative group:

England, Belgium, France, Holland, Denmark, and Scotland.

Within three months of its formation no less that 16 countries were represented in the Federation, either by formation of member sections or by the affiliation of existing clubs.

The objects of the Federation, as laid down at the time of its formation and still in force today, are to promote the sport of sea angling and maintain the list of European Sea Fish Records and to keep a watching brief on all commercial fishing activities in European waters.

One of our rules, which we are proud of because it was ahead of its time when promulgated in 1961, and which we still rigidly enforce, is that the Federation shall have no restrictions or limitations based on race, colour or creed.

One of the functions of the Federation is to stage the European Sea Angling Championships. These championships have been held annually since 1962 and are held in a different country each year. Host countries have included Gibraltar, Scotland, Iceland, France, Norway, Sweden, Denmark, England, Holland and Wales. In addition to the European Championships a European Tope Festival and a European Cod Festival are held each year, with the more recent addition of the European Game Championships and Shore Championships.

10 GOOD REASONS TO JOIN EFSA

1. Regular updates on European Records.
2. Annual International Tournament Calendar.
3. Periodic releases on items of interest to sportsfishermen through newsletters in your own language.
4. Annual European Open and Line Class Championships, Boat, Shore and Big Game.
5. Listing of all EFSA rules and regulations including updates
6. Assistance through EFSA representatives all over Europe.
7. Information on fishing areas and facilities such as boats and accommodation.
8. Scientific information on game fish and 'hotspots'.
9. Embroidered blazer badge, EFSA membership pins and membership cards.
10. Free Yearbook.

For further information contact your National Secretary as listed in the EFSA Yearbook, or write to the General Secretary -

Hamish   Holmes
Inglewood, Braal Road
Halkirk, Cathness, Scotland KW12 6XE

Fly Rodders Make News, New Zealand a Hot Spot

By Mike Leech

Coming off an *El Nino* year as we were this year, you might not expect too much, but you would be wrong. The fish may have shifted with the warm water currents, but they didn't go away. Traditional locations were a disappointment in some areas, but great fishing took place in others. Here is some of the best of 1998.

Watamu, Kenya is an unlikely place for a milestone in fishing history to occur, but nonetheless, on April 5, flyfisherman Jeremy Block became the first person ever to land a swordfish on fly. Using 20-lb tippet and drifting strip teasers, his mates lured a 54-lb 10-oz broadbill that took Block's squid fly, and 35 minutes later, Block was in the book of "firsts." He was fishing aboard the *Eclare* with Capt. Richard Moller and mates Lewis Mwarere, Gabriel Bomu, and Wilson Mwarere. In our opinion, definitely the Catch of the Year.

Like the 4-minute mile, once the swordfish on fly barrier was broken, and anglers knew it was possible, others have started to follow. The second fly fisherman to catch a swordfish (actually two swordfish) was Fouad Sahiaoui from Morocco. Trolling teasers with lightsticks, he was able to hook a 49 lb 13 oz broadbill, and after a battle of over three hours, landed the fish on 16 lb tippet. Three nights later, using 12-lb tippet, he again hooked up, and this time only took 25 minutes to land an 89 lb 15 oz broadbill. He was fishing aboard the *B's Nest* with Capt. Ali Al-Harazi and Nixon and Daniel as crew in December. Once again, the catches were made at Watamu, Kenya. These potential world records were pending at press time.

Three Catches 32 Times Strength of Line

Leading the pack with the heaviest fish in relation to the strength of their line, were three well-known world record holders: Mike Levitt, Raleigh Werking and Leo Cloostermans. All had catches of 32 times the strength of their line. Levitt thought he was fishing with 6-lb line, but due to mislabeling, ended up with a 12-lb line class record for this 296-lb striped marlin and a 32-to-1 catch. He was fishing at Three Kings, New Zealand. Werking racked up his 32-to-1 catch at New Smyrna Beach, Florida with his 66 lb black drum on 2-lb line.

Leo Cloostermans' 76 lb white marlin caught at Horta, Faial, Azores was also on line testing slightly over 2 lb; and at 32-to-1, put him in IGFA's 20-to-1 Club with plenty to spare.

Carl Angus made a great catch at North Cape, New Zealand with his 148 lb 9 oz striped marlin on line of less than 6-lb strength. His 26-to-1 catch took well over two hours. New Zealand was hot this year and produced a 138 lb 10 oz porbeagle shark for Dave Carr on 6-lb line for a 24-to-1 catch in May.

Raleigh Werking made the 20-to-1 Club again with his 21-to-1 black drum world record weighing 90 lb 8 oz on 4-lb test line. Want to see it? It's hanging in the IGFA World Fishing Hall of Fame.

Another impressive New Zealand catch was made by Grant Collings from a 21-foot boat. Using 8-lb line, he hooked and landed a 27-to-1 mako shark weighing 206 lb 2 oz after a battle of 40 minutes.

One more outstanding catch from New Zealand in

Outstanding catch of the year was Jeremy Block's first-ever swordfish caught on a fly rod. The catch was made on 20-lb tippet at Watamu, Kenya and weighed 54 lb 10 oz.

February was Ian O'Brien's 643 lb swordfish. It took him 3 hours and 40 minutes to land the fish on 50-pound line for a new world record and a place in IGFA's 10-to-1 Club.

The ladies continued to turn in amazing catches in 1998. Perhaps the best catch was Karen Heldts' first-ever blue marlin on 6-lb test line by a woman. After many attempts, Karen finally landed a 112 lb blue to fill in the long vacant record. She made the catch on May 8 while fishing at La Guaira, Venezuela aboard the *Heldter Skelter* with Capt. Chuck Barnett and mate Curt Schloderer. The fight lasted more than two hours.

Another long 2-hour fight was experienced by Barbara Woodull with her 366 lb 6 oz striped marlin. A world record in the women's 30-lb line class caught in February at, you guessed it, New Zealand.

Liz Hogan is a glutton for punishment. She has fought tarpon for 8 hours, striped marlin for 9 hours, and black marlin for 12 hours. In January, she traveled from her home in Florida to Hatteras, North Carolina for a shot at the women's 30-lb record for bluefin tuna. Her first day she lost three tuna after battles of 2 hours 10 minutes, 48 minutes, and 5 hours. On day two she was again hooked up before 9 a.m.; and after about 2½ hours, boated a 350 lb bluefin for a new world record on 30-lb line. The catch was made aboard the *Suspense* with Capt. Peter Dubose.

60 Records Plus!

To set a world record can be impressive, but how about more than 60 records? That's the elite plateau that Gene H. DuVal reached in 1998. The variety and widespread locations of her catches is amazing. Usually fishing with her husband Bill, who has a bunch of records also, she uses light tackle and fly rod and now holds more world records than any woman in history. We look for more impressive catches from her in 1999.

Now, back to New Zealand where Stephane Uzan used a fly with 20-lb tippet to set a new world record for southern yellowtail with his 55 lb 8 oz fish. Nice catch!

Before catching his two swordfish on fly, Fouad Sahiaoui spent some time in Port Stephens, Australia in March. He wasted no time in setting world records on March 10, 16 and 19 for two black marlin and a striped marlin. The blacks were on 12- and 20-lb tippets (123 lb 7 oz and 112 lb 6 oz respectively), and the striped marlin was 211 lb 10 oz on 20 lb tippet. He was fishing with Capt. Craig Denham on the *Warrigol*.

Port Stephens was also the site of Brian Kane's record catch of a 222 lb 10 oz black marlin on 20 lb tippet on March 26. He also was guided to his two-hour fight by Capt. Denham. Want to see the video? It's in the IGFA library.

There was no shortage of very impressive fly rod catches this year as Charlie Tombras traveled to the Cape Verde Islands to fish aboard *The Hooker* with Capt. Trevor Cockle. Tombras hooked a blue marlin on 16-lb tippet and after a 1 hour 45 minute fight, boated a record 208 blue for a 13-to-1 catch.

Rare Spearfish on Fly

A rare spearfish on fly record was set in 1998, half a world away at Kona, Hawaii. The angler was Warren Keinath and his fish was caught on 16-tippet and weighed 41 lb. His catch was made on March 12. Capt. Marlin Parker on *Marlin Magic* with mate Kevin Nakamaru guided Keinath to his record.

Baby black marlin were at Cairns, Australia in August, and Charles D. Owen, Jr. and Cary C. Owen took advantage to land two world fly rod records. His was 44 lb 1 oz on 4-lb tippet. Hers was 35 lb 4 oz on 16-lb tippet.

One more impressive and unusual fly rod catch was Dr. Michael Nonnenmann's 56-lb cubera snapper on 20-lb tippet at Honduras in October. A rare species on fly!

We mentioned Trevor Cockle was captain of *The Hooker* for Charlie Tombras' world record, but Capt. Cockle also won the 1998 running of the prestigious Blue Marlin World Cup held each 4th of July around the world. Fishing with only the regular crew, they landed a 458-lb blue to beat out close to 100 anglers. The boat's engineer, Rusty Armbrecht, was the angler. For the spring season from March through June 9, *The Hooker* and Capt. Cockle raised 256 marlin and caught 97, which isn't bad considering they fished several fly rod anglers and spent several days with Guy Harvey to dive with and film free-swimming marlin.

1998 seemed to be a slow year for really big fish, as fewer than usual were reported to IGFA headquarters. The largest marlin we heard caught was Mark Mylius' 1,092-lb blue caught in July in the Cape Verde Islands. He was using 80-lb line aboard the *Happy Hooker* with Capt. Berno Niebuhr. It's the largest blue ever for the Cape Verde Islands.

First Grander of '98

The first grander of 1998 was Walter Goday's 1,061-lb blue caught on the first day of the Cabo Frio Brazil Tournament in January. Unfortunately it only took 3rd Place for the *Andesa* and Capt. Jose Thomas Britto. Other teams released several smaller blues.

One of New Zealand's biggest blues was Tony Harding's 1,007-pounder. It

The heaviest catch reported to IGFA in 1998 was Mark Mylius' 1,092 lb blue marlin caught on 80-lb line. He was fishing in the Cape Verde Islands aboard the "Happy Hooker" with Capt. Berno Niebuhr. It was the largest marlin ever caught in the Cape Verde Islands.

Thirteen-year-old Gayle Steiner's 62 1/2 lb king mackerel gave her the IGFA junior girl's world record. She made the catch while fishing off Miami Beach on 20-lb line during a local tournament. Needless to say, she walked away with the trophy for the heaviest king.

was also caught during a tournament while fishing aboard the *Reel Passion* with Capt. Bob Ash in 50 minutes on 80-lb line.

The Azores produced one grander blue marlin on August 16. Capt. Joseph Franck, an IGFA rep, was aboard his *Shanghai* with angler David Lauzen when the big blue hit. Back at the scales, the marlin topped out at 1,001 lb.

Epic Battle at Midway

An epic battle took place at Midway Island in the Pacific in August aboard Capt. Chris Sheeders' *Yorktown*. The first angler fought the 1,000-lb plus blue marlin for 4 hours before handing over the rod to the second angler for two hours. After a total of 8 hours, the leader broke 25 feet from the transom. And that's why they call it "fishing" and not "catching."

Mike Wallis got into the fight of his life off St. Augustine, Florida in September. While tarpon fishing with Capt. Whit Whitlock, they hooked a 100-lb plus tarpon in the morning of what was supposed to be a half-day charter. Six hours, four miles and many blisters later at 3:30 p.m., the 20-lb class tippet parted and another great fish story came to an end.

George Handgis was on the winning end of a 4-hour 40-minute battle with a 167 lb yellowfin tuna at Kona, Hawaii in July. When he finally got it to the boat on 20-lb line, he discovered it had been hooked in the tail. Not a good thing for anglers using light line!

Tarpon figured in another epic battle at Islamorada in Florida's middle keys. Diana Owen Harris was flyfishing with Capt. William Bassett when she hooked a very feisty 83-lb tarpon on 16-lb tippet. After 4½ hours

Cary C. Owen took advantage of the new ladies saltwater fly rod record category and put her name in the record book with this 35 lb 4 oz black marlin caught on 16-lb tippet at Cairns, Australia.

The largest freshwater catch officially weighed in accordance with IGFA requirements was Darren Robert Lord's 210 lb Nile perch. Lord was using 50-lb line while fishing in Lake Nasser, Egypt.

she landed the women's fly record in that category. We'd say she earned that one.

Freshwater Action

On the freshwater scene, some nice catches were made in 1998. Chris Brandt's 19 lb 4 oz largemouth bass was the largest in 10 years in the San Diego, California area Miramar Lake, and the 13th largest bass ever. He made the catch on 10 lb line on March 22 and later released it alive.

Unquestionably the biggest officially weighed freshwater catch of the year was a 210 lb Nile perch taken from Lake Nasser, Egypt on June 24. Angler Darren Robert Lord from England used 50 lb line to land the 6-foot 4-inch monster. It becomes the new world record in that line class.

The largest flathead catfish ever caught was taken on May 14 from Elk City Lake in Kansas. Ken Paulie was fishing for crappie with a Zebco reel and 17-lb test line when he hooked the 123 lb 9 oz catfish. It took about 15 minutes for Paulie, who was fishing from shore, to make the catch.

Rob Lewis was targeting catfish in the Cumberland River, Tennessee, when he hooked a 112 lb blue catfish in June. It exceeded the state record by almost 30 lb. Lewis was fishing from shore, and when his landing net broke under the weight of the fish, he had to go into the water and wrap his arms around the giant cat to land it.

Outstanding Juniors

Since the inception of the IGFA Junior Angler World Record Program, kids have turned up some very impressive catches. One of the most outstanding junior catches of the year was 13-year-old Gayle Steiner's 62½-lb

king mackerel. It took the Miami girl 25 minutes to make her world record catch off Miami Beach, Florida on 20-lb line. It was a family affair with her dad and two brothers as crew. They were fishing in the South Florida Fishing Club Kingfish Tournament. She not only had heaviest king, but the junior girl's world record as well.

Jessica Harvey may be only 7 years old, but when she's around, the fish better watch out! Her famous artist dad, Dr. Guy Harvey, took her to Tropic Star Lodge, Panama in January; and between January 4 and 9 she racked up seven world records. They included three amberjack to 52 lb, a 42 lb grouper, a 23½ lb yellowfin tuna, and a couple of Sierra mackerel. Who knows what records she will catch by the time she's too old for the junior girl's small fry division at age 11.

There were plenty of other outstanding achievements in 1998. New York billfish angler David Lawrence became one of the few people in the world to land all nine

20-to-1 Plus

These are the 1998 entries into **IGFA's 20 to 1 Club**; where the weight of the catch exceeds the breaking strength of the line by more than 20 times.

RATIO	ANGLER	WEIGHT	SPECIES	LOCATION
32 to 1	Mike Levitt	296 lb	striped marlin	Three Kings Islands, New Zealand
32 to 1	Raleigh Werking	66 lb	black drum	New Smyrna Beach, Florida
32 to 1	Leo R. Cloostermans	76 lb 8 oz	white marlin	Horta, Faial, Azores
28 to 1	Grant Collings	206 lb 2 oz	mako shark	Lebore Bay, New Zealand
26 to 1	Carl Angus	148 lb 9 oz	striped marlin	North Cape, New Zealand
24 to 1	Dave Carr	138 lb 10 oz	porbeagle shark	Otago Heads, New Zealand
21 to 1	Raleigh Werking	90 lb 8 oz	black drum	New Smyrna Beach, Florida
20 to 1	Edward C. Davis	52 lb	flathead catfish	Fayetteville, North Carolina

HEAVIEST CATCHES OF THE YEAR

These catches, made in 1998, exceeded 1,000 lb. Additional catches may have been made, but not reported to IGFA.

Wt.	Species	Angler	Location	Date	CAPTAIN	BOAT
1092	blue marlin	Mark Mylius	Sao Vicente, Cape Verde Islands	July 7, 1998	Berno Niebuhr	Happy Hooker
1061	blue marlin	Walter Godoy	Cabo Frio, Brazil	January 21, 1998	Jose Thomas Britto	Andesa
1007	blue marlin	Tony Harding	North Cape, New Zealand	March 18, 1998	Bob Ash	Reel Passion
1001	blue marlin	David Lauzen	Azores Bank, Azores	August 16, 1998	Joseph Franck	Shanghai

Warren Keinath, standing on right, made this rare catch of a spearfish on fly. The 41 lb fish is the new 16-lb tippet world record. Mate Kevin Nakamaru, on the left, and Capt. Marlin Parker, second from left, help him hold up the catch made at Kona, Hawaii aboard the "Marlin Magic".

Light tackle specialist Liz Hogan set a new bluefin tuna record in the 30-lb line class category with this 350 lb bluefin taken at Hatteras after a 2 1/2 hour battle. The catch was made from the "Suspense" with Capt. Peter Dubose.

billfish species. His quest culminated in the catch of a swordfish at La Guaira, Venezuela in September. Fishing on one of the Gigi fleet's boats with Capt. Alexander Barreto and mate David Hernandez, he tagged and released his broadbill by using the daytime deep drop technique that has become both popular and productive in Venezuela. Lawrence's other catches were spearfish and Pacific blue marlin in Hawaii, Atlantic blue and white marlin, plus sailfish in Venezuela; striped marlin and Pacific sail in Ecuador, and black marlin in Panama. All his catches have been made since 1996.

Super Grand Slam

A super grand slam is rare, and off Florida is almost unheard of. However, on August 7, Capt. Steven Seaman aboard *Jester* headed 100 miles offshore from Port Canaveral. First they caught a sailfish on a lure and an hour later, a spearfish estimated at 20 lb. Next came a blue marlin estimated at 175 lb. They decided to fish for swordfish at night, and after losing one swordfish, released an estimated 65 lb sword to complete the super slam. Oh, yes, they also caught a bunch of dolphin, yellowfin tuna, and a wahoo.

A new all-tackle record for oceanic whitetip shark was set aboard Capt. Bert Klein's *Silver Rod-O* in January. Reid Hodges landed the 369 lb brute on 60 lb line in a little over a hour while fishing out of San Salvador, Bahamas.

Another all-tackle record for the colorful opah was set by Thomas Foran in October. He was fishing out of San Luis Obispo, California on the Portside Marine Sport Launch, *Avila*. Feeling lucky, he entered the jackpot, but after

Raleigh Werking's 90 1/2 lb black drum on 4-lb test not only put him in the 20 to 1 Club but set the world record in the 4-lb line category. A replica of his catch currently hangs in the IGFA World Fishing Hall of Fame.

boating the huge opah, the largest fish by far, he was told that species didn't count. Some days are like that.

Applause for Circle Hooks

Rick Princenthal has caught all nine billfish species, but perhaps his most exciting day was while fishing out of Fins 'N Feathers Lodge in Guatemala's Pacific Coast in late November. In one day he and two other anglers raised about 150 sailfish, got 109 bites, and released 58 sails - all on circle hooks! The following day, Princenthal, Susan and Burt Moss decided to fly fish for sails for the first time. The score: 51 sails raised, 27 strikes, and 8 released.

All three anglers released their first sails on fly.

Fishing at Fins 'N Feathers Lodge in November was nothing short of phenomenal. Capt. John Fox raised 272 billfish in 8 days; Capt. Ron Hamlin, a strong advocate of circle hooks, averaged 41 per day raised, catching 56 sails on his best day in November. Capt. Bud Gramer aboard his *Intensity* averaged over 50 billfish raised for the nine days he fished in November. It was Capt. Hamlin running the *Capt. Hook*, however, who set the record for most releases in a day with 71 sailfish out of 97 raised on December 9.

Heartbreakers

A couple of heartbreakers that happened during the year deserve mention. While fishing in Nkumba Bay, Entebbe, Uganda, Sarel Du Plessis hooked a giant 251 lb 5 oz Nile perch, far exceeding the current record. Unfortunately, due to the remoteness of the area, no certified scale could be located and the catch could not be certified as a record.

Dieter Vogel was fishing in the Canary Islands in July when he hooked and landed a blue marlin of 1,084 lb on 50-lb line, but could not qualify for the IGFA Thousand Pound Club or the 20-to-1 Club since the fish was mutilated while trying to get it on board.

Anything Can Happen

What great catches, heartbreakers and first-ever accomplishments will take place in 1999? Nobody knows, but if we get out there and keep a bait in the water, anything can happen. Just getting out on lake, stream, bay or ocean is reward unto itself, catching fish is just a nice bonus.

I believe if all the world's leaders were required to spend one day a month in a tuna tower on a calm day on any of the world's oceans, to contemplate the beauty and wonder of nature, perhaps we could achieve world peace. Tight lines and good fishing in 1999.

RECORD APPLICATIONS
The IGFA world record and contest application is on page 145, and the Junior Angler world record application is on page 243. Copies of these applications can be made for your convenience.

Mexico's New Bass Hotspot: Lake Huites

By Gary Laden

From daybreak to mid-morning, we had been casting shallow running crankbaits, suspending jerkbaits and flashy spinnerbaits to steep banks, targeting every piece of potential fish-holding cover and structure we could identify. Our strategy was to saturate the best looking areas with a variety of baits to trigger strikes from aggressive shallow water oriented largemouth bass.

And the fish were coming at an astonishing rate, literally one in every eight to 10 casts. Long-time Mexican bass fishing guide Rene Salazar's pattern was working to perfection as Atlanta homebuilder Jim Kennedy and I had landed an incredible amount of 1-1/2 to 3 pound bass in just a few hours of fishing. "You've caught plenty of little fish," said the personable second generation fishing guide, "now it's time to move offshore and see if we can get a trophy for Jim."

Jim Kennedy methodically worked the Texas-rigged 10-inch chartreuse colored plastic worm on top of a stump-laden hump in 22 feet of water. After fishing the hump for 20 minutes or so without a bass, Kennedy began questioning our guide's decision to leave the shallow biting fish.

Any further speculation on Kennedy's behalf that Rene Salazar's deep-water pattern would produce was answered rather abruptly a moment later, when a fish took his plastic offering and literally tore the rod from his grasp. There was little doubt that this was a bass of large proportions as the 62-year-old angler's stout casting rod arched as if it was a 4-weight fly rod after he set the hook. His casting reel's drag screamed in protest as the fish made two strong runs for the protective confines of the flooded timber below. After a three-minute duel, angler bested bass that day and the "pescado grande" (Spanish for big fish) was led to the guide's outstretched net.

Although Kennedy has fished for largemouth bass for the better part of 50 years, he had never actually landed a double-digit bass. Within a half hour of fishing Rene Salazar's deep water pattern, the elated angler was now weighing what he considered as his first true trophy largemouth, a 10-1/2 pounder.

Florida-strain largemouths stocked in the lake decades ago have multiplied to make 100-catch days ordinary instead of rare for visiting anglers.

"We can leave now and head back for the states," joked Kennedy, who still yearned to catch more trophy bass during the remaining two days of fishing on Mexico's Lake Huites, considered by some to be the hottest bass lake in the world. "I'm skeptical when I hear claims of 100 fish days and trophy bass as the norm rather than the exception, but in only a half day or so

of fishing, you don't have to convince me any longer. I'd be happy if I didn't catch another fish on this trip."

Kennedy's fishing success on Huites is not an isolated incident. Since the lake first opened to American anglers three years ago, most have reported astonishing catches of bass on Huites, a 30,000-acre reservoir (at full pool) located in the foothills of the majestic Sierra Madre mountain range of northwestern Mexico in the state of Sinaloa. Lake Huites was constructed in 1993 for the purposes of irrigation to neighboring farmlands and to generate hydroelectric power. But the damming of the Chinipas and Fuertes rivers also created a world class bass fishery.

Back to the Glory Years

Mexico has had a storied past for yielding high quality largemouth bass fisheries. Unfortunately, due to a variety of circumstances, many of these fabled lakes have become just a shadow of their former selves. Not understanding the concept of fishery conservation, or simply ignoring it, meat-hunting American anglers had once hauled countless coolers full of bass filets back to the states. Fishing publications often revealed what now would be considered sickening photos of elated anglers holding up stringers of 100 trophy bass or more. Several years of severe drought conditions at many of these former bass factories caused

problems with water quality and poor oxygen concentrations, resulting in a dramatic decline in both the numbers and size of bass that they once produced.

"In the last two years, one lake has emerged that might restore the glamour days of Mexican bass fishing," says Mexican bass fishing promoter Terry Hollan. "Although countless tales of virgin bass fisheries abound, few anglers have actually experienced a body of water where aggressive fish have not yet grown wary of artificial lures or flies. These are those rare destinations where active fish literally devour a plug, plastic worm or spinner bait on just about any well placed cast. I would say that Huites is the closest thing to the mythical virgin fishery that I have ever encountered.

"In the early 1970's, Lake Guerrero of northeastern Mexico was a true virgin bass fishery, one that set the standard by which all future Mexican bass fishing lakes would be judged. I believe it was the first bass lake in Mexico that would consistently yield 100 plus bass days, with the average fish exceeding three pounds. Lake Huites is as good, or better, than any Mexican bass lake I have ever fished, including Guerrero, and I've visited them all in the past 13 years. For those that missed out on the glory days of

The author with a nice largemouth bass taken on a plastic worm, and released.

lakes like Guerrero, Bacarrac and El Salto in their prime, they've been given a second chance. Lakes like Huites become available to American bass anglers maybe once or twice in a lifetime."

One of the primary reasons for the success of Huites lies in the fact that it was initially stocked with a reported 80,000 Florida strain largemouth bass fingerlings that have matured at a rapid rate and visiting anglers have been astounded by their success.

According to Hollan, when you combine fast growing, aggressive Florida strain largemouth bass, optimal water quality, relatively light fishing pressure and an abundant supply of shad and tilapia, you have the ingredients to allow those bass to grow faster and larger than they would in the states.

"I have never encountered such girth in largemouth bass before," offered Spence Petros of McHenry, Illinois following his first trip to Huites, a clear, deep mountain reservoir. "These fish resemble overfilled footballs. Not only is the average size of the fish I caught quite impressive, but these fish are extremely aggressive as well. I'd often observe six or eight fish trying to take a lure or plastic worm from a hooked fish. In some cases you'd catch two fish on the same plug and this is a common occurrence."

Fishing Patterns

According to Rene Salazar, who gleaned years of bass fishing experience from his father Jose (himself a pioneer in hosting American anglers in Mexico), there are two distinct patterns that exist on Huites. You can fish for large numbers of one to three pound bass fishing visible targets and structure along the steep banks or hunt for larger fish, ranging from four to 12 pounds, by fishing deep, offshore structure.

"If you really want some fast and furious action, I would fish a crankbait, such as a chrome Bill Lewis Rat-L-Trap, shad-colored Bill Dance Fat Free Shad, Smithwick Suspending Pro Rattlin' Rogues, plastic worm or a spinnerbait at the bank," advises Salazar. "These are nice, stout fish, but not the trophies many are looking for. The banks on Huites are steep and you won't find many flats in this lake. For lots of fish, you need to cast at shallow bushes, trees, points and bluff banks."

Salazar targets trophy bass on Lake Huites, those in excess of four pounds, on main lake deep structure, in water ranging from 20 to 40 feet deep. He seeks out abundant old roadbeds, humps, points and flooded timber and advises visiting anglers to fish 10-inch long plastic worms and deep diving crankbaits for best results.

When fishing plastic worms for deep Lake Huites largemouths, it is advisable to use a stout casting or spinning rod, 20-pound monofilament, 3/8 to ½-ounce slip sinkers and strong offset shank worm hooks. "These fish have a tendency to head for cover, like trees or stump roots, when hooked," points out Salazar, "so you need some heavy duty equipment to horse these fish out of deep water."

For deep diving crankbaits, consider seven-foot long fiberglass rods and 12-14 pound test to insure maximum diving capabilities of the plugs.

At times, the fish will be schooling on these structures and it is not unusual to catch numerous trophy bass on consecutive casts. In some instances a ¾-ounce jigging spoon fished vertically beneath the boat will trigger strikes from these deep oriented fish as well

Big fish can also be taken on topwater baits fished over standing timber, brush and across deep points. Prime baits include the Rebel Pop-R, Hedden Zara Spook and Luhr-Jensen Woodchopper.

Two anglers are paired with an experienced local guide (all trained by Salazar) and share a 17-1/2 foot boat, equipped with 65hp outboard and trolling motor.

Preservation of the Fishery

According to Hollan, owner of the Lake Huites Lodge, the original agreements with local Mexican officials called for Huites to be designated as a "sportfish only" catch-and-release fishery. Many of the locals who relied on this lake as a source of food for their families were instrumental in repealing the catch-and-release only policy and now a three-fish limit per day is in effect.

Another potential problem for lodge owners and American bass fishing promoters was the fact that there were numerous netting operations throughout the lake in search of tilapia, a highly prized fish for table-fare and fertilizer.

"Right now, myself and many of the lodge owners are on the verge of signing an agreement that will call for us to pay the local commercial fishermen an amount that would, at least, equal what they would have earned netting tilapia," reports Hollan. "Huites has the strongest chance of any lake in Mexico of actually having a no-net policy strictly enforced by local officials. This would be fantastic for the long-term health of the bass fishery."

Getting There

Anglers can reach the lodge by flying commercially to the airport at Los Mochis, Mexico, or they may elect to fly to Dallas and take a twin-engine turbo prop charter flight to the town of El Fuerte. They are then transferred via air conditioned Suburbans and vans to the Lake Huites Lodge, one of only a handful of lodges that are actually located on the lake.

Lake Huites Lodge was opened in October of 1998 and can house up to 20 anglers. The lodge construction is angled so that visitors have a view of the lake from their room and they also have their own covered porch. A palapa is in the center of the lodge where meals are prepared by one of the best chefs in the area. Each room is air-conditioned, offers private bathrooms and has daily maid service. The water is filtered via a reverse osmosis process and is safe to drink out of the tap. For untrusting visitors, however, bottled water is available.

Anglers are greeted each morning with a pot of hot coffee left at their bungalow door. Three excellent meals are served daily and the coolers that accompany the anglers on the boats are crammed with ice, water, soft drinks and beer.

"I believe that there is no other lake in the world where anglers can catch as many three to eight pound fish," says Hollan. "I believe it can be considered a bass angler's dream lake."

For more information call 1-888-891-3474.

GARY LADEN, a freelance angling writer and photographer, is a regular contributor to IGFA's *World Record Game Fishes*. A former outdoor writer for the Atlanta *Journal* and *Constitution* newspapers, Laden's passion is angling adventure and travel. Photos in this article were courtesy of the author.

Anglers' Check List ForTrip to Mexico

- Passport, birth certificate, or voters registration and drivers license.
- Travel rods (breakdown rods to carry on plane).
- Fishing cap
- Camera and film
- Sunglasses
- Rain gear
- Prescriptions
- Sunscreen, lip screen
- Rods, reels, tackle
- Line clippers
- Needle nose pliers

At right, Jim Kennedy brings in one of his many largemouth bass caught during stay at Lake Huites in Mexico.

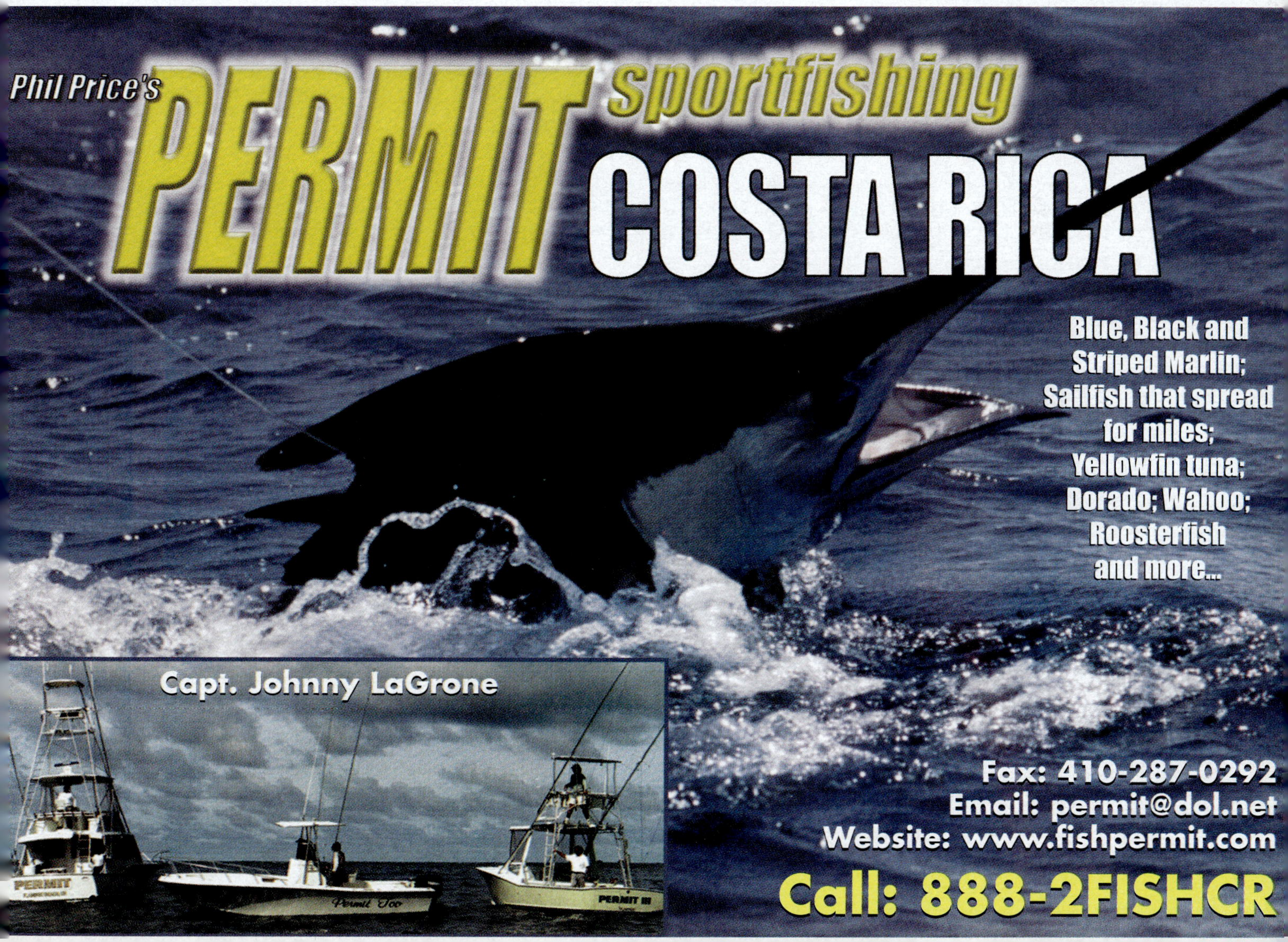

STEVE'S MARINE DESIGNS

WORLD CLASS NAUTICAL FURNITURE AND CUSTOM WORK

MARINE ARTIST: STEVEN LEE

CUSTOM MARINE FURNITURE --CUSTOM MIRRORS--CARVED GLASS--TROPHIES--GLASS SCULPTURES--GIFT IDEAS--CUSTOM DOOR DESIGNS--FISH WALL MOUNTS--FISH SCULPTURES.

VISIT OUR WEB SITE
www.stevesmarinedesigns.com

E MAIL US AT
info@stevesmarinedesigns.com

MARINE ART STUDIOS
LOCATED AT:
3653 N. W. 124 AVE.
CORAL SPRINGS, FLORIDA
33065

TELEPHONE: 954-752-4360

FAX: 954-340-3083

Fly Fishermen Will Travel to End of Earth In Search of These Hard-Hitting Salmon

If you have ever wondered where the "end of the earth" is, I think I've found it. It's a town called Quinhagak on the Bering Sea on the northwest coast of Alaska. It's what they call "rural Alaska" to put it mildly. It's about 350 miles from Anchorage in distance and several centuries in time.

You can only get there by plane. First you get to Anchorage, then hop a semi-commercial flight to Bethel, then the lodge charters you a rather "personal" aircraft from Bethel to Quinhagak. When you set down on a dirt runway that looks about 50 yards long from the air, you're there.

It's a desolate, flat, fishing village where winter temperatures routinely drop to 80 below zero and the first sign you see says "Beware: seal hunters are lousy shots" or something to that effect. I think it means don't go fishing when seal hunting season is underway.

All this was running through my mind as Rick Murphy, Stu Apte and I stepped off the plane. One does not accidentally visit Quinhagak and we did have a purpose. Rick has a TV show called *"Sportsman's Adventures with Captain Rick Murphy"* and he and Stu were there to do a show. I was enticed with the promise of a spot in the show if Stu happened to fall into the river and drown, but came along anyway.

Rick had been there before and what really perked my interest was the

Noted fly fisherman Stu Apte and guide Derek Fergus pose with a big king salmon caught in Alaska's Kanektok River during filming for Rick Murphy's television show.

chance of a 50 lb king salmon on a fly. Mike Zimmer and Barkey Haddad, who produce the show, and Paul Wingrove, another observer like myself, completed our group.

We were headed for Alaska West, a tent camp that is situated on the Kanektok River. The Kanektok is part of the 4.5 million acres of the Togiak Wildlife Refuge. It originates in the Ahklun Mountains and empties into Kuskokwim Bay at the Bering Sea. The only reason Quinhagak exists is because of the huge runs of salmon that enter the Kanektok every summer. The kings (chinook salmon) arrive in

June, the sockeyes and chums in early July and the silvers (coho salmon) in early August.

Alaska West is just a few minutes by boat up River from the village on one of the best "runs" in the entire area. I'd fished for king salmon on Kodiak Island and the Nushaqak with some success but the Kanektok is a relatively small river, 60 to 100 feet wide in most places, and its gravel bottom is easy to wade. Dale DePriest took all these things into consideration when he set up Alaska West as a premiere fly fishing destination for all five kinds of Pacific salmon.

It didn't take long for us to dump our gear in the boat for the short run to the camp. I could see that the river was clear and cold but lower than I'd expected. In several places king salmon scurried out of our way as the jet boat blew past.

Bad News: 70 Degrees and Sunny

On the way up our guide explained that it had been an unusual year. Instead of the normal cloudy, cold, rainy and generally inclement weather typical of an Alaskan June, this year it had been 70 degrees and sunny most every day. In fact there had been so little rain that the river was 4 or 5 feet lower than usual.

This in turn had a major impact on the kings and it had not been good.

Guide Derek Fergus releases a chromer king salmon back into the Kanektok.

our work cut out for us. We had arrived on July 4, the last week of the king run, but Rick and Stu didn't need a lot of fish for their program and the great weather was going to make filming a lot easier. Paul and I had a whole week to figure things out so there was little anyone could say to dampen our enthusiasm.

As soon as lunch was finished, we were fishing. We were the first of the week's guests to arrive, so this afternoon I had a boat and guide to myself. I didn't know much about fishing for kings but I had caught a few and I knew they were big and strong. The thought of catching several of them a day on fly on a relatively small, accessible river was what lured me to Alaska West in the first place. That there would be a group of us from South Florida made it even more fun.

The only drawback that I could see was that I'd be sharing a tent with Murphy who threatened me with severe bodily harm if I snored even half as much as my wife told him I did. With all this behind us, it was not long before my guide, Mike White, dropped anchor just above a pool not far from the river mouth. There was still a fair amount of current because the tide was just beginning to come in. As the tide rises it almost completely offsets the natural flow of the river and the salt water literally replaces the fresh.

Mike, like all of Alaska West's guides, was an expert fly fisherman. He looked over my tackle with approval and in retrospect I can safely say that the perfect outfit for king salmon is a 10 weight rod with a reel that has a smooth drag and lots of

The rainbow fishing however had been the best ever. It's always a bad sign when you come to a fishing camp for one species and they start talking about another before you've even unpacked.

It didn't take long for us to complete a tour of the camp, unpack our waders and fishing gear, and meet at the dining tent for lunch where guides described our situation. The lack of rain had lowered the water to record levels. The numbers of king salmon were still good and they would push into the mouth of the river on the incoming tide. As the salt water receded the kings would find themselves in fresh water that was lower and warmer than normal and this sent them one message, "time to spawn."

Instead of holding in the several pools and runs at the mouth for a few days, the salmon would take off upstream literally on the first tide change. Almost immediately their bright chrome coloring would fade to red and once that happened it was much harder to trick them with a fly. Anyone interested in fishing plugs and spoons on conventional gear could take all the fish they could handle, but as fly fisherman we were going to have

Barkey Haddad with a "buck" king.

backing. I was using a 9' Sage RPL+ and a Tibor Riptide reel. A 40 lb salmon may not seem like much compared to a 100 lb tarpon, but when you combine the river current with 30 to 50 pounds of silver muscle that decides it wants to return to an ocean a half mile away, you can watch 250 yards of backing melt off your reel in a matter of seconds. I brought several different outfits and I found the 9 weight too light for the big fish in current and that there really was no need for an 11 or 12 weight. Also the continued casting required to dredge up a big king was far more enjoyable with the 10 weight. Sinking Lines were a must and I found a Teeny 300 to be perfect for almost all conditions except for the fast water areas where I went to a 400. The leaders were short and stout, about three feet of 20 lb was fine.

'Monster Fur Ball' Fly Worked

The camp supplied the flies but naturally I'd brought several pounds of my own. The lodge flies were basically giant steelhead patterns called "LC prawns" which fascinated me. I had my own creation called a "monster fur ball" which was basically a muddy water tarpon fly converted to chartreuse or pink instead of purple and black. Naturally, I started with my own my flies. It's more fun to catch a fish on one of your own creations.

The plan was quite simple. Cast across the river, let the line sink with the current and sweep across till it was directly downstream, then retrieve in short strips. After a while I began to feel the rhythm of the sinking line and actually impressed myself with the distance I could muster with each cast. Every so often we would see some salmon break the surface porpoise fashion as they headed upstream. Just as we spotted one pod of fish, one of my "sweeps" was interrupted by a jolt that nearly took the rod from my hand. King salmon strikes are not subtle.

Setting the hook was not a problem and I somehow managed to clear all the line from around my feet. Once I was on the reel, things settled down. Mike pulled the anchor and we drifted after the fish, only to watch it pass us heading back upstream. This meant I had probably 40 yards of belly in my line and a lot of frantic reeling was necessary to reacquire a direct connection to the fish. By now Mike had the Yamaha going and soon thereafter my first Kanektok king was in the net, a chromer weighing about 30 pounds. She was a hen, fresh from the sea and full of spunk. It was a pleasure to set her free and get the skunk out of the boat.

The rest of the afternoon provided several strikes, a few short runs, but no more fish in the net. Rick and Stu were fun fishing that afternoon and Mike and Barkey had gone upstream to look for chums and sockeyes. They probably caught 40 fish each, but Stu's and Rick's search for kings was pretty much the same as mine. Stu had a good beginning but nothing exceptional and Rick couldn't rent a fish. For some reason kings don't hit well on sunny days and unfortunately it had been sunny for a month.

Back at camp, dinner was served family style in the main tent. The guests' tents are more like canvas

Author Pat Ford with a red "hen" king salmon.

CUSTOM
J&M TACKLE
SPORTFISHING OUTFITTERS
1-800-483-7069
www.jmtackle.com

MERLIN
GEOSONICS
POLU KAI
BLACK BART
BOB SCHNEIDER

At J&M Tackle, CUSTOM outfitting anglers and sportfishermen of the world is our business. Because we are devoted anglers ourselves, we recognize that precision equipment is the key to successful fishing. From professionally rigged lures to fighting chairs to tournament rod sets, we can outfit your boat with the finest in quality fishing products.

In celebration of our tenth anniversary, we are proud to announce the arrival of our full-color mail order catalog. In it you will find all the products you already use, plus a lot more. At J&M, we carry those hard-to-find items.

Come discover our new line of custom-designed rods, along with thousands of other products — all at your fingertips, all at great prices. Just call toll free or log on at www.jmtackle.com for your FREE copy.

As always, when you entrust your fishing experience to J&M Tackle, our commitment becomes evident. "We aren't satisfied until you are."

J&M TACKLE
SPORTFISHING OUTFITTERS
25125 Canal Road • Orange Beach, AL 36561
Phone: (334)981-5460 Fax: (334)981-5515
Toll FREE Orders 1-800-483-7069
We ship UPS Daily!
ALL MAJOR CREDIT CARDS ACCEPTED
www.jmtackle.com

Call for FREE CATALOG

David Rainer

MARLIN AND SUNSET PHOTO ©1999 RICHARD GIBSON

houses complete with heat, comfortable beds and 10 pounds of covers. I was worried about sleeping in a light colored tent in Alaska in July where there is only about two hours of darkness a day. The camp is located right on the river bank so fishing is only a few steps away. Some guests were still fishing at 2 a.m. Luckily, I had no trouble sleeping in spite of the constant sun light and Rick's snoring, which was pretty impressive for a young guy. He'll be tournament material when he's my age.

The next few days were a blast. Breakfast was served at 7 a.m. and the boats left at 8 a.m. Everyone went in different directions since there were plenty of pools and runs that held fish. We spent most our time at the mouth of the river with Stu, Rick, and the camera boat. Every once in a while I'd hook up and have to drift by them fighting the fish. The kings were not being kind to Stu so it wasn't too long before we left the TV group and moved upstream. After all, they knew where we lived.

The Kanektok's braids vary from three-foot side channels to 200-foot estuary waters and most of our fishing was done from shore. We stopped at one spot next to what Quinhagak calls its airport. There was a gravel bar in the center and the back channel was full of big red kings. I managed to hook a half dozen that afternoon and that's when I discovered I was outgunned with a 9 weight. I'd hook a fish and it would simply saunter over to the fast water and swim away. We'd race back to the boat and try to catch up with it usually without success.

I finally learned that king salmon have two textures in their mouths-- very hard (so your hook doesn't penetrate) and very soft (so the hook pulls out.) On several occasions I watched a fish hang downstream from me, face directly into the current, open its mouth and shake its head sharply from side to side in a wide arch. Almost every time I saw this tactic, the hook pulled out. If you wanted to catch these brutes you had to stay on top of them. The farther they got away from you, the less chance you had of landing them. And, they could get pretty far away, fast.

We Were in Control

After a few days we had things control. The chromers down at the mouth were selective but Stu landed

some beauties for their show. Paul took a 40 lb chromer right next to Stu and Rick, and as usual we took great pleasure drifting right by them while fighting it. Fortunately, they reserved the rocks for me. Occasionally we'd hook a big fresh chum salmon that fought so hard we could not tell the difference between it and the smaller kings.

Later that day we stopped at a gravel bank called the "Puppy Bar" where we could see dozens of red kings holding in the current in a channel about 4 feet deep that ran right

next to the shore. These fish were frustrating because they were in their spawning mode and pretty much ignored every fly we threw at them. Yet, they always stayed in the same place like tomato-colored logs.

That evening Stu and I discussed these fish because it would be a real coup to have both the chrome bright kings in the same show as the red spawning fish. The only difference was the color. These "Puppy Bar" fish were still hot and full of fight. Mike White pointed out that while the red fish weren't really feeding, they were still very protective of their territory and had several natural enemies such as sculpin and leeches that routinely stole eggs from their nests. Hence the origin of the egg-sucking-leech fly. Stu had a collection of flies with him and he promptly came up with an oversized version of his "Apte Too" pattern that he had tied for Homosassa tarpon many years back. The guides took one look at it and said "sculpin." The fly looked a great deal like a large egg-stealing sculpin, so we had a plan.

The next morning dawned typical Alaska--cold, cloudy, and rainy. Stu, Rick, Barkey and Mike took off for the Puppy Bar and set up shop. Paul and I came by a little later to see how things were going and to watch the guys at work. Mike had the cameras set up while Rick and Stu worked the fish. The logistics of the Puppy Bar were perfect. The channel was close to the bank, so a cast into the river let the fly sweep down into and across the channel where the kings were holding.

You could see the fish easily and could position yourself above them, measure your cast, and thus swing the fly directly in front of the fish. By the time we got there Stu had already enticed two solid strikes. As we watched, Stu sent a long cast out into the current. He was using one of his interchangeable sink tip lines and we could watch the floating section swing the sinking tip through the current into the channel just a few feet from shore.

An explosion in the water plus Murphy's shouts told the whole story. Stu was into a big fish and it wasn't happy. The "Apte Too" had done it again. If you ever want to learn how to dominate a big fish on a fly rod, watch Stu at work. His tarpon video that he made with Rick Murphy several years ago describes and shows his fighting style in detail and believe me it works. I follow Stu's technique on all my fish, especially tarpon, and one day last Spring I boated three tarpon in the 120 lb range with Rick and none of them took more than 20 minutes. If you want to do something right learn from the Master.

This poor king salmon never had a chance. Its mistake was giving up on its downstream run and trying to cross the river and head up current. Stu had the fish pretty well whipped by the time it got back to him, but the current was still a factor. Rather than risk pulling the hook, everyone hopped into the boat and beached the fish at the next gravel bar about 100 yards downstream. It was a majestic male about 40 lb with a mouth that looked like it could take a major chunk out of your leg. Barkey held Stu's prize up with great satisfaction. It had made his show. Now everyone could relax.

Stu and I decided to fish together the last day now that the pressure was off. The number of chromer kings had been disappointing but the sockeyes and chums had just started entering the river in droves. Pools that were empty when we arrived now had hundreds of fish stacked in them. Our plan was to start out at the Puppy Bar for the kings and then work upstream for chums and sockeyes. It was my turn at the kings and I landed two in the first hour.

Once again they hit my monster fur ball in the original dark color that resembled a leech. My second was a pretty 25 lb hen with a brown and red coloring that I had never seen before. Our next stop was a little farther upstream where we could see chum and sockeye salmon holding in a pool just below a bend in the river. The chums were big and fresh. Several I landed were in the 15 lb range and on my six weight Sage RPL+, they were a blast. Stu and I caught chum and sockeye all day long and finally we let our guide take us on a sightseeing trip upriver.

Author Pat Ford with a sockeye salmon.

I was amazed at the number of kings that had infiltrated the entire river. Naturally, we had to stop at a back channel for a few minutes to try for some of the Kanektok's famous "leopard" rainbows. I hooked several bows and landed a beautiful 26-inch prize. The coloring on this strain of rainbow is fantastic. On our way back that afternoon we passed Jim Teeny who fishes the Kanektok every spring. That gives you a pretty good idea of the quality of the fishing in the system.

It seemed like our week was over just as it had began. We had all caught king up to 40 lb on fly both chromers and reds. On the way home Stu had 70 lb of fillets which probably kept the Upper Keys in salmon for the rest of the summer. Rick, Barkey and Mike had their TV show with plenty of time left over to enjoy themselves. I survived sharing a tent with Murphy who proceeded to throw shoes at me whenever my snoring woke him up. The tents were as comfortable as any motel I've ever been in and the food and hospitality were exceptional. But as we left everyone was apologizing for the poor fishing. We'd probably averaged hooking a half dozen kings a day when the camp thought we should have hooked a couple of dozen.

Hooking is one thing, catching is another. These fish are powerful and present quite a challenge on a fly, The hope of a 50 pounder brings most of Alaska West's guest back year after year. There is probably no better river for taking king salmon on a fly. And as an aside, don't forget a 6 or 7 weight for the chums and sockeyes. They're just about as much fun as the kings on the light rods and a lot more user friendly.

Anyone interested in Alaska West should call 1-800-344-3628 for details. Reservations must be made early because most of the guests are repeat customers.

Addendum: fly tips

The Alaska West Prawn is not as complicated to tie as one might think. For kings you need a long shank 2/0 hook. The tail is bucktail and mylar, followed by five wraps of chenille. A schlappen feather is then palmered around the hook followed by a marabou spey hackle.

Five more wraps of chenille are followed by another schlappen and marabou spey. A pheasant crest feather is added as a "back" followed by more marabou and a second pheasant crest. Colors can be varied to suit your fancy, and wrap-around lead wire is optional.

The "monster fur ball" is a zonker strip, followed by palmered marabou spey hackle, followed by Dan Bailey's body fur. Bead eyes are optional. I prefer the bead eyes on salmon flies but not on tarpon flies. This was 1997's "secret fly" during Florida Bay's tarpon season.

PAT FORD, a Miami lawyer, is a long-time IGFA member and an ardent fly fisherman who has traveled to many exotic spots in search of his quarry. He has been featured on several TV outdoors shows, and his articles appear regularly in fishing publications. All photos were courtesy of the author.

IGFA Plays Major Role in Conservation

Most serious anglers around the world are well aware of the International Game Fish Association (IGFA) and its role as the world's accepted authority as recordkeeper for all freshwater and saltwater gamefish, and as the world's respected arbiter of angling ethics.

What is less known is IGFA's role in fishery conservation around the world. IGFA's conservation efforts, although low profile, are increasing annually and have helped conserve fishery resources internationally.

Catch and release - tag and release: For more than 50 years, IGFA has been encouraging the world's anglers to release all but their few trophy catches or what they intend to use for personal consumption. IGFA does this through its publications, conferences and worldwide network of more than 300 representatives and trustees. This international network in dozens of countries is active in nearly 1,000 fishing-related organizations. This gives IGFA an unequaled opportunity to spread the word on conservation. In most areas, IGFA representatives are the conservation leaders in their communities. In a growing number of areas around the world, it has been IGFA representatives that have converted kill tournaments to a release format. Efforts in this area are increasing.

IGFA donated 7,000 tags to the National Marine Fisheries Service (NMFS) for free distribution to anglers intending to tag billfish and other pelagic species. IGFA has also given financial support to efforts to place archival tags in bluefin tuna off Hatteras, North Carolina. These tags, when recovered, will actually trace a tuna's movements throughout its range.

A single IGFA representative has tagged more than 7,500 game fish including more than 1,000 striped bass in 1996, and IGFA has printed countless articles in the promotion of catch and release and tag and release. The IGFA *World Record Game Fishes* book contains the only directory of the world's tagging programs, which is updated annually.

Promoting Conservation efforts: In order to promote and encourage conservation efforts, IGFA created their prestigious annual conservation awards. These awards are presented before 700 guests at IGFAs annual banquet in January. We also allow the banquet to be used to present awards to the winners of the popular Aftco Tag Flag Contest, recognizing those who have tagged and released the most gamefish in the Atlantic. IGFA also contributes some of the trophies. These efforts have expanded to the Pacific.

Promoting Conservation Zones: It was IGFA that initially proposed no longlining or conservation zones in the Atlantic back in the 1980's. IGFA recommended an area extending from shore to approximately 75 miles offshore where longlining would be prohibited. Although initially accepted as part of the swordfish management plan, it was later eliminated through strong lobbying by commercial fishing interests. Now, IGFA supports time and area closures to longlining, although we feel it will not be as effective as IGFA's initial proposal.

In other areas, IGFA representatives and trustees have been successful in working to set up conservation zones where commercial fishing is prohibited or severely restricted. These areas include Venezuela, Bahamas, Panama, Hawaii, Mexico, Australia, and New Zealand. Several other areas are currently being worked on.

Billfish Conservation: IGFA was a major player in the enactment of the current very conservative Atlantic Billfish Management Plan. The plan

prohibits the possession or landing of billfish by U.S. commercial vessels in the Atlantic and places strict size limits on recreational anglers. IGFA provided data to help convince fishery managers this plan was necessary and provided testimony at many of the hearings. Commercial interests would like to overturn this plan so they can land billfish and IGFA has been opposing these efforts.

IGFA held the first-ever World Angling Conference in France which addressed international concerns regarding billfish and other species, and also co-sponsored the International Billfish Symposium held in Hawaii.

It was IGFA in 1990 that started a program of writing to restaurants and markets reported to be selling sailfish and marlin to convince them to stop the practice. This program is ongoing and has been very successful.

Conservation networking: IGFA exchanges information and publications with most major conservation and scientific organizations in the world. We support their conservation efforts and ask them to support ours. IGFA trustees and representatives serve on many of the boards of directors of these organizations. IGFA trustees helped create such organizations as the Pacific Ocean Research Foundation, The Caribbean Forum, and others.

Snook success story: IGFA took the initiative when snook stocks in Florida were at an all time low by organizing two snook symposiums. IGFA brought scientists, fishery managers, government officials, conservationists and recreational anglers together, and identified the problems and facilitated strong conservation measures that have rebuilt snook populations to near all-time highs. Over the years, IGFA has been co-sponsor of many other conferences that have addressed various fishery problems in an effort to promote more conservative fishery management.

Bycatch and overfishing: IGFA considers bycatch and overfishing two of the worst enemies of recreational angling. By shining the spotlight of publicity on these abuses through many articles, testimony and letter writing, we keep pressure on fishery managers to end or at least reduce these terrible abuses of our fishery resources. In the Gulf of Mexico, more than 100 fish die for every pound of shrimp harvested, and the Gulf's bottom species are at least 70% depleted. IGFA thinks the public should know this, because only widespread public pressure will ever get the politicians and fishery managers to stop these abusive practices. Worldwide 25% to 35% of all commercial landings are discarded. IGFA wants it to stop.

Monitoring fisheries: It was IGFA that first found out about illegal large-scale drift netting in the Caribbean and blew the whistle on the fleet, causing the netters to retreat to the Pacific. IGFA helped publicize these walls of death until the practice of large-scale drift netting was outlawed by the United Nations.

IGFA strongly supported efforts to eliminate the destructive practice of pair trawling in the Atlantic which has now been prohibited, and IGFA is working on protecting artificial reef sites from commercial fishing. These artificial reefs have been paid for by recreational fishing interests to enhance sport fishing, yet many are being overfished by commercial fishermen. IGFA has taken the initiative to push for strong restrictions on commercial fishing at some of these sites.

IGFA is constantly reviewing reports, attending hearings, and commenting on proposed fishery management measures to push for better fishery management. IGFA represents the recreational anglers and the fish, who can't do these things themselves.

Conservation information: IGFA is unique as an information source of last resort. With a huge library, computer databases and international network of representatives, IGFA is tuned in to the world's fishery problems. IGFA constantly provides information

of these problems, scientific information on over 12,000 species of fish and management measures that have worked or failed in various parts of the world. No other source of this data is available to the world's anglers.

More conservation efforts: IGFA is working to reverse the severe decline in stocks of sharks, swordfish, billfish, and tuna, all of which are at or near their all time lows. IGFA strongly supported the ban on nets in Florida which has proven extremely successful in improving recreational fishing opportunities. IGFA has a program of scale certification so anglers can weigh their catch and release it alive and still qualify for a world record. IGFA's line testing

program is designed to let anglers know if their line will test correctly so they won't needlessly kill a potential world record, should they choose to release the fish. To encourage conservation among young anglers, IGFA's Junior Angler World Record Program allows for the catch, weighing and release of record fish in the boat, as does IGFA's 10-lb Bass Club. IGFA's Grand Slam Clubs also allow the release of all fish.

IGFA is devoted to promoting conservation and education so that future generations of anglers will have a better world to fish in.

MAXIMA IGFA TOURNAMENT SILVER

Choice of Tournament Anglers Throughout the World.

Tournament Silver IGFA class line is available in 2-30 lb. test One Shot spools, 2-130 lb. test Maxi Spools and in large Service Spools ranging from 2-130 lb. test sizes. To set records, spool up with Maxima.

IGFA Corporate Member

©1997 MAXIMA AMERICA

Maxima America, 180 McCormick Ave., Costa Mesa, CA 92626 • Tel: 714-850-5966 • Fax: 714-850-5963

There are many advantages to ùsing my next generation product:

1. 100% freedom from all leader chafe -- guaranteed.

2. The only soft lure with hand-tied skirts, no glue needed.

3. Head and skirt colors developed for maximum reflectivity.

4. Balance, weight, design action = more fish, big fish.

5. Durable. Drop them on the deck, slam them against the boat, they won't crack or break.

6. Each lure comes with my new hook lock device allowing you to position your hook and trust that it will stay locked.

7. The softness was tested over and over. They are perfect. Take the challenge, fish my new lures and teasers!

Black Bart's winning weighs. Aloha. Captain Bart Miller

Dealer Enquiries welcome.   Please visit our website at www.blackbartlures.com
207 East Blue Heron Blvd., Riviera Beach, Florida 33404. Phone/fax 561-844-4722

ELWOOD K. HARRY FELLOWSHIP AWARD

One of Elwood Harry's goals for the International Game Fish Association (IGFA) when he became president in 1973 was to create an extensive library on fishing and related subjects.

By the time of his death in June, 1992 the library had become one of the largest in the world on the subject of fishing. The trustees named the library the Elwood K. Harry Reference Library of Fishes.

To further honor the man who led the growth of IGFA for 20 years, IGFA created the "Elwood K. Harry Fellowship Award." The award consists of a beautiful certificate featuring a full-color painting of Elwood Harry in his favorite pose: pulling on a giant bluefin tuna. The award includes a bronze medallion with stained wood desk stand plus a lapel pin or tie tack contained in a beautiful presentation box.

Any IGFA individual member, IGFA member club, or tournament committee may designate a recipient of the Elwood K. Harry Fellowship Award by making a $1,000 donation or more to the Library Fund.

The fellowship award is the single most prestigious award that IGFA can bestow on an individual. Honorees are recognized for lifetime achievement or significant acts in the sport of fishing, or conservation.

Nineteen persons have been honored since the award was conceived in July 1993. They are: Peter Goadby, John O'Brien, Ted Naftzger, Peter Fithian, Jack Anderson, George Matthews, Pierre Clostermann, Terri Kittridge Andrews, Irby Basco, Ted Williams, Capt. Jimmy Albright, Homer Circle, Lefty Kreh, George Hommell, Mina Hemingway, Loren Grey, Hidenori (Hank) Onishi, Dade Thornton, and Raleigh Werking.

Those interested in further details for sponsoring an individual for the Elwood K. Harry Fellowship Award should contact IGFA headquarters, phone (954) 927-2628 or Fax (954) 924-4299.

Don Ray Studio

"Horned Out"   Courtesy of Jack Newman *Buddy Boy*

**For more information on Don Ray Prints, Originals and Commissions
please write or call Don Ray Studio, PO Box 490, Sebastian, FL 32967
Phone 561-388-2477 Fax 561-388-0176
Http://www.donraystudio.com**

J.D.'s BIG GAME CATALOG

Order your copy now! 1-800-660-5030

CHECK OUT OUR WEBSITE AT: http://www.jdsbiggame.com

New products, new prices.
50 pages of full color.

U.S. $7.00
(includes $5.00 credit on purchases)

International $15.00
(includes $10.00 credit on purchases)

**J.D.'s
Big Game Tackle**
406 So. Bayfront
Balboa Island, CA 92662
USA
(714) 723-0883
Fax (714) 723-0810
email: jdsbiggame@aol.com

BogaGrip

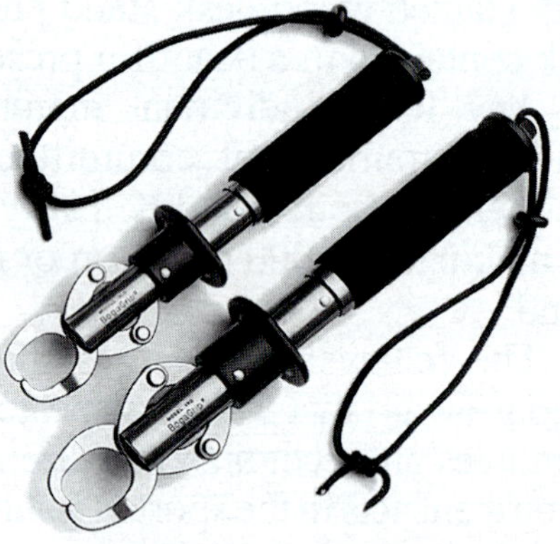

The BogaGrip is a time tested - saltwater tough fish landing, handling and weighing tool. It is designed for the sport fisherman who practices catch and release. The BogaGrip's accurate and durable scales can be certified by IGFA for your potential world record catches. 15 and 30 pound models available.

For more information or the name of a dealer in your area contact:

**Eastaboga Tackle Mfg. Co., Inc.
261 Mudd Street
Eastaboga, AL 36260
256-831-9682   Fax 256-835-2524**

IGFA's World Fishing Center Collection

Sportsman's Classic Windbreaker by Bimini Bay. Logo embroidered fine detail jacket, including a double collar configuration, twin-tandem pockets, inner breathable mesh liner, elastic waist, full-yoke back and two button adjustable cuff. Easy care polyester/cotton. Available in khaki with navy collar, and navy. **Sizes**: S, M, L, XL, XXL Price $65, **Member price $58.50** Item #FP1

Fishing Skills by Tony Whieldon. This comprehensive, easy-to-follow guide gives an introduction to all aspects of fishing. Sections on freshwater and saltwater fishing illustrate the tackle, rigs, and baits to use as well as the species, fish location, casting and fishing techniques. Price $9.99. **Member price $8.99** Item #FP2

Action optics. Combination of glare reduction, UV protection makes these the perfect eyewear for your outdoor fun. Choose Alturas, bronze monel frame with spring hinges and silicone nose pads, brown lenses. Optimum performance in medium to bright conditions. Price $149. **Member price $134.10** Item #FP3

Wire Wraps. Gunmetal monel frame with spring hinges and silicone nose pads. Medium-dark grey lenses preserve natural hues. Great for the open ocean! Price $139.95. **Member price $125.95** Item #FP4

The Angler's Book of Daily Inspiration by Kevin Nelson filled with the wisdom of anglers past and present. Price $14.95 **Member price $13.45** Item #TL1 **Embroidered IGFA logo tournament shirt** by Bimini Bay. Short sleeved, prewashed 100% cotton. Color sage. Price $40 **Member price $36** Item #TL2 **Bone fish full chest detailed embroidery.** Lofty cotton with a hint of poly to retain shape. Sweatshirt or tee. Color stone. Price sweatshirt $48 **Member price $43.20,** tee shirt $25 **Member $22.50** Item #TL3 **A Tribute to Zane Grey,** video. Spectacular archive fishing footage. 60 min. B/W. Price $19.95 **Member price $17.95** Item #TL4 **Bass Fisherman's Bible and Freshwater Fisherman's Bible.** Both are filled with how, when and where to catch fish. Price $12.95 each **Member price $11.65** Item #TL5 **Classic bass fish logo embroidery** 100% cotton French rib crew by Camp David. Charcoal, natural, or pebble. Price $60 **Member price** $54 Item #TL6 **Garments** come in sizes S, M, L, XL, XXL.

Comfortable 100% cotton pique polo with IGFA World Fishing Center logo. Colors stone, white or putty. Price $40 **Member price $36** Item #TR1 **Embroidered cotton tee** by Camp David with choice of IGFA logo or World Fishing Center logo. Specify logo when ordering. Putty, stone or white. Price $18 **Member price $16.20** Items #TR2 and TR5 **Leather gift items** with IGFA logo. **Tri Fold Wallet** (not shown) price $39.95 **Member price $35.95 Money Clip Wallet** Price $24.95 **Member price $22.45 Key Fob** Price $12.95 **Member price $11.65** Set of six **leather coasters** imprinted with IGFA logo in gift tin. Price $16 **Member price $14.40** Item #TR4 **The Quotable Fisherman** compiled by Nick Lyons. A collection of 350 memorable quotations about fishing. Illustrated. Price $20 **Member price $18** Item#TR6

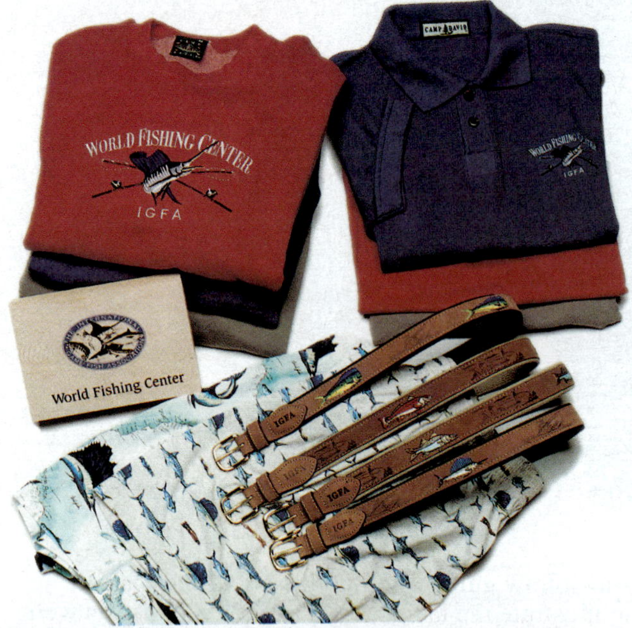

Classic Camp David pique polo. Sailfish design, IGFA logo on left chest. 100% cotton, colors denim, berry, putty. Price $40 **Member price $36** Item #BL1 **Embroidered leather belts** with brass buckle and IGFA logo. Specify dolphin, redfish, snook or sailfish. Sizes 30-44. Price $32, **Member price $28.80 Boxer shorts** by Bimini Bay. Elastic waist, "Fish of Champions" brushed cotton, "Grand Slam" in polished cotton. Price $15 **Member price $13.50** Item # BL4 **Alaska Smokehouse salmon,** 4 oz packed in IGFA cedar gift box Price $15.95 **Member price $14.35** Item #BL4 **Sailfish design embroidered** on Camp David washed fleece. Berry, denim, putty. Price $50 **Member price $45**

Cool-Tek short sleeve fishing shirt by Bimini Bay. Embroidered IGFA World Fishing Center logo. White. Price $40 **Member price $36** Item #BR2 **McClane's New Standard Fishing Encyclopedia.** Most authoritative book on fishing, originally $75, 1100 pages. Price $29.99 **Member price $26.99** Item #BR2 **Embroidered dog collar** with marlin design and IGFA logo. Sueded leather lined with nylon. Measure dog's neck for accurate fit. Price $22 **Member price $19.80** Item #BR3 **Hiker/fishing shorts** by Bimini Bay. Rugged construction, 100% cotton. Khaki or blue. Price $28 **Member price $25.20** Item #BR4 **The Hemingway Cookbook** by Craig Boreth is a feast with more than 125 recipes. Price $24 **Member price $21.60** Item #BR5 **Bimini Bay challenger short sleeve shirt.** Extra large shirt pockets, 100% cotton, canvas color. Price $42, **Member price $37.80.** Item #BR6

Special Merchandise for IGFA Members

IGFA Logo Sweatshirt 100% cotton, logo on chest and back, colors fleece, grey, and navy. Sizes S, M, L, XL, XXL. Price $38 **Member price $34.20** Item #100

IGFA Logo Pocket Tee 100% cotton, IGFA logo front and back, available in long and short sleeves. Sizes S, M, L, XL, XXL.Prices, long sleeve $19 **Member price $17.10** Item #105 Short sleeve $18 **Member price $16.20** Item #106 Available for juniors sizes S, M, L, XL Price $14 **Member price $12.60** Item #107

IGFA Seven Billfish Pocket Tee 100% cotton, logo front and back, available in long and short sleeves. Sizes S, M, L, XL, XXL. Prices, long sleeve $19 **Member price $17.10** item # 101, short sleeve $18 **member price $16.20** Item #102

Mouse Pads Historic photo or IGFA logo. Historic photo item #400A, IGFA logo Item #400B. Price $9.95 **Member price $8.95**

Collectible Ornament Gold-plated brass etched on faux ivory made exclusively for IGFA World Fishing Center to commemorate grand opening. Limited supply gift boxed. Price $16, **Member price $14.40** Item #108

IGFA Member Crest Denim Jacket Stone washed, embroidered front & back, khaki sleeves. Sizes S, M, L, XL, XXL Price $120 **Member price $114.95** Item #291

Freshwater Gamefish of North America By Dick Sternberg, filled with hundreds of photographs of fish in their natural habitat. Price $19.95, **Member price $17.95** Item #109

Junior Angler Club Merchandise

Mouse Pad Junior Angler Club logo to bring your favorite sport to the computer. Price $9.95 **Member price $8.95** Item #110

Junior Angler Club Hat with embroidered logo. Price $12.95 **Member price $11.55**

Junior Angler Club Logo Tee Shirt Pre-shrunk 100% quality cotton, full-color screen print logo, full cut for comfort. Price $14 **Member price $12.50** Item #111

Junior Angler Club Logo Sweatshirt Screen printed on heavy cotton with a hint of poly to retain shape. Available in ash or white, sizes S (4-6), M (6-8) L (12-14) Adult small (14-16). Price $26 **Member price $23.40**

First Cast Teaching Kids to Fly-Fish By Phil Genova. Takes kids to the tying bench and to the stream from their first half hitches and wooly buggers, to long casts over rising trout or stripers in the surf. Price $19.95 **Member price $17.95**

Moving on Specials (While Supplies Last!)

In Celebration of the *New* IGFA Fishing Hall of Fame and Museum

IGFA Crest Embroidered Sports Shirt
IGFA crest logo with gold metallic thread embroidered on soft pique 100% cotton sports shirt! **Colors**: White, Turquoise, Jade, Navy. **Sizes**: M, L, XL, *XXL Price: $32.95
Member Price $29.95. *XXL add $2 Item #200
Special Price $19.95

IGFA Crest Embroidered Tee
IGFA crest logo with gold metallic thread! **Colors**: White, Black, Jade, Turquoise. **Sizes**: M, L, XL. Price: $19.95 - **Member Price** $17.95. Item #210
Special Price $9.95

IGFA Embroidered Captain's Shirt   IGFA crest with gold metallic thread or classic logo embroidered on our classic sportfishing shirt, made for comfort and functionality! Fabric is poly/cotton blend. **Colors**: white, khaki, chambray- (light blue). Please specify logo choice. **Sizes**: M, L, XL, *XXL. Price: $38.95 - **Member Price:** $35.25. (*XXL add $2) Item #205   **Special Price $19.95**

IGFA Crest Tee
IGFA crest logo printed on front of heavy-weight 100% cotton tee! **Colors**: White or Ash Gray. Sizes: M, L, XL, XXL. Price: $13.50
Member Price $11.95 Item #100
Special Price $9.95

Classic IGFA Logo Hat Classic IGFA logo embroidered on 100% cotton hat! **Colors**: White, Jade. Items #305A & 305B

Classic IGFA 2 / Tone Logo Hat Embroidered on cool 100% nylon supplex hat! **Colors**: White/ Royal. Item #306

IGFA Crest Embroidered Hat New IGFA Crest Logo embroidered with gold metallic thread on cool nylon supplex hat. **Colors**: Jade, White, Black. Items #300A, 300B, 300C.

All Hats Price: $13.50
Member price: $11.95

Special Price $9.95

The Mariner
Pullover jacket - 100% waterproof nylon shell, zip pockets with elastic cuffs and bottom. **Colors**: Jade Body with Navy Trim; Royal Body, Purple Trim.

Sizes: S, M. L, XL, XXL. Price: $69.95
Member Price: $62.95   Item #270
Special Price $49.95

Sportfisherman Jacket

Nylon shell with polar fleece and nylon lining that is water resistant. Embroidered with IGFA crest logo front and back. **Colors**: Khaki Body with Tartan/Navy combination; Navy Body with Royal/Jade combination or White Body with Jade/Navy combination (not shown). **Sizes**: S, M, L, XL, XXL. Price $150 **Member Price** $129.95. Item #280 Special Price: Front and back logos $99.95

Captain's Jacket

Water resistant nylon shell with polar fleece and nylon lining. Khaki Body with navy and tartan trim. **Sizes**: S,M, L, XL, XXL. Embroidered front only $93.95, **Member Price $89.95**. Embroidered front & back: $124.95, **Members: $119.95** - Item #157. Special Price front logo only $69.95; front and back logos $99.95

Crest 2-Tone Hat

Brushed cotton twill, embroidered logo. **Colors**: Black/Saddle; Hunter Green/Silver; Royal/Silver. Price: $15.95, **Member Price: $14.95**. Item #155. Special Price $9.95

Tri-Color Sport Shirt

100% cotton pique with color coordinated collar and placket. Embroidered logo. **Colors**: Cherry / Royal / Jade. **Sizes**: M, L, XL, XXL Price $37.50 **Member Price $34.95** Item #153 Special Price $19.95

Two Tone Hat Brushed cotton twill, embroidered logo.

Colors: Hunter Green/Silver; Saddle/Navy. Price $15.95, **Member Price $14.95** Items #152A / 152B Special Price $9.95

IGFA Crest Sweat Shirt

IGFA crest logo printed on premium weight 50/50 sweatshirt with set in sleeves. White only. **Sizes**: M, L, XL, XXL. Price: $19.95 - **Member Price $17.95**. Item #225 Special Price $13.95

Denim Jackets

Casual comfort in stone-washed denim with saddle cotton twill sleeves, lined with cotton sheeting. Embroidered with IGFA Crest or World Record Logos, front and back. **Sizes**: S, M, L, XL, XXL. Price: $124.95 - **Member Price $119.95**. Special Price: Front and back logos $99.95

Harmony Image Size: 16" x 37" Limited Edition size of: 500 - $200.00

Grande Image Size: 16" x 36" Limited Edition size of: 500 - $200.00

Grand Slam Image Size-Small: 18" x 30"
Limited Edition Repligraph size of: 199 - $400.00
Artist Proof size of: 29 - add $100.00
Image Size-Large: 28" x 46"
Limited Edition Repligraph size of: 199 - $650.00
Artist Proof size of: 29 - add $100.00
Repligraph is a new technology that reproduces an original work onto fine art canvas. Each piece is hand signed and numbered by the artist.

Silver Kings
Image Size: 16" x 36"
Limited Edition size of: 500 - $200.00

Line Dance Image Size: 18" x 20"
Limited Edition size of: 950 - $95.00

Remarque: Full water color sketch applied to the border of a limited edition print-$225.00 additional to the print price.

Artist Proof: A smaller edition of a limited edition print series. It is considered a very elite edition and highly collectable. $100.00 additional to the print price.

Canvas Transfer: A new technique that actually transfers an image of a limited edition print onto art canvas, giving the image an almost three dimensional look. $300.00 additional to the print price.

Ghost Flats Image Size: 28" x 21"
Limited Edition size of: 500 - $150.00

Guy Harvey Publishing, Inc.
P.O. Box 50078, Lighthouse Point, Florida 33064 • (800) 245-2223, (954) 783-2223, Fax: (954) 783-0091 • www.guyharveyart.com

Don Ray

"Frequent Flyers"
Limited edition
of 500
Image size:
22 x 33 inches
Price: $150
Remarqued $300
50 Canvas
editions: $375
Item #DR1

"Chasing the Carrot"
Limited edition of 500
Image size: 30 x 40 inches
Price: $200, Remarqued $350
50 Canvas editions: $395
Item #DR3

"Dropping Back"
Limited edition
of 500
Image size:
24 x 36 inches
Price: $150
Remarqued $300
50 Canvas
editions: $375
Item #DR2

Al Barnes

"Deep Hunter"
Limited edition of 600
Image size: 26 x 19 inches
Price $90
Remarqued: $140
Item #010

"Adios"
Limited edition of 1000
Image size: 28 x 21 inches
Price: $165, remarqued: $215
Item #009

"Palm Beach Live Baiting"
Limited edition
of 650 prints
Image size:
13 ½ x 18 inches
Price: $90,
remarqued $140
Item #AP1

Randall McKissick

"Breaker Blues"
Limited edition of 700
image size:
36 x 12 1/2 inches
price: $125
remarqued $225
Item #017

A limited number of "Breaker Blues" prints are available. The prints were gifts at the 1996 IGFA International Auction and Banquet, and only those who attended were able to obtain one until this special offering.

"Squaring Off"
Limited edition of 500
image size: 30 x 10 1/2 inches
price: $125
remarqued: $225
Item #018

"Jaruco Blue"
Limited edition of 1,500
image size: 36 x 12 1/2 inches
price: $85
remarqued: $185
Item #019

"Blue Water Sails"
Limited edition of 500
image size: 24 x 16 inches
price: $125
remarqued: $225
Item #020

BLUEWATER WEAR

"Tuna Lure"
Men's traditional short-sleeve shirt.
100% cotton. Sizes M, L, XL, XXL.
Price $49.95 **Item #569**

"Fish Stamps"
Men's marine theme short-sleeve shirt.
100% cotton. Sizes M, L, XL, XXL.
Price $49.95 **Item #562**

"Multi-Fish"
Men's short-sleeve knit polo shirt.
100% cotton. Sizes M, L, XL, XXL
Price $39.95 **Item #570**

A Quality Product Made for Anglers By Other Anglers

The IGFA Sportswear features designs targeted to please the avid angler, and all shirts are 100% cotton. The traditional short-sleeve shirts on this page have button-down collars, and offer a full-button placket, cross-stitched buttons, and a box pleat in the back for extra comfort. The marine theme print designs have a full-button front, matching chest pocket, cross-stitched buttons, and box pleat in the back. The short-sleeve knit polo shirts have a casual, roomy cut for freedom of movement with ribbed collar and sleeves and cross-stitched buttons.

"Tuna Club"
Men's traditional short-sleeve shirt.
(Print features historic scenes as shown).
100% cotton. Sizes M, L, XL, XXL.
Price $49.95 **Item #563**

"Retro Fish Scenes"
Men's traditional short-sleeve shirt.
100% cotton. Sizes M, L, XL, XXL.
Price $49.95 **Item #561**

BLUEWATER WEAR®
IGFA
Sportswear

The International Game Fish Association has chosen AFTCO Bluewater Wear® to design, manufacture, and market a new line of IGFA sportswear, which we are pleased to announce in this catalog. The "IGFA Collection" targets the serious fisherman and is centered around printed woven and polo shirts that feature scenes and elements depicting the rich history of the IGFA and sportfishing. This exclusive clothing line is distinguished by its own IGFA label and hang tag.

The IGFA is respected worldwide as the keeper for freshwater, saltwater and fly fishing world record information, while formulating the tackle guidelines and standards for the sportfishing world. For 60 years, the IGFA has been instrumental in fishery research, education, conservation and fishery management, and in late 1998 opened the $30 million IGFA World Fishing Center in Dania, Florida, which houses the World Fishing Hall of Fame and museum.

IGFA World Record Watch

24k Gold-plated face, water resistant to 100 feet, stainless steel case, Swiss quartz movement, one-year guarantee, genuine leather strap. Price: $145
Item: men's #038 - women's #039

039   038

IGFA Member Watch

24k Gold-plated face price: $145 - **Item: men's #040 women's #041** (not shown, same shape as Ladies World Record). Men's nickle-plated price: $145 - **Item: #042**

042   040

IGFA Rings

These hand-crafted gold rings were designed for IGFA by sculptor Randy Buck. Available in 10, 14 or 18 karat gold, the rings come in two finishes, "high-polish" or scratch-resistant "Sportsman." Available in Member, World Record Holder, Grand Slam Clubs, 1,000-Lb, 5, 10, 15, or 20-1 Clubs, 10-lb Bass, and 25-lb Snook clubs. Price: 10k-$325 / 14k-$395 / 18k-$485 **Item: #043**

IGFA Game Fish Glassware

Tumblers

Steins and Double Old-Fashioned Glasses

The rugged, versatile IGFA tumblers are sure to make a hit with anglers whether on the boat or at home. These acrylic tumblers, 16 oz each, are double walled and dishwasher safe. The tumblers come in sets of four. The steins and double old-fashioned glasses are extremely popular with IGFA members.

There's something special about drinking from a glass with a leaping largemouth bass, a bull dolphin, or the famed "grand slam" in your hand. The 14-oz double old-fashioned glasses come in sets of four, and the 15-oz steins are sold individually. When ordering, please specify choice: largemouth, bull dolphin, or "grand slam."

Old-fashioned glasses, price $24.95, **Item #056**; Steins, price $9.95, **Item #057**; IGFA Tumblers, price $17.95, **Item #058**

Fly your colors proudly with the bold IGFA emblem at your masthead. This sturdy double-stitched nylon pennant affirms your dedication to ethical sportfishing rules and practices, and identifies you as a member of IGFA. The *IGFA Member* flag comes in two sizes: 12 x 18 inches and 8 x 12 inches. Price: small $10, large $12. **Item #060**

The *IGFA Tag and Release* flag, 8 x 12 inches, can be flown to indicate that you have tagged and released a game fish. Price: $10. **Item #061**

The high quality *Game Fish Flags* fly true and clean at the halyard because of the velcro headings. Simply open the velcro, wrap it around the halyard, and close it. These extra strong cotton/polyester flags come in size 12 x 18 inches. Choose from the wide variety of species shown above. Note: if you order a marlin flag, please indicate background color, blue or white. Price: $12. **Item #062**

1936 Photo and Replica of Tommy Gifford's Telegram Describing Michael Lerner's Historic Swordfish Catch

From 1936, this collectible framed photograph and telegraph message describe the first rod and reel caught swordfish in the north Atlantic by IGFA founder Michael Lerner. On August 7, 1936, Captain Tommy Gifford sent a telegram to outdoor editor Earl Roman of the *Miami Herald* describing the day's swordfishing success off Nova Scotia and providing details of Lerner's historic catch. The old telegram recovered from the IGFA archives was so carefully reproduced that it is near impossible to distinguish between the original and the copy. A limited edition of 199 has been issued at a price of $275 each, including mat and frame.

IGFA's Original Game Fish Print & Stamp Series

"Sail at Dawn" by Russ Smiley

"Spring Creek Nymphing" by Don Ray

For the first time, IGFA is offering commemorative saltwater and freshwater game fish stamps and matching prints signed and numbered by the artists. In 1997, Russ Smiley was commissioned to paint "Sail at Dawn" and Don Ray was selected to create "Spring Creek Nymphing" for the original stamps and prints in this collectors' series.

The limited edition of 499 full color prints (image size 6 1/2" x 9") reproduced on fine art paper, numbered and signed by the artists sell for $130. The stamps (1 1/4" x 2 1/16") are $6 each, and $60 for a sheet of 10. Prints and stamps with matching numbers will be sold in sets for $136. Matching stamps and prints showcased in a beautiful wood frame as pictured above are $230. Prints will be remarqued by the artists for an additional $100 per print.

This special stamp and print creation gives collectors an opportunity to become involved from the start of this original IGFA limited edition series. To receive the lowest number available, order today!

THE ARTISTS...

Russ Smiley's limited edition prints have been featured by IGFA and well received by anglers. A member of the Society of Animal Artists, Smiley has been painting fish, birds, animals and landscapes for more than 45 years. He has published over 40 limited edition prints which have sold worldwide, and many of his original paintings hang in private collections.

Don Ray's paintings appear regularly in and on covers of popular wildlife magazines and sporting catalogs. He won first place in the 1992 and 1995 Florida snook print and stamp competitions. He was selected to paint the Texas saltwater fishing stamp and print in 1996-1997. He has earned the Society of Animal Artists' Award of Excellence.

When ordering, please give name of print/stamp and describe which presentation you want: individual print or stamp, matched set, framed set, remarqued, etc. on the order form on the last page of this brochure.

053

054

055

TO ORDER FROM THE IGFA COLLECTION
MAIL THIS FORM TO IGFA OR
CALL TOLL FREE 1-800-442-4665 • FAX (954) 924-4220

PAGE	ITEM #	QTY.	SIZE	DESCRIPTION AND COLOR	ITEM PRICE	TOTAL AMOUNT

MERCHANDISE TOTAL	SHIPPING & HANDLING
$0.00 - 20.00	ADD $5.00
$21.00 - 50.00	ADD $10.00
$51.00 - 100.00	ADD $12.00
$101.00 - 200.00	ADD $15.00
To the above charges:	
Canada	ADD $15.00
Worldwide International	ADD $30.00
2nd Day Air (US Only)	ADD $15.00

SUBTOTAL	
FLORIDA RESIDENTS ADD 6% SALES	
ADD SHIPPING SEE CHART AT LEFT	
TOTAL AMOUNT OF ORDER	

PLEASE ALLOW 4 - 6 WEEKS FOR DELIVERY. ALL U.S. DELIVERIES ARE MADE BY UPS GROUND UNLESS OTHERWISE REQUESTED.

ADDITIONAL SHIPPING CHARGES WILL BE INCURRED FOR FOREIGN SHIPMENTS WEIGHING 4 POUNDS OR MORE.

ENCLOSED IS MY CHECK / MONEY ORDER FOR $________________
(MAKE CHECKS PAYABLE TO: INTERNATIONAL GAME FISH ASSOCIATION, US DOLLARS ONLY)

GIFT WRAP AVAILABLE ON MOST ITEMS FOR $5.00 (INCLUDES BOX, RIBBON & GIFT PAPER)

CHARGE TO MY: ☐ VISA ☐ MASTERCARD ☐ AMERICAN EXPRESS ☐ DISCOVER

ACCOUNT NO. ☐☐☐☐☐☐☐☐☐☐☐☐☐☐☐☐ EXP. DATE______

SIGNATURE____________________________________

MEMBER IDENTIFICATION #________________DAYTIME TELEPHONE________________

NAME ____________________________________

ADDRESS____________________________________

CITY____________________STATE____________ZIP________

☐ PLEASE SEND MEMBERSHIP INFORMATION   **My e-mail address is:**________________

SECTION 3
ANGLING RULES

Rules for Fishing In Fresh and Salt Water — 134

Rules for Fly Fishing — 138

WORLD RECORD REQUIREMENTS

Record Categories — 139

Record Catch Regulations — 141

Preparation of Claims — 142

Conversion Formulas for Weights & Measures — 143

CONTEST & CLUB REQUIREMENTS

Grand Slam Clubs — 143

10 Pound Bass Club — 143

25 Pound Snook Club — 143

1000 Pound Club — 143

Annual IGFA Fishing Contest — 144

5 to 1, 10 to 1, 15 to 1, & 20 to 1 Clubs — 144

APPLICATION FORMS

World Record and Fishing Contest — 145

10 Pound Bass Club — 147

International Angling Rules

The following angling rules have been formulated by the International Game Fish Association to promote ethical and sporting angling practices, to establish uniform regulations for the compilation of world game fish records, and to provide basic angling guidelines for use in fishing tournaments and any other group angling activities.

The word "angling" is defined as catching or attempting to catch fish with a rod, reel, line, and hook as outlined in the international angling rules. There are some aspects of angling that cannot be controlled through rule making, however. Angling regulations cannot insure an outstanding performance from each fish, and world records cannot indicate the amount of difficulty in catching the fish. Captures in which the fish has not fought or has not had a chance to fight do not reflect credit on the fisherman, and only the angler can properly evaluate the degree of achievement in establishing the record.

Only fish caught in accordance with IGFA international angling rules, and within the intent of these rules, will be considered for world records.

Following are the rules for freshwater and saltwater fishing and a separate set of rules for fly fishing.

RULES FOR FISHING IN FRESH AND SALT WATER

(Also see *Rules for Fly fishing*)

Equipment Regulations

A. LINE

1. Monofilament, multifilament, and lead core multifilament lines may be used. For line classes, see *World Record Requirements*.

2. Wire lines are prohibited.

B. LINE BACKING

1. Backing not attached to the fishing line is permissible with no restrictions as to size or material.

2. If the fishing line is attached to the backing, the catch shall be classified under the heavier of the two lines. The backing may not exceed the 130 lb (60 kg) line class and must be of a type of line approved for use in these angling rules.

C. DOUBLE LINE

The use of a double line is not required. If one is used, it must meet the following specifications:

1. A double line must consist of the actual line used to catch the fish.

2. Double lines are measured from the start of the knot, braid, roll or splice making the double to the farthermost end of the knot, splice, snap, swivel or other device used for securing the trace, leader, lure or hook to the double line.

Saltwater species: In all line classes up to and including 20 lb (10 kg), the double line shall be limited to 15 feet (4.57 meters). The combined length of the double line and leader shall not exceed 20 feet (6.1 meters).

The double line on all classes of tackle over 20 lb (10 kg) shall be limited to 30 feet (9.14 meters). The combined length of the double line and leader shall not exceed 40 feet (12.19 meters).

Freshwater species: The double line on all classes of tackle shall not exceed 6 feet (1.82 meters). The combined length of the double line and the leader shall not exceed 10 feet (3.04 meters).

D. LEADER

The use of a leader is not required. If one is used, it must meet the following specifications:

1. The length of the leader is the overall length including any lure, hook arrangement or other device. The leader must be connected to the line with a snap, knot, splice, swivel or other device. Holding devices are prohibited. There are no regulations regarding the material or strength of the leader.

Saltwater species: In all line classes up to and including 20 lb (10 kg), the leader shall be limited to 15 feet (4.57 meters). The combined length of the double line and leader shall not exceed 20 feet (6.1 meters).

The leader on all classes of tackle over 20 lb (10 kg) shall be limited to 30 feet (9.14 meters). The combined length of the double line and leader shall be limited to 40 feet (12.19 meters).

Freshwater species: The leader on all classes of tackle shall be limited to 6 feet (1.82 meters). The combined length of the double line and leader shall not exceed 10 feet (3.04 meters).

E. ROD

1. Rods must comply with sporting ethics and customs. Considerable latitude is allowed in the choice of a rod, but rods giving the angler an unfair advantage will be disqualified. This rule is intended to eliminate the use of unconventional rods.

2. The rod tip must be a minimum of 40 inches (101.6 cm) in length. The rod butt cannot exceed 27 inches (68.58 cm) in length. These measurements must be made from a point directly beneath the center of the reel. A curved butt is measured in a straight line. (The above measurements do not apply to surf casting rods.)

F. REEL

1. Reels must comply with sporting ethics and customs.

2. Power driven reels of any kind are prohibited. This includes motor, hydraulic, or electrically driven reels, and any device which gives the angler an unfair advantage.

3. Ratchet handle reels are prohibited.

4. Reels designed to be cranked with both hands at the same time are prohibited.

G. HOOKS FOR BAIT FISHING

1. For live or dead bait fishing no more than two single hooks may be used. Both must be firmly imbedded in or securely attached to the bait. The eyes of the hooks must be no less than a hook's length (the length of the largest hook used) apart and no more than 18 inches (45.72 cm) apart. The only exception is that the point of one hook may be passed through the eye of the other hook.

2. The use of a dangling or swinging hook is prohibited. Double or treble hooks are prohibited.

3. A two-hook rig for bottom fishing is acceptable if it consists of two single hooks on separate leaders or drops. Both hooks must be imbedded in the respective baits and separated sufficiently so that a fish caught on one hook cannot be foul-hooked by the other.

4. All record applications made for fish caught on two-hook tackle must be accompanied by a photograph or sketch of the hook arrangement.

H. HOOKS AND LURES

1. When using an artificial lure with a skirt or trailing material, no more than two single hooks may be attached to the line, leader, or trace. The hooks need not be attached separately. The eyes of the hooks must be no less than an overall hook's length (the overall length of the largest hook used) apart and no more than 12 inches (30.48 cm) apart. The only exception is that

the point of one hook may be passed through the eye of the other hook. The trailing hook may not extend more than a hook's length beyond the skirt of the lure. A photograph or sketch showing the hook arrangement must accompany a record application.

2. Gang hooks are permitted when attached to plugs and other artificial lures that are specifically designed for this use. Gang hooks must be free swinging and shall be limited to a maximum of three hooks (either single, double, or treble, or a combination of any three). Baits may not be used with gang hooks. A photograph or sketch of the plug or lure must be submitted with record applications.

I. OTHER EQUIPMENT

1. *Fighting chairs* may not have any mechanically propelled devices which aid the angler in fighting a fish.

2. *Gimbals* must be free swinging, which includes gimbals that swing in a vertical plane only. Any gimbal that allows the angler to reduce strain or to rest while fighting the fish is prohibited.

3. *Gaffs and nets* used to boat or land a fish must not exceed 8 feet (2.44 meters) in overall length. In using a flying or detachable gaff the rope may not exceed 30 feet (9.14 meters). The gaff rope must be measured from the point where it is secured to the detachable head to the other end. Only the effective length will be considered. If a fixed head gaff is used, the same limitations shall apply and the gaff rope shall be measured from the same location on the gaff hook. Only a single hook is permitted on any gaff. Harpoon or lance attachments are prohibited. Electrified gaffs are prohibited. Tail ropes are limited to 30 feet (9.14 meters). (When fishing from a bridge, pier, or other high platform or structure, this length limitation does not apply.)

4. *Floats* are prohibited with the exception of any small flotation device attached to the line or leader for the sole purpose of regulating the depth of the bait. The flotation device must not in any way hamper the fighting ability of the fish.

5. *Entangling devices*, either with or without a hook, are prohibited and may not be used for any purpose including baiting, hooking, fighting, or landing the fish.

6. *Outriggers, downriggers, and kites* are permitted to be used provided that the actual fishing line is attached to the snap or other release device, either directly or with some other material. The leader or double line may not be connected to the release mechanism either directly or with the use of a connecting device.

7. *Umbrella or spreader rigs, daisy chains and similar devices* may only be used if they do not unfairly hamper or inhibit the normal swimming or fighting ability of the fish, thereby giving the angler or crew an unfair advantage in fighting, landing or boating the fish.

8. *A safety line* may be attached to the rod provided that it does not in any way assist the angler in fighting the fish.

Angling Regulations

1. From the time that a fish strikes or takes a bait or lure, the angler must hook, fight, and land or boat the fish without the aid of any other person, except as provided in these regulations.

2. If a rod holder is used and a fish strikes or takes the bait or lure, the angler must remove the rod from the holder as quickly as possible. The intent of this rule is that the angler shall strike and hook the fish with the rod in hand.

3. In the event of a multiple strike on separate lines being fished by a single angler, only the first fish fought by the angler will be considered for a world record.

4. If a double line is used, the intent of the regulations is that the fish will be fought on the single line most of the time that it takes to land the fish.

5. A harness may be attached to the reel or rod, but not to the fighting chair. The harness may be replaced or adjusted by a person other than the angler.

6. Use of a rod belt or waist gimbal is permitted.

7. When angling from a boat, once the leader is brought within the grasp of the mate, or the end of the leader is wound to the rod tip, more than one person is permitted to hold the leader.

8. One or more gaffers may be used in addition to persons holding the leader. The gaff handle must be in hand when the fish is gaffed.

9. The angling and equipment regulations shall apply until the fish is weighed.

The following acts will disqualify a catch:

1. Failure to comply with equipment or angling regulations.

2. The act of persons other than the angler in touching any part of the rod, reel, or line (including the double line) either bodily or with any device, from the time a fish strikes or takes the bait or lure, until the fish is either landed or released, or in giving any aid other than that allowed in the rules and regulations. If an obstacle to the passage of the line through the rod guides has to be removed from the line, then the obstacle (whether chum, floatline, rubber band, or other material) shall be held and cut free. Under no circumstances should the line be held or touched by anyone other than the angler during this process.

3. Resting the rod in a rod holder, on the gunwale of the boat, or any other object while playing the fish.

4. Handlining or using a handline or rope attached in any manner to the angler's line or leader for the purpose of holding or lifting the fish.

5. Shooting, harpooning, or lancing any fish (including sharks and halibuts) at any stage of the catch.

6. Chumming with or using as bait the flesh, blood, skin, or any part of mammals other than hair or pork rind used in lures designed for trolling or casting.

7. Using a boat or device to beach or drive a fish into shallow water in order to deprive the fish of its normal ability to swim.

8. Changing the rod or reel while the fish is being played.

9. Splicing, removing, or adding to the line while the fish is being played.

10. Intentionally foul-hooking a fish.

11. Catching a fish in a manner that the double line never leaves the rod tip.

12. Using a size or kind of bait that is illegal to possess.

13. Attaching the angler's line or leader to part of a boat or other object for the purpose of holding or lifting the fish.

14. If a fish escapes before gaffing or netting and is recaptured by any method other than as outlined in the angling rules.

The following situations will disqualify a catch:

1. When a rod breaks (while the fish is being played) in a manner that reduces the length of the tip below minimum dimensions or severely impairs its angling characteristics.

2. Mutilation to the fish, prior to landing or boating the catch, caused by sharks, other fish, mammals, or propellers that remove or penetrate the flesh. (Injuries caused by leader or line, scratches, old healed scars or regeneration deformities are not considered to be disqualifying injuries.) Any mutilation on the fish must be shown in a photograph and fully explained in a separate report accompanying the record application.

3. When a fish is hooked or entangled on more than one line.

Illustrated Guide to Equipment Regulations

DOUBLE LINES AND LEADERS

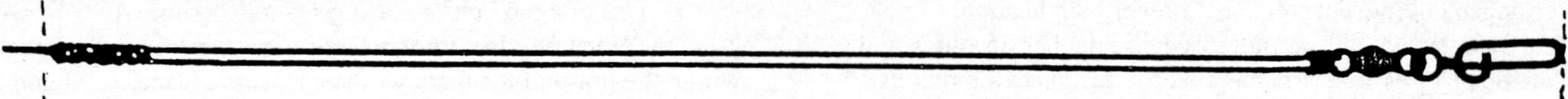

Double lines are measured from the start of the knot, braid, roll or splice making the double to the farthermost end of the knot, splice, snap, swivel or other device used for securing the trace, leader, lure or hook to the double line. For saltwater species the double line shall be limited to 15 feet (4.57 meters) for all line classes up to and including 20 lb (10 kg); and shall be limited to 30 feet (9.14 meters) for line classes over 20 lb (10 kg). For freshwater species the double line on all classes of tackle shall not exceed 6 feet (1.82 meters).

The leader shall be limited to 15 feet (4.57 meters) for saltwater species in line classes up to 20 lb (10 kg), and 30 feet (9.14 meters) for all line classes over 20 lb (10 kg). For freshwater species the leader on all classes of tackle shall be limited to 6 feet (1.82 meters).

The length of the leader is the overall length including any lure, hook arrangements or other device.

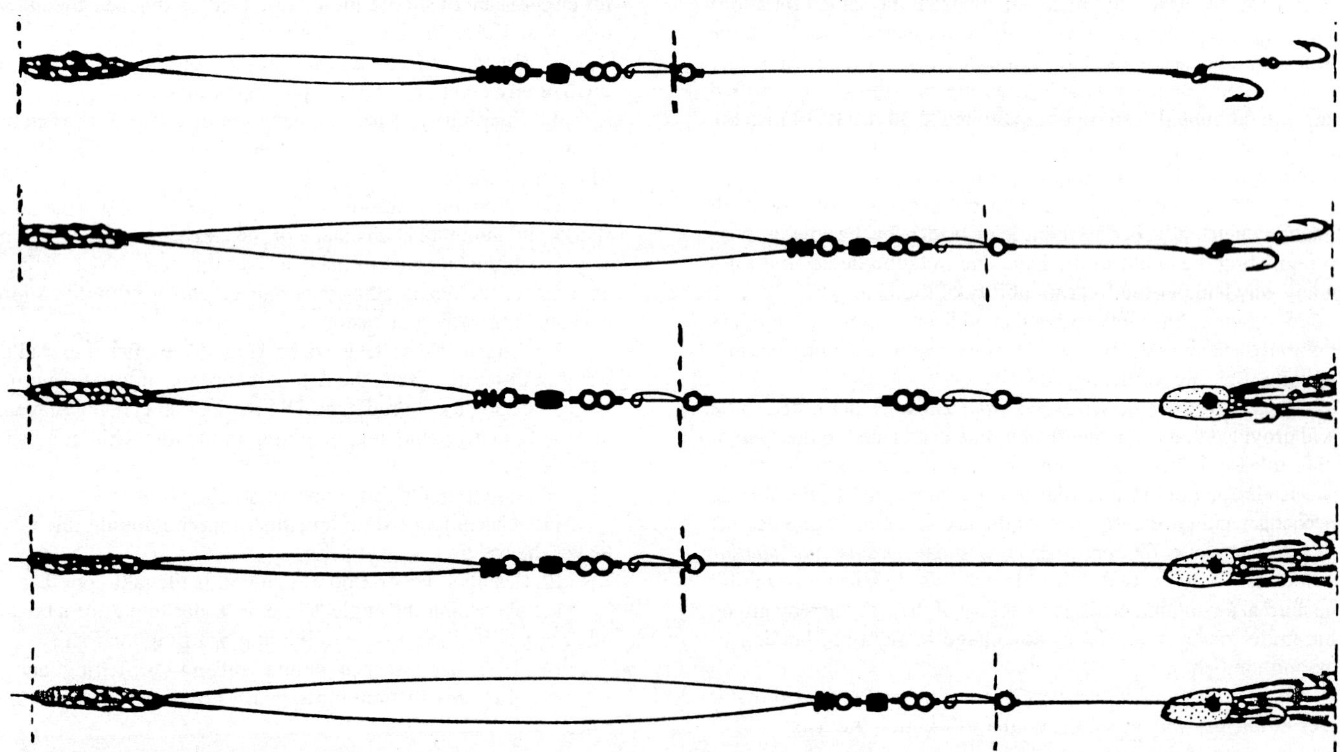

The combined length of the double line and leader shall not exceed 20 feet (6.1 meters) in line classes up to and including 20 lb (10 kg) and 40 feet (12.19 meters) in line classes over 20 lb (10 kg) for saltwater species. The combined length of the double line and leader shall not exceed 10 feet (3.04 meters) for freshwater species.

HOOKS

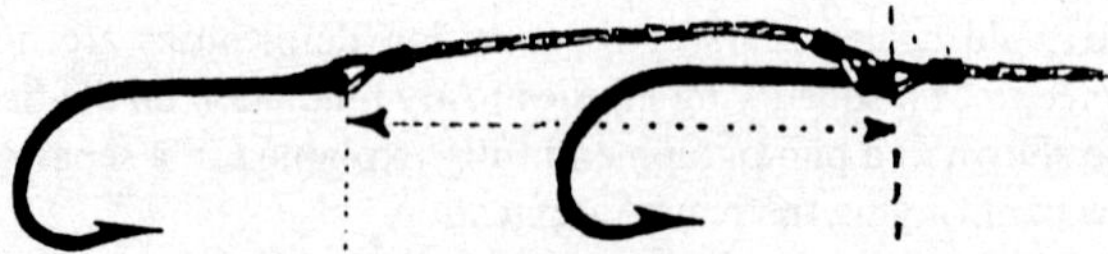

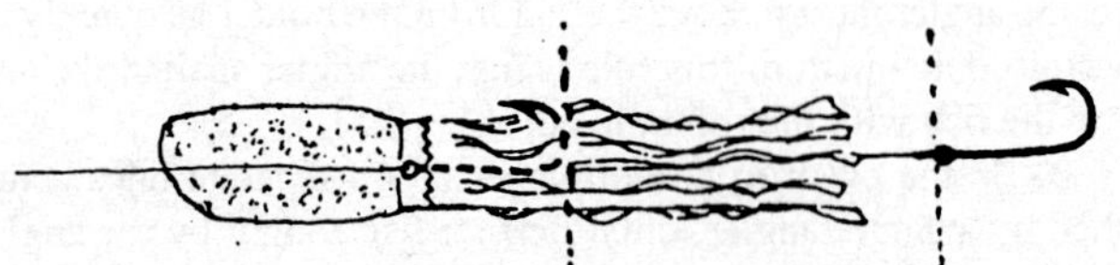

LEGAL if eyes of hooks no more than 18 inches (45.72 cm) apart in baits and no more than 12 inches (30.45 cm) apart in lures. ILLEGAL if eyes further apart than these distances.

NOT LEGAL as the second or trailing hook extends more than the hook's length beyond skirt. See also two hook rigs.

NOT LEGAL in bait or lures as eyes of hooks are less than hook's length (the length of the largest hook) apart.

LEGAL as eyes of hooks are no less than a hook's length apart and no more than 18 inches (45.72 cm) in baits and 12 inches (30.45 cm) in lures.

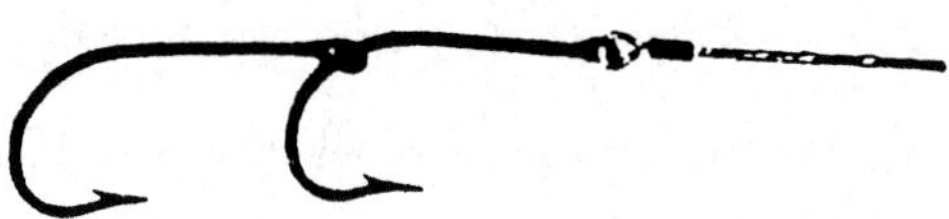

LEGAL in bait and lures. The point of one hook is passed through the eye of the other hook.

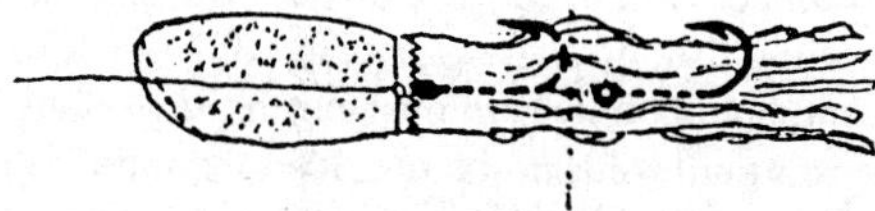

LEGAL as eyes of hooks are no less than a hook's length apart and no more than 12 inches (30.45 cm) apart, and the trailing hook does not extend more than a hook's length beyond the skirt.

LEGAL as hook is contained within skirt.

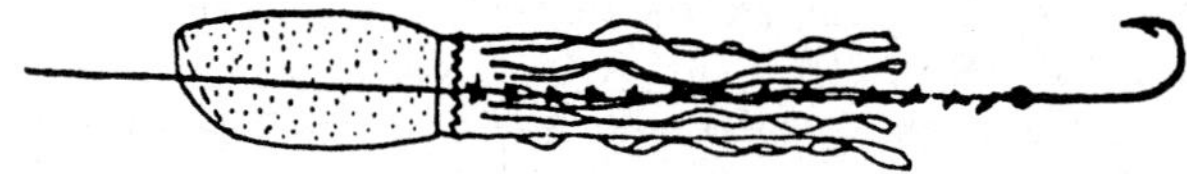

NOT LEGAL as the single hook extends more than its length beyond the skirt.

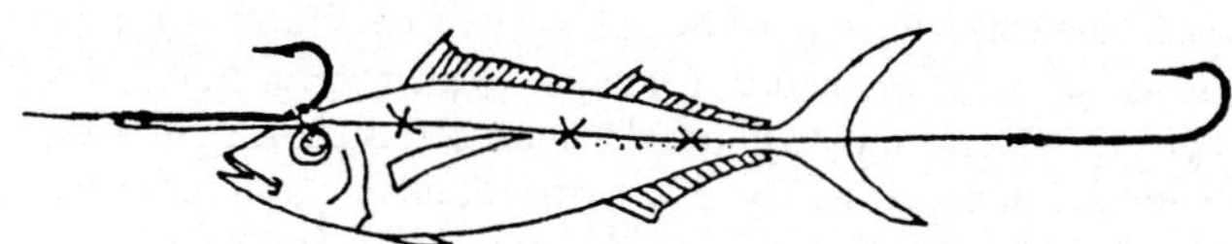

NOT LEGAL as back hook is not firmly imbedded in or securely attached to bait and is a dangling or swinging hook.

LEGAL as both hooks are firmly imbedded or securely attached to bait. Would not be legal if eyes of hooks were more than 18 inches (45.72 cm) apart.

GAFFS

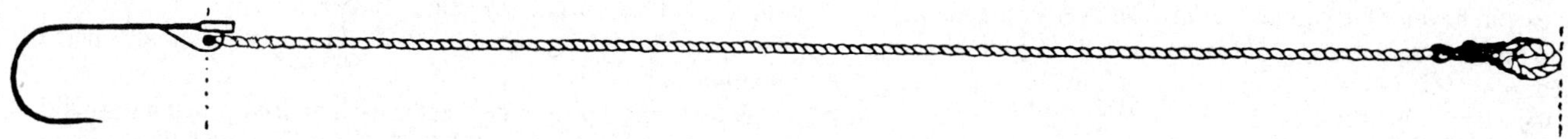

LEGAL on boats if effective length does not exceed 30 feet (9.15 meters).

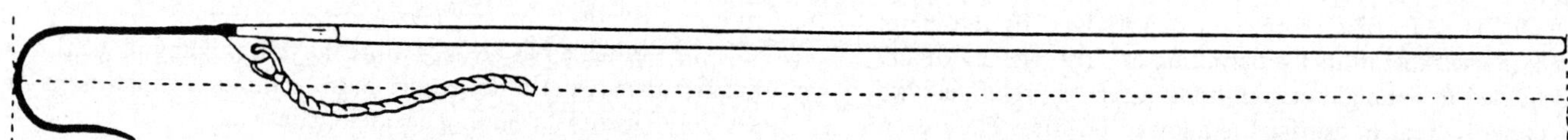

LEGAL on boats if overall length does not exceed 8 feet (2.44 meters).

RULES FOR FLY FISHING

Equipment Regulations

A. LINE

Any type of fly line and backing may be used. The breaking strength of the fly line and backing are not restricted.

B. LEADER

Leaders must conform to generally accepted fly fishing customs.

A leader includes a class tippet and, optionally, a shock tippet. A butt or taper section between the fly line and the class tippet shall also be considered part of the leader and there are no limits on its length, material, or strength.

A class tippet must be made of nonmetallic material and either attached directly to the fly or to the shock tippet if one is used. The class tippet must be at least 15 inches (38.10 cm) long (measured inside connecting knots). With respect to knotless, tapered leaders, the terminal 15 inches (38.10 cm) will also determine tippet class. There is no maximum length limitation.

A shock tippet, not to exceed 12 inches (30.48 cm) in length, may be added to the class tippet and tied to the lure. It can be made of any type of material, and there is no limit on its breaking strength. The shock tippet is measured from the eye of the hook to the single strand of class tippet and includes any knots used to connect the shock tippet to the class tippet.

In the case of a tandem hook fly, the shock tippet shall be measured from the eye of the leading hook.

C. ROD

Regardless of material used or number of sections, rods must conform to generally accepted fly fishing customs and practices. A rod shall not measure less than 6 feet (1.82 meters) in overall length. Any rod that gives the angler an unsporting advantage will be disqualified. Extension butts are limited to 6 inches (15.24 cm).

D. REEL

The reel must be designed expressly for fly fishing. There are no restrictions on gear ratio or type of drag employed except where the angler would gain an unfair advantage. Electric or electronically operated reels are prohibited.

E. HOOKS

A conventional fly may be dressed on a single or double hook or two single hooks in tandem. The second hook in any tandem fly must not extend beyond the wing material. The eyes of the hooks shall be no farther than 6 inches (15.24 cm) apart. Treble hooks are prohibited.

F. LURES

The lure must be a recognized type of artificial fly, which includes streamer, bucktail, tube fly, wet fly, dry fly, nymph, popper and bug. The use of any other type of lure or natural or preserved bait, either singularly or attached to the fly, is expressly prohibited. Only a single fly is allowed. Dropper flies are prohibited. The fact that a lure can be cast with a fly rod is not evidence in itself that it fits the definition of a fly. The use of any lure designed to entangle or foul-hook a fish is prohibited. No scent, either natural or artificial is allowed on flies. The use of scented material in a fly is prohibited.

G. GAFFS & NETS

Gaffs and nets used to boat or land a fish must not exceed 8 feet (2.44 meters) in overall length. (When fishing from a bridge, pier or other high stationary structure, this length limitation does not apply.) The use of a flying gaff is not permitted. Only a single hook is permitted on any gaff. Harpoon or lance attachments are prohibited. A rope or any extension cannot be attached to the gaff.

Angling Regulations

1. The angler must cast, hook, fight, and bring the fish to gaff or net unaided by any other person. No other person may touch any part of the tackle during the playing of the fish or give aid other than taking the leader for gaffing or netting purposes.

2. Casting and retrieving must be carried out in accordance with normal customs and generally accepted practices. The major criterion in casting is that the weight of the line must carry the fly rather than the weight of the fly carrying the line. Trolling a fly behind a moving water craft is not permitted. The craft must be completely out of gear both at the time the fly is presented to the fish and during the retrieve. The maximum amount of line that can be stripped off the reel is 120 feet (36.57 meters) from the fly.

3. Once a fish is hooked, the tackle may not be altered in any way, with the exception of adding an extension butt.

4. Fish must be hooked on the fly in use. If a small fish takes the fly and a larger fish swallows the smaller fish, the catch will be disallowed.

5. One or more people may assist in gaffing or netting the fish.

6. The angling and equipment regulations shall apply until the fish is weighed.

The following acts will disqualify a catch:

1. Failure to comply with equipment or angling regulations.

2. The act of persons other than the angler in touching any part of the rod, reel, or line either bodily or with any device during the playing of the fish, or in giving any aid other than that allowed in the rules and regulations. If an obstacle to the passage of the line through the rod guides has to be removed from the line, then the obstacle shall be held and cut free. Under no circumstances should the line be held or touched by anyone other than the angler during this process.

3. Resting the rod on any part of the boat, or on any other object while playing the fish.

4. Handlining or using a handline or rope attached in any manner to the angler's line or leader for the purpose of holding or lifting the fish.

5. Intentionally foul-hooking or snagging a fish.

6. Shooting, harpooning, or lancing any fish (including sharks and halibut) at any stage of the catch.

7. Chumming with the flesh, blood, skin, or any part of mammals.

8. Using a boat or device to beach or drive a fish into shallow water in order to deprive the fish of its normal ability to swim.

9. Attaching the angler's line or leader to part of a boat or other object for the purpose of holding or lifting the fish.

10. If a fish escapes before gaffing or netting and is recaptured by any method other than as outlined in the angling rules.

11. When a rod breaks (while the fish is being played) in a manner that reduces its length below minimum dimensions or severely impairs its angling characteristics.

12. When a fish is hooked or entangled on more than one line.

13. Mutilation to the fish, prior to landing or boating the catch, caused by sharks, other fish, mammals, or propellers that remove or penetrate the flesh. (Injuries caused by leader or line, scratches, old healed scars or regeneration deformities are not considered to be disqualifying injuries.) Any mutilation on the fish must be shown in a photograph and fully explained in a separate report accompanying the record application.

World Record Requirements

Game fish catches can only be considered for world record status if they are caught according to International Angling Rules. Following is information on world record categories, requirements, and procedures for filing claims, effective January 1, 1999. An application fee of $10 for U.S. members and $25 U.S. for non-members is required for each claim. All materials submitted become the property of IGFA.

World Record Categories

GENERAL INFORMATION

IGFA maintains world records for both freshwater and saltwater game fishes in line class, tippet class and all-tackle categories.

In order to qualify for a record, a catch must be a minimum of 1 pound (.453 kg) in weight, and must out weigh the existing record by the required amount or meet the minimum weight requirements, if any, for vacant records.

No applications will be accepted for fish caught in hatchery waters or sanctuaries. The catch must not be at variance with any laws or regulations governing the species or the waters in which it was caught.

When an additional species of game fish is made eligible for IGFA world records, the effective date will be announced. Fishes caught on or after the effective date will be eligible for records. Announcement of an additional species in the *World Record Game Fishes* book or in other IGFA publications will be considered proper notification in lieu of any other notice.

ALL-TACKLE CATEGORY

All-tackle world records are kept for the heaviest fish of a species caught by an angler in any line class up to 130 lb (60 kg). Fish caught on lines designed to test over the 130 lb (60 kg) class will not be considered for record claims.

All-tackle record claims are considered for all species of fish caught according to IGFA angling rules.

Applications for species not currently included in the IGFA line class and tippet class listings must meet the following criteria:

1. The fish must represent a valid species with a recognized scientific name.

2. The fish must be a species commonly fished for with rod and reel in the general area where the catch is made.

3. The fish must be identifiable based on photos and other supporting data presented with the application.

4. The fish must be considered "trophy-sized." A rule of thumb is that the weight must fall within the top half of the estimated maximum weight of the species.

FLY ROD CATEGORIES

Fly rod world records are maintained according to tippet strength. Records are kept for the same species listed for line class records in the following tippet classes:

Metric	U.S. Customary
1 kg	2 lb
2 kg	4 lb
3 kg	6 lb
4 kg	8 lb
6 kg	12 lb
8 kg	16 lb
10 kg	20 lb

LINE CLASS CATEGORIES

Line class records are kept according to the strength of the line. Records are kept in these line classes:

Metric	U.S. Customary
1 kg	2 lb
2 kg	4 lb
3 kg	6 lb
4 kg	8 lb
6 kg	12 lb
8 kg	16 lb
10 kg	20 lb
15 kg	30 lb
24 kg	50 lb
37 kg	80 lb
60 kg	130 lb

With the exception of all-tackle claims, line classes are limited for many species. Listed below are the maximum line classes acceptable for world record purposes in each species category:

Freshwater Species

Species listed under the "freshwater" category are also eligible for world records if caught in salt or brackish water. The catch must be made in accordance with freshwater equipment regulations.

	Maximum Line Class
Barramundi / *Lates calcarifer*	37 kg (80 lb)
Bass, largemouth / *Micropterus salmoides*	10 kg (20 lb)
Bass, redeye / *Micropterus coosae*	6 kg (12 lb)
Bass, rock / *Ambloplites rupestris*	6 kg (12 lb)
Bass, smallmouth / *Micropterus dolomieu*	8 kg (16 lb)
Bass, spotted / *Micropterus punctulatus*	10 kg (20 lb)
Bass, striped (landlocked) / *Morone saxatilis*	24 kg (50 lb)
Bass, white / *Morone chrysops*	6 kg (12 lb)
Bass, whiterock / *Morone saxatilis x Morone chrysops*	10 kg (20 lb)
Bass, yellow / *Morone mississippiensis*	6 kg (12 lb)
Bluegill / *Lepomis macrochirus*	6 kg (12 lb)
Bowfin / *Amia calva*	15 kg (30 lb)
Buffalo, bigmouth / *Ictiobus cyprinellus*	37 kg (80 lb)
Buffalo, smallmouth / *Ictiobus bubalus*	24 kg (50 lb)
Bullhead, black / *Ameiurus melas*	6 kg (12 lb)
Bullhead, brown / *Ameiurus nebulosus*	6 kg (12 lb)
Bullhead, yellow / *Ameiurus natalis*	6 kg (12 lb)
Burbot / *Lota lota*	10 kg (20 lb)
Carp, common / *Cyprinus carpio*	24 kg (50 lb)
Catfish, blue / *Ictalurus furcatus*	60 kg (130 lb)
Catfish, channel / *Ictalurus punctatus*	37 kg (80 lb)
Catfish, flathead / *Pylodictis olivaris*	60 kg (130 lb)
Catfish, white / *Ameiurus catus*	10 kg (20 lb)
Char, Arctic / *Salvelinus alpinus*	15 kg (30 lb)
Crappie, black / *Pomoxis nigromaculatus*	6 kg (12 lb)

Species	Line Class
Crappie, white / *Pomoxis annularis*	6 kg (12 lb)
Dolly Varden / *Salvelinus malma*	6 kg (12 lb)
Dorado / *Maxillosus spp.*	24 kg (50 lb)
Drum, freshwater / *Aplodinotus grunniens*	37 kg (80 lb)
Gar, alligator / *Lepisosteus spatula*	60 kg (130 lb)
Gar, Florida / *Lepisosteus platyrhincus*	10 kg (20 lb)
Gar, longnose / *Lepisosteus osseus*	37 kg (80 lb)
Gar, shortnose / *Lepisosteus platostomus*	10 kg (20 lb)
Gar, spotted / *Lepisosteus oculatus*	10 kg (20 lb)
Grayling, Arctic / *Thymallus arcticus*	10 kg (20 lb)
Huchen / *Hucho hucho*	60 kg (130 lb)
Inconnu / *Stenodus leucichthys*	24 kg (50 lb)
Kokanee / *Oncorhynchus nerka*	6 kg (12 lb)
Muskellunge / *Esox masquinongy*	37 kg (80 lb)
Muskellunge, tiger / *Esox Masquinongy x Esox lucius*	24 kg (50 lb)
Payara / *Hydrolicus scomberoides*	10 kg (20 lb)
Peacock, blackstriped / *Cichla intermedia*	10 kg (20 lb)
Peacock, butterfly / *Cichla ocellaris*	10 kg (20 lb)
Peacock, speckled / *Cichla temensis*	10 kg (20 lb)
Perch, Nile / *Lates niloticus*	60 kg (130 lb)
Perch, white / *Morone americana*	6 kg (12 lb)
Perch, yellow / *Perca flavescens*	6 kg (12 lb)
Pickerel, chain / *Esox niger*	6 kg (12 lb)
Pike, northern / *Esox lucius*	24 kg (50 lb)
Redhorse, shorthead / *Moxostoma macrolepidotum*	6 kg (12 lb)
Redhorse, silver / *Moxostoma anisurum*	6 kg (12 lb)
Salmon, Atlantic / *Salmo salar*	24 kg (50 lb)
Salmon, chinook / *Oncorhynchus tshawytscha*	60 kg (130 lb)
Salmon, chum / *Oncorhynchus keta*	15 kg (30 lb)
Salmon, coho / *Oncorhynchus kisutch*	24 kg (50 lb)
Salmon, pink / *Oncorhynchus gorbuscha*	15 kg (30 lb)
Salmon, sockeye / *Oncorhynchus nerka*	15 kg (30 lb)
Sauger / *Stizostedion canadense*	8 kg (16 lb)
Shad, American / *Alosa sapidissima*	6 kg (12 lb)
Splake / *Salvelinus namaycush x Salvelinus fontinalis*	15 kg (30 lb)
Sturgeon / *Acipenseridae family*	60 kg (130 lb)
Sunfish, green / *Lepomis cyanellus*	6 kg (12 lb)
Sunfish, redbreast / *Lepomis auritus*	6 kg (12 lb)
Sunfish, redear / *Lepomis microlophus*	6 kg (12 lb)
Taimen / *Hucho taimen*	60 kg (130 lb)
Tigerfish / *Hydrocynus vittatus*	15 kg (30 lb)
Tigerfish, giant / *Hydrocynus goliath*	60 kg (130 lb)
Trout, brook / *Salvelinus fontinalis*	10 kg (20 lb)
Trout, brown / *Salmo trutta*	24 kg (50 lb)
Trout, bull / *Salvelinus confluentus*	10 kg (20 lb)
Trout, cutthroat / *Oncorhynchus clarki*	10 kg (20 lb)
Trout, golden / *Oncorhynchus aguabonita*	6 kg (12 lb)
Trout, lake / *Salvelinus namaycush*	37 kg (80 lb)
Trout, rainbow / *Oncorhynchus mykiss*	24 kg (50 lb)
Trout, tiger / *Salmo trutta x Salvelinus fontinalis*	15 kg (30 lb)
Walleye / *Stizostedion vitreum*	10 kg (20 lb)
Warmouth / *Lepomis gulosus*	6 kg (12 lb)
Whitefish, lake / *Coregonus clupeaformis*	8 kg (16 lb)
Whitefish, mountain / *Prosopium williamsoni*	6 kg (12 lb)
Whitefish, round / *Prosopium cylindraceum*	6 kg (12 lb)

Saltwater Species

Species	Maximum Line Class
Albacore / *Thunnus alalunga*	37 kg (80 lb)
Amberjack, greater / *Seriola dumerili*	60 kg (130 lb)
Barracuda, great / *Sphyraena barracuda*	37 kg (80 lb)
Bass, black sea / *Centropristis striata*	15 kg (30 lb)
Bass, European / *Dicentrarchus labrax*	15 kg (30 lb)
Bass, giant sea / *Stereolepis gigas*	60 kg (130 lb)
Bass, kelp (calico) / *Paralabrax clathratus*	10 kg (20 lb)
Bass, striped / *Morone saxatilis*	37 kg (80 lb)
Bluefish / *Pomatomus saltatrix*	24 kg (50 lb)
Bonefish / *Albula spp.*	15 kg (30 lb)
Bonito, Atlantic / *Sarda sarda*	15 kg (30 lb)
Bonito, Pacific / *Sarda spp.*	15 kg (30 lb)
Cobia / *Rachycentron canadum*	37 kg (80 lb)
Cod, Atlantic / *Gadus morhua*	37 kg (80 lb)
Cod, Pacific / *Gadus macrocephalus*	24 kg (50 lb)
Conger / *Conger conger*	60 kg (130 lb)
Dentex / *Dentex dentex*	15 kg (30 lb)
Dolphinfish / *Coryphaena hippurus*	37 kg (80 lb)
Drum, black / *Pogonias cromis*	37 kg (80 lb)
Drum, red / *Sciaenops ocellatus*	37 kg (80 lb)
Flounder, summer / *Paralichthys dentatus*	15 kg (30 lb)
Halibut, Atlantic / *Hippoglossus hippoglossus*	60 kg (130 lb)
Halibut, California / *Paralichthys californicus*	37 kg (80 lb)
Halibut, Pacific / *Hippoglossus stenolepis*	60 kg (130 lb)
Jack, crevalle / *Caranx hippos*	24 kg (50 lb)
Jack, horse-eye / *Caranx latus*	24 kg (50 lb)
Jack, Pacific crevalle / *Caranx caninus*	24 kg (50 lb)
Jewfish / *Epinephelus itajara*	60 kg (130 lb)
Kahawai / *Arripis trutta*	15 kg (30 lb)
Kawakawa / *Euthynnus affinis*	15 kg (30 lb)
Leerfish (Garrick) / *Lichia amia*	24 kg (50 lb)
Lingcod / *Ophiodon elongatus*	24 kg (50 lb)
Mackerel, cero / *Scomberomorus regalis*	10 kg (20 lb)
Mackerel, king / *Scomberomorus cavalla*	37 kg (80 lb)
Mackerel, narrowbarred / *Scomberomorus commerson*	37 kg (80 lb)
Mackerel, Spanish / *Scomberomorus maculatus*	10 kg (20 lb)
Madai / *Pagrus major*	24 kg (50 lb)
Marlin, black / *Makaira indica*	60 kg (130 lb)
Marlin, blue (Atlantic) / *Makaira nigricans*	60 kg (130 lb)
Marlin, blue (Pacific) / *Makaira nigricans*	60 kg (130 lb)
Marlin, striped / *Tetrapturus audax*	60 kg (130 lb)
Marlin, white / *Tetrapturus albidus*	60 kg (130 lb)
Permit / *Trachinotus falcatus*	24 kg (50 lb)
Pollack, European / *Pollachius pollachius*	24 kg (50 lb)
Pollock / *Pollachius virens*	24 kg (50 lb)
Pompano, African / *Alectis ciliaris*	24 kg (50 lb)
Queenfish / *Scomberoides commersonnianus & Scomberoides lysan*	24 kg (50 lb)
Roosterfish / *Nematistius pectoralis*	60 kg (130 lb)
Runner, rainbow / *Elagatis bipinnulata*	24 kg (50 lb)
Sailfish, Atlantic / *Istiophorus platypterus*	37 kg (80 lb)
Sailfish, Pacific / *Istiophorus platypterus*	60 kg (130 lb)
Seabass, blackfin / *Lateolabrax latus*	15 kg (30 lb)
Seabass, Japanese / *Lateolabrax japonicus*	15 kg (30 lb)
Seabass, white / *Atractoscion nobilis*	37 kg (80 lb)
Seatrout, spotted / *Cynoscion nebulosus*	15 kg (30 lb)
Shark, blue / *Prionace glauca*	60 kg (130 lb)
Shark, hammerhead / *Sphyrna spp.*	60 kg (130 lb)
Shark, mako / *Isurus spp.*	60 kg (130 lb)
Shark, porbeagle / *Lamna nasus*	60 kg (130 lb)
Shark, thresher / *Alopias spp.*	60 kg (130 lb)
Shark, tiger / *Galeocerdo cuvier*	60 kg (130 lb)
Shark, tope / *Galeorhinus galeus*	37 kg (80 lb)
Shark, white / *Carcharodon carcharias*	60 kg (130 lb)
Skipjack, black / *Euthynnus lineatus*	15 kg (30 lb)
Snapper (squirefish) / *Pagrus auratus*	24 kg (50 lb)
Snapper, cubera / *Lutjanus cyanopterus*	60 kg (130 lb)

Snapper, mutton / *Lutjanus analis*	15 kg (30 lb)
Snapper, Pacific cubera / *Lutjanus novemfasciatus*	60 kg (130 lb)
Snook / *Centropomus spp.*	24 kg (50 lb)
Spearfish / *Tetrapturus spp.*	37 kg (80 lb)
Swordfish / *Xiphias gladius*	60 kg (130 lb)
Tarpon / *Megalops atlanticus*	60 kg (130 lb)
Tautog / *Tautoga onitis*	15 kg (30 lb)
Threadfin, king / *Polynemus sheridani*	15 kg (30 lb)
Trevally, bigeye / *Caranx sexfasciatus*	37 kg (80 lb)
Trevally, bluefin / *Caranx melampygus*	15 kg (30 lb)
Trevally, giant / *Caranx ignobilis*	60 kg (130 lb)
Tripletail / *Lobotes surinamensis*	24 kg (50 lb)
Tuna, bigeye (Atlantic) / *Thunnus obesus*	60 kg (130 lb)
Tuna, bigeye (Pacific) / *Thunnus obesus*	60 kg (130 lb)
Tuna, blackfin / *Thunnus atlanticus*	24 kg (50 lb)
Tuna, bluefin / *Thunnus thynnus*	60 kg (130 lb)
Tuna, dogtooth / *Gymnosarda unicolor*	60 kg (130 lb)
Tuna, longtail / *Thunnus tonggol*	37 kg (80 lb)
Tuna, skipjack / *Katsuwonus pelamis*	24 kg (50 lb)
Tuna, southern bluefin / *Thunnus maccoyi*	60 kg (130 lb)
Tuna, yellowfin / *Thunnus albacares*	60 kg (130 lb)
Tunny, little / *Euthynnus alletteratus*	15 kg (30 lb)
Wahoo / *Acanthocybium solandri*	60 kg (130 lb)
Weakfish / *Cynoscion regalis*	15 kg (30 lb)
Yellowtail, California / *Seriola lalandi dorsalis*	37 kg (80 lb)
Yellowtail, southern / *S. lalandi lalandi*	60 kg (130 lb)

LINE TESTING

IGFA tests all line and tippet samples submitted with world record claims in accordance with the metric line class designations, which vary slightly from the standard U.S. customary designations. For example, the U.S. customary equivalent of 4 kilograms is 8.81 pounds. Thus, line designated by the manufacturer as 8 lb class line may test up to 8.81 pounds (4 kg) to qualify for an 8 lb line class record. The U.S. customary equivalents in pounds for the metric line classes are as follows:

Metric	U.S. Customary Equivalent
1 kg	2.20 lb
2 kg	4.40 lb
3 kg	6.61 lb
4 kg	8.81 lb
6 kg	13.22 lb
8 kg	17.63 lb
10 kg	22.04 lb
15 kg	33.06 lb
24 kg	52.91 lb
37 kg	81.57 lb
60 kg	132.27 lb

Line and tippet samples submitted with record claims are uniformly tested in accordance with Government specifications which have been modified and supplemented by IGFA.

Note: **IGFA offers a line and tippet testing service for members only.**

Record Catch Regulations

GENERAL INFORMATION

1. Protested applications or disputed existing records will be referred to the IGFA Executive Committee for review. Its decisions will be final. IGFA reserves the right to refuse to consider an application or grant a claim for a record or fishing contest application. All IGFA decisions will be based upon the intent of the regulations.

2. When a substantial award is specifically offered for a world record catch in *any* line or tippet class, only a claim for an all-tackle record will be considered.

3. In some instances, an IGFA officer or member of the International Committee or a deputy from a local IGFA member club may be asked to recheck information supplied on a claim. Such action is not to be regarded as doubt of the formal affidavit, but rather as evidence of the extreme care with which IGFA investigates and maintains its records.

SPECIES IDENTIFICATION

1. Photographs must be submitted by which positive identification of the exact species can be made. Read the rules on photographs at the end of this section, and refer to the Species Identification section in the *World Record Game Fishes* book to determine which features must show to identify your fish. Applications without photographs will not be accepted.

2. If there is the slightest doubt that the fish cannot be properly identified from the photographs and other data submitted, the fish should be examined by an ichthyologist or qualified fishery biologist before a record or contest application is submitted to IGFA. The scientist's signature and title (or qualifications) should appear on the IGFA application form or on a separate document confirming the identification of the species.

3. If a scientist is not available, the fish should be retained in a preserved or frozen condition until a qualified authority can verify the species or until notified by IGFA that the fish need no longer be retained.

4. If no decision can be made from the photographs and the angler can provide no further proof of the identification of the species, the record claim will not be considered.

WITNESSES TO CATCH

On all record claims, witnesses to the catch are highly desirable if at all possible. Unwitnessed catches may be disallowed if questions arise regarding their authenticity. It is important that the witnesses can attest to the angler's compliance with the IGFA International Angling Rules and Equipment Regulations.

MINIMUM WEIGHT REQUIREMENTS FOR VACANT RECORDS

The minimum acceptance weight for any record catch claim is 1 pound (.453 kg).

WEIGHTS NEEDED TO DEFEAT OR TIE EXISTING RECORDS

1. To replace a record for a fish weighing less than 25 pounds (11.33 kg), the replacement must weigh at least 2 ounces (56.69 gm) more than the existing record.

2. To replace a record fish weighing 25 pounds (11.33 kg) or more, the replacement must weigh at least one half of 1 percent more than the existing record. *Ex:* At 100 pounds (45.35 kg) the additional weight required would be 8 ounces (226.7 gm); at 200 pounds (90.71 kg) the additional weight required would be 1 pound (.45 kg).

3. A catch which matches the weight of an existing record or exceeds the weight by less than the amount required to defeat the record will be considered a tie. In case of a tie claim involving more than two catches, weight must be compared with the original record (first fish to be caught). Nothing weighing less than the original record will be considered.

4. Estimated weights will not be accepted. (See *Weighing Requirements.*) Fractions of ounces or their metric equivalents will not be considered.

TIME LIMIT ON CLAIMS

With the exception of *all-tackle records* only, claims for record fish caught in U.S. continental waters must be received by IGFA within 60 days of the date of catch. Claims for record fish caught in other waters must be received by IGFA within three months of the date of catch.

Claims for all-tackle records only are considered for catches made in past years if (1) acceptable photographs are submitted, (2) the weight of the fish can be positively verified, and (3) the method of catch can be substantiated. For these catches, as much information as possible must be submitted on an IGFA world record application form with any additional substantiating data.

If an incomplete record claim is submitted, it must be accompanied by an explanation of why certain portions are incomplete. An incomplete claim will be considered for a record if the following conditions are met:

1. The incomplete claim with explanations of why portions are incomplete must be received by IGFA within the time limits specified above.

2. Missing data must be due to circumstances beyond the control of the angler making the record claim.

3. All missing data must be supplied within a period of time considered to be reasonable in view of the particular circumstances.

Final decisions on incomplete claims will be made by IGFA's Executive Committee.

WEIGHING REQUIREMENTS

1. The fish must be weighed by an official weighmaster (if one is available) or by an IGFA official or by a recognized local person familiar with the scale. Disinterested witnesses to the weight should be used whenever possible.

2. The weight of the sling, platform, or rope (if one is used to secure the fish on the scales) must be determined and deducted from the total weight.

3. At the time of weighing, the actual tackle used by the angler to catch the fish must be exhibited to the weighmaster and the weight witness.

4. No estimated weights will be accepted. Fish weighed only at sea or on other bodies of water will not be accepted.

5. Only weights indicated by the graduations on the scale will be accepted. Visual fractionalizing of these graduations is not allowed. Any weights that fall between two graduations on the scale must be rounded to the lower of the two.

6. All record fish should be weighed on scales that have been checked and certified for accuracy by government agencies or other qualified and accredited organizations. All scales must be regularly checked for accuracy and certified in accordance with applicable government regulations at least once every twelve months. If at the time of weighing the fish, the scale has not been properly certified within twelve months, it should be checked and certified for accuracy as quickly as possible, and an official report stating the findings of the inspection prior to any adjustment of the scale must be included with the record application.

SCALE CERTIFICATION

1. If there is no official government inspector or accredited commercial scales representative available in the area where the fish is weighed, the scales must be checked by weighing objects of recognized and proven weight. Objects weighed must be at least equal to the weight of the fish. Substantiation of the correct weight of these objects must be submitted to IGFA along with the names and complete addresses of accredited witnesses to the entire procedure.

2. In extremely remote areas where no weighing scales are available, it will be permissible for the angler to use his own scales providing that they are of a quality type and have been properly certified both before and after returning from the fishing trip.

3. IGFA reserves the right to require any scale to be recertified for accuracy if there are any indications that the scale might not have weighed correctly.

Note: **IGFA now offers a scale testing service for members only.**

Preparation of Claims

To apply for a world record, the angler must submit a completed IGFA application form, the mandatory length of line and terminal tackle (described below) used to catch the fish, and acceptable photographs of the fish, the tackle used to catch the fish, the scale used to weigh the fish, and the angler with the fish.

APPLICATION FORM

The official IGFA world record application form or a reproduction must be used for record claims. This form may be reproduced as long as all items are included.

The angler must fill in the application personally. IGFA also recommends that the angler personally mail the application, line sample or fly leader and photographs.

When making any record claim, the angler must indicate the specified strength of the line or tippet used to catch the fish. In the cases of line class and tippet class records, this will place the claim in an IGFA line or tippet class category (see *World Record Categories*). All lines will be examined by IGFA to verify the specified strength of the line. If the line or tippet over tests its particular category, the application will be considered where the line tests; if it under tests into a lower line or tippet class category, the application will not be considered for the lower line class. The heaviest line class permitted for both freshwater and saltwater records is 60 kg (130 lb) class. The heaviest tippet class permitted for fly fishing records is 10 kg (20 lb). If the line or tippet over tests these maximum strengths, the claim will be disallowed.

Extreme care should be exercised in measuring the fish as the measurements are often important for weight verification and scientific studies. See the measurement diagram on the record application to be sure you have measured correctly.

The angler is responsible for seeing that the necessary signatures and correct addresses of the boat captain, weighmaster and witnesses are on the application. If an IGFA officer or representative, or an officer or member of an IGFA club is available, he or she should be asked to witness the claim. The name of a boatman, guide, or weighmaster repeated as witness is not acceptable.

The angler must appear in person to have his application notarized. In territories where notarization is not possible or customary, the signature of a government commissioner or resident, a member of an embassy, legation or consular staff or an IGFA officer or International Committee member may replace notarization.

Any deliberate falsification of an application will disqualify the applicant for any future IGFA world record, and any existing records will be nullified.

LINE OR TIPPET SAMPLE

All applications for fly fishing records must be accompanied by the fly, the entire tippet, and the entire leader along with one inch of the fly line beyond the attachment to the leader. These components must be intact and connected.

All applications for freshwater and saltwater line class records must be accompanied by the entire leader, the double line, and at least 50 feet (15.24 meters) of the single line closest to the double line, leader or hook. All line samples and the leader (if one is used) must be submitted in one piece. If a lure is used with the leader, the leader should be cut at the eye attachment to the lure.

Each line sample must be in one piece. It must be submitted in a manner that it can be easily unwound without damage to the line. A recommended method is to take a rectangular piece of stiff cardboard and cut notches in two opposite ends. Secure one end of the line to the cardboard and wind the line around the cardboard through the notched areas. Secure the other end, and write your name and the specified strength of the line on the cardboard. Any line sample submitted that is tangled or cannot be easily unwound will not be accepted.

PHOTOGRAPHS

Photographs showing the full length of the fish, the rod and reel used to make the catch, and the scale used to weigh the fish must accompany each record application. A photograph of the angler with the fish is also required.

For species identification, the clearest possible photos should be submitted. This is especially important in the cases of hybrids and fishes that may be confused with similar species. Shark applications should include a photograph of the shark's teeth, and of the head and back taken from above in addition to the photographs taken from the side. Whether the shark has or does not have a ridge between the dorsal fins should be clearly evident in this photograph.

In all cases, photographs should be taken of the fish in a hanging position and also lying on a flat surface on its side. The fish should be broadside to the camera and no part of the fish should be obscured. **The fins must be fully extended and not obscured with the hands, and the jaw or bill clearly shown. Avoid obscuring the keels of sharks and tunas with a tail rope.**

When photographing a fish lying on its side, the surface beneath the fish should be smooth and a ruler or marked tape place beside the fish if possible. Photographs from various angles are most helpful. An additional photograph of the fish on the scale with actual weight visible helps to expedite the application.

Photos taken by daylight with a reproducible-type negative film are highly recommended if at all possible.

Conversion Formulas for Weights & Measures

Persons submitting world record and contest claims are only required to provide the weights and measurements of the fish in the units in which they were taken. The following formulas are provided for your information.

WEIGHTS

Ounces	x	28.349	= Grams
Ounces	x	0.02835	= Kilograms
Pounds	x	453.59	= Grams
Pounds	x	0.45359	= Kilograms
Grams	x	0.0353	= Ounces
Grams	x	0.002	= Pounds
Kilograms	x	35.2736	= Ounces
Kilograms	x	2.2046	= Pounds

MEASURES

Inches	x	25.4	= Millimeters
Inches	x	2.54	= Centimeters
Feet	x	30.48	= Centimeters
Feet	x	0.3048	= Meters
Millimeters	x	0.03937	= Inches
Centimeters	x	0.3937	= Inches
Centimeters	x	0.0328	= Feet
Meters	x	39.37	= Inches

Grand Slam Clubs

The four Grand Slam Clubs honor the outstanding accomplishment of multiple catches of designated species by one angler in a single day. The clubs are: **Offshore Super Grand Slam, Inshore Super Grand Slam, Offshore Grand Slam, Inshore Grand Slam.**

To qualify for the **Offshore Super Grand Slam Club** the angler must catch any four of the following: blue marlin, black marlin, sailfish, swordfish and/or spearfish in one day. Catching three of the billfish will qualify the angler for the **Offshore Grand Slam Club.**

The targeted species for the inshore clubs are bonefish, permit, tarpon and snook. Catching all four species in one day will earn a place in the **Inshore Super Grand Slam Club.** Three catches in one day will qualify for the **Inshore Grand Slam Club.** Past catches in one day are eligible. Also, in line with IGFA's conservation policy, fish do not have to be landed or weighed to qualify.

The club members will receive a personalized certificate of recognition featuring the work of renowned game fish artist Dave McHose, an embroidered jacket patch identifying the club with individual chevrons featuring each species of the slam, and recognition in the Special Clubs section of the *World Record Game Fishes* book. To participate angler must obtain a Grand Slam Club application from IGFA and there is a $50 (US) registration fee. For more information contact IGFA.

10 Pound Bass Club

The 10 Pound Bass Club acknowledges freshwater bass catches of 10 pounds or more. Eligible species are largemouth, smallmouth, spotted and peacock bass. Catches past and present are eligible as long as they can be documented to the satisfaction of the IGFA.

For conservation reasons, catches may be weighed on the boat on small portable scales. They can be quickly photographed and released. Scales must be certified prior to the weighing, or as quickly after the weighing as possible.

Anglers wishing to enter their bass should submit a 10 Pound Bass Club application with a photograph of the catch and a fee of $25 (US) to cover postage, handling and cost of material.

Club members will receive a beautiful certificate suitable for framing, a multicolored jacket emblem featuring a leaping bass and special recognition in the *World Record Game Fishes* book.

Thousand Pound Club

The Thousand Pound Club recognizes anglers who have fought and subdued fish weighing 1,000 pounds or more. The club is open to any angler who had legitimately caught with regulation tackle a black marlin, blue marlin, bluefin tuna, mako shark, tiger shark, or white shark weighing 1,000 lb (453.50 kg) or more.

Applications must be submitted on the standard IGFA World Record form or a reproduction. The angler must submit sufficient information to positively identify the catch and verify the weight. There will be no limitation on when the fish was caught.

Those who qualify will receive a gold embossed certificate to substantiate their membership in the club. Members also will receive a handsome gold crest jacket emblem, along with a distinctive jacket/cap pin.

The one-time charge to become a member of the Thousand Pound Club is $100 (US) currency.

25 Pound Snook Club

IGFA's most recent addition to the Special Clubs is the **25 Pound Snook Club.** Any angler that submits an application for the club and documents such a catch will receive a beautiful, full-color certificate for framing, plus an embroidered snook emblem. Anglers wishing to register their 25 pound or larger snook catches with **IGFA** should contact Patricia Brown, Executive Administrator, Special Clubs, at IGFA for a **25 Pound Snook Club** application form. Fill it out and send it to **IGFA** with a photo of the catch and a registration fee of $35 US to cover postage, handling and cost of the awards.

Annual Fishing Contest

Freshwater and saltwater anglers worldwide can enter their prize catches in the Annual Fishing Contest. Entries are accepted for all species taken on rod and reel according to IGFA angling rules. First, second and third place certificates are awarded for the heaviest fish of each species taken during the contest year plus all entrants receive a certificate of catch.

In addition to recognizing many of the great catches made by anglers each year the contest is designed to document these catches and make the statistics available to fishery scientists and other interested parties. IGFA also recognizes that the current world record listings may fail to include some species caught in substantial numbers throughout the world.

CONTEST DATES

Entries are accepted for catches made on or after August 1 of each year. The deadline for submitting claims is October 31 of each year.

ELIGIBILITY

The contest is open to all anglers. There is no charge for processing an entry.

All freshwater and saltwater species caught on rod and reel are eligible for consideration.

Official contest winners are determined according to the three heaviest approved catches of each species caught on any line up to 130 lb (60 kg) strength or any tippet up to 20 lb (10 kg).

The line or tippet sample strength used to catch the fish *must be* designated on the entry form. This is especially important in the case of species not currently listed in the IGFA world records as the contest entry may determine a new line class record category.

CONTEST REGULATIONS

1. All catches must be made in accordance with IGFA International Angling Rules and Equipment Regulations.

2. The minimum acceptance weight for any fish entered in the contest is 1 pound (.453 kg).

3. Applications will not be accepted for fish caught in hatchery waters or sanctuaries. The catch must not be at variance with any laws or regulations governing the species or the waters in which it was caught.

4. Weighing requirements must comply with those currently in affect for world record catches.

5. In the case of a tie for first place or second place, the first fish caught will be placed in the higher category. In the case of a tie for third place, only the first fish caught will be listed as a contest winner.

SUBMISSION OF ENTRIES

When submitting a contest entry, anglers must supply the same information and materials (line or tippet sample and photographs) as required for a world record. The standard IGFA application form must be used. Catches submitted for world record claims are automatically included in the annual fishing contest within the time frame limitations.

Due to the amount of paperwork involved in following up on claims, incomplete applications will not be accepted. The angler must insure that photographs, line samples, and a completed application are sent to IGFA.

CONTEST DECISIONS

All decisions involving applications in this contest will be made by the IGFA Executive Committee. Their decisions will be final.

ENTRY FORMS & ANGLING RULES

Contest applications and copies of the IGFA angling rules may be obtained from IGFA.

IGFA 5, 10, 15 & 20 to 1 Clubs

The International Game Fish Association has established a program to give special recognition to catches where the weight of the fish far exceeds the breaking strength of the line or tippet used to catch the fish. This program gives recognition for catches where the weight of the fish is five, ten, fifteen or twenty times the breaking strength of the line or tippet. Approved applications will be recognized as members of the IGFA 5 to 1, 10 to 1, 15 to 1 or 20 to 1 Clubs.

ELIGIBILITY

All anglers worldwide fulfilling the "Club catch requirements" are eligible. Catches made in the past will be considered if reputable data can be submitted to substantiate the breaking strength of the line or tippet. All previous IGFA record holders are eligible. There is no limit on the number of entries submitted by the angler but each entry must be accompanied by the designated entry fee.

CLUB CATCH REQUIREMENTS

1. All catches must be made in accordance with IGFA International Angling Rules and Equipment Regulations.

2. The minimum weight for any fish entered is 10 lb (4.5 kg)

3. The weight of the catch must exceed the breaking strength of the line by 5, 10 , 15 or 20 times, depending on the club category for which the application is being made. For example, in order to apply for the 10 to 1 club, an angler using 8-lb test line would have to catch a fish weighing at least 80 pounds, while an angler using 50-lb test line would have to catch a fish weighing a minimum of 500 pounds.

4. All freshwater and saltwater species are eligible, provided the fish can be positively identified from the data and photographs submitted. Entries will not be accepted for fish caught in hatchery waters or sanctuaries. The catch must not be at variance with any laws or regulations governing the species or the waters in which it was caught.

5. Weighing requirements must comply with those currently in effect for IGFA world record claims.

APPLICATION FORM

When submitting an entry anglers must supply the same information and materials (line or tippet sample and photographs) as required for a world record. The standard "IGFA World Record & Fishing Contest Application" form must be used. If an earlier application form is used, the angler must indicate in the form the club for which the application is being made.

ENTRY FEE

Each entry shall be accompanied by a registration fee of U.S. $25 to help cover the costs of processing the application, award items and other cost incurred in establishing and maintaining the award program. If an entry is not approved, the fee will be refunded.

AWARDS

When an IGFA 5, 10, 15, or 20 to 1 Club entry is approved, the angler will receive a certificate, an embroidered jacket emblem, and a pin, each denoting the appropriate club category.

ADDITIONAL COPIES

Entry forms and/or IGFA International Angling Rules and World Record Requirements may be obtained from IGFA.

IGFA World Record & Fishing Contest Application
FORM FOR RECORDING FRESHWATER & SALTWATER GAME FISH CATCHES

Read all IGFA angling rules and world record requirements before completing and signing this application. The angler's signature on the completed form must be witnessed by a notary. This application must be accompanied by line or tippet samples and photographs as specified in the World Record Requirements. Hybrids and other species which may pose a problem of identity should be examined by an ichthyologist or qualified fishery biologist.

I AM SUBMITTING THIS ENTRY FOR:

☐ An all-tackle world record.

☐ A world record in the following line class:

_____________ lb/ _____________ kg

☐ A fly rod world record in the following tippet class:

_____________ lb/ _____________ kg

☐ Annual Contest ☐ Catch & Release ☐ State record

☐ 5-1 Club ☐ 10-1 Club ☐ 15-1 Club ☐ 20-1 Club

☐ 10 Pound Bass Club ☐ Thousand Pound Club

SPECIES

Common name: _________________________

Scientific name: _________________________

WEIGHT: Fish was weighed in ☐ lbs ☐ kgs.

lbs: _____________ oz: _____________ kg: _____________

Digital weight (if weighed on electronic scales, give weight exactly as shown): _________________________

DATE OF CATCH: _________________________

PLACE OF CATCH: _________________________

____

LENGTH (See measurement diagrams)

inches: x to x _____________ xx to xx _____________

cm: x to x _____________ xx to xx _____________

GIRTH (See measurement diagrams)

inches: _____________ cm: _____________

METHOD OF CATCH (trolling, casting, fly fishing, etc.): _________________________

FIGHTING TIME: _________________________

Was this catch recorded on video? _____________

ANGLER (Print name as you wish it to appear on your record or contest certificate:

____

Daytime phone _________________________

Permanent address
(Include country and address code):

____

____

____

Age if 16 or under _____________

Angler's fishing club affiliation (if any):

____

EQUIPMENT

Rod

Make: _________________________

Tip length (center of reel to end of tip): _____________

Butt length (center of reel to lower end of butt):

____

Reel

Make: _____________ Size: _____________

Line or tippet

Make: _____________ Size as stated on label: _____________

☐ I am an IGFA member, enclosed is $10.
☐ I am not an IGFA member, enclosed is $35.
☐ Enclosed is $45 for membership and processing fee.

Enclosed is $_________ check or money order for the World Record application processing fee.

Or please charge to my:

___Visa ___Mastercard ___American Express ___Discover

Account No. ☐☐☐☐☐☐☐☐☐☐☐☐☐☐☐☐☐

Expiration date _________ Signature _________________________

☐ Please send ___ extra copies of my record certificate at $5 each

Note: All items must be filled in. If an item does not apply, write "none used". Do not leave any spaces blank.

Length of double line: _______________________

Make of backing: _________________ Size: _________

Other equipment:

Type of gaff: _____________ Length: ___________

Length of trace or leader: _________________

Number and type of hooks : _________________

Name of lure, fly or bait: _________________

BOAT (if used)

Name: _________________________________

Make: ________________ Length: ___________

Captain's name: _____________________

Signature: _________________________

Address: _________________________________

____

Mate's name: _______________________

Signature: _________________________

Address: _________________________

____

SCALES

Location: _________________________

Type: _________________________

Manufacturer: _____________________

Date last certified: _______________

Person and/or agency that certified scales:

____

Weighmaster: _____________________________

Signature: _______________________________

Address: _________________________________

____

WITNESSES

Witness to weighing (other than angler, captain or

weighmaster): ___________________________

Address: _______________________________

____

Witnesses to catch (other than captain). List two names and
addresses if possible.

1. _____________________________________

____

2. _____________________________________

____

Number of persons witnessing catch: ___________

**VERIFICATION OF SPECIES IDENTITY
(See world record requirements.)**

Signature of examining ichthyologist:

____

Title, degree, or qualifications: _______________

Address: _________________________________

Anglers are encouraged to write a detailed description of the catch and in some cases this may be required. The description may be used in a future IGFA publication.

AFFIDAVIT

I, the undersigned, hereby take oath and attest that the fish described in this application was hooked, fought, and brought to gaff by me without assistance from anyone, except as specifically provided in the regulations; and that it was caught in accordance with IGFA angling rules; and that the line submitted with this application is the actual line used to catch the fish on the stated date. I further declare that all the information in this application is true and correct to the best of my knowledge. I understand that IGFA reserves the right to employ verification procedures. I agree to be bound by any ruling of the IGFA relative to this application.

Signature of angler: ____

Sworn before me this _________________ day of _____________________________ 19________

Notary signature and seal:____

When completely filled out and signed, mail this application with photos and line sample by quickest means to:

IGFA, 300 Gulf Stream Way, Dania Beach, Florida 33004 USA

(This application may be reproduced.)

IGFA
10 LB BASS CLUB

Species_______________________________

Weight

Fish weighed in: ❑ lbs ❑ kgs

__________lbs _________oz _______________kgs

Digital weight:_____________ **Released: Yes___ No___**

Scales

Location:_________________________________
Type:____________________________________
Manufacturer:_____________________________
Date last certified: _______________________

Person Who Weighed Catch

Name:____________________________________
Address:__________________________________
____

Length
inches: x to x_______________ xx to xx_______________
cm: x to x_______________ xx to xx _______________

Girth
inches:_______________ cm:_______________

Date of Catch_______________________

Place of Catch_______________________

____

Angler
(Print name as you wish it to appear on certificate):

____

Permanent address (include country and postal code)

____

____

____

Witnesses:
Witness to weighing:_______________________

Address:__________________________________

____

Witnesses to catch:
(Please provide name and mailing address)

1._______________________________________
____
____
2._______________________________________
____
____

Method of Catch
(trolling, casting, fly fishing, etc.):

____

Fighting Time:

____

Equipment

Rod

Make_______________________________________

Tip length (center of reel to end of tip):

____

Butt length: (center of reel to lower end of butt):

____

Reel

Make:_________________ Size:_______________

Line or tippet

Make:_______________________________________

Size as stated on label:___________________________

Length of trace or leader:___________________________

Number and type of hooks:___________________________

Name of lure, fly or bait:___________________________

❑ I am a member of IGFA
❑ Please send me IGFA membership information

Boat (if used)

Name:_______________________________________

Make:_______________________________________

Length:_______________________________________

Captain

Name:_______________________________________

Address:_______________________________________

____

Species Measurements:

x to x = length from lower lip to fork in tail
xx to xx = length from upper lip to point of tail
G = girth measures around fish at widest location

Eligible species include largemouth, smallmouth, spotted and peacock basses. All 10 lb catches, past and present are eligible as long as they can be documented and have been caught in accordance with IGFA rules. Anglers will not have to kill their bass to be eligible. Fish may be weighed in the boat, photographed and released alive. Scales should be certified for accuracy prior to the weighing or as quickly as possible after the weighing. Send completed application, photos and $25.00 registration fee to IGFA.

AFFIDAVIT

I the undersigned, hereby take oath and attest that the fish described in this application was hooked, fought, and boated by me without assistance from anyone, except as specifically provided in the regulations; and that it was caught in accordance with IGFA angling rules. I further declare that all the information in this application is true and correct to the best of my knowledge. I agree to be bound by any ruling of the IGFA relative to this application.

Signature of angler:_______________________________________

Sworn before me this _______________ day of_______________________________________ 19_____________

Notary signature and seal:_______________________________________

Mail to:

International Game Fish Association
300 Gulf Stream Way
Dania Beach, Florida 33004 USA
Phone (954) 927-2628 Fax (954) 924-4299

Enclosed is $25 check or money order for the 10 Pound Bass Club application processing fee. Or please charge to my:

___Visa ___Mastercard ___American Express ___Discover

Account No.

Expiration date_________Signature_______________

SECTION 4
WORLD RECORDS

In an effort to constantly maintain the most up-to-date and accurate listing of records, we have changed the names of several species as recommended in the 1991 editions of the American Fisheries Society Special Publications 20 and 21.

Freshwater Line Class Records — 150

Saltwater Line Class Records — 160

Freshwater Fly Rod Records — 186

Saltwater Fly Rod Records — 196

Freshwater & Saltwater All-Tackle Records — 215

Junior Angler Records — 234
Junior Angler World Record Application — 243

All records are listed alphabetically according to common names of species

IGFA Freshwater Line Class World Records

The following are world freshwater records granted in IGFA line class categories as of January 1, 1999. The records are listed alphabetically according to the common names of species.

Barramundi / *Lates calcarifer*

LINE CLASS	WEIGHT	PLACE	DATE	ANGLER
01 kg (2 lb)	8.85 kg (19 lb 8 oz)	Hodel Lagoon, Townsville, Queensland, Australia	June 2, 1982	Bruce Glanville
02 kg (4 lb)	19.20 kg (42 lb 5 oz)	False Cape, Cairns, Australia	Feb. 1, 1993	Billy Fairbairn
03 kg (6 lb)	17.30 kg (38 lb 2 oz)	Lake Tinaroo, Queensland, Australia	May 26, 1995	Jack Leighton
04 kg (8 lb)	22.20 kg (48 lb 15 oz)	South Alligator River, Northern Territory, Australia	Mar. 16, 1990	Richard De Groot
06 kg (12 lb)	27.10 kg (59 lb 11 oz)	Mary River, Northern Territory, Australia	Apr. 10, 1994	Richard Creswick
08 kg (16 lb)	28.65 kg (63 lb 2 oz)	Normah River, Normahton, Queensland, Australia	Apr. 28, 1991	Scott Barnsley
10 kg (20 lb)	27.50 kg (60 lb 10 oz)	Aroa River, Papua New Guinea	May 24, 1987	Manfred A.H. Birner
15 kg (30 lb)	24.40 kg (53 lb 12 oz)	Galley Reach, Port Moresby, Papua New Guinea	Dec. 8, 1993	Nathan J.T.W. Chang
24 kg (50 lb)	21.40 kg (47 lb 2 oz)	Laloki River, Port Moresby, Papua New Guinea	Oct. 3, 1991	Manfred A.H. Birner
37 kg (80 lb)	Vacant			

Bass, largemouth / *Micropterus salmoides*

LINE CLASS	WEIGHT	PLACE	DATE	ANGLER
01 kg (2 lb)	6.70 kg (14 lb 12 oz)	Castaic Lake, Castaic, California, USA	June 1, 1992	Robert J. Crupi
02 kg (4 lb)	7.76 kg (17 lb 1 oz)	Castaic Lake, Castaic, California, USA	Dec. 28, 1990	Robert J. Crupi
03 kg (6 lb)	7.51 kg (16 lb 9 oz)	Lake Isabella, California, USA	Mar. 18, 1998	Terry McAbee
04 kg (8 lb)	9.61 kg (21 lb 3 oz)	Oakview, California, USA	Mar. 4, 1980	Raymond D. Easley
06 kg (12 lb)	9.53 kg (21 lb 0 oz)	Castaic Lake, Castaic, California, USA	Mar. 9, 1990	Robert J. Crupi
08 kg (16 lb)	9.98 kg (22 lb 0 oz)	Castaic Lake, Castaic, California, USA	Mar. 12, 1991	Robert J. Crupi
10 kg (20 lb)	8.63 kg (19 lb 0 oz)	Lake Castaic, California, USA	Jan. 8, 1989	Dan T. Kadota

Bass, redeye / *Micropterus coosae*

LINE CLASS	WEIGHT	PLACE	DATE	ANGLER
01 kg (2 lb)	2.40 kg (5 lb 5 oz)	Flint River, Warwick, Georgia, USA	Feb. 16, 1986	Larry M. Guilbeau
02 kg (4 lb)	3.16 kg (6 lb 15 oz)	Flint River, Warwick, Georgia, USA	Apr. 8, 1990	Larry Guilbeau
03 kg (6 lb)	3.17 kg (7 lb 0 oz)	Flint River, Georgia, USA	Nov. 24, 1995	Jimmy Pearson
04 kg (8 lb)	3.40 kg (7 lb 8 oz)	Flint River, Albany, Georgia, USA	Apr. 24, 1986	Robert Hall
06 kg (12 lb)	3.55 kg (7 lb 13 oz)	Apalachicola River, Chattahoochee, Florida, USA	Feb. 18, 1989	Bill Johnston

Bass, rock / *Ambloplites rupestris*

LINE CLASS	WEIGHT	PLACE	DATE	ANGLER
01 kg (2 lb)	0.90 kg (2 lb 0 oz)	Lake Erie, Pennsylvania, USA	June 18, 1998	Herbert G. Ratner, Jr.
02 kg (4 lb)	0.90 kg (2 lb 0 oz)	Lake Erie, Pennsylvania, USA	June 18, 1998	Herbert G. Ratner, Jr.
03 kg (6 lb)	1.13 kg (2 lb 8 oz)	Lake Erie, Pennsylvania, USA	June 18, 1998	Herbert G. Ratner, Jr.
04 kg (8 lb)	1.36 kg (3 lb 0 oz)	Lake Erie, Pennsylvania, USA	June 18, 1998	Herbert G. Ratner, Jr.
06 kg (12 lb)	0.56 kg (1 lb 4 oz)	Big Toad Lake, Minnesota, USA	May 27, 1985	Roland Kotowski
06 kg (12 lb) Tie	0.57 kg (1 lb 4 oz)	Crow Wing River, Pillager, Minnesota, USA	June 22, 1985	Gilbert Wettstein
06 kg (12 lb) Tie	0.61 kg (1 lb 5 oz)	O'Brien Lake, Nashwauk, Minnesota, USA	Sept. 30, 1987	Ricky Jansen

Bass, smallmouth / *Micropterus dolomieu*

LINE CLASS	WEIGHT	PLACE	DATE	ANGLER
01 kg (2 lb)	3.15 kg (7 lb 0 oz)	Pickwick Lake, Tennessee, USA	June 2, 1997	Herbert G. Ratner, Jr.
02 kg (4 lb)	3.43 kg (7 lb 9 oz)	Pickwick Lake, Florence, Alabama, USA	Jan. 5, 1991	Charles I. Dunlap
03 kg (6 lb)	3.90 kg (8 lb 9 oz)	Pickwick Lake, Counce, Tennessee, USA	Mar. 11, 1998	E. Scott Yarbro, MD
04 kg (8 lb)	4.76 kg (10 lb 8 oz)	Hendricks Creek, Kentucky, USA	Apr. 14, 1986	Paul E. Beal
06 kg (12 lb)	3.85 kg (8 lb 8 oz)	Watts Bar Lake, Spring City, Tennessee, USA	Apr. 6, 1984	Lenny Cecil
08 kg (16 lb)	3.81 kg (8 lb 6 oz)	Pickwick Lake, Florence, Alabama, USA	Jan. 4, 1988	Terrell D. Nail

Bass, spotted / *Micropterus punctulatus*

LINE CLASS	WEIGHT	PLACE	DATE	ANGLER
01 kg (2 lb)	2.87 kg (6 lb 5 oz)	Lake Perris, California, USA	Mar. 17, 1985	Gilbert J. Rowe
02 kg (4 lb)	3.34 kg (7 lb 5 oz)	Lake Perris, California, USA	Mar. 27, 1986	Gilbert J. Rowe
03 kg (6 lb)	4.19 kg (9 lb 4 oz)	Lake Perris, California, USA	Jan. 24, 1987	Steven M. West
04 kg (8 lb)	4.19 kg (9 lb 4 oz)	Lake Perris, California, USA	Apr. 1, 1987	Gilbert J. Rowe
06 kg (12 lb)	4.33 kg (9 lb 9 oz)	Pine Flat Lake, California, USA	Oct. 12, 1996	Kirk M. Sakamoto
08 kg (16 lb)	4.28 kg (9 lb 7 oz)	Pine Flat Lake, California, USA	Feb. 25, 1994	Bob E. Shelton
10 kg (20 lb)	3.92 kg (8 lb 10 oz)	Smith Lake, Alabama, USA	Feb. 25, 1972	Billy Henderson

Bass, striped (landlocked) / *Morone saxatilis*

LINE CLASS	WEIGHT	PLACE	DATE	ANGLER
01 kg (2 lb)	14.51 kg (32 lb 0 oz)	Norfork Lake, Mountain Home, Arkansas, USA	Jan. 24, 1998	Bill Fitzgerald
02 kg (4 lb)	19.95 kg (44 lb 0 oz)	Watts Bar Lake, Spring City, Tennessee, USA	Feb. 2, 1987	Rufus S. Morgan, MD
03 kg (6 lb)	19.95 kg (44 lb 0 oz)	Melton Hill Lake, Oak Ridge, Tennessee, USA	Mar. 22, 1995	Glen Roberts
04 kg (8 lb)	24.04 kg (53 lb 0 oz)	Bull Shoals, Arkansas, USA	May 1, 1987	William G. Sligar
06 kg (12 lb)	30.61 kg (67 lb 8 oz)	O'Neill Forebay, Los Banos, California, USA	May 7, 1992	Hank Ferguson
08 kg (16 lb)	29.93 kg (66 lb 0 oz)	O'Neill Forebay, Los Banos, California, USA	June 29, 1988	Theodore H. Furnish
10 kg (20 lb)	28.91 kg (63 lb 12 oz)	Melton Hill Lake, Tennessee, USA	Feb. 2, 1998	Willis L. Marsh
15 kg (30 lb)	21.64 kg (47 lb 11 oz)	Flint River, Albany, Georgia, USA	Mar. 7, 1986	Don Allen Fowler
24 kg (50 lb)	23.81 kg (52 lb 8 oz)	Elephant Butte Reservoir, New Mexico, USA	Jan. 16, 1991	Johnny Carl Dickerson

Bass, white / *Morone chrysops*

LINE CLASS	WEIGHT	PLACE	DATE	ANGLER
01 kg (2 lb)	1.58 kg (3 lb 8 oz)	Frio River, Texas, USA	Feb. 26, 1988	David R. Gentry
02 kg (4 lb)	2.43 kg (5 lb 6 oz)	Grenada, Mississippi, USA	Apr. 21, 1979	W. C. Mulvihill
03 kg (6 lb)	1.72 kg (3 lb 12 oz)	Sabine River, Carthage, Texas, USA	Feb. 17, 1998	Keith Warren
04 kg (8 lb)	2.52 kg (5 lb 9 oz)	Colorado River, Texas, USA	Mar. 31, 1977	David S. Cordill
06 kg (12 lb)	3.09 kg (6 lb 13 oz)	Lake Orange, Orange, Virginia, USA	July 31, 1989	Ronald L. Sprouse

Bass, whiterock / *Morone saxatilis x Morone chrysops*

LINE CLASS	WEIGHT	PLACE	DATE	ANGLER
01 kg (2 lb)	4.72 kg (10 lb 6 oz)	Little Red River, Heber Spring, Arkansas, USA	Sept. 5, 1988	Gary Lee Evans
02 kg (4 lb)	8.21 kg (18 lb 1 oz)	Sooner Lake, Redrock, Oklahoma, USA	Jan. 28, 1988	Neil K. Jackson

Bass, whiterock / *(continued)*

03 kg (6 lb)	8.64 kg (19 lb 1 oz)	Lake Hamilton, Hot Springs, Arkansas, USA	Mar. 1, 1995	Mike T. Smith
04 kg (8 lb)	8.02 kg (17 lb 11 oz)	Lake Austin, Austin, Texas, USA	June 21, 1989	Jerry D. Coddington
06 kg (12 lb)	10.57 kg (23 lb 5 oz)	Lake Lugert, Aitus, Oklahoma, USA	Apr. 1, 1997	Paul G. Hollister
08 kg (16 lb)	11.78 kg (25 lb 15 oz)	Warrior River, Alabama, USA	Sept. 13, 1996	E.H. (Sonny) Hodges
10 kg (20 lb)	11.56 kg (25 lb 8 oz)	Lake Chatuge, Georgia, USA	May 1, 1995	David C. Hobby

Bass, yellow / *Morone mississippiensis*

LINE CLASS	WEIGHT	PLACE	DATE	ANGLER
01 kg (2 lb)	Vacant			
02 kg (4 lb)	0.53 kg (1 lb 2 oz)	Canyon Lake, Arizona, USA	Feb. 16, 1985	Adolph W. Zeugner, Sr.
03 kg (6 lb)	Vacant			
04 kg (8 lb)	0.51 kg (1 lb 2 oz)	Canyon Lake, Arizona, USA	Aug. 7, 1988	John H. Melisko
06 kg (12 lb)	0.47 kg (1 lb 0 oz)	Canyon Lake, Arizona, USA	June 2, 1995	William Warman, II

Bluegill / *Lepomis macrochirus*

LINE CLASS	WEIGHT	PLACE	DATE	ANGLER
01 kg (2 lb)	0.73 kg (1 lb 10 oz)	Lake Perris, Perris, California, USA	Oct. 3, 1986	Gary Edward Smith
02 kg (4 lb)	1.24 kg (2 lb 12 oz)	Vaughn Lake, Michigan, USA	June 30, 1983	Gary Saylor
03 kg (6 lb)	0.66 kg (1 lb 7 oz)	Pace, Florida, USA	June 5, 1998	Zac Cooper
03 kg (6 lb) Tie	0.68 kg (1 lb 8 oz)	Pace, Florida, USA	June 5, 1998	Lori Cooper
04 kg (8 lb)	1.36 kg (3 lb 0 oz)	Bledsoe County, Tennessee, USA	Dec. 19, 1987	H. Brad Pendergrass
06 kg (12 lb)	1.89 kg (4 lb 3 oz)	Hopkins County, Kentucky, USA	Aug. 5, 1980	Phil Moore Conyers

Bowfin / *Amia calva*

LINE CLASS	WEIGHT	PLACE	DATE	ANGLER
01 kg (2 lb)	4.37 kg (9 lb 10 oz)	Chickahominy River, Virginia, USA	Feb. 21, 1998	Eddy Johnston
02 kg (4 lb)	7.45 kg (16 lb 7 oz)	Lake Tohopekaliga, Florida, USA	Dec. 12, 1984	Neil W. Shelhorn
03 kg (6 lb)	3.06 kg (6 lb 12 oz)	Chickahominy River, Virginia, USA	Mar. 24, 1996	J. Parks Rountrey
04 kg (8 lb)	7.17 kg (15 lb 12 oz)	Watertown Lake, Lake City, Florida, USA	Jan. 19, 1989	Arthur M. McIver
06 kg (12 lb)	6.10 kg (13 lb 7 oz)	Withlacoochee River, Florida, USA	Dec. 18, 1981	Donald Kimbel
06 kg (12 lb) Tie	6.10 kg (13 lb 7 oz)	Lake Washington, Melbourne, Florida, USA	June 16, 1996	Charles A. Petersen
08 kg (16 lb)	6.54 kg (14 lb 7 oz)	Diascund Reservoir, Virginia, USA	Apr. 21, 1984	Belvin C. Palmer, Jr.
10 kg (20 lb)	9.75 kg (21 lb 8 oz)	Forest Lake, Florence, South Carolina, USA	Jan. 29, 1980	Robert L. Harmon
15 kg (30 lb)	8.61 kg (18 lb 15 oz)	Lake Kissimmee, Florida, USA	Nov. 5, 1984	Jim Brown

Buffalo, bigmouth / *Ictiobus cyprinellus*

LINE CLASS	WEIGHT	PLACE	DATE	ANGLER
01 kg (2 lb)	5.86 kg (12 lb 15 oz)	Comas Dam, Delavan, Wisconsin, USA	Dec. 30, 1985	Brent A. Cummings
02 kg (4 lb)	15.42 kg (34 lb 0 oz)	Last Resort, Lake Ozark, Missouri, USA	June 30, 1985	John F. Roasio
03 kg (6 lb)	4.14 kg (9 lb 3 oz)	Rock River, Machoney Park, Illinois, USA	Dec. 7, 1997	Dustin Genin
04 kg (8 lb)	23.58 kg (52 lb 0 oz)	City Park Lagoon, Louisiana, USA	July 21, 1976	Tommy Descant
06 kg (12 lb)	31.89 kg (70 lb 5 oz)	Bastrop, Louisiana, USA	Apr. 21, 1980	Delbert Sisk
08 kg (16 lb)	23.81 kg (52 lb 8 oz)	Toledo Bend Reservoir, Zwolle, Louisiana, USA	Apr. 24, 1994	William Holland, Jr.
10 kg (20 lb)	23.58 kg (52 lb 0 oz)	Long Lake, Columbia, Louisiana, USA	Oct. 21, 1987	Doug Wheelington
15 kg (30 lb)	18.96 kg (41 lb 13 oz)	Lake Sam Rayburn, Texas, USA	Feb. 8, 1985	Gary Kennedy
24 kg (50 lb)	3.51 kg (7 lb 12 oz)	Lake Delavan, Wisconsin, USA	Dec. 29, 1984	Richard E. LaBouy
37 kg (80 lb)	10.54 kg (23 lb 3 oz)	Comas Dam, Delavan, Wisconsin, USA	Dec. 30, 1985	Michael H. Cummings

Buffalo, smallmouth / *Ictiobus bubalus*

LINE CLASS	WEIGHT	PLACE	DATE	ANGLER
01 kg (2 lb)	7.93 kg (17 lb 8 oz)	Trinity River, Lake Ray, Hubbard, Texas, USA	Mar. 12, 1995	Scott S. Nichols
02 kg (4 lb)	7.82 kg (17 lb 4 oz)	Lake Texoma, Texas, USA	July 13, 1993	John Hardin
03 kg (6 lb)	12.90 kg (28 lb 8 oz)	Chickamauga Reservoir, Chattanooga, Tennessee, USA	June 1, 1996	James L. Henderson
04 kg (8 lb)	17.46 kg (38 lb 8 oz)	Lake Palestine, Texas, USA	May 20, 1990	Tim Rose
06 kg (12 lb)	37.29 kg (82 lb 3 oz)	Athens Lake, Texas, USA	May 6, 1993	Randy Collins
08 kg (16 lb)	29.25 kg (64 lb 8 oz)	Sabine River, Easton, Texas, USA	Mar. 28, 1987	Gaylon L. Cole
10 kg (20 lb)	19.02 kg (41 lb 15 oz)	Owensboro, Kentucky, USA	June 26, 1980	John M. Lewis
15 kg (30 lb)	9.88 kg (21 lb 12 oz)	Nickajack Dam, Tennessee, USA	Nov. 11, 1986	Terri Adams
24 kg (50 lb)	8.77 kg (19 lb 5 oz)	Lake of the Ozarks, Missouri, USA	Aug. 4, 1984	Rick A. Severs

Bullhead, black / *Ameiurus melas*

LINE CLASS	WEIGHT	PLACE	DATE	ANGLER
01 kg (2 lb)	1.28 kg (2 lb 13 oz)	Washington, Iowa, USA	May 26, 1985	Richard Greiner
02 kg (4 lb)	0.87 kg (1 lb 15 oz)	Andrew County, Missouri, USA	Mar. 31, 1984	Larry Lowdon
03 kg (6 lb)	3.37 kg (7 lb 7 oz)	Mill Pond, Wantagh, Long Island, NY	Aug. 25, 1993	Kevin Kelly
04 kg (8 lb)	0.90 kg (2 lb 0 oz)	Huddle Bay, Lake George, New York, USA	Aug. 19, 1995	John Boesenberg
06 kg (12 lb)	3.32 kg (7 lb 5 oz)	Havana, Kansas, USA	May 13, 1985	David A. Tremain

Bullhead, brown / *Ameiurus nebulosus*

LINE CLASS	WEIGHT	PLACE	DATE	ANGLER
01 kg (2 lb)	1.12 kg (2 lb 7 oz)	Argyle Lake, West Babylon, New York, USA	June 1, 1997	John Boesenberg
02 kg (4 lb)	2.21 kg (4 lb 14 oz)	Eatonton, Georgia, USA	June 5, 1988	Ron R. Cranford
03 kg (6 lb)	2.74 kg (6 lb 1 oz)	Waterford, New York, USA	Apr. 26, 1998	Bobby Triplett
04 kg (8 lb)	0.79 kg (1 lb 12 oz)	Argyle Lake, West Babylon, New York, USA	May 16, 1997	John Boesenberg
06 kg (12 lb)	Vacant			

Bullhead, yellow / *Ameiurus natalis*

LINE CLASS	WEIGHT	PLACE	DATE	ANGLER
01 kg (2 lb)	1.04 kg (2 lb 5 oz)	Morman Lake, Arizona, USA	May 17, 1984	Carl Battali
02 kg (4 lb)	0.92 kg (2 lb 0 oz)	Oklahoma River, Florida, USA	Nov. 2, 1984	Alice Meyer
03 kg (6 lb)	1.37 kg (3 lb 0 oz)	Nelson Lake, Wisconsin, USA	May 8, 1977	Mark Nessmann
04 kg (8 lb)	Vacant			
06 kg (12 lb)	0.99 kg (2 lb 3 oz)	Morman Lake, Arizona, USA	May 17, 1984	Loree Bruce

Burbot / *Lota lota*

LINE CLASS	WEIGHT	PLACE	DATE	ANGLER
01 kg (2 lb)	4.06 kg (8 lb 15 oz)	Missouri River, North Dakota, USA	Dec. 21, 1986	Greg J. Magrum
02 kg (4 lb)	4.63 kg (10 lb 3 oz)	Missouri River, North Dakota, USA	Nov. 26, 1987	Kent B. Stillwell

Burbot / *(continued)*

LINE CLASS	WEIGHT	PLACE	DATE	ANGLER
03 kg (6 lb)	7.03 kg (15 lb 8 oz)	Riverdale, North Dakota, USA	June 10, 1979	Irvin E. Glanville
04 kg (8 lb)	7.19 kg (15 lb 13 oz)	Black River Bay, Lake Ontario, New York, USA	Feb. 6, 1994	David Dewey
06 kg (12 lb)	6.37 kg (14 lb 1 oz)	Grand Rapids, Minnesota, USA	Feb. 2, 1980	Leonard L. Lundeen
08 kg (16 lb)	2.49 kg (5 lb 8 oz)	Lake Erie, Erie, Pennsylvania, USA	Nov. 27, 1997	Richard E. Faler, Jr.
10 kg (20 lb)	6.39 kg (14 lb 1 oz)	River Faxalven, Sweden	Oct. 5, 1987	Per Torstensson

Carp, common / *Cyprinus carpio*

LINE CLASS	WEIGHT	PLACE	DATE	ANGLER
01 kg (2 lb)	13.15 kg (29 lb 0 oz)	Patuxent River, Maryland, USA	May 13, 1983	Jean E. Ward
02 kg (4 lb)	16.00 kg (35 lb 4 oz)	Deventer, The Netherlands	Feb. 12, 1989	P. Vroegindewey
03 kg (6 lb)	14.82 kg (32 lb 11 oz)	Sterling Pond, Lake Ontario, Canada	May 16, 1996	Kevin Kelly
04 kg (8 lb)	21.77 kg (48 lb 0 oz)	Mecklenburg County, North Carolina, USA	Mar. 11, 1986	William Houston, Jr.
06 kg (12 lb)	34.35 kg (75 lb 11 oz)	Lac de St. Cassien, France	May 21, 1987	Leo van der Gugten
08 kg (16 lb)	25.85 kg (57 lb 0 oz)	Lake Cassein, France	Nov. 1, 1985	Richie McDonald
10 kg (20 lb)	26.22 kg (57 lb 13 oz)	Potomac River, Washington, DC, USA	June 19, 1983	David Nikolow
15 kg (30 lb)	37.30 kg (82 lb 3 oz)	Lake Roduta, Romania	May 26, 1998	Christian Baldemair
24 kg (50 lb)	12.14 kg (26 lb 12 oz)	Hassleholm, Sweden	Aug. 18, 1986	Kristian Wennberg

Catfish, blue / *Ictalurus furcatus*

LINE CLASS	WEIGHT	PLACE	DATE	ANGLER
01 kg (2 lb)	11.33 kg (25 lb 0 oz)	Rockfish Creek, Fayetteville, North Carolina, USA	Dec. 8, 1995	Edward C. Davis
02 kg (4 lb)	21.31 kg (47 lb 0 oz)	Rockfish Creek, Fayetteville, North Carolina, USA	Mar. 26, 1998	Edward C. Davis
03 kg (6 lb)	26.30 kg (58 lb 0 oz)	Hal's Lake, Alabama, USA	Dec. 9, 1995	Timothy Ray Wilks
04 kg (8 lb)	32.20 kg (71 lb 0 oz)	Osage River, Jefferson City, Missouri, USA	Dec. 21, 1994	Virgil D. Agee
06 kg (12 lb)	34.01 kg (75 lb 0 oz)	Lake Guntersville, Guntersville, Alabama, USA	Sept. 6, 1997	Jim Kitchens, Sr.
08 kg (16 lb)	45.81 kg (101 lb 0 oz)	Osage River, Jefferson City, Missouri, USA	Oct. 20, 1994	Virgil Dale Agee
10 kg (20 lb)	49.55 kg (109 lb 4 oz)	Cooper River, Moncks Corner, South Carolina, USA	Mar. 14, 1991	George A. Lijewski
15 kg (30 lb)	50.34 kg (111 lb 0 oz)	Wheeler Reservoir, Tennessee River, Alabama, USA	July 5, 1996	William P. McKinley
24 kg (50 lb)	31.29 kg (69 lb 0 oz)	Lake Texoma, Oklahoma, USA	Sept. 6, 1977	W. H. Kirk
37 kg (80 lb)	36.28 kg (80 lb 0 oz)	Lake Texoma, Durant, Oklahoma, USA	Nov. 28, 1980	Ron J. Smith
60 kg (130 lb)	9.07 kg (20 lb 0 oz)	Trailer Lake, Bucksville, Alabama, USA	July 7, 1998	Troy Beatty

Catfish, channel / *Ictalurus punctatus*

LINE CLASS	WEIGHT	PLACE	DATE	ANGLER
01 kg (2 lb)	9.27 kg (20 lb 6 oz)	Red River, Manitoba, Canada	Aug. 28, 1985	Jeff C. Suggitt
02 kg (4 lb)	15.64 kg (34 lb 8 oz)	Merritt Reservoir, Valentine, Nebraska, USA	June 26, 1988	Lynn L. Stockall
03 kg (6 lb)	10.45 kg (23 lb 0 oz)	Lake Quassapaus, Middlebury, Connecticut, USA	July 2, 1996	Richard J. Tavares
04 kg (8 lb)	20.41 kg (45 lb 0 oz)	St. Croix River, Wisconsin, USA	Sept. 18, 1993	Hector M. Perez
06 kg (12 lb)	17.07 kg (37 lb 10 oz)	La Due Reservoir, Geauge County, Ohio, USA	Aug. 15, 1992	Gus Gronowski
08 kg (16 lb)	19.95 kg (44 lb 0 oz)	Irvine Lake, Irvine, California, USA	Oct. 12, 1995	David H. Heine
10 kg (20 lb)	19.61 kg (43 lb 4 oz)	Kaweah Lake, Lemon Cove, California, USA	Dec. 3, 1995	Roxie A. Davenport
15 kg (30 lb)	18.82 kg (41 lb 8 oz)	Snake River, Valentine, Nebraska, USA	Aug. 11, 1986	Heather Jo Cunning
24 kg (50 lb)	14.96 kg (33 lb 0 oz)	Snake River, Valentine, Nebraska, USA	Aug. 15, 1986	Johnnie F. Cunning
37 kg (80 lb)	18.42 kg (40 lb 10 oz)	Merritt Res., Nebraska, USA	Sept. 9, 1989	John L. Snelling

Catfish, flathead / *Pylodictis olivaris*

LINE CLASS	WEIGHT	PLACE	DATE	ANGLER
01 kg (2 lb)	14.96 kg (33 lb 0 oz)	Cape Fear River, Fayetteville, North Carolina, USA	Sept. 21, 1995	Edward C. Davis
02 kg (4 lb)	30.39 kg (67 lb 0 oz)	Pomona Reservoir, Kansas, USA	May 19, 1987	Charles F. Miller
03 kg (6 lb)	18.99 kg (41 lb 14 oz)	St. Croix River, Minnesota, USA	Oct. 20, 1995	Richard Grzywinski
04 kg (8 lb)	29.59 kg (65 lb 4 oz)	Pickwick Lake, Mississippi, USA	Mar. 21, 1987	Wade Arnold
06 kg (12 lb)	41.39 kg (91 lb 4 oz)	Lake Lewisville, Texas, USA	Mar. 28, 1982	Mike Rogers
08 kg (16 lb)	55.79 kg (123 lb 9 oz)	Elk City Reservoir, Independence, Kansas, USA	May 19, 1998	Ken Paulie
10 kg (20 lb)	38.27 kg (84 lb 6 oz)	San Jacinto River, Houston, Texas, USA	May 27, 1987	Stacy Small
15 kg (30 lb)	36.85 kg (81 lb 4 oz)	Marais des Cygnes River, Kansas, USA	July 8, 1982	Douglas C. Wyatt
24 kg (50 lb)	28.09 kg (61 lb 15 oz)	Lake Marian, South Carolina, USA	May 10, 1987	Cathy Shannon Bookhart
37 kg (80 lb)	31.29 kg (69 lb 0 oz)	Cape Fear River, Fayetteville, North Carolina, USA	July 27, 1994	Edward C. Davis
60 kg (130 lb)	29.03 kg (64 lb 0 oz)	Lake Tawakoni, Texas, USA	Aug. 1, 1989	Marianne E. Willaby

Catfish, white / *Ameiurus catus*

LINE CLASS	WEIGHT	PLACE	DATE	ANGLER
01 kg (2 lb)	3.40 kg (7 lb 8 oz)	Connecticut River, Hartford, Connecticut, USA	Mar. 11, 1988	William L. Bechard
02 kg (4 lb)	6.73 kg (14 lb 13 oz)	Lake Wallenpaupack, Pennsylvania, USA	July 1, 1986	Richard A. Olenchak, Jr.
03 kg (6 lb)	3.28 kg (7 lb 4 oz)	Occoquan Reservoir, Fairfax Station, Virginia, USA	Oct. 13, 1994	Thomas F. Elkins
04 kg (8 lb)	7.59 kg (16 lb 12 oz)	Caloosahatchee River, Alva, Florida, USA	Apr. 24, 1984	Shawn J. Williams
06 kg (12 lb)	7.22 kg (15 lb 15 oz)	Chester, Virginia, USA	Apr. 20, 1982	Earl D. Hartman
06 kg (12 lb) Tie	7.23 kg (15 lb 15 oz)	Broward County, Florida, USA	Sept. 23, 1984	Robert M. Buda
08 kg (16 lb)	7.90 kg (17 lb 7 oz)	Success Lake, Tulare, California, USA	Nov. 15, 1981	Chuck Idell
10 kg (20 lb)	3.79 kg (8 lb 5 oz)	High Rock Lake, North Carolina, USA	Oct. 14, 1996	Stephen Stallings

Char, Arctic / *Salvelinus alpinus*

LINE CLASS	WEIGHT	PLACE	DATE	ANGLER
01 kg (2 lb)	7.82 kg (17 lb 4 oz)	Kugaryak River, N.W.T., Canada	Aug. 26, 1981	Raymond Goodrich
02 kg (4 lb)	9.52 kg (21 lb 0 oz)	Kugaryak River, N.W.T., Canada	Aug. 26, 1981	Raymond Goodrich
03 kg (6 lb)	4.08 kg (9 lb 0 oz)	Coppermine River, Canada	Aug. 4, 1997	Marlin A. Coulombe
04 kg (8 lb)	10.20 kg (22 lb 8 oz)	Kugaryak River, N.W.T., Canada	Aug. 28, 1978	Ruby A. Goodrich
06 kg (12 lb)	11.34 kg (25 lb 0 oz)	Kugaryak River, N.W.T., Canada	Aug. 28, 1978	Raymond Goodrich
08 kg (16 lb)	12.70 kg (28 lb 0 oz)	Tree River, N.W.T., Canada	Aug. 21, 1985	Robert J. Frost, M.D.
10 kg (20 lb)	10.88 kg (24 lb 0 oz)	Hadley Bay, Victoria Island, N.W.T., Canada	July 30, 1985	Chuck McCauley
15 kg (30 lb)	9.75 kg (21 lb 8 oz)	Victoria Island, N.W.T., Canada	Aug. 1, 1981	Robert W. Kitchen

Crappie, black / *Pomoxis nigromaculatus*

LINE CLASS	WEIGHT	PLACE	DATE	ANGLER
01 kg (2 lb)	1.44 kg (3 lb 2 oz)	Chickahominy Lake, Lanexa, Virginia, USA	Oct. 10, 1986	Max Tongier, Jr.
02 kg (4 lb)	1.92 kg (4 lb 4 oz)	Lake Weddington, Arkansas, USA	Dec. 26, 1982	Jack L. Ferguson
03 kg (6 lb)	2.05 kg (4 lb 8 oz)	Kerr Lake, Virginia, USA	Mar. 1, 1981	L. Carl Herring, Jr.

Crappie, black / *(continued)*

LINE CLASS	WEIGHT	PLACE	DATE	ANGLER
04 kg (8 lb)	1.64 kg (3 lb 10 oz)	Lake Logan Martin, Alabama, USA	Mar. 21, 1998	Mark E. Williamson
06 kg (12 lb)	1.92 kg (4 lb 4 oz)	Paint Creek, Coosa River, Alabama, USA	Mar. 18, 1984	Sherril S. Harris

Crappie, white / *Pomoxis annularis*

LINE CLASS	WEIGHT	PLACE	DATE	ANGLER
01 kg (2 lb)	1.31 kg (3 lb 9 oz)	Cape Fear River, Fayetteville, North Carolina, USA	Nov. 4, 1994	Edward C. Davis
02 kg (4 lb)	1.36 kg (3 lb 0 oz)	Delaware River, Morrisville, Pennsylvania, USA	Apr. 21, 1985	John J. Phillips, Jr.
03 kg (6 lb)	0.70 kg (1 lb 9 oz)	Bull Shoals Lake, Arkansas, USA	May 13, 1996	Gary Nelson
04 kg (8 lb)	1.70 kg (3 lb 12 oz)	Alabama River, Alabama, USA	Mar. 31, 1982	James E. Black
06 kg (12 lb)	1.81 kg (4 lb 0 oz)	Rome, Georgia, USA	Mar. 19, 1980	Ken Wright

Dolly Varden / *Salvelinus malma*

LINE CLASS	WEIGHT	PLACE	DATE	ANGLER
01 kg (2 lb)	3.26 kg (7 lb 3 oz)	Noatak River, Alaska, USA	July 8, 1988	Kenneth T. Alt
02 kg (4 lb)	5.47 kg (12 lb 1 oz)	Sagavanirktok River, Pruedoe Bay, Alaska, USA	July 8, 1991	George Wm. West
03 kg (6 lb)	7.37 kg (16 lb 4 oz)	Noatuk River, Alaska, USA	July 30, 1994	John L. Nicholson
04 kg (8 lb)	7.96 kg (17 lb 9 oz)	Wulik River, Alaska, USA	Sept. 14, 1995	Robert H. Mace
06 kg (12 lb)	8.41 kg (18 lb 9 oz)	Kivalina River, Alaska, USA	July 13, 1993	Richard B. Evans

Dorado / *Salminus maxillosus*

LINE CLASS	WEIGHT	PLACE	DATE	ANGLER
01 kg (2 lb)	4.30 kg (9 lb 7 oz)	Vallemi, Paraguay River, Paraguay	Dec. 4, 1984	Jorge E. Xifra
02 kg (4 lb)	6.09 kg (13 lb 7 oz)	Parana River, Coratei, Paraguay	Apr. 20, 1984	Jorge E. Xifra
03 kg (6 lb)	Vacant			
04 kg (8 lb)	7.54 kg (16 lb 10 oz)	Parana River, Coratei, Paraguay	Apr. 21, 1984	Jorge E. Xifra
06 kg (12 lb)	8.25 kg (18 lb 3 oz)	Pena Hermosa River, Paraguay	Sept. 1, 1984	Jorge E. Xifra
08 kg (16 lb)	11.20 kg (24 lb 11 oz)	Parana River, Ayolas, Paraguay	Nov. 10, 1991	Bill Blackwell
10 kg (20 lb)	16.80 kg (37 lb 0 oz)	Parana River, Ayolas, Paraguay	Nov. 6, 1989	Gilberto Fernandes
15 kg (30 lb)	23.30 kg (51 lb 5 oz)	Toledo (Corrientes), Argentina	Sept. 27, 1984	Armando Giudice
24 kg (50 lb)	13.80 kg (30 lb 6 oz)	Ayolas, Paraguay	Mar. 29, 1990	Juan Francisco Xifra

Drum, freshwater / *Aplodinotus grunniens*

LINE CLASS	WEIGHT	PLACE	DATE	ANGLER
01 kg (2 lb)	8.64 kg (19 lb 1 oz)	Nickajack Dam, Tennessee, USA	Apr. 14, 1985	Richard C. Hamrick
02 kg (4 lb)	12.30 kg (27 lb 2 oz)	Lake Barkley, Trigg County, Kentucky, USA	Oct. 12, 1981	Danny J. Leasure
03 kg (6 lb)	5.13 kg (11 lb 5 oz)	Kentucky Lake, Kentucky, USA	Oct. 26, 1997	Steve Wendt
04 kg (8 lb)	15.98 kg (35 lb 4 oz)	Mississippi River, Wisconsin, USA	Aug. 29, 1992	Raymond L. Childs
06 kg (12 lb)	13.60 kg (30 lb 0 oz)	Pickwick Lake, Florence, Alabama, USA	May 9, 1987	James G. Pickle
08 kg (16 lb)	14.23 kg (31 lb 6 oz)	Nickajack Reservoir, Tennessee, USA	Mar. 12, 1988	Joseph E. Willard, Jr.
10 kg (20 lb)	10.09 kg (22 lb 4 oz)	Table Rock Lake, Missouri, USA	June 16, 1985	Grant W. Bailey
15 kg (30 lb)	12.18 kg (26 lb 13 oz)	Nickajack Dam, Tennessee, USA	May 18, 1986	James Adams
24 kg (50 lb)	9.83 kg (21 lb 10 oz)	Nickajack Dam, Tennessee, USA	Apr. 8, 1987	Richard C. Hamrick
37 kg (80 lb)	9.09 kg (20 lb 0 oz)	Nickajack Dam, Tennessee, USA	Apr. 18, 1987	James Adams

Gar, alligator / *Lepisosteus spatula*

LINE CLASS	WEIGHT	PLACE	DATE	ANGLER
01 kg (2 lb)	15.64 kg (34 lb 8 oz)	Houston Ship Channel, Texas, USA	Nov. 1, 1981	Dale Leverone
02 kg (4 lb)	30.61 kg (67 lb 8 oz)	Blakeley River, Spanish Fort, Alabama, USA	Aug. 19, 1984	James Adams
03 kg (6 lb)	Vacant			
04 kg (8 lb)	35.60 kg (78 lb 8 oz)	Blakeley River, Spanish Fort, Alabama, USA	Aug. 17, 1984	Richard C. Hamrick
06 kg (12 lb)	56.24 kg (124 lb 0 oz)	Bacliff, Texas, USA	June 26, 1987	Tripp Hill
08 kg (16 lb)	50.34 kg (111 lb 0 oz)	Lake Sam Rayburn, Jasper, Texas, USA	Mar. 8, 1985	Ron Coleman
10 kg (20 lb)	78.03 kg (150 lb 8 oz)	Power & Light Channel, Texas, USA	Apr. 30, 1976	William L. Carter, Jr.
15 kg (30 lb)	84.45 kg (186 lb 3 oz)	Nassau Bay, Texas, USA	Oct. 14, 1995	Johnny L. Gilbert
24 kg (50 lb)	53.84 kg (118 lb 11 oz)	Escambia Bay, Pensacola, Florida, USA	July 5, 1997	Gregory Lewis Barnes
37 kg (80 lb)	53.07 kg (117 lb 0 oz)	Fish River, Alabama, USA	July 27, 1988	Perry Puckett
60 kg (130 lb)	50.00 kg (110 lb 4 oz)	Blakeley River, Alabama, USA	July 14, 1985	Winston H. Baker

Gar, Florida / *Lepisosteus platyrhincus*

LINE CLASS	WEIGHT	PLACE	DATE	ANGLER
01 kg (2 lb)	2.69 kg (5 lb 15 oz)	Alligator Alley, Florida, USA	May 16, 1984	Rick Earle
02 kg (4 lb)	2.92 kg (6 lb 7 oz)	Alligator Alley, Florida, USA	Mar. 9, 1984	Robert Janzer
03 kg (6 lb)	1.26 kg (2 lb 12 oz)	Merritt Island, Florida, USA	June 9, 1996	Randy Morgan
04 kg (8 lb)	3.28 kg (7 lb 4 oz)	Boca Raton, Florida, USA	May 7, 1988	Dean K. Watson
06 kg (12 lb)	2.60 kg (5 lb 12 oz)	Alligator Alley, Florida, USA	May 15, 1984	Phillip O. Lloyd, Jr.
08 kg (16 lb)	2.72 kg (6 lb 0 oz)	Alligator Alley, Florida, USA	June 4, 1984	Rick Earle
10 kg (20 lb)	2.60 kg (5 lb 12 oz)	Alligator Alley, Florida, USA	Dec. 30, 1984	Rick Earle

Gar, longnose / *Lepisosteus osseus*

LINE CLASS	WEIGHT	PLACE	DATE	ANGLER
01 kg (2 lb)	11.02 kg (24 lb 5 oz)	Sardis Reservoir, Mississippi, USA	Aug. 26, 1984	James Adams
02 kg (4 lb)	11.08 kg (24 lb 7 oz)	Sardis Reservoir, Mississippi, USA	Aug. 25, 1984	James Adams
03 kg (6 lb)	7.45 kg (16 lb 7 oz)	Westernbranch Reservoir, Suffolk, Virginia, USA	Oct. 20, 1994	Charles Frank Forbes
04 kg (8 lb)	11.90 kg (26 lb 4 oz)	Chattahoochee River, Alabama, USA	Apr. 26, 1989	Stephen L. Taylor
06 kg (12 lb)	13.60 kg (30 lb 0 oz)	Lake Henderson, Inverness, Florida, USA	May 16, 1988	Glenn Dishman
08 kg (16 lb)	12.38 kg (27 lb 5 oz)	Sardis Reservoir, Mississippi, USA	Sept. 2, 1984	Richard C. Hamrick
10 kg (20 lb)	19.95 kg (44 lb 0 oz)	Lake Bistineau, Bassier Parish, Louisiana, USA	Sept. 22, 1991	Fred Elliott
15 kg (30 lb)	16.32 kg (36 lb 0 oz)	St. John River, Astor, Florida, USA	Apr. 1, 1993	Kitty Strauss
24 kg (50 lb)	12.87 kg (28 lb 6 oz)	Flint River, Georgia, USA	Jan. 28, 1995	Richard Johnson
37 kg (80 lb)	11.73 kg (25 lb 14 oz)	Sardis Reservoir, Mississippi, USA	Sept. 2, 1984	Richard C. Hamrick

Gar, shortnose / *Lepisosteus platostomus*

LINE CLASS	WEIGHT	PLACE	DATE	ANGLER
01 kg (2 lb)	1.47 kg (3 lb 4 oz)	Lake Francis Case, South Dakota, USA	Aug. 28, 1987	Andrew William Williamson
02 kg (4 lb)	1.28 kg (2 lb 13 oz)	Lake Francis Case, South Dakota, USA	June 4, 1987	Andrew William Williamson
03 kg (6 lb)	1.53 kg (3 lb 6 oz)	Cottonwood River, Emporia, Kansas, USA	Apr. 27, 1987	Joe Hanlon
04 kg (8 lb)	0.90 kg (1 lb 15 oz)	Red Rock Dam, Pella, Iowa, USA	July 26, 1998	Dan Lopez

Gar, shortnose / *(continued)*

LINE CLASS	WEIGHT	PLACE	DATE	ANGLER
06 kg (12 lb)	2.08 kg (4 lb 9 oz)	Mississippi River, Minnesota, USA	July 22, 1984	Matthew (Dewy) Ocel
08 kg (16 lb)	1.58 kg (3 lb 8 oz)	New Madrid, Missouri, USA	July 11, 1984	Michael John Bobersky
10 kg (20 lb)	2.26 kg (5 lb 0 oz)	Sally Jones Lake, Vian, Oklahoma, USA	Apr. 26, 1985	Buddy Croslin

Gar, spotted / *Lepisosteus oculatus*

LINE CLASS	WEIGHT	PLACE	DATE	ANGLER
01 kg (2 lb)	3.04 kg (6 lb 11 oz)	Cotaco Creek, Decatur, Alabama, USA	Aug. 14, 1984	Winston H. Baker
02 kg (4 lb)	3.14 kg (6 lb 15 oz)	Tennessee River, Alabama, USA	Sept. 1, 1986	Carol Baker
03 kg (6 lb)	2.86 kg (6 lb 5 oz)	Buzz's Lake, Mount Vernon, Alabama, USA	July 19, 1998	Robert T. Cunningham, Jr.
04 kg (8 lb)	3.21 kg (7 lb 1 oz)	Tennessee River, Alabama, USA	Aug. 30, 1987	Linda R. Baker
04 kg (8 lb) Tie	3.22 kg (7 lb 1 oz)	Marlin City, Marlin Lake, Texas, USA	Dec. 31, 1994	Rick Rivard
06 kg (12 lb)	3.13 kg (6 lb 14 oz)	Cotaco Creek, Decatur, Alabama, USA	Aug. 14, 1984	April Kilpatrick
08 kg (16 lb)	4.44 kg (9 lb 12 oz)	Lake Mexia, Mexia, Texas, USA	Apr. 7, 1994	Rick Rivard
10 kg (20 lb)	3.96 kg (8 lb 12 oz)	Tennessee River, Alabama, USA	Aug. 26, 1987	Winston H. Baker

Grayling, Arctic / *Thymallus arcticus*

LINE CLASS	WEIGHT	PLACE	DATE	ANGLER
01 kg (2 lb)	1.64 kg (3 lb 10 oz)	Great Bear Lake, N.W.T., Canada	July 13, 1990	Allen Fraser
01 kg (2 lb) Tie	1.64 kg (3 lb 10 oz)	Great Bear Lake, N.W.T., Canada	Aug. 3, 1993	Marlin A. Coulombe
02 kg (4 lb)	2.09 kg (4 lb 10 oz)	Great Bear Lake, N.W.T., Canada	Aug. 9, 1984	Carol B. Bull
03 kg (6 lb)	1.81 kg (4 lb 0 oz)	Great Bear Lake, N.W.T., Canada	July 19, 1995	Harold M. Ball
04 kg (8 lb)	2.38 kg (5 lb 4 oz)	Great Bear Lake, N.W.T., Canada	Aug. 1, 1986	Silvio Ronconi
06 kg (12 lb)	1.92 kg (4 lb 4 oz)	Port Radium, N.W.T., Canada	Aug. 21, 1978	Raymond Goodrich
08 kg (16 lb)	1.64 kg (3 lb 10 oz)	Great Bear Lake, N.W.T., Canada	Aug. 2, 1993	Marlin A. Coulombe
10 kg (20 lb)	1.61 kg (3 lb 9 oz)	Great Bear Lake, N.W.T., Canada	Aug. 5, 1987	Marlin A. Coulombe

Huchen / *Hucho hucho*

LINE CLASS	WEIGHT	PLACE	DATE	ANGLER
01 kg (2 lb)	Vacant			
02 kg (4 lb)	Vacant			
03 kg (6 lb)	Vacant			
04 kg (8 lb)	Vacant			
06 kg (12 lb)	Vacant			
08 kg (16 lb)	Vacant			
10 kg (20 lb)	34.80 kg (76 lb 11 oz)	Gemeinde Spittal/Drau, Osterreich (Austria)	Feb. 19, 1985	Hans Offermanns
15 kg (30 lb)	32.09 kg (70 lb 12 oz)	Carinthia, Austria	Jan. 1, 1980	Martin F.P. Esterl
24 kg (50 lb)	Vacant			
37 kg (80 lb)	Vacant			
60 kg (130 lb)	Vacant			

Inconnu / *Stenodus leucichthys*

LINE CLASS	WEIGHT	PLACE	DATE	ANGLER
01 kg (2 lb)	18.71 kg (41 lb 4 oz)	Kobuk River, Alaska, USA	Aug. 10, 1987	Lawrence E. Hudnall
02 kg (4 lb)	17.57 kg (38 lb 12 oz)	Kobuk River, Alaska, USA	Aug. 8, 1987	Lawrence E. Hudnall
03 kg (6 lb)	7.93 kg (17 lb 8 oz)	Kobuk River, Alaska, USA	July 21, 1997	Ronald Paul Spencer, MD
04 kg (8 lb)	17.69 kg (39 lb 0 oz)	Kobuk River, Alaska, USA	Aug. 20, 1986	Daniel J. Hudnall
06 kg (12 lb)	15.87 kg (35 lb 0 oz)	Kobuk River, Alaska, USA	Aug. 7, 1987	Daniel J. Hudnall
08 kg (16 lb)	16.32 kg (36 lb 0 oz)	Kobuk River, Alaska, USA	Aug. 7, 1987	Lawrence E. Hudnall
10 kg (20 lb)	24.04 kg (53 lb 0 oz)	Pah River, Alaska, USA	Aug. 20, 1986	Lawrence E. Hudnall
15 kg (30 lb)	15.42 kg (34 lb 0 oz)	Kobuk River, Alaska, USA	Aug. 10, 1987	Daniel J. Hudnall
24 kg (50 lb)	14.51 kg (32 lb 0 oz)	Kobuk River, Alaska, USA	Aug. 12, 1987	Daniel J. Hudnall

Kokanee / *Oncorhynchus nerka*

LINE CLASS	WEIGHT	PLACE	DATE	ANGLER
01 kg (2 lb)	2.40 kg (5 lb 5 oz)	Flaming Gorge Reservoir, Utah, USA	Dec. 11, 1984	Ray Johnson
02 kg (4 lb)	2.86 kg (6 lb 4 oz)	Turquoise Lake, Leadville, Colorado, USA	Sept. 22, 1987	Jim Hewlett
03 kg (6 lb)	Vacant			
04 kg (8 lb)	2.80 kg (6 lb 3 oz)	Spinney Mountain Reservoir, Colorado, USA	Sept. 6, 1986	Arthur J. Beck
06 kg (12 lb)	2.57 kg (5 lb 11 oz)	Spinney Mountain Reservoir, Colorado, USA	May 31, 1986	Adolph Aragon

Muskellunge / *Esox masquinongy*

LINE CLASS	WEIGHT	PLACE	DATE	ANGLER
01 kg (2 lb)	5.66 kg (12 lb 7 oz)	Lake Tremblant, Canada	Nov. 24, 1986	Guy Daniel Lefebvre
02 kg (4 lb)	16.55 kg (36 lb 8 oz)	Allegheny River, Armstrong, Pennsylvania, USA	June 2, 1988	Anthony Valance
03 kg (6 lb)	19.61 kg (43 lb 4 oz)	Cedar Lake, Ontario, Canada	Aug. 18, 1989	Joe Alan See
04 kg (8 lb)	18.48 kg (40 lb 12 oz)	Piedmont Lake, Ohio, USA	June 2, 1997	Pete Provan
06 kg (12 lb)	29.48 kg (65 lb 0 oz)	Blackstone Harbor, Ontario, Canada	Oct. 16, 1988	Kenneth J. O'Brien
08 kg (16 lb)	20.41 kg (45 lb 0 oz)	1000 Island Lake, Michigan, USA	July 26, 1980	Dr. William H. Pivar
10 kg (20 lb)	23.70 kg (52 lb 4 oz)	St. Lawrence River, Quebec, Canada	Nov. 12, 1994	George McQuillen
15 kg (30 lb)	25.59 kg (56 lb 7 oz)	Manitou Lake, Ontario, Canada	Aug. 30, 1984	Gene Borucki
24 kg (50 lb)	24.94 kg (55 lb 0 oz)	Moon River, MacTier, Ontario, Canada	Oct. 11, 1981	Gary Ishii
37 kg (80 lb)	17.69 kg (39 lb 0 oz)	Lake of the Woods, Ontario, Canada	Aug. 13, 1987	Richard R. Zebleckis

Muskellunge, tiger / *Esox Masquinongy x Esox lucius*

LINE CLASS	WEIGHT	PLACE	DATE	ANGLER
01 kg (2 lb)	Vacant			
02 kg (4 lb)	10.68 kg (23 lb 9 oz)	Lake Rolard, Twin Lakes, Michigan, USA	Aug. 8, 1987	Bryan Guzek
03 kg (6 lb)	Vacant			
04 kg (8 lb)	13.83 kg (30 lb 8 oz)	Round Lake, Wisconsin, USA	May 12, 1976	Leonard S. Grunow
06 kg (12 lb)	11.87 kg (26 lb 2 oz)	Lake Summerset, Davis, Illinois, USA	Aug. 4, 1989	David Pan
08 kg (16 lb)	16.10 kg (35 lb 8 oz)	Tioughnioga River, New York, USA	May 25, 1990	Brett Arthur Gofgosky
10 kg (20 lb)	14.45 kg (31 lb 14 oz)	St. Lawrence River, New York, USA	Oct. 1, 1979	George C. Pifer
15 kg (30 lb)	16.15 kg (35 lb 10 oz)	Quincy River, Aurora, Colorado, USA	July 10, 1994	Paul R. Framsted
24 kg (50 lb)	12.87 kg (28 lb 6 oz)	Leech Lake, Minnesota, USA	July 3, 1987	Jerry Kelm

Payara / *Hydrolicus scomberoides*

LINE CLASS	WEIGHT	PLACE	DATE	ANGLER
01 kg (2 lb)	1.50 kg (3 lb 4 oz)	Orinoco River, Puerto Ayacucho, Venezuela	Jan. 20, 1997	Eric Ostmark
02 kg (4 lb)	8.16 kg (18 lb 1 oz)	Uraima Falls, Venezuela	Feb. 9, 1998	Shoichiro Kawai
03 kg (6 lb)	7.99 kg (17 lb 10 oz)	Uraima Falls, Venezuela	Feb. 8, 1998	Shoichiro Kawai
04 kg (8 lb)	10.43 kg (23 lb 0 oz)	Uraima Falls, Venezuela	Apr. 14, 1996	Lance Glaser
06 kg (12 lb)	14.51 kg (32 lb 0 oz)	Uraima Falls, Venezuela	Apr. 14, 1996	Lance Glaser
08 kg (16 lb)	14.76 kg (32 lb 8 oz)	Uraima Falls, Venezuela	Apr. 13, 1996	Lance Glaser
10 kg (20 lb)	14.74 kg (32 lb 8 oz)	Uraima Falls, Venezuela	Dec. 27, 1995	Ronald C. Snody

Peacock, blackstriped / *Cichla intermedia*

LINE CLASS	WEIGHT	PLACE	DATE	ANGLER
01 kg (2 lb)	Vacant			
02 kg (4 lb)	1.13 kg (2 lb 8 oz)	Rio Cinaruco, Venezuela	Mar. 11, 1998	Norman Earl Bean
02 kg (4 lb) Tie	1.13 kg (2 lb 8 oz)	Cinaruco River, Venezuela	Mar. 14, 1998	Glenn Webb
03 kg (6 lb)	0.95 kg (2 lb 1 oz)	Rio Tomo, Orinoco, Colombia	Feb. 22, 1997	Carlos Aristeguieta L.
04 kg (8 lb)	1.20 kg (2 lb 10 oz)	Rio Tomo, Orinoco, Colombia	Feb. 22, 1997	Carlos Aristeguieta L.
06 kg (12 lb)	1.70 kg (3 lb 12 oz)	Rio Cinaruco, Venezuela	Mar. 11, 1998	Dot Bean
08 kg (16 lb)	1.02 kg (2 lb 4 oz)	Rio Tomo, Orinoco, Colombia	Feb. 21, 1997	Carlos Aristeguieta L.
10 kg (20 lb)	1.07 kg (2 lb 5 oz)	Rio Tomo, Orinoco, Colombia	Feb. 21, 1997	Carlos Aristeguieta L.

Peacock, butterfly / *Cichla ocellaris*

LINE CLASS	WEIGHT	PLACE	DATE	ANGLER
01 kg (2 lb)	2.49 kg (5 lb 8 oz)	Miami, Florida, USA	Apr. 15, 1998	Herbert G. Ratner, Jr.
02 kg (4 lb)	2.65 kg (5 lb 13 oz)	Rio Sipapo, Amazonas, Venezuela	Nov. 20, 1996	Carlos Aristeguieta L.
03 kg (6 lb)	2.49 kg (5 lb 8 oz)	Miami, Florida, USA	Mar. 4, 1998	Herbert G. Ratner, Jr.
04 kg (8 lb)	3.06 kg (6 lb 12 oz)	Lake Catalina, Florida, USA	Mar. 11, 1997	Chelsey Dawn Contillo
06 kg (12 lb)	2.49 kg (5 lb 8 oz)	Miami, Florida, USA	Apr. 30, 1998	Herbert G. Ratner, Jr.
08 kg (16 lb)	3.50 kg (7 lb 11 oz)	Camatagua, Venezuela	Sept. 12, 1998	Claudia Lavegas
10 kg (20 lb)	2.72 kg (6 lb 0 oz)	Miami, Florida, USA	Apr. 9, 1998	Herbert G. Ratner, Jr.

Peacock, speckled / *Cichla temensis*

LINE CLASS	WEIGHT	PLACE	DATE	ANGLER
01 kg (2 lb)	6.35 kg (14 lb 0 oz)	Rio Cinaruco, Venezuela	Feb. 5, 1986	Forrest I. Townsend, Jr.
02 kg (4 lb)	7.32 kg (16 lb 2 oz)	Mamori Lake, Amazonas, Brazil	Oct. 18, 1997	Gilberto Fernandes
03 kg (6 lb)	9.37 kg (20 lb 10 oz)	Rio Sipapo, Amazonas, Venezuela	Jan. 6, 1995	Carlos A. Aristeguieta L.
04 kg (8 lb)	9.18 kg (20 lb 3 oz)	Jatapu River, Amazon, Brazil	Sept. 6, 1992	Gilberto Fernandes
06 kg (12 lb)	12.02 kg (26 lb 8 oz)	Mataveni River, Orinoco, Colombia	Jan. 26, 1982	Rod Neubert, D.V.M.
08 kg (16 lb)	10.43 kg (23 lb 0 oz)	Rio Pasimoni, Venezuela	Mar. 6, 1992	Bert Bookout
08 kg (16 lb) Tie	10.48 kg (23 lb 1 oz)	Pasimoni River, Venezuela	Jan. 22, 1993	T.O. McLean
10 kg (20 lb)	10.88 kg (24 lb 0 oz)	Mataveni River, Orinoco, Colombia	Jan. 15, 1982	J. Hatcher James III
10 kg (20 lb) Tie	10.88 kg (24 lb 0 oz)	Rio Pasimoni, Venezuela	Mar. 6, 1992	Ami Nash

Perch, Nile / *Lates niloticus*

LINE CLASS	WEIGHT	PLACE	DATE	ANGLER
01 kg (2 lb)	12.50 kg (27 lb 8 oz)	Rusinga Island, Victoria, Kenya	Mar. 22, 1989	Hal Neibling
02 kg (4 lb)	11.00 kg (24 lb 4 oz)	South Island, Lake Turkana, Kenya	May 15, 1997	Gai Cullien
03 kg (6 lb)	22.50 kg (49 lb 9 oz)	Ngodhe Island, Lake Victoria, Kenya	Nov. 4, 1994	Derek Brink
04 kg (8 lb)	37.00 kg (81 lb 9 oz)	Rusinga Island, Victoria, Kenya	Mar. 22, 1989	Debi Neibling
06 kg (12 lb)	75.84 kg (167 lb 3 oz)	Rusinga Island, Lake Victoria, Kenya	Oct. 15, 1992	Gerhard von Bonde
08 kg (16 lb)	69.00 kg (152 lb 1 oz)	Spider Island, Entebbe Bay, Entebbe, Uganda	July 17, 1994	Phil Clouston
10 kg (20 lb)	61.00 kg (134 lb 7 oz)	Magogaye Island, Lake Victoria, Uganda	May 24, 1992	Gunnar Thomsen
15 kg (30 lb)	96.61 kg (213 lb 0 oz)	Lake Nasser, Egypt	Dec. 18, 1997	Adrian Brayshaw
24 kg (50 lb)	95.25 kg (210 lb 0 oz)	Lake Nasser, Egypt	June 24, 1998	Darren Robert Lord
37 kg (80 lb)	77.50 kg (170 lb 13 oz)	Entebbe, Uganda	Dec. 26, 1993	Joe Fernandes
60 kg (130 lb)	56.50 kg (124 lb 8 oz)	Lake Victoria, Kenya	Mar. 31, 1994	Derek Brink

Perch, white / *Morone americana*

LINE CLASS	WEIGHT	PLACE	DATE	ANGLER
01 kg (2 lb)	1.13 kg (2 lb 8 oz)	W. Kingston, Rhode Island, USA	Sept. 28, 1982	Albert Stephen Ferris
02 kg (4 lb)	1.35 kg (2 lb 15 oz)	Nantucket Island, Massachusetts, USA	Dec. 31, 1988	Jeffrey C. Beamish
03 kg (6 lb)	1.24 kg (2 lb 12 oz)	Barnagat, New Jersey, USA	Apr. 15, 1998	Michael A. King
04 kg (8 lb)	1.38 kg (3 lb 1 oz)	Forest Hill Park, New Jersey, USA	May 6, 1989	Edward Tango
06 kg (12 lb)	1.07 kg (2 lb 6 oz)	W. Kingston, Rhode Island, USA	Sept. 25, 1982	Frances Eileen Ferris

Perch, yellow / *Perca flavescens*

LINE CLASS	WEIGHT	PLACE	DATE	ANGLER
01 kg (2 lb)	1.18 kg (2 lb 9 oz)	Yuba Reservoir, Fayette, Utah, USA	July 5, 1984	Ray Johnson
02 kg (4 lb)	1.23 kg (2 lb 11 oz)	Yuba Reservoir, Fayette, Utah, USA	July 4, 1984	Ray Johnson
03 kg (6 lb)	0.82 kg (1 lb 13 oz)	North River, Currituck, North Carolina, USA	Feb. 11, 1995	Thomas F. Elkins
03 kg (6 lb) Tie	0.82 kg (1 lb 13 oz)	Whippoorwill Lake, Roundtop, New York, USA	July 29, 1995	John Boesenberg
04 kg (8 lb)	1.05 kg (2 lb 5 oz)	Yuba Reservoir, Fayette, Utah, USA	July 6, 1984	Ray Johnson
06 kg (12 lb)	0.87 kg (1 lb 15 oz)	Barbers Pond, W. Kingston, Rhode Island, USA	Sept. 26, 1986	Holly Kristen Ferris
06 kg (12 lb) Tie	0.90 kg (2 lb 0 oz)	North River, Currituck, North Carolina, USA	Feb. 15, 1989	Roy Cahoon

Pickerel, chain / *Esox niger*

LINE CLASS	WEIGHT	PLACE	DATE	ANGLER
01 kg (2 lb)	3.47 kg (7 lb 10 oz)	Lake Shawnee, Powhatan, Virginia, USA	Dec. 29, 1996	Reginald L. White
02 kg (4 lb)	2.83 kg (6 lb 4 oz)	Lee Hall Reservoir, Newport News, Virginia, USA	Dec. 7, 1986	Keith Tongier
02 kg (4 lb) Tie	2.83 kg (6 lb 4 oz)	Forest Lake, Methuen, Massachusetts, USA	May 19, 1994	Frank Howard
03 kg (6 lb)	1.87 kg (4 lb 2 oz)	Cape Fear River, North Carolina, USA	Dec. 21, 1995	Arnold Lee Rose
04 kg (8 lb)	3.28 kg (7 lb 4 oz)	Nanticoke River, Maryland, USA	Feb. 22, 1987	Paul D. Boggs
06 kg (12 lb)	3.11 kg (6 lb 14 oz)	Lee Hall Reservoir, Newport News, Virginia, USA	Jan. 3, 1982	Max Tongier, Jr.
06 kg (12 lb) Tie	3.11 kg (6 lb 14 oz)	Stockbridge, Massachusetts, USA	July 6, 1987	Rod Teehan

Pike, northern / *Esox lucius*

LINE CLASS	WEIGHT	PLACE	DATE	ANGLER
01 kg (2 lb)	10.85 kg (23 lb 15 oz)	Innoko River, Alaska, USA	Aug. 10, 1990	Rick Townsend
02 kg (4 lb)	11.56 kg (25 lb 8 oz)	Yukon River, Alaska, USA	Aug. 14, 1991	Craig Johnston, MD
03 kg (6 lb)	15.10 kg (33 lb 4 oz)	Smith Bay, Ontario, Canada	July 7, 1996	Marion M. Heffren
04 kg (8 lb)	19.60 kg (43 lb 3 oz)	Ascona, Lago Maggiore, Switzerland	Dec. 10, 1990	Giacomo Pinotti
06 kg (12 lb)	21.45 kg (47 lb 4 oz)	Lodde, Sweden	Jan. 28, 1989	Ake Nilsson
08 kg (16 lb)	18.05 kg (39 lb 12 oz)	Tenhultasjon, Sweden	Nov. 1, 1990	Thomas Lindwall
10 kg (20 lb)	18.10 kg (39 lb 14 oz)	Osthammar, Sweden	Nov. 20, 1993	Benny Pettersson
15 kg (30 lb)	15.64 kg (34 lb 8 oz)	Yukon, Alaska, USA	Aug. 10, 1991	Bill Tenney
24 kg (50 lb)	14.74 kg (32 lb 8 oz)	Gator Lake, Alaska, USA	Aug. 1, 1995	David Flicek

Redhorse, shorthead / *Moxostoma macrolepidotum*

LINE CLASS	WEIGHT	PLACE	DATE	ANGLER
01 kg (2 lb)	3.76 kg (8 lb 4 oz)	North River, Ontario, Canada	May 24, 1988	Bruce E. Johnstone
02 kg (4 lb)	3.99 kg (8 lb 12 oz)	North River, Ontario, Canada	May 23, 1988	Bruce E. Johnstone
03 kg (6 lb)	0.76 kg (1 lb 11 oz)	French Creek, Franklin, Pennsylvania, USA	Mar. 8, 1997	Richard E. Faler, Jr.
04 kg (8 lb)	3.77 kg (8 lb 5 oz)	North River, Ontario, Canada	May 23, 1988	Kimberley F. Fielder
06 kg (12 lb)	2.21 kg (4 lb 14 oz)	Rainy River, Loman, Minnesota, USA	Apr. 19, 1986	Joel M. Anderson

Redhorse, silver / *Moxostoma anisurum*

LINE CLASS	WEIGHT	PLACE	DATE	ANGLER
01 kg (2 lb)	3.30 kg (7 lb 4 oz)	Limestone Creek, Mooresville, Alabama, USA	Mar. 17, 1986	Randall Paulk
02 kg (4 lb)	3.27 kg (7 lb 3 oz)	Rainy River, Loman, Minnesota, USA	Sept. 18, 1987	Joel M. Anderson
03 kg (6 lb)	5.18 kg (11 lb 7 oz)	Plum Creek, Wisconsin, USA	May 29, 1985	Neal D.G. Long
04 kg (8 lb)	1.64 kg (3 lb 10 oz)	Thornapple River, Grand Rapids, Michigan, USA	Apr. 29, 1996	Leroy W. Baldwin
06 kg (12 lb)	3.94 kg (8 lb 11 oz)	Belle River, Michigan, USA	Mar. 26, 1986	Frank Jon Ruszkiewicz

Salmon, Atlantic / *Salmo salar*

LINE CLASS	WEIGHT	PLACE	DATE	ANGLER
01 kg (2 lb)	4.27 kg (9 lb 6 oz)	Lac Tremblant, Quebec, Canada	May 3, 1987	Pierre Lefebvre
02 kg (4 lb)	7.85 kg (17 lb 4 oz)	Lake Mattawa, Orange, Massachusetts, USA	Apr. 19, 1996	David Agocs
03 kg (6 lb)	8.14 kg (17 lb 15 oz)	Bay of Hano, Baltic Sea, Sweden	June 20, 1996	Leif Colleen
04 kg (8 lb)	11.73 kg (25 lb 13 oz)	Morrum Pool 16, Sweden	May 22, 1983	Bjarke Schmidt
06 kg (12 lb)	15.40 kg (33 lb 15 oz)	Namsen River, Norway	June 7, 1984	Rolf Hagstrom
08 kg (16 lb)	24.47 kg (53 lb 15 oz)	Bay of Punkavik, Baltic Sea, Sweden	May 9, 1994	Team Karlsson
10 kg (20 lb)	26.72 kg (58 lb 14 oz)	Bay of Punkavik, Baltic Sea, Sweden	May 13, 1993	Thommy Bengtsson
15 kg (30 lb)	27.48 kg (60 lb 9 oz)	Kasen, Bay of Punkavik, Baltic Sea, Sweden	May 9, 1995	Kenneth Olsson
24 kg (50 lb)	26.36 kg (58 lb 1 oz)	Baltic Sea, Sweden	Apr. 10, 1992	Lars Scharin

Salmon, chinook / *Oncorhynchus tshawytscha*

LINE CLASS	WEIGHT	PLACE	DATE	ANGLER
01 kg (2 lb)	20.32 kg (44 lb 12 oz)	Kenai River, Alaska, USA	Apr. 1, 1995	Raleigh Werking
02 kg (4 lb)	27.10 kg (59 lb 12 oz)	Skeena River, British Columbia, Canada	July 31, 1987	C.F. Rick Ream
03 kg (6 lb)	22.79 kg (50 lb 4 oz)	Kenai River, Alaska, USA	June 7, 1996	Deryk Anderson
04 kg (8 lb)	28.34 kg (62 lb 8 oz)	Queen Charlotte Islands, British Columbia, Canada	June 29, 1987	Albert Heimenberg
06 kg (12 lb)	30.50 kg (67 lb 4 oz)	Kenai River, Sterling, Alaska, USA	July 31, 1986	Michael J. Fenton
08 kg (16 lb)	35.15 kg (77 lb 8 oz)	Kenai River, Alaska, USA	July 18, 1985	Jerry Downey
10 kg (20 lb)	38.78 kg (85 lb 8 oz)	Odlom Point Lighthouse, British Columbia, Canada	Aug. 4, 1987	Robert Paul Carter
15 kg (30 lb)	44.11 kg (97 lb 4 oz)	Kenai River, Alaska, USA	May 17, 1985	Les Anderson
24 kg (50 lb)	36.85 kg (81 lb 4 oz)	Deep Creek, Alaska, USA	July 15, 1985	Dale C. Anderson
37 kg (80 lb)	32.31 kg (71 lb 4 oz)	Kenai River, Alaska, USA	June 30, 1988	Nathanel J. Anderson
60 kg (130 lb)	28.62 kg (63 lb 1 oz)	Kenai River, Alaska, USA	July 2, 1994	Raleigh Werking

Salmon, chum / *Oncorhynchus keta*

LINE CLASS	WEIGHT	PLACE	DATE	ANGLER
01 kg (2 lb)	7.00 kg (15 lb 7 oz)	Fish Creek, Alaska, USA	Aug. 1, 1986	Jeff Trom
02 kg (4 lb)	7.85 kg (17 lb 5 oz)	Fish Creek, Alaska, USA	Aug. 1, 1986	Martin Vanderploeg
03 kg (6 lb)	Vacant			
04 kg (8 lb)	9.03 kg (19 lb 14 oz)	Satsop River, Washington, USA	Nov. 7, 1986	William J. Harris, DDS
06 kg (12 lb)	8.61 kg (19 lb 0 oz)	Ketchikan, Alaska, USA	July 18, 1987	Lee W. Putman
08 kg (16 lb)	11.77 kg (25 lb 15 oz)	Satsop River, Washington, USA	Oct. 19, 1997	Johnnie R. Wilson
10 kg (20 lb)	15.87 kg (35 lb 0 oz)	Edye Pass, British Columbia, Canada	July 11, 1995	Todd A. Johansson
15 kg (30 lb)	12.13 kg (26 lb 12 oz)	Rivers Inlet, British Columbia, Canada	Oct. 28, 1989	Robert P. Caldow

Salmon, coho / *Oncorhynchus kisutch*

LINE CLASS	WEIGHT	PLACE	DATE	ANGLER
01 kg (2 lb)	7.29 kg (16 lb 1 oz)	Kenai River, Alaska, USA	Oct. 9, 1988	Pat K. Johnson
02 kg (4 lb)	8.20 kg (18 lb 1 oz)	Karluk River, Alaska, USA	Sept. 15, 1990	Burton R. Leed
03 kg (6 lb)	8.36 kg (18 lb 7 oz)	Camp Kiklukh, Kiklukh River, Alaska, USA	Oct. 10, 1995	George R. Davis
04 kg (8 lb)	8.84 kg (19 lb 8 oz)	Situk River, Yakutat, Alaska, USA	Sept. 20, 1984	Melvin E. Snook
06 kg (12 lb)	9.97 kg (22 lb 0 oz)	Kiklukh River, Alaska, USA	Sept. 22, 1994	Harold F. Baritell, Sr.
08 kg (16 lb)	12.08 kg (26 lb 10 oz)	Oakville, Ontario, Canada	Aug. 7, 1987	Glenn Osborne
10 kg (20 lb)	13.94 kg (30 lb 12 oz)	Salmon River, Pulaski, New York, USA	Sept. 12, 1985	Bub Cornish
15 kg (30 lb)	15.08 kg (33 lb 4 oz)	Salmon River, Pulaski, New York, USA	Sept. 27, 1989	Jerry Lifton
24 kg (50 lb)	7.82 kg (17 lb 4 oz)	Kenai River, Alaska, USA	Sept. 14, 1984	Paul W. Pearson

Salmon, pink / *Oncorhynchus gorbuscha*

LINE CLASS	WEIGHT	PLACE	DATE	ANGLER
01 kg (2 lb)	4.64 kg (10 lb 4 oz)	Karluk River, Kodiak Island, Alaska, USA	July 13, 1984	Rod Neubert, D.V.M.
02 kg (4 lb)	3.90 kg (8 lb 9 oz)	Kenai River, Alaska, USA	Aug. 20, 1988	Pat K. Johnson
03 kg (6 lb)	5.21 kg (11 lb 8 oz)	Karluk River, Kodiak Island, Alaska, USA	July 13, 1984	Rod Neubert, D.V.M.
04 kg (8 lb)	3.23 kg (7 lb 2 oz)	Kenai River, Alaska, USA	Aug. 22, 1998	Steven N. Davis
06 kg (12 lb)	5.69 kg (12 lb 9 oz)	Moose & Kenai Rivers, Alaska, USA	Aug. 17, 1974	Steven Alan Lee
08 kg (16 lb)	4.60 kg (10 lb 2 oz)	Snohomish River, Washington, USA	Sept. 13, 1985	F. John Erickson
10 kg (20 lb)	5.94 kg (13 lb 1 oz)	St. Mary's River, Ontario, Canada	Sept. 23, 1992	Ray Higaki
15 kg (30 lb)	5.32 kg (11 lb 11 oz)	St. Mary's River, Detour, Michigan, USA	July 13, 1992	David R. Comba

Salmon, sockeye / *Oncorhynchus nerka*

LINE CLASS	WEIGHT	PLACE	DATE	ANGLER
01 kg (2 lb)	5.61 kg (12 lb 5 oz)	Russian River, Alaska, USA	Aug. 20, 1987	Martin Vanderploeg
02 kg (4 lb)	4.96 kg (10 lb 15 oz)	Russian River, Alaska, USA	Aug. 14, 1984	Martin Vanderploeg
03 kg (6 lb)	5.50 kg (12 lb 2 oz)	Russian River, Alaska, USA	Aug. 20, 1987	Dale Hallman
04 kg (8 lb)	4.30 kg (9 lb 8 oz)	Nonvinack River, Alaska, USA	Sept. 10, 1996	Paul Marvin Adams
06 kg (12 lb)	6.69 kg (14 lb 12 oz)	Coktuli River, Alaska, USA	July 17, 1993	Warren J. Redmond
08 kg (16 lb)	6.57 kg (14 lb 8 oz)	Kenai River, Alaska, USA	Aug. 2, 1994	Archer J. Richardson
10 kg (20 lb)	5.89 kg (13 lb 0 oz)	Kenai River, Alaska, USA	July 3, 1990	Jesse J. Zalonis
15 kg (30 lb)	6.88 kg (15 lb 3 oz)	Kenai River, Alaska, USA	Aug. 9, 1987	Stan Roach

Sauger / *Stizostedion canadense*

LINE CLASS	WEIGHT	PLACE	DATE	ANGLER
01 kg (2 lb)	3.54 kg (7 lb 12 oz)	Saskatchewan River, Saskatoon, Canada	Sept. 9, 1990	Alex D. Foster
02 kg (4 lb)	3.06 kg (6 lb 12 oz)	Saskatchewan River, Saskatoon, Canada	Sept. 7, 1990	Alex D. Foster
03 kg (6 lb)	1.58 kg (3 lb 8 oz)	Pittsburgh, Pennsylvania, USA	Mar. 13, 1997	Herbert G. Ratner, Jr
04 kg (8 lb)	3.43 kg (7 lb 9 oz)	Fort Peck Lake, Montana, USA	Dec. 15, 1993	Rodney Kelm
06 kg (12 lb)	2.99 kg (6 lb 9 oz)	Yellowstone River, Terry, Montana, USA	Mar. 16, 1988	Gerald Frank
08 kg (16 lb)	3.37 kg (7 lb 7 oz)	Lake Cumberland, Kentucky, USA	Apr. 27, 1983	Rastie O. Andrew

Shad, American / *Alosa sapidissima*

LINE CLASS	WEIGHT	PLACE	DATE	ANGLER
01 kg (2 lb)	3.54 kg (7 lb 13 oz)	Pond Eddy, Delaware River, New York, USA	June 22, 1993	John Boesenberg
02 kg (4 lb)	4.02 kg (8 lb 14 oz)	Delaware River, New Jersey, USA	Apr. 29, 1984	Andre Moirano
03 kg (6 lb)	1.84 kg (4 lb 1 oz)	Delaware River, Easton, Pennsylvania, USA	May 14, 1997	John Boesenberg
04 kg (8 lb)	5.01 kg (11 lb 1 oz)	Delaware River, Columbia, New Jersey, USA	May 5, 1984	Charles J. Mower
06 kg (12 lb)	5.10 kg (11 lb 4 oz)	Connecticut River, S. Hadley, Massachusetts, USA	May 19, 1986	Bob Thibodo

Splake / *Salvelinus namaycush x Salvelinus fontinalis*

LINE CLASS	WEIGHT	PLACE	DATE	ANGLER
01 kg (2 lb)	2.16 kg (4 lb 12 oz)	Green Bay, Lake Michigan, Michigan, USA	Mar. 9, 1989	Keith Thomas Grabowski
02 kg (4 lb)	3.06 kg (6 lb 12 oz)	Harrow Lake, Canada	May 23, 1976	Leo Warner Pirak
03 kg (6 lb)	1.77 kg (3 lb 14 oz)	St. Mary's River, Sault Ste Marie, Michigan, USA	May 3, 1997	Joe S. Krzykwa
04 kg (8 lb)	9.39 kg (20 lb 11 oz)	Georgian Bay, Ontario, Canada	May 17, 1987	Paul S. Thompson
06 kg (12 lb)	3.31 kg (7 lb 5 oz)	Crystal Falls, Michigan, USA	May 27, 1979	Warren A. Dellies
08 kg (16 lb)	2.21 kg (4 lb 14 oz)	Meaford, Ontario, Canada	May 31, 1990	James Ross Nixon
10 kg (20 lb)	2.56 kg (5 lb 10 oz)	Georgian Bay, Ontario, Canada	May 14, 1990	Bruce E. Turner
15 kg (30 lb)	1.07 kg (2 lb 5 oz)	Deerfield Lake, Deerfield, South Dakota, USA	Feb. 11, 1989	Terry J. Hulm

Sturgeon / *Acipenseridae family*

LINE CLASS	WEIGHT	PLACE	DATE	ANGLER
01 kg (2 lb)	16.32 kg (36 lb 0 oz)	Honker Bay, California, USA	Feb. 14, 1985	Walt Peterson
02 kg (4 lb)	17.87 kg (39 lb 6 oz)	Santa Ana River Lakes, California, USA	Mar. 21, 1998	Robert Vandevelde
03 kg (6 lb)	26.39 kg (58 lb 3 oz)	Suisin Bay, Pittsburg, California, USA	Nov. 5, 1995	Joe Hawkins
04 kg (8 lb)	37.19 kg (82 lb 0 oz)	San Francisco Bay, California, USA	Mar. 25, 1983	Ronald L. Johnson
06 kg (12 lb)	76.20 kg (168 lb 0 oz)	Georgian Bay, Ontario, Canada	May 29, 1982	Edward Paszkowski
08 kg (16 lb)	81.53 kg (179 lb 12 oz)	Suisin Bay, California, USA	Nov. 15, 1989	Ron Bernhardt
10 kg (20 lb)	107.50 kg (237 lb 0 oz)	Sacramento River, Antioch, California, USA	Sept. 20, 1989	Alvin L. Threet
15 kg (30 lb)	176.90 kg (390 lb 0 oz)	Honker Bay, California, USA	Nov. 7, 1981	William A. Stratton
24 kg (50 lb)	146.17 kg (322 lb 4 oz)	Sacramento River, Pittsburg, California, USA	Dec. 8, 1985	Pete M. Anderson
37 kg (80 lb)	212.28 kg (468 lb 0 oz)	Benicia, California, USA	July 9, 1983	Joey Pallotta, III
60 kg (130 lb)	23.75 kg (52 lb 6 oz)	Rainy River, Loman, Minnesota, USA	Sept. 19, 1987	Joel M. Anderson

Sunfish, green / *Lepomis*

LINE CLASS	WEIGHT	PLACE	DATE	ANGLER
01 kg (2 lb)	0.60 kg (1 lb 5 oz)	Great Bear Lake, Michigan, USA	June 2, 1988	David W. Rose
02 kg (4 lb)	Vacant			
03 kg (6 lb)	Vacant			
04 kg (8 lb)	Vacant			
06 kg (12 lb)	Vacant			

Sunfish, redbreast / *Lepomis auritus*

LINE CLASS	WEIGHT	PLACE	DATE	ANGLER
01 kg (2 lb)	0.48 kg (1 lb 1 oz)	Suwannee River, Florida, USA	June 29, 1986	Winston Baker
02 kg (4 lb)	0.77 kg (1 lb 11 oz)	Suwannee River, Florida, USA	May 10, 1987	Leon H. Bath
03 kg (6 lb)	Vacant			
04 kg (8 lb)	0.79 kg (1 lb 12 oz)	Suwannee River, Florida, USA	May 29, 1984	Alvin Buchanan
06 kg (12 lb)	0.51 kg (1 lb 2 oz)	Suwannee River, Chiefland, Florida, USA	July 23, 1986	Bernard L. Schultz
06 kg (12 lb) Tie	0.51 kg (1 lb 2 oz)	South River, Cumberland Co., North Carolina, USA	Apr. 22, 1990	Dr. R. D. Snipes

Sunfish, redear / *Lepomis microlophus*

LINE CLASS	WEIGHT	PLACE	DATE	ANGLER
01 kg (2 lb)	1.06 kg (2 lb 5 oz)	Callaway Gardens, Pine Mountain, Georgia, USA	May 22, 1996	Charley H. Jones
02 kg (4 lb)	1.26 kg (2 lb 12 oz)	Conyers, Georgia, USA	June 22, 1979	Loy P. Croker
03 kg (6 lb)	0.53 kg (1 lb 2 oz)	Steelwood Lake, Alabama, USA	Sept. 14, 1997	Robert T. Cunningham, Jr.
04 kg (8 lb)	2.35 kg (5 lb 3 oz)	Folsum South Canal, Sacramento, California, USA	June 27, 1994	Anthony H. White, Sr.
06 kg (12 lb)	2.20 kg (4 lb 13 oz)	Merritt's Mill Pond, Marianna, Florida, USA	Mar. 13, 1986	Joey M. Floyd

Taimen / *Hucho taimen*

LINE CLASS	WEIGHT	PLACE	DATE	ANGLER
01 kg (2 lb)	Vacant			
02 kg (4 lb)	3.81 kg (8 lb 6 oz)	Dyanyshka, Jukutsk, Siberia, Russia	Aug. 4, 1991	Scott T. Wride
03 kg (6 lb)	Vacant			
04 kg (8 lb)	16.28 kg (35 lb 14 oz)	Dyanyshka, Jukutsk, Siberia, Russia	Aug. 12, 1991	Scott T. Wride
06 kg (12 lb)	19.50 kg (43 lb 0 oz)	Keta River, Russian Far East, Siberia, Russia	Aug. 7, 1993	David L. Stoick
08 kg (16 lb)	41.95 kg (92 lb 0 oz)	Keta River, Russia	Aug. 11, 1993	Yuri Orlov
10 kg (20 lb)	34.47 kg (76 lb 0 oz)	Tugar River, Russia	Aug. 24, 1992	Goo Vogt
15 kg (30 lb)	188.49 kg (85 lb 8 oz)	Keta River, Siberia, Russia	Aug. 10, 1993	Greg Stoick

Taimen / *(continued)*

24 kg (50 lb)	7.20 kg (15 lb 13 oz)	Maya River, Siberia, Russia	Sept. 15, 1992	Hakan Brugard
37 kg (80 lb)	Vacant			
60 kg (130 lb)	Vacant			

Tigerfish / *Hydrocynus vittatus*

LINE CLASS	WEIGHT	PLACE	DATE	ANGLER
01 kg (2 lb)	6.47 kg (14 lb 4 oz)	Zambezi River, Chirundo, Zimbabwe	Jan. 22, 1993	Graham Law
02 kg (4 lb)	8.07 kg (17 lb 12 oz)	Zambezi River, Zimbabwe	May 22, 1989	Graham Law
03 kg (6 lb)	7.00 kg (15 lb 6 oz)	Tiger Camp, Zambezi River, Zambia	Nov. 23, 1994	Bernard Esterhuyse
04 kg (8 lb)	9.90 kg (21 lb 13 oz)	Zambezi River, Zimbabwe	July 31, 1986	Brent Reg Gavin Hudson
06 kg (12 lb)	8.45 kg (18 lb 10 oz)	Royal Zambezi Lodge, Chiawa, Zambia	Nov. 1, 1995	Brett Hickman
08 kg (16 lb)	9.50 kg (20 lb 15 oz)	Zambezi River, Zambia	Aug. 11, 1985	Reg Hughes
10 kg (20 lb)	8.90 kg (19 lb 9 oz)	Tiger Camp, Zambezi River, Zambia	Aug. 2, 1997	Ryuichi Takahashi
15 kg (30 lb)	8.20 kg (18 lb 1 oz)	Tiger Camp, Zambezi River, Zambia	Aug. 29, 1994	T.F. Ashworth

Tigerfish, giant / *Hydrocynus goliath*

LINE CLASS	WEIGHT	PLACE	DATE	ANGLER
01 kg (2 lb)	Vacant			
02 kg (4 lb)	Vacant			
03 kg (6 lb)	Vacant			
04 kg (8 lb)	18.60 kg (41 lb 0 oz)	Zaire River, Kinshasa, Zaire	July 23, 1989	Raymond Houtmans
06 kg (12 lb)	44.00 kg (97 lb 0 oz)	Zaire River, Kinshasa, Zaire	July 9, 1988	Raymond Houtmans
08 kg (16 lb)	42.00 kg (92 lb 9 oz)	Zaire River, Zaire	July 19, 1987	Raymond Houtmans
10 kg (20 lb)	40.00 kg (88 lb 2 oz)	Zaire River, Kinshasa, Zaire	June 28, 1987	Jean van Loock
15 kg (30 lb)	32.50 kg (71 lb 10 oz)	Zaire River, Kinshasa, Zaire	July 28, 1985	Raymond Houtmans
24 kg (50 lb)	Vacant			
37 kg (80 lb)	Vacant			
60 kg (130 lb)	Vacant			

Trout, brook / *Salvelinus fontinalis*

LINE CLASS	WEIGHT	PLACE	DATE	ANGLER
01 kg (2 lb)	3.40 kg (7 lb 8 oz)	Misstassini, Quebec, Canada	Sept. 1, 1982	Bill Atwood
02 kg (4 lb)	4.08 kg (9 lb 0 oz)	Lake Nipigon, Ontario, Canada	July 1, 1996	Paul J. Heytons
03 kg (6 lb)	3.28 kg (7 lb 4 oz)	Osprey Lake, Labrador, Canada	June 24, 1998	Robert A. King
04 kg (8 lb)	3.85 kg (8 lb 8 oz)	Minonipi Lake, Labrador, Canada	July 6, 1989	Jeffery S. Andrews
06 kg (12 lb)	3.45 kg (7 lb 10 oz)	Round Lake, Saskatchewan, Canada	May 4, 1993	Richard Myers, III
08 kg (16 lb)	4.87 kg (10 lb 12 oz)	Osprey Lake, Labrador, Newfoundland, Canada	June 24, 1996	William A. Trendler
10 kg (20 lb)	3.85 kg (8 lb 8 oz)	Osprey Lake, Labrador, Canada	July 4, 1997	Joseph P. Trendler

Trout, brown / *Salmo trutta*

LINE CLASS	WEIGHT	PLACE	DATE	ANGLER
01 kg (2 lb)	9.41 kg (20 lb 12 oz)	White River, Arkansas, USA	Sept. 19, 1987	Carl H. Jones
02 kg (4 lb)	18.25 kg (40 lb 4 oz)	Little Red River, Heber Springs, Arkansas, USA	May 9, 1992	Howard L. (Rip) Collins
03 kg (6 lb)	12.92 kg (28 lb 8 oz)	Niagara River, Niagara Falls, Canada	Nov. 16, 1996	Glenn A. Taggart
04 kg (8 lb)	15.59 kg (34 lb 6 oz)	Lake Ontario, Mississauga, Ontario, Canada	Sept. 9, 1994	Richard Matusiak
06 kg (12 lb)	15.59 kg (34 lb 6 oz)	Bar Lake, Arcadia, Michigan, USA	May 16, 1984	Robert Henderson
08 kg (16 lb)	17.00 kg (37 lb 7 oz)	Lake Storsjon, Lapland, Sweden	Oct. 16, 1991	Kurt Stenlund
10 kg (20 lb)	13.83 kg (30 lb 8 oz)	Platt Bay, Lake Michigan, USA	Apr. 18, 1994	Tim W. Kammer
15 kg (30 lb)	8.00 kg (17 lb 10 oz)	Stockholm Stream, Stockholm, Sweden	Nov. 3, 1983	Magnus Herou
24 kg (50 lb)	6.46 kg (14 lb 4 oz)	Lake Ontario, New York, USA	Apr. 29, 1986	Paul Loquasto

Trout, bull / *Salvelinus confluentus*

LINE CLASS	WEIGHT	PLACE	DATE	ANGLER
01 kg (2 lb)	4.35 kg (9 lb 9 oz)	Flathead River, Montana, USA	Aug. 18, 1989	James P. Landwehr
02 kg (4 lb)	3.55 kg (7 lb 13 oz)	McKenzie River, Oregon, USA	July 12, 1988	Mike McCoy
03 kg (6 lb)	Vacant			
04 kg (8 lb)	5.55 kg (12 lb 4 oz)	Flathead River, Montana, USA	July 4, 1987	William J. Harris, DDS
06 kg (12 lb)	10.48 kg (23 lb 2 oz)	Lake Billy Chinook, Culver, Oregon, USA	Mar. 25, 1989	Don Yow
08 kg (16 lb)	8.78 kg (19 lb 6 oz)	Lake Pend Oreille, Idaho, USA	May 2, 1981	Jack W. Klein
10 kg (20 lb)	6.01 kg (13 lb 4 oz)	Kootenay Lake, British Columbia, Canada	Nov. 10, 1986	Michael V. Higgins
10 kg (20 lb) Tie	6.01 kg (13 lb 4 oz)	Lake Pend Oreille, Idaho, USA	June 6, 1987	R. Kendall McDowell

Trout, cutthroat / *Oncorhynchus clarki*

LINE CLASS	WEIGHT	PLACE	DATE	ANGLER
01 kg (2 lb)	5.72 kg (12 lb 10 oz)	Pyramid Lake, Nevada, USA	Nov. 12, 1989	Richard D. Hanes
02 kg (4 lb)	4.95 kg (10 lb 14 oz)	Pyramid Lake, Nevada, USA	July 21, 1984	Ray Johnson
03 kg (6 lb)	6.46 kg (14 lb 4 oz)	Pyramid Lake, Nevada, USA	Feb. 28, 1988	Gordie Morris
04 kg (8 lb)	8.18 kg (18 lb 0 oz)	Omak Lake, Washington, USA	July 1, 1993	Dan Beardslee
06 kg (12 lb)	5.32 kg (11 lb 12 oz)	Pyramid Lake, Nevada, USA	Nov. 8, 1985	John A. F. Gorzelny
08 kg (16 lb)	5.32 kg (11 lb 12 oz)	Pyramid Lake, Nevada, USA	Feb. 16, 1986	Robert C. Brunner
10 kg (20 lb)	5.16 kg (11 lb 6 oz)	Pyramid Lake, Nevada, USA	July 30, 1984	Ray Johnson

Trout, golden / *Oncorhynchus aguabonita*

LINE CLASS	WEIGHT	PLACE	DATE	ANGLER
01 kg (2 lb)	2.55 kg (5 lb 10 oz)	Golden Lake, Wyoming, USA	June 22, 1989	Bob Shettel
02 kg (4 lb)	2.09 kg (4 lb 10 oz)	Golden Lake, Wyoming, USA	June 19, 1989	Bob Shettel
03 kg (6 lb)	1.64 kg (3 lb 10 oz)	Thumb Lake, Wyoming, USA	July 2, 1996	Sean Moran
04 kg (8 lb)	2.09 kg (4 lb 10 oz)	Golden Lake, Wyoming, USA	June 20, 1989	Chip Hane
06 kg (12 lb)	1.98 kg (4 lb 6 oz)	Golden Lake, Wyoming, USA	June 20, 1989	Bob Shettel

Trout, lake / *Salvelinus namaycush*

LINE CLASS	WEIGHT	PLACE	DATE	ANGLER
01 kg (2 lb)	12.84 kg (28 lb 5 oz)	Flaming Gorge Reservoir, Utah, USA	Oct. 31, 1984	Ray Johnson
02 kg (4 lb)	14.28 kg (31 lb 8 oz)	Flaming Gorge Reservoir, Utah, USA	Nov. 5, 1984	Ray Johnson
03 kg (6 lb)	12.08 kg (26 lb 8 oz)	Lac La Martre, Canada	July 2, 1998	Gerald Chesin
04 kg (8 lb)	22.22 kg (49 lb 0 oz)	Great Bear Lake, N.W.T., Canada	July 5, 1987	Robert J. Vallee
06 kg (12 lb)	22.90 kg (50 lb 8 oz)	Great Bear Lake, N.W.T., Canada	Aug. 22, 1984	Marco J. Zonni

Trout, lake / *(continued)*

LINE CLASS	WEIGHT	PLACE	DATE	ANGLER
08 kg (16 lb)	24.15 kg (53 lb 4 oz)	Great Bear Lake, N.W.T., Canada	July 19, 1986	Richard J. Simourd
10 kg (20 lb)	28.83 kg (63 lb 9 oz)	Great Bear Lake, N.W.T., Canada	July 31, 1986	Mike Kroening
15 kg (30 lb)	32.65 kg (72 lb 0 oz)	Great Bear Lake, N.W.T., Canada	Aug. 19, 1995	Lloyd E. Bull
24 kg (50 lb)	24.94 kg (55 lb 0 oz)	Great Bear Lake, N.W.T., Canada	July 9, 1989	Massey Lombardi
37 kg (80 lb)	16.78 kg (37 lb 0 oz)	Great Bear Lake, N.W.T., Canada	July 30, 1998	Marlin A. Coulombe

Trout, rainbow / *Oncorhynchus mykiss*

LINE CLASS	WEIGHT	PLACE	DATE	ANGLER
01 kg (2 lb)	8.27 kg (18 lb 4 oz)	Cowlitz River, Washington, USA	July 4, 1981	Larry Johnson
02 kg (4 lb)	10.77 kg (23 lb 12 oz)	Bowmanville Creek, Ontario, Canada	Apr. 28, 1984	Brett Elliott
03 kg (6 lb)	8.21 kg (18 lb 12 oz)	Lake Pend Oreille, Idaho, USA	Oct. 24, 1995	Gene Grimes
04 kg (8 lb)	12.04 kg (26 lb 9 oz)	Lake Pend Oreille, Idaho, USA	Oct. 18, 1982	Robert E. Pugh
06 kg (12 lb)	13.18 kg (29 lb 1 oz)	Skeena River, Canada	Nov. 12, 1976	Day B. Karr
08 kg (16 lb)	14.34 kg (31 lb 10 oz)	Lake Pend Oreille, Idaho, USA	Oct. 26, 1992	Ron Provience
10 kg (20 lb)	14.20 kg (31 lb 5 oz)	Lake Pend Oreille, Idaho, USA	Nov. 19, 1983	Gilbert Norlen
15 kg (30 lb)	14.25 kg (31 lb 6 oz)	Lake Michigan, Wheaton, Illinois, USA	July 10, 1993	Kyle C. Johnson
24 kg (50 lb)	9.01 kg (19 lb 14 oz)	Burns Harbor, Portage, Indiana, USA	June 11, 1987	Joshua M. Davis

Trout, tiger / *Salmo trutta x Salvelinus fontinalis*

LINE CLASS	WEIGHT	PLACE	DATE	ANGLER
01 kg (2 lb)	0.57 kg (1 lb 4 oz)	Blue Lakes, Nevada, USA	Oct. 17, 1998	D. Scott Scovira
02 kg (4 lb)	1.91 kg (4 lb 3 oz)	Lake Michigan, Illinois, USA	May 19, 1976	Tom Musil
03 kg (6 lb)	Vacant			
04 kg (8 lb)	5.25 kg (11 lb 9 oz)	Lake Michigan, Wisconsin, USA	July 16, 1976	John E. Schmidt
06 kg (12 lb)	Vacant			
08 kg (16 lb)	1.02 kg (2 lb 4 oz)	Westfield River, Massachusetts, USA	May 9, 1998	John J. Regan
10 kg (20 lb)	9.44 kg (20 lb 13 oz)	Lake Michigan, Wisconsin, USA	Aug. 12, 1978	Pete M. Friedland
15 kg (30 lb)	Vacant			

Walleye / *Stizostedion vitreum*

LINE CLASS	WEIGHT	PLACE	DATE	ANGLER
01 kg (2 lb)	4.70 kg (10 lb 6 oz)	Branched Oak Lake, Lincoln, Nebraska, USA	Apr. 18, 1984	Thomas G. Bitting
02 kg (4 lb)	8.27 kg (18 lb 4 oz)	Little Red River, Arkansas, USA	Mar. 14, 1983	Mark Steven Wallace
03 kg (6 lb)	5.44 kg (12 lb 0 oz)	Bay of Quinte, Ontario, Canada	Nov. 10, 1995	James J. Sloyka
04 kg (8 lb)	8.98 kg (19 lb 13 oz)	Forsyth, Missouri, USA	Feb. 8, 1991	Pete Gleason
06 kg (12 lb)	10.29 kg (22 lb 11 oz)	Greers Ferry Lake, Arkansas, USA	Mar. 14, 1982	Al Nelson
08 kg (16 lb)	8.27 kg (18 lb 4 oz)	Greers Ferry Lake, Arkansas, USA	Jan. 12, 1982	Howard L. Brierly
10 kg (20 lb)	9.35 kg (20 lb 9 oz)	Devils Fork Branch, Heber Springs, Arkansas, USA	Feb. 10, 1989	Tom Evans

Warmouth / *Lepomis gulosus*

LINE CLASS	WEIGHT	PLACE	DATE	ANGLER
01 kg (2 lb)	0.53 kg (1 lb 2 oz)	Lee Hall Reservoir, Newport News, Virginia, USA	Aug. 29, 1985	Max Tongier, Jr.
02 kg (4 lb)	0.50 kg (1 lb 1 oz)	Lee Hall Reservoir, Newport News, Virginia, USA	Aug. 29, 1985	Max Tongier, Jr.
03 kg (6 lb)	0.96 kg (2 lb 2 oz)	Coteau Holmes, Louisiana, USA	July 26, 1987	Frank E. Dean, Jr.
04 kg (8 lb)	Vacant			
06 kg (12 lb)	1.10 kg (2 lb 7 oz)	Guess Lake, Yellow River, Holt, Florida, USA	Oct. 19, 1985	Tony David Dempsey

Whitefish, lake / *Coregonus clupeaformis*

LINE CLASS	WEIGHT	PLACE	DATE	ANGLER
01 kg (2 lb)	3.88 kg (8 lb 9 oz)	Great Bear Lake, N.W.T., Canada	Aug. 16, 1988	Larry R. Barr
02 kg (4 lb)	6.52 kg (14 lb 6 oz)	Meaford, Ontario, Canada	May 21, 1984	Dennis M. Laycock
03 kg (6 lb)	1.48 kg (3 lb 4 oz)	St. Mary's River, Ste Sault Mary, Ontario, Canada	Nov. 26, 1997	John Gausas, PhD.
04 kg (8 lb)	6.32 kg (13 lb 15 oz)	Meaford, Ontario, Canada	Apr. 19, 1981	Wayne Caswell
06 kg (12 lb)	5.92 kg (13 lb 1 oz)	Meaford, Ontario, Canada	Apr. 28, 1978	Denis J. Bouchard
08 kg (16 lb)	3.99 kg (8 lb 13 oz)	Great Bear Lake, N.W.T., Canada	Aug. 11, 1988	John B. Johnson

Whitefish, mountain / *Prosopium williamsoni*

LINE CLASS	WEIGHT	PLACE	DATE	ANGLER
01 kg (2 lb)	1.67 kg (3 lb 11 oz)	Roaring Fork River, Colorado, USA	Sept. 19, 1987	Jack L. Hester
02 kg (4 lb)	1.75 kg (3 lb 14 oz)	Provo River, Utah, USA	Sept. 25, 1977	Kay M. Zabriskie
03 kg (6 lb)	1.40 kg (3 lb 1 oz)	Clarks Fork, Yellowstone River, Clark, Wyoming, USA	Aug. 10, 1998	Hooper Cassidy Flanigan
04 kg (8 lb)	2.32 kg (5 lb 2 oz)	Columbia River, Washington, USA	Nov. 30, 1983	Steven W. Becken
06 kg (12 lb)	2.51 kg (5 lb 8 oz)	Elbow River, Calgary, Alberta, Canada	Aug. 1, 1995	Randy G. Woo

Whitefish, round / *Prosopium cylindraceum*

LINE CLASS	WEIGHT	PLACE	DATE	ANGLER
01 kg (2 lb)	0.73 kg (1 lb 10 oz)	Lake Michigan, Michigan, USA	Nov. 2, 1983	Kenneth R. Darwin
02 kg (4 lb)	1.84 kg (4 lb 0 oz)	Grand Haven, Michigan, USA	Nov. 19, 1992	Kenneth E. Bilski
03 kg (6 lb)	Vacant			
04 kg (8 lb)	2.72 kg (6 lb 0 oz)	Putahow River, Manitoba, Canada	June 14, 1984	Allan J. Ristori
06 kg (12 lb)	1.47 kg (3 lb 4 oz)	Leland Harbor, Michigan, USA	Nov. 2, 1977	Vernon A. Bauer

IGFA Saltwater Line Class Records

The following are men's and women's world saltwater records granted in IGFA line class categories as of January 1, 1999. The records are listed alphabetically according to the common names of the species.

Albacore / *Thunnus alalunga*

LINE CLASS	WEIGHT	PLACE	DATE	ANGLER
M-01 kg (2 lb)	7.10 kg (15 lb 10 oz)	Cape Point, Cape Town, South Africa	Jan. 16, 1993	Sean Todd
M-02 kg (4 lb)	22.68 kg (50 lb 0 oz)	Kona, Hawaii, USA	Sept. 15, 1994	Ronald J. Freitas
M-03 kg (6 lb)	15.75 kg (34 lb 11 oz)	Broken Bay Sydney, Australia	Sept. 21, 1980	Tim Simpson
M-04 kg (8 lb)	27.55 kg (60 lb 11 oz)	Hout Bay, Cape Town, Republic of South Africa	Apr. 30, 1992	Hubert Meyer
M-06 kg (12 lb)	31.18 kg (68 lb 12 oz)	Port San Luis, California, USA	Nov. 7, 1984	Kevin J. Crow
M-08 kg (16 lb)	32.54 kg (71 lb 12 oz)	Catalina Channel, California, USA	Nov. 14, 1984	Roy R. Ludt
M-10 kg (20 lb)	34.47 kg (76 lb 0 oz)	San Pedro, California, USA	Nov. 14, 1984	Michael E. Bradley
M-15 kg (30 lb)	35.00 kg (77 lb 2 oz)	Cape Point, Republic of South Africa	Sept. 4, 1988	Barrie Rose
M-24 kg (50 lb)	38.00 kg (83 lb 12 oz)	Miyake Island, Tokyo, Japan	Jan. 20, 1986	Yuji Sato
M-37 kg (80 lb)	40.00 kg (88 lb 2 oz)	Gran Canaria, Canary Islands, Spain	Nov. 19, 1977	Siegfried Dickemann
W-01 kg (2 lb)	Vacant			
W-02 kg (4 lb)	9.07 kg (20 lb 0 oz)	San Clemente Island, California, USA	Aug. 11, 1984	Lorraine Carlton
W-03 kg (6 lb)	11.79 kg (26 lb 0 oz)	San Diego, California, USA	Sept. 12, 1976	Lorraine Carlton
W-04 kg (8 lb)	19.50 kg (42 lb 15 oz)	Hout Bay, Republic of South Africa	Sept. 4, 1988	Maureen K. Colyn
W-06 kg (12 lb)	26.19 kg (57 lb 12 oz)	Point Loma, California, USA	Nov. 2, 1982	Jean S. Hinckley
W-08 kg (16 lb)	27.20 kg (59 lb 15 oz)	Hout Bay, Republic of South Africa	Aug. 21, 1988	Maureen K. Colyn
W-10 kg (20 lb)	34.01 kg (75 lb 0 oz)	Catalina Channel, San Pedro, California, USA	Nov. 8, 1984	Frances Gowen Kennedy
W-15 kg (30 lb)	32.65 kg (72 lb 0 oz)	San Diego, California, USA	Sept. 5, 1983	Kelly Sale
W-24 kg (50 lb)	32.50 kg (71 lb 10 oz)	Hout Bay, Republic of South Africa	May 10, 1987	Maureen K. Colyn
W-37 kg (80 lb)	29.00 kg (63 lb 14 oz)	Gran Canaria, Canary Islands, Spain	Oct. 11, 1977	Mrs. Genevieve Margoulies

Amberjack, greater / *Seriola dumerili*

LINE CLASS	WEIGHT	PLACE	DATE	ANGLER
M-01 kg (2 lb)	12.02 kg (26 lb 8 oz)	Key West, Florida, USA	Dec. 6, 1984	Jim Anson
M-02 kg (4 lb)	21.09 kg (46 lb 8 oz)	Charleston, South Carolina, USA	Sept. 11, 1986	Thomas R. Wynne
M-03 kg (6 lb)	30.39 kg (67 lb 0 oz)	Ft. Pierce Inlet, Florida, USA	Jan. 15, 1976	Dave Chermanski
M-04 kg (8 lb)	37.98 kg (83 lb 12 oz)	Virginia Beach, Virginia, USA	Aug. 8, 1987	Marion E. Hutson
M-06 kg (12 lb)	40.82 kg (90 lb 0 oz)	Key West, Florida, USA	Mar. 4, 1982	Jim Anson
M-08 kg (16 lb)	48.98 kg (108 lb 0 oz)	Key West, Florida, USA	Jan. 12, 1984	Jim Anson
M-10 kg (20 lb)	54.17 kg (119 lb 7 oz)	Bermuda	June 16, 1980	Willard R. Watson
M-15 kg (30 lb)	67.58 kg (149 lb 0 oz)	Bermuda	June 21, 1964	Peter Simons
M-24 kg (50 lb)	58.06 kg (128 lb 0 oz)	Islamorada, Florida, USA	Mar. 16, 1994	Joseph Gazia
M-37 kg (80 lb)	70.59 kg (155 lb 10 oz)	Challenger Bank, Bermuda	June 24, 1981	Joseph Dawson
M-37 kg (80 lb) Tie	70.64 kg (155 lb 12 oz)	Bermuda	Aug. 16, 1992	Larry Trott
M-60 kg (130 lb)	64.41 kg (142 lb 0 oz)	Islamorada, Florida, USA	Feb. 3, 1979	W. A. Colbert, Jr.
W-01 kg (2 lb)	10.09 kg (22 lb 4 oz)	Key West, Florida, USA	May 27, 1992	Terry L. Maconi
W-02 kg (4 lb)	10.65 kg (23 lb 8 oz)	Key West, Florida, USA	May 27, 1992	Terry L. Maconi
W-03 kg (6 lb)	25.74 kg (56 lb 12 oz)	Key West, Florida, USA	Feb. 5, 1979	Dixie Lee Burns
W-04 kg (8 lb)	32.38 kg (71 lb 6 oz)	Port Canaveral, Florida, USA	Feb. 6, 1989	Christine A. Currie
W-06 kg (12 lb)	41.73 kg (92 lb 0 oz)	Bimini, Bahamas	Jan. 30, 1978	Bess Greenberg
W-08 kg (16 lb)	30.61 kg (67 lb 8 oz)	Oregon Inlet, North Carolina, USA	Sept. 24, 1983	Mrs. Stephen R. Hutchins
W-10 kg (20 lb)	45.13 kg (99 lb 8 oz)	Palm Beach, Florida, USA	May 7, 1978	Katie Adamson
W-15 kg (30 lb)	50.80 kg (112 lb 0 oz)	Islamorada, Florida, USA	Apr. 22, 1983	Peggy Knapton
W-24 kg (50 lb)	48.98 kg (108 lb 0 oz)	Palm Beach, Florida USA	Dec. 30, 1967	Peggy Kester Mumford
W-37 kg (80 lb)	39.46 kg (87 lb 0 oz)	Miami, Florida, USA	Mar. 9, 1991	Heidi Mason
W-60 kg (130 lb)	38.55 kg (85 lb 0 oz)	Palm Beach, Florida, USA	Apr. 29, 1971	Mrs. Cynthia Boomhower

Barracuda, great / *Sphyraena barracuda*

LINE CLASS	WEIGHT	PLACE	DATE	ANGLER
M-01 kg (2 lb)	13.49 kg (29 lb 12 oz)	Key West, Florida, USA	Jan. 10, 1985	Jim Anson
M-02 kg (4 lb)	14.74 kg (32 lb 8 oz)	Key West, Florida, USA	May 8, 1985	Bill Riesenfeld
M-03 kg (6 lb)	24.04 kg (53 lb 0 oz)	Marathon, Florida, USA	Mar. 28, 1987	Donald L. Lampus
M-04 kg (8 lb)	26.50 kg (58 lb 6 oz)	Mission Beach, Queensland, Australia	Nov. 7, 1993	Bruce Shepherd
M-06 kg (12 lb)	29.03 kg (63 lb 15 oz)	Lizard Island, Queensland, Australia	Sept. 4, 1983	Kenneth Raymond Carnie
M-08 kg (16 lb)	29.80 kg (65 lb 11 oz)	Port Michel, Gabon	Jan. 22, 1984	Anestis Arnopoulos
M-10 kg (20 lb)	29.50 kg (65 lb 0 oz)	Bonee Sifflante, Cameroon	Oct. 5, 1986	Pierre Boursier
M-15 kg (30 lb)	36.00 kg (79 lb 5 oz)	Libreville, Gabon	Aug. 25, 1991	Robert Courdesses
M-24 kg (50 lb)	37.64 kg (83 lb 0 oz)	Lagos, Nigeria	Jan. 13, 1952	K. J. W. Hackett
M-37 kg (80 lb)	38.50 kg (84 lb 14 oz)	Scarborough Shoals, Philippines	Mar. 1, 1991	Jessie D. Cordova
M-37 kg (80 lb) Tie	38.55 kg (85 lb 0 oz)	Christmas Island, Republic of Kiribati	Apr. 11, 1992	John W. Helfrich
W-01 kg (2 lb)	15.87 kg (35 lb 0 oz)	Marathon Key, Florida, USA	May 12, 1992	Elizabeth Hogan
W-02 kg (4 lb)	20.00 kg (44 lb 1 oz)	Groote Eylandt, N.T., Australia	Nov. 30, 1987	Jeanne Woods
W-03 kg (6 lb)	16.32 kg (36 lb 0 oz)	Key West, Florida, USA	Feb. 2, 1981	Dixie Lee Burns
W-04 kg (8 lb)	21.30 kg (46 lb 15 oz)	Groote Eylandt, Australia	Oct. 16, 1994	Jane Manton
W-06 kg (12 lb)	31.25 kg (68 lb 14 oz)	Cairns, Queensland, Australia	Sept. 26, 1982	Marianne Pearce
W-08 kg (16 lb)	31.60 kg (69 lb 10 oz)	Coral Bay, W.A., Australia	Sept. 4, 1984	Katherine Webber
W-10 kg (20 lb)	32.00 kg (70 lb 8 oz)	Innisfail, Queensland, Australia	Aug. 3, 1979	Anne See Poy
W-15 kg (30 lb)	27.50 kg (60 lb 10 oz)	Bom Bom Island, West Africa	May 24, 1993	Ursula Marais
W-24 kg (50 lb)	28.30 kg (62 lb 6 oz)	Serua, Fiji Islands	July 28, 1988	Sharon Anne Light
W-37 kg (80 lb)	30.05 kg (66 lb 4 oz)	Cape Lopez, Gabon	July 17, 1955	Mme. M. Halley

Bass, black sea / *Centropristis striata*

LINE CLASS	WEIGHT	PLACE	DATE	ANGLER
M-01 kg (2 lb)	1.61 kg (3 lb 9 oz)	East Matunuck, Rhode Island, USA	July 20, 1984	Albert (Butch) Ferris
M-02 kg (4 lb)	2.43 kg (5 lb 6 oz)	Virginia Beach, Virginia, USA	Aug. 24, 1986	Scott D. Williams

Bass, black sea / *(continued)*

LINE CLASS	WEIGHT	PLACE	DATE	ANGLER
M-02 kg (4 lb) Tie	2.43 kg (5 lb 6 oz)	Ocean City, Maryland, USA	Oct. 28, 1992	Gary F. Rantz
M-03 kg (6 lb)	2.35 kg (5 lb 3 oz)	Virginia Beach, Virginia, USA	May 1, 1974	Harry L. Hall, Jr.
M-04 kg (8 lb)	3.28 kg (7 lb 3 oz)	Nags Head, North Carolina, USA	Dec. 19, 1992	James H. Sheffield
M-06 kg (12 lb)	3.40 kg (7 lb 8 oz)	Virginia Beach, Virginia, USA	Apr. 25, 1990	Jimmy Kolb
M-08 kg (16 lb)	3.28 kg (7 lb 4 oz)	Virginia Beach, Virginia, USA	Oct. 25, 1998	Denny P. Dobbins
M-10 kg (20 lb)	4.08 kg (9 lb 0 oz)	Montauk, New York, USA	Oct. 10, 1983	Salvatore Vicari
M-15 kg (30 lb)	4.30 kg (9 lb 8 oz)	Virginia Beach, Virginia, USA	Dec. 22, 1990	Jack G. Stallings, Jr.
W-01 kg (2 lb)	1.70 kg (3 lb 12 oz)	Oregon Inlet, North Carolina, USA	May 30, 1988	Mrs. William B. DuVal
W-02 kg (4 lb)	2.15 kg (4 lb 12 oz)	Oregon Inlet, North Carolina, USA	May 24, 1987	Mrs. William B. DuVal
W-03 kg (6 lb)	2.43 kg (5 lb 6 oz)	Virginia Beach, Virginia, USA	June 15, 1986	Linda M. Williams
W-04 kg (8 lb)	0.99 kg (2 lb 3 oz)	Montauk, New York, USA	June 20, 1997	Lorry Mangan
W-06 kg (12 lb)	2.40 kg (5 lb 5 oz)	Fire Island, New York, USA	July 31, 1983	Linda Jean Panciarello
W-08 kg (16 lb)	2.21 kg (4 lb 14 oz)	Oregon Inlet, North Carolina, USA	May 30, 1988	Mrs. William B. DuVal
W-10 kg (20 lb)	2.32 kg (5 lb 2 oz)	Virginia Beach, Virginia, USA	May 17, 1971	Mrs. Charlotte J. Wright
W-15 kg (30 lb)	2.66 kg (5 lb 14 oz)	Cape Henry, Virginia, USA	Oct. 2, 1972	Marylou Penny Durney

Bass, European / *Dicentrarchus labrax*

LINE CLASS	WEIGHT	PLACE	DATE	ANGLER
M-01 kg (2 lb)	4.87 kg (10 lb 12 oz)	Baggy Point, North Devon, England	Aug. 15, 1987	Raymond John White
M-02 kg (4 lb)	5.04 kg (11 lb 2 oz)	Gosport, England	Sept. 5, 1985	Ted Legg
M-03 kg (6 lb)	3.00 kg (6 lb 9 oz)	Isle of Graciosa, Canary Islands, Spain	Oct. 10, 1997	Nicola Zingarelli
M-04 kg (8 lb)	7.41 kg (16 lb 5 oz)	Bahia de Rosas, Spain	Oct. 26, 1989	Christian Schimmel
M-06 kg (12 lb)	8.24 kg (18 lb 2 oz)	Bahia de Rosas, Spain	Oct. 26, 1989	Christian Schimmel
M-08 kg (16 lb)	8.53 kg (18 lb 12 oz)	Bahia de Rosas, Spain	June 27, 1987	Christian Schimmel
M-10 kg (20 lb)	9.40 kg (20 lb 11 oz)	Stes Maries de la Mer 13, France	May 6, 1986	Jean Baptiste Bayle
M-15 kg (30 lb)	7.89 kg (17 lb 6 oz)	Bahia de Rosas, Spain	June 22, 1987	Christian Schimmel
W-01 kg (2 lb)	3.28 kg (7 lb 4 oz)	Instow Beach, Devon, England	Sept. 12, 1986	Mrs. Ruth Caroline White
W-02 kg (4 lb)	5.44 kg (12 lb 0 oz)	Gosport, England	Aug. 16, 1995	Pat Gillies
W-03 kg (6 lb)	Vacant			
W-04 kg (8 lb)	4.50 kg (9 lb 15 oz)	Gosport, Hampshire, England	Aug. 16, 1995	Pat Gillies
W-06 kg (12 lb)	4.82 kg (10 lb 10 oz)	Arzon, France	Aug. 2, 1986	Mrs. Dominique Guillois
W-08 kg (16 lb)	6.40 kg (14 lb 1 oz)	Salin de Giraud, France	Dec. 13, 1987	Michele Ebejer
W-10 kg (20 lb)	5.86 kg (12 lb 15 oz)	Herne Bay, Kent, England	Aug. 17, 1988	Yvonne Rowley
W-15 kg (30 lb)	5.47 kg (12 lb 1 oz)	Langney Point, Sussex, England	Aug. 17, 1984	Pat Whippy

Bass, giant sea / *Stereolepis gigas*

LINE CLASS	WEIGHT	PLACE	DATE	ANGLER
M-01 kg (2 lb)	Vacant			
M-02 kg (4 lb)	Vacant			
M-03 kg (6 lb)	Vacant			
M-04 kg (8 lb)	41.50 kg (91 lb 8 oz)	San Quintin, Mexico	July 10, 1988	Dr. John F. Whitaker
M-06 kg (12 lb)	51.02 kg (112 lb 8 oz)	San Francisco Island, Baja California, Mexico	June 12, 1957	David B. Rosenthal
M-08 kg (16 lb)	35.24 kg (77 lb 11 oz)	Cedros Island, Mexico	June 18, 1996	Russ Hampton
M-10 kg (20 lb)	192.77 kg (425 lb 0 oz)	Point Mugu, California, USA	Oct. 1, 1960	C. C. Joiner
M-15 kg (30 lb)	203.21 kg (448 lb 0 oz)	Coronado Islands, Mexico	Apr. 13, 1975	R. H. Gautier
M-24 kg (50 lb)	252.73 kg (557 lb 3 oz)	Catalina Island, California, USA	July 1, 1962	Richard M. Lane
M-37 kg (80 lb)	255.60 kg (563 lb 8 oz)	Anacapa Island, California, USA	Aug. 20, 1968	James D. McAdam, Jr.
M-60 kg (130 lb)	233.14 kg (514 lb 0 oz)	San Clemente, California, USA	Aug. 29, 1955	J. Patterson
M-60 kg (130 lb) Tie	233.14 kg (514 lb 0 oz)	San Clemente, California, USA	Nov. 15, 1961	Joe M. Arve
W-01 kg (2 lb)	Vacant			
W-02 kg (4 lb)	Vacant			
W-03 kg (6 lb)	Vacant			
W-04 kg (8 lb)	Vacant			
W-06 kg (12 lb)	Vacant			
W-08 kg (16 lb)	Vacant			
W-10 kg (20 lb)	54.43 kg (120 lb 0 oz)	Malibu, California, USA	Jan. 6, 1957	Jane D. Hill
W-15 kg (30 lb)	155.58 kg (343 lb 0 oz)	Catalina Island, California, USA	May 30, 1981	Lillian R. Scott
W-24 kg (50 lb)	205.93 kg (454 lb 0 oz)	Catalina Island, California, USA	Sept. 16, 1980	Lillian R. Scott
W-37 kg (80 lb)	205.02 kg (452 lb 0 oz)	Coronado Islands, Mexico	Oct. 8, 1960	Lorene Wheeler
W-60 kg (130 lb)	Vacant			

Bass, kelp (calico) / *Paralabrax clathratus*

LINE CLASS	WEIGHT	PLACE	DATE	ANGLER
M-01 kg (2 lb)	2.57 kg (5 lb 11 oz)	Palos Verdes, California, USA	June 20, 1993	Peter R. Wight
M-02 kg (4 lb)	3.25 kg (7 lb 2 oz)	Laguna Beach, California, USA	July 5, 1993	Peter R. Wight
M-03 kg (6 lb)	3.91 kg (8 lb 9 oz)	Palos Verdes, California, USA	Sept. 16, 1995	Peter R. Wight
M-04 kg (8 lb)	3.62 kg (8 lb 2 oz)	La Jolla, California, USA	June 17, 1994	John W. Fiedler
M-06 kg (12 lb)	4.87 kg (10 lb 12 oz)	Paradise Cove, California, USA	June 1, 1997	Keith K. Denette
M-08 kg (16 lb)	5.32 kg (11 lb 12 oz)	Federal Breakwater, L.A. Harbor, California, USA	May 22, 1994	Eric D. Kim
M-10 kg (20 lb)	4.73 kg (10 lb 4 oz)	Oxnard, Ventura, California, USA	July 25, 1993	John Turner
W-01 kg (2 lb)	1.08 kg (2 lb 6 oz)	Catalina Island, California, USA	May 6, 1993	Linda M. Hicks
W-02 kg (4 lb)	0.88 kg (1 lb 15 oz)	Catalina Island, California, USA	May 6, 1993	Linda M. Hicks
W-03 kg (6 lb)	1.41 kg (3 lb 2 oz)	San Clemente Island, California, USA	June 10, 1995	Miss Jaime Harrison
W-04 kg (8 lb)	2.57 kg (5 lb 11 oz)	Guadalupe Island, Mexico	June 11, 1994	Sandra "Honey" Beazley
W-06 kg (12 lb)	3.57 kg (7 lb 15 oz)	Laguna Beach, California, USA	Aug. 29, 1993	Cheryl Stiewel
W-08 kg (16 lb)	3.68 kg (8 lb 2 oz)	South Laguna, California, USA	Aug. 30, 1993	Betty Burkart
W-10 kg (20 lb)	3.37 kg (7 lb 7 oz)	Hen Rock, Catalina Island, California, USA	July 17, 1994	Kathy Craine

Bass, striped / *Morone saxatilis*

LINE CLASS	WEIGHT	PLACE	DATE	ANGLER
M-01 kg (2 lb)	9.53 kg (21 lb 0 oz)	San Francisco Bay, California, USA	Jan. 20, 1992	Kirk E. Campbell

Bass, striped / *(continued)*

LINE CLASS	WEIGHT	PLACE	DATE	ANGLER
M-02 kg (4 lb)	18.37 kg (40 lb 8 oz)	Cape Cod Bay, Massachusetts, USA	May 25, 1985	Christopher Van Duzer
M-03 kg (6 lb)	25.79 kg (56 lb 14 oz)	Gay Head, Massachusetts, USA	Oct. 15, 1981	Richard C. Landon
M-04 kg (8 lb)	18.82 kg (41 lb 8 oz)	Fisher's Island, New York, USA	Aug. 27, 1995	Alan Golinski
M-06 kg (12 lb)	30.27 kg (66 lb 12 oz)	Bradley Beach, New Jersey, USA	Nov. 1, 1979	Steven R. Thomas
M-08 kg (16 lb)	31.29 kg (69 lb 0 oz)	Sandy Hook, New Jersey, USA	Nov. 18, 1982	Thomas James Russell
M-10 kg (20 lb)	35.60 kg (78 lb 8 oz)	Atlantic City, New Jersey, USA	Sept. 21, 1982	Albert R. McReynolds
M-15 kg (30 lb)	32.20 kg (71 lb 0 oz)	Norwalk, Connecticut, USA	July 14, 1980	John Baldino
M-24 kg (50 lb)	34.47 kg (76 lb 0 oz)	Montauk, Long Island, New York, USA	July 17, 1981	Robert A. Rocchetta
M-37 kg (80 lb)	31.75 kg (70 lb 0 oz)	Orient Point, New York, USA	Sept. 5, 1987	Chester A. Berry
W-01 kg (2 lb)	4.36 kg (9 lb 10 oz)	Cape Cod Bay, Massachusetts, USA	June 7, 1986	Sharyn Guggino
W-02 kg (4 lb)	13.77 kg (30 lb 6 oz)	Cape Cod Bay, Massachusetts, USA	May 24, 1985	Sharyn Guggino
W-03 kg (6 lb)	21.20 kg (46 lb 12 oz)	Fisher's Island, New York, USA	Sept. 4, 1995	Emme Golinski
W-04 kg (8 lb)	18.20 kg (40 lb 2 oz)	Millicoma River, Oregon, USA	Apr. 5, 1985	Edna Skinner
W-06 kg (12 lb)	22.02 kg (48 lb 9 oz)	Deal, New Jersey, USA	July 27, 1980	Edna Yates
W-08 kg (16 lb)	21.99 kg (48 lb 8 oz)	Monomoy Island, Cape Cod, Massachusetts, USA	July 16, 1991	Connie Codner
W-10 kg (20 lb)	26.08 kg (57 lb 8 oz)	Block Island Sound, New York, USA	Aug. 28, 1959	Mary R. Aubry
W-15 kg (30 lb)	29.25 kg (64 lb 8 oz)	North Truro, Massachusetts, USA	Aug. 14, 1960	Rosa O. Webb
W-24 kg (50 lb)	29.03 kg (64 lb 0 oz)	Sea Bright, New Jersey, USA	June 27, 1971	Mrs. Asie Espenak
W-37 kg (80 lb)	25.96 kg (57 lb 4 oz)	Watch Hill, Rhode Island, USA	Aug. 24, 1997	Janice Masciarelli

Bluefish / *Pomatomus saltatrix*

LINE CLASS	WEIGHT	PLACE	DATE	ANGLER
M-01 kg (2 lb)	7.82 kg (17 lb 4 oz)	Kill Devil Hills, North Carolina, USA	Dec. 1, 1992	Steven J. Benson
M-02 kg (4 lb)	9.30 kg (20 lb 8 oz)	Horta, Faial, Azores, Portugal	July 7, 1995	Jurgen Oeder
M-03 kg (6 lb)	9.10 kg (20 lb 1 oz)	Montauk, New York, USA	Nov. 13, 1977	Jeff Schneider
M-04 kg (8 lb)	9.07 kg (20 lb 0 oz)	Horta, Faial, Azores, Portugal	July 5, 1995	Jurgen Oeder
M-06 kg (12 lb)	10.97 kg (24 lb 3 oz)	San Miguel, Azores, Portugal	Aug. 27, 1953	M. A. da Silva Veloso
M-08 kg (16 lb)	11.65 kg (25 lb 10 oz)	Isle of Graciosa, Spain	Aug. 10, 1996	Fulvio Monticone
M-10 kg (20 lb)	11.11 kg (24 lb 8 oz)	Buxton, North Carolina, USA	Dec. 3, 1986	Gregory R. Wojciechowski
M-15 kg (30 lb)	14.40 kg (31 lb 12 oz)	Hatteras, North Carolina, USA	Jan. 30, 1972	James M. Hussey
M-24 kg (50 lb)	14.40 kg (31 lb 12 oz)	Hatteras, North Carolina, USA	Jan. 30, 1972	James M. Hussey
W-01 kg (2 lb)	6.60 kg (14 lb 9 oz)	Oregon Inlet, North Carolina, USA	Nov. 16, 1991	Mrs. William B. DuVal
W-01 kg (2 lb) Tie	6.63 kg (14 lb 10 oz)	Oregon Inlet, North Carolina, USA	Nov. 16, 1991	Mrs. Stephen R. Hutchins
W-02 kg (4 lb)	7.59 kg (16 lb 12 oz)	Nags Head, North Carolina, USA	Nov. 2, 1987	Joan W. Hinson
W-03 kg (6 lb)	7.03 kg (15 lb 8 oz)	Hatteras, North Carolina, USA	Nov. 21, 1996	Mrs. William B. DuVal
W-04 kg (8 lb)	9.10 kg (20 lb 0 oz)	Faial, Azores	July 31, 1996	Patricia Braun
W-06 kg (12 lb)	8.95 kg (19 lb 12 oz)	Rodanthe, North Carolina, USA	Nov. 24, 1983	Joan Hinson
W-08 kg (16 lb)	9.52 kg (21 lb 0 oz)	Oregon Inlet, North Carolina, USA	Dec. 3, 1984	Peggy B. McCaskill
W-10 kg (20 lb)	11.11 kg (24 lb 8 oz)	Nags Head, North Carolina, USA	Nov. 12, 1971	Mrs. Rita Mizelle
W-15 kg (30 lb)	11.45 kg (25 lb 4 oz)	Chesapeake Bay, Hampton, Virginia, USA	May 11, 1986	Gayle E. Cozzens
W-24 kg (50 lb)	10.85 kg (23 lb 15 oz)	Nags Head, North Carolina, USA	Nov. 19, 1970	Mrs. Joyce Payne Bell

Bonefish / *Albula spp*

LINE CLASS	WEIGHT	PLACE	DATE	ANGLER
M-01 kg (2 lb)	5.44 kg (12 lb 0 oz)	Islamorada, Florida, USA	Nov. 4, 1998	Mark Cockerham
M-02 kg (4 lb)	6.12 kg (13 lb 8 oz)	Chub Cay, Berry Islands, Bahamas	Aug. 24, 1997	Wayne M. Sandlin, Jr.
M-03 kg (6 lb)	6.32 kg (13 lb 15 oz)	Islamorada, Florida, USA	Apr. 9, 1978	Dick Moeller
M-04 kg (8 lb)	7.14 kg (15 lb 12 oz)	Key Biscayne, Florida, USA	Feb. 27, 1997	Ken Pittman
M-06 kg (12 lb)	7.25 kg (16 lb 0 oz)	Bimini, Bahamas	Feb. 25, 1971	Jerry Lavenstein
M-08 kg (16 lb)	5.78 kg (12 lb 12 oz)	Islamorada, Florida, USA	Oct. 11, 1989	Vic Gaspeny
M-10 kg (20 lb)	7.71 kg (17 lb 0 oz)	Mabibi, Zululand, Republic of South Africa	May 24, 1976	Peter F. Mason
M-15 kg (30 lb)	8.61 kg (19 lb 0 oz)	Zululand, Republic of South Africa	May 26, 1962	Brian W. Batchelor
W-01 kg (2 lb)	4.53 kg (10 lb 0 oz)	Islamorada, Florida, USA	Apr. 18, 1990	Kathleen Meyer
W-02 kg (4 lb)	5.61 kg (12 lb 6 oz)	Islamorada, Florida, USA	Aug. 9, 1986	JoAnn Kenyon
W-03 kg (6 lb)	5.95 kg (13 lb 2 oz)	Islamorada, Florida, USA	Apr. 5, 1973	Charlotte Rowland
W-04 kg (8 lb)	6.46 kg (14 lb 4 oz)	Islamorada, Florida, USA	Oct. 18, 1988	Harriet Masinter
W-06 kg (12 lb)	6.80 kg (15 lb 0 oz)	Bimini, Bahamas	Mar. 20, 1961	Andrea Tose
W-08 kg (16 lb)	5.84 kg (12 lb 14 oz)	Tavernier Key, Florida, USA	Nov. 23, 1987	Pauline Froelich
W-10 kg (20 lb)	6.23 kg (13 lb 12 oz)	Exuma, Bahamas	Jan. 3, 1956	Mrs. B. A. Garson
W-15 kg (30 lb)	2.94 kg (6 lb 8 oz)	Biscayne Bay, Florida, USA	Oct. 24, 1997	Susanne I. Gill

Bonito, Atlantic / *Sarda sarda*

LINE CLASS	WEIGHT	PLACE	DATE	ANGLER
M-01 kg (2 lb)	4.33 kg (9 lb 8 oz)	Martha's Vineyard, Massachusetts, USA	Oct. 29, 1994	Stan Brown
M-02 kg (4 lb)	6.26 kg (13 lb 13 oz)	Barnagat, New Jersey, USA	Nov. 14, 1982	Ross J. Giarratana
M-03 kg (6 lb)	4.74 kg (10 lb 7 oz)	Siracusa, Italy	Dec. 26, 1997	Giovanni Grimaldi
M-04 kg (8 lb)	5.55 kg (12 lb 3 oz)	Dakar, Senegal	Mar. 7, 1974	Dr. J. P. Terrisse
M-06 kg (12 lb)	6.15 kg (13 lb 8 oz)	Machico, Madeira Islands, Portugal	June 6, 1980	Kurt Muskat
M-08 kg (16 lb)	5.64 kg (12 lb 7 oz)	Martha's Vineyard, Massachusetts, USA	Oct. 13, 1994	Gary R. Look
M-10 kg (20 lb)	7.60 kg (16 lb 12 oz)	Gran Canaria, Canary Islands, Spain	Dec. 6, 1980	Rolf Fedderies
M-15 kg (30 lb)	8.15 kg (17 lb 15 oz)	Isla Graciosa, Canary Islands, Spain	Jan. 2, 1993	Pierangelo Dellabona
W-01 kg (2 lb)	2.86 kg (6 lb 4 oz)	Puerto Rico, Canary Island, Spain	Apr. 3, 1995	Andrea Probst
W-02 kg (4 lb)	4.79 kg (10 lb 9 oz)	Martha's Vineyard, Massachusetts, USA	Oct. 24, 1993	Leslie Storer Smith
W-03 kg (6 lb)	3.10 kg (6 lb 13 oz)	Puerto Rico, Canary Island, Spain	Mar. 29, 1995	Andrea Probst
W-04 kg (8 lb)	4.24 kg (9 lb 5 oz)	Martha's Vineyard, Massachusetts, USA	Oct. 10, 1987	Mary Wynne Wynter
W-06 kg (12 lb)	4.25 kg (9 lb 6 oz)	Martha's Vineyard, Massachsetts, USA	Sept. 21, 1993	Leslie Storer Smith
W-08 kg (16 lb)	6.56 kg (14 lb 7 oz)	Faial, Azores, Portugal	July 21, 1997	Kori Ann Valenta
W-10 kg (20 lb)	6.00 kg (13 lb 3 oz)	Gran Canaria, Canary Islands, Spain	Aug. 22, 1979	Renate Reichel
W-15 kg (30 lb)	4.40 kg (9 lb 11 oz)	Garajou, Madeira Islands, Portugal	May 17, 1980	Elisabet Alm-Sieurin

Bonito, Pacific / *Sarda spp*

LINE CLASS	WEIGHT	PLACE	DATE	ANGLER
M-01 kg (2 lb)	3.62 kg (8 lb 0 oz)	San Martin Island, Mexico	Nov. 28, 1982	Jerry Wells, Sr.
M-02 kg (4 lb)	4.71 kg (10 lb 6 oz)	Flinders Bay, Augusta, W.A., Australia	Mar. 27, 1989	John Williams
M-03 kg (6 lb)	5.47 kg (12 lb 10 oz)	Balboa, California, USA	May 14, 1997	Jim Duncan
M-04 kg (8 lb)	5.95 kg (13 lb 2 oz)	La Jolla, California, USA	July 23, 1983	Thomas W. Edmunds
M-06 kg (12 lb)	6.69 kg (14 lb 12 oz)	San Benitos Island, Baja California, Mexico	Oct. 12, 1980	Jerome H. Rilling
M-08 kg (16 lb)	10.07 kg (21 lb 3 oz)	Malibu, California, USA	July 30, 1978	Gino M. Picciolo
M-10 kg (20 lb)	Vacant			
M-15 kg (30 lb)	9.40 kg (20 lb 11 oz)	Montague Island, N.S.W., Australia	Apr. 1, 1978	Bruce Conley
W-01 kg (2 lb)	3.78 kg (8 lb 5 oz)	Toothbrush Island, Port Kembla, Australia	Mar. 5, 1989	Natasha Anne Bonetig
W-02 kg (4 lb)	3.57 kg (7 lb 14 oz)	Santa Monica Bay, California, USA	Nov. 5, 1983	Andrea Lawson
W-03 kg (6 lb)	2.72 kg (6 lb 0 oz)	Cape Matapalo, Golfito, Costa Rica	Feb. 13, 1976	Jean A. Lovetang
W-04 kg (8 lb)	4.30 kg (9 lb 8 oz)	Santa Monica Bay, California, USA	July 21, 1992	Laura Tanaka
W-06 kg (12 lb)	7.50 kg (16 lb 8 oz)	Sir Joseph Young Banks, N.S.W., Australia	Apr. 24, 1979	Mrs. Aileen Malone
W-08 kg (16 lb)	5.35 kg (11 lb 13 oz)	Newport Beach, California, USA	Apr. 12, 1992	Cheryl Duncan
W-10 kg (20 lb)	5.26 kg (11 lb 9 oz)	San Diego, California, USA	July 16, 1983	Christine Ann Clark
W-15 kg (30 lb)	7.00 kg (15 lb 6 oz)	Greenwell Point, N.S.W., Australia	Mar. 25, 1978	Betty Solomon

Cobia / *Rachycentron canadum*

LINE CLASS	WEIGHT	PLACE	DATE	ANGLER
M-01 kg (2 lb)	20.97 kg (46 lb 4 oz)	Key West, Florida, USA	Feb. 26, 1985	Pete Peacock
M-02 kg (4 lb)	22.99 kg (50 lb 11 oz)	Destin, Florida, USA	Apr. 3, 1997	George E. Hogan, Jr.
M-03 kg (6 lb)	30.39 kg (67 lb 0 oz)	Miami, Florida, USA	Jan. 8, 1979	Jay Wright, Jr.
M-04 kg (8 lb)	34.07 kg (75 lb 2 oz)	Gulf of Mexico, Alabama, USA	Apr. 26, 1995	Robert T. Cunningham, Jr.
M-06 kg (12 lb)	44.45 kg (98 lb 0 oz)	Key West, Florida, USA	Jan. 24, 1982	Herbert G. Ratner, Jr.
M-08 kg (16 lb)	58.42 kg (128 lb 12 oz)	Pensacola Beach, Florida, USA	Apr. 19, 1995	Thomas Hardy
M-10 kg (20 lb)	51.93 kg (114 lb 8 oz)	Pensacola, Florida, USA	Apr. 10, 1994	John Paul Whibbs
M-15 kg (30 lb)	61.50 kg (135 lb 9 oz)	Shark Bay, W.A., Australia	July 9, 1985	Peter William Goulding
M-24 kg (50 lb)	52.05 kg (114 lb 12 oz)	Perdido Pass, Alabama, USA	Apr. 30, 1986	Paul D. Eberly
M-37 kg (80 lb)	48.98 kg (108 lb 0 oz)	Mombasa, Kenya	Sept. 20, 1980	Luigino Trebucci
W-01 kg (2 lb)	16.38 kg (36 lb 2 oz)	Marathon, Florida, USA	Nov. 2, 1991	Elizabeth Hogan
W-02 kg (4 lb)	24.49 kg (54 lb 0 oz)	Key West, Florida, USA	Dec. 4, 1984	Eileen Peacock
W-03 kg (6 lb)	24.94 kg (55 lb 0 oz)	Key West, Florida, USA	Mar. 8, 1976	Mrs. William B. Du Val
W-04 kg (8 lb)	29.93 kg (66 lb 0 oz)	Key Biscayne, Florida, USA	Jan. 29, 1995	Heidi Mason
W-06 kg (12 lb)	34.13 kg (75 lb 4 oz)	Key West, Florida, USA	Feb. 2, 1985	Betty Wilde
W-08 kg (16 lb)	36.20 kg (79 lb 12 oz)	Moreton Island, Queensland, Australia	June 18, 1989	Olga Mack
W-10 kg (20 lb)	31.93 kg (70 lb 6 oz)	Gulf of Mexico, Destin, Florida, USA	May 4, 1996	Sherry Lynn Brown
W-15 kg (30 lb)	36.51 kg (80 lb 8 oz)	Destin, Florida, USA	Apr. 20, 1979	Judy McCarley
W-24 kg (50 lb)	48.42 kg (106 lb 12 oz)	Orange Beach, Alabama, USA	May 4, 1990	Kim C. Chaney
W-37 kg (80 lb)	46.44 kg (103 lb 8 oz)	Dauphin Island, Alabama, USA	Apr. 24, 1995	Wendy C. Kennedy

Cod, Atlantic / *Gadus morhua*

LINE CLASS	WEIGHT	PLACE	DATE	ANGLER
M-01 kg (2 lb)	11.70 kg (25 lb 12 oz)	Helsingborg, Sweden	Aug. 21, 1986	H. Jacob Nyholm
M-02 kg (4 lb)	15.35 kg (33 lb 13 oz)	Helsingborg, Sweden	Aug. 20, 1986	Peter Madholm
M-03 kg (6 lb)	4.75 kg (32 lb 8 oz)	Denmark	Feb. 12, 1982	Gorm Siiger
M-04 kg (8 lb)	27.25 kg (60 lb 12 oz)	Perkins Cove, Ogunquit, Maine, USA	June 19, 1991	Donald F.X. Angerman
M-06 kg (12 lb)	25.62 kg (56 lb 8 oz)	Hampton Beach, New Hampshire, USA	May 22, 1988	Robert H. Withee
M-08 kg (16 lb)	28.97 kg (63 lb 14 oz)	Perkins Cove, Ogunquit, Maine, USA	June 23, 1992	Jim Mailea
M-10 kg (20 lb)	44.79 kg (98 lb 12 oz)	Isle of Shoals, New Hampshire, USA	June 8, 1969	Alphonse J. Biclevich
M-15 kg (30 lb)	36.74 kg (81 lb 0 oz)	Brielle, New Jersey, USA	Mar. 15, 1967	Joseph Chesla
M-24 kg (50 lb)	38.55 kg (85 lb 0 oz)	Montauk Point, New York, USA	Feb. 25, 1984	Frederick Shay, Jr.
M-37 kg (80 lb)	34.92 kg (77 lb 0 oz)	Perkins Cove, Ogunquit, Maine, USA	June 22, 1989	Dave LaRue
W-01 kg (2 lb)	7.82 kg (17 lb 4 oz)	Marblehead, Massachusetts, USA	Nov. 20, 1983	Mrs. Lillian D. LaBrie
W-02 kg (4 lb)	9.41 kg (20 lb 12 oz)	Middlebank, Massachusetts, USA	Apr. 12, 1986	Mrs. Lillian D. LaBrie
W-03 kg (6 lb)	7.96 kg (17 lb 9 oz)	Jones Inlet, Freeport, Long Island, New York, USA	Jan. 7, 1976	Ronnie Deluca
W-04 kg (8 lb)	8.52 kg (18 lb 8 oz)	Middlebank, Massachusetts, USA	May 29, 1988	Mrs. Lillian D. LaBrie
W-06 kg (12 lb)	15.42 kg (34 lb 0 oz)	Middlebank, Massachusetts, USA	Apr. 19, 1980	Mrs. Lillian D. LaBrie
W-08 kg (16 lb)	23.95 kg (52 lb 13 oz)	Nauset, Cape Cod, Massachusetts, USA	Sept. 10, 1988	Lori Jean Murphy
W-10 kg (20 lb)	32.43 kg (71 lb 8 oz)	Cape Cod, Massachusetts, USA	Aug. 2, 1964	Muriel Betts
W-15 kg (30 lb)	28.63 kg (63 lb 2 oz)	Georges Bank, New York, USA	June 12, 1985	Ann Houseknecht
W-24 kg (50 lb)	34.13 kg (75 lb 4 oz)	Perkins Cove, Ogunquit, Maine, USA	June 18, 1984	Marjory Kerr
W-37 kg (80 lb)	37.08 kg (81 lb 12 oz)	Middlebank, Massachusetts, USA	Sept. 24, 1970	Mrs. Sophie Karwa

Cod, Pacific / *Gadus macrocephalus*

LINE CLASS	WEIGHT	PLACE	DATE	ANGLER
M-01 kg (2 lb)	5.32 kg (11 lb 12 oz)	Cook Inlet, Alaska, USA	July 29, 1985	Rick Townsend
M-02 kg (4 lb)	7.25 kg (16 lb 0 oz)	Kodiak, Alaska, USA	June 9, 1998	Paul Leader
M-03 kg (6 lb)	7.71 kg (17 lb 0 oz)	Kodiak, Alaska, USA	June 9, 1998	Paul Leader
M-04 kg (8 lb)	9.07 kg (20 lb 0 oz)	Kodiak, Alaska, USA	June 9, 1998	Eric Stirrup
M-06 kg (12 lb)	7.25 kg (17 lb 0 oz)	Kodiak, Alaska, USA	June 9, 1998	Paul Leader
M-08 kg (16 lb)	12.02 kg (26 lb 8 oz)	Dutch Harbor, Alaska, USA	July 18, 1997	Raleigh Werking
M-10 kg (20 lb)	7.82 kg (17 lb 4 oz)	Gustavus, Alaska, USA	July 25, 1985	Bill Rice
M-15 kg (30 lb)	5.21 kg (11 lb 8 oz)	Shelter Island, Juneau, Alaska, USA	Aug. 21, 1985	George Tanaka
M-24 kg (50 lb)	13.15 kg (28 lb 0 oz)	Marmot Bay, Kodiak Island, Kodiak, Alaska, USA	Aug. 2, 1995	Lucas William Wright
W-01 kg (2 lb)	5.78 kg (12 lb 12 oz)	Cook Inlet, Alaska, USA	July 28, 1986	Lori Townsend
W-02 kg (4 lb)	5.44 kg (12 lb 0 oz)	Kodiak, Alaska, USA	Sept. 5, 1995	Ruth C. Stoky
W-03 kg (6 lb)	6.80 kg (15 lb 0 oz)	Kodiak, Alaska, USA	June 9, 1998	Jacqueline Leader
W-04 kg (8 lb)	9.07 kg (20 lb 0 oz)	Sequal Point, Kodiak Island, Alaska, USA	May 22, 1998	Sally Magnuson
W-06 kg (12 lb)	7.25 kg (16 lb 0 oz)	Kodiak, Alaska, USA	June 9, 1998	Jacqueline Leader

Cod, Pacific / *(continued)*

LINE CLASS	WEIGHT	PLACE	DATE	ANGLER
W-08 kg (16 lb)	8.61 kg (19 lb 0 oz)	Dutch Harbor, Alaska, USA	June 23, 1998	Fariba Zand
W-10 kg (20 lb)	10.88 kg (24 lb 0 oz)	Cape Grevelle, Kodiak Island, Alaska, USA	July 28, 1997	Sally Magnuson
W-15 kg (30 lb)	4.87 kg (10 lb 12 oz)	Chichagof Island, Alaska, USA	June 18, 1990	Marjorie Cushman
W-24 kg (50 lb)	9.52 kg (21 lb 0 oz)	Marmot Bay, Kodiak Island, Alaska, USA	May 15, 1994	Kelley R. Nicholson

Conger / *Conger conger*

LINE CLASS	WEIGHT	PLACE	DATE	ANGLER
M-01 kg (2 lb)	9.12 kg (20 lb 2 oz)	Gosport, Hampshire, England	Aug. 19, 1987	Denis J. Froud
M-02 kg (4 lb)	13.01 kg (28 lb 11 oz)	Plymouth Sound, Devon, England	Aug. 25, 1985	Gary Avery
M-03 kg (6 lb)	17.90 kg (39 lb 7 oz)	Poanichet-La, Baulc, France	May 26, 1980	Jean Claude Guilmineau
M-04 kg (8 lb)	19.39 kg (42 lb 12 oz)	Folkestone, England	June 14, 1989	Denis J. Froud
M-06 kg (12 lb)	26.50 kg (58 lb 6 oz)	Folkestone, England	Sept. 16, 1990	Denis J. Froud
M-08 kg (16 lb)	26.08 kg (57 lb 6 oz)	Hoo Bank, Littlehampton, Sussex, England	May 25, 1991	Peter Ronald Blondell
M-10 kg (20 lb)	25.91 kg (57 lb 2 oz)	Folkestone, England	June 14, 1989	Denis J. Froud
M-15 kg (30 lb)	47.74 kg (105 lb 4 oz)	Dartmouth, Devon, England	June 25, 1992	Ray Goldsmith
M-24 kg (50 lb)	50.12 kg (110 lb 8 oz)	English Channel, Plymouth, England	Aug. 20, 1991	Hans Christian Clausen
M-37 kg (80 lb)	60.44 kg (133 lb 4 oz)	Berry Head, South Devon, England	June 5, 1995	Vic Evans
M-60 kg (130 lb)	29.03 kg (64 lb 0 oz)	Herd's Deep, British Channel, England	Aug. 31, 1990	Malte Astrom
W-01 kg (2 lb)	Vacant			
W-02 kg (4 lb)	9.17 kg (20 lb 3 oz)	Langney Point, Eastbourne, England	July 17, 1987	Pat Whippy
W-03 kg (6 lb)	Vacant			
W-04 kg (8 lb)	14.57 kg (32 lb 2 oz)	Gosport, Hampshire, England	Mar. 20, 1994	Pat Gillies
W-06 kg (12 lb)	20.86 kg (46 lb 0 oz)	Gosport, Hampshire, England	Mar. 1, 1996	Pat Gillies
W-08 kg (16 lb)	33.90 kg (74 lb 12 oz)	Gosport, Hampshire, England	Feb. 28, 1992	Pat Gillies
W-10 kg (20 lb)	25.68 kg (56 lb 10 oz)	Gosport, Hampshire, England	Feb. 28, 1992	Pat Gillies
W-15 kg (30 lb)	36.10 kg (79 lb 9 oz)	La Grande Motte, Mediterranean, France	Aug. 15, 1986	Marielle Gabrielli
W-24 kg (50 lb)	36.06 kg (79 lb 8 oz)	English Channel, Plymouth, England	Aug. 20, 1991	Vivienne Milden
W-37 kg (80 lb)	21.10 kg (46 lb 8 oz)	St. Gilles, Croix de Vie, France	Nov. 28, 1987	Jacqueline Rainjard
W-60 kg (130 lb)	12.70 kg (28 lb 0 oz)	Pevensey Bay, Sussex, England	Oct. 12, 1985	Salina Whippy

Dentex / *Dentex dentex*

LINE CLASS	WEIGHT	PLACE	DATE	ANGLER
M-01 kg (2 lb)	4.25 kg (9 lb 5 oz)	Isla Graciosa, Canary Islands, Spain	Jan. 8, 1994	Giuseppe Omegna
M-02 kg (4 lb)	6.50 kg (14 lb 5 oz)	Isla Graciosa, Canary Islands, Spain	Nov. 15, 1993	Giuseppe Omegna
M-03 kg (6 lb)	5.15 kg (11 lb 5 oz)	Porto Cervo, Sardinia, Italy	July 10, 1998	Luca Bonfanti
M-04 kg (8 lb)	6.08 kg (13 lb 6 oz)	Porto Cervo, Sardinia, Italy	July 7, 1998	Ottavio Bonfanti
M-06 kg (12 lb)	8.01 kg (17 lb 10 oz)	Porto Cervo, Sardinia, Italy	July 2, 1994	Ottavio Bonfanti
M-08 kg (16 lb)	7.95 kg (17 lb 8 oz)	Isla Graciosa, Canary Islands, Spain	Nov. 10, 1993	Paolo Boccardo
M-10 kg (20 lb)	7.45 kg (16 lb 6 oz)	Isle of Lanzarote, Canary Islands, Spain	Aug. 3, 1998	Sergio Bacchetti
M-15 kg (30 lb)	7.00 kg (15 lb 6 oz)	Isle of Lanzarote, Italy	Nov. 6, 1997	Nicola Vallani
W-01 kg (2 lb)	Vacant			
W-02 kg (4 lb)	Vacant			
W-03 kg (6 lb)	Vacant			
W-04 kg (8 lb)	Vacant			
W-06 kg (12 lb)	Vacant			
W-08 kg (16 lb)	5.05 kg (11 lb 2 oz)	Isle of Lanzarote, Canary Islands, Spain	Sept. 2, 1998	Elide Legnani
W-10 kg (20 lb)	4.36 kg (10 lb 14 oz)	Porto Ottiolu, Sardenia, Centor Pesca, Italy	June 16, 1994	Sabine Sluka
W-15 kg (30 lb)	Vacant			

Dolphinfish / *Coryphaena hippurus*

LINE CLASS	WEIGHT	PLACE	DATE	ANGLER
M-01 kg (2 lb)	18.82 kg (41 lb 8 oz)	Pinas Bay, Panama	Jan. 13, 1992	Jerry Dunaway
M-02 kg (4 lb)	24 kg (52 lb 14 oz)	Cabo San Lucas, Baja California Sur, Mexico	Sept. 11, 1989	George E. Hogan, Jr.
M-03 kg (6 lb)	26.30 kg (58 lb 0 oz)	Mona Passage, Mayaguez, Puerto Rico	May 26, 1984	Luis A. Battistini, Sr.
M-04 kg (8 lb)	24.04 kg (53 lb 0 oz)	Tropic Star Lodge, Pinas Bay, Panama	Dec. 5, 1995	Raleigh Werking
M-06 kg (12 lb)	34.98 kg (77 lb 2 oz)	Islamorada, Florida, USA	Jan. 2, 1982	Monte W. Green
M-08 kg (16 lb)	28.25 kg (62 lb 4 oz)	Mazatlan, Mexico	Nov. 2, 1989	Jeronimo Jergins
M-10 kg (20 lb)	34.70 kg (76 lb 8 oz)	Lake Worth Inlet, Florida, USA	May 23, 1993	Rene R. Viau
M-15 kg (30 lb)	36.00 kg (79 lb 5 oz)	Saly, Senegal	Aug. 1, 1996	Francois Collomb
M-24 kg (50 lb)	39.46 kg (87 lb 0 oz)	Papagallo Gulf, Costa Rica	Sept. 25, 1976	Manuel Salazar
M-37 kg (80 lb)	36.28 kg (80 lb 0 oz)	Walker's Cay, Bahamas	Nov. 26, 1989	Walter C. Quick
W-01 kg (2 lb)	18.37 kg (40 lb 8 oz)	Pinas Bay, Panama	Mar. 24, 1992	Deborah Maddux Dunaway
W-02 kg (4 lb)	19.05 kg (42 lb 0 oz)	Pinas Bay, Panama	Jan. 29, 1991	Deborah Maddux Dunaway
W-03 kg (6 lb)	24.72 kg (54 lb 8 oz)	Tropic Star Lodge, Pinas Bay, Panama	Dec. 28, 1997	Trish Werking
W-04 kg (8 lb)	29.25 kg (64 lb 8 oz)	Dry Tortugas, Florida, USA	Dec. 19, 1990	Mrs. Stephen R. Hutchins
W-06 kg (12 lb)	25.00 kg (55 lb 2 oz)	Mazatlan, Mexico	Oct. 18, 1964	Marguerite H. Barry
W-08 kg (16 lb)	25.74 kg (56 lb 12 oz)	Key West, Florida, USA	June 5, 1984	Rita L. Pierce
W-10 kg (20 lb)	37.81 kg (83 lb 6 oz)	Mazatlan, Mexico	Apr. 24, 1972	Mrs. Eugene W. Wooten
W-15 kg (30 lb)	33.42 kg (73 lb 11 oz)	Cabo San Lucas, Baja California Sur, Mexico	July 12, 1962	Barbara Kibbee Jayne
W-24 kg (50 lb)	34.01 kg (75 lb 0 oz)	Cabo San Lucas, Baja California Sur, Mexico	Nov. 30, 1997	Betty Ann Mehl
W-37 kg (80 lb)	37.25 kg (82 lb 2 oz)	Cabo San Lucas, Baja California Sur, Mexico	Aug. 16, 1993	Tera Allegri

Drum, black / *Pogonias cromis*

LINE CLASS	WEIGHT	PLACE	DATE	ANGLER
M-01 kg (2 lb)	29.93 kg (66 lb 0 oz)	New Smyrna Beach, Florida, USA	Mar. 29, 1998	Raleigh Werking
M-02 kg (4 lb)	41.05 kg (90 lb 8 oz)	New Smyrna Beach, Florida, USA	Mar. 29, 1998	Raleigh Werking
M-03 kg (6 lb)	29.93 kg (66 lb 0 oz)	Cape Charles, Virginia, USA	Apr. 28, 1976	Joe Fielder
M-03 kg (6 lb) Tie	29.93 kg (66 lb 0 oz)	New Smyrna Beach, Florida, USA	Mar. 13, 1997	Raleigh Werking
M-04 kg (8 lb)	37.42 kg (82 lb 8 oz)	Chesapeake Bay Bridge Tunnel, Virginia, USA	June 11, 1994	Ellyson S. Robinson, IV
M-06 kg (12 lb)	40.37 kg (89 lb 0 oz)	Delaware Bay, New Jersey, USA	May 14, 1971	John K. Osborne, Jr.
M-08 kg (16 lb)	41.27 kg (91 lb 0 oz)	Wildwood, New Jersey, USA	Sept. 18, 1993	Anthony Buck Sheeran

M-10 kg (20 lb)	44.45 kg (98 lb 0 oz)	Ocean City, New Jersey, USA	July 20, 1980	Raymond George Fessler
M-15 kg (30 lb)	48.53 kg (107 lb 0 oz)	Cape Charles, Virginia, USA	Apr. 29, 1974	Everette M. Masten, Jr.
M-24 kg (50 lb)	51.28 kg (113 lb 1 oz)	Lewes, Delaware, USA	Sept. 15, 1975	Gerald M. Townsend
M-37 kg (80 lb)	50.34 kg (111 lb 0 oz)	Cape Charles, Virginia, USA	May 3, 1974	G. L. Hopkins
W-01 kg (2 lb)	5.44 kg (12 lb 0 oz)	Banana River, Merritt Island, Florida, USA	Mar. 15, 1994	Christine Perez
W-02 kg (4 lb)	9.63 kg (21 lb 4 oz)	Sylvan Beach, Texas, USA	Nov. 2, 1984	Viola J. Hernandez
W-03 kg (6 lb)	25.00 kg (55 lb 2 oz)	Villas, New Jersey, USA	May 27, 1977	Ruth B. Verity
W-04 kg (8 lb)	8.39 kg (18 lb 8 oz)	Merritt Island, Florida, USA	Dec. 16, 1996	Christine Perez
W-06 kg (12 lb)	36.74 kg (81 lb 0 oz)	Delaware Bay, New Jersey, USA	Sept. 19, 1980	Catherine M. Reider
W-08 kg (16 lb)	34.92 kg (77 lb 0 oz)	Broad River, South Carolina, USA	Mar. 30, 1986	Sharon Linker
W-10 kg (20 lb)	36.51 kg (80 lb 8 oz)	Cape Charles, Virginia, USA	Apr. 27, 1974	Louise M. Gaskill
W-15 kg (30 lb)	36.28 kg (80 lb 0 oz)	Cape Charles, Virginia, USA	May 24, 1975	Diane Dattoli
W-24 kg (50 lb)	42.18 kg (93 lb 0 oz)	Fernandina Beach, Florida, USA	Mar. 28, 1957	Mrs. Stella Moore
W-37 kg (80 lb)	50.34 kg (111 lb 0 oz)	Cape Charles, Virginia, USA	May 20, 1973	Betty D. Hall

Drum, red / *Sciaenops ocellatus*

LINE CLASS	WEIGHT	PLACE	DATE	ANGLER
M-01 kg (2 lb)	18.82 kg (41 lb 8 oz)	Ocracoke, North Carolina, USA	Nov. 15, 1995	George E. Hogan, Jr.
M-02 kg (4 lb)	23.74 kg (52 lb 5 oz)	Indian River Lagoon, Florida, USA	Feb. 24, 1996	George E. Hogan, Jr.
M-03 kg (6 lb)	20.86 kg (46 lb 0 oz)	Ocracoke, North Carolina, USA	Nov. 6, 1995	William B. DuVal
M-04 kg (8 lb)	27.44 kg (60 lb 8 oz)	Oregon Inlet, North Carolina, USA	June 7, 1987	Stuart C. Lee
M-06 kg (12 lb)	31.38 kg (69 lb 3 oz)	Gwynn's Island, Virginia, USA	July 10, 1975	John Oscar Everett
M-08 kg (16 lb)	26.76 kg (59 lb 0 oz)	Ocracoke, North Carolina, USA	Nov. 1, 1993	William B. DuVal
M-10 kg (20 lb)	32.85 kg (72 lb 7 oz)	Hatteras Island, North Carolina, USA	Nov. 27, 1973	Wayne Plageman
M-15 kg (30 lb)	40.82 kg (90 lb 0 oz)	Rodanthe, North Carolina, USA	Nov. 7, 1973	Elvin Hooper
M-24 kg (50 lb)	42.69 kg (94 lb 2 oz)	Avon, North Carolina, USA	Nov. 7, 1984	David G. Deuel
M-37 kg (80 lb)	19.16 kg (42 lb 4 oz)	Oriental, North Carolina, USA	Aug. 27, 1997	Raleigh Werking
W-01 kg (2 lb)	16.66 kg (36 lb 12 oz)	Ocracoke, North Carolina, USA	Nov. 13, 1995	Elizabeth M. Hogan
W-02 kg (4 lb)	18.14 kg (40 lb 0 oz)	Ocracoke, North Carolina, USA	Nov. 4, 1995	Mrs. William B. DuVal
W-03 kg (6 lb)	19.73 kg (43 lb 8 oz)	Indian River Lagoon, Florida, USA	Sept. 5, 1995	Elizabeth Hogan
W-04 kg (8 lb)	21.09 kg (46 lb 8 oz)	Ocracoke, North Carolina, USA	Nov. 14, 1989	Mrs. William B. DuVal
W-06 kg (12 lb)	23.36 kg (51 lb 8 oz)	Cape Hatteras, North Carolina, USA	Nov. 19, 1958	Joan S. Dull
W-08 kg (16 lb)	27.32 kg (60 lb 4 oz)	Avon, North Carolina, USA	Nov. 5, 1984	Joan Hinson
W-10 kg (20 lb)	29.48 kg (65 lb 0 oz)	Cape Hatteras, North Carolina, USA	Nov. 11, 1983	Lyn Gottert
W-15 kg (30 lb)	31.52 kg (69 lb 8 oz)	Cape Hatteras, North Carolina, USA	Nov. 16, 1958	Jean Browning
W-24 kg (50 lb)	31.86 kg (70 lb 4 oz)	Oregon Inlet, North Carolina, USA	May 28, 1985	Elizabeth Zavislak Pomory
W-37 kg (80 lb)	15.81 kg (34 lb 14 oz)	Virginia Beach, Virginia, USA	Oct. 10, 1998	Cheryl B. Paige

Flounder, summer / *Paralichthys dentatus*

LINE CLASS	WEIGHT	PLACE	DATE	ANGLER
M-01 kg (2 lb)	2.97 kg (6 lb 8 oz)	Virginia Beach, Virginia, USA	May 31, 1997	J. Parks Rountrey
M-02 kg (4 lb)	5.50 kg (12 lb 2 oz)	Robins Island, Peconic Bay, New York, USA	June 23, 1989	Alan Flexer
M-03 kg (6 lb)	8.24 kg (18 lb 3 oz)	Fire Island, New York, USA	Dec. 11, 1974	Dr. Einar F. Grell
M-04 kg (8 lb)	3.23 kg (7 lb 2 oz)	Greenport, New York, USA	May 24, 1996	Al "The Hat" Lama
M-06 kg (12 lb)	9.29 kg (20 lb 8 oz)	Carolina Beach, North Carolina, USA	Oct. 29, 1980	Harold W. Auten
M-08 kg (16 lb)	8.33 kg (18 lb 6 oz)	Barnagat Bay, New Jersey, USA	Aug. 2, 1988	John S. Patterson, Sr.
M-10 kg (20 lb)	9.07 kg (20 lb 0 oz)	Oak Beach, Long Island, New York, USA	Sept. 7, 1948	F. Howard Kessel
M-15 kg (30 lb)	9.12 kg (20 lb 2 oz)	Montauk, Long Island, New York, USA	Sept. 20, 1958	Gay F. Schwinzer
W-01 kg (2 lb)	6.57 kg (14 lb 8 oz)	Charlestown, Rhode Island, USA	June 15, 1985	Jill Caddick
W-02 kg (4 lb)	3.07 kg (6 lb 12 oz)	Montauk, Long Island, New York, USA	Sept. 5, 1984	Diane Lynne Mellish
W-03 kg (6 lb)	3.85 kg (8 lb 8 oz)	Montauk Point, Long Island, New York, USA	Sept. 25, 1976	Ronnie Deluca
W-04 kg (8 lb)	5.44 kg (12 lb 0 oz)	Montauk, New York, USA	Sept. 15, 1987	Lorry Mangan
W-06 kg (12 lb)	5.49 kg (12 lb 2 oz)	Avalon, New Jersey, USA	Sept. 8, 1957	Mrs. Alfred Bernstein
W-06 kg (12 lb) Tie	5.51 kg (12 lb 2 oz)	Horton's Pt., Long Island Sound, New York, USA	June 15, 1986	Jane Kilthau
W-08 kg (16 lb)	6.17 kg (13 lb 9 oz)	Montauk, New York, USA	Sept. 14, 1987	June Heath
W-10 kg (20 lb)	8.58 kg (18 lb 15 oz)	Jones Beach, New York, USA	Sept. 7, 1977	Mabel M. Andretta
W-15 kg (30 lb)	6.20 kg (13 lb 11 oz)	Long Branch, New Jersey, USA	Aug. 20, 1953	Mrs. Leslie H. Taylor

Halibut, Atlantic / *Hippoglossus hippoglossus*

LINE CLASS	WEIGHT	PLACE	DATE	ANGLER
M-01 kg (2 lb)	Vacant			
M-02 kg (4 lb)	Vacant			
M-03 kg (6 lb)	Vacant			
M-04 kg (8 lb)	3.64 kg (8 lb 0 oz)	Holsteinsborg, Greenland	Aug. 19, 1982	Peter W. Kogebohn
M-06 kg (12 lb)	23.15 kg (51 lb 0 oz)	Holsteinsborg, Greenland	Aug. 21, 1982	Peter W. Kogebohn
M-08 kg (16 lb)	15.87 kg (35 lb 0 oz)	Gulf of Maine, Massachusetts, USA	July 28, 1985	Donald F.X. Angerman
M-10 kg (20 lb)	6.04 kg (13 lb 5 oz)	Ilsoyfluin, Trondelag, Norway	July 15, 1986	Bo Jerdmyr
M-15 kg (30 lb)	31.29 kg (69 lb 0 oz)	Gloucester, Massachusetts, USA	May 31, 1987	Bill Monte, Jr.
M-24 kg (50 lb)	115.78 kg (255 lb 4 oz)	Gloucester, Massachusetts, USA	July 28, 1989	Sonny Manley
M-37 kg (80 lb)	161.20 kg (355 lb 6 oz)	Valevag, Norway	Oct. 20, 1997	Odd Arve Gunderstad
M-60 kg (130 lb)	Vacant			
W-01 kg (2 lb)	Vacant			
W-02 kg (4 lb)	Vacant			
W-03 kg (6 lb)	Vacant			
W-04 kg (8 lb)	Vacant			
W-06 kg (12 lb)	5.50 kg (12 lb 2 oz)	Holsteinsborg, Greenland	Aug. 24, 1982	Katharina Graul
W-08 kg (16 lb)	3.10 kg (6 lb 13 oz)	Holsteinsborg, Greenland	Aug. 8, 1982	Katharina Graul
W-10 kg (20 lb)	Vacant			
W-15 kg (30 lb)	10.85 kg (23 lb 14 oz)	Holsteinsborg, Greenland	Aug. 24, 1982	Katharina Graul
W-24 kg (50 lb)	6.60 kg (14 lb 8 oz)	Holsteinsborg, Greenland	Aug. 10, 1982	Katharina Graul

Halibut, Atlantic / *(continued)*

LINE CLASS	WEIGHT	PLACE	DATE	ANGLER
W-37 kg (80 lb)	Vacant			
W-60 kg (130 lb)	Vacant			

Halibut, California / *Paralichthys californicus*

LINE CLASS	WEIGHT	PLACE	DATE	ANGLER
M-01 kg (2 lb)	8.82 kg (19 lb 7 oz)	San Quintin, Mexico	July 10, 1988	Dr. John F. Whitaker
M-02 kg (4 lb)	9.46 kg (20 lb 14 oz)	Catalina Island, California, USA	Apr. 20, 1991	Scott Houghton
M-03 kg (6 lb)	12.93 kg (28 lb 8 oz)	Torrance Beach, California, USA	Feb. 14, 1996	Alexey K. Haussmann
M-04 kg (8 lb)	14.40 kg (31 lb 12 oz)	Oceanside Harbor, California, USA	May 5, 1990	Steve T. Mares
M-06 kg (12 lb)	23.81 kg (52 lb 8 oz)	Morro Bay, California, USA	Nov. 9, 1993	Ken G. Scott
M-08 kg (16 lb)	22.67 kg (50 lb 0 oz)	Marina Del Rey, Santa Monica Bay, California, USA	Aug. 15, 1996	John J. Bourget
M-10 kg (20 lb)	24.17 kg (53 lb 4 oz)	Santa Rosa Island, California, USA	July 7, 1988	Russell J. Harmon
M-15 kg (30 lb)	22.31 kg (49 lb 3 oz)	Marina Del Rey, California, USA	Sept. 16, 1993	Wm. R. Sands
M-24 kg (50 lb)	19.50 kg (43 lb 0 oz)	Santa Monica Bay, California, USA	Feb. 5, 1997	Hunter Von Leer
M-37 kg (80 lb)	18.50 kg (40 lb 12 oz)	Guadalupe Island, Mexico	July 15, 1987	Ralph A. Mikkelsen
W-01 kg (2 lb)	2.83 kg (6 lb 4 oz)	Torrance Beach, California, USA	Aug. 13, 1989	Sydney Marie Whitaker
W-02 kg (4 lb)	7.99 kg (17 lb 10 oz)	Coronado Islands, Baja California, Mexico	June 2, 1985	Shirley M. Blackman
W-03 kg (6 lb)	17.46 kg (38 lb 8 oz)	Coronado Islands, Baja California, Mexico	July 8, 1995	Shirley M. Blackman
W-04 kg (8 lb)	17.23 kg (38 lb 0 oz)	Santa Cruz Island, California, USA	May 30, 1982	Kathy E. Smith
W-06 kg (12 lb)	19.45 kg (42 lb 14 oz)	Redondo Beach, California, USA	Jan. 28, 1998	Roberta Stotesbury
W-08 kg (16 lb)	18.59 kg (41 lb 0 oz)	Cornado Islands, Baja California, Mexico	July 3, 1994	Shirley M. Blackman
W-10 kg (20 lb)	19.27 kg (42 lb 8 oz)	Huntington Flats, California, USA	July 25, 1985	Nancy Reiko Ogino
W-15 kg (30 lb)	18.59 kg (41 lb 0 oz)	Catalina Island, California, USA	June 26, 1988	Beverly K. Phillips
W-24 kg (50 lb)	Vacant			
W-37 kg (80 lb)	5.64 kg (12 lb 7 oz)	Catalina Island, California, USA	July 22, 1998	Sandy Peck

Halibut, Pacific / *Hippoglossus stenolepis*

LINE CLASS	WEIGHT	PLACE	DATE	ANGLER
M-01 kg (2 lb)	33.74 kg (72 lb 3 oz)	Cook Inlet, Homer, Alaska, USA	July 11, 1994	George E. Hogan, Jr.
M-02 kg (4 lb)	40.37 kg (89 lb 0 oz)	Kodiak, Alaska, USA	Aug. 2, 1994	Robert C. Stoky
M-03 kg (6 lb)	56.24 kg (124 lb 0 oz)	Kodiak, Alaska, USA	Aug. 6, 1997	Paul Leader
M-04 kg (8 lb)	110.67 kg (244 lb 0 oz)	Basket Bay, Chichagof Island, Alaska, USA	Aug. 18, 1988	Gene Grimes
M-06 kg (12 lb)	78.01 kg (172 lb 0 oz)	Langara Island, British Columbia, Canada	June 21, 1992	Glen A. Oliver
M-08 kg (16 lb)	74.84 kg (165 lb 0 oz)	Resurrection Bay, Seward, Alaska, USA	May 28, 1989	Earl D. Cagle
M-10 kg (20 lb)	109.95 kg (242 lb 6 oz)	Funter Bay, Juneau, Alaska, USA	July 27, 1988	Greg Anderson
M-15 kg (30 lb)	161.70 kg (356 lb 8 oz)	Castineau Channel, Juneau, Alaska, USA	Nov. 8, 1986	Gregory C. Olsen
M-24 kg (50 lb)	156.03 kg (344 lb 0 oz)	Thomas Bay, Petersburg, Alaska, USA	Sept. 13, 1986	Gordon S. Newhouse
M-37 kg (80 lb)	179.17 kg (395 lb 0 oz)	Unalaska Bay, Bering Sea, Russia	June 21, 1995	Michael James Golat
M-60 kg (130 lb)	208.20 kg (459 lb 0 oz)	Dutch Harbor, Alaska, USA	June 11, 1996	Jack Tragis
W-01 kg (2 lb)	11.79 kg (26 lb 0 oz)	Cape Muzon, Alaska, USA	May 26, 1990	Marjorie Cushman
W-02 kg (4 lb)	31.75 kg (70 lb 0 oz)	Yasha Island, Alaska, USA	July 25, 1991	Dorothy A. Loros
W-03 kg (6 lb)	39.91 kg (88 lb 0 oz)	Kodiak Island, Alaska, USA	Aug. 1, 1996	Sally Magnuson
W-04 kg (8 lb)	55.79 kg (123 lb 0 oz)	Basket Bay, Chichagof Island, Alaska, USA	Aug. 12, 1988	Susan McCarty Grimes
W-06 kg (12 lb)	67.81 kg (149 lb 8 oz)	Deep Creek, Cook Inlet, Alaska, USA	June 26, 1989	Jocelyn J. Everette
W-08 kg (16 lb)	100.69 kg (222 lb 0 oz)	Dutch Harbor, Alaska, USA	June 24, 1998	Fariba Zand
W-10 kg (20 lb)	75.07 kg (165 lb 8 oz)	Sullivan Bay, British Columbia, Canada	July 17, 1979	Stephanie Pollard
W-15 kg (30 lb)	97.18 kg (214 lb 4 oz)	Gustavus, Alaska, USA	Aug. 24, 1987	Roxanna M. Andrews
W-24 kg (50 lb)	119.74 kg (264 lb 0 oz)	St. Lazaria Island, Sitka Sound, Alaska, USA	Aug. 24, 1986	Elaine M. Loopstra
W-37 kg (80 lb)	166.92 kg (368 lb 0 oz)	Gustavus, Alaska, USA	July 5, 1991	Celia H. Dueitt
W-60 kg (130 lb)	107.50 kg (237 lb 0 oz)	Flat Island, Homer, Alaska, USA	Aug. 19, 1988	Brenda K. Hearnsberger

Jack, crevalle / *Caranx hippos*

LINE CLASS	WEIGHT	PLACE	DATE	ANGLER
M-01 kg (2 lb)	12.32 kg (27 lb 2 oz)	Pensacola Bay, Pensacola, Florida, USA	Sept. 5, 1991	Carl E. Cole
M-02 kg (4 lb)	12.31 kg (27 lb 2 oz)	Pensacola Bay, Pensacola, Florida, USA	Aug. 29, 1991	James G. Fuller
M-03 kg (6 lb)	14.17 kg (31 lb 4 oz)	Lake Worth, Florida, USA	Sept. 18, 1980	Ralph O. Cannon, Jr.
M-04 kg (8 lb)	16.78 kg (37 lb 0 oz)	Key West, Florida, USA	Mar. 4, 1985	Alex M. Jernigan
M-06 kg (12 lb)	9.50 kg (43 lb 0 oz)	Lake Worth, Florida, USA	Dec. 9, 1996	Joseph C. Bogdan, MD
M-08 kg (16 lb)	20.20 kg (44 lb 8 oz)	Barra do Kwanza, Angola	May 11, 1995	Fergus Kiernan
M-10 kg (20 lb)	21.31 kg (47 lb 0 oz)	Jupiter, Florida, USA	Mar. 25, 1982	Bert Jorgensen
M-15 kg (30 lb)	26.00 kg (57 lb 5 oz)	Barra do Kwanza, Angola	Oct. 10, 1992	Cam Nicolson
M-24 kg (50 lb)	24.04 kg (53 lb 0 oz)	Gulf of Mexico, Louisiana, USA	Aug. 17, 1990	Julius Martin
W-01 kg (2 lb)	10.99 kg (24 lb 4 oz)	Pensacola Bay, Pensacola, Florida, USA	Sept. 11, 1993	Wendy A. Fuller
W-02 kg (4 lb)	11.42 kg (25 lb 3 oz)	Pensacola Bay, Pensacola, Florida, USA	July 25, 1992	Mrs. Wendy A. Fuller
W-03 kg (6 lb)	13.72 kg (30 lb 4 oz)	West Palm Beach, Florida, USA	Sept. 19, 1980	Doris J. Williams
W-04 kg (8 lb)	13.06 kg (28 lb 12 oz)	Pensacola Bay, Pensacola, Florida, USA	Aug. 30, 1994	Ellen W. Sims
W-06 kg (12 lb)	18.05 kg (39 lb 13 oz)	Haulover Cut, Miami, Florida, USA	Sept. 21, 1985	June A. Mick
W-08 kg (16 lb)	15.87 kg (35 lb 0 oz)	Lake Worth Inlet, Florida, USA	Jan. 12, 1994	Karen Dixon
W-10 kg (20 lb)	19.05 kg (42 lb 0 oz)	Barra del Colorado, Costa Rica	Oct. 1, 1978	Marilyn Mattson
W-15 kg (30 lb)	16.55 kg (36 lb 8 oz)	Palm Beach, Florida, USA	Sept. 9, 1979	Darlene Marie Labens
W-24 kg (50 lb)	13.69 kg (30 lb 3 oz)	Pensacola Bay, Pensacola Florida USA	Sept. 5, 1993	Ellen W. Sims

Jack, horse-eye / *Caranx latus*

LINE CLASS	WEIGHT	PLACE	DATE	ANGLER
M-01 kg (2 lb)	4.30 kg (9 lb 8 oz)	West End Grand Bahama, Bahamas	July 17, 1996	Colin Rose
M-02 kg (4 lb)	6.23 kg (13 lb 12 oz)	Key West, Florida, USA	July 10, 1987	Herbert G. Ratner, Jr.
M-03 kg (6 lb)	7.28 kg (16 lb 1 oz)	Dry Tortugas, Key West, Florida, USA	Nov. 10, 1994	Kristof Cloostermans
M-04 kg (8 lb)	9.97 kg (22 lb 0 oz)	Dry Tortugas, Florida, USA	Mar. 5, 1995	Jose Rodriguez
M-06 kg (12 lb)	11.68 kg (25 lb 12 oz)	Palm Beach, Florida, USA	Oct. 31, 1997	David Leavitt
M-08 kg (16 lb)	10.43 kg (23 lb 0 oz)	Long Reef, Miami, Florida, USA	Jan. 3, 1988	Frank Cullen
M-10 kg (20 lb)	10.88 kg (24 lb 0 oz)	Fowey Light, Miami, Florida, USA	Jan. 10, 1987	Buddy Tompkins

M-15 kg (30 lb)	10.50 kg (23 lb 2 oz)	Cancun, Mexico	Oct. 2, 1981	Norman A. Carpenter
M-24 kg (50 lb)	13.38 kg (29 lb 8 oz)	Ascencion Island, South Atlantic Ocean	May 28, 1993	Mike Hanson
W-01 kg (2 lb)	3.85 kg (8 lb 8 oz)	Key West, Florida, USA	Oct. 2, 1988	Mrs. William B. DuVal
W-02 kg (4 lb)	6.86 kg (15 lb 2 oz)	Key West, Florida, USA	Aug. 17, 1986	Mrs. William B. DuVal
W-03 kg (6 lb)	5.29 kg (11 lb 12 oz)	Bimini, Bahamas	Aug. 4, 1997	Pamela Marmin
W-04 kg (8 lb)	8.13 kg (17 lb 15 oz)	Palm Beach, Florida, USA	Feb. 6, 1995	Shannon R. Griste
W-06 kg (12 lb)	10.20 kg (22 lb 8 oz)	Argus Bank, Bermuda	July 17, 1990	Mrs. Wally Beauchamp
W-08 kg (16 lb)	10.77 kg (23 lb 12 oz)	Key West, Florida, USA	Oct. 8, 1983	Rita Pierce
W-10 kg (20 lb)	10.88 kg (24 lb 0 oz)	Puerto Aventuras, Mexico	Apr. 16, 1997	Susan Gooch
W-15 kg (30 lb)	7.13 kg (15 lb 11 oz)	Ocean Reef, Key Largo, Florida, USA	July 4, 1995	Sherry Jumonville
W-24 kg (50 lb)	9.07 kg (20 lb 0 oz)	Pompano Beach, Florida, USA	Nov. 13, 1984	Jan Amis

Jack, Pacific crevalle / *Caranx caninus*

LINE CLASS	WEIGHT	PLACE	DATE	ANGLER
M-01 kg (2 lb)	3.17 kg (7 lb 0 oz)	Playa Zancudo, Costa Rica	Dec. 20, 1995	Craig Whitehead, MD
M-02 kg (4 lb)	8.50 kg (18 lb 7 oz)	Puerto Vallarta, Jalisco, Mexico	May 17, 1993	Federico Del Toro
M-03 kg (6 lb)	10.03 kg (22 lb 2 oz)	Cabo San Lucas, Baja California Sur, Mexico	Dec. 25, 1997	Stephen Jansen
M-04 kg (8 lb)	9.20 kg (20 lb 4 oz)	Puerto Vallarta, Jalisco, Mexico	July 26, 1994	Federico Del Toro Gomez
M-06 kg (12 lb)	10.41 kg (22 lb 15 oz)	Salinas, Ecuador	Nov. 19, 1983	Emilio Kronfle
M-08 kg (16 lb)	10.20 kg (22 lb 8 oz)	Cabo San Lucas, Baja California Sur, Mexico	June 5, 1992	Jeff Klassen
M-10 kg (20 lb)	12.13 kg (26 lb 12 oz)	Golfito, Costa Rica	Aug. 2, 1992	Dr. Jerome N. Matthews
M-15 kg (30 lb)	10.43 kg (23 lb 0 oz)	Isla de la Plata, Ecuador	Jan. 13, 1990	Roberto Estrada
M-24 kg (50 lb)	14.06 kg (31 lb 0 oz)	Playa Zancudo, Costa Rica	Dec. 17, 1997	Roy Ventura Roig
W-01 kg (2 lb)	0.54 kg (1 lb 3 oz)	Zihuatanejo, Mexico	Nov. 11, 1989	Irene McDonald Johnson
W-02 kg (4 lb)	10.88 kg (24 lb 0 oz)	Cabo San Lucas, Baja California Sur, Mexico	Apr. 30, 1987	Sharon R. Swanson
W-03 kg (6 lb)	5.05 kg (11 lb 2 oz)	Zihuatanejo, Mexico	Apr. 3, 1995	Irene McDonald Johnson
W-04 kg (8 lb)	6.49 kg (14 lb 5 oz)	Zihuatanejo, Mexico	Apr. 4, 1994	Irene McDonald Johnson
W-06 kg (12 lb)	9.42 kg (20 lb 12 oz)	Zihuatanejo, Mexico	Sept. 15, 1987	Irene McDonald Johnson
W-08 kg (16 lb)	8.30 kg (18 lb 5 oz)	Puerto Vallarta, Jalisco, Mexico	Mar. 15, 1998	Irene McDonald Johnson
W-10 kg (20 lb)	8.35 kg (18 lb 6 oz)	Zihuatanejo, Mexico	Dec. 6, 1990	Irene McDonald Johnson
W-15 kg (30 lb)	9.29 kg (20 lb 8 oz)	Isla Cerralvo, Baja California, Mexico	Mar. 25, 1991	Sandy Peck
W-24 kg (50 lb)	10.65 kg (23 lb 8 oz)	Playa Zancudo, Costa Rica	Dec. 23, 1992	Judy M. Sypniecki

Jewfish / *Epinephelus itajara*

LINE CLASS	WEIGHT	PLACE	DATE	ANGLER
M-01 kg (2 lb)	Vacant			
M-02 kg (4 lb)	Vacant			
M-03 kg (6 lb)	140.38 kg (309 lb 8 oz)	Flamingo, Florida, USA	Jan. 15, 1977	Kenny Bittner
M-04 kg (8 lb)	Vacant			
M-06 kg (12 lb)	165.78 kg (365 lb 8 oz)	Flamingo, Florida, USA	Mar. 31, 1975	Kenny Bittner
M-08 kg (16 lb)	43.54 kg (96 lb 0 oz)	Iles de Salut, French Guiana	Aug. 21, 1994	Dr. Francis Maquin
M-10 kg (20 lb)	156.37 kg (344 lb 12 oz)	Flamingo, Florida, USA	Jan. 11, 1976	Al Polofsky
M-15 kg (30 lb)	195.04 kg (430 lb 0 oz)	Ft. Lauderdale, Florida, USA	Apr. 25, 1967	Curt Johnson
M-24 kg (50 lb)	167.37 kg (369 lb 0 oz)	Marathon, Florida, USA	Apr. 25, 1956	C. F. Mann
M-37 kg (80 lb)	308.44 kg (680 lb 0 oz)	Fernandina Beach, Florida, USA	May 20, 1961	Lynn Joyner
M-60 kg (130 lb)	308.44 kg (680 lb 0 oz)	Fernandina Beach, Florida, USA	May 20, 1961	Lynn Joyner
W-01 kg (2 lb)	Vacant			
W-02 kg (4 lb)	Vacant			
W-03 kg (6 lb)	Vacant			
W-04 kg (8 lb)	Vacant			
W-06 kg (12 lb)	49.89 kg (110 lb 0 oz)	Islamorada, Florida, USA	Aug. 2, 1961	Mrs. Gar Wood, Jr.
W-08 kg (16 lb)	Vacant			
W-10 kg (20 lb)	39.91 kg (88 lb 0 oz)	Key West, Florida, USA	Dec. 11, 1980	Dawn S. Maconi
W-15 kg (30 lb)	144.24 kg (318 lb 0 oz)	Dry Tortugas, Florida, USA	Mar. 14, 1966	Dottie Hall
W-24 kg (50 lb)	131.54 kg (290 lb 0 oz)	Marathon, Florida, USA	May 5, 1967	Mrs. Leslie Lear
W-37 kg (80 lb)	166.01 kg (366 lb 0 oz)	Guayabo, Panama	Feb. 8, 1965	Betsy B. Walker
W-60 kg (130 lb)	148.32 kg (327 lb 0 oz)	Flamingo, Florida, USA	June 24, 1969	Helen Robinson

Kahawai / *Arripis trutta*

LINE CLASS	WEIGHT	PLACE	DATE	ANGLER
M-01 kg (2 lb)	3.20 kg (7 lb 0 oz)	Almonta Beach, Pt. Lincoln, Australia	June 30, 1986	Desmond Barry Woolford
M-02 kg (4 lb)	4.40 kg (9 lb 11 oz)	Sleaford Bay, S.A., Australia	Sept. 4, 1988	Roger K. Sinclair
M-03 kg (6 lb)	3.15 kg (6 lb 15 oz)	Clare Bay, Australia	Sept. 24, 1997	John Marsh
M-04 kg (8 lb)	5.20 kg (11 lb 7 oz)	Wyadup, W.A., Australia	Mar. 12, 1988	Brian Robert Anderson
M-06 kg (12 lb)	8.46 kg (18 lb 10 oz)	North Island, New Zealand	Mar. 19, 1990	Olivier S. Kapetanakos
M-08 kg (16 lb)	4.30 kg (9 lb 7 oz)	Rottnest Island, W.A., Australia	Mar. 29, 1987	Hal Harvey
M-10 kg (20 lb)	8.74 kg (19 lb 4 oz)	Currarong, Australia	Apr. 9, 1994	Stephen Muller
M-15 kg (30 lb)	7.50 kg (16 lb 8 oz)	Jarvis Bay, N.S.W., Australia	Feb. 16, 1986	Michael Davies
W-01 kg (2 lb)	2.30 kg (5 lb 1 oz)	Coromandel, New Zealand	Jan. 27, 1991	Tracy Cramond
W-02 kg (4 lb)	2.66 kg (5 lb 14 oz)	Kaipara Harbour, North Island, New Zealand	Jan. 13, 1990	Philippa M. Nash
W-03 kg (6 lb)	3.06 kg (6 lb 11 oz)	Tauranga, New Zealand	Jan. 25, 1997	Debbie McNamara
W-04 kg (8 lb)	3.25 kg (7 lb 2 oz)	Whakatane, New Zealand	Mar. 12, 1987	Judi Thomson
W-06 kg (12 lb)	3.12 kg (6 lb 14 oz)	Otago Heads, Dunedin, New Zealand	Jan. 6, 1991	Jackie Roos
W-08 kg (16 lb)	5.77 kg (12 lb 11 oz)	North Cape, Australia	May 3, 1986	Stephanie Newman
W-10 kg (20 lb)	3.76 kg (8 lb 4 oz)	Whanganei, Nelson, New Zealand	Jan. 22, 1986	Linley Butler
W-15 kg (30 lb)	2.68 kg (5 lb 14 oz)	Parengarenga Harbor, New Zealand	Dec. 28, 1991	Catana Sue Reber

Kawakawa / *Euthynnus affinis*

LINE CLASS	WEIGHT	PLACE	DATE	ANGLER
M-01 kg (2 lb)	3.55 kg (7 lb 13 oz)	Coffs Harbour, N.S.W., Australia	Sept. 29, 1986	Jim Wray
M-02 kg (4 lb)	8.41 kg (18 lb 8 oz)	Port Stephens, N.S.W., Australia	Oct. 19, 1985	Peter Richardson

Kawakawa / *(continued)*

LINE CLASS	WEIGHT	PLACE	DATE	ANGLER
M-03 kg (6 lb)	8.84 kg (19 lb 8 oz)	Port Stephens, N.S.W. Australia	Aug. 3, 1975	Jonathan M. Rowley
M-04 kg (8 lb)	9.10 kg (20 lb 0 oz)	Moreton Bay, Brisbane, Australia	Oct. 27, 1984	Darryl J. Steel
M-06 kg (12 lb)	10.00 kg (22 lb 0 oz)	Nowra, N.S.W., Australia	Mar. 23, 1980	Stephen Goatcher
M-08 kg (16 lb)	11.00 kg (24 lb 4 oz)	Port Stephens, N.S.W., Australia	Oct. 4, 1987	Andrew Fuller
M-10 kg (20 lb)	11.04 kg (24 lb 5 oz)	St. Lucia, Zululand, South Africa	Jan. 20, 1995	Hendrik Acker
M-15 kg (30 lb)	13.15 kg (29 lb 0 oz)	Isla Clarion, Revillagigedo Islands, Mexico	Dec. 17, 1986	Ronald Nakamura
W-01 kg (2 lb)	2.00 kg (4 lb 6 oz)	Moreton Island, Queensland, Australia	Mar. 4, 1985	Anne Dalling
W-02 kg (4 lb)	5.60 kg (12 lb 5 oz)	Dampier, Australia	Jan. 25, 1998	Tammy Yates
W-03 kg (6 lb)	8.10 kg (17 lb 13 oz)	Bustard Head, Queensland, Australia	Mar. 14, 1981	Raelene Babs Anderson
W-04 kg (8 lb)	9.30 kg (20 lb 8 oz)	Bribie Island, Brisbane, Queensland, Australia	May 4, 1987	Kathy Maguire
W-06 kg (12 lb)	8.20 kg (18 lb 1 oz)	Kosi Bay, Zululand, Republic of South Africa	Sept. 23, 1986	Linda Denton
W-08 kg (16 lb)	7.90 kg (17 lb 6 oz)	Orpheus Island, Queensland, Australia	Oct. 26, 1987	Jane S. Blaxland
W-10 kg (20 lb)	8.30 kg (18 lb 4 oz)	Coffe Bay, Transkei, Republic of South Africa	July 31, 1983	Anette Sparg
W-15 kg (30 lb)	7.00 kg (15 lb 6 oz)	Cape Moreton, Queensland, Australia	Apr. 28, 1985	Anne Dalling

Leerfish (Garrick) / *Lichia amia*

LINE CLASS	WEIGHT	PLACE	DATE	ANGLER
M-01 kg (2 lb)	8.50 kg (18 lb 11 oz)	Algoa Bay, Port Elizabeth, Republic of South Africa	Dec. 22, 1985	George Rodocanachi
M-02 kg (4 lb)	11.50 kg (25 lb 5 oz)	Algoa Bay, Port Elizabeth, Republic of South Africa	May 27, 1989	George Rodocanachi
M-03 kg (6 lb)	13.00 kg (28 lb 10 oz)	Jeffrey's Bay, South Africa	May 1, 1998	Trevor Hansen
M-04 kg (8 lb)	16.15 kg (35 lb 9 oz)	Riomar, Spain	Aug. 23, 1989	Joachim Billstein
M-06 kg (12 lb)	17.10 kg (37 lb 11 oz)	Algoa Bay, Republic of South Africa	Mar. 12, 1988	Peter D. Matthews
M-08 kg (16 lb)	14.50 kg (31 lb 15 oz)	Baie de L'Etoile, Nouadhibou	Oct. 2, 1996	Regis Jeannicot
M-10 kg (20 lb)	18.80 kg (41 lb 7 oz)	Port Shepstone, Republic of South Africa	Sept. 16, 1990	James A. Westoby
M-15 kg (30 lb)	23.79 kg (52 lb 3 oz)	Catania, Italy	Oct. 17, 1991	Massimo Brogna
M-24 kg (50 lb)	12.20 kg (26 lb 4 oz)	Mapelane, Natal, Republic of South Africa	July 22, 1994	Charles Stewart
W-01 kg (2 lb)	Vacant			
W-02 kg (4 lb)	4.30 kg (9 lb 7 oz)	Algoa Bay, Port Elizabeth, Republic of South Africa	May 18, 1994	Santie Beukes
W-03 kg (6 lb)	2.85 kg (6 lb 4 oz)	Nouadhibou, Africa	Nov. 10, 1996	Lorella Burroni
W-04 kg (8 lb)	11.00 kg (24 lb 4 oz)	Algoa Bay, Port Elizabeth, Republic of South Africa	June 4, 1986	Catherine Erene Jarman
W-06 kg (12 lb)	10.50 kg (23 lb 2 oz)	Nouadhibou, Africa	Nov. 9, 1996	Antonella Pirazzoli
W-08 kg (16 lb)	12.60 kg (27 lb 12 oz)	Nouadhibou, Mauritania	Dec. 2, 1994	Antonella Pirazzoli
W-10 kg (20 lb)	10.30 kg (22 lb 11 oz)	St. Lucia, Republic of South Africa	Aug. 18, 1990	Dorothy Uys
W-15 kg (30 lb)	10.50 kg (23 lb 2 oz)	Port Elizabeth, Republic of South Africa	Feb. 4, 1990	Mrs. John H. Hanan, II
W-24 kg (50 lb)	Vacant			

Lingcod / *Ophiodon elongatus*

LINE CLASS	WEIGHT	PLACE	DATE	ANGLER
M-01 kg (2 lb)	7.25 kg (16 lb 0 oz)	Kodiak, Alaska, USA	July 31, 1996	Paul Leader
M-02 kg (4 lb)	14.96 kg (33 lb 0 oz)	Kodiak, Alaska, USA	Sept. 11, 1995	Paul Leader
M-03 kg (6 lb)	16.78 kg (37 lb 0 oz)	Kodiak, Alaska, USA	Sept. 11, 1995	William J. Hillgardner
M-04 kg (8 lb)	19.62 kg (43 lb 4 oz)	Seward, Alaska, USA	Sept. 2, 1996	Andrew Mezirow
M-06 kg (12 lb)	17.40 kg (38 lb 6 oz)	San Juan Island, Washington, USA	Aug. 10, 1982	Doug Olander
M-08 kg (16 lb)	23.58 kg (52 lb 0 oz)	East Chugach, Alaska, USA	July 17, 1998	Stephen P. Cushman
M-10 kg (20 lb)	31.29 kg (69 lb 0 oz)	Langara Island, British Columbia, Canada	June 16, 1992	Murray M. Romer
M-15 kg (30 lb)	28.12 kg (62 lb 0 oz)	Elfin Cove, Alaska, USA	June 18, 1991	Robert E. Webster
M-24 kg (50 lb)	29.03 kg (64 lb 0 oz)	Elfin Cove, Alaska, USA	Aug. 2, 1988	David L. Bauer
W-01 kg (2 lb)	5.44 kg (12 lb 0 oz)	Pt. Helen, Knight Island, Alaska, USA	Aug. 11, 1998	Marjorie L. Cushman
W-02 kg (4 lb)	9.80 kg (21 lb 10 oz)	Resurrection Bay, Seward, Alaska, USA	May 26, 1991	J. Laurie Cagle
W-03 kg (6 lb)	24.04 kg (53 lb 0 oz)	Kodiak, Alaska, USA	Sept. 11, 1995	Ruth C. Stoky
W-04 kg (8 lb)	17.23 kg (38 lb 0 oz)	Aialik Bay, Alaska, USA	July 1, 1995	Theda Cagle
W-06 kg (12 lb)	19.50 kg (43 lb 0 oz)	East Chugach, Alaska, USA	July 17, 1998	Marjorie L. Cushman
W-08 kg (16 lb)	21.77 kg (48 lb 0 oz)	East Chugach, Alaska, USA	July 9, 1998	Marjorie L. Cushman
W-10 kg (20 lb)	21.54 kg (47 lb 8 oz)	Queen Charlotte Sound, British Columbia, Canada	Aug. 22, 1985	Deborah Olander
W-15 kg (30 lb)	24.94 kg (55 lb 0 oz)	Queen Charlotte Islands, British Columbia, Canada	Sept. 23, 1990	Frances Claire Gibbs
W-24 kg (50 lb)	24.94 kg (55 lb 0 oz)	Elfin Cove, Alaska, USA	July 7, 1986	Christine Olivas

Mackerel, cero / *Scomberomorus regalis*

LINE CLASS	WEIGHT	PLACE	DATE	ANGLER
M-01 kg (2 lb)	3.96 kg (8 lb 12 oz)	Key West, Florida, USA	Mar. 9, 1993	Tom Pierce
M-02 kg (4 lb)	5.32 kg (11 lb 12 oz)	Key West, Florida, USA	Jan. 23, 1997	Herbert G. Ratner, Jr.
M-03 kg (6 lb)	5.66 kg (12 lb 8 oz)	Bimini, Bahamas	May 2, 1997	Lawrence B. Fitzpatrick
M-04 kg (8 lb)	5.49 kg (12 lb 2 oz)	Key West, Florida, USA	May 23, 1993	Dale Bittner
M-06 kg (12 lb)	6.69 kg (14 lb 12 oz)	Key West, Florida, USA	Feb. 6, 1993	Peter Wintersdorf
M-08 kg (16 lb)	6.35 kg (14 lb 0 oz)	Key West, Florida, USA	Jan. 28, 1996	Mark S. Peters
M-10 kg (20 lb)	7.39 kg (16 lb 4 oz)	Bimini, Bahamas	May 15, 1996	Bert Caskill
W-01 kg (2 lb)	3.17 kg (7 lb 0 oz)	Key West, Florida, USA	Dec. 17, 1996	Mrs. William B. DuVal
W-02 kg (4 lb)	4.19 kg (9 lb 4 oz)	Key West, Florida, USA	Mar. 10, 1993	Rita L. Pierce
W-03 kg (6 lb)	4.30 kg (9 lb 8 oz)	Key West, Florida, USA	Jan. 21, 1995	Mrs. William B. DuVal
W-04 kg (8 lb)	5.21 kg (11 lb 8 oz)	Key West, Florida, USA	Feb. 6, 1995	Emme (Emily) Golinski
W-06 kg (12 lb)	4.08 kg (9 lb 0 oz)	Key West, Florida, USA	Jan. 21, 1995	Mrs. William B. DuVal
W-08 kg (16 lb)	5.90 kg (13 lb 0 oz)	Key West, Florida, USA	Jan. 6, 1994	Emily Golinski
W-10 kg (20 lb)	4.76 kg (10 lb 8 oz)	Puerto Aventuras, Mexico	Apr. 16, 1997	Susan Gooch

Mackerel, king / *Scomberomorus cavalla*

LINE CLASS	WEIGHT	PLACE	DATE	ANGLER
M-01 kg (2 lb)	10.95 kg (24 lb 2 oz)	Indian Rocks Beach, Florida, USA	Nov. 28, 1990	Ken Krohel
M-02 kg (4 lb)	17.57 kg (38 lb 12 oz)	Key West, Florida, USA	Jan. 5, 1997	Jerome N. Matthews
M-03 kg (6 lb)	24.72 kg (54 lb 8 oz)	Empire, Louisana, USA	Apr. 8, 1978	Maumus F. Claverie, Jr.
M-04 kg (8 lb)	28.80 kg (63 lb 8 oz)	Key West, Florida, USA	Jan. 18, 1985	James M. Eckhart
M-06 kg (12 lb)	34.01 kg (75 lb 0 oz)	Key West, Florida, USA	Jan. 13, 1987	Alan Lane

Mackerel, king / *(continued)*

LINE CLASS	WEIGHT	PLACE	DATE	ANGLER
M-08 kg (16 lb)	32.31 kg (71 lb 4 oz)	Dry Tortugas, Key West, Florida, USA	Mar. 17, 1995	Fred W. Gadd
M-10 kg (20 lb)	34.92 kg (77 lb 0 oz)	Bimini, Bahamas	May 12, 1957	Clinton Olney Potts
M-15 kg (30 lb)	34.01 kg (75 lb 0 oz)	Walker's Cay, Bahamas	May 22, 1966	Thomas J. Sims, Jr.
M-24 kg (50 lb)	35.72 kg (78 lb 12 oz)	La Romana, Dominican Republic	Nov. 26, 1971	Fernando Viyella
M-37 kg (80 lb)	40.82 kg (90 lb 0 oz)	Key West, Florida, USA	Feb. 16, 1976	Norton I. Thomton
W-01 kg (2 lb)	12.92 kg (28 lb 8 oz)	Marathon, Florida, USA	Apr. 5, 1992	Elizabeth M. Hogan
W-02 kg (4 lb)	16.78 kg (37 lb 0 oz)	Key West, Florida, USA	Feb. 22, 1987	Donna Campbell Zequeira
W-03 kg (6 lb)	19.73 kg (43 lb 8 oz)	Stuart, Florida, USA	Dec. 31, 1976	Janey Franklin
W-04 kg (8 lb)	18.59 kg (41 lb 0 oz)	Dry Tortugas, Florida, USA	Feb. 12, 1995	Mrs. William B. DuVal
W-06 kg (12 lb)	24.72 kg (54 lb 8 oz)	Dry Tortugas, Florida, USA	Mar. 16, 1992	Mrs. William B. DuVal
W-08 kg (16 lb)	24.12 kg (53 lb 3 oz)	Long Beach, North Carolina, USA	Apr. 27, 1991	Katherine W. Davis
W-10 kg (20 lb)	31.52 kg (69 lb 8 oz)	Islamorada, Florida, USA	Jan. 15, 1979	Florence R. Austin
W-15 kg (30 lb)	30.53 kg (67 lb 5 oz)	Tortola, British Virgin Islands	May 4, 1980	Elizabeth B. Clark
W-24 kg (50 lb)	35.38 kg (78 lb 0 oz)	Guayanilla, Puerto Rico	May 25, 1963	Ruth M. Coon
W-37 kg (80 lb)	35.49 kg (78 lb 4 oz)	Grand Isle, Louisiana, USA	Nov. 29, 1981	Debra R. Sebastian

Mackerel, narrowbarred / *Scomberomorus commerson*

LINE CLASS	WEIGHT	PLACE	DATE	ANGLER
M-01 kg (2 lb)	8.84 kg (19 lb 8 oz)	Hayman Island, Queensland, Australia	June 16, 1982	Peter Bruce
M-02 kg (4 lb)	16.10 kg (35 lb 7 oz)	Exmouth, Australia	Nov. 8, 1995	Dave Barrow
M-03 kg (6 lb)	24.60 kg (54 lb 0 oz)	Peron Islands, N.T., Australia	Mar. 24, 1978	Graeme Copley
M-04 kg (8 lb)	33.00 kg (72 lb 12 oz)	Lee Point, Darwin, N.T., Australia	Aug. 24, 1985	Henry J. Fehres
M-06 kg (12 lb)	33.20 kg (73 lb 3 oz)	Cape Cuvier, W.A., Australia	Aug. 27, 1982	Shane Quinlan
M-08 kg (16 lb)	36.40 kg (80 lb 3 oz)	Coral Bay, W.A., Australia	July 1, 1987	Bob Burdinat
M-10 kg (20 lb)	42.00 kg (92 lb 9 oz)	Cairns, Queensland, Australia	Aug. 8, 1993	Christopher Leishman
M-15 kg (30 lb)	38.25 kg (84 lb 5 oz)	Cairns, Queensland, Australia	Aug. 1, 1990	Alan Jorgensen
M-24 kg (50 lb)	44.90 kg (99 lb 0 oz)	Scottburgh, Natal, Republic of South Africa	Mar. 14, 1982	Michael John Wilkinson
M-37 kg (80 lb)	38.00 kg (83 lb 12 oz)	Pig Island, Papua, New Guinea	Mar. 17, 1985	M. Tsang
W-01 kg (2 lb)	0.50 kg (1 lb 1 oz)	Arovo Island, Papua, New Guinea	Apr. 14, 1982	Susan Fuller
W-02 kg (4 lb)	13.60 kg (29 lb 15 oz)	Darwin, Northern Territory, Australia	May 23, 1983	Judy Jenkins
W-03 kg (6 lb)	22.80 kg (50 lb 4 oz)	Groote Eylandt, Australia	Feb. 10, 1997	Clare Pries
W-04 kg (8 lb)	29.40 kg (64 lb 13 oz)	Mackay, Queensland, Australia	Sept. 20, 1986	Janette Shuttleworth
W-06 kg (12 lb)	30.84 kg (68 lb 0 oz)	Cairns, Queensland, Australia	Aug. 25, 1976	Mrs. Wilma Childs
W-08 kg (16 lb)	25.00 kg (55 lb 1 oz)	Orpheus Island, Queensland, Australia	Oct. 23, 1987	Jane S. Blaxland
W-10 kg (20 lb)	29.50 kg (65 lb 0 oz)	Whitsunday's, Queensland, Australia	Aug. 7, 1986	Netta Smith
W-15 kg (30 lb)	30.84 kg (68 lb 0 oz)	Hayman Island, Queensland, Australia	May 14, 1969	Lady Joan Ansett
W-24 kg (50 lb)	34.00 kg (74 lb 15 oz)	Hayman Island, Queensland, Australia	May 26, 1979	Lady Joan Ansett
W-37 kg (80 lb)	29.03 kg (64 lb 0 oz)	Mozambique, East Africa	Sept. 12, 1959	A. C. Lee

Mackerel, Spanish / *Scomberomorus maculatus*

LINE CLASS	WEIGHT	PLACE	DATE	ANGLER
M-01 kg (2 lb)	2.77 kg (6 lb 1 oz)	Biscayne Bay, Miami, Florida, USA	Feb. 19, 1987	Jack D. Agramonte
M-02 kg (4 lb)	3.84 kg (8 lb 7 oz)	Tampa Bay, Tampa, Florida, USA	Oct. 22, 1985	James P. Wisner
M-03 kg (6 lb)	4.45 kg (9 lb 13 oz)	Key Largo, Florida, USA	Dec. 29, 1987	Robert A. Waller
M-04 kg (8 lb)	3.60 kg (7 lb 15 oz)	Stuart, Florida, USA	Dec. 4, 1995	Dennis O'Toole
M-06 kg (12 lb)	4.50 kg (9 lb 15 oz)	Miami, Florida, USA	Nov. 22, 1994	Joaquin Diaz
M-08 kg (16 lb)	4.43 kg (9 lb 12 oz)	Cape May, New Jersey, USA	Sept. 11, 1990	Donald Kohler
M-10 kg (20 lb)	5.44 kg (12 lb 0 oz)	Ft. Pierce, Florida, USA	Nov. 17, 1984	John F. Colligan
W-01 kg (2 lb)	2.72 kg (6 lb 0 oz)	Key West, Florida, USA	Jan. 6, 1989	Mrs. William B. DuVal
W-02 kg (4 lb)	3.06 kg (6 lb 12 oz)	Sunny Isles, Miami, Florida, USA	Nov. 30, 1996	Pamela W. Marmin
W-03 kg (6 lb)	3.17 kg (7 lb 0 oz)	Miami, Florida, USA	Oct. 21, 1995	Pamela W. Marmin
W-04 kg (8 lb)	4.59 kg (10 lb 2 oz)	Ocracoke, North Carolina, USA	Nov. 3, 1993	Mrs. William B. DuVal
W-06 kg (12 lb)	3.96 kg (8 lb 11 oz)	Hatteras Island, North Carolina, USA	Sept. 22, 1988	Dede Gaskins
W-08 kg (16 lb)	4.97 kg (10 lb 15 oz)	Oak Bluffs Wharf, Massachusetts, USA	Sept. 18, 1983	Heather J. Wadsworth
W-10 kg (20 lb)	2.94 kg (6 lb 8 oz)	Marathon, Florida, USA	Feb. 19, 1998	Janet F. Farish

Madai / *Pagrus major*

LINE CLASS	WEIGHT	PLACE	DATE	ANGLER
M-01 kg (2 lb)	Vacant			
M-02 kg (4 lb)	Vacant			
M-03 kg (6 lb)	Vacant			
M-04 kg (8 lb)	4.28 kg (9 lb 6 oz)	Tokyo Bay, Japan	June 23, 1997	Mikio Kambara
M-06 kg (12 lb)	4.90 kg (10 lb 12 oz)	Oura, Kochi, Japan	Feb. 14, 1998	Yuichi Ueno
M-08 kg (16 lb)	3.30 kg (7 lb 4 oz)	Kanzaki-oki, Kitaamabe-gun, Ooita-ken, Japan	July 31, 1997	Shinji Sato
M-10 kg (20 lb)	Vacant			
M-15 kg (30 lb)	Vacant			
M-24 kg (50 lb)	9.40 kg (20 lb 11 oz)	Muroto, Kouichi, Japan	Dec. 7, 1996	Ken Fukuba
W-01 kg (2 lb)	Vacant			
W-02 kg (4 lb)	Vacant			
W-03 kg (6 lb)	Vacant			
W-04 kg (8 lb)	Vacant			
W-06 kg (12 lb)	5.20 kg (11 lb 7 oz)	Shima Peninsula, Mie, Japan	Mar. 2, 1997	Rieko Ushikubo
W-08 kg (16 lb)	Vacant			
W-10 kg (20 lb)	Vacant			
W-15 kg (30 lb)	Vacant			
W-24 kg (50 lb)	Vacant			

Marlin, black / *Makaira indica*

LINE CLASS	WEIGHT	PLACE	DATE	ANGLER
M-01 kg (2 lb)	21.30 kg (46 lb 15 oz)	Cape Bowling Green, Townsville, Australia	Aug. 21, 1988	Mike Levitt
M-02 kg (4 lb)	52.00 kg (114 lb 10 oz)	Broughton Island, Port Stephens, Australia	Mar. 16, 1997	Mike Levitt

Marlin, black / *(continued)*

LINE CLASS	WEIGHT	PLACE	DATE	ANGLER
M-03 kg (6 lb)	110.67 kg (244 lb 0 oz)	Pinas Bay, Panama	Jan. 26, 1976	Edwin D. Kennedy
M-04 kg (8 lb)	209.56 kg (462 lb 0 oz)	Pinas Bay, Panama	Feb. 13, 1990	Jean Paul Richard
M-06 kg (12 lb)	334.50 kg (737 lb 7 oz)	Cairns, Queensland, Australia	Nov. 16, 1981	Michael J. Levitt
M-08 kg (16 lb)	235.64 kg (519 lb 8 oz)	Pinas Bay, Panama	Apr. 7, 1991	Jerry Dunaway
M-10 kg (20 lb)	476.73 kg (1051 lb 0 oz)	Cairns, Queensland, Australia	Oct. 7, 1976	Peter W. Mahood
M-15 kg (30 lb)	489.50 kg (1079 lb 2 oz)	Cairns, Queensland, Australia	Nov. 28, 1980	Bob Oliver
M-24 kg (50 lb)	509.84 kg (1124 lb 0 oz)	Cairns, Queensland, Australia	Oct. 31, 1969	Edward Seay
M-37 kg (80 lb)	611.00 kg (1347 lb 0 oz)	Lizard Island, Queensland, Australia	Nov. 1, 1979	Morton D. May
M-60 kg (130 lb)	707.61 kg (1560 lb 0 oz)	Cabo Blanco, Peru	Aug. 4, 1953	Alfred C. Glassell, Jr.
W-01 kg (2 lb)	11.00 kg (24 lb 4 oz)	Cape Bowling Green, Townsville, Australia	July 5, 1986	Anne Dalling
W-02 kg (4 lb)	29.50 kg (65 lb 0 oz)	Cape Bowling Green, Australia	Sept. 18, 1997	Anne Dalling
W-03 kg (6 lb)	73.00 kg (160 lb 0 oz)	Opal Reef, Cairns, Australia	Nov. 27, 1996	Christie Andrews
W-04 kg (8 lb)	108.40 kg (239 lb 0 oz)	Pinas Bay, Panama	Jan. 20, 1987	Deborah Maddux Dunaway
W-06 kg (12 lb)	160.11 kg (353 lb 0 oz)	Pinas Bay, Panama	Mar. 6, 1968	Evelyn Anderson
W-08 kg (16 lb)	201.85 kg (445 lb 0 oz)	Pinas Bay, Panama	Mar. 11, 1995	Elizabeth Hogan
W-10 kg (20 lb)	452.69 kg (998 lb 0 oz)	Lizard Island, Queensland, Australia	Oct. 23, 1982	Kay Mulholland
W-15 kg (30 lb)	369.22 kg (814 lb 0 oz)	Great Barrier Reef, Queensland, Australia	Nov. 4, 1983	Mrs. Jill Hooper
W-24 kg (50 lb)	396.44 kg (874 lb 0 oz)	Cairns, Queensland, Australia	Oct. 16, 1976	Kay Mulholland
W-37 kg (80 lb)	600.10 kg (1323 lb 0 oz)	Cairns, Queensland, Australia	Nov. 8, 1977	Georgette Douwma
W-60 kg (130 lb)	691.73 kg (1525 lb 0 oz)	Cabo Blanco, Peru	Apr. 22, 1954	Mrs. Charles E. Hughes

Marlin, blue (Atlantic) / *Makaira nigricans*

LINE CLASS	WEIGHT	PLACE	DATE	ANGLER
M-01 kg (2 lb)	Vacant			
M-02 kg (4 lb)	260.00 kg (573 lb 0 oz)	Horta, Faial, Azores	Aug. 1, 1995	Leo Cloostermans
M-03 kg (6 lb)	112.71 kg (248 lb 8 oz)	Horta, Faial, Azores	Aug. 14, 1994	Leo R. Cloostermans
M-04 kg (8 lb)	172.82 kg (381 lb 0 oz)	Horta, Faial, Azores	Aug. 20, 1993	Leo R. Cloostermans
M-06 kg (12 lb)	273.97 kg (604 lb 0 oz)	Horta, Faial, Azores	Aug. 15, 1992	Leo R. Cloostermans
M-08 kg (16 lb)	371.94 kg (820 lb 0 oz)	Grand Bereby, Ivory Coast	Apr. 9, 1992	Stewart N. Campbell
M-10 kg (20 lb)	324.09 kg (714 lb 8 oz)	Grand Bereby, Ivory Coast	Apr. 7, 1990	Stewart N. Campbell
M-15 kg (30 lb)	395.53 kg (872 lb 0 oz)	Madeira, Portugal	Aug. 29, 1995	Stewart N. Campbell
M-24 kg (50 lb)	520.00 kg (1146 lb 6 oz)	Horta, Faial, Azores	Sept. 17, 1988	Lawrence H. Furman
M-37 kg (80 lb)	540.00 kg (1189 lb 0 oz)	Azores Bank, Faial, Azores	Sept. 9, 1993	Jacky Delbrel
M-60 kg (130 lb)	636.00 kg (1402 lb 2 oz)	Vitoria, Brazil	Feb. 29, 1992	Paulo Roberto A. Amorim
W-01 kg (2 lb)	Vacant			
W-02 kg (4 lb)	Vacant			
W-03 kg (6 lb)	57.80 kg (112 lb 0 oz)	La Guaira, Venezuela	May 8, 1998	Karen Heldt
W-04 kg (8 lb)	133.81 kg (295 lb 0 oz)	St. Thomas, U.S. Virgin Islands	Sept. 7, 1992	Marg Love
W-06 kg (12 lb)	120.65 kg (266 lb 0 oz)	St. Thomas, U.S. Virgin Islands	Sept. 6, 1993	Marg Love
W-08 kg (16 lb)	166.47 kg (367 lb 0 oz)	Sao Vincente, Cape Verde	May 23, 1997	Annick Thorn-Chopin
W-10 kg (20 lb)	181.89 kg (401 lb 0 oz)	San Juan, Puerto Rico	Nov. 16, 1975	Carmina Miller
W-15 kg (30 lb)	321.14 kg (708 lb 0 oz)	Madeira, Portugal	June 28, 1996	Mrs. Stewart N. Campbell
W-24 kg (50 lb)	364.00 kg (802 lb 7 oz)	Gran Canaria, Canary Islands, Spain	Aug. 9, 1986	Ann Holmes
W-37 kg (80 lb)	480.35 kg (1059 lb 0 oz)	Madeira, Portugal	July 23, 1995	Shelby E. Rogers
W-60 kg (130 lb)	486.70 kg (1073 lb 0 oz)	St. Thomas, U.S. Virgin Islands	July 6, 1982	Annette (Maudi) Lopez

Marlin, blue (Pacific) / *Makaira nigricans*

LINE CLASS	WEIGHT	PLACE	DATE	ANGLER
M-01 kg (2 lb)	Vacant			
M-02 kg (4 lb)	64.00 kg (141 lb 1 oz)	Cabo San Lucas, Baja California Sur, Mexico	Sept. 8, 1989	George E. Hogan, Jr.
M-03 kg (6 lb)	64.41 kg (142 lb 0 oz)	Keahole Point, Hawaii, USA	Apr. 1, 1996	Steven Schumacher
M-04 kg (8 lb)	142.88 kg (315 lb 0 oz)	Punta Arenus, Baja California, Mexico	July 25, 1990	Jerry Dunaway
M-06 kg (12 lb)	179.93 kg (396 lb 11 oz)	Punta Colorado, Baja California, Mexico	June 6, 1981	Bernard A. Guentner
M-08 kg (16 lb)	204.11 kg (450 lb 0 oz)	Milolii, Hawaii, USA	May 2, 1985	Martin G. Abel
M-10 kg (20 lb)	348.67 kg (768 lb 10 oz)	Buena Vista, Mexico	Nov. 22, 1982	Eugene A. Nazarek
M-15 kg (30 lb)	500.54 kg (1103 lb 8 oz)	Kailua-Kona, Hawaii, USA	June 25, 1987	Kelley K. Everette
M-24 kg (50 lb)	528.89 kg (1166 lb 0 oz)	Kailua-Kona, Hawaii, USA	Aug. 19, 1993	Ray G. Hawkes
M-37 kg (80 lb)	459.94 kg (1014 lb 0 oz)	Manta, Ecuador	May 12, 1985	Jorge F. Jurado E.
M-60 kg (130 lb)	624.14 kg (1376 lb 0 oz)	Kaaiwi Pt., Kona, Hawaii, USA	May 31, 1982	Jay Wm. de Beaubien
W-01 kg (2 lb)	Vacant			
W-02 kg (4 lb)	73.66 kg (162 lb 6 oz)	Quepos, Costa Rica	Mar. 15, 1989	Marg Love
W-03 kg (6 lb)	Vacant			
W-04 kg (8 lb)	37.19 kg (82 lb 0 oz)	Bora Bora, French Polynesia	Apr. 11, 1990	Shannon T. Pitner
W-04 kg (8 lb) Tie	37.19 kg (82 lb 0 oz)	Kona Coast, Hawaii, USA	Nov. 7, 1996	Pam Basco
W-06 kg (12 lb)	137.43 kg (303 lb 0 oz)	Flamingo Bay, Costa Rica	Aug. 15, 1991	Deborah Maddux Dunaway
W-08 kg (16 lb)	287.01 kg (632 lb 12 oz)	Pinas Bay, Panama	May 8, 1984	Linda L. Miller
W-10 kg (20 lb)	184.16 kg (406 lb 0 oz)	Mazatlan, Mexico	May 18, 1972	Marguerite H. Barry
W-15 kg (30 lb)	289.84 kg (639 lb 0 oz)	Kailua-Kona, Hawaii, USA	Oct. 8, 1988	Jocelyn J. Everette
W-24 kg (50 lb)	325.00 kg (716 lb 7 oz)	Cape Karikari, New Zealand	Mar. 11, 1985	Irene Jamieson
W-37 kg (80 lb)	431.14 kg (950 lb 8 oz)	Kailua-Kona, Hawaii, USA	May 18, 1988	Louise Ann (Angel) Bowles
W-60 kg (130 lb)	430.92 kg (950 lb 0 oz)	Le Morne, Mauritius	Dec. 16, 1994	Maria Rosa Tomaini

Marlin, striped / *Tetrapturus audax*

LINE CLASS	WEIGHT	PLACE	DATE	ANGLER
M-01 kg (2 lb)	59.87 kg (132 lb 0 oz)	Cabo San Lucas, Baja California Sur, Mexico	June 7, 1989	George E. Hogan, Jr.
M-02 kg (4 lb)	74.16 kg (163 lb 8 oz)	Pinas Bay, Panama	Feb. 18, 1989	Jean Paul Richard
M-03 kg (6 lb)	92.98 kg (205 lb 0 oz)	Cabo San Lucas, Baja California Sur, Mexico	Apr. 3, 1972	W. Matt Parr
M-04 kg (8 lb)	116.20kg (256 lb 2 oz)	Middlesex Bank, New Zealand	June 8, 1997	Thomas Campbell Fraser
M-06 kg (12 lb)	134.26 kg (296 lb 0 oz)	Three Kings, New Zealand	May 17, 1998	Mike Levitt
M-08 kg (16 lb)	125.40 kg (276 lb 7 oz)	Middlesex Bank, New Zealand	May 27, 1997	Geoffrey Fraser

Marlin, striped / *(continued)*

LINE CLASS	WEIGHT	PLACE	DATE	ANGLER
M-10 kg (20 lb)	164.20 kg (361 lb 15 oz)	Waineare, Bay of Islands, New Zealand	May 4, 1994	Kirk Stoneman
M-15 kg (30 lb)	180.40 kg (397 lb 11 oz)	Cavalli Islands, New Zealand	May 29, 1996	Roy Sheard
M-24 kg (50 lb)	224.10 kg (494 lb 0 oz)	Tutukaka, New Zealand	Jan. 16, 1986	Bill Boniface
M-37 kg (80 lb)	206.50 kg (455 lb 4 oz)	Mayor Island, New Zealand	Mar. 8, 1982	Bruce Jenkinson
M-60 kg (130 lb)	180.53 kg (398 lb 0 oz)	Mayor Island, New Zealand	Dec. 30, 1974	John Kenneth Boyle
W-01 kg (2 lb)	50.50 kg (111 lb 5 oz)	Cabo San Lucas, Baja California Sur, Mexico	May 3, 1992	Elizabeth Hogan
W-02 kg (4 lb)	64.63 kg (142 lb 8 oz)	Pinas Bay, Panama	Feb. 21, 1991	Deborah Maddux Dunaway
W-03 kg (6 lb)	85.27 kg (188 lb 0 oz)	Cabo San Lucas, Baja California Sur, Mexico	June 8, 1974	Kathryn McGinnis
W-04 kg (8 lb)	85.95 kg (189 lb 8 oz)	Pinas Bay, Panama	Feb. 13, 1993	Deborah Maddux Dunaway
W-06 kg (12 lb)	142.00 kg (313 lb 0 oz)	Middlesex Bank, New Zealand	June 6, 1997	Ann Martin
W-08 kg (16 lb)	119.00 kg (262 lb 5 oz)	Stephensons Island, New Zealand	Apr. 25, 1982	Robyn Hall
W-10 kg (20 lb)	154.22 kg (340 lb 0 oz)	Bay of Islands, New Zealand	Jan. 21, 1977	Robyn Hall
W-15 kg (30 lb)	166.20 kg (366 lb 6 oz)	Mayor Island, New Zealand	Feb. 15, 1998	Barbara Woodill
W-24 kg (50 lb)	192.00 kg (423 lb 4 oz)	Whangamumu, New Zealand	June 5, 1983	Robyn Hall
W-37 kg (80 lb)	188.00 kg (414 lb 7 oz)	Tutukaka, New Zealand	May 1, 1981	Mrs. J. J. Main
W-60 kg (130 lb)	117.80 kg (259 lb 11 oz)	Cape Karikari, New Zealand	Apr. 19, 1996	Tessa Nicola Brasting

Marlin, white / *Tetrapturus albidus*

LINE CLASS	WEIGHT	PLACE	DATE	ANGLER
M-01 kg (2 lb)	39.46 kg (87 lb 0 oz)	Nantucket Island, Massachusetts, USA	Aug. 23, 1986	Ron Nation
M-02 kg (4 lb)	40.10 kg (88 lb 6 oz)	Vitoria, Brazil	Dec. 6, 1990	Mike Levitt
M-03 kg (6 lb)	41.00 kg (90 lb 6 oz)	Vitoria, Brazil	Dec. 4, 1994	Mike Levitt
M-04 kg (8 lb)	55.20 kg (121 lb 11 oz)	Vitoria, Brazil	Dec. 7, 1987	Mike Levitt
M-06 kg (12 lb)	64.41 kg (142 lb 0 oz)	Vitoria, Brazil	Dec. 5, 1992	Mike Levitt
M-08 kg (16 lb)	60.20 kg (132 lb 11 oz)	Rio de Janeiro, Brazil	Dec. 14, 1996	Mauricio Paixao
M-10 kg (20 lb)	79.00 kg (174 lb 2 oz)	Rio de Janeiro, Brazil	Dec. 3, 1997	Paulo Fabiano Ferreira Filho
M-15 kg (30 lb)	82.50 kg (181 lb 14 oz)	Vitoria, Brazil	Dec. 8, 1979	Evandro Luiz Coser
M-24 kg (50 lb)	80.00 kg (176 lb 5 oz)	Vitoria Espirito, Santo, Brazil	Dec. 4, 1993	Luiz Azevedo Franca
M-37 kg (80 lb)	73.80 kg (162 lb 11 oz)	Vitoria Espirito, Santo, Brazil	Dec. 6, 1986	Paulo Egydio Martins
M-60 kg (130 lb)	48.30 kg (106 lb 8 oz)	Algarve, Portugal	Aug. 30, 1997	Guido Fehr
W-01 kg (2 lb)	25.60 kg (56 lb 8 oz)	La Guaira, Venezuela	Nov. 28, 1993	Pamela S. Basco
W-02 kg (4 lb)	44.11 kg (97 lb 4 oz)	Nantucket, Massachusetts, USA	Sept. 2, 1986	Susan C. Goodwin
W-03 kg (6 lb)	33.60 kg (74 lb 1 oz)	Mohammedia, Morocco	Sept. 9, 1996	Odile Robelin
W-04 kg (8 lb)	36.70 kg (80 lb 14 oz)	Mohammedia, Morocco	Sept. 20, 1992	Odile Robelin
W-06 kg (12 lb)	55.33 kg (122 lb 0 oz)	Bimini, Bahamas	Mar. 30, 1953	Dorothy A. Curtice
W-08 kg (16 lb)	51.71 kg (114 lb 0 oz)	Nantucket Island, Massachusetts, USA	Sept. 1, 1986	Biddy Pauley
W-10 kg (20 lb)	58.62 kg (129 lb 4 oz)	Bimini, Bahamas	Apr. 11, 1963	Mrs. J. M. Watters
W-15 kg (30 lb)	54.71 kg (120 lb 10 oz)	Bimini, Bahamas	Mar. 29, 1956	Mrs. M. Meyer, Jr.
W-24 kg (50 lb)	67.13 kg (148 lb 0 oz)	Chub Cay, Berry Islands, Bahamas	Apr. 7, 1983	Barbara S. Greenfield
W-37 kg (80 lb)	64.41 kg (142 lb 0 oz)	Ft. Lauderdale, Florida, USA	Mar. 14, 1959	Marie Beneventi
W-60 kg (130 lb)	32.20 kg (71 lb 0 oz)	Horta, Faial, Azores	Aug. 14, 1997	Deborah Maddux Dunaway

Permit / *Trachinotus falcatus*

LINE CLASS	WEIGHT	PLACE	DATE	ANGLER
M-01 kg (2 lb)	11.53 kg (25 lb 7 oz)	Key West, Florida, USA	Mar. 28, 1988	Crawford W. Adams
M-02 kg (4 lb)	20.29 kg (44 lb 12 oz)	Key West, Florida, USA	Apr. 20, 1987	Bill Riesenfeld
M-03 kg (6 lb)	17.23 kg (38 lb 0 oz)	Key West, Florida, USA	Mar. 19, 1972	Stuart C. Apte
M-04 kg (8 lb)	19.27 kg (42 lb 8 oz)	Key West, Florida, USA	Apr. 13, 1993	Steven L. Lawyer
M-06 kg (12 lb)	22.67 kg (50 lb 0 oz)	Miami, Florida, USA	Mar. 27, 1965	Robert F. Miller
M-08 kg (16 lb)	20.97 kg (46 lb 4 oz)	Key West Harbor, Key West, Florida, USA	Apr. 10, 1994	Herbert G. Ratner, Jr.
M-10 kg (20 lb)	25.45 kg (56 lb 2 oz)	Ft. Lauderdale, Florida, USA	June 30, 1997	Thomas Sebestyen
M-15 kg (30 lb)	23.36 kg (51 lb 8 oz)	Lake Worth, Florida, USA	Apr. 28, 1978	William M. Kennedy
M-24 kg (50 lb)	24.15 kg (53 lb 4 oz)	Lake Worth, Florida, USA	Mar. 25, 1994	Roy Brooker
W-01 kg (2 lb)	8.73 kg (19 lb 4 oz)	Marquesas Keys, Florida, USA	Aug. 20, 1993	Joyce May Rehr
W-02 kg (4 lb)	11.90 kg (26 lb 4 oz)	Islamorada, Florida, USA	July 19, 1992	Kathleen Meyer
W-03 kg (6 lb)	15.05 kg (33 lb 3 oz)	Key West, Florida, USA	Aug. 13, 1981	Rita L. Pierce
W-04 kg (8 lb)	18.14 kg (40 lb 0 oz)	Key West, Florida, USA	Mar. 17, 1994	Lu Anne Liederman
W-06 kg (12 lb)	19.05 kg (42 lb 0 oz)	Matecumbe Key, Florida, USA	Apr. 23, 1981	Susan C. Riccardi
W-08 kg (16 lb)	18.25 kg (40 lb 4 oz)	Key West, Florida, USA	July 6, 1987	Cindy White
W-10 kg (20 lb)	20.86 kg (46 lb 0 oz)	Key West, Florida, USA	Apr. 15, 1988	Jeanne L. Harris
W-15 kg (30 lb)	19.05 kg (42 lb 0 oz)	Key West, Florida, USA	Mar. 25, 1993	Joyce Dolce
W-24 kg (50 lb)	17.69 kg (39 lb 0 oz)	Islamorada, Florida, USA	Apr. 2, 1966	Shelagh B. Richards

Pollack, European / *Pollachius pollachius*

LINE CLASS	WEIGHT	PLACE	DATE	ANGLER
M-01 kg (2 lb)	6.63 kg (14 lb 10 oz)	Brixham, Devon, England	Nov. 19, 1983	Albert King
M-02 kg (4 lb)	7.03 kg (15 lb 8 oz)	Brixham, Devon, England	Oct. 27, 1984	Barry Edward Stanley
M-03 kg (6 lb)	7.68 kg (16 lb 14 oz)	Berry Head, Brixham, England	Dec. 29, 1982	Brian Stewart Taylor
M-04 kg (8 lb)	9.79 kg (21 lb 9 oz)	Fedje, Norway	May 20, 1997	Jorgen Larsson
M-06 kg (12 lb)	11.56 kg (25 lb 8 oz)	Plymouth, Devon, England	Feb. 19, 1988	Darren Kester
M-08 kg (16 lb)	12.41 kg (27 lb 6 oz)	Salcombe, Devon, England	Jan. 16, 1986	Robert Samuel Milkins
M-10 kg (20 lb)	11.22 kg (24 lb 12 oz)	Salcombe, Devon, England	Feb. 22, 1988	Colin J. Davies
M-15 kg (30 lb)	11.80 kg (26 lb 0 oz)	Ile de Ouessant, France	Aug. 30, 1981	Loik Le Chat
M-24 kg (50 lb)	9.53 kg (21 lb 0 oz)	Plymouth, Devon, England	Feb. 26, 1983	Carel Boonen
W-01 kg (2 lb)	2.08 kg (4 lb 9 oz)	Helsingborg, Sweden	Oct. 24, 1984	Anna-Lena Andersson
W-02 kg (4 lb)	5.49 kg (12 lb 2 oz)	Gosport, Hampshire, England	June 30, 1992	Pat Gillies
W-03 kg (6 lb)	6.87 kg (15 lb 2 oz)	Plymouth, Devon, England	Mar. 10, 1973	Mrs. Rita Barrett
W-04 kg (8 lb)	Vacant			
W-06 kg (12 lb)	10.37 kg (22 lb 14 oz)	Plymouth, Devon, England	Feb. 11, 1989	Mrs. Pat Maunder
W-08 kg (16 lb)	7.14 kg (15 lb 12 oz)	Lund, Sweden	June 17, 1989	Birgitta Wall

Pollock, European / *(continued)*

LINE CLASS	WEIGHT	PLACE	DATE	ANGLER
W-10 kg (20 lb)	7.05 kg (15 lb 9 oz)	Berryhead, Devon, England	Mar. 6, 1985	Sandy Martin
W-15 kg (30 lb)	7.82 kg (17 lb 4 oz)	Plymouth, Devon, England	Dec. 28, 1984	Diana Mulder
W-24 kg (50 lb)	3.94 kg (8 lb 11 oz)	Tobermory, Isle of Mull, Scotland	Sept. 26, 1985	E. Jean Whittaker

Pollock / *Pollachius virens*

LINE CLASS	WEIGHT	PLACE	DATE	ANGLER
M-01 kg (2 lb)	3.75 kg (8 lb 4 oz)	Terrak, Norway	July 24, 1984	Jorg Marquard
M-02 kg (4 lb)	16.66 kg (36 lb 12 oz)	Perkins Cove, Ogunquit, Maine, USA	Oct. 18, 1984	Bradford A. Perkins
M-03 kg (6 lb)	13.15 kg (29 lb 0 oz)	Montauk Point, New York, USA	May 10, 1980	Thomas F. Cashman
M-04 kg (8 lb)	17.23 kg (38 lb 0 oz)	Perkins Cove, Ogunquit, Maine, USA	Sept. 25, 1990	Donald F.X. Angerman
M-06 kg (12 lb)	17.65 kg (38 lb 14 oz)	Meloysundet, Norway	Sept. 1, 1978	Roar Nilsen
M-08 kg (16 lb)	18.37 kg (40 lb 8 oz)	Isle of Shoals, New Hampshire, USA	Sept. 2, 1985	Donald F.X. Angerman
M-10 kg (20 lb)	19.68 kg (43 lb 6 oz)	Perkins Cove, Ogunquit, Maine, USA	Oct. 18, 1990	Robert H. Withee
M-15 kg (30 lb)	20.83 kg (45 lb 15 oz)	Fire Island, New York, USA	Aug. 26, 1988	Bruce A. Morabito
M-24 kg (50 lb)	22.55 kg (49 lb 11 oz)	Saltstraumen, Norway	Nov. 14, 1995	Geir Kristian Olsen
W-01 kg (2 lb)	0.74 kg (1 lb 10 oz)	Terrak, Norway	July 30, 1984	Sabine Niedrig
W-02 kg (4 lb)	12.14 kg (26 lb 12 oz)	Montauk, New York, USA	May 22, 1984	Diane Lynne Mellish
W-03 kg (6 lb)	Vacant			
W-04 kg (8 lb)	12.87 kg (28 lb 6 oz)	Green Harbor, Massachusetts, USA	Oct. 8, 1989	Diana Barry
W-06 kg (12 lb)	13.49 kg (29 lb 12 oz)	Perkins Cove, Ogunquit, Maine, USA	Nov. 10, 1985	Meg Tower
W-08 kg (16 lb)	16.95 kg (37 lb 6 oz)	Perkins Cove, Ogunquit, Maine, USA	Nov. 10, 1985	Madelyn J. Maguire
W-10 kg (20 lb)	17.23 kg (38 lb 0 oz)	Westport, Nova Scotia, Canada	Aug. 30, 1971	Ruth G. Verber
W-15 kg (30 lb)	17.05 kg (37 lb 9 oz)	Perkins Cove, Ogunquit, Maine, USA	Sept. 23, 1990	Linda M. Paul
W-24 kg (50 lb)	21.14 kg (46 lb 10 oz)	Perkins Cove, Ogunquit, Maine, USA	Oct. 24, 1990	Linda M. Paul

Pompano, African / *Alectis ciliaris*

LINE CLASS	WEIGHT	PLACE	DATE	ANGLER
M-01 kg (2 lb)	2.04 kg (4 lb 8 oz)	Nassau, Bahamas	Aug. 6, 1984	John R. Morley
M-02 kg (4 lb)	14.62 kg (32 lb 4 oz)	Palm Beach, Florida, USA	Apr. 1, 1985	Dave Hurst
M-03 kg (6 lb)	16.32 kg (36 lb 0 oz)	Miami Beach, Florida, USA	Jan. 31, 1997	Raleigh Werking
M-04 kg (8 lb)	18.37 kg (40 lb 8 oz)	Key West, Florida, USA	Feb. 24, 1996	Jim Waterman
M-06 kg (12 lb)	20.63 kg (45 lb 8 oz)	O'Quinns Channel, Stuart, Florida, USA	June 10, 1986	Dave Webb
M-08 kg (16 lb)	20.18 kg (44 lb 8 oz)	Jupiter, Florida, USA	Mar. 24, 1994	Ralph Kimball
M-10 kg (20 lb)	19.50 kg (43 lb 0 oz)	Hollywood, Florida, USA	Jan. 10, 1993	Neal Laue
M-15 kg (30 lb)	20.92 kg (46 lb 8 oz)	Jensen Beach, Florida, USA	Apr. 12, 1993	Kevyn R. Kaplowitz
M-24 kg (50 lb)	20.01 kg (44 lb 2 oz)	Stuart, Florida, USA	Jan. 5, 1991	Robin W. Frierson
W-01 kg (2 lb)	6.35 kg (14 lb 0 oz)	Key West, Florida, USA	May 13, 1994	Dixie Lee Burns
W-02 kg (4 lb)	9.72 kg (21 lb 8 oz)	Key West, Florida, USA	May 15, 1994	Sharan C. Kutner
W-03 kg (6 lb)	12.70 kg (28 lb 0 oz)	Miami Beach, Florida, USA	Jan. 21, 1995	Elizabeth Hogan
W-04 kg (8 lb)	17.23 kg (38 lb 0 oz)	Key Biscayne, Florida, USA	Dec. 18, 1993	Cornelia "Tomatoes" Schmitt
W-06 kg (12 lb)	15.87 kg (35 lb 0 oz)	Dry Tortugas, Florida, USA	Mar. 17, 1992	Mrs. William B. DuVal
W-08 kg (16 lb)	19.05 kg (42 lb 0 oz)	O'Quinn's Channel, Jupiter, Florida, USA	Feb. 23, 1997	Laurie Webb
W-10 kg (20 lb)	17.83 kg (39 lb 5 oz)	Ft. Pierce, Florida, USA	Apr. 27, 1985	Karen S. Hogan
W-15 kg (30 lb)	19.95 kg (44 lb 0 oz)	Jupiter, Florida, USA	Mar. 25, 1994	Renee Gamache
W-24 kg (50 lb)	16.10 kg (35 lb 8 oz)	Long Key, Florida, USA	Nov. 10, 1979	Mary Boggs

Queenfish / *Scomberoides commersonnianus & Scomberoides lysan*

LINE CLASS	WEIGHT	PLACE	DATE	ANGLER
M-01 kg (2 lb)	7.78 kg (17 lb 2 oz)	Russell Heads, N. Queensland, Australia	Aug. 16, 1986	G.A. Hart
M-02 kg (4 lb)	13.45 kg (29 lb 10 oz)	Port Douglas, Queensland, Australia	Mar. 19, 1989	Daniel Peter Bergamo
M-03 kg (6 lb)	9.00 kg (19 lb 13 oz)	Salt Creek, Groote Eylandt, Australia	May 26, 1998	Michael Ward-Grodd
M-04 kg (8 lb)	14.00 kg (30 lb 13 oz)	Townsville, Australia	July 10, 1983	Andrew Mead
M-06 kg (12 lb)	11.15 kg (24 lb 9 oz)	Sharker Point, N.T., Australia	Oct. 10, 1993	Chris Murdock
M-08 kg (16 lb)	10.00 kg (22 lb 0 oz)	Willie Creek, Broome, Australia	July 8, 1996	Laurie Chadder
M-10 kg (20 lb)	13.60 kg (30 lb 0 oz)	Endalgout Island, Australia	Oct. 20, 1996	Alan Richardson
M-15 kg (30 lb)	10.75 kg (23 lb 11 oz)	Colombo, Sri Lanka	Oct. 19, 1991	Harris N. De Lanerolle
M-24 kg (50 lb)	14.50 kg (31 lb 15 oz)	Bazaruto Island, Mozambique, Republic of South Africa	Jan. 18, 1991	Hilton Nichols
W-01 kg (2 lb)	4.80 kg (10 lb 9 oz)	Groote Eylandt, Australia	Feb. 2, 1993	Jane Manton
W-02 kg (4 lb)	6.60 kg (14 lb 8 oz)	Groote Eylandt, Australia	Aug. 5, 1988	Rosemary Riding
W-03 kg (6 lb)	7.50 kg (16 lb 8 oz)	Groote Eylandt, Australia	June 13, 1998	Melissa De Koning
W-04 kg (8 lb)	10.50 kg (23 lb 2 oz)	Dampier Archipelago, W.A., Australia	Apr. 14, 1991	Bron Rack
W-06 kg (12 lb)	15.60 kg (34 lb 6 oz)	Daintree River, North Queensland, Australia	Oct. 18, 1994	Kim Blackwell
W-08 kg (16 lb)	8.80 kg (19 lb 6 oz)	Groote Eylandt, Australia	June 13, 1998	Cheree Collins
W-10 kg (20 lb)	Vacant			
W-15 kg (30 lb)	Vacant			
W-24 kg (50 lb)	Vacant			

Roosterfish / *Nematistius pectoralis*

LINE CLASS	WEIGHT	PLACE	DATE	ANGLER
M-01 kg (2 lb)	13.00 kg (28 lb 10 oz)	Cabo San Lucas, Baja California Sur, Mexico	May 8, 1992	George E. Hogan, Jr.
M-02 kg (4 lb)	12.75 kg (28 lb 1 oz)	Zihuatanejo, Mexico	Sept. 28, 1992	H. Clay Johnson
M-03 kg (6 lb)	17.69 kg (39 lb 10 oz)	Buena Vista, B.C. Mexico	Aug. 10, 1977	Herbert R. Kameon
M-04 kg (8 lb)	19.05 kg (42 lb 0 oz)	Golfito, Costa Rica	May 19, 1990	Dr. Jerome N. Matthews
M-06 kg (12 lb)	32.00 kg (70 lb 8 oz)	Porto Escondito, Baja California, Mexico	June 12, 1992	Timothy S. O'Brien
M-08 kg (16 lb)	31.18 kg (68 lb 12 oz)	Gulf of Papagayo, Costa Rica	Oct. 9, 1992	John Porr
M-10 kg (20 lb)	38.92 kg (85 lb 13 oz)	La Paz, Baja California, Mexico	June 15, 1966	Willard E. Hanson
M-15 kg (30 lb)	51.71 kg (114 lb 0 oz)	La Paz, Baja California, Mexico	June 1, 1960	Abe Sackheim
M-24 kg (50 lb)	36.28 kg (80 lb 0 oz)	Cabo Blanco, Peru	June 13, 1954	Cloyce J. Tippett
M-37 kg (80 lb)	41.40 kg (91 lb 4 oz)	Manzanillo, Mexico	June 28, 1998	Eduardo Vergara Camou
M-60 kg (130 lb)	45.35 kg (100 lb 0 oz)	Cabo Blanco, Peru	Jan. 12, 1954	Miguel Barrenechea
W-01 kg (2 lb)	4.81 kg (10 lb 10 oz)	Isla Chame, Panama	Aug. 2, 1992	Renee M. Nellis

Roosterfish / *(continued)*

LINE CLASS	WEIGHT	PLACE	DATE	ANGLER
W-02 kg (4 lb)	11.79 kg (26 lb 0 oz)	Gulf of Papagayo, Costa Rica	Sept. 25, 1996	Beth Kleine
W-03 kg (6 lb)	19.73 kg (43 lb 8 oz)	Punta Colorado, Baja California Sur, Mexico	July 11, 1977	Pat Snyder
W-04 kg (8 lb)	27.21 kg (60 lb 0 oz)	Flamingo Bay, Costa Rica	Oct. 1, 1993	Virginia Jane Penley
W-06 kg (12 lb)	24.94 kg (55 lb 0 oz)	Cabo San Lucas, Baja California Sur, Mexico	Dec. 1, 1981	Susie Kritini
W-08 kg (16 lb)	28.60 kg (63 lb 0 oz)	Punta Colorado, Baja California Sur, Mexico	July 4, 1986	Pat Snyder
W-10 kg (20 lb)	40.00 kg (88 lb 2 oz)	Palmas de Cortez, Baja California, Mexico	May 27, 1982	Anne Purkis
W-15 kg (30 lb)	44.90 kg (99 lb 0 oz)	La Paz, Baja California, Mexico	Nov. 30, 1964	Lily Call
W-24 kg (50 lb)	38.61 kg (85 lb 2 oz)	La Paz, Baja California, Mexico	Nov. 24, 1956	Mrs. Esther Carle
W-37 kg (80 lb)	29.93 kg (66 lb 0 oz)	La Paz, Baja California, Mexico	Dec. 1, 1964	Lily Call
W-60 kg (130 lb)	19.50 kg (43 lb 0 oz)	Flamingo Bay, Costa Rica	July 16, 1992	Deborah Maddux Dunaway

Runner, rainbow / *Elagatis bipinnulata*

LINE CLASS	WEIGHT	PLACE	DATE	ANGLER
M-01 kg (2 lb)	4.53 kg (10 lb 0 oz)	Pinas Bay, Panama	Mar. 7, 1984	Marc Giraud
M-02 kg (4 lb)	5.89 kg (13 lb 0 oz)	Cozumel, Quintana Roo, Mexico	Apr. 4, 1982	Stephen Sloan
M-03 kg (6 lb)	7.99 kg (17 lb 10 oz)	Isla Coiba, Panama	Dec. 4, 1975	Stuart C. Apte
M-04 kg (8 lb)	8.84 kg (19 lb 8 oz)	Club Pacifico, Panama	Mar. 10, 1982	Kent M. Smith
M-06 kg (12 lb)	10.88 kg (24 lb 0 oz)	Tamarindo Beach, Costa Rica	Nov. 23, 1986	Anthony V. Spezzano
M-08 kg (16 lb)	9.97 kg (22 lb 0 oz)	Pinas Bay, Panama	Jan. 7, 1986	Adam Singer
M-10 kg (20 lb)	11.33 kg (25 lb 0 oz)	Pinas Bay, Panama	May 9, 1965	Donald J.S. Merten
M-15 kg (30 lb)	14.06 kg (31 lb 0 oz)	Isla Roca Partida, Revillagigedo Islands, Mexico	Dec. 3, 1981	Edward Gorecki
M-24 kg (50 lb)	15.25 kg (33 lb 10 oz)	Isla Clarion, Revillagigedo Islands, Mexico	Mar. 14, 1976	Ralph A. Mikkelsen
W-01 kg (2 lb)	3.74 kg (8 lb 4 oz)	Pinas Bay, Panama	July 1, 1984	Deborah L. McCollum
W-02 kg (4 lb)	6.46 kg (14 lb 4 oz)	Argus Bank, Bermuda	July 18, 1994	Mrs. William B. DuVal
W-03 kg (6 lb)	5.66 kg (12 lb 8 oz)	Pinas Bay, Panama	Dec. 10, 1975	Mary Wallace Josepho
W-04 kg (8 lb)	7.71 kg (17 lb 0 oz)	Key West, Florida, USA	Apr. 11, 1987	Ann Doan
W-06 kg (12 lb)	8.61 kg (19 lb 0 oz)	Club Pacifico, Panama	Jan. 21, 1982	Sue Kenyon
W-08 kg (16 lb)	10.16 kg (22 lb 6 oz)	Midway Islands	Sept. 2, 1998	Kater Bourdon
W-10 kg (20 lb)	8.76 kg (19 lb 5 oz)	Isla Roca Partida, Revillagigedo Islands, Mexico	Dec. 14, 1983	Sande Corey
W-15 kg (30 lb)	11.80 kg (26 lb 0 oz)	Buena Vista, Baja California, Mexico	Oct. 29, 1986	Marguerite E. Cascio
W-24 kg (50 lb)	10.43 kg (23 lb 0 oz)	Oahu, Hawaii, USA	May 9, 1961	Lila M. Neuenfelt

Sailfish, Atlantic / *Istiophorus platypterus*

LINE CLASS	WEIGHT	PLACE	DATE	ANGLER
M-01 kg (2 lb)	37.40 kg (82 lb 7 oz)	Dakar, Senegal	Aug. 5, 1990	Philippe Sleurs
M-02 kg (4 lb)	40.80 kg (89 lb 15 oz)	Dakar, Senegal	July 26, 1990	Philippe Sleurs
M-03 kg (6 lb)	39.00 kg (89 lb 15 oz)	Luanda, Angola	Feb. 14, 1974	A.de Jesus Gaspar dos Santos
M-04 kg (8 lb)	47.74 kg (105 lb 4 oz)	Key West, Florida, USA	Apr. 20, 1993	Christain Martin
M-06 kg (12 lb)	51.20 kg (112 lb 14 oz)	Sali Portudal, Senegal	Oct. 6, 1987	Pierre Laveissiere
M-08 kg (16 lb)	47.62 kg (105 lb 0 oz)	Key Largo, Florida, USA	Mar. 20, 1986	James E. Frasier
M-10 kg (20 lb)	58.00 kg (127 lb 13 oz)	Luanda, Angola	Mar. 30, 1975	Mario Rui Alves Da Silva
M-15 kg (30 lb)	55.20 kg (121 lb 11 oz)	Luanda, Angola	Feb. 25, 1996	Hakan Ekberg
M-24 kg (50 lb)	61.40 kg (135 lb 5 oz)	Lagos, Nigeria	Nov. 10, 1991	Ron King
M-37 kg (80 lb)	60.60 kg (133 lb 9 oz)	Luanda, Angola	Mar. 22, 1998	Eduardo Vale Moreira
W-01 kg (2 lb)	33.02 kg (72 lb 12 oz)	Dakar, Senegal	Aug. 5, 1988	Deborah Maddux Dunaway
W-02 kg (4 lb)	36.95 kg (81 lb 7 oz)	Hotel Esperon, Club de Saly, Senegal	Oct. 30, 1995	Odile Robelin
W-03 kg (6 lb)	41.20 kg (90 lb 13 oz)	Saly, Senegal	Sept. 19, 1996	Odile Robelin
W-04 kg (8 lb)	44.00 kg (97 lb 0 oz)	Vitoria Espirito, Santos, Brazil	Dec. 8, 1994	Ruth C. Stoky
W-06 kg (12 lb)	50.80 kg (112 lb 0 oz)	Cancun, Quintana Roo, Mexico	June 6, 1979	Gloria J. Applegate
W-08 kg (16 lb)	45.30 kg (99 lb 13 oz)	Dakar, Senegal	Aug. 23, 1984	Helene Tournier
W-08 kg (16 lb) Tie	45.34 kg (99 lb 15 oz)	Saly Portudal, Senegal	Oct. 5, 1987	Iomgard Laveissiere
W-10 kg (20 lb)	48.30 kg (106 lb 8 oz)	Luanda, Angola	Mar. 15, 1975	Mrs. Pamela Jean Durkin
W-15 kg (30 lb)	58.10 kg (128 lb 1 oz)	Luanda, Angola	Feb. 20, 1994	Bernadette O'Brien
W-24 kg (50 lb)	52.00 kg (114 lb 10 oz)	Principe Island, Sao Tome and Principe	Nov. 20, 1992	Annette Sparg
W-37 kg (80 lb)	41.27 kg (91 lb 0 oz)	Principe Island, Sao Tome and Principe	Oct. 21, 1993	Margot D. Vincent

Sailfish, Pacific / *Istiophorus platypterus*

LINE CLASS	WEIGHT	PLACE	DATE	ANGLER
M-01 kg (2 lb)	50.34 kg (111 lb 0 oz)	Flamingo Bay, Costa Rica	July 5, 1993	Jerry Dunaway
M-02 kg (4 lb)	64.18 kg (141 lb 8 oz)	Pinas Bay, Panama	Dec. 27, 1992	Raleigh Werking
M-03 kg (6 lb)	76.20 kg (168 lb 0 oz)	Salinas, Ecuador	Sept. 7, 1974	Santiago Maspons
M-04 kg (8 lb)	58.51 kg (129 lb 0 oz)	Coiba, Panama	Feb. 13, 1995	Jean Paul Richard
M-06 kg (12 lb)	77.79 kg (171 lb 8 oz)	Pinas Bay, Panama	Jan. 9, 1976	Felipe Estrada E.
M-06 kg (12 lb) Tie	77.95 kg (171 lb 13 oz)	Exmouth, W.A., Australia	Jan. 11, 1983	Vic Rayner
M-08 kg (16 lb)	63.50 kg (140 lb 0 oz)	Salinas, Ecuador	Jan. 30, 1983	Santiago Maspons
M-10 kg (20 lb)	87.54 kg (193 lb 0 oz)	Acapulco, Mexico	Jan. 8, 1978	Anthony T. Russo
M-15 kg (30 lb)	93.75 kg (206 lb 10 oz)	Tubbataha Reefs, Sulu Sea, Philippines	May 9, 1990	Noel R. Jones
M-24 kg (50 lb)	95.50 kg (210 lb 8 oz)	Eua Island, Kingdom of Tonga	July 7, 1990	Konrad Englberger
M-37 kg (80 lb)	89.81 kg (198 lb 0 oz)	Mazatlan, Mexico	Nov. 10, 1954	George N. Anglen
M-60 kg (130 lb)	100.24 kg (221 lb 0 oz)	Santa Cruz Island, Ecuador	Feb. 12, 1947	Carl W. Stewart
W-01 kg (2 lb)	46.26 kg (102 lb 0 oz)	Flamingo Bay, Costa Rica	July 19, 1992	Deborah Maddux Dunaway
W-02 kg (4 lb)	49.80 kg (109 lb 12 oz)	Golfito, Costa Rica	Jan. 25, 1989	Deborah Maddux Dunaway
W-03 kg (6 lb)	52.73 kg (116 lb 4 oz)	Pinas Bay, Panama	Aug. 19, 1975	Lovern K. Daniels
W-04 kg (8 lb)	58.96 kg (130 lb 0 oz)	Pinas Bay, Panama	Dec. 14, 1985	Marlene Vallarino
W-06 kg (12 lb)	66.45 kg (146 lb 8 oz)	Palmilla, Baja California, Mexico	Nov. 14, 1962	Evelyn M. Anderson
W-08 kg (16 lb)	60.00 kg (132 lb 4 oz)	Cape Moreton, N.S.W., Australia	Mar. 22, 1984	Lorrie Fay
W-10 kg (20 lb)	71.21 kg (157 lb 0 oz)	La Plata Island, Ecuador	Sept. 14, 1961	Jeannette Alford
W-15 kg (30 lb)	80.74 kg (178 lb 0 oz)	Santa Cruz Island, Ecuador	Feb. 27, 1955	Martha A. Hall
W-24 kg (50 lb)	87.09 kg (192 lb 0 oz)	La Paz, Baja California, Mexico	Sept. 6, 1950	Gay Thomas
W-37 kg (80 lb)	90.26 kg (199 lb 0 oz)	Pinas Bay, Panama	Jan. 17, 1968	Carolyn B. Steiner

Sailfish, Pacific / *(continued)*

LINE CLASS	WEIGHT	PLACE	DATE	ANGLER
W-60 kg (130 lb)	85.72 kg (189 lb 0 oz)	Yanuca, Fiji	Dec. 7, 1967	Mrs. C. L. Foster

Seabass, blackfin / *Lateolabrax latus*

LINE CLASS	WEIGHT	PLACE	DATE	ANGLER
M-01 kg (2 lb)	6.30 kg (13 lb 14 oz)	Shioya Port, Gobo-shi, Wakayama, Japan	Feb. 10, 1994	Toshinari Yoshimura
M-02 kg (4 lb)	7.70 kg (16 lb 15 oz)	Kawazu River, Shizuokaken, Japan	Mar. 15, 1996	Junichi Iso
M-03 kg (6 lb)	7.08 kg (15 lb 9 oz)	Chikura, Chiba, Japan	Apr. 18, 1998	Katsumi Shimada
M-04 kg (8 lb)	6.90 kg (15 lb 3 oz)	Azuchi Island, Nagasaki, Japan	Nov. 11, 1991	Sadao Sano
M-06 kg (12 lb)	9.10 kg (20 lb 0 oz)	Muroto, Kochi, Japan	July 13, 1997	Yuji Shimasaki
M-08 kg (16 lb)	8.30 kg (18 lb 4 oz)	Naminoura, Wakayama, Japan	Feb. 25, 1990	Takashi Tsujimoto
M-10 kg (20 lb)	7.85 kg (17 lb 4 oz)	Koza, Wakayama, Japan	Jan. 21, 1990	Toshimasa Yagi
M-15 kg (30 lb)	6.80 kg (14 lb 15 oz)	Shionomisaki, Kushimoto, Wakayama, Japan	Apr. 25, 1998	Shizuka Ueji
W-01 kg (2 lb)	Vacant			
W-02 kg (4 lb)	Vacant			
W-03 kg (6 lb)	Vacant			
W-04 kg (8 lb)	6.10 kg (13 lb 7 oz)	Azuchi Island, Nagasaki, Japan	Nov. 17, 1991	Mrs. Masako Tsurusaki
W-06 kg (12 lb)	3.35 kg (7 lb 6 oz)	Koza River, Wakayama, Japan	Sept. 11, 1993	Toshie Ikeda
W-08 kg (16 lb)	6.00 kg (13 lb 3 oz)	Koza River, Wakayama, Japan	Aug. 29, 1993	Toshie Ikeda
W-10 kg (20 lb)	Vacant			
W-15 kg (30 lb)	Vacant			

Seabass, Japanese / *Lateolabrax japonicus*

LINE CLASS	WEIGHT	PLACE	DATE	ANGLER
M-01 kg (2 lb)	7.10 kg (15 lb 10 oz)	Yakinoura Beach, Nagasaki, Japan	Apr. 2, 1990	Yoshitaka Tsurusaki
M-02 kg (4 lb)	7.90 kg (17 lb 6 oz)	Minato River, Chiba, Japan	Nov. 17, 1994	Yukio Yamazaki
M-03 kg (6 lb)	8.10 kg (17 lb 13 oz)	Yoshino River, Tokushima, Japan	May 3, 1995	Akira Miyoshi
M-04 kg (8 lb)	7.20 kg (15 lb 13 oz)	Sakata City, Yamagata, Japan	Nov. 2, 1990	Shinichi Kanai
M-06 kg (12 lb)	8.70 kg (19 lb 2 oz)	Kano River, Numazu-shi, Shizuoka, Japan	Nov. 26, 1988	Yasuaki Ohshio
M-08 kg (16 lb)	7.65 kg (16 lb 13 oz)	Karino River, Shizuoka, Japan	Dec. 22, 1983	Hiroshi Tokunaga
M-10 kg (20 lb)	6.52 kg (14 lb 5 oz)	Minato River, Futtsu-shi, Chiba, Japan	Dec. 29, 1995	Hiroya Sikegawa
M-15 kg (30 lb)	6.10 kg (13 lb 7 oz)	Minato River, Futtsu-shi, Chiba, Japan	Dec. 6, 1996	Akio Horie
W-01 kg (2 lb)	1.30 kg (2 lb 13 oz)	Kita Port, Osaka Bay, Osaka, Japan	May 29, 1991	Yukiko Matsumoto
W-02 kg (4 lb)	5.54 kg (12 lb 3 oz)	Kawasaki, Kanagawa, Japan	Nov. 29, 1993	Junko Tokunaga
W-03 kg (6 lb)	3.85 kg (8 lb 7 oz)	Ube Harbor, Chiba, Japan	Dec. 14, 1997	Tsuyako Ito
W-04 kg (8 lb)	4.45 kg (9 lb 12 oz)	Oi River, Shizuoka, Japan	Nov. 14, 1992	Yuko Suzuki
W-06 kg (12 lb)	8.30 kg (18 lb 4 oz)	Oi River, Shizuoka, Japan	Nov. 3, 1995	Yuko Suzuki
W-08 kg (16 lb)	Vacant			
W-10 kg (20 lb)	Vacant			
W-15 kg (30 lb)	Vacant			

Seabass, white / *Atractoscion nobilis*

LINE CLASS	WEIGHT	PLACE	DATE	ANGLER
M-01 kg (2 lb)	7.69 kg (16 lb 11 oz)	Catalina Island, California, USA	May 7, 1994	Thomas G. Pfleger
M-02 kg (4 lb)	9.59 kg (21 lb 2 oz)	Catalina Island, California, USA	Apr. 20, 1993	Tom Pfleger
M-03 kg (6 lb)	11.65 kg (25 lb 11 oz)	Catalina Island, California, USA	Apr. 7, 1995	Tom Pfleger
M-04 kg (8 lb)	17.69 kg (39 lb 0 oz)	Horseshoe Rock, Santa Barbara, California, USA	June 27, 1990	William S. Abel
M-06 kg (12 lb)	29.48 kg (65 lb 0 oz)	Ensenada, Baja California, Mexico	July 8, 1955	C. J. Aronis
M-08 kg (16 lb)	27.80 kg (61 lb 0 oz)	Imperial Beach, San Diego, California, USA	Apr. 24, 1993	Charles R. Rhodes
M-10 kg (20 lb)	33.56 kg (74 lb 0 oz)	San Clemente Island, California, USA	Dec. 29, 1982	Chris Brun
M-15 kg (30 lb)	37.98 kg (83 lb 12 oz)	San Felipe, Mexico	Mar. 31, 1953	Lyal C. Baumgardner
M-24 kg (50 lb)	35.04 kg (77 lb 4 oz)	San Diego, California, USA	Apr. 8, 1950	H. P. Bledsoe
M-37 kg (80 lb)	33.56 kg (74 lb 0 oz)	Catalina Island, California, USA	May 11, 1968	Allan D. Tromblay
W-01 kg (2 lb)	Vacant			
W-02 kg (4 lb)	7.37 kg (16 lb 4 oz)	Catalina Island, California, USA	May 15, 1992	Kathleen I. Franklin
W-03 kg (6 lb)	8.22 kg (18 lb 2 oz)	Catalina Island, California, USA	Apr. 21, 1995	Sandra "Honey" Beazley
W-04 kg (8 lb)	12.24 kg (27 lb 0 oz)	Catalina Island, California, USA	May 26, 1991	Alyson Gillett
W-06 kg (12 lb)	23.75 kg (52 lb 6 oz)	Newport Beach, California, USA	June 3, 1959	Ruth Jayred
W-08 kg (16 lb)	16.78 kg (37 lb 0 oz)	Catalina Island, California, USA	June 26, 1990	Magdelena Martinez
W-10 kg (20 lb)	28.12 kg (62 lb 0 oz)	Malibu, California, USA	Dec. 6, 1951	Mrs. D. W. Jackson
W-15 kg (30 lb)	26.98 kg (59 lb 8 oz)	Catalina Island, California, USA	May 2, 1968	Janice Jackson
W-24 kg (50 lb)	20.04 kg (44 lb 3 oz)	Catalina Island, California, USA	May 2, 1968	Gail Cruz
W-37 kg (80 lb)	Vacant			

Seatrout, spotted / *Cynoscion nebulosus*

LINE CLASS	WEIGHT	PLACE	DATE	ANGLER
M-01 kg (2 lb)	4.56 kg (10 lb 1 oz)	Daytona Beach, Florida, USA	Apr. 16, 1983	David Michael Fairbanks
M-02 kg (4 lb)	4.87 kg (10 lb 12 oz)	Halifax River, Ponce Inlet, Florida, USA	Apr. 12, 1983	Ben L. Britton
M-03 kg (6 lb)	5.98 kg (13 lb 3 oz)	Fort Pierce, Florida, USA	June 1, 1980	Winton P. McMillen
M-04 kg (8 lb)	6.12 kg (13 lb 8 oz)	Texas City Flats, Texas, USA	Nov. 17, 1984	Gerald Hernandez
M-06 kg (12 lb)	6.35 kg (14 lb 0 oz)	Ponce de Leon Inlet, Florida, USA	Aug. 10, 1972	Allen Kent Gibbens
M-08 kg (16 lb)	5.66 kg (12 lb 8 oz)	Crystal River, Florida, USA	Dec. 8, 1983	Tom E. Thorpe
M-08 kg (16 lb) Tie	5.69 kg (12 lb 9 oz)	Spruce Creek, Ponce Island, Florida, USA	Mar. 9, 1986	Lonnie L. Nelson
M-10 kg (20 lb)	7.92 kg (17 lb 7 oz)	Ft. Pierce, Florida, USA	May 11, 1995	Craig F. Carson
M-15 kg (30 lb)	6.97 kg (15 lb 6 oz)	Jensen Beach, Florida, USA	May 4, 1969	Michael J. Foremny
W-01 kg (2 lb)	4.36 kg (9 lb 10 oz)	Texas City Flats, Texas, USA	Oct. 27, 1984	Viola J. Hernandez
W-02 kg (4 lb)	4.70 kg (10 lb 6 oz)	Melbourne Beach, Florida, USA	Apr. 10, 1984	Barbara S. Arthur
W-03 kg (6 lb)	6.37 kg (14 lb 1 oz)	Satellite Beach, Florida, USA	Apr. 21, 1984	Sunae (Katie) Edwards
W-04 kg (8 lb)	6.52 kg (14 lb 6 oz)	Texas City Flats, Texas, USA	Nov. 17, 1984	Viola J. Hernandez
W-06 kg (12 lb)	5.49 kg (12 lb 2 oz)	Melbourne Beach, Florida, USA	May 6, 1986	Barbara Smith Arthur
W-08 kg (16 lb)	5.31 kg (11 lb 11 oz)	Melbourne Beach, Florida, USA	Jan. 11, 1987	Barbara Smith Arthur
W-10 kg (20 lb)	4.79 kg (10 lb 9 oz)	Banana River, Florida, USA	July 12, 1979	Jackie M. Patton

Seatrout, spotted / *(continued)*

LINE CLASS	WEIGHT	PLACE	DATE	ANGLER
W-15 kg (30 lb)	6.35 kg (14 lb 0 oz)	Stuart, Florida, USA	Apr. 25, 1970	Marilyn C. Albright

Shark, blue / *Prionace glauca*

LINE CLASS	WEIGHT	PLACE	DATE	ANGLER
M-01 kg (2 lb)	53.97 kg (119 lb 0 oz)	Shinnecock, Long Island, New York, USA	July 1, 1983	Stephen Sloan
M-02 kg (4 lb)	83.46 kg (184 lb 0 oz)	Montauk, Long Island, New York, USA	Oct. 7, 1984	Stephen Sloan
M-03 kg (6 lb)	113.85 kg (251 lb 0 oz)	Montauk, Long Island, New York, USA	Oct. 5, 1981	Stephen Sloan
M-04 kg (8 lb)	115.50 kg (254 lb 10 oz)	East Port Hacking, Australia	Nov. 20, 1983	Denis Pearce
M-06 kg (12 lb)	179.50 kg (395 lb 11 oz)	Port Hacking, Sydney, Australia	Nov. 3, 1992	Robert Egan
M-08 kg (16 lb)	189.00 kg (416 lb 10 oz)	Botany Bay, Sydney, Australia	Nov. 3, 1985	Jayson Heyward
M-10 kg (20 lb)	166.00 kg (365 lb 15 oz)	Wollongong, Australia	Oct. 3, 1993	Brad Major
M-15 kg (30 lb)	198.22 kg (437 lb 0 oz)	Catherine Bay, N.S.W., Australia	Oct. 2, 1976	Peter Hyde
M-24 kg (50 lb)	198.10 kg (436 lb 11 oz)	Mayor Island, Bay of Plenty, New Zealand	Feb. 8, 1993	Graeme Smith
M-37 kg (80 lb)	205.93 kg (454 lb 0 oz)	Martha's Vineyard, Massachusetts, USA	July 19, 1996	Pete Bergin
M-60 kg (130 lb)	181.43 kg (400 lb 0 oz)	Le Morne, Mauritius	Oct. 17, 1976	Philip Fleming
W-01 kg (2 lb)	39.46 kg (87 lb 0 oz)	Snug Harbor, Rhode Island, USA	July 18, 1997	Shawna M. Oliver
W-02 kg (4 lb)	70.00 kg (154 lb 5 oz)	Whakatane, New Zealand	Mar. 26, 1989	Cynthia Dreifuss
W-03 kg (6 lb)	87.54 kg (193 lb 0 oz)	Botany, N.S.W., Australia	Dec. 15, 1974	Dulcie Chee
W-04 kg (8 lb)	118.00 kg (260 lb 2 oz)	Port Hacking, N.S.W., Australia	Aug. 26, 1995	Kylie P. Daly
W-06 kg (12 lb)	140.00 kg (308 lb 10 oz)	Swansea, N.S.W., Australia	Sept. 29, 1990	Michelle Jones
W-08 kg (16 lb)	143.50 kg (316 lb 5 oz)	East Port Hacking, Sydney, Australia	Oct. 5, 1996	Danielle Williams
W-10 kg (20 lb)	167.00 kg (368 lb 2 oz)	Swansea, N.S.W., Australia	Nov. 3, 1984	Narelle Wanless
W-15 kg (30 lb)	191.80 kg (422 lb 13 oz)	Te Kaha, New Zealand	Feb. 23, 1994	Martha Walker
W-24 kg (50 lb)	170.60 kg (376 lb 1 oz)	Tutukaka, New Zealand	Mar. 19, 1984	Bernadette Brown
W-37 kg (80 lb)	185.97 kg (410 lb 0 oz)	Rockport, Massachusetts, USA	Aug. 17, 1967	Martha C. Webster
W-60 kg (130 lb)	151.50 kg (334 lb 0 oz)	Rockport, Massachusetts, USA	Sept. 4, 1964	Cassandra Webster

Shark, hammerhead / *Sphyrna spp*

LINE CLASS	WEIGHT	PLACE	DATE	ANGLER
M-01 kg (2 lb)	4.53 kg (10 lb 0 oz)	Biscayne Bay, Miami, Florida, USA	Sept. 10, 1983	Max L. Kamerman
M-02 kg (4 lb)	12.36 kg (27 lb 4 oz)	Port Canaveral, Florida, USA	July 12, 1984	Troy Perez
M-03 kg (6 lb)	46.20 kg (101 lb 13 oz)	Luanda, Angola	Dec. 29, 1974	M. Quintela Maia de Loureiro
M-04 kg (8 lb)	88.11 kg (194 lb 4 oz)	Key West, Florida, USA	Feb. 22, 1991	Herbert G. Ratner, Jr.
M-06 kg (12 lb)	151.95 kg (335 lb 0 oz)	Miami, Florida, USA	Mar. 19, 1977	Bill Peacock
M-08 kg (16 lb)	153.80 kg (339 lb 1 oz)	Takau Bay, Bay of Islands, New Zealand	Apr. 7, 1992	Geoff Stone
M-10 kg (20 lb)	184.00 kg (405 lb 10 oz)	East Botany Bay, Sydney, Australia	Jan. 29, 1984	Barry Yates
M-15 kg (30 lb)	258.00 kg (568 lb 12 oz)	Port Stephens, N.S.W., Australia	Feb. 27, 1994	Denis Castronini
M-24 kg (50 lb)	246.98 kg (544 lb 8 oz)	Boca Grande, Florida, USA	May 20, 1981	Clark Balsinger
M-37 kg (80 lb)	281.23 kg (620 lb 0 oz)	Freeport, Texas, USA	Aug. 15, 1976	Dan Wright
M-60 kg (130 lb)	449.50 kg (991 lb 0 oz)	Sarasota, Florida, USA	May 30, 1982	Allen Ogle
W-01 kg (2 lb)	3.17 kg (7 lb 0 oz)	Sugarloaf Key, Florida, USA	Sept. 17, 1983	Jacqueline Leader
W-02 kg (4 lb)	17.00 kg (37 lb 7 oz)	Whitsunday's, N. Queensland, Australia	Feb. 16, 1986	Teena Draper
W-03 kg (6 lb)	7.04 kg (15 lb 8 oz)	Hilton Head Island, South Carolina, USA	June 9, 1998	Tonya B. Jones
W-04 kg (8 lb)	15.08 kg (33 lb 4 oz)	Pinas Bay, Panama	Jan. 25, 1994	Deborah Maddux Dunaway
W-06 kg (12 lb)	139.00 kg (306 lb 7 oz)	Auckland, New Zealand	Dec. 29, 1986	Raewyn Curin
W-08 kg (16 lb)	111.00 kg (244 lb 11 oz)	Cape Brett, New Zealand	Feb. 1, 1985	Viki Johnson
W-10 kg (20 lb)	189.00 kg (416 lb 10 oz)	Port Stephens, N.S.W., Australia	Feb. 26, 1984	Monique Eady
W-15 kg (30 lb)	185.00 kg (407 lb 13 oz)	Bermagui, N.S.W., Australia	Jan. 21, 1984	Stephenie Newman
W-24 kg (50 lb)	340.19 kg (750 lb 0 oz)	Boca Grande, Florida, USA	June 8, 1986	Connie L. Cora
W-37 kg (80 lb)	210.01 kg (463 lb 0 oz)	Key Largo, Florida, USA	Apr. 30, 1993	Heidi Mason
W-60 kg (130 lb)	184.16 kg (406 lb 0 oz)	Lottin Point, New Zealand	Feb. 26, 1974	H. M. Wood

Shark, mako / *Isurus spp*

LINE CLASS	WEIGHT	PLACE	DATE	ANGLER
M-01 kg (2 lb)	37.00 kg (81 lb 9 oz)	Cabo San Lucas, Baja California Sur, Mexico	May 5, 1992	George E. Hogan, Jr.
M-02 kg (4 lb)	75.00 kg (165 lb 5 oz)	Port Hacking, N.S.W., Australia	Sept. 30, 1989	Edward Paul Caughlan
M-03 kg (6 lb)	155.13 kg (342 lb 0 oz)	Port Hacking, N.S.W., Australia	Sept. 22, 1974	Norman Richard Smith
M-04 kg (8 lb)	95.00 kg (209 lb 6 oz)	Kaikoura, New Zealand	Feb. 28, 1998	David W. Tattle
M-06 kg (12 lb)	296.00 kg (652 lb 8 oz)	Port Hacking, Australia	July 10, 1997	Jason Andrew Caughlan
M-08 kg (16 lb)	317.50 kg (699 lb 15 oz)	Sydney, Botany Bay, Australia	Oct. 30, 1993	Mark Johnston
M-10 kg (20 lb)	329.00 kg (725 lb 5 oz)	Swansea, N.S.W., Australia	Nov. 25, 1979	Neil Williamson
M-15 kg (30 lb)	443.50 kg (977 lb 11 oz)	Botany Bay, Sydney, Australia	Nov. 4, 1995	Andrew Nasr
M-24 kg (50 lb)	489.88 kg (1080 lb 0 oz)	Montauk, New York, USA	Aug. 26, 1979	James L. Melanson
M-37 kg (80 lb)	488.00 kg (1075 lb 13 oz)	Puerto Rico, Spain	July 22, 1997	Steven Courtney
M-60 kg (130 lb)	505.76 kg (1115 lb 0 oz)	Black River, Mauritius	Nov. 16, 1988	Patrick Guillanton
W-01 kg (2 lb)	19.00 kg (41 lb 14 oz)	Tutukaka, New Zealand	Mar. 26, 1995	Kelly Pou
W-02 kg (4 lb)	7.80 kg (17 lb 3 oz)	Tutukaka, New Zealand	Mar. 8, 1995	Kelly Pou
W-03 kg (6 lb)	52.16 kg (115 lb 0 oz)	Botany Bay, N.S.W., Australia	Oct. 27, 1974	Dulcie Chee
W-04 kg (8 lb)	48.90 kg (107 lb 12 oz)	Blackhead, Hawke Bay, New Zealand	Feb. 18, 1997	Tobi Jayne Henderson
W-06 kg (12 lb)	131.20 kg (289 lb 3 oz)	Port Hacking, Australia	Sept. 30, 1995	Kylie Daly
W-08 kg (16 lb)	150.50 kg (331 lb 12 oz)	Sydney, Australia	May 4, 1986	Connie Rolley
W-10 kg (20 lb)	181.00 kg (399 lb 0 oz)	Port Stephens, N.S.W., Australia	Mar. 3, 1990	Cheryl Adams
W-15 kg (30 lb)	288.00 kg (634 lb 14 oz)	Port Stephens, N.S.W., Australia	Feb. 29, 1992	Cheryl Adams
W-24 kg (50 lb)	316.20 kg (697 lb 0 oz)	Tutukaka, New Zealand	Feb. 9, 1986	Joy Clements
W-24 kg (50 lb) Tie	317.00 kg (698 lb 13 oz)	Redhead, N.S.W., Australia	Oct. 11, 1987	Lesley Martin
W-37 kg (80 lb)	399.16 kg (880 lb 0 oz)	Bimini, Bahamas	Aug. 3, 1964	Florence Lotierzo
W-60 kg (130 lb)	413.56 kg (911 lb 12 oz)	Palm Beach, Florida, USA	Apr. 9, 1962	Audrey Cohen

Shark, porbeagle / *Lamna nasus*

LINE CLASS	WEIGHT	PLACE	DATE	ANGLER
M-01 kg (2 lb)	Vacant			

Shark, porbeagle / *(continued)*

LINE CLASS	WEIGHT	PLACE	DATE	ANGLER
M-02 kg (4 lb)	48.75 kg (107 lb 7 oz)	Gosport, England	Aug. 8, 1984	Denis J. Froud
M-03 kg (6 lb)	62.90 kg (138 lb 10 oz)	Otago Heads, New Zealand	May 24, 1998	Dave Carr
M-04 kg (8 lb)	98.43 kg (217 lb 0 oz)	Padstow, Cornwall, England	July 11, 1984	Ian Bunney
M-06 kg (12 lb)	111.58 kg (246 lb 0 oz)	Padstow, Cornwall, England	Sept. 7, 1983	Ian Bunney
M-08 kg (16 lb)	173.27 kg (382 lb 0 oz)	Hartland Point, Devon, Cornwall, England	July 28, 1982	Brian Stewart Taylor
M-10 kg (20 lb)	152.40 kg (336 lb 0 oz)	Padstow, Cornwall, England	June 20, 1982	Ian Bunney
M-15 kg (30 lb)	188.69 kg (416 lb 0 oz)	Padstow, Cornwall, England	May 26, 1986	Ian Bunney
M-24 kg (50 lb)	188.00 kg (414 lb 7 oz)	Pentland Firth, Scotland	Mar. 9, 1992	Robert Richardson
M-37 kg (80 lb)	230.00 kg (507 lb 0 oz)	Pentland Firth, Caithness, Scotland	Mar. 9, 1993	Christopher Bennett
M-60 kg (130 lb)	210.92 kg (465 lb 0 oz)	Padstow, Cornwall, England	July 23, 1976	Jorge Potier
W-01 kg (2 lb)	Vacant			
W-02 kg (4 lb)	Vacant			
W-03 kg (6 lb)	Vacant			
W-04 kg (8 lb)	Vacant			
W-06 kg (12 lb)	39.68 kg (87 lb 8 oz)	Padstow, Cornwall, England	June 16, 1984	Pamela Jane Bunney
W-08 kg (16 lb)	Vacant			
W-10 kg (20 lb)	Vacant			
W-15 kg (30 lb)	100.92 kg (222 lb 8 oz)	Isle of Wight, England	Aug. 14, 1969	Mrs. Paula Everington
W-24 kg (50 lb)	108.18 kg (238 lb 8 oz)	Montauk, New York, USA	May 17, 1966	Bea Harry
W-37 kg (80 lb)	107.04 kg (236 lb 0 oz)	Padstow, Cornwall, England	Aug. 1, 1981	Mrs. Marie Potier
W-60 kg (130 lb)	167.37 kg (369 lb 0 oz)	Looe, Cornwall, England	July 20, 1970	Mrs. Patricia Winifred Smith

Shark, thresher / *Alopias spp*

LINE CLASS	WEIGHT	PLACE	DATE	ANGLER
M-01 kg (2 lb)	Vacant			
M-02 kg (4 lb)	16.32 kg (36 lb 0 oz)	Santa Monica Bay, California, USA	Apr. 12, 1989	Robert I. Levy
M-03 kg (6 lb)	41.50 kg (91 lb 8 oz)	Santa Monica Bay, California, USA	May 14, 1977	James D. Olson
M-04 kg (8 lb)	26.85 kg (59 lb 3 oz)	False Bay, South Africa	Feb. 22, 1997	Mike Casserley
M-06 kg (12 lb)	89.40 kg (197 lb 1 oz)	Kilcunda, Victoria, Australia	Dec. 4, 1997	Russell Taylor
M-08 kg (16 lb)	97.52 kg (215 lb 0 oz)	Santa Monica Bay, California, USA	Oct. 18, 1997	Donald McPherson, Jr.
M-10 kg (20 lb)	119.00 kg (262 lb 5 oz)	Mdumbi, Transkei	Dec. 16, 1991	Gregory Tew
M-15 kg (30 lb)	220.00 kg (485 lb 0 oz)	Albarella, Adriatic Sea	Aug. 14, 1996	Vittadello Massimo
M-24 kg (50 lb)	348.00 kg (767 lb 3 oz)	Bay of Islands, New Zealand	Feb. 26, 1983	D.L. Hannah
M-37 kg (80 lb)	335.20 kg (739 lb 0 oz)	Tutukaka, New Zealand	Feb. 17, 1975	Brian Galvin
M-60 kg (130 lb)	306.62 kg (676 lb 0 oz)	Mayor Island, New Zealand	Feb. 23, 1978	Robert Charles Faulkner
W-01 kg (2 lb)	Vacant			
W-02 kg (4 lb)	Vacant			
W-03 kg (6 lb)	15.42 kg (34 lb 0 oz)	Santa Monica Bay, California, USA	June 8, 1977	Ruth Kameon
W-04 kg (8 lb)	Vacant			
W-06 kg (12 lb)	62.59 kg (138 lb 0 oz)	Santa Monica Bay, California, USA	May 15, 1977	Sylvia A. Naibert
W-08 kg (16 lb)	63.95 kg (141 lb 0 oz)	Santa Monica Bay, California, USA	Oct. 20, 1987	Lisa Zipser Derr
W-10 kg (20 lb)	79.15 kg (174 lb 8 oz)	Santa Monica Bay, California, USA	May 28, 1977	Sylvia A. Naibert
W-15 kg (30 lb)	136.90 kg (302 lb 0 oz)	Kona Coast, Hawaii, USA	May 28, 1994	Jocelyn J. Everette
W-24 kg (50 lb)	203.21 kg (448 lb 0 oz)	Montauk, New York, USA	July 8, 1984	Lynnette M. Pintauro
W-37 kg (80 lb)	363.80 kg (802 lb 0 oz)	Tutukaka, New Zealand	Feb. 8, 1981	Dianne North
W-60 kg (130 lb)	330.67 kg (729 lb 0 oz)	Mayor Island, New Zealand	June 3, 1959	Mrs. V. Brown

Shark, tiger / *Galeocerdo cuvier*

LINE CLASS	WEIGHT	PLACE	DATE	ANGLER
M-01 kg (2 lb)	1.64 kg (3 lb 10 oz)	Boca Raton, Florida, USA	June 19, 1991	Jim Ingalls
M-02 kg (4 lb)	72.12 kg (159 lb 0 oz)	Key West, Florida, USA	Mar. 17, 1991	Herbert G. Ratner, Jr.
M-03 kg (6 lb)	115.89 kg (255 lb 8 oz)	Key West, Florida, USA	Feb. 20, 1990	Herbert G. Ratner, Jr.
M-04 kg (8 lb)	Vacant			
M-06 kg (12 lb)	164.42 kg (362 lb 8 oz)	Islamorada, Florida, USA	Apr. 1, 1983	Andrew A. MacGrath
M-08 kg (16 lb)	344.50 kg (759 lb 7 oz)	East Swansea, N.S.W., Australia	May 22, 1993	Peter David Noakes
M-10 kg (20 lb)	411.50 kg (907 lb 3 oz)	Swansea, N.S.W., Australia	Nov. 22, 1981	Gary Hoff
M-10 kg (20 lb) Tie	412.00 kg (908 lb 4 oz)	Broughton Island, Australia	June 7, 1986	Mick Volkens
M-15 kg (30 lb)	619.00 kg (1364 lb 10 oz)	Swansea, N.S.W., Australia	Sept. 29, 1990	Glen Kirkwood
M-24 kg (50 lb)	579.50 kg (1277 lb 9 oz)	Swansea, N.S.W., Australia	June 1, 1996	Trent Visscher
M-37 kg (80 lb)	591.94 kg (1305 lb 0 oz)	Sydney, N.S.W., Australia	May 17, 1959	Samuel Jamieson
M-60 kg (130 lb)	807.40 kg (1780 lb 0 oz)	Cherry Grove, South Carolina, USA	June 14, 1964	Walter Maxwell
W-01 kg (2 lb)	Vacant			
W-02 kg (4 lb)	7.70 kg (16 lb 15 oz)	Shute Harbour, Queensland, Australia	Apr. 11, 1987	Tracy Hallam
W-03 kg (6 lb)	Vacant			
W-04 kg (8 lb)	49.24 kg (108 lb 9 oz)	Key West, Florida, USA	Feb. 13, 1991	Dixie Lee Burns
W-06 kg (12 lb)	97.97 kg (216 lb 0 oz)	Key West, Florida, USA	Feb. 5, 1991	Barbara A. Martin
W-08 kg (16 lb)	163.29 kg (360 lb 0 oz)	Gulf of Mexico, Boca Grande, Florida, USA	May 30, 1988	Connie L. Cora
W-10 kg (20 lb)	194.00 kg (427 lb 11 oz)	Broken Bay, Sydney, Australia	Mar. 15, 1997	Sharon Hegner
W-15 kg (30 lb)	548.00 kg (1208 lb 1 oz)	N.S.W., Australia	Apr. 16, 1989	Leanne Grieves
W-24 kg (50 lb)	497.00 kg (1095 lb 10 oz)	Swansea, N.S.W., Australia	Mar. 17, 1985	Bronwyn L. Norris
W-37 kg (80 lb)	532.06 kg (1173 lb 0 oz)	Cronulla, N.S.W., Australia	Mar. 24, 1963	June Irene Turnbull
W-60 kg (130 lb)	596.02 kg (1314 lb 0 oz)	Cape Moreton, Queensland, Australia	July 27, 1953	Mrs. Robert Dyer

Shark, tope / *Galeorhinus galeus*

LINE CLASS	WEIGHT	PLACE	DATE	ANGLER
M-01 kg (2 lb)	22.30 kg (49 lb 2 oz)	Parengarenga Harbor, New Zealand	Jan. 14, 1990	Mark Feldman
M-02 kg (4 lb)	25.10 kg (55 lb 5 oz)	Parengarenga Harbor, New Zealand	Jan. 14, 1990	Mark Feldman
M-03 kg (6 lb)	Vacant			
M-04 kg (8 lb)	26.70 kg (58 lb 13 oz)	Parengarenga Harbor, New Zealand	Dec. 16, 1986	Mark L. Feldman
M-06 kg (12 lb)	29.00 kg (63 lb 14 oz)	Parengarenga Harbor, New Zealand	Dec. 16, 1986	Mark L. Feldman

Shark, tope / *(continued)*

M-08 kg (16 lb)	32.50 kg (71 lb 10 oz)	Parengarenga Harbor, New Zealand	Jan. 4, 1991	Toby Martens
M-10 kg (20 lb)	26.36 kg (58 lb 2 oz)	Baggy Pt., North Devon, England	Oct. 22, 1982	Raymond John White
M-15 kg (30 lb)	44.67 kg (98 lb 8 oz)	Santa Monica, California, USA	Oct. 20, 1994	Fred Oakley
M-24 kg (50 lb)	32.50 kg (71 lb 10 oz)	Knysna, Republic of South Africa	July 10, 1982	William F. De Wet
M-37 kg (80 lb)	30.25 kg (66 lb 11 oz)	Parengarenga Harbor, New Zealand	Jan. 1, 1987	Wes Martens
W-01 kg (2 lb)	16.50 kg (36 lb 6 oz)	Parengarenga Harbor, New Zealand	Jan. 29, 1987	Elizabeth M. Feldman
W-02 kg (4 lb)	17.50 kg (38 lb 9 oz)	Parengarenga Harbor, New Zealand	Jan. 30, 1987	Melanie Feldman
W-03 kg (6 lb)	Vacant			
W-04 kg (8 lb)	24.40 kg (53 lb 12 oz)	Parengarenga Harbor, New Zealand	Dec. 3, 1987	Laurel Martens
W-06 kg (12 lb)	31.00 kg (68 lb 5 oz)	Parengarenga Harbor, New Zealand	Dec. 20, 1987	Heather M. Morton
W-08 kg (16 lb)	28.40 kg (62 lb 9 oz)	Parengarenga Harbor, New Zealand	Nov. 29, 1987	Jennifer Sutton
W-10 kg (20 lb)	27.50 kg (60 lb 10 oz)	Parengarenga Harbor, New Zealand	Dec. 12, 1987	Jenepher Cummins
W-15 kg (30 lb)	24.00 kg (52 lb 14 oz)	Parengarenga Harbor, New Zealand	Dec. 3, 1985	Melanie Feldman
W-24 kg (50 lb)	33.00 kg (72 lb 12 oz)	Parengarenga Harbor, New Zealand	Dec. 19, 1986	Melanie B. Feldman
W-37 kg (80 lb)	30.50 kg (67 lb 3 oz)	Parengarenga Harbor, New Zealand	Nov. 28, 1987	Jessica Lightband

Shark, white / *Carcharodon carcharias*

LINE CLASS	WEIGHT	PLACE	DATE	ANGLER
M-01 kg (2 lb)	Vacant			
M-02 kg (4 lb)	Vacant			
M-03 kg (6 lb)	Vacant			
M-04 kg (8 lb)	Vacant			
M-06 kg (12 lb)	81.00 kg (178 lb 9 oz)	Dudley, N.S.W., Australia	May 5, 1991	David Ashman
M-08 kg (16 lb)	95.50 kg (210 lb 8 oz)	Swansea, N.S.W., Australia	Oct. 29, 1983	Gary Kenneth Hoff
M-10 kg (20 lb)	484.44 kg (1068 lb 0 oz)	Cape Moreton, Queensland, Australia	June 18, 1957	Robert Dyer
M-15 kg (30 lb)	699.50 kg (1542 lb 1 oz)	Port Lincoln, Australia	July 5, 1997	Rolf Czabayski
M-24 kg (50 lb)	850.94 kg (1876 lb 0 oz)	Cape Moreton, Queensland, Australia	Aug. 6, 1955	Robert Dyer
M-37 kg (80 lb)	1063.23 kg (2344 lb 0 oz)	Streaky Bay, South Australia	Nov. 6, 1960	Alfred Dean
M-60 kg (130 lb)	1208.38 kg (2664 lb 0 oz)	Ceduna, South Australia	Apr. 21, 1959	Alfred Dean
W-01 kg (2 lb)	Vacant			
W-02 kg (4 lb)	Vacant			
W-03 kg (6 lb)	Vacant			
W-04 kg (8 lb)	Vacant			
W-06 kg (12 lb)	Vacant			
W-08 kg (16 lb)	Vacant			
W-10 kg (20 lb)	167.37 kg (369 lb 0 oz)	Cape Moreton, Queensland, Australia	July 6, 1957	Mrs. Robert Dyer
W-15 kg (30 lb)	364.23 kg (803 lb 0 oz)	Cape Moreton, Queensland, Australia	July 5, 1957	Mrs. Robert Dyer
W-24 kg (50 lb)	363.33 kg (801 lb 0 oz)	Cape Moreton, Queensland, Australia	June 11, 1957	Mrs. Robert Dyer
W-37 kg (80 lb)	413.68 kg (912 lb 0 oz)	Cape Moreton, Queensland, Australia	Aug. 29, 1954	Mrs. Robert Dyer
W-60 kg (130 lb)	528.00 kg (1164 lb 0 oz)	The Pages, South Australia	Mar. 11, 1994	Janet Forster

Skipjack, black / *Euthynnus lineatus*

LINE CLASS	WEIGHT	PLACE	DATE	ANGLER
M-01 kg (2 lb)	2.58 kg (5 lb 11 oz)	Isla Roca Partida, Revillagigedo Islands, Mexico	Oct. 19, 1986	Butch Green
M-02 kg (4 lb)	4.63 kg (10 lb 3 oz)	Vinoramas, San Jose del Cabo, Baja Mexico	Apr. 21, 1994	George Bogen
M-03 kg (6 lb)	4.13 kg (9 lb 2 oz)	Isla Coiba, Panama	Aug. 1, 1979	Higinio Jiminez C.
M-04 kg (8 lb)	6.57 kg (14 lb 8 oz)	Cabo San Lucas, Baja California Sur, Mexico	May 25, 1990	Bill A. Young
M-06 kg (12 lb)	5.78 kg (12 lb 12 oz)	Alijos Rocks, Baja California, Mexico	Sept. 25, 1978	Fred Christopherson
M-08 kg (16 lb)	8.33 kg (18 lb 6 oz)	Isla Cerralvo, Baja California, Mexico	July 4, 1989	John P. Whalen
M-10 kg (20 lb)	7.14 kg (15 lb 12 oz)	Alijos Rocks, Mexico	Sept. 7, 1985	Roy R. Ludt
M-15 kg (30 lb)	11.79 kg (26 lb 0 oz)	Thetis Bank, Baja California, Mexico	Oct. 23, 1991	Clifford K. Hamaishi
W-01 kg (2 lb)	1.83 kg (4 lb 0 oz)	Zihuatanejo, Mexico	Apr. 7, 1995	Irene McDonald Johnson
W-02 kg (4 lb)	5.15 kg (11 lb 6 oz)	Bahia San Francisquito, Baja California, Mexico	Oct. 9, 1983	Susan Seefeldt
W-03 kg (6 lb)	6.57 kg (14 lb 8 oz)	Cabo San Lucas, Baja California Sur, Mexico	May 24, 1977	Lorraine Carlton
W-04 kg (8 lb)	2.50 kg (5 lb 8 oz)	Zihuatanejo, Mexico	Apr. 6, 1996	Irene McDonald Johnson
W-06 kg (12 lb)	7.71 kg (17 lb 0 oz)	La Paz, Baja California, Mexico	May 27, 1988	Agnes H. (Pug) Jones
W-08 kg (16 lb)	7.71 kg (17 lb 0 oz)	La Paz, Baja California, Mexico	May 27, 1988	Agnes H. (Pug) Jones
W-10 kg (20 lb)	5.95 kg (13 lb 2 oz)	Thetis Bank, Baja California, Mexico	Sept. 27, 1976	Barbara McKinney
W-10 kg (20 lb) Tie	5.98 kg (13 lb 3 oz)	Loreto, Baja California, Mexico	Aug. 20, 1988	Louise Prentice
W-15 kg (30 lb)	6.80 kg (15 lb 0 oz)	La Paz, Baja California, Mexico	May 27, 1988	Agnes H. (Pug) Jones

Snapper (squirefish) / *Pagrus auratus*

LINE CLASS	WEIGHT	PLACE	DATE	ANGLER
M-01 kg (2 lb)	Vacant			
M-02 kg (4 lb)	8.60 kg (18 lb 15 oz)	Roberton Island, Bay of Islands, New Zealand	Dec. 9, 1996	Tony Bird
M-03 kg (6 lb)	9.31 kg (20 lb 8 oz)	Pinnacles, Poor Knights, New Zealand	Oct. 6, 1996	Ken McDowall
M-04 kg (8 lb)	15.20 kg (33 lb 8 oz)	Outer Harbor, Australia	Sept. 22, 1997	Shaun Polley
M-06 kg (12 lb)	150 kg (33 lb 1 oz)	Deep Water Cave, Bay of Islands, New Zealand	Jan. 27, 1994	Kiyotaka Ikegami
M-08 kg (16 lb)	14.25 kg (31 lb 6 oz)	Omaio, Te Kaha, New Zealand	Jan. 15, 1995	Gordon C. Sutherland
M-10 kg (20 lb)	15.00 kg (33 lb 1 oz)	Outer Harbour, Port Adelaide, Australia	Sept. 22, 1997	Roger John Harrison, N.F.C.
M-15 kg (30 lb)	13.40 kg (29 lb 8 oz)	Pinnicals, New Zealand	Nov. 8, 1997	Daniel Hart
W-01 kg (2 lb)	Vacant			
W-02 kg (4 lb)	4.11 kg (9 lb 0 oz)	Bay of Islands, New Zealand	Dec. 1, 1997	Bonita Jane Lyn Koch
W-03 kg (6 lb)	7.40 kg (16 lb 5 oz)	Poor Knights, New Zealand	Sept. 11, 1996	Alana Sardelich
W-04 kg (8 lb)	7.49 kg (16 lb 8 oz)	Motiti Island, Mount Maunganui, New Zealand	Nov. 5, 1994	Cheryl A. Murphy
W-06 kg (12 lb)	11.00 kg (24 lb 4 oz)	Doubtless Bay, New Zealand	Jan. 2, 1996	Rachael Downs-Honey
W-08 kg (16 lb)	9.00 kg (19 lb 13 oz)	Mokohinau Islands, New Zealand	Nov. 1, 1997	Margaret Anderson
W-10 kg (20 lb)	12.60 kg (27 lb 12 oz)	Tutukaka, New Zealand	Aug. 13, 1995	Mandy Smith
W-15 kg (30 lb)	16.35 kg (36 lb 0 oz)	Slipper Island, New Zealand	Apr. 11, 1998	Dawn Irvine

Snapper, cubera / *Lutjanus cyanopterus*

LINE CLASS	WEIGHT	PLACE	DATE	ANGLER
M-01 kg (2 lb)	Vacant			
M-02 kg (4 lb)	8.66 kg (19 lb 1 oz)	Clearwater, Florida, USA	Oct. 21, 1984	Kenneth E. Roy
M-03 kg (6 lb)	Vacant			
M-04 kg (8 lb)	4.08 kg (9 lb 0 oz)	Rio Tinto, Honduras	Oct. 16, 1994	Ronald C. Snody
M-06 kg (12 lb)	31.29 kg (69 lb 0 oz)	Sebastian Inlet, Florida, USA	Sept. 4, 1995	Matthew S. Salmons
M-08 kg (16 lb)	29.93 kg (66 lb 0 oz)	Boca Raton, Florida, USA	Feb. 11, 1990	Victor I. Clayman
M-10 kg (20 lb)	36.31 kg (80 lb 1 oz)	Miami, Florida, USA	Feb. 4, 1990	Michael Mack
M-15 kg (30 lb)	34.24 kg (75 lb 8 oz)	Key Largo, Florida, USA	June 14, 1994	John Perrotta
M-24 kg (50 lb)	49.78 kg (109 lb 12 oz)	Madeira Beach, Florida, USA	Sept. 3, 1982	Ray Meader
M-37 kg (80 lb)	55.11 kg (121 lb 8 oz)	Cameron, Louisiana, USA	July 5, 1982	Mike Hebert
M-60 kg (130 lb)	38.55 kg (85 lb 0 oz)	Panama City, Florida, USA	June 20, 1984	Ted Harrell
W-01 kg (2 lb)	Vacant			
W-02 kg (4 lb)	Vacant			
W-03 kg (6 lb)	Vacant			
W-04 kg (8 lb)	Vacant			
W-06 kg (12 lb)	19.50 kg (43 lb 0 oz)	Rio Cricamola, Panama	May 24, 1983	Lila W. Kirkland
W-08 kg (16 lb)	Vacant			
W-10 kg (20 lb)	31.00 kg (68 lb 5 oz)	Tortuguero, Costa Rica	Aug. 27, 1988	Ruth Geraldine Roach
W-15 kg (30 lb)	20.41 kg (45 lb 0 oz)	Rio Cricamola, Panama	May 26, 1983	Clare P. Potter
W-24 kg (50 lb)	35.38 kg (78 lb 0 oz)	Cannon Key, Brus Laguna, Honduras	Jan. 19, 1995	Ruth Kryger
W-37 kg (80 lb)	14.85 kg (32 lb 12 oz)	Ocean Reef, Florida, USA	Aug. 24, 1991	Anita N. Haddad
W-60 kg (130 lb)	17.50 kg (38 lb 9 oz)	Ocean Reef, Florida, USA	Aug. 15, 1997	Diane Smolka

Snapper, mutton / *Lutjanus analis*

LINE CLASS	WEIGHT	PLACE	DATE	ANGLER
M-01 kg (2 lb)	5.78 kg (12 lb 12 oz)	Key West, Florida, USA	Apr. 6, 1989	Raymond A. Rizzuti, MD
M-02 kg (4 lb)	8.61 kg (19 lb 0 oz)	Dry Tortugas, Florida, USA	May 19, 1997	Wayne M. Sandlin, Jr.
M-03 kg (6 lb)	8.05 kg (17 lb 12 oz)	Key West, Florida, USA	Jan. 26, 1995	Herbert G. Ratner, Jr.
M-04 kg (8 lb)	8.27 kg (18 lb 4 oz)	Dry Tortugas, Florida, USA	Mar. 21, 1988	Franco D'Ascanio
M-06 kg (12 lb)	9.52 kg (21 lb 0 oz)	Tennessee Light, Florida, USA	Mar. 23, 1987	Chad Meuse
M-08 kg (16 lb)	10.54 kg (23 lb 4 oz)	Key West, Florida, USA	May 6, 1993	Dennis Lee Dyer
M-10 kg (20 lb)	11.90 kg (26 lb 4 oz)	North Key Largo, Florida, USA	June 24, 1993	M. Austin Forman
M-15 kg (30 lb)	12.78 kg (28 lb 3 oz)	Anna Maria, Florida, USA	July 18, 1997	Anthony Manali, Jr.
W-01 kg (2 lb)	1.24 kg (2 lb 12 oz)	Key West, Florida, USA	Jan. 6, 1989	Mrs. William B. DuVal
W-02 kg (4 lb)	4.19 kg (9 lb 4 oz)	Dry Tortugas, Florida, USA	Feb. 13, 1995	Mrs. William B. DuVal
W-03 kg (6 lb)	7.48 kg (16 lb 8 oz)	Key West, Florida, USA	Feb. 22, 1991	William B. DuVal
W-04 kg (8 lb)	7.48 kg (16 lb 8 oz)	Key West, Florida, USA	Apr. 25, 1992	Linda Denkert
W-06 kg (12 lb)	8.39 kg (18 lb 8 oz)	Dry Tortugas, Florida, USA	Feb. 10, 1995	Mrs. William B. DuVal
W-08 kg (16 lb)	9.97 kg (22 lb 0 oz)	Palm Beach, Florida, USA	May 8, 1994	Olga Melin
W-10 kg (20 lb)	8.50 kg (18 lb 12 oz)	Key West, Florida, USA	June 24, 1991	Jo Ann Cronin
W-15 kg (30 lb)	7.93 kg (17 lb 8 oz)	Islamorada, Florida, USA	May 25, 1998	Mary Katherine DeFoor

Snapper, Pacific cubera / *Lutjanus novemfasciatus*

LINE CLASS	WEIGHT	PLACE	DATE	ANGLER
M-01 kg (2 lb)	0.90 kg (2 lb 0 oz)	Playa Zancudo, Costa Rica	Dec. 8, 1995	Craig Whitehead, MD
M-02 kg (4 lb)	5.55 kg (12 lb 4 oz)	Golfito, Costa Rica	Mar. 23, 1991	Dr. Jerome N. Matthews
M-03 kg (6 lb)	2.72 kg (6 lb 0 oz)	Playa Zancudo, Costa Rica	Sept. 6, 1995	Craig Whitehead, MD
M-04 kg (8 lb)	21.86 kg (48 lb 3 oz)	Drake's Bay, Costa Rica	June 6, 1997	Bill Kirby
M-06 kg (12 lb)	23.13 kg (51 lb 0 oz)	Isla de Cano, Costa Rica	Mar. 14, 1989	Dick Love
M-08 kg (16 lb)	25.40 kg (56 lb 0 oz)	Pinas Bay, Panama	Dec. 20, 1984	Roberto R. Vallarino
M-10 kg (20 lb)	33.00 kg (72 lb 12 oz)	Frieles, Panama	Aug. 6, 1987	Gerald W. Coffey
M-15 kg (30 lb)	35.72 kg (78 lb 12 oz)	Bahia Pez Vela, Costa Rica	Mar. 23, 1988	Steven C. Paull
M-24 kg (50 lb)	30.90 kg (68 lb 1 oz)	Farllies Island, Panama	Mar. 24, 1985	Ralph A. Mikkelsen
M-37 kg (80 lb)	32.47 kg (71 lb 9 oz)	Isla de Cano, Costa Rica	Mar. 26, 1989	Eric D. Price
M-60 kg (130 lb)	24.04 kg (53 lb 14 oz)	Isla de Coiba, Panama	Mar. 4, 1994	Gary Gard
W-01 kg (2 lb)	Vacant			
W-02 kg (4 lb)	2.94 kg (6 lb 8 oz)	Golfito, Costa Rica	July 30, 1992	Cheri Ann Matthews
W-03 kg (6 lb)	Vacant			
W-04 kg (8 lb)	17.29 kg (38 lb 2 oz)	Golfito, Costa Rica	July 28, 1992	Cheri Ann Matthews
W-06 kg (12 lb)	9.52 kg (21 lb 0 oz)	Golfito, Costa Rica	Jan. 11, 1990	Cheri Ann Matthews
W-08 kg (16 lb)	16.21 kg (35 lb 12 oz)	Isla del Cano, Costa Rica	Jan. 23, 1991	Cheri Ann Matthews
W-10 kg (20 lb)	28.91 kg (63 lb 12 oz)	Pinas Bay, Panama	Dec. 18, 1984	Marlene Vallarino
W-15 kg (30 lb)	24.04 kg (53 lb 0 oz)	Pinas Bay, Panama	Jan. 22, 1985	Barbara Edgar
W-24 kg (50 lb)	22.22 kg (49 lb 0 oz)	Pinas Bay, Panama	Apr. 2, 1989	Julie Laver
W-37 kg (80 lb)	25.40 kg (56 lb 0 oz)	Isla de Coiba, Panama	Mar. 5, 1994	Suzy Matthews Gard
W-60 kg (130 lb)	25.85 kg (57 lb 0 oz)	Pinas Bay, Panama	Jan. 10, 1986	Terri Kittredge

Snook / *Centropomus spp*

LINE CLASS	WEIGHT	PLACE	DATE	ANGLER
M-01 kg (2 lb)	10.99 kg (24 lb 4 oz)	Jupiter, Florida, USA	Aug. 8, 1995	George E. Hogan, Jr.
M-02 kg (4 lb)	13.63 kg (30 lb 1 oz)	O'Quinns Channel, Stuart, Florida, USA	May 13, 1988	Jesse Webb
M-03 kg (6 lb)	18.82 kg (41 lb 8 oz)	Jupiter, Florida, USA	July 23, 1996	George E. Hogan
M-04 kg (8 lb)	15.42 kg (34 lb 0 oz)	Cabo San Lucas, Mexico	Sept. 27, 1997	Jeff Klassen
M-06 kg (12 lb)	25.20 kg (55 lb 8 oz)	Rio Parrita, Parrita, Costa Rica	May 23, 1992	Jose Manuel Brenes J.
M-08 kg (16 lb)	22.60 kg (49 lb 13 oz)	Rio Tulin, Costa Rica	May 20, 1990	Gerardo Cespedez
M-10 kg (20 lb)	24.32 kg (53 lb 10 oz)	Parismina Ranch, Costa Rica	Oct. 18, 1978	Gilbert Ponzi
M-15 kg (30 lb)	26.19 kg (57 lb 12 oz)	Rio Naranjo, Quepos, Costa Rica	Aug. 23, 1991	George Beck
M-24 kg (50 lb)	20.04 kg (44 lb 3 oz)	Ft. Myers Beach, Florida, USA	Apr. 25, 1984	Robert De Cosmo
W-01 kg (2 lb)	8.61 kg (19 lb 0 oz)	Jupiter, Florida, USA	Aug. 26, 1995	Elizabeth Hogan

Snook / *(continued)*

LINE CLASS	WEIGHT	PLACE	DATE	ANGLER
W-02 kg (4 lb)	9.43 kg (20 lb 12 oz)	Charlotte Harbor, Florida, USA	May 23, 1989	Deborah B. Miller
W-03 kg (6 lb)	10.43 kg (23 lb 0 oz)	Jupiter, Florida, USA	Aug. 8, 1995	Elizabeth Hogan
W-04 kg (8 lb)	12.47 kg (27 lb 8 oz)	Barra del Colorado, Costa Rica	Oct. 2, 1989	Donna L. Davenport
W-06 kg (12 lb)	15.78 kg (34 lb 12 oz)	Charlotte Harbor, Boca Grande, Florida, USA	Apr. 26, 1993	Sharon M. Weekes
W-08 kg (16 lb)	14.17 kg (31 lb 4 oz)	Caloosahatchee River, Ft. Myers, Florida, USA	Apr. 4, 1990	Maryvonne Hemming
W-10 kg (20 lb)	18.82 kg (41 lb 8 oz)	Fort Pierce, Florida, USA	Jan. 15, 1978	Barbara Hodges
W-15 kg (30 lb)	15.30 kg (33 lb 12 oz)	Ft. Lauderdale, Florida, USA	July 29, 1951	Mrs. Cecile G. Pollard
W-24 kg (50 lb)	14.28 kg (31 lb 8 oz)	Stuart, Florida, USA	July 17, 1951	Mrs. Boyd N. Fox

Spearfish / *Tetrapturus spp.*

LINE CLASS	WEIGHT	PLACE	DATE	ANGLER
M-01 kg (2 lb)	Vacant			
M-02 kg (4 lb)	15.64 kg (34 lb 8 oz)	Keahole Point, Kona Coast, Hawaii, USA	Apr. 23, 1994	Dennis Harris
M-03 kg (6 lb)	14.27 kg (42 lb 8 oz)	Keahole Point, Kona, Hawaii, USA	Jan. 19, 1995	Torben Frederiksen
M-04 kg (8 lb)	19.05 kg (42 lb 0 oz)	Kona Coast, Hawaii, USA	May 10, 1994	Jeffery W. Meyer
M-06 kg (12 lb)	28.48 kg (62 lb 12 oz)	Madeira, Portugal	Sept. 6, 1996	Stewart N. Campbell
M-08 kg (16 lb)	27.60 kg (60 lb 13 oz)	Dakar, Senegal	Nov. 1, 1994	Albert Chery
M-10 kg (20 lb)	30.00 kg (66 lb 2 oz)	Narooma, N.S.W., Australia	Mar. 1, 1981	Kevin M. Hawkins
M-15 kg (30 lb)	40.05 kg (88 lb 4 oz)	Puerto Rico, Gran Canaria, Spain	July 28, 1992	Dieter Vogel
M-24 kg (50 lb)	41.20 kg (90 lb 13 oz)	Madeira Island, Portugal	June 2, 1980	Joseph Larkin
M-37 kg (80 lb)	37.50 kg (82 lb 10 oz)	Puerto Rico, Gran Canaria, Spain	June 28, 1993	Gunter Schulz
W-01 kg (2 lb)	Vacant			
W-02 kg (4 lb)	12.02 kg (26 lb 8 oz)	Cape Cook, Kona, Hawaii, USA	Apr. 10, 1993	Deborah Maddux Dunaway
W-03 kg (6 lb)	12.70 kg (28 lb 0 oz)	Kona Coast, Hawaii, USA	May 16, 1996	Sharon Handgis
W-04 kg (8 lb)	14.28 kg (31 lb 8 oz)	Napoopoo, Kona Coast, Hawaii, USA	Aug. 9, 1993	Pamela Basco
W-06 kg (12 lb)	17.69 kg (39 lb 0 oz)	Kona, Hawaii, USA	Apr. 16, 1991	Janeen G. Davis
W-08 kg (16 lb)	18.14 kg (40 lb 0 oz)	Kailua, Kona, Hawaii, USA	July 30, 1983	Louise Hawkins
W-10 kg (20 lb)	29.00 kg (63 lb 14 oz)	Port Stephens, N.S.W., Australia	Mar. 1, 1984	Sharon Parkins
W-15 kg (30 lb)	28.40 kg (62 lb 9 oz)	Gable End, Foreland, Gisborne, New Zealand	Feb. 19, 1995	Glenys Knox
W-24 kg (50 lb)	29.20 kg (64 lb 5 oz)	Dakar, Senegal	Oct. 14, 1994	Chantal Romieu
W-37 kg (80 lb)	26.50 kg (58 lb 6 oz)	Funchal, Madeira, Portugal	July 8, 1997	Fonda Huizenga

Swordfish / *Xiphias gladius*

LINE CLASS	WEIGHT	PLACE	DATE	ANGLER
M-01 kg (2 lb)	Vacant			
M-02 kg (4 lb)	33.11 kg (73 lb 0 oz)	LaGuaira, Venezuela	Nov. 1, 1986	Marc Giraud
M-03 kg (6 lb)	48.30 kg (106 lb 8 oz)	Cabo San Lucas, Baja, Mexico	June 11, 1972	James Perry
M-04 kg (8 lb)	49.44 kg (109 lb 0 oz)	Pinas Bay, Panama	Feb. 24, 1986	Jerry Dunaway
M-06 kg (12 lb)	75.29 kg (166 lb 0 oz)	Pinas Bay, Panama	Feb. 21, 1986	Jerry Dunaway
M-08 kg (16 lb)	110.45 kg (243 lb 8 oz)	Ft. Lauderdale, Florida, USA	June 7, 1984	Robert Ray Goldsby
M-10 kg (20 lb)	140.61 kg (310 lb 0 oz)	Palmilla, Baja California, Mexico	May 24, 1979	David G. Nottage
M-15 kg (30 lb)	177.81 kg (392 lb 0 oz)	Nantucket, Massachusetts, USA	Aug. 3, 1976	John F. Willits
M-24 kg (50 lb)	291.90 kg (643 lb 0 oz)	Mercury Bay, New Zealand	Apr. 2, 1998	Ian O'Brien
M-37 kg (80 lb)	298.01 kg (657 lb 0 oz)	Algarrobo, Chile	Mar. 20, 1989	Fred Cameron
M-60 kg (130 lb)	536.15 kg (1182 lb 0 oz)	Iquique, Chile	May 7, 1953	L. Marron
W-01 kg (2 lb)	Vacant			
W-02 kg (4 lb)	Vacant			
W-03 kg (6 lb)	Vacant			
W-04 kg (8 lb)	Vacant			
W-06 kg (12 lb)	120.35 kg (265 lb 5 oz)	Gordon's Bay, Cape Point, South Africa	May 1, 1993	Marg Love
W-08 kg (16 lb)	78.92 kg (174 lb 0 oz)	Pinas Bay, Panama	Feb. 17, 1986	Deborah Maddux Dunaway
W-10 kg (20 lb)	128.40 kg (283 lb 1 oz)	Gordon's Bay, Cape Point, South Africa	May 4, 1993	Marg Love
W-15 kg (30 lb)	135.80 kg (297 lb 15 oz)	Hout Bay, Republic of South Africa	May 12, 1995	Maureen K. Colyn
W-24 kg (50 lb)	223.28 kg (492 lb 4 oz)	Montauk Point, New York, USA	July 4, 1959	Dorothea L. Cassullo
W-37 kg (80 lb)	350.17 kg (772 lb 0 oz)	Iquique, Chile	June 7, 1954	Mrs. L. Marron
W-60 kg (130 lb)	344.28 kg (759 lb 0 oz)	Iquique, Chile	June 30, 1952	Mrs. D. A. Allison

Tarpon / *Megalops atlanticus*

LINE CLASS	WEIGHT	PLACE	DATE	ANGLER
M-01 kg (2 lb)	48.08 kg (106 lb 0 oz)	Marathon Key, Florida, USA	June 10, 1992	George E. Hogan, Jr.
M-02 kg (4 lb)	58.28 kg (128 lb 8 oz)	Marathon Key, Florida, USA	Apr. 6, 1992	George E. Hogan, Jr.
M-03 kg (6 lb)	63.45 kg (139 lb 14 oz)	Marathon Key, Florida, USA	Apr. 10, 1997	George E. Hogan, Jr.
M-04 kg (8 lb)	66.84 kg (147 lb 6 oz)	Key West, Florida, USA	Mar. 26, 1982	Anton G. Zukas
M-06 kg (12 lb)	85.50 kg (188 lb 7 oz)	Sherbro Island, Sierra Leone	Apr. 18, 1997	Michel Delaunay
M-08 kg (16 lb)	92.00 kg (202 lb 13 oz)	Sherbro Island, Sierra Leone	Apr. 8, 1997	Daniel Lopuszanski
M-10 kg (20 lb)	110.22 kg (243 lb 0 oz)	Key West, Florida, USA	Feb. 17, 1975	Gus Bell
M-15 kg (30 lb)	128.36 kg (283 lb 0 oz)	Lake Maracaibo, Venezuela	Mar. 19, 1956	Mario Salazar
M-15 kg (30 lb) Tie	128.50 kg (283 lb 4 oz)	Sherbro Island, Sierra Leone	Apr. 16, 1991	Yvon Victor Sebag
M-24 kg (50 lb)	123.00 kg (271 lb 0 oz)	Sherbro Island, Sierra Leone	Mar. 31, 1993	Pierre Clostermann
M-37 kg (80 lb)	120.20 kg (265 lb 0 oz)	Sherbro Island, Sierra Leone	Mar. 22, 1993	Thomas F. Gibson
M-60 kg (130 lb)	110.00 kg (242 lb 8 oz)	Sherbro Island, Sierra Leone	Apr. 8, 1992	G.E. (Ged) Fleming
W-01 kg (2 lb)	25.40 kg (56 lb 0 oz)	Marathon, Florida, USA	May 18, 1991	Elizabeth Hogan
W-02 kg (4 lb)	60.87 kg (134 lb 3 oz)	Marathon Key, Florida, USA	Apr. 20, 1996	Elizabeth Hogan
W-03 kg (6 lb)	52.16 kg (115 lb 0 oz)	Conch Key, Florida, USA	May 30, 1995	Elizabeth Hogan
W-04 kg (8 lb)	64.22 kg (141 lb 9 oz)	Marathon Key, Florida, USA	Apr. 21, 1996	Elizabeth Hogan
W-06 kg (12 lb)	85.00 kg (187 lb 6 oz)	Sherbro Island, Sierra Leone	Mar. 19, 1997	Andree Delaunay
W-08 kg (16 lb)	75.00 kg (166 lb 7 oz)	Sherbro Island, Sierra Leone	Mar. 11, 1997	Andree Delaunay
W-10 kg (20 lb)	104.30 kg (230 lb 0 oz)	Sherbro Island, Sierra Leone	Mar. 24, 1994	Pascale Alarcon
W-15 kg (30 lb)	112.94 kg (249 lb 0 oz)	Sherbro Island, Sierra Leone	Apr. 1, 1994	Frederique Jarland
W-24 kg (50 lb)	102.06 kg (225 lb 0 oz)	Sherbro Island, Sierra Leone	Apr. 11, 1994	Andree Delaunay

Tarpon / *(continued)*

W-37 kg (80 lb)	99.00 kg (218 lb 4 oz)	Port Michel, Gabon	Jan. 12, 1984	Jeaninne Depuy
W-37 kg (80 lb) Tie	99.00 kg (218 lb 4 oz)	Sherbro Island, Sierra Leone	Mar. 21, 1997	Andree Delaunay
W-60 kg (130 lb)	100.50 kg (221 lb 8 oz)	Sherbro Island, Sierra Leone	Mar. 20, 1997	Andree Delaunay

Tautog / *Tautoga onitis*

LINE CLASS	WEIGHT	PLACE	DATE	ANGLER
M-01 kg (2 lb)	4.45 kg (9 lb 13 oz)	Sheffield Island, Norwalk, Connecticut, USA	June 17, 1988	Tony Contino
M-02 kg (4 lb)	4.70 kg (10 lb 6 oz)	Sheffield Island, Norwalk, Connecticut, USA	May 28, 1988	Tony Contino
M-03 kg (6 lb)	6.52 kg (14 lb 6 oz)	Virginia Beach, Virginia, USA	May 17, 1972	Linwood A. Martens
M-04 kg (8 lb)	7.71 kg (17 lb 0 oz)	Long Island Sound, Norwalk, Connecticut, USA	July 4, 1988	Christian J. Heise
M-06 kg (12 lb)	7.34 kg (16 lb 3 oz)	Buzzard's Bay, Marion, Massachusetts, USA	May 13, 1988	Roy Horwitz
M-08 kg (16 lb)	7.34 kg (16 lb 3 oz)	Long Island Sound, New York, USA	Oct. 31, 1984	Ian C. Lindsay
M-10 kg (20 lb)	9.52 kg (21 lb 0 oz)	Jamestown Island, Rhode Island, USA	Nov. 6, 1954	Conrad W. Sundquist
M-15 kg (30 lb)	10.88 kg (24 lb 0 oz)	Wachapreague, Virginia, USA	Aug. 25, 1987	Gregory Robert Bell
W-01 kg (2 lb)	1.75 kg (3 lb 14 oz)	Niantic, Connecticut, USA	Nov. 9, 1985	Mary S. Carlson
W-02 kg (4 lb)	3.62 kg (8 lb 0 oz)	Montauk, Long Island, New York, USA	Oct. 28, 1984	Mrs. Toby Grossman
W-03 kg (6 lb)	4.50 kg (9 lb 15 oz)	Mt. Sinai, New York, USA	Oct. 12, 1995	Mrs. Lorry Mangan
W-04 kg (8 lb)	4.64 kg (10 lb 4 oz)	Mt. Sinai, Long Island, New York, USA	June 11, 1988	Mrs. Lorry Mangan
W-06 kg (12 lb)	5.17 kg (11 lb 6 oz)	Montauk, New York, USA	Nov. 20, 1992	Mrs. Lorry Mangan
W-08 kg (16 lb)	6.20 kg (13 lb 11 oz)	Port Jefferson, Long Island, New York, USA	Dec. 8, 1993	Lorry Mangan
W-10 kg (20 lb)	5.78 kg (12 lb 12 oz)	Fisher's Island, New York, USA	Oct. 21, 1985	Donna M. Pratt
W-15 kg (30 lb)	6.40 kg (14 lb 2 oz)	Little Gull Island, New York, USA	Oct. 10, 1984	Marie Raycroft

Threadfin, king / *Polynemus sheridani*

LINE CLASS	WEIGHT	PLACE	DATE	ANGLER
M-01 kg (2 lb)	4.80 kg (10 lb 9 oz)	Port Hedland, Australia	Jan. 29, 1997	Anthony Boekhorst
M-02 kg (4 lb)	6.60 kg (14 lb 8 oz)	Port Hurd, Bathurst Island, N.T., Australia	Jan. 11, 1988	Wayne Andrew Ross
M-03 kg (6 lb)	6.00 kg (13 lb 3 oz)	Walker River, Australia	Mar. 25, 1998	Gregory Paul De Koning
M-04 kg (8 lb)	11.40 kg (25 lb 2 oz)	Dampier, Australia	Dec. 13, 1997	Mark Cottrell
M-06 kg (12 lb)	12.50 kg (27 lb 8 oz)	Dampier Creek, Broome, Australia	Apr. 24, 1996	Brian William Albert
M-08 kg (16 lb)	10.00 kg (22 lb 0 oz)	Port Hurd, Bathurst Island, N.T., Australia	Nov. 24, 1990	Wayne Andrew Ross
M-10 kg (20 lb)	10.60 kg (23 lb 5 oz)	Bathurst Island, N.T., Australia	May 4, 1991	Peter A. Taylor
M-15 kg (30 lb)	Vacant			
W-01 kg (2 lb)	1.40 kg (3 lb 1 oz)	Arnhem Land, N.T., Australia	Apr. 22, 1994	Carolyn Rosemary Caughlan
W-02 kg (4 lb)	Vacant			
W-03 kg (6 lb)	6.88 kg (15 lb 2 oz)	Dampier, Australia	Dec. 30, 1997	Nicole Livingstone
W-04 kg (8 lb)	Vacant			
W-06 kg (12 lb)	9.60 kg (21 lb 2 oz)	Port Hurd, Bathurst Island, N.T., Australia	Aug. 4, 1991	Dottie Wing
W-08 kg (16 lb)	8.80 kg (19 lb 6 oz)	Bathurst Island, N.T., Australia	June 16, 1986	Lorrie Fay
W-10 kg (20 lb)	Vacant			
W-15 kg (30 lb)	Vacant			

Trevally, bigeye / *Caranx sexfasciatus*

LINE CLASS	WEIGHT	PLACE	DATE	ANGLER
M-01 kg (2 lb)	3.11 kg (6 lb 13 oz)	Bahia Pez Vela, Costa Rica	Apr. 14, 1983	Yves F.M. Hentic
M-02 kg (4 lb)	4.50 kg (9 lb 14 oz)	Queensland, Australia	Dec. 30, 1990	John A. Kraschnefski
M-03 kg (6 lb)	6.30 kg (13 lb 14 oz)	Sandy Cape, Queensland, Australia	Dec. 27, 1995	Wayne Jeffers
M-04 kg (8 lb)	4.90 kg (10 lb 12 oz)	Futami Bay, Chichijima, Ogasawara, Tokyo, Japan	Nov. 28, 1997	Masanori Miyagawa
M-06 kg (12 lb)	6.60 kg (14 lb 8 oz)	Ishigaki Island, Okinawa, Japan	May 30, 1995	Takaomi Hashimoto
M-08 kg (16 lb)	6.70 kg (14 lb 12 oz)	Ishigaki Island, Okinawa, Japan	May 6, 1992	Noriaki Kamiya
M-10 kg (20 lb)	7.82 kg (17 lb 4 oz)	Clipperton Island	May 12, 1990	Dr. Robert H. Cassar
M-15 kg (30 lb)	7.50 kg (16 lb 9 oz)	Kikaijima, Amami Oshima, Kagoshima, Japan	Oct. 2, 1995	Yasuhira Tasaka
M-24 kg (50 lb)	7.80 kg (17 lb 3 oz)	Chichijima, Ogasawara, Tokyo, Japan	July 9, 1998	Hiroaki Shikunami
M-37 kg (80 lb)	14.30 kg (31 lb 8 oz)	Poivre Island, Seychelles	Apr. 23, 1997	Les Sampson
W-01 kg (2 lb)	2.20 kg (4 lb 13 oz)	Exmouth, Australia	Nov. 3, 1996	Jan Prince
W-02 kg (4 lb)	3.04 kg (7 lb 7 oz)	Mosquito Island, Papua, New Guinea	Nov. 27, 1988	Rebecca Jane Mallett
W-03 kg (6 lb)	2.80 kg (6 lb 2 oz)	Duke of York Island, Papua, New Guinea	Dec. 6, 1981	Dorothy Miles
W-04 kg (8 lb)	Vacant			
W-06 kg (12 lb)	Vacant			
W-08 kg (16 lb)	6.10 kg (13 lb 7 oz)	Higashijima, Chichijima, Ogasawara, Tokyo, Japan	Sept. 24, 1996	Michiru Moroe
W-10 kg (20 lb)	5.73 kg (12 lb 10 oz)	Clipperton Island	May 12, 1990	Patricia Ann Chase
W-15 kg (30 lb)	6.80 kg (15 lb 0 oz)	Isla Coiba, Panama	Jan. 18, 1984	Sally S. Timms
W-24 kg (50 lb)	6.90 kg (15 lb 3 oz)	Magojima, Ogasawara, Tokyo, Japan	Aug. 9, 1998	Mutsumi Shoji
W-37 kg (80 lb)	Vacant			

Trevally, bluefin / *Caranx melampygus*

LINE CLASS	WEIGHT	PLACE	DATE	ANGLER
M-01 kg (2 lb)	2.89 kg (6 lb 6 oz)	Isla San Benedicto, Revillagigedo Islands, Mexico	May 19, 1987	Butch Green
M-02 kg (4 lb)	5.90 kg (13 lb 0 oz)	Gangehi, Ari Atoll, Republic of Maldives	July 10, 1989	Roberto Ferrario
M-03 kg (6 lb)	7.25 kg (16 lb 0 oz)	Quepos, Costa Rica	Apr. 5, 1997	Michael R. Clark
M-04 kg (8 lb)	7.70 kg (16 lb 15 oz)	Oyster Reef, Cairns, Queensland, Australia	Mar. 16, 1989	Peter Richard Cooper
M-06 kg (12 lb)	9.07 kg (20 lb 0 oz)	Tamarindo Beach, Costa Rica	May 28, 1989	Lawrence A. Gordich
M-08 kg (16 lb)	8.60 kg (18 lb 15 oz)	Ogasawara Island, Meijima, Tokyo, Japan	Sept. 9, 1991	Seiichi Nagai
M-10 kg (20 lb)	10.84 kg (23 lb 14 oz)	Clipperton Island	May 12, 1996	W. Scott McKelvey
M-15 kg (30 lb)	10.12 kg (22 lb 5 oz)	Maalaea, Maui, Hawaii, USA	Nov. 28, 1989	Michael Sellinger
W-01 kg (2 lb)	0.68 kg (1 lb 8 oz)	Christmas Island, Republic of Kiribati	Dec. 30, 1986	Dixie Lewis van der Kamp
W-02 kg (4 lb)	2.50 kg (5 lb 8 oz)	Kosi Bay, Zululand, Republic of South Africa	Apr. 26, 1986	Fay Ashington
W-03 kg (6 lb)	7.71 kg (17 lb 0 oz)	Cocos Island, Costa Rica	Apr. 5, 1997	Marti Manser
W-04 kg (8 lb)	1.50 kg (3 lb 5 oz)	Christmas Island, Republic of Kiribati	Feb. 16, 1992	Andrea U. Warner
W-06 kg (12 lb)	10.00 kg (22 lb 1 oz)	Clipperton Island	May 14, 1990	Rebecca A. Mills
W-08 kg (16 lb)	8.19 kg (18 lb 1 oz)	Clipperton Island	May 2, 1987	Ruthanne Heidt

Trevally, bluefin / *(continued)*

LINE CLASS	WEIGHT	PLACE	DATE	ANGLER
W-10 kg (20 lb)	9.10 kg (20 lb 0 oz)	Inhaca Island, Mozambique	July 17, 1994	Danita Stanford
W-15 kg (30 lb)	9.00 kg (19 lb 13 oz)	Higashijima, Chichijima, Ogasawara, Tokyo, Japan	Oct. 16, 1996	Michiru Moroe

Trevally, giant / *Caranx ignobilis*

LINE CLASS	WEIGHT	PLACE	DATE	ANGLER
M-01 kg (2 lb)	14.20 kg (31 lb 4 oz)	Hervey Bay, Queensland, Australia	Dec. 8, 1996	Raymond Bruce Revill
M-02 kg (4 lb)	11.83 kg (26 lb 1 oz)	Cairns, N. Queensland, Australia	Dec. 13, 1987	Terry Holman
M-03 kg (6 lb)	13.00 kg (28 lb 10 oz)	Groote Eylandt, Australia	Oct. 19, 1997	Robert Nichells
M-04 kg (8 lb)	18.75 kg (41 lb 5 oz)	Port Heoland, Australia	Jan. 7, 1984	Ian Hornhardt
M-06 kg (12 lb)	30.20 kg (66 lb 9 oz)	Monte Bello Island, W.A., Australia	July 4, 1981	Warren B. Cornelius
M-08 kg (16 lb)	39.50 kg (87 lb 1 oz)	Exmouth, W.A., Australia	Nov. 9, 1989	Colin Barron
M-10 kg (20 lb)	40.23 kg (88 lb 11 oz)	Thetford Reef, Queensland, Australia	Oct. 18, 1987	Dennis Remedio
M-15 kg (30 lb)	47.67 kg (105 lb 1 oz)	Midway Island	Sept. 24, 1996	George Handgis
M-24 kg (50 lb)	54.10 kg (119 lb 4 oz)	Ile de la Reunion, France	Mar. 15, 1998	Hughes Savalli
M-37 kg (80 lb)	65.99 kg (145 lb 8 oz)	Makena, Maui, Hawaii, USA	Mar. 28, 1991	Russell Mori
M-60 kg (130 lb)	52.61 kg (116 lb 0 oz)	Pago Pago, American Samoa	Feb. 20, 1978	William G. Foster
W-01 kg (2 lb)	Vacant			
W-02 kg (4 lb)	4.94 kg (10 lb 14 oz)	Singaua, Huon Gulf, Papua, New Guinea	Sept. 24, 1989	Rebecca Jane Mallett
W-03 kg (6 lb)	17.54 kg (38 lb 11 oz)	Midway Island	May 10, 1997	Sharon Handgis
W-04 kg (8 lb)	14.50 kg (31 lb 15 oz)	Exmouth, Australia	Mar. 5, 1994	Belinda Barrow
W-06 kg (12 lb)	35.00 kg (77 lb 2 oz)	Seymour River Estuary, Queensland, Australia	June 12, 1996	Esme Rosalind Henderson
W-08 kg (16 lb)	24.94 kg (55 lb 0 oz)	Midway Island	Sept. 29, 1996	Susan Hays
W-10 kg (20 lb)	27.00 kg (59 lb 8 oz)	Dampier, W.A., Australia	Nov. 12, 1978	Melva Rack
W-15 kg (30 lb)	33.19 kg (73 lb 3 oz)	Christmas Island, Republic of Kiribati	July 12, 1987	Jeanette Foster
W-24 kg (50 lb)	53.50 kg (117 lb 15 oz)	Bassas da India, Mozambique	July 6, 1984	Elinor Bullen
W-37 kg (80 lb)	45.00 kg (99 lb 3 oz)	Lamu, Kenya	Oct. 14, 1985	Carol Anderson
W-60 kg (130 lb)	40.50 kg (89 lb 4 oz)	Port Vila, Republic of Vanuatu	Dec. 12, 1988	Mrs. Christiane Billaut

Tripletail / *Lobotes surinamensis*

LINE CLASS	WEIGHT	PLACE	DATE	ANGLER
M-01 kg (2 lb)	5.75 kg (12 lb 10 oz)	Naples, Florida, USA	Sept. 15, 1997	Erik J. Madison, DVM
M-02 kg (4 lb)	8.05 kg (17 lb 12 oz)	Indian River, Ft. Pierce, Florida, USA	Aug. 27, 1997	Tony Ortega
M-03 kg (6 lb)	10.60 kg (23 lb 6 oz)	Port Canaveral, Florida, USA	May 13, 1997	Steve V. Sigman
M-04 kg (8 lb)	11.79 kg (26 lb 0 oz)	Port Canaveral, Florida, USA	Oct. 14, 1993	Troy Perez
M-06 kg (12 lb)	11.90 kg (26 lb 4 oz)	Port Canaveral, Florida, USA	June 20, 1997	Jerome N. Matthews
M-08 kg (16 lb)	14.96 kg (33 lb 0 oz)	Port Canaveral, Florida, USA	May 7, 1997	Mark Nudds
M-10 kg (20 lb)	18.51 kg (40 lb 13 oz)	Ft. Pierce, Florida, USA	Mar. 4, 1998	Thomas D. Lewis
M-15 kg (30 lb)	15.42 kg (34 lb 0 oz)	Port Canaveral, Florida, USA	May 7, 1997	Doug Sagorski
M-24 kg (50 lb)	10.43 kg (23 lb 0 oz)	Jupiter Inlet, Florida, USA	Sept. 1, 1996	Mike Dinnen
W-01 kg (2 lb)	2.94 kg (6 lb 8 oz)	Port Canaveral, Florida, USA	Apr. 17, 1995	Christine Perez
W-02 kg (4 lb)	5.21 kg (11 lb 8 oz)	Port Canaveral, Florida, USA	Nov. 19, 1993	Christine Perez
W-02 kg (4 lb) Tie	5.21 kg (11 lb 8 oz)	Port Canaveral, Florida, USA	Nov. 19, 1993	Christine Perez
W-03 kg (6 lb)	8.02 kg (17 lb 11 oz)	Port Canaveral, Florida, USA	June 19, 1997	Christine Perez
W-04 kg (8 lb)	11.56 kg (25 lb 8 oz)	Port Canaveral, Florida, USA	June 3, 1997	Christine Perez
W-06 kg (12 lb)	10.20 kg (22 lb 8 oz)	Port Canaveral, Florida, USA	Oct. 12, 1993	Sandra A. Brkich
W-08 kg (16 lb)	10.27 kg (22 lb 10 oz)	Palocios Ship Channel, Matagorda Bay, Texas, USA	Sept. 9, 1995	Ruby M. Bocttcher
W-10 kg (20 lb)	11.79 kg (26 lb 0 oz)	Port Canaveral, Florida, USA	June 26, 1996	Christine Perez
W-15 kg (30 lb)	12.58 kg (27 lb 12 oz)	Cape Canaveral, Florida, USA	Sept. 23, 1993	Marti W. Schlegler
W-24 kg (50 lb)	11.33 kg (25 lb 0 oz)	Port Canaveral, Florida, USA	June 23, 1997	Christine Perez

Tuna, bigeye (Atlantic) / *Thunnus obesus*

LINE CLASS	WEIGHT	PLACE	DATE	ANGLER
M-01 kg (2 lb)	Vacant			
M-02 kg (4 lb)	Vacant			
M-03 kg (6 lb)	Vacant			
M-04 kg (8 lb)	7.37 kg (16 lb 4 oz)	Rio De Janeiro, Brazil	Jan. 5, 1992	Fernando A. Martins Salles
M-06 kg (12 lb)	59.10 kg (130 lb 4 oz)	Hout Bay, South Africa	May 8, 1994	Lionel Howson Willmore
M-08 kg (16 lb)	63.55 kg (140 lb 1 oz)	Cape Point, South Africa	Oct. 20, 1995	D.E.L. Carter
M-10 kg (20 lb)	97.52 kg (215 lb 0 oz)	Shinnecock, Long Island, New York, USA	July 26, 1980	Tred Barta
M-15 kg (30 lb)	149.25 kg (329 lb 0 oz)	Abidjan, Ivory Coast	May 4, 1986	Stewart N. Campbell
M-24 kg (50 lb)	178.00 kg (392 lb 6 oz)	Puerto Rico, Gran Canaria, Spain	July 25, 1996	Dieter Vogel
M-37 kg (80 lb)	161.02 kg (355 lb 0 oz)	Hudson Canyon, Long Island, New York, USA	Sept. 27, 1981	Rick Buechmann
M-60 kg (130 lb)	165.00 kg (363 lb 12 oz)	Puerto Rico, Gran Canaria, Canary Islands	Aug. 21, 1987	H. van Bemmel
W-01 kg (2 lb)	Vacant			
W-02 kg (4 lb)	Vacant			
W-03 kg (6 lb)	Vacant			
W-04 kg (8 lb)	Vacant			
W-06 kg (12 lb)	Vacant			
W-08 kg (16 lb)	53.32 kg (117 lb 8 oz)	Oregon Inlet, North Carolina, USA	Nov. 26, 1994	Mrs. Stephen R. Hutchins
W-10 kg (20 lb)	53.70 kg (118 lb 6 oz)	Cape Point, South Africa	Oct. 27, 1994	Denise Marguerite Milton
W-15 kg (30 lb)	111.00 kg (244 lb 11 oz)	Madeira, Portugal	Oct. 5, 1996	Andree Delaunay
W-24 kg (50 lb)	128.00 kg (282 lb 3 oz)	Madeira, Portugal	Oct. 2, 1996	Andree Delaunay
W-37 kg (80 lb)	144.13 kg (317 lb 12 oz)	Hudson Canyon, New Jersey, USA	July 23, 1978	Charlene Sanford
W-60 kg (130 lb)	151 kg (332 lb 14 oz)	Gran Canaria, Canary Islands, Spain	June 16, 1977	Mrs. Waltraud Lehmann

Tuna, bigeye (Pacific) / *Thunnus obesus*

LINE CLASS	WEIGHT	PLACE	DATE	ANGLER
M-01 kg (2 lb)	4.08 kg (9 lb 0 oz)	Palmas de Cortez, Baja California, Mexico	Apr. 28, 1984	Burton R. Leed
M-02 kg (4 lb)	9.97 kg (22 lb 0 oz)	Kona, Hawaii, USA	Apr. 16, 1994	George E. Hogan, Jr.
M-03 kg (6 lb)	13.38 kg (29 lb 8 oz)	Salinas, Ecuador	May 31, 1975	Luis Alberto Flores A.
M-04 kg (8 lb)	37.64 kg (83 lb 0 oz)	San Diego, California, USA	Oct. 13, 1990	Robert R. Kurz

Tuna, bigeye (Pacific) / *(continued)*

LINE CLASS	WEIGHT	PLACE	DATE	ANGLER
M-06 kg (12 lb)	65.09 kg (143 lb 8 oz)	Santa Cruz Island, California, USA	Oct. 12, 1984	David M. Denholm
M-08 kg (16 lb)	71.57 kg (157 lb 12 oz)	San Clemente Island, California, USA	Nov. 1, 1986	Jerry Wells, Sr.
M-10 kg (20 lb)	66.22 kg (146 lb 0 oz)	San Diego, California, USA	Sept. 14, 1991	Robert C. Newton
M-15 kg (30 lb)	107.04 kg (236 lb 0 oz)	Salinas, Ecuador	Jan. 17, 1993	Jorge F. Jorado
M-24 kg (50 lb)	137.87 kg (304 lb 0 oz)	Salinas, Ecuador	July 6, 1985	Antuan Taleb D
M-37 kg (80 lb)	154.67 kg (341 lb 0 oz)	Salinas, Ecuador	Jan. 17, 1988	Knud Holst
M-60 kg (130 lb)	197.31 kg (435 lb 0 oz)	Cabo Blanco, Peru	Apr. 17, 1957	Dr. Russel V. A. Lee
W-01 kg (2 lb)	1.13 kg (2 lb 8 oz)	Kailua, Kona, Hawaii, USA	Oct. 26, 1984	Diane Grantham
W-02 kg (4 lb)	2.25 kg (4 lb 15 oz)	Cabo Marzo, Choco, Colombia	May 9, 1991	Celine Rectenwald
W-03 kg (6 lb)	Vacant			
W-04 kg (8 lb)	10.88 kg (24 lb 0 oz)	Kona, Hawaii, USA	Apr. 15, 1994	Elizabeth Hogan
W-06 kg (12 lb)	22.90 kg (50 lb 8 oz)	San Diego, California, USA	Sept. 24, 1981	Mary Wallace Josepho
W-08 kg (16 lb)	37.87 kg (83 lb 8 oz)	San Diego, California, USA	July 21, 1985	Nicole L. Denholm
W-10 kg (20 lb)	71.21 kg (157 lb 0 oz)	San Clemente Island, California, USA	Aug. 15, 1987	Lorraine Carlton
W-15 kg (30 lb)	61.91 kg (136 lb 8 oz)	La Jolla, California, USA	Aug. 17, 1980	Carolyn B. Morris
W-24 kg (50 lb)	108.86 kg (240 lb 0 oz)	Salinas, Ecuador	Jan. 11, 1969	Helen C. King
W-37 kg (80 lb)	151.95 kg (335 lb 0 oz)	Cabo Blanco, Peru	Mar. 25, 1953	Mrs. Wendell Anderson, Jr.
W-60 kg (130 lb)	152.40 kg (336 lb 0 oz)	Cabo Blanco, Peru	Jan. 16, 1957	Mrs. Seymour Knox, III

Tuna, blackfin / *Thunnus atlanticus*

LINE CLASS	WEIGHT	PLACE	DATE	ANGLER
M-01 kg (2 lb)	4.98 kg (11 lb 0 oz)	San Juan, Puerto Rico	Dec. 23, 1997	Gustavo Ferrer
M-02 kg (4 lb)	12.70 kg (28 lb 0 oz)	Key West, Florida, USA	May 12, 1988	Bill Riesenfeld
M-03 kg (6 lb)	13.15 kg (29 lb 0 oz)	Challenger Bank, Bermuda	Aug. 6, 1972	Keith R. Winter
M-04 kg (8 lb)	14.51 kg (32 lb 0 oz)	Miami, Florida, USA	June 7, 1998	Joseph G. Singer
M-06 kg (12 lb)	17.94 kg (39 lb 9 oz)	Challenger Bank, Bermuda	June 27, 1987	Francis H.P. Patterson
M-08 kg (16 lb)	16.55 kg (36 lb 8 oz)	Clearwater, Florida, USA	May 10, 1997	Robert Lee Whitman, Jr.
M-10 kg (20 lb)	20.63 kg (45 lb 8 oz)	Key West, Florida, USA	May 4, 1996	Sam J. Burnett
M-15 kg (30 lb)	18.59 kg (41 lb 0 oz)	Bermuda	Sept. 19, 1990	James R.M. Parris
M-24 kg (50 lb)	19.05 kg (42 lb 0 oz)	Bermuda	June 2, 1978	Alan J. Card
W-01 kg (2 lb)	1.44 kg (3 lb 3 oz)	Islamorada, Florida, USA	Sept. 20, 1987	Barbara Edgar
W-02 kg (4 lb)	12.24 kg (27 lb 0 oz)	Key West, Florida, USA	May 2, 1983	Joan M. Garisto
W-03 kg (6 lb)	12.70 kg (28 lb 0 oz)	Islamorada, Florida, USA	Mar. 26, 1978	Ruth C. Stoky
W-04 kg (8 lb)	15.87 kg (35 lb 0 oz)	Key West, Florida, USA	Apr. 16, 1990	Mrs. William B. DuVal
W-06 kg (12 lb)	13.60 kg (30 lb 0 oz)	Key West, Florida, USA	May 9, 1991	Lisa Booth
W-08 kg (16 lb)	13.78 kg (30 lb 6 oz)	Boca Raton, Florida, USA	Apr. 28, 1998	Lynne W. Mitchem
W-10 kg (20 lb)	15.19 kg (33 lb 0 oz)	Miami Beach, Florida, USA	Apr. 25, 1997	Julie Armstrong
W-15 kg (30 lb)	17.23 kg (38 lb 0 oz)	Islamorada, Florida, USA	May 22, 1973	Elizabeth Jean Wade
W-24 kg (50 lb)	17.09 kg (37 lb 11 oz)	Northwest Edge, Bermuda	Aug. 25, 1982	Denise O'Toole

Tuna, bluefin / *Thunnus thynnus*

LINE CLASS	WEIGHT	PLACE	DATE	ANGLER
M-01 kg (2 lb)	Vacant			
M-02 kg (4 lb)	7.57 kg (16 lb 11 oz)	Cortes Bank, California, USA	Sept. 14, 1992	Tom Pfleger
M-03 kg (6 lb)	17.69 kg (39 lb 0 oz)	Montauk, Long Island, New York, USA	Oct. 8, 1983	Chuck Mallinson
M-04 kg (8 lb)	16.49 kg (36 lb 6 oz)	Montauk, Long Island, New York, USA	Sept. 14, 1994	Stephen Sloan
M-06 kg (12 lb)	37.19 kg (82 lb 0 oz)	Oregon Inlet, North Carolina, USA	May 26, 1991	John W. DuVal
M-08 kg (16 lb)	85.27 kg (188 lb 0 oz)	Montauk, Long Island, New York, USA	Sept. 5, 1982	Stephen Sloan
M-10 kg (20 lb)	83.00 kg (182 lb 15 oz)	Secche di Vada, Italy	May 16, 1994	Daniele Zingoni
M-15 kg (30 lb)	157.85 kg (348 lb 0 oz)	Hatteras, North Carolina, USA	Feb. 26, 1995	George B. Sowers
M-24 kg (50 lb)	407.00 kg (897 lb 4 oz)	Gran Canaria, Canary Islands, Spain	Mar. 25, 1977	Charles Chtivelman
M-37 kg (80 lb)	506.21 kg (1116 lb 0 oz)	North Lake, Prince Edward Island, Canada	Sept. 26, 1985	Dr. J. M. Steffey
M-60 kg (130 lb)	679.00 kg (1496 lb 0 oz)	Aulds Cove, Nova Scotia, Canada	Oct. 26, 1979	Ken Fraser
W-01 kg (2 lb)	Vacant			
W-02 kg (4 lb)	Vacant			
W-03 kg (6 lb)	18.82 kg (41 lb 8 oz)	Virginia Beach, Virginia, USA	July 3, 1977	Mrs. William B. DuVal
W-04 kg (8 lb)	20.41 kg (45 lb 0 oz)	Jackspot, Ocean City, Maryland, USA	Aug. 18, 1997	Karen Gilbreath
W-06 kg (12 lb)	22.67 kg (50 lb 0 oz)	Jackspot, Ocean City, Maryland, USA	July 21, 1995	Karen Gilbreath
W-08 kg (16 lb)	29.48 kg (65 lb 0 oz)	Twin Wrecks, Ocean City, Maryland, USA	July 12, 1995	Karen Gilbreath
W-10 kg (20 lb)	42.18 kg (93 lb 0 oz)	Provincetown, Massachusetts, USA	Sept. 14, 1958	Willia H. Mather
W-15 kg (30 lb)	158.75 kg (350 lb 0 oz)	Hatteras, North Carolina, USA	Jan. 21, 1998	Elizabeth Hogan
W-24 kg (50 lb)	234.96 kg (518 lb 0 oz)	Bimini, Bahamas	May 13, 1950	Mrs. Phyllis Bass
W-37 kg (80 lb)	442.00 kg (974 lb 6 oz)	Azores Bank, Azores, Portugal	Oct. 5, 1996	Jeannine Francois
W-60 kg (130 lb)	530.71 kg (1170 lb 0 oz)	North Lake, Prince Edward Island, Canada	Oct. 2, 1978	Colette Perras, MD

Tuna, dogtooth / *Gymnosarda unicolor*

LINE CLASS	WEIGHT	PLACE	DATE	ANGLER
M-01 kg (2 lb)	3.30 kg (7 lb 4 oz)	Kohama Island, Okinawa, Japan	Mar. 15, 1989	Fumio Suzuki
M-02 kg (4 lb)	5.20 kg (11 lb 7 oz)	Kohama Island, Okinawa, Japan	Mar. 9, 1989	Fumio Suzuki
M-03 kg (6 lb)	9.00 kg (19 lb 13 oz)	Tubai Island, Tahiti, French Polynesia	Jan. 1, 1976	Alban Ellacott
M-04 kg (8 lb)	17.50 kg (38 lb 9 oz)	Townsville, Queensland, Australia	Nov. 30, 1986	Peter Charles O'Brien
M-06 kg (12 lb)	49.00 kg (108 lb 0 oz)	Hahazima, Ogasawara, Tokyo, Japan	Aug. 8, 1988	Kyoji Uchimi
M-08 kg (16 lb)	57.00 kg (125 lb 10 oz)	Mwali Island, Comoros	Nov. 11, 1983	Nic de Kock
M-10 kg (20 lb)	45.58 kg (100 lb 8 oz)	Denis Island, Seychelles	Apr. 12, 1977	Pierre Burkhardt
M-15 kg (30 lb)	66.00 kg (145 lb 8 oz)	Passe de Dumbea, Noumea, New Caledonia	Oct. 6, 1990	Christian Kalinowski
M-24 kg (50 lb)	101.60 kg (224 lb 0 oz)	La Morne, Mauritius	Nov. 6, 1988	Armand Jean Orttner
M-37 kg (80 lb)	131.00 kg (288 lb 12 oz)	Kwan-Tall Island, Cheju-Do, Korea	Oct. 6, 1982	Boo-Il Oh
M-60 kg (130 lb)	104.32 kg (230 lb 0 oz)	LeMorne, Mauritius	Jan. 18, 1993	Roger Amand
W-01 kg (2 lb)	Vacant			
W-02 kg (4 lb)	13.78 kg (30 lb 6 oz)	Maccles Field Bank, South China	May 5, 1993	Cristina Marina B. Villavicenc

Tuna, dogtooth / *(continued)*

LINE CLASS	WEIGHT	PLACE	DATE	ANGLER
W-03 kg (6 lb)	Vacant			
W-04 kg (8 lb)	22.52 kg (49 lb 10 oz)	Maccles Field Bank, South China	May 4, 1993	Margarita Marina B.
W-06 kg (12 lb)	17.23 kg (38 lb 0 oz)	Denis Island, Seychelles	Mar. 27, 1976	Georgette Douwma
W-08 kg (16 lb)	26.40 kg (58 lb 3 oz)	Hangkow Reef, Madang	June 13, 1993	Jan Hardie
W-10 kg (20 lb)	29.93 kg (66 lb 0 oz)	Denis Island, Seychelles	Apr. 7, 1977	Georgette Douwma
W-15 kg (30 lb)	46.70 kg (102 lb 15 oz)	Christmas Island, Australia	Oct. 10, 1996	Marie MacFarlane
W-24 kg (50 lb)	57.46 kg (126 lb 11 oz)	Latham Island, Tanzania, East Africa	June 7, 1987	Lynn Hamilton Ommanney
W-37 kg (80 lb)	47.40 kg (104 lb 8 oz)	Cairns, Queensland, Australia	Sept. 11, 1974	Gloria J. Applegate
W-60 kg (130 lb)	41.20 kg (90 lb 13 oz)	Linden Harbour, Papua, New Guinea	Jan. 13, 1993	Diane Dean

Tuna, longtail / *Thunnus tonggol*

LINE CLASS	WEIGHT	PLACE	DATE	ANGLER
M-01 kg (2 lb)	Vacant			
M-02 kg (4 lb)	11.85 kg (26 lb 1 oz)	Hervey Bay, Queensland, Australia	June 2, 1990	Raymond Bruce Revill
M-03 kg (6 lb)	14.00 kg (30 lb 13 oz)	Moreton Island, Queensland, Australia	Apr. 18, 1977	Lawrie Munro
M-04 kg (8 lb)	23.50 kg (51 lb 10 oz)	Moreton Island, Brisbane, Queensland, Australia	July 26, 1987	Jim Maguire
M-06 kg (12 lb)	30.00 kg (66 lb 2 oz)	Coffs Harbour, Australia	Mar. 25, 1985	John Gary Cross
M-08 kg (16 lb)	27.50 kg (60 lb 10 oz)	Bermagui, N.S.W., Australia	May 5, 1985	Jim Uttleymoore
M-10 kg (20 lb)	31.76 kg (70 lb 0 oz)	Green Cape, N.S.W., Australia	Dec. 16, 1984	Wayne Hoyle
M-15 kg (30 lb)	35.90 kg (79 lb 2 oz)	Montague Island, N.S.W., Australia	Apr. 12, 1982	Tim Simpson
M-24 kg (50 lb)	Vacant			
M-37 kg (80 lb)	28.00 kg (61 lb 11 oz)	Morton Bay, Australia	Aug. 17, 1995	Steven Foster
W-01 kg (2 lb)	Vacant			
W-02 kg (4 lb)	4.80 kg (10 lb 9 oz)	Groote Eylandt, Australia	Apr. 15, 1995	Jenny Gibson
W-03 kg (6 lb)	Vacant			
W-04 kg (8 lb)	21.25 kg (46 lb 13 oz)	Bribie Island, Brisbane, Queensland, Australia	July 17, 1988	Kathy Maguire
W-06 kg (12 lb)	23.50 kg (51 lb 12 oz)	Moreton Island, Brisbane, Queensland, Australia	June 30, 1990	Kathy Maguire
W-08 kg (16 lb)	25.60 kg (56 lb 7 oz)	Moreton Island, Queensland, Australia	May 3, 1992	Olga Mack
W-10 kg (20 lb)	22.00 kg (48 lb 8 oz)	Moreton Island, Brisbane, Queensland, Australia	May 15, 1992	Kathy Maguire
W-15 kg (30 lb)	26.60 kg (58 lb 10 oz)	Bermagui, N.S.W., Australia	May 5, 1985	Roslyn Uttleymoore
W-24 kg (50 lb)	20.30 kg (44 lb 12 oz)	Moreton Island, Australia	May 9, 1993	Kathy Maguire
W-37 kg (80 lb)	Vacant			

Tuna, skipjack / *Katsuwonus pelamis*

LINE CLASS	WEIGHT	PLACE	DATE	ANGLER
M-01 kg (2 lb)	6.01 kg (13 lb 4 oz)	Miami Beach, Florida, USA	Aug. 6, 1985	John R. McCabe
M-02 kg (4 lb)	9.79 kg (21 lb 9 oz)	Freeport, Bahamas	Apr. 14, 1996	Colin Rose
M-03 kg (6 lb)	10.50 kg (23 lb 2 oz)	Black River, Mauritius	Jan. 19, 1998	Michael Bartels
M-04 kg (8 lb)	10.65 kg (23 lb 8 oz)	Keahole Pt., Kona, Hawaii, USA	Nov. 13, 1983	Rodger Spencer
M-06 kg (12 lb)	15.04 kg (33 lb 2 oz)	Sagami Bay, Kanagawa, Japan	Sept. 12, 1996	Makoto Urabe
M-08 kg (16 lb)	15.00 kg (33 lb 1 oz)	Black River, Mauritius	Feb. 18, 1996	Michael Bartels
M-10 kg (20 lb)	17.80 kg (39 lb 4 oz)	Challenger Bank, Bermuda	July 13, 1978	Keith R. Winter
M-15 kg (30 lb)	19.00 kg (41 lb 14 oz)	Pearl Beach, Mauritius	Nov. 12, 1985	Edmund K. R. Heinzen
M-24 kg (50 lb)	18.93 kg (41 lb 12 oz)	Black River, Mauritius	Mar. 13, 1982	Bruno de Ravel
W-01 kg (2 lb)	2.41 kg (5 lb 5 oz)	The Sisters, Tasmania, Australia	Apr. 2, 1984	Ann Self
W-02 kg (4 lb)	4.42 kg (9 lb 12 oz)	Boynton Beach, Florida, USA	June 11, 1985	Adrienne Sorg
W-03 kg (6 lb)	6.57 kg (14 lb 8 oz)	San Diego, California, USA	Sept. 3, 1976	Joanne Birtcher
W-04 kg (8 lb)	11.33 kg (25 lb 0 oz)	Kona, Hawaii, USA	June 7, 1991	Louise Hawkins
W-06 kg (12 lb)	11.79 kg (26 lb 0 oz)	Kaneohe, Oahu, Hawaii, USA	July 24, 1982	Charlotte T. Nottage
W-08 kg (16 lb)	10.31 kg (22 lb 11 oz)	Kona, Hawaii, USA	June 16, 1990	Pat Snyder
W-10 kg (20 lb)	15.08 kg (33 lb 4 oz)	Le Morne, Mauritius	Apr. 10, 1986	Monique Tyack
W-15 kg (30 lb)	16.05 kg (35 lb 6 oz)	Trou Aux Biches, Mauritius	Sept. 23, 1990	Marie Laure Krauze
W-24 kg (50 lb)	16.55 kg (36 lb 8 oz)	Isla Clarion, Revillagigedo Islands, Mexico	Oct. 29, 1987	Jan Satterfield

Tuna, southern bluefin / *Thunnus maccoyi*

LINE CLASS	WEIGHT	PLACE	DATE	ANGLER
M-01 kg (2 lb)	8.00 kg (17 lb 10 oz)	Port Lincoln, S.A., Australia	June 24, 1992	George Flourentzou
M-02 kg (4 lb)	11.00 kg (24 lb 4 oz)	Port Lincoln, S.A., Australia	June 25, 1992	George Flourentzou
M-03 kg (6 lb)	20.50 kg (45 lb 3 oz)	Ward Island, Australia	Feb. 19, 1997	George Flourentzou
M-04 kg (8 lb)	24.10 kg (53 lb 2 oz)	Cannon Reef, Streaky Bay, Australia	Feb. 21, 1996	George Flourentzou
M-06 kg (12 lb)	36.50 kg (80 lb 7 oz)	Cannon Reef, Streaky Bay, Australia	Feb. 5, 1997	David Young
M-08 kg (16 lb)	32.00 kg (70 lb 8 oz)	Streaky Bay, Australia	Jan. 22, 1994	George Mitris
M-10 kg (20 lb)	58.96 kg (130 lb 0 oz)	Hippolytes, Tasmania, Australia	Mar. 2, 1976	Anthony John Little
M-15 kg (30 lb)	106.50 kg (234 lb 12 oz)	Tasman Island, Tasmania, Australia	May 11, 1980	Jim Allen
M-24 kg (50 lb)	158.00 kg (348 lb 5 oz)	Whakatane, New Zealand	Jan. 16, 1981	Rex Wood
M-37 kg (80 lb)	138.00 kg (304 lb 3 oz)	White Island, New Zealand	Feb. 18, 1984	Brian Guy
M-60 kg (130 lb)	148.50 kg (327 lb 6 oz)	Westport, New Zealand	Aug. 7, 1981	Des Benson
W-01 kg (2 lb)	Vacant			
W-02 kg (4 lb)	Vacant			
W-03 kg (6 lb)	9.60 kg (21 lb 2 oz)	South West Rocks, Kangaroo, South Australia	Apr. 7, 1981	Kim Carolan
W-04 kg (8 lb)	14.50 kg (31 lb 15 oz)	Cabbage Patch, Australia	May 18, 1997	Xenia Nacevicius
W-06 kg (12 lb)	21.70 kg (47 lb 13 oz)	St. Helen's Island, Tasmania, Australia	Apr. 19, 1981	Anne Shaw
W-08 kg (16 lb)	17.20 kg (37 lb 14 oz)	Hippolyte Rocks, Tasmania, Australia	Apr. 2, 1988	Rebecca Hallam
W-10 kg (20 lb)	37.00 kg (81 lb 9 oz)	Tasman Island, Tasmania, Australia	Mar. 7, 1981	Nanette Lyall
W-15 kg (30 lb)	45.25 kg (99 lb 12 oz)	Eaglehawk Neck, Tasmania, Australia	May 3, 1981	Elizabeth Bracey
W-24 kg (50 lb)	26.64 kg (58 lb 11 oz)	Firodland, New Zealand	May 6, 1996	Donna Harris
W-37 kg (80 lb)	78.50 kg (173 lb 0 oz)	White Island, New Zealand	Feb. 12, 1981	Carolyn L. Thies
W-60 kg (130 lb)	Vacant			

Tuna, yellowfin / *Thunnus albacares*

LINE CLASS	WEIGHT	PLACE	DATE	ANGLER
M-01 kg (2 lb)	5.60 kg (12 lb 5 oz)	Malindi, Kenya	Feb. 28, 1983	Dieter Weber
M-02 kg (4 lb)	25.00 kg (55 lb 1 oz)	Mooloolaba, Queensland, Australia	Jan. 1, 1993	Mike Levitt
M-03 kg (6 lb)	28.91 kg (63 lb 12 oz)	Moriches, New York, USA	Aug. 26, 1978	Tred Barta
M-04 kg (8 lb)	39.50 kg (87 lb 1 oz)	Bermagui, N.S.W., Australia	June 17, 1992	Ken Stockton
M-06 kg (12 lb)	74.00 kg (163 lb 2 oz)	Montague Island, Australia	May 15, 1983	Phillip Volkens
M-08 kg (16 lb)	86.50 kg (190 lb 11 oz)	Bermagui, N.S.W., Australia	Apr. 13, 1987	Jim Morris
M-10 kg (20 lb)	97.00 kg (213 lb 13 oz)	Bellambi, N.S.W., Australia	Dec. 7, 1980	Gregory Phillip Clarke
M-15 kg (30 lb)	117.11 kg (258 lb 3 oz)	Isla San Benedicto, Revillagigedo Islands, Mexico	Apr. 26, 1994	Thomas G. Pfleger
M-24 kg (50 lb)	164.03 kg (361 lb 10 oz)	Isla Socorro, Revillagigedo Islands, Mexico	Dec. 6, 1981	Jim D. Nemlowill
M-37 kg (80 lb)	176.35 kg (388 lb 12 oz)	Isla San Benedicto, Revillagigedo Islands, Mexico	Apr. 1, 1977	Curt Wiesenhutter
M-60 kg (130 lb)	170.73 kg (376 lb 6 oz)	Clarion Island, Baja California, Mexico	Jan. 5, 1996	Kenneth "Corky" Yokoe
W-01 kg (2 lb)	6.35 kg (14 lb 0 oz)	Pinas Bay, Panama	Mar. 23, 1992	Deborah Maddux Dunaway
W-02 kg (4 lb)	9.07 kg (20 lb 0 oz)	Pinas Bay, Panama	Mar. 15, 1995	Elizabeth Hogan
W-03 kg (6 lb)	17.74 kg (39 lb 11 oz)	Challenger Bank, Bermuda	July 5, 1980	Janet M. Lines
W-04 kg (8 lb)	28.43 kg (62 lb 11 oz)	Challenger Bank, Bermuda	Aug. 28, 1987	Dylis Allison Pantry
W-06 kg (12 lb)	53.00 kg (116 lb 13 oz)	Sydney, N.S.W., Australia	Oct. 8, 1978	Dulcie Chee
W-08 kg (16 lb)	54.65 kg (120 lb 8 oz)	Kailua, Kona, Hawaii, USA	Aug. 5, 1986	Jocelyn Everette
W-10 kg (20 lb)	92.30 kg (203 lb 8 oz)	Kona, Hawaii, USA	July 16, 1992	Pamela S. Basco
W-15 kg (30 lb)	111.13 kg (245 lb 0 oz)	Kaaiwi Pt., Kona, Hawaii, USA	July 28, 1978	Ann Blumenfeld
W-24 kg (50 lb)	116.12 kg (256 lb 0 oz)	Kailua, Kona, Hawaii, USA	Aug. 6, 1979	Evangeline T. Komo
W-37 kg (80 lb)	122.47 kg (270 lb 0 oz)	Isla Roca Partida, Revillagigedo Islands, Mexico	Mar. 16, 1980	Caroline Layne
W-60 kg (130 lb)	138.00 kg (304 lb 4 oz)	San Benedicto Island, Mexico	Nov. 13, 1993	Joyce Corrigan

Tunny, little / *Euthynnus alletteratus*

LINE CLASS	WEIGHT	PLACE	DATE	ANGLER
M-01 kg (2 lb)	6.91 kg (15 lb 4 oz)	Key West, Florida, USA	May 1, 1984	Pete Peacock
M-02 kg (4 lb)	7.48 kg (16 lb 8 oz)	Cancun, Quintana Roo, Mexico	June 15, 1983	Joseph A. Webster, III
M-03 kg (6 lb)	9.29 kg (20 lb 8 oz)	Key West, Florida, USA	Apr. 22, 1978	David L. Vatter
M-04 kg (8 lb)	9.97 kg (22 lb 0 oz)	Challenger Bank, Bermuda	Dec. 31, 1989	David D. Barber
M-06 kg (12 lb)	12.80 kg (28 lb 3 oz)	Annaba, Cap de Garde, Algeria	Dec. 25, 1988	Raymond Madau
M-08 kg (16 lb)	10.61 kg (23 lb 6 oz)	Challenger Banks, Bermuda	Aug. 8, 1991	Bertie Lines
M-10 kg (20 lb)	12.81 kg (28 lb 4 oz)	Challenger Banks, Bermuda	July 2, 1994	Robert Charles Davies
M-15 kg (30 lb)	15.95 kg (35 lb 2 oz)	Cap de Garde, Algeria	Dec. 14, 1988	Jean Yves Chatard
W-01 kg (2 lb)	6.80 kg (15 lb 0 oz)	Key West, Florida, USA	May 23, 1984	Eileen Peacock
W-02 kg (4 lb)	7.48 kg (16 lb 8 oz)	Key West, Florida, USA	May 15, 1984	Eileen Peacock
W-03 kg (6 lb)	9.52 kg (21 lb 0 oz)	Cancun, Quintana Roo, Mexico	May 20, 1980	Gloria J. Applegate
W-04 kg (8 lb)	7.71 kg (17 lb 0 oz)	Saly, Senegal	Feb. 20, 1997	Odile Robelin
W-06 kg (12 lb)	7.71 kg (17 lb 0 oz)	Isla Mujeres, Quintana Roo, Mexico	May 7, 1995	Bibi Capozzi
W-08 kg (16 lb)	14.62 kg (32 lb 4 oz)	Challenger Bank, Bermuda	June 23, 1990	Susan D. Wilson
W-10 kg (20 lb)	9.63 kg (21 lb 4 oz)	Palm Beach, Florida, USA	Aug. 19, 1978	Joan Zeitlin
W-15 kg (30 lb)	9.29 kg (20 lb 8 oz)	Jupiter Inlet, Jupiter, Florida, USA	June 18, 1983	Doris D. Hawthorn

Wahoo / *Acanthocybium solandri*

LINE CLASS	WEIGHT	PLACE	DATE	ANGLER
M-01 kg (2 lb)	Vacant			
M-02 kg (4 lb)	15.59 kg (34 lb 6 oz)	Boynton Inlet, Florida, USA	June 19, 1986	Robert Joseph Sorg
M-03 kg (6 lb)	23.13 kg (51 lb 0 oz)	Mayaguez, Puerto Rico	Mar. 4, 1978	Leroy V. Battistini
M-04 kg (8 lb)	22.60 kg (49 lb 13 oz)	Ponta Barra, Mozambique	Sept. 29, 1997	Hennie Geldennuys
M-06 kg (12 lb)	36.93 kg (81 lb 7 oz)	North Rock, Bermuda	Dec. 22, 1984	Michael E. Midgett
M-08 kg (16 lb)	42.86 kg (94 lb 8 oz)	Gulf of Mexico, Gulf Breeze, Florida, USA	May 30, 1991	Michael D. Flowers
M-10 kg (20 lb)	52.16 kg (115 lb 0 oz)	Bermuda	July 2, 1961	Leo Barboza
M-15 kg (30 lb)	57.60 kg (127 lb 0 oz)	Buenavista, Baja California, Mexico	June 2, 1994	Dean D. Ettinger, MD
M-24 kg (50 lb)	71.89 kg (158 lb 8 oz)	Loreto, Baja California, Mexico	June 10, 1996	Keith Winter
M-37 kg (80 lb)	70.53 kg (155 lb 8 oz)	San Salvador, Bahamas	Apr. 3, 1990	William Bourne
M-60 kg (130 lb)	67.58 kg (149 lb 0 oz)	Cat Cay, Bahamas	June 15, 1962	John Pirovano
W-01 kg (2 lb)	Vacant			
W-02 kg (4 lb)	9.69 kg (21 lb 9 oz)	Destin, Florida, USA	Aug. 26, 1997	Melanie D. Mitchell
W-03 kg (6 lb)	12.81 kg (28 lb 4 oz)	Isla de la Plata, Ecuador	Nov. 3, 1975	Maria Isabel Maspons
W-04 kg (8 lb)	23.58 kg (52 lb 0 oz)	Dry Tortugas, Florida, USA	Mar. 6, 1993	Mrs. William B. DuVal
W-06 kg (12 lb)	37.19 kg (82 lb 0 oz)	Port Canaveral, Florida, USA	Jan. 2, 1989	Christine Currie
W-08 kg (16 lb)	33.56 kg (74 lb 0 oz)	San Salvador, Bahamas	Apr. 4, 1996	Melissa Carr
W-10 kg (20 lb)	37.64 kg (83 lb 0 oz)	St. Thomas, U.S. Virgin Islands	Mar. 5, 1968	Gloria J. Applegate
W-15 kg (30 lb)	49.24 kg (108 lb 9 oz)	Cape May, New Jersey, USA	July 17, 1977	Charlene Mascuch
W-24 kg (50 lb)	69.62 kg (153 lb 8 oz)	San Salvador, Bahamas	Mar. 1, 1996	Gabrielle Knapp
W-37 kg (80 lb)	59.87 kg (132 lb 0 oz)	San Salvador, Bahamas	Mar. 20, 1990	Suzan Packer
W-60 kg (130 lb)	51.25 kg (113 lb 1 oz)	San Salvador, Bahamas	Feb. 19, 1996	Suzan Packer Sellian

Weakfish / *Cynoscion regalis*

LINE CLASS	WEIGHT	PLACE	DATE	ANGLER
M-01 kg (2 lb)	5.32 kg (11 lb 12 oz)	Chesapeake Bay, Virginia, USA	May 16, 1982	Ellyson S. Robinson III
M-02 kg (4 lb)	6.49 kg (14 lb 5 oz)	Cape May, New Jersey, USA	May 25, 1986	Matthew D. Welsh
M-03 kg (6 lb)	7.93 kg (17 lb 8 oz)	Fire Island Inlet, New York, USA	Aug. 25, 1976	Joseph Giallanzo
M-04 kg (8 lb)	8.67 kg (19 lb 2 oz)	Jones Beach Inlet, Long Island, New York, USA	Oct. 11, 1984	Dennis Roger Rooney
M-06 kg (12 lb)	8.67 kg (19 lb 2 oz)	Delaware Bay, Delaware, USA	May 20, 1989	William E. Thomas
M-08 kg (16 lb)	8.05 kg (17 lb 12 oz)	Lewes, Delaware, USA	July 14, 1984	Frank M. Yodie
M-10 kg (20 lb)	8.61 kg (19 lb 0 oz)	Chesapeake Bay, Virginia, USA	May 19, 1983	Philip W. Halstead
M-15 kg (30 lb)	7.51 kg (16 lb 9 oz)	Fire Island, Babylon, New York, USA	Oct. 4, 1985	Al Lorenzetti
M-15 kg (30 lb) Tie	7.51 kg (16 lb 9 oz)	Chesapeake Bay, Virginia, USA	May 16, 1986	James E. Lester, Jr.
W-01 kg (2 lb)	4.16 kg (9 lb 3 oz)	Delaware Bay, Delaware, USA	May 13, 1985	Jill Marshall

Weakfish / *(continued)*

LINE CLASS	WEIGHT	PLACE	DATE	ANGLER
W-02 kg (4 lb)	5.75 kg (12 lb 11 oz)	Chesapeake Bay, Virginia, USA	June 3, 1987	JoAnn H. McInnis
W-03 kg (6 lb)	5.67 kg (12 lb 8 oz)	Peconic Bay, New York, USA	May 26, 1981	Toni Christ
W-04 kg (8 lb)	6.20 kg (13 lb 11 oz)	Long Island Sound, New York, USA	June 3, 1986	Josephine Alese
W-06 kg (12 lb)	6.68 kg (14 lb 11 oz)	Delaware Bay, Cape May, New Jersey, USA	June 1, 1989	Cheri Wallace
W-08 kg (16 lb)	8.10 kg (17 lb 14 oz)	Fayerweather Island, Bridgeport, Conn., USA	Sept. 13, 1986	June Andrejko
W-10 kg (20 lb)	7.28 kg (16 lb 1 oz)	Southold Bay, Greenport, New York, USA	May 24, 1990	Carole Mysliborski
W-15 kg (30 lb)	7.05 kg (15 lb 9 oz)	Fire Island, Long Island, New York, USA	May 18, 1986	Joy E. Librizzi Bonvino

Yellowtail, California / *Seriola lalandi*

LINE CLASS	WEIGHT	PLACE	DATE	ANGLER
M-01 kg (2 lb)	6.80 kg (15 lb 0 oz)	San Martin Island, Mexico	Nov. 28, 1982	Jerry Wells, Sr.
M-02 kg (4 lb)	11.96 kg (26 lb 6 oz)	Loreto, Baja California, Mexico	Apr. 12, 1989	Gordon C. Prentice
M-03 kg (6 lb)	17.17 kg (37 lb 14 oz)	Coronado Island, Baja California, Mexico	Oct. 25, 1988	Carl E. Root
M-04 kg (8 lb)	7.89 kg (17 lb 6 oz)	Guadalupe Island, Mexico	July 16, 1995	Tom Pfleger
M-06 kg (12 lb)	19.61 kg (43 lb 4 oz)	Point Vincente, California, USA	May 23, 1997	John R. Arbuckle
M-08 kg (16 lb)	25.80 kg (56 lb 14 oz)	Catalina Island, California, USA	Jan. 16, 1989	Ronald R. Howarth
M-10 kg (20 lb)	26.76 kg (59 lb 0 oz)	La Jolla, California, USA	Jan. 26, 1988	Stephen W. Whybrew
M-15 kg (30 lb)	24.72 kg (54 lb 8 oz)	San Benitos Island, Baja California, Mexico	Oct. 14, 1984	Danny Jackson
M-24 kg (50 lb)	35.38 kg (78 lb 0 oz)	Alijos Rocks, Baja California, Mexico	June 27, 1987	Richard W. Cresswell
M-37 kg (80 lb)	35.97 kg (79 lb 4 oz)	Alijos Rocks, Baja California, Mexico	July 22, 1991	Robert I. Welker
W-01 kg (2 lb)	Vacant			
W-02 kg (4 lb)	7.93 kg (17 lb 8 oz)	Loreto, Baja California, Mexico	Apr. 15, 1989	Louise Prentice
W-03 kg (6 lb)	9.83 kg (21 lb 11 oz)	La Paz, Baja California, Mexico	Mar. 1, 1981	Louise Prentice
W-04 kg (8 lb)	5.95 kg (13 lb 1 oz)	San Clemente Island, California, USA	Aug. 17, 1997	Sandy Peck
W-06 kg (12 lb)	13.26 kg (29 lb 4 oz)	San Clemente Island, California, USA	Aug. 12, 1988	Julie Ann Yates
W-08 kg (16 lb)	17.00 kg (37 lb 8 oz)	Guadalupe Island, Mexico	May 14, 1992	Sandra (Honey) Beazley
W-10 kg (20 lb)	15.15 kg (33 lb 6 oz)	Guadalupe Island, Mexico	Aug. 9, 1992	Sandra (Honey) Beazley
W-15 kg (30 lb)	21.77 kg (48 lb 0 oz)	Mission Bay, San Diego, California, USA	Aug. 11, 1991	Renee Shoberg
W-24 kg (50 lb)	25.67 kg (56 lb 9 oz)	Alijos Rocks, Baja California, Mexico	Apr. 10, 1988	Agnes H. (Pug) Jones
W-37 kg (80 lb)	16.78 kg (37 lb 0 oz)	Alijos Rocks, Baja California, Mexico	June 22, 1992	Yolanda Madrid Shelp

Yellowtail, southern / *Seriola lalandi lalandi*

LINE CLASS	WEIGHT	PLACE	DATE	ANGLER
M-01 kg (2 lb)	6.50 kg (14 lb 5 oz)	Bateman's Bay, N.S.W., Australia	July 26, 1991	Kev Behrens
M-02 kg (4 lb)	15.50 kg (34 lb 2 oz)	Mangonui, New Zealand	Sept. 23, 1984	Mark L. Feldman, MD
M-03 kg (6 lb)	17.23 kg (38 lb 0 oz)	Bangitoto Channel, New Zealand	Dec. 17, 1972	Gabriel D. Tetro
M-04 kg (8 lb)	25.00 kg (55 lb 1 oz)	Bay of Islands, New Zealand	Aug. 30, 1987	John Bolland
M-06 kg (12 lb)	33.60 kg (74 lb 7 oz)	Cape Brett, Auckland, New Zealand	Apr. 26, 1993	Guy Eady
M-08 kg (16 lb)	32.90 kg (72 lb 8 oz)	Ngunguru Reef, Tutukaka, New Zealand	Mar. 26, 1987	Mike MacGibbon
M-10 kg (20 lb)	42.00 kg (92 lb 9 oz)	Cavalli Islands, New Zealand	July 3, 1991	Graham Fraser
M-15 kg (30 lb)	52.00 kg (114 lb 10 oz)	Tauranga, New Zealand	Feb. 5, 1984	Mike Godfrey
M-24 kg (50 lb)	52.00 kg (114 lb 10 oz)	White Island, New Zealand	Jan. 9, 1987	David Lugton
M-37 kg (80 lb)	48.98 kg (108 lb 0 oz)	Cape Brett, New Zealand	Jan. 15, 1962	Robin O'Connor
M-60 kg (130 lb)	43.09 kg (95 lb 0 oz)	White Island, New Zealand	Apr. 11, 1975	James Victor Bayliss
W-01 kg (2 lb)	2.25 kg (4 lb 15 oz)	Bellambi, N.S.W., Australia	Jan. 10, 1988	Wendy Patricia Jordan
W-02 kg (4 lb)	4.20 kg (9 lb 4 oz)	Mangonui Harbor, New Zealand	Mar. 11, 1986	Elizabeth M. Feldman
W-03 kg (6 lb)	7.25 kg (16 lb 0 oz)	Sydney, N.S.W., Australia	Sept. 24, 1972	Pamela Hudspeth
W-04 kg (8 lb)	25.40 kg (55 lb 15 oz)	Kawau Island, New Zealand	June 7, 1987	Ingrid van der Linden
W-06 kg (12 lb)	29.40 kg (64 lb 13 oz)	Cape Brett, Bay of Islands, Russell, New Zealand	June 8, 1997	Sharon Oates
W-08 kg (16 lb)	24.80 kg (54 lb 10 oz)	Cavalli Island, Bay of Islands, New Zealand	Aug. 6, 1998	Karene Cates
W-10 kg (20 lb)	33.00 kg (72 lb 12 oz)	Waiwiri Rock, Bay of Islands, New Zealand	Sept. 8, 1987	Dale Williamson
W-15 kg (30 lb)	43.80 kg (96 lb 8 oz)	White Island, New Zealand	Dec. 13, 1997	Anita Syben
W-24 kg (50 lb)	47.00 kg (103 lb 9 oz)	Bay of Plenty, Tauranga, New Zealand	Feb. 23, 1991	Shirley Ruane
W-37 kg (80 lb)	43.20 kg (95 lb 3 oz)	White Island, Whakatane, New Zealand	Dec. 13, 1993	Pauline Adams
W-60 kg (130 lb)	36.74 kg (81 lb 0 oz)	Mayor Island, New Zealand	Apr. 8, 1966	Patricia E. Jack

IGFA Freshwater Fly Rod World Records

The following are world freshwater fly rod records granted in IGFA tippet class categories as of January 1, 1999. The records are listed alphabetically according to the common names of species.

Barramundi / *Lates calcarifer*

TIPPET	WEIGHT	PLACE	DATE	ANGLER
Tippet 01 kg (2 lb)	3.20 kg (7 lb 0 oz)	Barron River, Cairns, Australia	Feb. 24, 1994	Stephen N. Jackson
Tippet 02 kg (4 lb)	8.10 kg (17 lb 13 oz)	Northern Territory, Australia	May 31, 1992	Malcolm Domaille
Tippet 03 kg (6 lb)	Vacant			
Tippet 04 kg (8 lb)	12.00 kg (26 lb 7 oz)	Howard R., Darwin, N.T., Australia	Dec. 12, 1982	P. J. Crase
Tippet 06 kg (12 lb)	13.50 kg (29 lb 12 oz)	Cape York, Australia	Aug. 16, 1992	Guaita Daniele
Tippet 08 kg (16 lb)	13.15 kg (28 lb 15 oz)	Ingham, N. Queensland, Australia	June 23, 1992	Darryl J. Steel
Tippet 10 kg (20 lb)	6.40 kg (14 lb 1 oz)	Goose Creek, Melville Island, N.T., Australia	Aug. 11, 1992	Wayne Andrew Ross

Bass, largemouth / *Micropterus salmoides*

TIPPET	WEIGHT	PLACE	DATE	ANGLER
Tippet 01 kg (2 lb)	3.43 kg (7 lb 9 oz)	Arivaca Lake, Arizona, USA	Mar. 17, 1984	Paul (Corky) Dufek
Tippet 02 kg (4 lb)	4.28 kg (9 lb 7 oz)	Lake Park, Florida, USA	Apr. 6, 1988	Jim Sulser
Tippet 03 kg (6 lb)	4.59 kg (10 lb 2 oz)	Lake Dixon, Escondido, California, USA	May 30, 1995	Dennis L. Ditmars
Tippet 04 kg (8 lb)	6.15 kg (13 lb 9 oz)	Lake Morena, San Diego, California, USA	Apr. 4, 1984	Ned Sparks Sewell
Tippet 06 kg (12 lb)	5.70 kg (12 lb 9 oz)	Lake Tsala, Apopka, Florida, USA	Mar. 25, 1984	Robert M. Ekker
Tippet 08 kg (16 lb)	5.76 kg (12 lb 11 oz)	Lake Dixon, Escondido, California, USA	Apr. 30, 1998	Dennis Ditmars
Tippet 10 kg (20 lb)	4.22 kg (9 lb 5 oz)	Lake Poway, Poway, California, USA	Apr. 22, 1992	Dennis L. Ditmars

Bass, redeye / *Micropterus coosae*

TIPPET	WEIGHT	PLACE	DATE	ANGLER
Tippet 01 kg (2 lb)	Vacant			
Tippet 02 kg (4 lb)	0.96 kg (2 lb 2 oz)	Ocmulgee River, Butts County, Georgia, USA	Apr. 28, 1995	Steven G. Bailey
Tippet 03 kg (6 lb)	1.09 kg (2 lb 6 oz)	Flint River, Bainbridge, Georgia, USA	July 1, 1995	J. Galt Allee
Tippet 04 kg (8 lb)	1.25 kg (2 lb 12 oz)	Flat Shoals Creek, Georgia, USA	June 11, 1987	Dudley Guthrie
Tippet 06 kg (12 lb)	0.56 kg (1 lb 4 oz)	Flint River, Bainbridge, Georgia, USA	May 6, 1995	J. Galt Allee
Tippet 08 kg (16 lb)	0.73 kg (1 lb 10 oz)	Flint River, Bainbridge, Georgia, USA	Aug. 23, 1998	Danny Riley
Tippet 10 kg (20 lb)	0.58 kg (1 lb 4 oz)	Flint River, Bainbridge, Georgia, USA	July 4, 1995	J. Galt Allee

Bass, rock / *Ambloplites rupestris*

TIPPET	WEIGHT	PLACE	DATE	ANGLER
Tippet 01 kg (2 lb)	0.90 kg (2 lb 0 oz)	Lake Erie, Pennsylvania, USA	Aug. 21, 1998	Herbert G. Ratner, Jr.
Tippet 02 kg (4 lb)	0.68 kg (1 lb 8 oz)	Lake Erie, Pennsylvania, USA	Aug. 21, 1998	Herbert G. Ratner, Jr.
Tippet 03 kg (6 lb)	0.68 kg (1 lb 8 oz)	Lake Erie, Pennsylvania, USA	Aug. 21, 1998	Herbert G. Ratner, Jr.
Tippet 04 kg (8 lb)	0.90 kg (2 lb 0 oz)	Lake Erie, Pennsylvania, USA	Aug. 20, 1998	Herbert G. Ratner, Jr.
Tippet 06 kg (12 lb)	0.68 kg (1 lb 8 oz)	Lake Erie, Pennsylvania, USA	Aug. 21, 1998	Herbert G. Ratner, Jr.
Tippet 08 kg (16 lb)	0.45 kg (1 lb 0 oz)	Lake Erie, Pennsylvania, USA	July 14, 1998	Herbert G. Ratner, Jr.
Tippet 10 kg (20 lb)	0.45 kg (1 lb 0 oz)	Lake Erie, Pennsylvania, USA	Aug. 21, 1998	Herbert G. Ratner, Jr.

Bass, smallmouth / *Micropterus dolomieu*

TIPPET	WEIGHT	PLACE	DATE	ANGLER
Tippet 01 kg (2 lb)	1.84 kg (4 lb 1 oz)	Basswood Lake, Ontario, Canada	June 3, 1993	Steven J. Torok
Tippet 02 kg (4 lb)	2.09 kg (4 lb 10 oz)	Basswood Lake, Ontario, Canada	June 4, 1992	Steven J. Torok
Tippet 03 kg (6 lb)	2.26 kg (5 lb 0 oz)	Basswood Lake, Canada	June 1, 1997	Doug Miller
Tippet 04 kg (8 lb)	2.26 kg (5 lb 0 oz)	Lake Erie, Pennsylvania, USA	July 25, 1997	Herbert G. Ratner, Jr.
Tippet 06 kg (12 lb)	2.49 kg (5 lb 8 oz)	Pickwick Dam, Tennessee, USA	Oct. 2, 1996	Herbert G. Ratner, Jr.
Tippet 08 kg (16 lb)	2.83 kg (6 lb 4 oz)	Pine Lake, Michigan, USA	Aug. 12, 1995	Pamela Kinsey McClelland
Tippet 10 kg (20 lb)	3.06 kg (6 lb 12 oz)	Basswood Lake, Minnesota, USA/Canada	Aug. 30, 1997	John Herrick

Bass, spotted / *Micropterus punctulatus*

TIPPET	WEIGHT	PLACE	DATE	ANGLER
Tippet 01 kg (2 lb)	Vacant			
Tippet 02 kg (4 lb)	1.44 kg (3 lb 3 oz)	Neosho River, Oklahoma, USA	Aug. 2, 1986	Jim Dougherty
Tippet 03 kg (6 lb)	2.04 kg (4 lb 8 oz)	Coosa River, Alabama, USA	Jan. 24, 1997	Peter Daniel Kramer
Tippet 04 kg (8 lb)	1.44 kg (3 lb 2 oz)	Neosho River, Oklahoma, USA	July 19, 1986	Jim Dougherty
Tippet 06 kg (12 lb)	2.86 kg (6 lb 5 oz)	Logan Martin Lake, Talladega, Alabama, USA	Oct. 9, 1985	Daniel W. Watson
Tippet 08 kg (16 lb)	2.52 kg (5 lb 9 oz)	Coosa River, Alabama, USA	Oct. 29, 1995	Peter Daniel Kramer
Tippet 10 kg (20 lb)	1.40 kg (3 lb 1 oz)	Logan Martin Lake, Alabama, USA	May 5, 1996	Shaw Grigsby, Jr.

Bass, striped (landlocked) / *Morone saxatilis*

TIPPET	WEIGHT	PLACE	DATE	ANGLER
Tippet 01 kg (2 lb)	13.38 kg (29 lb 8 oz)	San Luis Reservoir, California, USA	Apr. 3, 1994	Alfred Whitehurst
Tippet 02 kg (4 lb)	14.85 kg (32 lb 12 oz)	San Luis Reservoir, California, USA	Nov. 28, 1993	Alfred L. Whitehurst
Tippet 03 kg (6 lb)	17.23 kg (38 lb 0 oz)	San Luis Reservoir, California, USA	May 4, 1991	Leonard B. Bearden, Jr.
Tippet 04 kg (8 lb)	17.90 kg (39 lb 8 oz)	San Luis Reservoir, California, USA	May 1, 1996	Alfred L. Whitehurst
Tippet 06 kg (12 lb)	18.25 kg (40 lb 4 oz)	O'Neill Forebay, Los Banos, California, USA	Dec. 10, 1989	Alfred L. Whitehurst
Tippet 08 kg (16 lb)	24.72 kg (54 lb 8 oz)	O'Neill Forebay, Los Banos, California, USA	Sept. 17, 1989	Alfred L. Whitehurst
Tippet 10 kg (20 lb)	22.23 kg (49 lb 0 oz)	San Luis Reservoir, California, USA	Jan. 28, 1995	Leonard B. Bearden, Jr.

Bass, white / *Morone chrysops*

TIPPET	WEIGHT	PLACE	DATE	ANGLER
Tippet 01 kg (2 lb)	1.18 kg (2 lb 9 oz)	Pomme de Terre River, Minnesota, USA	May 20, 1982	R. E. Massey
Tippet 02 kg (4 lb)	1.17 kg (2 lb 9 oz)	Lake Nacimiento, California, USA	Mar. 12, 1983	Butch Olson
Tippet 03 kg (6 lb)	1.07 kg (2 lb 6 oz)	Richland Creek, Goshen, Arkansas, USA	Apr. 20, 1996	J. Phillip Guffey
Tippet 04 kg (8 lb)	1.58 kg (3 lb 8 oz)	Lake Nacimiento, California, USA	Mar. 6, 1981	Cory Wells
Tippet 06 kg (12 lb)	1.41 kg (3 lb 2 oz)	Missouri River, South Dakota, USA	June 22, 1996	Rick Hayden
Tippet 08 kg (16 lb)	1.08 kg (2 lb 2 oz)	White River, Goshen, Arkansas, USA	Apr. 27, 1995	Phillip Guffey
Tippet 10 kg (20 lb)	1.19 kg (2 lb 10 oz)	Richland Creek, Goshen, Arkansas, USA	Apr. 20, 1996	J. Phillip Guffey

Bass, whiterock / *Morone saxatilis x Morone chrysops*

TIPPET	WEIGHT	PLACE	DATE	ANGLER
Tippet 01 kg (2 lb)	3.85 kg (8 lb 8 oz)	Anna Reservoir, Summer Lake, Oregon, USA	Oct. 28, 1989	James Allen Crofoot
Tippet 02 kg (4 lb)	4.45 kg (9 lb 13 oz)	Anna Reservoir, Summer Lake, Oregon, USA	Aug. 12, 1988	James A. Crofoot

Bass, whiterock / *(continued)*

TIPPET	WEIGHT	PLACE	DATE	ANGLER
Tippet 03 kg (6 lb)	3.29 kg (7 lb 4 oz)	Eagle Creek, Indianapolis, Indiana, USA	June 11, 1996	Shane V. Wilson
Tippet 04 kg (8 lb)	3.45 kg (7 lb 10 oz)	Milford Reservoir, Junction City, Kansas, USA	Sept. 10, 1998	Ken Wisby
Tippet 06 kg (12 lb)	5.44 kg (12 lb 0 oz)	Nockamixon Lake, Pennsylvania, USA	Oct. 14, 1990	Jonathan G. Greaser
Tippet 08 kg (16 lb)	4.98 kg (11 lb 0 oz)	Percy Priest, Nashville, Tennessee, USA	Apr. 7, 1992	Charles H. Moeling
Tippet 10 kg (20 lb)	3.81 kg (8 lb 6 oz)	Beaver Lake, Rogers, Arkansas, USA	Dec. 3, 1997	Mark Powell

Bass, yellow / *Morone mississippiensis*

TIPPET	WEIGHT	PLACE	DATE	ANGLER
Tippet 01 kg (2 lb)	Vacant			
Tippet 02 kg (4 lb)	Vacant			
Tippet 03 kg (6 lb)	Vacant			
Tippet 04 kg (8 lb)	Vacant			
Tippet 06 kg (12 lb)	Vacant			
Tippet 08 kg (16 lb)	Vacant			
Tippet 10 kg (20 lb)	Vacant			

Bluegill / *Lepomis macrochirus*

TIPPET	WEIGHT	PLACE	DATE	ANGLER
Tippet 01 kg (2 lb)	0.73 kg (1 lb 12 oz)	Daufuskie Island, South Carolina, USA	June 16, 1994	Gay Fowler
Tippet 02 kg (4 lb)	0.83 kg (1 lb 13 oz)	Colorado Springs, Colorado, USA	May 14, 1986	Raymond C. Sapp
Tippet 03 kg (6 lb)	0.79 kg (1 lb 12 oz)	Weldon's Pond, Florida, USA	June 12, 1995	J. Galt Alle
Tippet 04 kg (8 lb)	1.25 kg (2 lb 12 oz)	Guilford County, North Carolina, USA	Nov. 4, 1984	Curtis Ray Holmes, Jr.
Tippet 06 kg (12 lb)	0.68 kg (1 lb 8 oz)	Daufuskie Island, South Carolina, USA	June 15, 1994	Gay Fowler
Tippet 08 kg (16 lb)	0.62 kg (1 lb 6 oz)	Steelwood Lake, Alabama, USA	Sept. 22, 1997	Robert T. Cunningham, Jr.
Tippet 10 kg (20 lb)	0.68 kg (1 lb 8 oz)	Daufuskie Island, South Carolina, USA	June 15, 1994	Weston Fowler

Bowfin / *Amia calva*

TIPPET	WEIGHT	PLACE	DATE	ANGLER
Tippet 01 kg (2 lb)	3.06 kg (6 lb 12 oz)	Mobile River Delta, Alabama, USA	May 17, 1998	Robert T. Cunningham, Jr.
Tippet 02 kg (4 lb)	3.05 kg (6 lb 11 oz)	Mobile River Delta, Mobile, Alabama, USA	Aug. 17, 1997	Robert T. Cunningham, Jr.
Tippet 03 kg (6 lb)	5.21 kg (11 lb 8 oz)	Big MuddyRiver, Rend Lake, Illinois, USA	Aug. 31, 1996	Bill Willmert
Tippet 04 kg (8 lb)	2.83 kg (6 lb 4 oz)	Mobile River Delta, Alabama, USA	May 17, 1998	Robert T. Cunningham, Jr.
Tippet 06 kg (12 lb)	3.61 kg (7 lb 15 oz)	Oxbow Lake, South Carolina, USA	June 30, 1993	James D.P. Carter
Tippet 08 kg (16 lb)	2.94 kg (6 lb 8 oz)	Mobile River Delta, Alabama, USA	May 17, 1998	Robert T. Cunningham, Jr.
Tippet 10 kg (20 lb)	3.77 kg (8 lb 5 oz)	Buzz's Lake, Mount Vernon, Alabama, USA	July 12, 1998	Robert T. Cunningham, Jr.

Buffalo, bigmouth / *Ictiobus cyprinellus*

TIPPET	WEIGHT	PLACE	DATE	ANGLER
Tippet 01 kg (2 lb)	1.47 kg (3 lb 4 oz)	Rend Lake, Illinois, USA	Aug. 25, 1996	Bill Willmert
Tippet 02 kg (4 lb)	4.08 kg (9 lb 0 oz)	Rend Lake, Illinois, USA	Apr. 14, 1998	Rick Hayden
Tippet 03 kg (6 lb)	4.98 kg (11 lb 0 oz)	Oahe Tailwater, South Dakota, USA	May 2, 1998	Rick Hayden
Tippet 04 kg (8 lb)	Vacant			
Tippet 06 kg (12 lb)	2.26 kg (5 lb 0 oz)	Big Muddy River, Rend Lake, Illinois, USA	Sept. 15, 1996	Rick Hayden
Tippet 08 kg (16 lb)	1.70 kg (3 lb 12 oz)	Big Muddy River, Rend Lake, Illinois, USA	Sept. 10, 1995	Rick Hayden
Tippet 10 kg (20 lb)	Vacant			

Buffalo, smallmouth / *Ictiobus bubalus*

TIPPET	WEIGHT	PLACE	DATE	ANGLER
Tippet 01 kg (2 lb)	Vacant			
Tippet 02 kg (4 lb)	26.76 kg (59 lb 0 oz)	Town Lake, Austin, Texas, USA	Oct. 28, 1997	Gibbs Milliken
Tippet 03 kg (6 lb)	Vacant			
Tippet 04 kg (8 lb)	Vacant			
Tippet 06 kg (12 lb)	Vacant			
Tippet 08 kg (16 lb)	Vacant			
Tippet 10 kg (20 lb)	Vacant			

Bullhead, black / *Ameiurus melas*

TIPPET	WEIGHT	PLACE	DATE	ANGLER
Tippet 01 kg (2 lb)	Vacant			
Tippet 02 kg (4 lb)	Vacant			
Tippet 03 kg (6 lb)	Vacant			
Tippet 04 kg (8 lb)	Vacant			
Tippet 06 kg (12 lb)	Vacant			
Tippet 08 kg (16 lb)	Vacant			
Tippet 10 kg (20 lb)	Vacant			

Bullhead, brown / *Ameiurus nebulosus*

TIPPET	WEIGHT	PLACE	DATE	ANGLER
Tippet 01 kg (2 lb)	1.06 kg (2 lb 5 oz)	Kebert Pond, Pennsylvania, USA	May 9, 1992	Richard E. Faler, Jr.
Tippet 02 kg (4 lb)	1.14 kg (2 lb 8 oz)	Kebert Pond, Pennsylvania, USA	May 12, 1992	Richard E. Faler, Jr.
Tippet 03 kg (6 lb)	Vacant			
Tippet 04 kg (8 lb)	0.65 kg (1 lb 7 oz)	Kebert Pond, Pennsylvania, USA	May 17, 1993	Richard E. Faler, Jr.
Tippet 06 kg (12 lb)	0.82 kg (1 lb 13 oz)	Kebert Pond, Crawford County, Pennsylvania, USA	May 29, 1991	Richard E. Faler, Jr.
Tippet 08 kg (16 lb)	0.86 kg (1 lb 14 oz)	Kebert Pond, Pennsylvania, USA	May 9, 1992	Richard E. Faler, Jr.
Tippet 10 kg (20 lb)	1.02 kg (2 lb 4 oz)	Kebert Pond, Crawford County, Pennsylvania, USA	June 3, 1994	Richard E. Faler, Jr.

Bullhead, yellow / *Ameiurus natales*

TIPPET	WEIGHT	PLACE	DATE	ANGLER
Tippet 01 kg (2 lb)	Vacant			
Tippet 02 kg (4 lb)	Vacant			
Tippet 03 kg (6 lb)	Vacant			
Tippet 04 kg (8 lb)	Vacant			
Tippet 06 kg (12 lb)	Vacant			
Tippet 08 kg (16 lb)	Vacant			
Tippet 10 kg (20 lb)	Vacant			

Burbot / *Lota lota*

TIPPET	WEIGHT	PLACE	DATE	ANGLER
Tippet 01 kg (2 lb)	Vacant			
Tippet 02 kg (4 lb)	Vacant			
Tippet 03 kg (6 lb)	Vacant			
Tippet 04 kg (8 lb)	Vacant			
Tippet 06 kg (12 lb)	Vacant			
Tippet 08 kg (16 lb)	Vacant			
Tippet 10 kg (20 lb)	Vacant			

Carp, common / *Cyprinus carpio*

TIPPET	WEIGHT	PLACE	DATE	ANGLER
Tippet 01 kg (2 lb)	7.65 kg (16 lb 14 oz)	Carman's River, Long Island, New York, USA	Sept. 1, 1991	William A. Kuhle
Tippet 02 kg (4 lb)	9.45 kg (20 lb 13 oz)	St. Louis, Missouri, USA	June 29, 1992	Dan McClure
Tippet 03 kg (6 lb)	7.80 kg (17 lb 3 oz)	Lake Austin, Texas, USA	May 11, 1998	Gibbs Milliken
Tippet 04 kg (8 lb)	12.98 kg (28 lb 9 oz)	Private Lake, St. Louis, Missouri, USA	Apr. 19, 1992	Dan McClure
Tippet 06 kg (12 lb)	13.31 kg (29 lb 5 oz)	South Platte River, Colorado, USA	Mar. 11, 1995	Donald D. Jacobs
Tippet 08 kg (16 lb)	7.82 kg (17 lb 4 oz)	Carman's River, Long Island, New York, USA	June 4, 1992	William A. Kuhle
Tippet 10 kg (20 lb)	13.40 kg (29 lb 8 oz)	Town Lake, Austin, Texas, USA	May 5, 1998	Gibbs Milliken

Catfish, blue / *Ictalurus furcatus*

TIPPET	WEIGHT	PLACE	DATE	ANGLER
Tippet 01 kg (2 lb)	3.77 kg (8 lb 5 oz)	House Lake, Bucksville, Alabama, USA	Sept. 1, 1997	Troy Beatty
Tippet 02 kg (4 lb)	9.09 kg (20 lb 0 oz)	Pavillion Lake, Bucksville, Alabama, USA	June 29, 1997	Troy Beatty
Tippet 03 kg (6 lb)	13.01 kg (28 lb 11 oz)	Cape Fear River, Fayetteville, North Carolina, USA	Aug. 25, 1997	Edward C. Davis
Tippet 04 kg (8 lb)	6.63 kg (14 lb 9 oz)	Bucksville, Alabama, USA	July 10, 1997	Melanie Walton
Tippet 06 kg (12 lb)	7.47 kg (16 lb 7 oz)	House Lake, Bucksville, Alabama, USA	Aug. 15, 1997	Melanie Walton
Tippet 08 kg (16 lb)	19.05 kg (42 lb 0 oz)	Cape Fear River, Fayetteville, North Carolina, USA	July 11, 1997	Edward C. Davis
Tippet 10 kg (20 lb)	8.48 kg (18 lb 11 oz)	Cape Fear River, Fayetteville, North Carolina, USA	Aug. 8, 1997	Edward C. Davis

Catfish, channel / *Ictalurus punctatus*

TIPPET	WEIGHT	PLACE	DATE	ANGLER
Tippet 01 kg (2 lb)	5.66 kg (12 lb 8 oz)	Trailer Lake, Bucksville, Alabama, USA	July 5, 1998	Troy Beatty
Tippet 02 kg (4 lb)	9.12 kg (20 lb 2 oz)	Red River, Manitoba, Canada	May 14, 1992	Kastaway Kulis
Tippet 03 kg (6 lb)	4.74 kg (10 lb 7 oz)	Trailer Lake, Bucksville, Alabama, USA	June 14, 1996	Troy Beatty
Tippet 04 kg (8 lb)	10.57 kg (23 lb 5 oz)	Red River, Manitoba, Canada	May 22, 1992	Kastaway Kulis
Tippet 06 kg (12 lb)	13.66 kg (30 lb 2 oz)	Red River, Manitoba, Canada	May 13, 1992	Kastaway Kulis
Tippet 08 kg (16 lb)	10.58 kg (23 lb 5 oz)	Red River, Manitoba, Canada	May 13, 1992	Kastaway Kulis
Tippet 10 kg (20 lb)	12.70 kg (28 lb 0 oz)	Red River, Manitoba, Canada	May 12, 1992	Kastaway Kulis

Catfish, flathead / *Pylodictis olivaris*

TIPPET	WEIGHT	PLACE	DATE	ANGLER
Tippet 01 kg (2 lb)	Vacant			
Tippet 02 kg (4 lb)	Vacant			
Tippet 03 kg (6 lb)	Vacant			
Tippet 04 kg (8 lb)	Vacant			
Tippet 06 kg (12 lb)	17.00 kg (37 lb 8 oz)	Sooner Lake, Red Rock, Oklahoma, USA	Nov. 28, 1993	Rogers Fowler
Tippet 08 kg (16 lb)	Vacant			
Tippet 10 kg (20 lb)	Vacant			

Catfish, white / *Ameiurus catus*

TIPPET	WEIGHT	PLACE	DATE	ANGLER
Tippet 01 kg (2 lb)	Vacant			
Tippet 02 kg (4 lb)	Vacant			
Tippet 03 kg (6 lb)	Vacant			
Tippet 04 kg (8 lb)	Vacant			
Tippet 06 kg (12 lb)	5.46 kg (12 lb 0 oz)	Lake Talquin, Tallahassee, Florida, USA	July 5, 1990	Clayton C. Oaks, Sr.
Tippet 08 kg (16 lb)	Vacant			
Tippet 10 kg (20 lb)	Vacant			

Char, Arctic / *Salvelinus alpinus*

TIPPET	WEIGHT	PLACE	DATE	ANGLER
Tippet 01 kg (2 lb)	3.06 kg (6 lb 12 oz)	Basset Brook, Labrador, Canada	Sept. 1, 1983	Franklin F. Webb
Tippet 02 kg (4 lb)	4.98 kg (11 lb 0 oz)	Coppermine River, N.W.T., Canada	July 4, 1985	Thomas M. Bruno
Tippet 03 kg (6 lb)	6.12 kg (13 lb 8 oz)	Victoria Island, N.W.T., Canada	Aug. 16, 1994	Jefferey A. Trunsky
Tippet 04 kg (8 lb)	9.18 kg (20 lb 4 oz)	Tree River, N.W.T., Canada	Aug. 4, 1993	Ed Rice
Tippet 06 kg (12 lb)	6.80 kg (15 lb 0 oz)	Victoria Island, N.W.T., Canada	Sept. 2, 1980	Elmer M. Rusten
Tippet 08 kg (16 lb)	6.69 kg (14 lb 12 oz)	Kugaryuak River, N.W.T., Canada	Aug. 14, 1984	Jim Dixon
Tippet 10 kg (20 lb)	7.26 kg (16 lb 0 oz)	Tree River, Canada	Aug. 14, 1997	Ron Hickman

Crappie, black / *Pomoxis nigromaculatus*

TIPPET	WEIGHT	PLACE	DATE	ANGLER
Tippet 01 kg (2 lb)	1.01 kg (2 lb 3 oz)	Lee Hall Reservoir, Newport News, Virginia, USA	Mar. 20, 1985	Max Tongier
Tippet 02 kg (4 lb)	0.98 kg (2 lb 2 oz)	Alachua County, Florida, USA	Jan. 29, 1994	Wayne T. Mattox
Tippet 03 kg (6 lb)	1.14 kg (2 lb 8 oz)	Bull Shoals Lake, Arkansas, USA	Apr. 5, 1992	Gary Nelson
Tippet 04 kg (8 lb)	0.87 kg (1 lb 15 oz)	White Springs, Florida, USA	Jan. 18, 1998	Hamilton M. Franz
Tippet 06 kg (12 lb)	1.27 kg (2 lb 13 oz)	Custis Millpond, King William County, Virginia, USA	Apr. 4, 1994	T. Carter Hubard
Tippet 08 kg (16 lb)	0.82 kg (1 lb 13 oz)	Bull Shoals Lake, Arkansas, USA	Apr. 30, 1993	Gary Nelson
Tippet 10 kg (20 lb)	0.78 kg (1 lb 11 oz)	Pennington's Lake, Calvary, Georgia, USA	Mar. 1, 1996	J. Galt Allee

Crappie, white / *Pomoxis annularis*

TIPPET	WEIGHT	PLACE	DATE	ANGLER
Tippet 01 kg (2 lb)	0.59 kg (1 lb 5 oz)	Lake Marion, Eutawville, South Carolina, USA	Mar. 25, 1991	Robert McLain Nutting
Tippet 02 kg (4 lb)	1.13 kg (2 lb 8 oz)	Amelia County, Virginia, USA	Sept. 6, 1986	Adam S. Plotkin
Tippet 03 kg (6 lb)	0.54 kg (1 lb 3 oz)	Singleton Lake, Mobile River, Alabama, USA	Aug. 22, 1998	Robert T. Cunningham, Jr.
Tippet 04 kg (8 lb)	0.62 kg (1 lb 6 oz)	Lake Marion, Eutawville, South Carolina, USA	Mar. 25, 1991	Robert McLain Nutting
Tippet 06 kg (12 lb)	0.70 kg (1 lb 9 oz)	Smithville, Mississippi, USA	May 19, 1987	Johnny Harper
Tippet 08 kg (16 lb)	0.51 kg (1 lb 2 oz)	Lake Marion, Eutawville, South Carolina, USA	Mar. 25, 1991	Robert McLain Nutting

Crappie, white / *(continued)*

TIPPET	WEIGHT			
Tippet 10 kg (20 lb)	Vacant			

Dolly Varden / *Salvelinus malma*

TIPPET	WEIGHT	PLACE	DATE	ANGLER
Tippet 01 kg (2 lb)	5.37 kg (11 lb 13 oz)	Kelly River, Alaska, USA	July 13, 1998	Carl E. Brent
Tippet 02 kg (4 lb)	5.10 kg (11 lb 4 oz)	Kelly River, Alaska, USA	July 11, 1998	Jim Seegraves
Tippet 03 kg (6 lb)	6.49 kg (14 lb 5 oz)	Kivalina River, Alaska, USA	July 7, 1996	Martin Leibenguth
Tippet 04 kg (8 lb)	5.49 kg (12 lb 2 oz)	Wulik River, Alaska, USA	July 18, 1992	John A. Holland
Tippet 06 kg (12 lb)	5.78 kg (12 lb 12 oz)	Wulik River, Alaska, USA	July 17, 1992	Philip E. Driver
Tippet 08 kg (16 lb)	7.05 kg (15 lb 9 oz)	Kivalina River, Alaska, USA	July 1, 1997	Paulette "Polly" Kansagrad
Tippet 10 kg (20 lb)	6.12 kg (13 lb 8 oz)	Kivalina River, Alaska, USA	July 10, 1998	Phillip Wright

Dorado / *Salminus maxillosus*

TIPPET	WEIGHT	PLACE	DATE	ANGLER
Tippet 01 kg (2 lb)	Vacant			
Tippet 02 kg (4 lb)	4.87 kg (10 lb 12 oz)	Apa River, Paraguay	Nov. 5, 1991	Walter W. Fondren, III
Tippet 03 kg (6 lb)	Vacant			
Tippet 04 kg (8 lb)	Vacant			
Tippet 06 kg (12 lb)	Vacant			
Tippet 08 kg (16 lb)	7.80 kg (17 lb 3 oz)	Apa River, Paraguay	Nov. 3, 1991	Alex M. Jernigan
Tippet 10 kg (20 lb)	Vacant			

Drum, freshwater / *Aplodinotus grunniens*

TIPPET	WEIGHT	PLACE	DATE	ANGLER
Tippet 01 kg (2 lb)	3.91 kg (8 lb 10 oz)	Red River, Manitoba, Canada	May 16, 1990	John R. Starkell
Tippet 02 kg (4 lb)	2.89 kg (6 lb 6 oz)	False River, New Roads, Louisiana, USA	Apr. 19, 1994	R. Glen "Catch" Cormier
Tippet 03 kg (6 lb)	Vacant			
Tippet 04 kg (8 lb)	2.63 kg (5 lb 13 oz)	Red River, Manitoba, Canada	May 18, 1990	John R. Starkell
Tippet 06 kg (12 lb)	2.12 kg (4 lb 11 oz)	Red River, Manitoba, Canada	May 26, 1987	John R. Starkell
Tippet 08 kg (16 lb)	1.27 kg (2 lb 13 oz)	Red River, Manitoba, Canada	Sept. 17, 1988	John R. Starkell
Tippet 10 kg (20 lb)	4.64 kg (10 lb 4 oz)	Big Muddy River, Rend Lake, Illinois, USA	Sept. 14, 1996	Donna Willmert

Gar, alligator / *Lepisosteus spatula*

TIPPET	WEIGHT	PLACE	DATE	ANGLER
Tippet 01 kg (2 lb)	Vacant			
Tippet 02 kg (4 lb)	Vacant			
Tippet 03 kg (6 lb)	Vacant			
Tippet 04 kg (8 lb)	Vacant			
Tippet 06 kg (12 lb)	Vacant			
Tippet 08 kg (16 lb)	11.25 kg (24 lb 13 oz)	Buffalo Bayou, Houston, Texas, USA	June 18, 1995	Gregory L. Johnston
Tippet 10 kg (20 lb)	Vacant			

Gar, Florida / *Lepisosteus platyrhincus*

TIPPET	WEIGHT	PLACE	DATE	ANGLER
Tippet 01 kg (2 lb)	0.92 kg (2 lb 0 oz)	Alligator Alley, Florida, USA	Aug. 25, 1983	Rick Earle
Tippet 02 kg (4 lb)	1.33 kg (2 lb 15 oz)	Miami Canal, Broward Co., Florida, USA	Aug. 9, 1983	Rick Earle
Tippet 03 kg (6 lb)	1.22 kg (2 lb 11 oz)	Merritt Island, Florida, USA	June 8, 1996	Clifton C. Hodges
Tippet 04 kg (8 lb)	1.65 kg (3 lb 10 oz)	Everglades, Florida, USA	May 28, 1985	Gerry Suarez
Tippet 06 kg (12 lb)	1.30 kg (2 lb 14 oz)	Alligator Alley, Florida, USA	Aug. 25, 1983	Rick Earle
Tippet 08 kg (16 lb)	1.28 kg (2 lb 13 oz)	Lake Talquin, Tallahassee, Florida, USA	June 15, 1995	Clayton C. Oaks, Sr.
Tippet 10 kg (20 lb)	1.04 kg (2 lb 4 oz)	Merritt Island, Florida, USA	June 9, 1996	Randy Morgan

Gar, longnose / *Lepisosteus osseus*

TIPPET	WEIGHT	PLACE	DATE	ANGLER
Tippet 01 kg (2 lb)	Vacant			
Tippet 02 kg (4 lb)	1.75 kg (3 lb 14 oz)	Nickajack Dam, Tennessee, USA	May 10, 1987	Sarah Hamrick
Tippet 03 kg (6 lb)	0.56 kg (1 lb 4 oz)	St. Francis River, Missouri, USA	June 23, 1998	Donna Willmert
Tippet 04 kg (8 lb)	2.23 kg (4 lb 15 oz)	Tennessee River, Stevenson, Alabama, USA	Sept. 27, 1987	Terri Adams
Tippet 06 kg (12 lb)	3.33 kg (7 lb 5 oz)	Tennessee River, Stevenson, Alabama, USA	June 7, 1986	Sarah Hamrick
Tippet 08 kg (16 lb)	7.93 kg (17 lb 8 oz)	Lake Oliver, Georgia, USA	June 7, 1990	Trip Meine
Tippet 10 kg (20 lb)	0.85 kg (1 lb 14 oz)	St. Francis River, Missouri, USA	June 12, 1998	Bill Willmert

Gar, shortnose / *Lepisosteus platostomus*

TIPPET	WEIGHT	PLACE	DATE	ANGLER
Tippet 01 kg (2 lb)	0.90 kg (2 lb 0 oz)	Cinque Holmes Creek, Missouri, USA	May 26, 1996	Rick Hayden
Tippet 02 kg (4 lb)	1.19 kg (2 lb 10 oz)	Big Lake Bayou, Missouri, USA	June 26, 1994	Philip Willmert
Tippet 03 kg (6 lb)	1.36 kg (3 lb 4 oz)	Big Muddy River, Rend Lake, Illinois, USA	June 9, 1998	Rick Hayden
Tippet 04 kg (8 lb)	2.06 kg (4 lb 9 oz)	Big Lake Bayou, Missouri, USA	June 8, 1997	Donna K. Willmert
Tippet 06 kg (12 lb)	1.64 kg (3 lb 10 oz)	Lower Big Lake, Missouri, USA	July 15, 1997	Bill Willmert
Tippet 08 kg (16 lb)	1.58 kg (3 lb 8 oz)	Lower Big Lake, Charleston, Missouri, USA	July 7, 1995	Bill Willmert
Tippet 10 kg (20 lb)	2.60 kg (5 lb 12 oz)	Rend Lake, Illinois, USA	July 16, 1995	Donna Willmert

Gar, spotted / *Lepisosteus oculatus*

TIPPET	WEIGHT	PLACE	DATE	ANGLER
Tippet 01 kg (2 lb)	2.72 kg (6 lb 0 oz)	Buzz's Lake, Mobile, Alabama, USA	Aug. 23, 1998	Robert T. Cunningham, Jr.
Tippet 02 kg (4 lb)	2.38 kg (5 lb 4 oz)	Big Muddy River, Rend Lake, Illinois, USA	June 9, 1998	Rick Hayden
Tippet 03 kg (6 lb)	1.75 kg (3 lb 14 oz)	Big Muddy River, Rend Lake, Illinois, USA	Sept. 10, 1995	Rick Hayden
Tippet 04 kg (8 lb)	2.66 kg (5 lb 14 oz)	Rend Lake, Illinois, USA	Aug. 25, 1996	Bill Willmert
Tippet 06 kg (12 lb)	2.66 kg (5 lb 14 oz)	Big Muddy River, Rend Lake, Illinois, USA	Aug. 25, 1996	Rick Hayden
Tippet 08 kg (16 lb)	2.55 kg (5 lb 10 oz)	Mingo National Wildlife Refuge, Missouri, USA	May 25, 1996	Bill Willmert
Tippet 10 kg (20 lb)	2.94 kg (6 lb 8 oz)	Rend Lake, Illinois, USA	July 13, 1997	Bill Willmert

Grayling, Arctic / *Thymallus arcticus*

TIPPET	WEIGHT	PLACE	DATE	ANGLER
Tippet 01 kg (2 lb)	1.60 kg (3 lb 8 oz)	Great Slave Lake, N.W.T., Canada	Sept. 6, 1984	Don L. Guhlke
Tippet 02 kg (4 lb)	1.58 kg (3 lb 8 oz)	Great Bear Lake, N.W.T., Canada	Aug. 18, 1983	Joseph B. Doggett
Tippet 03 kg (6 lb)	1.33 kg (2 lb 15 oz)	Great Bear Lake, N.W.T., Canada	Aug. 3, 1997	Marlin A. Coulombe
Tippet 04 kg (8 lb)	1.58 kg (3 lb 8 oz)	Kasba Lake, Manitoba, N.W.T., Canada	Aug. 10, 1982	Iain P. MacDougall

Grayling, Arctic / *(continued)*

TIPPET	WEIGHT	PLACE	DATE	ANGLER
Tippet 06 kg (12 lb)	1.64 kg (3 lb 10 oz)	Kasan River, N.W.T., Canada	July 29, 1989	George A. Bernstein
Tippet 08 kg (16 lb)	1.53 kg (3 lb 6 oz)	Great Bear Lake, Canada	July 30, 1998	Marlin A. Coulombe
Tippet 10 kg (20 lb)	1.50 kg (3 lb 3 oz)	Niukluk River, Alaska, USA	Aug. 7, 1993	Mo Tidemanis

Huchen / *Hucho hucho*

TIPPET	WEIGHT	PLACE	DATE	ANGLER
Tippet 01 kg (2 lb)	Vacant			
Tippet 02 kg (4 lb)	Vacant			
Tippet 03 kg (6 lb)	Vacant			
Tippet 04 kg (8 lb)	Vacant			
Tippet 06 kg (12 lb)	Vacant			
Tippet 08 kg (16 lb)	Vacant			
Tippet 10 kg (20 lb)	Vacant			

Inconnu / *Stenodus leucichthys*

TIPPET	WEIGHT	PLACE	DATE	ANGLER
Tippet 01 kg (2 lb)	9.52 kg (21 lb 0 oz)	Kobuk River, Alaska, USA	Aug. 12, 1987	Lawrence E. Hudnall
Tippet 02 kg (4 lb)	12.47 kg (27 lb 8 oz)	Kobuk River, Alaska, USA	Aug. 14, 1987	Lawrence E. Hudnall
Tippet 03 kg (6 lb)	9.75 kg (21 lb 8 oz)	Holitna River, Alaska, USA	June 23, 1997	Jim Seegraves
Tippet 04 kg (8 lb)	15.08 kg (33 lb 4 oz)	Kobuk River, Alaska, USA	Aug. 13, 1987	Lawrence E. Hudnall
Tippet 06 kg (12 lb)	8.78 kg (19 lb 6 oz)	Kobuk River, Alaska, USA	July 20, 1997	Jim Seegraves
Tippet 08 kg (16 lb)	13.60 kg (30 lb 0 oz)	Kobuk River, Alaska, USA	Aug. 11, 1987	Daniel J. Hudnall
Tippet 10 kg (20 lb)	7.42 kg (16 lb 6 oz)	Kobuk River, Alaska, USA	July 21, 1997	Jim Seegraves

Kokanee / *Oncorhynchus nerka*

TIPPET	WEIGHT	PLACE	DATE	ANGLER
Tippet 01 kg (2 lb)	1.65 kg (3 lb 10 oz)	Missouri River, Montana, USA	Oct. 21, 1993	Jim Dixon
Tippet 02 kg (4 lb)	2.15 kg (4 lb 12 oz)	South Platte River, Hartsel, Colorado, USA	Nov. 16, 1997	Bill Perry
Tippet 03 kg (6 lb)	2.35 kg (5 lb 3 oz)	South Platte River, Hartsel, Colorado, USA	Nov. 16, 1997	Jim W. Williams
Tippet 04 kg (8 lb)	2.20 kg (4 lb 13 oz)	Missouri River, Montana, USA	Oct. 21, 1993	Jim Dixon
Tippet 06 kg (12 lb)	1.79 kg (3 lb 15 oz)	Missouri River, Montana, USA	Oct. 16, 1985	Jim Dixon
Tippet 08 kg (16 lb)	1.78 kg (3 lb 15 oz)	Missouri River, Montana, USA	Oct. 25, 1988	Jim Dixon
Tippet 10 kg (20 lb)	1.67 kg (3 lb 11 oz)	Missouri River, Montana, USA	Oct. 21, 1993	Jim Dixon

Muskellunge / *Esox masquinongy*

TIPPET	WEIGHT	PLACE	DATE	ANGLER
Tippet 01 kg (2 lb)	Vacant			
Tippet 02 kg (4 lb)	Vacant			
Tippet 03 kg (6 lb)	Vacant			
Tippet 04 kg (8 lb)	5.89 kg (13 lb 0 oz)	Susquehanna River, Pennsylvania, USA	Nov. 15, 1988	Boyd H. Walker
Tippet 06 kg (12 lb)	8.41 kg (18 lb 9 oz)	Pike Lake, Lac de Flambeau, Wisconsin, USA	June 28, 1989	Russell W. Fisher
Tippet 08 kg (16 lb)	8.39 kg (18 lb 8 oz)	Niagara River, New York, USA	June 18, 1995	Rick Kustich
Tippet 10 kg (20 lb)	6.23 kg (13 lb 12 oz)	Susquehanna River, Selinsgrove, Pennsylvania, USA	Oct. 23, 1993	Boyd H. Walker

Muskellunge, tiger / *Esox Masquinongy*

TIPPET	WEIGHT	PLACE	DATE	ANGLER
Tippet 01 kg (2 lb)	4.42 kg (9 lb 12 oz)	Susquehanna River, Pennsylvania, USA	Nov. 26, 1988	R. H. Lichtenwalner
Tippet 02 kg (4 lb)	2.60 kg (5 lb 12 oz)	Susquehanna River, Pennsylvania, USA	Dec. 9, 1987	R. H. Lichtenwalner
Tippet 03 kg (6 lb)	7.82 kg (17 lb 4 oz)	Freehold, New York, USA	July 29, 1983	Paul M. Schmookler
Tippet 04 kg (8 lb)	4.81 kg (10 lb 10 oz)	Horseshoe Lake, Walsenburg, Colorado, USA	May 15, 1997	John Brandstatter
Tippet 06 kg (12 lb)	13.80 kg (30 lb 6 oz)	St. Lawrence River, Montreal, Quebec, Canada	Oct. 20, 1985	Michel D. Croteau
Tippet 08 kg (16 lb)	Vacant			
Tippet 10 kg (20 lb)	Vacant			

Payara / *Hydrolicus scomberoides*

TIPPET	WEIGHT	PLACE	DATE	ANGLER
Tippet 01 kg (2 lb)	Vacant			
Tippet 02 kg (4 lb)	2.72 kg (6 lb 0 oz)	Uraima Falls, Venezuela	Mar. 27, 1998	Howard Wiles
Tippet 03 kg (6 lb)	Vacant			
Tippet 04 kg (8 lb)	Vacant			
Tippet 06 kg (12 lb)	Vacant			
Tippet 08 kg (16 lb)	Vacant			
Tippet 10 kg (20 lb)	Vacant			

Peacock, blackstriped / *Cichla intermedia*

TIPPET	WEIGHT	PLACE	DATE	ANGLER
Tippet 01 kg (2 lb)	Vacant			
Tippet 02 kg (4 lb)	Vacant			
Tippet 03 kg (6 lb)	Vacant			
Tippet 04 kg (8 lb)	Vacant			
Tippet 06 kg (12 lb)	Vacant			
Tippet 08 kg (16 lb)	Vacant			
Tippet 10 kg (20 lb)	Vacant			

Peacock, butterfly / *Cichla ocellaris*

TIPPET	WEIGHT	PLACE	DATE	ANGLER
Tippet 01 kg (2 lb)	1.81 kg (4 lb 0 oz)	Pembroke Pines, Florida, USA	Apr. 25, 1997	Jay Wright, Jr.
Tippet 02 kg (4 lb)	2.26 kg (5 lb 0 oz)	Pembroke Pines, Florida, USA	Feb. 15, 1997	Jay Wright, Jr.
Tippet 03 kg (6 lb)	Vacant			
Tippet 04 kg (8 lb)	4.53 kg (10 lb 0 oz)	Paragua River, Venezuela	Mar. 23, 1997	Scott Swartz
Tippet 06 kg (12 lb)	1.81 kg (4 lb 0 oz)	Miami, Florida, USA	Apr. 21, 1998	Herbert G. Ratner, Jr.
Tippet 08 kg (16 lb)	2.15 kg (4 lb 12 oz)	Snapper Creek, Miami, Florida, USA	Mar. 22, 1998	Al Karch
Tippet 10 kg (20 lb)	4.64 kg (10 lb 4 oz)	Mataveni River, Orinoco, Colombia	Feb. 26, 1998	Steven Jensen

Peacock, speckled / *Cichla temensis*

TIPPET	WEIGHT	PLACE	DATE	ANGLER
Tippet 01 kg (2 lb)	2.72 kg (6 lb 0 oz)	Cinaruco River, Venezuela	Feb. 5, 1986	Bert Bookout
Tippet 02 kg (4 lb)	5.90 kg (13 lb 0 oz)	Cinaruco River, Venezuela	Mar. 19, 1986	Walter W. Fondren, III

Peacock, speckled / *(continued)*

TIPPET	WEIGHT	PLACE	DATE	ANGLER
Tippet 03 kg (6 lb)	3.85 kg (8 lb 8 oz)	Paragua River, Venezuela	Mar. 28, 1997	Dr. Scott E. Swartz
Tippet 04 kg (8 lb)	7.50 kg (16 lb 5 oz)	Rio La Pica, Edo. Apure, Venezuela	Feb. 24, 1993	E.E. "Tex" Chandler
Tippet 06 kg (12 lb)	7.70 kg (16 lb 15 oz)	El Morichal, Rio Bita, Colombia	Apr. 16, 1988	Warren Brewster
Tippet 08 kg (16 lb)	8.61 kg (19 lb 0 oz)	Rio Pasimoni, Venezuela	Nov. 14, 1992	Elverton E. Clark, Jr.
Tippet 10 kg (20 lb)	11.56 kg (25 lb 8 oz)	Rio Pasimoni, Venezuela	Nov. 10, 1992	Bert Bookout

Perch, Nile / *Lates niloticus*

TIPPET	WEIGHT	PLACE	DATE	ANGLER
Tippet 01 kg (2 lb)	Vacant			
Tippet 02 kg (4 lb)	3.40 kg (7 lb 7 oz)	Rubondo Island, Lake Victoria, Africa	Nov. 9, 1993	Phillip P. de Moor
Tippet 03 kg (6 lb)	5.00 kg (11 lb 0 oz)	Rubondo Island, Lake Victoria, Africa	Oct. 24, 1994	Phillip P. de Moor
Tippet 04 kg (8 lb)	10.00 kg (22 lb 0 oz)	Rubondo Island, Lake Victoria, Africa	Oct. 9, 1993	Phillip P. de Moor
Tippet 06 kg (12 lb)	28.00 kg (61 lb 11 oz)	Rubondo Island, Lake Victoria, Tanzania	Oct. 29, 1994	Wayne John Haselau
Tippet 08 kg (16 lb)	50.00 kg (110 lb 3 oz)	Rubondo Island, Lake Victoria, Tanzania	Oct. 25, 1994	Wayne John Haselau
Tippet 10 kg (20 lb)	34.00 kg (74 lb 15 oz)	Rubondo Island, Lake Victoria, Tanzania	Oct. 26, 1994	Wayne John Haselau

Perch, white / *Morone americana*

TIPPET	WEIGHT	PLACE	DATE	ANGLER
Tippet 01 kg (2 lb)	0.66 kg (1 lb 7 oz)	Pawcatuck River, Rhode Island, USA	May 6, 1998	Alan Caolo
Tippet 02 kg (4 lb)	0.90 kg (2 lb 0 oz)	Nantucket, Massachusetts, USA	July 20, 1991	David Goodman
Tippet 03 kg (6 lb)	0.79 kg (1 lb 12 oz)	Pawcatuck River, Rhode Island, USA	May 3, 1997	Alan C. Caolo
Tippet 04 kg (8 lb)	0.54 kg (1 lb 3 oz)	Long Pond, Nantucket, Massachusetts, USA	Dec. 27, 1994	David Goodman
Tippet 06 kg (12 lb)	0.85 kg (1 lb 14 oz)	Miacomet Pond, Nantucket, Massachusetts, USA	Mar. 10, 1998	Chad Whitlock
Tippet 08 kg (16 lb)	0.77 kg (1 lb 11 oz)	Nantucket, Massachusetts, USA	Apr. 27, 1991	David Goodman
Tippet 10 kg (20 lb)	0.69 kg (1 lb 8 oz)	Nantucket, Massachusetts, USA	Apr. 28, 1991	David Goodman

Perch, yellow / *Perca flavescens*

TIPPET	WEIGHT	PLACE	DATE	ANGLER
Tippet 01 kg (2 lb)	Vacant			
Tippet 02 kg (4 lb)	Vacant			
Tippet 03 kg (6 lb)	0.63 kg (1 lb 6 oz)	North River, Currituck, North Carolina, USA	Feb. 5, 1995	Thomas F. Elkins
Tippet 04 kg (8 lb)	0.60 kg (1 lb 5 oz)	Blackwater Lake, Canada	June 23, 1997	Geoff J. Bernardo
Tippet 06 kg (12 lb)	0.56 kg (1 lb 4 oz)	Pakwash Lake, Ear Falls, Ontario, Canada	Oct. 16, 1985	Lawrence E. Hudnall
Tippet 08 kg (16 lb)	Vacant			
Tippet 10 kg (20 lb)	Vacant			

Pickerel, chain / *Esox niger*

TIPPET	WEIGHT	PLACE	DATE	ANGLER
Tippet 01 kg (2 lb)	1.52 kg (3 lb 5 oz)	Newport News, Virginia, USA	Apr. 12, 1984	Max Tongier, Jr.
Tippet 02 kg (4 lb)	1.92 kg (4 lb 4 oz)	Lovell's Pond, Cotuit, Massachusetts, USA	Oct. 24, 1985	Jeffrey Joiner
Tippet 03 kg (6 lb)	1.70 kg (3 lb 12 oz)	Nantucket, Massachusetts, USA	Dec. 8, 1991	David Goodman
Tippet 04 kg (8 lb)	2.38 kg (5 lb 4 oz)	Nockamixon Lake, Pennsylvania, USA	Mar. 8, 1997	Martin J. Haring
Tippet 06 kg (12 lb)	2.23 kg (4 lb 15 oz)	Nockamixon Lake, Pennsylvania, USA	Dec. 25, 1997	Martin J. Haring
Tippet 08 kg (16 lb)	1.95 kg (4 lb 5 oz)	Mingo National Wildlife Refuge, Missouri, USA	Oct. 21, 1995	Donna Willmert
Tippet 10 kg (20 lb)	1.53 kg (3 lb 6 oz)	Sand Bar, Hackettstown, New Jersey, USA	Sept. 20, 1993	Jerome J. McDonnell

Pike, northern / *Esox lucius*

TIPPET	WEIGHT	PLACE	DATE	ANGLER
Tippet 01 kg (2 lb)	10.97 kg (24 lb 3 oz)	Brabant Island, N.W.T., Canada	July 31, 1985	John A. Propp
Tippet 02 kg (4 lb)	12.24 kg (27 lb 0 oz)	Innoko River, Alaska, USA	Aug. 7, 1996	Bradley A. Befus
Tippet 03 kg (6 lb)	12.02 kg (26 lb 8 oz)	Innoko River, Hill Lake, Alaska, USA	Aug. 11, 1997	Barry Reynolds
Tippet 04 kg (8 lb)	12.24 kg (27 lb 0 oz)	Innoko River, Alaska, USA	Aug. 8, 1996	Bradley A. Befus
Tippet 06 kg (12 lb)	15.19 kg (33 lb 8 oz)	Nejanilini Lake, Manitoba, Canada	July 14, 1994	Barry D. Reynolds
Tippet 08 kg (16 lb)	14.51 kg (32 lb 0 oz)	Nejanilini Lake, Manitoba, Canada	July 13, 1994	Thomas W. Smith
Tippet 10 kg (20 lb)	13.83 kg (30 lb 8 oz)	Innoko River, Alaska, USA	Aug. 5, 1996	Bradley A. Befus

Redhorse, shorthead / *Moxostoma macrolepidotum*

TIPPET	WEIGHT	PLACE	DATE	ANGLER
Tippet 01 kg (2 lb)	Vacant			
Tippet 02 kg (4 lb)	Vacant			
Tippet 03 kg (6 lb)	Vacant			
Tippet 04 kg (8 lb)	Vacant			
Tippet 06 kg (12 lb)	0.90 kg (2 lb 0 oz)	Rock River, Illinois, USA	June 18, 1988	Mike Berg
Tippet 08 kg (16 lb)	Vacant			
Tippet 10 kg (20 lb)	Vacant			

Redhorse, silver / *Moxostoma anisurum*

TIPPET	WEIGHT	PLACE	DATE	ANGLER
Tippet 01 kg (2 lb)	Vacant			
Tippet 02 kg (4 lb)	Vacant			
Tippet 03 kg (6 lb)	Vacant			
Tippet 04 kg (8 lb)	1.44 kg (3 lb 3 oz)	Conneaut Marsh Outlet, Pennsylvania, USA	June 17, 1997	Richard E. Faler
Tippet 06 kg (12 lb)	Vacant			
Tippet 08 kg (16 lb)	Vacant			
Tippet 10 kg (20 lb)	Vacant			

Salmon, Atlantic / *Salmo salar*

TIPPET	WEIGHT	PLACE	DATE	ANGLER
Tippet 01 kg (2 lb)	9.97 kg (22 lb 0 oz)	Alta River, Norway	June 28, 1983	Darryl G. Behrman
Tippet 02 kg (4 lb)	17.46 kg (38 lb 8 oz)	Alta River, Norway	June 30, 1983	Darryl G. Behrman
Tippet 03 kg (6 lb)	11.49 kg (25 lb 5 oz)	Namsen River Grong, Norway	June 7, 1998	Dr. John B. Baldwin
Tippet 04 kg (8 lb)	14.28 kg (31 lb 8 oz)	Alta River, Norway	June 25, 1983	Darryl G. Behrman
Tippet 06 kg (12 lb)	20.29 kg (44 lb 12 oz)	Moisie River, Quebec, Canada	June 4, 1980	Leopold Miousse
Tippet 08 kg (16 lb)	23.20 kg (51 lb 2 oz)	Alta River, Norway	Aug. 7, 1994	Mort Seaman
Tippet 10 kg (20 lb)	22.20 kg (48 lb 15 oz)	Alta River, Norway	Aug. 16, 1993	W. Thorpe McKenzie

Salmon, chinook / *Oncorhynchus tshawytscha*

TIPPET	WEIGHT	PLACE	DATE	ANGLER
Tippet 01 kg (2 lb)	10.88 kg (24 lb 0 oz)	Salmon River, Pulaski, New York, USA	Sept. 3, 1996	Nunzio Incremona
Tippet 02 kg (4 lb)	16.44 kg (36 lb 4 oz)	Lake Marie Lodge, Lake Marie Creek, Alaska, USA	July 10, 1998	David L. Wilson
Tippet 03 kg (6 lb)	19.33 kg (42 lb 10 oz)	Lake Marie Lodge, Lake Marie Creek, Alaska, USA	July 9, 1998	Bobby W. Wilson
Tippet 04 kg (8 lb)	23.81 kg (52 lb 8 oz)	Chetco River, Oregon, USA	Nov. 10, 1982	Bob Byers
Tippet 06 kg (12 lb)	25.80 kg (56 lb 14 oz)	Kenai River, Alaska, USA	July 19, 1989	Walter E. Bottelsen
Tippet 08 kg (16 lb)	28.57 kg (63 lb 0 oz)	Trask River, Oregon, USA	Nov. 13, 1987	Bill Rhoades
Tippet 10 kg (20 lb)	21.77 kg (48 lb 0 oz)	Kenai River, Alaska, USA	June 3, 1992	Guido Rahr, III

Salmon, chum / *Oncorhynchus keta*

TIPPET	WEIGHT	PLACE	DATE	ANGLER
Tippet 01 kg (2 lb)	5.89 kg (13 lb 0 oz)	Pah River, Alaska, USA	Aug. 18, 1986	Lawrence E. Hudnall
Tippet 02 kg (4 lb)	6.15 kg (13 lb 9 oz)	Baranof Island, Alaska, USA	July 28, 1988	Lawrence E. Hudnall
Tippet 03 kg (6 lb)	6.69 kg (14 lb 12 oz)	Salmon River, Alaska, USA	Aug. 31, 1998	Mike Gallion
Tippet 04 kg (8 lb)	10.54 kg (23 lb 4 oz)	Dean River Channel, British Columbia, Canada	Aug. 19, 1983	Rod Neubert, D.V.M.
Tippet 06 kg (12 lb)	10.82 kg (23 lb 14 oz)	Stillaguamish River, Washington, USA	Dec. 7, 1985	Michael F. Graham
Tippet 08 kg (16 lb)	10.43 kg (23 lb 0 oz)	Kilchus River, Tillamook, Oregon, USA	Nov. 11, 1990	Roger C. Nelson
Tippet 10 kg (20 lb)	8.69 kg (19 lb 2 oz)	Satsop River, Washington, USA	Nov. 16, 1991	James J. Ames

Salmon, coho / *Oncorhynchus kisutch*

TIPPET	WEIGHT	PLACE	DATE	ANGLER
Tippet 01 kg (2 lb)	6.88 kg (15 lb 2 oz)	Kenai River, Alaska, USA	Jan. 23, 1991	Don A. Middleton
Tippet 02 kg (4 lb)	8.10 kg (17 lb 13 oz)	Karluk River, Alaska, USA	Sept. 15, 1990	Burton R. Leed
Tippet 03 kg (6 lb)	8.39 kg (18 lb 8 oz)	Kikluch River, Alaska, USA	Nov. 30, 1994	Alex Brant
Tippet 04 kg (8 lb)	8.89 kg (19 lb 9 oz)	Kodiak Island, Alaska, USA	Sept. 23, 1992	Paul Leader
Tippet 06 kg (12 lb)	9.52 kg (21 lb 0 oz)	Karluk River, Kodiak, Alaska, USA	Sept. 6, 1988	Gary R. Dubiel
Tippet 08 kg (16 lb)	9.75 kg (21 lb 8 oz)	Eyak River, Cordova, Alaska, USA	Sept. 7, 1996	George Halper, Jr.
Tippet 10 kg (20 lb)	8.73 kg (19 lb 4 oz)	Karluk River, Alaska, USA	Sept. 4, 1992	Burton R. Leed

Salmon, pink / *Oncorhynchus gorbuscha*

TIPPET	WEIGHT	PLACE	DATE	ANGLER
Tippet 01 kg (2 lb)	4.53 kg (10 lb 0 oz)	Karluk River, Kodiak Island, Alaska, USA	July 13, 1984	Rod Neubert, D.V.M.
Tippet 02 kg (4 lb)	5.21 kg (11 lb 8 oz)	Karluk River, Kodiak Island, Alaska, USA	July 10, 1984	Rod Neubert, D.V.M.
Tippet 03 kg (6 lb)	2.94 kg (6 lb 8 oz)	Alagnak River, Kodiak, Alaska, USA	Aug. 6, 1994	Terry Gunn
Tippet 03 kg (6 lb) Tie	2.94 kg (6 lb 8 oz)	Ungalikthluk River, Alaska, USA	Aug. 14, 1994	Robert M. Nutting
Tippet 03 kg (6 lb) Tie	2.94 kg (6 lb 8 oz)	American River, Kodiak, Alaska, USA	Aug. 21, 1994	Jonathan J. Wexler
Tippet 04 kg (8 lb)	3.08 kg (6 lb 12 oz)	Douglas Island, Alaska, USA	July 23, 1989	Andrea U. Warner
Tippet 06 kg (12 lb)	3.11 kg (6 lb 13 oz)	Salmon Creek, Juneau, Alaska, USA	July 31, 1985	Bob Garfield
Tippet 08 kg (16 lb)	2.69 kg (5 lb 15 oz)	Wolverine Creek, Alaska, USA	July 27, 1990	Lawrence E. Hudnall
Tippet 10 kg (20 lb)	2.49 kg (5 lb 8 oz)	Pybus Point, Alaska, USA	Aug. 8, 1998	John F. Whitaker

Salmon, sockeye / *Oncorhynchus nerka*

TIPPET	WEIGHT	PLACE	DATE	ANGLER
Tippet 01 kg (2 lb)	5.13 kg (11 lb 5 oz)	Baranof Island, Alaska, USA	July 29, 1988	Lawrence E. Hudnall
Tippet 02 kg (4 lb)	5.21 kg (11 lb 8 oz)	Prince of Wales Island, Alaska, USA	Aug. 3, 1989	Lawrence E. Hudnall
Tippet 03 kg (6 lb)	5.35 kg (11 lb 8 oz)	Kulik River, Alaska, USA	Aug. 10, 1994	Robert M. Nutting
Tippet 04 kg (8 lb)	5.34 kg (11 lb 12 oz)	Kenai River, Alaska, USA	Sept. 6, 1987	Galen (Skip) Perry
Tippet 06 kg (12 lb)	6.43 kg (14 lb 3 oz)	Russian River, Alaska, USA	Aug. 16, 1987	Marcy Yentzer
Tippet 08 kg (16 lb)	6.57 kg (14 lb 8 oz)	Mulchatna River, Alaska, USA	July 16, 1993	Alan Haynes
Tippet 10 kg (20 lb)	5.44 kg (12 lb 0 oz)	Clear Creek, Alaska, USA	Sept. 10, 1996	George Halper, Jr.

Sauger / *Stizostedion canadense*

TIPPET	WEIGHT	PLACE	DATE	ANGLER
Tippet 01 kg (2 lb)	1.58 kg (3 lb 8 oz)	Pittsburgh, Pennsylvania, USA	Apr. 11, 1997	Herbert G. Ratner, Jr.
Tippet 02 kg (4 lb)	0.90 kg (2 lb 0 oz)	Pittsburgh, Pennsylvania, USA	Apr. 11, 1997	Herbert G. Ratner, Jr.
Tippet 03 kg (6 lb)	1.13 kg (2 lb 8 oz)	Pittsburgh, Pennsylvania, USA	Apr. 11, 1997	Herbert G. Ratner, Jr.
Tippet 04 kg (8 lb)	1.81 kg (4 lb 0 oz)	Pittsburgh, Pennsylvania, USA	Nov. 17, 1997	Herbert G. Ratner, Jr.
Tippet 06 kg (12 lb)	1.81 kg (4 lb 0 oz)	Pittsburgh, Pennsylvania, USA	Dec. 7, 1997	Herbert G. Ratner, Jr.
Tippet 08 kg (16 lb)	1.13 kg (2 lb 8 oz)	Pittsburgh, Pennsylvania, USA	Dec. 7, 1997	Herbert G. Ratner, Jr.
Tippet 10 kg (20 lb)	1.36 kg (3 lb 0 oz)	Pittsburgh, Pennsylvania, USA	Dec. 7, 1997	Herbert G. Ratner, Jr.

Shad, American / *Alosa sapidissima*

TIPPET	WEIGHT	PLACE	DATE	ANGLER
Tippet 01 kg (2 lb)	3.28 kg (7 lb 4 oz)	Feather River, California, USA	June 30, 1983	Rod Neubert, D.V.M.
Tippet 02 kg (4 lb)	2.69 kg (5 lb 15 oz)	Delaware River, Pennsylvania, USA	May 24, 1990	Bill Howarth
Tippet 03 kg (6 lb)	2.60 kg (5 lb 12 oz)	Delaware River, New Jersey, USA	May 20, 1995	Jerome J. McDonnell
Tippet 04 kg (8 lb)	2.92 kg (6 lb 7 oz)	Yuba River, Marysville, California, USA	May 30, 1981	Eugene W. Schweitzer
Tippet 06 kg (12 lb)	3.06 kg (6 lb 12 oz)	Verona, California, USA	Apr. 26, 1988	James R. Humphrey
Tippet 08 kg (16 lb)	2.26 kg (5 lb 0 oz)	Columbia River, Washington, USA	June 14, 1986	William J. Harris
Tippet 10 kg (20 lb)	2.57 kg (5 lb 10 oz)	Delaware River, New Jersey, USA	May 12, 1992	Jerome J. McDonnell

Splake / *Salvelinus namaycush x Salvelinus fontinalis*

TIPPET	WEIGHT	PLACE	DATE	ANGLER
Tippet 01 kg (2 lb)	Vacant			
Tippet 02 kg (4 lb)	Vacant			
Tippet 03 kg (6 lb)	1.27 kg (2 lb 13 oz)	Folley Lake, La Reserve Beauc, Quebec, Canada	June 28, 1996	George A. Bernstein
Tippet 04 kg (8 lb)	1.41 kg (3 lb 1 oz)	Georgian Bay, Ontario, Canada	May 8, 1988	William J. Dettmar
Tippet 06 kg (12 lb)	Vacant			
Tippet 08 kg (16 lb)	Vacant			
Tippet 10 kg (20 lb)	Vacant			

Sturgeon / *Acipenseridae family*

TIPPET	WEIGHT	PLACE	DATE	ANGLER
Tippet 01 kg (2 lb)	Vacant			
Tippet 02 kg (4 lb)	Vacant			
Tippet 03 kg (6 lb)	Vacant			
Tippet 04 kg (8 lb)	Vacant			

Sturgeon / *(continued)*

Tippet 06 kg (12 lb)	Vacant			
Tippet 08 kg (16 lb)	Vacant			
Tippet 10 kg (20 lb)	Vacant			

Sunfish, green / *Lepomis*

TIPPET	WEIGHT	PLACE	DATE	ANGLER
Tippet 01 kg (2 lb)	Vacant			
Tippet 02 kg (4 lb)	Vacant			
Tippet 03 kg (6 lb)	0.45 kg (1 lb 0 oz)	Ute Reservoir, Logan, New Mexico, USA	Aug. 15, 1994	Marina M. Ellis
Tippet 04 kg (8 lb)	0.58 kg (1 lb 4 oz)	Lorman, Mississippi, USA	June 30, 1995	John Forrest
Tippet 06 kg (12 lb)	Vacant			
Tippet 08 kg (16 lb)	Vacant			
Tippet 10 kg (20 lb)	Vacant			

Sunfish, redbreast / *Lepomis auritus*

TIPPET	WEIGHT	PLACE	DATE	ANGLER
Tippet 01 kg (2 lb)	0.68 kg (1 lb 8 oz)	Leechburg, Pennsylvania, USA	Oct. 7, 1998	Herbert G. Ratner, Jr.
Tippet 02 kg (4 lb)	0.68 kg (1 lb 8 oz)	Leechburg, Pennsylvania, USA	Oct. 7, 1998	Herbert G. Ratner, Jr.
Tippet 03 kg (6 lb)	0.68 kg (1 lb 8 oz)	Leechburg, Pennsylvania, USA	Oct. 7, 1998	Herbert G. Ratner, Jr.
Tippet 04 kg (8 lb)	0.45 kg (1 lb 0 oz)	Leechburg, Pennsylvania, USA	Sept. 30, 1998	Herbert G. Ratner, Jr.
Tippet 06 kg (12 lb)	0.45 kg (1 lb 0 oz)	Leechburg, Pennsylvania, USA	Oct. 7, 1998	Herbert G. Ratner, Jr.
Tippet 08 kg (16 lb)	Vacant			
Tippet 10 kg (20 lb)	Vacant			

Sunfish, redear / *Lepomis microlophus*

TIPPET	WEIGHT	PLACE	DATE	ANGLER
Tippet 01 kg (2 lb)	0.58 kg (1 lb 4 oz)	Merritt's Mill Pond, Florida, USA	Sept. 30, 1986	Jerry Hill
Tippet 02 kg (4 lb)	0.85 kg (1 lb 14 oz)	St. John's River, Sanford, Florida, USA	Nov. 1, 1982	Marie Gardner
Tippet 03 kg (6 lb)	0.68 kg (1 lb 8 oz)	Callaway Gardens, Pine Mountain, Georgia, USA	Sept. 22, 1998	Carter Nelson
Tippet 04 kg (8 lb)	1.10 kg (2 lb 7 oz)	Merritt's Mill Pond, Marianna, Florida, USA	July 21, 1989	Chuck Deckerhoff
Tippet 06 kg (12 lb)	0.68 kg (1 lb 8 oz)	Daufuskie Island, South Carolina, USA	June 16, 1994	Frank Fowler
Tippet 08 kg (16 lb)	0.51 kg (1 lb 2 oz)	Escambia County, Florida, USA	Mar. 12, 1994	Thomas Hardy
Tippet 10 kg (20 lb)	0.43 kg (1 lb 0 oz)	Escambia County, Florida, USA	Mar. 12, 1994	Thomas Hardy

Taimen / *Hucho hucho taimen*

TIPPET	WEIGHT	PLACE	DATE	ANGLER
Tippet 01 kg (2 lb)	Vacant			
Tippet 02 kg (4 lb)	Vacant			
Tippet 03 kg (6 lb)	Vacant			
Tippet 04 kg (8 lb)	4.98 kg (11 lb 0 oz)	Sharlan River, Mongolia	June 21, 1990	Guido Rahr, III
Tippet 06 kg (12 lb)	Vacant			
Tippet 08 kg (16 lb)	9.75 kg (21 lb 4 oz)	Orhon River, Ovorhungai, Mongolia	Aug. 28, 1994	Christopher Bakwin
Tippet 10 kg (20 lb)	Vacant			

Tigerfish / *Hydrocyon vittatus*

TIPPET	WEIGHT	PLACE	DATE	ANGLER
Tippet 01 kg (2 lb)	0.70 kg (1 lb 8 oz)	Zambezi River, Zimbabwe	Nov. 2, 1993	Jean Van Loock
Tippet 02 kg (4 lb)	5.00 kg (11 lb 0 oz)	Zambezi River, Zimbabwe	Oct. 28, 1993	Phillip P. de Moor
Tippet 03 kg (6 lb)	2.75 kg (6 lb 1 oz)	Tiger Camp, Zambezi River, Zambia	Aug. 28, 1994	Skip Nielsen
Tippet 04 kg (8 lb)	7.10 kg (15 lb 10 oz)	Tiger Camp, Zambezi River, Zambia	Nov. 17, 1996	Bernard Esterhuyse
Tippet 06 kg (12 lb)	6.50 kg (14 lb 5 oz)	Tiger Camp, Zambezi River, Zambia	July 31, 1994	Bernard Esterhuyse
Tippet 08 kg (16 lb)	7.41 kg (16 lb 5 oz)	Charara, Kariba, Zimbabwe	Aug. 30, 1997	Stephen G. Mullett
Tippet 10 kg (20 lb)	7.40 kg (16 lb 5 oz)	Tiger Camp, Zambezi River, Zambia	Oct. 29, 1997	Roger A. Shepherd

Tigerfish, giant/ *Hydrocyon goliath*

TIPPET	WEIGHT	PLACE	DATE	ANGLER
Tippet 01 kg (2 lb)	Vacant			
Tippet 02 kg (4 lb)	Vacant			
Tippet 03 kg (6 lb)	Vacant			
Tippet 04 kg (8 lb)	Vacant			
Tippet 06 kg (12 lb)	Vacant			
Tippet 08 kg (16 lb)	Vacant			
Tippet 10 kg (20 lb)	Vacant			

Trout, brook / *Salvelinus fontinalis*

TIPPET	WEIGHT	PLACE	DATE	ANGLER
Tippet 01 kg (2 lb)	3.85 kg (8 lb 8 oz)	Minonipi Lake, Labrador, Canada	Aug. 15, 1989	Robert B. Ryan
Tippet 02 kg (4 lb)	4.53 kg (10 lb 0 oz)	Minonipi Lake, Labrador, Canada	June 29, 1987	Sal Borrelli
Tippet 03 kg (6 lb)	3.96 kg (8 lb 12 oz)	Minonipi, Labrador, Canada	July 11, 1995	Dan S. Edgerton
Tippet 04 kg (8 lb)	4.73 kg (10 lb 7 oz)	Assinica Broadback River, Quebec, Canada	Sept. 5, 1982	James Francis McGarry
Tippet 06 kg (12 lb)	4.28 kg (9 lb 7 oz)	Minonipi River, Labrador, Canada	Aug. 8, 1988	Robert B. Ryan
Tippet 08 kg (16 lb)	4.13 kg (9 lb 2 oz)	Minonipi River, Labrador, Canada	Aug. 11, 1987	Robert B. Ryan
Tippet 10 kg (20 lb)	2.83 kg (6 lb 4 oz)	Anne Marie Lake, Labrador, Canada	Aug. 1, 1991	Greg Marc Behrman

Trout, brown / *Salmo trutta*

TIPPET	WEIGHT	PLACE	DATE	ANGLER
Tippet 01 kg (2 lb)	5.55 kg (12 lb 4 oz)	Grindstone Creek, Pulaski, New York, USA	Nov. 2, 1995	Robert F. Jordan
Tippet 02 kg (4 lb)	8.61 kg (19 lb 0 oz)	Rio Grande, Tierra del Fuego, Argentina	Jan. 29, 1993	Robert C.K. Valtz
Tippet 03 kg (6 lb)	9.52 kg (21 lb 0 oz)	Rio Grande, Tierra del Fuego, Argentina	Mar. 7, 1995	Philip E. Carlin
Tippet 04 kg (8 lb)	12.70 kg (29 lb 0 oz)	Rio Grande, Tierra del Fuego, Argentina	Mar. 9, 1996	Charlie Blaquier
Tippet 06 kg (12 lb)	15.93 kg (35 lb 2 oz)	Rio Grande, Tierra del Fuego, Argentina	Mar. 1, 1998	Mark T. Gates, Jr.
Tippet 08 kg (16 lb)	13.50 kg (29 lb 12 oz)	Rio Grande, Tierra del Fuego, Argentina	Jan. 19, 1992	Randolph Harrison
Tippet 10 kg (20 lb)	8.84 kg (19 lb 8 oz)	Rio Grande, Tierra del Fuego, Argentina	Feb. 10, 1998	Richard L. Vainer

Trout, bull / *Salvelinus confluentus*

TIPPET	WEIGHT	PLACE	DATE	ANGLER
Tippet 01 kg (2 lb)	1.81 kg (4 lb 0 oz)	Flathead Lake, Montana, USA	May 17, 1986	William J. Harris, Jr.
Tippet 02 kg (4 lb)	2.15 kg (4 lb 12 oz)	Flathead River, Montana, USA	July 31, 1985	Burton R. Leed

Trout, bull / *(continued)*

TIPPET	WEIGHT	PLACE	DATE	ANGLER
Tippet 03 kg (6 lb)	Vacant			
Tippet 04 kg (8 lb)	5.40 kg (11 lb 14 oz)	Flathead River, Montana, USA	July 18, 1991	Burton R. Leed
Tippet 06 kg (12 lb)	Vacant			
Tippet 08 kg (16 lb)	Vacant			
Tippet 10 kg (20 lb)	Vacant			

Trout, cutthroat / *Oncorhynchus clarki*

TIPPET	WEIGHT	PLACE	DATE	ANGLER
Tippet 01 kg (2 lb)	3.88 kg (8 lb 9 oz)	Pyramid Lake, Nevada, USA	Apr. 20, 1987	Terry A. Baird
Tippet 02 kg (4 lb)	3.01 kg (6 lb 10 oz)	Pyramid Lake, Nevada, USA	Dec. 22, 1989	Ted Hartley
Tippet 03 kg (6 lb)	0.69 kg (1 lb 8 oz)	Round Lake, Tahoe Basin, California, USA	Aug. 16, 1998	Stephen L. Cognata
Tippet 04 kg (8 lb)	6.37 kg (14 lb 1 oz)	Pyramid Lake, Reno, Nevada, USA	Apr. 4, 1982	Donald R. Williamson
Tippet 06 kg (12 lb)	4.53 kg (10 lb 0 oz)	Pyramid Lake, Nevada, USA	Feb. 9, 1990	Chuck Echer
Tippet 08 kg (16 lb)	5.92 kg (13 lb 1 oz)	Pyramid Lake, Nevada, USA	Mar. 14, 1994	Roger Iveson
Tippet 10 kg (20 lb)	0.77 kg (1 lb 11 oz)	Red Lake, Hwy 88, California, USA	Aug. 20, 1998	Stephen L. Cognata

Trout, golden / *Oncorhynchus aguabonita*

TIPPET	WEIGHT	PLACE	DATE	ANGLER
Tippet 01 kg (2 lb)	2.26 kg (5 lb 0 oz)	Golden Lake, Wyoming, USA	June 22, 1989	Bob Shettel
Tippet 02 kg (4 lb)	2.06 kg (4 lb 9 oz)	Golden Lake, Wyoming, USA	June 29, 1989	Chip Hane
Tippet 03 kg (6 lb)	1.60 kg (3 lb 8 oz)	Thumb Lake, Wyoming, USA	July 12, 1997	Danny Kurttila
Tippet 04 kg (8 lb)	1.87 kg (4 lb 2 oz)	Golden Lake, Wyoming, USA	June 28, 1989	Chip Hane
Tippet 06 kg (12 lb)	1.87 kg (4 lb 2 oz)	Golden Lake, Wyoming, USA	June 26, 1989	Chip Hane
Tippet 08 kg (16 lb)	1.75 kg (3 lb 14 oz)	Golden Lake, Wyoming, USA	June 26, 1989	Chip Hane
Tippet 10 kg (20 lb)	1.09 kg (2 lb 6 oz)	Thumb Lake, Wyoming, USA	June 28, 1992	Daniel W. Kurttila

Trout, lake / *Salvelinus namaycush*

TIPPET	WEIGHT	PLACE	DATE	ANGLER
Tippet 01 kg (2 lb)	6.12 kg (13 lb 8 oz)	Wellesley Lake, Yukon Territory, Canada	Aug. 12, 1986	T. Jack Beeler
Tippet 02 kg (4 lb)	12.02 kg (26 lb 8 oz)	Great Bear Lake, N.W.T., Canada	Aug. 11, 1992	Roy McGraw
Tippet 03 kg (6 lb)	8.39 kg (18 lb 8 oz)	Nueltin Lake, Canada	June 20, 1996	James Boyer
Tippet 04 kg (8 lb)	12.02 kg (26 lb 8 oz)	Great Bear Lake, N.W.T., Canada	Aug. 11, 1992	Roy McGraw
Tippet 06 kg (12 lb)	11.05 kg (24 lb 6 oz)	Nueltin Lake, Manitoba, Canada	June 23, 1995	James Boyer
Tippet 08 kg (16 lb)	11.90 kg (26 lb 4 oz)	Whale River, Quebec, Canada	July 5, 1997	Stephen M. Carta
Tippet 10 kg (20 lb)	12.47 kg (27 lb 8 oz)	Nueltin Lake, Alonsa, Canada	June 24, 1994	James Boyer

Trout, rainbow / *Oncorhynchus mykiss*

TIPPET	WEIGHT	PLACE	DATE	ANGLER
Tippet 01 kg (2 lb)	7.48 kg (16 lb 8 oz)	Salmon River, Pulaski, New York, USA	Feb. 22, 1982	Francis J. Verdoliva, Jr.
Tippet 02 kg (4 lb)	9.00 kg (19 lb 13 oz)	Little Calumet River, Indiana, USA	Sept. 6, 1982	Roger D. Enyeart
Tippet 03 kg (6 lb)	10.46 kg (23 lb 1 oz)	Lakedown Trout Fishery, Heathfield, Sussex, England	June 24, 1996	Peter Reece
Tippet 04 kg (8 lb)	11.11 kg (24 lb 8 oz)	Sustut River, British Columbia, Canada	Sept. 22, 1982	Bruce Gernon
Tippet 06 kg (12 lb)	10.88 kg (24 lb 0 oz)	Skeena River, British Columbia, Canada	Oct. 20, 1987	Chuck Stephens
Tippet 08 kg (16 lb)	12.70 kg (28 lb 0 oz)	Skeena River, British Columbia, Canada	Oct. 20, 1985	Chuck Stephens
Tippet 10 kg (20 lb)	7.00 kg (15 lb 7 oz)	Kuiachak River, Alaska, USA	Oct. 9, 1995	George Halper, Jr.

Trout, tiger / *Salmo trutta x Salvelinus fontinalis*

TIPPET	WEIGHT	PLACE	DATE	ANGLER
Tippet 01 kg (2 lb)	Vacant			
Tippet 02 kg (4 lb)	2.35 kg (5 lb 3 oz)	Beaver Creek, Pennsylvania, USA	June 7, 1995	Robert McLain Nutting
Tippet 03 kg (6 lb)	4.64 kg (10 lb 4 oz)	Heathfield, Sussex, England	June 23, 1996	Keith R. Griffiths
Tippet 04 kg (8 lb)	4.47 kg (9 lb 14 oz)	Connetquat River, Oakdale, New York, USA	Sept. 3, 1988	Christian Eiler
Tippet 06 kg (12 lb)	1.92 kg (4 lb 4 oz)	Connetquat River, Oakdale, New York, USA	Aug. 14, 1989	Ronald LaChase
Tippet 08 kg (16 lb)	Vacant			
Tippet 10 kg (20 lb)	Vacant			

Walleye / *Stizostedion vitreum vitreum*

TIPPET	WEIGHT	PLACE	DATE	ANGLER
Tippet 01 kg (2 lb)	3.62 kg (8 lb 0 oz)	Pittsburgh, Pennsylvania, USA	Apr. 16, 1997	Herbert G. Ratner, Jr.
Tippet 02 kg (4 lb)	4.30 kg (9 lb 8 oz)	Pittsburgh, Pennsylvania, USA	Dec. 7, 1997	Herbert G. Ratner, Jr.
Tippet 03 kg (6 lb)	3.68 kg (8 lb 2 oz)	Chatfield State Park Reservoir, Colorado, USA	June 10, 1998	Robert E. Hix
Tippet 04 kg (8 lb)	4.25 kg (9 lb 6 oz)	Lake Gunasio, Manitoba, Canada	May 17, 1991	Kastaway Kulis
Tippet 06 kg (12 lb)	3.62 kg (8 lb 0 oz)	Chippewa River, Hayward, Wisconsin, USA	July 12, 1998	Dan Edwards
Tippet 08 kg (16 lb)	4.30 kg (9 lb 8 oz)	Chatfield State Park Reservoir, Colorado, USA	June 4, 1998	Robert E. Hix
Tippet 10 kg (20 lb)	4.13 kg (9 lb 2 oz)	Lake Gunasio, Manitoba, Canada	May 18, 1991	Kastaway Kulis

Warmouth / *Lepomis gulosus*

TIPPET	WEIGHT	PLACE	DATE	ANGLER
Tippet 01 kg (2 lb)	0.54 kg (1 lb 3 oz)	Lee Hall Reservoir, Newport News, Virginia, USA	Aug. 31, 1985	Keith Tongier
Tippet 02 kg (4 lb)	Vacant			
Tippet 03 kg (6 lb)	0.53 kg (1 lb 2 oz)	Lee Hall Reservoir, Newport News, Virginia, USA	Aug. 31, 1985	Keith Tongier
Tippet 04 kg (8 lb)	Vacant			
Tippet 06 kg (12 lb)	0.50 kg (1 lb 1 oz)	Lee Hall Reservoir, Newport News, Virginia, USA	Aug. 31, 1985	Max Tongier, Jr.
Tippet 08 kg (16 lb)	Vacant			
Tippet 10 kg (20 lb)	Vacant			

Whitefish, lake / *Coregonus clupeaformis*

TIPPET	WEIGHT	PLACE	DATE	ANGLER
Tippet 01 kg (2 lb)	2.02 kg (4 lb 7 oz)	Great Slave Lake, N.W.T., Canada	Sept. 5, 1984	Don L. Guhlke
Tippet 02 kg (4 lb)	1.84 kg (4 lb 0 oz)	Great Slave Lake, N.W.T., Canada	Sept. 6, 1984	William S. Pifer
Tippet 03 kg (6 lb)	0.56 kg (1 lb 3 oz)	St. Mary's River, Sault Ste Marie, Michigan, USA	June 5, 1995	Joe S. Krzykwa
Tippet 04 kg (8 lb)	2.25 kg (4 lb 15 oz)	Winnipeg River, Manitoba, Canada	July 4, 1986	Gerry G. Beck
Tippet 06 kg (12 lb)	1.98 kg (4 lb 5 oz)	Winnipeg River, Manitoba, Canada	July 4, 1986	Gerry G. Beck
Tippet 08 kg (16 lb)	1.01 kg (2 lb 3 oz)	St. Mary's River, Sault Ste Marie, Michigan, USA	June 18, 1995	Joe S. Krzykwa
Tippet 10 kg (20 lb)	0.86 kg (1 lb 14 oz)	St. Mary's River, Sault Ste Marie, Michigan, USA	June 9, 1995	Joe S. Krzykwa

Whitefish, mountain / *Prosopium williamsoni*

TIPPET	WEIGHT	PLACE	DATE	ANGLER
Tippet 01 kg (2 lb)	1.04 kg (2 lb 5 oz)	Big White Salmon River, Washington, USA	Mar. 28, 1992	Joe J. Warren
Tippet 02 kg (4 lb)	1.22 kg (2 lb 11 oz)	Roaring Fork River, Colorado, USA	Aug. 24, 1986	Robert J. Nicholas
Tippet 02 kg (4 lb) Tie	1.24 kg (2 lb 12 oz)	Roaring Fork River, Colorado, USA	Oct. 10, 1987	Robert D. van Dyke
Tippet 03 kg (6 lb)	1.36 kg (3 lb 0 oz)	Roaring Fork River, Colorado, USA	June 13, 1993	Michael Donovan
Tippet 04 kg (8 lb)	0.72 kg (1 lb 9 oz)	Bow River, Calgary, Alberta, Canada	May 6, 1997	Douglas Harvey Weitz
Tippet 06 kg (12 lb)	0.59 kg (1 lb 4 oz)	Wind River, Dubris, Wyoming, USA	Mar. 19, 1994	Daniel W. Kurttila
Tippet 08 kg (16 lb)	0.54 kg (1 lb 3 oz)	Fisher River, Montana, USA	Sept. 4, 1998	Stephen L. Cognata
Tippet 10 kg (20 lb)	0.63 kg (1 lb 6 oz)	Kootenai River, Montana, USA	Sept. 4, 1998	Stephen L. Cognata

Whitefish, round / *Prosopium cylindraceum*

TIPPET	WEIGHT	PLACE	DATE	ANGLER
Tippet 01 kg (2 lb)	Vacant			
Tippet 02 kg (4 lb)	0.62 kg (1 lb 6 oz)	Lake Marie Lodge, Lake Marie Creek, Alaska, USA	Aug. 7, 1998	Bobby W. Wilson
Tippet 03 kg (6 lb)	Vacant			
Tippet 04 kg (8 lb)	0.72 kg (1 lb 9 oz)	Kenai River, Soldotna, Alaska, USA	Apr. 27, 1986	Joe Ray Skrha
Tippet 06 kg (12 lb)	Vacant			
Tippet 08 kg (16 lb)	Vacant			
Tippet 10 kg (20 lb)	Vacant			

Bobby W. Wilson strains to heft this 42 lb 10 oz chinook salmon he caught July 9, 1998 while fly fishing at Lake Marie Creek in Alaska. It won the 6-lb tippet class record and first place in the 23rd annual IGFA fishing contest.

The look on Steven Jensen's face says it all: a fly rod world record for butterfly peacock in the 20-lb tippet class. This 10 lb 4 oz fish caught Feb. 26, 1998, was just four ounces less than the all-tackle record, and gave him first place in IGFA's 23rd annual fishing contest.

IGFA Saltwater Fly Rod World Records

The following are world saltwater fly rod records granted in IGFA tippet class categories as of January 1, 1999. The records are listed alphabetically according to the common names of species.

Albacore / *Thunnus alalunga*

TIPPET	WEIGHT	PLACE	DATE	ANGLER
Tippet M-01 kg (2 lb)	Vacant			
Tippet M-02 kg (4 lb)	Vacant			
Tippet M-03 kg (6 lb)	4.71 kg (10 lb 6 oz)	San Diego, California, USA	June 23, 1998	Gary Brettnacher
Tippet M-04 kg (8 lb)	9.85 kg (21 lb 11 oz)	Hout Bay, Republic of South Africa	Apr. 2, 1992	Simon Susman
Tippet M-06 kg (12 lb)	11.85 kg (26 lb 2 oz)	San Diego, California, USA	July 15, 1972	Les Eichhorn
Tippet M-08 kg (16 lb)	18.00 kg (39 lb 10 oz)	Hout Bay, Republic of South Africa	Apr. 6, 1987	Nic de Kock
Tippet M-10 kg (20 lb)	21.31 kg (47 lb 0 oz)	Hudson Canyon, New Jersey, USA	Sept. 7, 1992	Robert Lubarsky
Tippet W-01 kg (2 lb)	Vacant			
Tippet W-02 kg (4 lb)	Vacant			
Tippet W-03 kg (6 lb)	Vacant			
Tippet W-04 kg (8 lb)	Vacant			
Tippet W-06 kg (12 lb)	Vacant			
Tippet W-08 kg (16 lb)	Vacant			
Tippet W-10 kg (20 lb)	Vacant			

Amberjack, greater / *Seriola dumerili*

TIPPET	WEIGHT	PLACE	DATE	ANGLER
Tippet M-01 kg (2 lb)	1.02 kg (2 lb 4 oz)	Key West, Florida, USA	Feb. 20, 1990	Herbert G. Ratner, Jr.
Tippet M-02 kg (4 lb)	8.39 kg (18 lb 8 oz)	Key West, Florida, USA	Apr. 9, 1992	George L. Foti
Tippet M-03 kg (6 lb)	13.46 kg (29 lb 11 oz)	Sebastian Inlet, Florida, USA	Sept. 15, 1972	Dave Chermanski
Tippet M-04 kg (8 lb)	16.55 kg (36 lb 8 oz)	Dry Tortugas, Florida, USA	Mar. 16, 1992	William B. DuVal
Tippet M-06 kg (12 lb)	36.28 kg (80 lb 0 oz)	Fort Pierce, Florida, USA	Jan. 15, 1976	Dave Chermanski
Tippet M-08 kg (16 lb)	47.06 kg (103 lb 12 oz)	Key West, Florida, USA	Jan. 28, 1977	Dr. William J. Munro
Tippet M-10 kg (20 lb)	24.38 kg (53 lb 12 oz)	Dry Tortugas, Florida, USA	Mar. 6, 1993	William B. DuVal
Tippet W-01 kg (2 lb)	Vacant			
Tippet W-02 kg (4 lb)	Vacant			
Tippet W-03 kg (6 lb)	Vacant			
Tippet W-04 kg (8 lb)	0.90 kg (2 lb 0 oz)	Midway Island	July 25, 1998	Sharon Handgis
Tippet W-06 kg (12 lb)	Vacant			
Tippet W-08 kg (16 lb)	Vacant			
Tippet W-10 kg (20 lb)	Vacant			

Barracuda, great / *Sphyraena barracuda*

TIPPET	WEIGHT	PLACE	DATE	ANGLER
Tippet M-01 kg (2 lb)	9.18 kg (20 lb 4 oz)	Key West, Florida, USA	Feb. 24, 1991	Herbert G. Ratner, Jr.
Tippet M-02 kg (4 lb)	11.56 kg (25 lb 8 oz)	Key West, Florida, USA	Jan. 9, 1991	Herbert G. Ratner, Jr.
Tippet M-03 kg (6 lb)	14.40 kg (31 lb 12 oz)	Key West, Florida, USA	Oct. 31, 1979	Dallas Howard
Tippet M-04 kg (8 lb)	14.62 kg (32 lb 4 oz)	Biscayne Bay, Miami Beach, Florida, USA	Dec. 28, 1997	Joey "Tomatoes" Posnick
Tippet M-06 kg (12 lb)	17.12 kg (37 lb 12 oz)	Key West, Florida, USA	Dec. 19, 1978	Joe Machiorlatti
Tippet M-08 kg (16 lb)	16.89 kg (37 lb 4 oz)	Key West, Florida, USA	Dec. 16, 1975	Roy Terrell
Tippet M-10 kg (20 lb)	21.77 kg (48 lb 0 oz)	Ocracoke, North Carolina, USA	Aug. 9, 1996	Reginald L. White
Tippet W-01 kg (2 lb)	Vacant			
Tippet W-02 kg (4 lb)	Vacant			
Tippet W-03 kg (6 lb)	9.97 kg (22 lb 0 oz)	Key West, Florida, USA	Apr. 21, 1998	Glenda Kelley
Tippet W-04 kg (8 lb)	Vacant			
Tippet W-06 kg (12 lb)	9.97 kg (22 lb 0 oz)	Key West, Florida, USA	July 15, 1998	Christine Perez
Tippet W-08 kg (16 lb)	Vacant			
Tippet W-10 kg (20 lb)	Vacant			

Bass, black sea / *Centropristis striata*

TIPPET	WEIGHT	PLACE	DATE	ANGLER
Tippet M-01 kg (2 lb)	0.70 kg (1 lb 9 oz)	Ocracoke, North Carolina, USA	Oct. 31, 1992	William B. DuVal
Tippet M-02 kg (4 lb)	0.99 kg (2 lb 3 oz)	Ocracoke, North Carolina, USA	Oct. 31, 1992	William B. DuVal
Tippet M-03 kg (6 lb)	0.59 kg (1 lb 5 oz)	Ocracoke, North Carolina, USA	June 19, 1994	William B. DuVal
Tippet M-04 kg (8 lb)	Vacant			
Tippet M-06 kg (12 lb)	1.36 kg (3 lb 0 oz)	Ocracoke, North Carolina, USA	Oct. 31, 1992	William B. DuVal
Tippet M-08 kg (16 lb)	0.82 kg (1 lb 13 oz)	Ocracoke, North Carolina, USA	Oct. 31, 1992	William B. DuVal
Tippet M-10 kg (20 lb)	1.02 kg (2 lb 4 oz)	Ocracoke, North Carolina, USA	Aug. 12, 1994	William B. DuVal
Tippet W-01 kg (2 lb)	Vacant			
Tippet W-02 kg (4 lb)	Vacant			
Tippet W-03 kg (6 lb)	Vacant			
Tippet W-04 kg (8 lb)	0.73 kg (1 lb 10 oz)	Ocracoke, North Carolina, USA	Nov. 3, 1993	Mrs. William B. DuVal
Tippet W-06 kg (12 lb)	Vacant			
Tippet W-08 kg (16 lb)	Vacant			
Tippet W-10 kg (20 lb)	Vacant			

Bass, European / *Dicentrarchus labrax*

TIPPET	WEIGHT	PLACE	DATE	ANGLER
Tippet M-01 kg (2 lb)	Vacant			
Tippet M-02 kg (4 lb)	5.99 kg (13 lb 3 oz)	Pirou, France	Aug. 19, 1998	Philippe Boulet
Tippet M-03 kg (6 lb)	0.89 kg (1 lb 15 oz)	Ansedonia, Grosseto, Italy	July 22, 1995	Marco Sammicheli
Tippet M-04 kg (8 lb)	1.52 kg (3 lb 5 oz)	Alberese, Grosseto, Italy	Mar. 7, 1998	Marco Sammicheli
Tippet M-06 kg (12 lb)	0.91 kg (2 lb 0 oz)	Giannella, Grosseto, Italy	Nov. 24, 1994	Marco Sammicheli
Tippet M-08 kg (16 lb)	2.27 kg (5 lb 0 oz)	Ansedonia, Grosseto, Italy	May 13, 1995	Marco Sammicheli
Tippet M-10 kg (20 lb)	Vacant			
Tippet W-01 kg (2 lb)	Vacant			
Tippet W-02 kg (4 lb)	Vacant			
Tippet W-03 kg (6 lb)	Vacant			

Bass, European /*(continued)*

TIPPET	WEIGHT	PLACE	DATE	ANGLER
Tippet W-04 kg (8 lb)	Vacant			
Tippet W-06 kg (12 lb)	Vacant			
Tippet W-08 kg (16 lb)	Vacant			
Tippet W-10 kg (20 lb)	Vacant			

Bass, giant sea / *Stereolepis gigas*

TIPPET	WEIGHT	PLACE	DATE	ANGLER
Tippet M-01 kg (2 lb)	Vacant			
Tippet M-02 kg (4 lb)	Vacant			
Tippet M-03 kg (6 lb)	Vacant			
Tippet M-04 kg (8 lb)	Vacant			
Tippet M-06 kg (12 lb)	Vacant			
Tippet M-08 kg (16 lb)	Vacant			
Tippet M-10 kg (20 lb)	Vacant			
Tippet W-01 kg (2 lb)	Vacant			
Tippet W-02 kg (4 lb)	Vacant			
Tippet W-03 kg (6 lb)	Vacant			
Tippet W-04 kg (8 lb)	Vacant			
Tippet W-06 kg (12 lb)	Vacant			
Tippet W-08 kg (16 lb)	Vacant			
Tippet W-10 kg (20 lb)	Vacant			

Bass, kelp (calico) / *Paralabrax clathratus*

TIPPET	WEIGHT	PLACE	DATE	ANGLER
Tippet M-01 kg (2 lb)	0.45 kg (1 lb 0 oz)	Point Loma, San Diego, California, USA	June 22, 1994	Marshall Madruga
Tippet M-01 kg (2 lb)Tie	0.48 kg (1 lb 1 oz)	Palos Verdes, California, USA	July 19, 1996	Robert Levy
Tippet M-02 kg (4 lb)	0.70 kg (1 lb 9 oz)	Palos Verdes, California, USA	July 19, 1996	Robert Levy
Tippet M-03 kg (6 lb)	1.85 kg (4 lb 1 oz)	Palos Verdes, California, USA	June 23, 1998	Dr. John F. Whitaker
Tippet M-04 kg (8 lb)	1.13 kg (2 lb 8 oz)	Palos Verdes, California, USA	Mar. 22, 1996	John F. Whitaker
Tippet M-06 kg (12 lb)	2.38 kg (5 lb 4 oz)	Catalina Island, California, USA	Sept. 30, 1993	Nick R. Curcione
Tippet M-08 kg (16 lb)	2.75 kg (6 lb 1 oz)	Solana Beach, California, USA	July 8, 1994	Wesley G. Woll
Tippet M-10 kg (20 lb)	1.75 kg (3 lb 14 oz)	Palos Verdes, California, USA	July 27, 1997	Dr. John F. Whitaker, Jr.
Tippet W-01 kg (2 lb)	Vacant			
Tippet W-02 kg (4 lb)	Vacant			
Tippet W-03 kg (6 lb)	Vacant			
Tippet W-04 kg (8 lb)	Vacant			
Tippet W-06 kg (12 lb)	Vacant			
Tippet W-08 kg (16 lb)	Vacant			
Tippet W-10 kg (20 lb)	Vacant			

Bass, striped / *Morone saxatilis*

TIPPET	WEIGHT	PLACE	DATE	ANGLER
Tippet M-01 kg (2 lb)	5.44 kg (12 lb 0 oz)	Napatree Beach, Rhode Island, USA	Sept. 27, 1997	Alan Caolo
Tippet M-02 kg (4 lb)	8.84 kg (19 lb 8 oz)	Misquamicit Beach, Rhode Island, USA	Aug. 6, 1997	Alan Caolo
Tippet M-03 kg (6 lb)	11.22 kg (24 lb 12 oz)	American River, California, USA	Dec. 2, 1973	Alfred Perryman
Tippet M-04 kg (8 lb)	19.05 kg (42 lb 0 oz)	Sacramento River, Verona, California, USA	May 30, 1986	Ronald S. Hayashi
Tippet M-06 kg (12 lb)	29.25 kg (64 lb 8 oz)	Smith River, Oregon, USA	July 28, 1973	Beryl E. Bliss
Tippet M-08 kg (16 lb)	23.36 kg (51 lb 8 oz)	Smith River, Oregon, USA	May 18, 1974	Gary L. Dyer
Tippet M-10 kg (20 lb)	14.96 kg (33 lb 0 oz)	Chatham, Massachusetts, USA	July 23, 1996	David W. Rimmer
Tippet W-01 kg (2 lb)	Vacant			
Tippet W-02 kg (4 lb)	1.47 kg (3 lb 4 oz)	Chesapeake Bay, Virginia Beach, Virginia, USA	Nov. 10, 1998	Vivian M. Webb
Tippet W-03 kg (6 lb)	Vacant			
Tippet W-04 kg (8 lb)	0.85 kg (1 lb 14 oz)	Chesapeake Bay, Virginia Beach, Virginia, USA	Nov. 1, 1998	Vivian M. Webb
Tippet W-06 kg (12 lb)	1.13 kg (2 lb 8 oz)	Chesapeake Bay, Virginia Beach, Virginia, USA	Nov. 8, 1998	Vivian M. Webb
Tippet W-08 kg (16 lb)	1.02 kg (2 lb 4 oz)	Chesapeake Bay, Virginia Beach, Virginia, USA	Nov. 8, 1998	Vivian M. Webb
Tippet W-10 kg (20 lb)	5.89 kg (13 lb 0 oz)	Virginia Beach, Virginia, USA	Jan. 3, 1998	Stephanie Gooch

Bluefish / *Pomatomus saltatrix*

TIPPET	WEIGHT	PLACE	DATE	ANGLER
Tippet M-01 kg (2 lb)	6.52 kg (14 lb 6 oz)	Martha's Vineyard, Massachusetts, USA	Oct. 19, 1984	Danwin M. Purdy
Tippet M-02 kg (4 lb)	6.61 kg (14 lb 9 oz)	Lobsterville Beach, Massachusetts, USA	Oct. 19, 1984	Danwin M. Purdy
Tippet M-03 kg (6 lb)	7.00 kg (15 lb 7 oz)	Virginia Beach, Virginia, USA	Nov. 11, 1997	Dennis Cline
Tippet M-04 kg (8 lb)	8.35 kg (18 lb 6 oz)	Martha's Vineyard, Massachusetts, USA	Oct. 22, 1984	Gregory J. Essayan
Tippet M-06 kg (12 lb)	8.73 kg (19 lb 4 oz)	Virginia Beach, Virginia, USA	Nov. 6, 1980	Larry Greene
Tippet M-08 kg (16 lb)	8.95 kg (19 lb 12 oz)	Nags Head, North Carolina, USA	Nov. 2, 1987	Doug Hinson
Tippet M-10 kg (20 lb)	Vacant			
Tippet W-01 kg (2 lb)	Vacant			
Tippet W-02 kg (4 lb)	Vacant			
Tippet W-03 kg (6 lb)	Vacant			
Tippet W-04 kg (8 lb)	6.35 kg (14 lb 0 oz)	Cape Cod Bay, Massachusetts, USA	July 19, 1998	Acha Lord
Tippet W-06 kg (12 lb)	5.44 kg (12 lb 0 oz)	Oregon Inlet, North Carolina, USA	Mar. 2, 1998	Sarah M. Gardner
Tippet W-08 kg (16 lb)	5.71 kg (12 lb 9 oz)	Hatteras, North Carolina, USA	Jan. 5, 1998	Shawn C. Franklin
Tippet W-10 kg (20 lb)	8.48 kg (18 lb 11 oz)	Martha's Vineyard, Massachusetts, USA	Oct. 9, 1995	LoriLee VanDerlaske

Bonefish / *Albula spp*

TIPPET	WEIGHT	PLACE	DATE	ANGLER
Tippet M-01 kg (2 lb)	5.44 kg (12 lb 0 oz)	Bimini, Bahamas	Nov. 12, 1989	James B. Orthwein
Tippet M-02 kg (4 lb)	6.80 kg (15 lb 0 oz)	Bimini, Bahamas	Mar. 17, 1983	James B. Orthwein
Tippet M-03 kg (6 lb)	6.01 kg (13 lb 4 oz)	Islamorada, Florida, USA	Nov. 6, 1973	Jim Lopez
Tippet M-04 kg (8 lb)	7.03 kg (15 lb 8 oz)	Key Biscayne, Florida, USA	Feb. 27, 1997	Joe Pantorno
Tippet M-06 kg (12 lb)	6.90 kg (15 lb 4 oz)	Big Pine Key, Florida, USA	June 19, 1997	Gordon E. Hill
Tippet M-08 kg (16 lb)	6.37 kg (14 lb 1 oz)	Islamorada, Florida, USA	Apr. 17, 1998	Richard L. Bowers
Tippet M-10 kg (20 lb)	5.66 kg (12 lb 8 oz)	Key Biscayne, Florida, USA	Mar. 13, 1997	Jimmie Kline
Tippet W-01 kg (2 lb)	Vacant			

Bonefish / *(continued)*

Tippet W-02 kg (4 lb)	Vacant			
Tippet W-03 kg (6 lb)	Vacant			
Tippet W-04 kg (8 lb)	Vacant			
Tippet W-06 kg (12 lb)	Vacant			
Tippet W-08 kg (16 lb)	Vacant			
Tippet W-10 kg (20 lb)	Vacant			

Bonito, Atlantic / *Sarda sarda*

TIPPET	WEIGHT	PLACE	DATE	ANGLER
Tippet M-01 kg (2 lb)	2.71 kg (5 lb 15 oz)	Montauk, Long Island, New York, USA	Aug. 12, 1988	Stephen Sloan
Tippet M-02 kg (4 lb)	3.81 kg (8 lb 6 oz)	Weekapaug, Rhode Island, USA	Nov. 2, 1990	John F. Dickinson
Tippet M-03 kg (6 lb)	4.74 kg (10 lb 7 oz)	Fischer's Island, New York, USA	Oct. 27, 1994	David W. Skok
Tippet M-04 kg (8 lb)	4.79 kg (10 lb 9 oz)	Martha's Vineyard, Massachusetts, USA	Oct. 3, 1989	Kib Bramhall
Tippet M-06 kg (12 lb)	5.61 kg (12 lb 5 oz)	Martha's Vineyard, Massachusetts, USA	Oct. 23, 1994	Jim Lepage
Tippet M-08 kg (16 lb)	3.28 kg (7 lb 4 oz)	Mt. Sinai Inlet, New York, USA	Nov. 3, 1995	Christopher J. Catan
Tippet M-10 kg (20 lb)	3.51 kg (7 lb 12 oz)	Nantucket, Massachusetts, USA	Oct. 20, 1995	Pip Winslow
Tippet W-01 kg (2 lb)	Vacant			
Tippet W-02 kg (4 lb)	Vacant			
Tippet W-03 kg (6 lb)	2.49 kg (5 lb 8 oz)	Watch Hill, Rhode Island, USA	Aug. 15, 1998	Gail Greenwood Noyes
Tippet W-04 kg (8 lb)	2.49 kg (5 lb 8 oz)	Quonochontaug, Rhode Island, USA	Aug. 17, 1998	Gail Greenwood Noyes
Tippet W-06 kg (12 lb)	Vacant			
Tippet W-08 kg (16 lb)	3.17 kg (7 lb 0 oz)	Weekapaug, Rhode Island, USA	Aug. 14, 1998	Gail Greenwood Noyes
Tippet W-10 kg (20 lb)	2.49 kg (5 lb 8 oz)	Watch Hill, Rhode Island, USA	Aug. 14, 1998	Gail Greenwood Noyes

Bonito, Pacific / *Sarda spp*

TIPPET	WEIGHT	PLACE	DATE	ANGLER
Tippet M-01 kg (2 lb)	2.20 kg (4 lb 13 oz)	Wollongong, Australia	Mar. 2, 1996	Gregory Phillip Clarke
Tippet M-02 kg (4 lb)	4.08 kg (9 lb 0 oz)	San Diego, California, USA	Aug. 24, 1997	Don B. Walker
Tippet M-03 kg (6 lb)	2.70 kg (5 lb 15 oz)	La Jolla, California, USA	July 23, 1998	Paul Victor Deibel, II
Tippet M-04 kg (8 lb)	5.44 kg (12 lb 0 oz)	Flamingo, Costa Rica	May 24, 1994	Robert Rein
Tippet M-06 kg (12 lb)	7.03 kg (15 lb 8 oz)	Monterey Bay, California, USA	Sept. 15, 1972	Bob Edgley
Tippet M-08 kg (16 lb)	3.35 kg (7 lb 6 oz)	San Martin Island, Baja California, Mexico	Sept. 29, 1994	Jerry Wang
Tippet M-10 kg (20 lb)	4.62 kg (10 lb 3 oz)	13 Fathom Bank, Baja California, Mexico	Jan. 11, 1995	Bill F. Howe
Tippet W-01 kg (2 lb)	Vacant			
Tippet W-02 kg (4 lb)	Vacant			
Tippet W-03 kg (6 lb)	Vacant			
Tippet W-04 kg (8 lb)	Vacant			
Tippet W-06 kg (12 lb)	Vacant			
Tippet W-08 kg (16 lb)	Vacant			
Tippet W-10 kg (20 lb)	Vacant			

Cobia / *Rachycentron canadum*

TIPPET	WEIGHT	PLACE	DATE	ANGLER
Tippet M-01 kg (2 lb)	10.38 kg (22 lb 14 oz)	Destin, Florida, USA	June 5, 1996	George E. Hogan, Jr.
Tippet M-02 kg (4 lb)	16.87 kg (37 lb 3 oz)	Destin, Florida, USA	Apr. 26, 1995	George E. Hogan, Jr.
Tippet M-03 kg (6 lb)	17.91 kg (39 lb 8 oz)	Key West, Florida, USA	Mar. 15, 1972	Roy Terrel
Tippet M-04 kg (8 lb)	30.50 kg (67 lb 4 oz)	Key West, Florida, USA	Mar. 2, 1985	Pat Ford
Tippet M-06 kg (12 lb)	31.29 kg (69 lb 0 oz)	Florida Bay, Florida, USA	Dec. 9, 1967	Ralph Delph
Tippet M-08 kg (16 lb)	37.76 kg (83 lb 4 oz)	Key West, Florida, USA	Jan. 2, 1986	Jim Anson
Tippet M-10 kg (20 lb)	28.12 kg (62 lb 3 oz)	Gulf Shores, Alabama, USA	Apr. 27, 1994	Robert T. Cunningham, Jr.
Tippet W-01 kg (2 lb)	Vacant			
Tippet W-02 kg (4 lb)	Vacant			
Tippet W-03 kg (6 lb)	Vacant			
Tippet W-04 kg (8 lb)	Vacant			
Tippet W-06 kg (12 lb)	8.16 kg (18 lb 0 oz)	Key West, Florida, USA	Apr. 28, 1998	Mrs. William B. DuVal
Tippet W-08 kg (16 lb)	Vacant			
Tippet W-10 kg (20 lb)	Vacant			

Cod, Atlantic / *Gadus*

TIPPET	WEIGHT	PLACE	DATE	ANGLER
Tippet M-01 kg (2 lb)	1.25 kg (2 lb 12 oz)	Great Belt, Denmark	Apr. 22, 1984	Gorm Siiger
Tippet M-02 kg (4 lb)	1.23 kg (2 lb 11 oz)	Terrak, Norway	Aug. 4, 1984	Hans Joachim Wenzel
Tippet M-03 kg (6 lb)	2.66 kg (5 lb 14 oz)	Port Maitland, Nova Scotia, Canada	June 22, 1973	Lou Truppi
Tippet M-04 kg (8 lb)	8.35 kg (18 lb 6 oz)	Vikaer Beach, Jylland, Denmark	Feb. 15, 1983	John Anker
Tippet M-06 kg (12 lb)	4.02 kg (8 lb 14 oz)	Port Maitland, Nova Scotia, Canada	June 22, 1973	Lou Truppi
Tippet M-08 kg (16 lb)	1.58 kg (3 lb 8 oz)	Gloucester, Massachusetts, USA	June 28, 1990	Kenneth M. Lai
Tippet M-10 kg (20 lb)	Vacant			
Tippet W-01 kg (2 lb)	Vacant			
Tippet W-02 kg (4 lb)	Vacant			
Tippet W-03 kg (6 lb)	Vacant			
Tippet W-04 kg (8 lb)	Vacant			
Tippet W-06 kg (12 lb)	Vacant			
Tippet W-08 kg (16 lb)	Vacant			
Tippet W-10 kg (20 lb)	Vacant			

Cod, Pacific / *Gadus macrocephalus*

TIPPET	WEIGHT	PLACE	DATE	ANGLER
Tippet M-01 kg (2 lb)	Vacant			
Tippet M-02 kg (4 lb)	1.87 kg (4 lb 2 oz)	Dangerous Cape, Alaska, USA	June 20, 1993	E.Z. Marchant
Tippet M-03 kg (6 lb)	2.26 kg (5 lb 0 oz)	Kodiak, Alaska, USA	July 28, 1996	Paul Leader
Tippet M-04 kg (8 lb)	2.01 kg (4 lb 7 oz)	Dangerous Cape, Alaska, USA	June 20, 1993	E.Z. Marchant
Tippet M-06 kg (12 lb)	3.62 kg (8 lb 0 oz)	Kodiak, Alaska, USA	July 28, 1996	Paul Leader
Tippet M-08 kg (16 lb)	3.99 kg (8 lb 13 oz)	Dangerous Cape, Alaska, USA	June 20, 1993	Lance Anderson
Tippet M-10 kg (20 lb)	2.04 kg (4 lb 8 oz)	Dangerous Cape, Alaska, USA	June 20, 1993	Lindy Keirn

Tippet	Weight			
Tippet W-01 kg (2 lb)	Vacant			
Tippet W-02 kg (4 lb)	Vacant			
Tippet W-03 kg (6 lb)	Vacant			
Tippet W-04 kg (8 lb)	Vacant			
Tippet W-06 kg (12 lb)	Vacant			
Tippet W-08 kg (16 lb)	Vacant			
Tippet W-10 kg (20 lb)	Vacant			

Conger / *Conger conger*

TIPPET	WEIGHT	PLACE	DATE	ANGLER
Tippet M-01 kg (2 lb)	Vacant			
Tippet M-02 kg (4 lb)	Vacant			
Tippet M-03 kg (6 lb)	Vacant			
Tippet M-04 kg (8 lb)	Vacant			
Tippet M-06 kg (12 lb)	Vacant			
Tippet M-08 kg (16 lb)	Vacant			
Tippet M-10 kg (20 lb)	Vacant			
Tippet W-01 kg (2 lb)	Vacant			
Tippet W-02 kg (4 lb)	Vacant			
Tippet W-03 kg (6 lb)	Vacant			
Tippet W-04 kg (8 lb)	Vacant			
Tippet W-06 kg (12 lb)	Vacant			
Tippet W-08 kg (16 lb)	Vacant			
Tippet W-10 kg (20 lb)	Vacant			

Dentex / *Dentex dentex*

TIPPET	WEIGHT	PLACE	DATE	ANGLER
Tippet M-01 kg (2 lb)	Vacant			
Tippet M-02 kg (4 lb)	Vacant			
Tippet M-03 kg (6 lb)	Vacant			
Tippet M-04 kg (8 lb)	Vacant			
Tippet M-06 kg (12 lb)	Vacant			
Tippet M-08 kg (16 lb)	Vacant			
Tippet M-10 kg (20 lb)	Vacant			
Tippet W-01 kg (2 lb)	Vacant			
Tippet W-02 kg (4 lb)	Vacant			
Tippet W-03 kg (6 lb)	Vacant			
Tippet W-04 kg (8 lb)	Vacant			
Tippet W-06 kg (12 lb)	Vacant			
Tippet W-08 kg (16 lb)	Vacant			
Tippet W-10 kg (20 lb)	Vacant			

Dolphinfish / *Coryphaena hippurus*

TIPPET	WEIGHT	PLACE	DATE	ANGLER
Tippet M-01 kg (2 lb)	8.05 kg (17 lb 12 oz)	Petite Coupe, Mauritius	Nov. 29, 1990	Richard F. Flasch
Tippet M-02 kg (4 lb)	10.43 kg (23 lb 0 oz)	Gulf of Mexico, Alabama, USA	June 20, 1998	Robert T. Cunningham, Jr.
Tippet M-03 kg (6 lb)	15.42 kg (34 lb 0 oz)	Pinas Bay, Panama	Dec. 23, 1980	Tred Barta
Tippet M-04 kg (8 lb)	21.18 kg (46 lb 11 oz)	Freeport, Grand Bahama, Bahamas	May 19, 1997	Peter Rose
Tippet M-06 kg (12 lb)	26.30 kg (58 lb 0 oz)	Pinas Bay, Panama	Dec. 6, 1964	Stu Apte
Tippet M-08 kg (16 lb)	24.26 kg (53 lb 8 oz)	Isla Mujeres, Quintana Roo, Mexico	Apr. 29, 1990	Rufus Wakeman II
Tippet M-10 kg (20 lb)	26.08 kg (57 lb 8 oz)	Loreto, Mexico	July 23, 1997	Donald W. Childress, DDS
Tippet W-01 kg (2 lb)	Vacant			
Tippet W-02 kg (4 lb)	3.40 kg (7 lb 8 oz)	Islamorada, Florida, USA	June 14, 1998	Acha Lord
Tippet W-03 kg (6 lb)	8.98 kg (19 lb 13 oz)	Islamorada, Florida, USA	July 6, 1998	Annie Pope
Tippet W-04 kg (8 lb)	10.65 kg (23 lb 8 oz)	Islamorada, Florida, USA	July 6, 1998	Julie Pope Dantzler
Tippet W-06 kg (12 lb)	10.03 kg (22 lb 2 oz)	Islamorada, Florida, USA	June 13, 1998	Acha Lord
Tippet W-08 kg (16 lb)	12.47 kg (27 lb 8 oz)	Islamorada, Florida, USA	June 7, 1998	Courtney H. Scott
Tippet W-10 kg (20 lb)	Vacant			

Drum, black / *Pogonias cromis*

TIPPET	WEIGHT	PLACE	DATE	ANGLER
Tippet M-01 kg (2 lb)	5.55 kg (12 lb 4 oz)	Banana River, Cocoa Beach, Florida, USA	Nov. 4, 1994	Dave Chermanski
Tippet M-02 kg (4 lb)	13.83 kg (30 lb 8 oz)	Banana River, Cape Canaveral, Florida, USA	Jan. 14, 1996	Scott Nickels
Tippet M-03 kg (6 lb)	13.09 kg (28 lb 14 oz)	Banana River, Florida, USA	Dec. 23, 1996	Scott Nickels
Tippet M-04 kg (8 lb)	22.79 kg (50 lb 4 oz)	Indian River, Merritt Island, Florida, USA	July 12, 1986	Mark R. Marconi
Tippet M-06 kg (12 lb)	26.30 kg (57 lb 8 oz)	Chesapeake Bay Bridge Tunnel, Virginia, USA	June 25, 1995	Jon Holsenbeck
Tippet M-08 kg (16 lb)	20.29 kg (44 lb 12 oz)	Chesapeake Bay Bridge Tunnel, Virginia, USA	June 21, 1998	Jon Holsenbeck
Tippet M-10 kg (20 lb)	30.20 kg (66 lb 9 oz)	Chesapeake Bay Bridge Tunnel, Virginia, USA	June 24, 1998	Jon Holsenbeck
Tippet W-01 kg (2 lb)	Vacant			
Tippet W-02 kg (4 lb)	Vacant			
Tippet W-03 kg (6 lb)	Vacant			
Tippet W-04 kg (8 lb)	Vacant			
Tippet W-06 kg (12 lb)	Vacant			
Tippet W-08 kg (16 lb)	Vacant			
Tippet W-10 kg (20 lb)	Vacant			

Drum, red / *Sciaenops ocellatus*

TIPPET	WEIGHT	PLACE	DATE	ANGLER
Tippet M-01 kg (2 lb)	6.80 kg (15 lb 0 oz)	Pensacola, Florida, USA	Dec. 28, 1997	Robert T. Cunningham, Jr.
Tippet M-02 kg (4 lb)	12.47 kg (27 lb 8 oz)	Chandeleur Islands, Louisiana, USA	Jan. 16, 1993	Robert T. Cunningham, Jr.
Tippet M-03 kg (6 lb)	15.64 kg (34 lb 8 oz)	Banana River, Florida, USA	Oct. 29, 1994	Lance Crouch
Tippet M-04 kg (8 lb)	14.51 kg (32 lb 0 oz)	Banana River, Florida, USA	May 31, 1994	Lance Crouch
Tippet M-04 kg (8 lb)Tie	14.74 kg (32 lb 0 oz)	Grand Gosier Island, Louisiana, USA	Mar. 14, 1998	Rudolph A. Hall
Tippet M-06 kg (12 lb)	19.19 kg (42 lb 5 oz)	Oregon Inlet, North Carolina, USA	May 12, 1981	J. M. (Chico) Fernandez

Drum, red / *(continued)*

TIPPET	WEIGHT	PLACE	DATE	ANGLER
Tippet M-08 kg (16 lb)	19.50 kg (43 lb 0 oz)	Banana River Lagoon, Florida, USA	May 7, 1995	Greg Braunstein, MD
Tippet M-10 kg (20 lb)	17.80 kg (39 lb 4 oz)	Ocracoke, North Carolina, USA	Oct. 27, 1995	Doug Hinson
Tippet W-01 kg (2 lb)	Vacant			
Tippet W-02 kg (4 lb)	Vacant			
Tippet W-03 kg (6 lb)	Vacant			
Tippet W-04 kg (8 lb)	Vacant			
Tippet W-06 kg (12 lb)	2.10 kg (4 lb 10 oz)	Lake Salvadore, Lafitte, Louisiana, USA	Sept. 5, 1998	Susan K. Gros
Tippet W-08 kg (16 lb)	2.90 kg (6 lb 6 oz)	Lake Salvadore, Lafitte, Louisiana, USA	Sept. 5, 1998	Susan K. Gros
Tippet W-10 kg (20 lb)	Vacant			

Flounder, summer / *Paralichthys dentatus*

TIPPET	WEIGHT	PLACE	DATE	ANGLER
Tippet M-01 kg (2 lb)	1.87 kg (4 lb 2 oz)	Horton's Point, Long Island, New York, USA	Aug. 31, 1994	John Boesenberg
Tippet M-02 kg (4 lb)	1.08 kg (2 lb 6 oz)	Montauk, New York, USA	July 12, 1998	William Kuhle
Tippet M-03 kg (6 lb)	3.68 kg (8 lb 2 oz)	Greenwich, Connecticut, USA	Oct. 27, 1991	William N. Herold
Tippet M-04 kg (8 lb)	2.35 kg (5 lb 3 oz)	Montauk, New York, USA	June 25, 1998	William Kuhle
Tippet M-06 kg (12 lb)	1.58 kg (3 lb 8 oz)	Longport, New Jersey, USA	June 23, 1997	Joseph J. Cariosa, Jr.
Tippet M-08 kg (16 lb)	3.09 kg (6 lb 13 oz)	Asbescon Inlet, New Jersey, USA	June 18, 1996	Paul D. Ripperger
Tippet M-10 kg (20 lb)	2.32 kg (5 lb 1 oz)	Montauk Point, New York, USA	July 10, 1993	Mike Corblies
Tippet W-01 kg (2 lb)	Vacant			
Tippet W-02 kg (4 lb)	Vacant			
Tippet W-03 kg (6 lb)	Vacant			
Tippet W-04 kg (8 lb)	Vacant			
Tippet W-06 kg (12 lb)	Vacant			
Tippet W-08 kg (16 lb)	Vacant			
Tippet W-10 kg (20 lb)	Vacant			

Halibut, Atlantic / *Hippoglossus hippoglossus*

TIPPET	WEIGHT	PLACE	DATE	ANGLER
Tippet M-01 kg (2 lb)	Vacant			
Tippet M-02 kg (4 lb)	Vacant			
Tippet M-03 kg (6 lb)	Vacant			
Tippet M-04 kg (8 lb)	Vacant			
Tippet M-06 kg (12 lb)	Vacant			
Tippet M-08 kg (16 lb)	Vacant			
Tippet M-10 kg (20 lb)	Vacant			
Tippet W-01 kg (2 lb)	Vacant			
Tippet W-02 kg (4 lb)	Vacant			
Tippet W-03 kg (6 lb)	Vacant			
Tippet W-04 kg (8 lb)	Vacant			
Tippet W-06 kg (12 lb)	Vacant			
Tippet W-08 kg (16 lb)	Vacant			
Tippet W-10 kg (20 lb)	Vacant			

Halibut, California / *Paralichthys californicus*

TIPPET	WEIGHT	PLACE	DATE	ANGLER
Tippet M-01 kg (2 lb)	Vacant			
Tippet M-02 kg (4 lb)	2.52 kg (5 lb 9 oz)	Long Beach, California, USA	Dec. 13, 1997	Richard B. Jacobsen
Tippet M-03 kg (6 lb)	6.25 kg (13 lb 12 oz)	Macklyn Cove, Brookings, Oregon, USA	July 3, 1998	Michael Cowley
Tippet M-04 kg (8 lb)	2.94 kg (6 lb 8 oz)	Magdalena Bay, Baja California, Mexico	Mar. 13, 1989	Didier Van der Veecken
Tippet M-06 kg (12 lb)	3.56 kg (7 lb 13 oz)	Long Beach, California, USA	Jan. 3, 1998	Cecil F. Gamble
Tippet M-08 kg (16 lb)	3.09 kg (6 lb 13 oz)	Alameda Rockwall, San Francisco Bay, California, USA	June 3, 1995	Lance P. Anderson
Tippet M-10 kg (20 lb)	5.95 kg (13 lb 2 oz)	Palos Verdes, California, USA	May 20, 1995	Dr. John F. Whitaker
Tippet W-01 kg (2 lb)	Vacant			
Tippet W-02 kg (4 lb)	Vacant			
Tippet W-03 kg (6 lb)	Vacant			
Tippet W-04 kg (8 lb)	Vacant			
Tippet W-06 kg (12 lb)	Vacant			
Tippet W-08 kg (16 lb)	Vacant			
Tippet W-10 kg (20 lb)	Vacant			

Halibut, Pacific / *Hippoglossus stenolepis*

TIPPET	WEIGHT	PLACE	DATE	ANGLER
Tippet M-01 kg (2 lb)	4.98 kg (11 lb 0 oz)	Kodiak, Alaska, USA	Aug. 1, 1994	Paul Leader
Tippet M-02 kg (4 lb)	13.60 kg (30 lb 0 oz)	Kodiak, Alaska, USA	Aug. 7, 1997	Paul Leader
Tippet M-03 kg (6 lb)	15.42 kg (34 lb 0 oz)	Kodiak, Alaska, USA	Aug. 1, 1997	Paul Leader
Tippet M-04 kg (8 lb)	33.56 kg (74 lb 0 oz)	Port Armstrong, Alaska, USA	July 19, 1990	Dick DeMars
Tippet M-06 kg (12 lb)	33.56 kg (74 lb 0 oz)	Kodiak, Alaska, USA	Aug. 1, 1997	Paul Leader
Tippet M-08 kg (16 lb)	38.01 kg (83 lb 12 oz)	Gove Point, Alaska, USA	Aug. 6, 1994	Mike Hood
Tippet M-10 kg (20 lb)	38.10 kg (84 lb 0 oz)	Kodiak, Alaska, USA	Aug. 2, 1998	Paul Leader
Tippet W-01 kg (2 lb)	Vacant			
Tippet W-02 kg (4 lb)	Vacant			
Tippet W-03 kg (6 lb)	Vacant			
Tippet W-04 kg (8 lb)	Vacant			
Tippet W-06 kg (12 lb)	Vacant			
Tippet W-08 kg (16 lb)	7.85 kg (17 lb 5 oz)	Montague Island, Alaska, USA	Aug. 18, 1998	Donna Teeny
Tippet W-10 kg (20 lb)	Vacant			

Jack, crevalle / *Caranx hippos*

TIPPET	WEIGHT	PLACE	DATE	ANGLER
Tippet M-01 kg (2 lb)	4.98 kg (11 lb 0 oz)	Fort Lauderdale, Florida, USA	Feb. 23, 1983	Mark E. Krowka
Tippet M-02 kg (4 lb)	13.38 kg (29 lb 8 oz)	Sebastian River, Florida, USA	June 14, 1993	Dave Chermanski
Tippet M-03 kg (6 lb)	13.83 kg (30 lb 8 oz)	Pensacola Beach, Florida, USA	Aug. 13, 1994	Carl E. Cole
Tippet M-04 kg (8 lb)	14.06 kg (31 lb 0 oz)	Port Canaveral, Florida, USA	Apr. 28, 1983	Troy Perez

Jack, crevalle / *(continued)*

TIPPET	WEIGHT	PLACE	DATE	ANGLER
Tippet M-06 kg (12 lb)	17.00 kg (37 lb 8 oz)	Dry Tortugas, Florida, USA	Feb. 11, 1994	Carlos B. Solis
Tippet M-08 kg (16 lb)	19.95 kg (44 lb 0 oz)	Tortuguero, Costa Rica	Feb. 20, 1979	R. T. Miller
Tippet M-10 kg (20 lb)	15.42 kg (34 lb 0 oz)	Pensacola Bay, Pensacola, Florida, USA	Aug. 14, 1992	Carl E. Cole
Tippet W-01 kg (2 lb)	Vacant			
Tippet W-02 kg (4 lb)	Vacant			
Tippet W-03 kg (6 lb)	Vacant			
Tippet W-04 kg (8 lb)	7.25 kg (16 lb 0 oz)	Jupiter, Florida, USA	June 11, 1998	Jing Torn
Tippet W-06 kg (12 lb)	Vacant			
Tippet W-08 kg (16 lb)	9.07 kg (20 lb 0 oz)	Jupiter, Florida, USA	June 12, 1998	Jing Torn
Tippet W-10 kg (20 lb)	Vacant			

Jack, horse-eye / *Caranx latus*

TIPPET	WEIGHT	PLACE	DATE	ANGLER
Tippet M-01 kg (2 lb)	0.68 kg (1 lb 8 oz)	Andros Island, Bahamas	Oct. 18, 1997	Robert T. Cunningham, Jr.
Tippet M-02 kg (4 lb)	4.53 kg (10 lb 0 oz)	Bimini, Bahamas	Aug. 8, 1998	Ray Stormont
Tippet M-03 kg (6 lb)	2.81 kg (6 lb 3 oz)	West End, Grand Bahama, Bahamas	Oct. 25, 1996	Colin Rose
Tippet M-04 kg (8 lb)	6.57 kg (14 lb 8 oz)	Key West, Florida, USA	Sept. 7, 1986	Joseph M. Stehr, III
Tippet M-06 kg (12 lb)	8.84 kg (19 lb 8 oz)	Bimini, Bahamas	Aug. 14, 1997	Ray C. Stormont
Tippet M-08 kg (16 lb)	6.80 kg (15 lb 0 oz)	Bimini, Bahamas	June 19, 1998	Hance H. Oliver
Tippet M-10 kg (20 lb)	5.66 kg (18 lb 0 oz)	Bimini, Bahamas	June 7, 1997	Barry Dorf
Tippet W-01 kg (2 lb)	Vacant			
Tippet W-02 kg (4 lb)	Vacant			
Tippet W-03 kg (6 lb)	Vacant			
Tippet W-04 kg (8 lb)	4.08 kg (9 lb 0 oz)	Bimini, Bahamas	Aug. 8, 1998	Dixie Lee Burns
Tippet W-06 kg (12 lb)	Vacant			
Tippet W-08 kg (16 lb)	Vacant			
Tippet W-10 kg (20 lb)	3.85 kg (8 lb 8 oz)	Bimini, Bahamas	Aug. 9, 1998	Dixie Lee Burns

Jack, Pacific crevalle / *Caranx caninus*

TIPPET	WEIGHT	PLACE	DATE	ANGLER
Tippet M-01 kg (2 lb)	Vacant			
Tippet M-02 kg (4 lb)	3.40 kg (7 lb 8 oz)	Rincon de Guayabitos, Mexico	July 11, 1993	Terry Gunn
Tippet M-03 kg (6 lb)	Vacant			
Tippet M-04 kg (8 lb)	5.44 kg (12 lb 0 oz)	Cabo San Lucas, Baja California Sur, Mexico	Mar. 6, 1984	Didier Van der Veecken
Tippet M-06 kg (12 lb)	6.23 kg (13 lb 12 oz)	Rincon De Guayabitos, Mexico	July 11, 1993	Russell Sullivan
Tippet M-08 kg (16 lb)	7.37 kg (16 lb 4 oz)	Cabo San Lucas, Baja California Sur, Mexico	Apr. 29, 1988	Didier Van der Veecken
Tippet M-10 kg (20 lb)	7.71 kg (17 lb 0 oz)	Guatemala	Dec. 28, 1997	Ralph G. Bird
Tippet W-01 kg (2 lb)	Vacant			
Tippet W-02 kg (4 lb)	Vacant			
Tippet W-03 kg (6 lb)	Vacant			
Tippet W-04 kg (8 lb)	Vacant			
Tippet W-06 kg (12 lb)	Vacant			
Tippet W-08 kg (16 lb)	Vacant			
Tippet W-10 kg (20 lb)	10.34 kg (22 lb 12 oz)	Todos Santos, Baja California Sur, Mexico	Dec. 5, 1996	Karen Kukolich

Jewfish / *Epinephelus itajara*

TIPPET	WEIGHT	PLACE	DATE	ANGLER
Tippet M-01 kg (2 lb)	Vacant			
Tippet M-02 kg (4 lb)	Vacant			
Tippet M-03 kg (6 lb)	Vacant			
Tippet M-04 kg (8 lb)	Vacant			
Tippet M-06 kg (12 lb)	161.48 kg (356 lb 0 oz)	Islamorada, Florida, USA	Mar. 15, 1967	Bart Froth
Tippet M-08 kg (16 lb)	Vacant			
Tippet M-10 kg (20 lb)	Vacant			
Tippet W-01 kg (2 lb)	Vacant			
Tippet W-02 kg (4 lb)	Vacant			
Tippet W-03 kg (6 lb)	Vacant			
Tippet W-04 kg (8 lb)	Vacant			
Tippet W-06 kg (12 lb)	Vacant			
Tippet W-08 kg (16 lb)	Vacant			
Tippet W-10 kg (20 lb)	Vacant			

Kahawai / *Arripis trutta*

TIPPET	WEIGHT	PLACE	DATE	ANGLER
Tippet M-01 kg (2 lb)	2.60 kg (5 lb 11 oz)	Fantail Bay, Coromandel, New Zealand	Dec. 30, 1989	Phillip M. Lovell
Tippet M-02 kg (4 lb)	4.80 kg (10 lb 9 oz)	Rottnest Island, W.A., Australia	Apr. 5, 1986	Simon Gilbert
Tippet M-03 kg (6 lb)	2.17 kg (4 lb 12 oz)	"The Needles", Great Barrier Island, New Zealand	Oct. 18, 1996	Ian McFadzean
Tippet M-04 kg (8 lb)	4.00 kg (8 lb 13 oz)	Rottnest Island, W.A., Australia	Apr. 5, 1986	Simon Gilbert
Tippet M-06 kg (12 lb)	4.00 kg (8 lb 13 oz)	Rottnest Island, W.A., Australia	Apr. 5, 1986	Lou Rummer
Tippet M-08 kg (16 lb)	6.30 kg (13 lb 14 oz)	Jervis Bay, N.S.W., Australia	June 1, 1991	Steve Starling
Tippet M-10 kg (20 lb)	3.15 kg (6 lb 15 oz)	Ceduna, Australia	Sept. 25, 1997	John Marsh
Tippet W-01 kg (2 lb)	Vacant			
Tippet W-02 kg (4 lb)	Vacant			
Tippet W-03 kg (6 lb)	Vacant			
Tippet W-04 kg (8 lb)	Vacant			
Tippet W-06 kg (12 lb)	Vacant			
Tippet W-08 kg (16 lb)	Vacant			
Tippet W-10 kg (20 lb)	Vacant			

Kawakawa / *Euthynnus affinis*

TIPPET	WEIGHT	PLACE	DATE	ANGLER
Tippet M-01 kg (2 lb)	1.27 kg (2 lb 12 oz)	Sydney, N.S.W., Australia	Dec. 26, 1982	John G. Dow
Tippet M-02 kg (4 lb)	4.75 kg (10 lb 7 oz)	Dunk Island, Queensland, Australia	Sept. 28, 1984	Andrew A. MacGrath
Tippet M-03 kg (6 lb)	Vacant			

Kawakawa / *(continued)*

TIPPET	WEIGHT	PLACE	DATE	ANGLER
Tippet M-04 kg (8 lb)	8.46 kg (18 lb 8 oz)	Moreton Bay, Queensland, Australia	Oct. 22, 1987	Darryl J. Steel
Tippet M-06 kg (12 lb)	7.40 kg (16 lb 5 oz)	Onslow, W.A., Australia	Dec. 29, 1986	Jeffrey W. Grist
Tippet M-08 kg (16 lb)	8.60 kg (18 lb 15 oz)	Onslow, W.A., Australia	Dec. 29, 1986	Jeffrey W. Grist
Tippet M-10 kg (20 lb)	Vacant			
Tippet W-01 kg (2 lb)	Vacant			
Tippet W-02 kg (4 lb)	Vacant			
Tippet W-03 kg (6 lb)	Vacant			
Tippet W-04 kg (8 lb)	Vacant			
Tippet W-06 kg (12 lb)	Vacant			
Tippet W-08 kg (16 lb)	Vacant			
Tippet W-10 kg (20 lb)	Vacant			

Leerfish (Garrick) / *Lichia amia*

TIPPET	WEIGHT	PLACE	DATE	ANGLER
Tippet M-01 kg (2 lb)	Vacant			
Tippet M-02 kg (4 lb)	Vacant			
Tippet M-03 kg (6 lb)	Vacant			
Tippet M-04 kg (8 lb)	5.60 kg (12 lb 5 oz)	Nouadhibou, Mauritania	Aug. 12, 1994	Daniel Maury
Tippet M-06 kg (12 lb)	7.00 kg (15 lb 6 oz)	Port St. Johns, South Africa	Oct. 4, 1996	Richard Schumann
Tippet M-08 kg (16 lb)	Vacant			
Tippet M-10 kg (20 lb)	Vacant			
Tippet W-01 kg (2 lb)	Vacant			
Tippet W-02 kg (4 lb)	Vacant			
Tippet W-03 kg (6 lb)	Vacant			
Tippet W-04 kg (8 lb)	Vacant			
Tippet W-06 kg (12 lb)	Vacant			
Tippet W-08 kg (16 lb)	Vacant			
Tippet W-10 kg (20 lb)	Vacant			

Lingcod / *Ophiodon*

TIPPET	WEIGHT	PLACE	DATE	ANGLER
Tippet M-01 kg (2 lb)	Vacant			
Tippet M-02 kg (4 lb)	Vacant			
Tippet M-03 kg (6 lb)	8.16 kg (18 lb 0 oz)	Seward, Alaska, USA	July 2, 1998	John Aarnink
Tippet M-04 kg (8 lb)	2.49 kg (5 lb 8 oz)	Elfin Cove, Alaska, USA	Sept. 7, 1989	Paul Leader
Tippet M-06 kg (12 lb)	11.08 kg (24 lb 7 oz)	Depoe Bay, Oregon, USA	Aug. 21, 1993	Glenn W. Young
Tippet M-08 kg (16 lb)	59.11 kg (26 lb 13 oz)	Chugach Island, Alaska, USA	July 16, 1993	Lance P. Anderson
Tippet M-10 kg (20 lb)	16.32 kg (36 lb 0 oz)	Cross Sound, Alaska, USA	July 31, 1997	Russell Jensen
Tippet W-01 kg (2 lb)	Vacant			
Tippet W-02 kg (4 lb)	Vacant			
Tippet W-03 kg (6 lb)	Vacant			
Tippet W-04 kg (8 lb)	Vacant			
Tippet W-06 kg (12 lb)	Vacant			
Tippet W-08 kg (16 lb)	Vacant			
Tippet W-10 kg (20 lb)	Vacant			

Mackerel, cero / *Scomberomorus regalis*

TIPPET	WEIGHT	PLACE	DATE	ANGLER
Tippet M-01 kg (2 lb)	1.92 kg (4 lb 4 oz)	Key West, Florida, USA	Mar. 1, 1995	George L. Foti
Tippet M-02 kg (4 lb)	2.49 kg (5 lb 8 oz)	Key West, Florida, USA	Jan. 22, 1998	Jerome C. Matthews
Tippet M-03 kg (6 lb)	2.94 kg (6 lb 8 oz)	Key West, Florida, USA	Mar. 1, 1995	George L. Foti
Tippet M-04 kg (8 lb)	3.17 kg (7 lb 0 oz)	Key West, Florida, USA	Feb. 2, 1995	Al Golinski
Tippet M-06 kg (12 lb)	3.85 kg (8 lb 8 oz)	Walker's Cay, Bahamas	July 1, 1994	Greg Norman
Tippet M-08 kg (16 lb)	4.98 kg (11 lb 0 oz)	Walker's Cay, Abaco, Bahamas	June 23, 1993	David Webb
Tippet M-10 kg (20 lb)	3.51 kg (7 lb 12 oz)	Key West, Florida, USA	Feb. 2, 1995	Al Golinski
Tippet W-01 kg (2 lb)	Vacant			
Tippet W-02 kg (4 lb)	Vacant			
Tippet W-03 kg (6 lb)	Vacant			
Tippet W-04 kg (8 lb)	Vacant			
Tippet W-06 kg (12 lb)	Vacant			
Tippet W-08 kg (16 lb)	Vacant			
Tippet W-10 kg (20 lb)	Vacant			

Mackerel, king / *Scomberomorus cavalla*

TIPPET	WEIGHT	PLACE	DATE	ANGLER
Tippet M-01 kg (2 lb)	Vacant			
Tippet M-02 kg (4 lb)	6.69 kg (14 lb 12 oz)	Key West, Florida, USA	Feb. 4, 1997	Al Golinski
Tippet M-03 kg (6 lb)	10.88 kg (24 lb 0 oz)	Key West, Florida, USA	Feb. 5, 1997	George Foti
Tippet M-04 kg (8 lb)	13.04 kg (28 lb 12 oz)	Key West, Florida, USA	Feb. 5, 1997	George Foti
Tippet M-06 kg (12 lb)	17.23 kg (38 lb 0 oz)	Key West, Florida, USA	Jan. 12, 1971	Jim Lopez
Tippet M-08 kg (16 lb)	23.24 kg (51 lb 4 oz)	Key West, Florida, USA	Feb. 15, 1987	Rick Gunion
Tippet M-10 kg (20 lb)	24.94 kg (55 lb 0 oz)	Key West, Florida, USA	Mar. 20, 1995	Ben Bergeron
Tippet W-01 kg (2 lb)	Vacant			
Tippet W-02 kg (4 lb)	Vacant			
Tippet W-03 kg (6 lb)	Vacant			
Tippet W-04 kg (8 lb)	Vacant			
Tippet W-06 kg (12 lb)	4.08 kg (9 lb 0 oz)	Islamorada, Florida, USA	Jan. 13, 1998	Dianne Harbaugh
Tippet W-08 kg (16 lb)	Vacant			
Tippet W-10 kg (20 lb)	2.72 kg (6 lb 0 oz)	Miami, Florida, USA	Jan. 1, 1998	Pamela W. Marmin

Mackerel, narrowbarred / *Scomberomorus commerson*

TIPPET	WEIGHT	PLACE	DATE	ANGLER
Tippet M-01 kg (2 lb)	2.00 kg (4 lb 6 oz)	Torres Strait, Queensland, Australia	Mar. 7, 1990	Graham L. Plummer
Tippet M-02 kg (4 lb)	Vacant			

Mackerel, narrowbarred / *(continued)*

TIPPET	WEIGHT	PLACE	DATE	ANGLER
Tippet M-03 kg (6 lb)	Vacant			
Tippet M-04 kg (8 lb)	10.00 kg (22 lb 0 oz)	Exmouth, W.A., Australia	Aug. 25, 1988	Simon Gilbert
Tippet M-06 kg (12 lb)	16.80 kg (37 lb 0 oz)	Onslow, W.A., Australia	Sept. 11, 1987	Jeffrey W. Grist
Tippet M-08 kg (16 lb)	21.00 kg (46 lb 4 oz)	Exmouth, W.A., Australia	Sept. 2, 1991	Ken Ahmat
Tippet M-10 kg (20 lb)	18.50 kg (40 lb 12 oz)	Innisfail, Australia	Sept. 16, 1996	George Campbell
Tippet W-01 kg (2 lb)	Vacant			
Tippet W-02 kg (4 lb)	Vacant			
Tippet W-03 kg (6 lb)	Vacant			
Tippet W-04 kg (8 lb)	Vacant			
Tippet W-06 kg (12 lb)	Vacant			
Tippet W-08 kg (16 lb)	Vacant			
Tippet W-10 kg (20 lb)	Vacant			

Mackerel, Spanish / *Scomberomorus maculatus*

TIPPET	WEIGHT	PLACE	DATE	ANGLER
Tippet M-01 kg (2 lb)	1.95 kg (4 lb 4 oz)	Indian Rocks Beach, Florida, USA	Sept. 19, 1989	Doug Johnston
Tippet M-02 kg (4 lb)	2.94 kg (6 lb 8 oz)	Gulf of Mexico, Alabama, USA	Sept. 18, 1995	Robert T. Cunningham, Jr.
Tippet M-03 kg (6 lb)	2.49 kg (5 lb 7 oz)	New Port Richey, Florida, USA	Oct. 30, 1996	James P. Wisner
Tippet M-04 kg (8 lb)	2.94 kg (6 lb 7 oz)	New Port Richey, Florida, USA	Oct. 28, 1996	James P. Wisner
Tippet M-06 kg (12 lb)	3.94 kg (8 lb 11 oz)	Martha's Vineyard, Massachusetts, USA	Aug. 25, 1994	Donald T. MacGillivray, Jr.
Tippet M-08 kg (16 lb)	3.06 kg (6 lb 12 oz)	Key West, Florida, USA	Nov. 22, 1989	Ted Lund, III
Tippet M-10 kg (20 lb)	3.10 kg (6 lb 13 oz)	Tarpon Springs, Florida, USA	Nov. 7, 1995	James P. Wisner
Tippet W-01 kg (2 lb)	Vacant			
Tippet W-02 kg (4 lb)	1.24 kg (2 lb 12 oz)	Marathon, Florida, USA	Feb. 12, 1998	Jamie Callion
Tippet W-03 kg (6 lb)	1.81 kg (4 lb 0 oz)	Marathon, Florida, USA	Feb. 12, 1998	Jamie Callion
Tippet W-04 kg (8 lb)	1.58 kg (3 lb 8 oz)	Marathon, Florida, USA	Feb. 12, 1998	Jamie Callion
Tippet W-06 kg (12 lb)	1.58 kg (3 lb 8 oz)	Marathon, Florida, USA	Feb. 12, 1998	Jamie Callion
Tippet W-08 kg (16 lb)	Vacant			
Tippet W-10 kg (20 lb)	1.24 kg (2 lb 12 oz)	Marathon, Florida, USA	Feb. 12, 1998	Jamie Callion

Madai / *Pagrus major*

TIPPET	WEIGHT	PLACE	DATE	ANGLER
Tippet M-01 kg (2 lb)	Vacant			
Tippet M-02 kg (4 lb)	Vacant			
Tippet M-03 kg (6 lb)	Vacant			
Tippet M-04 kg (8 lb)	Vacant			
Tippet M-06 kg (12 lb)	Vacant			
Tippet M-08 kg (16 lb)	Vacant			
Tippet M-10 kg (20 lb)	Vacant			
Tippet W-01 kg (2 lb)	Vacant			
Tippet W-02 kg (4 lb)	Vacant			
Tippet W-03 kg (6 lb)	Vacant			
Tippet W-04 kg (8 lb)	Vacant			
Tippet W-06 kg (12 lb)	Vacant			
Tippet W-08 kg (16 lb)	Vacant			
Tippet W-10 kg (20 lb)	Vacant			

Marlin, black / *Makaira indica*

TIPPET	WEIGHT	PLACE	DATE	ANGLER
Tippet M-01 kg (2 lb)	Vacant			
Tippet M-02 kg (4 lb)	20.00 kg (44 lb 1 oz)	Cairns, Australia	Aug. 27, 1998	Charles D. Owen, Jr.
Tippet M-03 kg (6 lb)	20.97 kg (46 lb 4 oz)	Cairns, Queensland, Australia	Sept. 14, 1972	William W. Pate, Jr.
Tippet M-04 kg (8 lb)	27.50 kg (60 lb 10 oz)	Mooloolaba, Queensland, Australia	Jan. 9, 1996	Mark H. Carnegie
Tippet M-06 kg (12 lb)	56.00 kg (123 lb 7 oz)	Port Stephens, Australia	Mar. 19, 1998	Fouad Sahiaoui
Tippet M-08 kg (16 lb)	42.75 kg (94 lb 3 oz)	Cape Bowling Green, Townsville, Australia	July 27, 1987	Ray Beadle
Tippet M-10 kg (20 lb)	101.00 kg (222 lb 10 oz)	Port Stephens, Australia	Mar. 26, 1998	Brian E. Kane
Tippet W-01 kg (2 lb)	Vacant			
Tippet W-02 kg (4 lb)	Vacant			
Tippet W-03 kg (6 lb)	Vacant			
Tippet W-04 kg (8 lb)	Vacant			
Tippet W-06 kg (12 lb)	Vacant			
Tippet W-08 kg (16 lb)	16.00 kg (35 lb 4 oz)	Cairns, Australia	Aug. 29, 1998	Cary C. Owen
Tippet W-10 kg (20 lb)	52.88 kg (116 lb 9 oz)	Port Stephens, Australia	Mar. 14, 1998	Jodi Pate

Marlin, blue (Atlantic) / *Makaira nigricans*

TIPPET	WEIGHT	PLACE	DATE	ANGLER
Tippet M-01 kg (2 lb)	Vacant			
Tippet M-02 kg (4 lb)	Vacant			
Tippet M-03 kg (6 lb)	Vacant			
Tippet M-04 kg (8 lb)	Vacant			
Tippet M-06 kg (12 lb)	Vacant			
Tippet M-08 kg (16 lb)	94.34 kg (208 lb 0 oz)	Sao Nicolau, Cape Verde Island	Mar. 26, 1998	Charlie Tombras
Tippet M-10 kg (20 lb)	94.34 kg (208 lb 0 oz)	La Guaira Banks, Venezuela	May 20, 1994	Charlie Tombras
Tippet W-01 kg (2 lb)	Vacant			
Tippet W-02 kg (4 lb)	Vacant			
Tippet W-03 kg (6 lb)	Vacant			
Tippet W-04 kg (8 lb)	Vacant			
Tippet W-06 kg (12 lb)	Vacant			
Tippet W-08 kg (16 lb)	Vacant			
Tippet W-10 kg (20 lb)	Vacant			

Marlin, blue (Pacific) / *Makaira nigricans*

TIPPET	WEIGHT	PLACE	DATE	ANGLER
Tippet M-01 kg (2 lb)	Vacant			

Marlin, blue (Pacific) / *(continued)*

TIPPET	WEIGHT	PLACE	DATE	ANGLER
Tippet M-02 kg (4 lb)	Vacant			
Tippet M-03 kg (6 lb)	Vacant			
Tippet M-04 kg (8 lb)	Vacant			
Tippet M-06 kg (12 lb)	Vacant			
Tippet M-08 kg (16 lb)	92.30 kg (203 lb 8 oz)	Guanamar, Costa Rica	Feb. 12, 1991	Jim Gray
Tippet M-10 kg (20 lb)	117.93 kg (260 lb 0 oz)	Flamingo, Costa Rica	Aug. 6, 1991	Jim Gray
Tippet W-01 kg (2 lb)	Vacant			
Tippet W-02 kg (4 lb)	Vacant			
Tippet W-03 kg (6 lb)	Vacant			
Tippet W-04 kg (8 lb)	Vacant			
Tippet W-06 kg (12 lb)	Vacant			
Tippet W-08 kg (16 lb)	Vacant			
Tippet W-10 kg (20 lb)	Vacant			

Marlin, striped / *Tetrapturus audax*

TIPPET	WEIGHT	PLACE	DATE	ANGLER
Tippet M-01 kg (2 lb)	Vacant			
Tippet M-02 kg (4 lb)	Vacant			
Tippet M-03 kg (6 lb)	35.30 kg (78 lb 0 oz)	Cabo San Lucas, Baja California Sur, Mexico	Dec. 24, 1997	Tony Hedley
Tippet M-04 kg (8 lb)	47.62 kg (105 lb 0 oz)	Cocos Island, Costa Rica	June 28, 1996	Charles Owen, Jr.
Tippet M-06 kg (12 lb)	67.13 kg (148 lb 0 oz)	Salinas, Ecuador	May 1, 1967	Lee Wulff
Tippet M-08 kg (16 lb)	82.55 kg (182 lb 0 oz)	Cocos Island, Costa Rica	Aug. 27, 1995	Charles Tombras
Tippet M-10 kg (20 lb)	96 kg (211 lb 10 oz)	Port Stephens, Australia	Mar. 19, 1998	Fouad Sahiaoui
Tippet W-01 kg (2 lb)	Vacant			
Tippet W-02 kg (4 lb)	Vacant			
Tippet W-03 kg (6 lb)	Vacant			
Tippet W-04 kg (8 lb)	Vacant			
Tippet W-06 kg (12 lb)	Vacant			
Tippet W-08 kg (16 lb)	38.82 kg (85 lb 9 oz)	Potato Bank, Magdalena Bay, Baja California, Mexico	Jan. 13, 1998	Phyllis Kvinsland
Tippet W-10 kg (20 lb)	35.56 kg (78 lb 6 oz)	Potato Bank, Magdalena Bay, Baja California, Mexico	Jan. 11, 1998	Phyllis Kvinsland

Marlin, white / *Tetrapturus albidus*

TIPPET	WEIGHT	PLACE	DATE	ANGLER
Tippet M-01 kg (2 lb)	Vacant			
Tippet M-02 kg (4 lb)	Vacant			
Tippet M-03 kg (6 lb)	37.98 kg (83 lb 12 oz)	Mohammedia, Morocco	Oct. 25, 1997	Fouad Sahiaoui
Tippet M-04 kg (8 lb)	33.11 kg (73 lb 0 oz)	La Guaira, Venezuela	Sept. 22, 1984	Pat Ford
Tippet M-06 kg (12 lb)	39.60 kg (87 lb 4 oz)	Mohammedia, Morocco	Sept. 12, 1996	Fouad Sahiaoui
Tippet M-08 kg (16 lb)	47.36 kg (104 lb 6 oz)	Mohammedia, Morocco	Sept. 14, 1996	Billy Pate
Tippet M-10 kg (20 lb)	37.64 kg (83 lb 0 oz)	Vitoria, Brazil	Dec. 1, 1996	Charlie Tombras
Tippet W-01 kg (2 lb)	Vacant			
Tippet W-02 kg (4 lb)	Vacant			
Tippet W-03 kg (6 lb)	Vacant			
Tippet W-04 kg (8 lb)	Vacant			
Tippet W-06 kg (12 lb)	Vacant			
Tippet W-08 kg (16 lb)	23.81 kg (52 lb 8 oz)	Ilsa Mujeres, Mexico	May 19, 1998	Susan McCarthy
Tippet W-10 kg (20 lb)	28.16 kg (62 lb 1 oz)	Mohammedia, Morocco	Sept. 13, 1998	Jodi Pate

Permit / *Trachinotus falcatus*

TIPPET	WEIGHT	PLACE	DATE	ANGLER
Tippet M-01 kg (2 lb)	4.42 kg (9 lb 12 oz)	Sugarloaf Key, Florida, USA	Apr. 13, 1986	Del Brown
Tippet M-02 kg (4 lb)	10.88 kg (24 lb 0 oz)	Sugarloaf Key, Florida, USA	Mar. 9, 1992	Del Brown
Tippet M-03 kg (6 lb)	8.84 kg (19 lb 8 oz)	Isle of Pines, Cuba	May 16, 1957	Joseph W. Brooks
Tippet M-04 kg (8 lb)	18.82 kg (41 lb 8 oz)	Key West, Florida, USA	Mar. 13, 1986	Del Brown
Tippet M-06 kg (12 lb)	16.38 kg (36 lb 2 oz)	Marsh Harbor, Abaco, Bahamas	May 17, 1993	Carl Navarre, Jr.
Tippet M-08 kg (16 lb)	16.32 kg (36 lb 0 oz)	Key West, Florida, USA	Apr. 3, 1985	Kenneth Marlin
Tippet M-10 kg (20 lb)	14.74 kg (32 lb 8 oz)	Key West, Florida, USA	Apr. 15, 1994	James M. Eckhart
Tippet W-01 kg (2 lb)	Vacant			
Tippet W-02 kg (4 lb)	Vacant			
Tippet W-03 kg (6 lb)	Vacant			
Tippet W-04 kg (8 lb)	Vacant			
Tippet W-06 kg (12 lb)	Vacant			
Tippet W-08 kg (16 lb)	5.95 kg (13 lb 2 oz)	Islamorada, Florida, USA	May 6, 1998	Dianne Harbaugh
Tippet W-10 kg (20 lb)	13.15 kg (29 lb 0 oz)	Key West, Florida, USA	May 30, 1998	Susan Cocking

Pollack, European / *Pollachius pollachius*

TIPPET	WEIGHT	PLACE	DATE	ANGLER
Tippet M-01 kg (2 lb)	2.53 kg (5 lb 9 oz)	Pentland Firth, Scotland	Sept. 1, 1990	Stan Massey
Tippet M-02 kg (4 lb)	3.01 kg (6 lb 10 oz)	Sheephaven Bay, Eire	Sept. 6, 1996	Joe Nash
Tippet M-03 kg (6 lb)	1.76 kg (3 lb 13 oz)	Duesund, Norway	June 23, 1983	Rolf Van De Pavert
Tippet M-04 kg (8 lb)	2.15 kg (4 lb 11 oz)	Sheephaven Bay, Eire	Sept. 6, 1996	Joe Nash
Tippet M-06 kg (12 lb)	2.72 kg (6 lb 0 oz)	Ballantrae, Scotland	Sept. 25, 1993	Murdo B. Gunn
Tippet M-08 kg (16 lb)	5.59 kg (12 lb 5 oz)	Oygarden, Hordaland County, Norway	Oct. 27, 1990	Yngve Landro
Tippet M-10 kg (20 lb)	3.41 kg (7 lb 8 oz)	Sheephaven Bay, Eire	Sept. 11, 1996	Joe Nash
Tippet W-01 kg (2 lb)	Vacant			
Tippet W-02 kg (4 lb)	Vacant			
Tippet W-03 kg (6 lb)	Vacant			
Tippet W-04 kg (8 lb)	Vacant			
Tippet W-06 kg (12 lb)	Vacant			
Tippet W-08 kg (16 lb)	Vacant			
Tippet W-10 kg (20 lb)	Vacant			

Pollock / *Pollachius virens*

TIPPET	WEIGHT	PLACE	DATE	ANGLER
Tippet M-01 kg (2 lb)	0.82 kg (1 lb 13 oz)	East Boothbay, Maine, USA	May 8, 1982	Alan J. Campbell
Tippet M-02 kg (4 lb)	0.53 kg (1 lb 2 oz)	Fjellueroyo, Norway	July 21, 1990	Jorg Marquard
Tippet M-03 kg (6 lb)	4.02 kg (8 lb 14 oz)	Port Maitland, Nova Scotia, Canada	June 22, 1973	Louis Truppi
Tippet M-04 kg (8 lb)	Vacant			
Tippet M-06 kg (12 lb)	4.87 kg (10 lb 12 oz)	Newport, Rhode Island, USA	Nov. 27, 1968	R. H. Smith
Tippet M-08 kg (16 lb)	8.39 kg (18 lb 8 oz)	Port Maitland, Nova Scotia, Canada	June 22, 1973	Louis Truppi
Tippet M-10 kg (20 lb)	Vacant			
Tippet W-01 kg (2 lb)	Vacant			
Tippet W-02 kg (4 lb)	Vacant			
Tippet W-03 kg (6 lb)	Vacant			
Tippet W-04 kg (8 lb)	Vacant			
Tippet W-06 kg (12 lb)	Vacant			
Tippet W-08 kg (16 lb)	Vacant			
Tippet W-10 kg (20 lb)	Vacant			

Pompano, African / *Alectis ciliaris*

TIPPET	WEIGHT	PLACE	DATE	ANGLER
Tippet M-01 kg (2 lb)	Vacant			
Tippet M-02 kg (4 lb)	6.57 kg (14 lb 8 oz)	Key West, Florida, USA	May 2, 1994	Christian Martin
Tippet M-03 kg (6 lb)	Vacant			
Tippet M-04 kg (8 lb)	14.17 kg (31 lb 4 oz)	Key West, Florida, USA	Feb. 20, 1993	Carlos B. Solis
Tippet M-06 kg (12 lb)	15.19 kg (33 lb 8 oz)	Palm Beach, Florida, USA	Dec. 21, 1968	Gil Drake, Jr.
Tippet M-08 kg (16 lb)	13.74 kg (30 lb 5 oz)	Stuart, Florida, USA	Mar. 14, 1982	Paul F. Leader
Tippet M-10 kg (20 lb)	14.28 kg (31 lb 8 oz)	Jupiter, Florida, USA	July 24, 1993	Robert Follweiler
Tippet W-01 kg (2 lb)	Vacant			
Tippet W-02 kg (4 lb)	Vacant			
Tippet W-03 kg (6 lb)	Vacant			
Tippet W-04 kg (8 lb)	Vacant			
Tippet W-06 kg (12 lb)	Vacant			
Tippet W-08 kg (16 lb)	Vacant			
Tippet W-10 kg (20 lb)	Vacant			

Queenfish / *Scomberoides commersonnianus & Scomberoides lysan*

TIPPET	WEIGHT	PLACE	DATE	ANGLER
Tippet M-01 kg (2 lb)	0.51 kg (1 lb 2 oz)	Christmas Island, Republic of Kiribati	Mar. 2, 1997	Bud Korteweg
Tippet M-02 kg (4 lb)	5.00 kg (11 lb 0 oz)	Groote Eylandt, N.T., Australia	Aug. 3, 1989	Raz Reid
Tippet M-03 kg (6 lb)	3.20 kg (7 lb 0 oz)	Arnhem Land, Australia	Oct. 23, 1997	Laurie R. Chadder
Tippet M-04 kg (8 lb)	8.20 kg (18 lb 1 oz)	Onslow, W.A., Australia	Sept. 24, 1989	Simon Gilbert
Tippet M-06 kg (12 lb)	7.80 kg (17 lb 3 oz)	Onslow, W.A., Australia	Sept. 25, 1989	Simon Gilbert
Tippet M-08 kg (16 lb)	9.60 kg (21 lb 2 oz)	Inhaca Island, Mozambique	Mar. 20, 1997	Tim Briscoe
Tippet M-10 kg (20 lb)	8.80 kg (19 lb 6 oz)	Inhaca Island, Mozambique	Nov. 27, 1995	Garth Johnson
Tippet M-10 kg (20 lb) Tie	8.80 kg (19 lb 6 oz)	Cape York, Australia	Apr. 27, 1997	Greg Bethune
Tippet W-01 kg (2 lb)	Vacant			
Tippet W-02 kg (4 lb)	Vacant			
Tippet W-03 kg (6 lb)	Vacant			
Tippet W-04 kg (8 lb)	Vacant			
Tippet W-06 kg (12 lb)	Vacant			
Tippet W-08 kg (16 lb)	Vacant			
Tippet W-10 kg (20 lb)	Vacant			

Roosterfish / *Nematistius pectoralis*

TIPPET	WEIGHT	PLACE	DATE	ANGLER
Tippet M-01 kg (2 lb)	Vacant			
Tippet M-02 kg (4 lb)	3.50 kg (7 lb 11 oz)	Barra de Navidad, Jalisco, Mexico	Nov. 26, 1992	George Gehrke
Tippet M-03 kg (6 lb)	10.09 kg (22 lb 4 oz)	Los Frailes, Baja California, Mexico	Apr. 2, 1997	Grant Hartman
Tippet M-04 kg (8 lb)	13.26 kg (29 lb 4 oz)	Los Frailes, Baja California, Mexico	May 2, 1997	Grant Clifford Hartman
Tippet M-06 kg (12 lb)	18.82 kg (41 lb 8 oz)	Morro del Potosi, Zihuatanejo, Mexico	Apr. 19, 1998	Thomas B. Boyd
Tippet M-08 kg (16 lb)	14.40 kg (31 lb 12 oz)	Gulf of Papagayo, Guanacaste, Costa Rica	Aug. 20, 1988	Jack Samson
Tippet M-10 kg (20 lb)	18.14 kg (40 lb 0 oz)	Flamingo, Costa Rica	June 5, 1994	Robert Rein
Tippet W-01 kg (2 lb)	Vacant			
Tippet W-02 kg (4 lb)	Vacant			
Tippet W-03 kg (6 lb)	Vacant			
Tippet W-04 kg (8 lb)	Vacant			
Tippet W-06 kg (12 lb)	Vacant			
Tippet W-08 kg (16 lb)	Vacant			
Tippet W-10 kg (20 lb)	Vacant			

Runner, rainbow / *Elagatis bipinnulata*

TIPPET	WEIGHT	PLACE	DATE	ANGLER
Tippet M-01 kg (2 lb)	Vacant			
Tippet M-02 kg (4 lb)	3.20 kg (7 lb 0 oz)	Torres Strait, Queensland, Australia	Mar. 9, 1990	Graham L. Plummer
Tippet M-03 kg (6 lb)	2.72 kg (6 lb 0 oz)	Bermuda	June 29, 1972	Lefty Kreh
Tippet M-04 kg (8 lb)	3.78 kg (8 lb 5 oz)	Torres Strait, Queensland, Australia	Mar. 9, 1990	Graham L. Plummer
Tippet M-06 kg (12 lb)	3.91 kg (8 lb 10 oz)	Key West, Florida, USA	Jan. 18, 1980	John M. Ahearn
Tippet M-08 kg (16 lb)	5.46 kg (12 lb 0 oz)	Montousa Island, Republic of Panama	Oct. 12, 1994	John David McBride
Tippet M-10 kg (20 lb)	6.35 kg (14 lb 0 oz)	Clipperton Island	Mar. 20, 1997	Steve Abel
Tippet W-01 kg (2 lb)	Vacant			
Tippet W-02 kg (4 lb)	Vacant			
Tippet W-03 kg (6 lb)	Vacant			
Tippet W-04 kg (8 lb)	Vacant			
Tippet W-06 kg (12 lb)	Vacant			
Tippet W-08 kg (16 lb)	Vacant			

| Tippet W-10 kg (20 lb) | Vacant | | | |

Sailfish, Atlantic / *Istiophorus platypterus*

TIPPET	WEIGHT	PLACE	DATE	ANGLER
Tippet M-01 kg (2 lb)	Vacant			
Tippet M-02 kg (4 lb)	20.04 kg (44 lb 3 oz)	Puerto Quentaurus, Mexico	Apr. 20, 1998	Charles D. Owen, Jr.
Tippet M-03 kg (6 lb)	24.94 kg (55 lb 0 oz)	Bom Bom Island Resort, Principe	Nov. 12, 1996	Fouad Sahiaoui
Tippet M-04 kg (8 lb)	32.43 kg (71 lb 8 oz)	Cancun, Mexico	May 10, 1990	Charles D. Owen, Jr.
Tippet M-06 kg (12 lb)	Vacant			
Tippet M-08 kg (16 lb)	39.00 kg (86 lb 0 oz)	Bom Bom Island Resort, Principe	Nov. 6, 1996	Billy Pate
Tippet M-10 kg (20 lb)	46.26 kg (102 lb 0 oz)	Principe Island, Sao Tome & Principe	Oct. 22, 1993	Hugh S. Vincent, Jr.
Tippet W-01 kg (2 lb)	Vacant			
Tippet W-02 kg (4 lb)	Vacant			
Tippet W-03 kg (6 lb)	Vacant			
Tippet W-04 kg (8 lb)	Vacant			
Tippet W-06 kg (12 lb)	34.92 kg (77 lb 0 oz)	Bom Bom Island Resort, Principe	Oct. 20, 1995	Margot D. Vincent
Tippet W-08 kg (16 lb)	28.53 kg (62 lb 14 oz)	Saly Fishing Club, Senegal	Sept. 3, 1998	Jodi Pate
Tippet W-10 kg (20 lb)	28.34 kg (62 lb 8 oz)	Saly Fishing Club, Senegal	Sept. 2, 1998	Jodi Pate

Sailfish, Pacific / *Istiophorus platypterus*

TIPPET	WEIGHT	PLACE	DATE	ANGLER
Tippet M-01 kg (2 lb)	Vacant			
Tippet M-02 kg (4 lb)	42.86 kg (94 lb 8 oz)	Quepos, Costa Rica	Jan. 9, 1991	Jim Gray
Tippet M-03 kg (6 lb)	46.72 kg (103 lb 0 oz)	Quepos, Costa Rica	Feb. 16, 1995	Tony Hedley
Tippet M-04 kg (8 lb)	48.30 kg (106 lb 8 oz)	Quepos, Costa Rica	Jan. 2, 1991	Jim Gray
Tippet M-06 kg (12 lb)	61.68 kg (136 lb 0 oz)	Pinas Bay, Panama	June 25, 1965	Stu Apte
Tippet M-08 kg (16 lb)	56.24 kg (124 lb 0 oz)	Gulf of Papagayo, Guanacaste, Costa Rica	July 21, 1989	Eizo Maruhashi
Tippet M-10 kg (20 lb)	58.28 kg (128 lb 8 oz)	Quepos, Costa Rica	Jan. 10, 1993	Lee J. Dixon, II
Tippet W-01 kg (2 lb)	Vacant			
Tippet W-02 kg (4 lb)	Vacant			
Tippet W-03 kg (6 lb)	Vacant			
Tippet W-04 kg (8 lb)	26.76 kg (59 lb 0 oz)	Quepos, Costa Rica	Jan. 23, 1998	Jodi Pate
Tippet W-06 kg (12 lb)	Vacant			
Tippet W-08 kg (16 lb)	38.10 kg (84 lb 0 oz)	Quepos, Costa Rica	Jan. 20, 1998	Jodi Pate
Tippet W-10 kg (20 lb)	28.50 kg (62 lb 13 oz)	Mooloolaba, Australia	Apr. 27, 1998	Jodi Pate

Seabass, blackfin / *Lateolabrax latus*

TIPPET	WEIGHT	PLACE	DATE	ANGLER
Tippet M-01 kg (2 lb)	Vacant			
Tippet M-02 kg (4 lb)	2.50 kg (5 lb 8 oz)	Yugi, Tokushima, Japan	Mar. 16, 1997	Takeshi Nakamura
Tippet M-03 kg (6 lb)	5.00 kg (11 lb 0 oz)	Hiwasa, Kaifu-gun, Tokushima, Japan	Apr. 16, 1998	Takeshi Nakamura
Tippet M-04 kg (8 lb)	1.68 kg (3 lb 6 oz)	Wakamatsu, Nagasaki, Japan	Mar. 13, 1997	Tsunehisa Wake
Tippet M-06 kg (12 lb)	5.70 kg (12 lb 9 oz)	Aono River, Japan	Nov. 7, 1994	Osamu Matsumoto
Tippet M-08 kg (16 lb)	1.91 kg (4 lb 3 oz)	Chikura, Chiba, Japan	Dec. 18, 1983	Eizo Maruhashi
Tippet M-10 kg (20 lb)	2.76 kg (6 lb 1 oz)	Yugi, Tokushima, Japan	Feb. 16, 1997	Fukumi Wakisaka
Tippet W-01 kg (2 lb)	Vacant			
Tippet W-02 kg (4 lb)	Vacant			
Tippet W-03 kg (6 lb)	Vacant			
Tippet W-04 kg (8 lb)	Vacant			
Tippet W-06 kg (12 lb)	Vacant			
Tippet W-08 kg (16 lb)	Vacant			
Tippet W-10 kg (20 lb)	Vacant			

Seabass, Japanese / *Lateolabrax japonicus*

TIPPET	WEIGHT	PLACE	DATE	ANGLER
Tippet M-01 kg (2 lb)	1.62 kg (3 lb 9 oz)	Shibaura, Ninaata-ku, Tokyo, Japan	May 30, 1994	Koichi Kusunoki
Tippet M-02 kg (4 lb)	5.30 kg (11 lb 10 oz)	Sagami River, Kanagawa, Japan	Nov. 22, 1993	Tatsuhiko Sato
Tippet M-03 kg (6 lb)	4.50 kg (9 lb 14 oz)	Shin Yodogawa, Osaka-shi, Osaka, Japan	Nov. 1, 1995	Shoji Matsuura
Tippet M-04 kg (8 lb)	5.80 kg (12 lb 12 oz)	Sagami River, Kanagawa, Japan	Nov. 22, 1993	Tatsuhiko Sato
Tippet M-06 kg (12 lb)	5.76 kg (12 lb 11 oz)	Oita River, Oita, Japan	Nov. 1, 1997	Shigenori Kawanaka
Tippet M-08 kg (16 lb)	4.95 kg (10 lb 14 oz)	Sagami River, Kanagawa, Japan	Nov. 2, 1993	Kazuhiro Matsuishi
Tippet M-10 kg (20 lb)	5.25 kg (11 lb 9 oz)	Oita River, Oita, Japan	Jan. 1, 1998	Tomoaki Kutsukake
Tippet W-01 kg (2 lb)	Vacant			
Tippet W-02 kg (4 lb)	Vacant			
Tippet W-03 kg (6 lb)	Vacant			
Tippet W-04 kg (8 lb)	Vacant			
Tippet W-06 kg (12 lb)	Vacant			
Tippet W-08 kg (16 lb)	Vacant			
Tippet W-10 kg (20 lb)	Vacant			

Seabass, white / *Atractoscion nobilis*

TIPPET	WEIGHT	PLACE	DATE	ANGLER
Tippet M-01 kg (2 lb)	Vacant			
Tippet M-02 kg (4 lb)	Vacant			
Tippet M-03 kg (6 lb)	Vacant			
Tippet M-04 kg (8 lb)	Vacant			
Tippet M-06 kg (12 lb)	5.61 kg (12 lb 6 oz)	Santa Cruz Island, California, USA	Oct. 16, 1980	Roy Lawson
Tippet M-08 kg (16 lb)	7.92 kg (17 lb 7 oz)	Horseshoe Kelp, Long Beach, California, USA	June 20, 1995	Bill Matthews
Tippet M-10 kg (20 lb)	7.04 kg (15 lb 8 oz)	Carpenteria, California, USA	Aug. 11, 1996	Patt Wardlaw
Tippet W-01 kg (2 lb)	Vacant			
Tippet W-02 kg (4 lb)	Vacant			
Tippet W-03 kg (6 lb)	Vacant			
Tippet W-04 kg (8 lb)	Vacant			
Tippet W-06 kg (12 lb)	Vacant			

Seabass, white / *(continued)*

TIPPET	WEIGHT	PLACE	DATE	ANGLER
Tippet W-08 kg (16 lb)	Vacant			
Tippet W-10 kg (20 lb)	Vacant			

Seatrout, spotted / *Cynoscion nebulosus*

TIPPET	WEIGHT	PLACE	DATE	ANGLER
Tippet M-01 kg (2 lb)	3.94 kg (8 lb 11 oz)	South Padre Island, Texas, USA	July 8, 1989	Chuck Scates
Tippet M-02 kg (4 lb)	3.79 kg (8 lb 6 oz)	Arroyo City, Texas, USA	Apr. 12, 1988	Thomas P. Kilgore
Tippet M-03 kg (6 lb)	3.96 kg (8 lb 12 oz)	Banana River, Florida, USA	Dec. 5, 1974	Dave Chermanski
Tippet M-04 kg (8 lb)	5.21 kg (11 lb 8 oz)	Banana River, Merritt Island, Florida, USA	June 6, 1992	Dave Chermanski
Tippet M-06 kg (12 lb)	4.30 kg (9 lb 8 oz)	Stuart, Florida, USA	July 19, 1995	Jack Yanora
Tippet M-08 kg (16 lb)	5.65 kg (12 lb 7 oz)	Indian River, Sebastian, Florida, USA	Mar. 5, 1984	Sidney A. Freifeld
Tippet M-10 kg (20 lb)	3.81 kg (8 lb 6 oz)	Laguna Madre Beach, So. Padre Island, Texas, USA	Mar. 22, 1998	Kenny Brewer
Tippet W-01 kg (2 lb)	Vacant			
Tippet W-02 kg (4 lb)	Vacant			
Tippet W-03 kg (6 lb)	Vacant			
Tippet W-04 kg (8 lb)	Vacant			
Tippet W-06 kg (12 lb)	Vacant			
Tippet W-08 kg (16 lb)	Vacant			
Tippet W-10 kg (20 lb)	Vacant			

Shark, blue / *Prionace glauca*

TIPPET	WEIGHT	PLACE	DATE	ANGLER
Tippet M-01 kg (2 lb)	2.33 kg (5 lb 2 oz)	Taits Beach, Hawkes Bay, New Zealand	Feb. 27, 1993	Dennis Graham Niethe
Tippet M-02 kg (4 lb)	41.27 kg (91 lb 0 oz)	Montauk, Long Island, New York, USA	Sept. 14, 1989	Stephen Sloan
Tippet M-03 kg (6 lb)	52.05 kg (114 lb 12 oz)	Shinnecock, Long Island, New York, USA	June 28, 1980	Stephen Sloan
Tippet M-04 kg (8 lb)	34.00 kg (74 lb 15 oz)	Kaikoura, New Zealand	Feb. 16, 1997	Howard Lewis
Tippet M-06 kg (12 lb)	83.46 kg (184 lb 0 oz)	Montauk, Long Island, New York, USA	Sept. 28, 1989	Stephen Sloan
Tippet M-08 kg (16 lb)	68.40 kg (150 lb 12 oz)	Tutukaka, Poor Knights, New Zealand	Dec. 7, 1997	Sam Mossman
Tippet M-10 kg (20 lb)	75.20 kg (165 lb 12 oz)	Martha's Vineyard, Massachusetts, USA	July 20, 1997	Tom Taylor
Tippet W-01 kg (2 lb)	Vacant			
Tippet W-02 kg (4 lb)	Vacant			
Tippet W-03 kg (6 lb)	Vacant			
Tippet W-04 kg (8 lb)	Vacant			
Tippet W-06 kg (12 lb)	Vacant			
Tippet W-08 kg (16 lb)	31.20 kg (68 lb 12 oz)	North Reef, New Zealand	Feb. 8, 1998	Dianne Sands
Tippet W-10 kg (20 lb)	23.40 kg (51 lb 9 oz)	Kaikoura, New Zealand	Apr. 11, 1998	Jane Wilson

Shark, hammerhead / *Sphyrna spp*

TIPPET	WEIGHT	PLACE	DATE	ANGLER
Tippet M-01 kg (2 lb)	Vacant			
Tippet M-02 kg (4 lb)	4.88 kg (9 lb 0 oz)	Key West, Florida, USA	Mar. 12, 1998	Bennett Stern
Tippet M-03 kg (6 lb)	3.74 kg (8 lb 4 oz)	Key West, Florida, USA	Jan. 18, 1998	Bennett Stern
Tippet M-04 kg (8 lb)	2.83 kg (6 lb 4 oz)	Key West, Florida, USA	Mar. 25, 1996	Bennett M. Stern
Tippet M-06 kg (12 lb)	3.62 kg (8 lb 0 oz)	Islamorada, Florida, USA	Apr. 8, 1992	Ben Taylor
Tippet M-08 kg (16 lb)	48.30 kg (106 lb 8 oz)	Key West, Florida, USA	Feb. 11, 1987	Mike Stidham
Tippet M-10 kg (20 lb)	69.85 kg (154 lb 0 oz)	Key West, Florida, USA	Mar. 7, 1993	Rick Gunion
Tippet W-01 kg (2 lb)	Vacant			
Tippet W-02 kg (4 lb)	Vacant			
Tippet W-03 kg (6 lb)	Vacant			
Tippet W-04 kg (8 lb)	Vacant			
Tippet W-06 kg (12 lb)	Vacant			
Tippet W-08 kg (16 lb)	Vacant			
Tippet W-10 kg (20 lb)	Vacant			

Shark, mako / *Isurus spp*

TIPPET	WEIGHT	PLACE	DATE	ANGLER
Tippet M-01 kg (2 lb)	Vacant			
Tippet M-02 kg (4 lb)	12.45 kg (27 lb 8 oz)	Bellambi, Australia	Sept. 16, 1995	Gregory Phillip Clarke
Tippet M-03 kg (6 lb)	17.00 kg (7 lb 11 oz)	Tekaha, Bay of Plenty, New Zealand	Jan. 1, 1997	Andrew A. Macgrath
Tippet M-04 kg (8 lb)	18.60 kg (41 lb 0 oz)	Hawkes Bay, New Zealand	Jan. 25, 1995	Carl Angus
Tippet M-06 kg (12 lb)	29.80 kg (65 lb 11 oz)	Hawkes Bay, New Zealand	Mar. 11, 1990	Sam Mossman
Tippet M-08 kg (16 lb)	32.88 kg (72 lb 8 oz)	Anacapa Island, California, USA	July 21, 1991	Steve Abel
Tippet M-10 kg (20 lb)	31.20 kg (68 lb 12 oz)	Whakatane, New Zealand	Mar. 21, 1998	Sam Mossman
Tippet W-01 kg (2 lb)	Vacant			
Tippet W-02 kg (4 lb)	Vacant			
Tippet W-03 kg (6 lb)	Vacant			
Tippet W-04 kg (8 lb)	Vacant			
Tippet W-06 kg (12 lb)	Vacant			
Tippet W-08 kg (16 lb)	Vacant			
Tippet W-10 kg (20 lb)	Vacant			

Shark, porbeagle / *Lamna nasus*

TIPPET	WEIGHT	PLACE	DATE	ANGLER
Tippet M-01 kg (2 lb)	Vacant			
Tippet M-02 kg (4 lb)	Vacant			
Tippet M-03 kg (6 lb)	Vacant			
Tippet M-04 kg (8 lb)	Vacant			
Tippet M-06 kg (12 lb)	Vacant			
Tippet M-08 kg (16 lb)	Vacant			
Tippet M-10 kg (20 lb)	61.70 kg (136 lb 0 oz)	Otago Heads, New Zealand	June 7, 1998	Dave Carr
Tippet W-01 kg (2 lb)	Vacant			
Tippet W-02 kg (4 lb)	Vacant			
Tippet W-03 kg (6 lb)	Vacant			
Tippet W-04 kg (8 lb)	Vacant			

Shark, porbeagle / *(continued)*

TIPPET	WEIGHT	PLACE	DATE	ANGLER
Tippet W-06 kg (12 lb)	Vacant			
Tippet W-08 kg (16 lb)	Vacant			
Tippet W-10 kg (20 lb)	Vacant			

Shark, thresher / *Alopias spp*

TIPPET	WEIGHT	PLACE	DATE	ANGLER
Tippet M-01 kg (2 lb)	Vacant			
Tippet M-02 kg (4 lb)	Vacant			
Tippet M-03 kg (6 lb)	Vacant			
Tippet M-04 kg (8 lb)	Vacant			
Tippet M-06 kg (12 lb)	Vacant			
Tippet M-08 kg (16 lb)	Vacant			
Tippet M-10 kg (20 lb)	Vacant			
Tippet W-01 kg (2 lb)	Vacant			
Tippet W-02 kg (4 lb)	Vacant			
Tippet W-03 kg (6 lb)	Vacant			
Tippet W-04 kg (8 lb)	Vacant			
Tippet W-06 kg (12 lb)	Vacant			
Tippet W-08 kg (16 lb)	Vacant			
Tippet W-10 kg (20 lb)	Vacant			

Shark, tiger / *Galeocerdo cuvier*

TIPPET	WEIGHT	PLACE	DATE	ANGLER
Tippet M-01 kg (2 lb)	Vacant			
Tippet M-02 kg (4 lb)	Vacant			
Tippet M-03 kg (6 lb)	Vacant			
Tippet M-04 kg (8 lb)	46.26 kg (102 lb 0 oz)	Key West, Florida, USA	Mar. 15, 1996	Rick Gunion
Tippet M-06 kg (12 lb)	33.56 kg (74 lb 0 oz)	Key West, Florida, USA	Feb. 24, 1996	Rick Gunion
Tippet M-08 kg (16 lb)	28.00 kg (61 lb 12 oz)	Key West, Florida, USA	Feb. 23, 1992	Rick Gunion
Tippet M-10 kg (20 lb)	99.79 kg (220 lb 0 oz)	Key West, Florida, USA	Jan. 23, 1995	Gary Spence
Tippet W-01 kg (2 lb)	Vacant			
Tippet W-02 kg (4 lb)	Vacant			
Tippet W-03 kg (6 lb)	Vacant			
Tippet W-04 kg (8 lb)	Vacant			
Tippet W-06 kg (12 lb)	Vacant			
Tippet W-08 kg (16 lb)	Vacant			
Tippet W-10 kg (20 lb)	Vacant			

Shark, tope / *Galeorhinus galeus*

TIPPET	WEIGHT	PLACE	DATE	ANGLER
Tippet M-01 kg (2 lb)	Vacant			
Tippet M-02 kg (4 lb)	Vacant			
Tippet M-03 kg (6 lb)	Vacant			
Tippet M-04 kg (8 lb)	Vacant			
Tippet M-06 kg (12 lb)	Vacant			
Tippet M-08 kg (16 lb)	Vacant			
Tippet M-10 kg (20 lb)	Vacant			
Tippet W-01 kg (2 lb)	Vacant			
Tippet W-02 kg (4 lb)	Vacant			
Tippet W-03 kg (6 lb)	Vacant			
Tippet W-04 kg (8 lb)	Vacant			
Tippet W-06 kg (12 lb)	Vacant			
Tippet W-08 kg (16 lb)	Vacant			
Tippet W-10 kg (20 lb)	Vacant			

Shark, white / *Carcharodon carcharias*

TIPPET	WEIGHT	PLACE	DATE	ANGLER
Tippet M-01 kg (2 lb)	Vacant			
Tippet M-02 kg (4 lb)	Vacant			
Tippet M-03 kg (6 lb)	Vacant			
Tippet M-04 kg (8 lb)	Vacant			
Tippet M-06 kg (12 lb)	Vacant			
Tippet M-08 kg (16 lb)	Vacant			
Tippet M-10 kg (20 lb)	Vacant			
Tippet W-01 kg (2 lb)	Vacant			
Tippet W-02 kg (4 lb)	Vacant			
Tippet W-03 kg (6 lb)	Vacant			
Tippet W-04 kg (8 lb)	Vacant			
Tippet W-06 kg (12 lb)	Vacant			
Tippet W-08 kg (16 lb)	Vacant			
Tippet W-10 kg (20 lb)	Vacant			

Skipjack, black / *Euthynnus lineatus*

TIPPET	WEIGHT	PLACE	DATE	ANGLER
Tippet M-01 kg (2 lb)	0.70 kg (1 lb 8 oz)	Cabo Marzo, Choco, Colombia	Dec. 6, 1990	Gerard Aulong
Tippet M-02 kg (4 lb)	2.26 kg (5 lb 0 oz)	Pinas Bay, Panama	Apr. 12, 1983	Jorg Marquard
Tippet M-03 kg (6 lb)	6.15 kg (13 lb 9 oz)	Todos Santos, Baja California Sur, Mexico	Dec. 5, 1996	Ray Beadle
Tippet M-04 kg (8 lb)	5.24 kg (11 lb 9 oz)	Punta Taslo, Baja Mexico	Dec. 2, 1994	Terry Gunn
Tippet M-06 kg (12 lb)	6.23 kg (13 lb 12 oz)	Thetis Bank, Baja Mexico	Nov. 17, 1993	Carlos Solis
Tippet M-08 kg (16 lb)	6.49 kg (14 lb 5 oz)	Todos Santos, Baja California Sur, Mexico	Dec. 5, 1996	Trey Combs
Tippet M-10 kg (20 lb)	7.14 kg (15 lb 12 oz)	Thetis Bank, Baja California, Mexico	Nov. 16, 1993	Stuart M. Dunn
Tippet W-01 kg (2 lb)	Vacant			
Tippet W-02 kg (4 lb)	Vacant			
Tippet W-03 kg (6 lb)	Vacant			

Skipjack, black / *(continued)*

TIPPET	WEIGHT	PLACE	DATE	ANGLER
Tippet W-04 kg (8 lb)	Vacant			
Tippet W-06 kg (12 lb)	Vacant			
Tippet W-08 kg (16 lb)	Vacant			
Tippet W-10 kg (20 lb)	Vacant			

Snapper (squirefish) / *Pagrus auratus*

TIPPET	WEIGHT	PLACE	DATE	ANGLER
Tippet M-01 kg (2 lb)	Vacant			
Tippet M-02 kg (4 lb)	Vacant			
Tippet M-03 kg (6 lb)	Vacant			
Tippet M-04 kg (8 lb)	Vacant			
Tippet M-06 kg (12 lb)	Vacant			
Tippet M-08 kg (16 lb)	Vacant			
Tippet M-10 kg (20 lb)	Vacant			
Tippet W-01 kg (2 lb)	Vacant			
Tippet W-02 kg (4 lb)	Vacant			
Tippet W-03 kg (6 lb)	Vacant			
Tippet W-04 kg (8 lb)	Vacant			
Tippet W-06 kg (12 lb)	Vacant			
Tippet W-08 kg (16 lb)	Vacant			
Tippet W-10 kg (20 lb)	Vacant			

Snapper, cubera / *Lutjanus cyanopterus*

TIPPET	WEIGHT	PLACE	DATE	ANGLER
Tippet M-01 kg (2 lb)	Vacant			
Tippet M-02 kg (4 lb)	Vacant			
Tippet M-03 kg (6 lb)	Vacant			
Tippet M-04 kg (8 lb)	Vacant			
Tippet M-06 kg (12 lb)	0.90 kg (2 lb 0 oz)	Bobo's Lake, Andros Island, Bahamas	Feb. 24, 1998	Robert T. Cunningham, Jr.
Tippet M-08 kg (16 lb)	16.32 kg (36 lb 0 oz)	Pelican Cay, Turneffe Islands, Belize	Apr. 3, 1990	Burleigh J. Matthew, MD
Tippet M-10 kg (20 lb)	25.40 kg (56 lb 0 oz)	Brus Lagoon, Honduras	Oct. 2, 1998	Michael J. Nonnenmann
Tippet W-01 kg (2 lb)	Vacant			
Tippet W-02 kg (4 lb)	Vacant			
Tippet W-03 kg (6 lb)	Vacant			
Tippet W-04 kg (8 lb)	Vacant			
Tippet W-06 kg (12 lb)	Vacant			
Tippet W-08 kg (16 lb)	Vacant			
Tippet W-10 kg (20 lb)	Vacant			

Snapper, mutton / *Lutjanus analis*

TIPPET	WEIGHT	PLACE	DATE	ANGLER
Tippet M-01 kg (2 lb)	Vacant			
Tippet M-02 kg (4 lb)	6.18 kg (13 lb 10 oz)	Key West, Florida, USA	May 1, 1986	Del Brown
Tippet M-03 kg (6 lb)	6.57 kg (14 lb 8 oz)	Marsh Harbor, Abaco, Bahamas	June 3, 1997	Thomas Johnson
Tippet M-04 kg (8 lb)	6.74 kg (14 lb 14 oz)	Key West, Florida, USA	Apr. 15, 1985	Joseph A. Few, Jr.
Tippet M-06 kg (12 lb)	7.71 kg (17 lb 0 oz)	Key West, Florida, USA	May 31, 1990	Del Brown
Tippet M-08 kg (16 lb)	6.69 kg (14 lb 12 oz)	Key West, Florida, USA	Apr. 1, 1991	Rick Gunion
Tippet M-10 kg (20 lb)	3.51 kg (7 lb 12 oz)	Spanish Key, Abaco, Bahamas	Aug. 2, 1997	Robert Helmick
Tippet W-01 kg (2 lb)	Vacant			
Tippet W-02 kg (4 lb)	Vacant			
Tippet W-03 kg (6 lb)	Vacant			
Tippet W-04 kg (8 lb)	Vacant			
Tippet W-06 kg (12 lb)	Vacant			
Tippet W-08 kg (16 lb)	Vacant			
Tippet W-10 kg (20 lb)	Vacant			

Snapper, Pacific cubera / *Lutjanus novemfasciatus*

TIPPET	WEIGHT	PLACE	DATE	ANGLER
Tippet M-01 kg (2 lb)	Vacant			
Tippet M-02 kg (4 lb)	Vacant			
Tippet M-03 kg (6 lb)	Vacant			
Tippet M-04 kg (8 lb)	2.38 kg (5 lb 4 oz)	Cabo San Lucas, Baja California Sur, Mexico	Oct. 25, 1996	Terry Gunn
Tippet M-06 kg (12 lb)	2.26 kg (5 lb 0 oz)	Tropic Star Lodge, Pinas Bay, Panama	Apr. 14, 1998	Scott Jacobson
Tippet M-08 kg (16 lb)	9.07 kg (20 lb 0 oz)	Drake's Bay, Costa Rica	May 28, 1997	Collin Huff
Tippet M-10 kg (20 lb)	14.42 kg (31 lb 12 oz)	Drake's Bay, Costa Rica	May 21, 1997	Kevin Keith Ross Winter
Tippet W-01 kg (2 lb)	Vacant			
Tippet W-02 kg (4 lb)	Vacant			
Tippet W-03 kg (6 lb)	Vacant			
Tippet W-04 kg (8 lb)	Vacant			
Tippet W-06 kg (12 lb)	Vacant			
Tippet W-08 kg (16 lb)	Vacant			
Tippet W-10 kg (20 lb)	Vacant			

Snook / *Centropomus spp*

TIPPET	WEIGHT	PLACE	DATE	ANGLER
Tippet M-01 kg (2 lb)	4.98 kg (11 lb 0 oz)	Chokoloskee, Florida, USA	Aug. 19, 1996	Andy G. Novak
Tippet M-02 kg (4 lb)	7.03 kg (15 lb 8 oz)	Chokoloskee, Florida, USA	July 1, 1998	Andy G. Novak
Tippet M-03 kg (6 lb)	10.06 kg (22 lb 3 oz)	Sebastian River, Florida, USA	July 24, 1971	Dave Chermanski
Tippet M-04 kg (8 lb)	11.11 kg (24 lb 8 oz)	Indian River Lagoon, Vero Beach, Florida, USA	Dec. 14, 1995	Robert "Radar" Orth
Tippet M-06 kg (12 lb)	12.92 kg (28 lb 8 oz)	Stuart, Florida, USA	July 10, 1972	Martin Gottschalk
Tippet M-08 kg (16 lb)	11.79 kg (26 lb 0 oz)	Barra del Colorado, Costa Rica	Oct. 19, 1980	Bill Barnes
Tippet M-10 kg (20 lb)	13.72 kg (30 lb 4 oz)	Chokoloskee Island, Florida, USA	Apr. 4, 1993	Rex Garrett
Tippet W-01 kg (2 lb)	Vacant			
Tippet W-02 kg (4 lb)	Vacant			

Snook / *(continued)*

TIPPET	WEIGHT	PLACE	DATE	ANGLER
Tippet W-03 kg (6 lb)	Vacant			
Tippet W-04 kg (8 lb)	6.35 kg (14 lb 0 oz)	Jupiter, Florida, USA	June 26, 1998	Jing Torn
Tippet W-06 kg (12 lb)	Vacant			
Tippet W-08 kg (16 lb)	Vacant			
Tippet W-10 kg (20 lb)	6.35 kg (14 lb 0 oz)	Jupiter, Florida, USA	June 25, 1998	Jing Torn

Spearfish / *Tetrapturus*

TIPPET	WEIGHT	PLACE	DATE	ANGLER
Tippet M-01 kg (2 lb)	Vacant			
Tippet M-02 kg (4 lb)	Vacant			
Tippet M-03 kg (6 lb)	16.04 kg (35 lb 6 oz)	Keahole Point, Hawaii, USA	Mar. 21, 1997	Glenn L. Scott
Tippet M-04 kg (8 lb)	25.57 kg (56 lb 6 oz)	Cozumel, Mexico	Apr. 18, 1991	Charles D. Owen, Jr.
Tippet M-06 kg (12 lb)	15.64 kg (34 lb 8 oz)	Kailua, Hawaii, USA	Mar. 17, 1997	Glenn L. Scott
Tippet M-08 kg (16)	Vacant			
Tippet M-10 kg (20 lb)	16.78 kg (37 lb 0 oz)	Kona Coast, Hawaii, USA	Mar. 5, 1995	David M. Linkiewicz
Tippet W-01 kg (2 lb)	Vacant			
Tippet W-02 kg (4 lb)	Vacant			
Tippet W-03 kg (6 lb)	Vacant			
Tippet W-04 kg (8 lb)	Vacant			
Tippet W-06 kg (12 lb)	Vacant			
Tippet W-08 kg (16 lb)	Vacant			
Tippet W-10 kg (20 lb)	Vacant			

Swordfish / *Xiphias*

TIPPET	WEIGHT	PLACE	DATE	ANGLER
Tippet M-01 kg (2 lb)	Vacant			
Tippet M-02 kg (4 lb)	Vacant			
Tippet M-03 kg (6 lb)	Vacant			
Tippet M-04 kg (8 lb)	Vacant			
Tippet M-06 kg (12 lb)	Vacant			
Tippet M-08 kg (16 lb)	Vacant			
Tippet M-10 kg (20 lb)	24.80 kg (54 lb 10 oz)	Watamu, Kenya	Apr. 5, 1998	Jeremy Block
Tippet W-01 kg (2 lb)	Vacant			
Tippet W-02 kg (4 lb)	Vacant			
Tippet W-03 kg (6 lb)	Vacant			
Tippet W-04 kg (8 lb)	Vacant			
Tippet W-06 kg (12 lb)	Vacant			
Tippet W-08 kg (16 lb)	Vacant			
Tippet W-10 kg (20 lb)	Vacant			

Tarpon / *Megalops atlanticus*

TIPPET	WEIGHT	PLACE	DATE	ANGLER
Tippet M-01 kg (2 lb)	14.51 kg (32 lb 0 oz)	Sebastian River, Florida, USA	July 5, 1990	Dave Chermanski
Tippet M-02 kg (4 lb)	21.88 kg (48 lb 4 oz)	Islamorada, Florida, USA	June 25, 1997	Charles D. Owen, Jr.
Tippet M-03 kg (6 lb)	37.42 kg (82 lb 8 oz)	Flamingo, Florida, USA	June 25, 1977	Stu Apte
Tippet M-04 kg (8 lb)	57.60 kg (127 lb 0 oz)	Marathon, Florida, USA	Apr. 15, 1985	Del Brown
Tippet M-06 kg (12 lb)	80.28 kg (177 lb 0 oz)	Homosassa, Florida, USA	May 15, 1994	Clyde R. Balch, M.D.
Tippet M-08 kg (16 lb)	85.27 kg (188 lb 0 oz)	Homosassa, Florida, USA	May 13, 1982	William W. Pate, Jr.
Tippet M-10 kg (20 lb)	85.00 kg (187 lb 6 oz)	Sherbro Island, Sierra Leone	Apr. 9, 1992	Brian O'Keefe
Tippet W-01 kg (2 lb)	Vacant			
Tippet W-02 kg (4 lb)	Vacant			
Tippet W-03 kg (6 lb)	Vacant			
Tippet W-04 kg (8 lb)	Vacant			
Tippet W-06 kg (12 lb)	Vacant			
Tippet W-08 kg (16 lb)	37.64 kg (83 lb 0 oz)	Islamorada, Florida, USA	June 15, 1998	Diana Owen Harris
Tippet W-10 kg (20 lb)	41.78 kg (92 lb 2 oz)	Islamorada, Florida, USA	July 10, 1998	Jodi Pate

Tautog / *Tautoga onitis*

TIPPET	WEIGHT	PLACE	DATE	ANGLER
Tippet M-01 kg (2 lb)	Vacant			
Tippet M-02 kg (4 lb)	Vacant			
Tippet M-03 kg (6 lb)	0.73 kg (1 lb 10 oz)	Longport, Seaview Harbor, New Jersey, USA	Oct. 9, 1995	Frank S. Pecikonis
Tippet M-04 kg (8 lb)	1.30 kg (2 lb 13 oz)	Eaton Neck, Long Island, New York, USA	Nov. 5, 1992	William A. Kuhle
Tippet M-06 kg (12 lb)	0.79 kg (1 lb 12 oz)	Warwick, Rhode Island, USA	May 19, 1972	Dr. A. Chatowsky
Tippet M-08 kg (16 lb)	2.55 kg (5 lb 10 oz)	Lloyds Neck, New York, USA	June 22, 1978	Albert Apmann
Tippet M-10 kg (20 lb)	0.93 kg (2 lb 1 oz)	Margate City, New Jersey, USA	Oct. 9, 1993	Richard J. Embery
Tippet W-01 kg (2 lb)	Vacant			
Tippet W-02 kg (4 lb)	Vacant			
Tippet W-03 kg (6 lb)	Vacant			
Tippet W-04 kg (8 lb)	Vacant			
Tippet W-06 kg (12 lb)	Vacant			
Tippet W-08 kg (16 lb)	Vacant			
Tippet W-10 kg (20 lb)	Vacant			

Threadfin, king / *Polynemus sheridani*

TIPPET	WEIGHT	PLACE	DATE	ANGLER
Tippet M-01 kg (2 lb)	Vacant			
Tippet M-02 kg (4 lb)	Vacant			
Tippet M-03 kg (6 lb)	Vacant			
Tippet M-04 kg (8 lb)	1.80 kg (3 lb 15 oz)	Bathurst Island, N.T., Australia	June 22, 1991	Wayne Andrew Ross
Tippet M-06 kg (12 lb)	5.40 kg (11 lb 14 oz)	Port Hurd, Bathurst Island, N.T., Australia	May 6, 1987	Barry Anderson
Tippet M-08 kg (16 lb)	3.80 kg (8 lb 6 oz)	Port Hurd, Bathurst Island, N.T., Australia	July 26, 1991	Shane Third
Tippet M-10 kg (20 lb)	Vacant			
Tippet W-01 kg (2 lb)	Vacant			

Threadfin, king / *(continued)*

Tippet W-02 kg (4 lb)	Vacant			
Tippet W-03 kg (6 lb)	Vacant			
Tippet W-04 kg (8 lb)	Vacant			
Tippet W-06 kg (12 lb)	Vacant			
Tippet W-08 kg (16 lb)	Vacant			
Tippet W-20 kg (20 lb)	Vacant			

Trevally, bigeye / *Caranx sexfasciatus*

TIPPET	WEIGHT	PLACE	DATE	ANGLER
Tippet M-01 kg (2 lb)	Vacant			
Tippet M-02 kg (4 lb)	1.20 kg (2 lb 10 oz)	Onslow, W.A., Australia	Dec. 24, 1986	Jeffrey W. Grist
Tippet M-03 kg (6 lb)	3.65 kg (8 lb 1 oz)	Drake's Bay, Costa Rica	May 29, 1997	Collin Huff
Tippet M-04 kg (8 lb)	2.40 kg (5 lb 4 oz)	Onslow, W.A., Australia	Dec. 26, 1983	Richard N.H. Cooper
Tippet M-06 kg (12 lb)	3.40 kg (7 lb 7 oz)	Onslow, W.A., Australia	Dec. 23, 1986	Jeffrey W. Grist
Tippet M-08 kg (16 lb)	5.44 kg (12 lb 0 oz)	Drake's Bay, Costa Rica	Jan. 9, 1997	Andrew Moyes
Tippet M-10 kg (20 lb)	6.12 kg (13 lb 4 oz)	Isla Coiba, Panama	May 4, 1995	Rick Killgore
Tippet W-01 kg (2 lb)	Vacant			
Tippet W-02 kg (4 lb)	Vacant			
Tippet W-03 kg (6 lb)	Vacant			
Tippet W-04 kg (8 lb)	Vacant			
Tippet W-06 kg (12 lb)	Vacant			
Tippet W-08 kg (16 lb)	Vacant			
Tippet W-10 kg (20 lb)	Vacant			

Trevally, bluefin / *Caranx melampygus*

TIPPET	WEIGHT	PLACE	DATE	ANGLER
Tippet M-01 kg (2 lb)	1.81 kg (4 lb 0 oz)	Christmas Island, Republic of Kiribati	Feb. 27, 1996	Bud Korteweg
Tippet M-02 kg (4 lb)	1.98 kg (4 lb 6 oz)	Christmas Island, Republic of Kiribati	Mar. 3, 1994	Bud Korteweg
Tippet M-03 kg (6 lb)	3.40 kg (7 lb 8 oz)	Christmas Island, Republic of Kiribati	Feb. 24, 1996	Bud Korteweg
Tippet M-04 kg (8 lb)	2.76 kg (6 lb 1 oz)	Christmas Island, Republic of Kiribati	Mar. 13, 1998	Bud Korteweg
Tippet M-06 kg (12 lb)	4.90 kg (10 lb 12 oz)	Hahajima, Ogasawara Island, Japan	Apr. 29, 1991	Hiroshi Okada
Tippet M-08 kg (16 lb)	7.40 kg (16 lb 5 oz)	Watamu, Kenya	Apr. 7, 1994	James Philip Warne
Tippet M-10 kg (20 lb)	8.43 kg (18 lb 9 oz)	Clipperton Island	May 5, 1996	Douglas W. Alfers
Tippet W-01 kg (2 lb)	Vacant			
Tippet W-02 kg (4 lb)	Vacant			
Tippet W-03 kg (6 lb)	Vacant			
Tippet W-04 kg (8 lb)	Vacant			
Tippet W-06 kg (12 lb)	Vacant			
Tippet W-08 kg (16 lb)	Vacant			
Tippet W-10 kg (20 lb)	Vacant			

Trevally, giant / *Caranx ignobilis*

TIPPET	WEIGHT	PLACE	DATE	ANGLER
Tippet M-01 kg (2 lb)	0.90 kg (2 lb 0 oz)	Christmas Island, Republic of Kiribati	Mar. 1, 1994	Bud Korteweg
Tippet M-02 kg (4 lb)	4.71 kg (10 lb 6 oz)	Christmas Island, Republic of Kiribati	Mar. 17, 1998	Bud Korteweg
Tippet M-03 kg (6 lb)	6.57 kg (14 lb 8 oz)	Christmas Island, Republic of Kiribati	Feb. 27, 1995	Bud Korteweg
Tippet M-04 kg (8 lb)	15.87 kg (35 lb 0 oz)	Christmas Island, Republic of Kiribati	Feb. 27, 1995	Bud Korteweg
Tippet M-06 kg (12 lb)	24.26 kg (53 lb 8 oz)	Midway Island	Apr. 11, 1996	R.M. Pete Parker
Tippet M-08 kg (16 lb)	29.48 kg (65 lb 0 oz)	Christmas Island, Republic of Kiribati	Oct. 14, 1995	Richard Humphrey
Tippet M-10 kg (20 lb)	34.24 kg (75 lb 8 oz)	Christmas Island, Republic of Kiribati	Apr. 16, 1996	Stephen Collis
Tippet W-01 kg (2 lb)	Vacant			
Tippet W-02 kg (4 lb)	Vacant			
Tippet W-03 kg (6 lb)	Vacant			
Tippet W-04 kg (8 lb)	0.45 kg (1 lb 0 oz)	Midway Island	July 27, 1998	Sharon Handgis
Tippet W-06 kg (12 lb)	Vacant			
Tippet W-08 kg (16 lb)	Vacant			
Tippet W-10 kg (20 lb)	Vacant			

Tripletail / *Lobotes surinamensis*

TIPPET	WEIGHT	PLACE	DATE	ANGLER
Tippet M-01 kg (2 lb)	3.62 kg (8 lb 0 oz)	Flamingo, Florida, USA	June 20, 1994	Martin Arostegui
Tippet M-02 kg (4 lb)	4.53 kg (10 lb 0 oz)	Flamingo, Florida, USA	June 20, 1994	Martin Arostegui
Tippet M-03 kg (6 lb)	7.03 kg (15 lb 8 oz)	Collier County, Florida, USA	Nov. 6, 1996	Erik J. Madison, D.V.M.
Tippet M-04 kg (8 lb)	6.61 kg (14 lb 12 oz)	Islamorada, Florida, USA	July 11, 1996	Rusty Albury
Tippet M-06 kg (12 lb)	8.61 kg (19 lb 0 oz)	Sebastian, Florida, USA	Jan. 3, 1997	Rodney Smith
Tippet M-08 kg (16 lb)	9.07 kg (20 lb 0 oz)	Duck Key, Florida, USA	Oct. 3, 1995	Robert Chandler Schwartz
Tippet M-10 kg (20 lb)	7.42 kg (16 lb 6 oz)	Barra Colorado, Costa Rica	Oct. 17, 1995	Jim Gray
Tippet W-01 kg (2 lb)	Vacant			
Tippet W-02 kg (4 lb)	Vacant			
Tippet W-03 kg (6 lb)	0.90 kg (2 lb 0 oz)	Flamingo, Florida, USA	June 16, 1998	Acha Lord
Tippet W-04 kg (8 lb)	2.72 kg (6 lb 0 oz)	Port Canaveral, Florida, USA	June 10, 1998	Christine Perez
Tippet W-06 kg (12 lb)	Vacant			
Tippet W-08 kg (16 lb)	Vacant			
Tippet W-10 kg (20 lb)	Vacant			

Tuna, bigeye (Atlantic) / *Thunnus obesus*

TIPPET	WEIGHT	PLACE	DATE	ANGLER
Tippet M-01 kg (2 lb)	Vacant			
Tippet M-02 kg (4 lb)	Vacant			
Tippet M-03 kg (6 lb)	Vacant			
Tippet M-04 kg (8 lb)	Vacant			
Tippet M-06 kg (12 lb)	Vacant			
Tippet M-08 kg (16 lb)	4.50 kg (9 lb 14 oz)	Mauritania	Oct. 23, 1991	Christian Benazeth
Tippet M-10 kg (20 lb)	Vacant			

Tuna, bigeye (Atlantic) / *(continued)*

Tippet W-01 kg (2 lb)	Vacant			
Tippet W-02 kg (4 lb)	Vacant			
Tippet W-03 kg (6 lb)	Vacant			
Tippet W-04 kg (8 lb)	Vacant			
Tippet W-06 kg (12 lb)	Vacant			
Tippet W-08 kg (16 lb)	Vacant			
Tippet W-10 kg (20 lb)	Vacant			

Tuna, bigeye (Pacific) / *Thunnus obesus*

TIPPET	WEIGHT	PLACE	DATE	ANGLER
Tippet M-01 kg (2 lb)	Vacant			
Tippet M-02 kg (4 lb)	3.70 kg (8 lb 2 oz)	Kume Island, Okinawa, Japan	June 8, 1994	Tomoyoshi Kagami
Tippet M-03 kg (6 lb)	4.08 kg (9 lb 0 oz)	Island of Hawaii, Hawaii, USA	Jan. 8, 1982	Terry A. Baird
Tippet M-04 kg (8 lb)	10.45 kg (23 lb 0 oz)	Kume Island, Okinawa, Japan	June 7, 1994	Hiroaki Aoyagi
Tippet M-06 kg (12 lb)	14.30 kg (31 lb 8 oz)	Kume Island, Okinawa, Japan	July 7, 1994	Tomoyoshi Kagami
Tippet M-08 kg (16 lb)	12.40 kg (27 lb 5 oz)	Ishigaki Island, Okinawa, Japan	May 25, 1996	Takeshi Kamei
Tippet M-10 kg (20 lb)	10.40 kg (22 lb 14 oz)	Kume Island, Okinawa, Japan	June 7, 1994	Hisao Yamada
Tippet W-01 kg (2 lb)	Vacant			
Tippet W-02 kg (4 lb)	Vacant			
Tippet W-03 kg (6 lb)	Vacant			
Tippet W-04 kg (8 lb)	Vacant			
Tippet W-06 kg (12 lb)	Vacant			
Tippet W-08 kg (16 lb)	Vacant			
Tippet W-10 kg (20 lb)	Vacant			

Tuna, blackfin / *Thunnus atlanticus*

TIPPET	WEIGHT	PLACE	DATE	ANGLER
Tippet M-01 kg (2 lb)	Vacant			
Tippet M-02 kg (4 lb)	0.90 kg (2 lb 0 oz)	Islamorada, Florida, USA	June 30, 1988	Vic Gaspeny
Tippet M-03 kg (6 lb)	2.94 kg (6 lb 8 oz)	Gulf of Mexico, Venice, Louisiana, USA	Aug. 25, 1998	Scott A. Harness
Tippet M-04 kg (8 lb)	13.16 kg (29 lb 0 oz)	Tarpon Springs, Florida, USA	May 14, 1995	Luis R. Oliver
Tippet M-06 kg (12 lb)	13.72 kg (30 lb 4 oz)	Key West, Florida, USA	May 26, 1996	John D. Kreinces
Tippet M-08 kg (16 lb)	15.50 kg (34 lb 3 oz)	Islamorada, Florida, USA	Dec. 17, 1977	Rip Cunningham
Tippet M-10 kg (20 lb)	13.6 0kg (30 lb 0 oz)	Walker's Cay, Bahamas	June 20, 1992	David Webb
Tippet W-01 kg (2 lb)	Vacant			
Tippet W-02 kg (4 lb)	Vacant			
Tippet W-03 kg (6 lb)	Vacant			
Tippet W-04 kg (8 lb)	Vacant			
Tippet W-06 kg (12 lb)	Vacant			
Tippet W-08 kg (16 lb)	9.75 kg (21 lb 8 oz)	Key West, Florida, USA	Jan. 27, 1998	Emily Golinski
Tippet W-10 kg (20 lb)	10.20 kg (22 lb 8 oz)	Key West, Florida, USA	Apr. 28, 1998	Mrs. William B. DuVal

Tuna, bluefin / *Thunnus thynnus*

TIPPET	WEIGHT	PLACE	DATE	ANGLER
Tippet M-01 kg (2 lb)	Vacant			
Tippet M-02 kg (4 lb)	Vacant			
Tippet M-03 kg (6 lb)	6.35 kg (14 lb 0 oz)	Montauk, Long Island, New York, USA	Aug. 30, 1981	Stephen Sloan
Tippet M-04 kg (8 lb)	12.92 kg (28 lb 8 oz)	Indian River, Delaware, USA	Aug. 7, 1997	Rich Winnor
Tippet M-06 kg (12 lb)	19.27 kg (42 lb 8 oz)	Virginia Beach, Virginia, USA	July 20, 1997	David M. Limroth
Tippet M-08 kg (16 lb)	46.01 kg (101 lb 8 oz)	Hatteras, South Carolina, USA	Feb. 22, 1996	Raz Reid
Tippet M-10 kg (20 lb)	58.06 kg (128 lb 0 oz)	Hatteras, North Carolina, USA	Jan. 23, 1996	Michael Reid
Tippet W-01 kg (2 lb)	Vacant			
Tippet W-02 kg (4 lb)	Vacant			
Tippet W-03 kg (6 lb)	Vacant			
Tippet W-04 kg (8 lb)	Vacant			
Tippet W-06 kg (12 lb)	Vacant			
Tippet W-08 kg (16 lb)	Vacant			
Tippet W-10 kg (20 lb)	Vacant			

Tuna, dogtooth / *Gymnosarda unicolor*

TIPPET	WEIGHT	PLACE	DATE	ANGLER
Tippet M-01 kg (2 lb)	Vacant			
Tippet M-02 kg (4 lb)	Vacant			
Tippet M-03 kg (6 lb)	Vacant			
Tippet M-04 kg (8 lb)	Vacant			
Tippet M-06 kg (12 lb)	Vacant			
Tippet M-08 kg (16 lb)	Vacant			
Tippet M-10 kg (20 lb)	12.00 kg (26 lb 7 oz)	Madang, Papua, New Guinea	Nov. 13, 1995	Dean J. Butler
Tippet W-01 kg (2 lb)	Vacant			
Tippet W-02 kg (4 lb)	Vacant			
Tippet W-03 kg (6 lb)	Vacant			
Tippet W-04 kg (8 lb)	Vacant			
Tippet W-06 kg (12 lb)	Vacant			
Tippet W-08 kg (16 lb)	Vacant			
Tippet W-10 kg (20 lb)	Vacant			

Tuna, longtail / *Thunnus tonggol*

TIPPET	WEIGHT	PLACE	DATE	ANGLER
Tippet M-01 kg (2 lb)	Vacant			
Tippet M-02 kg (4 lb)	Vacant			
Tippet M-03 kg (6 lb)	Vacant			
Tippet M-04 kg (8 lb)	9.00 kg (19 lb 13 oz)	Carnarvon, W.A., Australia	Apr. 19, 1987	Simon Gilbert
Tippet M-06 kg (12 lb)	10.15 kg (22 lb 6 oz)	Cape Cuvier, W.A., Australia	May 21, 1981	Craig Radford
Tippet M-08 kg (16 lb)	13.00 kg (28 lb 10 oz)	Mooloolaba, Queensland, Australia	Apr. 22, 1998	Bryan Peterson

Tuna, longtail / *(continued)*

TIPPET	WEIGHT	PLACE	DATE	ANGLER
Tippet M-10 kg (20 lb)	12.60 kg (27 lb 12 oz)	Moreton Bay, Queensland, Australia	Mar. 28, 1998	Steve Morgan
Tippet W-01 kg (2 lb)	Vacant			
Tippet W-02 kg (4 lb)	Vacant			
Tippet W-03 kg (6 lb)	Vacant			
Tippet W-04 kg (8 lb)	Vacant			
Tippet W-06 kg (12 lb)	Vacant			
Tippet W-08 kg (16 lb)	Vacant			
Tippet W-10 kg (20 lb)	Vacant			

Tuna, skipjack / *Katsuwonus pelamis*

TIPPET	WEIGHT	PLACE	DATE	ANGLER
Tippet M-01 kg (2 lb)	5.95 kg (13 lb 2 oz)	Piton Pointe, Mauritius	Dec. 8, 1990	Richard F. Flasch
Tippet M-02 kg (4 lb)	4.98 kg (11 lb 0 oz)	Le Morne, Boye, Mauritius	Nov. 29, 1991	Richard F. Flasch
Tippet M-03 kg (6 lb)	6.69 kg (14 lb 12 oz)	Santa Barbara, California, USA	Dec. 7, 1975	Patt Wardlaw
Tippet M-04 kg (8 lb)	5.17 kg (11 lb 6 oz)	NE Whale Island, Whakatane, New Zealand	Feb. 9, 1996	Sam Mossman
Tippet M-06 kg (12 lb)	6.80 kg (15 lb 0 oz)	Santa Barbara, California, USA	Dec. 15, 1975	Patt Wardlaw
Tippet M-08 kg (16 lb)	7.03 kg (15 lb 8 oz)	Milolii, Kona, Hawaii, USA	Sept. 1, 1989	M. Schwartz
Tippet M-10 kg (20 lb)	7.30 kg (16 lb 1 oz)	Isla Clarion, Revillagigedo Islands, Mexico	Mar. 20, 1996	Walt Jennings
Tippet W-01 kg (2 lb)	Vacant			
Tippet W-02 kg (4 lb)	Vacant			
Tippet W-03 kg (6 lb)	Vacant			
Tippet W-04 kg (8 lb)	Vacant			
Tippet W-06 kg (12 lb)	Vacant			
Tippet W-08 kg (16 lb)	Vacant			
Tippet W-10 kg (20 lb)	Vacant			

Tuna, southern bluefin / *Thunnus maccoyi*

TIPPET	WEIGHT	PLACE	DATE	ANGLER
Tippet M-01 kg (2 lb)	Vacant			
Tippet M-02 kg (4 lb)	1.80 kg (3 lb 15 oz)	Rottnest Island, W.A., Australia	Jan. 16, 1983	Jeffrey W. Grist
Tippet M-03 kg (6 lb)	Vacant			
Tippet M-04 kg (8 lb)	5.00 kg (11 lb 0 oz)	Bunbury, W.A., Australia	Sept. 1, 1987	Adrian A. Pike
Tippet M-06 kg (12 lb)	Vacant			
Tippet M-08 kg (16 lb)	9.80 kg (21 lb 9 oz)	Port MacDonnell, South Australia	May 23, 1983	Bill Classon
Tippet M-10 kg (20 lb)	Vacant			
Tippet W-01 kg (2 lb)	Vacant			
Tippet W-02 kg (4 lb)	Vacant			
Tippet W-03 kg (6 lb)	Vacant			
Tippet W-04 kg (8 lb)	Vacant			
Tippet W-06 kg (12 lb)	Vacant			
Tippet W-08 kg (16 lb)	Vacant			
Tippet W-10 kg (20 lb)	Vacant			

Tuna, yellowfin / *Thunnus albacares*

TIPPET	WEIGHT	PLACE	DATE	ANGLER
Tippet M-01 kg (2 lb)	1.74 kg (3 lb 13 oz)	Cross Seamount, Hawaii, USA	Apr. 6, 1995	Kevin S. Nakamaru
Tippet M-02 kg (4 lb)	3.50 kg (7 lb 11 oz)	Ishigaki Island, Okinawa, Japan	June 6, 1998	Ken Suzuki
Tippet M-03 kg (6 lb)	8.61 kg (19 lb 0 oz)	Gulf of Mexico, Venice, Louisiana, USA	Aug. 25, 1998	Scott A. Harness
Tippet M-04 kg (8 lb)	19.20 kg (42 lb 5 oz)	Maiquetia, Venezuela	Jan. 10, 1991	A. C. Reuter
Tippet M-06 kg (12 lb)	30.61 kg (67 lb 8 oz)	Bermuda	July 7, 1973	Jim Lopez
Tippet M-08 kg (16 lb)	36.74 kg (81 lb 0 oz)	Bermuda	June 28, 1973	Jim Lopez
Tippet M-10 kg (20 lb)	32.40 kg (71 lb 6 oz)	Hout Bay, South Africa	Jan. 9, 1996	Nic de Kock
Tippet W-01 kg (2 lb)	Vacant			
Tippet W-02 kg (4 lb)	Vacant			
Tippet W-03 kg (6 lb)	Vacant			
Tippet W-04 kg (8 lb)	Vacant			
Tippet W-06 kg (12 lb)	Vacant			
Tippet W-08 kg (16 lb)	5.58 kg (12 lb 5 oz)	Quepos, Costa Rica	July 7, 1998	Wendy Don
Tippet W-10 kg (20 lb)	5.13 kg (11 lb 5 oz)	Quepos, Costa Rica	July 7, 1998	Wendy Don

Tunny, little / *Euthynnus alletteratus*

TIPPET	WEIGHT	PLACE	DATE	ANGLER
Tippet M-01 kg (2 lb)	2.35 kg (5 lb 3 oz)	Bayhead, New Jersey, USA	Sept. 26, 1998	Ron Mazzarella
Tippet M-02 kg (4 lb)	6.12 kg (13 lb 8 oz)	Key West, Florida, USA	July 23, 1983	Robert Steven Bass
Tippet M-03 kg (6 lb)	8.27 kg (18 lb 4 oz)	Cape Canaveral, Florida, USA	July 24, 1972	Dave Chermanski
Tippet M-04 kg (8 lb)	7.93 kg (17 lb 8 oz)	Jupiter, Florida, USA	July 7, 1996	Andy Mill
Tippet M-06 kg (12 lb)	8.05 kg (17 lb 12 oz)	Key West, Florida, USA	May 18, 1983	Luis de Hoyos
Tippet M-08 kg (16 lb)	8.39 kg (18 lb 8 oz)	Key West, Florida, USA	June 2, 1985	Jim Donnellan
Tippet M-10 kg (20 lb)	8.61 kg (19 lb 0 oz)	Dry Tortugas, Florida, USA	Apr. 12, 1995	Philip Caputo
Tippet W-01 kg (2 lb)	Vacant			
Tippet W-02 kg (4 lb)	0.90 kg (2 lb 0 oz)	Miami, Florida, USA	Jan. 1, 1998	Pamela W. Marmin
Tippet W-03 kg (6 lb)	3.53 kg (7 lb 12 oz)	Key West, Florida, USA	Apr. 21, 1998	Lisa Booth
Tippet W-04 kg (8 lb)	5.85 kg (12 lb 14 oz)	Key West, Florida, USA	Apr. 19, 1998	Bunny Eickelbeck
Tippet W-06 kg (12 lb)	5.55 kg (12 lb 4 oz)	Key West, Florida, USA	Apr. 28, 1998	Mrs. William B. DuVal
Tippet W-08 kg (16 lb)	5.66 kg (12 lb 8 oz)	Key West, Florida, USA	Apr. 28, 1998	Mrs. William B. DuVal
Tippet W-10 kg (20 lb)	6.40 kg (14 lb 2 oz)	Key West, Florida, USA	May 30, 1998	Linda Ann Luizza

Wahoo / *Acanthocybium solandri*

TIPPET	WEIGHT	PLACE	DATE	ANGLER
Tippet M-01 kg (2 lb)	Vacant			
Tippet M-02 kg (4 lb)	Vacant			
Tippet M-03 kg (6 lb)	7.99 kg (17 lb 10 oz)	Isla de Coiba, Panama	Oct. 12, 1975	Stu Apte
Tippet M-04 kg (8 lb)	17.19 kg (37 lb 14 oz)	Thetis Bank, Baja Mexico	Nov. 30, 1994	Ed Rice
Tippet M-06 kg (12 lb)	25.85 kg (57 lb 0 oz)	Gulf of Papagayo, Guancaste, Costa Rica	June 13, 1995	Hermann Fehringer

Wahoo / *(continued)*

TIPPET	WEIGHT	PLACE	DATE	ANGLER
Tippet M-08 kg (16 lb)	23.13 kg (51 lb 0 oz)	Baja California, Mexico	Dec. 3, 1992	Ed Rice
Tippet M-10 kg (20 lb)	30.05 kg (66 lb 4 oz)	Allejos Rocks, Baja California Sur, Mexico	Dec. 2, 1993	Trey Combs
Tippet W-01 kg (2 lb)	Vacant			
Tippet W-02 kg (4 lb)	Vacant			
Tippet W-03 kg (6 lb)	Vacant			
Tippet W-04 kg (8 lb)	Vacant			
Tippet W-06 kg (12 lb)	Vacant			
Tippet W-08 kg (16 lb)	Vacant			
Tippet W-10 kg (20 lb)	Vacant			

Weakfish / *Cynoscion regalis*

TIPPET	WEIGHT	PLACE	DATE	ANGLER
Tippet M-01 kg (2 lb)	1.41 kg (3 lb 2 oz)	State Channel, Captree, Long Island, New York, USA	Sept. 6, 1993	John Boesenberg
Tippet M-02 kg (4 lb)	6.40 kg (14 lb 2 oz)	Delaware Bay, Delaware, USA	June 5, 1987	Norman W. Bartlett
Tippet M-03 kg (6 lb)	4.64 kg (10 lb 4 oz)	Cape May Court House, New Jersey, USA	July 6, 1980	Gary L. Rudy
Tippet M-04 kg (8 lb)	2.35 kg (5 lb 3 oz)	Bayhead, New Jersey, USA	Sept. 30, 1998	Ron Mazzarella
Tippet M-06 kg (12 lb)	4.84 kg (10 lb 11 oz)	Chesapeake Bay, Virginia, USA	May 28, 1983	Lawrence E. Haack
Tippet M-08 kg (16 lb)	5.06 kg (11 lb 2 oz)	Loyd Point, Long Island, New York, USA	July 13, 1985	Howard F. Guja
Tippet M-10 kg (20 lb)	2.26 kg (5 lb 0 oz)	Staten Island, New York, USA	May 17, 1998	Vincent L. Trapani
Tippet W-01 kg (2 lb)	Vacant			
Tippet W-02 kg (4 lb)	Vacant			
Tippet W-03 kg (6 lb)	Vacant			
Tippet W-04 kg (8 lb)	1.81 kg (4 lb 0 oz)	Moriches Bay, East Moriches, New York, USA	July 13, 1998	Tom Cornicelli
Tippet W-06 kg (12 lb)	Vacant			
Tippet W-08 kg (16 lb)	Vacant			
Tippet W-10 kg (20 lb)	3.51 kg (7 lb 11 oz)	West Ocean City, Maryland, USA	May 25, 1998	Wanda S. Morgan

Yellowtail, California / *Seriola lalandi*

TIPPET	WEIGHT	PLACE	DATE	ANGLER
Tippet M-01 kg (2 lb)	Vacant			
Tippet M-02 kg (4 lb)	2.77 kg (6 lb 2 oz)	Santa Monica Bay, California, USA	Sept. 11, 1983	Roy Lawson
Tippet M-03 kg (6 lb)	6.88 kg (15 lb 3 oz)	Loreto, Baja California, Mexico	Jan. 30, 1973	Harry Kime
Tippet M-04 kg (8 lb)	7.99 kg (17 lb 10 oz)	Anacapa Island, California, USA	May 3, 1984	Roy Lawson
Tippet M-06 kg (12 lb)	14.74 kg (32 lb 8 oz)	Loreto, Baja California, Mexico	Mar. 14, 1972	Christy Blough
Tippet M-08 kg (16 lb)	14.51 kg (32 lb 0 oz)	Loreto, Baja California, Mexico	Mar. 27, 1973	Timothy W. Jewell
Tippet M-10 kg (20 lb)	5.21 kg (11 lb 8 oz)	Point Tosca, Baja California, Mexico	Jan. 13, 1995	Wayne A. Clark
Tippet W-01 kg (2 lb)	Vacant			
Tippet W-02 kg (4 lb)	Vacant			
Tippet W-03 kg (6 lb)	Vacant			
Tippet W-04 kg (8 lb)	Vacant			
Tippet W-06 kg (12 lb)	Vacant			
Tippet W-08 kg (16 lb)	Vacant			
Tippet W-10 kg (20 lb)	Vacant			

Yellowtail, southern / *Seriola lalandi lalandi*

TIPPET	WEIGHT	PLACE	DATE	ANGLER
Tippet M-01 kg (2 lb)	Vacant			
Tippet M-02 kg (4 lb)	2.08 kg (4 lb 9 oz)	White Island, Whakatane, New Zealand	Dec. 29, 1991	Louie Denolfo
Tippet M-03 kg (6 lb)	Vacant			
Tippet M-04 kg (8 lb)	8.19 kg (18 lb 1 oz)	Tauranga, New Zealand	July 8, 1982	Mike Godfrey
Tippet M-06 kg (12 lb)	14.51 kg (32 lb 0 oz)	Tauranga, New Zealand	May 12, 1979	Mike Godfrey
Tippet M-08 kg (16 lb)	19.75 kg (43 lb 8 oz)	Tauranga, New Zealand	June 8, 1986	Mike Godfrey
Tippet M-10 kg (20 lb)	25.20 kg (55 lb 8 oz)	Bay of Plenty, New Zealand	Jan. 21, 1998	Stephane Uzan
Tippet W-01 kg (2 lb)	Vacant			
Tippet W-02 kg (4 lb)	Vacant			
Tippet W-03 kg (6 lb)	Vacant			
Tippet W-04 kg (8 lb)	Vacant			
Tippet W-06 kg (12 lb)	Vacant			
Tippet W-08 kg (16 lb)	Vacant			
Tippet W-10 kg (20 lb)	Vacant			

IGFA Freshwater & Saltwater All-Tackle Records

All-Tackle records are kept for the heaviest of each species caught by an angler in any line class category up to 60 kg (130 lb). The following are records granted as of January 1, 1999.

SPECIES	SCIENTIFIC NAME	WEIGHT	PLACE	DATE	ANGLER
Albacore	*Thunnus alalunga*	40.00 kg / 88 lb 2 oz	Gran Canaria Canary Islands, Spain	Nov. 19, 1977	Siegfried Dickemann
Amberjack, greater (Tie)	*Seriola dumerili*	70.64 kg / 155 lb 12 oz	Bermuda	Aug. 16, 1992	Larry Trott
Amberjack, greater (Tie)	*Seriola dumerili*	70.59 kg / 155 lb 10 oz	Challenger Bank Bermuda	June 24, 1981	Joseph Dawson
Angler	*Lophius piscatorius*	57.70 kg / 126 lb 12 oz	Sagnefiorden Hoyanger, Norway	July 4, 1996	Gunnar Thorsteinsen
Arawana	*Osteoglossum bicirrhosum*	4.60 kg / 10 lb 2 oz	Puraquequara Lake Amazon, Brazil	Feb. 3, 1990	Gilberto Fernandes
Asp	*Aspius aspius*	5.66 kg / 12 lb 7 oz	Lake Vattern Sweden	Sept. 25, 1993	Jan-Erik Skoglund
Ayamekasago	*Sebasticus albofasciatus*	2.50 kg / 5 lb 8 oz	Irozaki, Shizuoka Japan	Aug. 13, 1998	Mikio Suzuki
Barenose, bigeye	*Monotaxis grandoculis*	5.89 kg / 13 lb 0 oz	Otec Beach, Kailua Kona, Hawaii, USA	July 12, 1992	Rex C. Bigg
Barracuda, blackfin	*Sphyraena qenie*	7.14 kg / 15 lb 12 oz	Puerto Quetzal Guatemala	June 10, 1995	Estuardo Vila S.
Barracuda, great (Tie)	*Sphyraena barracuda*	38.50 kg / 84 lb 14 oz	Scarborough Shoals Philippines	Mar. 1, 1991	Jessie D. Cordova
Barracuda, great (Tie)	*Sphyraena barracuda*	38.55 kg / 85 lb 0 oz	Christmas Island Republic of Kiribati	Apr. 11, 1992	John W. Helfrich
Barracuda, Guinean	*Sphyraena afra*	30.30 kg / 66 lb 12 oz	Mondia Branca Luanda, Angola	Feb. 24, 1998	Nisa Ekberg
Barracuda, Mexican	*Sphyraena ensis*	9.52 kg / 21 lb 0 oz	Phantom Isle Costa Rica	Mar. 27, 1987	E. Greg Kent
Barracuda, Pacific	*Sphyraena argentea*	3.48 kg / 7 lb 11 oz	Catalina Island California, USA	May 22, 1994	Jim Kingsmill
Barracuda, pickhandle	*Sphyraena jello*	11.50 kg / 25 lb 5 oz	Scottburgh, Natal Republic of South Africa	July 3, 1996	Demetrios Stamatis
Barracuda, yellowmouth	*Sphyraena viridensis*	8.20 kg / 18 lb 1 oz	Isla Graciosa Canary Islands, Spain	Aug. 26, 1994	Guiseppe Parini
Barramundi	*Lates calcarifer*	28.65 kg / 63 lb 2 oz	Normah River, Normahton Queensland, Australia	Apr. 28, 1991	Scott Barnsley
Bass, barred sand	*Paralabrax nebulifer*	5.98 kg / 13 lb 3 oz	Huntington Beach California, USA	Aug. 29, 1988	Robert Halal
Bass, black sea (Tie)	*Centropristis striata*	4.30 kg / 9 lb 8 oz	Virginia Beach Virginia, USA	Dec. 22, 1990	Jack G. Stallings, Jr.
Bass, black sea (Tie)	*Centropristis striata*	4.30 kg / 9 lb 8 oz	Rudee Inlet, Virginia Beach Virginia, USA	Jan. 9, 1987	Joe Mizelle, Jr.
Bass, European	*Morone labrax*	9.40 kg / 20 lb 11 oz	Stes Maries de la Mer 13 France	May 6, 1986	Jean Baptiste Bayle
Bass, giant sea	*Stereolepis gigas*	255.60 kg / 563 lb 8 oz	Anacapa Island California, USA	Aug. 20, 1968	James D. McAdam, Jr.
Bass, goldspotted rock	*Paralabrax auroguttatus*	2.72 kg / 6 lb 0 oz	San Francisco Baja California, Mexico	June 13, 1993	Charles F. Ulrich
Bass, Guadalupe	*Micropterus treculi*	1.67 kg / 3 lb 11 oz	Lake Travis Austin, Texas, USA	Sept. 25, 1983	Allen Christensen, Jr.
Bass, Guadalupe x smallmouth	*Micropterus treculi x dolomieu*	1.90 kg / 4 lb 3 oz	Blanco River Texas, USA	June 18, 1995	John Ryan Weaver
Bass, kelp (calico)	*Paralabrax clathratus*	6.54 kg / 14 lb 7 oz	Newport Beach California, USA	Oct. 2, 1993	Thomas Murphy
Bass, largemouth	*Micropterus salmoides*	10.09 kg / 22 lb 4 oz	Montgomery Lake Georgia, USA	June 2, 1932	George W. Perry
Bass, leather	*Dermatolepis dermatolepis*	12.47 kg / 27 lb 8 oz	Isla Clarion Revillagigedo Islands, Mexico	Jan. 26, 1988	Allan J. Ristori
Bass, Ozark	*Ambloplites constellatus*	0.45 kg / 1 lb 0 oz	Bull Shoals Lake Arkansas, USA	May 13, 1997	Gary Nelson
Bass, redeye	*Micropterus coosae*	3.99 kg / 8 lb 12 oz	Apalachicola River Florida, USA	Jan. 28, 1995	Carl W. Davis
Bass, Roanoke	*Ambloplites cavifrons*	3.30 kg / 1 lb 5 oz	Nottoway River, Southampton Co., Virginia, USA	Nov. 11, 1991	Thomas F. Elkins
Bass, rock	*Ambloplites rupestris*	1.36 kg / 3 lb 0 oz	York River Ontario, Canada	Aug. 1, 1974	Peter Gulgin
Bass, shadow	*Ambloplites ariommus*	0.62 kg / 1 lb 5 oz	Spring River Arkansas, USA	Oct. 19, 1994	Sam W. Barkley
Bass, smallmouth	*Micropterus dolomieu*	4.93 kg / 10 lb 14 oz	Dale Hollow Tennessee, USA	Apr. 24, 1969	John T. Gorman
Bass, splittail	*Hemanthias signifer*	0.68 kg / 1 lb 8 oz	Playa Zancudo Costa Rica	June 10, 1995	Craig Whitehead, MD

SPECIES	SCIENTIFIC NAME	WEIGHT	PLACE	DATE	ANGLER
Bass, spotted	*Micropterus punctulatus*	4.33 kg 9 lb 9 oz	Pine Flat Lake California, USA	Oct. 12, 1996	Kirk M. Sakamoto
Bass, spotted sand	*Paralabrax maculatofasciatus*	0.90 kg 2 lb 0 oz	Playa Hermosa Mexico	Mar. 30, 1997	William E. Favor
Bass, striped	*Morone saxatilis*	35.60 kg 78 lb 8 oz	Atlantic City New Jersey, USA	Sept. 21, 1982	Albert R. McReynolds
Bass, striped (landlocked)	*Morone saxatilis*	30.61 kg 67 lb 8 oz	O'Neill Forebay, Los Banos California, USA	May 7, 1992	Hank Ferguson
Bass, Suwannee	*Micropterus notius*	1.75 kg 3 lb 14 oz	Suwannee River Florida, USA	Mar. 2, 1985	Ronnie Everett
Bass, white	*Morone chrysops*	3.09 kg 6 lb 13 oz	Lake Orange Orange, Virginia, USA	July 31, 1989	Ronald L. Sprouse
Bass, whiterock	*Morone saxatilis x chrysops*	12.38 kg 27 lb 5 oz	Greers Ferry Lake Arkansas, USA	Apr. 24, 1997	Jerald C. Shaum
Bass, yellow	*Morone mississipiensis*	1.16 kg 2 lb 9 oz	Duck River Waverly, Tennessee, USA	Feb. 27, 1998	John T. Chappell
Bass, yellow hybrid	*Morone mississippiensis x M. chrysops*	1.04 kg 2 lb 5 oz	Kiamichi River Oklahoma, USA	Mar. 26, 1991	George R. Edwards
Biara	*Rhaphiodon vulpinas*	1.55 kg 3 lb 7 oz	Xingu River Estado Mato Grosso, Brazil	June 5, 1996	Sergio Roberto Rothier
Bicuda (pike characin)	*Boulengerella ocellata*	2.57 kg 5 lb 11 oz	Xingu River Estado Mato Grosso, Brazil	June 7, 1996	Sergio Roberto Rothier
Bigeye	*Priacanthus arenatus*	2.85 kg 6 lb 4 oz	Baja da Guanabara Rio de Janeiro, Brazil	Aug. 30, 1997	Jayme Garcia
Binga	*Dimidiochromis kiwinge*	0.51 kg 1 lb 2 oz	Maleri Island Lake Malawi, Malawi	Nov. 30, 1996	Garry Seymer Whitcher
Blackfish, smallscale	*Girella melanichthys*	3.40 kg 7 lb 7 oz	Hachijokojima Hachijo Island, Japan	Jan. 8, 1998	Papa Otsuru
Bludger	*Carangoides gymnostethus*	9.70 kg 21 lb 9 oz	Bartholmeu Dias Mozambique	June 17, 1997	Joh Haasbroek
Blue, big	*Buccochromis spp.*	0.55 kg 1 lb 3 oz	Maleri Island Lake Malawi, Malawi	July 5, 1997	Brendon Garry Whitcher
Bluefish	*Pomatomus saltatrix*	14.40 kg 31 lb 12 oz	Hatteras North Carolina, USA	Jan. 30, 1972	James M. Hussey
Bluegill	*Lepomis macrochirus*	2.15 kg 4 lb 12 oz	Ketona Lake Alabama, USA	Apr. 9, 1950	T. S. Hudson
Bocaccio	*Sebastes paucispinis*	9.63 kg 21 lb 4 oz	Swiftsure Bank, Neah Bay Washington, USA	July 29, 1986	Terry Rudnick
Bonefish	*Albula spp.*	8.61 kg 19 lb 0 oz	Zululand Republic of South Africa	May 26, 1962	Brian W. Batchelor
Bonito, Atlantic	*Sarda sarda*	8.30 kg 18 lb 4 oz	Faial Island Azores	July 8, 1953	D. Gama Higgs
Bonito, Australian	*Sarda australis*	9.40 kg 20 lb 11 oz	Montague Island N.S.W., Australia	Apr. 1, 1978	Bruce Conley
Bonito, leaping	*Cybiosarda elegans*	0.96 kg 2 lb 2 oz	Macleay River Australia	May 7, 1995	Wayne Colling
Bonito, Pacific	*Sarda chiliensis lineolatus*	10.07 kg 21 lb 3 oz	Malibu California, USA	July 30, 1978	Gino M. Picciolo
Bonito, striped	*Sarda orientalis*	10.65 kg 23 lb 8 oz	Victoria, Mahe Seychelles	Feb. 19, 1975	Anne Cochain
Bowfin	*Amia calva*	9.75 kg 21 lb 8 oz	Forest Lake, Florence South Carolina, USA	Jan. 29, 1980	Robert L. Harmon
Bream	*Abramis brama*	6.01 kg 13 lb 3 oz	Hagbyan Creek Sweden	May 11, 1984	Luis Kilian Rasmussen
Bream, African red	*Pagrus africanus*	5.55 kg 12 lb 3 oz	Nouadhibou Mauritania	Mar. 13, 1986	Bernard Defago
Bream, black	*Hephaestus fuliginosus*	6.17 kg 13 lb 9 oz	Lake Tinaroo Queensland, Australia	Jan. 16, 1997	Brian G. Seawright
Bream, gilthead	*Sparus auratus*	5.84 kg 12 lb 13 oz	Gibraltar Bay Gibraltar	Mar. 31, 1996	John Michael Chappory
Bream, twoband	*Diplodus vulgaris*	1.30 kg 2 lb 13 oz	Europa Point Gibraltar	Sept. 3, 1995	Ernest Borrell
Bream, white	*Abramis bjoerkna*	0.58 kg 1 lb 4 oz	Nok Germany	May 19, 1998	Holger Damerius
Brotula, bearded	*Brotula barbata*	7.98 kg 17 lb 9 oz	Destin Florida, USA	Aug. 16, 1997	William G. Siedow
Buffalo, bigmouth	*Ictiobus cyprinellus*	31.89 kg 70 lb 5 oz	Bastrop Louisiana, USA	Apr. 21, 1980	Delbert Sisk
Buffalo, black	*Ictiobus niger*	25.17 kg 55 lb 8 oz	Cherokee Lake Tennessee, USA	May 3, 1984	Edward H. Mc Lain
Buffalo, smallmouth	*Ictiobus bubalus*	37.29 kg 82 lb 3 oz	Athens Lake Alabama, USA	June 6, 1993	Randy Collins
Bulleye	*Cookeolus japonicus*	2.08 kg 4 lb 9 oz	Rio de Janeiro Brazil	Apr. 4, 1996	Eduardo Baumeier
Bullhead, black	*Ameiurus melas*	3.37 kg 7 lb 7 oz	Mill Pond, Wantagh Long Island, New York, USA	Aug. 25, 1993	Kevin Kelly

SPECIES	SCIENTIFIC NAME	WEIGHT	PLACE	DATE	ANGLER
Bullhead, brown	*Ameiurus nebulosus*	2.74 kg 6 lb 1 oz	Waterford New York, USA	Apr. 26, 1998	Bobby Triplett
Bullhead, yellow	*Ameiurus natalis*	1.92 kg 4 lb 4 oz	Mormon Lake Arizona, USA	May 11, 1984	Emily Williams
Burbot	*Lota lota*	8.50 kg 18 lb 11 oz	Angenmanalren Sweden	Oct. 22, 1996	Margit Agren
Buri (Japanese amberjack)	*Seriola quinqueradiata*	9.50 kg 20 lb 15 oz	Miyazu, Kyoto Japan	Apr. 29, 1998	Toshiyuki Fujioka
Burrfish, striped	*Cyclichthys schoepfi*	0.63 kg 1 lb 6 oz	Delaware Bay New Jersey, USA	Aug. 13, 1989	Donna L. Ludlam
Cabezon	*Scorpaenichthys marmoratus*	10.43 kg 23 lb 0 oz	Juan De Fuca Strait Washington, USA	Aug. 4, 1 990	Wesley S. Hunter
Captainfish	*Pseudotolithus senegalensis*	12.00 kg 26 lb 7 oz	Archipelago of Bijago Guinea-Bissau	May 17, 1998	Eric Legris
Carp, bighead	*Aristichthys nobilis*	9.07 kg 20 lb 0 oz	Cinque Holmes Creek Mentro, Missouri, USA	July 26, 1996	Rick Hayden
Carp, common	*Cyprinus carpio*	37.30 kg 82 lb 3 oz	Lake Roduta Romania	May 26, 1998	Christian Baldemair
Carp, crucian	*Carassius carassius*	2.30 kg 5 lb 1 oz	Lago Caldaro Kalterersee, Italy	July 16, 1997	Jorg Marquand
Carp, grass	*Ctenopharyngodon idella*	31.18 kg 68 lb 12 oz	Somerland's Pond North Carolina, USA	June 8, 1998	David Stowell
Carp, silver	*Hypophthalmichthys spp.*	16.00 kg 35 lb 4 oz	Danube River Austria	Nov. 10, 1983	Josef Windholz
Carpsucker, river	*Carpiodes carpio*	3.48 kg 7 lb 11 oz	Canadian County Oklahoma, USA	Apr. 18, 1990	W.C. (Bill) Kenyon
Catfish, blue	*Ictalurus furcatus*	50.34 kg 111 lb 0 oz	Wheeler Reservoir Tennesee River, Alabama, USA	July 5, 1996	William P. McKinley
Catfish, channel	*Ictalurus punctatus*	26.30 kg 58 lb 0 oz	Santee Cooper Reservoir South Carolina, USA	July 7, 1964	W. B. Whaley
Catfish, Eurasian	*Silurus biwaensis*	17.20 kg 37 lb 14 oz	Imazuhama Lake Biwa, Shiga, Japan	July 4, 1997	Shoji Matsuura
Catfish, flathead	*Pylodictis olivaris*	55.79 kg 123 lb 9 oz	Elk City Reservoir Independence, Kansas, USA	May 14, 1998	Ken Paulie
Catfish, flatwhiskered	*Pinirampus pinirampu*	4.19 kg 9 lb 4 oz	Caceres, Rio Paraguai Brazil	Sept. 11, 1996	Cavour Pieranti
Catfish, gafftopsail	*Bagre marinus*	4.02 kg 8 lb 14 oz	Indian River Florida, USA	Sept. 21, 1996	Larry C. Jones
Catfish, gilded	*Brachyplatystoma flavicans*	38.80 kg 85 lb 8 oz	Amazon River Amazon, Brazil	Nov. 15, 1986	Gilberto Fernandes
Catfish, hardhead	*Arius felis*	1.50 kg 3 lb 5 oz	Mays Marina Sebastian, Florida, USA	Apr. 18, 1993	Amanda Steed
Catfish, redtail (pirarara)	*Phractocephalus hemioliopterus*	44.20 kg 97 lb 7 oz	Amazon River Amazon, Brazil	July 16, 1988	Gilberto Fernandes
Catfish, sharptoothed	*Clarias gariepinus*	36.00 kg 79 lb 5 oz	Orange River Upington, Republic of South Africa	Dec. 5, 1992	Hennie Moller
Catfish, walking	*Clarias batrachus*	0.45 kg 1 lb 0 oz	Dade County Florida, USA	Mar. 9, 1997	Stephen H. Helvin
Catfish, white	*Ameiurus catus*	8.56 kg 18 lb 14 oz	Withlacoochee River Inverness, Florida, USA	Sept. 21, 1991	Jim Miller
Catshark, smallspotted	*Scyliorhinus canicula*	0.90 kg 1 lb 15 oz	Holmestrand Norway	May 23, 1998	Bjoers Borgensen
Char, Arctic	*Salvelinus alpinus*	14.77 kg 32 lb 9 oz	Tree River Canada	July 30, 1981	Jeffery L. Ward
Char, whitespotted	*Salvelinus leucomaenis*	7.37 kg 16 lb 9 oz	Samarga River Russia	Aug. 20, 1994	Pete Moring
Chilipepper	*Sebastes goodei*	1.13 kg 2 lb 8 oz	San Clemente Island California, USA	Feb. 14, 1998	Stephen D. Grossberg
Chinamanfish	*Symphorus nematophorus*	13.20 kg 29 lb 1 oz	Dampier Australia	Mar. 8, 1996	Mark Cotrell
Chub, Bermuda	*Kyphosus sectatrix*	6.01 kg 13 lb 4 oz	Fort Pierce Inlet Florida, USA	Mar. 5, 1997	Sam Baum
Chub, European	*Leuciscus cephalus*	2.62 kg 5 lb 12 oz	Helige Gemla, Sweden	July 26, 1987	Luis Kilian Rasmussen
Chub, gray sea	*Kyphosus bigibbus*	1.85 kg 4 lb 1 oz	Midway Island	July 26, 1998	George Handgis
Chub, yellow	*Kyphosus incisor*	3.85 kg 8 lb 8 oz	Sabine Pass Texas, USA	May 29, 1994	Stephen L. McDonald
Cisco	*Coregonus artedi*	3.35 kg 7 lb 6 oz	North Cross Bay Cedar Lake, Manitoba, Canada	Apr. 11, 1986	Randy K. Huff
Cobia	*Rachycentron canadum*	61.50 kg 135 lb 9 oz	Shark Bay W.A., Australia	July 9, 1985	Peter William Goulding
Cod, Atlantic	*Gadus morhua*	44.79 kg 98 lb 12 oz	Isle of Shoals New Hampshire, USA	June 8, 1969	Alphonse J. Bielevich
Cod, Pacific	*Gadus macrocephalus*	14.51 kg 32 lb 0 oz	Unalaska Bay Alaska, USA	June 29, 1997	Donald Boston

SPECIES	SCIENTIFIC NAME	WEIGHT	PLACE	DATE	ANGLER
Conger	*Conger*	60.44 kg	Berry Head	June 5, 1995	Vic Evans
	conger	133 lb 4 oz	South Devon, England		
Coralgrouper, blacksaddled	*Plectropomus*	24.20 kg	Hahajima, Ogasawara Island	Sept. 27, 1997	Hideo Morishita
	laevis	53 lb 5 oz	Tokyo, Japan		
Coralgrouper, highfin	*Plectropomus*	1.20 kg	Buso Point	May 1, 1994	Justin Mallett
	oligacanthus	2 lb 10 oz	Huon Gulf, Papua, New Guinea		
Corbina, California	*Minticirrhus*	2.95 kg	Dana Harbor	May 23, 1997	Scott Matthews
	undulatus	6 lb 8 oz	California, USA		
Coris, yellowstripe	*Coris*	4.62 kg	Keahole Point	Jan. 1, 1996	Rex C. Bigg
	flavovittata	10 lb 3 oz	Kailua Kona, Hawaii, USA		
Corvina, hybrid	*Cynoscion xanthulus x*	4.76 kg	Calaveras Lake	Jan. 27, 1987	Norma E. Cleary
	C. nebulosus	10 lb 8 oz	San Antonio, Texas, USA		
Corvina, orangemouth	*Cynoscion*	24.60 kg	Sabana Grande	July 29, 1992	Felipe Estrada E.
	xanthulus	54 lb 3 oz	Guayaquil, Ecuador		
Corvina, shortfin	*Cynoscion*	3.15 kg	Playa Hermosa	Apr. 26, 1998	William E. Favor
	parvipinnis	6 lb 15 oz	Mexico		
Corvina, striped	*Cynoscion*	0.90 kg	Playa Hermosa	Apr. 5, 1998	William E. Favor
	reticulatus	2 lb 0 oz	Mexico		
Crappie, black	*Pomoxis*	2.05 kg	Kerr Lake	Mar. 1, 1981	L. Carl Herring, Jr.
	nigromaculatus	4 lb 8 oz	Virginia, USA		
Crappie, white	*Pomoxis*	2.35 kg	Enid Dam	July 31, 1957	Fred L. Bright
	annularis	5 lb 3 oz	Mississippi, USA		
Croaker, Atlantic	*Micropogonias*	1.70 kg	Escambia River	Sept. 29, 1992	Tina Marie Jeffers
	undulatus	3 lb 12 oz	Pensacola, Florida, USA		
Croaker, long neck	*Pseudotolithus*	15.02 kg	Banjul	Mar. 25, 1998	Alberto Madaria Hernandez
	typus	33 lb 2 oz	Gambia		
Croaker, silver	*Plagioscion*	4.08 kg	Sao Benedito River	Aug. 17, 1997	Larry Larsen
	squamossimus	9 lb 0 oz	Brazil		
Croaker, yellowfin	*Umbrina*	0.93 kg	Dana Point	Aug. 3, 1995	Scott Crooke
	roncador	2 lb 1 oz	California, USA		
Cui-ui	*Chasmistes*	2.72 kg	Pyramid Lake	June 30, 1997	Mike Berg
	cujus	6 lb 0 oz	Arizona, USA		
Cunner	*Tautogolabrus*	0.45 kg	Brielle	Mar. 12, 1994	Alex Gerus
	adspersus	1 lb 9 oz	New Jersey, USA		
Cusk	*Brosme*	16.30 kg	Langesund	Apr. 26, 1998	Fredrik Amdal
	brosme	35 lb 14 oz	Norway		
Cutlassfish, Atlantic	*Trichiurus*	3.68 kg	Rio de Janeiro	Sept. 6, 1997	Felipe Ricciulli Soares
	lepturus	8 lb 1 oz	Brazil		
Dab (Kliesche)	*Limanda*	0.57 kg	East Sea, Kappeln	Sept. 20, 1998	Holger Damerius
	limanda	1 lb 4 oz	Germany		
Dentex	*Dentex*	9.85 kg	Cecina	May 21, 1993	Ermini Sergio
	dentex	21 lb 11 oz	Secche DiVada		
Dentex, pink	*Dentex*	13.80 kg	Italy	Apr. 5, 1996	P.A. Dunham
	gibbosus	30 lb 6 oz	Gibraltar		
Doctorfish	*Acanthurus*	0.57 kg	Steson Rock	Apr. 14, 1997	Jerry Dee McCullin
	chirurgus	1 lb 4 oz	Texas, USA		
Dogfish, smooth	*Mustelus*	12.15 kg	Galveston	Mar. 2, 1998	George A. Flores
	canis	26 lb 12 oz	Texas, USA		
Dogfish, spiny	*Squalus*	7.14 kg	Kenmare Bay	May 26, 1989	Horst Willi Muller
	acanthias	15 lb 12 oz	Kerry, Ireland		
Dolly Varden	*Salvelinus*	8.73 kg	Unnamed River	Sept. 4, 1998	Gary D. Ordway
	malma	19 lb 4 oz	Alaska, USA		
Dolphinfish	*Coryphaena*	39.91 kg	Highbourne Cay	May 5, 1998	Richard D. Evans
	hippurus	88 lb 0 oz	Exuma, Bahamas		
Dorado	*Salminus*	23.30 kg	Toledo (Corrientes)	Sept. 27, 1984	Armando Giudice
	maxillosus	51 lb 5 oz	Argentina		
Drum, black	*Pogonias*	51.28 kg	Lewes	Sept. 15, 1975	Gerald M. Townsend
	cromis	113 lb 1 oz	Delaware, USA		
Drum, freshwater	*Aplodinotus*	24.72 kg	Nickajack Lake	Apr. 20, 1972	Benny E. Hull
	grunniens	54 lb 8 oz	Tennessee, USA		
Drum, red	*Sciaenops*	42.69 kg	Avon	Nov. 7, 1984	David G. Deuel
	ocellatus	94 lb 2 oz	North Carolina, USA		
Eel, American	*Anguilla*	4.21 kg	Cape May	Nov. 9, 1995	Jeff Pennick
	rostrata	9 lb 4 oz	New Jersey, USA		
Eel, European (Tie)	*Anguilla*	3.60 kg	River Aare	July 10, 1992	Christoph Lave
	anguilla	7 lb 14 oz	Buren, Switzerland		
Eel, European (Tie)	*Anguilla*	3.59 kg	River Lyckeby	Aug. 8, 1988	Luis Kilian Rasmussen
	anguilla	7 lb 14 oz	Sweden		
Eel, king snake	*Ophichthus*	23.58 kg	Gulf of Mexico	Feb. 11, 1997	Patrick L. Lemire
	rex	52 lb 0 oz	Texas, USA		
Eel, marbled	*Anguilla*	16.36 kg	Hazelmere Dam	June 10, 1984	Ferdie Van Nooten
	marmorata	36 lb 1 oz	Durban, South Africa		
Emperor, longface	*Lethrinus*	4.85 kg	Christmas Island	Oct. 16, 1988	Jeff Konn
	elongatus	10 lb 11 oz	Republic of Kiribati		
Emperor, spangled	*Lethrinus*	8.40 kg	Anijima, Ogasawara Island	Dec. 16, 1996	Osamu Toji
	nebulosus	18 lb 8 oz	Tokyo, Japan		

SPECIES	SCIENTIFIC NAME	WEIGHT	PLACE	DATE	ANGLER
Emperor, yellowlip	*Lethrinus xanthochilus*	5.44 kg 12 lb 0 oz	Lifuka Island Kingdom of Tonga	Nov. 25, 1991	Peter Dunn-Rankin
Escolar	*Lepidocybuim flavobrunneum*	28.50 kg 62 lb 13 oz	El Hiero Spain	Sept. 8, 1996	Joep Stolwyk
Fallfish	*Semotilus corporalis*	1.61 kg 3 lb 8 oz	Lake Winnipesaukee Gilford, New Hampshire, USA	July 12, 1991	John Conti
Filefish, scrawled	*Aluterus scriptus*	2.15 kg 4 lb 11 oz	Pompano Beach Florida, USA	Jan. 20, 1998	Jonathan Mark Angel
Filefish, unicorn	*Aluterus monoceros*	2.71 kg 5 lb 15 oz	Orange Beach Alabama, USA	Mar. 10, 1993	Yvonne Hanek
Flathead, bar-tailed	*Platycephalus indicus*	2.15 kg 4 lb 11 oz	Shirahama Chiba, Japan	Sept. 27, 1992	Yukihiro Inoue
Flathead, dusky	*Platycephalus fuscus*	6.33 kg 13 lb 15 oz	Wallis Lake, Forster N.S.W., Australia	June 7, 1997	Glen Edwards
Flier	*Centrarchus macropterus*	0.56 kg 1 lb 4 oz	Lowndes County Georgia, USA	Feb. 26, 1996	Curt Anthony Brooks
Flier	*Centrarchus macropterus*	0.56 kg 1 lb 4 oz	Little River, Spring Lake North Carolina, USA	Aug. 24, 1988	Dr. R. D. Snipes
Flounder, European	*Platichthys flesus*	1.20 kg 2 lb 10 oz	Bua Harbor Halland County, Sweden	Sept. 3, 1993	Henning Madsen
Flounder, gulf	*Paralichthys albigutta*	2.83 kg 6 lb 4 oz	Dauphin Island Alabama, USA	Nov. 2, 1996	Don Davis
Flounder, olive	*Paralichthys olivaceus*	5.36 kg 11 lb 13 oz	Muroto, Kochi Japan	Aug. 9, 1998	Hiroyuki Nakanishi
Flounder, southern	*Paralichthys lethostigma*	9.33 kg 20 lb 9 oz	Nassau Sound Florida, USA	Dec. 23, 1983	Larenza W. Mungin
Flounder, summer	*Paralichthys dentatus*	10.17 kg 22 lb 7 oz	Montauk New York, USA	Sept. 15, 1975	Charles Nappi
Flounder, winter	*Pleuronectes americanus*	3.17 kg 7 lb 0 oz	Fire Island New York, USA	May 8, 1986	Einar F. Grell
Forkbead	*Phycis phycis*	2.57 kg 5 lb 10 oz	Detached Mole Gibraltar	Apr. 5, 1996	Brian Anthony Soiza
Forkbeard, greater	*Phycis blennoides*	3.54 kg 7 lb 12 oz	Straits of Gibraltar	July 12, 1997	Susan Anne Holgado
Gar, alligator	*Lepisosteus spatula*	126.55 kg 279 lb 0 oz	Rio Grande Texas, USA	Dec. 2, 1951	Bill Valverde
Gar, Florida	*Lepisosteus platyrhincus*	9.61 kg 21 lb 3 oz	Boca Raton Florida, USA	June 3, 1981	Jeff Sabol
Gar, longnose	*Lepisosteus osseus*	22.82 kg 50 lb 5 oz	Trinity River Texas, USA	July 30, 1954	Townsend Miller
Gar, shortnose	*Lepisosteus platostomus*	2.60 kg 5 lb 12 oz	Rend Lake Illinois, USA	July 16, 1995	Donna Willmert
Gar, spotted	*Lepisosteus oculatus*	4.44 kg 9 lb 12 oz	Lake Mexia Mexia, Texas, USA	Apr. 7, 1994	Rick Rivard
Gar, tropical	*Lepisosteus tropicus*	2.89 kg 6 lb 6 oz	Rio Frio Los Chiles, Costa Rica	Nov. 22, 1994	John A. Corry
Garfish	*Belone belone*	0.70 kg 1 lb 8 oz	Detached Mole Gibraltar	Aug. 31, 1997	R.H. Chichon
Geelbek	*Atractoscion aequidens*	14.91 kg 32 lb 14 oz	Algoa Bay, Port Elizabeth South Africa	June 16, 1994	Carel Saunders
Globefish	*Ephippion guttifer*	4.30 kg 9 lb 7 oz	Nouadhibou Mauritania	Mar. 10, 1986	Raphael Levy
Goldeye	*Hiodon alosoides*	1.72 kg 3 lb 13 oz	Pierre South Dakota, USA	Aug. 9, 1987	Gary Wayne Heuer
Goldfish	*Carassius auratus*	3.00 kg 6 lb 10 oz	Lake Hodges California, USA	Apr. 17, 1996	Florentino M. Abena
Goldfish, Asian	*Carassius auratus langsdorfil*	1.14 kg 2 lb 8 oz	Kako River Hyogo, Japan	Oct. 29, 1994	Masahiro Oomori
Goldfish/Carp hybrid	*Carassius auratus x Cyprinus carpio*	1.58 kg 3 lb 8 oz	Cermak Quarry Lyons, Illinois, USA	Aug. 22, 1990	Donald A. Czyzewski
Goosefish	*Lophius americanus*	22.56 kg 49 lb 12 oz	Perkins Cove Ogunquit, Maine, USA	July 9, 1991	Nancy Lee Regimbald
Grayling	*Thymallus thymallus*	1.69 kg 3 lb 11 oz	Dessau Bavaria, Germany	Sept. 12, 1991	Jean-Paul Pequegnot
Grayling, Arctic	*Thymallus arcticus*	2.69 kg 5 lb 15 oz	Katseyedie River N.W.T., Canada	Aug. 16, 1967	Jeanne P. Branson
Graysby	*Cephalopholis cruentata*	1.13 kg 2 lb 8 oz	Stetson Rock Texas, USA	Mar. 2, 1998	George A. Flores
Greenling, fat (ainame)	*Hexagrammos otaki*	2.41 kg 5 lb 5 oz	Todogasaki, Iwate, Japan	Dec. 29, 1997	Akira Tazawa
Greenling, kelp	*Hexagrammos decagrammus*	1.42 kg 3 lb 2 oz	Rivers Inlet British Columbia, Canada	June 23, 1990	Dave Vedder
Greenling, rock	*Hexagrammos lagocephalus*	0.83 kg 1 lb 13 oz	Adak Alaska, USA	Aug. 15, 1988	George D. Cornish
Grenadier, roundnose	*Coryphaenoides rupestris*	1.69 kg 3 lb 11 oz	Trondheimsfjorden Norway	Nov. 26, 1993	Knut Nilsen

SPECIES	SCIENTIFIC NAME	WEIGHT	PLACE	DATE	ANGLER
Grouper, black	*Mycteroperca bonaci*	51.71 kg 114 lb 0 oz	Galveston Texas, USA	Jan. 2, 1997	Stanely W. Sweet
Grouper, blue & yellow	*Epinephelus flavocaeruleus*	3.60 kg 7 lb 14 oz	Sardunia Bay Port Elizabeth, South Africa	Mar. 22, 1995	Mario Enzio Bruno
Grouper, broomtail	*Mycteroperca xenarcha*	40.37 kg 89 lb 0 oz	El Muerto Island Ecuador	June 20, 1997	Jorge Jurado
Grouper, convict	*Epinephelus septemfasciatus*	62.80 kg 138 lb 7 oz	Amamioshima Kagoshima, Japan	Sept. 24, 1997	Shinichi Tsurumi
Grouper, dusky	*Epinephelus marginatus*	21.25 kg 46 lb 13 oz	Porto Cervo Sardinia, Italy	Nov. 15, 1990	Luca Bonfanti
Grouper, gag	*Mycteroperca microlepis*	36.46 kg 80 lb 6 oz	Gulf of Mexico, Destin Florida, USA	Oct. 14, 1993	Bill Smith
Grouper, giant	*Mycteroperca lanceolatus*	119.00 kg 263 lb 7 oz	Anguruki Creek Groote Eylandt, N.T., Australia	Sept. 9, 1988	Peter C. Norris
Grouper, goldblotch	*Epinephelus costae*	1.35 kg 2 lb 15 oz	Detached Mole Gibraltar	Apr. 9, 1995	Joseph Anthony Triay
Grouper, gulf	*Mycteroperca jordani*	50.30 kg 110 lb 14 oz	Uncle Sam Bank Baja California, Mexico	Oct. 24, 1996	Donnie L. Smith
Grouper, Hawaiian	*Epinephelus quernus*	10.65 kg 23 lb 8 oz	Midway Island	July 27, 1998	George Handgis
Grouper, Hong Kong	*Epinephelus akaara*	1.05 kg 2 lb 5 oz	Kyuroku Island Aomori, Japan	Aug. 1, 1997	Shoji Sakuri
Grouper, leopard	*Mycteroperca rosacea*	9.64 kg 21 lb 4 oz	Cabo San Lucas Baja California, Mexico	July 11, 1995	Jeff Klassen
Grouper, longtooth	*Epinephelus bruneus*	33.00 kg 72 lb 12 oz	Hachijo Island Tokyo, Japan	July 16, 1998	Yasuhiko Nagasaka
Grouper, Malabar	*Epinephelus malabaricus*	10.00 kg 22 lb 0 oz	Emerald River N.T., Australia	Mar. 8, 1987	Andrew Brelsford
Grouper, marbled	*Dermatolepis inermis*	4.77 kg 10 lb 8 oz	Gulf of Mexico Galveston, Texas, USA	Aug. 11, 1998	Adolf Schulz
Grouper, mottled	*Mycteroperca rubra*	49.70 kg 109 lb 9 oz	East Side Gibraltar	Aug. 13, 1996	Albert Peralta
Grouper, moustache	*Epinephelus chabaudi*	55.00 kg 121 lb 3 oz	Desroches Island Seychelles	Jan. 1, 1998	Charles-Antoine Roucayrol
Grouper, Nassau	*Epinephelus striatus*	17.46 kg 38 lb 8 oz	Bimini Bahamas	Feb. 14, 1994	Lewis Goodman
Grouper, olive	*Epinephelus cifuentesi*	22.31 kg 49 lb 3 oz	Clarion Island Baja California, Mexico	Apr. 18, 1994	Norman Y. Taniguchi
Grouper, red	*Epinephelus morio*	19.16 kg 42 lb 4 oz	St. Augustine Florida, USA	Mar. 9, 1997	Del Wiseman, Jr.
Grouper, snowy	*Epinephelus niveatus*	10.43 kg 23 lb 0 oz	Miami Florida, USA	Oct. 10, 1993	Julio A. Mila
Grouper, speckled blue	*Epinephelus cyanopodus*	16.30 kg 35 lb 14 oz	Chichijima, Ogasawara Tokyo, Japan	Apr. 10, 1998	Takeshi Uesugi
Grouper, spotted (cabrilla)	*Epinephelus analogus*	22.31 kg 49 lb 3 oz	Cedros/Natividad Islands Baja California, Mexico	Nov. 18, 1990	Barry T. Morita
Grouper, tiger	*Mycteroperca tigris*	6.57 kg 14 lb 8 oz	Bimini Bahamas	May 30, 1993	Michael John Meeker
Grouper, Warsaw	*Epinephelus nigritus*	198.10 kg 436 lb 12 oz	Gulf of Mexico Destin, Florida, USA	Dec. 22, 1985	Steve Haeusler
Grouper, white	*Epinephelus aeneus*	6.85 kg 15 lb 1 oz	Dakar Senegal	Jan. 24, 1984	Michel Calendini
Grouper, yellowedge	*Mycteroperca veneosa*	18.64 kg 41 lb 1 oz	Gulf of Mexico Destin, Florida, USA	May 24, 1998	Christopher D. Allen
Grouper, yellowfin	*Mycteroperca venenosa*	18.48 kg 40 lb 12 oz	Gulf of Mexico Texas, USA	Nov. 15, 1995	Karl O. Loessin
Grouper, yellowmouth	*Mycteroperca interstitialis*	3.69 kg 8 lb 2 oz	Gulf of Mexico Tampa, Florida, USA	May 4, 1991	Skip Busto
Grunt, burrito	*Anisotremus interruptus*	3.57 kg 7 lb 14 oz	Morro Santo Domingo Baja Norte, Mexico	July 5, 1996	Bryan M. Cupp
Grunt, burro	*Pomadasys crocro*	1.85 kg 4 lb 1 oz	Los Chiles, Rio Fio Costa Rica	Dec. 4, 1995	John A. Corry
Grunt, Pacific roncador	*Pomadasys bayanus*	1.58 kg 3 lb 8 oz	Rio Grande de Terraba Costa Rica	Jan. 28, 1990	Craig Whitehead, MD
Grunt, rubberlip	*Plectorhinchus mediterraneus*	7.92 kg 17 lb 7 oz	Europa Point Gibraltar	Sept. 10, 1996	Michael Berllaque
Grunt, white	*Haemulon plumieri*	2.94 kg 6 lb 8 oz	North Brunswick Georgia, USA	May 6, 1989	J.D. Barnes, Jr.
Grunter, saddle	*Pomadasys maculatus*	3.20 kg 7 lb 0 oz	St. Lucia Republic of South Africa	Dec. 11, 1991	J.J. van Rensburg
Guapote	*Cichlasoma dovii*	5.70 kg 12 lb 9 oz	Laguna Echandi Costa Rica	Apr. 13, 1991	Rick Killgore
Guapote, jaguar	*Cichlasoma managuense*	0.75 kg 1 lb 10 oz	Barro Colorado Costa Rica	Sept. 9, 1997	John C. Taylor

SPECIES	SCIENTIFIC NAME	WEIGHT	PLACE	DATE	ANGLER
Guitarfish, blackchin	*Rhinobatos certiculos*	49.90 kg 110 lb 0 oz	Batanga Gabon	June 11, 1998	Philippe Le Danff
Guitarfish, giant	*Rhynchobatus djeddensis*	54.00 kg 119 lb 0 oz	Bird Island Seychelles	Oct. 9, 1995	Peter Lee
Guitarfish, shovelnose	*Rhinobatos productus*	9.75 kg 21 lb 8 oz	Manhattan Beach California, USA	Sept. 22, 1996	Robert B. Young
Gurnard, flying	*Dactylopterus volitans*	1.81 kg 4 lb 0 oz	Gulf of Mexico Panama City, Florida, USA	June 7, 1986	Vernon Carl Allen
Gurnard, grey	*Eutrigla gurnardus*	0.62 kg 1 lb 5 oz	La Middleground Kattegatt, Sweden	Apr. 20, 1998	Lars Kraemer
Haddock	*Melanogrammus aeglefinus*	6.80 kg 14 lb 15 oz	Saltraumen Germany	Aug. 15, 1997	Heike Neblinger
Hake, gulf	*Urophycis cirratus*	2.54 kg 5 lb 9 oz	Gulf of Mexico Texas, USA	Apr. 16, 1996	Patrick Lemire
Hake, Pacific	*Merluccius productus*	0.98 kg 2 lb 2 oz	Tatoosh Island Washington, USA	June 26, 1988	Steven D. Garnett
Hake, red	*Urophycis chuss*	3.60 kg 7 lb 15 oz	Mud Hole New Jersey, USA	Mar. 23, 1994	Stephen Schauermann
Hake, silver	*Merluccius bilinearis*	2.04 kg 4 lb 8 oz	Perkins Cove Ogunquit, Maine, USA	Aug. 8, 1995	Erik M. Callahan
Hake, white	*Urophycis tenuis*	20.97 kg 46 lb 4 oz	Perkins Cove Ogunquit, Maine, USA	Oct. 26, 1986	John Audet
Halibut, Atlantic	*Hippoglossus hippoglossus*	115.78 kg 255 lb 4 oz	Gloucester Massachusetts, USA	July 28, 1989	Sonny Manley
Halibut, California	*Paralichthys californicus*	24.17 kg 53 lb 4 oz	Santa Rosa Island California, USA	July 7, 1988	Russell J. Harmon
Halibut, Pacific	*Hippoglossus stenolepis*	208.20 kg 459 lb 0 oz	Dutch Harbor Alaska, USA	June 11, 1996	Jack Tragis
Happy, pink	*Sargochromis giardi*	2.45 kg 5 lb 6 oz	Upper Zambezi Zambia, Africa	Aug. 14, 1998	Graham J. Glasspool
Hawkfish, giant	*Cirrhitus rivulatus*	4.16 kg 9 lb 3 oz	Salinas Ecuador	Aug. 21, 1993	Hugo Tobar
Herring, Atlantic	*Clupea harangus*	0.48 kg 1 lb 1 oz	Magnolia Pier Long Beach, New York, USA	Apr. 17, 1995	John Boesenberg
Herring, skipjack	*Alosa chrysochloris*	1.70 kg 3 lb 12 oz	Watts Bar Lake Kingston, Tennessee, USA	Feb. 14, 1982	Paul D. Goddard
Hind, red	*Epinephelus guttatus*	2.74 kg 6 lb 1 oz	Dry Tortugas Florida, USA	Jan. 23, 1993	Mark Johnson
Hind, rock	*Epinephelus adscensionis*	4.08 kg 9 lb 0 oz	Ascension Island South Atlantic	Apr. 25, 1994	William F. Kleinfelder
Hind, speckled	*Epinephelus drummondhayi*	23.81 kg 52 lb 8 oz	Destin Florida, USA	Oct. 21, 1994	Russell George Perry
Hogfish	*Lachnolaimus maximus*	8.84 kg 19 lb 8 oz	Daytona Beach Florida, USA	Apr. 28, 1962	Robert E. Batson
Hottentot	*Pachymetopon blochii*	1.70 kg 3 lb 12 oz	Cape Point Republic of South Africa	May 28, 1989	Byron Ashington
Houndfish	*Tylosurus crocodilus*	3.34 kg 7 lb 6 oz	Victory Reef Bahamas	June 22, 1998	Rick Lundell
Houndfish, Mexican	*Tylosurus crocodilus fodiator*	9.86 kg 21 lb 12 oz	Cabo San Lucas Baja California Sur, Mexico	Aug. 10, 1993	John J. Kovacevich
Huchen	*Hucho hucho*	34.80 kg 76 lb 11 oz	Gemeinde Spittal/Drau Osterreich (Austria)	Feb. 19, 1985	Hans Offermanns
Huchen, Japanese	*Hucho perryi*	3.35 kg 7 lb 6 oz	Poronuma Hokkaido, Japan	May 23, 1998	Takashi Yamada
Ide	*Leuiscus idus*	2.87 kg 6 lb 5 oz	Grangshammaran, Borlange Sweden	June 27, 1998	Sonny Pettersson
Inconnu	*Stenodus leucichthys*	24.04 kg 53 lb 0 oz	Pah River Alaska, USA	Aug. 20, 1986	Lawrence E. Hudnall
Jack, almaco (Atlantic)	*Seriola rivoliana*	35.38 kg 78 lb 0 oz	Argus Bank Bermuda	July 11, 1990	Joey Dawson
Jack, almaco (Pacific)	*Seriola rivoliana*	59.87 kg 132 lb 0 oz	La Paz Baja California, Mexico	July 21, 1964	Howard H. Hahn
Jack, black	*Caranx lugubris*	17.94 kg 39 lb 9 oz	Isla Roca Partida Revillagigedo Islands, Mexico	Apr. 13, 1995	Calvin R. Sheets
Jack, cornish	*Mormyrops anguilloides*	11.25 kg 24 lb 12 oz	Zambezi River Zambia	Aug. 24, 1996	Pieter Willem Jacobsz
Jack, cottonmouth	*Uraspis secunda*	2.04 kg 4 lb 8 oz	Cat Island Bahama	May 17, 1991	Linda R. Cook
Jack, crevalle	*Caranx hippos*	26.25 kg 57 lb 14 oz	Southwest Pass Louisiana, USA	Aug. 15, 1997	Leon D. Richard
Jack, horse-eye	*Caranx latus*	13.38 kg 29 lb 8 oz	Ascencion Island South Atlantic Ocean	May 28, 1993	Mike Hanson
Jack, island	*Caranx orthogrammus*	6.61 kg 14 lb 9 oz	Oahu Hawaii, USA	Jan. 2, 1995	Alex Ancheta
Jack, mangrove	*Lutjanus argentimaculatus*	8.70 kg 19 lb 2 oz	Fish Rock, N.S.W. Australia	Apr. 22, 1994	Ken Lyons

SPECIES	SCIENTIFIC NAME	WEIGHT	PLACE	DATE	ANGLER
Jack, Pacific crevalle	*Caranx caninus*	14.06 kg 31 lb 0 oz	Playa Zancudo Costa Rica	Dec. 17, 1997	Roy Ventura Roig
Jack, yellow	*Caranx bartholomaei*	8.81 kg 19 lb 7 oz	Alligator Light Islamorada, Florida, USA	Sept. 14, 1985	Peter Lee Ernst
Janamecem	*Crenecichla spp.*	1.38 kg 3 lb 1 oz	Cuibara River Mato Grosso, Brazil	Aug. 12, 1996	Sandy Blum
Jandia	*Rhamdia sebae*	4.02 kg 8 lb 14 oz	St. Benedicto River Brazil	Aug. 17, 1996	Rogerio E. Cabral de Menezes
Jau	*Paulicea luetkeni*	25.00 kg 55 lb 1 oz	Mato Grosso Piguiri River, Brazil	Apr. 16, 1998	Romulo Coutinho
Jawfish, finespotted	*Opistognathus punctatus*	1.13 kg 2 lb 8 oz	Turner Island Sonora, Mexico	June 11, 1988	Lorna R. Garrod
Jewfish	*Epinephelus itajara*	308.44 kg 680 lb 0 oz	Fernandina Beach Florida, USA	May 20, 1961	Lynn Joyner
Jobfish, green	*Aprion virescens*	13.70 kg 30 lb 1 oz	Amami Oshima Kagoshima, Japan	July 12, 1998	Kei Hiramatsu
Jobfish, lavender	*Pristipomoides sieboldii*	8.40 kg 18 lb 8 oz	Chichijima, Ogasawara Tokyo, Japan	Apr. 5, 1998	Yusuke Nakamura
Jurupoca	*Hemisorubim platyrhynchos*	1.47 kg 3 lb 4 oz	Caceres, Paraguai River Brazil	Sept. 9, 1996	Alacyr Beghini de Moraes
Kahawai (Australian salmon)	*Arripis trutta*	8.74 kg 19 lb 4 oz	Currarong Australia	Apr. 9, 1994	Stephen Muller
Kasago	*Sebastiscus marmoratus*	2.80 kg 6 lb 2 oz	Niijima Tokyo, Japan	June 23, 1996	Osamu Hida
Kawakawa	*Euthynnus affinis*	13.15 kg 29 lb 0 oz	Isla Clarion Revillagigedo Islands, Mexico	Dec. 17, 1986	Ronald Nakamura
Kingfish, northern	*Menticirrhus saxatilis*	0.73 kg 1 lb 10 oz	West End, Long Branch New Jersey, USA	Aug. 5, 1998	Joseph R. Anelli
Kingfish, southern	*Menticirrhus americanus*	0.85 kg 1 lb 14 oz	Dauphin Island Alabama, USA	Sept. 9, 1997	Marcus R. Kennedy
Kob	*Argyrosomus hololepidotus*	54.40 kg 119 lb 14 oz	Knysna Republic of South Africa	Jan. 25, 1988	Colin Stewart Vowles
Kobudai	*Semicossyphus reticulatus*	9.25 kg 20 lb 6 oz	Kyuroku Island Aomori, Japan	Aug. 1, 1997	Hitoshi Suzuki
Kokanee	*Oncorhynchus nerka*	4.27 kg 9 lb 6 oz	Okanagan Lake Vernon, B.C., Canada	June 18, 1988	Norm Kuhn
Ladyfish	*Elops saurus*	2.72 kg 6 lb 0 oz	Loxahatchee River Jupiter, Florida, USA	Dec. 20, 1997	Michael Baz
Ladyfish, Senegalese	*Elops senegalensis*	5.90 kg 12 lb 9 oz	Guinea-Bissau Bijagos Isles	Apr. 12, 1994	Gerard Cittadini
Ladyfish, springer	*Elops machnata*	10.80 kg 23 lb 12 oz	Ilha do Bazaruio Mozambique	Oct. 28, 1993	Zaqueu Paulo
Largemouth, humpback	*Serranochromis altus*	3.30 kg 7 lb 4 oz	Tiger Camp Zambezi River, Zambezi	Aug. 23, 1996	Colin Snyman
Lates, forktail	*Lates microlepis*	8.30 kg 18 lb 4 oz	Lake Tanganyika Zambia	Dec. 1, 1987	Steve Robinson
Lates, Japanese (akame)	*Lates japonicus*	33.00 kg 72 lb 12 oz	Shimanto River Kochi, Japan	May 31, 1996	Yoshio Murasaki
Lau lau (piraiba)	*Brachyplatystoma filamentosum*	116.40 kg 256 lb 9 oz	Solimoes River Amazon, Brazil	Apr. 3, 1981	Gilberto Fernandes
Leatherjack, longjaw	*Oligoplites altus*	1.58 kg 3 lb 8 oz	Playa Zancudo Costa Rica	May 27, 1995	Craig Whitehead, MD
Leatherjack, longjaw	*Oligoplites altus*	1.58 kg 3 lb 8 oz	Rio Coto Puntarenas, Costa Rica	Feb. 6, 1990	Craig Whitehead, MD
Leerfish (Garrick)	*Lichia amia*	24.80 kg 54 lb 10 oz	Nice France	Jan. 20, 1997	Dominique Loiseau
Lenok	*Brachymystax lenok*	2.45 kg 5 lb 6 oz	Maya River Siberia, Russia	Sept. 13, 1992	Hakan Brugard
Ling, blue	*Molva dypterygia*	16.05 kg 35 lb 6 oz	Trondheimsfjorden Norway	Nov. 23, 1993	Oyvind Braa
Ling, European	*Molva molva*	37.20 kg 82 lb 0 oz	Langesund Norway	May 4, 1993	Peter Arvidsson
Lingcod	*Ophiodon elongatus*	31.29 kg 69 lb 0 oz	Langara Island British Columbia, Canada	June 16, 1992	Murray M. Romer
Lizardfish, inshore (Tie)	*Synodus foetens*	0.90 kg 2 lb 0 oz	Boca Grande Florida, USA	Oct. 25, 1994	Robert L. Hill, Jr.
Lizardfish, inshore (Tie)	*Synodus foetens*	0.90 kg 2 lb 0 oz	Bellair Shores Florida, USA	Nov. 17, 1990	Todd Staley
Lookdown	*Selene vomer*	2.10 kg 4 lb 10 oz	Angra dos Reis, Rio de Janeiro, Brazil	Nov. 11, 1993	Adolpho A. Mayer Neto
Lord, Red Irish	*Hemilepidotus hemilepidotus*	1.11 kg 2 lb 7 oz	Depoe Bay Oregon, USA	Apr. 26, 1992	Ronald L. Chatham
Machaca	*Brycon guatemalensis*	4.32 kg 9 lb 8 oz	Barra del Colorado Costa Rica	Nov. 24, 1991	Barbara Ann Fields
Mackerel, Atlantic	*Scomber scombrus*	1.20 kg 2 lb 10 oz	Kraakvaag Fjord Norway	June 29, 1992	Jorge Marquard

SPECIES	SCIENTIFIC NAME	WEIGHT	PLACE	DATE	ANGLER
Mackerel, broadbarred	*Scomberomorus semifasciatus*	9.30 kg 20 lb 8 oz	The Patch, Dampier Australia	June 12, 1997	Tammy Denise Yates
Mackerel, cero	*Scomberomorus regalis*	7.76 kg 17 lb 2 oz	Islamorada Florida, USA	Apr. 5, 1986	G. Michael Mills
Mackerel, chub	*Scomber japonicus*	2.17 kg 4 lb 12 oz	Guadalupe Island Mexico	June 5, 1986	Roy R. Ludt
Mackerel, frigate	*Auxis thazard*	1.72 kg 3 lb 12 oz	Hat Head, N.S.W. Australia	Apr. 17, 1998	Glen Beers
Mackerel, king	*Scomberomorus cavalla*	40.82 kg 90 lb 0 oz	Key West Florida, USA	Feb. 16, 1976	Norton I. Thomton
Mackerel, narrowbarred	*Scomberomorus commerson*	44.90 kg 99 lb 0 oz	Scottburgh, Natal Republic of South Africa	Mar. 14, 1982	Michael John Wilkinson
Mackerel, Pacific sierra (Tie)	*Scomberomorus sierra*	8.16 kg 18 lb 0 oz	Salinas Ecuador	Sept. 15, 1990	Luis Alberto Flores A.
Mackerel, Pacific sierra (Tie)	*Scomberomorus sierra*	8.16 kg 18 lb 0 oz	Isla de la Plata Ecuador	Mar. 24, 1990	Jorge Begue W.
Mackerel, shark	*Grammatorcynus bicarinatus*	12.30 kg 27 lb 1 oz	Bribie Island, Brisbane Queensland, Australia	Mar. 24, 1989	Kathy Maguire
Mackerel, Spanish	*Scomberomorus maculatus*	5.89 kg 13 lb 0 oz	Ocracoke Inlet North Carolina, USA	Nov. 4, 1987	Robert Cranton
Mackerel, west African Spanish	*Scomberomorus tritor*	4.98 kg 11 lb 0 oz	Ada Ghana	July 30, 1995	E. Leon Buckles
Madai	*Pagrus major*	9.72 kg 21 lb 6 oz	Kouzu Island Tokyo, Japan	Aug. 18, 1998	Yoshiaki Nakajima
Mahseer	*Tor tor*	43.09 kg 95 lb 0 oz	Cauvery River India	Mar. 26, 1984	Robert Howitt
Manduba	*Ageneiosus brevifilis*	2.35 kg 5 lb 3 oz	Caceres, Paraguai River Brazil	Sept. 11, 1996	Cicero I. Kurtz Filho
Margate, black	*Anisotremus surinamensis*	5.78 kg 12 lb 12 oz	Ft. Pierce Inlet Florida, USA	May 28, 1994	Carol Napierala
Margate, white	*Haemulon album*	7.14 kg 15 lb 12 oz	Reef Point, San Pedro Ambergris Cay, Belize	Feb. 14, 1996	Carol Barrows
Marlin, black	*Makaira indica*	707.61 kg 1560 lb 0 oz	Cabo Blanco Peru	Aug. 4, 1953	Alfred C. Glassell, Jr.
Marlin, blue (Atlantic)	*Makaira nigricans*	636.00 kg 1402 lb 2 oz	Vitoria Brazil	Feb. 29, 1992	Paulo Roberto A. Amorim
Marlin, blue (Pacific)	*Makaira nigricans*	624.14 kg 1376 lb 0 oz	Kaaiwi Pt. Kona, Hawaii, USA	May 31, 1982	Jay Wm. de Beaubien
Marlin, striped	*Tetrapturus audax*	224.10 kg 494 lb 0 oz	Tutukaka New Zealand	Jan. 16, 1986	Bill Boniface
Marlin, white	*Tetrapturus albidus*	82.50 kg 181 lb 14 oz	Vitoria Brazil	Dec. 8, 1979	Evandro Luiz Coser
Matrincha (Tie)	*Brycon hilarii*	3.31 kg 7 lb 5 oz	Sao Benedicto River Para, Brazil	Apr. 26, 1997	Luiz Carlos Nolasco
Matrincha (Tie)	*Brycon hilarii*	3.36 kg 7 lb 6 oz	Rio Arinos Brazil	Sept. 3, 1997	Marcio Mattos Borges de Oliveira
Mcheni/lake tiger	*Rhamphochromis spp.*	0.65 kg 1 lb 6 oz	Maleri Islands Lake Malawi, Malawi	May 31, 1997	Brendon Garry Whitcher
Meagre	*Argyrosomus regius*	48.00 kg 105 lb 13 oz	Nouadhibou Mauritania	Mar. 30, 1986	Laurent Morat
Mebaru	*Sebastes inermis*	0.67 kg 1 lb 7 oz	Koshigoe Port Kanagawa, Japan	June 4, 1998	Yusuke Furuta
Medai (Japanese butterfish)	*Hyperoglyphe japonica*	7.75 kg 17 lb 1 oz	Ashizuri, Kochi Japan	July 12, 1998	Akira Sato
Menada	*Liza haematocheila*	3.40 kg 7 lb 8 oz	Hanami RIver Chiba City, Chiba, Japan	Aug. 20, 1995	Kazuyoshi Nagasawa
Mihara-hanadai	*Giganthias immaculatus*	1.00 kg 2 lb 3 oz	Irozaki, Shizuoka Japan	Aug. 13, 1998	Mikio Suzuki
Milkfish	*Chanos chanos*	11.11 kg 24 lb 8 oz	Hilo Bay Hilo, Hawaii, USA	Aug. 25, 1991	Rory Tokeshi
Mojarra, striped	*Diapterus plumieri*	1.02 kg 2 lb 4 oz	West Palm Beach Florida, USA	Aug. 21, 1987	James B. Black, Jr.
Monkfish, European(angelshark)	*Squatina squatina*	25.96 kg 57 lb 4 oz	Fenit, Tralee Bay County Kerry, Ireland	May 20, 1989	Jim Dooley
Mooneye	*Hiodon tergisus*	0.56 kg 1 lb 3 oz	Rainy River Ontario, Canada	May 28, 1994	Marguarette Vaughan
Moray, blacktail	*Gymnothorax kolpos*	1.09 kg 2 lb 6 oz	Gulf of Mexico Texas, USA	Mar. 24, 1998	George A. Flores
Moray, green	*Gymnothorax funebris*	15.19 kg 33 lb 8 oz	Marathon Keys Florida, USA	Mar. 15, 1997	Rene De Dios
Moray, purplemouth	*Gymnothorax vicinus*	0.75 kg 1 lb 10 oz	Port Everglades Reef Florida, USA	June 19, 1998	Rene G. De Dios
Moray, slender giant	*Thyrsoidea macrura*	5.35 kg 11 lb 12 oz	St. Lucia Republic of South Africa	Aug. 29, 1987	Graham Vollmer
Moray, viper	*Enchelycore nigricans*	1.32 kg 2 lb 14 oz	Fowey Light Florida, USA	May 25, 1998	Rene G. De Dios

SPECIES	SCIENTIFIC NAME	WEIGHT	PLACE	DATE	ANGLER
Mullet, hog	*Joturus pichardi*	3.25 kg 7 lb 2 oz	Rio Sarapiqui Costa Rica	Aug. 9, 1995	Carlos M. Barrantes R.
Mullet, striped	*Mugil cephalus cephalus*	3.14 kg 6 lb 15 oz	Hanami River Chiba City, Chiba, Japan	Sept. 4, 1995	Makoto Hanaki
Mullet, thicklip (Tie)	*Chelon labrosus*	3.52 kg 7 lb 12 oz	Zuid Pier Ymudien	Aug. 20, 1996	Frits Kromhout vander Meer
Mullet, thicklip (Tie)	*Chelon labrosus*	3.48 kg 7 lb 11 oz	Barseback Sweden	Mar. 16, 1991	Bengt Olsson
Mullet, thinlip	*Liza ramada*	2.38 kg 5 lb 4 oz	River Taw Barnstaple, England	June 14, 1984	Raymond John White
Muskellunge	*Esox masquinongy*	30.60 kg 67 lb 8 oz	Lake Court Oreilles Hayward, Wisconsin, USA	July 24, 1949	Cal Johnson
Muskellunge, tiger	*Esox masquinongy x Esox lucius*	23.21 kg 51 lb 3 oz	Lac Vieux-Desert Wisconsin/ Michigan., USA	July 16, 1919	John A. Knobla
Musselcracker, black	*Cymatoceps nasutus*	32.20 kg 70 lb 15 oz	Richards Bay South Africa	Aug. 25, 1996	John Rex Harvey
Needlefish, Agujon	*Tylosurus acus*	3.71 kg 8 lb 3 oz	Nags Head North Carolina, USA	Aug. 31, 1986	Keith Tongier
Needlefish, Atlantic	*Strongylura marina*	1.47 kg 3 lb 4 oz	Brigantine New Jersey, USA	July 18, 1990	Charlie Trost
Needlefish, flat	*Ablennes hians*	4.80 kg 10 lb 9 oz	Zavora Mozambique	Dec. 25, 1997	Leon Paul deBeer
Nembwe	*Serranochromis robustus*	3.00 kg 6 lb 9 oz	Tiger Camp Zambezi River, Zambia	Aug. 28, 1994	Skip Nielsen
Oilfish	*Ruvettus pretiosus*	63.50 kg 139 lb 15 oz	White Island New Zealand	Apr. 12, 1986	Tim Wallace
Opah	*Lampris guttatus*	73.93 kg 163 lb 0 oz	Port San Luis Obispo California, USA	Oct. 8, 1998	Thomas R. Foran
Oscar	*Astronotus ocellatus*	1.36 kg 3 lb 3 oz	Snake Creek Channel Florida, USA	Nov. 1, 1993	Carlos Rodriguez
Otolithe	*Pseudotolithus brachygnathus*	11.34 kg 25 lb 0 oz	Bijagos Guinea-Bissau	Apr. 19, 1995	Ernest Lopez
Oxeye	*Megalops cyprinoides*	1.67 kg 3 lb 10 oz	Amami Oshima Kagoshima, Japan	July 19, 1998	Yuichiro Kawabata
Pacu	*Colossoma spp.*	9.58 kg 21 lb 2 oz	Parana River Paso de la Patria, Argentina	Jan. 3, 1993	Ken Bohling
Pacu, black	*Colossoma brachypomum*	12.81 kg 28 lb 4 oz	Pompano Beach Florida, USA	Jan. 12, 1998	James L. Cohen, Sr.
Palometa	*Trachinotus goodei*	0.55 kg 1 lb 3 oz	Bimini Bahamas	Feb. 3, 1991	Dan Kipnis
Pandora	*Pagellus erythrinus*	3.24 kg 7 lb 2 oz	Monte Gordo Portugal	May 16, 1996	Geoff Flores
Parrotperch, Japanese	*Oplegnathus fasciatus*	6.40 kg 14 lb 1 oz	Hatusima, Sizuoka Japan	Sept. 11, 1993	Yoshikatu Higuchi
Parrotperch, spotted	*Oplegnathus punctatus*	12.08 kg 26 lb 10 oz	Hachijo Island Tokyo, Japan	May 5, 1978	Tsunehisa Kanayama
Payara	*Hydrolicus scomberoides*	17.80 kg 39 lb 4 oz	Uraima Falls Venezuela	Feb. 10, 1996	Bill Keeley
Peacock, blackstriped	*Cichla intermedia*	1.50 kg 3 lb 4 oz	Rio Cinaruco Estado Apure, Venezuela	Mar. 3, 1995	Carlos Aristeguieta L.
Peacock, butterfly	*Cichla ocellaris*	4.76 kg 10 lb 8 oz	Rio Branco Raraima, Brazil	Mar. 21, 1994	Larry Larsen
Peacock, speckled	*Cichla temensis*	12.24 kg 27 lb 0 oz	Rio Negro Brazil	Dec. 4, 1994	Gerald "Doc" Lawson
Pellona, Amazon	*Pellona castelneana*	6.15 kg 13 lb 8 oz	Cuara River Edo Bolivar, Venezuela	Oct. 28, 1997	Carlos Aristeguieta L.
Perch, European	*Perca fluviatilis*	1.50 kg 3 lb 4 oz	Eidsvoll Norway	June 13, 1998	Johnny Hogli
Perch, Nile	*Lates niloticus*	96.61 kg 213 lb 0 oz	Lake Nasser Egypt	Dec. 18, 1997	Adrian Brayshaw
Perch, Sacramento	*Archoplites interruptus*	1.44 kg 3 lb 3 oz	Crowley Lake California, USA	Sept. 22, 1995	Richard J. Fischer
Perch, white	*Morone americana*	2.15 kg 4 lb 12 oz	Messalonskee Lake Maine, USA	June 4, 1949	Earl Small
Perch, yellow	*Perca flavescens*	1.91 kg 4 lb 3 oz	Bordentown New Jersey, USA	May, 1865	Dr. C. C. Abbot
Permit	*Trachinotus falcatus*	25.45 kg 56 lb 2 oz	Ft. Lauderdale Florida, USA	June 30, 1997	Thomas Sebestyen
Piau	*Leporinus piau*	0.62 kg 1 lb 6 oz	Sao Francisco River Minas Gerais, Brazil	Aug. 18, 1993	Tobias Rothier
Pickerel, chain	*Esox niger*	4.25 kg 9 lb 6 oz	Homerville Georgia, USA	Feb. 17, 1961	Baxley McQuaig, Jr.
Pickerel, grass	*Esox americanus vermiculatus*	0.45 kg 1 lb 0 oz	Dewart Lake Indiana, USA	June 9, 1990	Mike Berg
Pickerel, redfin	*Esox americanus americanus*	1.02 kg 2 lb 4 oz	Gall Berry Swamp St. Pauls, North Carolina, USA	June 27, 1997	Edward C. Davis

SPECIES	SCIENTIFIC NAME	WEIGHT	PLACE	DATE	ANGLER
Pike, northern	*Esox lucius*	25.00 kg 55 lb 1 oz	Lake of Grefeern Germany	Oct. 16, 1986	Lothar Louis
Pike-conger, common	*Muraenesox bagio*	7.10 kg 15 lb 10 oz	Markham River, LAE Huon Gulf, Papua, New Guinea	Mar. 7, 1993	Barry Mallett
Pinook (Tie)	*Oncorhynchus gorbuscha x tshawytscha*	6.58 kg 14 lb 8 oz	Garden River, Sault Ste Marie Ontario, Canada	Sept. 22, 1997	Scott R. Smith
Pinook (Tie)	*Oncorhynchus gorbuscha x tshawytscha*	6.57 kg 14 lb 8 oz	Garden River Sault Ste Marie, Canada	Sept. 23, 1997	Larry Cory
Piranha, black	*Pygocentrus piraya*	3.17 kg 6 lb 15 oz	Rio Autana Venezuela	Feb. 27, 1995	Alejandro Mata
Piranha, black spot	*Pygocentrus cariba*	0.56 kg 1 lb 4 oz	Hato Cedral Apure, Venezuela	Jan. 18, 1991	William T. Miller
Piranha, Manualis	*Serrasalmus manueli*	2.15 kg 4 lb 12 oz	Rio Cinaruco Venezuela	Jan. 12, 1998	Eric Ostmark
Piranha, red	*Serrasalmus nattereri*	1.55 kg 3 lb 7 oz	Cuiaba River Brazil	July 9, 1994	H. Lauren Siegel
Piraputanga	*Brycon orbignyanus*	0.62 kg 1 lb 6 oz	Mato Grosso Piguiri River, Brazil	Apr. 16, 1998	Helder Coutinho
Pirarucu	*Arapaima gigas*	67.13 kg 148 lb 0 oz	Rupununi River Karanambu, Guyana	Apr. 1, 1953	Ed Migdalski
Pollack, European	*Pollachius pollachius*	12.41 kg 27 lb 6 oz	Salcombe Devon, England	Jan. 16, 1986	Robert Samuel Milkins
Pollock	*Pollachius virens*	22.70 kg 50 lb 0 oz	Salstraumen Norway	Nov. 30, 1995	Thor-Magnus Lekang
Pompano, African	*Alectis ciliaris*	22.90 kg 50 lb 8 oz	Daytona Beach Florida, USA	Apr. 21, 1990	Tom Sargent
Pompano, Florida	*Trachinotus carolinus*	3.67 kg 8 lb 1 oz	Flagler Beach Florida, USA	Mar. 19, 1984	Chester E. Dietrick
Pompano, gafftopsail	*Trachinotus rhodopus*	1.30 kg 2 lb 14 oz	Cabo San Lucas Mexico	Apr. 16, 1997	Bruce Coale
Porcupinefish	*Diodon hystrix*	2.80 kg 6 lb 3 oz	Oakhill Florida, USA	May 22, 1997	Bill Whipple
Porgy, black (Tie)	*Acanthopagrus schlegeli*	3.20 kg 7 lb 0 oz	West Port Niigata, Japan	Mar. 30, 1992	Yoichi Suzuki
Porgy, black (Tie)	*Acanthopagrus schlegeli*	3.20 kg 7 lb 0 oz	Daisan-kaiho Tokyo Bay, Japan	Mar. 30, 1995	Shigenobu Takahashi
Porgy, bluepointed	*Pagrus caeruleostictus*	9.40 kg 20 lb 11 oz	Europa Point Gibraltar	Mar. 17, 1996	Derek Apap
Porgy, Canary	*Dentex canariensis*	8.06 kg 17 lb 12 oz	Monte Gordo Portugal	July 14, 1997	Joseph Anthony Triay
Porgy, jolthead	*Calumus bajonado*	10.61 kg 23 lb 4 oz	Madeira Beach Florida, USA	Mar. 14, 1990	Harm M. Wilder
Porgy, red	*Pagrus pagrus*	7.72 kg 17 lb 0 oz	Gibraltar	July 12, 1997	Richard Gomila
Powan	*Coregonus lavaretus*	5.39 kg 11 lb 14 oz	Skrabean Nymolla, Sweden	Dec. 15, 1994	Allan Englund
Puffer, oceanic	*Lagocephalus lagocephalus*	3.17 kg 7 lb 0 oz	Sandy Hook New Jersey, USA	Aug. 28, 1991	Jane Lee Jagen
Puffer, smooth	*Lagocephalus laevigatus*	2.99 kg 6 lb 9 oz	Orange Beach Alabama, USA	June 3, 1998	Randall H. Atherton
Puffer, whitespotted	*Arothron hispidus*	2.01 kg 4 lb 7 oz	Iroquois Point Hawaii, USA	Oct. 31, 1992	George D. Cornish
Pumpkinseed	*Lepomis gibbosus*	0.63 kg 1 lb 6 oz	Mexico New York, USA	Apr. 27, 1985	Heather Ann Finch
Queenfish, doublespotted	*Scomberoides lysan*	1.13 kg 2 lb 8 oz	Lifuka Island, Ha-apai Kingdom of Tonga	Nov. 27, 1991	Norbert H. Watanabe
Queenfish, talang	*Scomberoides commersonianus*	15.60 kg 34 lb 6 oz	Daintree River North Queensland, Australia	Oct. 18, 1994	Kim Blackwell
Quillback	*Carpiodes cyprinus*	2.94 kg 6 lb 8 oz	Lake Michigan Indiana, USA	Jan. 15, 1993	Mike Berg
Raven, sea	*Hemitripterus americanus*	1.47 kg 3 lb 4 oz	Manasquan Inlet New Jersey, USA	Jan. 17, 1996	Allan Ristori
Ray, backwater butterfly	*Gymnura natalensis*	82.60 kg 182 lb 1 oz	Knysna Lagoon Republic of South Africa	July 11, 1992	Hilton Gervais
Ray, bat	*Myliobatis californica*	82.10 kg 181 lb 0 oz	Huntington Beach Pier California, USA	June 30, 1978	Bradley A. Dew
Ray, black	*Dasyatis thetidis*	37.50 kg 82 lb 10 oz	Weston Point Bay Newhaven, Australia	Jan. 20, 1993	Peter Ronald Blondell
Ray, blonde	*Raja brachyura*	14.28 kg 31 lb 8 oz	Jersey Channel Islands United Kingdom	Apr. 3, 1989	John Thompson
Ray, bull	*Pteromylaeus bovinus*	36.50 kg 80 lb 7 oz	Nouadhibou Mauritania	Sept. 16, 1986	Pierre Cluck
Ray, bull (Australian)	*Myliobatis australis*	56.50 kg 124 lb 8 oz	Neptune Island, Port Lincoln S.A., Australia	Apr. 13, 1991	Rolf Czabayski
Ray, painted	*Raja microocellata*	4.50 kg 9 lb 15 oz	Jersey Channel Islands, England	Aug. 2, 1988	Andrew R. J. Mitchell

SPECIES	SCIENTIFIC NAME	WEIGHT	PLACE	DATE	ANGLER
Ray, pale	*Raja lintea*	10.85 kg 23 lb 14 oz	South Langesund Norway	May 11, 1995	Per Markusson
Ray, southern fiddler	*Trygonorrhina fasciata*	6.70 kg 14 lb 12 oz	Marion Bay S.A., Australia	Aug. 11, 1990	Marcel Vandergoot
Ray, spiny butterfly	*Gymnura altavela*	60.00 kg 132 lb 4 oz	Nouadhibou Mauritania	May 5, 1984	Robin Michel
Ray, thornback	*Raja clavata*	7.59 kg 16 lb 12 oz	Jersey, Channel Islands United Kingdom	July 11, 1988	John Thompson
Rebeca	*Megalodoras irwini*	2.23 kg 4 lb 15 oz	Xingu River Estado Mato Grosso, Brazil	June 6, 1996	Sergio Roberto Rothier
Redfish (ocean perch)	*Sebastes marinus*	4.69 kg 10 lb 5 oz	Sorvfer Finnmark, Norway	July 16, 1990	Ole-Einar Jakobsen
Redhorse, black	*Moxostoma duquesnei*	1.02 kg 2 lb 4 oz	French Creek Franklin, Pennsylvania, USA	Feb. 22, 1998	Richard E. Faler, Jr.
Redhorse, golden	*Moxostoma erythrurum*	1.85 kg 4 lb 1 oz	French Creek Franklin, Pennsylvania, USA	Feb. 9, 1997	Richard E. Faler, Jr.
Redhorse, greater	*Moxostoma valenciennesi*	4.16 kg 9 lb 3 oz	Salmon River Pulaski, New York, USA	May 11, 1985	Jason A. Wilson
Redhorse, river	*Moxostoma carinatum*	3.96 kg 8 lb 11 oz	Trent River Ontario, Canada	Aug. 6, 1997	Geoff J. Bernado
Redhorse, shorthead	*Moxostoma macrolepidotum*	3.99 kg 8 lb 12 oz	North River Ontario, Canada	May 23, 1988	Bruce E. Johnstone
Redhorse, silver	*Moxostoma anisurum*	5.18 kg 11 lb 7 oz	Plum Creek Wisconsin, USA	May 29, 1985	Neal D.G. Long
Roach	*Rutilus rutilus*	1.84 kg 4 lb 1 oz	Colwick Nottingham, England	June 16, 1975	R. G. Jones
Rockfish, bank	*Sebastes rufus*	1.98 kg 4 lb 6 oz	San Clemente Island California, USA	Feb. 14, 1998	Stephen D. Grossberg
Rockfish, black	*Sebastes melanops*	4.56 kg 10 lb 0 oz	Puget Sound Washington, USA	July 20, 1986	William J. Harris, DDS
Rockfish, blue	*Sebastes mystinus*	3.79 kg 8 lb 6 oz	Whaler's Cove Alaska, USA	July 27, 1994	Dr. John F. Whitaker
Rockfish, canary	*Sebastes pinniger*	4.53 kg 10 lb 0 oz	Westport Washington, USA	May 17, 1986	Terry Rudnick
Rockfish, China	*Sebastes nebulosus*	1.67 kg 3 lb 11 oz	Tatoosh Island Neah Bay, Washington, USA	Aug. 24, 1992	Edward Schultz
Rockfish, copper	*Sebastes caurinus*	2.74 kg 6 lb 1 oz	Mink Bay Alaska, USA	June 17, 1995	Jack. H. Simon
Rockfish, dusky	*Sebastes ciliatus*	1.81 kg 4 lb 0 oz	Kodiak Alaska, USA	Sept. 27, 1997	Sally Magnuson
Rockfish, quillback	*Sebastes maliger*	3.28 kg 7 lb 4 oz	Depoe Bay Oregon, USA	Mar. 18, 1990	Kelly H. Canaday
Rockfish, shortraker	*Sebastes borealis*	16.24 kg 35 lb 13 oz	Ketchikan Alaska, USA	June 28, 1994	Jeffrey A. Hendrickson
Rockfish, silvergray	*Sebastes brevispinis*	0.82 kg 1 lb 13 oz	Yakutat Bay Alaska, USA	June 24, 1998	George Bogen
Rockfish, tiger	*Sebastes nigrocinctus*	2.22 kg 4 lb 14 oz	Depoe Bay Oregon, USA	Sept. 4, 1993	Ronald L. Chatham
Rockfish, vermillion	*Sebastes miniatus*	5.45 kg 12 lb 0 oz	Depoe Bay Oregon, USA	June 2, 1990	Joseph William Lowe
Rockfish, yelloweye	*Sebastes ruberrimus*	15.05 kg 33 lb 3 oz	Dall Island Alaska, USA	Aug. 17, 1995	Tom Fox
Rockfish, yellowtail	*Sebastes flavidus*	2.51 kg 5 lb 8 oz	Cape Flattery Washington, USA	Aug. 28, 1988	Steven D. Garnett
Roosterfish	*Nematistius pectoralis*	51.71 kg 114 lb 0 oz	La Paz Baja California, Mexico	June 1, 1960	Abe Sackheim
Rosefish, blackbelly	*Helicolenus dactylopteras*	1.49 kg 3 lb 4 oz	Hitra Norway	Aug. 12, 1997	Fredrik Meyer
Rudd	*Scardinius erytrophthalmus*	1.58 kg 3 lb 7 oz	Ljungan River Sweden	July 31, 1988	Luis Kilian Rasmussen
Runner, blue	*Caranx crysos*	5.05 kg 11 lb 2 oz	Dauphin Island Alabama, USA	June 28, 1997	Stacey Michele Moiren
Runner, rainbow	*Elagatis bipinnulata*	17.05 kg 37 lb 9 oz	Isla Clarion Revillagigedo Islands, Mexico	Nov. 21, 1991	Tom Pfleger
Sabalo	*Brycon melanopterus*	4.35 kg 9 lb 9 oz	Rio Tambopata Peru	Oct. 10, 1992	James B. Wise, MD
Sailfish, Atlantic	*Istiophorus platypterus*	64.00 kg 141 lb 1 oz	Luanda Angola	Feb. 19, 1994	Alfredo de Sousa Neves
Sailfish, Pacific	*Istiophorus platypterus*	100.24 kg 221 lb 0 oz	Santa Cruz Island Ecuador	Feb. 12, 1947	Carl W. Stewart
Salmon, Atlantic	*Salmo salar*	35.89 kg 79 lb 2 oz	Tana River Norway	1928	Henrik Henriksen
Salmon, chinook	*Oncorhynchus tshawytscha*	44.11 kg 97 lb 4 oz	Kenai River Alaska, USA	May 17, 1985	Les Anderson
Salmon, chum	*Oncorhynchus keta*	15.87 kg 35 lb 0 oz	Edye Pass British Columbia, Canada	July 11, 1995	Todd A. Johansson

SPECIES	SCIENTIFIC NAME	WEIGHT	PLACE	DATE	ANGLER
Salmon, coho	*Oncorhynchus kisutch*	15.08 kg 33 lb 4 oz	Salmon River Pulaski, New York, USA	Sept. 27, 1989	Jerry Lifton
Salmon, pink	*Oncorhynchus gorbuscha*	5.94 kg 13 lb 1 oz	St. Mary's River Ontario, Canada	Sept. 23, 1992	Ray Higaki
Salmon, sockeye	*Oncorhynchus nerka*	6.88 kg 15 lb 3 oz	Kenai River Alaska, USA	Aug. 9, 1987	Stan Roach
Samsonfish	*Seriola hippos*	36.50 kg 80 lb 7 oz	Cape Naturaliste Western Australia	Jan. 31, 1993	Terry Coote
Sandperch, namorado	*Pseudopercis numida*	20.20 kg 44 lb 8 oz	Rio de Janeiro Brazil	Mar. 7, 1998	Eduardo Baumeier
Sauger	*Stizostedion canadense*	3.96 kg 8 lb 12 oz	Lake Sakakawea North Dakota, USA	Oct. 6, 1971	Mike Fischer
Saugeye	*Stizostedion vitreum x S. canadense*	5.63 kg 12 lb 6 oz	Lake Logan Ohio, USA	Mar. 29, 1993	Daniel Louis D'Amore
Sawfish	*Pristis spp.*	403.92 kg 890 lb 8 oz	Fort Amador Canal Zone, Panama	May 26, 1960	Jack D. Wagner
Scabbardfish, silver	*Lepidopus caudatus*	6.40 kg 14 lb 1 oz	Europa Point Gibraltar	July 16, 1995	Ernest Borrell
Scamp	*Mycteroperca phenax*	14.17 kg 29 lb 0 oz	Dauphin Island Alabama, USA	June 2, 1995	Brett Rutledge
Scombrops, Atlantic	*Scombrops oculatus*	9.88 kg 21 lb 12 oz	Bimini Bahamas	July 15, 1997	Doug Olander
Scorpionfish, black	*Scorpaena porcus*	0.87 kg 1 lb 14 oz	Detached Mole Gibraltar	Feb. 3, 1997	Julius Gafan
Scorpionfish, red	*Scorpaena scrofa*	2.96 kg 6 lb 8 oz	Gibraltar	May 30, 1996	Stuart Brown-Giraldi
Scorpionfish, spotted	*Scorpaena plumieri*	1.55 kg 3 lb 7 oz	Angra Dor Reis Bay Rio de Janeiro, Brazil	May 25, 1997	Pedro L.D. Cabral de Menezes
Scup	*Stenotomus chrysops*	2.06 kg 4 lb 9 oz	Nantucket Sound Massachusetts, USA	June 3, 1992	Sonny Richards
Seabass, blackfin	*Lateolabrax latus*	9.10 kg 20 lb 0 oz	Muroto, Kochi Japan	July 13, 1997	Yuji Shimasaki
Seabass, Japanese (suzuki)	*Lateolabrax japonicus*	8.70 kg 19 lb 2 oz	Kano River, Numazu-shi Shizuoka, Japan	Nov. 26, 1988	Yasuaki Ohshio
Seabass, white	*Atractoscion nobilis*	37.98 kg 83 lb 12 oz	San Felipe Mexico	Mar. 31, 1953	Lyal C. Baumgardner
Seabream, black	*Spondyliosoma cantharus*	1.22 kg 2 lb 11 oz	Detached Mole Gibraltar	Jan. 14, 1996	Albert Ward
Seabream, daggerhead	*Chrysoblephus cristiceps*	7.30 kg 16 lb 1 oz	Algora Bay Port Elizabeth, South Africa	Oct. 10, 1993	Eddie De Reuck
Seabream, Okinawa	*Acanthopagrus sivicolus*	2.15 kg 4 lb 11 oz	Amami-oshima Kagoshima, Japan	Apr. 29, 1998	Hidehira Ike
Seabream, redbanded (murudai)	*Pagrus auriga*	3.00 kg 6 lb 9 oz	Nouadhibou Mauritania	Mar. 9, 1986	Serge Bensa
Seabream, Scotsman	*Polysteganus praeorbitalis*	7.80 kg 17 lb 3 oz	St. Lucia Estuary South Africa	Nov. 25, 1994	G.J. Van Der Westhuizen
Seabream, sharpsnout	*Diplodus puntazzo*	1.68 kg 3 lb 11 oz	La Sela Gibraltar Bay, Gibraltar	Nov. 23, 1996	Brian Anthony Soiza
Seabream, white	*Diplodus sargus*	1.84 kg 4 lb 1 oz	Gibraltar Bay Gibraltar	Apr. 28, 1996	Anthony William Loddo
Seabream, yellowfin	*Acanthopagrus latus*	1.50 kg 3 lb 4 oz	Nishinomiya Port Hyogo, Japan	June 1, 1998	Tsunehisa Wake
Seabream, zebra	*Diplodus cervinus cervinus*	2.60 kg 5 lb 11 oz	North Mole Gibraltar Bay	Dec. 31, 1995	Brian Anthony Soiza
Seaperch, spotted scale	*Lutjanus johni*	10.50 kg 23 lb 2 oz	Cairns Queensland, Australia	Mar. 2, 1986	Mac Mankowski
Searobin, striped	*Prionotus evolans*	1.55 kg 3 lb 6 oz	Mt. Sinai, Long Island New York, USA	June 22, 1988	Michael B. Greene, Jr.
Seatrout, sand	*Cynoscion arenarius*	2.78 kg 6 lb 2 oz	Dauphin Island Alabama, USA	May 24, 1997	Steve V. Scoggin
Seatrout, spotted	*Cynoscion nebulosus*	7.92 kg 17 lb 7 oz	Ft. Pierce Florida, USA	May 11, 1995	Craig F. Carson
Seerfish, Australian	*Scomberomorus munroi*	9.25 kg 20 lb 6 oz	South West Rocks N.S.W., Australia	July 5, 1987	Greg Laarkamp
Seerfish, Chinese	*Scomberomorus sinensis*	59.67 kg 131 lb 9 oz	Lema Islands Hong Kong	May 31, 1998	Peter Sprung
Seerfish, kanadi	*Scomberomorus plurilineatus*	12.00 kg 26 lb 7 oz	Mapelane, Zululand Natal, South Africa	July 11, 1997	Daniel J. Van Tonder
Sennet, southern	*Sphyraena picudilla*	0.93 kg 2 lb 1 oz	Lake Worth Florida, USA	Jan. 30, 1988	William J. White, Sr.
Seventy-four	*Polysteganus undulosus*	16.00 kg 35 lb 4 oz	Mapuzi, Transkei Republic of South Africa	Aug. 17, 1985	Nolan Sparg
Shad, American	*Alosa sapidissima*	5.10 kg 11 lb 4 oz	Connecticut River S. Hadley, Massachusetts, USA	May 19, 1986	Bob Thibodo
Shad, gizzard	*Dorosoma cepedianum*	1.98 kg 4 lb 6 oz	Lake Michigan Indiana, USA	Mar. 2, 1996	Mike Berg

SPECIES	SCIENTIFIC NAME	WEIGHT	PLACE	DATE	ANGLER
Shad, Mediterranean	*Alosa fallax nilotica*	0.76 kg 1 lb 10 oz	Ombrone River Grosseto, Italy	Apr. 16, 1994	Marco Sammicheli
Shark, Atlantic sharpnose	*Rhizoprionodon terraenovae*	7.25 kg 16 lb 0 oz	Port Mansfield Texas, USA	Oct. 12, 1994	R. Bruce Shields
Shark, bigeye thresher	*Alopias superciliosus*	363.80 kg 802 lb 0 oz	Tutukaka New Zealand	Feb. 8, 1981	Dianne North
Shark, bignose	*Carcharhinus altimus*	167.80 kg 369 lb 14 oz	Markham River Papua, New Guinea	Oct. 23, 1993	Lester J. Rohrlach
Shark, blackmouth cat	*Galeus melastomus*	1.37 kg 3 lb 0 oz	Mausundvar Trondheim, Norway	Sept. 17, 1994	Per Arne Hagen
Shark, blacknose	*Carcharhinus acronotus*	18.86 kg 41 lb 9 oz	Little River South Carolina, USA	July 30, 1992	Jon-Paul Hoffman
Shark, blacktail	*Carcharhinus wheeleri*	33.70 kg 74 lb 4 oz	Kosi Bay, Zululand Republic of South Africa	May 25, 1987	Trevor Ashington
Shark, blacktip	*Carcharhinus limbatus*	122.75 kg 270 lb 9 oz	Malindi Bay Kenya	Sept. 21, 1984	Jurgen Oeder
Shark, blacktip reef	*Carcharhinus melanopterus*	13.55 kg 29 lb 13 oz	Coco Island Indian Ocean	Oct. 22, 1995	Dr. Joachim Kleidon
Shark, blue	*Prionace glauca*	205.93 kg 454 lb 0 oz	Martha's Vineyard Massachusetts, USA	July 19, 1996	Pete Bergin
Shark, bonnethead	*Sphyrna tiburo*	10.76 kg 23 lb 11 oz	Cumberland Sound Georgia, USA	Aug. 5, 1994	Chad Wood
Shark, bull	*Carcharhinus leucas*	222.26 kg 490 lb 0 oz	Dauphin Island Alabama, USA	Aug. 30, 1986	Phillip Wilson
Shark, Caribbean reef	*Carcharhinus perezi*	69.85 kg 154 lb 0 oz	Molasses Reef Florida, USA	Dec. 29, 1996	Rene G. De Dios
Shark, dusky	*Carcharhinus obscurus*	346.54 kg 764 lb 0 oz	Longboat Key Florida, USA	May 28, 1982	Warren Girle
Shark, great hammerhead	*Sphyrna mokarran*	449.50 kg 991 lb 0 oz	Sarasota Florida, USA	May 30, 1982	Allen Ogle
Shark, Greenland	*Somniosus microcephalus*	775.00 kg 1708 lb 9 oz	Trondheimsfjord Norway	Oct. 18, 1987	Terje Nordtvedt
Shark, gulper	*Centrophorus uyato*	7.34 kg 16 lb 3 oz	Bimini Bahamas	July 15, 1997	Doug Olander
Shark, gummy	*Mustelus antarcticus*	30.80 kg 67 lb 14 oz	Mcloughins Beach Victoria, Australia	Nov. 15, 1992	Neale Blunden
Shark, lemon	*Negaprion brevirostris*	183.70 kg 405 lb 0 oz	Buxton North Carolina, USA	Nov. 23, 1988	Colleen D. Harlow
Shark, leopard	*Triakis semifasciata*	18.42 kg 40 lb 10 oz	Oceanside California, USA	May 13, 1994	Fred Oakley
Shark, narrowtooth	*Carcharhinus brachyurus*	242.00 kg 533 lb 8 oz	Cape Karikari New Zealand	Jan. 9, 1993	Gaye Harrison-Armstrong
Shark, night	*Carcharhinus signatus*	76.65 kg 169 lb 0 oz	Bimini Bahamas	July 13, 1997	Ron Schatman
Shark, nurse	*Ginglymostoma cirratum*	95.25 kg 210 lb 0 oz	Bahia Honda Channel Bridge Florida Keys, USA	Apr. 6, 1997	Rene De Dios
Shark, oceanic whitetip	*Carcharhinus longimanus*	167.37 kg 369 lb 0 oz	San Salvador Bahamas	Jan. 24, 1998	Reid Hodges
Shark, porbeagle	*Lamna nasus*	230.00 kg 507 lb 0 oz	Pentland Firth Caithness, Scotland	Mar. 9, 1993	Christopher Bennet
Shark, sand tiger	*Odontaspis taurus*	158.81 kg 350 lb 2 oz	Charleston Jetty Charleston, South Carolina, USA	Apr. 29, 1993	Mark Thawley
Shark, sandbar	*Carcharhinus plumbeus*	117.93 kg 260 lb 0 oz	Gambia Coast Gambia	Jan. 2, 1989	Paul Delsignore
Shark, scalloped hammerhead	*Sphyrna lewini*	152.40 kg 335 lb 15 oz	Latham Island Tanzania	Dec. 3, 1995	Jack Reece, Q.P.M.
Shark, sevengill	*Notorynchus cepedianus*	32.80 kg 72 lb 4 oz	Weymouth Channel Manukou Harbour, New Zealand	Oct. 23, 1995	Shane Sowerby
Shark, shortfin mako	*Isurus oxyrinchus*	505.76 kg 1115 lb 0 oz	Black River Mauritius	Nov. 16, 1988	Patrick Guillanton
Shark, silky	*Carcharhinus falciformis*	346.00 kg 762 lb 12 oz	Port Stephen's N.S.W., Australia	Feb. 26, 1994	Bryce Robert Henderson
Shark, silvertip	*Carcharhinus albimarginatus*	150.00 kg 330 lb 11 oz	Watamu Kenya	Oct. 22, 1991	Christopher Wood
Shark, sixgilled	*Hexanchus griseus*	485.00 kg 1069 lb 3 oz	Faial Azores	Oct. 18, 1990	Jack Reece
Shark, smallfin gulper	*Centrophorus moluccensis*	2.40 kg 5 lb 4 oz	Lae, Huon Gulf Papua, New Guinea	Feb. 13, 1993	Justin Mallett
Shark, smooth hammerhead	*Sphyrna zygaena*	148.10 kg 326 lb 7 oz	Lachlan Ridge Hawke Bay, New Zealand	Feb. 24, 1994	Tony Hill
Shark, spinner	*Carcharhinus brevipinna*	86.18 kg 190 lb 0 oz	Flagler Beach Florida, USA	Apr. 3, 1986	Mrs. Gladys Prior
Shark, thresher	*Alopias vulpinus*	348.00 kg 767 lb 3 oz	Bay of Islands New Zealand	Feb. 26, 1983	D.L. Hannah
Shark, tiger	*Galeocerdo cuvier*	807.40 kg 1780 lb 0 oz	Cherry Grove South Carolina, USA	June 14, 1964	Walter Maxwell

SPECIES	SCIENTIFIC NAME	WEIGHT	PLACE	DATE	ANGLER
Shark, white	*Carcharodon carcharias*	1208.38 kg 2664 lb 0 oz	Ceduna South Australia	Apr. 21, 1959	Alfred Dean
Shark, whitetip reef	*Triaenodon obesus*	18.25 kg 40 lb 4 oz	Isla Coiba Panama	Aug. 8, 1979	Jack Kamerman
Sharksucker	*Echeneis naucrates*	2.30 kg 5 lb 1 oz	Buso Point Huon Gulf, Papua, New Guinea	Mar. 27, 1994	Barry Mallett
Sheephead, California	*Semicossyphus pulcher*	9.75 kg 21 lb 8 oz	Huntington Beach California, USA	Dec. 2, 1992	Jack Dalla Corte
Sheepshead	*Archosargus probatocephalus*	9.63 kg 21 lb 4 oz	Bayou St. John New Orleans, Louisiana, USA	Apr. 16, 1982	Wayne Desselle
Sierra, Atlantic	*Scomberomorus brasiliensis*	6.10 kg 13 lb 7 oz	Maracaibo Venezuela	May 12, 1985	Edgar C. Jimenez
Skate	*Raja batis*	97.07 kg 214 lb 0 oz	Scapa Flow Orkney, Great Britain	July 16, 1968	Jan A. E. Olsson
Skate, big	*Raja binoculata*	41.27 kg 91 lb 0 oz	Humbolt Bay Eureka, California, USA	Mar. 6, 1993	Scotty A. Krick
Skate, starry	*Raja radiata*	4.25 kg 9 lb 5 oz	Hvasser Norway	Oct. 10, 1982	Knut Hedlund
Skipjack, black	*Euthynnus lineatus*	11.79 kg 26 lb 0 oz	Thetis Bank Baja California, Mexico	Oct. 23, 1991	Clifford K. Hamaishi
Smoothhound, Florida	*Mustelus norrisi*	13.78 kg 30 lb 6 oz	Gulf of Mexico Destin, Florida, USA	Apr. 1, 1992	Stephen L. Wilson
Smoothhound, star-spotted	*Mustelus manazo*	5.72 kg 12 lb 9 oz	Lae, Huon Gulf Papua, New Guinea	Feb. 13, 1993	Justin Mallett
Smoothhound, starry	*Mustelus asterias*	4.76 kg 10 lb 8 oz	Nab Rocks Isle of Wight, England	July 18, 1984	Sylvia M. Steed
Snakehead	*Channa argus*	6.10 kg 13 lb 7 oz	Yazawanuma Yamagata, Japan	May 13, 1990	Kazuhiro Takeda
Snapper (squirefish)	*Pagrus auratus*	17.20 kg 37 lb 14 oz	Mottiti Island New Zealand	Nov. 2, 1992	Mark Hemingway
Snapper, black	*Apsilus dentatus*	3.17 kg 7 lb 0 oz	Little San Salvador Bahamas	Apr. 24, 1992	Donald E. May
Snapper, blackfin	*Lutjanus buccanella*	3.28 kg 7 lb 3 oz	Bimini Bahamas	Aug. 25, 1993	Ron Mallet
Snapper, Colorado	*Lutjanus colorado*	9.29 kg 20 lb 8 oz	Playa Zancudo Costa Rica	Mar. 19, 1993	Craig Whitehead, MD
Snapper, cubera	*Lutjanus cyanopterus*	55.11 kg 121 lb 8 oz	Cameron Louisiana, USA	July 5, 1982	Mike Hebert
Snapper, dog (Atlantic)	*Lutjanus jocu*	10.90 kg 24 lb 0 oz	Hole in the Wall Abaco, Bahamas	May 28, 1994	Wayne Barder
Snapper, emperor	*Lutjanus sebae*	16.00 kg 35 lb 4 oz	Chichijima, Ogasawara Tokyo, Japan	Apr. 10, 1998	Takeshi Uesugi
Snapper, gray	*Lutjanus griseus*	7.71 kg 17 lb 0 oz	Port Canaveral Florida, USA	June 14, 1992	Steve Maddox
Snapper, greenbar	*Hoplopagrus guentheri*	9.58 kg 21 lb 2 oz	Solmar Beach Baja California, Mexico	June 15, 1994	Walt Geiger
Snapper, Guinean (Afr.cubera)	*Lutjanus agennes*	40.80 kg 89 lb 15 oz	Blieron, Cavally River Ivory Coast	Mar. 3, 1987	Daniel Pichard
Snapper, lane	*Lutjanus synagris*	3.17 kg 7 lb 0 oz	Gulf of Mexico Perdido Pass, Alabama, USA	June 23, 1991	Suzanne Ridgon
Snapper, Malabar	*Lutjanus malabaricus*	7.91 kg 17 lb 7 oz	Cairns Queensland, Australia	Aug. 3, 1989	Gregory Ronald Albert
Snapper, mullet	*Lutjanus aratus*	14.96 kg 33 lb 0 oz	Cano Island Costa Rica	Sept. 23, 1997	Jose Francisco Reyes Astorga
Snapper, mutton	*Lutjanus analis*	12.85 kg 28 lb 5 oz	Gulf of Mexico Florida, USA	Sept. 4, 1993	Bennie D. Kilgore
Snapper, Pacific cubera	*Lutjanus novemfasciatus*	35.72 kg 78 lb 12 oz	Bahia Pez Vela Costa Rica	Mar. 23, 1988	Steven C. Paull
Snapper, Pacific red	*Lutjanus peru*	4.86 kg 10 lb 11 oz	San Luis, San Jose Del Cabo Baja California, Mexico	June 18, 1996	George Bogen
Snapper, Papuan black	*Lutjanus goldiei*	19.20 kg 42 lb 5 oz	Fly River Papua, New Guinea	Sept. 22, 1992	Len Bradica
Snapper, queen	*Etelis oculatus*	5.30 kg 11 lb 11 oz	Bimini Bahamas	July 15, 1997	Jeff Dry
Snapper, red	*Lutjanus campechanus*	22.79 kg 50 lb 4 oz	Gulf of Mexico Louisiana, USA	June 23, 1996	Doc Kennedy
Snapper, schoolmaster	*Lutjanus apodus*	1.95 kg 4 lb 5 oz	Walker's Cay Bahamas	Nov. 10, 1995	Ken Blanchard
Snapper, silk	*Lutjanus vivanus*	8.32 kg 18 lb 5 oz	Gulf of Mexico Venice, Florida, USA	July 12, 1986	James M. Taylor
Snapper, twospot red	*Lutjanus bohar*	12.50 kg 27 lb 8 oz	Ogasawara Islands, Hahajima Tokyo, Japan	Aug. 9, 1990	Fujiko Shimazaki
Snapper, vermillion	*Rhomboplites aurorubens*	3.17 kg 7 lb 3 oz	Gulf of Mexico Mobile, Alabama, USA	May 31, 1987	John W. Doss
Snapper, yellow	*Lutjanus argentiventris*	5.44 kg 12 lb 0 oz	Golfito Costa Rica	Aug. 11, 1998	John Gunnar Olson

SPECIES	SCIENTIFIC NAME	WEIGHT	PLACE	DATE	ANGLER
Snapper, yellowtail (Tie)	*Ocyurus chrysurus*	3.85 kg 8 lb 8 oz	Gulf of Mexico, Ft. Myers Florida, USA	July 24, 1992	Suzanne Axel
Snapper, yellowtail (Tie)	*Ocyurus chrysurus*	3.88 kg 8 lb 9 oz	Gulf of Mexico Ft. Myers, Florida, USA	Sept. 13, 1996	William M. Howard
Snook, blackfin	*Centropomus medius*	3.15 kg 7 lb 0 oz	Playa Zancudo Costa Rica	Mar. 31, 1998	Stuart A. Schleujener
Snook, common	*Centropomus undecimalis*	24.32 kg 53 lb 10 oz	Parismina Ranch Costa Rica	Oct. 18, 1978	Gilbert Ponzi
Snook, fat	*Centropomus parallelus*	3.65 kg 8 lb 1 oz	St. Lucie River Stuart, Florida, USA	Nov. 15, 1997	Paul Strauss
Snook, Pacific black	*Centropomus nigrescens*	26.19 kg 57 lb 12 oz	Rio Naranjo Quepos, Costa Rica	Aug. 23, 1991	George Beck
Snook, Pacific blackfin	*Centropomus medius*	3.14 kg 6 lb 24 oz	Rio Parrita Costa Rica	Dec. 7, 1997	Victor Miranda Golfin
Snook, Pacific white	*Centropomus viridis*	17.83 kg 39 lb 8 oz	Cabo San Lucas Mexico	July 8, 1994	Billy Howell
Snook, swordspine	*Centropomus ensiferus*	0.60 kg 1 lb 5 oz	Stuart Florida, USA	Apr. 6, 1997	Robert R. Pelosi, Sr.
Snook, tarpon	*Centropomus pectinatus*	1.42 kg 3 lb 2 oz	Dona Bay Nokomis, Florida, USA	Sept. 19, 1996	David B. Coudal
Sole	*Solea solea*	0.80 kg 1 lb 12 oz	North Sea Netherlands	July 12, 1997	P.C. Ouwendijk
Sorubim, spotted	*Pseudoplatystoma coruscans*	25.00 kg 55 lb 1 oz	Mato Grosso Piguiri River, Brazil	Apr. 18, 1998	Romulo Coutinho
Sorubim, tiger	*Pseudoplatystoma tigrinum*	16.55 kg 36 lb 8 oz	Rupinuni River Karanambo, Guyana	Dec. 4, 1981	William T. Miller
Spadefish, Atlantic	*Chaetodipterus faber*	6.35 kg 14 lb 0 oz	Chesapeake Bay Virginia, USA	May 23, 1986	Geo. F. Brace
Spearfish, longbill	*Tetrapturus pfluegeri*	43.00 kg 94 lb 12 oz	Puerto Rico Gran Canaria, Spain	July 28, 1994	Siegfried Schmidt
Spearfish, Mediterranean	*Tetrapturus belone*	41.20 kg 90 lb 13 oz	Madeira Island Portugal	June 2, 1980	Joseph Larkin
Splake	*Salvelinus namaycush x S. fontinalis*	9.39 kg 20 lb 11 oz	Georgian Bay Ontario, Canada	May 17, 1987	Paul S. Thompson
Squirrelfish, sabre	*Sargocentron spiniferum*	2.55 kg 5 lb 10 oz	Keahole Point Kailua Kona, Hawaii, USA	Mar. 26, 1995	Rex C. Bigg
Stargazer	*Uranoscopus scaber*	0.94 kg 2 lb 1 oz	Gibraltar United Kingdom	Dec. 4, 1994	Albert Ward
Stargazer, northern	*Astroscotus guttatus*	4.87 kg 10 lb 12 oz	Cape May New Jersey, USA	June 20, 1998	John E. Jacobsen
Steed, barbel (nigoi)	*Hemibarbus barbus*	2.15 kg 4 lb 11 oz	Ibo-River, Hyogo Japan	Feb. 18, 1996	Masahiro Oomori
Steenbras, red	*Petrus rupestris*	56.60 kg 124 lb 12 oz	Aston Bay South Africa	May 8, 1994	Terry Colin Goldstone
Stingray, Atlantic	*Dasyatis sabina*	4.87 kg 10 lb 12 oz	Galveston Bay Texas, USA	July 3, 1994	David Lee Anderson
Stingray, black	*Dasyatis thetidis*	57.50 kg 126 lb 12 oz	Laurieton N.S.W., Australia	July 3, 1994	David Shearing
Stingray, diamond	*Dasyatis brevis*	46.26 kg 102 lb 0 oz	Mission Bay San Diego, California, USA	Aug. 7, 1993	Roger Ehlers
Stingray, roughtail	*Dasyatis centroura*	183.70 kg 405 lb 0 oz	Islamorada Florida, USA	February 1979	Geoff Flores
Stingray, round	*Urolophus halleri*	1.36 kg 3 lb 0 oz	Santa Clara River Ventura, California, USA	Sept. 3, 1989	Paul David Bodtke
Stingray, S.A. freshwater	*Potomotrygon motoro*	3.51 kg 7 lb 12 oz	Rio Araguaia Estado Goia's, Brazil	June 28, 1996	Sergio Roberto Rothier
Stingray, southern	*Dasyatis americana*	111.58 kg 246 lb 0 oz	Galveston Bay Complex Galveston County, Texas, USA	June 30, 1998	Carissa Egger
Stumpnose, red	*Chrysoblephus gibbiceps*	5.80 kg 12 lb 12 oz	St. Croix Island Port Elizabeth, South Africa	Dec. 20, 1993	Craig Saunders
Sturgeon, beluga	*Huso huso*	102.00 kg 224 lb 13 oz	Guryev Kazakhstan	May 3, 1993	Merete Lehne
Sturgeon, lake	*Acipenser fulvescens*	76.20 kg 168 lb 0 oz	Georgian Bay Ontario, Canada	May 29, 1982	Edward Paszkowski
Sturgeon, shortnose	*Acipenser brevirostrum*	5.04 kg 11 lb 2 oz	Kennebacis River New Brunswick, Canada	July 31, 1988	Lawrence Guimond
Sturgeon, shovelnose	*Scaphirhynchus platorynchus*	4.88 kg 10 lb 12 oz	Missouri River Loma, Montana, USA	June 14, 1985	Arthur James Seal
Sturgeon, white	*Acipenser transmontanus*	212.28 kg 468 lb 0 oz	Benicia California, USA	July 9, 1983	Joey Pallotta, III
Sucker, flannelmouth	*Catostomus latipinnis*	0.92 kg 2 lb 6 oz	Colorado River Colorado, USA	July 7, 1990	Karen A. DeVine
Sucker, longnose	*Catostomus catostomus*	2.97 kg 6 lb 9 oz	St. Joseph River Michigan, USA	Dec. 2, 1989	Ben Knoll
Sucker, northern hog	*Hypentelium nigricans*	0.48 kg 1 lb 1 oz	Clarion River Portland Mills, Pennsylvania, USA	Oct. 8, 1994	Richard E. Faler, Jr.

SPECIES	SCIENTIFIC NAME	WEIGHT	PLACE	DATE	ANGLER
Sucker, spotted	*Minytrema melanops*	1.23 kg 2 lb 11 oz	Hall's Lake Rome, Georgia, USA	Mar. 6, 1985	J. Paul Diprima, Jr.
Sucker, white	*Catostomus commersoni*	2.94 kg 6 lb 8 oz	Rainy River, Loman Minnesota, USA	Apr. 20, 1984	Joel M. Anderson
Sunfish, green	*Lepomis cyanellus*	0.96 kg 2 lb 2 oz	Stockton Lake Missouri, USA	June 18, 1971	Paul M. Dilley
Sunfish, green (hybrid)	*Lepomis Cyanellus x macrochirus*	0.97 kg 2 lb 2 oz	Patagonia Lake State Park Arizona, USA	June 5, 1998	Mikey A. Porter
Sunfish, longear	*Lepomis megalotis*	0.79 kg 1 lb 12 oz	Elephant Butte Lake New Mexico, USA	May 9, 1985	Patricia Stout
Sunfish, redbreast	*Lepomis auritus*	0.79 kg 1 lb 12 oz	Suwannee River Florida, USA	May 29, 1984	Alvin Buchanan
Sunfish, redear (Tie)	*Lepomis microlophus*	2.35 kg 5 lb 3 oz	Folsum South Canal Sacramento, California, USA	June 27, 1994	Anthony H. White, Sr.
Sunfish, redear (Tie)	*Lepomis microlophus*	2.40 kg 5 lb 4 oz	Diversion Canal Santee Cooper Cross, South Carolina, USA	June 18, 1998	Ray Lee
Surfperch, barred	*Amphistichus argenteus*	1.87 kg 4 lb 2 oz	Oxnard California, USA	Mar. 30, 1996	Fred Oakley
Sweetlip, painted	*Plectorhinchus pictus*	6.90 kg 15 lb 3 oz	Moreton Island Queensland, Australia	July 24, 1993	Kathy Maguire
Swordfish	*Xiphias gladius*	536.15 kg 1182 lb 0 oz	Iquique Chile	May 7, 1953	L. Marron
Taimen	*Hucho taimen*	41.95 kg 92 lb 8 oz	Keta River Russia	Aug. 11, 1993	Yuri Orlov
Tarpon (Tie)	*Megalops atlanticus*	128.36 kg 283 lb 0 oz	Lake Maracaibo Venezuela	Mar. 19, 1956	Mario Salazar
Tarpon (Tie)	*Megalops atlanticus*	128.50 kg 283 lb 4 oz	Sherbro Island Sierra Leone	Apr. 16, 1991	Yvon Victor Sebag
Tautog	*Tautoga onitis*	11.33 kg 25 lb 0 oz	Ocean City New Jersey, USA	Jan. 20, 1998	Anthony R. Monica
Tench	*Tinca tinca*	4.64 kg 10 lb 3 oz	Ljungbyan Sweden	July 2, 1985	Dan Dellerfjord
Threadfin, African	*Alectis alexandrinus*	3.17 kg 7 lb 0 oz	Guinea-Bissau	May 21, 1996	Yvon Mabileau
Threadfin, king	*Polynemus sheridani*	12.50 kg 27 lb 8 oz	Dampier Creek Broome, Australia	Apr. 24, 1996	Brian William Albert
Threadfin, moi	*Polydactylus sexfilis*	3.17 kg 7 lb 0 oz	Hanalei Hawaii, USA	Sept. 3, 1988	Harry H. Paik
Tigerfish	*Hydrocynus vittatus*	9.90 kg 21 lb 13 oz	Zambezi River Zimbabwe	July 31, 1986	Brent Reg Gavin Hudson
Tigerfish, giant	*Hydrocynus goliath*	44.00 kg 97 lb 0 oz	Zaire River Kinshasa, Zaire	July 9, 1988	Raymond Houtmans
Tilapia	*Oreochromis niloticus*	2.86 kg 6 lb 5 oz	Lake Arenal Costa Rica	Feb. 10, 1995	Marvin C. Smith
Tilapia, Mozambique	*Oreochromis mozambicus*	1.13 kg 2 lb 8 oz	Delray Beach Florida, USA	Nov. 10, 1997	Nick Cardella
Tilapia, redbreast	*Tilapia rendalli*	1.62 kg 3 lb 9 oz	Zambezi River Namibia	Nov. 14, 1994	Bill Staveley
Tilapia, threespot	*Oreochromis andersonii*	4.30 kg 9 lb 7 oz	Tiger Camp Zambezi River, Zambia	Nov. 2, 1997	Michael Harris
Tilefish, blueline	*Caulolatilus microps*	1.08 kg 2 lb 6 oz	Pompano Beach Florida, USA	May 24, 1992	Gabriel David Olander
Tilefish, golden-eyed	*Caulolatilus affinis*	0.68 kg 1 lb 8 oz	Playa Zancudo Costa Rica	Mar. 10, 1993	Craig Whitehead, MD
Tilefish, sand	*Malacanthus plumieri*	1.02 kg 2 lb 4 oz	Key Largo Florida, USA	June 23, 1991	Rachel S. Olander
Toadfish, oyster	*Opsanus tau*	2.23 kg 4 lb 15 oz	Ocracoke North Carolina, USA	June 4, 1994	David R. Tinsley
Tope	*Galeorhinus galeus*	44.67 kg 98 lb 8 oz	Santa Monica California, USA	Oct. 20, 1994	Fred Oakley
Torpedo, Atlantic	*Torpedo nobiliana*	16.01 kg 35 lb 4 oz	Perkins Cove Ogunquit, Maine, USA	Aug. 24, 1995	Don Carignan
Trahira	*Hoplias malabaricus*	1.41 kg 3 lb 2 oz	Rio Piqueri Mato Grosso, Brazil	Aug. 11, 1996	Sandy Blum
Trahira, giant	*Hoplias macrophthalmus*	10.25 kg 22 lb 9 oz	Rio Libindade Mato Grosso, Brazil	Sept. 3, 1996	Francisco Jose Melaga
Trevally, bigeye	*Caranx sexfasciatus*	14.30 kg 31 lb 8 oz	Poivre Island Seychelles	Apr. 23,1997	Les Sampson
Trevally, blue	*Caranx ferdau*	1.06 kg 2 lb 5 oz	Iroquois Point Hawaii, USA	Oct. 4, 1992	George D. Cornish
Trevally, bluefin	*Caranx melampygus*	11.99 kg 26 lb 7 oz	Clipperton Island	Mar. 24, 1997	Tom Taylor
Trevally, brassy	*Caranx papuensis*	4.40 kg 9 lb 11 oz	Isigaki Island Okinawa, Japan	Apr. 12, 1991	Fumio Suzuki
Trevally, giant	*Caranx ignobilis*	65.99 kg 145 lb 8 oz	Makena, Maui Hawaii, USA	Mar. 28, 1991	Russell Mori

SPECIES	SCIENTIFIC NAME	WEIGHT	PLACE	DATE	ANGLER
Trevally, golden	*Gnathanodon speciosus*	14.15 kg 31 lb 3 oz	Port Hedland Australia	Aug. 16, 1997	Tammy Yates
Trevally, longnose	*Carangoides chrysophrys*	4.35 kg 9 lb 9 oz	Midway Island	Aug. 9, 1997	Allan Durham
Trevally, white	*Caranx dentex*	15.25 kg 33 lb 9 oz	Hahajima, Ogasawara Tokyo, Japan	July 6, 1998	Kazuhiko Adachi
Trevally, yellowspotted	*Caranx fulvoguttatus*	11.20 kg 24 lb 11 oz	Inhaca Island Maputo	Mar. 4, 1998	Peter Kidd
Triggerfish, gray	*Balistes capriscus*	6.15 kg 13 lb 9 oz	Murrells Inlet South Carolina, USA	May 3, 1989	Jim Hilton
Triggerfish, ocean	*Canthidermis sufflamen*	6.12 kg 13 lb 8 oz	Pompano Beach Florida, USA	Mar. 7, 1995	Frederick J. Lauriello
Triggerfish, queen	*Balistes vetula*	5.44 kg 12 lb 0 oz	Ponce Inlet Florida, USA	Aug. 11, 1985	Cindy Pitts
Tripletail	*Lobotes surinamensis*	19.20 kg 42 lb 5 oz	Zululand Republic of South Africa	June 7, 1989	Steve Hand
Trout, Apache	*Oncorhynchus apache*	2.36 kg 5 lb 3 oz	White Mtn. Apache Reservation Arizona, USA	May 29, 1991	John (TRES) Baldwin
Trout, aurora	*Salvelinus fontinalis timagaiensis*	2.21 kg 4 lb 14 oz	Carol Lake Ontario, Canada	Oct. 8, 1996	Robert J. Bernardo
Trout, biwamasu	*Oncorhynchus masou* rhodurus	1.25 kg 2 lb 12 oz	Lake Biwa Shiga, Japan	May 21, 1993	Shoji Matsuura
Trout, brook	*Salvelinus fontinalis*	6.57 kg 14 lb 8 oz	Nipigon River Ontario, Canada	July, 1916	Dr. W. J. Cook
Trout, brown	*Salmo trutta*	18.25 kg 40 lb 4 oz	Little Red River Heber Springs, Arkansas, USA	May 9, 1992	Howard L. (Rip) Collins
Trout, bull	*Salvelinus confluentus*	14.51 kg 32 lb 0 oz	Lake Pond Orielle Idaho, USA	Oct. 27, 1949	N. L. Higgins
Trout, cutbow	*Oncorhynchus mykiss x O. clarki*	4.36 kg 9 lb 10 oz	Crystal Lake Colorado, USA	Mar. 22, 1997	Steven J. Mudra
Trout, cutthroat	*Oncorhynchus clarki*	18.59 kg 41 lb 0 oz	Pyramid Lake Nevada, USA	Dec. 1925	John Skimmerhorn
Trout, golden	*Oncorhynchus aguabonita*	4.98 kg 11 lb 0 oz	Cooks Lake Wyoming, USA	Aug. 5, 1948	Chas. S. Reed
Trout, lake	*Salvelinus namaycush*	32.65 kg 72 lb 0 oz	Great Bear Lake N.W.T., Canada	Aug. 19, 1995	Lloyd E. Bull
Trout, masu	*Oncorhynchus masou masou*	5.25 kg 11 lb 9 oz	Kuzuryu River Fukui, Japan	May 6, 1995	Takeshi Matsuura
Trout, ohrid (Tie)	*Salmo letnica*	6.49 kg 14 lb 4 oz	Watauga Lake Tennessee, USA	Mar. 28, 1986	Richard L. Carter
Trout, ohrid (Tie)	*Salmo letnica*	6.46 kg 14 lb 4 oz	Platte River Wyoming, USA	Jan. 26, 1986	Kim Darwin Durfee
Trout, rainbow	*Oncorhynchus mykiss*	19.10 kg 42 lb 2 oz	Bell Island Alaska, USA	June 22, 1970	David Robert White
Trout, red-spotted masu	*Oncorhynchus masou* macrostomus	1.54 kg 3 lb 6 oz	Yoshino River Tokushima, Japan	May 17, 1998	Akihiko Masutani
Trout, sand	*Cynoscion arenarius*	1.95 kg 4 lb 5 oz	Pensacola Bay Florida, USA	Oct. 26, 1996	Eric Gill
Trout, tiger	*Salmo trutta x Salvelinus fontinalis*	9.44 kg 20 lb 13 oz	Lake Michigan Wisconsin, USA	Aug. 12, 1978	Pete M. Friedland
Trunkfish	*Lactophrys trigonus*	2.68 kg 5 lb 14 oz	Tavernier Creek Key Largo, Florida, USA	Nov. 24, 1985	Edward Shaw
Tuna, bigeye (Atlantic)	*Thunnus obesus*	178.00 kg 392 lb 6 oz	Puerto Rico Gran Canaria, Spain	July 25, 1996	Dieter Vogel
Tuna, bigeye (Pacific)	*Thunnus obesus*	197.31 kg 435 lb 0 oz	Cabo Blanco Peru	Apr. 17, 1957	Dr. Russel V. A. Lee
Tuna, blackfin	*Thunnus atlanticus*	20.63 kg 45 lb 8 oz	Key West Florida, USA	May 4, 1996	Sam J. Burnett
Tuna, bluefin	*Thunnus thynnus*	679.00 kg 1496 lb 0 oz	Aulds Cove Nova Scotia, Canada	Oct. 26, 1979	Ken Fraser
Tuna, dogtooth	*Gymnosarda unicolor*	131.00 kg 288 lb 12 oz	Kwan-Tall Island Cheju-Do, Korea	Oct. 6, 1982	Boo-Il Oh
Tuna, longtail	*Thunnus tonggol*	35.90 kg 79 lb 2 oz	Montague Island N.S.W., Australia	Apr. 12, 1982	Tim Simpson
Tuna, skipjack	*Katsuwonus pelamis*	20.54 kg 45 lb 4 oz	Flathead Bank Baja California, Mexico	Nov. 16, 1996	Brian Evans
Tuna, slender	*Allothunnus fallai*	10.80 kg 23 lb 13 oz	North Whale Island Whakatane, New Zealand	Oct. 5, 1995	Alan Craig
Tuna, southern bluefin	*Thunnus maccoyi*	158.00 kg 348 lb 5 oz	Whakatane New Zealand	Jan. 16, 1981	Rex Wood
Tuna, yellowfin	*Thunnus albacares*	176.35 kg 388 lb 12 oz	Isla San Benedicto Revillagigedo Islands, Mexico	Apr. 1, 1977	Curt Wiesenhutter
Tunny, little	*Euthynnus alletteratus*	15.95 kg 35 lb 2 oz	Cap de Garde Algeria	Dec. 14, 1988	Jean Yves Chatard
Tuskfish, blackspot	*Choerodon schoenleinii*	9.50 kg 20 lb 15 oz	Bribie Island Queensland, Australia	June 19, 1988	Olga Mack

ALL TACKLE

SPECIES	SCIENTIFIC NAME	WEIGHT	PLACE	DATE	ANGLER
Ugui (Tie)	*Tribolodon hakonensis*	0.81 kg 1 lb 12 oz	Shimoda Port Shizuoka, Japan	July 20, 1995	Motoshi Aihara
Ugui (Tie)	*Tribolodon hakonensis*	0.85 kg 1 lb 13 oz	Kuzuryu River Fukui, Japan	May 13, 1996	Kaoru Hosoe
Ugui (Tie)	*Tribolodon hakonensis*	0.80 kg 1 lb 12 oz	Ibi River, Gifu Japan	June 23, 1995	Kaoru Hosoe
Vimba (Zahrte) (Tie)	*Vimba vimba*	1.14 kg 2 lb 8 oz	Olandsan Sweden	May 1, 1990	Sonny Pettersson
Vimba (Zahrte) (Tie)	*Vimba vimba*	1.11 kg 2 lb 7 oz	Hossmoan Kalmar, Sweden	June 9, 1987	Luis Kilian Rasmussen
Wahoo	*Acanthocybium solandri*	71.89 kg 158 lb 8 oz	Loreto Baja California, Mexico	June 10, 1996	Keith Winter
Walleye	*Stizostedion vitreum*	11.34 kg 25 lb 0 oz	Old Hickory Lake Tennessee, USA	Aug. 2, 1960	Mabry Harper
Warmouth	*Lepomis gulosus*	1.10 kg 2 lb 7 oz	Guess Lake, Yellow River Holt, Florida, USA	Oct. 19, 1985	Tony David Dempsey
Weakfish (Tie)	*Cynoscion regalis*	8.67 kg 19 lb 2 oz	Delaware Bay Delaware, USA	May 20, 1989	William E. Thomas
Weakfish (Tie)	*Cynoscion regalis*	8.67 kg 19 lb 2 oz	Jones Beach Inlet Long Island, New York, USA	Oct. 11, 1984	Dennis Roger Rooney
Weakfish, acoupa	*Cynoscion acoupa*	17.00 kg 37 lb 7 oz	Canal do Boqueirao Ilha do Governador, Brazil	Aug. 23, 1997	Gilberto Ferreira
Weever, greater	*Trachinus draco*	1.67 kg 3 lb 11 oz	Gran Canaria Canary Islands, Spain	Mar. 31, 1984	Arild J. Danielsen
Wels	*Silurus glanis*	36.28 kg 80 lb 0 oz	River Erbo Aldover, Spain	July 7, 1998	Valerie Hall
Wenchman	*Pristipomoides aquilonaris*	1.99 kg 4 lb 6 oz	Bimini Bahamas	July 13, 1997	Dan Upton
Whipray, pink	*Himanturua fai*	18.50 kg 40 lb 12 oz	Bali Beach Bali	July 20, 1995	Bo T. Johansson
Whitefish, broad	*Coregonus nasus*	4.08 kg 9 lb 0 oz	Tozitna River Alaska, USA	July 17, 1989	Al Mathews
Whitefish, lake	*Coregonus clupeaformis*	6.52 kg 14 lb 6 oz	Meaford Ontario, Canada	May 21, 1984	Dennis M. Laycock
Whitefish, mountain	*Prosopium williamsoni*	2.51 kg 5 lb 8 oz	Elbow River, Calgary Alberta, Canada	Aug. 1, 1995	Randy G. Woo
Whitefish, round	*Prosopium cylindraceum*	2.72 kg 6 lb 0 oz	Putahow River Manitoba, Canada	June 14, 1984	Allan J. Ristori
Whiting, blue	*Micromesistius poutassou*	0.78 kg 1 lb 11 oz	Mausundvar Norway	Jan. 6, 1996	Odd Inge Oyas
Whiting, European	*Merlangius merlangus*	3.11 kg 6 lb 13 oz	Dypdalen Norway	June 10, 1997	John Kafoed
Wolffish, Atlantic	*Anarhichas lupus*	23.58 kg 52 lb 0 oz	Georges Bank Massachusetts, USA	June 11, 1986	Frederick Gardiner
Wolffish, northern	*Anarhichas denticulatus*	17.00 kg 37 lb 7 oz	Holsteinsborg Greenland	Aug. 19, 1982	Jens Ploug Hansen
Wolffish, spotted	*Anarhichas minor*	23.35 kg 51 lb 7 oz	Holsteinsborg Greenland	Aug. 20, 1982	Jens Ploug Hansen
Wrasse, ballan	*Labrus bergylta*	4.35 kg 9 lb 9 oz	Clogher Head Co. Kerry, Ireland	Aug. 20, 1983	Bertrand Kron
Wrasse, humphead Maori	*Cheilinus undulatus*	19.80 kg 43 lb 10 oz	Platt Island Seychelles	Apr. 4, 1997	Vincent Yeo Hock Boon
Wrasse, purple (hou)	*Thalassoma purpureum*	1.21 kg 2 lb 9 oz	Kalapana Hawaii, USA	Feb. 8, 1992	Chris Hara
Wreckfish	*Polyprion americanus*	71.00 kg 156 lb 8 oz	White Island Whakatane, New Zealand	Nov. 2, 1990	Ian Grindle
Yellowtail, Asian	*Seriola lalandi aureovittata*	21.40 kg 47 lb 2 oz	Chichijima, Ogasawara Tokyo, Japan	July 4, 1998	Gakusei Ikeda
Yellowtail, California	*Seriola lalandi dorsalis*	35.97 kg 79 lb 4 oz	Alijos Rocks Baja California, Mexico	July 2, 1991	Robert I. Welker
Yellowtail, southern	*Seriola lalandi lalandi*	52.00 kg 114 lb 10 oz	Tauranga New Zealand	Feb. 5, 1984	Mike Godfrey
Zander	*Stizostedion lucioperca*	11.42 kg 25 lb 2 oz	Trosa Sweden	June 12, 1986	Harry Lee Tennison

Junior World Records

The following are boys' and girls' Junior world records granted in fresh and salt water by IGFA as of January 1, 1999.
They are listed by the common names of species.

Amberjack / *Seriola dumerili*

LINE CLASS	WEIGHT	PLACE	DATE	ANGLER
F-Junior	11.79 kg (26 lb 0 oz)	Kailua-Kona, Hawaii, USA	Oct. 11, 1997	Maryann Rogers
F-Smallfry	23.81 kg (52 lb 8 oz)	Tropic Star Lodge, Pinas Bay, Panama	Jan. 9, 1998	Jessica C. Harvey
M-Junior	39.68 kg (87 lb 8 oz)	Key West, Florida, USA	Jan. 17, 1998	K.C. Knudsen
M-Smallfry	22.90 kg (50 lb 8 oz)	Kailua-Kona, Hawaii, USA	Oct. 11, 1997	Peter E. Purdy

Barracuda / *Sphyraena spp.*

LINE CLASS	WEIGHT	PLACE	DATE	ANGLER
F-Junior	7.90 kg (17 lb 6 oz)	Shimoni, Kenya	Aug. 17, 1998	Lyndsay Hemphill
F-Smallfry	9.52 kg (21 lb 0 oz)	Key West, Florida, USA	Apr. 26, 1998	Trish A. Wise
M-Junior	19.64 kg (43 lb 4 oz)	Palm Beach, Florida, USA	July 11, 1998	Travis P. Hagler
M-Smallfry	15.50 kg (34 lb 3 oz)	Flamingo, Florida, USA	Nov. 16, 1997	Austin Porter

Barramundi / *Lates calcarifer*

LINE CLASS	WEIGHT	PLACE	DATE	ANGLER
F-Junior	Vacant			
F-Smallfry	Vacant			
M-Junior	3.64 kg (8 lb 0 oz)	Karratha, Australia	Nov. 23, 1997	Matthew Hall
M-Smallfry	Vacant			

Bass, black sea / *Centropristis striata*

LINE CLASS	WEIGHT	PLACE	DATE	ANGLER
F-Junior	Vacant			
F-Smallfry	0.65 kg (1 lb 7 oz)	Ocean City, Maryland, USA	Nov. 23, 1997	Jamie Lyn Burkholder
M-Junior	0.51 kg (1 lb 2 oz)	Flyn's Knoll, Sandy Hook, New Jersey, USA	Aug. 8, 1997	Mark Robert Musser
M-Smallfry	0.99 kg (2 lb 3 oz)	Bass Grounds, Selbyville, Delaware, USA	Aug. 16, 1998	Franklin Timothy Brinker

Bass, kelp (calico) / *Paralabrax clathratus*

LINE CLASS	WEIGHT	PLACE	DATE	ANGLER
F-Junior	0.63 kg (1 lb 6 oz)	La Jolla, California, USA	June 21, 1997	Christina Weitzel
F-Smallfry	1.17 kg (2 lb 9 oz)	La Jolla, California, USA	June 21, 1997	Kathryn Orida
M-Junior	2.44 kg (5 lb 6 oz)	Mexico	Dec. 30, 1997	Richard T. Maxa
M-Smallfry	2.12 kg (4 lb 11 oz)	San Diego, California, USA	July 13, 1997	Christien J Marcogliese

Bass, largemouth / *Micropterus salmoides*

LINE CLASS	WEIGHT	PLACE	DATE	ANGLER
F-Junior	5.72 kg (12 lb 10 oz)	Richland Chambers Reservoir, Corsicana, Texas, USA	Feb. 23, 1997	Kristy Ruthann Cox
F-Smallfry	2.49 kg (5 lb 8 oz)	Holiday Park, Ft. Lauderdale, Florida, USA	Apr. 27, 1998	Christina Wright
M-Junior	4.30 kg (9 lb 5 oz)	Lake O' The Pines, Texas, USA	June 2, 1997	Clint Grammer
M-Smallfry	6.35 kg (14 lb 0 oz)	Castaic Lake, California, USA	Jan. 2, 1998	Ryan P. Barnes

Bass, smallmouth / *Micropterus dolomieu*

LINE CLASS	WEIGHT	PLACE	DATE	ANGLER
F-Junior	Vacant			
F-Smallfry	1.07 kg (2 lb 6 oz)	Green Lake, Quebec, Canada	July 28, 1998	Cameron McLain Nutting
M-Junior	1.47 kg (3 lb 4 oz)	Lake Erie, Ohio, USA	Oct. 11, 1998	Christopher Lee Rose
M-Smallfry	2.13 kg (4 lb 11 oz)	Trout Lake, North Bay, Ontario, Canada	Oct. 25, 1998	Mitchell Manso

Bass, striped / *Morone saxatilis*

LINE CLASS	WEIGHT	PLACE	DATE	ANGLER
F-Junior	3.28 kg (7 lb 4 oz)	Boston Harbor, Massachusetts, USA	May 31, 1998	Whitney Carelton Hawkins
F-Smallfry	13.60 kg (30 lb 0 oz)	Chatham, Massachusetts, USA	Aug. 13, 1997	Erin Kathleen Landry
M-Junior	12.31 kg (27 lb 2 oz)	Well's Harbor, Maine, USA	July 2, 1998	Walter F. Evans, III
M-Smallfry	13.01 kg (28 lb 11 oz)	Ditch Pains Beach, Montauk, New York, USA	Aug. 9, 1998	Samuel E. Viemeister

Bass, striped (landlocked) / *Morone saxatilis*

LINE CLASS	WEIGHT	PLACE	DATE	ANGLER
F-Junior	7.46 kg (16 lb 7 oz)	Smith Lake, Alabama, USA	June 18, 1997	Felicia A. Cannon
F-Smallfry	6.96 kg (15 lb 5 oz)	Elephant Butte Lake, New Mexico, USA	July 22, 1998	Jackie Smith
M-Junior	23.42 kg (51 lb 10 oz)	Elephant Butte Lake, New Mexico, USA	Apr. 21, 1997	Jason Wedel
M-Smallfry	10.61 kg (23 lb 6 oz)	Smith Lake, Alabama, USA	Mar. 31, 1998	William Seth Lucas

Bass, whiterock / *Morone saxatilis x Morone chrysops*

LINE CLASS	WEIGHT	PLACE	DATE	ANGLER
F-Junior	0.90 kg (2 lb 0 oz)	Pavillion Lake, Bucksville, Alabama, USA	July 23, 1998	Jessica Foree Beatty
F-Smallfry	Vacant			
M-Junior	Vacant			
M-Smallfry	Vacant			

Bluefish / *Pomatomus saltatrix*

LINE CLASS	WEIGHT	PLACE	DATE	ANGLER
F-Junior	1.36 kg (3 lb 0 oz)	Buzzard's Bay, Massachusetts, USA	Sept. 4, 1998	Whitney C. Hawkins
F-Smallfry	9.07 kg (20 lb 0 oz)	Palm Beach, Florida, USA		Cristal Cameron
M-Junior	10.20 kg (22 lb 8 oz)	Hortons Beach, Horton's Point, New York, USA	Oct. 24, 1998	Joseph Marino
M-Smallfry	6.86 kg (15 lb 2 oz)	Shrewsbury Rocks, New Jersey, USA	Aug. 12, 1997	Dylan Robert Chayes

Bluegill / *Lepomis macrochirus*

LINE CLASS	WEIGHT	PLACE	DATE	ANGLER
F-Junior	Vacant			
F-Smallfry	0.45 kg (1 lb 0 oz)	Hawkins Pond, Indiana, USA	Aug. 31, 1997	Christina Berg
M-Junior	Vacant			
M-Smallfry	0.66 kg (1 lb 7 oz)	Pace, Florida, USA	June 5, 1998	Zac Cooper

Bonefish / *Albula spp.*

LINE CLASS	WEIGHT	PLACE	DATE	ANGLER
F-Junior	2.04 kg (4 lb 8 oz)	Bimini, Bahamas	July 13, 1998	Gayle Steiner
F-Smallfry	7.08 kg (15 lb 8 oz)	Islamorada, Florida, USA	May 10, 1997	Alexandra Beuckman

Bonefish / *(continued)*

LINE CLASS	WEIGHT	PLACE	DATE	ANGLER
M-Junior	5.89 kg (13 lb 0 oz)	Islamorada, Florida, USA	Aug. 15, 1998	Timothy Collins Forman
M-Smallfry	4.62 kg (10 lb 3 oz)	Biscayne Bay, Florida, USA	Feb. 25, 1998	David E. Melnikoff

Bonito / *Sarda spp.*

LINE CLASS	WEIGHT	PLACE	DATE	ANGLER
F-Junior	Vacant			
F-Smallfry	3.40 kg (7 lb 8 oz)	La Jolla, California, USA	Aug. 23, 1997	Kathryn Orida
M-Junior	4.64 kg (10 lb 4 oz)	Woods Hole, Massachusetts, USA	Sept. 2, 1998	Michael Murphy
M-Smallfry	Vacant			

Bowfin / *Amia calva*

LINE CLASS	WEIGHT	PLACE	DATE	ANGLER
F-Junior	Vacant			
F-Smallfry	3.62 kg (8 lb 0 oz)	Holiday Park, Ft. Lauderdale, Florida, USA	Apr. 27, 1997	Christina Wright
M-Junior	3.12 kg (6 lb 14 oz)	Western Broward County, Florida, USA	Oct. 10, 1998	Matthew Melchiorre
M-Smallfry	5.64 kg (12 lb 7 oz)	Rhodes Pond, North Carolina, USA	Dec. 26, 1997	Christopher Lee Rose

Bream / *Abramis spp.*

LINE CLASS	WEIGHT	PLACE	DATE	ANGLER
F-Junior	Vacant			
F-Smallfry	Vacant			
M-Junior	Vacant			
M-Smallfry	Vacant			

Buffalo / *Ictiobus spp.*

LINE CLASS	WEIGHT	PLACE	DATE	ANGLER
F-Junior	Vacant			
F-Smallfry	3.45 kg (7 lb 10 oz)	Rock River, Loves Park, Illinois, USA	Feb. 23, 1997	Leah R. Pratt
M-Junior	Vacant			
M-Smallfry	Vacant			

Bullhead / *Ameiurus spp.*

LINE CLASS	WEIGHT	PLACE	DATE	ANGLER
F-Junior	Vacant			
F-Smallfry	0.66 kg (1 lb 7 oz)	Argyle Lake, West Babylon, New York, USA	May 24, 1997	Kristin Boesenberg
M-Junior	0.97 kg (2 lb 2 oz)	Argyle Lake, West Babylon, New York, USA	May 24, 1997	Joe Rivilli, Jr.
M-Smallfry	0.96 kg (2 lb 2 oz)	Country Lake, Delray Beach, Florida, USA	Aug. 5, 1997	Jeffrey Price

Burbot / *Lota lota*

LINE CLASS	WEIGHT	PLACE	DATE	ANGLER
F-Junior	Vacant			
F-Smallfry	2.52 kg (5 lb 8 oz)	Big Lake, Wasillia, Alaska, USA	Apr. 4, 1998	Nicole R. Tarnowski
M-Junior	Vacant			
M-Smallfry	Vacant			

Carp / *Cyprinus spp.*

LINE CLASS	WEIGHT	PLACE	DATE	ANGLER
F-Junior	7.37 kg (16 lb 4 oz)	Sudbury River, Concord, Massachusetts, USA	July 30, 1997	Ashley B. Hyotte
F-Smallfry	9.97 kg (22 lb 0 oz)	Pembroke Pines, Florida, USA	Oct. 10, 1998	Christina Wright
M-Junior	10.50 kg (23 lb 2 oz)	Klein Strand, Belgium	Oct. 14, 1998	Marco Solar
M-Smallfry	17.83 kg (39 lb 5 oz)	Eagle's Landing Park, Hunter's Creek, Orlando, Florida, USA	May 2, 1997	Patrick J. Simmons, Jr.

Catfish, (blue/channel) / *Ictalurus spp.*

LINE CLASS	WEIGHT	PLACE	DATE	ANGLER
F-Junior	7.03 kg (15 lb 8 oz)	House Lake, Bucksville, Alabama, USA	Aug. 10, 1998	Jessica Foree Beatty
F-Smallfry	6.49 kg (14 lb 4 oz)	Cabin Lake, Bucksville, Alabama, USA	Jan. 22, 1997	Jessica Foree Beatty
M-Junior	3.74 kg (8 lb 4 oz)	Lakeland, Florida, USA	June 12, 1997	Blake Smith
M-Smallfry	9.61 kg (21 lb 3 oz)	James River, Richmond, Virginia, USA	July 16, 1998	Damon Fender

Catfish, flathead / *Pylodictis olivaris*

LINE CLASS	WEIGHT	PLACE	DATE	ANGLER
F-Junior	8.50 kg (18 lb 12 oz)	Rock River, Loves Park, Illinois, USA	June 22, 1998	Leah Pratt
F-Smallfry	Vacant			
M-Junior	14.51 kg (32 lb 0 oz)	Lake Moultrie, South Carolina, USA	May 16, 1998	Thomas Murray
M-Smallfry	7.52 kg (16 lb 9 oz)	James River, Richmond, Virginia, USA	Aug. 31, 1998	Jarrett Lee White

Catfish, white / *Ameiurus catus*

LINE CLASS	WEIGHT	PLACE	DATE	ANGLER
F-Junior	Vacant			
F-Smallfry	Vacant			
M-Junior	Vacant			
M-Smallfry	Vacant			

Char (Arctic Char & Dolly Varden) / *Salvelinus alpinus, S. malma*

LINE CLASS	WEIGHT	PLACE	DATE	ANGLER
F-Junior	Vacant			
F-Smallfry	Vacant			
M-Junior	Vacant			
M-Smallfry	0.96 kg (2 lb 2 oz)	Petersburg, Alaska, USA	July 4, 1997	Bryn B. Mueller

Cobia / *Rachycentron canadum*

LINE CLASS	WEIGHT	PLACE	DATE	ANGLER
F-Junior	8.64 kg (19 lb 1 oz)	Port Mansfield, Texas, USA	Aug. 9, 1998	Julie Lynn Whitis
F-Smallfry	Vacant			
M-Junior	34.69 kg (76 lb 8 oz)	Timberlair Island, Louisiana, USA	Apr. 19, 1997	Brian P. Dupont
M-Smallfry	30.73 kg (67 lb 12 oz)	Ocklocknee Bay, Florida, USA	Aug. 31, 1998	Christopher McCoy

Cod / *Gadus spp.*

LINE CLASS	WEIGHT	PLACE	DATE	ANGLER
F-Junior	1.44 kg (3 lb 3 oz)	Boston Harbor, Massachusetts, USA	May 31, 1998	Whitney Carelton Hawkins
F-Smallfry	10.06 kg (22 lb 2 oz)	Kraakvaag Fjord, Norway	July 22, 1998	Sandra Marquard
M-Junior	16.47 kg (36 lb 5 oz)	Point Lookout Marina, New York, USA	Jan. 18, 1998	Marshall Sklar

LINE CLASS	WEIGHT	PLACE	DATE	ANGLER
M-Smallfry	Vacant			

Crappie (black/white) / *Pomoxis nigromaculatus, P. annularis*

LINE CLASS	WEIGHT	PLACE	DATE	ANGLER
F-Junior	0.56 kg (1 lb 4 oz)	Smith Lake, Alabama, USA	June 19, 1997	Felicia A. Cannon
F-Junior Tie	0.61 kg (1 lb 5 oz)	Gainesville Lake, Tombigbec River, Alabama, USA	Jan. 3, 1998	Brittany N. Tubbs
F-Smallfry	0.59 kg (1 lb 5 oz)	Dewart Lake, Indiana, USA	Apr. 1, 1997	Nicole N. Berg
M-Junior	Vacant			
M-Smallfry	1.29 kg (2 lb 13 oz)	Farm Pond, Clanton, Alabama, USA	June 12, 1998	Matthew William Hill

Dolphinfish / *Coryphaena hippurus*

LINE CLASS	WEIGHT	PLACE	DATE	ANGLER
F-Junior	13.60 kg (30 lb 0 oz)	Tropic Star Lodge, Pinas Bay, Panama	Dec. 16, 1998	Lauren Ledermann
F-Smallfry	12.24 kg (27 lb 0 oz)	Jupiter, Florida, USA	May 24, 1998	Jessica Lynn DeVries
M-Junior	26.08 kg (57 lb 8 oz)	San Juan, Puerto Rico	Jan. 7, 1998	Alejandro M. Rosas Salgado
M-Smallfry	24.49 kg (54 lb 0 oz)	San Juan, Puerto Rico	Mar. 21, 1997	Jose Carlos Ramirez Marchand
M-Smallfry tie	24.49 kg (54 lb 0 oz)	Salinas, Ecuador	Oct. 11, 1997	Andres Cucalon Calderon

Drum (black/red) / *Sciaenops ocellatus, Pogonias cromis*

LINE CLASS	WEIGHT	PLACE	DATE	ANGLER
F-Junior	Vacant			
F-Smallfry	15.30 kg (33 lb 12 oz)	Port Mansfield, Texas, USA	Mar. 11, 1997	Jennifer Lee Nagelhout
M-Junior	47.62 kg (105 lb 0 oz)	Virginia Beach, Virginia, USA	Aug. 16, 1997	Kevin C. Brown
M-Smallfry	12.47 kg (27 lb 8 oz)	Galveston Bay, Texas, USA	Aug. 23, 1997	Joshua Daniel Parrott

Drum, freshwater / *Aplodinotus grunniens*

LINE CLASS	WEIGHT	PLACE	DATE	ANGLER
F-Junior	Vacant			
F-Smallfry	1.55 kg (3 lb 6 oz)	Red Rock Dam, Pella, Iowa, USA	July 18, 1998	Miranda Lopez
M-Junior	2.72 kg (6 lb 0 oz)	Lake Jackson, Oak Hill, Ohio, USA	July 13, 1998	Waylon Strickland
M-Smallfry	0.56 kg (1 lb 4 oz)	Lake Erie, Madison, Ohio, USA	July 8, 1997	Patrick Hall

Flounder (flatfishes) / *Pleuronectes, Platichthys Paralichthys spp.*

LINE CLASS	WEIGHT	PLACE	DATE	ANGLER
F-Junior	2.60 kg (5 lb 12 oz)	Montauk, New York, USA	July 4, 1997	Kristen Golfo
F-Smallfry	1.47 kg (3 lb 4 oz)	Mt. Sinai, New York, USA	June 28, 1998	Christina Riviezzo
M-Junior	3.17 kg (7 lb 0 oz)	Montauk, New York, USA	July 1, 1997	Gregory Golfo
M-Smallfry	3.17 kg (7 lb 0 oz)	Montauk, New York, USA	Aug. 17, 1997	Ross A. Smith

Gar (Florida, longnose, shortnose, spotted) / *Lepisosteus spp.*

LINE CLASS	WEIGHT	PLACE	DATE	ANGLER
F-Junior	Vacant			
F-Smallfry	1.47 kg (3 lb 4 oz)	Tamiami Trail Canal, Collier County, Florida, USA	Aug. 21, 1998	Danielle Arostegui
M-Junior	10.99 kg (24 lb 4 oz)	Caloosahatchee River, Florida, USA	June 27, 1997	Dan Forrester
M-Smallfry	1.60 kg (3 lb 8 oz)	Canal in Wellington, Florida, USA	Oct. 4, 1998	Grant Heffley

Grayling (Arctic/European) / *Thymallus arcticus, T. thymallus*

LINE CLASS	WEIGHT	PLACE	DATE	ANGLER
F-Junior	Vacant			
F-Smallfry	Vacant			
M-Junior	Vacant			
M-Smallfry	0.48 kg (1 lb 1 oz)	Svensen Creek, Redoubt, Yukon, Canada	June 8, 1997	Bryce Mueller

Grouper / *Epinephelus/Mycteroperca spp.*

LINE CLASS	WEIGHT	PLACE	DATE	ANGLER
F-Junior	Vacant			
F-Smallfry	19.05 kg (42 lb 0 oz)	Tropic Star Lodge, Pinas Bay, Panama	Jan. 9, 1998	Jessica C. Harvey
M-Junior	9.75 kg (21 lb 8 oz)	Ft. Lauderdale, Florida, USA	Oct. 4, 1997	Rhett Clark
M-Smallfry	11.33 kg (25 lb 0 oz)	Marathon, Florida, USA	May 28, 1997	John Callion

Grunt / *Haemulon spp.*

LINE CLASS	WEIGHT	PLACE	DATE	ANGLER
F-Junior	0.59 kg (1 lb 4 oz)	Bradenton, Florida, USA	May 24, 1998	Misty Flanagan
F-Smallfry	1.02 kg (2 lb 4 oz)	Bimini, Bahamas	July 13, 1998	Jaclyn Hirsch
M-Junior	Vacant			
M-Smallfry	0.45 kg (1 lb 0 oz)	Gulf of Mexico, Florida, USA	Nov. 21, 1997	Mark R. Roehrs

Halibut (Atlantic/California/Pacific) / *Hippoglossus, Paralichthys spp.*

LINE CLASS	WEIGHT	PLACE	DATE	ANGLER
F-Junior	Vacant			
F-Smallfry	6.30 kg (13 lb 14 oz)	San Francisco Bay, California, USA	June 15, 1998	Angela A.S. Weber
M-Junior	2.60 kg (5 lb 12 oz)	Point Loma, California, USA	Aug. 30, 1998	Jason Jocher
M-Smallfry	10.31 kg (22 lb 12 oz)	Catalina Island, California, USA	Feb. 8, 1997	Charlie Albright

Jack (black/crevalle/horse-eye/island/Pacific crevalle/yellow) / *Caranx spp.*

LINE CLASS	WEIGHT	PLACE	DATE	ANGLER
F-Junior	13.77 kg (30 lb 6 oz)	Santa Rosa Beach, Florida, USA	Oct. 12, 1997	Elizabeth Ann Dalton
F-Smallfry	6.91 kg (15 lb 4 oz)	Galveston Bay, Texas, USA	Aug. 23, 1997	Danielle Renee Parrott
M-Junior	17.23 kg (38 lb 0 oz)	Palm Beach, Florida, USA	Jan. 24, 1998	K.C. Knudsen
M-Smallfry	12.51 kg (28 lb 4 oz)	Orange Beach, Florida, USA	May 29, 1998	Cory Michael Bolton

Kahawai / *Arripis trutta*

LINE CLASS	WEIGHT	PLACE	DATE	ANGLER
F-Junior	2.14 kg (4 lb 11 oz)	Plate Island, Tauranga, New Zealand	Mar. 3, 1997	Kirsty Robinson
F-Smallfry	3.05 kg (6 lb 11 oz)	Matata, New Zealand	Dec. 7, 1997	Lisa Papuni
M-Junior	3.30 kg (7 lb 4 oz)	Hauraki Gulf, New Zealand	Apr. 13, 1998	Marin Hobson
M-Smallfry	Vacant			

Kokanee / *Oncorhynchus nerka*

LINE CLASS	WEIGHT	PLACE	DATE	ANGLER
F-Junior	Vacant			
F-Smallfry	Vacant			

Kokanee / *(continued)*

M-Junior	Vacant			
M-Smallfry	Vacant			

Mackerel / *Scomberomorus, Scomber spp.*

LINE CLASS	WEIGHT	PLACE	DATE	ANGLER
F-Junior	5.00 kg (11 lb 4 oz)	Bimini, Bahamas	June 13, 1998	Marie Jagusztyn
F-Smallfry	4.08 kg (9 lb 0 oz)	Pinas Bay, Panama	Jan. 9, 1998	Amanda Ruth Forman
M-Junior	5.10 kg (11 lb 4 oz)	Fowey Light, Florida, USA	July 23, 1998	Sean L. Mirmelli
M-Smallfry	6.57 kg (14 lb 8 oz)	Alligator Light, Florida, USA	Mar. 29, 1998	Cory Hebert

Mackerel (king/narrowbarred) / *Scomberomorus cavalla, S. commerson*

LINE CLASS	WEIGHT	PLACE	DATE	ANGLER
F-Junior	28.34 kg (62 lb 8 oz)	Miami Beach, Florida, USA	Mar. 22, 1998	Gayle Steiner
F-Smallfry	11.11 kg (24 lb 8 oz)	Gulf of Mexico, Florida, USA	Oct. 10, 1998	Mackenzie T. LaRoe
M-Junior	27.40 kg (60 lb 6 oz)	Brombie Islets, Australia	Oct. 5, 1997	Leigh Jones
M-Smallfry	20.23 kg (44 lb 9 oz)	Ft. Pierce, Florida, USA	July 26, 1997	Michael DiFrancesisco

Madai / *Pagrus major*

LINE CLASS	WEIGHT	PLACE	DATE	ANGLER
F-Junior	Vacant			
F-Smallfry	Vacant			
M-Junior	Vacant			
M-Smallfry	Vacant			

Marlin (black/blue/striped/white) / *Makaira spp., Tetrapterus spp.*

LINE CLASS	WEIGHT	PLACE	DATE	ANGLER
F-Junior	149.91 kg (330 lb 8 oz)	North Drop, British Virgin Islands	Oct. 18, 1997	Cari R. Loveland
F-Smallfry	152.40 kg (335 lb 15 oz)	Tutukaka, New Zealand	Apr. 1, 1997	Abbie Hamilton
M-Junior	370.00 kg (815 lb 11 oz)	Funchal, Madeira, Portugal	Aug. 12, 1997	Brent Malyon
M-Smallfry	148.32 kg (327 lb 0 oz)	Black River, Mauritius	Apr. 14, 1998	Phillip Vosloo

Muskellunge / *Esox masquinongy*

LINE CLASS	WEIGHT	PLACE	DATE	ANGLER
F-Junior	Vacant			
F-Smallfry	Vacant			
M-Junior	11.92 kg (26 lb 4 oz)	Shadow Lakes, Braidwood, Illinois, USA	Sept. 23, 1997	Brian Belke
M-Smallfry	Vacant			

Oscar / *Astronotus ocellatus*

LINE CLASS	WEIGHT	PLACE	DATE	ANGLER
F-Junior	Vacant			
F-Smallfry	0.56 kg (1 lb 4 oz)	Holiday Park, Florida, USA	May 17, 1998	Christina Wright
M-Junior	Vacant			
M-Smallfry	0.76 kg (1 lb 11 oz)	C-14 Canal, Ft. Lauderdale, Florida, USA	Sept. 26, 1998	Kyle Hoefer

Peacock, butterfly / *Cichla ocellaris*

LINE CLASS	WEIGHT	PLACE	DATE	ANGLER
F-Junior	3.17 kg (7 lb 0 oz)	Miami, Florida, USA	Sept. 10, 1998	Leslie Estrada
F-Smallfry	1.87 kg (4 lb 2 oz)	Pembroke Pines, Florida, USA	Apr. 27, 1997	Christina Wright
M-Junior	1.81 kg (4 lb 0 oz)	Cinaruco River, Venezuela	Mar. 18, 1998	Javier (Gordo) Garcia
M-Smallfry	2.26 kg (5 lb 0 oz)	Holiday Park, Ft. Lauderdale, Florida, USA	Apr. 27, 1998	Shawn A. Wright

Peacock, speckled / *Cichla temensis*

LINE CLASS	WEIGHT	PLACE	DATE	ANGLER
F-Junior	Vacant			
F-Smallfry	Vacant			
M-Junior	4.82 kg (10 lb 10 oz)	Cano La Pica, Estado Apure, Venezuela	Apr. 7, 1998	Felix Henrique Lairet
M-Smallfry	Vacant			

Perch (European/yellow) / *Perca fluviatilis, P. flavescens*

LINE CLASS	WEIGHT	PLACE	DATE	ANGLER
F-Junior	Vacant			
F-Smallfry	0.48 kg (1 lb 1 oz)	Red Cedar Lake, Wisconsin, USA	Aug. 11, 1998	Christina C. Berg
M-Junior	0.48 kg (1 lb 1 oz)	Country Lakes, Browns Mills, New Jersey, USA	Aug. 6, 1997	Joey Giafaglione
M-Smallfry	0.45 kg (1 lb 0 oz)	Red Cedar Lake, Wisconsin, USA	Aug. 11, 1998	Steven M. Berg

Perch, Nile / *Lates niloticus*

LINE CLASS	WEIGHT	PLACE	DATE	ANGLER
F-Junior	Vacant			
F-Smallfry	Vacant			
M-Junior	Vacant			
M-Smallfry	19.5 kg (42 lb 15 oz)	Lake Victoria, Entebbe, Uganda	Sept. 21, 1997	Shane Moldenhauer

Perch, white / *Morone americana*

LINE CLASS	WEIGHT	PLACE	DATE	ANGLER
F-Junior	Vacant			
F-Smallfry	Vacant			
M-Junior	0.70 kg (1 lb 9 oz)	Lake Winnipesaukee, New Hampshire, USA	Aug. 20, 1998	Joey Giafaglione
M-Smallfry	0.51 kg (1 lb 2 oz)	Derickson's Creek, Delaware, USA	Mar. 29, 1998	Franklin Timothy Brinker

Permit / *Trachinotus falcatus*

LINE CLASS	WEIGHT	PLACE	DATE	ANGLER
F-Junior	7.25 kg (16 lb 0 oz)	Key West, Florida, USA	June 16, 1997	Carly Brownlee
F-Smallfry	5.21 kg (11 lb 8 oz)	Ft. Pierce, Florida, USA	Aug. 4, 1998	Meagan Hart Benbow
M-Junior	14.96 kg (33 lb 0 oz)	Ft. Pierce, Florida, USA	July 19, 1997	Christian Poppell
M-Smallfry	11.79 kg (26 lb 0 oz)	Biscayne Bay, Florida, USA	July 19, 1997	Will Conner Davenport

Pickerel / *Esox spp.*

LINE CLASS	WEIGHT	PLACE	DATE	ANGLER
F-Junior	Vacant			
F-Smallfry	1.02 kg (2 lb 4 oz)	Holiday Park, Ft. Lauderdale, Florida, USA	Mar. 25, 1997	Christina Wright
M-Junior	0.90 kg (2 lb 0 oz)	Country Lakes, New Jersey, USA	July 31, 1997	Joey Giafaglione

Pickerel / *(continued).*

M-Smallfry	0.90 kg (2 lb 0 oz)	Holiday Park, Ft. Lauderdale, Florida, USA	May 23, 1997	Shawn A. Wright

Pike, northern / *Esox lucius*

LINE CLASS	WEIGHT	PLACE	DATE	ANGLER
F-Junior	Vacant			
F-Smallfry	Vacant			
M-Junior	6.60 kg (14 lb 9 oz)	Lac Laronge, Saskatchewan, Canada	June 1, 1997	Charlie Benson
M-Smallfry	5.78 kg (16 lb 13 oz)	Lac Laronge, Saskatchewan, Canada	May 31, 1997	Marcus Benson

Pollack, European / *Pollachius pollachius*

LINE CLASS	WEIGHT	PLACE	DATE	ANGLER
F-Junior	Vacant			
F-Smallfry	2.21 kg (4 lb 14 oz)	Kraakvaag Fjord, Norway	July 14, 1998	Sandra Marquard
M-Junior	Vacant			
M-Smallfry	Vacant			

Pollock / *Pollachius virens*

LINE CLASS	WEIGHT	PLACE	DATE	ANGLER
F-Junior	Vacant			
F-Smallfry	1.44 kg (3 lb 2 oz)	Kraakvaag Fjord, Norway	July 18, 1998	Sandra Marquard
M-Junior	15.42 kg (34 lb 0 oz)	Perkins Cove, Ogunquit, Maine, USA	Aug. 11, 1997	Andrew M. Tuttle
M-Smallfry	Vacant			

Queenfish / *Scomberoides spp.*

LINE CLASS	WEIGHT	PLACE	DATE	ANGLER
F-Junior	4.40 kg (9 lb 11 oz)	Exmouth, Australia	Apr. 23, 1997	Jaimie Snook
F-Smallfry	Vacant			
M-Junior	4.65 kg (10 lb 14 oz)	Mackerel Islands, Onslow, Australia	July 7, 1997	Carl Peter Barbarskas
M-Smallfry	2.74 kg (6 lb 0 oz)	Dampier, Australia	Feb. 2, 1998	Dean Lucas

Redhorse / *Moxostoma spp.*

LINE CLASS	WEIGHT	PLACE	DATE	ANGLER
F-Junior	Vacant			
F-Smallfry	Vacant			
M-Junior	Vacant			
M-Smallfry	Vacant			

Roach / *Rutilus spp.*

LINE CLASS	WEIGHT	PLACE	DATE	ANGLER
F-Junior	Vacant			
F-Smallfry	Vacant			
M-Junior	Vacant			
M-Smallfry	Vacant			

Rockfish / *Sebastes spp.*

LINE CLASS	WEIGHT	PLACE	DATE	ANGLER
F-Junior	Vacant			
F-Smallfry	Vacant			
M-Junior	3.03 kg (6 lb 11 oz)	San Diego, California, USA	Jan. 19, 1997	Scott Reidt
M-Smallfry	Vacant			

Roosterfish / *Nematistius pectoralis*

LINE CLASS	WEIGHT	PLACE	DATE	ANGLER
F-Junior	Vacant			
F-Smallfry	Vacant			
M-Junior	15.42 kg (34 lb 0 oz)	Buena Vista, Guatemala	June 11, 1997	Timothy Choate
M-Smallfry	9.75 kg (21 lb 8 oz)	East Cape, Baja California Sur, Mexico	June 25, 1998	Michael Anthony Fishman

Runner, rainbow / *Elagatis bipinnulata*

LINE CLASS	WEIGHT	PLACE	DATE	ANGLER
F-Junior	Vacant			
F-Smallfry	Vacant			
M-Junior	3.17 kg (7 lb 0 oz)	Pinas Bay, Panama	Feb. 2, 1997	Daniel Dunaway
M-Smallfry	5.08 kg (11 lb 3 oz)	Dauphin Island, Alabama, USA	Aug. 30, 1997	Jonathan Joseph Doss

Sailfish / *Istiophorus platypterus*

LINE CLASS	WEIGHT	PLACE	DATE	ANGLER
F-Junior	51.93 kg (114 lb 8 oz)	Pinas Bay, Panama	Aug. 10, 1997	Jana Cunningham
F-Smallfry	23.40 kg (51 lb 9 oz)	Cozumel, Mexico	Mar. 27, 1997	Katrina Patchin
M-Junior	67.00 kg (147 lb 11 oz)	El Tamarindo, La Union, El Salvador	Apr. 19, 1998	Jorge Francisco Saca Bahaia
M-Smallfry	47.50 kg (104 lb 11 oz)	Fua'amotu, Kingdom of Tonga	July 11, 1997	Bagus Setyo Perdana

Salmon (chum/coho/pink/sockeye) / *Oncorhynchus keta, O. kisutch, O. gorbuscha, O. nerka*

LINE CLASS	WEIGHT	PLACE	DATE	ANGLER
F-Junior	Vacant			
F-Smallfry	Vacant			
M-Junior	4.30 kg (9 lb 8 oz)	Goodnews River Lodge, Alaska, USA	Sept. 21, 1997	Chris Molle
M-Smallfry	5.44 kg (12 lb 0 oz)	Resurrection Bay, Seward, Alaska, USA	Aug. 29, 1998	Justin Deis

Salmon, Atlantic / *Salmo salar*

LINE CLASS	WEIGHT	PLACE	DATE	ANGLER
F-Junior	Vacant			
F-Smallfry	Vacant			
M-Junior	Vacant			
M-Smallfry	Vacant			

Salmon, chinook / *Oncorhynchus tshawytscha*

LINE CLASS	WEIGHT	PLACE	DATE	ANGLER
F-Junior	22.90 kg (50 lb 8 oz)	Kenai River, Alaska, USA	July 2, 1998	Keira Tomblinson
F-Smallfry	15.11 kg (33 lb 5 oz)	Deshka River, Alaska, USA	June 4, 1998	Veronica Tomblinson
M-Junior	14.06 kg (31 lb 0 oz)	Sitka Sound, Sitka, Alaska, USA	Aug. 15, 1998	Koby Huntington
M-Smallfry	12.92 kg (28 lb 8 oz)	Kenai River, Alaska, USA	July 14, 1998	Justin Deis

Sauger / *Stizostedion canadense*

LINE CLASS	WEIGHT	PLACE	DATE	ANGLER
F-Junior	Vacant			
F-Smallfry	Vacant			
M-Junior	Vacant			
M-Smallfry	Vacant			

Seabass, blackfin / *Lateolabrax latus*

LINE CLASS	WEIGHT	PLACE	DATE	ANGLER
F-Junior	Vacant			
F-Smallfry	Vacant			
M-Junior	Vacant			
M-Smallfry	Vacant			

Seabass, Japanese / *Lateolabrax japonicus*

LINE CLASS	WEIGHT	PLACE	DATE	ANGLER
F-Junior	Vacant			
F-Smallfry	Vacant			
M-Junior	1.85 kg (4 lb 1 oz)	Keihin-unga, Yokohama, Kanagawara, Japan	Mar. 21, 1998	Hayato Wakabayashi
M-Smallfry	1.04 kg (2 lb 5 oz)	Keihin-unga, Yokohama, Kanagawara, Japan	May 5, 1998	Kentaro Hara

Seabass, white / *Atractoscion nobilis*

LINE CLASS	WEIGHT	PLACE	DATE	ANGLER
F-Junior	Vacant			
F-Smallfry	8.49 kg (18 lb 11 oz)	Dana Point, California, USA	Sept. 13, 1998	Justine Ricigliano
M-Junior	18.14 kg (40 lb 0 oz)	Horseshoe Kelp, San Pedro, California, USA	May 23, 1997	Michael Snyder
M-Smallfry	24.52 kg (54 lb 1 oz)	Redondo Beach, California, USA	Mar. 14, 1998	Andrew J. Eddy

Seatrout/Weakfish / *Cynoscion spp.*

LINE CLASS	WEIGHT	PLACE	DATE	ANGLER
F-Junior	5.01 kg (11 lb 1 oz)	St. Lucie River, Stuart, Florida, USA	May 24, 1997	Chris Kirkhart
F-Smallfry	3.62 kg (8 lb 0 oz)	South Jetty, Ocean City, Maryland, USA	July 29, 1998	Sarah E. Trattner
M-Junior	3.71 kg (8 lb 3 oz)	Palm City C-23, Florida, USA	Apr. 11, 1997	K.C. Knudsen
M-Smallfry	3.68 kg (8 lb 2 oz)	Elizabeth River, Chesapeake, Virginia, USA	Oct. 8, 1997	Steven J. Bennett

Shad, American / *Alosa sapidissima*

LINE CLASS	WEIGHT	PLACE	DATE	ANGLER
F-Junior	Vacant			
F-Smallfry	Vacant			
M-Junior	Vacant			
M-Smallfry	1.68 kg (3 lb 11 oz)	Shanghai Bend, Feather River, California, USA	May 26, 1997	Reuben M. Bosch

Shark / *any species*

LINE CLASS	WEIGHT	PLACE	DATE	ANGLER
F-Junior	152.00 kg (335 lb 1 oz)	Pahaoa, Wairarapa, New Zealand	Feb. 28, 1998	Georgina A. Reid
F-Smallfry	46.40 kg (102 lb 4 oz)	Stanwell Park Canyons, N.S.W., Australia	Oct. 4, 1998	Pascale O. M. Paton
M-Junior	322.00 kg (709 lb 14 oz)	Port Stephens, Australia	Jan. 19, 1997	Steven J. Leonard
M-Smallfry	312.00 kg (687 lb 13 oz)	Port Stephens, Australia	Apr. 27, 1997	Ian Hissey

Sheepshead / *Archosargus probatocephalus*

LINE CLASS	WEIGHT	PLACE	DATE	ANGLER
F-Junior	Vacant			
F-Smallfry	1.04 kg (2 lb 5 oz)	Terra Ceia Bay, Florida, USA	Mar. 21, 1998	Lauren Baird Hawkins
M-Junior	1.02 kg (2 lb 4 oz)	Stuart, Florida, USA	June 10, 1997	John T. Snipes, Jr.
M-Smallfry	3.40 kg (7 lb 8 oz)	Sabine Lake, Texas, USA	June 26, 1998	Joseph Persohn, IV

Snapper / *Lutjanus spp.*

LINE CLASS	WEIGHT	PLACE	DATE	ANGLER
F-Junior	7.93 kg (17 lb 8 oz)	Islamorada, Florida, USA	May 25, 1998	Mary Katherine DeFoor
F-Smallfry	3.21 kg (7 lb 1 oz)	Galveston, Texas, USA	Aug. 4, 1997	Danielle Renee Parrott
M-Junior	18.59 kg (41 lb 0 oz)	28 Fathom Ledge, Florida, USA	July 24, 1998	Joshua S. Thompson
M-Smallfry	14.62 kg (32 lb 4 oz)	Isla de Cano, Costa Rica	Mar. 20, 1997	Burleson Smith

Snapper (squirefish) / *Pagrus auratus*

LINE CLASS	WEIGHT	PLACE	DATE	ANGLER
F-Junior	5.55 kg (12 lb 3 oz)	Fairway Reef, Doubtless Bay, New Zealand	Jan. 24, 1998	Stephanie L. Dickson
F-Smallfry	8.30 kg (18 lb 4 oz)	Slipper Island, New Zealand	Apr. 11, 1998	Monique Frances Thomas
M-Junior	12.20 kg (26 lb 14 oz)	Great Barrier Island, New Zealand	Feb. 24, 1997	Joseph Moselen
M-Smallfry	15.20 kg (33 lb 8 oz)	Outer Harbor, Australia	Sept. 22, 1997	Shaun Polley

Snook / *Centropomus spp.*

LINE CLASS	WEIGHT	PLACE	DATE	ANGLER
F-Junior	5.89 kg (13 lb 0 oz)	Fort Pierce, Florida, USA	July 4, 1997	Meredith Hickman
F-Smallfry	8.16 kg (18 lb 0 oz)	Fort Pierce, Florida, USA	July 25, 1998	Meagan Hart Benbow
M-Junior	11.42 kg (25 lb 3 oz)	Boynton Spillway, Florida, USA	May 26, 1997	William E. Kennedy
M-Smallfry	14.87 kg (32 lb 8 oz)	St. Lucie River, Stuart, Florida, USA	Apr. 3, 1998	James A. Bellavia

Sturgeon / *Acipenseridae spp.*

LINE CLASS	WEIGHT	PLACE	DATE	ANGLER
F-Junior	Vacant			
F-Smallfry	Vacant			
M-Junior	Vacant			
M-Smallfry	Vacant			

Sunfish (green/longear/redbreast/redear/spotted) / *Lepomis spp.*

LINE CLASS	WEIGHT	PLACE	DATE	ANGLER
F-Junior	Vacant			
F-Smallfry	0.45 kg (1 lb 0 oz)	Hawkins Pond, Indiana, USA	Aug. 31, 1998	Christina Berg
M-Junior	0.97 kg (2 lb 2 oz)	Patagonia Lake State Park, Arizona, USA	June 5, 1998	Mikey A. Porter
M-Smallfry	0.70 kg (1 lb 9 oz)	Mt. Pleasant, South Carolina, USA	Apr. 23, 1997	Jadie James

Tarpon / *Megalops atlanticus*

LINE CLASS	WEIGHT	PLACE	DATE	ANGLER
F-Junior	30.84 kg (68 lb 0 oz)	Cannon Island, Brus Lagoon, Honduras	July 10, 1997	Melissa Noviello
F-Smallfry	8.61 kg (19 lb 0 oz)	Red Hook, St. Thomas, US Virgin Islands	Oct. 11, 1998	Darcy Loveland
M-Junior	73.48 kg (162 lb 0 oz)	Boca Grande Pass, Boca Grande, Florida, USA	June 23, 1998	Drew White
M-Smallfry	27.21 kg (60 lb 0 oz)	Captiva Island, Florida, USA	May 19, 1997	John Martin Landry

Tautog / *Tautoga onitis*

LINE CLASS	WEIGHT	PLACE	DATE	ANGLER
F-Junior	2.26 kg (5 lb 0 oz)	Barrington, Rhode Island, USA	June 7, 1998	Becky Hiller
F-Smallfry	1.36 kg (3 lb 0 oz)	Buzzards Bay, Massachusetts, USA	June 9, 1997	Lauren B. Hawkins
M-Junior	5.55 kg (12 lb 4 oz)	New Jersey, USA	Dec. 17, 1997	Ariel J. Berman
M-Smallfry	1.36 kg (3 lb 0 oz)	Long Island Sound, New York, USA	Dec. 29, 1997	Bryan Boesenberg

Tigerfish / *Hydrocynus spp.*

LINE CLASS	WEIGHT	PLACE	DATE	ANGLER
F-Junior	Vacant			
F-Smallfry	Vacant			
M-Junior	7.70 kg (16 lb 15 oz)	Tiger Camp, Zambezi River, Zambia	Aug. 26, 1997	Anderson Mazoka
M-Smallfry	7.10 kg (15 lb 10 oz)	Tiger Camp, Zambezi River, Zambia	Aug. 29, 1997	George Sokota, Jr.

Tilapia / *Tilapia/Oreochromis spp.*

LINE CLASS	WEIGHT	PLACE	DATE	ANGLER
F-Junior	Vacant			
F-Smallfry	Vacant			
M-Junior	1.36 kg (3 lb 0 oz)	Wellington, Florida, USA	July 4, 1997	Scott Watson
M-Smallfry	1.56 kg (3 lb 8 oz)	Wellington, Florida, USA	July 4, 1997	Zachary Nicholas

Trevally (bluefin/giant) / *Caranx melampygus, C. ignobilis*

LINE CLASS	WEIGHT	PLACE	DATE	ANGLER
F-Junior	26.80 kg (59 lb 1 oz)	Midway Island	June 20, 1997	Kibbie Bone
F-Smallfry	Vacant			
M-Junior	20.21 kg (44 lb 9 oz)	Midway Island	Aug. 2, 1997	Robert C. Grant
M-Smallfry	Vacant			

Trevally, other / *Caranx spp.*

LINE CLASS	WEIGHT	PLACE	DATE	ANGLER
F-Junior	6.20 kg (13 lb 10 oz)	Groote Eylandt, Australia	Nov. 2, 1997	Jessica Thumwood
F-Smallfry	5.07 kg (11 lb 3 oz)	Midway Island	July 12, 1998	Hunter Doughty
M-Junior	10.00 kg (22 lb 0 oz)	Dampier, Australia	Apr. 17, 1998	Dean Lucas
M-Smallfry	2.00 kg (4 lb 6 oz)	Pinnacles, New Zealand	Feb. 21, 1998	Ben McFarlane

Tripletail / *Lobotes surinamensis*

LINE CLASS	WEIGHT	PLACE	DATE	ANGLER
F-Junior	5.04 kg (11 lb 2 oz)	Port Canaveral, Florida, USA	Oct. 31, 1997	Katrina Johnson Berrey
F-Smallfry	Vacant			
M-Junior	6.57 kg (14 lb 8 oz)	Punta Gorda, Florida, USA	June 17, 1998	Daniel Thompson
M-Smallfry	8.39 kg (18 lb 8 oz)	Port Canaveral, Florida, USA	Sept. 13, 1998	David C. Baggett

Trout, brook / *Salvelinus fontinalis*

LINE CLASS	WEIGHT	PLACE	DATE	ANGLER
F-Junior	Vacant			
F-Smallfry	Vacant			
M-Junior	Vacant			
M-Smallfry	1.55 kg (3 lb 7 oz)	Paulins Kill River, New Jersey, USA	May 31, 1997	Dylan Robert Chayes

Trout, brown / *Salmo trutta*

LINE CLASS	WEIGHT	PLACE	DATE	ANGLER
F-Junior	Vacant			
F-Smallfry	1.13 kg (2 lb 8 oz)	Lake Michigan, Michigan, USA	Apr. 28, 1998	Juliana Jackoviak
M-Junior	Vacant			
M-Smallfry	2.38 kg (5 lb 4 oz)	Paulins Kill River, New Jersey, USA	May 24, 1997	Dylan Robert Chayes

Trout, cutthroat / *Oncorhynchus clarki*

LINE CLASS	WEIGHT	PLACE	DATE	ANGLER
F-Junior	Vacant			
F-Smallfry	2.21 kg (4 lb 15 oz)	Pyramid Lake, Nevada, USA	June 30, 1997	Nicole N. Berg
M-Junior	1.64 kg (3 lb 10 oz)	Lake Lenore, Washington, USA	Apr. 6, 1998	Brady Foreman
M-Smallfry	2.26 kg (5 lb 0 oz)	Pyramid Lake, Nevada, USA	June 30, 1997	Steven M. Berg

Trout, lake / *Salvelinus namaycush*

LINE CLASS	WEIGHT	PLACE	DATE	ANGLER
F-Junior	Vacant			
F-Smallfry	0.70 kg (1 lb 8 oz)	Lake Niemegk, Germany	May 13, 1998	Sandra Marquard
M-Junior	25.45 kg (56 lb 2 oz)	Macintosh Bay, Great Bear Lake, Canada	July 13, 1997	Alex Rich
M-Smallfry	5.66 kg (12 lb 8 oz)	Lake Michigan, Manestee, Michigan, USA	June 2, 1998	Mark Wesley Johnston

Trout, rainbow / *Oncorhynchus mykiss*

LINE CLASS	WEIGHT	PLACE	DATE	ANGLER
F-Junior	1.36 kg (3 lb 0 oz)	Nielson Ranch Spring Creek Pond, Checkerboard, Montana, USA	Aug. 25, 1998	Mary Cathleen Connell
F-Smallfry	2.04 kg (4 lb 8 oz)	Boone, North Carolina, USA	May 16, 1997	Taylor Hauenstein
M-Junior	1.36 kg (3 lb 0 oz)	Bishop Creek, California, USA	Aug. 29, 1997	Andrew Craig Yamashita
M-Smallfry	6.53 kg (14 lb 6 oz)	Santa Ana Lakes, California, USA	Apr. 20, 1998	Dominick Ricigliano

Tuna (larger) / *Thunnus thynnus, T. albacares, T. maccoyi, T. obesus*

LINE CLASS	WEIGHT	PLACE	DATE	ANGLER
F-Junior	52.20 kg (115 lb 1 oz)	NE Whale Island, Whakatane, New Zealand	Jan. 7, 1997	Louise McCracken
F-Smallfry	25.20 kg (55 lb 8 oz)	NE Whale Island, Whakatane, New Zealand	Jan. 6, 1998	Ashlee Lang
M-Junior	293.47 kg (647 lb 0 oz)	Azores, Portugal	Aug. 4, 1997	Joffrey Grilli Francois
M-Smallfry	52.60 kg (115 lb 15 oz)	Hout Bay, South Africa	Mar. 23, 1997	Tom De Kock

Tuna (smaller) / *Thunnus alalunga, T. atlanticus, T. tonggol, Katsuwonus pelamis*

LINE CLASS	WEIGHT	PLACE	DATE	ANGLER
F-Junior	19.50 kg (42 lb 15 oz)	Tauranga, New Zealand	Sept. 13, 1997	Tyler Ross
F-Smallfry	6.40 kg (14 lb 1 oz)	Tutukaka, New Zealand	Apr. 12, 1998	Courtney Wood
M-Junior	27.21 kg (60 lb 0 oz)	Hudson Canyon, New York, USA	Oct. 12, 1997	Nicholas Calandra
M-Smallfry	28.30 kg (62 lb 6 oz)	Hout Bay, South Africa	Mar. 30, 1997	Tom De Kock

Tunny, little / *Euthynnus alletteratus*

LINE CLASS	WEIGHT	PLACE	DATE	ANGLER
F-Junior	6.35 kg (14 lb 0 oz)	Delray Beach, Florida, USA	June 14, 1997	Jacquelyn Rubio-Myatt
F-Smallfry	7.71 kg (17 lb 0 oz)	Haulover Inlet, Miami Beach, Florida, USA	July 18, 1998	Jaclyn Hirsch
M-Junior	7.37 kg (16 lb 4 oz)	Alligator Reef, Islamorada, Florida, USA	Aug. 20, 1997	Andrew Carter
M-Smallfry	8.64 kg (19 lb 0 oz)	Boca Raton, Florida, USA	May 2, 1998	John Bassett

Wahoo / *Acanthocybium solandri*

LINE CLASS	WEIGHT	PLACE	DATE	ANGLER
F-Junior	39.02 kg (86 lb 0 oz)	Gulf of Mexico, Texas, USA	June 4, 1997	Sarah Rothermel
F-Smallfry	17.91 kg (39 lb 8 oz)	Walker's Cay, Bahamas	Apr. 24, 1998	Sarah Grace King Black
M-Junior	37.87 kg (83 lb 8 oz)	Beaufort Inlet, North Carolina, USA	Sept. 14, 1997	Nicholas Greg Harrison
M-Smallfry	26.50 kg (58 lb 6 oz)	Solo Reef, Fiji Islands	July 24, 1998	Zane Southwick

Walleye / *Stizostedion vitreum*

LINE CLASS	WEIGHT	PLACE	DATE	ANGLER
F-Junior	Vacant			
F-Smallfry	Vacant			
M-Junior	1.19 kg (2 lb 10 oz)	Rainy Lake, Ontario, Canada	Aug. 10, 1998	Hunter Morris
M-Smallfry	0.79 kg (1 lb 12 oz)	Kelly's Island, Ohio, USA	July 20, 1997	Eddie Twyford

Warmouth / *Lepomis gulosus*

LINE CLASS	WEIGHT	PLACE	DATE	ANGLER
F-Junior	Vacant			
F-Smallfry	Vacant			
M-Junior	Vacant			
M-Smallfry	Vacant			

Wels / *Silurus glanis*

LINE CLASS	WEIGHT	PLACE	DATE	ANGLER
F-Junior	Vacant			
F-Smallfry	Vacant			
M-Junior	Vacant			
M-Smallfry	Vacant			

Whitefish (lake/mountain/round) / *Prosopium williamsoni, P. cylindraceum, Coregonus clupeaformis*

LINE CLASS	WEIGHT	PLACE	DATE	ANGLER
F-Junior	0.68 kg (1 lb 8 oz)		Aug. 25, 1998	Mary Cathleen Connell
F-Smallfry	Vacant			
M-Junior	Vacant			
M-Smallfry	Vacant			

Whiting / *Sillaginidae spp.*

LINE CLASS	WEIGHT	PLACE	DATE	ANGLER
F-Junior	Vacant			
F-Smallfry	1.95 kg (4 lb 5 oz)	Kraakvaag Fjord, Norway	July 24, 1998	Sandra Marquard
M-Junior	Vacant			
M-Smallfry	Vacant			

Yellowtail / *Seriola lalandi spp.*

LINE CLASS	WEIGHT	PLACE	DATE	ANGLER
F-Junior	24.80 kg (54 lb 10 oz)	Cavalli Island, Bay of Islands, New Zealand	Aug. 6, 1998	Karene Cates
F-Smallfry	5.89 kg (13 lb 0 oz)	San Diego, California, USA	May 22, 1997	Danielle Barnett
M-Junior	26.80 kg (59 lb 1 oz)	Cavalli Islands, New Zealand	June 22, 1997	Todd Lowry
M-Smallfry	20.32 kg (44 lb 12 oz)	Flat Rock, Kawau Island, New Zealand	Apr. 12, 1998	Mark Colville

IGFA

Get a Youngster Hooked on Fishing

Teach your boys or girls to fish and see how much fun they have. A Junior Membership in the International Game Fish Association costs only $15. IGFA's Junior Angler world record program officially kicked off on January 1, 1997. Catches made after that date are eligible for junior angler world record status.

There are four record divisions. Records will be maintained for males and females in a "small-fry" division through age 10 and for "junior anglers" 11 through 16 for 120 of the most popular species, 60 freshwater and 60 saltwater.

There's no better way to get your children interested in conservation of nature's resources, and give them an understanding of ethical fishing practices at an early age. Junior Angler membership includes:

- Junior Angler Club cap.
- Embroidered jacket emblem.
- Subscription to the *International Junior Angler.*
- Regular record updates.
- A Junior Angler Club decal.
- Individual membership card.

For junior membership information, call (954) 927-2628, or write: IGFA, 300 Gulf StreamWay, Dania Beach, FL 33004.

Please check the membership category for which you are applying.
[ ] $15 Junior Membership
[ ] $35 Regular Membership
[ ] $45 Family Membership
(Regular and family memberships include annual 352-page *World Record Game Fishes* book and subscription to *International Angler* newsletter. Family memberships do not include Junior membership.)

Enclosed is $__________ for IGFA Membership(s) indicated.
Charge to my [ ] VISA [ ] MASTERCARD [ ]AMEX [ ]DISCOVER

Account No. [ ][ ][ ][ ][ ][ ][ ][ ][ ][ ][ ][ ][ ][ ][ ][ ]

Expiration date__________ Signature__________________________

NAME ____

STREET ADDRESS____

CITY/STATE ____

COUNTRY ____

Mail to: IGFA,   300 Gulf Stream Way, Dania Beach, FL 33004

International Game Fish Association

IGFA Junior Angler World Record Application

FORM FOR RECORDING FRESHWATER AND SALTWATER GAME FISH CATCHES

Read all IGFA angling rules and world record requirements before completing and signing this application. The angler's signature on the completed form must be witnessed by a parent or guardian. This application must be accompanied by photographs as specified in the World Record Requirements. Junior anglers are governed by the same IGFA rules as adult anglers with the exception that junior anglers may weigh their fish in a boat on certified scales in order to facilitate live release when desired.

I AM SUBMITTING THIS ENTRY FOR:

☐ Small fry record category (age 10 and under)

☐ Junior angler record category (age 11 through 16 yrs)

☐ Male

☐ Female

Age at time of catch________years

SPECIES

Common name: _______________________

Scientific name: _______________________

WEIGHT:

lb: _________ oz: _________ kg: _____________
Digital weight (if weighed on electronic scales, give weight exactly as shown):_______________________

DATE OF CATCH: _______________________

PLACE OF CATCH:_______________________

____

FISH WAS WEIGHED ON ☐ Land ☐ Boat

FISH WAS RELEASED ☐ Yes ☐ No

METHOD OF CATCH (trolling, fly fishing, etc.):

____

FIGHTING TIME: _______________________
Was the catch recorded on video? _______________

LENGTH (See measurement diagrams)

inches:x to x________ cm:x to x _______________

GIRTH (See measurement diagrams)
inches_______________ cm:_______________

ANGLER (Print name as you wish it to appear on your record certificate):

Name _______________________

Address _______________________

____

Daytime phone _______________________

Angler's date of birth_______________________

EQUIPMENT

Rod
Make: _______________________

Tip length (center of reel to end of tip): _____________

Butt length (Center of reel to lower end of butt):_______

Reel
Make:_______________ Size: _______________

Line or tippet
Make:_______________ Size as stated on label: _______________

☐ I am a junior member of IGFA

☐ Please send me information on junior membership

☐ Enclosed is $15 U. S. for a junior membership

There is no charge for Junior angler record applications. However, contributions to support this program will be gratefully accepted.
Enclosed is $ ____ check or money order in support of the Junior Angler World Record program

Or please charge to my:

___Visa ___Mastercard ___American Express ___Discover

Account No. [ ][ ][ ][ ][ ][ ][ ][ ][ ][ ][ ][ ][ ][ ][ ][ ][ ]

Expiration Date________

Signature_______________________

PLEASE SEND information on corporate sponsorship opportunities in the Junior Angler world record program.
Name_______________________
Address_______________________

____

Note: All items must be filled in. If an item does not apply, write "none used". Do not leave any spaces blank.

Length of double line:_______________________

Make of backing(if any): __________ Size: _________

Other equipment:

Type of gaff: _____________ Length: _____________

Length of trace or leader: _________________________

Number and type of hooks: _________________________

Name of lure, fly or bait: _________________________

BOAT (if used)
Name: _________________________________

Make:_________________ Length: _____________

Captain's name: _________________________________

Address: _________________________________

____

Mate's name:_________________________________

Address: _________________________________

____

SCALES

Location: _________________________________

Type: _________________________________

Manufacturer: _________________________________

Date last certified: _________________________________

Person and/or agency that certified scales:

____

Weighmaster:_________________________________

Address: _________________________________

____

WITNESSES
Witnesses to catch (other than captain). List two names and addresses if possible.

1._________________________________

____

2._________________________________

____

Number of persons witnessing the catch: __________

VERIFICATION OF SPECIES IDENTITY
(only required if species ID from photos will be difficult)

Signature of examining ichthyologist:

____

Title, degree, or qualifications:_________________

Address: _________________________________

____

Anglers are encouraged to write a detailed description of the catch and include it with the application form. In some cases this may be required. The description may be used in a future IGFA publication.

Affidavit

I, the undersigned, hereby take oath and attest that the fish described in this application was hooked, fought and landed by me without assistance from anyone, except as specifically provided in the regulations; and that it was caught in accordance with IGFA angling rules. I further declare that all the information in this application including date of birth is true and correct to the best of my knowledge. I agree to be bound by any ruling of the IGFA relative to this application.

Signature of angler: _________________________________

Signature of parent or guardian: _________________________________

When completely filled out and signed, mail this application with photos by quickest means to:

IGFA, 300 Gulf Stream Way, Dania Beach, Florida 33004 USA
Phone (954) 927-2628 Fax (954) 924-4299 E-Mail: IGFAHQ@aol.com

SECTION 5
GUIDE TO FISHES

Species Identification   **246**

Species Illustration Credits   **295**

Species Identification

This illustrated guide to freshwater and saltwater species contains information on distribution, major identification characteristics, habitats, recreational and commercial value, and more. The species are listed alphabetically according to their standard common names. In the case of North American species, these names agree with those established by the Committee on Names of Fishes (a joint committee of the American Fisheries Society of Ichthyologists and Herpetologists) in *Common and Scientific Names of Fishes from the Unites States and Canada*, Fifth Edition (1991, American Fisheries Special Publication #20) and *World Fishes Important to North Americans*, (1991, American Fisheries Special Publication #21). In all other cases, the name most often used in the area(s) where the species occur was selected for this listing. Also see "Index to Common and Scientific Names of Fishes" at the back of this book.

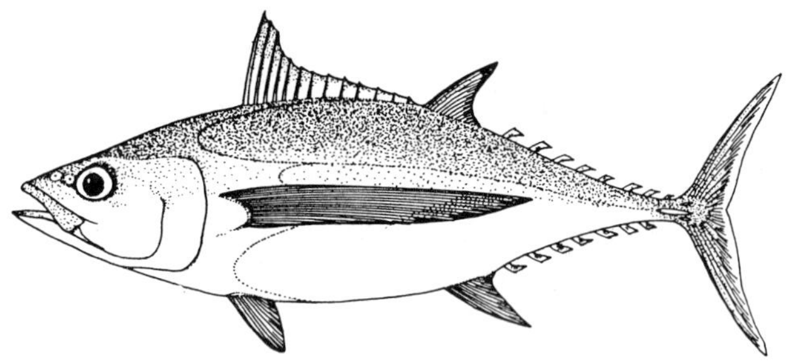

ALBACORE / *Thunnus alalunga* (Bonnaterre, 1788); SCOMBRIDAE FAMILY; also called longfin tuna, long-finned tunny

Found worldwide in tropical and warm temperate seas, including the Mediterranean, and seasonally in colder zones. Pelagic and migratory. Usually remains in deep, clear blue tropical or warm waters, but makes seasonal migrations into colder zones (New England, South Brazil, northern Gulf of Mexico).

The most distinguishing feature of this member of the tuna and mackerel family is its very long pectoral fins that reach to a point beyond the anal fin. The pectoral fins of other adult tunas may also be moderately long, but never extend all the way to the anal fin. Though the very long pectoral fins readily distinguish the adult albacore from other adult tunas, it should be noted that juvenile albacore may have shorter pectoral fins than similar-sized yellowfin tuna (*T. albacares*) or bigeye tuna (*T. obesus*). The albacore can be distinguished from these species at any age by the lack of stripes or spots on its lower flanks and belly and by the presence of a thin, white trailing edge on the margin of the tail fin. Gill rakers number from 25-32 on the first arch. The liver is striated on the ventral surface. The deepest part of the albacore's body is near the second dorsal fin, rather than near the middle of the first dorsal fin as in other tunas, and the vent is round rather than oval or teardrop shaped. The fins are dark yellowish, except for the white trailing edge of the tail. The anal finlets are dark.

Fishing methods include trolling with feathered jigs, spoons and lures; live and whole bait fishing with mullet, sardines, squid, herring, anchovies, sardines and other small fishes. The albacore is considered by anglers to be an excellent light-tackle game fish. In the United States the albacore is probably the most valuable tuna in terms of quality and profit. Its white meat is canned and sold commercially throughout the country, and, with the blackfin tuna, is the only kind that can carry the label "white meat tuna".

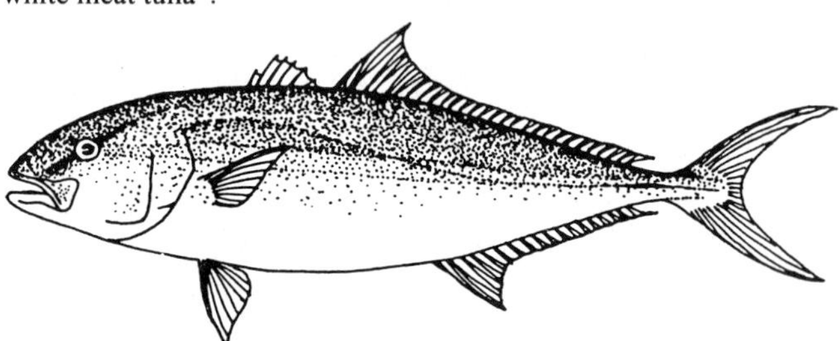

AMBERJACK, greater / *Seriola dumerili* (Risso, 1810); CARANGIDAE FAMILY

Found in the Indo-Pacific around Japan, China, and the Philippines, in the central Pacific off Hawaii, throughout the western Atlantic Ocean, in portions of the eastern Atlantic Ocean (Madeira and southern and western Africa), and in the Mediterranean Sea in tropical and warm temperate waters. It is found mainly near the surface in open waters, but can be found at considerable depths and around off shore reefs, wrecks, buoys, etc.

They bear a resemblance to the bluefish (*Pomatomus saltatrix*),

from which it can be distinguished by the more incavated tail. The amberjack has small teeth in bands, while the bluefish has large, triangular teeth. The greater amberjack can be distinguished from other related species by the gill raker count: greater amberjack over 8 inches long have only 11-16 developed gill rakers on the lower limb of the first branchial arch (the count may be higher in smaller specimens), whereas yellowtails have 21-28. The first dorsal fin consists of 6 or 7 small, fragile spines connected by a membrane; juveniles have an additional detached spine before the first dorsal fin. The second dorsal fin has one spine and 29-35 soft rays. The anal fin has three spines, the first two of which are detached, and 19-22 soft rays. In adults the two detached spines are sometimes covered with skin. There is a low keel on the caudal peduncle.

A dark olive-colored diagonal stripe reaches from the mouth across the eye to about the first dorsal fin, and a broad amber-colored stripe runs horizontally along the flanks. The amber stripe often causes anglers to confuse this species with the yellowtails.

The greater amberjack is the largest of the jacks and the most sought after by sport fishermen because of its qualities as a game fish. It strikes fast, fights hard, and often dives for the bottom. Frequently when one amberjack is brought to the boat, others will follow it to the surface. Fishing methods include trolling near the surface with lures, spoons, plugs, jigs or strip baits. Also live bait fishing with mullet, grunts, pinfish, or other small fishes. Many incidental catches of amberjack are made while fishing the bottom for snappers and groupers.

The amberjack is high on the list of 300 or more species of tropical marine fishes suspected of causing ciguatera poisoning. The great barracuda has the dubious distinction of leading that list. (See also barracuda, great).

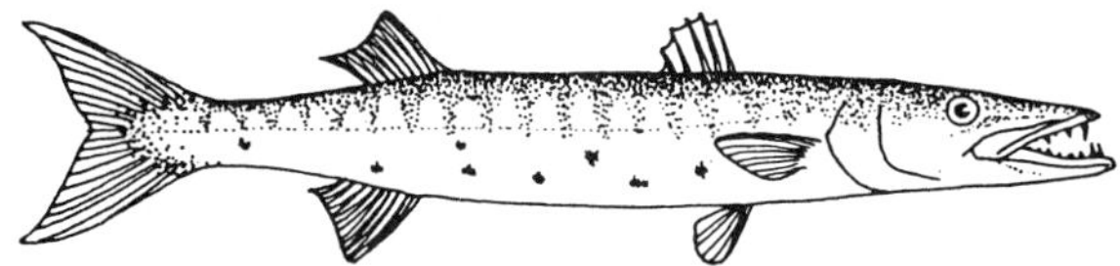

BARRACUDA, great / *Sphyraena barracuda* (Walbaum, 1792); SPHYRAENIDAE FAMILY; also called cuda, sea pike, giant sea pike

Occurs in all tropical seas except the East Pacific. Found offshore and inshore around reefs, piers, wrecks, sandy and grassy flats, and wherever smaller fish congregate. Smaller barracudas sometimes school, but the large ones are almost invariably loners.

The first dorsal fin has 5 spines; the second, 10 soft rays. The first rays of the second dorsal and anal fins reach to or beyond the tips of the last rays when the fins are depressed. There are 75-90 scales along the lateral line. The preopercle is rounded. The maxilla extends back as far as the eyes. The adult great barracuda has irregular black blotches on the lower flanks, especially near the tail. It is the only species of barracuda that has blotches. These features distinguish the great barracuda from the twenty or more smaller species of barracuda.

The barracuda eats whatever is available. Apparently curious, the great barracuda often follows divers. Its habit of "tagging along" while opening and closing its mouth and grinding its teeth has given more than one diver the faith to walk on water; nevertheless, barracudas do not usually attack unless speared or provoked. Sometimes they will attack a shiny object, which they may mistake for the silvery flash of a small fish. The barracuda should be regarded as dangerous because of its ability to inflict serious injury, in or out of water. Its bite is straight and clean, unlike the ragged, crescent-shaped bite of a shark.

Fishing methods include trolling with plugs, spoons, and prepared baits; live bait fishing with small fishes; casting and retrieving live and strip baits as well as plugs and spoons. The cast should not land too near the barracuda, but should be retrieved past it at a fast, erratic speed.

The great barracuda leads a list of over 300 tropical marine fishes suspected of causing ciguatera (a nerve poisoning) when eaten. Ciguatera is not caused by spoilage. Dr. Takeshi Yasumoto, in a 1977 report from the World Health Organization claims that the poison is caused by a microscopic plant (a dinoflagellate organism) eaten by smaller fishes and passed on in the food chain. There is no simple way to determine whether or not a barracuda is toxic. Silver coins turning black when boiled with a toxic barracuda, and other such "tests" are not reliable. The toxin can only be detected in laboratory tests.

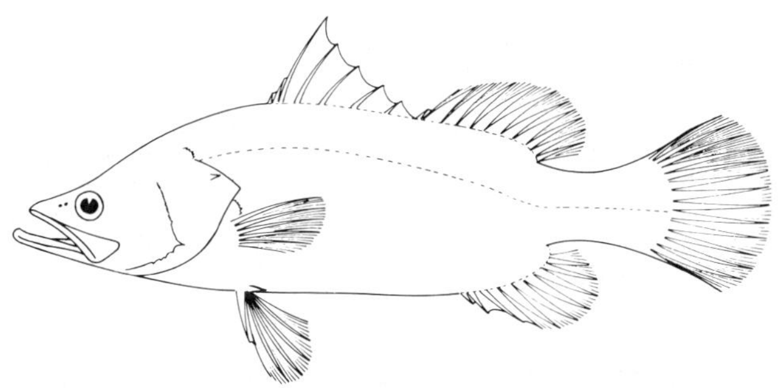

BARRAMUNDI / *Lates calcarifer* (Bloch, 1792); CEN-TROPOMIDAE FAMILY; also called silver barramundi, giant perch, palmer, cock-up, barra, anama (indigenous name, Port Moresby)

The barramundi occurs from northern Australia (primarily north of the Tropic of Capricorn, but rarely as far south as the Maroochy River) to the Philippines and southern China and around the coasts of India to the Persian Gulf. It is a catadromous fish, growing to maturity in fresh water and moving downstream with the onset of the summer monsoon season in October to spawn on the mud flats and in the mouths of estuaries in water of about 2 to 3 percent salinity.

Although the onset of the wet season stimulates spawning behavior in barramundi, only those fish which have access to the sea can spawn initially. The subsequent rainfall and floods allow movement of previously landlocked adult fish, and a second spawning peak occurs later. Through spawning usually ends in November, larvae have been found as late as January and, in one case at least, February. Each female may produce upward of a half a million eggs. The newly hatched larvae are spread randomly by the tidal flow, but soon seek out suitable sheltered habitats in lagoons, swamps, and the saltwater mangrove creeks. After 6 to 8 months the juveniles begin migrating back upstream, and are entering freshwater streams by the end of their first year. Dispersal throughout rivers and estuaries occurs during the second year. When the rains return, most will move back downstream with the help of the tidal flow, and those that are mature will spawn. Contrary to this general pattern, a few barramundi will swim upstream against the tidal flow while others appear to remain in salt or brackish water year round. Fish seen swimming upstream are not, as was once believed, going upstream to spawn; barramundi will not spawn in fresh water or impoundments (dams).

The barramundi is a distinctive fish that bears a noticeable resemblance to its relative the snook, (*Centropomus undecimalis*). It is also closely related to the huge Nile perch, (*Lates niloticus*). One of the it's most noticeable characteristics is its startling pinkish-red eyes, which glow brilliantly at night and even reflect in sunlight. The sides are silvery and the back has a greenish grey tint. The maxillae of the huge mouth extend back beyond the eyes. The head is relatively long and flattened on top, much like a snook's. The forehead is concave and the back rounded. The tongue is smooth, distinguishing it from the much smaller but closely related sand bass, (*Psammoperca waigiensis*) which is often confused with juvenile barramundi.

Many anglers are quick to notice that the barramundi's gill flaps are particularly sharp-edged and will slice through fishing line and nets readily. The two dorsal fins are set close together. The tail is more or less rounded (convex), in contrast to the snook's forked tail. The lateral line is a highly developed sensory organ in the barramundi that can detect vibrations in the water. Consequently, some anglers suggest that a lure should "swim" through the water with an action resembling that of a wounded fish. This creates a vibration that the barramundi can detect and identify.

Live mullets, minnows, barra frogs, and prawns are the barramundi's natural prey and are generally accepted as the best live baits; but certain lures, including rubber barra frog imitations, minnow lures, and some improbable sounding homemade lures fashioned from shotgun shell casings, tooth brushes, and shoe soles are also touted as being "deadly" to "barras" at times. Trolling along the banks is probably the most popular fishing method, but by casting from shore, an angler can work in among the snags and brush where barramundi hide and where a trolled lure won't reach. The barramundi is not an open water feeder; rather, it lies in ambush under cover along the banks, attacking its prey with lightening swiftness as it comes within range, inhaling it into its huge mouth. Because the barramundi "sucks" in its prey and mouths it before swallowing, a pause is recommended before striking.

Barramundi are hermaphrodites; they start life as males, then transform into females after about the second year when they weigh around 11 lb (5 kg). According to research officers D.L. Grey & R.K. Griffin in *A Review of the Northern Territory Barramundi Fishery* (N.T. Fisheries, March 1979), "Anecdotal records indicate that fish of up to 595 lb (270 kg) have been taken." Fish of about 120 lb (55 kg) and 5 ft (1.52 m) in length may be the largest officially recorded. In Australian waters barramundi of 50 lb (22.6 kg) or more are considered large and the average size caught by most anglers is more in the range of 11-22 lb (5-10 kg).

The barramundi is an excellent food fish, reported to be "of gourmet quality, "that attracts high prices in all fish markets. This species should not be confused with another Australian fish, also called "barramundi", which is strictly a freshwater species of the genus *Scleropages*; nor should it be confused with the so-called "barramundi cod", a saltwater fish of the genus *Cromileptes*.

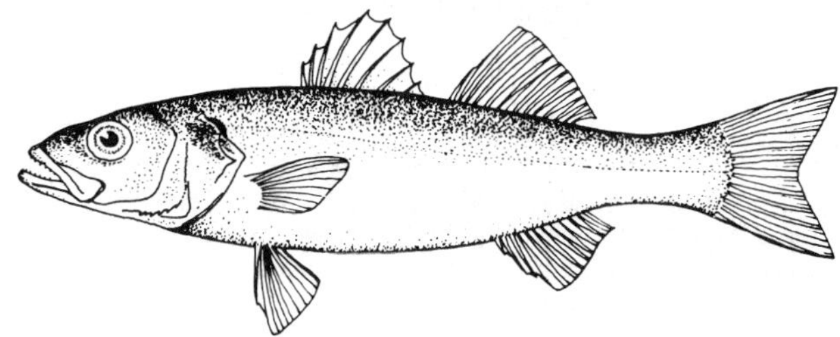

BASS, European / *Dicentrarchus labrax* (Linnaeus, 1758); SERRANIDAE FAMILY

The European bass, known simply as the "bass" in Europe, is a warm and temperate water marine species that is relatively restricted to the European coast from England to northern Africa and the Mediterranean and Black Sea. It is generally found inshore near the surf zone and is somewhat tolerant of fresh water, like its close North American relative, the striped bass (*Morone saxatilis*). In fact, some scientists believe that the European bass should be placed in the same genus (*Morone*) and family (Percichthyidae) as the striped bass. In behavior and appearance the two species are very much alike. The European bass lacks the stripes that characterize *M. saxatilis*, but their body shapes are very similar.

In late October or November, when the surf begins to cool, European bass migrate out to sea, returning when the water begins to warm between February and May. It is considered by many British sea anglers to be the best of all European game fish species, and may grow to over 30 lb (14 kg). Its average weight, however, is 2-9 lb (1-4 kg).

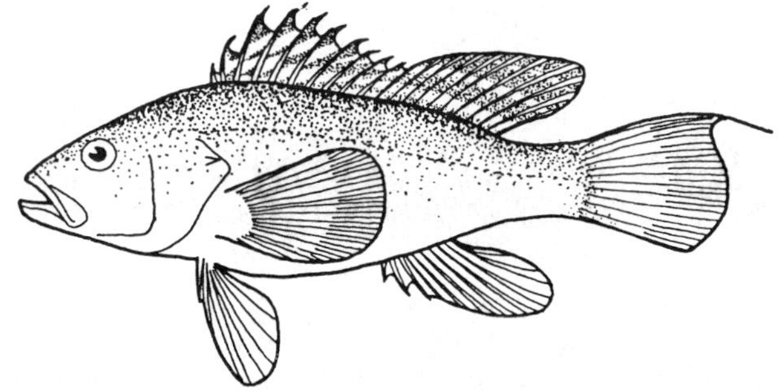

BASS, black sea / *Centropristis striata* (Linnaeus, 1758); SERRANIDAE FAMILY; also called sea bass, black bass, rockbass, common sea bass, humpback (large males)

Found in the western North Atlantic Ocean along the United States east coast from Massachusetts to the Gulf of Mexico; most common from about Long Island, New York to South Carolina. The black sea bass is a bottom species found around wrecks, reefs, piers, breakwaters, and over beds of shells, coral, rock, etc.

The continuous dorsal fin (both dorsal fins are joined into one) is composed of 10 spines followed by 11 soft rays. The anal fin has 3 spines and 7 soft rays. The tail or caudal fin is rounded (convex), and the top ray of the tail fin is typically very elongated in larger specimens. The lateral line has a scale count of 50-60. The dorsal fin is marked by several oblique, white spots arranged into stripes, and there is a large dark spot on the last dorsal spine. Large males of the species are sometimes known as "humpbacks" because of the visible rise or hump just behind their heads.

The best fishing is in depths of 6 to 20 fathoms from May to June and from November to December, though they can be caught all year round. When hooked on light tackle, the sea bass fights hard all the way to the surface. The action is fast and vigorous, and in spite of its small size, it is very much a game fish. Most are caught from anchored or drifting boats by bottom fishing with baits or by jigging with small metal jigs. Some are caught from docks, piers, or the shore. Baits include fishes, shrimp, squid, crabs, worms, clams and mackerel jigs.

Black sea bass are hermaphrodites; most begin their lives as females and change to males. The flesh is firm and white and makes excellent eating; the flavor is delicate.

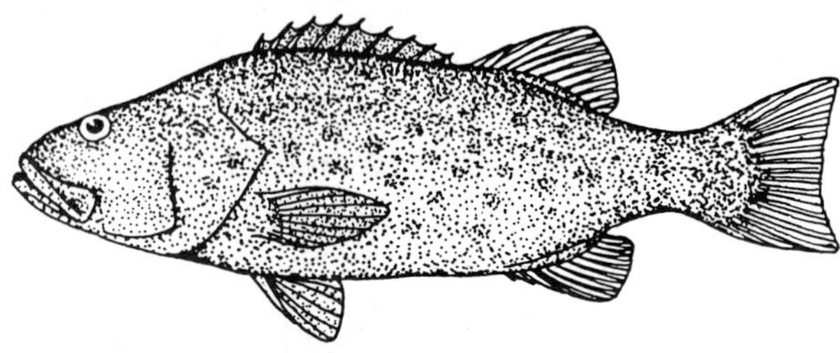

BASS, giant sea / *Stereolepis gigas* Ayres, 1859; PERCICHTHYIDAE FAMILY; also called California black sea bass, California jewfish

Occurs in tropical and subtropical inshore waters of the northeast Pacific off the California and Mexican coasts. Also known on the Asiatic Pacific coast. Despite its great size, the giant sea bass is an inhabitant of near-shore waters, particularly over hard, rocky bottoms and around kelp beds. The young can be found in depths of about 6 to 15 fathoms. Larger specimens can generally be found in depths of 15 to 25 fathoms. Diet includes crustaceans and a wide variety of fishes.

The first dorsal fin is very low and consists of 11 spines. The second dorsal fin is higher than the first, and consists of 10 soft rays. The presence of more dorsal spines than soft rays distinguishes the giant sea bass from any similar related species, including the jewfish (*Epinephelus itajara*). All the fins are black (though the ventral fins appear lighter because the white membrane shows clearly between the black spines). Juveniles are brick red with conspicuous dark spots and a few pale yellow blotches on the body; the fins are black or transparent.

Fishing methods are live or dead bait fishing from an anchored or drifting boat with large natural baits. Fishing is best in the 10 to 25 fathom range.

The giant sea bass and its close relative the jewfish are the giants of the bass family. It is believed that some very large specimens may be 75 years old or even older. American ichthyologists John E. Fitch and Robert J. Lavenberg estimated the age of one 434 lb (197 kg) specimen to be 72-75 years, and larger specimens have been taken. The fish reaches maturity at the age of 11 or 12, at which time it weighs about 50 lb (23 kg).

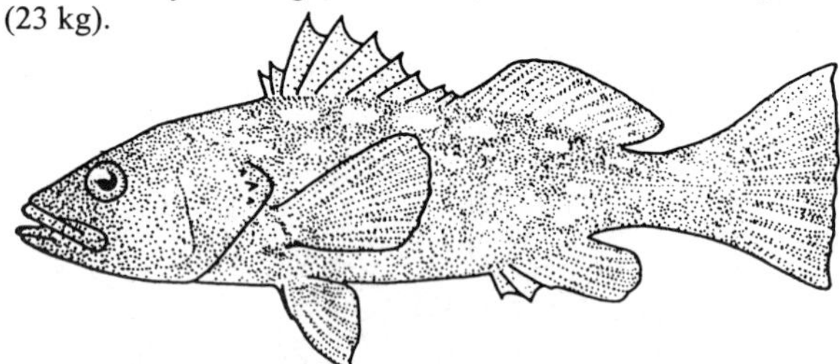

BASS, kelp (calico) / *Paralabrax clathratus* (Girard, 1854); SERRANIDAE FAMILY; also called calico bass, California kelp bass, rock bass, sand bass, bull bass, kelp salmon, cabrilla

The kelp bass is common along the central and southern California coast and northeastern Baja, and ranges from the Columbia River, Washington to Magdalena Bay, Baja California. It is usually found in or near kelp beds, over reefs, around rock jetties and breakwaters or structures in shallow water and to about 150 ft. (46 m). While it is found throughout the water column, larger specimens usually occur in deeper waters.

The kelp bass, a member of a large group of seabasses which inhabit the eastern Pacific, is a robust fish with a typical, well-known bass shape. Most anglers in its territory readily recognize the kelp bass as it is one of the most important targets among southern California's light tackle anglers. It is also a mainstay of the half-day and full-day party boats and 3 and 4 day trips to northern Baja.

The color of is brown to olive green with pale blotches on the back, becoming lighter below. They are easily be distinguished from the sand basses by the fact that the third, fourth and fifth dorsal spines are about the same length, whereas the third dorsal spine of the sand basses is much longer than the fourth and fifth.

Because it is considered to be among the best eating fish and a powerful fighter, it is highly sought by sport fishermen. An omnivorous feeder, it will take most of the local live baits such as anchovies, queenfish, mackerel, and squid, along with a variety of artificial lures. A favorite rig is a metal jig and whole squid, the bait most preferred by experienced kelp bass fishermen. The best fishing is summer to fall although it can be fished year round in some areas. It is caught from breakwaters, and trolling, drifting or anchored in boats.

Kelp bass are slow growing, taking 5 to 6 years before reaching the minimum legal size limit of 12 inches, at which time nearly all are capable of spawning. A larger fish, in the 8 to 10 pound range, could be 15 to 20 years old, with the largest exceeding 15 lb (6.8 kg). Since they do not migrate and tend to be territorial, they are susceptible to fishing pressure and can be depleted by over fishing in an area.

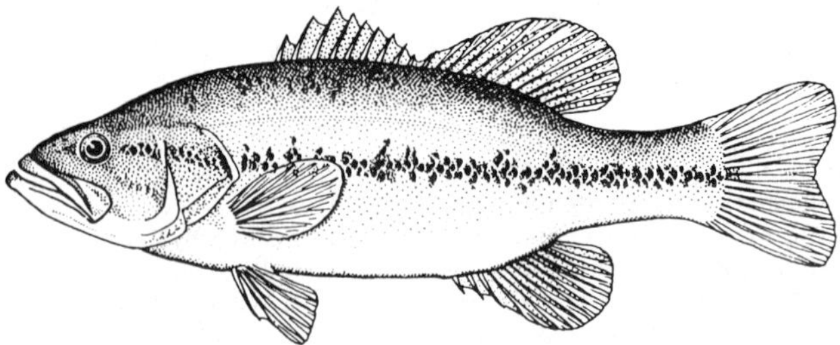

BASS, largemouth / *Micropterus salmoides* (Lacepede, 1802); CENTRARCHIDAE FAMILY; also called black bass, Oswego bass, green bass, green trout, Florida bass, Florida (or southern) largemouth, northern largemouth

Originally confined primarily to the eastern United States of American and portions of northern Mexico and southern Canada, this member of the sunfish family can be found in every state in the U.S.A., throughout Mexico and Central America, and in many other countries throughout the world.

The largemouth bass very closely resembles the smallmouth bass (*Micropterus dolomieu*) and other species of the genus Micropterus (i.e., spotted bass, redeye bass, etc.). Together these fishes form a group that is referred to as the black basses. The largemouth can be distinguished from most similar species by the fact that its mouth extends at least to, and often beyond the rear edge of the eyes. Also, its first and second dorsal fins are almost separated by an obvious deep dip, and there are no scales on the soft-rayed second dorsal fin. These characters are equally true of the Florida largemouth bass and the northern largemouth bass. In all other species of *Micropterus* the mouth does not extend to the back of the eyes, the two dorsal fins are clearly connected, usually with a slight dip between them, and the scales overlap the base portion of the second dorsal fin.

They are the most popular freshwater game fish. Much of its popularity is due to its pugnacious attitude and willingness to strike a lure or bait with explosive force. Research indicates that the largemouth bass is also the most intelligent freshwater fish, able to distinguish and avoid a particular type of lure after only one encounter with it. In fact, some bass lakes believed to be "fished out" contain plenty of bass but the fish have learned to recognize virtually all the lures in common use on the lake. In such cases, a lure that is new to them will often work where others have failed. By comparison the brook trout will strike a particular lure two, three or four times before it learns; sunfish and crappies will take the same lure repeatedly.

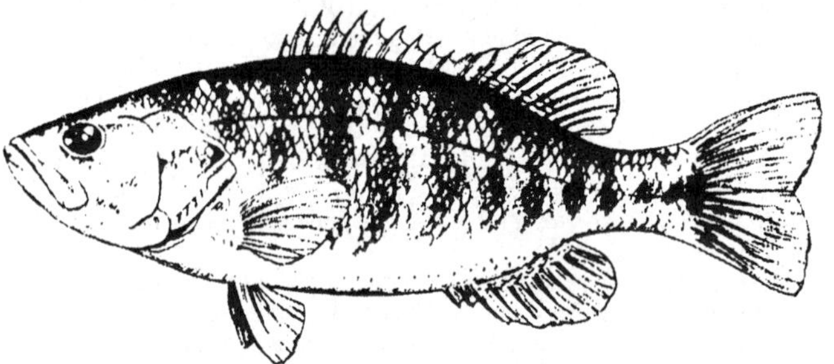

BASS, redeye / *Micropterus coosae* Hubbs & Bailey, 1940; CENTRARCHIDAE FAMILY; also called black bass, shoal bass

Apparently native only to the central and northern portions of Alabama and Georgia (Alabama, Chattahoochee, Coosa, Savannah and Warrior River systems) and southeastern Tennessee (Conasauga drainage), the redeye bass has been introduced to a limited degree in

California, Puerto Rico, and Kentucky's upper Cumberland River drainage as well as into other river systems near its native range.

At present there is some disagreement as to whether the "shoal bass", found in the Apalachicola River system in Florida and in the Chattahoochee, Chestatee, and Flint Rivers in Georgia, is the same as the redeye bass (Alabama River form) or a different species. Externally, the "shoal bass" can normally be distinguished by the presence of a prominent spot right before the tail and another on the edge of the gill cover. These basicaudal and opercular spots are much fainter or entirely absent in the Alabama River form. John S. Ramsey of Auburn University has strongly defended the status of the "shoal bass" as a new species, but it has yet to be fully described or given a scientific name, and most scientists consider it to be a variety of redeye bass, often referred to as the Apalachicola form.

The redeye bass is also superficially quite similar to the spotted bass (*M. punctulatus*) and the smallmouth bass (*M. dolomieu*) which are believed to be its closest relatives. All have red eyes or a considerable amount of red in the eyes, scales on the base portion of the soft-rayed second dorsal fin, clearly connected first and second dorsal fins, and an upper jaw bone that does not extend beyond the eyes. These features distinguish the above three Micropterus species from the largemouth bass (*M. salmoides*) although underwater photography has shown clearly that the eyes of the largemouth often will "light up and take on a reddish glow" when it is about to feed. The fins of redeye bass are noticeably redder in color than in other species, and this, together with location of the catch and all other facts, usually forms the basis of identification by the angler.

The redeye is a good game fish and a scrappy fighter that is hard to catch. Some have been known to reach more than 8 lb (3.70 kg).

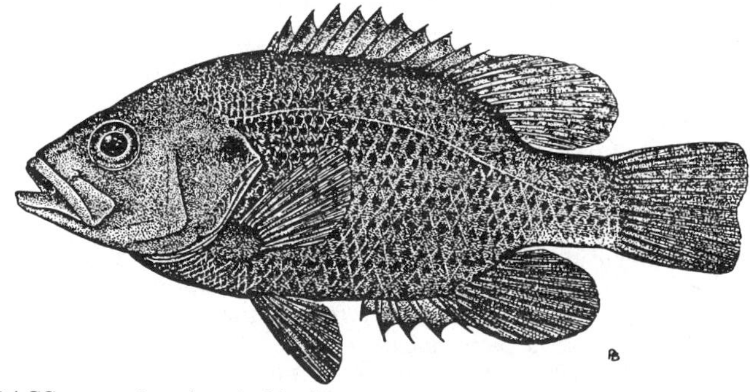

BASS, rock / *Ambloplites rupestris* (Rafinesque, 1817); CENTRARCHIDAE FAMILY; also called black perch, goggle-eye, red-eye, rock sunfish

Native to the northeastern U.S.A. and southeastern Canada, from Ontario and Quebec southward through the Great Lakes region as far as Tennessee an possibly Alabama. Rock bass have also been introduced into other states including some western states. They prefer small, cool, weedy lakes and streams and the outer edges of larger lakes, always over rocky bottoms (hence the name "rock" bass) where no silt is present, turbidity is low and cover is extensive. They are scrappy fighters but tire quickly. The flesh is firm, white, and makes excellent eating.

This is a large and robust sunfish that looks like a cross between a bluegill and one of the black basses. Its body is less compressed than most sunfishes of the genus Lepomis, including the bluegill, and longer in profile looking somewhat more like a black bass than a sunfish. It has been known to reach 3 lb (1.36 kg) but the more common size is about 8 oz (226 g). There is a black spot at the edge of the gill cover. The mouth is larger and more "basslike" than in most small sunfishes, the upper jaw reaching beyond the beginning of the eye, but not to the back of the eye. The two dorsal fins are clearly connected. The eyes are red.

The rock bass is frequently confused with the warmouth (*Lepomis gulosus*), it can be distinguished by the number of spines in front of the soft-rayed anal fin; 3 spines in the warmouth, but 6 in the rock bass. Also, the warmouth has teeth on the tongue unlike the rock bass.

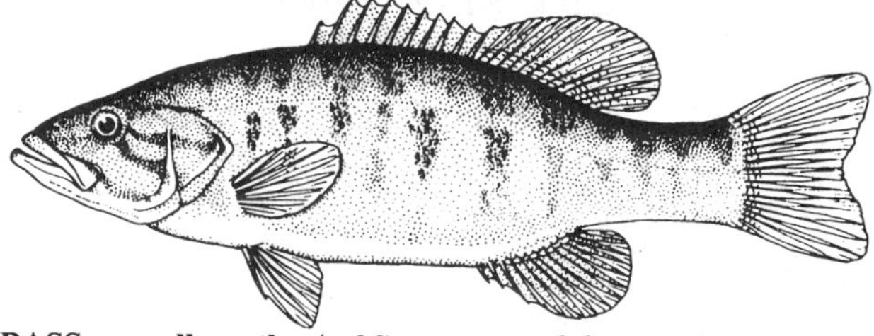

BASS, smallmouth / *Micropterus dolomieu* Lacepede, 1802; CENTRARCHIDAE FAMILY; also call black bass

The smallmouth bass is native to the eastern half of the U.S.A. and southeastern Canada from Manitoba and Quebec south to the Tennessee River system in Alabama and west to eastern Oklahoma. It has been widely transplanted so that today it occurs in almost every state and many other countries. It is not as widespread as the largemouth bass, (*Micropterus salmoides*).

The smallmouth bass is the second largest member of the sunfish family Centrarchidae, attaining a weight of almost 12 lb (5.45 kg). Only the largemouth bass, which reaches a weight of over 20 lb (9.08 kg), is heavier. The smallmouth is easily distinguished from the largemouth by its clearly connected dorsal fins, the scales on the base portion of the soft-rayed second dorsal fin, and the upper jaw bone which extends only to about the middle of the eye. The coloration is also distinctive being usually more brownish in the smallmouth and more greenish in the largemouth. The smallmouth also has faint bars on the body (prominent in the young), while the largemouth has a fairly wide streak of oval or diamond shaped markings or blotches down the midline of the sides. In either species the colors may vary and the markings may be inconspicuous or absent in individuals based on time of year and various biological factors. Generally, the smallmouth has bars radiating back from the eyes, and though similar bars may be present in individuals of other species, including the largemouth, they seem to be more prominent and more consistently present in the smallmouth. The eyes are red or orangish. In young smallmouths there is a distinctive band of orange at the base of the tail. This is followed by a black band with the tip of the tail being white or yellow.

They prefers deeper water than the largemouth and areas of clear, fast-flowing streams and pools with gravel/rubble bottom. In waters cohabited by both smallmouth and largemouth, the largemouth bass will spawn a little earlier due to the fact that the shallower nesting sites they choose in protected areas with emergent vegetation warm to the optimum temperature sooner than the deeper, rockier sites chosen by the smallmouths.

There are many who say that the smallmouth bass is gamer than the largemouth. There is no doubt that it rivals the largemouth in popularity. The flesh is white, flaky and of excellent quality.

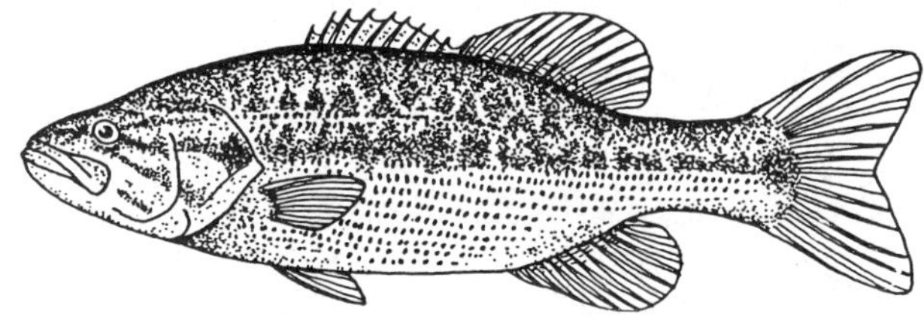

BASS, spotted / *Micropterus punctulatus* (Rafinesque, 1819); CENTRARCHIDAE FAMILY; also called Kentucky bass, Kentucky spotted bass, northern spotted bass, Alabama spotted bass, Wichita spotted bass, black bass

There are three recognized subspecies of the spotted bass: the northern spotted bass (*Micropterus punctulatus punctulatus*), the Alabama spotted bass (*Micropterus p. henshalli*), and the Wichita spotted bass (*Micropterus p. wichitae*). spotted bass can be found throughout the central and lower Mississippi basin to the Gulf of Mexico (from Texas to the Florida panhandle), including Georgia, Alabama, Tennessee, Kentucky and other nearby states where it occurs naturally or has been introduced. The Wichita spotted bass appears to be limited to the West Cache Creek, Oklahoma. The Alabama spotted bass has been introduced into California.

Many anglers who catch a spotted bass believe they have caught a largemouth bass (*M salmoides*), undoubtedly because the coloration is similar, both having a greenish hue and a broad stripe of diamonds or blotches along the midline of the body. The spotted bass, like all black basses except the largemouth, has scales on the base portion of the second dorsal fin, its first and second dorsal fin are clearly connected, and its upper jaw bone does not extend back to or beyond the rear edge of the eyes. The spotted bass is also often confused with the smallmouth bass (*M. dolomieu*), but it lacks the vertical bars that are present on the sides of the body in the smallmouth. The spotted bass also has small black spots below the lateral line (the rear edges of certain scales are black) unlike either the largemouth or the smallmouth. Juveniles of the species resemble the young of smallmouth bass in having a broad band of orange at the base of the tail, followed by a broad black band and white edge. Because of the difficulty in recognizing the species, it is probable that record-size specimens of spotted bass have gone unnoticed.

According to W.B. Scott & E.J. Crossman, the smallmouth bass is known to hybridize in nature with the spotted bass, which could make identification of some specimens where both species are known to occur, even more difficult. Where depth permits it appears that spotted bass usually stay deeper than smallmouths. In one lake in the TVA system in Tennessee, spotted bass have been taken at depths of up to 100 ft (30.4 m). Smallmouth bass, on the other hand, were not caught below 60 ft (18.2 m), and largemouths were always caught right near the surface

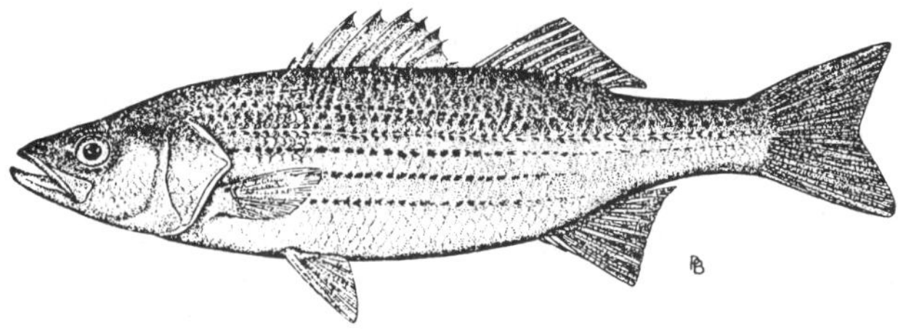

BASS, striped / *Morone saxatilis* (Walbaum, 1792); PERCICHTHYIDAE FAMILY; also called striper, rock, rockfish, squid hound, greenhead

The striped bass, or "rockfish" as it is known in North and South Carolina, occurs from the St. Lawrence River to northern Florida on the Atlantic coast of the United States; off Florida, Louisiana, Alabama and Mississippi in the Gulf of Mexico; and along the U.S. Pacific coast from Washington to California. Striped bass were unknown on the Pacific coast until they were introduced there in 1879 and 1882. On the east coast they have been well known to saltwater anglers and one of the most important food fishes since at least the early 1600's, both in terms of eating quality and commercial importance. In saltwater, the striped bass is anadromous and migratory. Some migrate from North Carolina, Virginia, or Maryland to more northern climates in the summer and return when the summer season is over. Others remain non-migratory within estuarine river systems such as the St. Lawrence, the Santee-Cooper, or the Savannah. To most freshwater anglers, this very important game fish is relatively new. The species moves far upstream in rivers during spawning migrations. It has a native range (in freshwater) from the St. Lawrence River, N.Y., south to St. John's River, Florida, and also from the Suwannee River in Florida, to Lake Pontchartrain in Louisiana. In some of these waters populations have become landlocked due to artificial impoundments that blocked their return to the sea. In recent years, striped bass have been introduced into freshwater systems in most of the states, and today many have grown to quite large sizes.

The striped bass' closest freshwater relatives are the white bass (*Morone chrysops*), the yellow bass (*M. mississippiensis*), and the white "perch" (*M. americana*). The striped bass is easily recognized by the 7 or 8 prominent black stripes that run along the scale rows on each side of its long, sleek, silvery body. One stripe runs along the lateral line, and the remainder are about equally divided above and below it. The first dorsal fin has 8-10 spines and the second, 10-13 soft rays. The anal fin has 3 spines followed by 7-13 soft rays. The dorsal fins are completely separated. The striped bass is longer and sleeker and has a larger head than its close and similar looking relative, the white bass. The striped and white basses have been crossed to create a hybrid known as the whiterock or sunshine (in Florida) bass. Striped bass can be distinguished from hybrids by the regularity of stripes while the hybrid usually has interrupted or broken stripes. A voracious and opportunistic predator, the striped bass will consume all types of fishes. Spawning occurs in fresh or brackish waters from late April to early June. A wide variety of fishing methods are successfully employed, including trolling, jigging, bait fishing, surf casting, fly fishing, and spinning. Baits and lures include mullet, squid, eels, crabs, clams, bloodworms, plugs, spoons, flies, and casting lures.

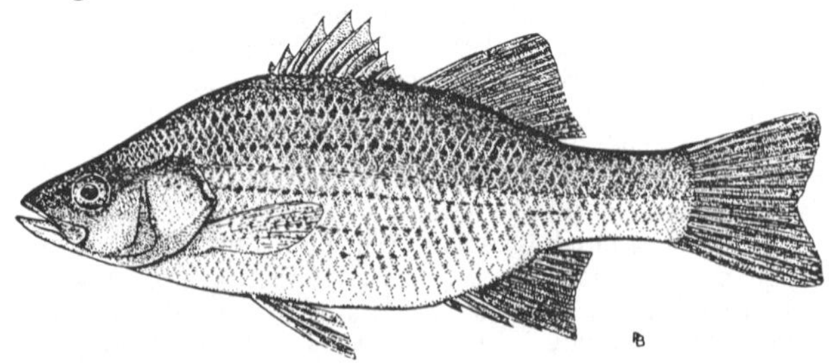

BASS, white / *Morone chrysops* (Rafinesque, 1820); PERCICHTHYIDAE FAMILY

White bass are widely distributed throughout river systems of the Mississippi and Ohio valleys and the Great Lakes. They are native from the St. Lawrence River in the east, to Lake Winnipeg in the north, and to the Rio Grande in the west. Most abundant in clear lakes and reservoirs, they have been transplanted into the systems of various states including California. They are an excellent light tackle fish that will take a bait or lure readily. The white bass looks quite a bit like a shortened version of its larger relative, the striped bass (*Morone saxatilis*). It has the same silvery white sides and black stripes. It differs most noticeably in being shorter and stockier with a smaller head, and the dorsal fins are set closer together. They can be distinguished from the yellow bass (*M. mississippiensis*), by its more silvery color and regular, unbroken stripes as well as by its protruding, pugnacious looking, basslike lower jaw (in the yellow bass the jaws are about equal). It can be distinguished from the white perch (*M. americana*) by the latter's lack of prominent stripes on the sides (though stripes may be present in very small juveniles).

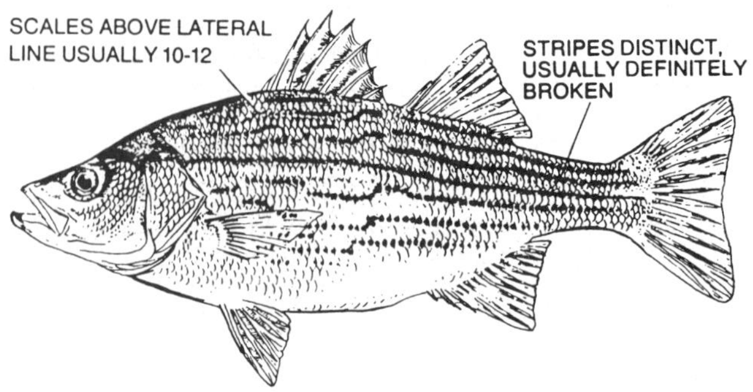

BASS, whiterock / *Morone saxatilis x Morone chrysops* PERCICHTHYIDAE FAMILY; also called sunshine bass (Florida), hybrid bass

The whiterock bass is a hybrid produced by a female striped bass (*Morone saxatilis*) and a male white bass (*Morone chrysops*). In Florida, the sunshine bass is the reverse cross of the same two species, and the two are therefore the same hybrid. Hybrids are not given their own scientific names, but are designated by the names of the two parent species.

The whiterock or sunshine bass looks like a stocky striped bass. It can be distinguished from its larger parent primarily by this shorter, stockier body, and by the interrupted or broken stripes on the sides. The interrupted lines will also distinguish it from its smaller parent, the white bass, as will its size in many cases.

It has been widely stocked in the lakes of various states, providing a new challenge for the angler. It is reputed to be an excellent game fish.

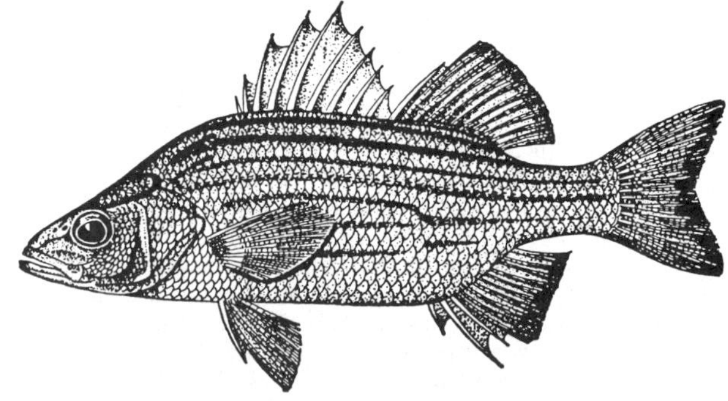

BASS, yellow / *Morone mississippiensis* Jordan and Eigenmann, 1887; PERCICHTHYIDAE FAMILY; also called barfish, brassy bass, stripe, striped bass (erroneously), streaker

The yellow bass can be found in quiet pools and backwaters of large streams, lakes, and reservoirs from Minnesota, Wisconsin, and Michigan south to Louisiana, eastern Texas, and the lower Coosa and Mobile Bay drainages. It is relatively confined to the central Mississippi Valley area and has not been extensively transplanted, though it has been introduced to some degree into other areas of the states within its native range as well as Arizona.

The yellow bass resembles its close relative, the white bass (*Morone chrysops*), but can be recognized by its golden yellow sides and more irregular stripes (of the 6-7 stripes the 3-4 that lie below the lateral line are broken or interrupted toward the tail). The usual size caught by anglers is only about 4-12 oz (340 g). It is even smaller than the largest bluegills, but has a distinctly basslike body as opposed to the rounder, flatter shape of the bluegill (in profile).

The yellow bass is a scrappy fighter and a popular species among light-tackle and panfish anglers. The flesh is white, flaky and better tasting than the white bass.

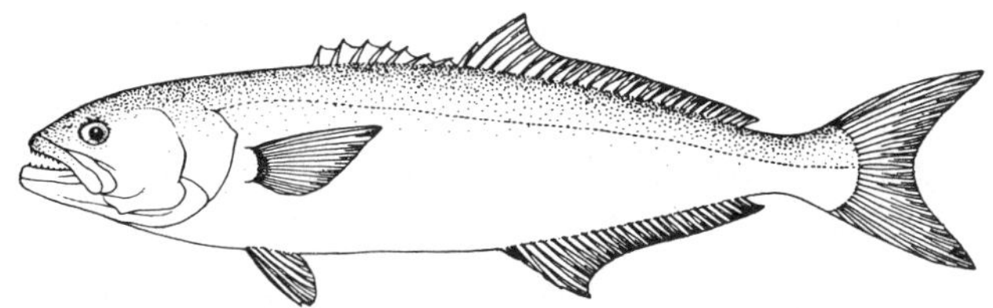

BLUEFISH / *Pomatomus saltatrix* (Linnaeus, 1766); POMATOMIDAE FAMILY; also called blue, tailor, elf, chopper, marine piranha, rock salmon, snapper blue, Hatteras blue

Found worldwide, including the Mediterranean and Black Seas, in temperate to tropical waters. Sporadic in occurrence and location.

The bluefish is the only member of the family Pomatomidae. The mouth has extremely sharp teeth. The existence of a spine in the second dorsal fin, the absence of head markings, and the lack of an interspace between the dorsal fins distinguish the bluefish from the similar looking greater amberjack (*Seriola dumerili*). The bluefish's lack of finlets immediately distinguishes it from the mackerels. The first dorsal fin with 6-8 spines is low and short. The second dorsal fin is long and consists of one spine and 23-28 soft rays. The anal fin has two spines and 25-27 soft rays. There is a recognizable dark spot or blotch at the base of the pectoral fins. The voracious bluefish richly deserves the nicknames "marine piranha" and"chopper" because it swims in large schools through shoals of bait fish, slashing and destroying everything in its path, including smaller individuals of its own kind. When in a feeding frenzy, migrating bluefish have been known to suddenly overwhelm the waters of public beaches. They will bite anything, including any swimmers unlucky enough to be in the water at the time, and will sometimes strand themselves on the beach after chasing the prey fish inshore. The "chopper'" bite can easily sever a finger or a toe and inflict other serious wounds even when the fish is out of water; as many a careless fisherman has learned.

Some anglers "sniff out" bluefish by their smell, which is something like fresh cucumbers. Fishing methods include trolling, chumming, casting, jigging, and live and dead bait fishing from boats, shores or piers. Live baits are best, but plugs, lures or feathers are also used. The flesh tends to become soft if not eaten soon after capture. It does not keep well if frozen.

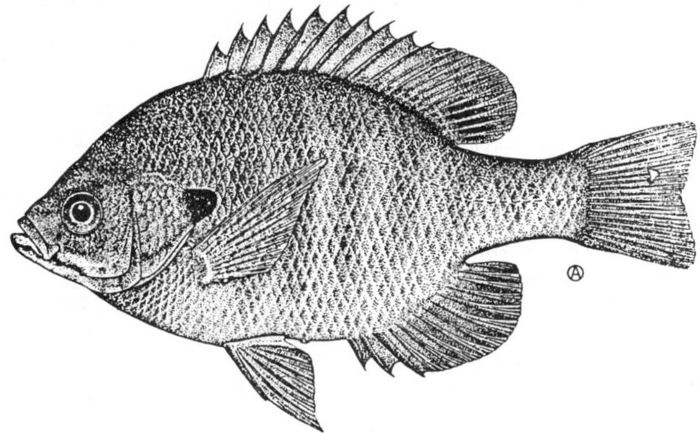

BLUEGILL / *Lepomis macrochirus* Rafinesque, 1819; CENTRARCHIDAE FAMILY; also called bream, sun perch, blue sunfish, copperbelly

Native to approximately the eastern half of the U.S.A. and a small portion of northeastern Mexico, the bluegill has been widely introduced elsewhere in North America as well as into Europe and South Africa. Today it is one of the most popular panfish species in North America. It has a greatly compressed, roundish (in profile) body that is typical of the sunfishes. Its color is highly variable and many range from dark blue or bluish-purple to yellow, and in some cases (notably in quarry holes) it may even appear to be clear and colorless. Usually, there are 6-8 vertical bars on the sides, which may or may not be prominent. The gill cover (operculum) peaks into a broad, roundish flap that is black in color; however, it is not surrounded by a lighter colored trim as it is in some other sunfishes. It has the small mouth and head that are typical of sunfish species. The pectoral fins are pointed. Fly fishing for bluegills has become increasingly popular and light tackle anglers have long found it to be one of the best action fish, ounce for ounce, that can be caught.

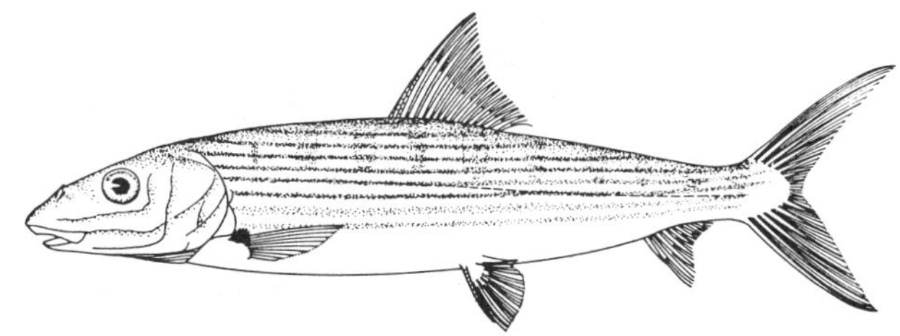

BONEFISH / *Albula spp.* (Linnaeus, 1758); ALBULIDAE FAMILY; also called banana fish, phantom, silver ghost, ladyfish, grubber

Occurs worldwide in shallow tropical and subtropical waters around flats and intertidal areas.

The dorsal fin consists of 17-19 soft rays. The anal fin has 8-9 soft rays, the ventral fins have 9, and the pectoral fins have 15-17. There are 65-73 scales along the lateral line—none on the head. The sides and belly of the fish are bright silver. Parts of the fins and the snout may show a yellowish or dusky color. Bonefish are basically schooling fish. The smaller ones can be seen in large schools on the flats. The larger ones tend to form smaller schools or groups. They feed on crabs, shrimp, clams, sea worms, sea urchins, and small fish that inhabit the sandy flats and intertidal areas. They are often seen rooting in the sand for mollusks, their tails breaking the surface of the shallow water; an action commonly known as "trailing". At other times they will plough the bottom stirring up silt and marl, known as "mudding". They are powerful and run very fast and hard when hooked. Fishing methods include plug, fly or spin casting from a skiff or while wading on tidal flats, using shrimp, crabs, clams, squid, sand bugs, conch or similar baits. Most bonefish are caught in depths from 6 inches to 10 ft (15 cm to 3 m).

This species begins life looking more like an eel than a fish and undergoes a leptocephalus larval stage during which it grow to a length of about 2 ½ in (6.3 cm); then during a period of metamorphosis the eel-like larva shrinks to half its former size. As it shrinks, fins begin to appear, and after 10-12 days the eel has become a 1½ in (3.81 cm) miniature bonefish, and begins to grow again. Tarpon and ladyfish undergo similar stages of development. As one might expect from the name, the bonefish has an abundance of bones (some of which are quite tiny), for which reason this fish is less than popular as table fare.

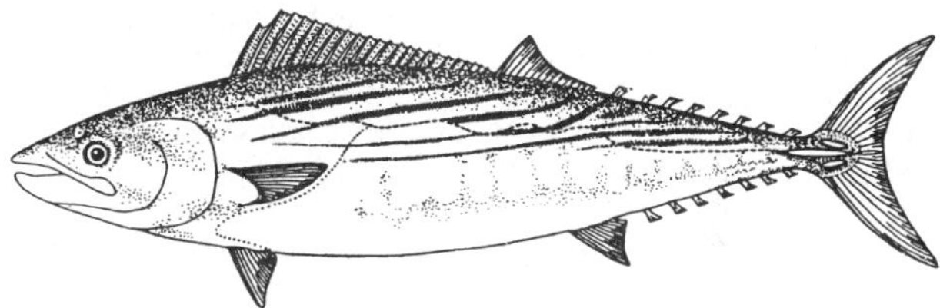

BONITO, Atlantic / *Sarda sarda* (Bloch, 1793); SCOMBRIDAE FAMILY; also called common bonito, katonkel, belted bonito

Occurs in tropical and temperate waters of the Atlantic Ocean from Argentina to Nova Scotia and from South Africa to Norway. It is apparently rare in the Caribbean Sea and Gulf of Mexico, and is common in the Mediterranean and Black Seas. It is replaced in the Pacific by other *Sarda* species. The Atlantic bonito is often confused with the skipjack or with other Atlantic *Scombroid* species. The bonitos have stripes on the back, not the belly. The first dorsal fin has 20-23 spines. The second dorsal fin consists of 13-18 rays followed by 7-10 finlets. The anal fin consists of 14-17 rays followed by 6-8 finlets. The caudal peduncle has a lateral keel on either side. As with all *Scombroid* fishes, there are also two smaller keels farther back, above and below the main keel. The *Sarda* species have no teeth on the tongue and no swim bladder. Also, the intestine is straight, rather than folded in the middle. There is a total of 16-23 gill rakers on the first gill arch. The back is steel blue or blue-green. The lower flanks and belly are silvery.

This species is pelagic, schooling, migratory and feeds on smaller fishes and squids usually at or near the surface. A strong, fast swimmer the it is known to skip or leap on the surface when in pursuit of prey. It is usually found in schools 15-20 miles offshore. Best fishing methods include trolling at or near the surface, casting, jigging, or live bait fishing. Baits include small pelagic schooling fishes and squid as well as cut fish, strip baits, or any of a variety of artificial lures. This species is of some importance in the eastern Atlantic where it is fished for commercially. In the western Atlantic it has little commercial value except off southern Brazil and Argentina. The flesh is light colored and of good quality, though held in low esteem by some.

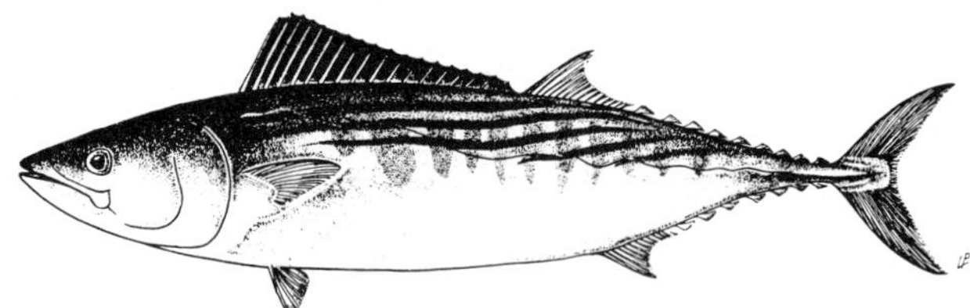

Pacific Bonito *(Sarda chiliensis)*

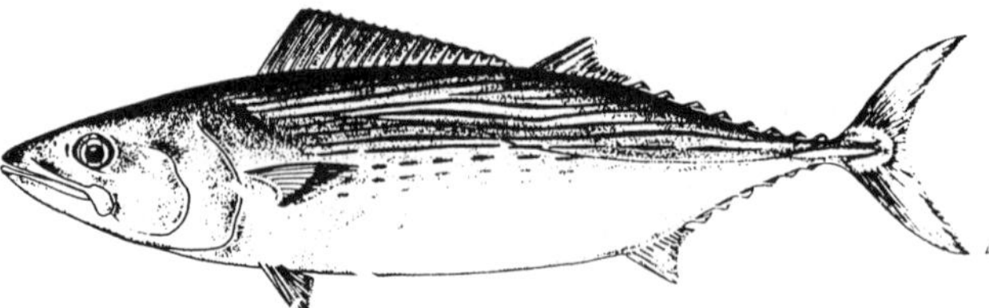

Striped Bonito *(Sarda orientalis)*

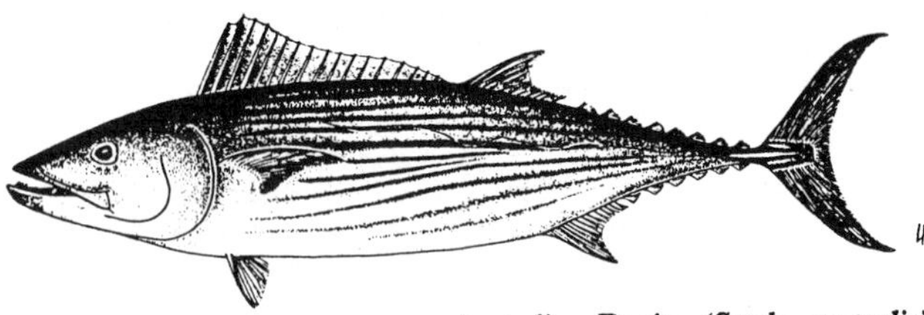

Australian Bonito *(Sarda australis)*

BONITO, Pacific

/ *Sarda orientalis* (Temminck & Schlegel, 1844);
/ *Sarda chiliensis* (Cuvier, 1831); and
/ *Sarda australis* (Macleay, 1880); SCOMBRIDAE FAMILY; also called
California bonito, striped bonito, Australian bonito

    Sarda chiliensis is restricted to the eastern Pacific Ocean. Its range is divided into two separate populations. The northern population *(Sarda chiliensis lineolata)* ranges from Alaska to southern Baja and the Revillagigedo Islands off Mexico. The southern population *(Sarda chiliensis chiliensis)* ranges from Peru to Chile. The two populations are replaced from Baja, California to Peru by *Sarda orientalis* (the most widespread of the species of *Sarda* listed above) which also occur in scattered populations throughout the Pacific and Indian Oceans. *Sarda australis* has the most restricted range of the three occurring only off the eastern coast of Australia. Distinguishing the Pacific bonitos from each other and from other Pacific *Scombroid* species has been confusing for many anglers. Superficially, many of the species resemble each other closely. The *Sarda* species differ from all other bonitos (with the exception of *Allothunnus fallai*, the so-called slender tuna) in having no teeth on the tongue and in having a straight intestine with no fold in the middle. The *Sarda* species are not normally confused with *Allothunnus* and can be easily distinguished by the number of gill rakers: *Sarda* has 8-27 on the first arch *(S. orientalis*, 8-13; *S. australis*, 19-21; *S. chiliensis*, 23-27) whereas *Allothunnus* had 72-80. The *Sarda* species are further characterized by the first dorsal fin which has 17-19 spines. Like all bonitos (with the exception of *Gymnosarda*, the dogtooth tuna) *Sarda* has no swim bladder. *Sarda australis* has stripes on the belly as well as on the back, but other *Sarda* species lack any sort of stripes, lines, or spots on the belly.

    Bonitos are migratory, schooling, pelagic fishes. They feed on smaller pelagic fishes and on squid, usually near the surface. Fishing methods include trolling at or near the surface; also casting, jigging, or live bait fishing with small pelagic fishes, squid, cut or strip baits, or with any of a variety of small artificial lures. They are certainly edible and have some commercial value, though much less than the tunas. The flesh is light colored and of good quality.

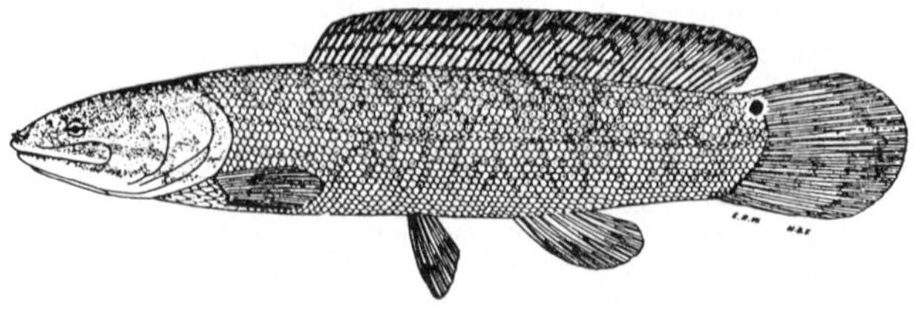

BOWFIN / *Amia calva* Linnaeus, 1766; AMIIDAE FAMILY; also called
mudfish, mud pike, dogfish, griddle, grinnel, cypress trout

    Inhabits the eastern U.S.A. from the Mississippi River basin eastward to the St. Lawrence River in the north, and southward from Minnesota to the Gulf Coast; from eastern Texas to and including all of Florida. The bowfin is easily recognized by its flattened head; long, stout body; large mouth full of small, sharp teeth; long dorsal fin that extends along most of the back; and rounded tail. Also, the pelvic fins are set far back on the belly near the middle of the body and the pectoral fins are low on the sides so that the overall appearance is one of three sets of fins in a row; the pectorals behind the head, the pelvics near the midbody, and the anal fin near the tail. In the males there is a spot surrounded by an orange-yellow halo on the upper area of the caudal peduncle. In the females the spot either is not ocellated or is lacking entirely.

    This is the sole surviving representative of the *Amiiformes* and is considered a living fossil. Its genus, *Amia*, is known to date back to the upper Cretaceous period and the early Tertiary period in North America. It is able to gulp air from the surface directly into the air bladder, which is connected to the throat and can be used as a lung. It can also withstand high temperatures, for which reasons it survives in waters unsuited to most other fishes. It is considered poor as a food fish, but an excellent fighter, better than some highly rated game fish.

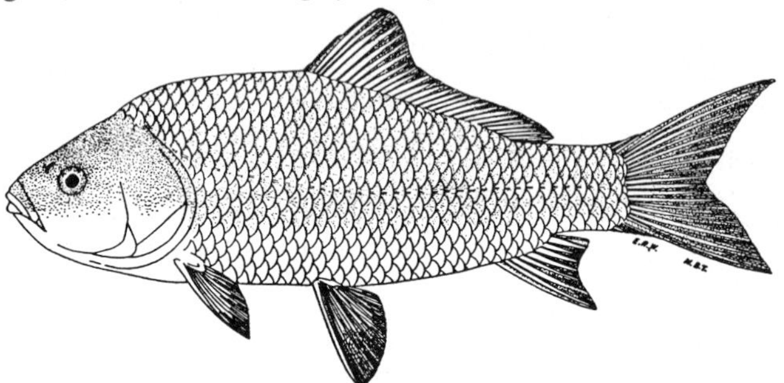

BUFFALO, bigmouth / *Ictiobus cyprinellus* (Valenciennes, 1844); CATOSTOMIDAE FAMILY

    Found in the Lake Erie, Ohio, and Mississippi drainages from Canada to the Gulf of Mexico, the bigmouth buffalo has also been introduced into Arizona and California.

    It is the largest member of the sucker family, growing to over 70 lb (31 kg). In general body shape it very much resembles the carp. The dorsal fin is similar, beginning with a taller lobe near the middle of the back and continuing in a lower portion nearly to the tail. The carp has a single serrated spine at the beginning of the dorsal fin, while the bigmouth buffalo has no spines in any of the fins, only soft rays. The toothless mouth is relatively large and wide, and slants downward when closed. The upper lip begins almost on a level with the eyes. In comparison the mouth of the smallmouth buffalo *(Ictiobus bubalus)*, in addition to being smaller, is almost horizontal when closed, subterminal, and protracts downward in typical sucker fashion. The body of the bigmouth buffalo is coppery olive-brown to slate-blue above, becoming lighter toward the belly, which is white.

    About 90 percent of the bigmouth buffalo's diet consists of small crustaceans. It also feeds on algae and other plant matter, but very seldom eats insects, insect larvae, or other fish. Consequently, the species does not form a large sport fishery since it will not take the normal types of baits. It does, however, form a fairly important freshwater commercial fishery. The flesh is white and of excellent quality.

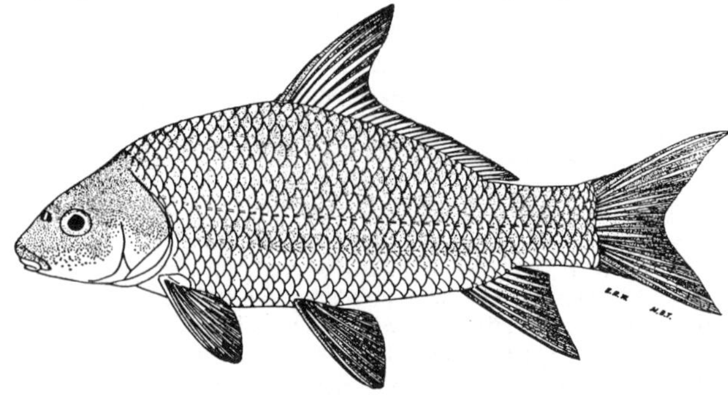

BUFFALO, smallmouth / *Ictiobus bubalus* (Rafinesque, 1818); CATOSTOMIDAE FAMILY; also called razorback buffalo, roachback, thicklipped buffalo

    Second in size in the sucker family the smallmouth buffalo is found in the same general areas of North America as the bigmouth buffalo *(Ictiobus cyprinellus)*, and has been introduced into Arizona.

    It resembles its large relative, the bigmouth buffalo, closely in most respects, but can be distinguished by a number of factors. It is generally lighter in color than other buffalos, having an olive-bronze cast. Also the body is somewhat more compressed with a higher arch in the back, and the small, subterminal mouth is almost horizontal instead of slanted, though it protracts downward in typical sucker fashion when the fish is feeding.

It is reputed to be an even better food fish than the bigmouth buffalo, but the species is less abundant and therefore less important commercially than the bigmouth. To the sports angler the species is of little importance, not because it isn't worthy as a sport fish, but because it is caught only occasionally or by accident.

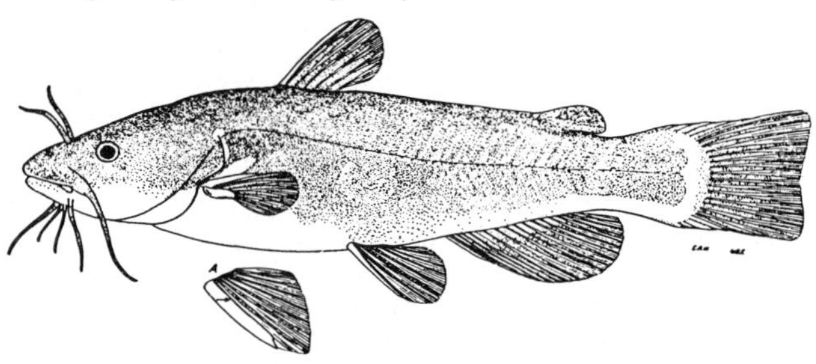

BULLHEAD, black / *Ameiurus melas* (Rafinesque, 1820); ICTALURIDAE FAMILY

The black bullhead is found from southern Ontario through the Great Lakes and St. Lawrence River, south to the Gulf of Mexico. It occurs from Montana in the west to the Appalachians in the east, and has been introduced into Arizona, California, and various other western states as well as a few states east of the Appalachians.

Despite the common names, black bullhead *(Ameiurus melas)*, brown bullhead *(A. nebulosus)*, and yellow bullhead *(A. natalis)*, color is not the best way to identify these fish. The "black" bullhead may be dark green, olive, brown, yellowish-green, or black on top, green or gold on the sides, and white or bright yellow below. Spawning males are jet black, as are the very young (the young of brown and yellow bullheads are also usually black). The surest way to distinguish this fish from the brown or yellow bullheads is by the pectoral fins. In the brown and yellow bullheads the rear edge of the pectoral fin spine is serrated with numerous sharp tooth-like projections, while in the black bullhead the serrations are extremely weak or absent altogether. Also, the black bullhead has dark-colored chin barbels which may be gray, black, or black-spotted, and its body and head are deeper and more massive than in the brown and yellow bullheads. The tail fin is squarish (truncate) or slightly emarginate, which will readily distinguish the black bullhead from the channel catfish *(Ictalurus punctatus)*, the white catfish *(Ameiurus catus)*, and the blue catfish *(Ictalurus furcatus)*, all of which have deeply forked tails.

It is a small catfish at around 8 lb (3.62 kg) especially compared to the blue catfish which may reach over 100 lb (45 kg), but it is an extremely popular sport fish that, like the bluegill, is often stocked in farm ponds. It is considered excellent as a food fish.

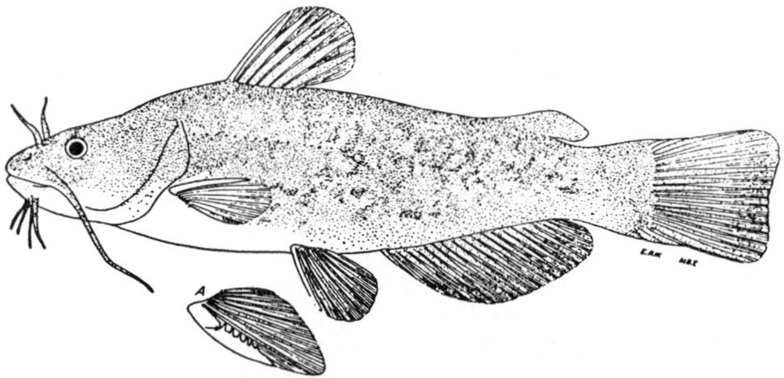

BULLHEAD, brown / *Ameiurus nebulosus* (Lesueur, 1819); ICTALURIDAE FAMILY

The brown bullhead is native to the eastern U.S.A. (both sides of the Appalachians) and southern Canada, but has been widely introduced elsewhere. It occurs in larger and deeper waters than other bullheads.

The "brown" bullhead may vary from yellow-brown or chocolate brown to olive, gray, or bluish-black. The sides are often lighter and may be mottled with brown blotches. The belly is yellow or white. Very round brown bullheads are jet black and are often mistakenly believed to be black bullheads *(A. melas)*. Color is an undependable distinguishing characteristic at best and it is important to observe other physical characteristics in order to make a positive identification. The brown bullhead and the yellow bullhead *(A. natalis)* have sharp, tooth-like serrations along the rear edge of the pectoral spine at the top of the

pectoral fin. The black bullhead lacks any such serrations or has only extremely weak serrations that are negligible by comparison. In the brown and black bullheads, the tail is squarish (truncate) or slightly emarginate, while in the yellow bullhead it is slightly rounded. The brown bullhead is frequently mottled while the yellow is never mottled and its chin barbels are yellow, buff, or pale pink in color (the upper barbels are light to dark brown). In the brown bullhead all of the barbels are dark brown to nearly black, but in some cases there may be pale yellow or white at the base only of the chin barbels.

It is small at around 5 lb (2.27 kg), but is an extremely popular panfish and has some commercial importance. The meat is firm, reddish to pink, and of excellent quality and taste. It is also a popular fish stocked in farm ponds.

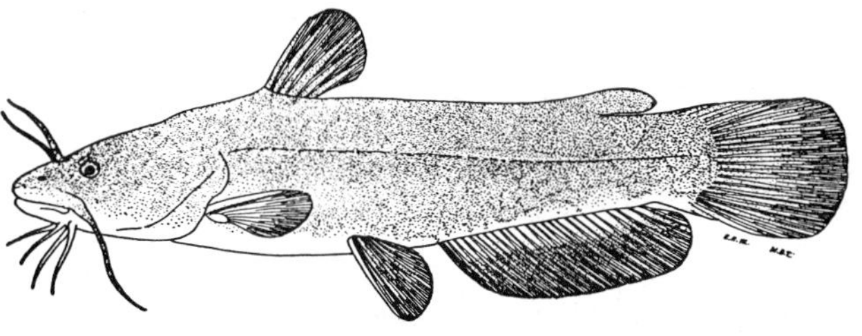

BULLHEAD, yellow / *Ameiurus natalis* (Lesueur, 1819); ICTALURIDAE FAMILY

Occurs natively throughout most of the eastern and central U.S.A. (both sides of the Appalachians). In the southern portion of its range, the yellow bullhead extends further west (western Texas) than the brown bullhead (Alabama), and tends to occur in smaller, weedier and shallower waters. Like the other bullheads it has also been introduced outside its native range.

The yellow bullhead ranges in color from olive to brown to almost black dorsally with a yellow or white belly and yellow or brown sides that are never mottled as they often are in the brown bullhead *(A. nebulosus)*. Juveniles usually have dark brown to jet black bodies. It is the only bullhead in which the chin barbels are yellow, buff, or pale pink instead of dark in color. The upper barbels are brown. The tail is rounded which helps to distinguish the yellow bullhead from the brown bullhead and the black bullhead *(A. melas)*, which have truncate or slightly emarginate tails. An even better distinction between the yellow and black bullheads is the spine at the top of the pectoral fins. In the yellow bullhead, as in the brown, this spine has sharp, tooth-like serrations along the back edge. In the black bullhead it is either not serrated at all or only very weakly serrated.

The flesh of this small catfish is whiter than that of the brown bullhead, and has been described as cream-colored. It is of excellent quality, but the species does not play a large role in either the commercial or sport fisheries.

BURBOT / *Lota lota* (Linnaeus, 1758); GADIDAE FAMILY; also called cusk, eel pout, ling, lawyer

Widely distributed around the world above 40°N. The burbot is common throughout Canada, the northern U.S.A., and Europe within this range, with the notable exceptions of Scotland and Ireland, the Kamchatka Peninsula, the west coast of Norway, extreme western British Columbia, Nova Scotia, and the Atlantic Islands. It commonly occurs in deep, cold waters (up to 116 fathoms, almost 700 feet), and is one of the few fishes that spawn in midwinter under the ice. Spawning always occurs at night, usually in shallow bays, on gravel shoals, or sometimes in rivers in 1-10 ft (0.3-3.0 m) of water.

This is an unusually distinctive fish with its long, almost eel-like body; single, slender, cod-like barbel under the chin; rounded paddle-like tail; large rounded pectoral fins; small, short first dorsal fin (8-16 rays); and long second dorsal fin (60-79 rays) and anal fin (59-76 rays) that start near the middle of the body and run all the way back to the tail. The body is yellow, light brown, or tan with a mottled appearance due to a darker brown or black pattern over the lighter body color. Some individuals, noticeably adults from deep lakes in the far north, may be entirely dark brown or black.

It is most frequently caught incidentally by anglers who are ice-fishing for lake trout *(Salvelinus namaycush)*. While it is both a good sportfish and a good quality food fish, it is not generally popular.

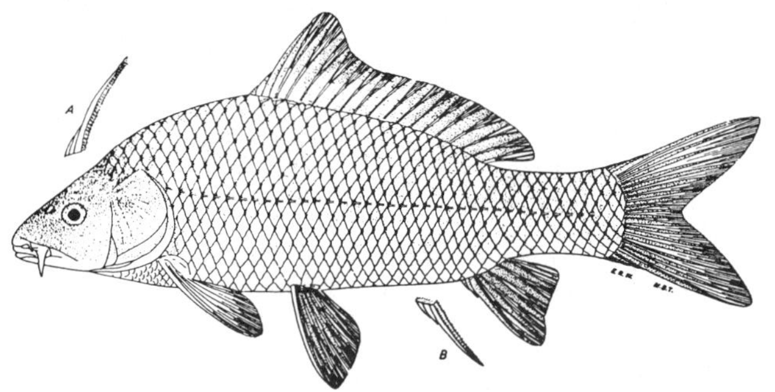

CARP, common / *Cyprinus carpio* Linnaeus, 1758; CYPRINIDAE FAMILY

The carp's original range was limited to temperate Asia and the rivers of the Black Sea and Aegean basins, notably the Danube, in Europe. It was introduced into England during the reign of Henry VIII, and was brought to America from Germany by the United States Fish Commission in 1876 or 1877. From Washington D.C., distribution was made on request to applicants throughout the U.S. and parts of Canada until 1896, by which time it had become thoroughly established on this continent. Today, they are widely distributed in North America below the 50th parallel south to the Florida panhandle. Besides North America, Europe, and Asia, it is also now found in South America, Africa, Australia and New Zealand.

This is one of the largest members of the "minnow" family, Cyprinidae, and a close relative of the goldfish *(Carassius auratus)*, with which it hybridizes freely in nature. In addition to carp, goldfish, and of course minnows, the "minnow" family includes shiners, chubs, daces, and—in Europe—the tench *(Tinca tinca)*, the bream *(Abramis brama)*, the roach *(Rutilus rutilus)*, and the rudd *(Scardinius erythrophthalmus)*, as well as a few other species. The carps closest look-alikes may be the bigmouth and smallmouth buffalos *(Ictiobus cyprinellus* and *I. bubalus)*, which despite their almost clonish resemblance to the carp, belong to an entirely different family, Catostomidae (the "sucker" family). The carp, the goldfish, and the buffalos all grow fairly large (the goldfish to about 16 inches; the carp and buffalos much larger); all have deep bodies; relatively small, protractile mouths; a forked tail; a single, long dorsal fin on the back; and large scales. The coloration of their bodies is also similar, ranging from olive brown to gold. Still, all these species can be quite easily distinguished. The carp and the goldfish both have a single serrated spine at the beginning of the dorsal and anal fins. All the fins are soft on the buffalos, with no spines at all, only soft rays. The carp has two fleshy barbels on each side of the mouth, distinguishing it from the goldfish, which lacks barbels. In Europe the tench, roach, rudd, and bronze bream are easily set apart from the carp, most obviously, by their dorsal fin which is much shorter along the base.

It is very prolific, excellent survivor, and is able to tolerate a wide range of conditions and bottom types, therefore making it an excellent species for pond culture. In Europe and Asia it has always been highly regarded as a game and food fish, but such has not been its destiny in the New World. Its bottom feeding activity muddies the water, occasionally causing loss of plants and habitat of native game fish. This fact, together with its unchecked, rapid spread throughout the country, has earned it disrepute among many.

In Europe, where the carp is highly regarded, farmed, and selectively bred, cultivated carp (referred to as "king" carp as opposed to wild carp) come in a variety of body shapes and squamation patterns. They may be fully scaled, partially scaled ("mirror" carp), or completely nude ("leather" carp). They are still the same species and after a few generations in the wild, will revert to their normal wild form. They are selectively bred to produce forms that are faster growing or more cold resistant (such as the form the Russians produced for stocking in Arctic waters), or ornamental (such as the "golden" carp or "Hi-goi" which resembles the goldfish). Its most attractive attribute may be that it is an excellent and inexpensive source of protein, and will produce a relatively high yield per acre of water even with little or no care.

CATFISH, blue / *Ictalurus furcatus* (Lesueur, 1840); ICTALURIDAE FAMILY

This native species of the Mississippi, Missouri, and Ohio River basin systems frequents deep areas of large rivers, swift chutes, and pools with swift currents. It is confined to the major rivers of the aforementioned systems, extending north into South Dakota and southern Minnesota, and south into Mexico and northern Guatemala. It has been introduced into Virginia.

This is the largest catfish of the family Ictaluridae, reported to grow to 120 lb (54 kg). The only larger catfish is the wels *(Silurus glanis)*, a member of the Siluridae family, which is found in central and eastern Europe and southern Russia, and may grow to 440 lb (200 kg). The blue catfish, the channel catfish *(Ictalurus punctatus)*, and the white catfish *(Ameiurus catus)* are the only three catfishes in the U.S.A. that have distinctly forked tails, setting them apart from the bullheads and the flathead catfish *(Pylodictis olivaris)*, which have squarish or slightly emarginate tails. The blue catfish can be distinguished from the channel and white catfish by its noticeably longer anal fin, which has a more even depth and a straighter edge than in the other two species. There are 30-36 rays in the fin, versus 24-30 rays in the channel catfish and 19-23 rays in the white catfish. Internally, the blue catfish can be identified by the fact that it has three chambers in the swim bladder, whereas the channel catfish has two chambers. All three forked tail species may be almost uniformly pale blue or silvery in color, though white catfish may show a more distinct difference between the bluish back and white belly. Channel catfish frequently have spots.

The blue catfish is considered an excellent food and game fish. It prefers clean, swift-moving waters where it feeds primarily on fish and crayfish. It is a strong, well-toned fish with a fine, delicate flavor and has commercial value throughout its range.

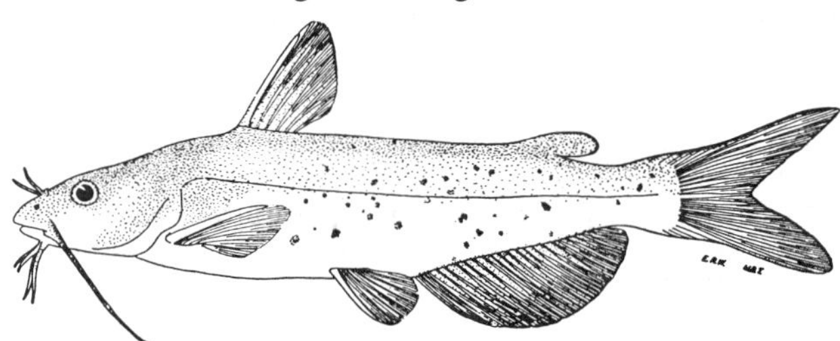

CATFISH, channel / *Ictalurus punctatus* (Rafinesque, 1818); ICTALURIDAE FAMILY

The channel catfish is very highly regarded for its food and sports value, and is reared commercially and transported throughout the country. Its current distribution includes most of the U.S. and parts of southern Canada and northern Mexico. In the U.S. it is most abundant in the central part of the country east to the Appalachians. Its occurrence is sparser and mostly by introduction along the west coast and east of the Appalachians.

Channel catfish prefer clean bottoms of sand or gravel in larger lakes and rivers. They feed mainly on crayfish, fishes, and insects generally at night in swifter moving currents. At spawning time they will enter and ascend small tributaries and streams.

The distinctive channel catfish can often be recognized at a glance. It is safe to say that a catfish with a deeply forked tail and spots on the body is a channel catfish (though not all specimens have them). The only other catfish with forked tails occurring in U.S. waters are the blue catfish *(Ictalurus furcatus)* and the white catfish *(Ameiurus catus)*, neither of which is ever spotted. The yaqui catfish *(I. pricei)* also has a forked tail, but currently is only found in the Yaqui River drainage in Mexico; though at one time it extended slightly into southern Arizona.

In addition to the spotted specimens, some channel catfish may be entirely black dorsally (males during the spawning season), or dark blue without spots, or even uniformly light blue or silvery exactly like a blue catfish or white catfish. In the latter cases, the species can be identified by the number of rays in the anal fin. White catfish have 19-23 rays, channel catfish have 24-30, and blue catfish have the longest anal fin with 30-36 rays. Internally, the channel catfish has two chambers in the swim bladder and the blue catfish has three.

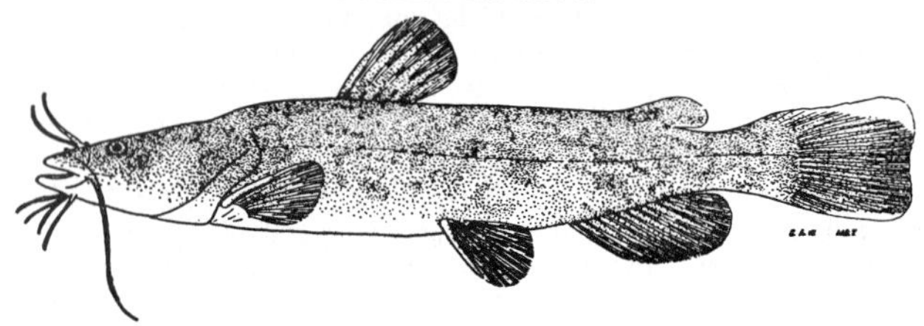

CATFISH, flathead / *Pylodictis olivaris* (Rafinesque, 1818); ICTALURIDAE FAMILY

254

Native to the large rivers of the Mississippi, Missouri, and Ohio basins from southern North Dakota, south into northern Mexico, and east as far as Lake Erie's southeast coast and the western most tip of the Florida panhandle. It occurs broadly over this entire area, but has not been widely introduced outside its native range.

The flathead catfish is very distinctive in appearance and not easily confused with any other species. It is one of the largest catfish in its family, possibly reaching 100 lb (45 kg), second in size only to the blue catfish *(Ictalurus furcatus)*. It has a squarish, rather than forked, tail. Its body is long and its head is wide and distinctly flattened. The eyes accentuate the flatness of the head with their distinctly flat-looking, oval shape and the lower jaw further accentuates it by protruding beyond the upper jaw. The anal fin is short along its base, 14-17 rays, compared to other catfish, especially the blue catfish which has 30-36 rays. Even the bullheads usually have 20-27 rays in the anal fin. In general coloration, the flathead catfish is mottled with varying shades of brown and yellow.

This popular food fish has an excellent flavor. It frequents deep sluggish pools with hard bottoms in large rivers. It seems to have a distinct culinary preference for fish, it is omnivorous and will eat most anything that suits its fancy. Its large size makes it especially popular with anglers.

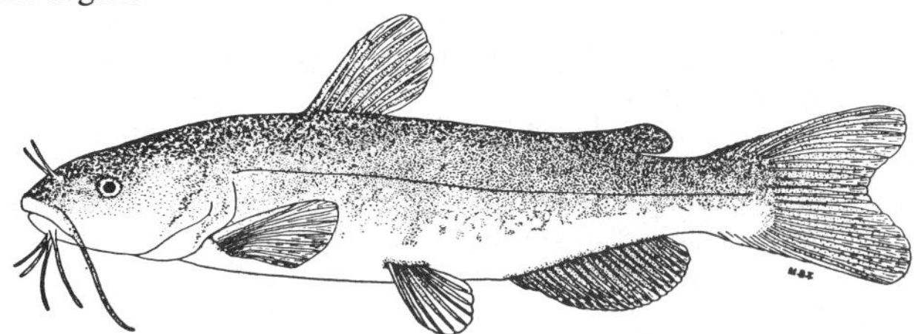

CATFISH, white / *Ameiurus catus* (Linnaeus, 1758); ICTALURIDAE FAMILY

The white catfish is native to the U.S. Atlantic coastal states from about Palm Beach, Florida, to New York. It has been introduced outside this range southward into Texas and on the west coast.

It is the smallest of the four catfish in the U.S.A. and Mexico that have forked tails, reaching about 17 lb (7.70 kg). In all other species the tail is either rounded, squarish, or slightly emarginate. Despite the names white catfish and blue catfish, any of the species with a forked tail maybe light silvery blue with a white belly, though in the white catfish there is sometimes a sharper contrast between the bluish back and the white of the belly. It usually has numerous dark spots on the body, except in older individuals and spawning males.

The surest way to identify the white catfish is to count the rays in the anal fin. The white catfish has 19-23 rays and the fin is rounded along the bottom edge. The channel catfish has 24-30 rays and also has a rounded anal fin. The blue catfish has a longer and much straighter edged anal fin with 30-36 rays.

Like all the catfish listed here the white catfish is a delicious food fish. Its flesh is firm and white. It is easily caught on live bait, less nocturnal than some species, and an excellent survivor. It has therefore become a very popular anglers' fish and a popular stock fish in private lakes and ponds.

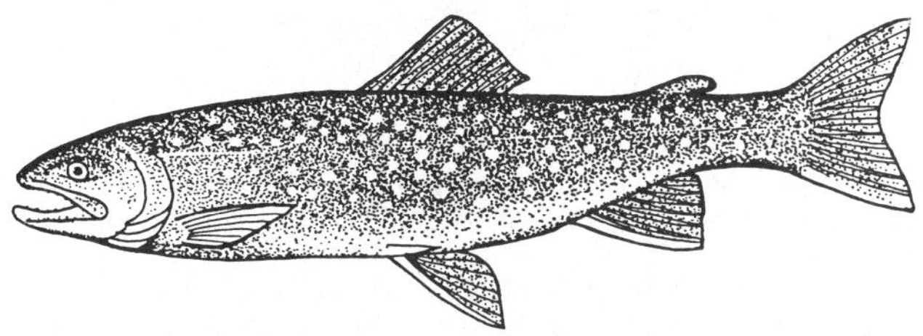

CHAR, Arctic / *Salvelinus alpinus* (Linnaeus, 1758); SALMONIDAE FAMILY; also called blueback char, blueback trout, Sunapee trout, golden trout (Sunapee).

The most northerly of all freshwater fish, the Arctic char is circumpolar in distribution, occurring around the globe from Maine and New Hampshire in the United States northward across northern Canada, Alaska and the Aleutian Islands, and from northern Russia south to Lake Baikal and Kamchatka as well as in Iceland, Great Britain, Scandinavia, the Alps, and Spitsbergen, among other places. An anadromous species (except where it has become landlocked), the Arctic char always returns from the sea to spawn in fresh water, usually in lakes or quiet pools of rivers over gravel bottom. It spawns in autumn or winter when water temperatures reach 4°C or less.

Like all chars (members of the genus *Salvelinus*), the Arctic char has light colored spots on the body and the leading edges of all the fins on the lower part of the body are milk white. These features set the chars apart from the salmons and trouts, which are the chars' closest relatives and similar in body shape. There is an adipose fin between the dorsal fin and the tail, and an axillary process at the base of each pelvic fin. It has a squarish or slightly forked tail.

The species most often confused with the Arctic char is an extremely close relative (also a char), the Dolly Varden *(Salvelinus malma)*. Often it is virtually impossible to distinguish between the two species except by laboratory analysis, and even today there are few scientists who know how to make a positive identification. Much erroneous material has been published concerning the distribution of each species, and consequently anglers and scientists alike have made many false identifications based on the mistaken belief that only Arctic char or only Dolly Varden occurred in a given area, lake, or river in Alaska. An individual who is familiar with both species may be able to make an identification based on the size of the spots, which are larger in the Arctic char. However, fish returning from the sea are often silvery with no spots at all, making external identification all but impossible. Gill raker counts are helpful. In Canada, Victoria Island (Northwest Territory) char have about 25-30 gill rakers on the first left gill arch. Dolly Varden have 21-22. Arctic char have 40-45 pyloric caeca (worm-like appendages on the pylorus, the section of intestine directly after the stomach), while Dolly Varden have about 30.

As in all salmon, trout and char, both the color of the body and the shape of the head vary considerably in different forms of the fish; landlocked, seagoing, and most of all, spawning males which develop "kype", (a deformation or mutation of the lower and sometimes upper jaw into a hook at spawning time). The tremendous variation makes it almost impossible for one to make an identification based on coloration. Even if an individual is thoroughly familiar with all the color variations of all salmonids occurring in the area, color is not a factor that will distinguish the Arctic char from the Dolly Varden.

The Arctic char is a food and game fish par excellence. It would be difficult to over estimate its value to the sport fishery. According to A.J. McClane (McClane's New Standard Fishing Encyclopedia), a prime char (one that is not spent from its journey upstream) taken on fly "typically...moves with rapier like speed for about one hundred feet, then leaps clear of the water and runs again. A four-or five-pound fish jumps a half-dozen times in swift currents and goes well down into the backing before it can be turned."

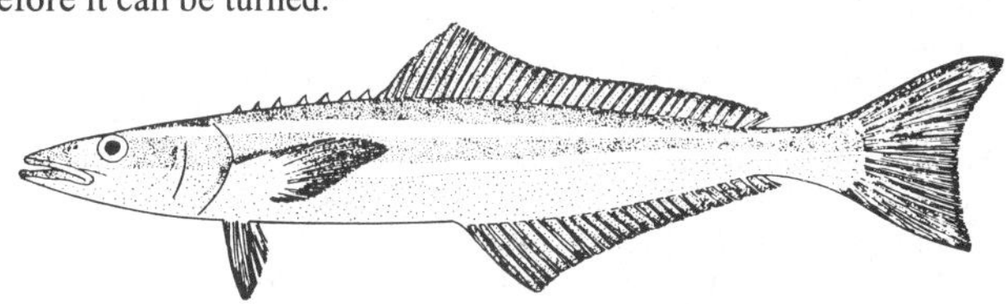

COBIA / *Rachycentron canadum* (Linnaeus, 1766); RACHYCENTRIDAE FAMILY; also called ling, lemonfish, black salmon, black kingfish, sergeant fish, crab-eater, runner, cabio.

Worldwide in tropical and warm temperate waters both offshore and inshore. Adult cobia seem to prefer shallow continental shelf waters. They particularly like buoys, pilings, wrecks, anchored boats, flotsam, etc., and will sometimes congregate around these objects.

It is the only known member of the family Rachycentridae. It has a long, broad, depressed head. The first dorsal fin consists of 8-10 short, depressible spines which are not connected by a membrane. The second dorsal fin has 1 spine and 27-33 soft rays. The anal fin has 1-2 spines and 22-27 soft rays. The overall appearance of the fish is similar to that of a small shark, given the shape of the body, the powerful tail fin, and the elevated anterior portion of the second dorsal fin. Even more striking is it's resemblance to the remora. The most noticeable difference between these two species is the suction pad on the remora's head. The cobia is known to swim with sharks and other large species as the remora does.

The cobia's coloration and markings are distinctive. The back is dark chocolate brown while the sides are lighter with alternate horizontal stripes of brown and silver or bronze and white. The markings on smaller specimens are more vivid; the black and dark stripes are blacker, making the lighter areas stand out more.

The cobia is a highly rated, hard-hitting game fish that is prone to long, powerful, determined runs and occasional leaps. Often when one is hooked the entire school will surface along with it. Preferred fishing methods are trolling with lures or baits, bottom fishing, jigging, chumming, and spin casting. They can be caught on crustaceans (which is why they are nicknamed "crab-eaters" in Australia) as well as on smaller fishes. Good baits are squid, crabs, small live fishes, cut baits, and strip baits. Spoons, plugs, and weighted feathers can also be used. They rate high as table fare.

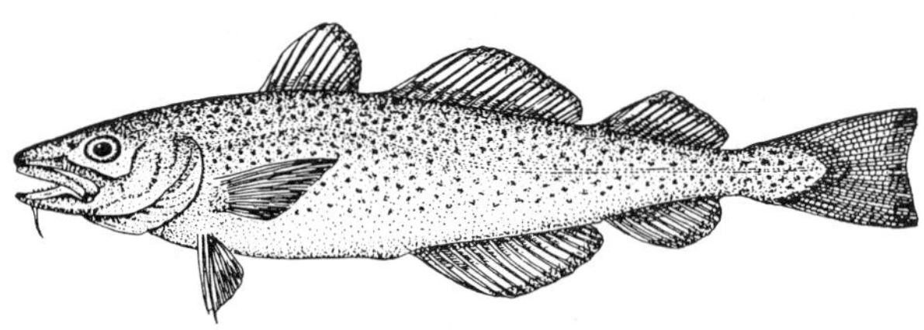

COD, Atlantic / *Gadus morhua* Linnaeus, 1758; GADIDAE FAMILY; also called codfish, codling

Occurs in subarctic and cool temperate waters of the North Atlantic from Greenland to North Carolina, including the Hudson Strait, and from Novaya Zemlya, in the former U.S.S.R., to the northern reaches of the Bay of Biscay, including the Baltic and North seas and Iceland. The cod is basically ademersal species with a preference for rough bottoms composed of sand and rock or of shells. It can be found in depths of up to 200 fathoms. It is migratory though the extent of its migration varies among stocks.

The cod can be distinguished from other members of its family by the large barbel on the chin and the arch in the lateral line. Like many other members of its family they have three separate dorsal fins and two separate anal fins, none of which contain any spines. The back and sides are highly variable in color (ranging from brownish or sandy to gray, yellow, reddish, greenish, or any combination), and mottled with numerous lighter spots. The belly is white, the lateral line is pale, and all the fins are dark.

Largely omnivorous, they feed on herring, sprat, capelin, sand eels, Irish moss, etc. Many unusual items have also been found in the stomachs of adult cod, including an oil can, a rubber doll, finger rings, clothing, and some very rare deep-sea shells that were previously unknown to science.

Most cod taken by anglers are caught by bait fishing on the bottom from a drifting or anchored boat, but many are taken by jigging and deep trolling as well. Cod have large mouths, so hook size may vary, but the bait need not be large—a good sized ocean clam will do for almost any size cod. Other good baits include strip baits of squid, hake, cunner, or mackerel as well as herring, crabs, sand eels, and capelin. When clams are used as bait, the shells are often used for chum. Artificial lures such as chrome diamond jigs, spinners, bucktails, spoons, and shiny metal squids may also be used.

The largest cod known to have been caught weighed 211 lb 8 oz (95.90 kg) and was taken in May of 1895 off the coast of Massachusetts. It was over 6 ft (1.8 m) long. Possibly due to relentless fishing pressure, the average size of cod today is only 4-15 lb (2-7 kg) and specimens weighing over 60 lb (27 kg) are unusual.

It would be difficult to overstate the cod's value as a food fish. The Basques fished the Banks of Newfoundland centuries before Columbus discovered America, and cod bones have been found in coastal dwelling sites dating back to the Mesolithic Age. So important was the cod in colonial America that it appeared in the state seal of Massachusetts. Today, the U.S. takes 40 to 70 million pounds (20,000 metric tons) of cod yearly, and other nations take another 2.5 million metric tons. Cod meat is white and is marketed fresh, frozen, dried, and salted.

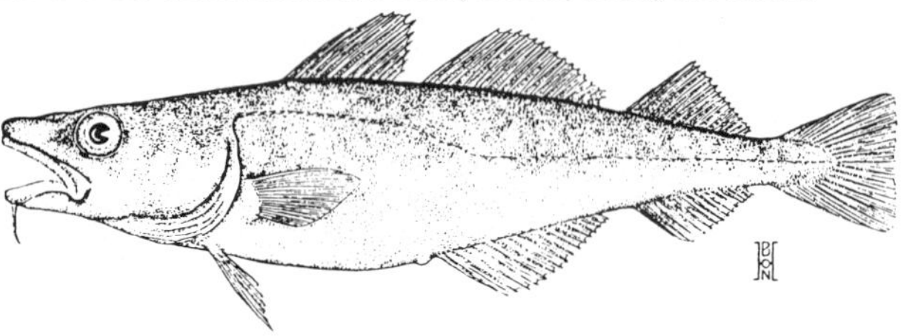

COD, Pacific / *Gadus macrocephalus* Tilesius, 1810; GADIDAE FAMILY; also called cod, gray cod, true cod

Occurs along the U.S. Pacific coast from Santa Monica, California to northwestern Alaska, and in Asia from the Chukchi Sea to the Yellow Sea and Lushun (Port Arthur), China. It is a common species off the U.S. northwest coast (Oregon, Washington and Alaska) and is most abundant at spawning time (winter and early spring) in coastal waters.

The Pacific cod is usually caught in waters deeper than 60 ft (18.3 m) up to 300 fathoms (550 m). It is a slightly smaller, but close relative of the Atlantic cod *(Gadus morhua)*. Both are members of the true cod family (Gadidae) having three separate and distinct dorsal fins, two anal fins, and a single barbel under the chin. All the fins are soft-rayed and the chin barbel is at least as long as the diameter of the eye. The scales are small and cycloid. Coloration ranges from gray to brown dorsally, lightening on the sides and belly. There are numerous brown spots on the

sides and back. All the fins are dusky and the unpaired fins are edged with white on their outer margins (especially obvious on the caudal and anal fins).

Reported to weigh at least 40 lb (18.1 kg) with a length of 3 ft 9 in (114 cm) the average size is considerably smaller. The larger Atlantic species has been recorded to over 211 lb 8 oz (95.9 kg) for a specimen caught in 1895, but today it is considered rare over 60 lb (27 kg) and averages 15 lb (7 kg) or less in most areas.

An excellent food fish and a good sport fish the Pacific cod is usually taken by anglers using fish or cut bait. It is the most important trawl caught bottom fish in British Columbia, with millions of pounds landed there alone. It is marketed commercially as fish sticks and fillets.

CONGER / *Conger conger* ([Artedi, 1738] Linnaeus, 1758); CONGRIDAE FAMILY; also called sea eel, eel pout

Endemic to the coasts of northern Europe and the Mediterranean, British authority Alwyne Wheeler states, "Its range is believed to extend south to South African waters, but there is a possibility that two species are involved in this range."

The conger is a large eel known to reach a length of 9 ft (2.4 m) and a weight of 143 lb (65 kg). It is easily distinguished from the moray eel by the presence of pectoral fins, which the moray lacks. It also has a longer snout, its upper jaw is slightly longer than its lower jaw, the head is narrower in appearance, and the dorsal fin does not extend quite as far forward as in the moray.

They inhabit relatively shallow waters in the vicinity of cover material such as rocks, reefs, pier pilings, and especially shipwrecks or other submerged objects suitable as hiding places. They are known to eat octopus, lobsters, crabs, and many types of reef fishes.

Fishing for conger is extremely popular in Britain. It's great strength, sharp teeth, ability to swim backward, and propensity for remaining in or near cover make it a formidable foe and account for many broken lines. Because it remains in sheltered places, it is almost exclusively an anglers' fish since it is highly unlikely to be taken in a net. Skin and scuba divers sometimes spear congers, but this does not account for a great portion of the catch. They should be considered dangerous when boated or speared as their teeth are strong and sharp. They are considered excellent food fish.

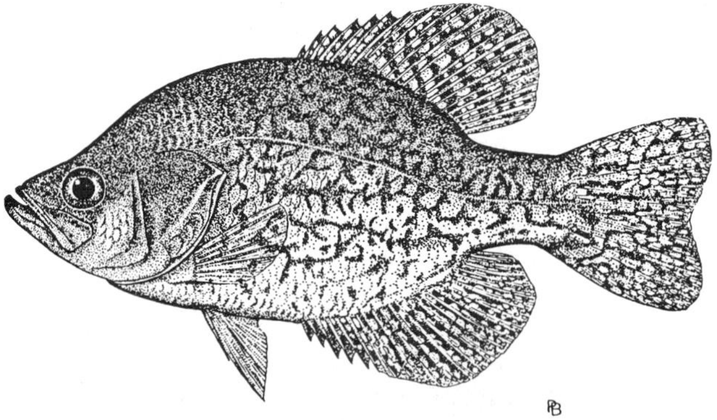

CRAPPIE, black / *Pomoxis nigromaculatus* (Lesueur, 1829); CENTRARCHIDAE FAMILY; also called calico bass, papermouth, bachelor perch

Native to most of the eastern half of the U.S.A., the black crappie has been so extensively transplanted that today it almost entirely blankets the U.S. and reaches up into southern Manitoba, Ontario and Quebec in Canada. It is only noticeably scarce in a swathe of the midwest stretching from western Texas up through Nevada, Colorado, Utah, Wyoming, Idaho and western Montana, and even these states have black crappies either along their borders or in limited internal areas.

Crappies are members of the sunfish and black bass family, and though they show a definite family resemblance, they are distinctive enough that they shouldn't be confused with any other species. The black crappie and the white crappie *(Pomoxis annularis)* are most often confused with each other, and this is where the real need for positive identification characteristics arise. Despite their common names both species are the same color (dark olive or black dorsally with silvery sides) and both have spots on the sides. However, the pattern of the spotting is distinctly different. In the black crappie the spots are more or less irregular and scattered while in the white crappie the spots may be more vague and are clearly arranged into 7-9 vertical bars on the sides. Another distinction is the number of spines in the dorsal fin. The black crappie has 7-8 dorsal spines while the white crappie has only 6, the same number as in its anal fin. In body shape the black crappie is somewhat deeper than the white crappie, but both species resemble the sunfish in profile with greatly compressed bodies.

Several features will readily distinguish the crappies from the sunfishes. In the crappies, the gill cover has a sharp point instead of ending in a little ear-like flap. The scientific name, *Pomoxis*, means "sharp opercle", or gill cover. Crappies also have larger, more bass-like mouths than most sunfish, and can be distinguished even at a distance by their coloration and distinctive dorsal and anal fins. The dorsal fin is positioned directly above the anal fin and both are almost exactly the same size and shape. The fact that the spines and rays of the dorsal fins run together is typical of the Sunfish family. But in the crappies more than in most other sunfish, the rays and spines give the appearance of forming a single fin rather than two fins that are connected.

The black crappie inhabits large ponds and shallow areas of lakes, with sandy or muddy bottoms and usually in areas of abundant vegetation. It requires a deeper, clearer, somewhat cooler habitat than does the white crappie. It is an abundant species (though in smaller concentrations than the white crappie), and is important both commercially and as a sport fish. The flesh is white, flaky, and of excellent quality and the fish are easily caught, often as fast as the hook can be rebaited. According to tests performed by Elgin Ciampi (as reported in Bass by Robert H. Boyle), of eight fish tested for "intelligence" based on how fast they learned to avoid a particular lure, the crappie ranked seventh, with only the gar being slower to learn.

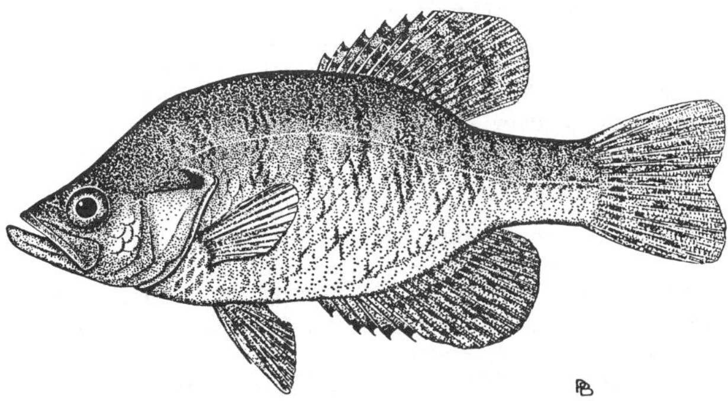

CRAPPIE, white / *Pomoxis annularis* Rafinesque, 1818; CENTRARCHIDAE FAMILY; also called papermouth, bachelor perch

Native to the eastern half of the U.S. and southern Ontario west of the Appalachians, this species has also been introduced east of the Appalachians along the southern U.S. border into northern Mexico and all along the west coast. It is missing from most of peninsular Florida and from some north, central and midwestern states.

The white crappie and black crappie *(Pomoxis nigromaculatus)* are two of the most distinctive members of the sunfish and black bass family. Crappies closely resemble the sunfish with their deep, roundish (in profile), greatly compressed bodies and small heads. The crappies can be identified even at a distance by their lighter colored bodies (olive to black above, with silvery sides) generously covered with black spots (though the spots are often more vague in the white crappie), and by their almost identical dorsal and anal fins. In most of the sunfish the dorsal fin, which has more spines than a crappie, is clearly longer and reaches further forward than the anal fin. In the crappie the dorsal and anal fins are almost exactly alike in size and shape and the dorsal fin is located almost directly above the anal fin. The crappies also differ from the sunfish in having a pointed gill cover edge, rather than the little ear-like flap that is typical of sunfish, and in having a larger, more bass-like mouth than most sunfish.

Crappies can be distinguished from each other by the number of spines in the dorsal fin; 6 in the white crappie and 7-8 in the black crappie. The white crappie is the only sunfish with the same number of spines in both the dorsal and anal fins. Also, the spots on the white crappie are neatly arranged into 7-9 vertical bars on the sides, whereas in the black crappie the spots are scattered in an irregular fashion. In the white crappie the spots are sometimes vaguer, which may explain the names "white" and "black" crappie since in fact both fish are essentially the same color. The dorsal, anal, and tail fins are also spotted or mottled in both species, but the paired fins (pectorals and ventrals) are never spotted. As in all the sunfishes, the dorsal spines run together with the dorsal rays, but in the crappies, the spines and rays look distinctly like a single fin rather than like two connected fins.

The white crappie is not a bottom dweller and prefers shallower water than the black crappie. It is also better able to tolerate areas of high turbidity, being found in warm, weedy bays, silted streams, lakes, ponds, and muddy, slow-moving areas of larger rivers. Like the black crappie, it is considered an excellent food and sport fish and has white flaky meat that is of excellent quality.

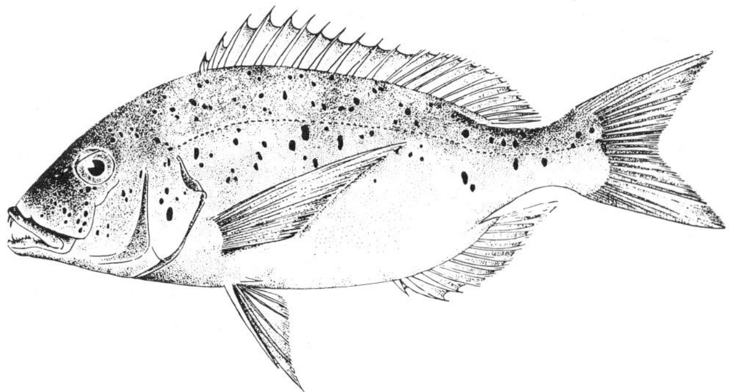

DENTEX / *Dentex dentex* (Linnaeus, 1758); SPARIDAE FAMILY; also called dentice, denton, or dente)

Occurs in the Mediterranean and Atlantic Ocean from the Bay of Biscay to West Africa north off Cape Blanc and Madeira. Occasionally, dentex are found as far north as the British Isles and as far south as Senegal.

While inhabiting hard bottoms (rock or rubble) down to 200 m (656 ft), dentex are more commonly found between 15 and 50 m (50 and 165 ft). Adults are generally solitary, the young gregarious. They are active predatory fish that feed on fish, mollusks, and cephalopods (octopus, cuttlefish, squid). In the summer they approach the shore, but in winter migrate to deeper water.

The dentex have oval-shaped rather deep bodies with a massive, smoothly rounded head in adults. Very large individuals have a profile with a slight frontal hump. Both jaws have well developed canine-like teeth plus several rows of smaller teeth of similar shape. The dorsal fin has 11 spines and 11 or 12 soft rays, the spines increasing in length from the first to the fourth or fifth then subequal. The lateral line has 62-68 scales. Color is variable but young are dentex are grayish, spotted with black on the back and upper sides, becoming pinkish with sexual maturity. Older individuals are bluish grey with spots becoming more or less diffuse with age. Some have a yellow tinge behind the mouth and on the gill cover.

They can be distinguished from other similar species by the dark spots which are always present and the several rows of canine-like teeth. Other species have more than one type of teeth or incisor-like teeth.

Fishing methods include trolling with dead bait, live bait like mackerel, garfish, boga and squid or artificials such as rapalas in 10 to 50 m (33 to 165 ft). Bottom fishing in deeper waters with both live and dead bait such as anchovies, sardines, octopus or squid is also productive. They are very clever fish, needing small hooks and light leaders. A very popular game fish and esteemed table fish, they reportedly reach a weight of around 15 kg (33 lb).

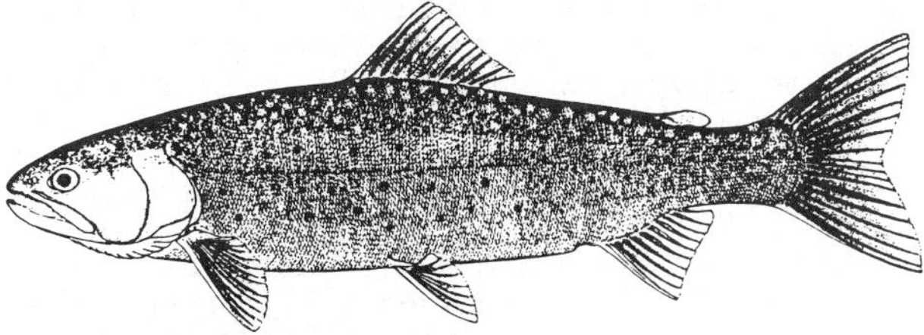

DOLLY VARDEN / *Salvelinus malma* (Walbaum, 1792); SALMONIDAE FAMILY

Known to occur from the Sea of Japan through the Kuril Islands to Kamchatka, through the Aleutian Islands and around Alaska to the Yukon and Northwest Territories (Canada) in the north and the northwestern United States in the south. Like the Arctic char *(Salvelinus alpinus)*, it is an anadromous fish (migrates to the sea and back), though some populations are landlocked.

The complex of chars composed of Arctic char *(S. alpinus)*, Dolly Varden *(S. malma)* and bull trout *(S. confluentus)* is a closely related group and difficult to distinguish from external characteristics. Due to past misidentification of species in various locales and lack of scientific knowledge, much of the available literature on these species is either misleading or incorrect, and there is still some disagreement among scientists on their distribution.

The Dolly Varden and bull trout can generally be distinguished by their size and habitat. The Dolly Varden is usually a coastal species whereas the larger bull trout is found inland in large, cold rivers and lakes draining high, mountainous areas. A much greater problem arises in trying to separate the Dolly Varden from the Arctic char. Much published information on the distribution of these species is incorrect and often presupposed that only one species or the other occurred in areas or rivers where it is now believed both species may occur. The two are outwardly almost identical in every respect and to complicate matters, significant variations occurs in both species. The spots on the Dolly Varden are usually smaller than the pupil of the eye, while on the Arctic char they are larger than the pupil. When returning from the sea both species are silvery and lack spots. Arctic char on the average have more gill rakers on the first left gill arch (25-30 as opposed to 21-22 in the Dolly Varden) and more pyloric caeca (40-45 as opposed to about 30 in the Dolly Varden), but fish with intermediate counts (i.e., 23 or 24 gill rakers and 35 pyloric caeca) are not at all uncommon in either species.

Fish that don't clearly "fit the pattern" will almost certainly have to be examined in a laboratory to determine their identity. Since the problem of identification was only very recently even diagnosed, there are at present very few scientists who are qualified to make a positive identification on an unusual specimen. IGFA recommends that all potential record chars that cannot be positively identified by external characteristics be frozen in case further study is needed.

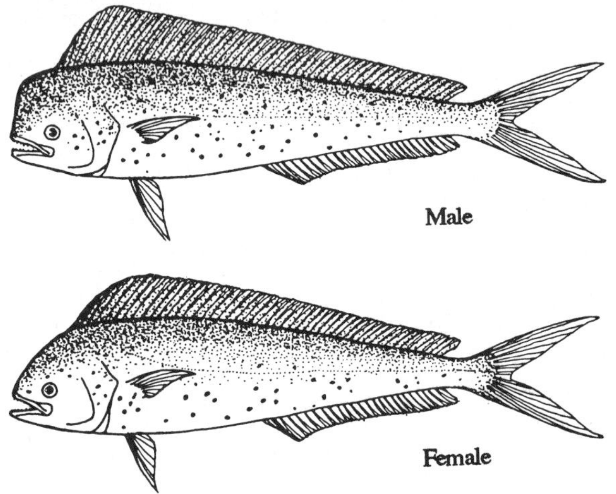

DOLPHIN / *Coryphaena hippurus* Linnaeus, 1758; CORYPHAENIDAE FAMILY; also called dolphinfish, mahi mahi, dorado

Found worldwide in tropical and warm temperate seas, the dolphin is pelagic, schooling, and migratory. Though occasionally caught from an ocean pier, it is basically a deep water species, inhabiting the surface of the open ocean.

The dolphin is a distinctive fish, both for its shape and its colors. Though it is among the most colorful fish in the sea, the colors are quite variable and defy an accurate, simple description. Generally, when the fish is alive in the water, the dolphin is rich iridescent blue or blue-green dorsally; gold, bluish gold, or silvery gold on the lower flanks; and silvery white or yellow on the belly. The sides are sprinkled with a mixture of dark and light spots, ranging from black or blue to golden. The dorsal fin is rich blue, and the anal fin is golden or silvery. The other fins are generally golden yellow, edged with blue. When removed from the water, the colors fluctuate between blue, green, and yellow. After death the fish usually turns uniformly yellow or silvery gray.

Large males have high, vertical foreheads, while the female's forehead is rounded. Males grow larger than females. There are no spines in any of the fins. The dorsal fin has 55-66 soft rays. The anal fin has 25-31 soft rays.

They are extremely fast swimmers and feed extensively on flying fish and squid as well as on other small fish. They have a particular affinity for swimming beneath buoys, seaweed, logs, and floating objects of almost any kind. One skipper reportedly made some very good catches while circling a ladder found drifting in the water.

Hooked dolphin may leap or tailwalk, darting first in one direction, then another. It is believed that they can reach speeds up to 50 mph (80.5 kph) in short bursts. Successful fishing methods include trolling surface baits (flying fish, mullet, balao, squid, strip baits) or artificial lures; also live bait fishing or casting. If the first dolphin caught is kept in the water, it will usually hold the school, and often others will come near enough to be caught by casting.

In addition to being a highly rated game fish, the dolphin is a delicious food fish. It is often referred to as the "dolphinfish" to distinguish it from the dolphin of the porpoise family, which is a mammal and in no way related.

The dolphin family (Coryphaenidae) consists of two species. The smaller variety, pompano dolphin (*Coryphaena equiselis*) often confused with females or small males of the larger dolphin (*C. hippurus*). The two species can be quickly distinguished because the greatest body depth of *C. equiselis* is near the middle of the body instead of up front close to the head. Also, its dorsal fin originates behind rather than directly above the eyes. The anal fin does not have an extended anterior lobe with a concave outline.

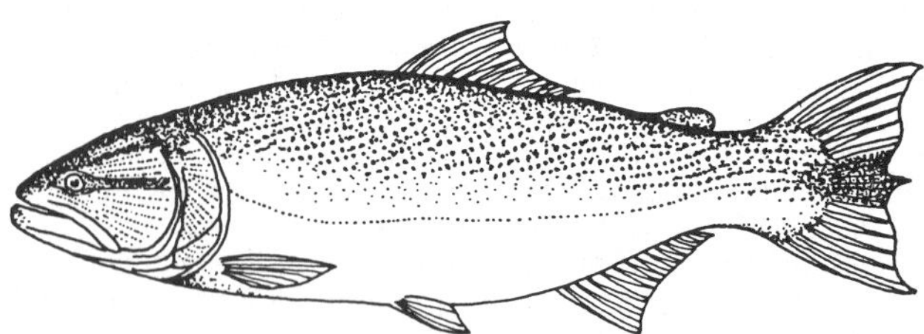

DORADO / *Salminus maxillosus*; Valenciennes, 1849 CHARACIDAE FAMILY

This South American fish is found in the rivers of the São Francisco River system of Brazil, the Paraguay and Uruguay River systems, the Magdalena River system of Colombia, and most importantly, the Paran River of Argentina. It also occurs in the Rio de la Plata and has been introduced into the Paralba and Doce rivers of Brazil. It apparently does not occur in the Amazon and Orinoco basins as once believed. This misconception, widespread in literature, appears to be due to confusion with another species that occurs in the Amazon and Orinoco and which is called dorado in that region, but is actually the piralba. The largest dorado species (there are at least 4 species) *Salminus maxillosus* seems to be most common to the south, especially in the Paran. While it is widespread, it is uncertain whether the dorados found in all these river systems, especially to the north, include this species.

The name "dorado" is Spanish for "golden" . The same name is used in Spanish language areas of the Caribbean for the dolphin (*Coryphaena hippurus*). Both species are predominantly golden in color with blue, orange, and yellow overtones or highlights. There is a shock of blue in the center of the tail. In general body shape the dorado greatly resembles a salmon with a golden body and a somewhat scalloped tail. The position and shape of the fins is also the same as in the salmons. There is an adipose fin after the dorsal fin, and an axillary process. The head looks like a bluefish's head, machine tooled in gold with blue highlights. The lower jaw is stout and strong, and there is a double row of teeth, the outer row consisting of strong canines.

Unlike the salmons, it does not die after spawning and never ventures beyond the river mouth into the open sea. It is a good food fish and an excellent sport fish. It is powerful and huge, and its mouth has been described as a "steel trap".

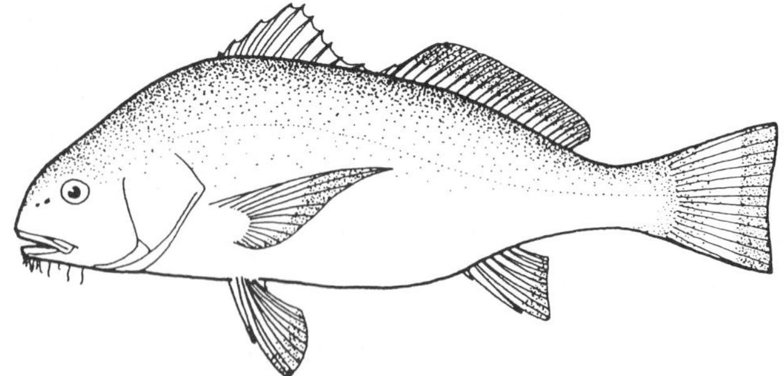

DRUM, black / *Pogonias cromis* (Linnaeus, 1766); SCIAENIDAE FAMILY; also called drum, sea drum, common drum

Found in the western Atlantic Ocean from Massachusetts, U.S.A. to Argentina, including the Gulf of Mexico. Occurring rarely north of New Jersey. An inshore, schooling fish, the black drum is known to inhabit areas near breakwaters, jetties, bridge and pier pilings, clam and oyster beds, channels, estuaries, bays, high marsh areas, and the shorelines over sandy bottoms.

Drums are members of the croaker family (Sciaenidae) which are comprised of 260 species including the weakfish, spotted seatrout, white seabass, Atlantic croaker, and California kingfish. The black drum is distinguished from similar species by the unusually large spine in the anal fin and numerous barbels on the chin. There are large pavement like teeth in the throat that are used to crush shellfish. The dorsal fin is continuous with the forward part having 10 spines and the posterior part

1 spine and 21 soft rays. The anal fin has 2 spines and 5-7 rays. There are 41-47 scales along the lateral line, which runs all the way to the end of the tail, and there are 16 gill rakers on the first branchial arch (4 on the upper limb and 12 on the lower limb). The tail is either truncate or slightly concave. Unlike the red drum *(Sciaenops ocellatus)*, the black drum has no dark spot on the tail base and usually lacks any oblique dark streaks along the scale rows. Juveniles have 4 or 5 broad, dark vertical bars on the body. They feed on mollusks and crustaceans which they locate in the sand with their sensitive chin barbels. Oyster growers report that this fish is very destructive to oyster beds.

Drums use their air bladder to create a sound similar to a drum beating. This "drumming" is largely associated with the breeding season and probably assists in locating and attracting members of the opposite sex. The drumming of the males is particularly loud while the sound of the females is softer.

The black drum is sluggish and does not strike quickly or with force, but when hooked, it puts up an exceedingly tough fight. Fishing methods include bottom fishing, casting from boats or shore, or slow trolling. Baits and lures include shrimp, clams, crabs, squid, cut fish, metal jigs, spoons, and weighted bucktails. Small drums of about 10-15 lb (5-7 kg) are said to be good eating, though they are often infested with parasites. The parasites are not harmful to man, and are killed by cooking, but they detract from the fish's appeal. The flesh is coarse, but tender and delicately flavored. The large, silvery scales, which are hard and difficult to remove, are often marketed as fish jewelry.

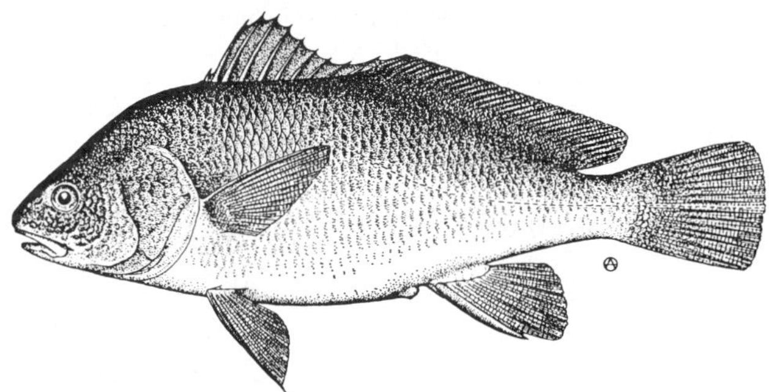

DRUM, freshwater / *Aplodinotus grunniens* Rafinesque, 1819; SCIAENIDAE FAMILY

A. grunniens is the only North American freshwater representative of the Sciaenidae family which includes the croakers, corbinas, drums, seatrout, etc. It also has the greatest north/south range of any North American freshwater fish, occurring over much of the U.S. between the Rockies and the Appalachians southward through eastern Mexico to Guatemala's Rio Usumacinta system and northward through Manitoba, Canada, all the way to the Hudson Bay. It also occurs in some areas of Ontario, Quebec, and Saskatchewan.

Though it is a fairly distinctive fish, its deep body, humped back, blunt snout and subterminal mouth have led some to confuse it with the carp and the buffalos. It can be easily distinguished by its two dorsal fins (only one in the carp and buffalos) and its rounded, rather than forked tail. Also, the first dorsal fin of the freshwater drum is composed of 8-9 spines, whereas the carp has only one spine at the beginning of its single soft rayed dorsal fin and the buffalos have no spines at all.

The freshwater drum is a bottom feeder; its diet consists of mollusks, insects, and fish. Huge otoliths, "ear bones", excavated from Indian village sites indicate that at one time they have grown as large as 200 lb (90 kg). Currently this species is known to reach about 50 lb (24 kg), and commercially marketed catches average 1.5-5 lb (0.68-2.26 kg).

Although a strong fighter with some commercial value, it is not generally highly regarded as either a sport or a food fish. The flesh is white with large, coarse flakes and its quality has been compared to that of the carp. Perhaps 5-10 million pounds are taken annually for commercial purposes, mostly from Lake Erie. It is utilized to a great extent as mink food.

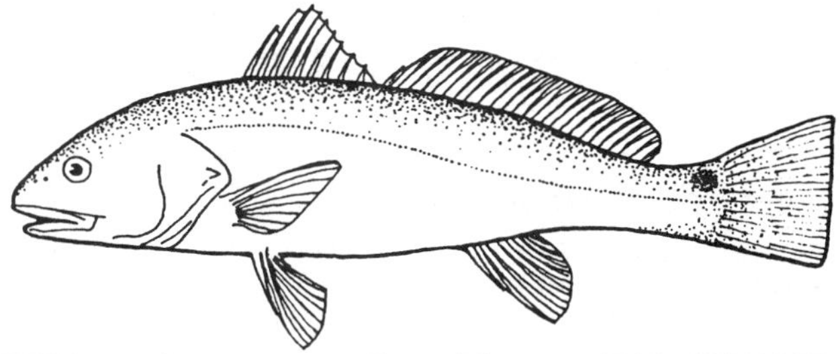

DRUM, red / *Sciaenops ocellatus* (Linnaeus, 1766); SCIAENIDAE

FAMILY; also called channel bass, redfish, spot-tail bass, red bass, red horse, school drum, puppy drum

Found in the western Atlantic Ocean from Maine to the Gulf of Mexico, but rare north of New Jersey. The red rum is a schooling species that occurs inshore over sandy or muddy bottoms. It inhabits both salt and brackish waters and can tolerate fresh water. It is found in inlets and channels, and smaller specimens may be found in shallow estuaries.

The red drum can be distinguished from the black drum *(Pogonias cromis)* by its lack of chin barbels and more elongated body. The first dorsal fin of the red drum has 9 or 10 spines; the second has 23-26 soft rays. The anal fin has 2 spines and 8 rays. The tail fin is either truncate or slightly concave. There are 40-45 scales along the lateral line and 8 or 9 gill rakers on the lower limb of the first gill arch. The body has coppery red overtones on a silvery gray background. The most obvious and characteristic marking on the red drum is a large black spot about the size of the eye on either side of the caudal peduncle, just before the tail fin. Sometimes there are two spots on each side, and occasionally there may be similar spots on the body.

It is a strong, hard fighter when hooked. Fishing methods include drifting or still fishing on the bottom, jigging or casting from boats or from the shore, and slow trolling. In some areas red drum may be stalked on the flats like bonefish. Baits and lures include crabs, shrimp, clams, mullet, worms, sandbugs, mossbunker, jigs, underwater plugs, spoons, weighted bucktails, strip bait, feathers, metal squids, and streamer flies. Large red drum can be taken from just about the breaker line on an incoming tide or near channels, inlets, shell beds, etc.

Very large specimens are often called "bull reds", although they are usually females. Red drum up to about 10-15 lb (5-7 kg) are very fine eating. Larger specimen may be coarse, stringy and unpalatable.

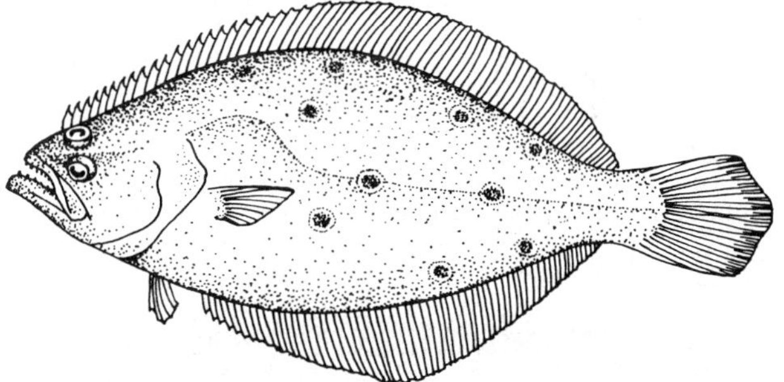

FLOUNDER, summer / *Paralichthys dentatus* (Linnaeus, 1766); BOTHIDAE FAMILY; also called fluke

Occurs in the western Atlantic from Maine to South Carolina and possibly to northeast Florida. It may be found in water as shallow as 6 in (15 cm) during the summer, though the largest specimens are found in depths of 8 to 10 fathoms. In the winter the large fish move offshore into depths of 25 to 80 fathoms.

The summer flounder is a left-eyed flatfish. The eyed side always blends in perfectly with the sea bed. There is usually a scattering of 10 to 14 eye-like spots on the body. As in other flatfish, the blind side is white and relatively featureless. The teeth are well developed on both sides of the jaws. The dorsal fin has 85-94 rays; the anal fin has 60-63 rays. There are only 5 or 6 gill rakers on the upper limb of the first arch and 11-21 on the lower limb.

Adults are largely piscivorous and highly predatory, feeding actively in midwater as well as on the bottom. They are often seen chasing bait fish at the surface. It is a rapid swimmer and a good light-tackle game fish that provides lively action. It prefers sandy or muddy bottoms and is common in the summer months in bays, harbors, estuaries, canals, creeks, and along shorelines as well as in the vicinity of piers and bridges.

Drift fishing is the most common fishing method and probably the most effective, since drifting covers more bottom and keeps the bait or lure in motion. Many are also taken by chumming while fishing at anchor, by trolling, or by casting with low retrievers from shore or pier. The most popular bait is a ½ to 3/4 inch strip of shark belly, fluke belly, or squid with the tail split for fluttering action; a killie or spearing (silverside) is often added to the strip. Other effective baits include strips cut from the undersides of menhaden, herring, porgy, young bluefish, or sea robin; or a piece of blue crab. Effective lures include a small spoon, spinner, or feather. Some time must be allowed between the moment the flounder picks up the bait and the strike, or the bail may simply be yanked away. Inshore fishing is best on a running tide, and the largest fish are caught late in the season.

It is an excellent food fish; the flesh is white firm, and succulent. It is by far the most important flatfish of the Atlantic states.

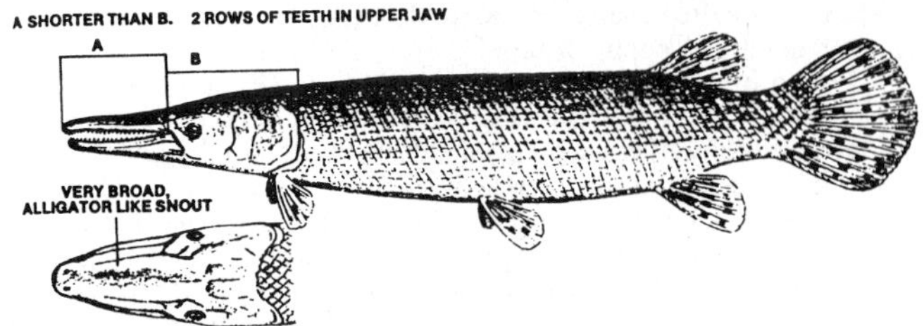

GAR, alligator / *Lepisosteus spatula* Lacepede, 1803; LEPISOSTEIDAE FAMILY

The alligator gar is an inhabitant of large rivers, bays, and coastal marine waters from the western Florida panhandle (the Econfina River) west along the Gulf of Veracruz, Mexico, and north in the Mississippi River drainage as far as the lower reaches of the Ohio and Missouri rivers. It has been reported from Lake Nicaragua and the Sapoa River.

Believed to grow to over 300 lb (136 kg) with a head that looks very much like an alligator's, it is certainly one of the most distinctive freshwater species. It can be distinguished from all other gars by the two rows of teeth in the upper jaw, its broader snout, and its size when fully grown. All other gars have one row of teeth in the upper jaw and the second largest gar does not usually exceed 50 lb (22 kg). In most other respects all gars are very similar in appearance, with a long body, a long, toothy snout, and a single dorsal fin that is far back on the body above the anal fin and just before the tail. The tail is rounded and the pectoral, ventral, and anal fins are fairly evenly spaced on the lower half of the body. The gars most closely resemble the fishes of the pike family (muskellunge, northern pike, and the pickerels, *Esox spp.)* in body shape and fin placement. In these fishes the tail is forked, not rounded.

Because of its huge size and great strength, the alligator gar is popular with anglers. Obviously, it is not a fish that is easily caught, as its sharp teeth will cut most lines in an instant. They are edible, but are not highly rated by most people. Gar are used to a slight extent as food, mostly in the south. The roe (eggs) should never be eaten as it is toxic to man, animals, and birds (but apparently not to other fish), and will cause severe illness in people and sometimes death in smaller animals.

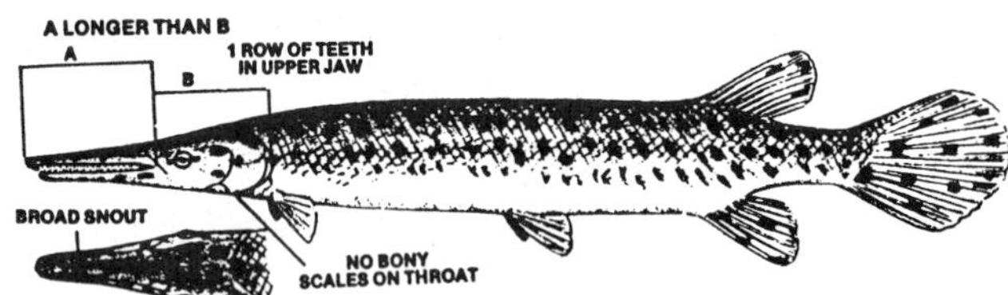

GAR, Florida / *Lepisosteus platyrhincus* DeKay, 1842; LEPISOSTEIDAE FAMILY

Found throughout peninsular Florida and in the panhandle as far as the Apalachicola River drainage, where there is evidence that it may hybridize with the spotted gar *(Lepisosteus oculatus)*, its closest relative. The Florida gar also occurs through part of southern Georgia to the Savannah River drainage. West of the Apalachicola River drainage in the western panhandle and throughout several states to the west and northwest of Florida, they are by the spotted gar. Apparently their ranges do not overlap except in the Apalachicola drainage. The Florida gar is relatively common in medium to large lowland streams and lakes with mud or sand bottoms and an abundance of underwater vegetation. It is also abundant in canals, such as the Tamiami. Over 2,000 gars have been taken from a stretch of canal only 300 feet long.

Like the spotted gar, it has spots on top of the head as well as over the entire body and on all the fins. Other gars have spots on the fins and usually on the posterior part of the body only. The Florida and spotted gars can be distinguished from each other mainly by the distance from the front of the eye to the back of the gill cover. In the Florida gar the distance is less than 2/3 the length of the snout, and in the spotted gar it is more than 2/3 the length. The only other gar that is known to occur within the Florida gar's range is the longnose gar *(L. osseus)* which is found throughout much of the eastern half of the U.S.A., including Florida, at least as far south as Lake Okeechobee. The longnose gar, however, lacks spots on top of its head and its beak is 18-20 times as long as it is wide (at its narrowest point), while the Florida gar's beak is probably less than 5 ½ times as long as it is wide.

Gars are popular as sport fish. Although edible, they are unpopular as food. The roe is highly toxic to humans, animals, and birds.

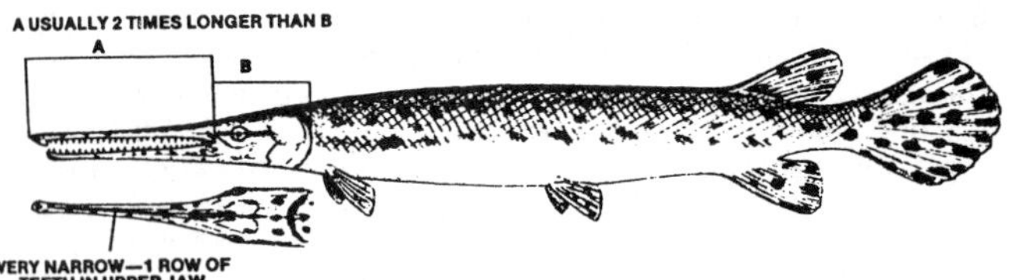

GAR, longnose / *Lepisosteus osseus* (Linnaeus, 1758); LEPISOSTEIDAE FAMILY

The longnose gar is the most common and widely distributed of all the gars. It is found throughout the eastern half of the U.S.A. through the Mississippi River system and other drainages in larger streams and brackish water coastal inlets. Its range extends at least as far south as Florida's Lake Okeechobee, the Gulf states, and the Rio Grande between Texas and Mexico; and as far north as Minnesota, the Great Lakes, and Quebec, Canada. It extends west to the border between Minnesota and south Dakota, and probably as far as Montana in the north and Pecos River in New Mexico to the south. It is found both east and west of the Appalachians, with large concentrations along the Atlantic coast.

This gar is generally distinguished from other gars by its longer, more slender body, and especially by its longer, narrower beak (18-20 times as long as it is wide at its narrowest point). The nostrils are located in a small, bulbous fleshy growth at the very tip of the beak (upper jaw). The bony, diamond shaped ganoid scales of the gars overlap to form a protective armor on the body that has been known to deflect arrows and, according to some sources, even rifle shot on occasion.

Although edible, it is not popular, and the eggs are poisonous, causing severe illness in humans and sometimes death in smaller animals and birds. Only fish seem to be able to consume them without harm.

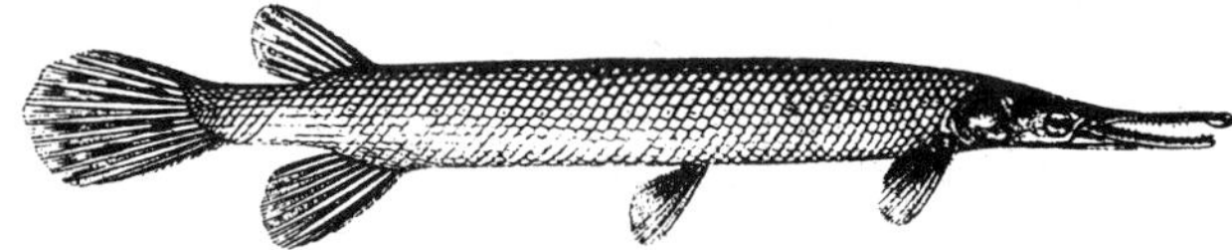

GAR, shortnose / *Lepisosteus platostomus* Rafinesque, 1820; LEPISOSTEIDAE FAMILY

This gar occurs from the Great Lakes south to the Gulf of Mexico, but is essentially limited to the low gradient portions of the Mississippi River basin. It can withstand higher turbidity than most gars, and is common in calm backwater areas of rivers as well as in lakes and other such waters, frequently where little or no aquatic vegetation is present. In U.S. it can be found from northern Alabama to Oklahoma and down through Louisiana to the Gulf. In the north, it has a broad range in the river systems that feed the Mississippi from southern Ohio to Montana.

Because the shortnose gar occurs in many of the same areas (specifically the fertile Mississippi drainage system) as the alligator gar *(Lepisosteus spatula)*, the spotted gar *(L. oculatus)*, and the longnose gar *(L. osseus)*, identifying it involves a process of elimination. It isn't what it is unique for, but rather what the other species have that sets them apart. The alligator gar has two rows of teeth in the upper jaw, while all other gars have only one row. The spotted gar and its close relative the Florida gar *(L. platyrhincus)* have spots on top of the head, over the entire body, and on all the fins. The spots on other gars are confined mainly to the rear portion of the bodies and on the fins, never on the head. The longnose gar is distinguished by its beak or snout which is 18-20 times as long as it is wide at its narrowest point, a considerably greater length to width ratio than in other species. The beak of the shortnose gar is only about 5½ times as long as its narrowest width.

Like all gars, the shortnose gar is a good sport fish. Though edible, it is not popular. The dark green eggs of the gars are poisonous, and cause violent illness in humans and death in small animals and birds. Fish seem to suffer no harm from them.

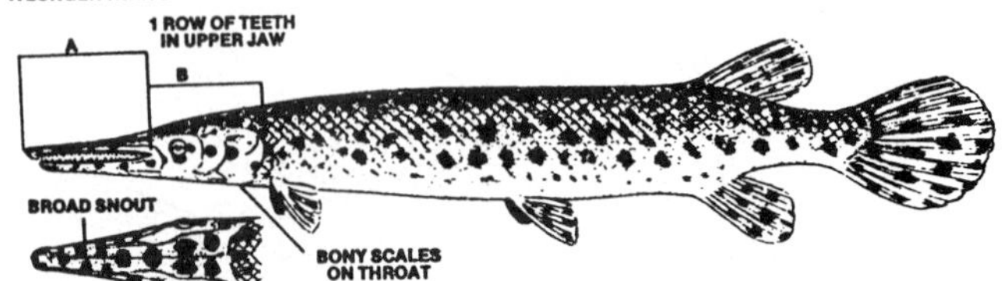

GAR, spotted / *Lepisosteus oculatus* (Winchell, 1864); LEPISOSTEIDAE FAMILY

The spotted gar can be found from the Great Lakes to the Gulf of Mexico down through the Mississippi River drainage system. It occurs all along the Gulf coast from central Texas to the western portion of the

Florida panhandle. East of the Apalachicola drainage, in the remainder of Florida, the spotted gar is replaced by its closest relative, the Florida gar *(L. platyrhincus)*. Both species occur in the Apalachicola drainage itself, where they are believed to hybridize to some extent. In the north of its range, it occurs eastward to the north and south shores of Lake Erie in northern Ohio, Michigan, and Ontario, but is not known to occur much west of Illinois.

The spotted gar and the Florida gar are the only two gars that have spots on top of the head as well as over the entire body and on all the fins. The spots on other gars are limited to the fins and the posterior portion of the body, usually after the pelvic (ventral) fins. The spotted and Florida gars, which both occur in the Apalachicola drainage, are generally distinguished by the distance between the front of the eye and the rear edge of the gill cover. If the distance is less than ⅔ the length of the snout, it is a Florida gar. If it is more than ⅔ the length of the snout, it is a spotted gar. Hybrids of the two may be less easily distinguished and may represent a problem that only a qualified ichthyologist can sort out. The spotted gar has a single row of teeth in each jaw, a characteristic common to all gars except the alligator gar *(L. spatula)* which has two rows of teeth in the upper jaw. Its snout is much broader than that of the longnose gar.

The gars are fine sport fish and their numerous, needle-like teeth can make short work of some lines, which is why wire leaders are often used. Though edible, the gars are not popular as food, and the dark green eggs are poisonous.

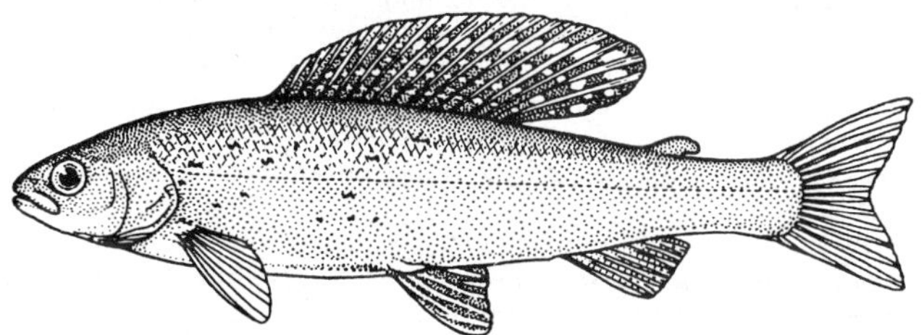

GRAYLING, Arctic / *Thymallus arcticus* (Pallas, 1776); SALMONIDAE FAMILY; also called American grayling

As its name implies, the Arctic grayling is primarily an inhabitant of northern waters. It can be found from the Hudson Bay west through northern and central Canada to Alaska as well as in Siberia. It once occurred in some of the rivers feeding Lakes Huron, Michigan, and Superior in northern Michigan, but has been considered extinct there since 1936. Small natural populations occur in Montana and Idaho, and transplanted populations occur in these states as well as in Vermont, Wyoming, Colorado, Utah, Arizona, Nevada, and California. The best fishing for this species, however, is in Alaska's and northern Canada's rivers and lakes, including Great Bear Lake, Great Slave Lake, Reindeer Lake, and others. It was once believed that four separate species of *Thymallus* occurred in North America, but these are now generally accepted to be only subspecies of *T. arcticus.*

It is easily recognized by its distinctive sail-like dorsal fin which is followed by a small adipose fin that identifies this fish as a member of the salmon family. In males the dorsal fin is higher and rounded in the rear portion, and in females it is higher in front and somewhat smaller overall.

It is a handsome fish due to its graceful lines, large fin, and coloration. Although the colors are considerably variable, the body is generally grayish-silver in appearance, usually with faint to prominent overtones or highlights of gold and/or lavender. The following part of the body generally has several dark spots, which may be shaped like X's or V's in some specimens. The dorsal fin is also spotted. Occasionally a fish may have an entirely golden or silvery appearance, or may be dark blue.

They are superb sport and food fish. They are primarily taken by fly fishing. The firm, white flesh has a uniquely delicate flavor.

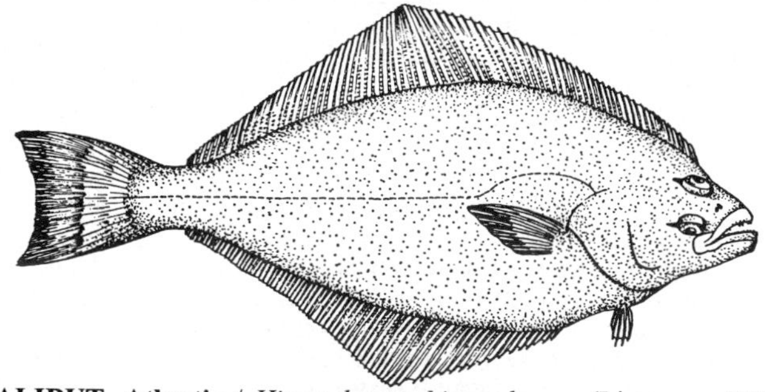

HALIBUT, Atlantic / *Hippoglossus hippoglossus* (Linnaeus, 1758); PLEURONECTIDAE FAMILY; also called common halibut, giant halibut, righteye flounder

Inhabits cold and boreal waters of the North Atlantic, including the Barents Sea, Iceland, and Greenland. It is also found in very deep, cold waters as far south as Virginia on the American side and southwest Ireland on the European side. This species does not occur in near freezing polar waters as many people believe, but is replaced there by the Greenland halibut *(Reinhardtius hippoglossoides)*.

The Atlantic halibut is among the largest bony fishes in the sea. The largest known specimen was taken off Sweden and weighed 720 lb (326.6 kg). Halibut weighing 350 lb (158.76 kg) are about 7-8 ft (2-2.5 m) long and 4 ft (1.2 m) wide.

The lateral line, which has a scale count of about 160, arches strongly above the pectoral fin. The dorsal fin has 98-106 rays and the anal fin has 73-80 rays. The teeth are equally well developed in both sides of the jaw. This species is usually pearly white and featureless on the blind side. Some specimens, nicknamed "cherry-bellies", have a reddish tint on the blind side.

They make extensive migrations and interchanges between stocks in North America and Iceland, and among stocks in Iceland, the Faeroe Islands and the North Sea. Their local movements are usually related to spawning, feeding, water temperature and other factors.

From the eighth or ninth year on the females grow larger and more numerous than the males, mature later (at about 9-10 years of age), and live longer (maximum age is believed to be 35-45 years).

They feed in midwater as well as on the bottom. The best fishing method is drift fishing on the bottom with heavy tackle. Baits include haddock, cod, herring, mackerel, redfish, capelin, crabs, squid and mollusks. Large specimens are often caught while jigging with large diamond jigs.

The halibut is a strong fighter and a valuable food fish. Commercially it is taken predominantly on longlines, but many are also caught on otter trawls. The flesh is of good quality and texture.

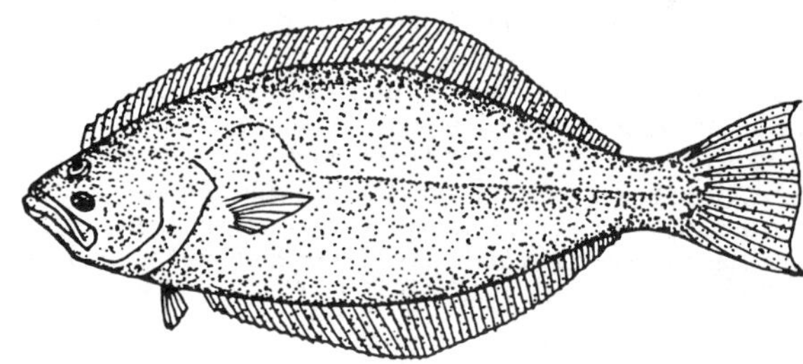

HALIBUT, California / *Paralichthys californicus* (Ayres, 1859); BOTHIDAE FAMILY; also called chicken halibut, southern halibut, bastard halibut, portsider, alabato Monterey halibut

Occurs along the Pacific coast of North America from San Francisco, California, to Baja California, Mexico. There are scattered records of its occurrence as far north as the State of Washington. It is usually found on sandy bottoms in depths of 10 to 20 fathoms or less, though it may occasionally be found in depths up to 100 fathoms. It is not known to make any extensive migrations such as its larger northern relatives do.

This is the largest and most abundant flatfish within its normal range (south of San Francisco), growing to a weight of 60 lb (27 kg) and a length of 5 ft (1.97 m). Females grow larger, live longer, and are more numerous than males. Although is a member of the lefteye flounder family (Bothidae), it appears that nearly half of the population has both eyes on the right side of the body. The sighted side of the fish is usually brownish and the blind side white. Rare specimens may be either brown or white on both sides or have partial coloration on both sides. The gill rakers are slender and numerous totaling about 29 on the first arch.

They feed on anchovies, small fishes, crustaceans, squid, and mollusks. Drift fishing with live anchovies, shrimp, or queenfish is the most successful sportfishing method, though slow trolling has also been known to be effective. This species is not overly finicky and will sometimes take almost any kind of bait or lure.

The firm, white flesh is excellent eating making this fish a target for commercial fisheries, anglers, and spear fishermen in both California and Mexico. It is frequently preyed upon by sharks, rays, porpoises, and especially sea lions.

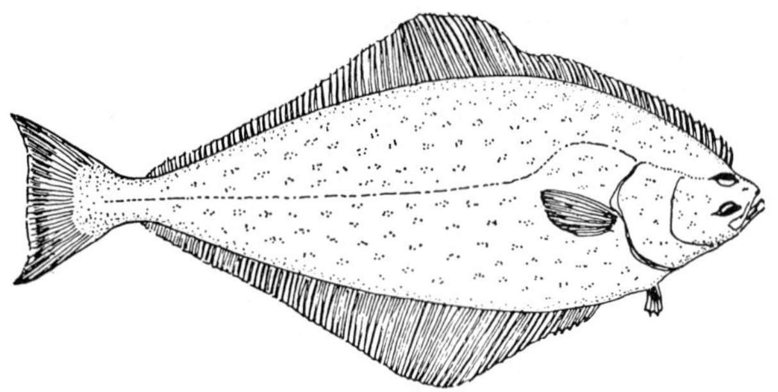

HALIBUT, Pacific / *Hippoglossus stenolepis* Schmidt, 1904; PLEURONECTIDAE FAMILY; also called northern halibut, right halibut, alabato

Occurs in cold waters of the North Pacific from the Bering Sea south to about Santa Rosa Island, California, on the American side and to northern Japan (including the Okhotsk Sea) on the Asian side. The Pacific halibut is highly migratory. Tagging operations have shown that some adult specimens travel 2,000 miles or more, though others appear to remain near the spawning grounds. In northern areas large halibut can be found in relatively shallow waters, but in the warmer southern portions of their range they may go as deep as 600 fathoms or more.

This is the largest Pacific flatfish and very much resembles the Atlantic halibut *(Hippoglossus hippoglossus)*. The teeth are strong and equally well developed on both sides of the jaws. Coloration is uniformly dark brown or gray on the top side (often with small, lighter spots), and white and relatively featureless on the blind side.

Females grow to weights of over 470 lb (213 kg), live to a maximum age of 35-45 years and may attain a length of 9 ft (3 m). By comparison, males probably do not exceed 40 lb (18 kg) or 55 in (140 cm), and their maximum life expectancy appears to be about 25 years. The females are more numerous than the males and grow faster, except during the early stages of development.

The young feed primarily on crustaceans. Adults are piscivorous but will consume large crustaceans, squid, and other mollusks. Stomach contents indicate that large halibut feed in midwater as well as near the bottom. They can be caught while drift fishing on the bottom with heavy tackle, using baits like cod, herring, squid, mackerel or smaller flatfishes.

The flesh is of excellent quality. There is no commercial fishery specifically for halibut other than that of the U.S. and Canada.

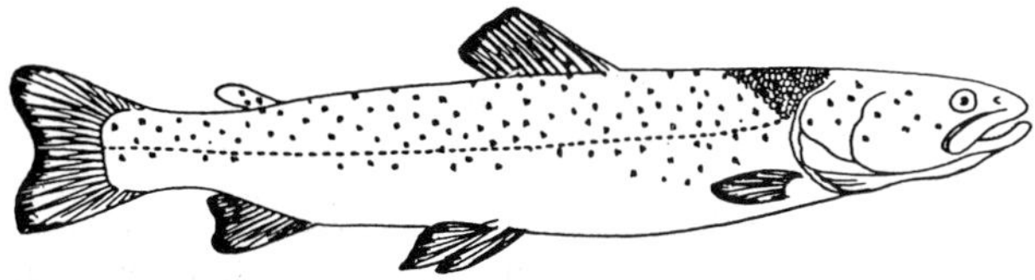

HUCHEN / *Hucho hucho* (Linnaeus, 1758); SALMONIDAE FAMILY; also called huchon, Danube salmon, Danube trout, sulec, mladica

Endemic to Europe, where it is restricted to the Danube River and its tributaries, and occasionally in lakes within the Danube basin. It also occurs in the basin of the Prut River. Introduced into other European rivers early in the 1900's, it was largely unsuccessful. In the Thames River in England it was established at least until the 1930's. Some believe it still exists there with a few being caught each year but misidentified as brown trout *(Salmo trutta)*. Unlike the brown trout and the Atlantic salmon *(Salmo salar)*, both of which the huchen resembles, it stays in the river systems and does not migrate to the sea.

Within Europe, it will not be confused with any species except the brown trout or the Atlantic salmon, which are also members of the Salmonidae family. The huchen can be identified by counting the scales along the lateral line. It has by far the smallest scales numbering 180-200 as compared to 110-120 in the brown trout (called sea trout in Europe), and 120-130 in the Atlantic salmon. It is completely covered with minute black speckles, but never has the red spots which may be present on the brown trout and Atlantic salmon.

This is a popular fish. Part of its popularity is due to the fact that it grows to at least 114 lb (52 kg), making it one of the largest species in the salmon family. A larger fish, also a subspecies of the genus Huch, the taimen, <u>Hucho hucho taimen</u>, reportedly grows to over 200 lb (91 kg).

Because it is relatively rare, it is not common food fish, nor is it as highly valued as other salmonids. However, it is of good quality and is certainly edible. In all of its range, the huchen is presently endangered by commercialization and habitat deterioration.

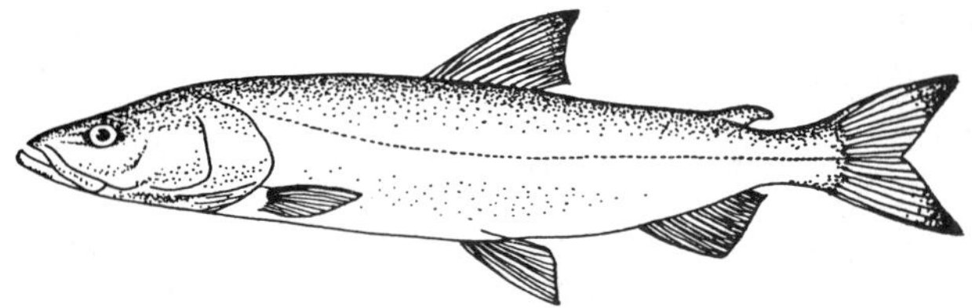

INCONNU / *Stenodus leucichthys* (Guldenstadt, 1772); SALMONIDAE FAMILY; also called sheefish, connie (or conny) Eskimo tarpon. Inconnu is a French name meaning "unknown."

This member of the salmon family is found in of Alaska from the Kuskokwim River (Bering Sea drainage) north, throughout the Yukon River into Canada as well as the MacKenzie River and Great Bear and Great Slave Lakes in Canada's Northwest Territories as far as the Anderson River near Cape Bathurst, and in isolated areas of extreme northern British Columbia. On the Asian side, it occurs westward as far as the White Sea, and an isolated population inhabits the Caspian Sea. In coastal areas this species is anadromous, but in many inland lakes it has become strictly a freshwater fish.

The inconnu belongs to the salmon subfamily Coregoninae, which includes the whitefishes and ciscoes. Its general body shape is very similar to that of char or whitefish, but the head is relatively long, pointed, and depressed on the top. Its mouth is large, and the lower jaw clearly projects outward beyond the upper jaw. The maxillary, or upper jaw bone, extends back at least as far as the middle of the eye. Its small, fine teeth are found on the anterior part of the lower jaw, on the tongue, the premaxillaries, the head of the maxillaries (upper jaw bones), the vomer, and on the palatines (bones of the roof of the mouth). The tail is distinctly forked.

The only predatory member of the whitefish group in Northern America, it is highly favored as a sport fish. Its silvery coloring and tendency to leap high out of the water when hooked have earned it the name "Eskimo tarpon" As a food fish opinion is mixed. It is certainly edible, and a good number are taken commercially in gill nets from Great Slave Lake (and perhaps other areas) and sold both fresh and frozen. The somewhat oily flesh tastes best when smoked. Inconnu are known to grow to 55 lb (25 kg).

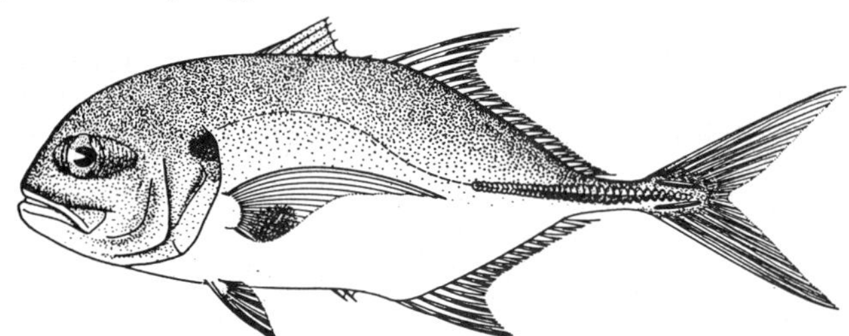

JACK, crevalle / *Caranx hippos* (Linnaeus, 1766); CARANGIDAE FAMILY; also called common jack, toro, cavally, cavalla, horse crevalle

Occurs only in the western Atlantic Ocean from Nova Scotia, Canada, to Uruguay, including the Gulf of Mexico and, occasionally in the West Indies. It was previously believed that this species also occurred in the eastern Atlantic and in parts of the Pacific, but current scientific information shows that these populations are other jack species and not *Caranx hippos*.

The crevalle jack is the common jack of in shore oceanic waters. The species apparently can tolerate a wide range of salinities and occurs around off shore reefs, in coastal waters, harbors and protected bays, over highly saline shallow flats, in brackish waters at river mouths, and has even been known to travel up coastal rivers.

The straight portion of the lateral line on the crevalle jack has 26-35 scutes, whereas in the Pacific species, recently designated *C. caninus*, there may be up to 42 scutes. The arched portion of the lateral line is equal to 66-100 percent of the length of the straight portion. There are 16-19 gill rakers on the lower limb of the first branchial arch, fewer than the blue runner *(C. crysos)* with 23-28 or the bar jack *(C. ruber)* which has 31-35. Closely resembling its relative the horse-eye jack *(C. latus)*, it can be easily distinguished by the small patch of scales on its otherwise bare chest (the entire chest is covered with scales in the horse-eye jack). There is a distinct black spot or blotch on the pectoral fin and another on the operculum. Juveniles typically have about five broad, black bands on the body and one on the head.

A voracious predator, it feeds primarily on smaller fishes which it often chases onto beaches, against seawalls, or into boats. In open water, jacks will herd bait fish into a tight mass, then rush in from all sides, choosing their prey and doggedly pursuing it. The crevalle jack also feeds on shrimp and other invertebrates and on garbage dumped from boats.

This superb light tackle species can be taken by spinning, fly fishing, trolling, or surf casting, generally with live mullet or pinfish as bait. Lures should be retrieved at a fast pace without pausing or stopping as jacks tend to lose interest in anything that doesn't act normally.

Most jacks are not highly valued as food, though they are edible. The small fish taste best; larger specimens can be dark and tasteless. Bleeding the fish may improve the taste. Jacks are among the many species of tropical fishes which have been implicated in ciguatera poisonings (see barracuda, great).

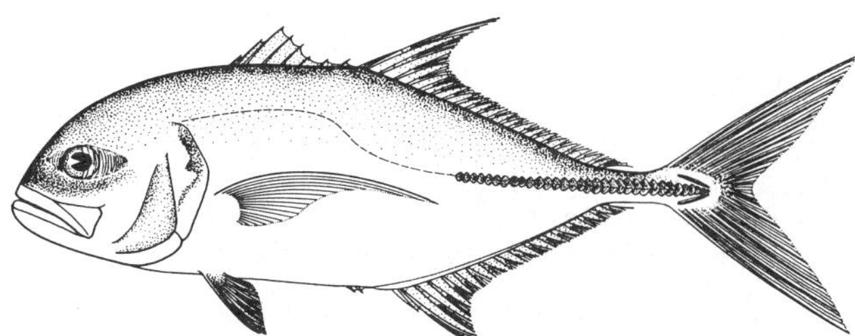

JACK, horse-eye / *Caranx latus* Agassiz, 1831; CARANGIDAE FAMILY; also called goggle-eye

Occurs throughout the Atlantic Ocean New Jersey on the U.S. coast to Rio de Janeiro, Brazil, including Bermuda, the Bahamas and West Indies in the western Atlantic and off the coast of Africa in the eastern Atlantic. In the Pacific and Indian oceans it is replaced by its close relative, the bigeye trevally *(Caranx (Caranx) sexfasciatus)*.

It occurs in small schools around off shore islands and reefs, deep bluewater holes, channels adjacent to flats, and in shore along sandy beaches. It is also known in brackish water and, occasionally, in freshwater coastal rivers and streams.

The chest in front of the pelvic fins is completely covered with scales, distinguishing this species from the crevalle jack *(C. hippos)*, which has a small patch of scales on its otherwise bare chest. The second dorsal and anal fins have 19-22 and 16-18 rays respectively. The body is compressed, though the profile of the head is not as vertical or as blunt as in large crevalle jacks. The eyes are characteristically large and have thick, adipose eyelids. The curved portion is equal to about 55-65 percent of the length of the straight portion (as opposed to 66-100 percent of the length in the crevalle jack). The straight portion of the lateral line has 32-39 scutes, and the scale count of the total lateral line is 84-92. There are 16-18 gill rakers on the lower limb of the first branchial arch and 6-7 on the upper limb. There is a small black spot on the operculum, but there is no spot on the pectoral fin as in the crevalle jack.

It feeds primarily on fish, but also on shrimp, crabs, and other invertebrates. It is a good light-tackle game fish that can be taken with live baits such as mullet, pinfish, or other small fishes, as well as with plugs, jigs, spoons, flies, or other small artificial lures. Lures should be retrieved at a fast pace without slowing or stopping.

Like other jacks, it is edible but not highly esteemed as a food fish. The flesh is dark and relatively tasteless, though this can be improved by cutting off the tail and bleeding the fish immediately after capture. It is one of many tropical species which have been implicated in ciguatera poisonings (see barracuda, great).

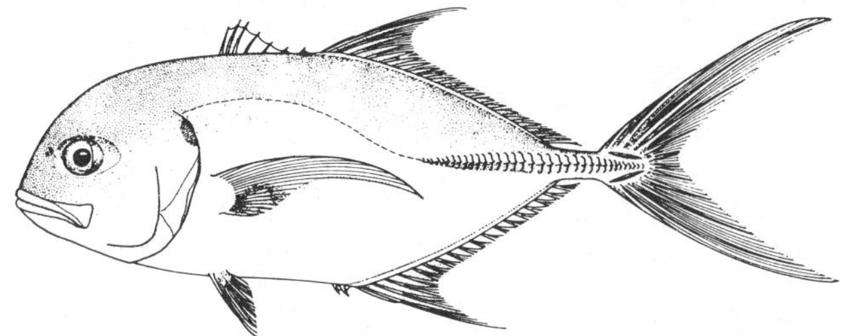

JACK, Pacific crevalle / *Caranx caninus* Gunther, 1868; CARANGIDAE FAMILY; also called toro, crevally, cavalla, jiguagua

This eastern Pacific species is identical in most respects to the crevalle jack *(Caranx hippos)* of the western Atlantic, including the characteristic black spot or blotch on the operculum (gill cover) and on the pectoral fins. The Pacific species is distinguished externally only by the presence of a larger maximum number of scutes (up to 42, as opposed to 26-35 in *C. hippos*). This and other differences documented by scientists have led to classification of the Pacific crevalle jack in recent years as a separate and valid species.

Behavior patterns, edibility and the general appearance of *C. caninus* are the same as for its Atlantic counterpart (see Jack, crevalle).

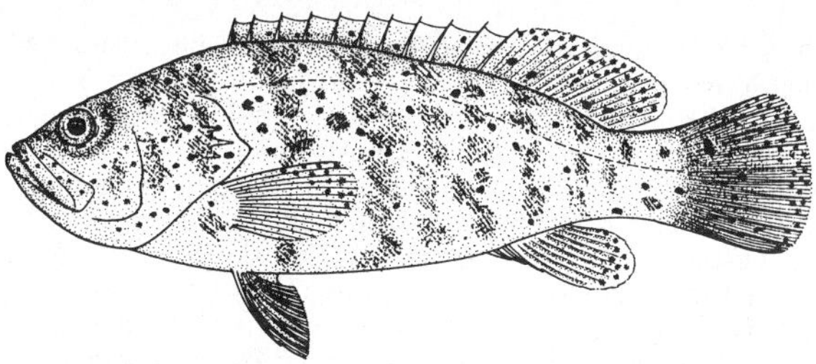

JEWFISH / *Epinephelus itajara* (Lichtenstein, 1822); SERRANIDAE FAMILY; also called spotted jewfish, southern jewfish, junefish, Florida jewfish

Known to occur in the western Atlantic Ocean from Florida to Brazil, including the Gulf of Mexico and the West Indies. It is also known in the eastern Pacific from Costa Rica to Peru. This species is usually found inside of the 12 fathom bottom contour, though it may occur in deeper waters. It favors areas near rocky shores and islands, reefs, ledges, dock and bridge pilings, and wrecks, where caves and holes offer refuge.

The jewfish is the largest of the groupers, attaining a length of up to 8 ft (2.5 m) and a weight of 700 lb (320 kg). It has a short anal fin with only 8 rays; 22-24 gill rakers, including rudiments, on the first arch; and a lateral line scale count of 95-135. The body, including the head and fins, is mottled with dark brown blotches and blackish spots. As the fish grows older, the body becomes darker and the spots and blotches become more numerous and less distinct. Very large specimens may appear also uniformly olive-brown.

It can be easily distinguished from the giant sea bass *(Stereolepis gigas)* because it has more soft rays (15-16) than spines (11) in the dorsal fin. The giant sea bass also has 11 spines, but only 10 soft rays. The jewfish can also be distinguished from the giant sea bass by its rounded tail fin, large, rounded pectoral fins, and different color pattern. The warsaw grouper *(Epinephelus nigritus)* differs from the jewfish in having 10 long dorsal spines, 9 anal rays, a more laterally compressed body, and different coloration.

Jewfish feed primarily on crustaceans, but also on fishes and even an occasional turtle, which is inhaled" into the jewfish's enormous mouth. It is a very sluggish fish and an opportunistic feeder. Some very large specimens show an extraordinary degree of curiosity and will leave their caves to swim up to a diver or any other intruder in their domain. There are reliable reports of jewfish or giant sea bass interfering with diving operations and occasionally even attempting to swallow divers.

Despite poor fighting ability, its great size and weight and its habit of swimming into a hole or between rocks when hooked, make it difficult to land. They can be taken on live or dead bait fished on the bottom from boats, bridges, or shore. Slow trolling also works on occasion. Baits include crabs, spiny lobster, mullet, grunts, mackerel, conch, clams, fish heads, and cut bait.

It is an excellent food fish at any size. The flesh is finely grained, white, and succulent. During World War II the flesh of the jewfish was salted, dried, and sold in the West Indies as imported salt cod.

Evidence indicates that the jewfish begins life as a female and becomes a functional male later in life. A number of grouper species are known to undergo such a sex change.

KAHAWAI (Australian Salmon)
/ *Arripis trutta* (Forster, 1801) and
/ *Arripis esper* (Whitley, 1951); ARRIPIDAE FAMILY; also called Australian salmon, blackback, colonial salmon, cockie salmon, buck salmon

This an in shore pelagic species found around New Zealand, Tasmania, and the southern portions of Australia. Possibly three species of *Arripis* occur in this range, the two listed above and the smaller tommy rough *(A. georgianus)*. The "eastern" Australian salmon *(A. trutta)*, is found off New Zealand, Tasmania, Victoria, New South Wales, Southern Queensland, and Lord Howe Island. The "Western" Australian salmon or "buck salmon" *(A. esper)* occurs off South and Western Australia, Victoria, New South Wales, and Tasmania. Kahawai nursery grounds exist off Tasmania, where the fish move into shallow water and are common along rocky shores in March and April. *A. trutta* is also known to spawn off eastern Victoria and New South Wales in late spring and early summer, and *A. esper* off Western Australia.

They grow to at least 3 ft (1 m) and 33 lb (15 kg), resembling a cross between a bluefish (tailor) and a southern yellowtail (called kingfish in Australia and New Zealand). The body varies from blue-green or greenish to silvery with scattered dark gray, brown, or golden spots. Often mistaken for southern yellowtail, the it can be quickly and easily distinguished by its lack of a yellow stripe along the body and its high first dorsal fin. The name "Australian salmon" is something of a misnomer, as it is in no way related to the true salmon or their relatives (Salmonidae), and is only found in the most southerly ranges of Australia. Even so, some very large fish have come from Australia and northern New Zealand.

They are highly prized by anglers and commercial fishermen. Commercially, they are netted, caught by purse seine or trolling, and canned. They feed actively on anchovies and other small fish and can be caught on these or on fast moving lures. *A. trutta* is known to consume large amounts of krill, while *A. esper* is a major predator on pilchards *(Sardinops neopilchardus)*.

Large concentrations of feeding birds often indicate the presence of kahawai, which go into surface feeding frenzies similarto those of bluefish (tailor). On light tackle, the kahawai is a very sporting catch and will leap repeatedly. Fly fishermen might take note of B.W.Kane's words,...indeed is a fish ideally suited to fly fishing. For the keen angler who is not handy to trout water, but is close to the sea, the kahawai is an excellent substitute for the rainbow." *(Complete Book of Australian Fishing*, ed. Roger Hungerford).

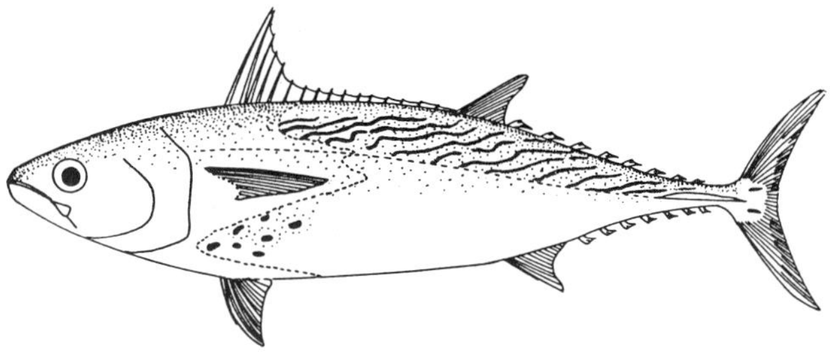

KAWAKAWA / *Euthynnus affinis* (Cantor, 1849); SCOMBRIDAE FAMILY; also called wavyback skipjack, eastern little tuna, mackerel, tuna, Pacific little tunny, false albacore.

Widespread in tropical and temperate waters of the Indo-Pacific from the Red Sea and South Africa east to Indonesia and Australia, and from Japan and the Philippines through Oceania to the Hawaiian Islands. It is accidental in the eastern Pacific where it is replaced by the closely related black skipjack *(Euthynnus lineatus)*. This pelagic and migratory species stays fairly close to land. It may be found near reefs and in estuaries as well as in open waters.

The dorsal fin has 14-16 spines and the second dorsal fin, 12-13 rays. The anal fin has 12-14 rays. There are no scales on the body, except on the corselet and lateral line. There are 29-34 gill rakers on the first arch, as compared to 53-63 in the skipjack tuna *(Katsuwonnus pelamis)* and 32-41 in the black skipjack *(E. lineatus)*. On the back, beginning near the midpoint of the dorsal fin, there are a number of oblique, wavy lines over a turquoise background. These squiggly lines run from the lateral line back towards the dorsal fins. Some live specimens may display dark, prominent longitudinal stripes on the venter. These stripes tend to disappear quickly once the fish is removed from the water, leaving only a number of dark spots showing between the pectoral fins and the ventral fins.

More than half of the food ingested by the kawakawa consists of crustaceans, though squid and pelagic fish also form a large part of its diet. Fishing methods include trolling lures or whole or cut baits, live bait fishing, casting, and spin fishing. Some effective baits include squid, herring, sauri, mullet, anchovy, mackerel, half-beaks and yellowtail.

The flesh is dark red. In some places it is highly valued as food, though there is no specific commercial market for it. In Hawaii it is often served as sashimi.

The kawakawa was once classified as *Euthynnus alletteratus affinnis* when it was thought to be a subspecies of the Atlantic little tunny *(Euthynnus alletteratus)*. It is now considered a separate species.

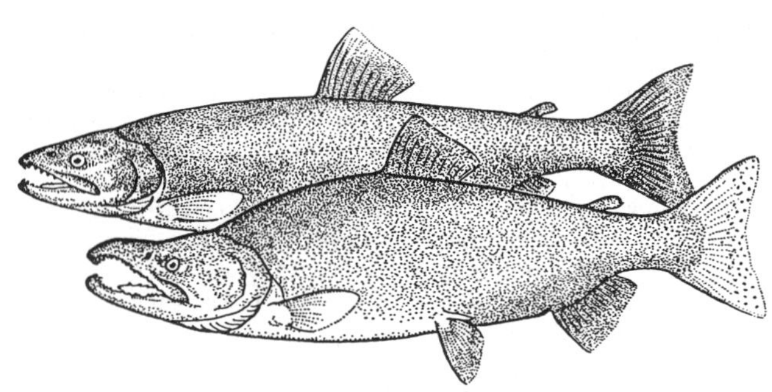

KOKANEE / *Oncorhynchus nerka* (Walbaum, 1792); SALMONIDAE FAMILY; also called sockeye salmon (anadromous form), landlocked sockeye salmon, little redfish, Kennerly's salmon or Kennerly's trout, landlocked red salmon, and other names, including "silver trout".

Kokanee are known to occur in Japan, Russia, British Columbia and the Yukon in Canada, and the states of Alaska, Washington, Idaho and Oregon in the U.S.A. They have been introduced into other U.S. states of the northeast and west coasts, including Maine, New York, Vermont, Connecticut, California, Colorado, Montana, North Dakota, Wyoming, Utah and Nevada; and in Canada into Alberta, Saskatchewan, Manitoba and Ontario.

This is a non-anadromous, or "landlocked", form of the sockeye salmon; and although the two are the same species and morphologically alike, there are individual differences. The strictly freshwater kokanee does not grow as large as the anadromous sockeye. When landlocked in fresh water, the species reaches adulthood at a length of 6-11 in (15-28 cm), while the sockeye reaches adulthood at a length of 24-28 in (60-71 cm). Maximum size is variable depending on environmental conditions. In one lake in Vermont, for example, stocked kokanee grew to 21 in (53 cm), while eggs from the very same source, used to stock other Vermont lakes, produced kokanee that did not exceed 11 in (28 cm).

Males turn from silvery to red at spawning time, while females become a somewhat darker grayish or grayish red color. Rarely, some freshwater populations, and even more rarely, some anadromous populations turn dull green or yellow instead of red. Both male and female die after spawning just like anadromous Pacific salmon. The kokanee is the only Pacific salmon species that is able to mature and spawn in fresh water without an access to the sea.

The kokanee is an extremely popular food and sport fish, but its diet consists primarily of planktonic matter (mostly small aquatic crustaceans like "water flies" and a few insects) which makes it a difficult fish to catch with traditional angling gear and baits. However, using a small piece of worm, a kernel of corn, a salmon egg, or insect larva such as a maggot as bait, or fly fishing with similar imitations have been successful. It is considered a delicacy when smoked.

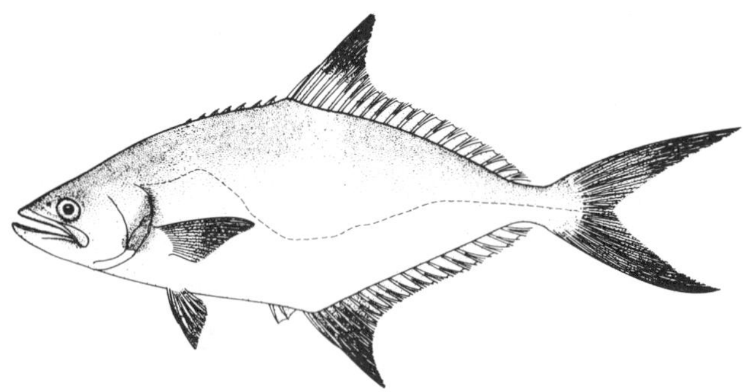

LEERFISH (GARRICK) / *Lichia amia* (Linnaeus, 1758); CARANGIDAE FAMILY; also known as garrick, leervis

It is found throughout the Mediterranean Sea and in the eastern Atlantic Ocean along the entire coasts of the Iberian Peninsula and western Africa to the Cape, then north along the eastern African coast to Delagoa Bay (Maputo, Mozambique). It is a coastal species forming small schools in the surf zone off beaches and rocky promontories. The leerfish is seasonally migratory, some populations moving south to the Cape in summer and north to Natal in winter, possibly following the sardine run which occurs at the same time.

A large species of the jack and trevally family, it attains a weight of at least 71 lb (32.2 kg), the South African angling record for the species. If the body ahead of the prominent second dorsal and anal fin lobes were shorter, the leerfish would look very much like a permit or pompano, but the body is extended considerably to the point that this fish looks like a cross between a permit and a mackerel. The silvery, dart-like body is further identified by the unusually curvy, sinuous lateral line, which arches high over the pectoral fins, then dips to or below the pectoral fins, then rises back to the midline as it nears the tail. The first dorsal fin consists of 8 very short, almost detached spines. The second dorsal fin has 1 spine and 19-21 rays. The anal fin has 3 spines, two of them separate, preceding the rest of the fin, and 17-21 rays. There is a prominent lobe at the beginning of the long second dorsal and anal fins, a characteristic typical of many species of the jack and trevally family. Unlike many members of the family, however, the leerfish has short pectoral fins and no scutes.

Overall, this is a silvery fish with a leathery, scaleless appearance, though in fact it does possess minute embedded scales. The back is dusky to brown or blue-gray, and the lower surface of the belly is white. The fin lobes may be black or dusky-tipped. Juveniles less than 4 in (10 cm) long have orangish to brownish-black bars on the sides.

The leerfish is a highly-rated sport fish that can be caught by angling from the rocks or shore. It takes both live baits, such as mullets or sardines, and lures with zeal. Bluefish (elf) are one of its favorite foods as it aggressively forages along the coasts, and it is not uncommon to see leerfish pursuing mullet on the surface. It is rated fair for edibility and has only limited commercial food value. It is marketed mostly fresh.

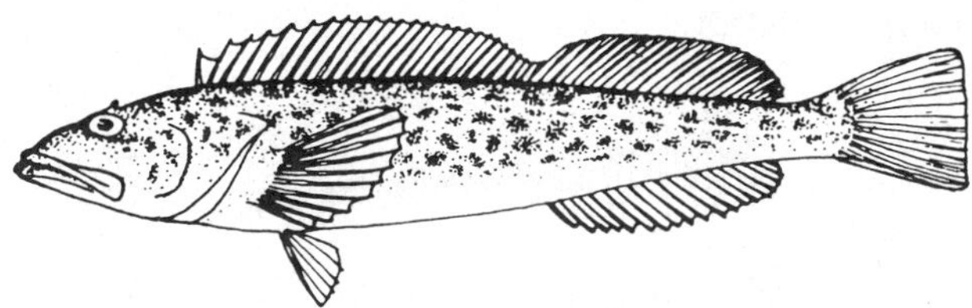

LINGCOD / *Ophiodon elongatus* Girard, 1854; HEXAGRAMMIDAE FAMILY; also called ling, cultus cod, green cod, buffalo cod

Endemic to the eastern Pacific Ocean from Point San Carlos, Baja California, Mexico, north to Kodiak Island, Alaska. Juveniles may be caught near kelp beds and rocky areas. Adults tend to remain in deeper water, and have been taken as deep as 1,381 ft (421 m), although they are most common at depths less than 350 ft (106 m).

It is recognized by a combination of characteristics. The mouth is large and slightly upward directed with a projecting lower jaw; the maxillae (upper jaw bones) extend back beyond the posterior margin of the eyes. The large canine teeth are responsible for the genus name *Ophiodon*, derived from the greek words "ophis" (snake) and "odons" (tooth). There is a single, continuous dorsal fin with a dip between the spiny anterior portions (24-27 spines) and soft-rayed posterior part (21-24 rays). The pectoral fins are large and fan-like (typical of greenling and rockfish). The single anal fin has three spines (usually embedded under the skin in adults) and 21-24 rays. The head and body are covered with small, smooth, cycloid scales, giving the fish a smooth look. Color is highly variable with habitat and may be almost any shade of brown, black, gray, blue or green with darker mottling.

A highly regarded sport fish and food fish, it supports several well established commercial fisheries that take millions of pounds annually. They are voracious feeders that readily devour flounders, hake, herring, rockfish, cod, and even their own species, as well as crustacean and octopus. They can be taken on heavy jigs fished in 30-700 ft (9-213 m) of water, and were once taken by Indians with a sort of shuttlecock (called a "hee hee") made out of wood and feathers, which was pushed to the bottom on the end of a long spear. The lingcod would follow the spinning lure as it rose to the surface, whereupon the fish were deftly speared.

They have been known to chase down and inhale hooked salmon and other fish being played by anglers, often refusing to let go until lifted out of the water.

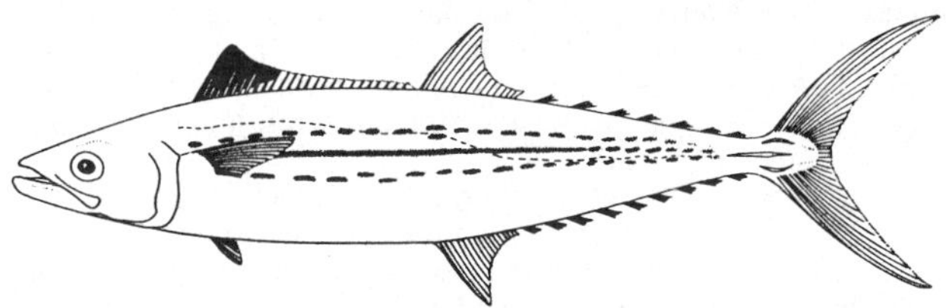

MACKEREL, cero / *Scomberomorus regalis* (Bloch, 1793); SCOMBRIDAE FAMILY; also called cero, spotted cero, king mackerel, black spotted Spanish mackerel, sierra, pintada, cavalla

While known from New England to Brazil, cero are primarily fish of the tropical and sub-tropical reefs. They are common throughout the Florida Keys, West Indies, and Cuba. It is the most common *Scomberomorus* species in the West Indies.

Cero differ from the king mackerel and Spanish mackerel in having a pattern of both yellow spots, yellow-orange streaks, and a dark color line running the length of the body, and a lateral line that gradually curves down toward the caudal peduncle. The anterior third of the first dorsal fin is black like the Spanish mackerel. The pectoral fins are covered with small scales like the king mackerel.

They are an epipelagic species that are most abundant in the clear waters around coral reefs, usually found solitary or in small groups. They feed mainly on small schooling fishes, especially sardines, herrings, pilchards, anchovies and silversides and sometimes squids and shrimps.

They are popular game fish and are frequently taken by commercial fishermen. Sometimes, cero are used as rigged bait for larger game fish. Fishing methods are identical for cero and Spanish mackerel. As with any mackerel fishing, fast trolling while looking for bait fish is a good way to find ceros. Common lures include small silver spoons and white jigs. They also hit surface swimming plugs, chuggers, and shallow running plugs. They have sharp teeth so a wire leader is essential.

Cero reportedly attain a weight in excess of 22 lb (10 kg), but most caught are much smaller. They are considered to be excellent table fare.

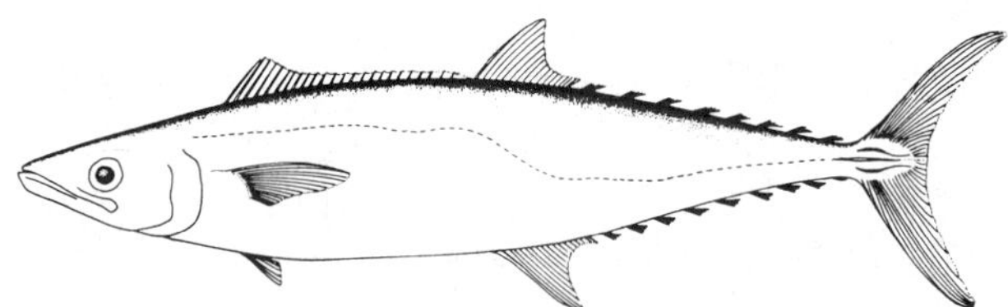

MACKEREL, king / *Scomberomorus cavalla* (Cuvier, 1829); SCOMBRIDAE FAMILY; also called kingfish, giant mackerel

Found in the western Atlantic Ocean in tropical and subtropical waters, it ranges from Maine in the U.S. to Rio de Janeiro, Brazil, including the Gulf of Mexico, and is common around south Florida in the winter months when northern waters drop below about 21°C. This migratory species is constantly on the move. Stocks wintering in Florida migrate as far west as Texas and as far north as Virginia during the summer. It also occurs around south Florida in the spring and early summer months.

A coastal, pelagic, schooling species, it is usually found in waters of 10-20 fathoms. Occasionally it may be caught from ocean piers and around inlets. Congregations often occur around wrecks, buoys, coral reefs, and other such areas where food is abundant. Schools vary in size and the largest individuals are usually loners.

They can be distinguished from other Spanish mackerels in the western Atlantic by the sharp dip in the lateral line under the second dorsal fin, by the relatively small number of spines in the first dorsal fin (14-16) and by the lower gill raker count (6-11 on the first arch). The young have spots similar to those in the Spanish mackerel *(Scomberomorus maculatus)*, but these spots disappear with age. The first dorsal fin is uniformly blue; the anterior third of this fin is never black as it is in the Spanish mackerel and the cero mackerel *(S. regalis)*.

This is an important species, both commercially and as a sport fish. The flesh is firm and of excellent quality. Fishing methods include trolling or drifting either deep or on the surface using strip baits, lures, or small whole baits as well as casting and live bait fishing. Balao, mullet, jacks, herring, pinfish, croakers, shrimp, spoons, feathers, jigs, and plugs have proven effective under various conditions, as have such combinations as feather strip bait and skirt strip bait. Chumming works well to attract and hold these fish.

The maximum age of this species is believed to be 14 years, but fish 7 years old or less are most often caught off Florida, where they enter the fishery at age 2.

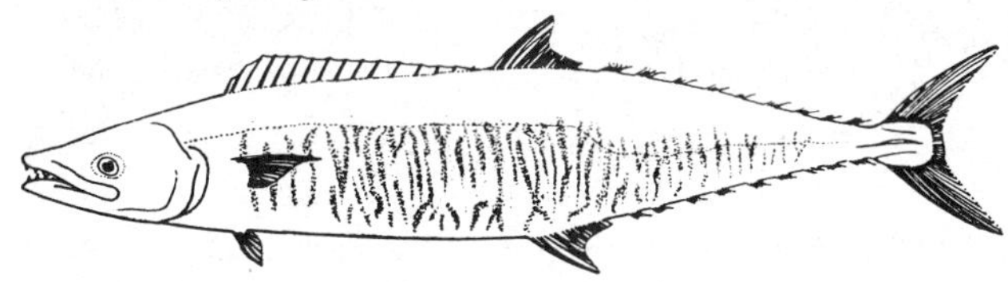

MACKEREL, narrowbarred / *Scomberomorus commerson* (Lacepede, 1800); SCOMBRIDAE FAMILY; also called tanguigue, giant mackerel, kingfish, serra, barracuta

Found in tropical and warm temperate waters of the Indian and Pacific oceans. Specimens have been found in the Red Sea and have migrated through the Suez Canal into the eastern Mediterranean.

The first dorsal fin has 16-17 moderate or low spines, and the second has 16-19 rays followed by 8-10 finlets. The anal fin has 17-20 rays and is also followed by 8-10 finlets. The body is more compressed than the similar looking wahoo's *(Acanthocybium solanderi)* and the lateral line dips below the second dorsal fin, rather than near the middle of the first dorsal fin. There are 3-6 gill rakers on the first arch, whereas the wahoo has none. The flanks display numerous irregular, vertical, wavy bars. As the fish grows the number of stripes increase.

This pelagic and migratory species is a schooling fish but large specimens often travel alone. Its diet consists of small, pelagic schooling fishes, such as sardines and anchovies. It also feeds on flying fish which it is adept at catching even in mid-flight.

The narrowbarred mackerel is a highly rated game fish that sounds often, runs hard and fast, and occasionally leaps. Fishing methods include surface or deep trolling with squid, mullet, sauries, flying fish, garfish and strip baits as well as with drone heads and other artificial lures. Live bait fishing near reefs with these and other baits is also productive. The best fishing is at dawn or dusk and at high or low slack tide.

It is an important commercial species in the areas where it occurs. The flesh is of excellent quality as table fare as well as for use as whole bait, strip bait or chum.

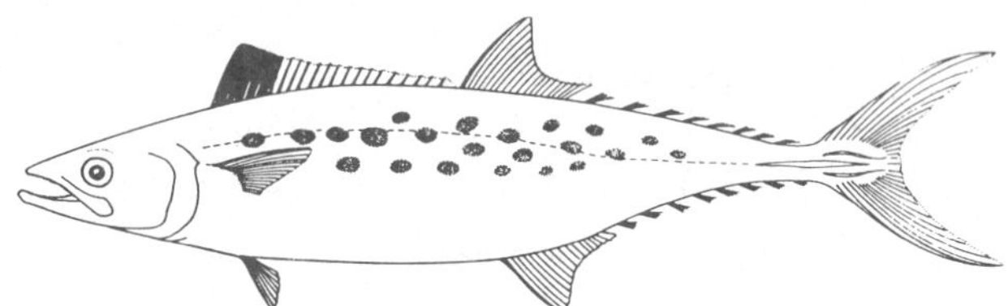

MACKEREL, Spanish / *Scomberomorus maculatus* (Mitchill, 1815); SCOMBRIDAE FAMILY

Occ urs in the western Atlantic north to the Chesapeake Bay and occasionally to Cape Cod, Massachusetts, and south to Yucatan, Mexico.

The Spanish mackerel can be distinguished from both the cero mackerel *(Scomberomorus regalis)* and the king mackerel *(S. cavalla)* by the presence of bronze or yellow spots but no stripes, on the sides and by the lack of scales on the pectoral fins. The cero, the Spanish mackerel's closest look-alike in the Atlantic, has both spots and stripes of bronze or yellow on the sides, and the king mackerel has neither spots nor stripes. Both the cero and the king mackerel have scales on the pectoral fins.

The anterior portion of the first dorsal fin in the Spanish mackerel is black (not true of the king mackerel), and the second dorsal fin and pectoral fins may be black tipped. There are 16-17 spines in the first dorsal fin and 15-18 soft rays in the second dorsal fin, followed by 8-9 finlets. The body is essentially silvery and typically mackerel-like. The back is bluish.

This is an excellent game fish that can be taken on a wide variety of lures and baits. Nylon jigs are considered one of the best lures, especially when retrieved rapidly with an occasional jerk of the rod tip to impact a darting motion to the jig. Feather lures and spoons are also successful, while minnows and live shrimp are the best natural baits. Occasionally almost any lure or bait will work, while at other times, nothing will.

Spanish mackerel are a good food fish and although they are considered large at 10 lb (4.53 kg) some record specimens will grow to more than twice that size.

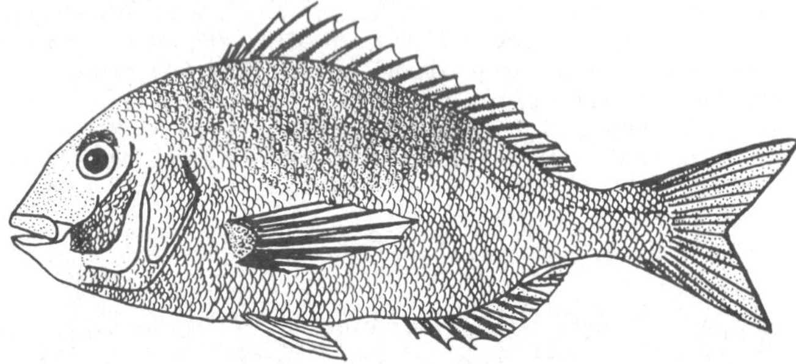

MADAI / *Pagrus major* (Temminck & Schlegel, 1843); SPARIDAE FAMILY; also called red seabream, red porgy, red tail, silver seabream, Japanese seabream, tai

In Japan, seabream, in the family Sparidae, are referred to generally by the term "tai," while the red seabream is called madai, a name inferring that it is the "true tai."

Madai are found distributed throughout Japanese waters with the exception of the Eastern and Northern coasts of Hokkaido and the waters of the Ryukyu Archipelago. They continue southward to the southern part of the Korean Peninsula, the East China Sea, the South China Sea and Taiwan.

The body of the madai is robust, high and moderately compressed. The lower jaw is slightly shorter than the upper. The single dorsal fish has 12 strong spines with 10-12 soft rays and the spines are **not** elongated into filaments. The head and upper body are red/brown and the sides and belly silvery. Numerous small bright blue spots are scattered over the body. The fins are red or faint red. A narrow black margin and a pale lower lobe of the caudal fin are characteristic.

Madai are bottom living at depths of 10 to 200 m deep, often on rough grounds, sand and mud. Adult fish migrate into shallower water to spawn in late spring and summer. Juvenile fish occur mainly in the shallower seas. Madai reportedly attain a length of 130 cm (50 inches), but most fish caught are considerably smaller.

Fishing methods vary from surfcasting and jetty fishing to drift fishing, jigging or anchoring to chum. They feed on wide range of bottom-living invertebrates and also on fishes, so bait selection should be fairly easy.

The red color of the fish and flesh, the shape and taste of the madai are particularly appealing and it is a popular food fish throughout its range. It is particularly high priced in Japan where it is much sought for ceremonies and celebrations. The madai is important both as a game fish and to the Japanese fishing industry, where much of the catch is the product of aquaculture.

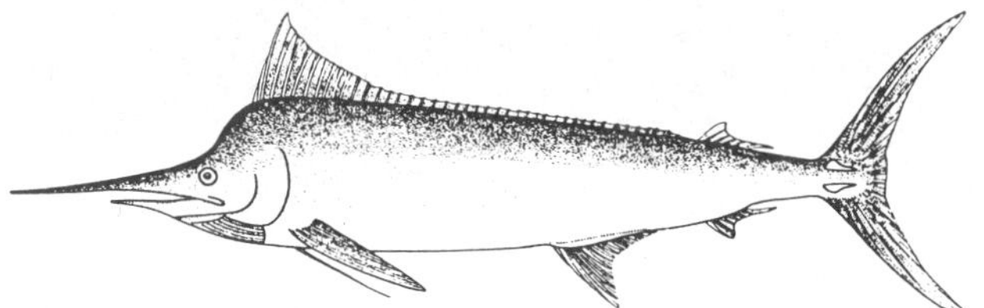

MARLIN, black / *Makaira indica* (Cuvier, 1831); ISTIOPHORIDAE FAMILY; also called white marlin (Japan), silver marlin (Hawaii)

Occurs in the tropical Indian and Pacific oceans. In tropical areas distribution is scattered but continuous in open waters; denser in coastal areas and near islands. In temperate waters occurrence is rare. A few stray black marlin travel around the Cape of Good Hope into the Atlantic, moving up the southwest coast of Africa until they reach the Ivory Coast. Some have been known to cross the ocean from there, traveling in a southwesterly direction as far as Rio de Janeiro, Brazil, or in a northwesterly direction as far as the Atlantic coasts of the Lesser Antilles. Such excursions are, however, regarded as exceptional and very rare. Little is known of the migrations of this pelagic species, but they do not appear to be extensive except in unusual cases.

It can be quickly and positively identified since it is the only marlin that have rigid pectoral fins that cannot be folded flat up against the body without breaking the joints. It is also set apart by the airfoil shape of the pectoral fins and by its very short ventral fins, which almost never exceed 12 in (30 cm) in length, regardless of the size of the fish. The lateral line, which is rarely visible in adults, is a straight double row of pores. The first dorsal fin is proportionately the lowest of any billfish, usually less than 50 percent of the body depth. The body is laterally compressed, rather than rounded; much more so than in similar sized blue marlin.

The body is slate blue dorsally, changing abruptly to silvery white below the lateral line. When feeding or leaping, the black marlin may display light blue vertical stripes on the sides (see striped marlin coloration). Slight variations in color cause some specimens to have a silvery haze over the body. In Hawaii this has led to the name "silver marlin" (once thought to be a separate species). The name "white marlin" applied in Japan refers to the color of the meat, rather than the external color of the fish.

A highly rated game fish, the black marlin has the power, size, and persistence of which anglers dream. Its diet consists of squid and pelagic fishes. Fishing methods include trolling with large, whole baits (mackerel, bonito, flying fish, squid and others) or with artificial lures. Live bait is also effective. The meat is firm and white and brings a high price on the commercial market.

Though there are some exceptions, giant black marlin are larger than giant blue marlin taken on rod and reel. This may be because large black marlin are more accessible and more often occur within the range of sportfishing vessels. Japanese longline fishermen contend that giant blue marlin taken far out at sea beyond the range of sportfishing boats are larger than giant blacks. Blue marlin, or any marlin, larger than 300 lb (136 kg) are almost always females. A 500 lb (226.7 kg) male is a rarity.

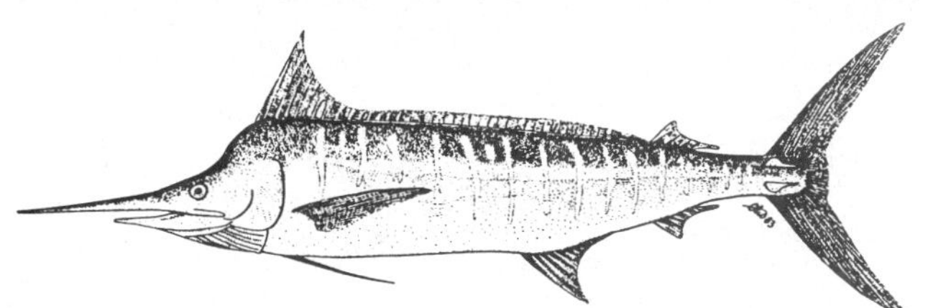

MARLIN, blue (Atlantic & Pacific) / *Makaira nigricans* Lacepede, 1802; ISTIOPHORIDAE FAMILY

This pelagic and migratory species occurs in tropical and warm temperate oceanic waters. In the Atlantic Ocean it is found from 45°N to 35°S, and in the Pacific Ocean from 48°N to 48°S. It is less abundant in the eastern portions of both oceans. In the Indian Ocean it occurs around Ceylon, Mauritius, and off the east coast of Africa. In the northern Gulf of Mexico its movements seem to be associated with the so called Loop Current, an extension of the Caribbean Current. Seasonal concentrations occur in the southwest Atlantic (5°-30°S) from January to April; in the northwest Atlantic (10°-35°N) from June to October; in the western and central North Pacific (2°-24°N) from May to October; in the equatorial Pacific (10°N-10°S) in April and November; and in the Indian Ocean (0°-13°S) from April to October.

Japanese longliners report that the blue marlin is the largest of the istiophorid fishes. It apparently grows larger in the Pacific. All giant marlins are females, and male blue marlin rarely exceed 300 lb (136 kg). The pectoral fins of blue marlin are never rigid, even after death, and can be folded completely flat against the sides. The dorsal fin is high and pointed anteriorly (rather than rounded) and its greatest height is less than the greatest body depth. The anal fin is relatively large and it too is pointed. Juveniles may not share all the characteristics listed above, but the peculiar lateral line system is usually visible in small specimens. In adults it is rarely visible unless the scales or skin are removed. The lateral line of a Pacific blue marlin is a series of large loops, like a chain, along the flanks. The lateral line of an Atlantic blue marlin is a reticulated network that is more complex than the simple loops of the Pacific specimens. The vent is just in front of the anal fin, as it is in all billfish except the spearfish. The back is cobalt blue and the flanks and belly are silvery white. There may be light blue or lavender vertical stripes on the sides, but these usually fade away soon after death, and they are never as obvious as those of the striped marlin. There are no spots on the fins.

They are known to feed on squid and pelagic fishes, including blackfin tuna and frigate mackerel. A powerful, aggressive fighter, they run hard and long, sound deep, and leap high into the air in a seemingly inexhaustible display of strength. Fishing methods include trolling large whole baits such as bonito, dolphin, mullet, mackerel, bonefish, ballyhoo, flying fish and squid as well as various types of artificial lures and sometimes strip baits. The flesh is pale and firm and makes excellent table fare. In the Orient it is often served as sashimi or in fish sausages.

Some taxonomists believe that the Atlantic and Pacific blue marlins are closely related but separate species. They apply the scientific name *Makaira nigricans*, Lacepede, 1892, to the Atlantic species only and the name *Nakaira mazara* (Jordan & Snyder, 1901) to the Pacific and Indian Ocean species. Others treat the two populations as subspecies, *Makaira nigricans nigricans* and *Makaira nigricans mazara*.

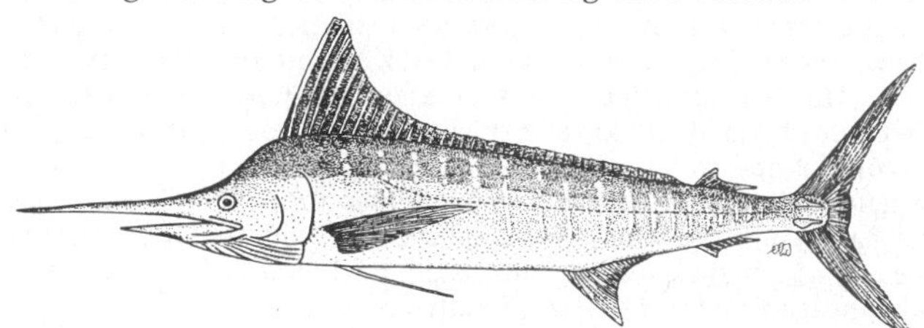

MARLIN, striped / *Tetrapturus audax* (Philippi, 1887); ISTIOPHORIDAE FAMILY; also called striper, red marlin (Japan).

Found in tropical and warm temperate waters of the Indian and Pacific oceans, the striped marlin is pelagic and seasonally migratory, moving toward the equator during the cold season and away again during the warm season.

The most distinguishing characteristic is its high, pointed first dorsal fin, which normally equals or exceeds the greatest body depth. Even in the largest specimens this fin is at least equal to 90 percent of the body depth. Like the dorsal fin, the anal and pectoral fins are pointed. They are also flat and movable and can easily be folded flush against the sides, even after death. The sides are very compressed. The lateral line is straight, single and clearly visible. The back is steely blue fading to

bluish silver on the upper flanks and white below the lateral line. There are a number of iridescent blue spots on the fins and pale blue or lavender vertical stripes on the sides. These may or may not be prominent, but they are normally more prominent than those of other marlins, and they persist after death, which is not always true on other marlins.

It is highly predatory, feeding extensively on pilchards, anchovies, mackerel, sauries, flying fish, squid, and whatever is abundant. It is well known for its fighting ability and has the reputation of spending more time in the air than in the water after it is hooked. In addition to long runs and tail walks, it will "greyhound" across the surface, making up to a dozen or more long, graceful leaps. It can be caught fairly close to shore, and lacking the size and weight of the blue marlin or the black marlin, it is more acrobatically inclined. Fishing methods include trolling whole fish, strip baits, or lures; also live bait fishing.

It has red meat, and many people consider it the least desirable of the billfish for food purposes. In some areas, however, it is highly esteemed and a commercially important species; such is the case in Japan and throughout most of its range in the Indian and Pacific oceans. It is reported to be the most common Indo-Pacific billfish species. As with other marlins, the majority of the catch is taken by commercial longlines.

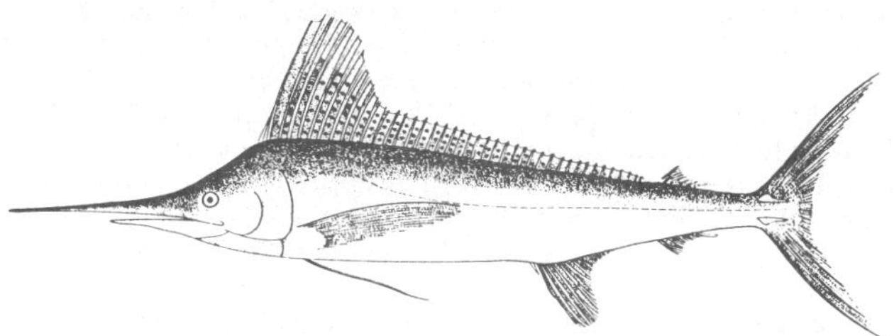

MARLIN, white / *Tetrapturus albidus* Poey, 1861; ISTIOPHORIDAE FAMILY; also called spikefish

Occurs throughout the Atlantic Ocean from latitudes 35°S to 45°N, including the Gulf of Mexico, the Caribbean Sea, and the western Mediterranean Sea. Stray specimens have been recorded outside this range. Though this pelagic and migratory species is usually found in deep blue tropical and warm temperate waters, it frequently comes in close to shore where waters aren't much deeper than 8 fathoms.

Its most characteristic feature is the rounded, rather than pointed, tips of the pectoral fins, first dorsal fin and first anal fin. Some specimens apparently vary from the norm in that the dorsal and pectoral fins may be more pointed; the anal fin is more consistently rounded than the others. The first dorsal fin resembles that of the striped marlin (*T. audax*) in that it is usually as high or higher than the greatest body depth. It differs from that of the striped marlin, or any other marlin, in that both margins are convex. The flat, movable pectoral fins can easily be folded flush against the sides of the body. The lateral line is visible and straight.

In overall appearance the white marlin is generally lighter in color and tends to show more green than do other marlins. Several light blue or lavender vertical bars may show on the flanks, especially when the fish is feeding or leaping (see striped marlin coloration). Some specimens have a scattering of black or purple spots on the first dorsal and anal fins.

A top rated light tackle game fish, the white marlin can be caught by trolling with small whole or strip baits as well as with small spoons, feathers or any of a variety of other artificial lures. Live bait fishing with squid, ballyhoo, mullet, bonefish, mackerel, anchovies, herring and other fish is also successful. It feeds on whatever species are locally abundant. The flesh is of good quality and is especially tasty when smoked.

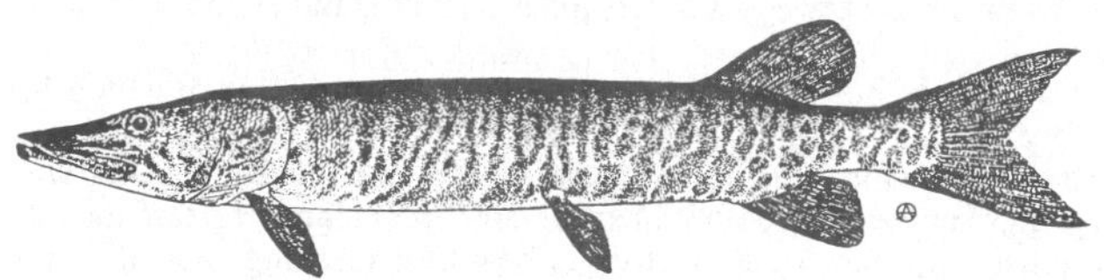

MUSKELLUNGE / *Esox masquinongy* Mitchill, 1824; ESOCIDAE FAMILY; also called maskinonge, muskallonge, muskie, musky, 'lunge, silver muskellunge, Great Lakes muskellunge, Ohio muskellunge, spotted muskellunge, barred muskellunge, great muskellunge, great pike, blue pike, etc. Occasionally, it is referred to as a "jack" in some areas.

It is endemic to the northeastern United States, throughout the area of the Great Lakes south to Georgia, and north to Quebec (St. Lawrence Seaway) and Ontario in Canada. It has been introduced into Manitoba west of Lake Winnipeg. It rarely ventures far from cover, and prefers shallow, heavily vegetated waters less than 40 ft (12 m) deep, usually along rocky shorelines in slow moving streams and larger rivers.

At one time, it was believed that there were at least four species of muskellunge, but these "varieties" are now considered to be one species, *Esox masquinongy*. The exception to this is the tiger musky, which is a hybrid, a cross between a muskellunge and a northern pike *(E. lucius)*.

The musky and all other species belonging to the *Esox genus* (northern pike, the various smaller pickerels, the hybrid tiger musky, and the exotic Amur pike) have a distinctive body that is long and sleek with a single dorsal fin located very far back near the tail (the various species of Esox do not have a spiny first dorsal fin). The pelvic (ventral) fins are located relatively far back on the belly, about half way between the pectoral fins and the tail, instead of directly under the pectoral fins. The mouth is large with the maxillae reaching back at least to the middle of the eyes, and broad, like a duck's bill, but full of teeth.

It can be distinguished from the pike and the pickerels by several factors. It may be barred, spotted, or have no markings at all, but any markings that do occur will be darker than the background of the body. The northern pike, by comparison, has light-colored, oblong spots against a darker body, and the chain pickerel *(E. niger)* has a unique chain-like pattern on the sides, though the spaces between the "links" of the chain may be seen as large oblong spots, depending upon one's point of view. The redfin and grass pickerels (subspecies of *E. americanus*) look much more like the musky in their markings, but they only grow to about 15 in (38 cm) long. The musky can also be distinguished from other *Esox* species by the fact that both the cheeks and the gill cover are usually scaled only on the top half. In pickerels the cheeks and gill covers are fully scaled, and in the pike the cheeks are fully scaled, but the gill cover is usually only scaled on the top half. Another distinction occurs in the number of pores under the lower jaw. In the musky there are 6-9 along each side (rarely 5 or 10 on one side only). In the northern pike there are 5 along each side (rarely 3, 4, or 6 on one side only). In the pickerels, there are 4 along each side (occasionally 3 or 5 on one side only).

This is a very popular game fish, and many anglers dedicate themselves almost exclusively to its pursuit. The musky is very elusive, and is not a common catch, even for those who constantly seek it out. W.B. Scott and E.J. Crossman, in *Freshwater Fishes of Canada*, estimate that the capture of a legal size musky requires 100 man hours of angling in the known haunts of the species. They further estimate that anglers spend several million dollars annually in pursuit of the musky. The flesh is white and flaky and of excellent quality, but many caught by anglers are either mounted or released.

MUSKELLUNGE, tiger / *Esox masquinongy x Esox lucius*; ESOCIDAE FAMILY

The tiger musky is a hybrid produced when a male northern pike *(Esox lucius)* fertilizes the eggs spawned by a female muskellunge *(E. masquinongy)*. Consequently, it is conceivable that one might find a tiger musky anywhere that both muskellunge and northern pike occur together, though it is not a common fish anywhere. They may also be found in areas where they have been introduced, but such populations are naturally self-limiting since the tiger musky is sterile, like the mule (which is a cross between a horse and a donkey), and cannot reproduce itself.

It should not be confused with the true muskellunge which has long been called tiger musky in Minnesota. In most respects, notably in size and appearance, the hybrid is very much like the true muskellunge and anglers universally hold it in equal, and often higher, esteem than the true musky because of its rarity, its beautiful markings and its game nature. It differs from the true muskellunge most noticeably in the markings on its sides. The true musky may have either bars or spots on the sides or no markings at all, but it is rarely as strikingly beautiful as the tiger musky with its wavering tiger stripes.

For many years the tiger musky was believed to be a separate species until scientists succeeded in crossing a northern pike with a muskellunge to discover its true origin. Today it is one of the most prized freshwater catches that an angler can make. Most tiger muskies are either released or mounted, but some are also eaten. The excellent quality of the flesh is white and flaky and comparable to that of the muskellunge.

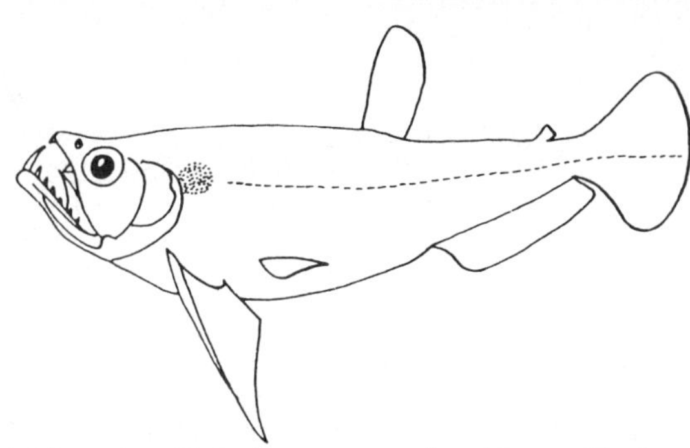

PAYARA / *Hydrolycus scomberoides* (Cuvier 1819); CYNODONTIDAE FAMILY; also called peixe-cachorro, dog fish, saber toothed dogfish, tiger fish, guapeta

Payara inhabit freshwater rivers and lakes in South America from the Orinoco to Paraguay River basins. The distribution of large payara is limited to a few places in Columbia, Venezuela, Brazil, Guyana, Peru and probably Ecuador. They prefer fast-moving water, but are found in still waters of lakes and rivers as well.

The outstanding characteristic of this fish is the pair of enormous saber-like teeth protruding from the lower jaw of the broad upturned mouth. The upper jaw contains two corresponding holes to accommodate the four to six inch teeth when the mouth is closed. In addition, there is one row of numerous, acute, caniniform and conical teeth in each jaw; the gill rakers are spinous. There are 100-125 lateral line scales and 31-40 branched anal rays. The payaras elongated, compressed body and enlarged pectoral fins are ideal for the violently turbulent water that these topendpredators seem to prefer. Payara are generally dark blue to olivaceous dorsally, blending to silver along the sides and belly.

Payara are among the gamest of South Americas freshwater fishes, leaping when hooked and making long fast runs. They are picivorous predators that attack upward, stabbing prey with the large canine teeth and then swallowing them whole and head first.

While not particularly tasty, local populations fish for them and eat them regularly. Though plentiful now, the distribution of payara is limited, and anglers must be cautious to preserve this fantastic fishery, taking care to release fish in good condition.

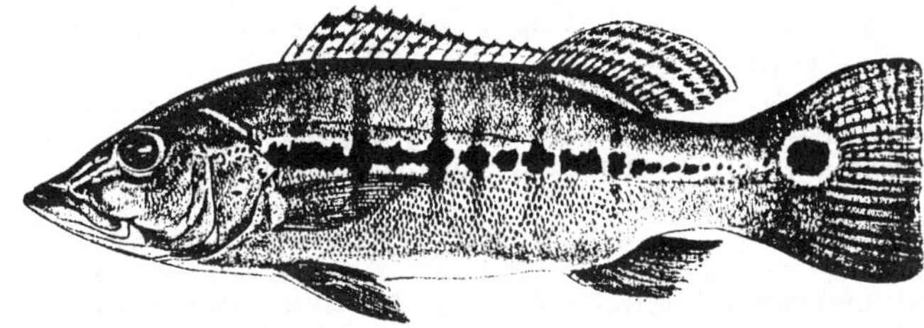

PEACOCK, blackstripe / *Cichlaintermedia*Ogilvie, 1966; CICHLIDAE FAMILY; also known as pavón real or royal pavón

The blackstripe peacock is limited to the Orinoco watershed in Venezuela south of San Fernando.

Blackstripe peacocks are characterized by an irregular black stripe which runs laterally along the full length of the midsection of the fish and is crossed intermittently by a series of six to eight fainter black oval shaped spots. This the only Cichlid that has more than three black bars.

The blackstripe peacock will rarely weigh more than 10 pounds, although 12 pound fish have been caught. As a point of interest, while the blackstripe pavon is less frequently encountered by anglers, most experienced pavón fishermen feel that pound for pound *C. intermedia* is the gamest of the pavónes. Like the speckled and butterfly peacocks, it is easily caught on spinning, bait-casting or fly rod tackle. And, like the other peacocks, it is a superior foodfish.

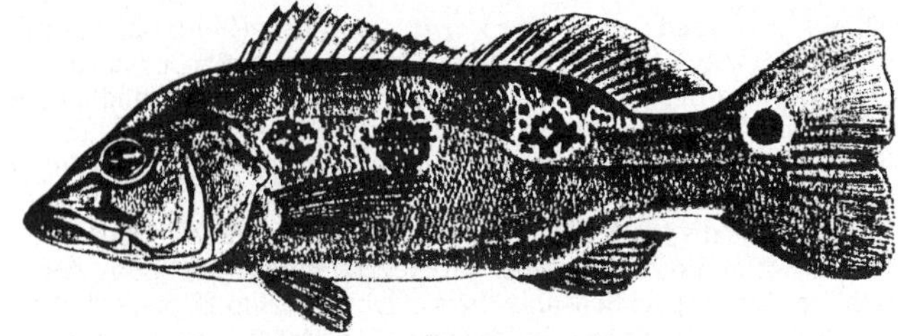

PEACOCK, butterfly / *Cichla ocellaris* Bloch & Schneider, 1801; CICHLIDAE FAMILY; also known as pavón mariposa, pavón amarillo, marichapa or pavón tres estrellas, tucunare, lukanani

The butterfly peacock is native to tropical South America. It was introduced in Hawaii in 1957 and in Florida in 1984 and 1986. It has also been stocked in many other countries including Puerto Rico, Panama, Kenya, Guam and the Dominican Republic.

Of all the peacock basses, the butterfly peacock has the greatest variation in color. They are yellowish green, with three dark, yellow-fringed blotches along the lateral midsection, or bars that typically fade in fish larger than three or four pounds. A smaller "eyespot" spot, characteristic of all "pavónes," appears at the beginning of the caudal fin. The iris of the eye is frequently deep reddish in color. They are also distinguished by the absence of black markings on the opercula. This species is believed to attain weights of 11 to 12 pounds.

The butterfly peacock's powerful, laterally compressed body and aggressive temperament make it pound for pound one of the hardest fish to handle on light tackle, but because of the size, light spinning, bait casting, or fly fishing outfits are recommended. Small fishes such as shiners or threadfin shad are the best bait, but light spinning lures and surface lures that resemble small fish are also highly effective. The butterfly peacock has rapidly become the one of the most popular game fish in the areas where it has been introduced. It is more than just a fighter. It is not only beautifully colored but tasty as well.

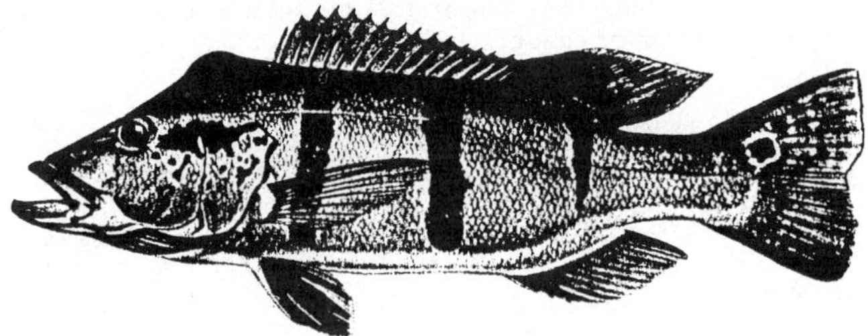

PEACOCK, speckled / *Cichla temensis* Humbolt, 1821; CICHLIDAE FAMILY; also known as pavón cinchado, pavón pintado, pavón trucha, tucunare, and pavón venado

The speckled peacock is a world-class warm-water sportfish native to South America's Orinoco and Amazon River Basins. It has been introduced into other countries and is established in southeastern Florida as a result of a deliberate introduction made in 1985.

Adult speckled peacocks are distinguished by blotches on the opercula and three vertical black bars on the body which become more pronounced with age. Juveniles less than 14 inches are generally darker than adults. Another color phase may have 4-6 horizontal rows of light colored dashes along the sides and speckling over the rest of the body and fins. The above description may be confusing, but it combines what was thought to be two different species until 1981. This species is the largest of the *Cichla* genus and fish in excess of 30 pounds have been speared, handlined or netted by local fishermen. This is the only *Cichla* spp. which has broken longitudinal lines and spots on the head, opercula and in caudal/dorsal fins, resulting in a speckled appearance.

An excellent game fish, the speckled peacock can be caught on spin, bait-casting or fly tackle. Their pound-for-pound power is brutal, even when matched to heavy tackle. They will strike plugs, spoons, spinners, streamer flies and popping bugs. Their top water strikes are stunning in ferocity and they make spectacular jumps and strong runs. The larger they get, the more fiercely they fight. Considering they can grow to more than 30 pounds, be prepared for a battle when you hook into a speckled peacock!

An excellent food fish, the flesh of the speckled peacock is firm in texture and varies from white to a creamy white in color.

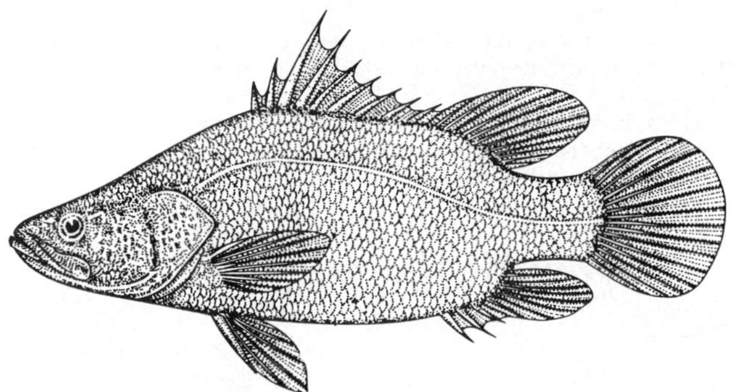

PERCH, Nile / *Lates niloticus*; (Linneaus, 1758); CENTROPOMIDAE FAMILY; also called giant perch, Niger perch

Endemic to the African continent, they can be found in rivers and lakes in tropical regions. It is known to be present in the Blue and White Niles, the Niger and Benue rivers, and in lakes Rudolph, Albert, Tanganyika, Fayoum, and Menzaleh. Good Nile perch fishing is well-known below the Aswan Dam and at the junction of the Blue and White Niles. Until recently, there were no Nile perch in Lake Victoria, but recent introductions of this species into Lake Victoria have been extremely successful, and the species is said to be prolific there now due to the availability of plentiful forage fish.

It looks very much like a larger version of the barramundi, in fact, they are close relatives in the Centropomidae Family. Juveniles are mottled brown and silver. By the time they are about a year old, measuring 8 in (20 cm) long, they are completely silver. Adults are generally brown to greenish-brown above and silvery below. The top of the head is strongly depressed, as in the barramundi and its relative across the sea, the snook. It has a rounded (convex) tail. The first dorsal fin consists of 7 or 8 strong spines, and the second dorsal fin, which immediately follows the first without a complete break, has 1 or 2 spines and 12 to 13 soft, branched rays.

Fish of 6.5 ft (2 m) long and weighing 176 lb (80 kg) have been caught and recorded by native fishermen and are said to be common. Much larger ones, up to 500 lb (226.8 kg) are said to have been taken in nets but have gone unrecorded.

Nile perch grow about 9 or 10 in (25 cm) a year the first 2 or 3 years, then growth slows. They reach maturity at a length of about 20 to 24 in (50-60 cm), the females being the larger at maturity. A 3.3 ft (1 m) fish is about 8 years old.

Fishing for Nile perch is best early or late in the day. Tigerfish and tilapia are common baits. Known for long, hard, powerful runs, the Nile perch provides the angler with the added benefit of being an excellent and popular eating fish with a tasty white meat.

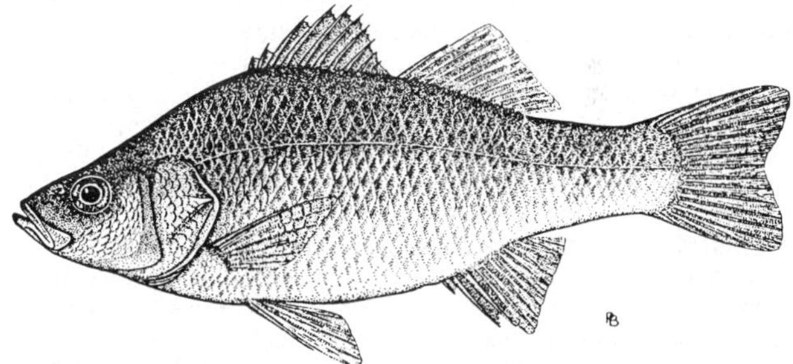

PERCH, white / *Morone americana* (Gmelin, 1788); PERCICHTHYIDAE FAMILY; also called narrow-mouthed bass, sea perch

The white perch is most commonly found in brackish waters of the Atlantic coast of North America from South Carolina north to the upper St. Lawrence River and the southern Gulf of St. Lawrence (rare in other areas of the Gulf) as well as throughout Nova Scotia to Cape Breton Island, Prince Edward Island, and New Brunswick. It is especially abundant in the Hudson River and the Chesapeake Bay area, and is quite common in Lake Ontario. In Lake Erie, only three captures of white perch are known to have been made (all in 1954), where it seems to be replaced by the white bass *(Morone chrysops)*.

Despite its common name, the white perch is actually a bass and a close relative of the white bass and the striped bass *(M. saxatilis)*. It is smaller, shorter, and stockier than the striped bass, but is very similar in appearance to the white bass. The most noticeable difference is that the white perch lacks the stripes that are present on both of the other species. The deepest part of the body of the white perch is at the beginning of the dorsal fin, whereas on the white and striped basses, it is nearer the middle of the back. The white perch is far more coastal in occurrence than the white bass (though the latter can be found southward on the Gulf coast), and most of the overlap in their distributions occurs in the area of the Great Lakes and upper St. Lawrence River. The white perch is more variable in coloration than is the white bass, ranging from pale olive or silvery green on the sides and silvery white on the belly to a much darker tone with a little hint of silver, especially in inland freshwater specimens.

As a food and game fish, it rates very high. It seems to be under utilized since their populations continue to increase. In some areas the fish are becoming stunted due to overpopulation, and are causing an equally adverse effect on other desirable species in the same waters. As to their edibility, Al McClane states without hesitation in *McClane's New Standard Fishing Encyclopedia*, "There is no finer fish to eat than the white perch. It has firm white meat and makes a delectable fish chowder...can be fried in the usual way by coating the fillets with corn meal, bread crumbs, or just plain flour (or as 'finger' fillets)...in a tempura batter."

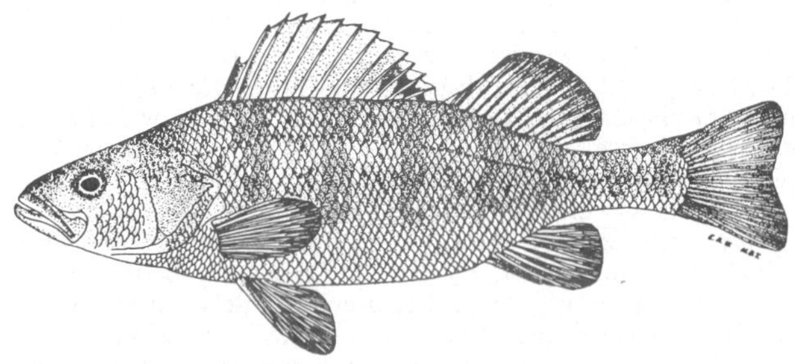

PERCH, yellow / *Perca flavescens* (Mitchill, 1814); PERCIDAE FAMILY; also called lake perch, American perch, ringed perch, striped perch, coon perch, jack perch

The yellow perch is a widespread species in the northern United States and in Canada. Although it occurs in nearly every U.S. state today, due to stocking, it is sparsely distributed in the South and through most of the West and Midwest, except for the northern portions. It blankets the northern U.S.A. and Canada, except British Columbia and the northern territories. In the east it ranges from Nova Scotia to the Santee River drainage, South Carolina and west through the Great Lakes states to the edge of British Columbia and into Washington. A narrow contingent extends north through Great Slave Lake almost to Great Bear Lake in the Northwest Territories, Canada.

The yellow perch, unlike the so-called "white perch" *(Morone americana)*, is a true perch, not a bass. Although it resembles the basses in many ways it is more closely related to the walleye *(Stizostedion vitreum)* and sauger *(S. canadense)*, also members of the Percidae family. Its most striking characteristic is its golden yellow body with 6-8 dark "fingers" or bands which extend from the back towards the belly. The body is also longer than in any but the striped bass *(Morone saxatilis)*, and is somewhat sway-backed in appearance. The deepest part of the body is at the beginning of the first dorsal fin; then it tapers slightly until the beginning of the second dorsal fin. Both dorsally and ventrally there then appears to be a slight swell beneath the second dorsal fin and above the anal fin, tapering down to a moderately narrow caudal peduncle.

Although the average size caught by anglers is 4-12 oz (0.1-0.34 kg) it provides fast action and can be caught all year long. It will devour almost any natural bait and many types of artificials, including flies, and is an active feeder even in the winter when it is caught while ice fishing. It is found in a wide variety of habitats over a vast range of territory and is available to a large number of anglers. The flesh is white, flaky and delicious, and has had some commercial importance, especially where larger specimens are caught. Commercial fishermen from Canada and the United States harvested 30 million pounds in Lake Erie worth $3.2 million according to W.B. Scott and E.J. Crossman in *Freshwater Fishes of Canada*.

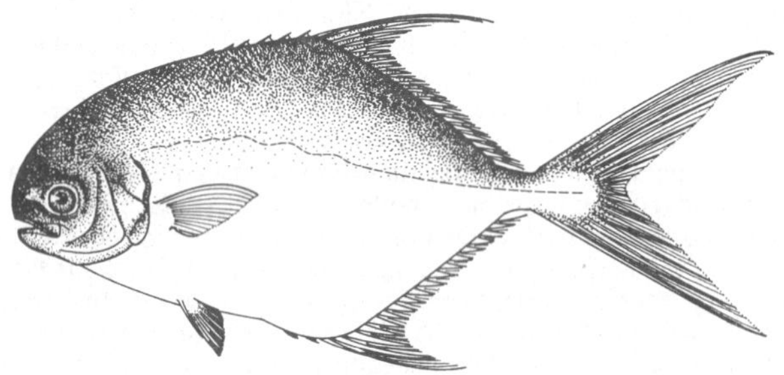

PERMIT / *Trachinotus falcatus* (Linnaeus, 1758); CARANGIDAE FAMILY; also called round pompano, great pompano, Indian River permit

Occurs in the western Atlantic Ocean from Massachusetts, USA to Brazil, including the Gulf of Mexico and the West Indies. The greatest concentrations are off south Florida and it is there that the biggest specimens are taken. Permit are essentially shallow water, schooling fish occurring over sandy flats and reefs in depths of from 1 to 17 fathoms. They travel in schools of ten or more fish, though occasionally they may be seen in great numbers. They tend to become more solitary with age.

It is distinguished from the common pompano *(Trachinotus carolinus)* by having fewer soft rays in the dorsal and anal fins. The second dorsal fin has 1 spine and 17-21 soft rays (22-27 in the pompano). The body is laterally compressed and the second and third ribs are prominent—often as big around as one's thumb in fish weighing over 10 lb (4-5 kg). These larger ribs can be felt through the sides of the fish and help in distinguishing the permit from the pompano. Juveniles are

roundish and adults are oblong. In overall appearance it is a silvery fish with dusky fins, though the back is usually bluish or grayish. The ventral fins and the anterior margin of the anal fin may be orange in some specimens. Often there is a triangular yellow patch before the anal fin.

They feed in much the same way as bonefish, rooting in the sand on shallow flats, though they rarely stir much mud or marl. Their diet consists primarily of mollusks, crustaceans, sea urchins, and less commonly, of smaller fish. They are often attracted to areas where the bottom is being stirred up.

It is a tough fighter on light tackle. When hooked it makes an initial long, fast run towards deep water, twisting and pausing to bump its head on the bottom or rub its mouth in the sand in an effort to disengage the hook. If there is coral, a sea fan, or any other obstacle on which the permit can snag the line, it will. To complicate matters, its mouth is as tough as shoe leather and it simply spits out the hook the first time there is a slack in the line.

Fishing methods include casting to fish sighted in shallow water, bottom fishing, fishing over inshore wrecks, and jigging from boats or while wading. Baits and lures include crabs, shrimp, clams, conch, streamer flies, bonefish jigs, weighted bucktails, plugs, etc. Because of the permit's tough mouth it helps to strike hard several times when the fish has taken the bait; half a dozen strikes is not too many. The permit is considered excellent eating.

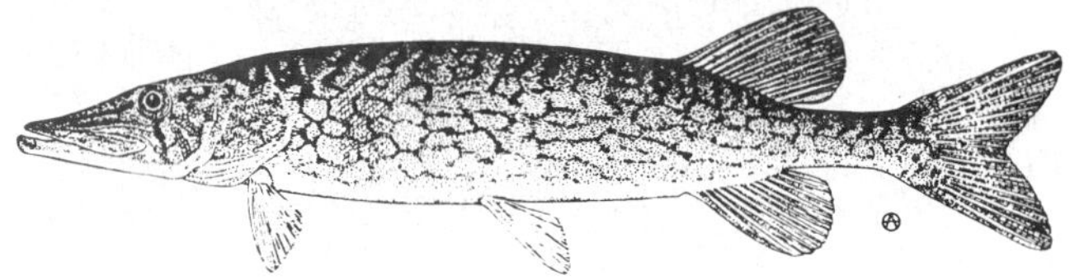

PICKEREL, chain / *Esox niger* Lesueur, 1818; ESOCIDAE FAMILY; also called eastern pickerel, eastern chain pickerel, lake pickerel, reticulated pickerel, federation pickerel, mud pickerel, green pike, black chain pike, duck-billed pike, picquerelle.

It inhabits the eastern United States and Canada, from Nova Scotia southward through all of the Atlantic coast states and most of Florida, and westward through Georgia, Alabama, and Louisiana to as far as the Navasota River in eastern Texas. From Louisiana, it extends northward in the Mississippi River drainage through eastern Arkansas to southeastern Missouri and southwestern Kentucky.

The pickerels, pikes, and muskies (all members of the genus Esox) have essentially identical body shapes and look very much alike, especially when young. The chain pickerel can be recognized by its markings. The sides which are yellowish to greenish (almost black when young) are overlaid with a reticulated, or chain-like, pattern of black lines that is unlike the bars, wavy "tiger" stripes, or spots present on other *Esox* species. The pattern on the chain pickerel can be viewed as very large, light oval areas. This may be confused with the northern pike *(Esox lacius)* which has a dark background (usually greenish or yellowish) with small, light colored oval spots on the sides. These spots never appear large in relation to the background whereas, in the chain pickerel, the lighter areas dominate the sides. Also, the pickerels (including the redfin and grass pickerels both subspecies of *E. americanus)*, have fully scaled cheeks and gill covers. The northern pike usually has no scales on the bottom half of the gill cover, and the muskellunge *(E. masquinongy)* usually has no scales on the bottom half of either the gill cover or the cheek. All species of the pike group have only one dorsal fin, which is located very far back on the body near the caudal peduncle.

The flesh is white and flaky, and very tasty during the winter months. In summer, however, the taste is not as good. Removing the skin before cooking may remedy this. It is not an especially popular sport fish, except in some localized areas. It can be caught in winter at a time when the number of species available to anglers is relatively low. Size and bag limits are often imposed.

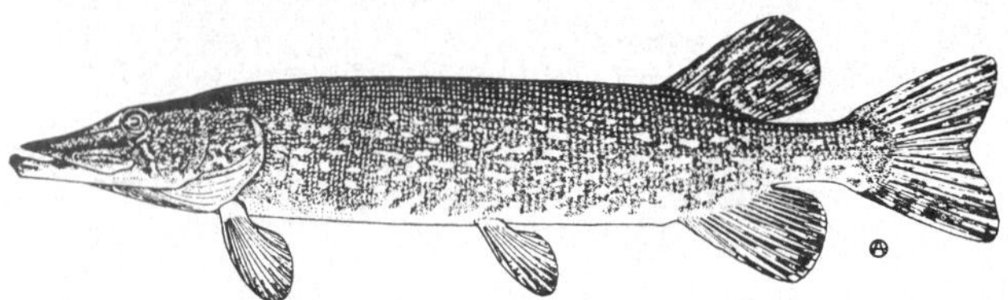

PIKE, northern / *Esox lucius* (Linnaeus, 1758); ESOCIDAE FAMILY; also called great northern pike, great northern pickerel, jack, jackfish

This is a Holarctic species, meaning that it occurs around the world in northern, or Arctic waters, extending from northwestern Europe, across northern Asia to northern North America. It is densely distributed throughout Alaska with the exception of the off shore islands. Northern pike are widespread throughout Canada and the Arctic islands above the Hudson Bay, and conspicuously absent from the coastal plains (most of British Columbia and the Atlantic coast east of the St. Lawrence). In the U.S. it can be found below Maine through New Hampshire, Vermont and Massachusetts (except along the coast) and in all the Great Lakes states (though largely absent from lower Michigan and Indiana) as well as west of the Great Lakes in Minnesota, Wisconsin, Iowa, Illinois, Missouri, Nebraska and Montana. It is restricted primarily to the extreme eastern portions of North and South Dakota. It has been widely introduced outside this native range, even into southern and western states, but there is little information on the long term success of these transplants.

Like the muskellunge *(Esox masquinongy)* and the pickerels *(E. niger* and *E. americanus)*, it is a long, sleek, predatory fish with a broad, flat mouth resembling a duck's bill, and a single dorsal fin located on the posterior portion of the body. In body shape the members of the pike group are all identical, but the northern pike can be distinguished from its relatives by three main features. Most noticeably the greenish or yellowish sides of the fish are covered with lighter colored oblong horizontal spots or streaks, whereas all other species have darker markings (spots, bars, stripes or reticulations) than the background color. Its markings are most likely to be confused with those of the chain pickerel. The second distinction is the scalation pattern on the gill cover and cheek. In the northern pike the cheek is fully scaled, but the bottom half of the gill cover is scaleless. In the larger muskellunge, both the bottom half of the gill cover and the bottom half of the cheek are scaleless. In the smaller pickerels the gill cover and the cheek are both fully scaled. The third distinctive feature is the number of pores under each side of the lower jaw; usually 5 in the northern pike (rarely 3, 4 or 6 on one side), 6-9 in the muskellunge (rarely 5 or 10 on one side), and 4 in the smaller pickerels (occasionally 3 or 5 on one side only).

It is considered a delicious food fish. The flesh is sweet, white and flaky, but like other members of its genus, it sometimes has a "weedy" or "muddy" taste during the summer months. This taste is probably due to the skin mucus and can be eliminated by removing the skin prior to cooking. It has considerable commercial value and is an excellent sport fish. Pike are usually taken by trolling with large spoons, plugs or natural baits, but casting and still fishing are also frequently successful.

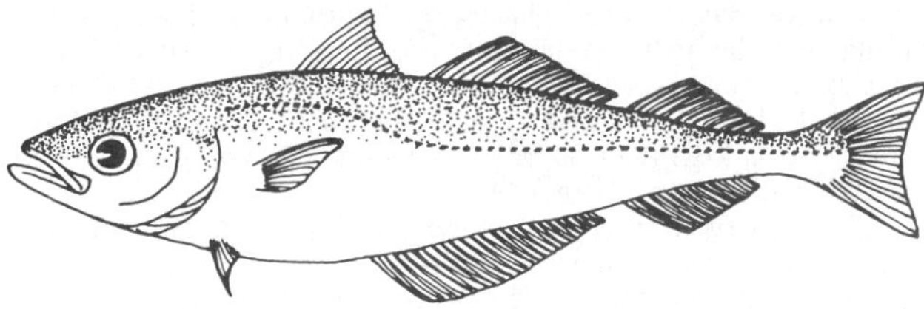

POLLACK, European / *Pollachius pollachius* (Linnaeus, 1758); GADIDAE FAMILY; also called billet, lythe, black jack

It is strictly a European species, occurring in the eastern Atlantic Ocean from Norway to Spain and Portugal, including the English Channel, the North Sea, Iceland, and more rarely the northern coast of the western Mediterranean. It is mainly an in shore species found near rocky coasts and over rocky bottoms. Though a bottom feeder it may also be found swimming in shoals in midwaters.

It is a member of the cod family Gadidae and can be distinguished from similar looking species in its own family (about 59 species) by a combination of features. Its lower jaw projects beyond the upper jaw, its tail is concave, its lateral line is dark greenish brown and arches sharply above the pectoral fins, and the chin lacks barbels. There are 26-27 gill rakers on the first branchial arch. The first dorsal fin has 12 rays, the second has 19-20 rays, and the third has 17-10 rays. The first anal fin has 29 rays and the second has 17-20. Coloration of this species is usually dark brown or olive dorsally. The sides of the fish change rather abruptly to a paler, yellowish color. Sometimes dark yellow or orange spots or stripes are apparent on the upper flanks.

It is a good sport fish and a strong fighter. It is in the words of one author "a crash dive artist par excellence" and is difficult to stop before it reaches sanctuary. Its diet includes sand eels, sprats, herring, smaller cod-like fish, wrasses, rocklings, blennies, squid, worms and large crustaceans. Bait fishing, casting, jigging or trolling are all successful fishing methods. Baits and lures include diamond jigs, squid, herring, clams, worms, smaller cod species, crabs, shrimp, and prawns, spoons, tub lures, spinners, plugs and flies.

Pollack usually attain a length of about 20-21 in (52 cm) by the fifth year. They are an excellent table fish and except for a relatively small number that are taken by trawlers and longliners, they are not a commercially important species.

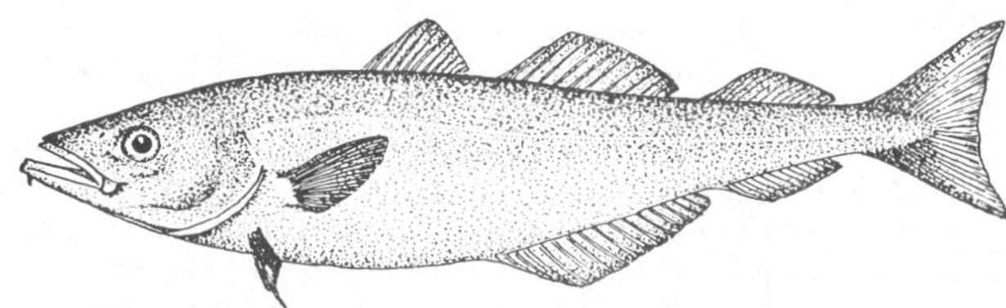

POLLOCK / *Pollachius virens* (Linnaeus, 1758): GADIDAE FAMILY; also called coalfish, Boston bluefish, green cod, blisterback, saithe, coley

Found on both sides of the Atlantic, from Greenland and Labrador to Virginia on the west side, and on the east, from Iceland to northern Spain, including the Bay of Biscay, the English Channel, and western Baltic and North Sea.

It is said to be the most active member of the cod family Gadidae. Though it occurs in shallower waters than either the cod or haddock, it is generally a deep or midwater fish occurring in depths of up to 100 fathoms. It will sometimes chase bait fish to the surface and smaller individuals are often seen milling about at the surface in large, tightly packed schools. In the western Atlantic south of Cape Cod, Massachusetts, off the U.S. east coast, pollock can be taken from depths of 25 fathoms to as little as 4 fathoms. North of Cape Cod where most of the fish are taken, they have even been caught by surf fishermen.

They can be distinguished from other members of the cod family by three features. Its lower jaw projects beyond the upper jaw, its tail is forked, and its lateral line is quite straight, not arching above the pectoral fins. The first dorsal fin has 13-14 rays, the second has 20-22, and the third has 19-24. The first anal fin has 24-28 rays and the second has 19-23. There are 35-40 gill rakers on the first arch. Young pollock have cod-like barbels on the chin, but these are small and usually disappear with age. The back varies from olive green to greenish brown. The flanks are a lighter yellowish green or gray.

Its diet consists of smaller pelagic fishes, sand eels and various crustaceans. Fishing methods include bait fishing or jigging with shrimp, herring, squid, clams, worms, or diamond jigs (reported to be very successful in large schools), trolling or casting with spoons, tube lures, spinners, plugs, or flies. It makes strong, powerful runs and occasionally leaps and shakes. The flesh is of good quality and is commercially important.

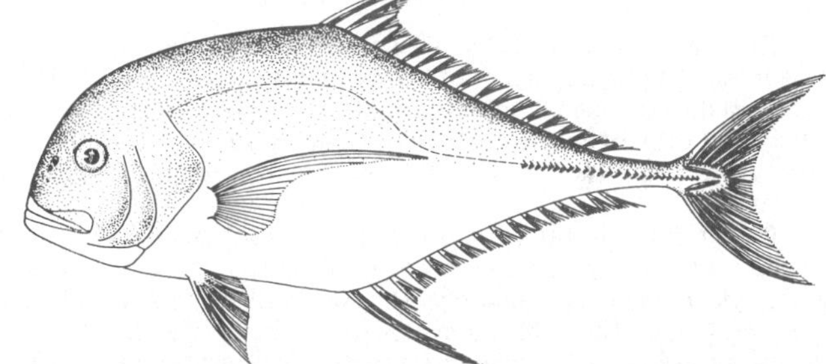

POMPANO, African / *Alectis ciliaris* (Bloch, 1787); CARANGIDAE FAMILY; also called Cuban jack, Atlantic threadfin, threadfin, pennantfish, cobblerfish

Occurring worldwide the smallest specimens have been taken in offshore waters from July through September. Larger specimens are usually found off shore around the outer reefs and in "ocean holes" in the sea bed.

The African pompano is the largest and most widespread species of the genus *Alectis*. It can be distinguished from other members of the genus by the lower number of gill rakers on the first branchial arch (18-22 as opposed to 30-35 in *A. indicus* of the Indo-Pacific and even more in *A. alexandrinus* of Mediterranean and West African waters).

It is characterized by 4-6 elongated, thread-like rays in the front part of the second dorsal and anal fins. In juveniles the first two of these rays may be four times as long as the fish. Normally, the rays tend to disappear or erode away as the fish grows. It also undergoes changes in body shape as it grows. The body of juveniles is short and deep. The spines of the first dorsal fin are visible, though not very prominent at this stage. By the time the fish is 14 in (35-36 cm) long, the body is more elongated and the forehead is steeper. In both juveniles and adults of *A. ciliaris* the body is strongly compressed. The lateral line, which has 24-38 relatively weak scutes in the straight portion and a total scale count of 120-140, arches smoothly but steeply above the pectoral fins. Larger specimens are light bluish green above and silvery over most of the remainder of the body. They may have dark blotches on the operculum on the dorsal side of the caudal peduncle, and on the anterior portion of the second dorsal and anal fins. Juveniles are banded with 5-6 ventral bars over the silvery flanks.

It is a strong fighter and an excellent light tackle game fish. It will take small live or dead baits, as well as lures, jigs and feathers. It is usually caught incidentally while trolling for other species.

The name African pompano is misleading, since the fish is actually a member of the jack family. The species has been surrounded by a great deal of myth and confusion. Until recently the adults and juveniles were classified as entirely different species with the adults being given the scientific name *Hynnis cubensis*, which is no longer used. Also, the species named *Alectis crinitus* which is widely used for the western Atlantic population, is incorrect as *Alectis crinitus* and *Alectis ciliaris* are the same species.

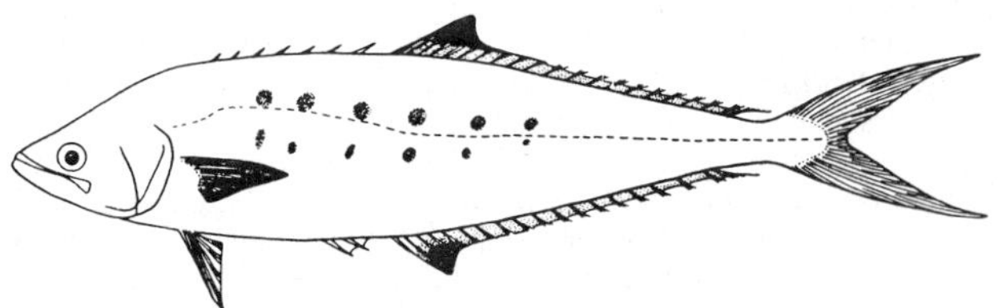

Doublespotted Queenfish (*Scomberoides lysan*)

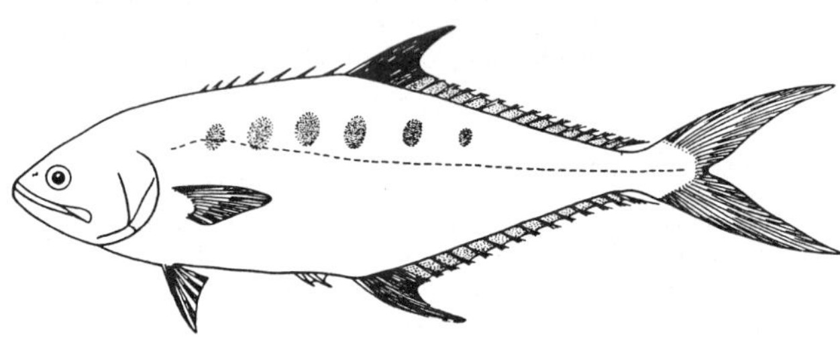

Talang Queenfish (*Scomberoides commersonnianus*)

QUEENFISH
/ *Scomberoides commersonnianus* Lacepede, 1802; and
/ *Scomberoides lysan* (Forsskal, 1775); CARANGIDAE FAMILY;
also called leatherskin, spotted leatherskin, giant dart, white fish, skinny fish

The talang and the doublespotted queenfish range widely over the Indo-Pacific. The talang has been verified from the Gulf of Thailand, Okinawa, Indonesia, the Philippines, Papua New Guinea, Australia, and the east coast of Africa. The doublespotted has a similar range and also occurs in the Hawaiian Islands, but is unconfirmed in the Gulf of Thailand.

The queenfish has an oblong to elliptical profile with a very short head and a strongly compressed body (from whence the name "skinny fish". Its lateral line is straight except for a weak, slightly wavy arch over the pectoral fins. The scales are partially embedded and lanceolate (broadly lanceolate in *S. commersonnianus*, more sharply in *S. lysan*). The tail is deeply forked as is typical of carangids and the second dorsal and anal fins are prominent anterior lobes. The first dorsal fin consists of 6-7 short spines with very little visible membrane. The spines are depressible into a groove on the back. The second dorsal fin has one spine and 19-21 soft rays.

The talang has a greater number of elements in the anal fin (two detached spines, one attached spine and 19-21 soft rays). The doublespotted has two detached spines and 17-19 soft rays. It also has more total gill rakers on the upper and lower first arch 21-27 and may grow to 2 ft (58.5 cm). The talang has 8-15 gill rakers and may grow to almost 4 ft (120 cm).

The mouth is large on the talang extending well back beyond the eyes. The forehead is slightly rounded (convex) or may have a small bump over the eyes, and the fin lobes are twice as high as in the doublespotted. It has a single row of 5-8 round spots above the lateral line, with the first two possibly touching or intersecting the lateral line.

The doublespotted has a double row of round spots, 5-8 above the lateral line and a parallel row of 5-8 below the line. The mouth extends back only to the back of the eye or scarcely beyond it and the forehead is slightly but noticeably indented (concave).

Both fish are generally dusky green to bluish above, fading to gray, silvery or white below. The high second dorsal and anal fin lobes of the talang are uniformly pigmented (dusky or light) from the body to the tip, whereas in the part of the lobes that extends above the finlets in the doublespotted (the distal half) is distinctly and abruptly darker.

All Scomberoides (queenfish) can be distinguished from other carangids (jacks, trevallies, amberjacks, etc) by three characteristics. The upper lip is jointed to the snout at midline, the posterior portion of the soft dorsal and anal fins is formed by semiattached finlets, and there are no scutes along the lateral line.

They generally frequent in shore lagoons, reefs, and off shore islands. They may enter estuaries, but the talang does not tolerate low salinity well, nor does it like turbid water. Queenfish are daytime feeders and prefer small pelagic fish, squids, and other fast-moving prey. Occasionally they may also feed on crustaceans.

The queenfish is extremely popular as a sport fish and is an excellent fighter on light tackle. Small live baits and trolled lures are preferred. Queenfish do have some commercial value and are taken by drift net, gill net and seine and marketed fresh or dried and salted. Many anglers say that the coarse flesh is rather tasteless and is better smoked, while others that it is quite good when very fresh. In any event, the leathery skin is best removed before cooking and one should avoid touching the spines of the dorsal and anal fins, as they are poisonous and can inflict very painful wounds.

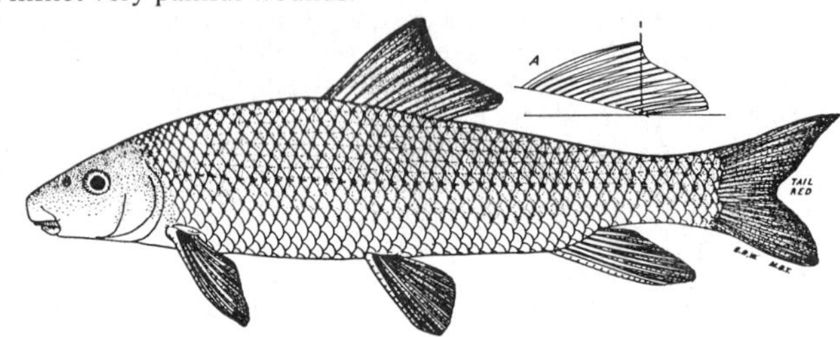

REDHORSE, shorthead / *Moxostoma macrolepidotum* (Lesueur, 1817); CATOSTOMIDAE FAMILY; also called northern redhorse, northern shorthead redhorse, common redhorse, red sucker, short-headed mullet, redfin, redfin sucker, bigscale sucker

The shorthead redhorse is a relatively widespread species of the northeastern U.S. and Canada. Three subspecies are recognized. One is widespread in the Ohio basin, another in the Ozark uplands and adjacent areas, and the third throughout the remainder of the species' range. Their combined distribution extends throughout the Great Lakes region north to the Hudson Bay, east to Montreal and Vermont, and south to South Carolina and the extreme northern portions of Georgia, Alabama, Mississippi, Arkansas, and Oklahoma. Found as far west as Oklahoma in the southern U.S., Montana in the northern U.S. and Alberta in Canada. A small disjunct population occurs at a point on the border between Oklahoma and Texas.

This is by far the most wide ranging and common species of sucker as well as being one of the most colorful. The fins range from bright orange to deep red and the sides from silver to gold or bronze. The belly is lighter, ranging from dusky yellow to milk white. The fins contain only soft rays and there are no teeth. Typical of the redhorse is the single dorsal fin located near the middle of the back. The edge of the dorsal fin on the shorthead is emarginate or concave, distinguishing it from the silver redhorse *(Moxostoma anisurum)*, in which the top edge of the dorsal fin is rounded (convex). As its name indicates the shorthead has an unusually short head (17-19% of the fish's total length). There are no scales on the head.

It has little commercial value at present, although it was held in high esteem in the early 1900's by farmers who snared, seined and trapped great numbers of them in the spring and salted them away for winter. It does have some value as a sport fish today and is actively sought by a good number of anglers. The flesh of the shorthead is tasty and sweet, but contains many small bones.

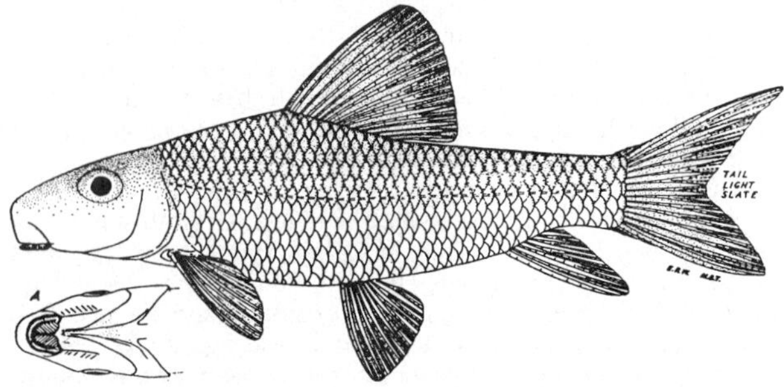

REDHORSE, silver / *Moxostoma anisurum* (Rafinesque, 1820); CATOSTOMIDAE FAMILY; also called silver mullet, white nose redhorse, white nose mullet, white nose sucker

The silver redhorse while found in the same general areas as the shorthead redhorse *(Moxostoma macrolepidotum)* is not as wide ranging. It occurs from the Great Lakes northeast to about Quebec, Canada and south to southern Georgia, northern Alabama and Oklahoma. From there it extends to Lake Superior, northwestward to just across the border into Alberta, Canada. In the U.S. it does not extend very far west or east of the Great Lakes, except in Georgia and the Carolinas where it occurs all the way to the coast. It occurs northwest of the Great Lakes through the lower two-thirds of Lake Winnipeg to as far north as central Manitoba and Saskatchewan.

It has no teeth and no dorsal spines. The single dorsal fin contains only soft rays and is located approximately in the middle of the back. The top edge of the dorsal fin is rounded (convex), whereas in the shorthead redhorse it is emarginate or concave. It is generally silvery in appearance, except for its bronze-toned or olive green back. The fins are either white or grayish or pale red, but they may appear bright red in netted fish because they hemorrhage easily. The nose is white.

Though not particularly sought after as a sport fish, it has some potential and is probably under utilized in this respect. The flesh is tasty and similar to that of the shorthead redhorse, but like the shorthead redhorse, it has many small bones.

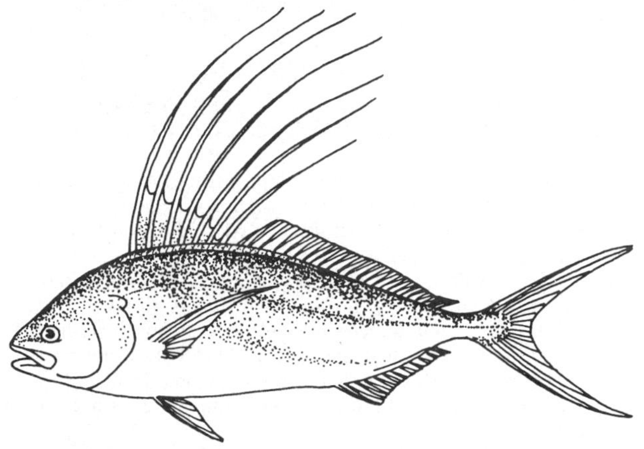

ROOSTERFISH / *Nematistius pectoralis* Gill, 1862; NEMATISTIIDAE FAMILY

Occurs in the eastern Pacific Ocean from the Gulf of California to Peru., most commonly off Ecuador. An in shore species, it is found in the surf, over sandy bottoms, and in moderate depths., the maximum movement being about 300 miles (483 km).

The second dorsal fin has one spine and 25-28 soft rays. The dorsal fins normally remain retracted in a deep groove along the fish's back, but when the fish is excited the fins rise. There are no bony scutes along the caudal peduncle. There are two dark blue or black, curved bands on the flanks. One beginning from the front and the other from the back of the first dorsal fin. Both run diagonally down the flanks towards the front of the anal fin then curve smoothly and run along the flanks to the tail base. The dorsal spines are banded with alternate dark and light stripes and the lower base of the pectoral fins is black.

It is a predator of small fishes. When hooked or in pursuit of prey it will raise its dorsal fin like a flag and leap repeatedly, greyhounding over the surface. Fishing methods are trolling or casting baits and lures, or live bait fishing from a boat or shore.

The roosterfish has strong local commercial value. The flesh is tasty and of good quality.

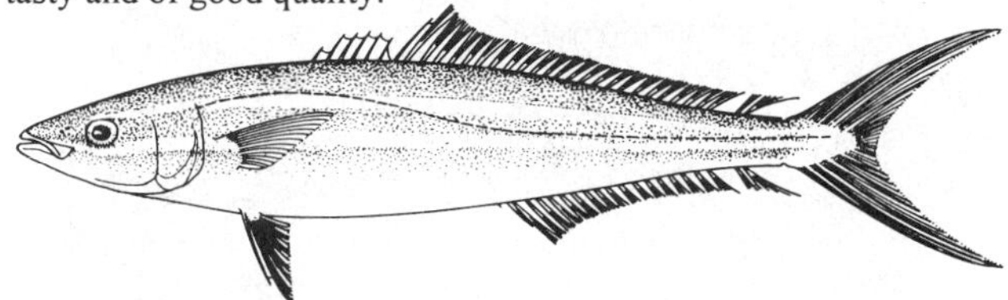

RUNNER, rainbow / *Elagatis bipinnulata* (Quoy & Gaimard, 1824); CARANGIDAE FAMILY; also called runner, rainbow yellowtail, skipjack, shoemaker, Hawaiian salmon, prodigal son

Occurs worldwide in tropical and warm temperate waters particularly temperatures of 70°-80°F (21°-30°C). Young are known to occur in the vicinity of floating rafts or debris and have been seen swimming with large sharks accompanied by pilotfish. It is rarely found in shore being more an inhabitant of the open sea. Young fish probably swim in relatively loose, small schools; older fish are more solitary.

There is a groove on the back and another on the venter in front of the tail fin of this species, but there are no bony scutes on the sides. The first dorsal fin has six spines. The second dorsal fin has one spine and 25-27 connected soft rays, followed by a 2-rayed finlet. The anal fin consists of a single detached spine that is covered by skin in most specimens over 1 ft (30 cm) long, followed by another spine with 16-18 connect soft rays and a 2-rayed finlet.

It resembles the cobia *(Rachycentron canadum)* in shape, but can be distinguished by its coloration as well as the finlet after the dorsal and anal fins. The back is blue-green. On each side there is a broad, dark blue, horizontal stripe near the back and one or two narrower, light blue stripe(s) beneath the broader one. Between and around these blue stripes, the sides are a cadmium yellow. The belly is white or silver, often with a yellow or pink tint. The tail is yellow and the other fins are a greenish or olive yellow.

Fishing methods include trolling with small baits and lures or live bait fishing. The rainbow runner is sometimes caught on heavy tackle intended for larger fish, but its fighting ability is reduced when this happens. When hooked on light tackle, it is an excellent game fish and a tough fighter prone to fast surface runs.

It is an excellent food fish with firm white flesh. In Japan it is cooked with a special sauce or eaten raw and considered a delicacy.

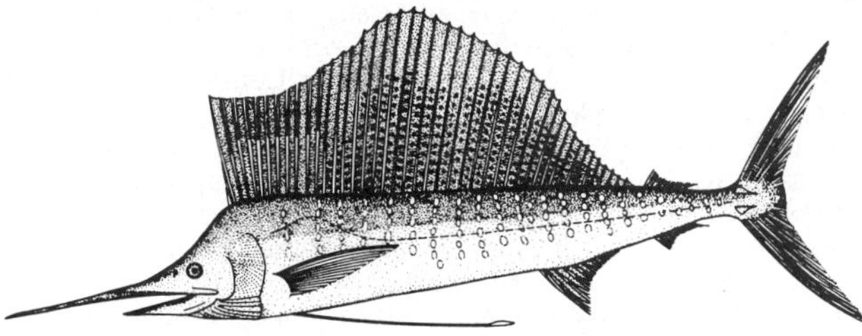

SAILFISH (Atlantic & Pacific) / *Istiophorus platypterus* (Shaw & Nodder, 1791); ISTIOPHORIDAE FAMILY; also called spindlebeack, bayonetfish

Inhabits tropical and subtropical waters near land masses, usually in depths over 6 fathoms, but occasionally caught in lesser depths and from ocean piers. Pelagic and migratory, sailfish usually travel alone or in small groups. They appear to feed mostly in midwater along the edges of reefs or current eddies.

Its outstanding feature is the long, high first dorsal fin (37-49 total elements). The second dorsal fin is very small with 6-8 rays. The lateral line along the median line of the flanks is single and prominent. The bill is longer than that of the spearfish, usually a little more than twice the length of the elongated lower jaw. The vent is just forward of the first anal fin. The sides often have pale, bluish gray vertical bars or rows of spots. The sail-like first dorsal fin is slate or cobalt blue with a scattering of black spots.

The most action is found where sailfish are located on or near the surface. They eat squid, octopus, mackerels, tunas, jacks, herring, ballyhoo, needlefish, flying fish, mullet and other small fishes.

Its fighting ability and spectacular aerial acrobatics endear the sailfish to the saltwater angler, but it tires quickly and is considered a light tackle species. Fishing methods include trolling with strip baits, whole mullet or ballyhoo, plastic lures, feathers or spoons, as well as live bait fishing and kite fishing from boats using jacks, mullet and other small live baits. Recent acoustical tagging and tracking experiments suggest that this species is quite hardy and that survival of released specimens is good.

Although present taxonomy suggests that the Atlantic and Pacific sailfish are the same species, some experts are not yet convinced. It has long been believed that Indo-Pacific specimens of sailfish attain a much greater size than their Atlantic counterparts, but a recent study of size data from the Japanese longline fishery by Dr. Grant L. Beardsley of the National Marine Fisheries Service, Miami Laboratory, provides evidence that eastern Atlantic specimens can reach much larger sizes than previously recorded.

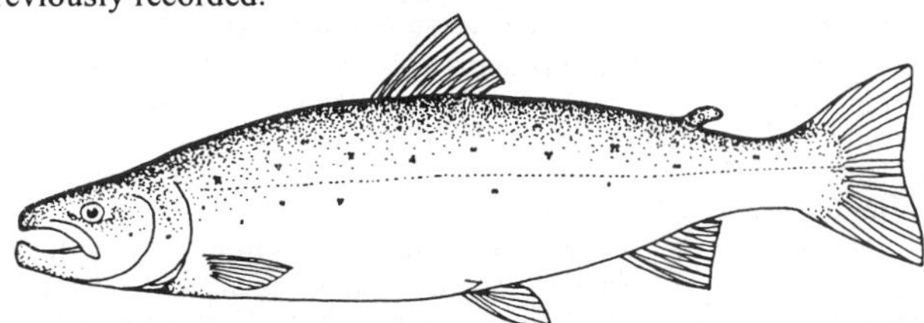

SALMON, Atlantic / *Salmo salar* Linnaeus, 1758; SALMONIDAE FAMILY; also called landlocked salmon, ouananiche, Kennebec salmon, Sebago salmon, black salmon, grilse, kelt, grayling, smolt, parr, slink

The Atlantic salmon is native to the northern Atlantic from the Connecticut River to Quebec, Iceland and southern Greenland. It also occurs from the Arctic Circle to Portugal. Inland, there are a number of landlocked populations that must be considered strictly freshwater fish. Otherwise, the species is anadromous (migrates to the sea and back, and spawns in fresh water). Unlike Pacific salmons (*Oncorhynchus spp.*), Atlantic salmon spawn more than once before dying.

It has the body shape of a trout, and is distinguished from trouts of the genus *Oncorhynthus* by coloration, size, and location of occurrence, among other things. At sea it is a silvery fish with a sparse scattering of small black spots often shaped like X's or Y's on the upper half of the body, and sometimes with a few spots on the cheek and gill cover. In inland waters, especially at spawning time, the Atlantic salmon turns a much darker color of bronze or dark brown. This change may be accompanied by the appearance of red spots on the head and body, making this fish look remarkably like a brown trout *(Salmo trutta)*, its closest relative. Often brown trout may have circles, or halos, around some of its spots and the spotting may be heavier than in the Atlantic salmon, extending onto the lower half of the sides and the fins including the adipose fin. The spots do not normally take the form of X's or Y's.

The fact that the Atlantic salmon is classified taxonomically as a member of the "trout" genus *Salmo*, rather than the Pacific salmon genus *Oncorhynchus*, is confusing to those who do not know the history of the common names. The name "salmon" arose in Europe and originally applied to the Atlantic salmon. American settlers carried the name with them from the Old World and applied it not only to the Atlantic salmon on the east coast, but also to the fishes of the same family Salmonidae, but different genus *Oncorhynchus*, on the west coast. The Atlantic salmon's closest relative in North America is the brown trout, *Salmo trutta*. Though some have proposed that the name Atlantic salmon be changed to end confusion concerning its taxonomical relationship to the trouts, the name is deeply rooted in history and published in literature worldwide. It is also regulated under the name Atlantic salmon in most places, and to change the name at this point in time would not only cause greater confusion, but would some argue, be an injustice to the species with which the same "salmon" originated.

The value of the Atlantic salmon both as a sports fish and as a commercial and food fish cannot be exaggerated. As W.B. Scott and E.J. Crossman stated in *Freshwater Fishes of Canada*, the Atlantic salmon was "Prized by the Gauls, then by the Romans, an abundant commercial fish in the British Isles, mentioned in the Magna Charta, revered by the sportsman and esteemed by gourmets..."

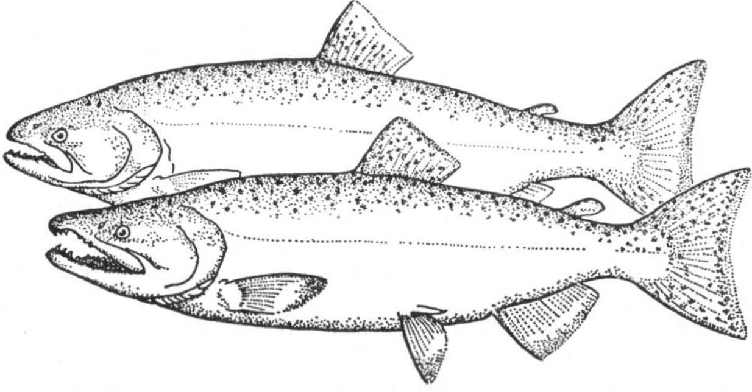

SALMON, chinook / *Oncorhynchus tshawytscha* (Walbaum, 1792); SALMONIDAE FAMILY; also called king salmon, spring salmon, tyee, quinnat, blackmouth

It is a member of the Pacific salmon genus Oncorhynchus and is both largest and least abundant of this group. It is endemic to the Pacific and rarely, the Arctic Ocean as well as the Bering Sea, the Okhotsk Sea, the Sea of Japan, and most of the rivers that flow into these waters; from Hokkaido in northern Japan to the Anadyr River in the former U.S.S.R., and from the Ventura River in southern California to Point Hope, Alaska. Since as early as 1872, it has been introduced into other waters around the world including the Great Lakes, Atlantic and Gulf states of the U.S., some areas of Central and South America, Europe, and the South Pacific. These transplanted populations apparently failed due to an inability to maintain spawning levels, with the exceptions of South Island in New Zealand, and to some degree in the Great Lakes. In Chile more recent transplants have shown hope of becoming established with some chinook returning to spawn.

Its body is typical of the Pacific salmon group (see "Salmons, Trouts, and Chars"). At sea, it is basically a silvery fish with spotting on the back, upper sides, top of the head, and all the fins including both the top and bottom half of the tail fin. Spawning chinooks are darker (olive brown to purplish or even red) and undergo a radical metamorphosis, especially the males which develop a large kype. The young have 6-12 long, wide parr marks and no spots on the dorsal fin. One way to distinguish the chinook from other species is by its black mouth and gums. The very similar looking coho salmon (*Oncorhynchus kisutch*) has a black mouth, but white gums, except in the Great Lakes population where the gums may be gray or black.

It is the largest salmonid in North America, growing to at least 5 ft (1.52 m) and 126 lb (57 kg). It is an extremely important food and commercial fish, and due to its large size and game nature, an important sport fish. It is the only Pacific salmon in which the meat may be regularly either red or white. While white meat is rare, red meat commands a higher price in any Pacific salmon species. It is sold either fresh, fresh-frozen, canned, or smoked.

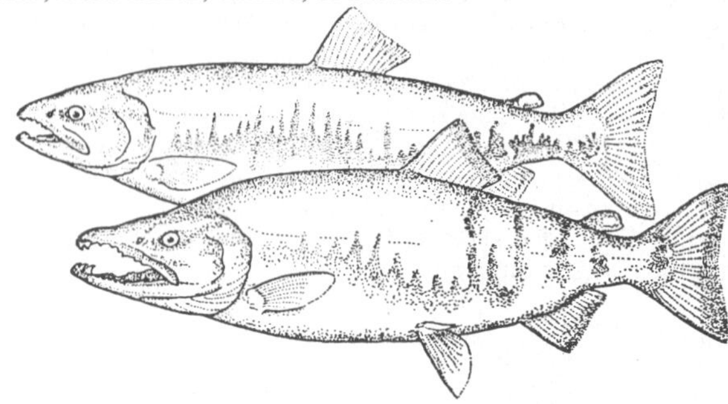

SALMON, chum / *Oncorhynchus keta* (Walbaum, 1792), SALMONIDAE FAMILY; also called dog salmon, fall salmon, autumn salmon

Endemic to the Pacific and Arctic Oceans, the Bering Sea, the Sea of Japan, and the Okhotsk Sea. In North America it occurs from the San Lorenzo River, California, to northwest Alaska, and east to the Peel, MacKenzie and possibly Anderson Rivers. During spawning it is known to ascend some rivers for considerable distances (1,242 mi or 2,000 km). In the MacKenzie River, N.W.T., Canada, it travels all the way to the mouth of the Hay River and to the rapids below Forth Smith on the Salve River, entering both Great Bear and Great Slave Lakes and traveling through the Northwest Territories to the edge of Alberta. Like all Pacific salmons, with the exception of landlocked specimens, the chum salmon is anadromous.

At sea, it is silvery and has no distinct black spots, though it may have fine black speckling on the upper sides and back. Spawning males turn olive green with blood red vertical markings reaching up the sides, making this one of the most easily recognized Pacific salmon species. The color of spawning females is less vivid, but essentially the same. Breeding males of the species have large, bared teeth, which may be the origin of the name "dog salmon," though it is also said that this name evolved because this species was often fed to sled dogs. They may grow to at least 33 lb (15 kg); however, the more usual weight is about 5-20 lb (2-9 kg).

The flesh is creamy white and the lowest of all the salmons in fat content. It is sold fresh, frozen, dry salted, smoked, or canned. It is not as popular or as desirable as other Pacific salmons.

Together with the pink salmon (*Oncorhynchus gorbuscha*), it is sometimes called "autumn salmon" or "fall salmon" because it is the last salmon to make its spawning run. It begins entering the river mouths after mid-June and reaches some spawning grounds as late as November or December. This late run severely affects its utilization as a sport fish, and it is not one of the most sought after by anglers. The chum salmon is believed to hybridize in nature with pink salmon.

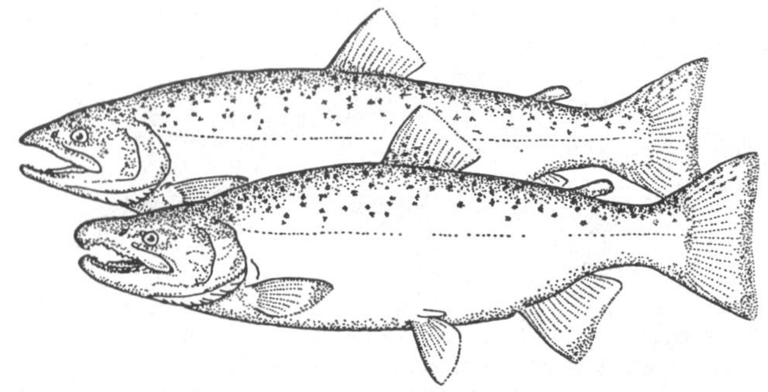

SALMON, coho / *Oncorhynchus kisutch* (Walbaum, 1792); SALMONIDAE FAMILY; also called silver salmon, silver sides, hooknose, sea trout, blueback

Endemic to the Pacific Ocean and the rivers flowing into it from northern Japan to the Anadyr River, Russia, and from Point Hope, Alaska south to Monterey Bay, California. Infrequently, it has been reported at sea as far south as Baja California. It has been transplanted into the Great Lakes and into freshwater lakes in Alaska and along the U.S. Pacific coast as well as into Maine, Maryland, and Louisiana in the east, Alberta in Canada, Argentina, and Chile. Natural successful spawning has not noticeably occurred in these transplanted populations (with the possible exception of the Great Lakes in Michigan) and most have been perpetuated through successive stockings.

This is a silvery fish when at sea and has small black spots on the back, upper sides, base of the dorsal fin, and upper lobe of the tail. It can be distinguished from both the chinook salmon *(Oncorhynchus tshawytscha)* and the steelhead, or rainbow trout *(O. mykiss)* by the fact that it only has spots on the upper half of the tail while the latter two have spots over the entire tail. Also, it generally has pale or white gums and a black mouth (some Great Lakes specimens may have gray or black gums) while the chinook always has black gums and a black mouth.

Spawning females change very little. Males exhibit less dramatic color changes than do other Pacific salmons, and generally only tend to turn somewhat darker on the back and a duller silver on the sides. During the spawning run they may also exhibit a red stripe along the sides, like that of the rainbow trout. The males develop a kype, both the upper and lower jaw becoming extended and "hooked" toward each other so that it becomes impossible to close its mouth. Like all Pacific salmon, it does not feed once it enters freshwater on the spawning run. Although most coho do not seem to migrate extensively, tagged individuals have been recovered up to 1,200 mi (1.931 km) from the tagging site. Some remain in freshwater lakes and streams, never venturing to sea. These specimens do not spawn and are replenished only by successive runs of migratory coho. An estimated 85 percent of native Pacific coho return to spawn in the same stream where they began their life. Great Lakes cohos have a higher percentage of strays that seek out new streams in which to breed.

It is a very important commercial species and is marketed fresh, fresh-frozen, mild cured, smoked, and canned. The usual commercial catch weighs about 6-12 lb (2-5 kg) with 20 lb (9 kg) not uncommon. They can reach weights of at least 33 lb (15 kg).

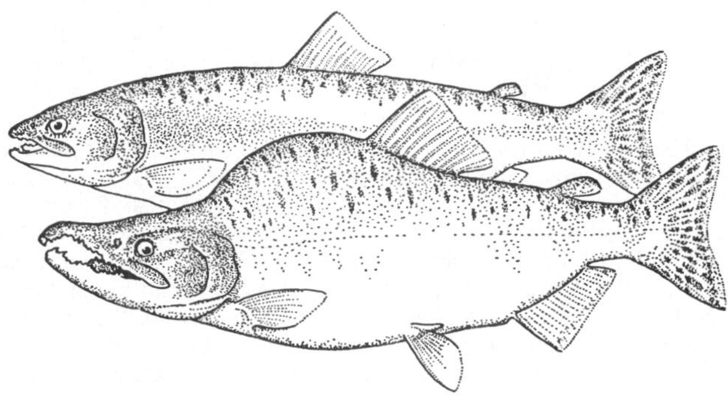

SALMON, pink / *Oncorhynchus gorbuscha* (Walbaum, 1792); SALMONIDAE FAMILY; also called humpback salmon, fall salmon

Endemic to the Pacific and Arctic oceans, Bering and Okhotsk seas, the Sea of Japan, and the rivers that flow into these waters. It occurs from Alaska south to the Sacramento River, California, throughout the Aleutian Islands, and northeast into the MacKenzie River, N.W.T., Canada. It has been introduced to Newfoundland and to the western coast of Lake Superior and is maintaining populations in these locations. Since the introduction into Newfoundland there have been sporadic reports of pink salmon in Labrador, Nova Scotia, and Quebec. It has spread through Lake Superior and is now spawning in tributaries of Lake Huron.

The smallest of the Pacific salmons, the usual size is 3-5 lb (1-2 kg). At sea they are silvery, as are all salmons. They can be identified by the large, black, oval-shaped spots on both halves of the tail and large spots on the back and the adipose fin. At spawning time the male is easily recognized by its distorted, extremely humpbacked appearance, which is much more pronounced than in the males of other Pacific salmon species. The male develops a kype at spawning time. The body of breeding males is pale red or "pink" on the sides with brown to olive-green blotches. The young have no parr marks and no spots on the fins.

The flesh is pink, rather than red or white, and although large numbers are caught commercially the pink salmon is regarded as less desirable than most other Pacific salmon.

The pink salmon and the chum salmon *(Oncorhynchus keta)* are often referred to as "autumn salmon" or "fall salmon" because of their late spawning runs. They can hybridize with each other.

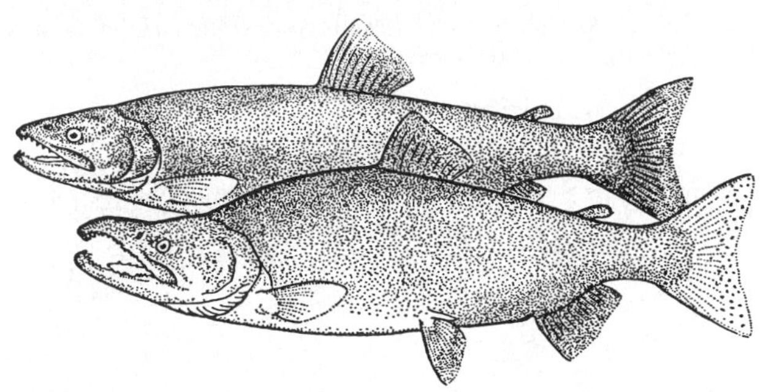

SALMON, sockeye / *Oncorhynchus nerka* (Walbaum, 1792); SALMONIDAE FAMILY; also called sockeye, red salmon, blueback salmon, kokanee

The sockeye salmon (anadromous form of *Oncorhynchus nerka*) is endemic to the Pacific Ocean and its tributaries from Hokkaido in Japan to the Anadyr River, Russia, and from the Sacramento River, California to Point Hope, Alaska. Freshwater, non-migratory populations, known as kokanee, occur naturally in Japan, Russia, Alaska, Washington, Oregon and Idaho, the Yukon and British Columbia and have been introduced elsewhere, but largely unsuccessfully.

The body of breeding males is bright red with small black speckling (spots not large or distinct) on the back. The totally red body will distinguish the sockeye from the otherwise similar chum salmon *(O. keta)*, and the lack of large, distinct spots will distinguish it from the other three Pacific salmons.

Sockeye are plankton feeders. They can be caught on a small hook baited with salmon eggs, a piece of worm, a maggot, or a small, flashy metal troll such as a willow leaf troll. The landlocked kokanee can be taken by fly fishing at times when they are feeding on insects at the surface. Anadromous salmon rarely feed after entering fresh water on their spawning run.

The flesh is deep red and high in oil content. It is the most commercially valuable of all the Pacific salmons. The meat is delicious whether smoked or prepared in any of a variety of ways. Most of the commercial catch is canned.

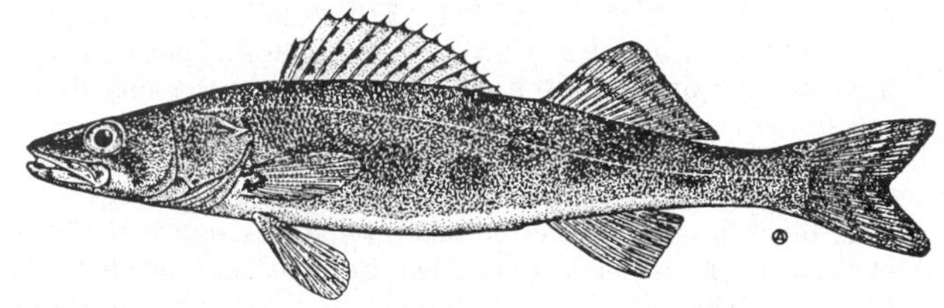

SAUGER / *Stizostedion canadense* (Smith, 1834); PERCIDAE FAMILY; also called blue pickerel, sand pickerel, sand pike, gray pike, blue pike, river pike, pike-perch, blue pike-perch, sand pike-perch, gray pike-perch, spotfin pike, jackfish, jack salmon

It has a general distribution in Canada and the U.S. from Quebec to Tennessee and Arkansas, and from northwestward through Montana to about central Alberta. Between Alberta and Quebec it occurs in southern Saskatchewan and Ontario and throughout the Great Lakes to James Bay. It does not occur east of the Appalachians or much south of Tennessee except in a few drainages where it has been introduced, principally from the Carolinas around through the lower coastal states to as far as Texas on the Gulf.

It is the closely related to the walleye *(Stizostedion vitreum)* and the two appear almost identical. They can be distinguished by several factors, most noticeably, the sauger has distinct dark spots on the dorsal fin. The walleye may have dark streaks or blotches on the dorsal fin, but they are less distinct than the spots of the sauger and may not be present. Also, the walleye has one large dark blotch at the base of the last few spines of the dorsal fin which is not present in the sauger. The sauger has 17-20 soft-rays in the second dorsal fin versus 19-22 in the walleye. Identification is complicated by the fact that the sauger is known to hybridize in nature with the walleye. This hybrid is commonly referred to as a "saugeye".

The sauger is smaller than the walleye. The maximum size of the hybrid is between a sager and a walleye and it is believed that reports of very large saugers may in fact be the hybrid.

The sauger is important commercially and as a sport fish in the north. Although the average size of commercially caught sauger is only about 1 lb (0.45 kg), it is the third most important fish after the walleye and whitefish in Manitoba, Canada and has considerable importance elsewhere in the north as well. The flesh is firm, white and delicious. It is sold as fresh or frozen boneless fillets.

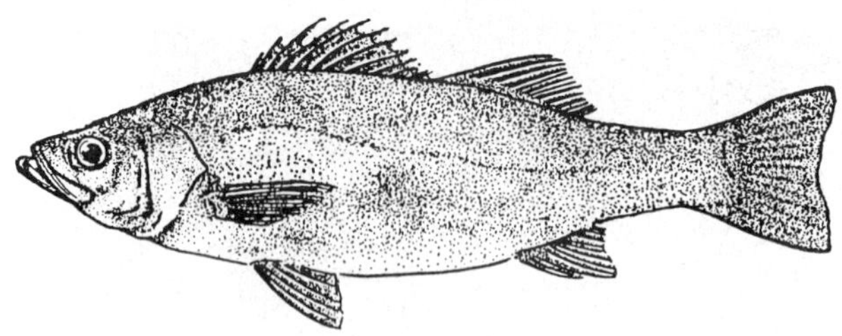

SEABASS, blackfin / *Lateolabrax latus* Katayama, 1957; PERCICHTHYIDAE FAMILY

The blackfin seabass is endemic to the north eastern Pacific from the Shizuoka and Chiba Prefectures in central Japan southward to the Nagasaki Prefecture and the East China Sea. In southern waters of Japan, it is caught more often than its close relative, the Japanese seabass *(Lateolabrax japonicus)*. Large fish are often caught in the area of shallow rocks and reefs and, in southern Japan even in the brackish waters of river mouths.

It is similar in shape to the striped bass *(Morone saxatilis)* of coastal U.S. waters and some inland U.S. waters. It has an elongate, compressed, silvery body, a large mouth of which the lower jaw projects beyond the upper jaw, and a slightly forked tail. It does, however, lack the stripes of *Morone saxatilis*. According to Hideya Suzuki, senior biologist with the National Research Institute of Fisheries Engineering in Tokyo, the blackfin seabass differs from the Japanese seabass in having a deeper body, a row of scales on the lower jaw, and a more silvery body color. In addition, the meristic counts of dorsal and anal fin elements differ. The blackfin seabass has 12 dorsal fin spines with 15-16 soft rays and 3 anal fin spines with 9-10 soft rays. The Japanese seabass has 12-15 dorsal fin spines with 12-14 soft rays and 3 anal fin spines with 7-9 soft rays. The lateral line pore count is 71-76 for the blackfin seabass.

Based on information submitted to the IGFA, the blackfin seabass appears to be noticeably stockier than the Japanese seabass. Its eyes appear to be slightly larger and more laterally situated on the sides of the head, perhaps because of the deeper body. The dorsal spines appear to be black, but not the membranes in between. The anal fin appears to have a slightly concave outline at the extremity, whereas the anal fin of the Japanese seabass sometimes appears to have a truncate or even convex outline of the extremity. The Japanese seabass sometimes has spots on the body whereas the blackfin seabass almost never has spots.

The blackfin seabass can be taken by surfcasting with flashy, minnow shaped artificial lures or metal jigs, or by fly fishing with feather streamers as well as by bait fishing with small live baits. The species grows to at least 40 in (101.6 cm) total length and a weight of 23 lb (10.43 kg). It is highly regarded both as a food fish and as a game fish.

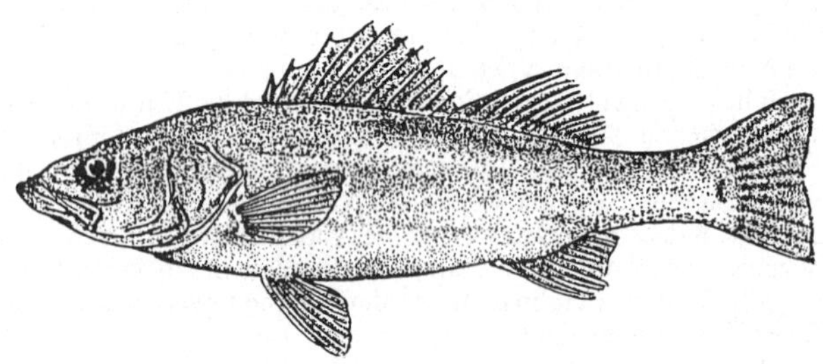

SEABASS, Japanese (suzuki) / *Lateolabrax japonicus* (Cuvier, 1828); PERCICHTHYIDAE FAMILY

Endemic to the northeastern Pacific from Japan south to Taiwan and the East and South China seas. It is known to frequent river mouths and shallow inshore bays, surf, and rocky reef areas as well as deeper waters. The young occasionally ascend rivers in summer. Although apparently more wide-ranging than its very close "cousin" the blackfin seabass *(Lateolabrax latus)*, the blackfin is a more frequent catch, at least in southern Japanese waters.

It is elongate and compressed, resembling the weakfish or spotted seatrout *(Cynoscion spp.)* in shape. Its body is less deep and stocky than is that of the blackfin seabass or the American striped bass *(Morone saxatilis)*. It somewhat resembles the European bass *(Dicentrarchus labrax)*. The tail is slightly forked and the mouth is large with the lower jaw projecting beyond the upper. Young fish have small black spots on the back and dorsal fin. These tend to disappear in larger fish, although specimens from the Ariake Sea, Japan, seem to retain the small spots.

Large specimens taken in the Yellow Sea and Gulf of Po-Hai have been found to have large, distinct black spots.

The first dorsal fin has 12-15 spines followed by 12-14 soft rays in the second dorsal fin. The anal fin has 3 spines and 7-9 soft rays. The lateral line pore count is 71-86. The Japanese seabass differs from the blackfin seabass in meristics (fin ray counts), body depth, and other characteristics. (See blackfin seabass.)

Claims submitted to IGFA for record consideration have shown white, clear, or dusky (but not black) dorsal fin spines and membranes. The body above the midline is generally darker than in the "blackfin" species which is more silvery and usually lacks spots. The eyes of the Japanese seabass often appear to be more dorsally positioned (higher on the head) than in the blackfin seabass, possibly due to the fact that the body is not as deep. All information on Japanese seabass submitted to IGFA has shown a truncate to slightly convex edge at the extremity of the anal fin, but illustrations in Japanese books indicate that it may also be concave. The blackfin seabass, on the other hand, has a slight concave edge visible both in photographs and in book illustrations.

Japanese seabass spawn from November to January in the deeper rocky reef areas near bays. After spawning they move into shallow waters to feed. Their diet includes sardines, anchovies and shrimp, as well as other small fishes and crustaceans. They can be taken by bait fishing with small fish or crustaceans, or by slow trolling, jigging, or casting with feathers or minnow-type artificial lures, flashy jigs or spoons at any level from the bottom to the surface. Best fishing is said to be at night and dawn near the surface. The largest fish are caught in fall and winter. As a food fish or a game fish the Japanese seabass is very highly rated. Its flesh is white and it is the object of Japanese commercial fisheries as well as anglers. Adult fish attain sizes of at least 23 lb (10.43 kg) and 40 in (101.6. cm).

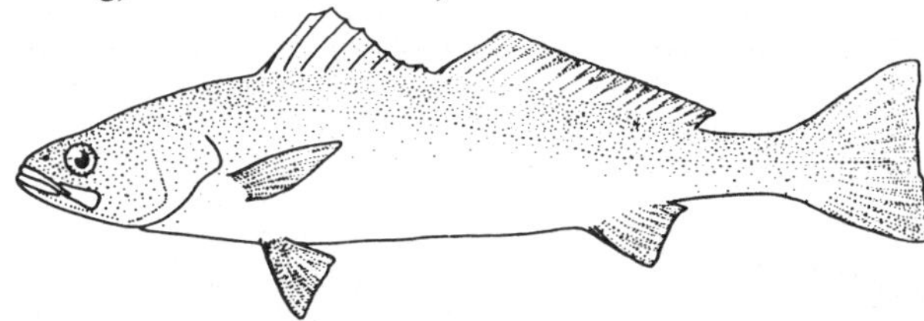

SEABASS, white / *Atractoscion nobilis* (Ayres, 1860); SCIAENIDAE FAMILY; also called Catalina salmon

Inhabits the eastern Pacific mainly between San Francisco, California and Baja California, Mexico and in the northern Gulf of California. It may be as far north as Vancouver Island, Canada or even southern Alaska, and as far south as Chile. They are usually found near kelp beds in depths of 12 to 25 fathoms, but they may also be found in shallow surf or deeper waters.

The white seabass lacks the two enlarged, recurvate canine teeth that are usually present in its Atlantic relatives, the weakfish and spotted seatrout. The first dorsal fin has 9 spines and the second dorsal fin has 2 spines and 20 soft rays. There are 2 spines and 10 soft rays in the anal fin. The lateral line pore count is 70-90 and the scale count 85-150. There are no barbels on the chin. A characteristic raised ridge exists along the midline of the belly between the vent and the base of the pelvic (ventral) fins. There is a black spot at the base of the pectoral fin. Young fish up to about 18 in (45 cm) may have 3-6 broad, dark vertical bars on the flanks, but these disappear with age.

It may be taken by drift fishing or still fishing with live baits or by slow trolling, jigging or casting with feathers or small, flashy metal lures. They eat sardines, anchovies, squid, small mackerel and other small fishes and crustaceans. Most are caught near the mainland shore and around Catalina and San Clemente Islands. The best fishing is said to be at night near the bottom. Off California the species is most numerous from about May to September.

The white seabass and its relatives are weakfishes. The name "weakfish" refers to the tender, easily torn mouth tissues characteristic of these fishes, not their fighting ability. "Seabass" and "seatrout" are misnomers for *Atractoscion* and *Cynoscion* species which are not related to either bass or trout.

The flesh is white and tender and the fish is the object of commercial fisheries as well as anglers. It spoils quickly, and should be eaten soon after capture.

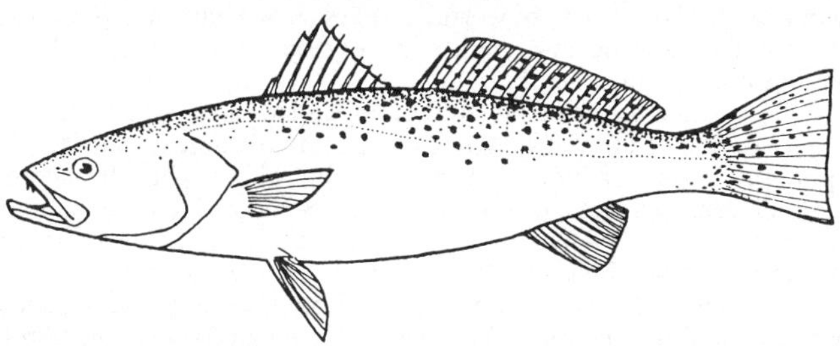

SEATROUT, spotted / *Cynoscion nebulosus* (Cuvier, 1830); SCIAENIDAE FAMILY; also called spotted weakfish, spotted squeteague, speckled trout, gator trout, winter trout, salmon trout, black trout

Occurs in the western Atlantic Ocean from New York to the Gulf of Mexico, from Virginia southward, particularly off the coasts of North Carolina and Texas. An in shore, schooling species, it usually inhabits the shallow areas of bays and estuaries. In the winter some fish leave the bays but the majority seem to remain and may be killed by the low temperatures. Adults, though not highly migratory, are more migratory than other members of the same genus. They range as far north as Long Island in late spring.

Two large, recurvate canine teeth in the front of the upper jaw stand out noticeably. The first dorsal fin has 10 spines (rarely 11), and the second dorsal fin has 1 spine and 24-27 soft rays. The anal fin has 2 spines and 10-11 soft rays. There are 8 or 9 short, stubby gill rakers on the lower limb of the first gill arch as opposed to 11-13 in the weakfish *(Cynoscion regalis)*. There are no barbels on the chin. There are round black spots on the back and upper flanks and on the tail and second dorsal fin. In the weakfish the spots do not extend onto the fins.

This bottom dwelling, predatory fish feeds at any level. It may be taken at any level by chumming from a drifting or anchored boat, by trolling, jigging, or surf casting. Conventional or spinning tackle may be used. Shrimp is the most popular and effective bait. Whenever shrimp are abundant, spotted seatrout feed on them almost exclusively. Crabs, small live fishes, cut mullet, clams, worms, or small flashy artificial lures may also be used. It may be caught in salt or brackish water and shows a preference for shallow waters of estuaries. They rate highly as a food fish, but tend to spoil rapidly so should be eaten soon after capture.

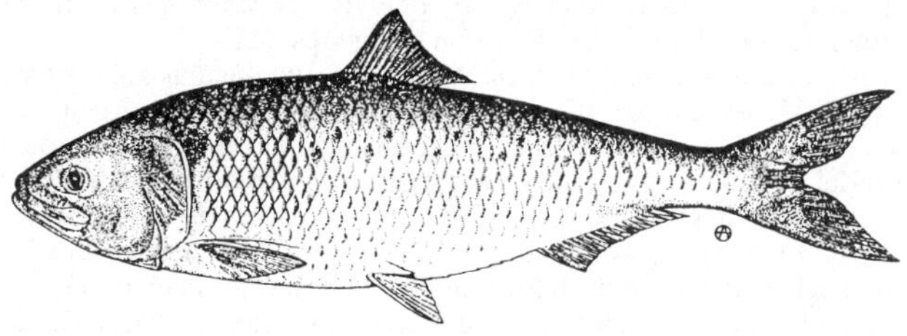

SHAD, American / *Alosa sapidissima* (Wilson, 1811); CLUPEIDAE FAMILY; also called common shad, Atlantic shad, Connecticut River shad, North River shad, Potomac shad, Susquehanna shad, white shad, Delaware shad, alose

The American shad occurs natively east of the Appalachians along the Atlantic coast of North America from Sand Hill River, Labrador to the St. John's River, Florida. Also, in the St. Lawrence River to Lakes Huron and Erie. Between 1871 and 1881 it was introduced into the Sacramento River, California and is today found in numerous spots up and down the Pacific coast as far south as Bahia de Todos Santos in upper Baja California, Mexico and as far north as Alaska and the Kamchatka Peninsula, formerly the U.S.S.R., on the Asiatic side. Like the salmons, the American shad is an anadromous fish that ascends coastal rivers to spawn.

This is a silvery fish with a single dorsal fin in the middle of the back. There is a large black spot directly behind the top of the gill cover, followed by 4-27 spots, which are generally smaller than the first. Sometimes there may be a second row of spots below the first, and more rarely, a third row below the second.

They closely resemble the hickory shad *(Alosa mediocris)*. The most important physical distinction is in the lower jaw. In the American shad this jaw fits easily into a deep notch under the upper jaw, whereas, in the hickory shad the lower jaw protrudes noticeably beyond the upper jaw. Also, the normal size of American shad is 2-8 lb (0.9-3.6 kg) with a maximum size of possibly 12 lb (5.4 kg). The normal size of the hickory shad is 1-3 lb (0.4-1.3 kg) with a maximum of about 6 lb (2.7 kg). Both occur up and down the coasts, but the American shad is predominant in more northerly climates (most abundant from North Carolina to Connecticut) and the hickory shad is predominant in southern climates.

The American shad is highly regarded by some as a game fish and its white, flaky flesh supports a considerable commercial fishery. It is taken in weirs, traps and gill nets during its spawning migration in rivers and estuaries. The roe is esteemed by some as a substitute caviar.

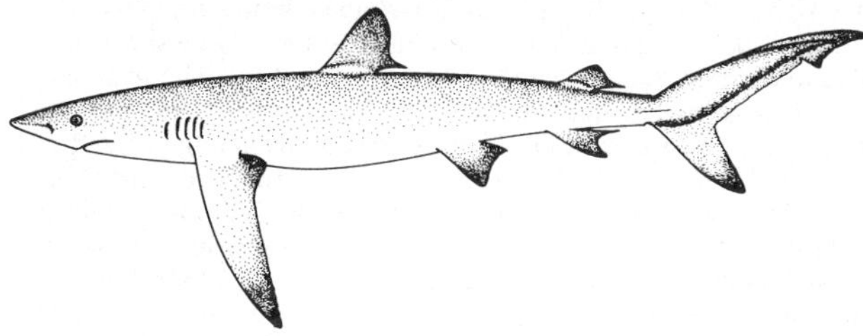

SHARK, blue / *Prionace glauca* (Linnaeus, 1758); CARCHARHINIDAE FAMILY; also called blue whaler, great blue shark, bluedog

Inhabits cool temperate seas, often near the surface, but usually submerged to depths of 110 to 170 fathoms in the tropics or in areas with warm water currents, 50°-68°F (10°-20°C). It is usually replaced as the common large pelagic shark by the white-tip in areas of warm surface water. It is present in the Mediterranean, absent from the Baltic and Red Seas, and extremely rare in the Gulf of Mexico.

It is recognizable by its brilliant blue color. It is dark cobalt or indigo blue dorsally, lightening to bright blue on the flanks and white on the belly. It is unique among sharks in that the larger teeth of the upper jaw are "saber-shaped", with one margin broadly convex, the other concave. The teeth are serrated along the edges. Those in the lower jaw are narrower and very sharp. Caudal keels and spiracles are absent.

They are pelagic, migratory and travel alone as well as in packs. They follow whaling ships, feeding in a frenzy on the carcasses of whales and ships' garbage, they earned the name "blue whaler". Fishes, sea birds, squid and other sharks are prey to the blue shark. While not considered one of the most dangerous sharks, they have been implicated in unprovoked attacks on both humans and boats. They were responsible for some attacks on shipwrecked sailors during World War II, since they are an abundant species.

Fishing methods include chumming with live or dead baits or trolling. Baits include squid, eels, mackerel, herring and other live or whole fishes as well as cut baits.

The blue shark is viviparous, giving birth to 50 or more young at a time. They mature at a length of 7 or 8 feet (2.0 to 2.3 m). It does not rate high as table fare. Sharks begin to smell strongly of ammonia once urea decomposition sets in and, they require prompt preparation if they are to be eaten.

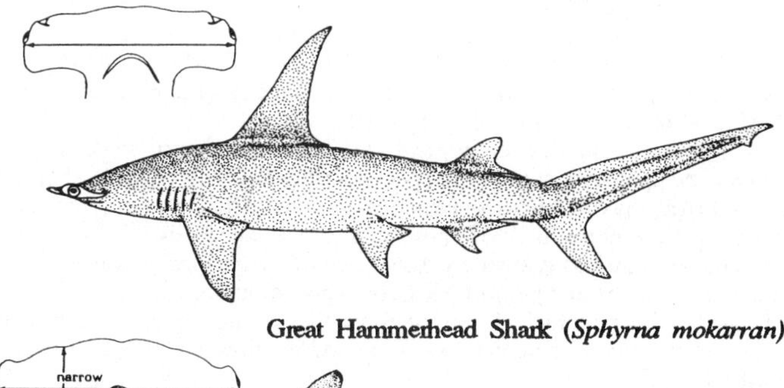

Great Hammerhead Shark *(Sphyrna mokarran)*

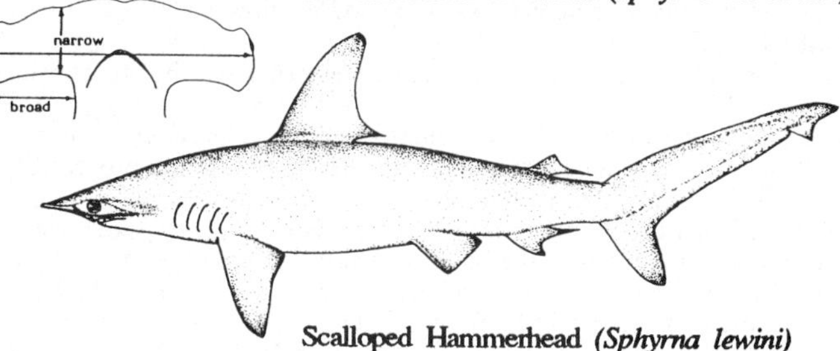

Scalloped Hammerhead *(Sphyrna lewini)*

SHARK, hammerhead / *Sphyrna spp.* collective SPHYRNIDAE FAMILY; also called great hammerhead, smooth or common hammerhead, scalloped hammerhead

The hammerheads occur worldwide, but some species have more restricted ranges. The most widely distributed species is probably the smooth, or common, hammerhead *(Sphyrna zygaena)*. They inhabit shallow waters along the coasts, bays and harbors where the water is calm and the bottom sandy.

The eyes are located at the ends of two thin protrusions, resembling a hammer. The caudal peduncle lacks keels. In some species the pectoral fins are black tipped. Of the nine species of hammerhead sharks, the largest is the great hammerhead *(S. mokarran)* which may reach a length of 20 ft (6 m). Its head is T-shaped, being almost straight along the front edge and notched in the center. Another large species, the smooth hammerhead *(S. zygaena)*, grows to 14 ft (4 m). The front edge of its head is rounded and unnotched in the center. The scalloped hammerhead *(S. lewini)*, grows to 10 ft (3 m). The front edge of its head is rounded and notched. Of the lesser known hammerheads, there is *S. couardi*, a large West African species that resembles *S. lewini*, and the strange-looking *S. blochii*, whose head lobes often measure 50 percent of the body length and are swept back like the wings of an airplane. The remainder of the species, *S. tiburo, S. media, S. corona* and *S. tudes*, known as the bonnetheads, are only 3-6 ft (1-2 m) long and have very short lobed, shovel shaped heads.

It swings its broad, flat head back and forth over the bottom in a scanning pattern, in the same way as one uses a metal detector. Tiny organs called the ampullae of Lorenzini, located in the head, function as electroreceptors that enable the shark to detect food buried beneath the sand. Stingray may be their favorite food. According to scientist Perry Gilbert one large hammerhead was found to have 96 stingray barbs imbedded in its jaw, mouth and head. Though all sharks have ampullae of Lorenzini which also serve to detect chemical, physical and thermal changes in the water, the head of the hammerhead seems ideally shaped to achieve optimum advantage from them.

Hammerheads fight hard making long surface and midwater runs and thrashing about causing a great deal of commotion. Fishing methods include slow trolling, drifting or still fishing with chum and baits that are oily or bloody. Mackerel, jack, squid and other baits, as well as artificial lures, may also work on occasion.

They are viviparous and prolific giving birth to as many as 30 or 40 young at a time. Some are known to be man eaters. In fact, the first fatal shark attack recorded in American waters was by a hammerhead off Long Island, New York in 1815. The meat of the hammerhead is of good quality if fresh and properly prepared. The fins are used in soup in some areas.

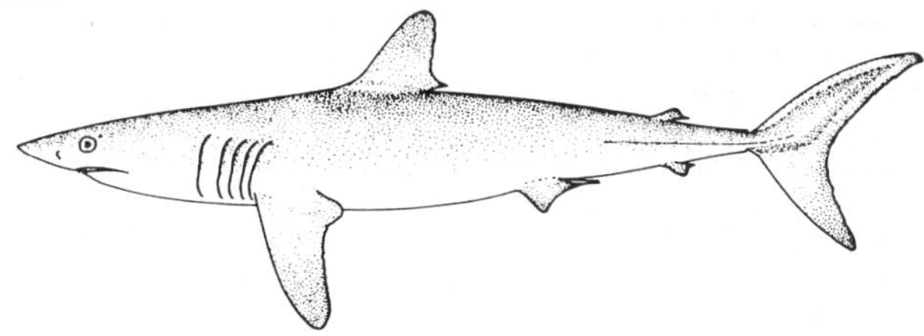

SHARK, mako

/ *Isurus oxyrinchus* Rafinesque, 1810; and
/ *Isurus paucus* Guitart Manday, 1965; LAMNIDAE FAMILY; also called shortfin mako shark, longfin mako shark, blue pointer, short-nosed mackerel shark, bonito shark

Found worldwide in tropical and warm temperate seas, these solitary, pelagic, fast swimming species rarely come in close to shore. The shortfin mako *(Isurus oxyrinchus)* is most often encountered by anglers as it is more likely to move in-shore on occasion. The longfin mako *(Isurus paucus)* is a widely distributed off shore species considered rare in the Atlantic and Gulf of Mexico, except along the coast of Cuba. It is taken almost exclusively on longlines though there is a record of at least one specimen being caught on rod and reel in the Gulf stream off south Florida.

It resembles its close relatives the porbeagle and the great white sharks, with a streamlined, well proportioned body and a conical pointed snout. The longfin mako has a blunter snout and a larger eye than the shortfin and much longer pectoral fins. There is a large, prominent, flattened keel on either side of the caudal peduncle. It can be easily distinguished from all other sharks by its teeth, which are like curved daggers with no cusps at the base or serrations along the razor shark edges. The front surface is flat and the teeth are curved inward. The back of the shortfin mako is a brilliant blue-gray or cobalt blue and the sides are light blue, changing to snowy white on the belly including the lower jaw. The longfin mako is also blue above with light blue sides, and is white below except for the jaw. In life the mako's colors are the most strikingly beautiful of all the mackerel sharks. After death the colors fade to grayish brown.

The mako is a known enemy of the broadbill swordfish. In one case a 730 lb (331 kg) mako was found to have swallowed a 120 lb (54 kg) swordfish whole. The mako, like the white shark and the porbeagle, swims with short, stiff, powerful strokes of its tail and presents a stiff-bodied, majestic appearance in contrast to the lithe, slithering motions of most other sharks.

It has been implicated in attacks on humans and is the undisputed leader in attacks on boats. A hooked mako will unleash all its fury, reportedly leaping as high as 30 ft (10 m) out of the water. It may roll, shake, dive, and charge the boat. It has also been known to bite the boat and occasionally to leap into it, causing severe injuries to the angler and wreaking havoc in the cockpit.

Fishing methods include trolling with whole tuna, mullet, squid, mackerel, or lures and also, chumming or live bait fishing with similar baits. Many are hooked incidentally while trolling for marlins. The flesh is excellent and said to be similar to swordfish.

The mako and its relatives, the white shark and the porbeagle shark, differ from most sharks in that they are warm-blooded. As the blood circulates the heat is trapped and retained, allowing the shark to maintain a body temperature higher than the temperature of the surrounding water.

The mackerel sharks (mako, white and porbeagle) are all ovoviviparous, the eggs hatch inside the mother and the young are born alive. One female was found to contain ten babies (five males and five females) each measuring 25 to 27.5 in (63.5 to 69.8 cm).

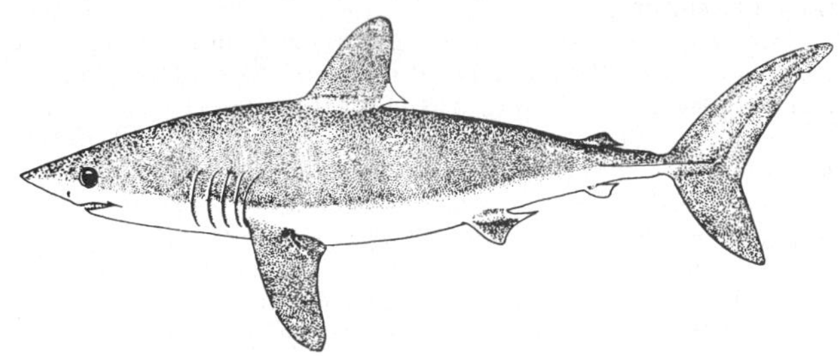

SHARK, porbeagle / *Lamna nasus* (Bonnaterre, 1788); LAMNIDAE FAMILY; also called mackerel shark, salmon shark, herring shark, bonito shark, blue dog, beaumaris shark

It inhabits cool temperate waters of the North Atlantic from South Carolina to Newfoundland, and from North Africa to Norway and Iceland. It also inhabits the Mediterranean Sea and the cool temperate waters of the southern Pacific. A pelagic, oceanic shark, it has nevertheless been found near shore on occasions.

It is of the same family as the great white and the mako sharks and they resemble each other. The snout is perfectly conical and ends in a point, and there is a large, very prominent flattened keel on either side of the caudal peduncle. It is easily distinguished from other sharks by its teeth, which are smooth and have little cusps on each side of the base. It has a small secondary keel that the white and mako sharks lack. The smaller keel is located beneath the main keel but farther back on the tail. The first dorsal fin is farther forward than on the mako or white sharks. Its anal fin is directly beneath the second dorsal fin, whereas the mako's anal fin originates near the midpoint of the second dorsal fin. It has a distinguishing white patch on the free-trailing base portion of the first dorsal fin.

It follows the migrations of mackerels, herring, cod, bonitos, etc., which is the reason it is often called mackerel shark, bonito shark, herring shark, etc. It also eats squid, flounder, hake and dogfish.

The porbeagle is reported to be an excellent sport fish and may leap when hooked. The flesh is of good quality and texture and is said to taste somewhat like swordfish. Fishing methods include trolling or bait fishing while chumming. Baits include mackerel, herring, bonito, squid and other fishes.

They inhabit colder waters than its relatives, which may account for the fact that there are no recorded instances of it ever attacking humans or boats. It is considered a potentially dangerous species.

The porbeagle is warm-blooded and ovoviviparous, though it has fewer babies, up to four measuring 19 ½ in (50 cm) long at birth.

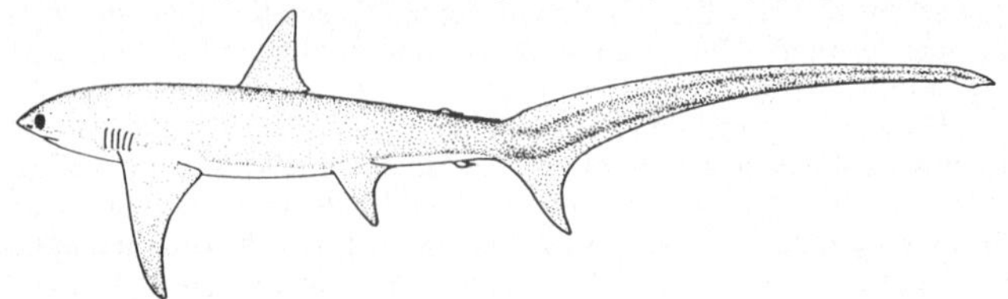

SHARK, thresher

/ *Alopias vulpinus* (Bonnaterre, 1788);
/ *Alopias pelagicus* Nakamura, 1935;
/ *Alopias superciliosus* (Lowe, 1840);
/ *Alopias profundus* Nakamura, 1935; ALOPIIDAE FAMILY; also

called longtail thresher, pelagic thresher, Atlantic bigeye thresher, Pacific bigeye thresher, fox shark, sea fox, swiveltail, swingletail, thrasher shark

The pelagic thresher shark *(A. pelagicus)* and the Pacific bigeye thresher *(A. profundus)* are found in the northwestern Pacific Ocean. The Atlantic bigeye thresher *(A. superciliosus)* occurs in the Atlantic. The longtail thresher *(A. vulpinus)* is found worldwide in warm to cool temperate zones. They are generally pelagic though they do come in close to shore. The longtail and pelagic threshers occur near the surface and the bigeye threshers inhabit deep waters, their large eyes undoubtedly aiding them in seeing at greater depths.

They are easily recognized because the upper lobe of the tail is usually as long as the rest of the body (appreciably longer in *A. vulpinus).* The caudal peduncle lacks keels, the teeth are small and pointed with broad bases, and the skin is smoother than that of most other sharks. The longtail thresher and the pelagic thresher have moderate sized eyes (1.2-1.5 percent of the total body length). The first dorsal fin is located almost squarely in the middle of the back, well forward of the origin of the pelvic fins. The Atlantic and Pacific bigeye threshers have much larger eyes (2.8-4.1 percent of the total body length) and the rear margin of the dorsal fin is located at least as far back as the origin of the pelvic fins. The belly and lower flanks of thresher sharks may be mottled.

Threshers are a solitary species but it is not uncommon for them to congregate when large schools of bait fish are available and occasionally hunt in pairs. Their diet is known to include mackerel, menhaden, garfish, needlefish and bluefish. Typically a thresher will slap or thrash the water with its tail to herd bait fish into a mass then use its tail to stun or injure individual fish before swallowing them. An angler may see his bait slapped out of the water then swallowed as it settles back in again, which is why threshers are often hooked in the tail. They are very active fighters when hooked and the longtail thresher has been known to leap clear of the water. Fishing methods include trolling in marlin fashion or deep trolling or drifting, depending on the species to be caught. Whole baits, strip baits, live yellowtail, snapper, or mullet may be used as well as feathers, Konaheads, knuckleheads, or other baits or lures which are generally used for marlin or tuna.

They are ovoviviparous and give birth to larger babies about 5 ft (1.5 m) long. However, there are only 2 to 4 young in a litter as opposed to forty or more in other species.

There is no record of a thresher shark ever attacking a person, though there are cases of threshers attacking boats. One is recorded in New Jersey off the U.S. east coast and another off South Africa.

The flesh is of good quality and commands a high price in southern California but more often used as bait or chum to catch other sharks than as food.

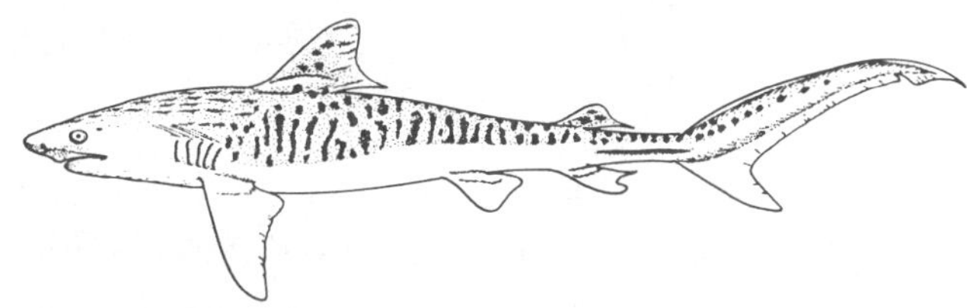

SHARK, tiger / *Galeocerdo cuvieri* (Peron and Lesueur, 1822); CARCHARHINIDAE FAMILY; also called leopard shark

Occurs worldwide in tropical and warm temperate seas, but has been found during the summer season as far north as Massachusetts in the western Atlantic and Iceland in the eastern Atlantic.

The tiger shark can be readily identified by its cockscomb-shaped, serrated teeth, which are recurvate and deeply notched on the inner margin. The teeth are the same in both jaws. The first two of the five gill slits are above the pectoral fin. There is a long, prominent keel along either side of the caudal peduncle. The young characteristically have very prominent, dark brown tiger stripes and leopard spots on the upper body and tail, but adults have less prominent markings and usually are just plain brownish gray or dusky ocher in color.

It is especially dangerous to man because of its proneness to attack, its undiscerning habits, and its tendency to frequent shallow waters where people swim. It is a sluggish swimmer under normal conditions, but comes alive in the presence of food, which considering the objects found in the stomachs of captured specimens, can be almost anything. The list includes fishes, crabs, turtles, stingrays, birds, other sharks, porpoises, dogs, rats, a crocodile's head, a tom-tom, articles of clothing, boat cushions, driftwood, lumps of coal, a two pound coil of copper wire, assorted nuts and bolts, the hind leg of a sheep and human flesh and limbs. In Australia, and Florida this shark has been responsible for many fatal attacks.

It is a hard fighting, highly rated game fish. Fishing methods include live bait fishing while chumming from boats or trolling. Whole or cut fish or scrap meat is effective. Many tiger sharks have been caught after attacking fish being played by anglers.

The tiger shark may give birth to from 10 to as many as 80 young in one litter. The flesh is not usually eaten, though it is certainly edible. Commercially, the hide is used to make leather, and fishermen use the flesh and liver for chumming.

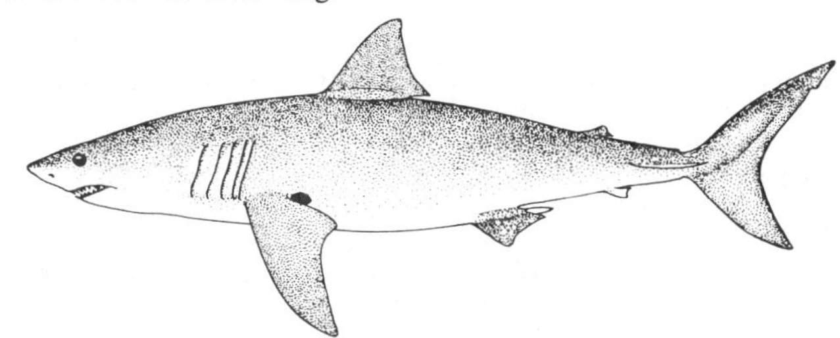

SHARK, white / *Carcharodon carcharias* (Linnaeus, 1758); LAMNIDAE FAMILY; also called great white shark, white pointer, white death, man-eater

Occurs worldwide, most commonly in cool temperate seas. It is best known in parts of the central and western Pacific, especially off Australia and New Zealand. On the Pacific coast of the U.S. it stays in the cool, southbound in shore current off California, but does not occur in California's warmer off shore waters. It is known to occur as far north as Nova Scotia in the western Atlantic and northern Spain in the eastern Atlantic. In the winter it occurs south of Florida, the Gulf of Mexico and the West Indies, but it apparently migrates north in the summer. It is also known to enter the Mediterranean Sea.

Though basically a deep water oceanic species, it does come in fairly close to shore off California because of the cool current and to feed on marine mammals. It also frequents Australian and South African beaches and is suspected of entering saltwater creeks. Three attacks, two of them fatal, occurred in Matawan Creek, New Jersey, USA in 1916, 11 mi (6 km) from the open ocean. The attacks were attributed to an 8.5 ft (2.5 m) white shark caught two days later in Raritan Bay.

It resembles the mako and the porbeagle. The snout is conical and ends in a point, hence the name "white pointer". There is a large, very prominent, flattened keel on either side of the caudal peduncle. It can be distinguished from all other sharks by its teeth, which are large and triangular like stone arrowheads, with sharp, serrated cutting edges. The great "white" shark is actually a grayish brown color above, fading to an off-white on the belly. The pectoral fins are black-tipped, and there is a black oval spot on the body just above them.

Its diet includes fish, squid and other sharks as well as sea turtles, seals, sea lions, and sea gulls. Many unusual items have also been found in their stomachs, including whole sheep, a bulldog, a cuckoo clock, glass, bottles, tin cans and parts of porpoises, whales, horses and humans. This shark has attacked small boats, sometimes sinking them, and has been known to take a larger boat by the propeller and shake it like a dog shaking a toy.

Fishing methods include bait fishing with large fish chunks while chumming. Also trolling. Baits include tuna, snapper, mullet and other fishes, especially those that are oily.

Despite its infamy, the great white shark is a relatively uncommon species. It reaches sexual maturity at a length of 11-14 ft (3-4 m). Like the other mackerel sharks (mako and porbeagle), it is warm-blooded. It is probably the most dangerous of all sharks as far as size, strength, ability and disposition to attack are concerned. The flesh is edible, though rarely eaten.

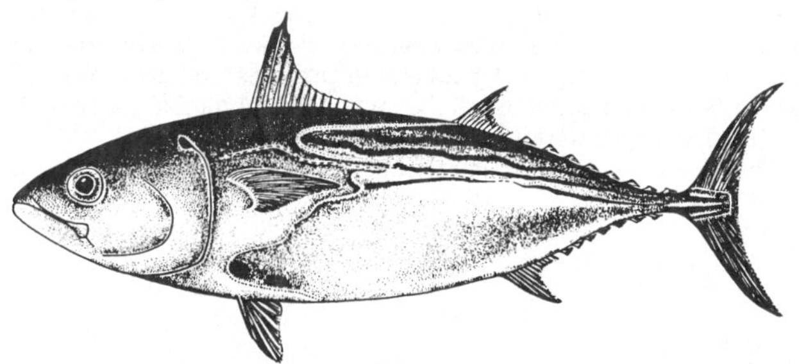

SKIPJACK, black / *Euthynnus lineatus* Kishinouye, 1920; SCOMBRIDAE FAMILY; also called little tuna, false albacore, spotted tuna, mackerel tuna, skipjack

They inhabit tropical and warm temperate waters of the eastern

Pacific Ocean from California to Peru, and rarely the central Pacific.

The dorsal fin has 13-15 spines and is high anteriorly. This distinguishes it from the bonito *(Sarda)* which have a relatively long and low first dorsal fin. The anal fin, which has 11-13 rays is similar to the second dorsal fin in size and shape. The body lacks scales, except on the anterior corselet and along the lateral line. This is the only species of *Euthynnus* with 37, instead of the usual 39, vertebrae. Each jaw has 20-40 small, conical teeth. Bonitos have fewer and larger conical teeth. Mackerels have flat, triangular teeth.

It is distinguished from similar species by the 4 or 5 broad, straight, black stripes which run horizontally along the back and by the dark spots between the pectoral and ventral fins. In live specimens, stripes may be visible on the venter as well as on the back, which has frequently led to confusion with the skipjack tuna *(Katsuwonus pelamis)*. The stripes on the belly rarely persist long after death in the black skipjack, however, whereas they remain prominent in the skipjack tuna.

It is pelagic, schooling and migratory, feeding predominantly on small surface fishes, squids, and crustaceans. It can be hooked by trolling or casting small whole baits or strip baits, or small lures such as spoons, plugs, jigs, and feathers. It has been said that the black skipjack will strike any lure trolled at speeds up to 8 or 10 miles per hour (12-16 km).

It is rated as a good food fish by some and disdained by others. Its flesh is dark red and the taste is strong. It does have some commercial value.

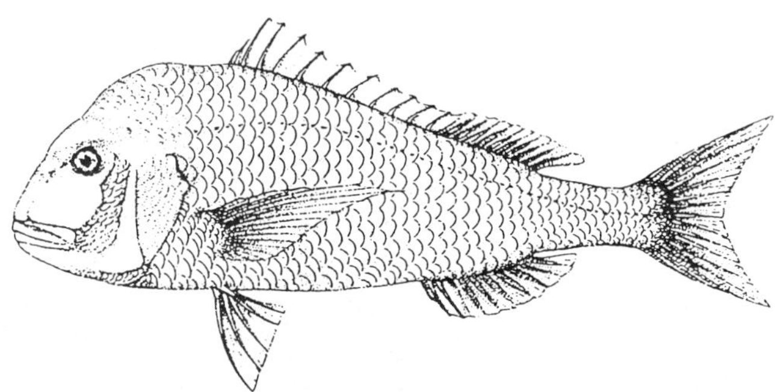

SNAPPER (Squirefish) / *Pagrus auratus* (Bloch & Schneider) (formerly *Chrysophrys auratus* or *Pagurus major*); SPARIDAE FAMILY; also called pink snapper,

Widely distributed off the southern half of Australia, Lord Howe and Norfolk Islands, and the northern two-thirds of New Zealand.

To avoid confusion with snappers in the family Lutjanidae, the American Fisheries Society refers to *Pagrus auratus* as a squirefish. In Australia, the names cockney, red bream, squire, and snapper or pink snapper are used for progressively larger fish. The name old man snapper refers to very large individuals with a distinctive bony hump on the head and a fleshy bulge on the snout.

The coloration of fresh-caught snapper is generally reddish-pink with a golden sheen, but color varies somewhat with habitat. Reef-dwelling fish are much darker reddish-brown where open water fish are a brighter pink, and snapper from soft muddy bottoms can be pale silvery pink.

They inhabit a variety of habitats at all ages, and a moderate depth range as adults. They are coastal fish, commonly found from 20-100 meters but may be right at the surface or down to at least 656 ft (200 m). They reportedly attains a weight of 43 lb (19.5 kg).

Fishing methods vary from surfcasting and jetty fishing to drift fishing, jigging or anchoring and using burley either presented at the surface or attached to an anchor chain. Hooks vary with the size of the fish targeted, from 4/0 for small snapper to 8/0 for real monsters. The hook must be razor sharp for the hard-mouthed snapper. They are omnivorous feeders, eating nearly any kind of marine animals, making bait selection fairly easy. Pilchards, skipjack tuna, kahawai, bonito, soldier crabs, or something tough like octopus or cuttlefish work well, but the best baits (and burley) should be reasonably fresh.

They are considered an excellent table fish in New Zealand and Australia.

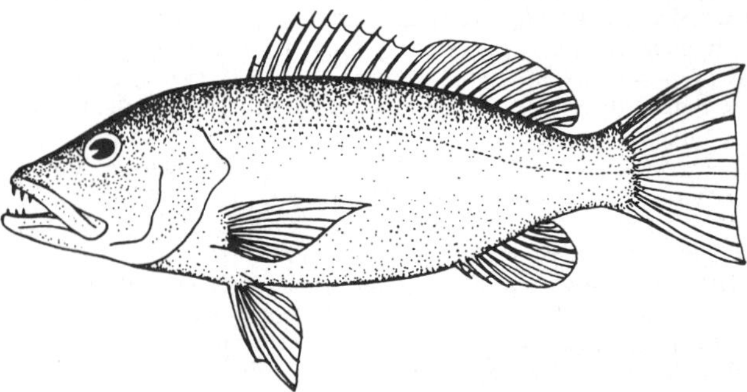

SNAPPER, cubera / *Lutjanus cyanopterus* (Cuvier, 1828); LUTJANIDAE FAMILY; also called Cuban snapper

It is found throughout the western Atlantic from Florida and Cuba southward to Brazil. It is the giant of all the snappers, attaining weights in excess of 100 lb (45 kg) and an overall length in excess of 4 ft (1.21 m). The snapper family Lutjanidae consists of some 250 different species in 25 genera. At least fifteen species are found in the waters of North America, and ten of these belong to the genus *Lutjanus*.

Dorsal fins are connected and consist of 10 spines, followed by 14 rays. The anal fin is roundish and consists of 8 rays. There are 5-7 gill rakers (not including rudiments) on the lower limb of the first branchial arch. The pectoral fins do not quite reach to the origin of the anal fin. The eyes are dark red and the body ranges from gray to greenish, often tinged with red. Its closest look-alike may be the gray, or "mangrove", snapper *(L. griseus)*. Like most snappers the gray snapper has more gill rakers on the average (7-9 on the lower limb of the first branchial arch) than does the cubera. It rarely exceeds 10 lb (22 kg). The red snapper differs not only in color and size, but in having 9 anal rays and 8-10 gill rakers on the lower limb of the first arch. Also, its pectoral fin reaches to or beyond the origin of its anal fin, which is angular, not roundish.

It ranges in depths from 2-3 ft (0.92 m) to 120 ft (36 m). It is a hard fighter, particularly on light tackle, and a fine food fish, though the flesh of larger fish may be coarse.

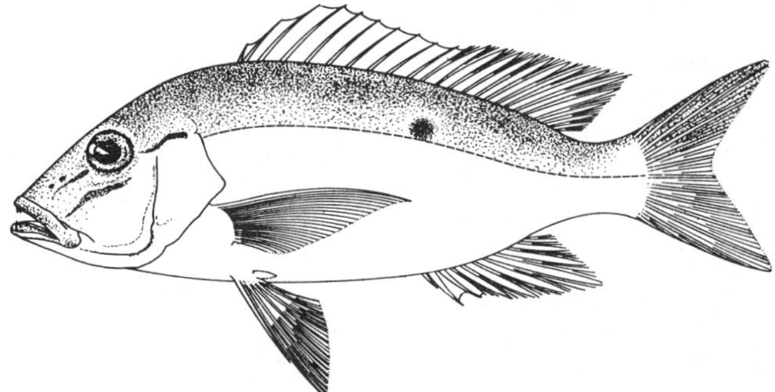

SNAPPER, mutton / *Lutjanus analis* (Cuvier, 1828); LUTJANIDAE FAMILY

It is one of the most common snapper from Florida to South America. Occasionally, it reaches as far north as Massachusetts and as far south as southeastern Brazil.

It is a handsome fish, varying from orangish to reddish-yellow with small blue streaks on the head, back and flanks, and orangish fins. The colors may vary, as with most species of fish. A combination of factors distinguish it from other snappers. There is a black, oval shaped spot on the upper flank on each side, the anal fin and rear edge of the dorsal fin is angulate (pointed rather than rounded), the tail is lunate, and the dorsal fin has ten spines and fourteen rays.

Although at first glance the mutton snapper and the lane snapper may look exactly alike, both having similar coloration, a lunate tail and even the same oval spot on the upper flanks, a closer look will reveal that the lane snapper has yellow streaks or horizontal stripes on the body, whereas the mutton snapper has small, oblique, blue streaks on a yellowish background, though these tend to disappear with age. Also, the anal fin and rear edge of the dorsal fin of the lane snapper are not sharply pointed but appear to be squarish or even rounded. Of all the species of Lutjanidae having a dark spot on the flanks below the dorsal fin, the mutton snapper *(L. analis)* is the only one in which the tooth patch in the roof of the mouth has no median extension and resembles a crescent rather than an anchor shape. Large mutton snappers take on a reddish coloration and are often mistaken for red snappers.

They attain weights in excess of 25-30 lb (11-14 kg). They are strong fighters on light tackle and can be taken on natural baits or small lures fished or slowly trolled near the bottom. Normally associated with reefs, wrecks, holes, and channels, they are nevertheless occasionally found on the flats and can be caught there by fly fishing. They may also be lured to the surface and caught on a fly.

The flesh is firm and white and is excellent eating whether baked, broiled, or prepared by any other method.

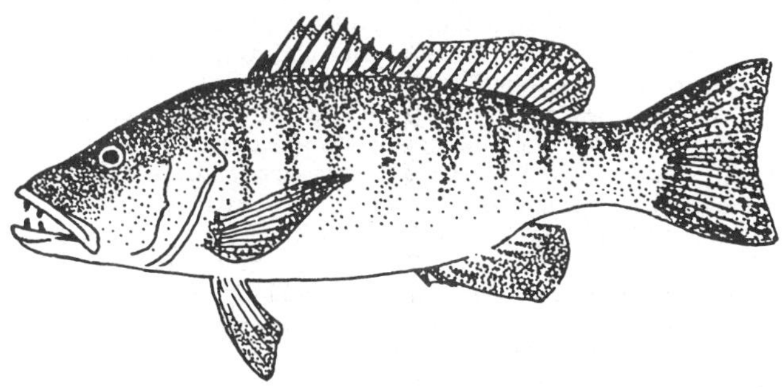

SNAPPER, Pacific cubera / *Lutjanus novemfasciatus* Gill, 1863; LUTJANIDAE FAMILY; also called black snapper, dog snapper

It is common throughout the Gulf of California (Sea of Cortez) from at least Laguna San Ignacio south to Panama, and probably Peru. It is an in shore Pacific species, frequenting reefs and caves from shallow waters to 100 ft (30 m) or more.

Growing to at least 80 lb (36 kg), it is the largest of the nine species of snapper that occur in its range. The most prominent and recognizable feature is the 4 large canine teeth, two in the upper jaw and two in the lower jaw. They are slightly larger than the diameter of the pupil of the eye and are the largest teeth of any snapper in its range. There is a crescent shaped patch of teeth in the roof of the mouth and other small ones are on the jaws.

As a juvenile, it is purplish-brown with a light spot in the center of each scale, but adults and older fish become deep reddish in color. There is sometimes a blue streak under the eye, and about 9 dusky bars may or may not be evident to varying degrees on the flanks. The tail is almost truncate, usually being very slightly forked to crescent shaped. The dorsal fin has 10 spines followed by 14 soft rays, the anal fin rounded with 3 spines and 8 rays. The pectoral fins do not reach to the anal fin, nor do they reach as far as the vent in adults.

The Pacific cubera snapper looks quite like the cubera snapper *(Lutjanus cyanopterus)* of the western Atlantic, the "river" or "mangrove red" snapper *(Lutjanus argentimaculatus)* of the western Indo-Pacific, and an African snapper *(Lutjanus spp.)*. These three snappers and some others around the world, grow to sizes approaching or exceeding 100 lb (45 kg). All have deep reddish bodies, 4 large canine teeth, stubby gill rakers, and almost identical body and fin shapes, habitat, and behavior. These similarities and others are suggestive of a worldwide complex of large cubera-type snappers that may be more closely related to each other than to most other members of the genus Lutjanus.

It is an strong fighter and sport fish that can be caught on live baits, jigs, spoons, feathers, plugs, or pork rind fished or trolled at up to 5 miles per hour. It is an active night predator of smaller fishes and crustaceans. It is excellent eating and is greatly prized as a sports catch.

Common Snook (Centropomus undecimalis)

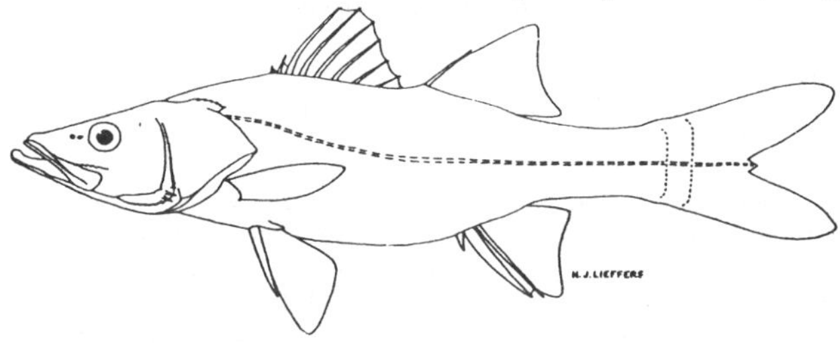

Black Snook (Centropomus nigrescens)

SNOOK / *Centropomus spp.* Lacepede (1802) (12 species);

CENTROPOMIDAE FAMILY; also called robalo

The genus *Centropomus* is confined to the American tropics and subtropics. Six species occur in the Atlantic and six in the Pacific. None occur in both oceans. They inhabit shallow coastal waters, estuaries and brackish lagoons, often penetrating far inland in fresh water. Their movements between fresh and salt water are seasonal, but they stay close to shore and never stray far from estuaries.

They are very distinctive and it would be difficult to confuse them with any other fishes. The lower jaw protrudes and a highly prominent black lateral line runs from the top of the gill cover along the sides and all the way through the tail. The body is compressed and the snout depressed and pike-like. Two dorsal fins are separated by a gap. The second anal spine is conspicuous, spurlike, much thicker than the first and third. The margin of the preopercle is serrate, with 1-5 enlarged denticles at angle.

One of the axioms relating to fish species is that the colors will likely be variable depending on season, habitat, and/or any number of other conditions. The snook is no exception. The back of the snook may be brown, brown-gold, olive green, dark gray, greenish silver, or black, depending largely on the areas the fish inhabits. The flanks and belly are silvery.

Its diet consists mainly of fish and crustaceans. Fishing methods include trolling or casting artificial lures or still fishing with live baits like pinfish, mullet, shrimp, crabs, or other small fish. Best fishing is said to be on the changing tide, especially high falling tide around river mouths and coastal shores and night fishing from bridges and in ocean inlets. A flooding or rising tide is more productive at creek heads.

An excellent table fish with delicate, white, flaky meat, it is a member of the Centropomidae family, which also includes the 200 lb (90.72 kg) Nile perch *(Lates niloticus)* and the barramundi *(Lates calcarifer)*. It usually matures by the third year and has a life span of at least seven years. It is very sensitive to temperature and may not survive at temperatures below about 60°F (15°C).

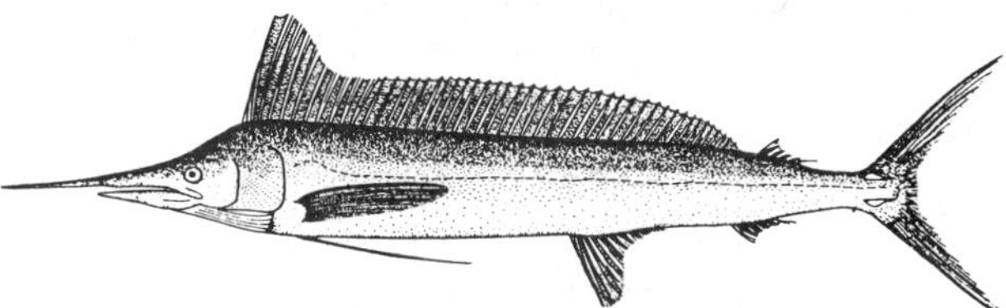

Longbill Spearfish *(Tetrapturus pfluegeri)*

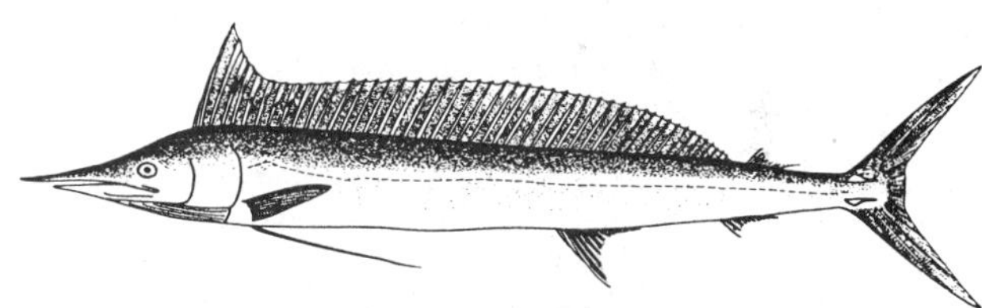

Shortbill Spearfish *(Tetrapturus angustirostris)*

SPEARFISH
/ *Tetrapturus pfluegeri* Robins & de Sylva, 1963;
/ *Tetrapturus angustirostris* Tanaka, 1914; and
/ *Tetrapturus belone* Rafinesque, 1810; ISTIOPHORIDAE FAMILY; also called longbill spearfish, shortbill spearfish, shortnose spearfish, slender spearfish, Mediterranean spearfish

The spearfishes are cosmopolitan, but nowhere are they abundant. The longbill spearfish *(Tetrapturus pfluegeri)* is known to occur in the northwest Atlantic from New Jersey to Venezuela, including the Gulf of Mexico. Japanese longliners have also recorded its occurrence in the north central Atlantic, in the south Atlantic, and off South Africa. The shortbill spearfish *(T. angustirostris)* is known in the Pacific and Indian Oceans. It is not reported to occur in the Mediterranean, but has been captured in the Atlantic Ocean west of the Cape of Good Hope, South Africa. The Mediterranean spearfish *(T. belone)* is known to occur only in the Mediterranean Sea.

It can be distinguished from other billfishes by its slender, lightweight body, short bill, and its dorsal fin which is highest anteriorly (higher than in the marlins and lower than in the sailfish). The vent is located well in front of the anal fin, in all other billfish it is located close to it. The bill of the shortbill spearfish is barely longer than its lower jaw, whereas in the longbill spearfish it is about twice as long, but still quite short by billfish standards. The pectoral fins of the shortbill and Mediterranean spearfishes barely reach to the curve of the lateral line. In the longbill spearfish they extend beyond the curve. The longbill spearfish has more elements (45 to 53) in the first dorsal fin than any other Atlantic billfish. The shortbill spearfish of the Pacific has approximately the same count (47-50 elements), but the Mediterranean spearfish has fewer (39-46). The lateral line is single and arches above the pectoral fins. The dorsal fin is bright blue and has no spots. The vertical bars on the body are never as prominent as in other billfish and may show only slightly or not at all.

They are pelagic, off shore, deep-water fishes. They feed at or near the surface, mainly on small and medium-sized fishes and squids, including dolphin, sauries, flying fish, needlefish and pilot fish. They appear to be available all year in small numbers. Fishing methods are the same as for other billfish, but with lighter tackle. Most are taken incidentally. Spearfishes are fairly good eating, though the flesh is dark.

Available data indicate that the longbill spearfish matures by the age of two and rarely lives past three years of age. Maximum age may be four to five years. Some scientists believe that a fourth species of spearfish *(Tetrapturus georgei*; Lowe, 1840) exists. Called the roundscale spearfish, it occurs around Sicily, Portugal, and Spain and is said to resemble the so-called hatchet marlin. The hatchet marlin has not yet been proven to be a separate species, however, and is presently considered to be a variation of the white marlin, which may also be the fate of the roundscale spearfish.

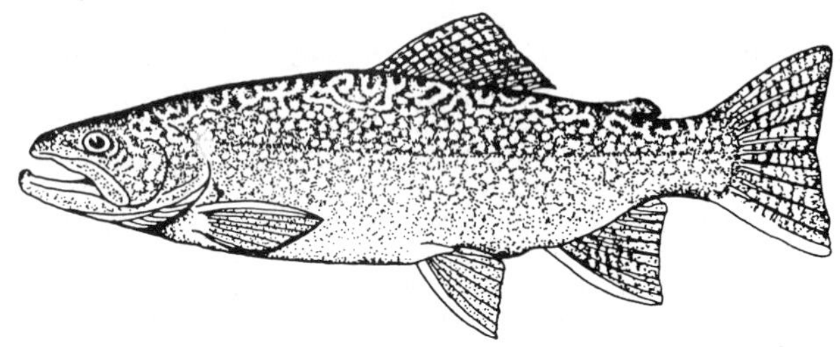

SPLAKE / *Salvelinus namaycush x Salvelinus fontinalis*; hybrid SALMONIDAE FAMILY; also called wendigo

It is a fertile cross between two chars, the lake trout *(Salvelinus namaycush)* and the brook trout *(S. fontinalis)*. This hybridization does not occur in nature, but is propagated by man. Once crossed, however, this hybrid can reproduce itself. It has been "planted" in the Great Lakes and various other parts of North America, particularly in Ontario, Canada where a program for selective breeding of this hybrid has been underway for some time with considerable success. The first cross between the lake trout and the brook trout was made in the United States. Because of the splake's fast growth rate, it has been seen as an excellent candidate for restocking waters where lake trout stocks have been decimated by the sea lamprey, as occurred in some of the Great Lakes.

The splake is difficult to identify externally because it resembles both parents in different aspects. The body shape is intermediate between the heavier lake trout and the slimmer brook trout. The shape of the tail is also intermediate. It is not as deeply forked as that of the lake trout, and more closely resembles the slightly indented tail of the brook trout. In coloration and markings, the splake more closely resembles the brook trout. It can be positively identified by the number of pyloric caeca, the worm-like appendages on the intestinal tract right after the stomach. The brook trout, which is the smaller parent, has only 23-55 (usually less than 50) pyloric caeca, while the intermediate-sized hybrid has 65-85, and the lake trout, the larger parent, has 93-208 (usually 120-180).

The quality of the splake as a food fish is excellent, and due to its initial fast growth rate and game nature it is highly regarded by anglers as well. The name "splake" is a combination of the words "speckled" from speckled trout, which is an alternate common name for brook trout, and "lake" from lake trout.

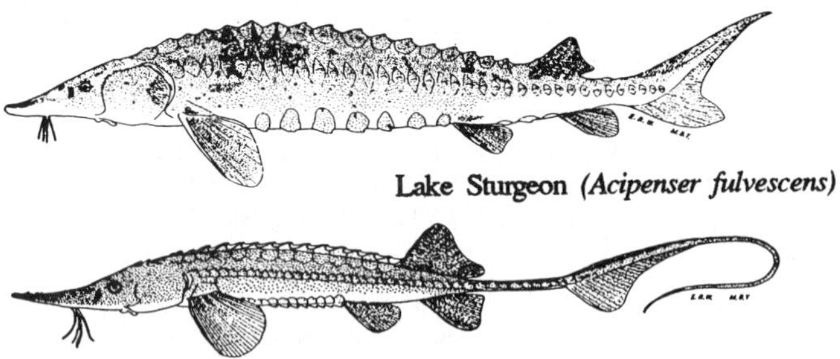

Lake Sturgeon *(Acipenser fulvescens)*

Shovelnose Sturgeon *(Scaphirhynchus platorynchus)*

STURGEON

 / *Acipenser spp.* (16 species)
 / *Scaphirhynchus spp.* (2 species)
 / *Huso spp.* (2 species)

 / *Pseudoscaphirhynchus spp.* (3 species); collective, ACIPENSERIDAE FAMILY

All sturgeons are either anadromous or freshwater fishes. Shortnose sturgeon *(Acipenser brevirostrum)* are found along the Atlantic coast from New Brunswick, Canada to Florida, U.S.A. Lake sturgeon *(A. fulvescens)* are found from the Hudson Bay, Canada to the Gulf of Mexico, U.S.A. Green sturgeon *(A. medirostris)* are found along the coastal North Pacific from the Gulf of Alaska to southern California, U.S.A., as well as in China, Japan, Korea and Russia. Atlantic sturgeon *(A.. oxyrhynchus)* are found from Labrador, Canada to Florida, U.S.A., with a subspecies in the Gulf of Mexico. White sturgeon *(A.. transmontanus)* are found along the Pacific coast from the Aleutian Islands to California, U.S.A. The pallid sturgeon *(Scaphirhynchus albus)* and the shovelnose sturgeon *(S, platorhynchus)* occur only in the U.S.A., primarily in the Missouri and Mississippi River systems.

They are easy to identify as a group. Some species grow to a length of over 20 ft (6 m) and well over 2,000 lb (907 kg) and may live to be over 100 years old. The body is long and heavy and is covered with 5 rows of large, heavy scutes. One row runs along the middle of each side, one along the back and two along the belly. The scutes become smoother as the sturgeon grows older and in some species, they may gradually disappear by absorption. On each side of the head there is a huge bony plate that serves as the gill cover. This plate is actually an expanded subopercle bone (the opercle bone and branchiostegal rays are absent in the sturgeon). The rest of the head is covered with smaller bony plates. The "nose" or snout is long, more so in some species than in others. The mouth is protrusible, like a sucker's, and is preceded by four barbels resembling a mustache. The eyes are small by comparisons to the overall size of the body. The single dorsal fin is located far back on the body near the tail and directly above the anal fin. The tail is heterocercal, resembling the tail of some sharks. The upper lobe is longer than the lower lobe.

The sturgeon roe is the only true caviar. The largest and most highly prized eggs come from the beluge *(Huso huso)* in Russia. This species has been recorded up to a weight of 3,359 lb (1,524 kg) and a female weighing 2,707 lb (1,228 kg) caught in 1924 yielded 542 lb (246 kg) of roe. A smaller, highly desirable, sturgeon from Russia is the osietr *(A. sturio)* which produces a golden-brown caviar preferred by some European gourmets. The sterlet *(A. ruthenus)*, which is almost extinct, produces the legendary "gold caviar of the Czars".

The most highly regarded North American species is the white sturgeon, both for its flesh and its roe. It may produce up to 200 lb (90.72 kg) of eggs, which are readily marketed as caviar. Two other North American species, the lake sturgeon and the Atlantic sturgeon, are also well regarded. The latter is often referred to as "Albany beef" and the roe of both species is sold as caviar. The green sturgeon although edible is said to have dark flesh with an unpleasant odor and a strong, disagreeable taste.

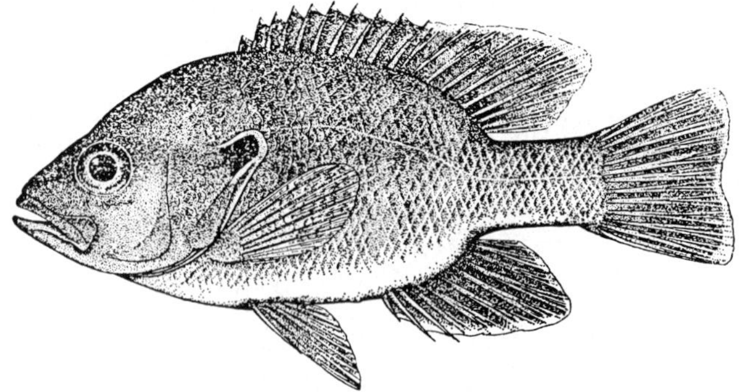

SUNFISH, green / *Lepomis cyanellus* Rafinesque, 1819; CENTRARCHIDAE FAMILY; also called green perch, sand bass, blue-spotted sunfish, rubbertail

Occurs naturally west of the Appalachians throughout the eastern and central U.S.A. and into Ontario, Canada and northern Mexico. Its range has been extended so that it is found east of the Appalachians in Oregon, Nevada, and California, as well as throughout the southwestern U.S.A. and Germany. It is absent from peninsular Florida and most of the northwest portion of the U.S.A.

It has a larger mouth and a thicker longer body than most sunfishes of the genus *Lepomis*, and in this respect more closely resembles the warmouth *(L. gulosus)* or its larger relatives of the genus *Micropterus*, such as the smallmouth bass. Most species of sunfish in the genus Lepomis are deep-bodied, notably roundish in profile, and extremely compressed laterally. As in other sunfishes the dorsal fins are connected and there is an extended gill cover flat, or "ear lobe", which is black edged with light red, pink, or yellow. The body is usually brown to olive green with a bronze to emerald green sheen, paling to yellow-green on the lower sides and yellow or white on the belly. There are emerald or bluish spots on the head and sometimes, wavy or radiating lines of the same color. Seven to twelve dark bars are vaguely visible on the back.

This is a panfish with white, flaky flesh. it is taken by angling with worms or other small live baits, flies, spinners, or poppers.

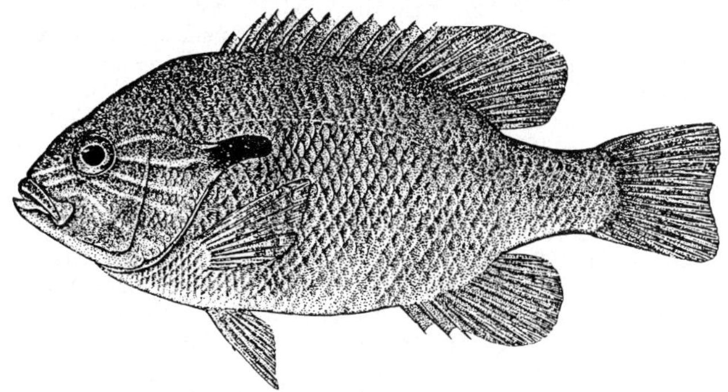

SUNFISH, redbreast / *Lepomis auritus* (Linnaeus, 1758); CENTRARCHIDAE FAMILY; also called yellowbelly sunfish, sun perch, redbreast bream, longear sunfish (not to be confused with Lepomis megalotis which goes by that name)

It is native to the east coast of North America from New Brunswick in Canada south along the Atlantic slope, east of the Appalachians, to about central Florida, but only as far west in the Florida panhandle as the Apalachicola River. It has been introduced into nearby states, and into lakes in northern Italy.

The belly, or ventral surface, ranges in color from yellow to orange-red or crimson red and the "ear lobe" (a lobe or flat on the gill cover) is usually long and narrow. In adult males of this species the lobe is actually longer than in the longear sunfish *(L. megalotis)*. The two species are readily distinguished by the fact that the gill cover lobe of the redbreast sunfish is completely black (or blue-black) all the way to the tip and is narrower than the eyes. The lobe of the longear sunfish is much wider and is bordered by a thin margin of pale red or yellow around the black. The pectoral fins of both species are short and roundish as compared to the longer, pointed pectoral fins of redear sunfish *(L. microlophus)*, and the opercular flaps are softer and more flexible than the rigid flaps of species such as the pumpkinseed sunfish *(L. gibbosus)*.

This is an excellent panfish and a scrappy fighter. It can be caught with baits or lures and it can even be taken at night.

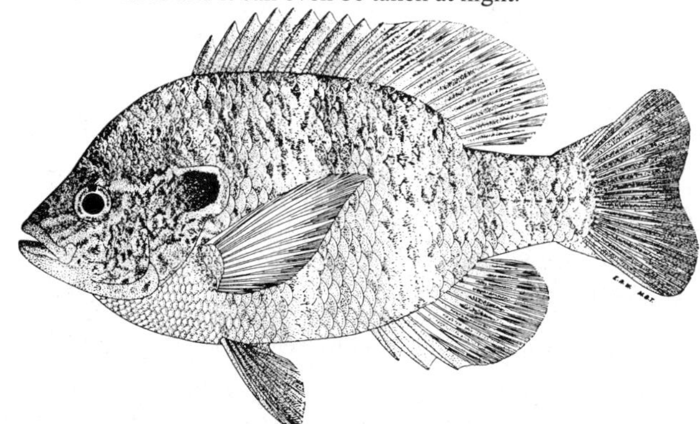

SUNFISH, redear / *Lepomis microlophus* (Gunther, 1859); CENTRARCHIDAE FAMILY; also called shellcracker, stump-knocker, yellow bream

This species is native to the U.S. Gulf states from Texas to Florida, including all of the Florida peninsula, and north to Indiana and North Carolina. Through introductions, the redear's range has been extended northward to the Great Lakes and transplanted populations also exist in the West.

This is a rather large sunfish known to reach over 4.5 lb (2.04 kg). As is typical of sunfishes, the redear has a small mouth, connected dorsal fins and a roundish, laterally compressed body. Its long, pointed, slightly falcate pectoral fins distinguish it from both the longear sunfish *(Lepomis megalotis)* and the redbreast sunfish *(L. auritus)*, which have short, roundish pectoral fins. The opercular flap is also much shorter than in the other two species and is black, with a red spot or margin at the tip. It can be distinguished from the similar looking pumpkinseed *(L. gibbosus)* by the fact that its gill cover flap is semi-flexible and can be bent at least to right angles, whereas the flap on the pumpkinseed is rigid. It also lacks

the spots on the dorsal fin and the bluish emerald lines on the sides of the head that are characteristic of the pumpkinseed. The body is slightly less compressed than that of the bluegill *(L. macrochirus)*, which differs from the redear most noticeably in the fact that its gill cover flap is entirely black without any spot or trim.

Like the bluegill and other sunfishes, it is an excellent panfish with white, flaky meat. It is less likely to be caught on artificials, such as spinners or poppers, than the other sunfishes. It prefers small live baits such as worms, grubs, insects and sometimes shrimp. Rarely, the redear will take a small fly or other small lure. It is strictly an angler's fish and has no commercial value.

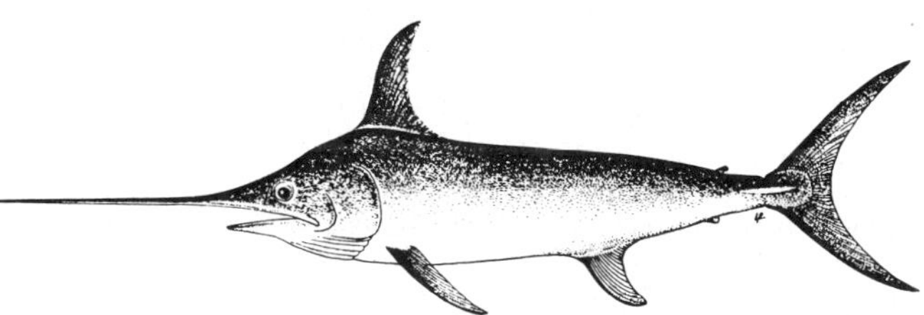

SWORDFISH / *Xiphias gladius* Linnaeus, 1758; XIPHIIDAE FAMILY; also called broadbill, broadbill swordfish

Found worldwide in temperate and tropical oceanic and continental shelf waters from the surface to depths of 400-500 fathoms or more. Except when spawning, females prefer cool, deep waters near submarine canyons or coral banks. Males prefer to remain in somewhat warmer waters.

Characteristically, it has a smooth, very broad, flattened sword (broadbill) that is significantly longer and wider than the bill of any other billfish. It also has a nonretractable dorsal fin, rigid, nonretractable pectoral fins, and a single, but very large keel on either side of the caudal peduncle. Adults lack scales and swordfish of all sizes lack ventral fins. The back may be dark brown, bronze, dark metallic purple, grayish blue or black. The sides may be dark like the back or dusky. The belly and lower sides of the head are dirty white or light brown.

This pelagic, migratory species usually travels alone. It uses its sword for defense and to kill or stun food such as squid, dolphin, mackerel, bluefish and various other midwater and deep-sea pelagic species. Occasional attacks on boats have been authenticated by the recovery of swords found broken off in wooden hulls. One swordfish attacked Alvin, the Woods Hole Oceanographic Institute submarine, at a depth of 330 fathoms and wedged its sword so tightly into a seam that it could not be withdrawn.

Fishing methods include presenting trolling baits or deep drifting at night with bait such as squid. They often bask on the surface with their dorsal and tail fins protruding from the water, making them susceptible to harpooners and longliners who make the majority of swordfish catches. They are finicky, easily frightened by an approaching boat, and rarely strike blindly. Usually the bait must be presented carefully and repeatedly before the swordfish will take it. The soft mouth makes hookup uncertain and the slashing bill can make short work of an angler's line or leader. Once a swordfish has been spotted the speed of the boat should not be changed appreciably and the bait should be eased quietly and gently in front of the fish. Squid is the most popular bait, though Spanish mackerel, eel, mullet, herring, tuna and live or dead bonito are also used. To land a broadbill is considered by many to be the highest achievement in angling.

Very large swordfish are always females. The males seldom exceed 200 lb (90 kg). The meat of the swordfish is excellent eating, making this fish the object of large commercial fisheries.

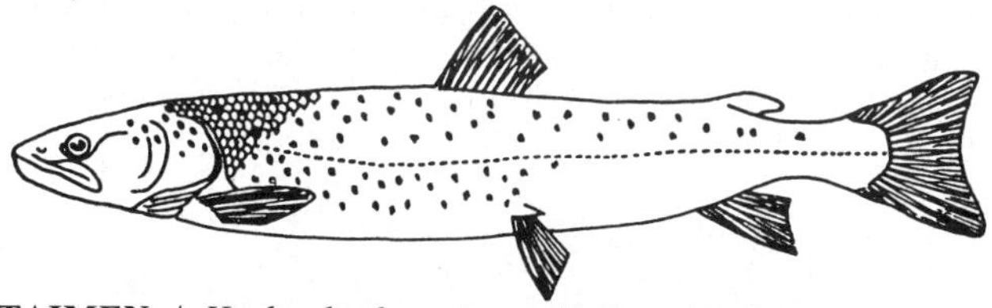

TAIMEN / *Hucho hucho taimen* (Pallas, 1773); SALMONIDAE FAMILY; also called taimen salmon

There are four species of the genus Hucho, which include the species *Hucho hucho*, the huchen and *Hucho hucho taimen,* the taimen. While the two subspecies of *Hucho hucho* cannot be separated on the basis of morphology or meristics, their geographical separation allows us to distinguish between the two.

The huchen is restricted to the Danube River drainage and the taimen to the Ural-Siberian-Amur drainages, most of which flow into the Arctic Ocean. Ranges of the huchen and taimen are disjunct (do not overlap) and are separated by the Eastern European Flatland.

The taimen inhabits large rivers with fast currents, often to their estuaries. It also occurs in lakes. In spring, it ascends the rivers and enters shallow creeks, spawning in May.

They probably attain the largest sizes of any salmonid fish. A report exists of a 231 lb specimen taken in a commercial net in 1943, but the largest authenticated record is 123 lb (55.8 kg), slightly less than a commercially caught 126 lb (57.2 kg) Chinook salmon.

Physically, they resemble a northern pike. The body is round and elongated and the head flattened with an enormous terminal mouth. Like huchen, taimen are specked with dark spots over the entire body, predominating on the upper portions, including the head and fins. The tail and anal fins are a crimson red. During the spawning period, almost all the body becomes copper-red.

Taimen fishing is similar to that of huchen, flies, plugs, large spoons, and spinners are all highly effective, and of coarse, any live bait should be productive. The voracious taimen reportedly will strike at anything resembling wounded prey. Just as large prey are sought by large fish, lure size should match the size of fish sought by the angler, monster fish require monster baits!

While huchen populations have diminished rapidly with over-exploitation and habitat deterioration, taimen are just emerging as a popular sportfish. Hopefully, with due care from concerned anglers, the taimen population will not suffer the same fate.

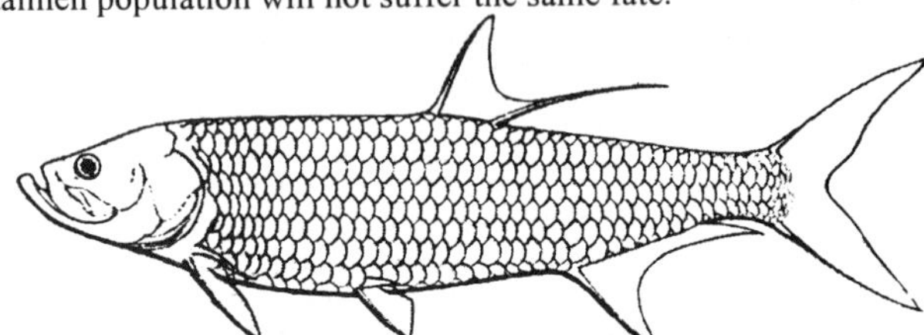

TARPON / *Megalops atlanticus* Valenciennes, 1846; ELOPIDAE FAMILY; also called silver king, cuffum

Occurs in warm temperate tropical and subtropical waters of the Atlantic Ocean. This coastal fish can be found both inshore and offshore. Because of its ability to gulp air directly into the air bladder by "rolling" at the surface, the tarpon is able to enter brackish and fresh waters that are stagnant and virtually depleted of oxygen. Such areas are relatively free of predators, thus offering a convenient refuse for the young.

The body is compressed and covered with very large scales. The lower jaw juts out and up. The teeth are small and fine, and the throat is covered by a bony plate. The dorsal fin consists of 12-16 soft rays (no spines) the last of which is greatly elongated. The anal fin has 19-25 soft rays. The lateral line is straight, even along the anterior portion with a scale count of 41-48. The back is greenish or bluish varying in darkness from silvery to almost black. The sides and belly are brilliant silver. Inland, brackish water tarpons frequently have a golden or brownish color because of tannic acid.

They may shed up to 12 million eggs. The eggs hatch at sea and the eel-like larvae drift in shore where they undergo a metamorphosis, shrinking to half the size previously attained and taking on the more recognizable features of the tarpon as they begin to grow again. Tarpon, bonefish, ladyfish and eels all undergo a similar leptocephalus stage, but the first three fish all have forked tails even at the larval state, whereas the eel does not. Tarpon grow rather slowly and usually don't reach maturity until they are six or seven years old and about 4 ft (1.2 m) long.

Fishing methods are still fishing with live mullet, pinfish, crabs, shrimp, etc., or casting or trolling with spoons, plugs, or other artificial lures. The best fishing is at night when the tarpon is feeding. They are hard to hook because of their hard, bony mouths. Once hooked they put up a stubborn and spectacular fight, often leaping up to 10 feet out of the water. It was one of the first saltwater species to be declared a game fish. It is edible, though it does not rate high as table fare with most people.

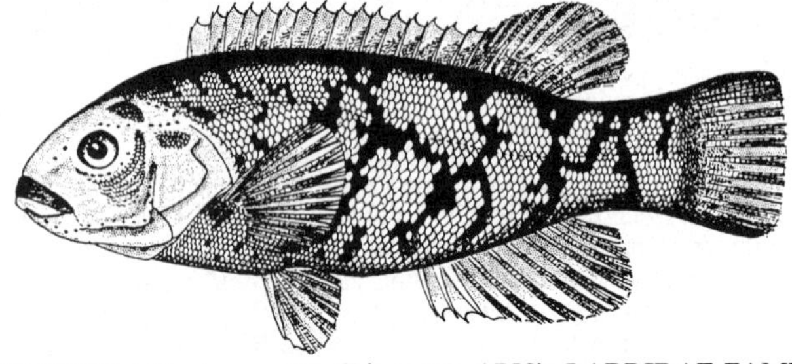

TAUTOG / *Tautoga onitis* (Linnaeus, 1758); LABRIDAE FAMILY; also called blackfish, tog, Molly George, chub, oysterfish

Occurs in the western Atlantic Ocean from Nova Scotia, Canada to South Carolina, U.S.A., with the greatest abundance between Cape Cod, Massachusetts and Delaware Bay. It is known to move in and out of bays or in shore and off shore according to the water temperature, but it does not make extensive migrations up and down the coast. It prefers shallow waters over rocky bottoms, shell beds, inshore wrecks, etc., which it often inhabits year-round.

It is a member of the wrasse family which, with 450 species in 60 known genera, is one of the largest families of fishes. It includes, the cunner *(Tautogolabrus adspersus)*, the hogfish *(Lachnolaimus maximus)* and the California redfish *(Pimelometo-pon pulcher)*.

The first dorsal fin has 16-17 spines of almost equal length. The short second dorsal fin consists of 10 somewhat longer soft rays. The anal fin has 3 spines and 7-8 soft rays. There is a detached area of small scales behind and beneath the eye, but none of the opercle. The lateral line is arched more or less following the contour of the back and has a scale count of 69-73. There are 9 gill rakers on the first branchial arch, 3 on the upper limb and 6 on the lower limb. A number of small teeth are present along the sides of the jaws and there are 2-3 large canine teeth in the tips. Young are generally brown or greenish brown with irregular dark mottling or blotching on the flanks. Larger specimens may be entirely black or charcoal gray, sometimes with greenish overtones, or they may be mottled with brown, black or white. The belly and chin are white or gray and there may be spots on the chin. Females develop a white saddle down the middle of each side during spawning.

Its diet is mainly of mollusks and crustaceans, the blue mussel being the most abundant food item. Fishing methods include bait fishing over rocky bottoms, shell beds, or in shore wrecks from an anchored boat, as well as bottom fishing from the shore in the late spring and fall months. Baits include crabs, clams, worms, mussels, shrimp and sand bugs. It is not a fast or extremely active species, but it puts up a very stubborn fight. Its year-round availability, together with its large size and stubborn disposition, make it a popular sport fish. The flesh is edible and of good quality.

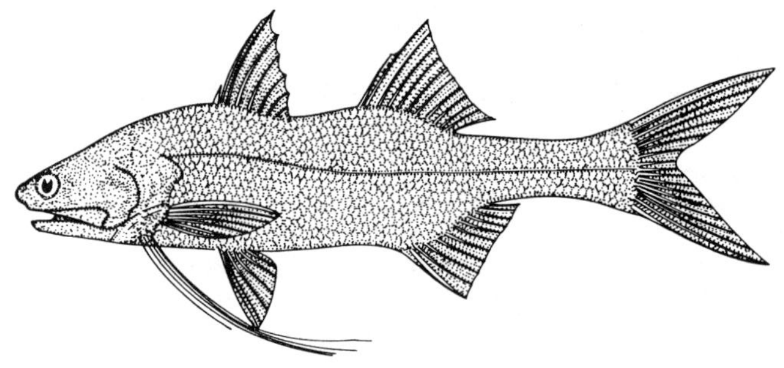

THREADFIN, king / *Polynemus sheridani* (Macleay); POLYNEMIDAE FAMILY; also known as threadfin salmon, Burnett salmon, Cooktown salmon, tassel-fish, putty-nose

It is found from the Queensland coast of Australia to the Gulf of Papua. Most abundant in the Northern Territory and northern part of Western Australia, it is a species of shallow coastal waters, occurring over muddy bottoms and in rivers, bays, and estuaries.

Its most obvious feature is the long, trailing filaments that extend from the pectoral area (around the throat), and which serve as feelers in the murky, discolored waters with which threadfins typically are associated.

It is one of the largest threadfin species, attaining weights of over 66 lb (30 kg). It is distinguished from similar species of its family by the fact that is has five filaments (as opposed to three or four in most Indo-Pacific species) and by its pectoral fin rays, which are simple instead of branched. The Indian threadfin *(Polynemus indicus)*, another large species, also has five filaments, but its pectoral rays are branched, each ray forming a pair at the extremity.

Its color is generally silvery with a darker, blue-grayish back. The pectoral fins are orangish; the dorsal fins and tail, slaty gray. Live fish may have a golden to pinkish flush over the silvery sides, and this is believed by some to have led to the misnomer, "salmon" In fact, the threadfins are in no way related to the salmons or to their relatives of the Salmonidae family.

It has a deeply-forked tail and two fairly large dorsal fins of approximately equal size. The tail lobes are long but do not end in extended filaments as they do in the Indian threadfin. The single anal fin is similar in size and shape to the second dorsal fin.

Fishing for threadfins is best when a run-in or run-out tide is underway, clouding and muddying up the waters, at the mouths of estuaries and saltwater creeks. It seems to prefer foraging for its food (crabs, prawns, and the like) under the cover of a top layer of sediment. Live baits fished at night have also been known to catch large specimens, as have poppers and plugs at dusk. It is a "lazy" swimmer like the bonefish when foraging, but might be described as a tornado on a string once hooked, seemingly going in all directions at once. It may also leap from the water or streak off on long runs.

It is frequently compared with the barramundi for its eating quality. Unscrupulous netters have been known to include threadfin fillets with barramundi fillets at market. The taste is excellent and there is a healthy commercial market for it.

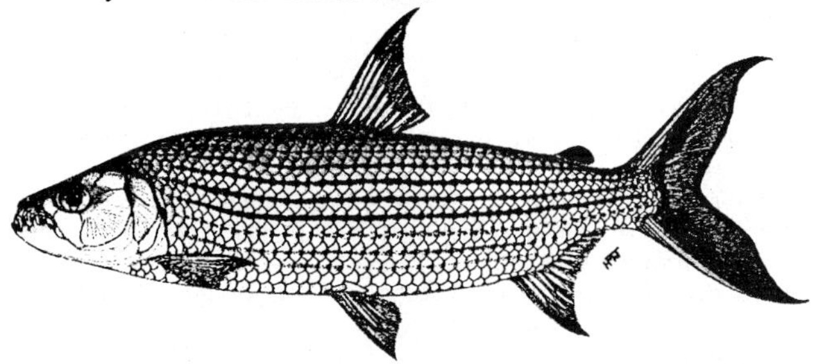

TIGERFISH / *Hydrocynus vittatus* (Castelnau, 1861) CHARACIDAE FAMILY; also called tiervis, ngweshi, maluvali, mcheni, muvanga, manga, shabani, simu-kuta, uthlangi, uluthlangi

Vittatus tigerfish has a wide distribution from west Africa to the Nile and southward to the Zaire, Zambezi, and Limpopo systems. It occurs in Lake Turkana (L. Rudolph) which was once connected to the Nile but has not been able to cross the Murchison Falls and reach Lake Victoria nor has it been able to colonize Lake Kivu from Lake Tanganyika.

The tigerfishes belong to the Characidae family, a large and diverse family containing "toothy critters" such as the potentially dangerous piranhas, biara and payara found in South America and the beautiful tetras and pacus familiar to home aquarists.

They are more vividly colored than the larger goliath tigerfish with silvery flanks and a bluish sheen on the back. The deeply forked caudal fin is red edged with black, the adipose fin is black anteriorly, clear posteriorly. The pectoral and pelvic fins are tinged with red or orange as is the anterior part of the anal fin. Black horizontal stripes run through each scale row and persist long after death. They also have gill rakers that are long, approximately equal to the gill filaments. They grow to about 34 lbs (15.5 kg).

They are efficient active predators, feeding on fish up to 40% of their own length. They have fantastic appetites, and readily take artificial lures, live bait such as the Lake Tanganyika sardines (kapenta) and even prey on their own species.

The tigerfishes are among the best known and most important game fishes in Africa, commanding high respect amongst anglers, and as such, an important asset to the tourist industry. They are one of the most important components of commercial catches<$&tigerfish, giant[-]>

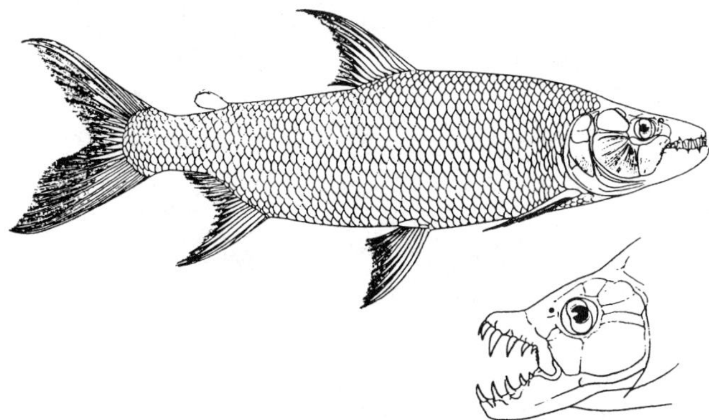

TIGERFISH, giant / *Hydrocynus goliath* (Boulenger, 1898) CHARACIDAE FAMILY; also called goliath tigerfish

The giant tigerfish is restricted to the Zaire River system, Lualaba River, Lake Upemba and Lake Tanganyika.

It is overall silvery in color with no conspicuous stripes. A few broad stripes may show up under the scales after death. It has fourteen or more teeth in the upper jaw and very short gill rakers, less than one-third the length of the gill filaments. The largest giant tigerfish may exceed 110 lbs (50 kg) but stories of fish weighing up to 132 lb (60 kg) have yet to be authenticated.

Its ferocious appearance gives ample indication of its predatory

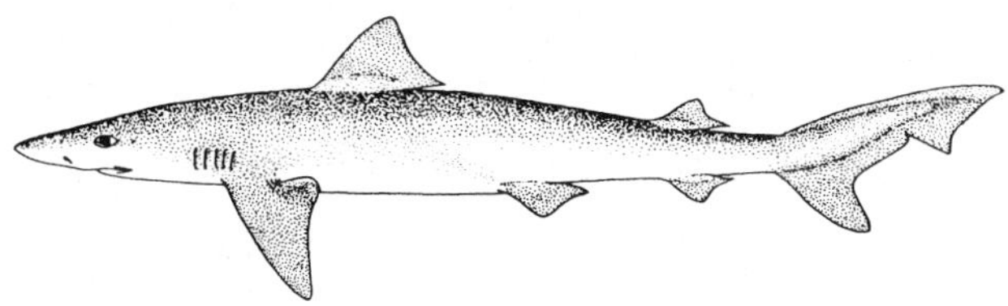

habits. This strong fighter is one of the great freshwater game fish species. It jumps repeatedly when hooked, will take almost any kind of bait, including artificial and is powerful even when taken on heavy tackle. A wire leader is essential due to the sharp teeth.

TOPE / *Galeorhinus galeus* (Linnaeus, 1758); TRIAKIDAE FAMILY; also called toper, school shark, soupfin, oil shark, vitamin shark

There are several populations of tope sharks that are isolated from one another but they probably represent only a single species.

Topes are moderately large, wide ranging, active, schooling sharks found in coastal continental waters of the Eastern Pacific, Western South Atlantic (not in North American waters), Eastern Atlantic, Southwestern Indian Ocean and Western South Pacific.

They are characterized by a rather long, pointed snout and oval eye and distinctive teeth, which have a sharp oblique cusp and 3-5 coarse basal serrations. The second dorsal fin is nearly over the anal fin and about the same size. The terminal lobe of the caudal fin is extremely large, about half the length of the upper lobe. Tope are sometimes confused with the spiny dogfish *(Squalus acanthias)* in some European waters, but unlike the spiny dogfish, they have no spines in the dorsal fins.

This is a frequent, popular catch of anglers, commonly taken by rod and reel particularly in the British Isles, off South Africa, California, and southern Australia. It is also fished in other areas where it occurs, although the stocks are depleted in some regions.

Primarily an opportunistic predator on moderate-sized bony fishes (taken alive), this shark readily feeds on some invertebrates and in some areas crabs and squid may be important prey items. It has a strong preference for very fresh fish or squid bait over slightly stale or even fresh-frozen bait presented on hooks. It will fight actively when hooked, and may give a far better fight on light tackle than its relative the blue shark *(Prionace glauca)*.

Tope are ovoviviparous, giving birth to 6 to 52 (average 35) young per litter, the number increasing with the size of the female. While the average weight of most tope is about 22-44 lbs (12-20 kg) the maximum weight is about 100 lb (45.36 kg).

Its meat is eaten fresh, fresh frozen, or dried salted, its fins are used for sharkfin soup. Tope were once intensively fished for the exceptionally high concentrations of Vitamin A found in the liver.

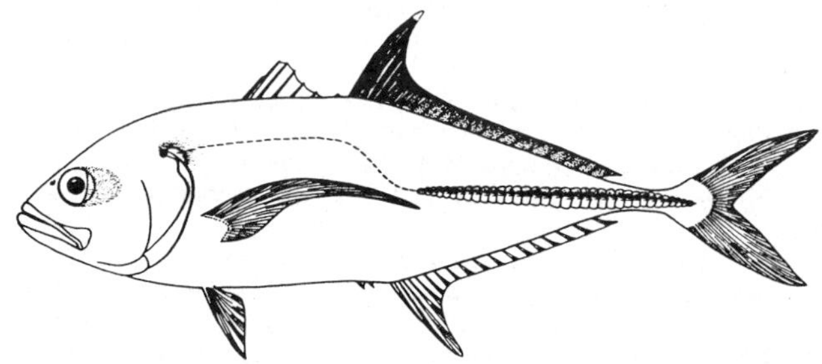

TREVALLY, bigeye / *Caranx (Caranx) sexfasciatus* Quoy & Gaimard, 1825; CARANGIDAE FAMILY; also called turrum, ulua, previously known by the misnomers giant or great trevally

Broadly found in tropical waters throughout the Indian and Pacific Oceans from east Africa to western America. It is found in rocky areas near shore as well as at outside reef drop-offs on the edge of deep tide-running channels, and in the deeper waters beyond the reef. This species is replaced in the Atlantic Ocean by its close relative the horse-eye jack *(Caranx latus)*.

The maximum verified size is 30 in (757 mm) fork length. The breast is completely scaled. The body is not very deep (more elongated) with the head curved to a slightly pointed snout. The eyes are relatively large. The lateral line is strongly curved anteriorly. The straight portion consists of 28-37 scutes. The first dorsal fin has 8 spines (rarely 7). The second has 1 spine and 19-22 soft rays and the anal fin has 3 spines (2 are detached) and 15-17 soft rays. There is a total of 20-25 gill rakers on the first branchial arch. There is a pair of lateral keels on either side of the caudal peduncle. Body color ranges from silvery to dusky or dark, especially along the back. The dorsal fin lobe is dark with a white tip and none on the pectoral fins. Juveniles are golden yellow and have 4-7 broad, dark vertical bars on the body.

Adults feed most actively at night, especially very dark nights. Diet includes eels and crustaceans, blennies *(pao'o)*, damselfish *(mamo)*, and other fishes. Fishing methods include trolling baits and lures, angling with live or cut baits while drifting or at anchor, and surf fishing. Trolled lure or bait should be moved slowly among other bait fish or along the outside drop-offs of reefs or rocky ledges. Mullet, herring, sauri, garfish, anchovy, squid, or strip baits are used as well as Konaheads, knuckleheads, bulletheads, feathers, plastic jigs, plastic fish and squid, drone spoons and rope lures.

The flesh is pinkish and is rated fair in taste and quality. In some areas of the Pacific, it is highly esteemed as food. It is also frequently used for strip baits, cut baits, or as chum.

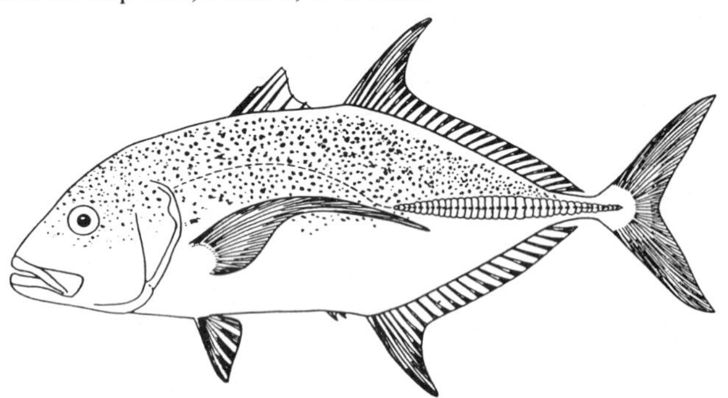

TREVALLY, bluefin / *Caranx (Caranx) melampygus* Cuvier & Valenciennes, 1833; CARANGIDAE FAMILY; also called blue-spotted jack, starry jack, blue crevally, omilu, bluefin kingfish

The bluefin trevally is widely distributed in the tropical and subtropical waters of the Indian and Pacific oceans. It can be found on the Pacific coast of America from Cabo San Lucas on the southern tip of Baja, California, Mexico, and the Islas Revillagigedos and Tres Marias to Panama. It is common throughout Hawaii and Polynesia, occurring in harbors, channels, and on outer reefs. From Australia where it is known along the entire Queensland and northern coasts, it ranges northward through the Philippines and Micronesia to Japan. Young fish are abundant in the bays of Okinawa during September. Schools of thousands gather to spawn at the southern tip of Peleliu, in Palau, during the new moon in April. *C. melampygus* is also known from east Africa, the Ryukus, Mauritius, New Caledonia, India, Sir Lanka, Indonesia and Papua New Guinea. It almost certainly occurs in other parts of this range as well.

A large species growing to at least 3 ft (1 m) in length, it is among the most beautiful of the jacks or trevallys. In adults the back and flanks are a brilliant turquoise blue, silvery blue, or greenish blue, generously covered with small blue or black spots. The tail and other fins may be an even more striking blue than the body. The anal and dorsal fin lobes often are white-tipped and the tail black edged. Young fish lack spots (including the opercular spot), and have a silvery-yellow body much like that of any other jack species. Even these juveniles are distinctive with their bright yellow pectoral fins and deep blue second dorsal and anal fins.

Adults are deep-bodied and have strong scutes. The dorsal fin is moderately low, with 8 spines plus 1 very small spine ahead of the fin. The second dorsal and anal fins are long with prominent anterior lobes. The tail is deeply forked and the pectoral fins are long and falcate. The sloping forehead of the is distinctive giving this fish a profile that is readily recognizable to those who are familiar with them. Males are slightly larger than females and sexual maturity occurs at a fork length of about 15 in (40 cm).

They frequent deeper lagoon and outer reef waters during the day. In evening they enter harbors, channels, and shallow reef areas to feed, then retreat to the deeper areas. They feed actively on smaller pelagic fishes and other fishes and crustaceans. In the late evening and early morning, they can be caught by surf casters using small fish baits, crustaceans, or lures. They are also taken from boats over the in shore reefs with similar baits and jigs, and with spoons and feathers trolled at 3 to 6 miles per hour.

The flesh is firm and very good table fare, prized over most of the other species of ulua.

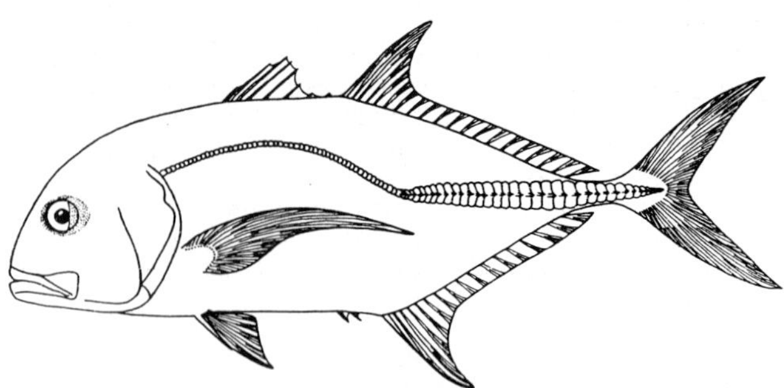

TREVALLY, giant / *Caranx (Caranx) ignobilis* (Forsskal, 1775); CARANGIDAE FAMILY; also called turrum or ulua, previously known by the misnomers "lowly" or "lesser" trevally

Inhabits coral and rock reefs in warm coastal waters of the Indian and central Pacific Oceans, eastward to the Hawaiian and Marquesas Islands. Common in the waters off Kenya and other parts of Africa as well as off Australia, New Zealand, the Philippines, Malaysia, and Hawaii. This is the most common of the trevallys found in Hawaii's and Kenya's waters.

The giant trevally, which grows to over 130 lb (62 kg), is the largest of the eight *Caranx* species which occur in the Indo-Pacific region. It has a small oval-shaped patch of scales in the center of the larger scaleless area on the breast in front of the ventral fins, distinguishing it from the bigeye trevally *(Caranx (Caranx) sexfasciatus)* whose breast is fully scaled. In some specimens (about 5%) this oval patch of scales is extensive enough to make detection of the scaleless area difficult. The body and head are usually very deep with a blunt snout. The lateral line is strongly curved anteriorly. The straight portion is covered with scutes; 25-33 in the giant trevally and 28-37 in the bigeye. The first dorsal fin consists of 8 spines, the second of 17-21 soft rays, and anal fin of 3 spines and 15-17 soft rays. Gill rakers on the first arch total 18-23. There is no spot on the operculum such as is found on the bigeye trevally, nor is there a spot at the base of the pectoral fins such as appears on the crevalle jacks (*Caranx hippos* and *Caranx caninus*), the close Atlantic and eastern Pacific relatives of this species.

Adults are sedentary, prefer rocky areas near shore or outside reef drop-offs, and feed most actively at night. Hawaiian anglers report that the darker the night the more actively they feed. It is a highly rated sport fish in the waters of Hawaii and Kenya both for its large size and for the hard fight it gives. Fishing methods include surf fishing, drifting, or still fishing using live or cut baits. Trolling with baits and lures can also bring results. Baits and lures include mullet, herring, sauri, garfish, anchovy, squid, cut strip baits, Konaheads, knuckleheads, bulletheads, feathers, plastic jigs, plastic fish and squids, drone spoons, and rope lures. The pinkish flesh is highly esteemed as food in some areas and is also frequently used for strip baits, cut baits or chum.

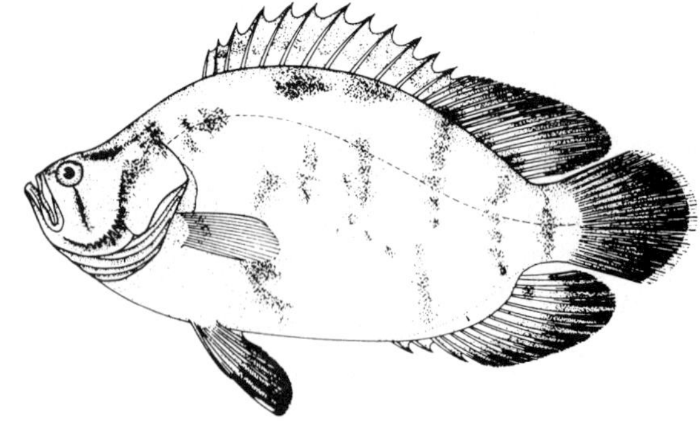

TRIPLETAIL / *Lobotes surinamensis* (Bloch, 1790); LOBOTIDAE FAMILY; also called buoy fish, buoy bass, blackfish, chobie, triplefin, flasher, lumpfish, snagdrifter, croupia roche, matsudai, dormilona, black perch, jumping cod

A cosmopolitan fish, tripletail live in tropical and subtropical seas worldwide. Their range is widespread through the Atlantic, Pacific and Indian Oceans.

They are deep-bodied perch-like fish with rounded dorsal and anal fins extending almost to the tail. At first glance they appear to have three tails, hence the most commonly used name, tripletail. Their color varies widely, from shades of yellow brown, to dark brown or black with ill defined spots and mottling.

They are most often found floating on or near the surface, hanging very near buoys (hence buoy fish or buoy bass), pier pilings or floating debris, or drifting along with currents imitating other buoyant objects.

They can also be found lurking around bottom structure such as wrecks.

All types of tackle can be used but a 30 or 40 lb (15 or 20 kg) leader or shock tippet is desirable, because once hooked tripletail will almost invariably head back to the barnacle covered refuge where found. While live shrimp seem to be the preferred bait of many anglers, tripletails will hit dead baits, jigs, plugs or shrimp pattern flies and popping bugs.

They may look like a lazy, slow fish floating at the surface, but they can move quickly when they strike, and can exhibit surprisingly powerful lunges and occasional jumps when hooked. They also grow to a substantial size, possibly reaching a weight of 50 lbs (22.68 kg) and the white, fine textured fillets are excellent eating.

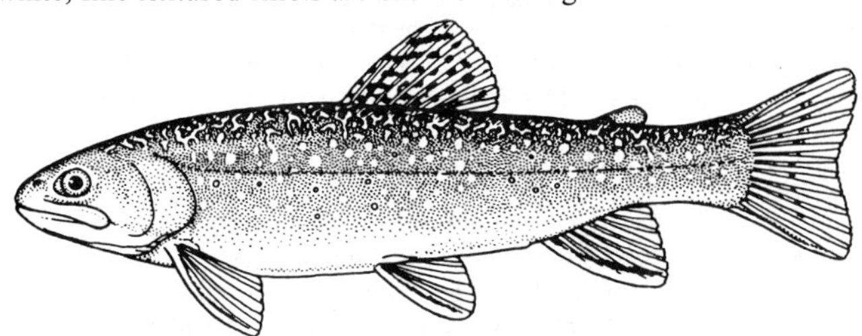

TROUT, brook / *Salvelinus fontinalis* (Mitchill, 1814); SALMONIDAE FAMILY; also called eastern brook trout, speckled or spotted trout, aurora trout, mountain trout, speckled char, brook char, salter, sea trout, square tailed trout, square-tail, mud trout, brookie, breac, coaster, native trout

It is native to northeastern North America, primarily from the Great Lakes north to the Hudson Bay and east to the Atlantic and Arctic coasts. It occurs in the Appalachians southeast of the Great Lakes to the northeastern corner of Georgia. It inhabits clear, cold mountain streams and lakes, prefering water temperatures of approximately 57°-61°F (13°-16°C). It is rarely found in waters exceeding 68°F (20°C) and temperatures of 77°-80°F (25°-27°C) are fatal. It has been introduced into areas of high elevation throughout most of western North America. Today it can be found in scattered locations from the central portions of the lower Canadian Provinces south almost to Mexico (west of Texas). It has also been introduced to other continents, notably South America (Argentina), and Europe.

It is a typical char of the Salvelinus genus. The lower fins (pectoral, pelvic and anal) of chars have a milk-white leading edge, distinguishing them from trouts. It is often identified by the light green to cream-colored wavy lines (vermiculations) on the back and top of the head, and by the pale yellowish or greenish spots and the red spots with blue halos (ocelli) on the sides. The dorsal fin has heavy black vermiculations. The basic color of the back is olive-green to dark brown, lightening to white on the belly. At spawning time, the lower flanks and belly of the males turn bright orange-red with a black edge on the lower sides. Sea-run specimens turn silvery, often with a light iridescent purplish sheen, and with only the red spots showing. The tail is squarish or only very slightly indented. All the fins are soft rayed, without spines.

As a food and game fish it rates extremely high. The flesh is white to bright orange and delicious. It is one of the most popular game fishes in northeastern North America, actively sought by both fly fishing and spinning enthusiasts. In some areas it is protected from commercial sale because of its status as a game fish.

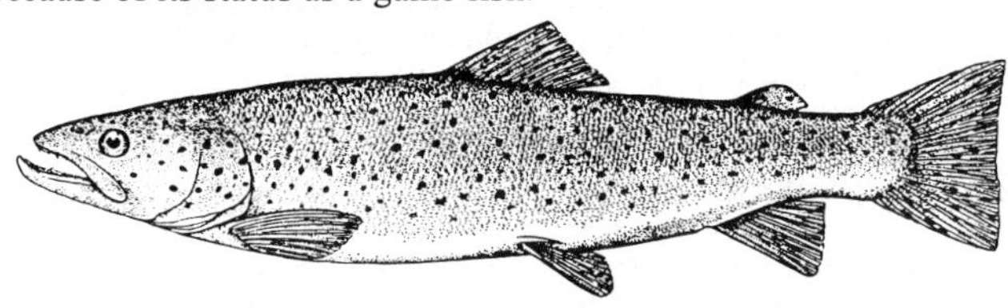

TROUT, brown / *Salmo trutta* Linnaeus, 1758; SALMONIDAE FAMILY; also called German brown trout, European brown trout, sea trout, lake trout, brook trout, river trout, bull trout, English trout, von Behr trout, Lochleven trout, German trout, breac, gealag, brownie

Native to Europe and parts of Asia, from Afghanistan and the Aral Sea across Europe to the British Isles and Iceland, and back across Scandinavia to Poluostrov Kanin (Cape Kanin), in Russia, on the Barents Sea. It has been introduced in other areas, notably, Newfoundland, Canada, U.S.A., South America, New Zealand, and Africa. Today it is found throughout the U.S.A. in the Great Lakes area, south in the Appalachians to the northern edge of Georgia, south in some high gradient streams and rivers of the Mississippi River drainage system, throughout much of Nebraska, and in every state west of Texas and Nebraska to the Pacific coast.

It resembles its relative, the Atlantic salmon *(Salmo salar)*. Despite the historical common names "salmon" and "trout", these two species belong to the same genus *Salmo* (see Salmon, Atlantic). Both have black spots on the back, upper sides, and on the gill cover, and sometimes have red spots. In fresh water especially near spawning time, both species are bronze to dark brown in general coloration, with black and (usually) red spots on the body and head. In salt water both species tend to become silvery with fewer black spots and no red spots.

Though both often occur in the same areas, they can usually be distinguished without laboratory analysis. In fresh water, brown trouts as a rule, are more heavily spotted than Atlantic salmon and usually a good number of these spots are surrounded by lighter halos. The spots on the Atlantic salmon have no halos and usually some of the spots will take the shape of X's or Y's, which is not usually the case in the brown trout. The brown trout also has dark spots on the dorsal and adipose fins and vague spots on the tail, though nothing like the prominent radiating spots on the tail of the rainbow trout *(Oncorhynchus mykiss)*. The Atlantic salmon has no clear spots on any of these fins. Also, the brown trout's tail is squarish or very slightly concave or convex, while the Atlantic salmon's tail is slightly forked or indented. In juveniles the difference is much more obvious. The tail is slightly forked in the brown trout and deeply forked in the Atlantic salmon. Otherwise, these parr (young Salmonids) look very much alike with small exceptions. A positive distinction between these two species, usually observed in the laboratory, is that the brown trout has well-developed vomerine teeth in a double zigzag row, while the Atlantic salmon has only a single row of poorly developed vomerine teeth.

The brown trout, like the Atlantic salmon, is one of the world's most widely distributed and highly esteemed freshwater (or anadromous) fish. It is a prime target of fly fishermen and one of the most difficult of trouts to catch by any angling method. It will sometimes be spooked by the bait or fly and at other times it will simply ignore it.

They sometimes hybridizes with the brook trout *(Salvelinus fontinalis)* producing a strikingly marked fish called a tiger trout. Few of the eggs or hatchlings of this cross survive due to genetic differences between the two genera, and the offspring is unable to reproduce. The anadromous brown trout can also be successfully crossed with the Atlantic salmon to produce a fertile hybrid, sometimes called a "trousal".

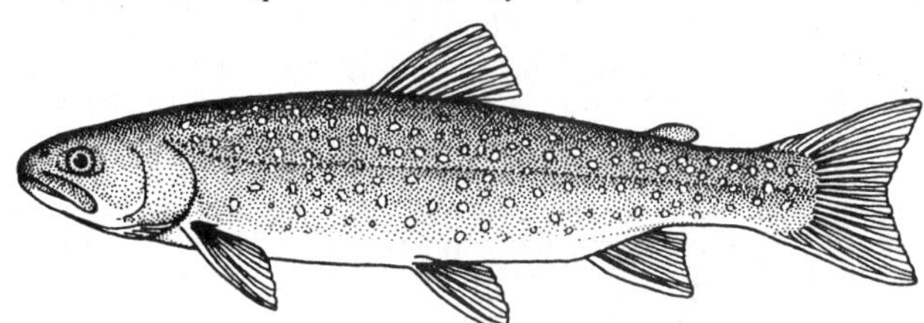

TROUT, bull / *Salvelinus confluentus* (Suckley, 1858); SALMONIDAE FAMILY; also called western brook trout, Rocky Mountain trout, red spotted salmon-trout, red spotted char

Endemic to the Pacific northwest, it inhabits most of the major drainages on both sides of the Continental Divide. It seems to prefer large, cold rivers and lakes draining high mountainous areas, and tends to frequent the bottoms of deep pools. It has been recorded in northern California, Oregon, Washington, northern Nevada, Idaho, western Montana, Alberta and British Columbia.

Though described and named by Suckley in 1858, for over a century it was confused with the Dolly Varden *(Salvelinus malma)* and much of the literature on the Dolly Varden is actually based in part or whole on the bull trout. In 1978, Ted M. Cavender, a fishery scientist, published scientific proof that the bull trout is a separate species [Calif. Fish & Game 64 (3): 139-74]. According to Cavender, separation of the two species is"based primarily on characteristics of the head and cranial skeleton". He further states that "some of the characters that have been employed for many years in *Salvelinus* taxonomy, such as numbers of gill rakers and pyloric caeca, will not separate *S. malma* and *S. confluentus*. This is one reason why it has not been recognized as a distinct form".

It resembles the Dolly Varden in external characters, and will probably require laboratory analysis by a scientist familiar with the species to be positively identified. As a rule one can be fairly certain that any char other than the lake trout *(S. namaycush)* or the brook trout *(S. fontinalis)*, weighing over 12 lb (5.44 kg) and taken in the areas mentioned, will prove to be a bull trout. (See "Salmons, Trouts & Chars".)

The bull trout and the Dolly Varden are not as highly rated as game fish as most other members of the Salmonidae family, but they do have considerable sporting and food value and are gaining esteem. It was thought that their predatory nature posed a threat to other salmons and trouts, and one writer went so far as to state that "...they mostly hang around the estuaries, waiting to mug any smaller fish or other unsuspecting prey that happens along". Anglers attempted to eradicate them and loggers even dynamited pools where bull trout and/or Dolly Varden congregated. In defense of these species, the aforementioned writer aptly pointed out that salmon and steelhead had somehow managed to survive for thousands of years despite the predatory habits of the bull trout and Dolly Varden.

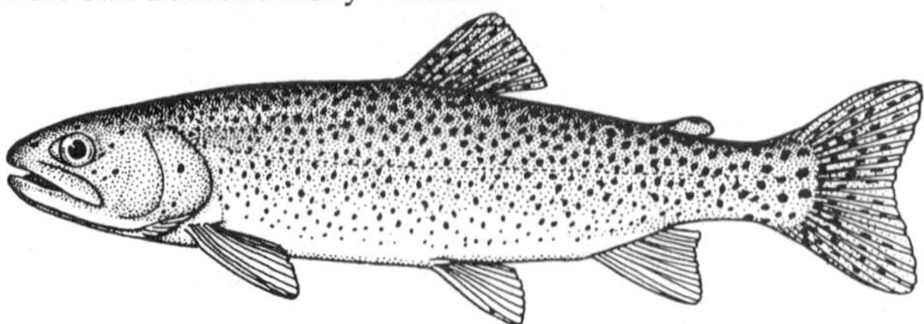

TROUT, cutthroat / *Oncorhynchus clarki* (Richardson, 1836); SALMONIDAE FAMILY; also called Clark's trout, red-throated trout, short-tailed trout, lake trout, sea trout, brook trout, native trout, Yellowstone cutthroat, Snake River cutthroat, Lahontan cutthroat, coastal cutthroat, Rio Grande cutthroat, Colorado cutthroat, Utah cutthroat, Piute cutthroat, harvest trout

Cutthroat trout are the most widely distributed of all the western trouts of North America prooven by the many names that refer to rivers, states, or drainages where unique forms occur. Anadromous (sea-run) forms of the cutthroat trout normally do not exist more than 100 miles (161 km) inland. They are known from the Eel River, California north to Prince William Sound, Alaska. Inland non-anadromous forms occur from southern Alberta, Canada to as far south as New Mexico, as far east as Colorado and most of Montana and west as far as Alberta and eastern California. A small, disjunct population which may have been transplanted, occurs in northern Baja California, Mexico. The species has been transplanted to other locations, including the east coast of Quebec, Canada (1942), where it began to appear in fishermen's catches in 1966.

This is a highly variable fish, in coloration and size. The characteristic that gave the cutthroat its name is the yellow, orange, or red streak in the skin fold on each side under the lower jaw. The color of the body ranges from cadmium blue and silvery (sea-run) to olive-green or yellowish green. There may or may not be red on the sides of the head, front part of the body, and the belly. In some specimens there may be a narrow pink streak along the sides, but not as broad as in the rainbow trout *(Oncorhynchus mykiss)*. The body is covered with black spots, which extend onto the dorsal fin, adipose fin, and the tail. Some are literally covered with spots, while in others the spots are sparse and larger, being more numerous on the posterior part of the body. On the tail, the spots radiate evenly outward as they do in such species as the rainbow trout, golden trout *(O. aguabonita)*, and Arizona native trout *(O. apache)*. While all of these species are very similar and closely related, only the cutthroat trout has hyoid teeth (teeth on the back of the tongue). These may be difficult to see or obsolete in some specimens. The tail of the cutthroat is slightly forked and all the fins are soft-rayed.

The largest form (or subspecies) of *O. clarki* was once the Lahontan cutthroat, which was native to the Lahontan drainage system of Nevada and California, including Lake Tahoe, Pyramid Lake, and the Truckee River. These specimens had an average weight of about 20 lb (9.07 kg) and in 1925 a 41 lb (18.59 kg) Lahontan cutthroat was recorded from Pyramid Lake. In 1938 water was diverted from the Truckee River and the Lahontan became extinct except for populations maintained by stocking, none of which attain the large sizes they once did. The smallest cutthroat occurs only in the upper Silver King Creek, California and does not exceed 12 in (30 cm). Coastal anadromous cutthroats have been recorded to 17 lb (7.71 kg) but average under 5 lb (2.26 kg). Most inland forms do not much exceed 5 lb (2.26 kg).

It hybridizes freely in nature with rainbow, golden trout, and other close relatives. The flesh varies from white to red and is highly regarded.

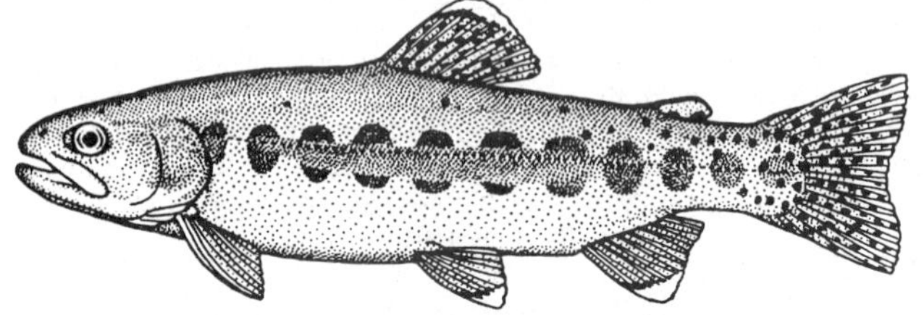

TROUT, golden / *Oncorhynchus aguabonita* (Jordan, 1893);

SALMONIDAE FAMILY; also called Kern River trout

Native only to the upper Kern River basin in Tulare and Kern Counties, California, the golden trout occurs in clear, cool waters at elevations higher than 6,890 ft (2100 m). Despite its limited distribution, there are two recognized subspecies of golden trout: *Oncorhynchus aguabonita aguabonita*, which is confined to the south fork of the Kern River and Golden Trout Creek, and *Oncorhynchus aguabonita gilberti*, which is confined to the Main Kern and Little Kern Rivers. An area of warm water where the South Fork joins the Kern apparently serves as a natural barrier that keeps the two subspecies apart. Golden trout have been introduced to other areas, including the states of Washington, Idaho and Wyoming, which have self-sustaining populations. It is believed that most of these populations have hybridized with the cutthroat trout *(Oncorhynchus clarki)*. According to Schreck & Behnke (1971. J. Fish. Res. Board Can. 28:987-98), most trouts in the Kern River basin are also hybrids of recent origin and the only pure populations of golden trout are those limited to the headwater areas.

Due to its coloration and markings it is considered one of the most beautiful of all freshwater game fishes. It is the only species of Salmonidae in which the parr marks on the sides typically remain prominent throughout life rather than disappearing at an early age. A red streak similar to that of a rainbow trout runs along the sides through the ten or so parr marks. The tail is golden yellow (as is most of the body) and is covered with large black spots that radiate outward toward the edge as in the rainbow, cutthroat, and some other closely related species. Usually the posterior part of the body is heavily spotted. The forward part of the body may have spots above the lateral line on the back and top of the head, but not always. The upper fins are golden yellow and heavily spotted. The lower fins are orangish or reddish with no spots. The dorsal fin and the ventral and anal fins have white tips (in some specimens) that are often separated from the rest of the fin by a broad black line. The sides of the head and "throat" are a blend of rosy red and golden yellow. When this species is brought down from its high altitude habitat and propagated at low altitudes, it loses its brilliant colors and becomes steely blue.

It is considered to be a highly desirable and almost mystical species. Fly fishermen and other anglers have to match their lures to the types of food items available at the high altitudes where the golden trout occurs. Caddisflies and midges are most effective, through goldens have been caught with spoons, spinners, worms, salmon eggs, small crustaceans, and various small insects. The flesh is slightly oilier than most trouts, but firm, finely textured, and delicious. It does not keep for extended periods of time and should be cooked soon after capture or well iced and properly packed.

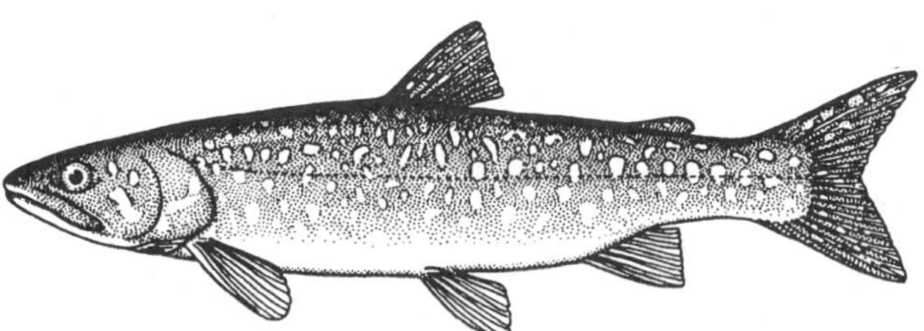

TROUT, lake / *Salvelinus namaycush* (Walbaum, 1792); SALMONIDAE FAMILY; also called mackinaw, Great Lakes trout or char, salmon trout, landlocked salmon, gray trout, great gray trout, mountain trout, laker, tongue, taque, namaycush or masamacush, siscowet, fat, paperbelly, bank trout, humper

It is found throughout most of Canada and well into Alaska as well as the Great Lakes and in sections of the western U.S. where it has been introduced. In the southern portions of its range, or where introduced south of its native range, it seeks out the cooler waters of deep lakes. In northern lakes it may occur in either shallow or deep water. The siscowet *(Salvelinus namaycush siscowet)*, one of three recognized subspecies, is found in Lake Superior at a depth of 300-600 ft (91-183 m). It is called a "fat" by commercial fishermen because the flesh is exceedingly fat and oily compared to the other two subspecies. Of all the chars, it is the least tolerant of salt water and is the only freshwater fish ranging into the far north of Canada and Alaska that has apparently not crossed the Bering Strait.

It is classified taxonomically with the chars (genus *Salvelinus*), although some scientists prefer to place it in a genus of its own *(Cristivomer)*. Like other chars it has white leading edges on all the lower fins and light colored spots on a dark background, instead of the dark spots on a light background which is characteristic of salmons and trouts. The body is typically grayish to brownish with white or nearly white spots which extend onto the dorsal, adipose and caudal fins. There are no red, black or haloed spots of any kind. It has a more deeply forked tail than other chars, and several rows of strong basibranchial teeth which are weak, less numerous, or absent in other chars. It is a very large char known to grow over 100 lb (45 kg).

It has been crossed with the brook trout *(Salvelinus fontinalis)* to produce a hybrid known as the "splake" or "wendigo trout". The hybrid lacks the deep fork in the tail and more closely resembles the brook trout in most respects. There are 65-85 pyloric caeca in the hybrid versus 93-208 in the lake trout and 23-55 in the brook trout.

It has considerable value both as a sport fish and a food fish. The flesh may be white, pink, orange or nearly red, depending on the fish's diet, and is excellent regardless of color. The fatty siscowets are best smoked, but other lake trout are delicious prepared in any manner.

It is extremely vulnerable to pollution, particularly DDT, and this together with the introduction of the sea lamprey into the Great Lakes through the Welland Canal has had a devastating effect on populations. A campaign to control the sea lamprey and the level of pollution has helped restore the stocks in more recent years.

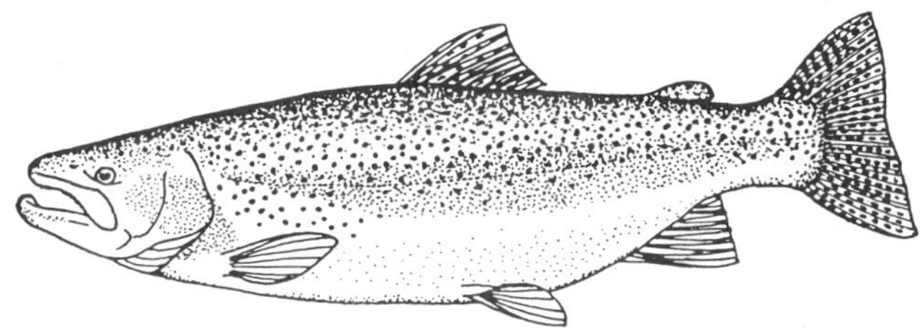

TROUT, rainbow / *Oncorhynchus mykiss* (Walbaum, 1792); SALMONIDAE FAMILY; also called steelhead, Kamloops, redband trout, Eagle Lake trout, Kern River trout, Shasta trout, San Gorgonio trout, Nelson trout, Whitney trout, silver trout

It is native to the west coast of North America from southern Alaska to Durango, Mexico and inland as far as central Alberta in Canada and Idaho and Nevada in the U.S. It has been extensively introduced across the lower Canadian provinces and throughout the area of the Great Lakes to the Atlantic coast, south in the Appalachians to northern Georgia and Alabama, east in the southern U.S. to western Texas and sporadically in the central U.S. as well as above the Great Lakes on the Atlantic coast. It has been transplanted to New Zealand, Australia, South America, Africa, Japan, southern Asia, Europe and Hawaii. An Asian species known as the Kamchatka trout is believed to be a form of the rainbow trout. It is native to the Amur River in the eastern part of Russia as well as Kamchatka and the Commander Islands.

Coloration varies greatly with size, habitat and spawning periods. For example, stream dwellers and spawners usually show the darkest and most vivid colors and markings, while the steelhead is silvery when it returns from the sea. Though noted for the broad red or pink stripe along the middle of its sides, this stripe may not be present on all forms, particularly the sea-run steelhead and immature specimens in clear lakes. A similar stripe is sometimes present on the golden trout *(Oncorhynchus aguabonita)* and the cutthroat trout *(O. clarki)*, though the golden trout usually has about 10 prominent parr marks on the sides through adulthood (uncommon but not unheard of in adult rainbows). The cutthroat can usually be distinguished by the yellow, orange, or red streak in the skin fold on each side under the lower jaw. In some waters rainbow trout may faintly display this streak in the skin fold, but most do not.

The rainbow and its closest relatives in the Pacific salmon group (cutthroat, golden, Mexican golden, Arizona native or Apache, and gila trout) are known as the "black-spotted" trouts because they are covered with numerous prominent black spots. These spots may cover the entire body or may be more abundant near the tail. The spots characteristically extend onto the dorsal fin, the adipose fin, and the tail. Those on the tail radiate outward in an even, orderly pattern. Spots may or may not be present on any of the lower fins and there are never any red spots such as occur on freshwater and spawning specimens of brown trout *(Salmo trutta)* and Atlantic salmon *(S. salar)*. The rainbow trout readily hybridizes with other "black-spotted" trout, especially with the cutthroat and golden trout. In fact, all these trout hybridize wherever they occur together producing fertile offspring with all manner of confusing color combinations and intermediate characteristics.

This is an extremely valuable species in any and all of its forms. It is the fly fisherman's delight as it takes a fly readily, leaps often, and fights hard. Though there is no direct commercial demand for the rainbow it is taken by Pacific salmon fishermen and it is pond-reared in Europe and Japan to be sold as frozen whole fish. The flesh ranges from bright red in small lake and stream populations to pink or white in large lake, stream, and steelhead populations in which the diet is primarily piscivorous. It is excellent regardless of color and may be cooked in any manner desired.

TROUT, tiger / *Salmo trutta x Salvelinus fontinalis*; SALMONIDAE FAMILY

This is a cross between a female brown trout *(Salmo trutta)* and a male brook trout *(Salvelinus fontinalis)*. It is primarily an artificial cross, though it has been known to occur in nature. Because of genetic differences between the two genera (the brook trout is actually a char), mortality of the eggs and alevin is high. About 65% of hatchery specimens do not survive and the loss is higher in the wild where the majority of normal eggs and alevin perish due to predation. Hybrid specimens that survive are unable to reproduce. They have primarily been produced only on a small scale in private hatcheries for stocking in European club waters and in a few limited areas on an experimental basis. Theoretically, they might occur anywhere that brook trout and brown trout inhabit the same waters.

The wavy tiger-like markings on the sides of this hybrid give it a unique beauty. It does not substantially resemble either of the parent species or any other salmonid. The overall color of the tiger trout is brownish on the back, lightening on the sides and belly to a golden yellow with a brown or orange wash. The back and sides both above and below the lateral line display large prominent sunshine yellow vermiculations, or worm-like markings, that are much more vivid and extensive than those of the brook trout. The dorsal fin is also brownish with yellow vermiculations. Large brown spots may be present on the adipose fin. The tail is dusky with brown or black markings and yellow visible beneath the dusky color. The rear margin of the tail has a thin black edge. The lower fins are brownish to orange with char-like white leading edges. The anterior part of the belly may be white.

Overall, it is stockier and more aggressive than either parent and thus more easily caught. It is a surface feeder and is highly regarded by anglers in waters where it is stocked.

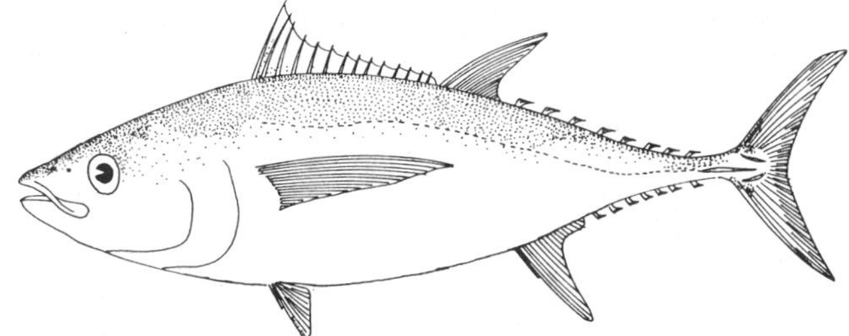

TUNA, bigeye (Atlantic and Pacific) *Thunnus obesus* (Lowe, 1836); SCOMBRIDAE FAMILY

Found in warm temperate waters of the Atlantic, Pacific and Indian Oceans, this schooling, pelagic, seasonally migratory species is suspected of making rather extensive migrations. Schools bigeye tuna generally run deep during the day. Schools of bluefin, yellowfin and some others are known to occasionally swim at the surface, especially in warm water.

The pectoral fins may reach to the second dorsal fin. The second dorsal and anal fins never reach back as far as those of large yellowfin tuna *(Thunnus albacares)*. It has a total of 23-31 gill rakers on the first arch. The margin of the liver is striated. The two dorsal fins are close-set, the first having 13-14 spines and the second, 14-16 rays. The anal fin has 11-15 rays. On either side of the caudal peduncle there is a strong lateral keel between two small keels that are located slightly farther back on the tail. The scales are small except on the anterior corselet. The vent is oval or teardrop shaped, not round as in the albacore. The first dorsal fin is deep yellow. The second dorsal fin and the anal fin are blackish brown or yellow and may be edged with black. The finlets are bright yellow with narrow black edges. The tail does not have a white trailing edge like that of the albacore. Generally, there are no special markings on the body, but some specimens may have vertical rows of whitish spots on the venter.

At one time it was not recognized as a separate species but

considered a variation of the yellowfin tuna. They are similar in many respects, but the bigeye's second dorsal and anal fins never grow as long as those of the yellowfin. In the bigeye tuna the margin of the liver is striated and the right lobe is about the same size as the left lobe, in the yellowfin tuna the liver is smooth and the right lobe is clearly longer than either the left or the middle lobe.

Its diet includes squid, crustaceans, mullet, sardines, small mackerels and some deep water species. Fishing methods are trolling deep with squid, mullet or other small baits, or artificial lures and live bait fishing in deep waters with similar baits. It is an excellent food or sport fish, an important commercial species taken mainly by longlines and sometimes by purse seines. It is marketed canned, frozen and salt-dried. In Hawaii it is marketed fresh.

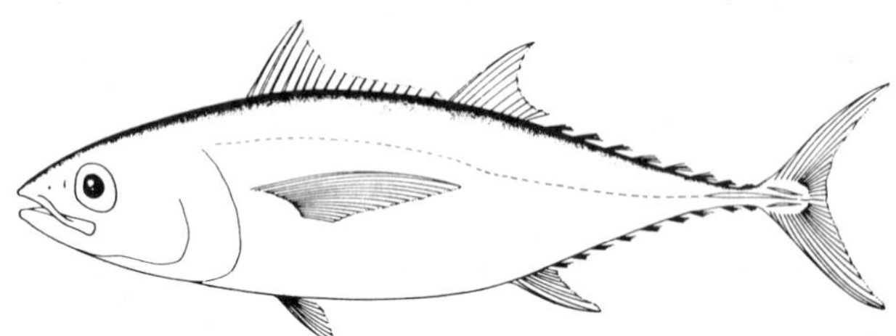

TUNA, blackfin / *Thunnus atlanticus* (Lesson, 1830); SCOMBRIDAE FAMILY; also called Bermuda tuna, blackfinned albacore

Occurs in tropical and warm-temperate waters of the western Atlantic Ocean. There are scattered records of blackfin tuna occurring as far north as Martha's Vineyard, Massachusetts, but the usual range is from North Carolina to Rio de Janeiro, Brazil, including the Caribbean Sea and the Gulf of Mexico.

The pectoral fins reach to somewhere between the twelfth dorsal spine and the origin of the second dorsal fin but they never extend beyond the second dorsal fin as in the albacore. There is a total of 19-25 (usually 21-23) gill rakers on the first arch (15-19 are on the lower limb), which is fewer than in any other species of *Thunnus*. The finlets are uniformly dark, without a touch of the bright lemon yellow usually present in those of other tunas. Light bars alternate with light spots on the lower flanks.

This is a pelagic, schooling fish that generally feeds near the surface. Its diet consists of small fishes, squid, crustaceans, and plankton. An excellent light tackle species, it can be taken by trolling or casting small baits or lures, including ballyhoo, mullet and other small fishes as well as strip baits, spoons, feathers, jigs, or plugs; or by live bait fishing from boats at the surface of deep waters one to two miles offshore. It has some local commercial importance, but is predominantly an angler's fish. It is a spunky game species and the flesh is of good quality and flavor.

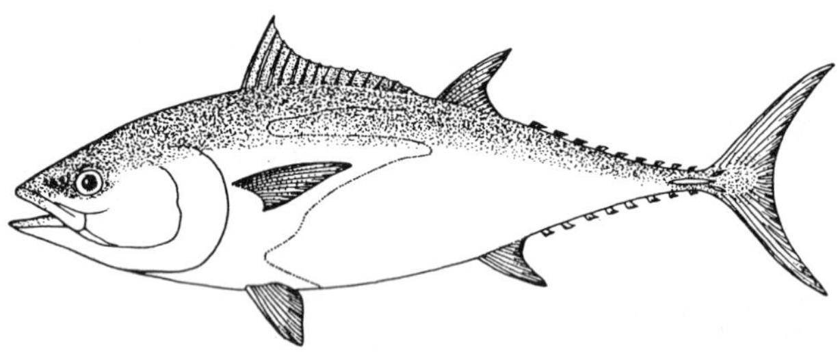

TUNA, bluefin / *Thunnus thynnus* (Linnaeus, 1758); SCOMBRIDAE FAMILY; also called Atlantic bluefin tuna, tunny fish, horse-mackerel

Occurs in subtropical and temperate waters of the north Pacific Ocean, the North Atlantic Ocean, and in the Mediterranean and Black seas.

It is a pelagic, schooling, highly migratory species. The smallest fish form the largest schools and vice versa. Its extensive migrations of all fish, appear to be tied to water temperature, spawning habits, and the seasonal movements of fishes on which the bluefin feeds. Specimens tagged in the Bahamas have been recaptured as far north as Newfoundland and Norway and as far south as Uruguay. In some cases the recaptured fish had traveled 5,000 mi (8050 km) in 50 days. The giants of the species make the longest migrations. Reportedly, some can be found as far north as northern Siberia. However, the water temperature must be above 50°F (10°C).

This is the largest tuna and one of the largest true bony fish. It can be distinguished from almost all others by its rather short pectoral fins which extend only as far back as the eleventh or twelfth spine in the first dorsal fin. There are 12-14 spines in the first dorsal fin and 13-15 rays in the second. The anal fin has 11-15 rays. It has the highest gill raker count of any species of *Thunnus* with 34-43 on the first arch. The ventral

surface of the liver is striated and the middle lobe is usually the largest. The anal fin and the finlets are dusky yellow edged with black. The lateral keel is black in adults.

Its diet consists of squid, eels and crustaceans as well as pelagic schooling fish such as mackerel, flying fish, herring, whiting, and mullet. During spawning which occurs in the summer or spring, a giant female may shed 25 million or more eggs. Bluefins grow rapidly and may be 2 ft (0.6 m) in length and weigh 9 lb (4 kg) by the end of their first year. By age 14 they may be over 8 ft (2 m) long and weigh 700 lb (318 kg).

Fishing methods include still fishing or trolling with live or dead bait such as mackerel, herring, mullet, or squid; and trolling with artificial lures including spoons, plugs, or feathers.

Bluefin tuna are supreme in their size, strength and speed, and are a very important game fish. They are also extremely important commercially in many parts of the world. The flesh is of good quality and the annual world catch is significant. Their red flesh is prized in Japan more than that of any other tuna, especially late in the season when the meat contains the most fat. It commands premium prices in Japanese restaurants, where it is served raw.

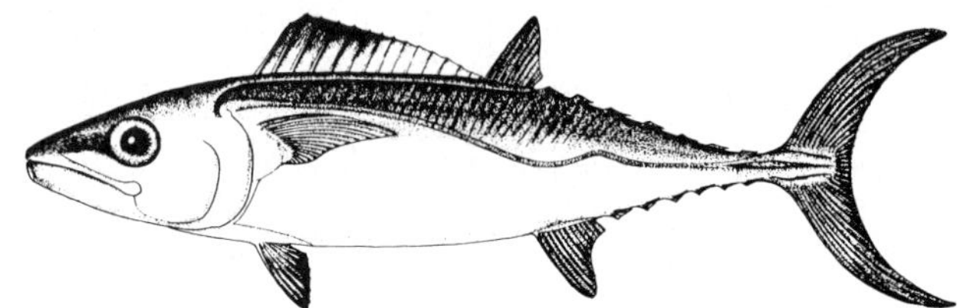

TUNA, dogtooth / *Gymnosarda unicolor* (Ruppell, 1836); SCOMBRIDAE FAMILY; also called scaleless tuna, lizard-mouth tuna, white tuna

Inhabits tropical and subtropical areas of the Indian and western Pacific Oceans around coral reefs. It has been taken in the Red Sea and sporadically in southern Japanese waters as well as around Papua New Guinea, the Marshall Islands, the Society Islands, the Marquesas Islands and from East Africa to Australia. It is a pelagic and migratory species, but is known to enter in shore waters during the warm season.

It is noted for its lack of scales (except on the corselet and along either side of the lateral line) and for its large conical teeth--features which have given it the names "scaleless tuna" and "dogtooth tuna" respectively. It is actually a bonito. The first dorsal fin has 13-15 spines, the second is higher and has 12-14 rays followed by 6-7 dorsal finlets. The anal fin has 12-13 rays. There are 11-14 gill rakers on the first arch. The lateral line is prominent and wavy, ending in a keel on the caudal peduncle. It is the only bonito that has a swim bladder and a large, single interpelvic process. It is similar to the Australian *Cybiosarda* in having two patches of teeth on the tongue. There are no dark stripes or spots on the body. The second dorsal and anal fins are tipped with white.

It is usually found around or reefs, channels, passes or rocky areas, where it feeds extensively on reef fish. Tunas and most bonitos feed more often on pelagic, schooling fishes, but no tuna or bonito feeds exclusively on any one type of prey. The dogtooth will readily consume a smaller mackerel, squid or other pelagic fish.

When hooked its first run is fast and long and is followed by a deep, circling, tough fight. It is usually taken incidentally while deep trolling or deep live or dead bait fishing for other species in the vicinity of an off shore reef, though some are caught on rigs trolled on or near the surface. It has been known to take mackerel, mullet, squid, strip baits, spoons, plugs, feathers and plastic lures.

The dogtooth is reported to be excellent both as a sport fish and as table fare, but in spite of the quality of the flesh, there is no major commercial fishery for this species owing to its relative scarcity. The flesh is white and in some areas the dogtooth tuna is known as the white tuna. In various islands of the southwest Pacific it is called *vau*, *atu*, *kidukidu* or *dadori*.

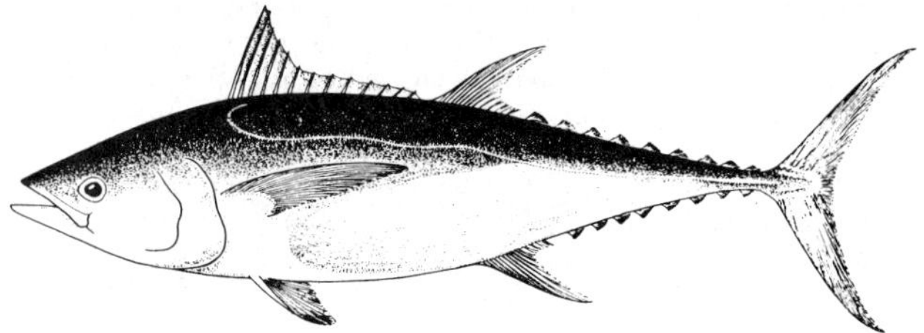

TUNA, longtail / *Thunnus tonggol* (Bleeker, 1851); SCOMBRIDAE FAMILY; also called northern bluefin tuna, oriental bonito

Occurs in the tropical and subtropical central Pacific Ocean

Though largely coastal, it avoids low salinity areas near the mouths of rivers. It is also seasonally migratory, occurring in large feeding schools off the western and northeastern coasts of Australia. Smaller schools occur off the coasts of India.

It is less robust and more elongated than the southern bluefin tuna *(Thunnus maccoyi)*. Other traits which separate this species from the southern bluefin are colorless oval spots on the belly, the absence of a swim bladder, the lack of striations on the liver surface, and the lower gill raker count, 20-23 mean total. The ventral surface from about the pectoral fin to the anal is covered with colorless elongated spots. The tips of the second dorsal and anal fins are yellow. The finlets are yellow and edged with gray.

Its diet consists of a wide variety of crustaceans, cephalopods (squid) and fish, including hardyheads and garfish. Longtail tuna are often observed making dashing bursts through dense shoals of bait fish, showering spray as they do so.

A major tournament is held each year in April at Tangalooma in Queensland, Australia, when longtail tuna, usually around the 28-44 lb (13-20 kg) mark, appear in large numbers. Big schools can often be seen on the surface but are often virtually impossible to hook. At other times this fish will take lures and baits without any previous indication of its presence. The fight is a tough one, both on the surface and deep down.

Trolling small feathers over "holes" in the bottom and between coral reefs at high tide produces strikes. Also, trolling live or dead baits through dumped trash fish behind trawlers will bring boiling masses of feeding "blues" to the surface and they will then readily take baits. Spinning or casting saltwater flies is also popular. Live baits include small whiting, mullet, yellowtail, slimy mackerel, crabs and squid. Lures include feathers, knuckleheads, bulletheads, plastic fish and squid replicas.

The flesh is pink and of good quality. Fillets can be bleached by immersing in hot water and then frying, in which case their flavor compares favorably with that of mackerel.

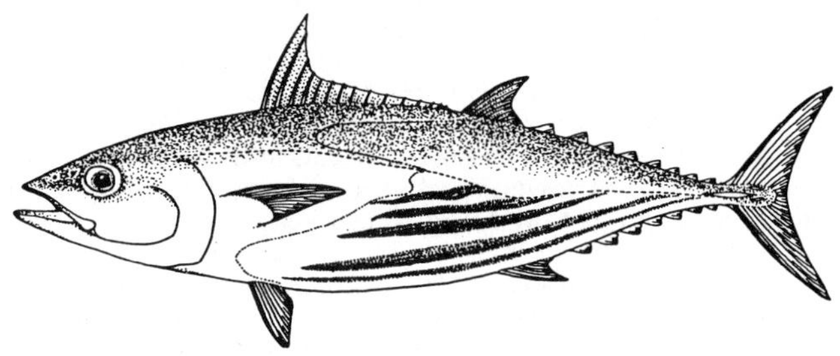

TUNA, skipjack / *Katsuwonus pelamis* (Linnaeus, 1758); SCOMBRIDAE FAMILY; also called skipjack, ocean bonito, Arctic bonito, striped tuna, watermelon tuna

Cosmopolitan in tropical and subtropical seas, usually in deep coastal and oceanic waters. It is common throughout the tropical Atlantic, south to Argentina and may range as far north as Cape Cod, Massachusetts in the summer months. A pelagic, migratory, deep water species, it may form schools composed of 50,000 or more individuals. In the western Atlantic, skipjack tuna frequently school with blackfin tuna *(Thunnus atlanticus)* and in the Pacific and Indian Oceans they often school with yellowfin tuna *(Thunnus albacares)*. The common name Arctic bonito which is sometimes applied to the skipjack is a misnomer. The fish does not range into Arctic waters and is not a bonito, but a tuna.

The presence of stripes on the belly and the absence of markings on the back are sufficient to distinguish the skipjack tuna from all similar species. The lower flanks and belly are silvery with 4 to 6 prominent, dark longitudinal stripes running from just behind the corselet back towards the tail, ending when they come into contact with the lateral line. Though some other species do have stripes on the belly, they have markings on the back as well, and the latter remain the most prominent after death.

The first dorsal fin has 14-16 spines. The pectoral and ventral fins are short. The body is scaleless except on the corselet and along the lateral line. On each side of the caudal peduncle there is a strong lateral keel. There are about 30 or 40 small conical teeth in each jaw. The teeth are smaller and more numerous than those of the bonitos and are unlike the triangular, compressed teeth of the mackerels. There are 53-63 gill rakers on the first arch, which is more than in any other species of tuna except the slender tuna *(Allothunnus)*.

This is a gregarious fish and a fast swimmer. It feeds near the surface and its diet consists of clupeoids, squids, small scombroids, lanternfish, euphausiid shrimps and crustaceans. It will strike trolled strip baits, feathers, spoons, plugs, or small whole baits. Some are taken by casting, jigging or live bait fishing off shore.

In addition to being an esteemed light tackle species, it has great commercial value. It is a mainstay of the California tuna fishery and is of tremendous importance in Japan, Hawaii, Cuba, the Dominican Republic and other areas of both oceans. It is marketed canned, frozen, smoked, fresh, and dried-salted. In the U.S. it is canned with yellowfin and bigeye tuna and sold as light meat tuna.

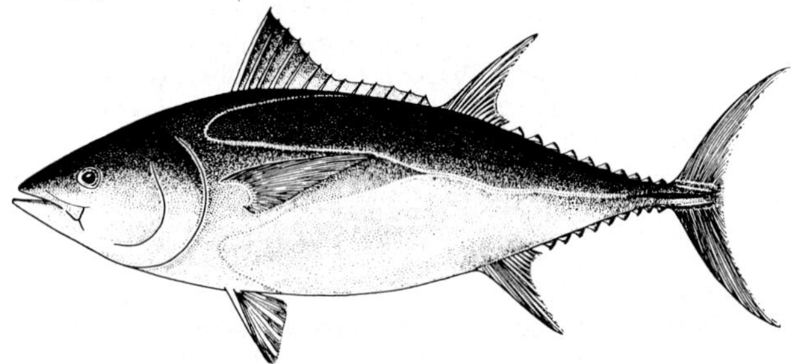

TUNA, southern bluefin / *Thunnus maccoyi* (Castelnau, 1872); SCOMBRIDAE FAMILY; also called Japanese Central Pacific bluefin tuna

A species of the southern ocean found worldwide from 30°S to about 50°S latitude occurring in oceanic to coastal waters below thermoclines. Southern bluefin are commonly found off the southern and eastern coasts of Australia and New Zealand.

This pelagic and seasonally migratory species has been studied quite extensively in Australian waters due to its commercial importance. They spawn in the eastern Indian Ocean with one and two year old fish appearing off Western Australia in summer. Three and four year olds appear off Southern Australia in summer and New South Wales in winter. The migratory route from the Indian Ocean to the Pacific splits into two routes off southern Tasmania. Fish move either to northern New Zealand via South Island or up the Australian coast.

They closely resemble the Atlantic bluefin *(Thunnus thynnus)*, and was once thought to be the same species. The difference is the number of gill rakers. The southern bluefin has a total of 31-40 on the first arch while the Atlantic bluefin has a total of 34-43. Both have in common striations on the ventral surface of the liver, short pectoral fins that do not reach to the interspace between the first and second dorsal fins, and moderate second dorsal and anal fins that are never elongated like those of the yellowfin tuna *(T. albacares)*. The finlets are dusky yellow edged with black. It is the only species of *Thunnus* in which the caudal keels are bright yellow except in fish larger than 150 lb (68 kg) where the caudal keels tend to be darker.

They travel in schools of similar-sized fish. Their diet consists of a variety of crustaceans, cephalopods, and fish including anchovies and pilchards. They are believed to attain an age of at least 20 years.

The most popular method of catch is trolling with Konaheads, knuckleheads, spoons, jigs, feathers or other artificial lures. It can also be taken from boats or from the shore using live scombroid fishes (mackerels and little tunas) for bait. It is rarely taken on dead baits although very large specimens have been landed by this method. Hooked fish are prone to fast surface runs, deep sounding, and plugging.

They are excellent both as a sport fish and as table fare. It is a powerful, hard fighting fish and its red meat is marketed canned or frozen. The raw flesh is highly prized for sashimi and draws a high price on the commercial market. A large commercial fishery for southern bluefin tuna exists in southern Australian waters where schools of larger fish are caught on the surface by purse seining, and smaller fish are caught by chumming and poling.

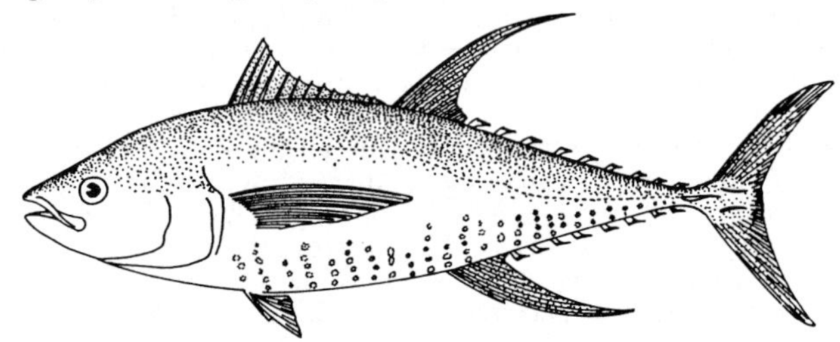

TUNA, yellowfin / *Thunnus albacares* (Bonnaterre, 1788); SCOMBRIDAE FAMILY; also called Allison tuna

Occurs worldwide in deep, warm temperate oceanic waters. It is both pelagic and seasonally migratory, but has been known to come fairly close to shore.

Just as the albacore *(Thunnus alalunga)* has characteristically overextended pectoral fins, the yellowfin has overextended second dorsal and anal fins that may reach more than halfway back to the tail base in some large specimens. In smaller specimens under about 60 lb (27 kg) and in some very large specimens as well, this may not be an accurate distinguishing factor since the fins do not appear to be as long in all specimens. The pectoral fins in adults reach to the origin of the second dorsal fin, but never beyond the second dorsal fin to the finlets as in the albacore. The bigeye tuna *(T. obesus)* and the blackfin tuna *(T. atlanticus)* may have pectoral fins similar in length to those of the yellowfin. The yellowfin can be distinguished from the blackfin by the black margins on its finlets. Blackfin tuna, like albacore, have white margins on the finlets. It can be distinguished from the bigeye tuna by the lack of striations on the ventral surface of the liver. The yellowfin tuna has a total of 25-35 gill rakers on the first arch, and has an air bladder as do all species of *Thunnus* except the longtail tuna *(T. tonggol).* There is no white, trailing margin on the tail.

This is probably the most colorful of all the tunas. The back is blue-black, fading to silver on the lower flanks and belly. A golden yellow or iridescent blue stripe runs from the eye to the tail, though this is not always prominent. All the fins and finlets are golden yellow though in some very large specimens the elongated dorsal and anal fins may be silver edged with yellow. The finlets have black edges. The belly frequently shows as many as 20 vertical rows of whitish spots.

Previously, large yellowfins with long second dorsal and anal fins were called Allison tunas or long-finned yellowfin tunas, and the smaller specimens were called short-finned yellowfin tunas in the mistaken belief that they were a separate species. It is now the general consensus that there is only one species of yellowfin tuna.

The diet depends largely on local abundance, and includes flying fish, other small fish, squid and crustaceans. Fishing methods include trolling with small fish, squid, or other trolled baits including strip baits and artificial lures as well as chumming with live bait fishing.

It is highly esteemed both as a sport fish and as table fare. Its flesh is very light compared to that of other tunas, with the exception of the albacore, which has white meat. Yellowfin tuna are an extremely valuable commercial fish and hundreds of thousands of tons are taken worldwide annually by longliners and purse seiners.

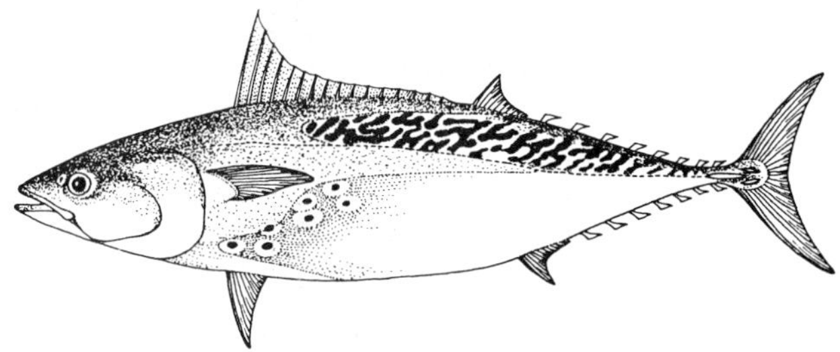

TUNNY, little / *Euthynnus alletteratus* (Rafinesque, 1810); SCOMBRIDAE FAMILY; also called little tuna, Atlantic little tunny, false albacore

Occurs in tropical and warm temperate waters of the Atlantic Ocean from the New England states and Bermuda to Brazil and from South Africa to Biscay or Great Britain. Also in the Mediterranean.

It is a pelagic, schooling, migratory species. Large schools may consist of many thousands of individuals. It is common in inshore waters near the surface where it feeds on squid, crustaceans, fish larvae, and large numbers of smaller pelagic fishes, especially clupeoids (herring and sardine species). The little tunny comes in closer to shore and is less migratory than the skipjack tuna.

It is most easily distinguished from similar species by its markings. It has a scattering of dark spots resembling fingerprints between the pectoral and ventral fins that are not present on any related Atlantic species. It also has wavy, "worm-like" markings on the back. These markings are above the lateral line within a well marked border, and never extend farther forward than about the middle of the first dorsal fin. The markings are the same as in the closely related Pacific kawakawa *(Euthynnus affinis)* but are unlike those of any other Atlantic species. The pectoral and ventral fins are short and broad. The body has no scales except on the corselet and along the lateral line. Unlike its close Pacific relatives the kawakawa and black skipjack *(E. lineatus)* it has no teeth on the vomer.

The little tunny is often confused with the Atlantic bonito *(Sarda sarda)*, the skipjack tuna *(Katsuwonus pelamis)*, and the frigate and bullet mackerels (genus *Auxis*). There are, however, differences among these species. The Atlantic bonito has a lower, sloping first dorsal fin. The frigate and bullet mackerels have the dorsal fins set apart. The skipjack tuna has broad, straight stripes on the belly and lacks markings on the back.

Flocks of diving seabirds are often indicative of the presence of a school of little tunny. Because this species feeds on small pelagic fishes near the surface, any school feeding action tends to attract and excite birds looking for a meal. Fishing methods include trolling or casting from boats using small whole baits, strip baits, or small lures such as spoons, plugs, jigs, and feathers. A few little tunny may be caught from shore. The dark flesh is esteemed by some and disdained by others. It has some commercial importance.

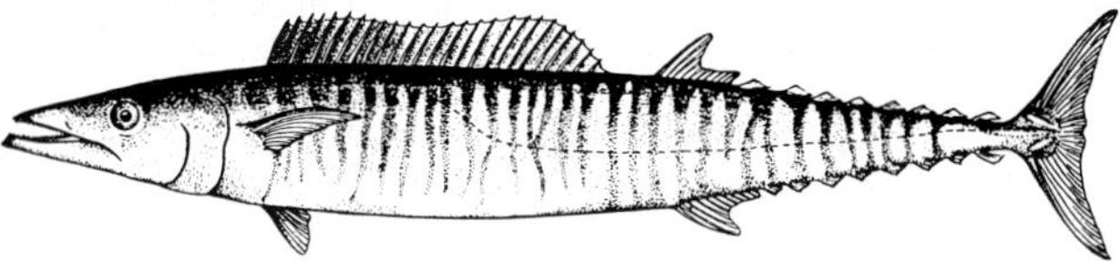

WAHOO / *Acanthocybium solandri* (Cuvier, 1832); SCOMBRIDAE FAMILY; also called oahu fish, Pacific kingfish

Worldwide in tropical and warm temperate seas. Pelagic and seasonally migratory, It tends to be a loner or travel in small groups of 2 to 6 fish. There are indications of seasonal concentrations off the Pacific coasts of Panama, Costa Rica and Baja California in the summer, off Grand Cayman (Atlantic) in the winter and spring, and off the western Bahamas and Bermuda in the spring and fall.

The upper jaw is movable and the teeth (45-64 on the upper jaw and 32-50 on the lower jaw) are large, strong and laterally compressed. The gill structure differs from that of other members of the tuna and mackerel family (Scombridae), most closely resembling the gill structure of the marlins. Additionally, it has no gill rakers. The well defined lateral line dips noticeably near the middle of the first dorsal fin, further forward than on the similar looking tanguigue *(Scomberomorus commerson)*, and is wavy back to the tail. The first dorsal fin is long with 23-27 spines. The second dorsal fin with 13-15 rays and the anal fin with 12-14 rays are very small. The back is a brilliant, deep, blue sometimes described as metallic or electric blue. Bright blue vertical bands, or "tiger stripes", flow down the sides onto the silver and sometimes join into pairs on the belly. These beautiful stripes are not, however, always prominent in large specimens and occasionally may be missing entirely.

It feeds on squid and pelagic fishes, including small mackerel and tuna, flying fish, puffers, and whatever appears desirable since few fish can escape. It is found around wrecks and reefs where smaller fish are abundant, but it may also be found far out at sea.

It is reputed to be one of the fastest fish in the sea, attaining speeds of 50 mph (80 km) and more. The first scorching run may peel off several hundred yards of line in seconds, and the heat generated by the friction has been known to burn out the drag on some reels. Occasionally this fish jumps on the strike and often shakes its head violently when hooked in an effort to free itself. Fishing methods include trolling with whole, rigged Spanish mackerel, mullet, ballyhoo, squid or other small baits as well as with strip baits or artificial lures. Live bait fishing and kite fishing are productive, but the wahoo is a relatively scarce species and is usually taken incidentally while fishing for other oceanic species. The wahoo has commercial importance in some countries. The flesh is finely grained and sweet and is considered excellent eating.

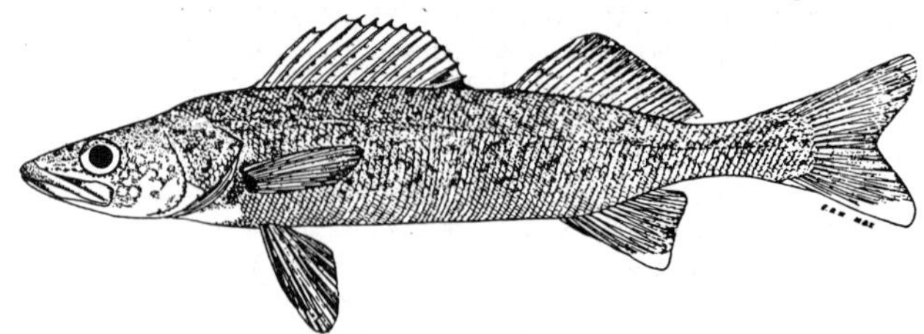

WALLEYE / *Stizostedion vitreum vitreum* (Mitchell, 1818); PERCIDAE FAMILY; also called yellow walleye, pike-perch, walleyed pike-perch, walleyed pickerel, yellow pickerel, yellow pike, yellow pike-perch, walleye pike

This wide-ranging North American species occurs from the Hudson Bay east to the St. Lawrence River, south to the Gulf coast of Alabama, and northwest of the Hudson Bay from Manitoba through the western Northwest Territories (including Great Slave and Great Bear Lakes) to the Beaufort Sea on the border of the Yukon Territory. In eastern drainages from Massachusetts southward it occurs all the way to the coast. It occurs from the Beaufort Sea south through Alberta, northeastern British Columbia and Montana to southern Arizona, the northern portions of Nevada and New Mexico, and then eastward to Georgia. Its western most limits are the states of Washington and Oregon where introduced populations occur.

The largest member of the perch family, it has been know to reach 25 lb (11 kg). Its closest relative and look-a-like is the sauger *(Stizostedion canadense)*. Both have the large, glassy, opaque eyes that gave the walleye its name. In shallow water at night the eyes glow eerily under lights, readily identifying these fishes even before they can be seen. They sauger can be distinguished by the markings on their dorsal fins. The walleye's dorsal fin may be streaked, blotched, or plain, but lacks any clear spots and there is a prominent blotch at the posterior edge. On the sauger the fin is spotted and lacks any large blotch at the back edge. The lower lobe of the tail in the walleye is white-tipped, a feature that is absent in the sauger. Internally, the walleye has 3 pyloric caeca each at least as long as the stomach, while the sauger has 3-9 (usually 5) pyloric caeca all considerably shorter than the stomach.

This is an extremely popular sport fish and an excellent food fish with considerable economic value. A survey in Ontario, Canada indicated that this is the species most often sought by anglers. The best fishing is at night when the walleye is feeding. The flesh is white to pink, firm and considered prime on the market.

The other walleye subspecies known as blue walleye or blue pike *(Stizostedion vitreum glaucum)* was declared an endangered species in the 1970's and may be extinct today. It occurred in Lake Erie, the lower Niagara River, and western Lake Ontario. It was also reported from Long Lake, Lake Nipissing and other inland lakes in Ontario, but scientists believe these reports to be based on misidentification of a gray mutant form of the yellow walleye.

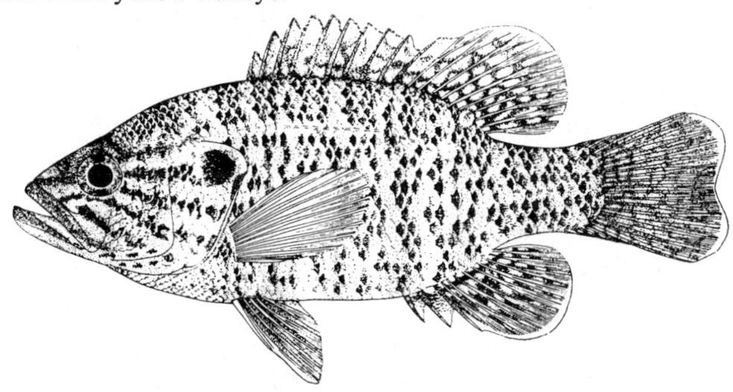

WARMOUTH / *Lepomis gulosus* (Cuvier, 1829); CENTRARCHIDAE FAMILY; also called stump-knocker, goggle-eye, goggle-eyed perch

Occurs throughout the eastern U.S. south of the Great Lakes from Wisconsin, Illinois, Indiana, Ohio and the states south of Pennsylvania through the entire lower eastern seaboard to and including all of the Florida peninsula. It ranges west from Florida to the Rio Grande, Texas and New Mexico and from there back to the Great Lakes. It is abundant in all the major drainages within these areas, including ponds, lakes, and streams, and has been introduced west of the Rockies. This small panfish can be found wherever dense weed beds and soft, muddy bottoms exist, and it is frequently caught near stumps. It is better able to tolerate turbid or muddy waters than most species.

It is a stocky, bass-like sunfish and like the rock bass *(Ambloplites rupestris)* and the green sunfish *(Lepomis cyanellus)*, its body is slightly thicker and longer than most sunfishes. It can be distinguished from the rock bass by the presence of three spines at the start of the anal fin. The rock bass has 5-7, usually 6, spines. Of these three species, the warmouth is the only one that has teeth on the tongue. Its color ranges from olive to gray with mottling on the sides and back, and small spots on the dorsal and anal fins.

Although it is an excellent panfish, it is not actively sought by a great many anglers.

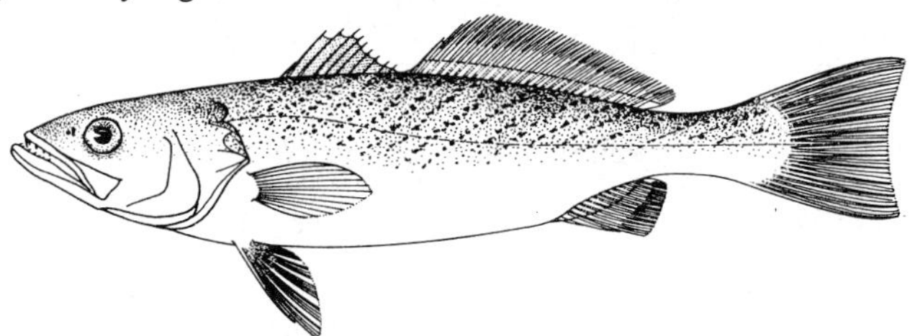

WEAKFISH / *Cynoscion regalis* (Bloch & Schneider, 1801); SCIAENIDAE FAMILY; also called squeteague, common weakfish, common sea trout, gray trout, summer trout, tiderunner

Inhabits the western Atlantic Ocean from Florida to Massachusetts, with isolated records of it occurring as far north as Nova Scotia. The centers of abundance are from North Carolina to Florida in the winter and from Delaware to New York in the summer. It is a schooling fish that occurs in shore over sandy bottoms in the summer and in deeper water,

up to 55 fathoms, in the winter. It may be found in the surf, in bays, or in estuaries of rivers and creeks, but does not venture into fresh water.

The name "weakfish" refers to the tender, easily-torn membrane of the fish's mouth, rather than to its fighting ability. The lower jaw of the weakfish clearly projects beyond the upper jaw. Two large, recurvant canine teeth in the front of the upper jaw stand out noticeably. There are no barbels on the chin. The first dorsal fin has 10 spines. The second has 1 spine and 26-29 soft rays. The anal fin has 2 spines and 11-12 rays. The scales are ctenoid and extend onto the soft dorsal and anal fins. In the similar looking spotted seatrout *(Cynoscion nebulosus)* the scales do not extend onto the fins. Also, there are 11-13 gill rakers on the lower limb of the first gill arch in the weakfish, but only 8-9 in the spotted seatrout. Numerous small spots of black, olive or bronze are set close together on the upper flanks of the weakfish and seem to form wavy diagonal lines. The spots do not extend onto the tail or the second dorsal fin as they do in the spotted seatrout, nor are they as large or as widely spaced. There is sometimes a black margin on the tip of the tongue.

It is omnivorous and feeds on crabs, shrimp, other crustaceans, mollusks and small fishes like herring, menhaden, silversides, killifish and butterfish which it may catch in midwater or at the surface.

They may be taken at any level from the bottom to the surface by chumming from a drifting or anchored boat or by trolling, jigging, or surf fishing. Conventional or spinning tackle may be used. Baits and lures include shrimp, sandworms, bloodworms, clams, squid strips, crabs, small metal jigs or squid, bucktails, spoons, surface and diving plugs, and small fish such as killy. They may also be taken from bridges, docks and piers. When hooked on light tackle the weakfish is prone to give a long initial run with sudden, unpredictable changes in direction. It is reputed to be the gamest species of the *Cynoscion* genus.

The meat is white and tender with a high moisture content and the flavor is excellent. The skin is usually left on during cooking to hold the meat together and the bones are easily removed once the meat is cooked. It does not keep well and should be eaten soon after capture.

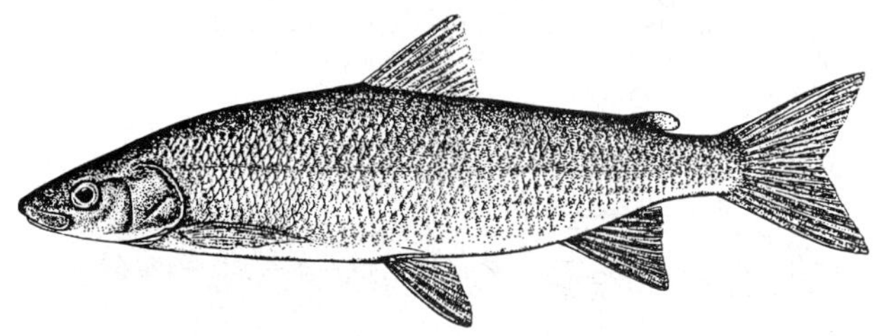

WHITEFISH, lake / *Coregonus clupeaformis* (Mitchell, 1818); SALMONIDAE FAMILY; also called high back, bow back, buffalo back, or humpback whitefish, common whitefish, eastern whitefish, Great Lakes whitefish, inland whitefish, Sault whitefish, gizzard fish

This species is found throughout Canada and Alaska and into the extreme northeastern portions of the U.S., throughout the Great Lakes as well as from New York to Maine. Transplanted populations exist in Washington, Idaho, and Montana in the northwestern U.S. The lake whitefish is much more widespread and attains a much larger size than either the mountain whitefish *(Prosopium williamsoni)* or the round whitefish *(P. cylindraceum)*.

This is a member of the salmon family, as can be noted by the presence of the adipose fin and pelvic axillary process. Overall coloration is silvery to satiny white with olive to pale greenish brown on the back. The back may be dark brown to black in some inland lake specimens. The mouth is subterminal and the snout protrudes beyond it. Because the head is small in relation to the length of the body, older fish may develop a hump behind the head; thus the name "humpback". The lake whitefish has more pyloric caeca, 140-222, than either the round with 50-130, or the mountain whitefish which has 50-146. The body is more laterally compressed than the round or mountain whitefish which belong to a group referred to as "round whitefishes".

More highly regarded as a game fish than the other whitefishes, it is one of the most valuable commercial freshwater fishes in Canada. The commercial catch has deteriorated considerably in places, however, notably in the Great Lakes. The flavor is considered supreme.

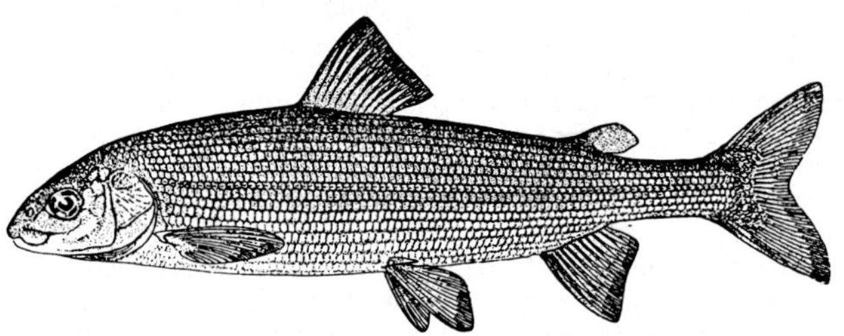

WHITEFISH, mountain / *Prosopium williamsoni* (Girard, 1856); SALMONIDAE FAMILY; also called Rocky Mountain whitefish, Williamson's whitefish, grayling

Endemic to the lakes and streams of the northwestern U.S. and southwestern Canada, from the Lahontan basin in Nevada north to the southern border of the Yukon Territory. It occurs inland into Alberta in Canada and Wyoming in the U.S. Its range overlaps that of the widespread lake whitefish *(Coregonus clupeaformis)* in British Columbia and Alberta, and slightly overlaps that of the round whitefish *(Prosopium cylindraceum)* in extreme northern British Columbia near the Yukon border.

Like other salmonids, it has an adipose fin and an axillary process. The mouth, however, is slightly subterminal with the snout extending clearly beyond it. The body is silvery overall. The back is brownish to olive. The scales often have pigmented borders, especially on the back. The ventral and pectoral fins may have an amber hue in adults. The body is nearly cylindrical, but not quite as cylindrical as the body of the round whitefish. It is nevertheless among the species referred to as "round whitefishes", and is therefore distinguishable from the lake whitefish which has a laterally compressed body.

Though not as important as the lake whitefish, the mountain whitefish has gained some popularity as a sport fish and can be taken by fly fishing or casting with small baits. It provides a considerable winter fishery in places, particularly where steelheads are absent. The flesh is tasty and of good quality.

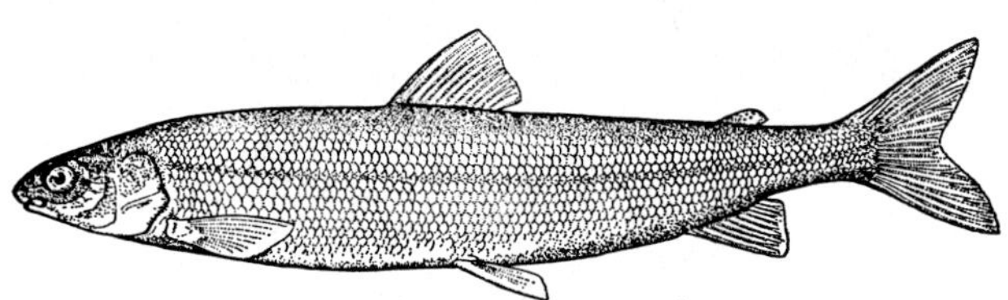

WHITEFISH, round / *Prosopium cylindraceum* (Pallas, 1784); SALMONIDAE FAMILY; also called menominee, round fish, frost fish, pilot fish, grayback

The round whitefish is a wide ranging species in the northern portions of North America and occurs in northeastern Asia from the Yanisea River to Kamchatka and the Bering Sea. In North America it can be found from the Great Lakes, with the exception of Lake Erie, north to the Arctic Ocean east of the Hudson Bay and throughout the northern Canadian Provinces and Alaska west of the Hudson Bay. It also occurs in limited areas directly south of the Hudson Bay and in East Twin Lake in Connecticut.

Although the range of the round whitefish naturally overlaps that of the lake whitefish *(Coregonus clupeaformis)* in parts of Canada and Alaska, the two can be easily distinguished. Aside from its small maximum size, the round whitefish is also a very cylindrical fish, whereas the body of the lake whitefish is laterally compressed. The body of the mountain whitefish *(Prosopium williamsoni)*, though almost cylindrical, is slightly compressed compared to the round whitefish. Coloration of the round whitefish is basically silvery, but the back is sepia brown to almost bronze with a greenish tinge. The scales, particularly on the back are edged with black. The lower fins are an amber shade becoming slightly more orange at spawning. The adipose fin is usually brown spotted. The round whitefish differs from all other North American whitefish and ciscoes in having only one flap between the openings of the nostrils, instead of two.

Because of its relative small size, seldom exceeding 2 lb (0.90 kg), the round whitefish has considerably less commercial value in Canada than the lake whitefish. It is sought to a limited degree by anglers and the flesh is of good quality.

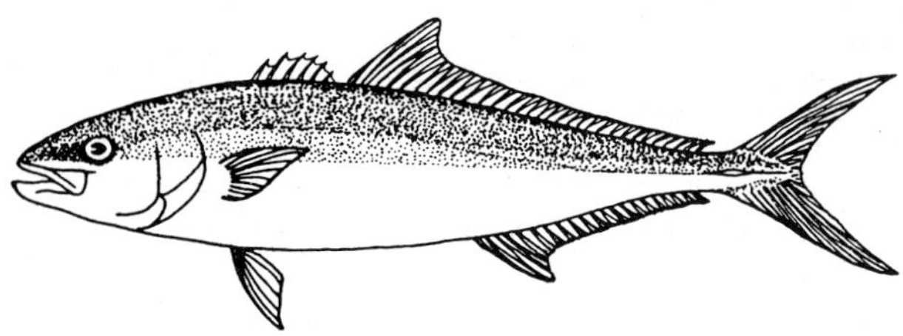

YELLOWTAIL California / *Seriola lalandi dorsalis* (Gill, 1863); CARANGIDAE FAMILY

Occurs in some abundance throughout the Gulf of California and along the Pacific coast of North America from Baja California, Mexico to Los Angeles, California. Less commonly, it has been reported farther north, and on rare occasions, as far north as Washington.

The yellowtail is a coastal, schooling fish that sometimes enters estuaries. It has been reported to occur occasionally in very large schools in the Gulf of California. It feeds predominantly in the morning and late afternoon on small fishes, invertebrates, and pelagic crabs. Small to medium size fish generally undertake seasonal migrations. Larger individuals are more solitary and less migratory.

The yellowtails are closely related to the greater amberjack, which also belongs to the genus *Seriola*, but can be distinguished by the higher number of gill rakers, 21-28 on the first branchial arch, whereas the greater amberjack has only 11-16. The small first dorsal fin consists of 6-7 spines connected to a membrane. The second dorsal fin contains 1 spine and 31-37 soft rays. The anal fin contains 3 spines, 2 of which are detached, and 19-23 soft rays. The caudal peduncle has a small keel on either side, but lacks scutes or finlets. The lateral line scale count is 156-203. The colors of the upper and lower body are separated abruptly by a light lemon yellow stripe that runs along the median line of the flanks from the tail to the eyes, becoming darker as it extends across the eyes to the tip of the snout. The tail is bright yellow.

The yellowtail is a fast swimmer. The strike is vicious and is followed by a long, hard run and sometimes two or three shorter runs before the fish is boated. Fishing methods include trolling or casting with live baits or with lures. The yellowtail's habit of driving bait fish up against the shore makes casting from the beach possible at times. The advice of experts is to allow time for the bait to be swallowed, then strike hard. The California yellowtail is of some commercial importance and is almost invariably described as delicious.

It is currently believed that the worldwide yellowtail complex is one species, *Seriola lalandi*. However, three subspecies are recognized, primarily because of their disjunct distribution and the fact that they do not interact. The subspecies are California yellowtail *(Seriola lalandi dorsalis)*, Asian yellowtail *(Seriola lalandi aureovittata)*, and southern yellowtail *(Seriola lalandi lalandi)*. There are five separate populations of southern yellowtail which were previously thought to be separate species. Interaction has since been shown to occur among these populations, and they are now known to be a single subspecies.

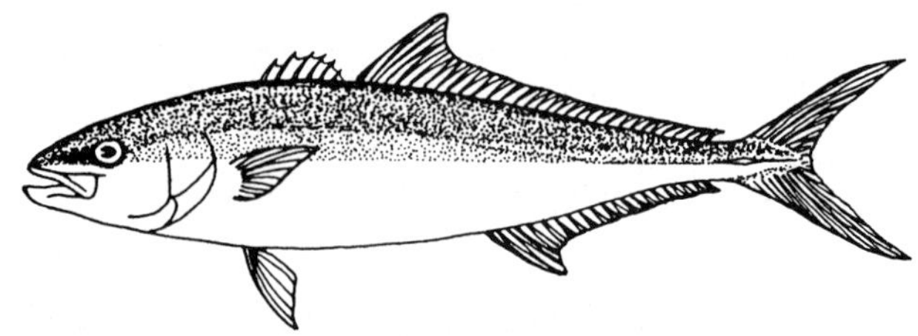

YELLOWTAIL, southern / *Seriola lalandi lalandi* Cuvier & Valenciennes, 1833; CARANGIDAE FAMILY; also called yellowtail kingfish, king yellowtail, northern kingfish, Cape yellowtail, amberfish, halfkoort

Occurs south of the equator (not in equatorial waters) off Argentina, southern Brazil, St. Helena, South Africa, Australia and North Island, New Zealand. North of the equator the southern yellowtail is replaced by the California yellowtail, *Seriola lalandi dorsalis* (Gill, 1863) and the Asian yellowtail, *Seriola lalandi aureovittata* Schlegel, 1844.

It is currently believed that the worldwide yellowtail complex consists of one species, *Seriola lalandi*. It has a disjunct distribution and little is known of its migrations. The three subspecies, southern, California and Asian, are recognized primarily because they are isolated from each other and do not appear to interact. There are five separate populations of southern yellowtail which were previously classified as separate species. There is reason to believe that these different populations do interact with each other and scientists are currently of the opinion that they are one subspecies, *Seriola lalandi lalandi*.

The yellowtail is easily recognized by its bright yellow tail and a characteristic brass colored stripe that runs along the median line of the flanks from the tip of the snout to the tail. It is closely related to the greater amberjack. It can be distinguished by the greater number of developed gill rakers, 21-28 on the first arch, while the amberjack has 11-16. The 6-7 spines in the first dorsal fin are connected by a membrane. The second dorsal fin has 1 spine and 31-37 rays. The anal fin has 3 spines, of which 2 are detached, and 19-23 rays. The lateral line has a scale count of 156-203. There are no scutes or finlets.

The yellowtail is a coastal schooling fish that sometimes enters estuaries. It feeds predominantly in morning and late afternoon on small fishes, invertebrates, and pelagic crabs. It can be taken with live baits or lures that are trolled or cast. The yellowtail's habit of driving bait fish up against the shore makes casting from the beach possible at times. A fast swimmer, the yellowtail strikes viciously, fights hard, and gives at least one long, hard run and sometimes two or three shorter runs when hooked.

Although opinions vary regarding the food value of this species, it is generally highly regarded, with the smaller specimens receiving the better ratings.

Species Illustration Credits

Ade, Robin. 1989. *The Trout and Salmon Handbook*, 122 p. (Facts on File, Inc.). — Page 275, trout, tiger.

American Fisheries Society, Vol. 17, No. 5, Sept./Oct. 1992, artist, Joe Tomelleri. — Page 246, gar, shortnose.

Allen, Roy. U.S. National Marine Fisheries Service, 1990.— Page 255, perch, Nile; 270, threadfin, king.

McGinnis, Samuel M., illustrations Doris Alcorn. 1985. *Freshwater Fishes of California*, (University of California Press.) — Page 234 bass, largemouth; 235 bass, smallmouth; 247 grayling, Arctic; 273 trout, brook; 273 trout, bull; 274 trout, cutthroat; 274 trout, golden; 274 trout, lake.

Hart, J.L. 1973. *Pacific Fishes of Canada*. 740 p. (Fisheries Research Board of Canada, Ottawa). — Page 242 cod, Pacific.

Illustrations courtesy of Hidenori Onishi, Japan Game Fish Association. 1987. — Page 262 seabass, blackfin; 262 seabass, Japanese (suzuki).

Illustrations by Wallace Hughes courtesy of the Florida Game and Fresh Water Fish Commission. — Page 234 bass, redeye; 246 gar, alligator; 246 gar, Florida; 246 gar, longnose; 246 gar, spotted

McClane, A.J. ed. 1974. *McClane's New Standard Fishing Encyclopedia*. 1156 p. (Holt, Rinehart and Winston, NY).— Page 232 bass, yellow; 242 cod, Atlantic; 247 halibut, Atlantic; 247 halibut, Pacific; 257 pollock; 270 tautog

Muskies, Inc., St. Paul, Minnesota. — Page 254 muskellunge, tiger.

Rivas, Luis R. 1986. *Systematic Review of the Perciform Fishes of the Genus* <u>Centropomus</u>, (Copeia, 1986(3), pp.579-611).— Page 267 snook.

Robins, C. Richard, G. Carlton Ray and John Douglas. 1986. *A Field Guide to Atlantic Coast Fishes of North America*. 354 p. (Houghton Mifflin Co., Boston).— Page 270 tarpon.

Scott, W.B. and E.J. Crossman. 1973. *Freshwater Fishes of Canada*, 966 p. (Fisheries Research Board of Canada, Ottawa). — Page 235 Bass, rock; 236 bass, striped; 236 bass, white; 237 bluegill; 241 char, Arctic; 242 crappie, black; 242 crappie, white; 243 Dolly Varden; 245 drum, freshwater; 250 kokanee; 253 muskellunge; 255 perch, white; 256 pickerel, chain; 256 pike, northern; 260 salmon, chinook; 260 salmon, chum; 260 salmon, coho; 261 salmon, pink; 261 salmon, sockeye; 261 sauger; 263 shad, American; 268 sturgeon; 268 sunfish, green; 269 sunfish, redbreast; 273 trout, brown; 279 whitefish, lake; 280 whitefish, mountain; 280 whitefish, round

Scott, Trevor D. 1962. *The Marine and Fresh Water Fishes of Southern Australia*. 338 p. (W.L. Hawes, Government Printer, Adelaide). — Page 249 kahawai (Australian salmon).

Marine Sportfish Identification, California, 1987. (California Department of Fish and Game, NOAA, California Sea Grant). — Page 234 bass, kelp (calico); 262 seabass, white.

Trautman, Milton B. 1981. *The Fishes of Ohio*. 782 p. (Ohio State University Press).—Page 238 bowfin; 238 buffalo, bigmouth; 238 buffalo, smallmouth; 239 bullhead, black; 239 bullhead, brown; 239 bullhead, yellow; 237 burbot; 237 carp, common; 238 catfish, blue; 238 catfish, channel; 240 catfish, flathead; 241 catfish, white; 255 perch, yellow; 258 redhorse, shorthead; 258 redhorse, silver; 269 sunfish, redear; 278 walleye; 279 warmouth

Brichard, Pierre, 1978. *Fishes of Lake Tanganyika*. TFH, Neptune City, New Jersey. — Page 271 tigerfish; 271 tigerfish, giant.

South Carolina Wildlife & Marine Resources Dept., Special Publications Coordinator, Columbia.— Page 236 bass, whiterock.

All other illustrations courtesy of Food and Agriculture Organization of the United Nations, *Species Identification Sheets for Fishery Purposes,* or Michelle Cox and Susan Smith of the U.S. National Marine Fisheris Service.

You, Too, Can Put Your Name in 'The Book'

Getting one's name in the *World Record Game Fishes* book isn't as difficult as many anglers believe. There are hundreds of millions of recreational fishermen in the world, yet only a small percentage, it seems, fish for world records.

Why does the majority allow the few to dominate the competition for world-record status? Every angler has the potential to catch a world-record fish. Phenomenal skill isn't always needed. Sometimes luck will go a long way.

The fish are out there waiting, but making the world record book depends on attention to a short list of details. The do's and don'ts fall into three categories: preparation, the catch, and the follow-up.

One should join IGFA to obtain the annual record book, rules, and forms required to enter your catch for record consideration.

Several matters must receive attention before the fishing day begins. To enter a catch in a line class, your line must test out at a breaking strength less than that figure.

Since IGFA records are set up in specific line-classes (except for all-tackle records) you should fish 2, 4, 6, 8, 12, 16, 20, 30, 50, 80, or 130-pound-test line. You should try to make sure the line will break at or less than the rated breaking strength on the package. Records are disallowed when the angler's line overtests.

There are several items that should accompany you on every excursion to waters that might produce a record fish. Your boat should contain a flexible tape measure at least 15 feet long, a camera, a length of heavy cord, a six-inch square of stiff cardboard to wind the line to submit to IGFA, and plastic bags.

Be sure the reels are spooled with fresh line, that rod guides and reel seats are in good repair, and that drags are smooth. Use hand scales to check the drag.

Check your terminal tackle. Be sure that swivels and swivel clips are ball-bearing types rather than barrel swivels which won't turn freely under load. Check all knots and crimped sleeves, as well as wire or monofilament leaders. Retie knots and re-do crimps with a crimping tool.

Are all hooks honed sharp enough, and is every bit of tackle between angler and fish matched to the possibility of a record-size catch?

If you're on a boat, make sure the crew knows about IGFA rules and that you're seeking a record. A crew member inadvertently handling an angler's line has disqualified many a potential record.

No one may touch the rod, reel, double line, or standing line from the moment of the strike to the landing. Once you bring the fish to the boat, a crew member may grab the leader — but only the leader and not the double line. You're on your own from the strike to the wiring.

It is your responsibility to see that the fish is weighed on properly certified scales, and you must measure the fork length and girth of the fish.

Clear photos are required by the IGFA to confirm your identification of the species. The IGFA rule book or the rules section in this book spell out in detail all procedures to apply for a record.

When everything on the checklist is gathered, the package containing the completed forms (including all necessary signatures of witnesses, weighmaster, and notary), the line, leader and terminal tackle samples, and photos should be mailed promptly to the IGFA headquarters in Dania Beach, Florida.

SECTION 6

IGFA SPECIAL CLUBS

1,000 Pound Club	298
10 Pound Bass Club	299
25 lb Snook Club	301
Grand Slam Clubs	302
20 to 1 Club	304
15 to 1 Club	306
10 to 1 Club	307
5 to 1 Club	310

23rd Annual Fishing Contest

First Place Winners	317
Second Place Winners	320
Third Place Winners	322

IGFA DISCOUNT PROGRAM

Participating Companies and Individuals	324

IGFA Special Clubs

These programs were established to give special recognition to catches where the weight of the fish far exceeds the breaking strength of the line or tippet. Each club recognizes catches made where the weight of the fish is five, ten, fifteen or twenty times the breaking strength of the line or tippet. The Thousand Pound Club recognizes anglers who have caught fish weighing 1,000 pounds or more. The Bass Club recognizes freshwater bass catches weighing 10 pounds or more (See the Club Requirements in Section 3.)

1,000 POUND CLUB

MARLIN, ATLANTIC BLUE

Amorim, Paulo Roberto A., 1,402 lb 2 oz, Vitoria, Brazil
Beard, Larry, 1,204 lb, Funchal, Madeira, Portugal
Bellant, Peter, 1,025 lb, Funchal, Madeira, Portugal
Campbell, Stewart N., 1,038 lb, Madeira, Portugal
Campbell, Stewart N., 1,141 lb, Madeira, Portugal
Cloostermans, Leo R., 1,020 lb, Horta, Faial, Azores
Corday, Kenneth R., 1,170 lb, Madeira, Portugal
Day, Francis O. "Mike", 1,005 lb, Madeira, Portugal
Delbrel, Jacky, 1,190 lb 7 oz, Azores Bank, Faial, Azores
Flinchum, Alan J., 1,021 lb 6 oz, Oregon Inlet, N.Carolina,USA
Fohey, Terry, 1,075 lb, Madeira Island, Portugal
Francois, Jeannine, 1,058 lb 3 oz, Azores, Portugal
Furman, Lawrence H., 1,146 lb 6 oz, Horta, Faial, Azores
Haselhorst, Jorg-Dieter, 1,051 lb 9 oz, Faial, Azores
Hernandez Palmerola, Angel, 1,040 lb, Algarve, Portugal
Jaen C., M.D., Ruben, 1,056 lb, Playa Grande, Venezuela
Jean, Francis, 1,118 lb 13 oz, Abidjan, Ivory Coast
Koerner, Linda, 1,018 lb 8 oz, Gulf of Mexico, Louisiana, USA
Latham, Michael, 1,011 lb, Madeira, Portugal
Lauzen, David, 1,001 lb, Azores Bank, Azores
Lemaitre, Daniel, 1,004 lb, Abidjan, Ivory Coast
Oberholz, Heinz, 1,062 lb 9 oz, Puerto Rico, Gran Canaria, Spain
Read, William A., 1,023 lb, La Guaira, Venezuela
Richard, Laurent, 1,046 lb, Madeira, Portugal
Richard, Jean-Paul, 1,093 lb, Madeira, Portugal
Richard, Jean-Paul, 1,157 lb, Madeira, Portugal
Rogers, Shelby E., 1,059 lb, Madeira, Portugal
Schamps, Francis, 1,008 lb, Madeira, Portugal
Seoane, David G., 1,162 lb, Bermuda

MARLIN, BLACK

Adams, Wally, 1,312 lb, Agincourt, Cairns, Australia
Andersen, Karl, 1,140 lb, Lizard Island, Australia
Anderson, II, John W., 1,307 lb 5 oz, Lizard Island, Australia
Archer, Claude, 1,127 lb, Linden Bank, Cairns, Australia
Astrom, Malte, 1,086 lb, Ruby Reef, Cairns, Australia
Baker, Graham, 1,078 lb, Ribbon Reef, Cairns, Australia
Ballantyne, Quint W., 1,086 lb, Lizard Island, Australia
Ballantyne, Quint W., 1,034 lb, Lizard Island, Australia
Barr, M.D., J. Larry, 1,212 lb, Cairns, Queensland, Australia
Bayliss, James Victor, 1,221 lb, Cairns, Australia
Benitez, Mike, 1,162 lb, Agincourt, Cairns, Australia
Bisgood, Anthony F., 1,356 lb, Linden Bank, Australia
Bisgood, Anthony F., 1,122 lb, Linden Bank, Australia
Carpenter, William K., 1,241 lb, Cabo Blanco, Peru
Caughlan, Craig Paul, 1,054 lb, Cairns, Queensland, Australia
Caughlan, Paul Edward, 1,179 lb, Grt. Barrier Reef, Qld., Australia
Cave, Dave, 1,066 lb 8 oz, Cairns, Australia
Cecil, Eric, 1,179 lb, Lizard Island, N. Qld., Australia
Chinn, Frank, 1,016 lb 8 oz, Ribbon Reef, Australia
Cochain, Dr. Jean-Pierre, 1,055 lb, Yonge Reef, Cairns, Australia
Connellan, Bob (Robt.), 1,291 lb, Grt. Barrier Reef, Qld., Australia
Critz, Jr., Dale C., 1,289 lb, Great Barrier Reef, Australia
Critz, Jr., Dale C., 1,080 lb, Great Barrier Reef, Australia
Curnock, Dave, 1,130 lb 15 oz, St. Crispins Reef, Cairns, Australia
Daito, Denya, 1,011 lb 14 oz, Ribbon Reef, Australia
De Gamboa, Luis F., 1,107 lb, Opal Reef, Australia
De Magalhaes Netto, J.P., 1,022 lb, Lizard Island, Australia
De Magalhaes Netto, J.P., 1,005 lb, Lizard Island, Australia
Denholm, Nicole L., 1,320 lb, Lizard Island, Australia
Denholm, David M., 1,172 lb, Lizard Island, Australia

Dryden, Doug, 1,179 lb 7 oz, Agincourt Reef, Cairns, Australia
Dunaway, Jerry, 1,060 lb, Great Barrier Reef, Australia
Dunkley, Bill, 1,100 lb, Great Barrier Reef, Australia
Elson, Jay M., 1,014 lb, Cairns, North Queensland, Australia
Elson, Jay M., 1,294 lb, Cairns, North Queensland, Australia
Elson, Jay M., 1,079 lb, Cairns, North Queensland, Australia
Elson, Jay M., 1,123 lb, Cairns, North Queensland, Australia
Estrada, Victor E., 1,025 lb, Cairns, Australia
Fawcett, David H., 1,025 lb, Agincourt Reef, Queensland, Australia
Fay, Gus, 1,203 lb, Yonge Reef, N.S.W., Australia
Fitzpatrick, Barry M., 1,177 lb, Great Barrier Reef, Qld., Australia
Fohey, Terry, 1,188 lb, Linden Bank, Great Barrier Reef, Australia
Forster, Janet, 1,052 lb, Lizard Island, Australia
Garrett, Gerald A., 1,219 lb, Linden Bank, Cairns, Australia
Gay, Christine, 1,121 lb, No. 7 Ribbon, Cairns, Australia
Gay, Patrick, 1,207 lb, Linden Bank, Cairns, Australia
Giraud, Marc, 1,160 lb, Ribbon Reef, Australia
Glass, George H., 1,055 lb, Onyx Reef, Cairns, Australia
Glassell, Jr., Alfred C., 1,560 lb, Cabo Blanco, Peru
Gutierrez, Jr., Raul, 1,025 lb 2 oz, Ribbon Reef, Cairns, Australia
Hall, Leon, 1,102 lb, Lizard Island, Queensland, Australia
Hamlin, Capt. Ron, 1,098 lb, Cairns, Australia
Harrison, Jaime, 1,102 lb, Ribbon Reef, Lizard Island, Australia
Heaton, James E., 1,168 lb, Cairns, Queensland, Australia
Heaton, James E., 1,212 lb, Cairns, Queensland, Australia
Heck, Roland G., 1,135 lb 5 oz, Cairns, Australia
Hill, Barry, 1,030 lb, Cairns, Australia
Hopper, Tony, 1,113 lb, Lizard Island, Australia
Houck, Joseph A., 1,014 lb, Ribbon Reef, Australia
Huerta G., Aurelio, 1,036 lb, Cairns, Australia
Huntsinger, Larry A., 1,075 lb, Linden Banks, Cairns, Australia
Immergut, Mel M., 1,204 lb, Lizard Island, Ribbon Reef, Australia
Inoue, Masahiko, 1,113 lb, Lizard Island, Australia
Isaacs, Richard A., 1,023 lb, Lizard Island, Australia
Jackson, John M., 1,087 lb, Lizard Island, Cairns, Qld., Australia
Jones, Rick, 1,236 lb, Lizard Island, Australia
Kilborn, III, Vincent, 1,000 lb, Linden Bank, Cairns, Australia
Lehr, Neill, 1,073 lb 6 oz, Lizard Island, Queensland, Australia
Levitt, Michael J., 1,058 lb, Great Barrier Reef, Australia
Lopuszanski, Daniel, 1,300 lb, St. Crispin Reef, Cairns, Australia
Lowe, Bob, 1,014 lb, Lizard Island, Australia
Lowery, Sr., Archie, 1,008 lb, Cairns, Australia
Marchandise, Michel, 1,070 lb, Great Barrier Reef, Qld., Australia
Marchandise, Michel, 1,025 lb, Great Barrier Reef, Qld., Australia
Marlin, Kenneth, 1,089 lb, Lizard Island, Australia
Martone, Alexander L., 1,179 lb, Grt. Barrier Reef, Australia
Maspons, Santiago, 1,114 lb, Agincourt, Cairns, Australia
McIntosh, Lin, 1,144 lb, Lizard Island, Cairns, Qld., Australia
Meyer, Jay W., 1,012 lb, Great Barrier Reef, Australia
Mote, William R., 1,180 lb, Cabo Blanco, Peru
Mulkey, Thomas F., 1,037 lb, Spur Reef, Queensland, Australia
Negley, William, 1,056 lb, Cabo Blanco, Peru
Nelson, Capt. Pat, 1,050 lb, Great Barrier Reef, Australia
Nye, Harold J., 1,075 lb 13 oz, North Queensland, Australia
Obach, Richard C., 1,064 lb, Cairns, Australia
Olivier, Clive, 1,109 lb, Lizard Island, Australia
Orthwein, James B., 1,006 lb 2 oz, Cairns, Australia
Owings, Osbourn, 1,128 lb, Cabo Blanco, Peru
Pfleger, Tom, 1,177 lb, Lizard Island, Australia
Philips, Jesse, 1,023 lb, Lizard Island, Australia
Pierce, T. L., 1,012 lb, Lizard Island, Australia
Pratt, Phil, 1,273 lb 2 oz, Cairns, Queensland, Australia
Ratanamangcla, Apiwat, 1,190 lb 7 oz, Cairns, Australia
Reid, Mark, 1,069 lb 3 oz, Lizard Island, Australia
Rivkin, Michael L., 1,226 lb, Great Barrier Reef, Cairns, Australia
Roccatti, Sergio, 1,036 lb, Lizard Island, Australia
Roush, Patrick, 1,177 lb, Spur Reef, Cairns, Qld., Australia

Roush, Jan S., 1,052 lb, Ribbon Reef, Cooktown, Qld., Australia
Russell, Jack, 1,255 lb, Great Barrier Reef, Cairns, Australia
Saragusa, Michael J., 1,047 lb, Ribbon Reef, Cairns, Qld., Australia
Sau-Ling Shi, Jeannette, 1,076 lb, Day Reef, North Qld., Australia
Schram, Jr., Gus W., 1,060 lb, Great Barrier Reef, Australia
Schram, Jr., Gus W., 1,392 lb, Cairns, Queensland, Australia
Silber, D. Robert, 1,220 lb, Lizard Island, Australia
Smith, Wilbur, 1,012 lb, Great Barrier Reef, Cairns, Australia
Stubbs, John Michael, 1,074 lb, Grt. Barrier Reef, Cairns, Australia
Takano, Tacky, 1,100 lb, Lizard Island, Australia
Thomasson, Burgess A., 1,067 lb, Great Barrier Reef, Australia
Thomson, David G., 1,109 lb, Great Barrier Reef, Australia
Turnbull, A. J., 1,271 lb, Lizard Island, Queensland, Australia
Tyson, Randal, 1,014 lb, Cairns, Australia
Tyson, John, 1,003 lb, Cairns, Australia
Tyson, Don, 1,124 lb, Cairns, Australia
Von Platen Luder, Shirley, 1,014 lb, Great Barrier Reef, Australia
Wallace, Dennis Capt., 1,058 lb, No. 3, Agincourt, Australia
Wallace, Dennis Capt., 1,022 lb, Linden Bank, Australia
Willits, John F., 1,031 lb, Lizard Island, Australia
Wilson, John H. M., 1,153 lb, Cairns, Australia
Wily, Hugh J., 1,047 lb, Lizard Island, Australia
Zehnder, John L., 1,007 lb, Great Barrier Reef, Australia
Zeitlin, Dr. Salvatore, 1,117 lb, Opal Reef, Australia

MARLIN, PACIFIC BLUE

Bento, Al, 1,207 lb, Kalaupapa, Molokai, Hawaii, USA
D'Hotman De Villiers, Andre, 1,100 lb, Le Morne, Mauritius
De Beaubien, Jay William, 1,376 lb, Kaaiwi Point, Kona, HI, USA
Everette, Kelley K., 1,103 lb 8 oz, Kailua, Kona, Hawaii, USA
Harding, Tony, 1,007 lb, The Hook, North Cape, New Zealand
Hawkes, Ray G., 1,166 lb, Kailua-Kona, Hawaii, USA
Jorgensen, Douglas, 1,201 lb 12 oz, Kahoolawe, Maui, Hawaii, USA
Jurado E., Jorge F., 1,014 lb, Manta, Ecuador
Kraemer, Gil, 1,062 lb 8 oz, Kona, Hawaii, USA
Marsh, Del, 1,000 lb, Kona, Hawaii, USA
Mau, Andrew, 1,101 lb 8 oz, Molokai, Hawaii, USA
Schonauer, K.F.J., 1,140 lb, Mauritius
Thalwitzer, T.M., 1,003 lb, Black River, Mauritius

SHARK, MAKO

Guillanton, Patrick, 1,115 lb, Black River, Mauritius
Kennedy, Leo, 1,014 lb, Black River, Mauritius
Shanaghan, Martin, 1,022 lb 7 oz, Hawke Bay, Napier, N.Z.

SHARK, SIXGILLED

Reece, W. P., 1,027 lb, Faial, Azores, Portugal
Reece, Jack Capt., 1,069 lb 3 oz, Faial, Azores, Portugal

SHARK, TIGER

Booth, Glen, 1,300 lb 11 oz, Port Hacking, N.S.W., Australia
Grieves, Leanne, 1,208 lb 1 oz, Lake Macquarie, N.S.W., Australia
Hezard, Philippe, 1,218 lb, Mauritius
McCarthy, Ian John, 1,138 lb 10 oz, Sydney, Australia
Meyer, Hans, 1,073 lb 10 oz, Swansea, N.S.W., Australia
Norris, Bronwyn L., 1,095 lb 10 oz, Swansea, N.S.W., Australia
Spruce, Robyn, 1,018 lb 8 oz, Swansea, N.S.W., Australia
Turnbull, June, 1,173 lb, Cronulla, N.S.W., Australia

SHARK, WHITE

Astrom, Malte, 1,946 lb 10 oz, Langton Isl., Pt. Lincoln, Australia
Caughlan, Jason Andrew, 2,026 lb, Port Lincoln, Australia
Colreavy, Stephen, 1,040 lb 9 oz, Port Stephens, N.S.W., Australia
Czabayski, Rolf, 1,542 lb 1 oz, Port Lincoln, Australia
Czabayski, Rolf, 1,102 lb 4 oz, Streaky Bay, Australia
Czabayski, Ralph Jeffrey, 1,195 lb 15 oz, Port Lincoln, Australia
Flourentzou, George, 1,058 lb 3 oz, Neptune Islands, Australia
Flourentzou, George, 1,272 lb, Cape Jervis, Australia
Forster, Janet, 1,164 lb, The Pages, Australia
Jenkins, Tom, 1,087 lb, The Pages, Australia
Morris, Steve, 1,684 lb 5 oz, Port Lincoln, Australia
Roccatti, Sergio, 1,037 lb, Port Lincoln, Australia
Sampson, Vic, 1,366 lb 13 oz, Australia
Sampson, Vic, 1,704 lb 2 oz, Kangaroo Island, Australia
Sampson, Vic, 1,340 lb 6 oz, Kangaroo Island, Australia

TUNA, BLUEFIN

Birkhead, Harry, 1,165 lb, North Lake, P.E.I., Canada
Braddick, Don, 1,112 lb, Prince Edward Island, North Lake, Canada
Carr, Jack, 1,020 lb, Havre Boucher, Nova Scotia, Canada
Cogswell, Charles D., 1,086 lb, Stellwagen B., Gloucester, MA, USA
Collins, John Michael, 1,092 lb, Prince Edward Island, Canada
Cunningham, Jr., Colin M., 1,115 lb, North Lake, P.E.I., Canada
Currie, Donald R., 1,060 lb, North Lake, P.E.I., Canada
Currie, Donald R., 1,055 lb, North Lake, P.E.I., Canada
Dackerman, Ray, 1,025 lb, Cape Cod Bay, Massachusetts, USA
De Gamboa, Luis F., 1,095 lb, Prince Edward Island, Canada
Dempsey, E. James, 1,140 lb 12 oz, Block Island, Rhode Island, USA
Drummond, Monty, 1,010 lb, North Lake, P.E.I., Canada
Fitzpatrick, Barry M., 1,115 lb, North Lake, P.E.I., Canada
Flores A., Luis Alberto, 1,170 lb, Prince Edward Island, Canada
Fraser, Ken, 1,496 lb, Auld's Cove, Nova Scotia, Canada
Gilliam, III, Robert L., 1,080 lb, Prince Edward Island, Canada
Immergut, Mel M., 1,040 lb, North Lake, P.E.I., Canada
Jacob, Bart M., 1,001 lb, Port Daniel, Gaspe, Canada
Jaen C., M.D., Ruben, 1,018 lb, North Lake, P.E.I., Canada
Lazcano, Raymond, 1,010 lb, Cape Cod Bay, Massachusetts, USA
Mans, Andrew J., 1,100 lb, North Lake, P.E.I., Canada
Marsay, Bill, 1,070 lb, North Lake, Prince Edward Island, Canada
Perras, M.D., Colette, 1,170 lb, North Lake, P.E.I., Canada
Slominski, Paul J., 1,140 lb, St. Georges Bay, Nova Scotia, Canada
Smith, Robert D., 1,020 lb, St. Georges Bay, Nova Scotia, Canada
Steffey, J. M. Dr., 1,116 lb, Prince Edward Island, Canada
Steffey, J. M. Dr., 1,230 lb, Prince Edward Island, Canada
Stott, Donald B., 1,120 lb, Harve Boucher, Nova Scotia, Canada
Stott, Donald B., 1,040 lb, Harve Boucher, Nova Scotia, Canada
Stott, Donald B., 1,100 lb, Harve Boucher, Nova Scotia, Canada
Stott, Donald B., 1,120 lb, Harve Boucher, Nova Scotia, Canada
Stott, Donald B., 1,256 lb, Harve Boucher, Nova Scotia, Canada
Stott, Donald B., 1,020 lb, Harve Boucher, Nova Scotia, Canada
Stott, Donald B., 1,132 lb, Harve Boucher, Nova Scotia, Canada
Tuit, Jaap, 1,105 lb, Prince Edward Island, Canada
Tuit, Jaap, 1,060 lb, Prince Edward Island, Canada
Tuit, Jaap, 1,211 lb, Prince Edward Island, Canada
Van Vleck, Perry B., 1,198 lb, North Lake, P.E.I., Canada
Van Vleck, Perry B., 1,085 lb, North Lake, P.E.I., Canada
Van Vleck, Perry B., 1,000 lb, North Lake, P.E.I., Canada

10 POUND BASS CLUB

LARGEMOUTH BASS

Allen, Dennis, 10 lb 4 oz, Lake Gaston, North Carolina, USA
Anderson, Eric, 11 lb 2 oz, Saguaro Lake, Arizona, USA
Arklin, Steve, 15 lb, Castaic Lake, Castaic, California, USA
Arklin, Phil, 15 lb 2 oz, Lake Casitas, Ventura, California, USA
Ashley, Rick E., 15 lb 1 oz, Private Lake, Texarkana, Arkansas, USA
Aumend, Dave, 10 lb 4 oz, Punta Gorda, Florida, USA
Bailey, Arthur E., 10 lb 1 oz, San Diego, California, USA
Ballas, Jr., Chuck, 11 lb 9 oz, Farm Pond, Burke Co., Girard, GA, USA
Barnes, Ryan P., 14 lb, Castaic, California, USA
Barrett, Kevin P., 11 lb 8 oz, Cooper River, South Carolina, USA
Benson, III, Joseph A., 12 lb 12 oz, Moran, Texas, USA
Bertken, Jim, 14 lb, Castaic Lake, Castaic, California, USA
Berwick, Pip, 12 lb 12 oz, Ashcott Farm Dam, Bindura, Zimbabwe
Besmer, Gary, 11 lb 8 oz, Lake Baccarac, Mexico
Blanton, C. E., 12 lb, Lake Casitas, Ventura, California, USA
Bohling, Ken, 10 lb, Hanabanilla Lake, Villa Clara, Cuba
Bozek, Steve, 13 lb 3 oz, Canyon Lake, Apache Junc., Arizona, USA
Bozek, Steve, 18 lb 1 oz, Canyon Lake, Apache Junc., Arizona, USA
Bozek, Steve, 13 lb 14 oz, Canyon Lake, Apache Junc., Arizona, USA
Bozek, Steve, 10 lb 15 oz, Canyon Lake, Apache Junc., Arizona, USA
Bradshaw, Leonard, 10 lb, Lake Cahoon, Suffolk, Virginia, USA
Brandon, Tom, 10 lb 10 oz, Compass Lake, Florida, USA
Breen, Jim, 10 lb 8 oz, Castaic Lake, Castaic, California, USA
Brewer, Norris, 11 lb 8 oz, Castaic Lake, Castaic, California, USA
Brown, Kennon, 12 lb 1 oz, Fall's Lake, Durham, N. Carolina, USA
Brown, Kennon, 10 lb 6 oz, Fall's Lake, Durham, N. Carolina, USA
Buckby, Bruce, 14 lb 5 oz, Private Dam, Centenary, Zimbabwe
Bunting, Don L., 10 lb 6 oz, Newnans Lake, Gainesville, FL, USA
Burnett, Pat, 10 lb, Bull Shoals Lake, Arkansas, USA
Carpenter, James R., 12 lb 3 oz, Lake Hodges, San Diego, CA, USA
Church, Dennis, 10 lb 12 oz, Castaic Lake, Castaic, California, USA
Clark, Jim, 10 lb 9 oz, Back Bay, Virginia, USA
Clines, Frank G., 10 lb 2 oz, Lake Mable, Florida, USA
Collis, John, 15 lb 4 oz, Castaic Lake, Castaic, California, USA
Coppola, Sr., Frank Paul, 11 lb 6, Hampstead, N. Hampshire, USA
Cormier, Jr, Tony, 10 lb 2 oz, Lake Fork, Little Caney, Texas, USA
Crupi, Bob, 17 lb 4 oz, Castaic Lake Lagoon, Castaic, CA, USA
Crupi, Bob, 10 lb 2 oz, Castaic Lake Lagoon, Castaic, CA, USA
Crupi, Bob, 10 lb 8 oz, Lake Casitas, Ventura, California, USA
Crupi, Bob, 10 lb Castaic Lake, Castaic, California, USA

Crupi, Bob, 10 lb 6 oz, Castaic Lake, Castaic, California, USA
Crupi, Bob, 11 lb 4 oz, Castaic Lake, Castaic, California, USA
Crupi, Bob, 10 lb 4 oz, Castaic Lake, Castaic, California, USA
Crupi, Bob, 16 lb 1 oz, Castaic Lake, Castaic, California, USA
Crupi, Bob, 13 lb 1 oz, Castaic Lake, Castaic, California, USA
Crupi, Bob, 10 lb 4 oz, Castaic Lake, Castaic, California, USA
Crupi, Bob, 10 lb 1 oz, Castaic Lake, Castaic, California, USA
Crupi, Bob, 13 lb 2 oz, Castaic Lake, Castaic, California, USA
Crupi, Bob, 11 lb 8 oz, Castaic Lake, Castaic, California, USA
Crupi, Bob, 10 lb 8 oz, Castaic Lake, Castaic, California, USA
Crupi, Bob, 10 lb 8 oz, Castaic Lake, Castaic, California, USA
Crupi, Bob, 10 lb 8 oz, Castaic Lake, Castaic, California, USA
Crupi, Bob, 13 lb 3 oz, Castaic Lake, Castaic, California, USA
Crupi, Bob, 17 lb 8 oz, Castaic Lake, Castaic, California, USA
Crupi, Bob, 22 lb, Castaic Lake, Castaic, California, USA
Crupi, Bob, 14 lb 12 oz, Castaic Lake, Castaic, California, USA
Crupi, Bob, 16 lb 14 oz, Castaic Lake, Castaic, California, USA
Crupi, Bob, 17 lb 1 oz, Castaic Lake, Castaic, California, USA
Crupi, Bob, 18 lb 9 oz, Castaic Lake, Castaic, California, USA
Crupi, Bob, 21 lb, Castaic Lake, Castaic, California, USA
Crupi, Bob, 12 lb 8 oz, Castaic Lake, Castaic, California, USA
Crupi, Bob, 10 lb 4 oz, Castaic Lake, Castaic, California, USA
Crupi, Bob, 11 lb, Castaic Lake, Castaic, California, USA
Crupi, Bob, 10 lb, Castaic Lake, Castaic, California, USA
Crupi, Bob, 11 lb 8 oz, Castaic Lake, Castaic, California, USA
Crupi, Bob, 10 lb 4 oz, Castaic Lake, Castaic, California, USA
Crupi, Bob, 11 lb, Castaic Lake, Castaic, California, USA
Crupi, Bob, 12 lb, Castaic Lake, Castaic, California, USA
Crupi, Bob, 12 lb, Castaic Lake, Castaic, California, USA
Crupi, Bob, 10 lb, Castaic Lake, Castaic, California, USA
Crupi, Bob, 10 lb 10 oz, Castaic Lake, Castaic, California, USA
Crupi, Bob, 10 lb 4 oz, Castaic Lake, Castaic, California, USA
Crupi, Bob, 10 lb 2 oz, Castaic Lake, Castaic, California, USA
Crupi, Bob, 10 lb, Castaic Lake, Castaic, California, USA
Crupi, Bob, 12 lb, Castaic Lake, Castaic, California, USA
Crupi, Bob, 10 lb 8 oz, Castaic Lake, Castaic, California, USA
Crupi, Bob, 10 lb, Castaic Lake, Castaic, California, USA
Crupi, Bob, 10 lb 2 oz, Castaic Lake, Castaic, California, USA
Crupi, Bob, 10 lb, Castaic Lake, Castaic, California, USA
Crupi, Bob, 11 lb 3 oz, Castaic Lake, Castaic, California, USA
Crupi, Bob, 11 lb, Castaic Lake, Castaic, California, USA
Crupi, Bob, 13 lb, Castaic Lake, Castaic, California, USA
Crupi, Bob, 11 lb, Castaic Lake, Castaic, California, USA
Crupi, Bob, 12 lb 2 oz, Castaic Lake, Castaic, California, USA
Crupi, Bob, 10 lb 1 oz, Castaic Lake, Castaic, California, USA
Crupi, Bob, 10 lb 8 oz, Castaic Lake, Castaic, California, USA
Crupi, Bob, 10 lb 1 oz, Castaic Lake, Castaic, California, USA
Crupi, Bob, 12 lb 12 oz, Castaic Lake, Castaic, California, USA
Crupi, Bob, 11 lb 12 oz, Castaic Lake, Castaic, California, USA
Crupi, Bob, 10 lb 12 oz, Castaic Lake, Castaic, California, USA
Crupi, Bob, 10 lb 8 oz, Castaic Lake, Castaic, California, USA
Crupi, Bob, 14 lb 7 oz, Castaic Lake, Castaic, California, USA
Crupi, Bob, 10 lb 8 oz, Lake Casitas, Ventura, California, USA
Crupi, Bob, 11 lb 12 oz, Castaic Lake, Castaic, California, USA
Crupi, Bob, 10 lb 8 oz, Castaic Lake, Castaic, California, USA
Crupi, Bob, 11 lb, Castaic Lake, Castaic, California, USA
Crupi, Bob, 13 lb 12 oz, Lake Casitas, Ventura, California, USA
Crupi, Bob, 11 lb, Castaic Lake, Castaic, California, USA
Crupi, Bob, 10 lb 4 oz, Castaic Lake, Castaic, California, USA
Crupi, Bob, 10 lb, Lake Casitas, Ventura, California, USA
Crupi, Bob, 12 lb, Castaic Lake, Castaic, California, USA
Crupi, Bob, 10 lb, Lake Casitas, Ventura, California, USA
Crupi, Bob, 12 lb 6 oz, Lake Miramar, San Diego, California, USA
Crupi, Bob, 10 lb, Castaic Lake, Castaic, California, USA
Crupi, Bob, 10 lb 10 oz, Castaic Lake, Castaic, California, USA
Crupi, Bob, 15 lb 10 oz, Lake Miramar, San Diego, California, USA
Crupi, Bob, 10 lb 8 oz, Lake Miramar, San Diego, California, USA
Crupi, Bob, 14 lb, Lake Miramar, San Diego, California, USA
Crupi, Bob, 12 lb 2 oz, Lake Miramar, San Diego, California, USA
Crupi, Bob, 14 lb 14 oz, Castaic Lake, Castaic, California, USA
Crupi, Bob, 13 lb, Lake Miramar, San Diego, California, USA
Crupi, Bob, 12 lb 3 oz, Castaic Lake, Castaic, California, USA
Crupi, Tiffany Noel, 10 lb 8 oz, Castaic Lake, Castaic, CA, USA
Davis, Jr., Preston, 12 lb, Castaic Lake, Castaic, California, USA
Davis, Mark, 10 lb 12 oz, Castaic Lake, Castaic, California, USA
Daye, Bob, 11 lb 9 oz, Okeechobee, Florida, USA
Deal, Larry S., 11 lb 4 oz, Farm Pond, Wake Co., N.Carolina, USA
Dilday, R. Burr, 11 lb, Dominguez Lake, El Fuerte, Mexico
Dingman, Brian, 11 lb 4 oz, Palm Bay, Florida, USA

Dowd, George, 10 lb 4 oz, Bull Shoals Lake, Arkansas, USA
Doyle, Billy Ross, 10 lb 2 oz, Bay Springs, Mississippi, USA
Drake, Don, 10 lb 8 oz, Lake El Salto, Mexico
Dunaway, Jerry, 10 lb 4 oz, Lake Casitas, Casitas, California, USA
Eads, Michael J., 11 lb 2 oz, Cane Creek Lake, Waxhaw, N.C., USA
Easter, Bill, 12 lb, Castaic Lake, Castaic, California, USA
Easter, Frank, 11 lb 12 oz, Castaic Lake, Castaic, California, USA
Evander, Scott Dixon, 11 lb, Rodman Reservoir, Palatka, Florida, USA
Evert, Thomas L., 10 lb, Water Mellon Pond, Newberry, Florida, USA
Fayard, Jr., John R., 10 lb 11 oz, Lake Billwaller, Mississippi, USA
Fedrowitz, George C., 12 lb 4 oz, Orlando, Florida, USA
Fern, Bob, 17 lb 6 oz, Lake Casitas, Ventura, California, USA
Frerking, William L., 10 lb, Castaic Lake, Castaic, California, USA
Frerking, William L., 10 lb, Castaic Lake, Castaic, California, USA
Fuhrmann, Judd Aaron, 10 lb 12 oz, Orange Springs, Florida, USA
Funke, III, Frank T., 11 lb 12 oz, Lake Okeechobee, Florida, USA
Gargan, Bill, 15 lb 9 oz, Kaweah Lake, Lemon Cove, California, USA
Gentry, John, 10 lb, Castaic Lake, Castaic, California, USA
Gifford, Allen, 10 lb 12 oz, Purcell City Lake, Oklahoma, USA
Goehrig, Gene A. "Lou", 10 lb 4 oz, Winter Park, Florida, USA
Grassi, Anthony, 11 lb 6 oz, Lake Casitas, Oakview, California, USA
Gritter, Jim, 11 lb 10 oz, Lake Kerr, Salt Springs, Florida, USA
Gunn, Jeff, 10 lb 4 oz, Lake Fork, Texas
Hall, Porter, 18 lb 5 oz, Lake Casitas, Oak View, California, USA
Hannon, Douglas, 16 lb 8 oz, Buck Lake, Ocala, Florida, USA
Hatcher, Rickey, 13 lb 15 oz, Lake Harris, Wedowee, Alabama, USA
Hendison, Brad, 12 lb 4 oz, Castaic Lake, Castaic, California, USA
Howle, Dan, 10 lb 13 oz, Lake Fork, Texas, USA
Hutchinson, R. J., 11 lb 12 oz, Private Dam, Mtepatepa, Zimbabwe
Jackson, Matt, 12 lb 8 oz, Castaic Lake, Castaic, California, USA
Johnson, Shain, 11 lb 2 oz, Triangle, Zimbabwe
Jones, Roger, 11 lb, Castaic Lake, Castaic, California, USA
Kaufman, Shep, 10 lb 6 oz, Lake Okeechobee, Okeechobee, FL, USA
Keener, Jeffrey L., 10 lb 12 oz, Santee, Cooper, S. Carolina, USA
Kuhens, Randy, 12 lb 14 oz, Rodman Reservoir, Palatka, FL, USA
Kunecke, Ron, 10 lb 2 oz, Castaic Lake, Castaic, California, USA
Lane, Dale A., 11 lb, Canyon Lake, California, USA
Larson, Jim 12 lb, Lake Sinclair, Georgia, USA
Lathem, J. Ernest, 12 lb, Greenville, South Carolina, USA
Lock, Jerry, 11 lb, St. Johns River, Florida, USA
Maggard, Bobby, 12 lb 6 oz, Stuart, Florida, USA
Manlin, Richard, 16 lb 4 oz, Lake Chambas, Cuba
Markert, Phil, 10 lb 4 oz, Castaic Lake, Castaic, California, USA
Martin, John, 10 lb 15 oz, Castaic Lake, Castaic, California, USA
Maruhashi, Eizo, 10 lb 2 oz, Lake Baccarac, Mexico
McAbee, Terry, 16 lb 9 oz, Lake Isabella, California, USA
McCurdy, Scott, 10 lb 1 oz, Lake Pickett, Oviedo, Florida, USA
McDaniel, Patric A., 10 lb, Lake Orlando, Orlando, Florida, USA
McLelland, Larry, 11 lb 3 oz, Lake Livingstone, Texas, USA
Medley, Ken H., 10 lb 2 oz, Farm Lake, Auxvasse, Florida, USA
Mikelson, Daniel J., 10 lb 5 oz, Lake Istokpoga, Florida, USA
Miller, Gary, 10 lb 1 oz, Castaic Lake, Castaic, California, USA
Moon, David, 12 lb 4 oz, Cabin Bluff, Georgia, USA
Moore, Richard, 13 lb, Castaic Lake, Castaic, California, USA
Mulvihill, Bill, 11 lb 8 oz, Castaic Lake, Castaic, California, USA
Murata, Hajime, 10 lb 11 oz, Ikehara Reservoir, Nara, Japan
Murata, Hajime, 11 lb 8 oz, Ikehara Reservoir, Nara, Japan
Murata, Hajime, 11 lb 1 oz, Ikehara Reservoir, Nara, Japan
Murata, Hajime, 10 lb 5 oz, Ikehara Reservoir, Nara, Japan
Murata, Hajime, 10 lb 6 oz, Ikehara Reservoir, Nara, Japan
Musbach, Alice, 11 lb 6 oz, Clearlake, California, USA
Nemec, Bill, 11 lb 4 oz, Lake Okeechobee, Clewiston, Florida, USA
Noonan, Dr. Dennis M., 14 lb 8 oz, Stuart, Florida, USA
Novelli, Terry, 14 lb, Castaic Lake, Castaic, California, USA
Nowell, Don R., 14 lb 2 oz, Lake Highland, Alford, Florida, USA
Okano, Kouichi, 15 lb 1 oz, Ikehara Reservoir, Nara, Japan
Patrick, Mike, 10 lb 6 oz, James Saha Pond, Frydek, Texas, USA
Patrick, Linda, 10 lb 6 oz, James Saha Pond, Frydek, Texas, USA
Patty, Betty J., 10 lb, Lake El Salto, Mazatlan
Pedneau, Ed, 14 lb, Lake Casitas, Ventura, California, USA
Pedneau, Francis, 11 lb 4 oz, Lake Casitas, Ventura, California, USA
Perkins, J. Wain, 11 lb 4 oz, Dripping Springs, Texas, USA
Petelik, Bill, 11 lb 2 oz, Table Rock Lake, Missouri, USA
Pickard, Mark, 13 lb 2 oz, L. Elizabeth, Ponte Vedra Bch., FL, USA
Pollock, Tony, 10 lb, Castaic Lake, Castaic, California, USA
Pompa, Samuel Yera, 13 lb 8 oz, Munoz L., Camaguey Prov., Cuba
Ratner, Jr., Herbert G., 10 lb 4 oz, Miami, Florida, USA
Ratner, Jr., Herbert G., 10 lb, Miami, Florida, USA
Richardson, Banks, 12 lb 1 oz, Lake Aumun, West End, NC, USA

Rodee, III, Walter F., 11 lb 6 oz, Lake Guerrero, Mexico
Rogers, Michael, 12 lb, Lake Kissimmee, Florida, USA
Roper, Bobby, 10 lb 14 oz, Lake Charles, Louisiana, USA
Rothhaar, Ron A., 11 lb 3 oz, Reedy Lake,Frostproof,Florida, USA
Rutherford, Steven W., 11 lb 1 oz, Dobson, North Carolina, USA
Samuels, Ricky Lee, 13 lb 8 oz, Farmville, Virginia, USA
Sanders, Jack M., 10 lb 8 oz, Lake Baccarac, Mexico
Sato, Darryl, 10 lb 2 oz, Castaic Lake, Castaic, California, USA
Savoie, Wayne, 10 lb 6 oz, Farm Pond, Louisiana, USA
Seki, Chitoshi, 10 lb 7 oz, Ikehara Reservoir, Nara, Japan
Sesto, Chris, 10 lb 4 oz, Castaic Lake, Castaic, California, USA
Shepard, Robert D., 11 lb, Belaire Canal,Dade County,Florida,USA
Sikora, Bruce T., 14 lb, Castaic Lake, Castaic, California, USA
Sikora, Bruce T., 13 lb 2 oz, Castaic Lake, Castaic,California, USA
Sikora, Bruce T., 10 lb 2 oz, Castaic Lake, Castaic,California, USA
Sikora, Bruce T., 11 lb 8 oz, Castaic Lake, Castaic,California, USA
Simmons, III, Ramsay, 10 lb 4 oz, Gretna, Florida, USA
Smith, Curt, 10 lb 2 oz, Sam Rayburn, Texas, USA
Smith, Ed, 10 lb 8 oz, Don Pedro Reservoir, California, USA
Smith, Jeffrey H., 13 lb 2 oz,Bienville Plant.,White Spg.,FL, USA
Smith, Jeffrey H., 12 lb, Bienville Plant., White Spg.,Florida, USA
Smith, Jeffrey H., 10 lb 2 oz,Bienville Plant.,White Spg.,FL, USA
Smith, Jeffrey H., 11 lb 4 oz, Winter Haven, Florida, USA
Smith, Jeffrey H., 16 lb 11 oz, Winter Haven, Florida, USA
Smith, Jeffrey H., 10 lb 7 oz, Winter Haven, Florida, USA
Smith, Jeffrey H., 10 lb 2 oz, Winter Haven, Florida, USA
Smith, Jeffrey H., 10 lb 9 oz, Orange Grove Lake, Bartow,FL,USA
Smith, Jeffrey H., 13 lb, Winter Haven, Florida, USA
Smith, Jeffrey H., 15 lb, Winter Haven, Florida, USA
Smith, Jeffrey H., 10 lb 8 oz, Stick Marsh Lake,Fellsmere, FL,USA
Smith, Sterling, 10 lb 8 oz, Orange Grove Lake, Bartow, FL, USA
Smith, Sterling, 10 lb 2 oz, Orange Grove Lake, Bartow, FL, USA
Smith, Steve, 13 lb, Polk County, Florida, USA
Smith, Steve, 10 lb 8 oz, Polk County, Florida, USA
Smith, Steve, 10 lb 8 oz, Polk County, Florida, USA
Smith, Steve, 15 lb 2 oz, Polk County, Florida, USA
Smith, Steve, 11 lb 12 oz, Polk County, Florida, USA
Smith, Steve, 10 lb 6 oz, Private Strip Pond, Missouri, USA
Smith, Steve, 11 lb 4 oz, Polk County, Florida, USA
Smith, Steve, 10 lb 2 oz, Polo, Missouri, USA
Steffes, James W., 10 lb 15 oz, Lake Hodges, San Diego,CA, USA
Stephens, Johnnie, 13 lb 7 oz, Hernando Lake, Hernando, FL, USA
Sterbinsky, Bill, 12 lb 6 oz,Lake Joy,Silver Springs Shores,FL,USA
Stevens, Skip, 15 lb 9 oz, Napa, California, USA
Stoner, Dave 10 lb 4 oz, Clear Lake, California, USA
Strangeway, Bruce, 10 lb 3 oz, Blue Cypress Lake, Florida, USA
Szymanik, Matthew J., 10 lb 8 oz, Pinelands, New Jersey, USA
Tait, Marilyn M., 10 lb 3 oz, Salt Springs, Florida, USA
Tangen, Joe, 10 lb 4 oz, Withlacoochee R.,Citrus County, FL, USA
Thodos, Dr. John R., 10 lb 4 oz,George's Lake,Florahome,FL,USA
Thodos, Dr. John R., 15 lb 4 oz, Stickmarsh, Fellsmere, FL, USA
Tokunaga, Kenzo, 11 lb 5 oz, Lake Baccarac, Mexico
Vice, Timothy J., 13 lb, Lake Espanola, Mexico
Vinzant, Herbert "Pat", 10 lb 4 oz, Dos Bocas, Puerto Rico
Visich, Dennis F., 10 lb 8 oz, Lake El Salto, Mazatlan, Mexico
Voss, Brendon, 10 lb 3 oz, Private Dam, Bindura, Zimbabwe
Waldow, Mitch, 10 lb, Castaic Lake, Castaic, California, USA
Walker, Joe, 11 lb 8 oz, Castaic Lake, Castaic, California, USA
Warman,Wm.J.(Bill)10 lb 12 oz,Canyon L.,Apache Junc.,AZ,USA
Warman,Wm. J.(Bill),13 lb 15 oz,Canyon L.,Apache Junc.,AZ,USA
Warman,Wm. J.(Bill),11 lb 14 oz,Canyon L.,Apache Junc.,AZ,USA
Warman,Wm. J.(Bill),11 lb 3 oz,Canyon L.,Apache Junc.,AZ,USA
Warman,Wm. J.(Bill),12 lb 2 oz,Canyon L.,Apache Junc.,AZ,USA
Warman,Wm. J.(Bill),10 lb 4 oz, Canyon L.,Apache Junc.,AZ,USA
Warman,Wm. J.(Bill),14 lb 6 oz,Canyon L.,Apache Junc.,AZ,USA
Warman,Wm. J.(Bill),11 lb 9 oz,Canyon L.,Apache Junc.,AZ,USA
Warman,Wm. J.(Bill),11 lb 11 oz,Canyon L.,Apache Junc.,AZ,USA
Warman,Wm. J.(Bill),10 lb 6 oz,Canyon L.,Apache Junc.,AZ,USA
Warman,Wm. J.(Bill),11 lb 14 oz,Canyon L.,Apache Junc.,AZ,USA
Warman,Wm. J.(Bill), 14 lb, Canyon L., Apache Junc., AZ, USA
Warman,Wm. J.(Bill),11 lb 15 oz,Canyon L.,Apache Junc.,AZ,USA
Warren, Charlie, 12 lb 8 oz, South Georgia Pond, GA, USA
Weizenecker, William, 10 lb 4 oz, Lake Baccarac, Mexico
Wetherald, Robt. E.,10 lb 2 oz,Currituck Sound,Knotts Is.,NC,USA
White, Jr., Harvey M., 10 lb 14 oz,L. Henderson,Inverness,FL,USA
Wiles, Charles B., 11 lb 2 oz, Lake George,Crescent City, FL,USA
Williams, Chris, 11 lb 8 oz, Lake Okeechobee, Clewiston, FL,USA
Woiczechowski, Charles, 10 lb 2 oz, Lake Conley,Holiday,FL,USA
Wolfe, Johnny D., 10 lb 1 oz, Lake Fork, Texas, USA

Wyatt, Dennis D., 10 lb 2 oz, Castaic Lake, Castaic, CA, USA
Young, Floyd D., 15 lb, Los Banos, California
Young, Robert B., 12 lb 4 oz, Castaic Lake, Castaic, CA, USA

PEACOCK

Aristeguieta L., Carlos A.,18 lb 15 oz, Rio Sipapo,Amazonas,Vene.
Aristeguieta L., Carlos A.,20 lb 10 oz, Rio Sipapo,Amazonas,Vene.
Arno, M.D., Irvin C., 13 lb 8 oz, Cinaruco, Venezuela
Berner, Daniel R., 25 lb, Rio Negro River, Amazonas, Brazil
Bershad, Goldie Goldon, 11 lb 8 oz, Cinaruco, Venezuela
Besmer, Gary, 12 lb 1 oz, Lake Guri, Venezuela
Campa G., Antonio, 21 lb, Rio Sipapo, Amazonas,Venezuela
Cittadini, Gerard, 20 lb, Rio Negro, Brazil
Cittadini, Gerard, 15 lb 13 oz, Rio Negro, Brazil
Costentin, Jauthier, 22 lb 7 oz, Rio Negro, Brazil
Dahlberg, Marilyn, 14 lb, Rio Negro, Brazil
Glaser, Lance, 20 lb, Pasimoni River, Venezuela
Gonzalez, Federico, 16 lb 8 oz, Pasimoni River, Venezuela
Hahn, Andrew J., 14 lb 5 oz, Rio Marmelos, Amazonas, Brazil
Ibarra, Frank, 17 lb 10 oz, Guri Lake, Venezuela
Jaen, Ruben J., 16 lb, Cano La Pica, Venezuela
Jaen U., Ruben E., 13 lb 7 oz, Cano La Pica, Venezuela
Kaufman, Shep, 14 lb, Manaka Lodge, Ventuari River, Venezuela
Kipnis, Capt. Dan, 19 lb 12 oz, Bita River, Colombia, S.America
Kossmann, Capt. Dietmar, 14 lb 8 oz, Guri Lake, Venezuela
Lairet S., Felix, 16 lb 6 oz, Cano La Pica,Estado Apure, Venezuela
Lairet S., Felix, 16 lb 8 oz, Cano La Pica,Estado Apure, Venezuela
Lairet T., Felix H., 15 lb 4 oz, Cano La Pica, Estado Apure, Vene.
Mata, Alejandro, 17 lb 5 oz, Rio Sipapo, Venezuela
Nickrass, Claude, 18 lb 8 oz, Rio Negro, Brazil
Olsen, Richard R., 22 lb 1 oz, Rio Preto, Brazil
Pestle, Lynn A., 21 lb, Rio Negro River, Amazonas, Brazil
Stohldrier, Don, 11 lb, Lake Guri, Venezuela
Thomas, Didier, 19 lb 13 oz, Rio Negro, Brazil
Whitehead, M.D., Craig, 16 lb 8 oz, Rio Preto, Brazil
Whitehead, M.D., Craig, 16 lb, Rio Negro, Brazil
Whitehead, M.D., Craig, 18 lb, Rio Negro, Brazil
Whitehead, M.D., Craig, 10 lb 8 oz, Rio Negro, Brazil
Whitehead, M.D., Craig, 19 lb, Rio Negro, Brazil
Whitehead, M.D., Craig, 17 lb, Rio Preto, Brazil
Whitehead, M.D., Craig, 21 lb, Rio Preto, Brazil
Yarboro, Thomas R., 22 lb 8 oz, Rio Negro, Amazonas, Brazil
Yatomi, Steven Zatoichi, 21 lb 8 oz, Rio Pasimoni,Amazonas,Vene.

25 POUND SNOOK CLUB

Bellavia, James A. 32 lb 8 oz, St. Lucie River, Stuart, FL, USA
Brandt, Buzz, 26 lb 2 oz, May Reef, Ft. Myers Beach, FL, USA
Brandt, Buzz, 29 lb 6 oz, Mullock Creek, Ft. Myers, FL, USA
Craft, Dana Duane, 30 lb, Miami Beach, Florida, USA
Cruce, Darrell L., 37 lb,Blind Pass,Sanibel/Captiva Island, FL,USA
Culp, Rick, 31 lb 8 oz, Plantation, Florida, USA
Davenport, Donna L., 27 lb 8 oz, Barra Del Colorado, Costa Rica
Dwyer, Richard J., 33 lb, Everglades National Park, FL, USA
Greene, Tom, 41 lb 8 oz, Flagler Bridge,West Palm Beach,FL,USA
Hagan, Dan, 46 lb, Cabo San Lucas, B.C.S., Mexico
Howell, Billy, 39 lb 8 oz, Cabo San Lucas, B.C.S., Mexico
Huegel, Peter, 25 lb, Jupiter Inlet, Florida, USA
Kirk, Chris E., 30 lb, Palm Beach, Florida, USA
McDonald, Jack, 37 lb, Palm Beach, Florida, USA
O'Toole, Dennis, 32 lb 11 oz, St. Lucie River, Stuart, FL, USA
Redington, David F., 26 lb 8 oz, Indian River, Ft. Pierce, FL, USA
Reichey, Capt. Michael J., 27 lb, Jupiter Inlet, Florida, USA
Reichey, Susan Hartl, 28 lb, Jupiter Inlet, Florida, USA
Robles Herrera, Dr. Luis Alonso, 63 lb 13 oz, Nayarit, Mexico
Routman, Alan S., 27 lb 7 oz, Ft. Lauderdale, FL, USA
Savko, Edward M., 32 lb, Playa Zancudo, Costa Rica
Strauss, Paul M., 27 lb, Indian River, Jensen Beach, FL, USA
Torn, Jing, 33 lb, Jupiter, Florida, USA
Vanderwerff, Eddie, 30 lb, Jupiter Inlet, Florida, USA
Whitehead, M.D., Craig, 27 lb, Boca Rio Colorado, Costa Rica
Whitehead, M.D., Craig, 26 lb, Chokoloskee, Florida, USA
Whitehead, M.D., Craig, 28 lb, Playa Zancudo, Costa Rica
Whitehead, M.D., Craig, 26 lb, Chokoloskee, Florida, USA

SUPER GRAND SLAM CLUB

INSHORE

Dunaway, Jerry, permit/tarpon/snook/bonefish, September 12, 1996, Marathon, Florida, USA

Gaver, Jr., John M., bonefish/permit/tarpon/snook, August 28, 1995, Biscayne Bay, Miami, Florida, USA

Gilardi, Luigi, bonefish/permit/tarpon/snook, August 20, 1998, Boca Paila Lodge, Yucatan, Mexico

Jocelyn, Rodney F., tarpon/permit/bonefish/snook, July 17, 1998, Boca Paila, Yucatan, Mexico

Muelrath, Don, bonefish/tarpon/permit/snook, November 23, 1993, Yucatan, Mexico

Pierce, Jerry C., permit/bonefish/snook/tarpon, May 28, 1997, Ascension Bay, Yucatan Peninsula, Mexico

Seymour, Stephen D., tarpon/snook/bonefish/permit, June 7, 1996, Biscayne Bay, Florida, USA

OFFSHORE

Amorim, Paulo, white marlin/blue marlin/sailfish/swordfish, February 2, 1996, Guarapari, E.S., Brazil

Breaux, Janice, white marlin/blue marlin/sailfish/swordfish, May 23, 1981, Cozumel, Mexico

Capozzi, Enrico, blue marlin/white marlin/sailfish/swordfish, July 2, 1987, La Guaira Bank, Venezuela

Davis, Janeen, black marlin/blue marlin/sailfish/striped marlin, September 5, 1996, Cocos Island, Costa Rica

Dunaway, Jerry, swordfish/blue marlin/white marlin/sailfish, May 19, 1982, Cozumel, Mexico

Ellender, Dr. S.E., blue marlin/sailfish/white marlin/swordfish, November 13, 1994, La Guaira Bank, Venezuela

Gallagher, Duke, blue marlin/white marlin/spearfish/sailfish, December 1, 1995, La Guaira, Venezuela

Hayes, Jr., C.J. Mickey, sailfish/white marlin/blue marlin/swordfish, November 5, 1985, La Guaira, Venezuela

Herder, Bob, sailfish/white marlin/blue marlin/swordfish, October 13, 1984, Venezuela

Keech, Gilbert W., sailfish/striped marlin/blue marlin/black marlin, January 26, 1994, Guanamar, Costa Rica

Manley, Hank, blue marlin/white marlin/sailfish/spearfish/swordfish, October 21, 1997, Caraballeda, Venezuela

Romero S., Calixto, striped marlin/blue marlin/black marlin/sailfish, August 6, 1996, Cocos Island, Costa Rica

GRAND SLAM CLUB

INSHORE

Anglesio-Farina, Aldo, permit/bonefish/tarpon, August 13, 1998, Jardines De La Reina, Cuba

Anglesio-Farina, Aldo, bonefish/tarpon/permit, August 25, 1997, Jardines De La Reina, Cuba

Bartz, Mary, permit/bonefish/tarpon, October 27, 1994, Marathon, Florida, USA

Berry, IV, George A., bonefish/permit/tarpon, May 17, 1996, Key Largo, Florida, USA

Bracher, Missy, bonefish/permit/tarpon, June 30, 1997, Cudjoe Key, Florida Keys, Florida, USA

Bracher, Missy, bonefish/permit/tarpon, May 22, 1998, Cudjoe Key, Florida Keys, Florida, USA

Bracher, Missy, bonefish/permit/tarpon, May 22, 1998, Cudjoe Key, Florida Keys, Florida, USA

Capra, Silvano, bonefish/permit/tarpon, May 5, 1997, Queen's Gardens, Cuba

Carter, Anthony C., tarpon/permit/bonefish, May 4, 1998, Islamorada, Florida, USA

Cohan, Ken, tarpon/permit/bonefish, January 9, 1999, Islamorada, Florida, USA

Cook, Jr., Donald C., bonefish/tarpon/permit, May 26, 1998, Islamorada, Florida, USA

Cook, Jr., Donald C., bonefish/permit/tarpon, May 7, 1997, Islamorada, Florida, USA

Costantini, Chip, tarpon/bonefish/permit, August 2, 1996, Islamorada, Florida, USA

De Cicco, Bruno R., bonefish/snook/tarpon, April 10, 1982, Belize River, Belize

Dunaway, Deborah Maddux, permit/tarpon/bonefish, September 13, 1996, Duck Key, Florida, USA

Dunaway, Jerry, permit/tarpon/bonefish, August 27, 1996, Duck Key, Florida, USA

Falwell, Beth Parnell, permit/tarpon/bonefish, October 9, 1998, Islamorada, Florida, USA

Floyd, Jason M., snook/bonefish/permit, June 26, 1996, Casa Blanca, Ascension Bay, Mexico

Grassi, Anthony, tarpon/snook/bonefish, June 10, 1997, Marathon, Florida, USA

Grassi, Anthony, permit/bonefish/tarpon, March 14, 1997, Espiritu Santo, Yucatan

Herstedt, Eric, permit/bonefish/tarpon, October 14, 1994, Islamorada, Florida, USA

Jocelyn, Rodney F., bonefish/permit/tarpon, July 22, 1997, Boca Paila, Quintana Roo, Mexico

Kilpatrick, Capt. Steve, tarpon/permit/bonefish, November 7, 1996, Casa Blanca Lodge, Ascension Bay, Mexico

Leavitt, David, permit/tarpon/snook, March 3, 1998, Lake Worth Inlet, Lake Worth, Florida, USA

McKain, Gini, tarpon/permit/bonefish, August 18, 1997, Duck Key, Florida, USA

McKinney, Howard, tarpon/permit/bonefish, June 21, 1998, Key West, Florida, USA

McKinney, Howard, bonefish/tarpon/permit, June 28, 1996, Key West, Florida, USA

Merly, Lawrence J., permit/tarpon/bonefish, April 16, 1997, Casa Blanca, Yucatan Peninsula, Mexico

Merly, Lawrence J., permit/bonefish/tarpon, April 19, 1996, Casa Blanca, Yucatan Peninsula, Mexico

Merly, Lawrence J., permit/bonefish/tarpon, May 17, 1994, Casa Blanca, Yucatan Peninsula, Mexico

Muelrath, Don, bonefish/tarpon/permit, November 25, 1993, Yucatan, Mexico

Muelrath, Don, bonefish/tarpon/permit, July 14, 1989, Yucatan, Mexico

Obstfeld, Malcolm, bonefish/permit/tarpon, July 20, 1996, Marathon, Florida, USA

Ragatz, Gary, tarpon/bonefish/permit, June 12, 1996, Islamorada, Florida, USA

Ragatz, Gary, tarpon/bonefish/permit, March 13, 1997, Islamorada, Florida, USA

Routman, Alan S., tarpon/bonefish/permit, June 9, 1997, Islamorada, Florida, USA

Rowland, Jr., Capt. Thomas Turner, permit/bonefish/tarpon, June 10, 1995, Key West, Florida, USA

Salisbury, Jr., John W., tarpon/bonefish/permit, May 20, 1998, Casa Blanca Lodge, Ascension Bay, Yucatan, Mexico

Salisbury, Jr., John W., tarpon/permit/bonefish, April, 1992, Casa Blanca Lodge, Ascension Bay, Yucatan, Mexico

Savko, Edward M., bonefish/permit/tarpon, June 4, 1996, Islamorada, Florida Keys, Florida. USA

Sedel, Arnold, tarpon/bonefish/permit, September 21, 1996, South Biscayne Bay, Key Largo, Florida, USA

Slavin, Gary L., permit/bonefish/tarpon, August 8, 1997, Big Pine Key, Florida, USA

Smith, Ralph, bonefish/permit/tarpon, February 23, 1996, Casa Blanca, Quintana Roo, Mexico

Solis, Carlos B., bonefish/tarpon/permit, August 7, 1994, Biscayne Bay, Florida, USA

Spear, John Hunter, tarpon/permit/bonefish, August 2, 1997, Duck Key, Florida, USA

Steinbrenner, Gerald W., tarpon/permit/bonefish, February 14, 1996, Ascension Bay, Mexico

Syn, D.D.S., Wayne J.W., tarpon/permit/bonefish, June 26, 1996, Florida Keys, Key West, Florida, USA

Taylor, Herman H., bonefish/permit/tarpon, July 10, 1997, Islamorada, Florida, USA

Thomas, Derek, permit/tarpon/bonefish, March 16, 1996, Islamorada, Florida, USA

Utigard, Philip R., bonefish/permit/tarpon, May 5, 1996, Marathon, Florida, USA

Vettore, Stefano, bonefish/permit/tarpon, September 3, 1998, The Queen's Garden, Cuba

Wilson, William M., bonefish/permit/tarpon, April 26, 1990, Marathon Key, Florida, USA

Zoll, Nicholas C., bonefish/permit/tarpon, June 17, 1996, Casa Blanca, Ascension Bay, Mexico

Zoll, Nicholas C., bonefish/permit/tarpon, April 23, 1996, Casa Blanca, Ascension Bay, Mexico

OFFSHORE

Adum, Jimmy, sailfish/blue marlin/striped marlin, November 22, 1998, Salinas, Ecuador

Allen, Richard B., sailfish, white marlin/blue marlin, November 6, 1995, La Guaira, Venezuela

Appling, Jr., Hefner, blue marlin/sailfish/striped marlin, June 2, 1996, Cocos Island, Costa Rica

Auman, Dinah, sailfish/white marlin/blue marlin, October 15, 1995, La Guaira, Venezuela

Auman, Robert, white marlin/sailfish/blue marlin, October 14, 1995, La Guaira, Venezuela

Beacher, Jon R., black marlin/blue marlin/sailfish, March 3, 1997, Tropic Star Lodge, Pinas Bay, Panama

Beard, Bernice D., blue marlin/white marlin/sailfish, September 10, 1980, Oregon Inlet, North Carolina, USA

Bierman, Marsha T., blue marlin/sailfish/striped marlin, November 12, 1998, Port Vila, Vanuatu

Bierman, Marsha T., black marlin/blue marlin/sailfish, May 31, 1992, Flamingo, Costa Rica

Bierman, Marsha T., sailfish/black marlin/blue marlin, August 19, 1990, Flamingo, Costa Rica

Bierman, Marsha T., blue marlin/sailfish/black marlin, August 20, 1990, Flamingo Bay, Costa Rica

Bierman, Marsha T., blue marlin/black marlin/sailfish, August 13, 1991, Flamingo, Costa Rica

Bierman, Marsha T., sailfish/black marlin/blue marlin, August 29, 1987, Flamingo, Costa Rica

Bierman, Marsha T., white marlin/blue marlin/sailfish, October 18, 1985, La Guaira, Venezuela

Biernat, Bob, black marlin/striped marlin/sailfish, August 11, 1998, Exmouth, W.A., Australia

Bouchard, Charles E., sailfish/white marlin/blue marlin, May 24, 1989, Isla Mujeres, Mexico

Capozzi, Enrico, blue marlin/white marlin/sailfish, September 23, 1996, La Guaira Bank, Venezuela

Capozzi, Enrico, sailfish/white marlin/blue marlin, September 28, 1996, La Guaira Bank, Venezuela

Capozzi, Enrico, blue marlin/white marlin/sailfish, October 1, 1996, La Guaira Bank, Venezuela

Capozzi, Enrico, white marlin/blue marlin/sailfish, October 3, 1996, La Guaira Bank, Venezuela

Capozzi, Enrico, blue marlin/white marlin/sailfish, October 8, 1996, La Guaira Bank, Venezuela

Capozzi, Enrico, blue marlin/white marlin/sailfish, October 11, 1996, La Guaira Bank, Venezuela

Capozzi, Enrico, blue marlin/white marlin/sailfish, October 17, 1996, La Guaira Bank, Venezuela

Capozzi, Enrico, blue marlin/white marlin/sailfish, October 11, 1994, La Guaira Bank, Venezuela

Capozzi, Enrico, blue marlin/white marlin/sailfish, November 7, 1995, La Guaira Bank, Venezuela

Capozzi, Enrico, white marlin/sailfish/spearfish, October 24, 1994, La Guaira Bank, Venezuela

Capozzi, Enrico, white marlin/sailfish/swordfish, October 10, 1995, La Guaira Bank, Venezuela

Carter, Gary A., blue marlin/white marlin/sailfish, December 5, 1998, La Guaira Bank, Venezuela

Casey, Clinton M., blue marlin/white marlin/sailfish, October 4, 1996, La Guaira, Venezuela

Clarke, M. John, white marlin/sailfish/spearfish, September 27, 1997, Caraballeda, Venezuela

Clarke, M. John, blue marlin/white marlin/sailfish, April 14, 1996, La Guaira, Venezuela

Cook, Jr., Donald C., blue marlin/white marlin/sailfish, September 25, 1998, Venezuela

Davenport, Larry W., blue marlin/white marlin/sailfish, August 12, 1994, Virginia Beach, Virginia, USA

Davis, Janeen, black marlin/blue marlin/striped marlin, July 29, 1994, Cocos Island, Costa Rica

Davis, Janeen, blue marlin/striped marlin/sailfish, July 30, 1994, Cocos Island, Costa Rica

Deerman, Kevin, black marlin/blue marlin/sailfish, January 30, 1992, Pinas Bay, Panama

Dias, Sondra, sailfish/blue marlin/striped marlin, August 24, 1994, East Cape, Baja, Mexico

Donald, Johan, blue marlin/striped marlin/sailfish, February 22, 1997, Pemba Channel, Shimoni, Kenya, Africa

Donestevez, Jr., Juan, sailfish/white marlin/blue marlin, October 29, 1993, La Guaira Bank, Venezuela

Donnelley, Jr., Thorne, sailfish/blue marlin/white marlin, May 30, 1994, Cancun, Mexico

Dunaway, Jerry, blue marlin/sailfish/white marlin, December 4, 1984, La Guaira, Venezuela

Dunaway, Jerry, black marlin/sailfish/swordfish, February 21, 1985, Pinas Bay, Panama

Dunaway, Jerry, sailfish/blue marlin/white marlin, June 5, 1982, Cozumel, Mexico

Dunaway, Jerry, blue marlin/white marlin/sailfish, November 8, 1983, La Guaira, Venezuela

Dunaway, Jerry, black marlin/sailfish/blue marlin, February 10, 1994, Pinas Bay, Panama

Dunnam, Russell M., sailfish/striped marlin/blue marlin, August 24, 1996, Cocos Island, Costa Rica

DuVal, Mrs. William B., white marlin/blue marlin/sailfish, October 14, 1994, La Guaira, Venezuela

Duvall, John P., (Jack), blue marlin/striped marlin/sailfish, July 24, 1996, East Cape, B.C.S., Mexico

Duvall, John P. (Jack), blue marlin/striped marlin/sailfish, July 17, 1996, East Cape, B.C.S., Mexico

Duvall, John P. (Jack), blue marlin/striped marlin/sailfish, July 16, 1996, East Cape, B.C.S., Mexico

Falcucci, Captain Jack, blue marlin/white marlin/sailfish, October 8, 1995, La Guaira, Venezuela

Fishman, Steven E., blue marlin/white marlin/sailfish, October 21, 1994, La Guaira, Venezuela

Fugler, Max, blue marlin/white marlin/sailfish, July 24, 1998, Freeport, Texas, USA

Gard, Ronald J., striped marlin/blue marlin/sailfish, June 23, 1997, Rancho Buena Vista, B.C.S., Mexico

Gilster, III, Ralph R., striped marlin/sailfish/blue marlin, August 26, 1996, Cocos Island, Costa Rica

Grassi, Anthony, black marlin/blue marlin/sailfish, April 6, 1997, Hannibal Bank, Panama

Grassi, Anthony, blue marlin/striped marlin/sailfish, July 5, 1995, East Cape, Mexico

Hages, Dr. Richard J., blue marlin/striped marlin/sailfish, November 4, 1994, Cabo San Lucas, B.C.S., Mexico

Haines, Stanley, blue marlin/white marlin/sailfish, May 3, 1989, Cancun, Mexico

Hamilton, Tim, swordfish/white marlin/sailfish, November 11, 1995, La Guaira, Venezuela

Harris, Sandra C., blue marlin/white marlin/sailfish, August 27, 1995, Freeport, Texas, USA

Harvey, PH.D., Guy C.M., blue marlin/striped marlin/sailfish, July 11, 1993, Cocos Island, Costa Rica

Harvey, PH.D., Guy C.M., blue marlin/black marlin/striped marlin, July 6, 1995, Cocos Island, Costa Rica

Harvey, PH.D., Guy C.M., white marlin/sailfish/swordfish, November 18, 1988, Venezuela

Harvey, PH.D., Guy C.M., black marlin/striped marlin/sailfish, January 23, 1992, Tropic Star Lodge, Pinas Bay, Panama

Herder, Vivian, sailfish/white marlin/blue marlin, October 15, 1993, Venezuela

Holt, Adriaan J., blue marlin/white marlin/sailfish, October 8, 1998, Caraballeda, Venezuela

James, Paula Jo, blue marlin/sailfish/white marlin, October 7, 1995, La Guaira, Venezuela

Jarvis, Richard D., white marlin/sailfish/blue marlin, February 7, 1996, La Guaira, Venezuela

Johnson, Frank W., blue marlin/sailfish/white marlin, November 4, 1989, La Guaira, Venezuela

Kennedy, Michael F., sailfish/blue marlin/white marlin, November 3, 1995, La Guaira, Venezuela

Lafair, Leonard, blue marlin/white marlin/sailfish, October 11, 1988, La Guaira Bank, Venezuela

Leach, Michael E., white marlin/blue marlin/sailfish, October 13, 1997, La Guaira, Venezuela

Lyons, Mark, blue marlin/white marlin/sailfish, July 3, 1996, Freeport, Texas, USA

Marmin, Pamela W., white marlin/sailfish/blue marlin, November 19, 1995, La Guaira, Venezuela

Melhuish, Steven J., sailfish/blue marlin/white marlin, September

26, 1995, La Guaira Bank, Venezuela
Moss, Burt, blue marlin/white marlin/sailfish, October 5, 1997, Caraballeda, Venezuela
Moss, Burt, white marlin/sailfish/blue marlin, October 4, 1997, Caraballeda, Venezuela
Moss, Burt, blue marlin/white marlin/sailfish, September 27, 1997, Caraballeda, Venezuela
Moss, Burt, blue marlin/white marlin/sailfish, September 20, 1996, Caraballeda, Venezuela
Moss, Burt, sailfish/white marlin/blue marlin, September 27, 1995, La Guaira, Venezuela
Moss, Burt, swordfish/sailfish/white marlin, September 26, 1995, La Guaira, Venezuela
Mundt, Ray B., sailfish/white marlin/blue marlin, May 29, 1998, Cancun, Mexico
Mundt, Ray B., sailfish/white marlin/blue marlin, May 28, 1998, Cancun, Mexico
Murray,II, James R., blue marlin/white marlin/sailfish, September 30, 1997, Caraballeda, Venezuela
Murray,II, James R., sailfish/white marlin/blue marlin, September 14, 1996, Caraballeda, Venezuela
Murray, II, James R., blue marlin/sailfish/white marlin, December 9, 1995, Caraballeda, Venezuela
Murray, II, James R., blue marlin/sailfish/white marlin, December 9, 1995, Caraballeda, Venezuela
Murray, II, James R., blue marlin/white marlin/sailfish, November 12, 1995, Caraballeda, Venezuela
Paley, Gregg M., sailfish/blue marlin/white marlin, October 23, 1998, La Guaira, Venezuela
Paley, Gregg M., blue marlin/white marlin/sailfish, November 17, 1994, La Guaira, Venezuela
Peacock, Myrtice, blue marlin/white marlin/sailfish, October 5, 1997, Caraballeda, Venezuela
Pharr, Charles, white marlin/sailfish/blue marlin, November 15, 1995, La Guaira Bank, Venezuela
Pimentel, Elio V., sailfish/white marlin/blue marlin, October 15, 1997, Vitoria, Brazil
Price, Phil, black marlin/sailfish/striped marlin, August 21, 1996, Cocos Island, Costa Rica
Price, Phil, blue marlin/striped marlin/sailfish, August 17, 1996, Cocos Island, Costa Rica
Princenthal, Rick, blue marlin/white marlin/sailfish, September 27, 1994, La Guaira Bank, Venezuela
Rabinsky, Israel, white marlin/blue marlin/sailfish, September 26, 1997, La Guaira, Venezuela
Raffo, Juan F., sailfish/striped marlin/blue marlin, August 8, 1996, Cocos Island, Costa Rica
Roden, Laura D., (2) blue marlin/(2) white marlin/(2) sailfish, September 22, 1997, La Guaira, Venezuela
Roland, Dick, blue marlin/white marlin/sailfish, October 22, 1997, La Guaira, Venezuela
Roversi, Dabney P., blue marlin/white marlin/sailfish, March 3, 1996, La Guaira, Venezuela
Schultz, Buddy, blue marlin/white marlin/sailfish, February 7, 1996, La Guaira, Venezuela
Schuttler, Kurtis W., blue marlin/white marlin/sailfish, October 14, 1998, Venezuela
Smith, IV, Oliver, blue marlin/striped marlin/sailfish, July 16, 1996, Cocos Island, Costa Rica
Spooner, Kevin, blue marlin/striped marlin/sailfish, July 29, 1994, Cocos Island, Costa Rica
Thomasson, Gary D., sailfish/blue marlin/white marlin, May 21, 1993, Puerto Adventuras, Mexico
Totura, Douglas B., blue marlin/white marlin/sailfish, October 9, 1998, Caraballeda, Venezuela
Totura, Douglas B., blue marlin/white marlin/sailfish, October 8, 1998, Caraballeda, Venezuela
Totura, Douglas B., sailfish/white marlin/blue marlin, October 5, 1997, Caraballeda, Venezuela
Totura, Douglas B., sailfish/white marlin/blue marlin, October 3, 1997, Caraballeda, Venezuela
Totura, Douglas B., blue marlin/white marlin/sailfish, October 5, 1995, La Guaira, Venezuela
Totura, Douglas B., blue marlin/white marlin/sailfish, October 2, 1995, La Guaira, Venezuela
Totura, Douglas B., blue marlin/white marlin/sailfish, September 4, 1995, La Guaira, Venezuela
Ullberg, Kent, sailfish/blue marlin/striped marlin, September 6, 1996, Cocos Island, Costa Rica

Varney, Nicholas L., blue marlin/white marlin/sailfish, September 19, 1996, La Guaira, Venezuela
Yeager, William, blue marlin/white marlin/sailfish, November 2, 1993, La Guaira Bank, Venezuela
Zimmer, Jr., Joseph M., white marlin/sailfish/swordfish, October 10, 1994, La Guaira, Venezuela
Zimmer, Jr., Joseph M., white marlin/blue marlin/sailfish, August 14, 1995, Norfolk Canyon, Virginia, USA
Zimmer, Jr., Joseph M., blue marlin/white marlin/sailfish, October 8, 1995, La Guaira, Venezuela

<u>20 TO 1 CLUB</u>

CATFISH, FLATHEAD
Davis, Edward C., 52 lb, Fayetteville, North Carolina, USA
COBIA
Ross, Barry, 40 lb 8 oz, Key West, Florida, USA
DOLPHIN
Dunaway, Jerry, 41 lb 8 oz, Pinas Bay, Panama
Dunaway, Deborah Maddux, 40 lb 8 oz, Pinas Bay, Panama
DRUM, BLACK
Werking, Raleigh, 90 lb 8 oz, New Smyrna Beach, Florida, USA
Werking, Raleigh, 66 lb, New Smyrna Beach, Florida, USA
HALIBUT, PACIFIC
Grimes, Gene, 244 lb, Basket Bay, Chichagof Island, Alaska, USA
Leader, Paul, 124 lb, Kodiak, Alaska, USA
Loros, Dorothy A., 70 lb, Yasha Island, Alaska, USA
Stoky, Robert C., 89 lb, Kodiak, Alaska, USA
INCONNU
Hudnall, Lawrence E., 41 lb 4 oz, Kobuk River, Alaska, USA
JEWFISH
Bittner, Kenny, 365 lb 8 oz, Flamingo, Florida, USA
Bittner, Kenny, 309 lb 8 oz, Flamingo, Florida, USA
LEERFISH
Rodocanachi, George, 18 lb 11 oz, Port Elizabeth, S. Africa
MARLIN, ATLANTIC BLUE
Buckmann, Claus, 604 lb, Rio de Janeiro, Brazil
Campbell, Mrs. Stewart N., 708 lb, Madeira, Portugal
Campbell, Stewart N., 144 lb 8 oz, Mayaguez, Puerto Rico
Campbell, Stewart N., 716 lb, San Pedro, Ivory Coast
Campbell, Stewart N., 249 lb, Grand Bereby, Ivory Coast
Campbell, Stewart N., 820 lb, Grand Bereby, Ivory Coast
Campbell, Stewart N., 714 lb 8 oz, Grand Bereby, Ivory Coast
Campbell, Stewart N., 872 lb, Madeira, Portugal
Campbell, Stewart N., 368 lb 13 oz, Abidjan, Ivory Coast
Campbell, Stewart N., 842 lb 6 oz, Grand Bereby, Ivory Coast
Cloostermans, Leo R., 604 lb, Horta, Faial, Azores
Cloostermans, Leo R., 381 lb, Horta, Faial, Azores
Cloostermans, Leo R., 573 lb, Horta, Faial, Azores
Cloostermans, Leo R., 248 lb 8 oz, Horta, Faial, Azores
Dunaway, Jerry, 672 lb 8 oz, San Pedro, Ivory Coast
Dunaway, Jerry, 231 lb 9 oz, San Pedro, Ivory Coast
Dunaway, Jerry, 409 lb 9 oz, Palmeira, Sal, Cape Verde Islands
Dunaway, Jerry, 93 lb 9 oz, St. Nicolao, Cape Verde Islands
Dunaway, Deborah Maddux, 194 lb 3 oz, San Pedro, Ivory Coast
Dunaway, Deborah Maddux,248 lb 12 oz,St.Nicolao,CapeVerde Isl.
Dunaway, Jerry, 392 lb, St. Thomas, U.S. Virgin Islands
Furman, Lawrence H., 1,146 lb 6 oz, Horta, Faial, Azores
Giraud, Marc, 165 lb, La Guaira, Venezuela
Sadler, John, 976 lb 10 oz, Faial, Azores
Thorn-Chopin, Annick, 367 lb, Sao Vicente, Cape Verde Islands
Vliegenthart, Dr. Don, 281 lb, St. Thomas, U.S. Virgin Islands
MARLIN, BLACK
Bishop, David A., 482 lb, Pinas Bay, Panama
Cochain, Dr. Jean-Pierre, 691 lb, Cairns, N. Queensland, Australia
Dunaway, Deborah Maddux, 239 lb, Pinas Bay, Panama
Dunaway, Jerry, 519 lb 8 oz, Pinas Bay, Panama
Dunaway, Deborah Maddux, 381 lb, Pinas Bay, Panama
Hogan, Elizabeth, 445 lb, Pinas Bay, Panama
Hooper, Mrs. Jill, 814 lb, Carter Reef, Great Barrier Reef, Australia
Kittredge, Terri, 364 lb, Pinas Bay, Panama
Levitt, Mike, 114 lb 10 oz,Broughton Island,Port Stephens,Australia
Levitt, Mike, 737 lb 7 oz, Escape Reef, Cairns, Australia
Levitt, Mike, 46 lb 15 oz,Cape Bowling Green,Townsville,Australia
Mulholland, Kay, 998 lb, Queensland, Australia

Naftzger, Roy E. (Ted), 1,046 lb, Great Barrier Reef, Australia
Sloan, Stephen, 862 lb, Lizard Island, Australia

MARLIN, PACIFIC BLUE
Abel, Martin G., 450 lb, Milolii, Hawaii, USA
Dunaway, Deborah Maddux, 303 lb, Flamingo Bay, Costa Rica
Dunaway, Deborah Maddux, 454 lb 8 oz, Pinas Bay, Panama
Dunaway, Jerry, 163 lb 12 oz, Quepos, Costa Rica
Dunaway, Jerry, 325 lb, Pinas Bay, Panama
Dunaway, Jerry, 315 lb, Punta Avenus, B.C.S., Mexico
Everette, Jocelyn, J., 639 lb, Kailua, Kona, Hawaii, USA
Everette, Kelley K., 1,103 lb 8 oz, Kailua, Kona, Hawaii, USA
Fahey, Terrence P., 156 lb 8 oz, Cabo San Lucas, B.C.S., Mexico
Fahey, Terrence P., 156 lb, Destiladeras, B.C.S., Mexico
Hawkes, Ray G., 1,166 lb, Kailua-Kona, Hawaii, USA
Hogan, Jr.,George E., 202 lb 13 oz,Cabo San Lucas,B.C.S., Mexico
Hogan, Jr.,George E., 141 lb 1 oz,Cabo San Lucas,B.C.S., Mexico
Kraemer, Gil, 1,062 lb 8 oz, Kona, Hawaii, USA
Love, Marg, 162 lb 6 oz, Quepos, Costa Rica
Miller, Linda L., 632 lb 12 oz, Pinas Bay, Panama
Nazarek, Eugene A., 768 lb 10 oz, B.C.S., Mexico
Schumacher, Steven, 142 lb, Keahole Point, Hawaii, USA
Spalding, Jr., Rufus P., 433 lb, Kailua, Kona, Hawaii, USA
Wenk, Rinaldo, 626 lb, Pinas Bay, Panama

MARLIN, STRIPED
Angus, Carl, 148 lb 9 oz, North Cape, New Zealand
Denholm, David M., 165 lb, Cabo San Lucas, B.C.S., Mexico
Dunaway, Jerry, 164 lb, Cocos Island, Costa Rica
Dunaway, Deborah Maddux, 142 lb 8 oz, Pinas Bay, Panama
Dunaway, Deborah Maddux, 189 lb 8 oz, Pinas Bay, Panama
Fraser, Thomas Campbell, 256 lb 2 oz,Middlesex Bank, N. Zealand
Garrett, Gerald A., 176 lb, Santa Catalina Island, California, USA
Hill, Barry, 271 lb 2 oz, Poor Knights Islands, New Zealand
Hogan, Elizabeth, 81 lb 9 oz, Cabo San Lucas, B.C.S., Mexico
Hogan, Elizabeth, 136 lb 10 oz, Cabo San Lucas, B.C.S., Mexico
Hogan, Elizabeth, 114 lb 10 oz,Cabo San Lucas,B.C.S., Mexico
Hogan, Jr., George E.,158 lb 11 oz,Cabo San Lucas,B.C.S., Mexico
Hogan, Jr., George E., 132 lb, Cabo San Lucas, B.C.S., Mexico
Levitt, Mike, 296 lb, Three Kings Islands, New Zealand
Martin, Ann, 313 lb, Three Kings Islands, New Zealand
Swanson, Sharon R., 140 lb, Cabo San Lucas, B.C.S., Mexico

MARLIN, WHITE
Basco, Pamela S., 56 lb 8 oz, La Guaira, Venezuela
Cloostermans, Leo R., 76 lb 8 oz, Horta, Faial, Azores
Dunaway, Deborah Maddux, 49 lb, La Guaira, Venezuela
Dunaway, Jerry, 29 lb 8 oz, La Guaira, Venezuela
Dunaway, Jerry, 48 lb 8 oz, La Guaira, Venezuela
Goodwin, Robert H., 58 lb 8 oz, Nantucket, Massachusetts, USA
Goodwin, Susan C., 97 lb 4 oz, Nantucket, Massachusetts, USA
Levitt, Mike, 88 lb 6 oz, Vitoria, Brazil
Nation, Ron, 87 lb, Nantucket Island, Massachusetts, USA
Schamroth, Michael, 81 lb, Caraballeda, Venezuela

RAY, BUTTERFLY
Gervais, Hilton, 182 lb 1 oz, Knysna Lagoon, Rep. of South Africa

SAILFISH, ATLANTIC
Basco, Pamela S., 45 lb 9 oz, Cancun, Mexico
Calendini, Michel, 69 lb, Dakar, Senegal
Calendini, Cyril, 79 lb 9 oz, Dakar, Senegal
Dunaway, Deborah Maddux, 72 lb 12 oz, Dakar, Senegal
Dunaway, Jerry, 65 lb, Isla Mujeres, Mexico
Dunaway, Deborah Maddux, 52 lb 14 oz, La Guaira, Venezuela
Manley, Gretchen H., Isla Mujeres, Quintana Roo, Mexico
Robelin, Odile, 81 lb 7 oz, Saly, Senegal
Sloan, Stephen, 58 lb 12 oz, Cozumel, Mexico

SAILFISH, PACIFIC
Aihara, Motoshi, 106 lb 8 oz, Bahia Pez Vela, Costa Rica
Cloostermans, Leo, 83 lb 8 oz, Pinas Bay, Panama
Dunaway, Deborah Maddux, 102 lb, Flamingo Bay, Costa Rica
Dunaway, Deborah Maddux, 97 lb 4 oz, Pinas Bay, Panama
Dunaway, Deborah Maddux, 109 lb 12 oz, Golfito, Costa Rica
Dunaway, Jerry, 111 lb, Flamingo Bay, Costa Rica
Elson, Jay M., 140 lb, Pinas Bay, Panama
Giraud, Marc, 97 lb 12 oz, Pinas Bay, Panama
Giraud, Marc, 91 lb, Pinas Bay, Panama
Giraud, Marc, 87 lb, Pinas Bay, Panama
Hedley, Tony, 103 lb, Quepos, Costa Rica
Kittredge, Terri, 96 lb 4 oz, Pinas Bay, Panama
Love, Marg, 98 lb 8 oz, Pinas Bay, Panama
Maspons, Santiago, 112 lb, Salinas, Ecuador

Miller, Dean D., 97 lb, Pinas Bay, Panama
Miller, Linda L., 89 lb, Pinas Bay, Panama
Miller, Linda L., 91 lb 4 oz, Pinas Bay, Panama
Miller, Linda L., 87 lb 8 oz, Pinas Bay, Panama
Mulholland, Kay, 106 lb, Pinas Bay, Panama
Nellis, Renee M., 107 lb, Pinas Bay, Panama
Touret, Jacques, 49 lb 6 oz, Sharjah, United Arab Emirates
Werking, Raleigh, 103 lb, Flamingo Bay, Costa Rica
Werking, Raleigh, 120 lb, Pinas Bay, Panama
Werking, Raleigh, 141 lb 8 oz, Pinas Bay, Panama
Werking, Raleigh, 85 lb, Pinas Bay, Panama
Yocum, Jr., George L., 113 lb, Pinas Bay, Panama

SALMON, CHINOOK
Werking, Raleigh, 37 lb 9 oz, Kenai River, Alaska, USA
Werking, Raleigh, 44 lb 12 oz, Kenai River, Alaska, USA

SHARK, BLUE
Caughlan, Craig Paul, 308 lb 10 oz, Cronulla, N.S.W., Australia
Caughlan, Jason Andrew, 362 lb 10 oz, Port Hacking, Australia
Caughlan, Paul Edward, 379 lb 3 oz,Port Hacking,N.S.W.,Australia
Dreifuss, Cynthia, 154 lb 5 oz, Whakatane, New Zealand
Egan, Robert, 395 lb 11 oz, Port Hacking, Sydney, Australia
Fitzpatrick, John, 313 lb, East Swansea, N.S.W., Australia
Heyward, Jayson, 416 lb 10 oz, Botany Bay, Sydney, Australia
Knight, Tony, 286 lb 9 oz, Port Hacking, Australia
Major, Brad, 365 lb 15 oz, Wollongong, Australia
Payne, Kim F., 84 lb 14 oz, Hippolyte Rocks, Tasmania, Australia
Pearce, Denis, 254 lb 10 oz, East Port Hacking, Australia
Sloan, Stephen, 119 lb, Long Island, New York, USA
Sloan, Stephen, 91 lb, Long Island, New York, USA
Sloan, Stephen, 184 lb, Long Island, New York, USA
Toohey, Peter T., 335 lb 1 oz, Long Reef Wide, Sydney, Australia
Williams, Danielle, 316 lb 5 oz,East Port Hacking,Sydney,Australia

SHARK, BULL
Eckhart, Cindy, 237 lb, Key West, Florida, USA
Gunion, Rick, 477 lb, Key West, Florida, USA
Matthews, Dr. Jerome N., 304 lb, Key West, Florida, USA
Peacock, Pete, 486 lb, Key West, Florida, USA
Solis, Carlos, 266 lb, Key West, Florida, USA
Spence, Gary, 218 lb 4 oz, Key West, Florida, USA
Wilde, Michael, 398 lb 4 oz, Key West, Florida, USA

SHARK, DUSKY
Reitano-Crompton, Evan, 592 lb 2 oz, Sydney, Australia

SHARK, HAMMERHEAD
Curin, Raewyn, 306 lb 7 oz, Auckland, New Zealand
Eady, Monique, 416 lb 10 oz, Port Stephens, Australia
Hogg, Paul, 213 lb 13 oz, Catherine Hill Bay, Australia
McWilliam, D.R., 279 lb 15 oz, Bay of Islands, New Zealand
Ratner, Jr., Herbert G., 194 lb 4 oz, Key West, Florida, USA
Stone, Geoff, 339 lb 1 oz, Takau Bay, Bay of Islands,New Zealand

SHARK, LEMON
Bittner, Dale, 294 lb, Key West, Florida, USA
Price, Jr., Robert D., 178 lb, Bahia Honda Key, Florida, USA
Riesenfeld, Bill, 101 lb, Key West, Florida, USA

SHARK, MAKO
Adams, Cheryl, 634 lb 14 oz, Port Stephens, N.S.W., Australia
Caughlan, Jason Andrew, 306 lb 8 oz, Port Hacking, Australia
Caughlan, Paul Edward, 165 lb 5 oz, Port Hacking, Australia
Caughlan, Paul Edward, 414 lb 7 oz, Port Hacking, Australia
Dagger, Les, 628 lb 4 oz, Port Stephens, N.S.W., Australia
Flett, G., 848 lb 12 oz, Hawke Bay, New Zealand
Johnston, Mark, 699 lb 15 oz, Sydney, Botany Bay, Australia
Lonsdale, Jamie, 959 lb, Norah Head, N.S.W., Australia
Male, Sharon J., 235 lb 14 oz, Bermagui, N.S.W., Australia
Markie, Steve, 69 lb 3 oz, Tolaga Bay, Gisborne, New Zealand
Rolley, Connie, 331 lb 12 oz, Sydney, Australia
Sloan, Stephen, 83 lb 8 oz, Long Island, New York, USA
Thomson, David G., 273 lb 6 oz, Bermagui, N.S.W., Australia

SHARK, NARROWTOOTH
Flourentzou, George, 341 lb 11 oz,Sceale Bay,Australia
Sowerby, Shane, 348 lb 5 oz, Manukau Harbour, New Zealand
Sowerby, Shane, 458 lb 3 oz, Manukau, New Zealand
Wakelin, Rick, 282 lb 3 oz, Auckland, New Zealand

SHARK, PORBEAGLE
Carr, Dave, 138 lb 10 oz, Otago Heads, New Zealand
Froud, Denis J., 107 lb 7 oz, Gosport, England
Taylor, Brian Stewart, 382 lb, Devon, Cornwall, England

SHARK, SILKY
Henderson, Bryce Robert, 762 lb 12 oz, Port Stephens, Australia
SHARK, SPINNER
Ratner, Jr., Herbert G., 95 lb, Key West, Florida, USA
SHARK, TIGER
Biffel, Michael T., 533 lb, Key West, Florida, USA
Booth, Glen, 1,300 lb 11 oz, Port Hacking, N.S.W., Australia
Brown, Garry, 679 lb, Port Hacking, N.S.W., Australia
Byrne, Mark, 665 lb 12 oz, Port Hacking, N.S.W., Australia
Coote, Terry, 526 lb 14 oz, Kendrew Island, Dampier, W. Australia
Dagger, Les, 725 lb 5 oz, Port Stephens, N.S.W., Australia
Daly, Kylie, 640 lb 6 oz, Port Hacking, N.S.W., Australia
Grieves, Leanne, 1,208 lb 1 oz, New South Wales, Australia
Gunion, Rick, 564 lb 4 oz, Key West, Florida, USA
Hegner, Sharon, 427 lb 11 oz, Sydney, N.S.W., Australia
Hilton, David, 741 lb 13 oz, Sydney, Australia
Leonard, Steven J., 709 lb 14 oz, Port Stephens, N.S.W., Australia
Meyer, Hans, 1,073 lb 10 oz, Swansea, N.S.W., Australia
Noakes, Peter David, 759 lb 7 oz, East Swansea, N.S.W., Australia
Norris, Bronwyn L., 1,095 lb 10 oz, Swansea, N.S.W., Australia
Ratner, Jr., Herbert G., 255 lb 8 oz, Key West, Florida, USA
Ratner, Jr., Herbert G., 159 lb, Key West, Florida, USA
Slack, Gordon C., 725 lb 5 oz, S.E. Port Stephens, Australia
Spruce, Robyn, 1,018 lb 8 oz, Swansea, N.S.W., Australia
SHARK, WHITE
Colreavy, Stephen, 1,040 lb 9 oz, Port Stephens, N.S.W., Australia
Czabayski, Rolf, 1,542 lb 1 oz, Port Lincoln, Australia
Czabayski, Rolf, 1,102 lb 4 oz, Streaky Bay, Australia
Morris, Steve, 1,684 lb 5 oz, Port Lincoln, Australia
TARPON
Adams, M.D., Crawford A., 41 lb, Florida Bay, Florida, USA
Adams, M.D., Crawford A., 41 lb, Florida Bay, Florida, USA
Davenport, Donna L., 83 lb, Casa Mar, Costa Rica
Judge, Joe, 54 lb, Rio Colorado, Costa Rica
Ratner, Jr., Herbert G., 42 lb 8 oz, Key West, Florida, USA
Riesenfeld, Bill, 108 lb 8 oz, Florida Bay, Florida, USA
TOPE
Feldman, Mark L., 40 lb 12 oz, Parengarenga Harbor, New Zealand

15 TO 1 CLUB

BASS, STRIPED - (LANDLOCKED)
Pack, Michael James, 22 lb 10 oz, Maynardville, Tennessee, USA
Whitehurst, Alfred L., 29 lb 8 oz, San Luis Reservoir, CA, USA
CATFISH, FLATHEAD
Davis, Edward C.,33 lb,Cape Fear River,Fayetteville,N.Carolina,USA
Miller, Charles F., 67 lb, Pomona Reservoir, Kansas, USA
COBIA
Hutchins, Mrs. Stephen R., 24 lb 12 oz, Key West, Florida, USA
Wright, Jr., Jay, 67 lb, Government Cut, Florida, USA
DOLPHIN
Dunaway, Deborah Maddux, 32 lb 8 oz, Pinas Bay, Panama
Meyer, Jr., John L., 36 lb, Cozumel, Quintana Roo, Mexico
Seroussi, Edouard, 37 lb, Pinas Bay, Panama
HALIBUT, PACIFIC
Carroll, David, 66 lb, Kodiak, Alaska, USA
Magnuson, Sally, 88 lb, Kodiak Island, Alaska, USA
INCONNU
Hudnall, Lawrence E., 24 lb, Pah River, Alaska, USA
MARLIN, ATLANTIC BLUE
Amorim, Paulo Roberto A., 1,402 lb 2 oz, Vitoria, Brazil
Carter, Dennis Michael, 446 lb, Treasure Cay, Bahamas
De Larroche, Patrick, 752 lb, Antigua, West Indies
De Silva, Gerard, 427 lb, Tobago, West Indies
Delaunay, Andree, 268 lb 15 oz, San Nicolau, Cape Verde Islands
Delbrel, Jacky, 1,190 lb 7 oz, Azores Bank, Faial, Azores
Dunaway, Deborah Maddux, 273 lb, St. Thomas, Virgin Islands
Dunaway, Jerry, 143 lb, La Guaira, Venezuela
Ekberg, Hakan, 736 lb 5 oz, Luanda, Angola
Fournillier, Murray R., 556 lb 8 oz, St. Georges, Grenada
Gray, Gloria, 560 lb, San Pedro, Ivory Coast
Guillanton, Patrick, 551 lb 2 oz, Dakar, Senegal
Holmes, Ann, 802 lb 7 oz, Gran Canaria, Canary Islands, Spain
Jaen C., M.D., Ruben, 802 lb 7 oz, Playa Grande, Venezuela

Nicolson, Cam, 507 lb, Luanda, Angola
Ratanamangcla, Apiwat, 978 lb, Madeira Island, Portugal
Robelin, Odile, 225 lb, Horta, Faial, Azores
Stoky, Ruth C., 124 lb 4 oz, Grand Cayman, British West Indies
Van Vliet, Robert, 803 lb 8 oz, Curacao, Netherland Antilles
MARLIN, BLACK
Beard, Jr., John A., 300 lb, Pinas Bay, Panama
Belk, Marilyn, 296 lb, Pinas Bay, Panama
Bishop, David A., 472 lb, Pinas Bay, Panama
Cunningham, Gerald L., 278 lb, Salinas, Ecuador
Elson, Jay M., 487 lb, Pinas Bay, Panama
Erskine, Jack, 72 lb 12 oz, Cape Moreton, Queensland, Australia
Erskine, Jack, 45 lb, Cairns, Queensland, Australia
Levitt, Mike, 79 lb 5 oz, Port Stephens, Australia
O'Brien, Val, 63 lb 14 oz, Townsville, Qld., Australia
Patterson, Mike, 441 lb 12 oz, Ocean Beach,Tutukaka,New Zealand
Saville, Charles W., 239 lb 3 oz, St. Lucia, Republic of S. Africa
MARLIN, PACIFIC BLUE
Basco, Pamela S., 341 lb 8 oz, Keauhou, Kona, Hawaii, USA
Basco, Pamela S., 182 lb 8 oz, Keahole Point, Kona, Hawaii, USA
Everette, Kelley K., 120 lb, Keahole Point, Hawaii, USA
Everette, Jocelyn J., 256 lb, Keahole Point, Kona, Hawaii, USA
Everette, Jocelyn J., 304 lb 8 oz, Mlholii, Kona, Hawaii, USA
Fann, Nancy Jo, 530 lb 8 oz, Kona, Hawaii, USA
Friend, John E., 496 lb, Keahole Point, Kona, Hawaii, USA
Gregg, Verna M., 462 lb, Cabo San Lucas, B.C.S., Mexico
Harding, Tony, 1,007 lb, The Hook, North Cape, New Zealand
Hemmings, Bob, 733 lb 8 oz, Kona, Hawaii, USA
Henry, Loren W., 878 lb, Kona, Hawaii, USA
Hogan, Elizabeth, 211 lb 10 oz, Cabo San Lucas, B.C.S., Mexico
Josepho, Mary Wallace, 502 lb, Cabo San Lucas, B.C.S., Mexico
Kormondy, Steven A., 440 lb, Cabo San Lucas, B.C.S., Mexico
Laverty, Roy, 831 lb 2 oz, Le Morne, Mauritius
Meyer, Jeffery, 631 lb 8 oz, Keahole Point, Kona, Hawaii, USA
Nishikawa, Neil N., 762 lb, Kona, Hawaii, USA
Spalding, Jr., Rufus P., 473 lb 9 oz, Kailua, Kona, Hawaii, USA
Stone, Catherine, 485 lb, Three Kings Islands, New Zealand
MARLIN, STRIPED
Fraser, Geoffrey, 276 lb 7 oz, Middlesex Bank, New Zealand
Hampton, Robert, 132 lb, Newport, California, USA
Hampton, Robert, 204 lb, San Clemente Island, California, USA
Henwood, Mark R., 131 lb, Catalina Island, California, USA
Houck, Joe, 179 lb 9 oz, Dana Point, California, USA
Lang, Peter A., 131 lb, Magdalena Bay, B.C.S., Mexico
Lopuszanski, Daniel, 140 lb, Cabo San Lucas, B.C.S., Mexico
Maccaferri, Luca, 130 lb, Cabo San Lucas, B.C.S., Mexico
Middleton, Ian, 254 lb, Madang, Papua, New Guinea
Mossman, Sam, 249 lb 1 oz, King Bank, New Zealand
Reed, Clive, 268 lb 8 oz, Three Kings Islands, New Zealand
Ross, Stephen A., 171 lb, Santa Catalina Island, California, USA
Stoneman, Kirk, 361 lb 15 oz, Bay of Islands, New Zealand
Tyson, Peter R., 231 lb 7 oz, Cape Brett, New Zealand
MARLIN, WHITE
Campbell, Stewart, 53 lb 8 oz, La Guaira, Venezuela
Cloostermans, Leo R., 35 lb, Horta, Faial, Azores
Levitt, Mike, 90 lb 6 oz, Vitoria, Brazil
Levitt, Mike, 121 lb 11 oz, Vitoria, Brazil
Storer, Sandra, 64 lb, La Guaira, Venezuela
PERCH, NILE
Von Bonde, Gerhard, 167 lb 3 oz, Lake Victoria, Kenya
SAILFISH, ATLANTIC
Basco, Pamela S., 57 lb 4 oz, Isla Contoy, Mexico
Baumeier, Eduardo, 53 lb 12 oz, Rio de Janeiro, Brazil
Critz, Dale C., 60 lb, Cancun, Q.R., Mexico
Dunaway, Deborah Maddux, 58 lb 8 oz, La Guaira, Venezuela
Dunaway, Deborah Maddux, 71 lb 3 oz, Dakar, Senegal
Dunaway, Deborah Maddux, 61 lb 3 oz, Dakar, Senegal
Dunaway, Jerry, 77 lb 6 oz, Dakar, Senegal
Leas, III, Donald Stewart, 60 lb 3 oz, Dakar, Senegal
Price, Gary R., 64 lb 3 oz, Dakar, Senegal
SAILFISH, PACIFIC
Beard, Bernice D., 120 lb, Pinas Bay, Panama
Billups, Guy C., 92 lb, Cabo San Lucas, B.C.S., Mexico
Cloostermans, Leo R., 73 lb, Pinas Bay, Panama
Levy, Alex, 110 lb, Pinas Bay, Panama
Levy, Alex, 91 lb, Pinas Bay, Panama
Rewalt, III, J. William, 150 lb, Acapulco, Mexico
Traversa, Giancarlo, 71 lb, Malindi, Kenya

Vander Hoek, Capt. Gene, 77 lb 8 oz, Pinas Bay, Panama
Werking, Raleigh, 118 lb, Tropic Star Lodge, Pinas Bay, Panama
Werking, Raleigh, 70 lb, Tropic Star Lodge, Pinas Bay, Panama
Whitehead, Craig, 90 lb, Playa Zancudo, Costa Rica

SALMON, CHINOOK
Hamilton, Robert E., 34 lb 10 oz, Chuitt River, Alaska, USA

SHARK, BLUE
Cairns, Diane, 212 lb 15 oz, Okains Bay, Canterbury, New Zealand
Caughlan, Craig Paul, 141 lb 1 oz, Marley, Australia
Flores, Geoff, 98 lb 12 oz, Tutukaka, Whangarei, New Zealand
Kabel, Adam P., 62 lb, Shinnecock Inlet, L.I., New York, USA
Knight, Tony, 288 lb 12 oz, Sydney, Australia
Murray, Colin D., 221 lb 12 oz, Hawke Bay, New Zealand
Paling, John, 166 lb 7 oz, Hawke Bay, New Zealand
Paling, John, 110 lb 10 oz, Hawke Bay, New Zealand
Shearman, Nick, 84 lb 14 oz, Tauranga, New Zealand
Sloan, Stephen, 61 lb, Long Island, New York, USA
Sloan, Stephen, 184 lb, Long Island, New York, USA
Yates, Adrian Richard, 363 lb 12 oz, Wollongong,N.S.W.,Australia

SHARK, HAMMERHEAD
Hall, Ashley, 485 lb, Bermagui, New South Wales, Australia
Miles, Mal, 169 lb 12 oz, Lee Point, Darwin, N.T., Australia

SHARK, LEMON
Gunion, Rick, 209 lb, Key West, Florida, USA
Spence, Gary, 275 lb, Key West, Florida, USA

SHARK, MAKO
Anderson, David Mark, 249 lb 1 oz, Botany Bay, Sydney, Australia
Broome, Mike, 412 lb 4 oz, Bay of Islands, New Zealand
Caughlan, Paul Edward, 268 lb 15 oz, Jibbon, N.S.W., Australia
Caughlan, Craig Paul, 339 lb 8 oz, Port Hacking, N.S.W., Australia
Jamieson, Bruce, 794 lb 12 oz,Cape Kari Kari,Auckland,N.Zealand
Levy, Robert I., 31 lb 12 oz, Catalina Channel, California, USA
Simpson, Tim, 432 lb 1 oz, Port Hacking, Sydney, Australia
Stannard, Darcy John, 180 lb 12 oz, Whitianga, New Zealand
Still, John L., 250 lb, Islamorada, Florida, USA
Tattersall, Frank, 884 lb, Cavalli Island, New Zealand
Thomson, David G., 396 lb 13 oz, Bermagui, N.S.W., Australia

SHARK, SILVERTIP
Zimmermann, Mike, 181 lb 14 oz, Bougainville,Papua,New Guinea

SHARK, SPOTTED RAGGED-TOOTH
Clausen, Hans Christian, 146 lb 6 oz,Port Elizabeth,Rep.ofS.Africa

SHARK, THRESHER
Gargiulo, Joe, 546 lb, Long Island, New York, USA
Hannah, D. L., 767 lb 3 oz,Cape Brett,Bay of Islands, N. Zealand
Massimo, Vittadello, 485 lb, Albarella, Adriatic Sea, Italy
Tew, Gregory, 262 lb 5 oz, Mdumbi, Transkei

SHARK, TIGER
Hezard, Philippe, 1,218 lb, Mauritius
Hissey, Ian, 745 lb 2 oz, Port Stephens, N.S.W., Australia
Martin, Barbara A., 216 lb, Key West, Florida, USA
Ratner, Jr., Herbert G., 242 lb, Cape May, New Jersey, USA
Turnbull, June, 1,173 lb, Cronulla, N.S.W., Australia

SHARK, WHITE
Astrom, Malte, 1,946 lb 10 oz, Port Lincoln, S.A., Australia
Caughlan, Jason Andrew, 2,026 lb, Port Lincoln, S.A., Australia
Sampson, Vic, 1,704 lb 2 oz, Kangaroo Island, Australia

STURGEON, WHITE
Peterson, Walt, 36 lb, Honker Bay, California, USA

SWORDFISH
Giraud, Marc, 73 lb, La Guaira, Venezuela
Goldsby, Robert Ray, 243 lb 8 oz, Ft. Lauderdale, Florida, USA
Perry, James, 106 lb 8 oz, Cabo San Lucas, B.C.S., Mexico

TARPON
Adams, Crawford W., 31 lb 6 oz, Florida Bay, Florida, USA
Balch, M.D., Clyde R., 177 lb, Homosassa, Florida, USA
Brown, Del, 127 lb, Marathon, Florida, USA
Chermanski, Dave, 32 lb, Sebastian River, Florida, USA
Delaunay, Andree, 187 lb 6 oz, Sherbro Island, Sierra Leone
Delaunay, Michel, 188 lb 7 oz, Sherbro Island, Sierra Leone
Fordyce, Pat, 120 lb, Islamorada, Florida, USA
Renton, Donald O., 72 lb, Marathon, Florida, USA
Zukas, Anton G., 147 lb 6 oz, Key West, Florida, USA

TROUT, LAKE
Johnson, Ray, 24 lb 13 oz, Flaming Gorge, Utah, USA

10 TO 1 CLUB

ALBACORE
Freitas, Ronald J., 50 lb, Kona, Hawaii, USA

AMBERJACK, GREATER
Chermanski, Dave, 67 lb, Ft. Pierce Inlet, Florida, USA
Hutson, Marion E., 83 lb 12 oz, Virginia Beach, Virginia, USA
Roy, Kenneth E., 45 lb 8 oz, Clearwater, Florida, USA
Wynne, Thomas R., 46 lb 8 oz, Charleston, South Carolina, USA

BARRACUDA, GREAT
Woods, Jeananne, 44 lb 1 oz, Groote-Eylandt, N.T., Australia

BASS, GIANT SEA
Whitaker, Dr. John F., 91 lb 8 oz, San Quintin, Mexico

BASS, STRIPED
Ballard, Hart (Sandy), 18 lb 6 oz, Suisun Bay, California, USA

BLUEFISH
Benson, Steven J., 17 lb 4 oz, Kill Devil Hills, North Carolina,USA

BUFFALO, SMALLMOUTH
Nichols, Scott S., 17 lb 8 oz, Trinity River, Hubbard, Texas, USA

CARP
Frash, James R., 21 lb 10 oz, Lake Irma, Florida, USA
McGraw, Roy, 24 lb 9 oz, Deer Point,Lake Tail Race,Florida, USA
Ward, Jean E., 29 lb, Patuxent River, Maryland, USA

CATFISH, BLUE
Davis, Edward C., 23 lb 8 oz, Cape Fear River, N. Carolina, USA

CATFISH, FLATHEAD
Robinson, IV, Ellyson S., 21 lb 6 oz, Richmond, Virginia, USA

COBIA
McAdam, J. D., 63 lb 14 oz, Escrauds, Nigeria
Porter, William T., 44 lb 13 oz, Flamingo, Florida, USA
Porter, William T., 25 lb, Key West, Florida, USA
Porter, William T., 25 lb, Flamingo, Florida, USA
Wilde, Michael, 25 lb, Key West, Florida, USA

CONGER
Froud, Denis J., 20 lb 2 oz, Gosport, Hampshire, England

DOLPHIN
Basco, Pamela S., 21 lb 12 oz, Cancun, Mexico
Basco, Pamela S., 19 lb 11 oz, Cancun, Mexico
Basco, Pamela S., 25 lb 1 oz, Cancun, Mexico
Basco, Pamela S., 18 lb 14 oz, Cancun, Mexico
Basco, Pamela S., 38 lb, Cancun, Mexico
Dunaway, Deborah Maddux, 42 lb, Pinas Bay, Panama
Flasch, Richard F., 17 lb 12 oz, Petite Coupe, Mauritius
Hogan, Jr., George E., 52 lb 16 oz,Cabo San Lucas,B.C.S.,Mexico
Miller, Linda L., 22 lb 12 oz, Pinas Bay, Panama

DRUM, BLACK
Noland, Buddy L., 75 lb 8 oz, Cape Charles, Virginia, USA
Porcelli, Capt. Joe, 43 lb, Indian River, Edgewater, Florida, USA
Robinson, IV, Ellyson S., 82 lb 8 oz,Chesapeake Bay,Virginia,USA
Werking, Raleigh, 56 lb, New Smyrna Beach, Florida, USA
Werking, Raleigh, 66 lb, New Smyrna Beach, Florida, USA

DRUM, RED
Currie, Christine, 22 lb 8 oz, Indian River, Cocoa, Florida, USA
Smith, Adam Lathrop, 24 lb 14 oz, Port St. Johns, Florida, USA
Werking, Raleigh, 27 lb 8 oz, Indian River Lagoon, Florida, USA
Werking, Raleigh, 39 lb 8 oz, Indian River Lagoon, Florida, USA

GAR, ALLIGATOR
Pickett, Jim C., 77 lb, Estes Flats, Rockport, Texas, USA

HALIBUT, PACIFIC
Anderson, Greg, 242 lb 6 oz, Funter Bay, Juneau, Alaska, USA
Cagle, Earl D., 165 lb, Resurrection Bay, Seward, Alaska, USA
Cushman, Marjorie, 26 lb, Cape Muzon, Alaska, USA
Everette, Jocelyn J., 149 lb 8 oz, Cook Inlet, Alaska, USA
Humphries, Jimmy Olen, 127 lb, Augustine Island, Alaska, USA
Sherwin, Betty-Jean, 68 lb, Douglas, Alaska, USA
Sherwin, Lee, 39 lb, Douglas, Alaska, USA
Stoky, Robert C., 82 lb, Kodiak, Alaska, USA
Thoreson, Maurice Dean, 122 lb, Chichagof Island, Alaska, USA
Vogt, Corolynn, 142 lb, Barren Islands, Homer, Alaska, USA
Zand, Fariba, 222 lb, Dutch Harbor, Alaska, USA

INCONNU
Hudnall, Lawrence E., 38 lb 12 oz, Kobuk River, Alaska, USA
Hudnall, Lawrence E., 21 lb, Kobuk River, Alaska, USA

JACK, CREVALLE

Chermanski, Dave, 29 lb 8 oz, Sebastian River, Florida, USA
Cole, Carl E., 27 lb 2 oz, Pensacola Bay, Pensacola, Florida, USA
Fuller, Wendy A., 24 lb 4 oz, Pensacola, Florida, USA

MACKEREL, KING

Hutchins, Mrs. Stephen R., 24 lb 8 oz, Key West, Florida, USA
Matthews, Dr. Jerome N., 38 lb 12 oz, Key West, Florida, USA

MARLIN, ATLANTIC BLUE

Baumgardner, Jr., L. P., 770 lb, Wachapreague, Virginia, USA
Bazin, Jean Claude, 849 lb 3 oz, Abidjan, Ivory Coast
Bierman, Marsha, 218 lb 8 oz, La Guaira, Venezuela
Bierman, Marsha, 168 lb, La Guaira, Venezuela
Borges De Sousa, Paulo, 815 lb 11 oz, Luanda, Angola
Calendini, Michel, 240 lb 4 oz, Dakar, Senegal
Calmon, Francoise, 521 lb 6 oz, Abidjan, Ivory Coast
Camp, Thomas J., 899 lb, Cape May, New Jersey, USA
Campbell, Stewart N., 1,038 lb, Madeira, Spain
Campbell, Stewart N., 1,141 lb, Madeira, Spain
Chery, Ronan, 250 lb, Dakar, Senegal
Cloostermans, Leo R., 1,020 lb, Horta, Faial, Azores
Colombani, Guy, 828 lb 14 oz, Libreville, Gabon
Corbin, David A., 478 lb, Grand Cayman, British West Indies
Corday, Kenneth R., 1,170 lb, Madeira, Portugal
Costa, Renato, 700 lb 6 oz, Vitoria, Brazil
Critz, Dale C., 531 lb 4 oz, Abidjan, Ivory Coast
De Silva, Henry J., 656 lb, Bermuda
De Silva, Henry J., 524 lb, Challenger Bank, Bermuda
De Silva, Henry, 805 lb, Challenger Bank, Bermuda
DeFeo, Donna, 888 lb, Ilheus, Brazil
Delaunay, Andree, 866 lb 6 oz, Abidjan, Ivory Coast
Destopelleire, Didier, 916 lb, Abidjan, Ivory Coast
Egitto, Frank, 921 lb 8 oz, Long Island, New York, USA
El-Hachem, Abdallah, 437 lb 2 oz, Lagos, Nigeria
Fernandez, III, Cruz, Ramon, 325 lb, Desecheo Island, Puerto Rico
Forstmann, Kenny, 678 lb, Oregon Inlet, North Carolina, USA
Foti, George L., 270 lb, Islamorada, Florida, USA
Francois, Jeannine, 1,058 lb 3 oz, Azores, Portugal
Harris, Jr., Audley C., 309 lb 8 oz, Grand Cayman, Cayman Islands
Haselhorst, Jorg-Dieter, 1,051 lb 9 oz, Faial, Azores
Hegmann, Karin, 685 lb 10 oz, Gran Canaria, Puerto Rico, Spain
Hegmann, Karin, 617 lb 4 oz, Gran Canary Island, Spain
Herrington, Jack, 1,142 lb, Nags Head, North Carolina, USA
Hutchins, Mrs. Stephen R., 183 lb, Caracas, Venezuela
Jean, Francis, 1,118 lb 13 oz, Abidjan, Ivory Coast
Karron, Richard, 920 lb, Boat Harbour, Abaco, Bahamas
Knight, II, William L., 602 lb, St. Thomas, Virgin Islands
Lambert, Rhonda, 502 lb, Port Eads, Louisiana, USA
Lauzen, David, 1,001 lb, Azores Bank, Azores
Lee, Stuart C., 213 lb, Oregon Inlet, North Carolina, USA
Lehmkuhl, Herbert, 306 lb 7 oz, Puerto Rico, Gran Canaria, Spain
Lemaitre, Daniel, 1,004 lb, Abidjan, Ivory Coast
Malyon, Brent, 815 lb 11 oz, Funchal, Madeira, Portugal
Martin, J. Andre, 956 lb 12 oz, Abidjan, Ivory Coast
Myers, Mark, 588 lb, Port Antonio, Jamaica
Nel, Danie, 498 lb 3 oz, Luanda, Angola
Nicolson, Iain, 500 lb 7 oz, Luanda, Angola
Northcutt, KayeLynne H., 530 lb, Chub Cay, Bahamas
Peacock, Myrtice, 885 lb, Marsh Harbour, Abaco, Bahamas
Perez, Jose L., 326 lb 12 oz, Tobago, West Indies
Perez, Juan Luis, 302 lb, Culebra, Puerto Rico
Piotrot, Raymond, 893 lb 15 oz, Abidjan, Ivory Coast
Ratanamangcla, Apiwat, 639 lb 5 oz, Funchal, Madeira, Portugal
Read, C. Greg, 297 lb, Key Biscayne, Florida, USA
Rogers, Shelby E., 1,059 lb, Madeira, Portugal
Simmons, Everard B., 686 lb, Challenger Bank, Bermuda
Siniscalchi, Anthony, 840 lb, Hudson Canyon, New York, USA
Soares, III, Eliseu, 930 lb 5 oz, Rio De Janeiro, Brazil
Sobrino-Catoni, Dr. Jose, 218 lb 4 oz, Higuey, Dominican Republic
Suarez, Rafael, 344 lb, San Juan, Puerto Rico
Tombras, Charlie, 208 lb, Sao Nicolau, Cape Verde Islands
Tombras, Charlie, 208 lb, La Guaira Bank, Brazil
Torruella, Juan Carlos, 241 lb, San Juan, Puerto Rico
Tri, M.D., Terry B., 943 lb 12 oz, Bom Bom Island Resort, Principe
Valdes, Jose A., 377 lb, El Pichincho, Mayaguez, Puerto Rico
Van Der Dijs, Papito, 347 lb, Curacao, Netherland Antilles
Van Vliet, Dirk, 347 lb, Curacao, Netherland Antilles
Vanbrugghe, Gerard, 860 lb 14 oz, Abidjan, Ivory Coast
Viyella, Luis, 895 lb 8 oz, San Juan, Puerto Rico
Vogel, Dieter, 595 lb 3 oz, Puerto Rico, Gran Canaria, Spain

Vogel, Dieter, 573 lb 3 oz, Gran Canaria, Spain
Vogel, Dieter, 578 lb 11 oz, Puerto Rico, Gran Canaria, Spain
Weber, Dr. Dieter, 507 lb, Puerto Rico, Gran Canaria, Spain
Wim, Keisers (Tommy), 652 lb 8 oz, Puerto Rico, Canary Isl., Spain

MARLIN, BLACK

Abel, Christopher H., 332 lb 14 oz, Bay of Islands, Russell, N. Zealand
Adams, Wally, 1,312 lb, Cairns, Queensland, Australia
Allison, Stuart W., 800 lb, Pemba Channel, Shimoni, Kenya
Anderson, II, John W., 1,307 lb 5 oz, Lizard Island, Australia
Anton, Jr., Jose, 540 lb 2 oz, Salinas, Ecuador
Anton, Jr., Jose, 600 lb, Salinas, Ecuador
Astrom, Malte, 1,086 lb, Ruby Reef, Cairns, Australia
Beard, Bernice D., 243 lb, Pinas Bay, Panama
Bloom, Ira J., 661 lb, Kona, Hawaii, USA
Canino, Michael A., 230 lb, Pinas Bay, Panama
Coombes, Lynne, 694 lb 14 oz, Cavalli Islands, New Zealand
Cooper, Arnold R., 295 lb, Pinas Bay, Panama
Cooper, Arnold R., 215 lb, Pinas Bay, Panama
Crane, Eddie, 155 lb 6 oz, Dunk Island, Queensland, Australia
Dalling, Anne, 93 lb 11 oz, Townsville, Australia
Elson, Jay M., 1,294 lb, Cairns, North Queensland, Australia
Erskine, Jack, 41 lb 1 oz, Cairns, Queensland, Australia
Erskine, Jack, 39 lb 14 oz, Cairns, Queensland, Australia
Fitzgerald, R. Curtis, 240 lb 4 oz, Acapulco, Mexico
Hatch, Charles, 455 lb, Pinas Bay, Panama
Joy, Ed, 868 lb, Queensland, Australia
Kane, Brian E., 222 lb 10 oz, Port Stephens, N.S.W., Australia
Knudsen, Robert, 596 lb 5 oz, Sodwana Bay, Republic of S. Africa
Limmer, Nina, 546 lb 11 oz, Red Head, Bay of Islands, N. Zealand
Lopuszanski, Daniel, 1,300 lb, St. Crispin Reef, Cairns, Australia
Obach, Richard C., 1,064 lb, Cairns, Australia
Princenthal, Rick, 826 lb, Ribbon Reef #10, Australia
Ratanamangcla, Apiwat, 1,190 lb 7 oz, Cairns, Australia
Rivera Garza, Mauricio, 202 lb 13 oz, Acapulco, Guerrero, Mexico
Sau-ling Shi, Jeannette, 1,076 lb, Day Reef, N. Qld., Australia
Simpson, Walter, 823 lb 10 oz, Motu River, New Zealand
Sola, Francisco, 568 lb, Salinas, Ecuador
Werking, Raleigh, 489 lb, Pinas Bay, Panama

MARLIN, PACIFIC BLUE

Andersen, Karl, 385 lb, Keahole, Kona, Hawaii, USA
Anton, Jr., Jose, 324 lb, Salinas, Ecuador
Barwick, Brigitte, 654 lb, Petit Coupe, Mauritius
Basco, Pamela S., 82 lb, Kona Coast, Hawaii, USA
Basco, Pamela S., 164 lb 8 oz, Kona Coast, Hawaii, USA
Campi, Adam, 475 lb 11 oz, Cape Kari Kari, Northland, N. Zealand
Canino, Michael A., 219 lb, Pinas Bay, Panama
Connor, Andrew, 559 lb 1 oz, Cape Kari Kari, New Zealand
Crosby, Patricia Parker, 215 lb, Cabo San Lucas, B.C.S., Mexico
Davies, Dennis, 552 lb 4 oz, Bay of Islands, Ninepin, New Zealand
Deanshaw, Graham, 811 lb 4 oz, Cape Moreton, Qld., Australia
Dunaway, Deborah Maddux, 190 lb, Cabo San Lucas, B.C.S., Mexico
Everette, Jocelyn J., 348 lb 8 oz, Keahole, Hawaii, USA
Farrell, Scott, 348 lb, Pinas Bay, Panama
Folkman, Daniel J., 584 lb, Kona, Hawaii, USA
Good, Elmer, 568 lb, Kailua-Kona, Hawaii, USA
Grassi, Anthony, 240 lb 6 oz, Sea of Cortez, B.C.S., Mexico
Handgis, George, 163 lb 8 oz, Kona, Hawaii, USA
Hayes, Reub, 588 lb 8 oz, Keauhou, Kona, Hawaii, USA
Jamieson, Irene, 716 lb 7 oz, Cape Kari Kari, New Zealand
Jenkins, Colin, 641 lb 8 oz, Bay of Islands, North Cape, N. Zealand
Jouvin, Ernesto, 903 lb, Salinas, Ecuador, South America
Jouvin, Ernesto, 880 lb, Salinas, Ecuador, South America
Koester, Heinz, 869 lb, Vavau Island, Kingdom of Tonga
Kraemer, Gil, 569 lb 8 oz, Keauhou Area, Hawaii, USA
Lipton, Jack, 328 lb 7 oz, Barra De Navidad, Jal., Mexico
Mann, Don, 810 lb, Manta, Ecuador
Mans, Andrew J., 965 lb, Le Morne, Mauritius
Maxwell, Peter, 252 lb 8 oz, Kona, Hawaii, USA
Maxwell, Peter, 203 lb, Keahole Point, Kona, Hawaii, USA
McFarlane, Brian, 518 lb 1 oz, Le Morne, Mauritius
McLaughlin, Steven M., 658 lb, Kona, Hawaii, USA
Neil, Mike, 862 lb 3 oz, Vava'u, Kingdom of Tonga
Pitner, Shannon T., 82 lb, Bora, Bora, French Polynesia
Salvat, Raymond, 564 lb 6 oz, Cabo Marzo, Choco, Colombia
Snyder, Tom, 558 lb, Kona, Hawaii, USA
Soubeyras, Marina, 540 lb 2 oz, Abidjan, Ivory Coast
Spalding, Michelle, 149 lb 8 oz, Kailua, Kona, Hawaii, USA
Spalding, Jr., Rufus P., 224 lb, Kealakekua, Kona, Hawaii, USA
Spalding, Michelle, 188 lb, Kailua, Kona, Hawaii, USA

Steffey, Dr. J. M., 353 lb, Kona Coast, Hawaii, USA
Stowe, Lindsay, 535 lb 4 oz, Tauranga, New Zealand
Taylor, M. Welby, 663 lb, Kona Coast, Hawaii, USA
Threadingham, Melvin A., 985 lb 7 oz, Nagara, Fiji Islands
Voelkel, M.D., A. Gene, 913 lb, Cabo San Lucas, B.C.S., Mexico
Walsh, Jr., Jim, 431 lb, Kona, Hawaii, USA
Waroquiers, Juan, 337 lb 8 oz, Kailua-Kona, Hawaii, USA
Weisson P., Ab. Enrique, 683 lb, Salinas, Ecuador

MARLIN, STRIPED

Abrego, Donald, 150 lb, San Diego, California, USA
Abrego, Donald L., 175 lb, San Diego, California, USA
Albright, Wally, 92 lb, Cabo San Lucas, B.C.S., Mexico
Albright, Wally, 110 lb, Cabo San Lucas, B.C.S., Mexico
Beadle, Ray, 110 lb, Cabo San Lucas, B.C.S., Mexico
Blumenthal, John, 242 lb 8 oz, Ninepin, Bay of Islands, N.Zealand
Boniface, Bill, 494 lb, Tutukaka, New Zealand
Bracken, Marge, 169 lb, Avalon, California, USA
Burtle, Jim, 157 lb 8 oz, Santa Barbara Island, California, USA
Butler, Dean, 199 lb 8 oz, Newcastle, N.S.W., Australia
Cottriall, Simon, 196 lb 8 oz, San Diego, California, USA
Cunningham, Gerald L., 175 lb, Salinas, Ecuador
Everard, Bruce, 377 lb 9 oz, Bermagui, N.S.W., Australia
Fink, David B., 132 lb 4 oz, Playa Hermosa, B.C.S., Mexico
Garrett, Gerald A., 130 lb, Santa Catalina Island, California, USA
Garrett, Victoria B., 167 lb, Catalina Island, California, USA
Gitmans, Mark, 363 lb 12 oz, Middle Ground, New Zealand
Gorrilla, Dr. L. Vincent, 222 lb, Mazatlan, Sinaloa, Mexico
Graham, Gary C., 98 lb, San Diego, California, USA
Graham, Yvonne, 129 lb, San Diego, California, USA
Griffith, John S., 167 lb 8 oz, Catalina Island, California, USA
Hall, William, 363 lb 12 oz, Home Point, Northland, N.Zealand
Hampton, Diana, 186 lb, Catalina Island, California, USA
Hampton, Diana, 135 lb 8 oz, Catalina Island, California, USA
Hampton, Robert, 144 lb, Catalina Island, California, USA
Hampton, Robert, 133 lb, Dana Point, California, USA
Hampton, Robert, 203 lb, San Diego, California, USA
Henricksen, T. N., 335 lb 1 oz,Middle Ground,Auckland,N.Zealand
Henricksen, Terry, 374 lb 4 oz, Bird Rock, New Zealand
Henry, Rowan, 127 lb, San Diego, California, USA
Herberts, Curtis, 145 lb 8 oz, Catalina Island, California, USA
Hill, Barry, 231 lb 7 oz, Redhead, Bay of Islands, New Zealand
Hinckley, Jean S., 124 lb 8 oz, Oceanside, California, USA
Ibey, Melvin C., 138 lb 8 oz, San Diego, California, USA
Kingsmill, Jim, 201 lb, Catalina Island, California, USA
Lank, Hank, 120 lb, Cabo San Lucas, B.C.S., Mexico
Liberti, Paul L., 256 lb, Santa Catalina Island, California, USA
Lynds, Phil, 355 lb 13 oz, Tutukaka, Whangarei, New Zealand
Moller, Graeme, 378 lb 1 oz, New Plymouth, Taranaki,N.Zealand
Neibling, Dr. Hal, 152 lb, Osbourne Bank, California, USA
Pearman, James A., 165 lb, Cabo San Lucas, B.C.S., Mexico
Price, Phil, 111 lb, Flamingo, Costa Rica
Rapp, Roy A., 147 lb, B.C.S., Mexico
Rilling, Gerald, 136 lb 10 oz, Cabo San Lucas, B.C.S., Mexico
Ross, Stephen A., 173 lb, San Clemente Island, California, USA
Royal, Ted, 131 lb 8 oz, Santa Catalina Island, California, USA
Shaw, John B., 199 lb, Pinas Bay, Panama
Sieminski, E. Richard, 163 lb, Dana Point, California, USA
Solovy, Mike, 120 lb, Cabo San Lucas, B.C.S., Mexico
Tombras, Charlie, 182 lb, Cocos Island, Costa Rica
Torre, Jack, 261 lb 12 oz, Cabo San Lucas, B.C.S., Mexico
Walter, Jody, 173 lb, San Diego, California, USA
Watson-Graham, Yvonne, 115 lb, San Diego, California, USA
Watson-Graham, Yvonne, 137 lb, San Diego, California, USA
Welch, Barbara Ruth, 181 lb, Cabo Falso, B.C.S., Mexico
Woodill, Barbara, 366 lb 6 oz, Mayor Island, New Zealand

MARLIN, WHITE

Knight, Jacqueline E., 64 lb, Walkers Cay, Bahamas
Robelin, Odile, 80 lb 14 oz, Mohammedia, Morocco
Robelin, Odile, 74 lb 1 oz, Mohammedia, Morocco
Sahiaoui, Fouad, 83 lb 12 oz, Mohammedia, Morocco

PERCH, NILE

Clouston, Phil, 152 lb 1 oz, Entebbe Bay, Entebbe, Uganda
Neibling, Debi, 81 lb 9 oz, Rusinga Island, Kenya
Neibling, Dr. Hal, 27 lb 8 oz, Rusinga Island, Kenya

PERMIT

Adams, Crawford W., 25 lb 7 oz, Key West, Florida, USA
Meyer, Kathleen, 26 lb 4 oz, Islamorada, Florida, USA
Riesenfeld, Bill, 41 lb 4 oz, Sugarloaf Key, Florida, USA
Riesenfeld, Bill, 44 lb 12 oz, Sugarloaf Key, Florida, USA
Ruilova, Sherril J., 23 lb, Sunshine Key, Florida, USA

PIKE, NORTHERN

Pearn, John, 23 lb 4 oz, Great Horden Lake, Kent, England

RAY, BACKWATER

Foster, Vivian Edwin, 87 lb 10 oz, Mossel Bay, R. of South Africa

SAILFISH, ATLANTIC

Agostini, Jean-Paul, 73 lb 10 oz, Saly, Senegal
Baratta, M.D., Robert O., 55 lb 6 oz, Dakar, Senegal
Baumeier, Eduardo, 59 lb 4 oz, Rio De Janeiro, Brazil
Critz, Dale C., 56 lb, Cancun, Q.R., Mexico
Gracie, Brian, 84 lb, Key West, Florida, USA
Hebert, Christine, 71 lb 3 oz, Saly, Senegal
Martin, Christian, 105 lb 4 oz, Key West, Florida, USA
Price, Gary R., 50 lb 6 oz, Dakar, Senegal
Robelin, Odile, 90 lb 13 oz, Saly, Senegal
Robelin, Odile, 88 lb 8 oz, Hotel Espadon, Club De Saly, Senegal
Wakeman, II, Rufus, 55 lb 9 oz, Dakar, Senegal
Webster, III, Joseph A., 43 lb 12 oz, Cancun, Q.R., Mexico

SAILFISH, PACIFIC

Adler, Steve, 81 lb, Pinas Bay, Panama
Bausman, III, Cooke, 75 lb, Rancho Leonero, B.C.S., Mexico
Bird, Charles A., 94 lb, Pinas Bay, Panama
Bird, Kay, 91 lb 8 oz, Pinas Bay, Panama
Bishop, David A., 97 lb, Tropic Star Lodge, Pinas Bay, Panama
Brumby, Russell, 48 lb 4 oz, Malindi, Kenya
Cloostermans, Leo R., 90 lb 8 oz, Pinas Bay, Panama
Cooper, Arnold R., 107 lb, Pinas Bay, Panama
De Villiers, D. G., 109 lb 5 oz,Cape Vidal,Natal,R. of South Africa
Del Torro, Federico, 98 lb 1 oz, Puerto Vallarta, Jalisco, Mexico
Dunaway, Jerry, 83 lb, Flamingo Bay, Costa Rica
Enneking, William F., 110 lb, Playa Zancudo, Golfito, Costa Rica
Gray, Jim, 84 lb, Quepos, Costa Rica
Handgis, Sharon, 93 lb 8 oz, Pinas Bay, Panama
Levy, Alex, 69 lb, Pinas Bay, Panama
Levy, Alex, 72 lb, Pinas Bay, Panama
Mack, Michael S., 99 lb 3 oz, Townsville, Australia
Miller, Judy, 99 lb 8 oz, Pinas Bay, Panama
Read, Chris, 76 lb, Rabaul, Papua, New Guinea
Rothenberger, John B., 100 lb, Panama
Tapson, Neil, 110 lb 3 oz, Cape Vidal, Republic of South Africa
Tracey, Claire, 89 lb 15 oz, Zululand, Republic of South Africa
Vander Hoek, Capt. Gene, 82 lb, Pinas Bay, Panama
Waring, Robert, 89 lb, Pinas Bay, Panama
Werking, Raleigh, 106 lb, Tropic Star Lodge, Pinas Bay, Panama
Werking, Raleigh, 85 lb 4 oz, Tropic Star Lodge,Pinas Bay,Panama

SALMON, ATLANTIC

Behrman, Darryl G., 22 lb, Alta River, Norway

SALMON, CHINOOK

Bottelsen, Walt, 51 lb, Kenai River, Alaska, USA
Chester, Douglas B., 24 lb 3 oz, Baldwin, Michigan, USA
Edwards, Gary P., 22 lb 9 oz,Salmon R.,Pulaski,New York, USA
Incremona, Nunzio, 24 lb, Salmon River, Pulaski, New York, USA
Judge, Joseph P., 28 lb 12 oz, Hakai Pass,British Columbia, Canada

SALMON, COHO

Leed, Burton R., 15 lb 12 oz, Karluck River, Alaska, USA

SHARK, BIGNOSE

Rohrlack, Lester J., 369 lb 14 oz, LAE, Papua, New Guinea

SHARK, BLACKTIP

Buitendag, Petrus C., 131 lb 2 oz,Sodwana Bay,Zululand, S. Africa

SHARK, BLUE

Bordner, Barry, 149 lb, Martha's Vineyard, Massachusetts, USA
Burt, Pauline, 112 lb 6 oz, Portland Island, Mahia, New Zealand
Chase, Mark, 93 lb 3 oz, Gulf of Maine, Maine, USA
Coleman, Tim, 176 lb, Martha's Vineyard, Massachusetts, USA
Pierce, Mrs. Sandy, 361 lb 12 oz, Tutukaka,Northland,New Zealand
Thomson, David G., 154 lb 5 oz, Bermagui, N.S.W., Australia
Wallis, Shaun, 177 lb 3 oz, Bay of Islands, New Zealand

SHARK, BULL

Pforr, Kenneth H., 165 lb, Key West, Florida, USA
Taylor, Ms. Brett, 354 lb 15 oz, Broken Bay, N.S.W., Australia

SHARK, GREENLAND

Nordtvedt, Terje, 1,708 lb 9 oz, Trondheimsfjord, Norway

SHARK, HAMMERHEAD

Bolland, John, 339 lb 8 oz, Cape Brett, New Zealand
Davies, Dennis, 340 lb 9 oz, Bay of Islands, Ninepin, New Zealand

Gunion, Rick, 88 lb 8 oz, Miami, Florida, USA
Hornhardt, Jason, 165 lb 12 oz, Flying Foam, Dampier, Australia

SHARK, MAKO
Butti, Philip, 335 lb, Jones Inlet, New York, USA
Clarke, M. J., 335 lb 1 oz, Bermagui, N.S.W., Australia
Federici, David, 560 lb,Nomans Isl.,Cape Cod, Massachusetts, USA
Flynn, Stephen A., 274 lb 8 oz, Ocean City, Maryland, USA
Harrington, Roy Dennis, 621 lb 4 oz, Bay of Islands, New Zealand
Jones, Niel Leonard, 356 lb, Bermuda
Mann, Ted, 542 lb 5 oz, Ninepin, Bay of Islands, New Zealand
Martin, Lesley, 698 lb 13 oz, Red Head, N.S.W., Australia
Meagher, Hugh A., 469 lb 9 oz, Broken Bay Wide, Australia
Murray, Kenneth, 542 lb 5 oz, Bird Rock, New Zealand
Paling, John, 92 lb 2 oz, Hawke Bay, New Zealand
Patterson, Kylie, 187 lb 6 oz, Wollowgong, N.S.W., Australia
Pescoe, B. J., 584 lb 3 oz, Red Head, New Zealand
Rewi, Dick, 88 lb 13 oz, Hawke Bay, New Zealand
Shanaghan, Martin, 1,022 lb 7 oz,Hawke Bay,Napier,N. Zealand
Spalding, Michelle, 167 lb, Kailua, Kona, Hawaii, USA
Stierhoff, Charles Scott, 373 lb, Ocean City, Maryland, USA
Stotesbury, Greg, 23 lb 3 oz, Newport Beach, California, USA
Watts, Karen Margaret,667 lb 1 oz,Poor Knights Islands,N. Zealand
Zand, Fariba, 83 lb 8 oz, Santa Monica, California, USA

SHARK, NARROWTOOTH
Haigh, Hamish, 372 lb 9 oz,(bronze whaler),Whangarei, N.Zealand

SHARK, SIXGILLED
Knight, Stuart, 103 lb 9 oz, Langebaan, South Africa
Reece, W. P., 1,027 lb, Faial, Azores

SHARK, THRESHER
Bartolini, Gabriele, 370 lb 5 oz, Adriatic Sea, Pesaro, Italy
Baxendell, Bill, 362 lb, Newport Beach, California, USA
Elm, Dave, 230 lb, Newport Beach, California, USA
McPherson, Jr., Donald, 215 lb, Santa Monica Bay,California, USA
Pintauro, Mrs. Lynnette M., 448 lb, Montauk, New York, USA
Secrest, Ben, 290 lb 2 oz, Dana Point, California, USA

SHARK, TIGER
Martin, Yves, 574 lb, Guinea-Bissau
Pantry, David G., 84 lb 4 oz, Bermuda
Spence, Gary, 220 lb, Key West, Florida, USA
Williams, Dolores V., 879 lb, Longboat Key, Florida, USA

SHARK, WHITE
Ashman, David, 178 lb 9 oz, Dudley, N.S.W., Australia
Flourentzou, George, 1,272 lb, Cape Jervis, Australia
Green, Tony, 890 lb 10 oz, Bank Struisbay, South Africa
Sampson, Vic, 1,366 lb 13 oz, Australia
Sampson, Vic, 1,340 lb 6 oz, Kangaroo Island, Australia
Stone, Christopher G., 583 lb 1 oz, Port Lincoln, Australia

SHARK, WHITETIP
Basco, Pamela S., 146 lb 8 oz, Kona, Hawaii, USA

SPEARFISH, SHORTBILL
Meyer, Jeffery W., 24 lb, Honokahua, Hawaii, USA

STEENBRAS, RED
Saunders, Craig, 89 lb 1 oz, Algoa Bay, Republic of South Africa

STURGEON, LAKE
Peterson,Everett Lee,135 lb 10 oz,Big Yellow Lake,Wisconsin,USA

STURGEON, WHITE
Barnard, John A., 162 lb 3 oz, San Rafael, California, USA
Hawkins, Joe, 58 lb 3 oz, Suisun Bay, Pittsburg, California, USA
Stratton, William A., 390 lb, Sacramento, California, USA

SWORDFISH
Colyn, Maureen K., 297 lb 15 oz,Hout Bay,Rep. of South Africa
Dunaway, Deborah Maddux, 114 lb, Pinas Bay, Panama
Dunaway, Deborah Maddux, 174 lb, Pinas Bay, Panama
Dunaway, Jerry, 109 lb, Pinas Bay, Panama
Dunaway, Jerry, 166 lb, Pinas Bay, Panama
McAdams, Craig, 533 lb 8 oz, Algarrobo, Chile
West, Olga N., 199 lb 12 oz, Key West, Florida, USA
Willits, John F., 392 lb, Nantucket, Massachusetts, USA

TARPON
Alarcon, Pascale, 230 lb, Sherbro Island, Sierra Leone
Botting, Paula S., 132 lb, Key West, Florida, USA
Delaunay, Andree, 166 lb 7 oz, Sherbro Island, Sierra Leone
Gibson, Jr., Thomas F., 223 lb 12 oz, Sherbro Island, Sierra Leone
Gibson, Jr., Thomas F., 64 lb, Isla Aguada, Campeche, Mexico
Kipnis, Capt. Dan, 121 lb 8 oz, Miami, Florida, USA
Levy, Bill, 42 lb 8 oz, Marathon, Florida, USA

Lopuszanski, Daniel, 198 lb 6 oz, Sherbro, Sierra Leone
Madaria H., Alberto, 173 lb, Port Michel, Gabon
Mason, Heidi, 139 lb 12 oz, Government Cut, Miami, Florida, USA
Price, Jr., Robert D., 86 lb 12 oz, Bahia Honda Key, Florida, USA
Ratner, Jr., Herbert G., 121 lb 8 oz, Key West, Florida, USA
Ross, Howard, 190 lb, Key West, Florida, USA
Schweitzer, H. George, 153 lb 8 oz, Florida Keys, Florida, USA
Storer, Sandra, 40 lb, Flamingo, Florida, USA
Thorn, Stephane, 170 lb, Sherbro Island, Sierra Leone

TREVALLY, GOLDEN
Lewin, Murray, 18 lb 15 oz, Exmouth, Australia
Ogg, John, 19 lb 6 oz, Exmouth, Australia

TROUT, BROWN
Salamon, Anthony J., 14 lb 6 oz, White River, Arkansas, USA

TUNA, ATLANTIC BIGEYE
Carter, D.E.L., 140 lb 1 oz, Cape Point, South Africa
Willmore, Lionel Howson, 130 lb 4 oz, Hout Bay, South Africa

TUNA, BLUEFIN
Fitzpatrick, Barry M., 820 lb,North Lake,Prince Edward Isl.,Canada
Fraser, Ken, 1,496 lb, Auld's Cove, Nova Scotia, Canada
Sowers, Jr., George B., 348 lb, Hatteras, North Carolina, USA
Steffey, Dr. J. M., 1,116 lb,North Lake,Prince Edward Isl., Canada

TUNA, PACIFIC BIGEYE
Denholm, David M., 143 lb 8 oz, Oxnard, California, USA
Kurz, Robert R., 83 lb, San Diego, California, USA
Wells, Sr., Capt. Jerry, 157 lb 12 oz, San Clemente Isl., CA, USA

TUNA, YELLOWFIN
Basco, Pamela S., 203 lb 8 oz, Kona, Hawaii, USA
Cik, J. O. (Hans), 173 lb, Kailua-Kona, Hawaii, USA
Denholm, David M., 183 lb 8 oz, Santa Cruz Isl.,Oxnard,CA, USA
Down, R. Andrew, 133 lb, Kona, Hawaii, USA
Harris, Capt. Dennis, 133 lb, Kona, Hawaii, USA
Morris, Jim, 190 lb 11 oz, Bermagui, N.S.W., Australia

YELLOWTAIL, SOUTHERN
Feldman, M.D., Mark L., 34 lb 2 oz, Mangonui, New Zealand

5 TO 1 CLUB

ALBACORE
Busby, R. J., 48 lb 6 oz, Hout Bay, Republic of South Africa
Crow, Kevin J., 68 lb 12 oz, Port San Luis, Avila Beach, CA,USA
Meyer, Hubert, 60 lb 11 oz,Hout Bay,Cape Town,Rep. of S. Africa

AMBERJACK, GREATER
Coleman, Tim, 84 lb 4 oz, Key West, Florida, USA
Flynn, Patrick, 75 lb 3 oz, Islamorada, Florida, USA
Porter, William T., 60 lb 4 oz, Islamorada, Florida, USA
Porter, William T., 46 lb 8 oz, Islamorada, Florida, USA
Porter, William T., 62 lb 8 oz, Islamorada, Florida, USA
Ross, Barry, 15 lb, Key West, Florida, USA

BARRACUDA, GREAT
Filios, Foxy, 74 lb 1 oz, Zanzibar, E. Africa
Manton, Jane, 46 lb 15 oz, Groote Eylandt, Australia
McAdam, J.D., 39 lb 10 oz, Escrauds, Nigeria
Micola, Justin, 27 lb 14 oz, Groote Eylandt, Australia
Riesenfeld, Bill, 32 lb 8 oz, Key West, Florida, USA
Robinson, III, Ellyson S., 43 lb 8 oz, Ocracoke, N. Carolina, USA
Sands, Patricia, 13 lb, Nassau, Bahamas
Shepherd, Bruce, 58 lb 6 oz, Mission Beach, Qld., Australia

BARRAMUNDI
De Groot, Richard, 48 lb 15 oz, S. Alligator River, N.T.,Australia

BASS, GIANT SEA
Coronado, Dr. Julius, 222 lb 4 oz, B.C.S., Mexico

BASS, LARGEMOUTH
Crupi, Robert J., 16 lb 14 oz, Castaic Lake,Castaic,California,USA
Crupi, Robert J., 14 lb 12 oz, Castaic Lake,Castaic,California,USA

BASS, PEACOCK
Townsend, Jr., D.V.M., Forrest I., 14 lb, Rio Cinaruco, Venezuela

BASS, STRIPED
Anderson, Gary S., 23 lb 6 oz,Smith Mountain Lake,Virginia, USA
Byer, Robert R., 60 lb, Feather River, California, USA
Duarte, David, 42 lb 8 oz, Martha's Vineyard, Massachusetts, USA
Golinski, Emme, 46 lb 12 oz, Fishers Island, New York, USA
Golinski, Alan, 41 lb 8 oz, Fishers Island, New York, USA
Hayashi, Ronald S., 42 lb, Sacramento River, Verona, CA, USA

Skinner, Edna, 40 lb 2 oz, Millicoma River, Oregon, USA

BASS, STRIPED - (LANDLOCKED)
Baker, Gene E., 64 lb 15 oz, Sutherland Lake, Nebraska, USA
Bearden, Jr., Leonard B., 38 lb, San Luis Reservoir, CA, USA
Brand, Jr., Fred, 55 lb, O'Neill Forebay, Santa Nella, CA, USA
Goodman, David, 23 lb 5 oz, Nantucket Island,Massachusetts, USA
Ratliff, Jimmy D., 11 lb 11 oz, Smith Mt.Lake, Moneta, VA, USA
Whitehurst, Alfred L., 22 lb 7 oz, San Luis Reservoir, CA, USA
Whitehurst, Alfred L., 32 lb 12 oz, San Luis Reservoir, CA, USA

BLUEFISH
DuVal, Mrs. William B., 14 lb 9 oz,Oregon Inlet,N. Carolina, USA
LaBrie, Mrs. Lillian D., 13 lb 2 oz, Boston, Massachusetts, USA
LaBrie, Mrs. Lillian D., 11 lb, Salem, Massachusetts, USA
Patenaude, Daniel, 12 lb, Narragansett Bay, Rhode Island, USA
Purdy, Danwin M., 14 lb 6 oz, Martha's Vineyard, MA, USA

BONEFISH
Adams, Crawford W., 11 lb 12 oz, Islamorada, Florida, USA
Orthwein, James Busch, 12 lb, Bimini, Bahamas

BUFFALO, BLACK
McLain, Edward H., 55 lb 8 oz, Rogersville, Tennessee, USA

BUFFALO, SMALLMOUTH
Dolezal, Jerry L., 68 lb 8 oz, Lake Hamilton, Arkansas, USA

CARP
Bonfadini, Michael A., 34 lb, Potomac River, Virginia, USA
Gross, John C., 32 lb 2 oz, Lake Madison, South Dakota, USA
Hershberger, Donald H., 18 lb, Schellsburg, Pennsylvania, USA
Kelly, Kevin, 32 lb 11 oz, Sterling Pond, Lake Ontario
McClure, Dan, 20 lb 13 oz, St. Louis, Missouri, USA
Regan, John J., 20 lb 12 oz, Springfield, Massachusetts, USA
Sedlarik, Jeffrey D., 14 lb 6 oz, Portage Lake, Michigan, USA
Vandergoot, Marcel, 11 lb 7 oz, Waikerie, Australia
Ward, Jean E., 25 lb 8 oz, Patuxent R.,Calvert Co.,Maryland, USA

CARPSUCKER, RIVER
Berg, Mike, 10 lb 2 oz, Lake Michigan, Indiana, USA

CATFISH, BLUE
Agee, Virgil Dale, 101 lb,Osage R.,Jefferson City, Missouri, USA
Bell, Glenn E., 58 lb 8 oz, Irvine Lake, Orange, California, USA
Davis, Edward C., 30 lb 8 oz,Cape Fear River,North Carolina,USA
Davis, Edward C., 47 lb, Cape Fear River, North Carolina, USA
Kitchens, Sr., Jim, 75 lb, Guntersville, Alabama, USA
Prieto, Edmund, 52 lb, Grassy L., St. Martin Parish,Louisiana,USA
Reece, Douglas H., 50 lb, Columbia, Missouri, USA

CATFISH, CHANNEL
Henkle, L. Steven, 31 lb, Rodman Reservoir, Florida, USA
Rowell, Danny R., 24 lb 10 oz, Heflin, Alabama, USA
Starkell, John R., 12 lb 8 oz, Red River, Manitoba, Canada

CATFISH, FLATHEAD
Anthony, Jr., Chuck, 80 lb, McAlpine Dam, Kentucky, USA
Armstrong, A. M., 52 lb, Lake Dardanelle, Dardanelle, AR, USA
Davidson, Charles L., 38 lb 4 oz,Sooner Lake,Ponce City,OK, USA
Davis, Edward C., 39 lb, Cape Fear River, North Carolina, USA
Jolley, Sandy, 38 lb, Pickwick Lake, Alabama, USA
Owens, Ray, 48 lb 2 oz, Rock Fork Lake, Hillsboro, Ohio, USA
Paulie, Ken, 123 lb, Elk City Reservoir, Independence, Kansas, USA

COBIA
DuVal, Mrs. William B., 55 lb, Key West, Florida, USA
Hardy, Thomas, 128 lb 12 oz, Pensacola Bay, Florida, USA
Mack, Olga, 70 lb 8 oz, Moreton Island, Qld., Australia
Mason, Heidi, 66 lb, Key Biscayne, Florida, USA
McCollester, Peter, 130 lb 1 oz, Destin, Florida, USA
Padron, Jorge L., 25 lb 8 oz, Flamingo, Florida, USA
Schultz, Harry C. "Buddy", 49 lb, Galveston, Texas, USA
Still, John Lee, 81 lb 8 oz, Key West, Florida, USA
Terrebonne, Brian A., 72 lb 8 oz, Grand Chernier, Louisiana, USA

COD, ATLANTIC
Angerman, Donald F.X., 41 lb, Perkins Cove,Ogunquit,Maine,USA
Angerman, Donald F.X., 60 lb 12 oz, Ogunquit, Maine, USA
LaBrie, Mrs. Lillian D.,20 lb 12 oz,Middlebank,Massachusetts,USA
LaBrie, Mrs. Lillian D., 17 lb 4 oz,Marblehead,Massachusetts, USA
Withee, Robert H., 40 lb 8 oz, Ammen Rock, Massachusetts, USA

DOLPHIN
Basco, Pamela S., 12 lb 12 oz, Cancun, Mexico
Basco, Pamela S., 21 lb 3 oz, Flamingo, Costa Rica
Basco, Pamela S., 16 lb, Cancun, Mexico
Basco, Pamela S., 22 lb 11 oz, Cancun, Mexico
Basco, Pamela S., 34 lb, Isla Mujeres, Mexico

Basco, Pamela S., 27 lb 1 oz, La Guaira, Venezuela
Basco, Pamela S., 22 lb, Isla Mujeres, Mexico
Basco, Pamela S., 11 lb 11 oz, Cancun, Mexico
Battistini, Sr., Luis A., 58 lb, Mayaguez, Puerto Rico
Baumeier, Eduardo, 11 lb 12 oz, Rio de Janeiro, Brazil
Carter, Richard G., 34 lb 4 oz, West Palm Beach, Florida, USA
Rose, Peter, 46 lb 11 oz, Freeport, Grand Bahama Island, Bahamas
Scott, Glenn L., 20 lb 8 oz, Islamorada, Florida, USA
Werking, Raleigh, 50 lb 8 oz,Tropic Star Lodge,Pinas Bay, Panama
Werking, Trish, 54 lb 8 oz, Tropic Star Lodge, Pinas Bay, Panama

DRUM, BLACK
Carlin, Harold D., 45 lb, Cape Hatteras, North Carolina, USA
Wisner, James P., 21 lb 15 oz, Tampa Bay, Florida, USA

DRUM, RED
Blaschke, Charles L., 46 lb, Cape Charles, Virginia, USA
Dean, Bill, 37 lb, Juniper Bay, Pamlico Sound,North Carolina,USA
DuVal, Mrs. William B., 46 lb 8 oz, Ocracoke,North Carolina,USA
DuVal, Mrs. William B., 34 lb 12 oz,Ocracoke,North Carolina,US
DuVal, Mrs. William B., 24 lb 8 oz, Ocracoke,North Carolina,USA
Fairbanks, David Michael, 12 lb 13 oz,New Smyrna Beach,FL,USA
Hernandez, Gerald E., 24 lb 8 oz, West Bay, Pasadena,Texas, USA
Lee, Stuart C., 60 lb 8 oz, Oregon Inlet, North Carolina, USA
Lund, Ted, 32 lb 8 oz, Cocoa Beach, Florida, USA
Rebstock, Sr., Charles E., 53 lb, Hatteras Island,N. Carolina, USA
Werking, Raleigh, 35 lb 4 oz, Indian River Lagoon, Florida, USA

GAR, ALLIGATOR
Gilbert, Johnny L., 186 lb 3 oz, Nassau Bay, Texas, USA

GAR, LONGNOSE
Rountrey, J. Parks, 15 lb 8 oz, Chickahominy,Lexana,Virginia,USA

GROPER, QUEENSLAND
Norris, Peter C., 263 lb 7 oz, Groote Eylandt, N.T., Australia

HALIBUT, CALIFORNIA
Walsh, Mike, 20 lb 9 oz, Santa Monica Bay, California, USA
Whitaker, Dr. John F., 19 lb 7 oz, San Quintin, Mexico

HALIBUT, PACIFIC
Blumhagen, Darcy, 182 lb 8 oz, Aaltanhash Inlet, B.C., Canada
Cagle, Earl D., 109 lb, Twin Rocks,Seward,Alaska,USA
Cushman, Marjorie, 40 lb, Langara Island, B.C., Canada
DeMars, Dick, 74 lb, Port Armstrong, Alaska, USA
Grimes, Susan McCarty, 26 lb 15 oz, Limestone Inlet,Alaska, USA
Gushiken, Jack N., 115 lb, Shelter Island, Juneau, Alaska, USA
Hillgardner, William J., 65 lb, Kodiak Island, Alaska, USA
Hillgardner, William J., 96 lb, Marmot Bay, Kodiak, Alaska, USA
Keller, William G., 91 lb, Vitskari Rocks, Sitka, Alaska, USA
Kubota, Masato, 133 lb, Shelter Lodge, Juneau, Alaska, USA
Leader, Paul, 108 lb, Kodiak, Alaska, USA
Loomis, Bob, 150 lb, Elfin Cove, Alaska, USA
Loopstra, Elaine M., 264 lb,St. Lazaria Isl.,Sitka Sound,AK, USA
Munk, Werner R., 121 lb, Chiniak Bay, Kodiak, Alaska,USA
Peck, Sandy, 166 lb, Glacier Bay, Alaska, USA
Raub, Jack G., 77 lb 8 oz,Point Lucan,Chicago Island,Alaska, USA
Shockley, Eleanor N., 236 lb, Icy Straits, Gustavus, Alaska, USA
Stoky, Robert C., 89 lb, Kodiak Island, Alaska, USA
Wolfe, Robert V., 130 lb, Prince William Sound, Alaska,USA
Wolfe, Ursula H. S., 114 lb, Prince William Sound, Alaska, USA

INCONNU
Hudnall, Daniel J., 39 lb, Kobuk River, Alaska, USA
Hudnall, Lawrence E., 27 lb 8 oz, Kobuk River, Alaska, US

JACK, CREVALLE, ATLANTIC
Fuller, James G., 27 lb 2 oz, Pensacola, Florida, USA
Prose, Albert B., 26 lb 4 oz, Crystal River, Florida, USA

JACK, CREVALLE, PACIFIC
Swanson, Sharon R., 24 lb, Cabo San Lucas, B.C.S., Mexico

JEWFISH
Maquin, Dr. Francis, 96 lb, Iles du Salut, French Guiana

KOB
Seymour, John Edward, 72 lb 12 oz, Bashee River, Transkei

LINGCOD
Cagle, J. Laurie, 21 lb 10 oz,Resurrection Bay,Seward,Alaska, USA
Mezirow, Andrew, 43 lb 4 oz, Seward, Alaska, USA

MACKEREL, KING
Cairo, Rinny, 32 lb, Key West, Florida, USA
Eckhart, James M., 63 lb 8 oz, Key West, Florida, USA
Kremser, Mike, 44 lb 8 oz, Stuart, Florida, USA
Zequeira, Donna Campbell, 37 lb, Key West, Florida, USA

MARLIN, ATLANTIC BLUE

Aleong, Roger, 631 lb 4 oz, Tobago, West Indies
Aleong, Roger, 358 lb, North Coast, Trinidad
Antun, Frank, 158 lb, Dominican Republic
Basch, Robert L., 568 lb, Bermuda
Beard, Larry, 1,204 lb, Funchal, Madeira
Bearden, Derry Lynn, 139 lb 5 oz, La Guaira, Venezuela
Bennett, David James, 809 lb 1 oz, Lagos, Nigeria
Capozzi, Enrico, 272 lb, La Guaira Bank, Venezuela
Cheong, Lindy Chu, 491 lb, Trinidad and Tobago
Culbertson, Warren, 980 lb 8 oz, Gulf of Mexico, Destin, FL, USA
Curtis, J.W. (Bill), 431 lb 8 oz, Greensboro, North Carolina, USA
Dahan, Marie-Therese, 165 lb,Rocher,Malendure,Guadeloupe,F.W.I.
Damerius, Holger, 414 lb 7 oz, Santa Maria, Azores, Portugal
Dapling, John, 524 lb 11 oz, Luanda, Angola, Africa
Delaunay, Andree, 222 lb 10 oz, San Nicolau, Cape Verde Islands
Deniz, Roberto, 449 lb 11 oz, Puerto Rico, Gran Canaria, Spain
Derom, Marie Josie, 375 lb, Abidjan, Ivory Coast
Dietze, Ulrich, 507 lb, Puerto De Mogan, Gran Canaria, Spain
Donestevez, Jr., Juan, 424 lb, Arecibo, Puerto Rico
Dupree, Chris, 569 lb, Pensacola, Florida, USA
Edwards, III, William R., 541 lb, Grand Cayman Island
El-Hachem, Abdallah, 176 lb 14 oz, Lagos, Nigeria
El-Hachem, Abdallah, 168 lb 10 oz, Lagos, Nigeria
El-Hachem, Miss Nawal, 306 lb 7 oz, Lagos, Nigeria
Ella, Desmond D., 338 lb 12 oz, Tobago
Elser, Otto K.,352 lb 4 oz, Rum Point, Grand Cayman Island
Fischer, Eric, 770 lb, Treasure Cay, Bahamas
Florio, William J., 748 lb, Challenger Bank, Bermuda
Formichella, Dianne C., 865 lb, Hudson Canyon, New Jersey, USA
Fulgueira, Johnny, 300 lb, Desecheo, Puerto Rico
Garcia Cabrera, Hector, 478 lb 6 oz, Gran Canaria, Spain
Gray, Jim, 106 lb, The Saddle, British Virgin Islands
Gunderson, Raymond Howard, 815 lb, Argus Bank, Bermuda
Haggerty, Sue, 413 lb, Abaco, Bahamas
Hegmann, Karin, 363 lb 12 oz, Gran Canaria, Spain
Hegmann, Helmut, 440 lb 14 oz, Gran Canaria, Spain
Hernandez Palmerola, Angel, 1,040 lb, Algarve, Portugal
Hernandez, Jr., Mario R., 503 lb, Playa Dorado, Puerto Rico
Highams, Pam, 157 lb 8 oz, Walkers Cay, Bahamas
Howe, Deering, 537 lb, Jupiter, Florida, USA
Hunnicutt, Dick, 417 lb, Hatteras, North Carolina, USA
Lohre, Bernhard, 460 lb 12 oz, Puerto Rico, Gran Canaria, Spain
Marsh, Ian C., 487 lb 3 oz, Luanda, Angola, Africa
Minors, Andrew G., 307 lb, Grenada, West Indies
Motley, Bertram A., 710 lb, North Carolina, USA
Perennes, Tanguy, 169 lb 4 oz, La Guaira, Venezuela
Perret Gentil, Oscar, 210 lb, Curacao, Netherland Antilles
Piotrot, Raymond, 893 lb 15 oz, Abidjan, Ivory Coast
Ricca, Richard J., 579 lb, Challenger Bank, Bermuda
Ringhaver, Randal L., 729 lb, Ocean City, Maryland, USA
Roper, Edward G., 540 lb, Port Eads, Louisiana, USA
Schamps, Fransis, 1,008 lb, Madeira, Portugal
Schwarzkopf, Mrs. Ailsa P., 301 lb 5 oz, Lagos, Nigeria
Shackelford, Mark, 407 lb, Hatteras, North Carolina, USA
Shealy, Dean H., 562 lb, Treasure Cay, Bahamas
Shields, Peter Kent, 281 lb 1 oz, Monrovia, Liberia
Smith, Terry, 672 lb, Ponta Delgada, Sao Miguel Island, Azores
Smith, Tom, 269 lb 4 oz, Challenger Bank, Bermuda
Stewart, John G., 527 lb, Hatteras, North Carolina, USA
Torruella, Juan Carlos, 676 lb, San Juan, Puerto Rico
Van Vliet, Dirk, 198 lb 6 oz, Aruba, Netherland Antilles
Vogel, Dieter, 339 lb 8 oz, Puerto Rico, Gran Canaria, Spain
Vogel, Dieter, 537 lb 14 oz, Puerto Rico, Gran Canaria, Spain
Vogel, Dieter, 511 lb 7 oz, Puerto Rico, Gran Canaria, Spain
Vogel, Dieter, 482 lb 12 oz, Puerto Rico, Gran Canaria, Spain
Vogel, Dieter, 359 lb 5 oz, Puerto Rico, Gran Canaria, Spain
Vogel, Dieter, 260 lb 2 oz, Puerto Rico, Gran Canaria, Spain
Zietsman, Johan, 827 lb, Ada Foah, Ghana, West Africa

MARLIN, BLACK

Beadle, Ray, 85 lb 15 oz,Cape Bowling Green,Townsville,Australia
Beadle, Ray, 94 lb 3 oz, Cape Bowling Green,Townsville, Australia
Braak, Joshua B. (Teddy), 440 lb, Albion, Mauritius
Bruckmann, Thomas Hollihan, 700 lb, Salinas, Ecuador
Brumby, Malcolm, 174 lb 2 oz, Malindi, Kenya
Caldow, Clark M., 264 lb 8 oz, Lord Howe Island, New Zealand
Carnegie, Mark H., 60 lb 10 oz, Mooloolaba, Queensland, Australia
Cecil, Eric, 1,179 lb, Lizard Island, North Queensland, Australia
Dunaway, Daniel, 338 lb, Pinas Bay, Panama

Elson, Jay M., 1,014 lb, Cairns, North Queensland, Australia
Fohey, Ann, 671 lb, Great Barrier Reef, Australia
Garrett, Gerald A., 1,219 lb, Linden Bank, Cairns, Qld., Australia
Glanninger, Horst R., 144 lb 6 oz, Beguela, Mozambique, Africa
Hall, Leon, 1,102 lb, Lizard Island, Queensland, Australia
Henderson, John J., 569 lb 8 oz, Kona, Hawaii, USA
Hill, Barry, 1,030 lb, Cairns, Australia
Jones, Mrs. Julie, 66 lb 2 oz, Cape Moreton, Queensland, Australia
Keresey, Thomas M., 260 lb, Pinas Bay, Panama
Kilborn, III, Vincent, 1,000 lb, Linden Bank,Cairns, Qld., Australia
Mulkey, Thomas F., 1,037 lb, Spur Reef, Queensland, Australia
Nelson, Capt. Pat, 1,050 lb, Great Barrier Reef, Australia
Pfleger, Tom, 1,177 lb, Lizard Island, Australia
Powis, Mark John, 125 lb 10 oz,Kokopo,Rabaul,Papua,New Guinea
Pretorius, K.J., 496 lb, Sodwana Bay, Republic of South Africa
Reid, Mark, 1,069 lb 3 oz, Lizard Island, Australia
Roccatti, Sergio, 1,036 lb, Lizard Island, Australia
Roegelein, Jr., William, 981 lb, Great Barrier Reef, Qld., Australia
Scharwenka, Mark H., 231 lb, Club Pacifico, Panama
Somers, Bruce, 917 lb, Cairns, Australia
Tamayo J., Rodrigo, 734 lb 2 oz, Cabo Marzo, Colombia
Taylor, Paul, 876 lb, Lizard Island, Queensland, Australia
Turnbull, A. J., 1,271 lb, Lizard Island, Queensland, Australia
Tyler, Walter, 517 lb, Bazaruto, Africa
Weinstock, Norman, 625 lb, San Jose del Cabo, B.C.S., Mexico

MARLIN, PACIFIC BLUE

Anderson, Alan W.G., 99 lb 3 oz,Pidgeon Isl.,Papua,New Guinea
Anton, Jr., Jose, 400 lb, Salinas, Ecuador
Bajakian, Richard L., 239 lb 8 oz, Kona, Hawaii, USA
Basco, Irby W., 207 lb, Kona, Hawaii, USA
Bento, Al, 1,207 lb, Kalaupapa, Molokai, Hawaii, USA
Berutich, Dave, 800 lb, Kailua, Kona, Hawaii, USA
Casillas, Chris, 411 lb, Kona, Hawaii, USA
Cecil, Eric, 287 lb 4 oz, Shimoni, Pemba Channel, Kenya
De Speville, Marc D., 958 lb, Le Morne, Mauritius
Dias, Sondra, 270 lb 6 oz, Los Barriles, B.C.S., Mexico
Diaz Gonzalez, Jesus Francisco, 203 lb 7 oz, Acapulco, Mexico
Dunaway, Daniel, 393 lb, Pinas Bay, Panama
Edmunds, Gilbert C., 692 lb 8 oz, Kona, Hawaii, USA
Elliopoulos, Margo, 306 lb 8 oz, Kailua, Kona, Hawaii, USA
Fann, Nancy, 158 lb, Kona, Hawaii, USA
Felger, Dan, 308 lb 10 oz, East Cape, Baja, Mexico
Gardner, Virginia L., 813 lb, Kailwi Point, Kona, Hawaii, USA
Garrett, Victoria B., 200 lb, Cabo San Lucas, B.C.S., Mexico
Gleason, Jerry, 464 lb, Kona, Hawaii, USA
Goldstein, Geoffrey Michael,300 lb,Cabo San Lucas,B.C.S.,Mexico
Harraway, Tony, 968 lb, Centre de Peche, Black River, Mauritius
Hawkes, Ray G., 491 lb 8 oz, Kona, Hawaii, USA
Henriksen, Lonnie R., 851 lb 8 oz, Kona, Hawaii, USA
Hugo, Marshall G., 628 lb, Cabo San Lucas, B.C.S., Mexico
Janssen, Irvin (Rusty), 286 lb, Cabo San Lucas, B.C.S., Mexico
Jones, Keith, 452 lb, Cabo San Lucas, B.C.S., Mexico
Jorgensen, Douglas, 1,201 lb 12 oz, Kahoolawe,Maui,Hawaii, USA
Koester, Heinz, 625 lb 10 oz, Vava'u Island, Kingdom of Tonga
Kurz, Robert R., 446 lb, Kona, Hawaii, USA
Lewandowski, Gordon, 176 lb, Kailua-Kona, Hawaii, USA
McElroy, Mike, 482 lb 8 oz, Kailua-Kona, Hawaii, USA
Meyer, Jeffery W., 221 lb 8 oz, Kailua-Kona, Hawaii, USA
Meyer, Jeffery W., 329 lb, Kailua-Kona, Hawaii, USA
Milmlow, Gloria, 682 lb 8 oz, Kona, Hawaii, USA
Monroe, Roger, 234 lb, Rancho Buena Vista, B.C.S., Mexico
Osier, Bill, 346 lb 8 oz, Kona, Hawaii, USA
Pavlik, Todd J., 389 lb, Kona, Hawaii, USA
Powis, Martin, 357 lb, Kona Coast, Hawaii, USA
Ratanamangcla, Apiwat, 440 lb, Black River, Mauritius
Roper, Justin C., 547 lb 12 oz, Port Eads, Louisiana, USA
Salomon, David, 336 lb 13 oz, Houma, Tongatapu, Tonga
Salomon, David, 311 lb 4 oz, Tongatapu, Tonga
Schaffer, Leo, 982 lb, Le Morne, Mauritius
Schonauer, K.F.J., 1,140 lb, Mauritius
Steinman, Joel, 290 lb, Spa Buena Vista, Baja, Mexico
Storino, Vincent D., 175 lb, Keahole Point, Kona, Hawaii, USA
Tate, Donnell A., 144 lb 8 oz, Palaoa Point, Lanai, Hawaii, USA
Terra, Richard, 162 lb 8 oz, Kona, Hawaii, USA
Wherlock, Terry, 437 lb, Kona, Hawaii, USA

MARLIN, STRIPED

Beadle, Ray, 105 lb, Uncle Sam Bank, B.C.S., Mexico
Beadle, Ray, 109 lb 11 oz, Uncle Sam Bank, B.C.S., Mexico
Boucaut, John, 315 lb 4 oz, Bay of Islands, New Zealand

Bustamante, Eduardo A., 96 lb 3 oz, Buenavista, B.C.S., Mexico
Cecil, Eric, 160 lb 12 oz, Shimoni, Pemba Channel, Kenya
Clark, Wayne A., 146 lb, Uncle Sam Bank, B.C.S., Mexico
Cornelius, Ian P., 222 lb 10 oz, Bay of Islands, New Zealand
Davis, Andrew T., 152 lb 8 oz, California, USA
Dulin, Ronald H., 164 lb, Catalina Channel, California, USA
Fischer, Barry S., 165 lb 5 oz, Cabo San Lucas, B.C.S., Mexico
Goldstein, M.D., Edward M., 146 lb, San Diego, California, USA
Graham, Gary C., 121 lb 6 oz, San Diego, California, USA
Griffith, Jr., John S., 143 lb 8 oz, Newport Beach, California, USA
Hampton, Diana, 154 lb 8 oz, San Diego California, USA
Hampton, Robert, 154 lb, San Diego, California, USA
Hanvold, Wendy R., 136 lb 4 oz, Uncle Sam Bank, B.C.S., Mexico
Howe, Kate L., 112 lb 1 oz, Uncle Sam Bank, B.C.S., Mexico
Hutchins, Mrs. Stephen R., 20 lb 6 oz, Nags Head,N. Carolina,USA
Jasper, Gary R., 339 lb, Avalon, California, USA
Kidd, Bradley, 155 lb 6 oz, Hemingways, Watamu, Kenya, Africa
Koester, Heinz, 357 lb 2 oz, Vava'u, Kingdom of Tonga
Lievers, Chip, 129 lb, Santa Catalina Island, California, USA
Lussa, Ray, 244 lb, San Diego, California, USA
Lynds, Phil, 230 lb 9 oz, Tutukaka, Whangarei, New Zealand
Mack, Michael S., 269 lb 6 oz, Bermagui, N.S.W., Australia
Neff, Jr., Walter G., 199 lb, Pinas Bay, Panama
Nelson, Bud D., 89 lb, Kona, Hawaii, USA
Pattinson, Paula, 80 lb, Kailua-Kona, Hawaii, USA
Peterson, Bryan, 105 lb 5 oz, Uncle Sam Bank, B.C.S., Mexico
Princenthal, Rick, 150 lb, Cabo San Lucas, B.C.S., Mexico
Proulx, Blair Marcus, 154 lb 8 oz, Catalina Island, California, USA
Proulx, Dixie, 169 lb 8 oz, Catalina Island, California, USA
Reilly, Jeannie, 138 lb, Newport Beach, California, USA
Rilling, Gerald, 110 lb, Cabo San Lucas, B.C.S., Mexico
Ross, Stephen A., 145 lb, San Diego, California, USA
Schuller, Anthony, 145 lb, Cabo San Lucas, B.C.S., Mexico
Smith, Charles D., 195 lb, Cabo San Lucas, B.C.S., Mexico
Sovinsky, Joseph F., 126 lb, Coronado, California, USA
Tenace, Merinda, 168 lb, Sea of Cortez, B.C.S., Mexico
Tombras, Charlie, 185 lb, Cocos Island, Costa Rica
Verdugo, R. David, 108 lb, Point Loma, California, USA
Von Quilich, Michael, 125 lb 10 oz,Cabo San Lucas,B.C.S.,Mexico
Worsley, Philip, 209 lb 6 oz, Botany Bay, Sydney, Australia

MARLIN, WHITE

Basco, Pamela S., 58 lb 9 oz, La Guaira, Venezuela
Cloostermans, Kristof, 57 lb, Horta, Faial, Azores
Ferreira Filho, Paulo Fabiano, 174 lb 2 oz, Rio de Janeiro, Brazil
Giangio, Massimo, 106 lb, Mohammedia, Morocco
Paixao, Capt. Mauricio, 132 lb 11 oz, Rio de Janeiro, Brazil
Pauley, Biddy, 114 lb, Nantucket Island, Massachusetts, USA
Pelissard, Louis, 113 lb 5 oz, Mohammedia, Morocco
Sahiaoui, Fouad, 87 lb 4 oz, Mohammedia, Morocco
Stoky, Ruth C., 70 lb 8 oz, Vitoria, Brazil

MUSKELLUNGE

Moen, Charles L., 38 lb 4 oz, Rathbun Lake, Iowa, USA
See, Joe Alan, 43 lb 4 oz, Cedar Lake, Ontario, Canada

MUSKELLUNGE, TIGER

Guzek, Bryan, 23 lb 9 oz, Lake Rolard,Twin Lakes,Michigan, USA

NEEDLEFISH, MEXICAN

Nellis, Renee M., 13 lb, Tortolla Island, Panama Bay, Panama

PERCH, NILE

Brink, Derek, 38 lb 9 oz, Ngodhe Island, Lake Victoria, Kenya
Brink, Derek, 49 lb 9 oz, Ngodhe Island, Lake Victoria, Kenya
Brink, Derek, 23 lb 2 oz, Lake Victoria, Kenya
Cartwright, Andrew J., 137 lb 12 oz, Lake Victoria, Uganda
De Mello, Arthur, 78 lb 4 oz, Bussi Bay, Entebbe, Uganda
Foley, Garry, 185 lb 2 oz, Mfangano Island, Lake Victoria, Kenya
Glaser, Lance, 41 lb, Lake Victoria, Kenya
Huckle, Dave, 132 lb 4 oz, Ngodhe Island, Lake Victoria, Kenya
Lewallen, Melvin E., 102 lb 8 oz, Lake Victoria, Kenya
Magri, Henri, 41 lb 14 oz, Comoe River, Abidjan, Ivory Coast
Neibling, Debi, 17 lb 10 oz, Rusinga Island, Kenya
Neibling, Dr. Hal, 42 lb 15 oz, Rusinga Island, Kenya
Neibling, Dr. Hal, 121 lb 4 oz, Rusinga Island, Kenya
Winter, Keith R., 124 lb 8 oz, Mfangano Isl.,Lake Victoria, Kenya

PERMIT

Boone, William P., 29 lb, Sugarloaf Key, Florida, USA
Brown, Del, 41 lb 8 oz, Key West, Florida, USA
Helo, Jr., Al, 20 lb 6 oz, Marquesas Keys, Florida, USA
Liederman, LuAnne, 40 lb, Key West, Florida, USA
Rehr, Joyce May, 24 lb 4 oz, Marquesas Keys, Florida, USA

Ruilova, Sherril J., 12 lb 4 oz, Marathon, Florida, USA
Tate, Michel, 11 lb 7 oz, Marathon, Florida, USA

PIKE, NORTHERN

Atwood, Kitty, 17 lb, Mitassihi, Quebec, Canada
Befus, Bradley A., 27 lb, Innoko River, Alaska, USA
Bell, John R., 24 lb 12 oz, Engler Lake, Saskatchewan, Canada
Johnston, M.D., Craig, 25 lb 8 oz, Yukon River, Alaska, USA
Pinotti, Giacomo, 43 lb 3 oz, Ascona, Lago Maggiore, Switzerland
Schulman, Alan, 14 lb 4 oz, Reindeer Lake, Canada

POLLOCK

LaBrie, Jack, 21 lb, Middle Bank, Massachusetts, USA
Mellish, Diane Lynne, 26 lb 12 oz, Montauk, New York, USA

POMPANO, AFRICAN

Kutner, Sharan C., 21 lb 8 oz, Key West, Florida, USA
Robinson, III, Ellyson S., 33 lb 8 oz,Ocracoke Isl.,N.Carolina, USA
Waterman, Jim, 40 lb 8 oz, Key West, Florida, USA
Werking, Raleigh, 36 lb, Miami Beach, Florida, USA

QUEENFISH, LEATHERSKIN

Husband, Fred, 14 lb 8 oz, Groote Eylandt, N.T., Australia
Kordt, Jan, 11 lb 7 oz, Cape Keraudren, Australia

QUEENFISH, TALANG

Manton, Jane, 10 lb 9 oz, Groote Eylandt, Australia

RAY, BAT

Kendrick, Joyce, 65 lb, Benicia, California, USA
Leach, Darrell T., 70 lb 2 oz, South Laguna, California, USA

RAY, EAGLE

Stone, Christine, 22 lb, Boston Bay, Port Lincoln, S.A., Australia

RAY, SOUTHERN FIDDLER

Vandergoot, Marcel, 14 lb 12 oz, Marion Bay, S.A., Australia

ROOSTERFISH

Matthews, Dr. Jerome N., 42 lb, Golfito, Costa Rica
Nellis, Renee M., 10 lb 10 oz, Isla Chame, Panama
O'Brien, Timothy S., 70 lb 8 oz, Porto Escondito, B.C.S., Mexico
Penley, Virginia Jane, 60 lb, Flamingo Bay, Costa Rica
Snyder, Pat, 43 lb 8 oz, Punta Colorada, B.C.S., Mexico
Snyder, Tom, 63 lb 14 oz, Punta Colorada, B.C.S., Mexico
Whitehead, M.D., Craig, 38 lb, Playa Zancudo, Costa Rica

SAILFISH, ATLANTIC

Amon, Guy, 89 lb, Dakar, Senegal
Basco, Pamela S., 35 lb 4 oz, Isla Contoy, Mexico
Buitendag, Petrus C., 52 lb 7 oz, Sodwana Bay, Rep. of S. Africa
Capozzi, Bibi, 64 lb, La Guaira Bank, Venezuela
Carter, Richard G., 80 lb, Key Largo, Florida, USA
Forman, Joe, 76 lb 12 oz, Miami, Florida, USA
Frasier, James E., 105 lb, Key Largo, Florida, USA
Gerner, Jeff, 60 lb, Dania, Florida, USA
Knight, Jacqueline E., 53 lb, Islamorada, Florida, USA
Leas, III, Donald Stewart, 53 lb 6 oz, Dakar, Senegal
Perennes, Tanguy, 68 lb 5 oz, Dakar, Senegal
Perennes, Tanguy, 79 lb 5 oz, Dakar, Senegal
Sherman, Gary J., 72 lb 12 oz, Dakar, Senegal, West Africa
Wakeman, II, Rufus, 65 lb 9 oz, Dakar, Senegal

SAILFISH, PACIFIC

Barnard, Pierre, 114 lb 6 oz,Cape Vidal,Natal,Rep. of South Africa
Basco, Pamela S., 59 lb 6 oz, Cabo San Lucas, B.C.S., Mexico
Cunningham, Gerald L., 135 lb 8 oz, Salinas, Ecuador
Dias, Sondra, 109 lb 1 oz, Los Barriles, B.C.S., Mexico
Dickson, Lily, 66 lb 2 oz, Rabaul, Papua, New Guinea
Enneking, William F., 103 lb 9 oz, Golfito, Costa Rica
Fay, Lorrie, 132 lb 4 oz, Cape Moretown, N.S.W., Australia
Jones, Noel R., 206 lb 10 oz, Tubbataha Reefs,Sulu Sea,Philippines
Maruhashi, Eizo, 124 lb, Gulf of Papagayo, Guanacaste, Costa Rica
McCabe, Brian, 89 lb, Playa Zancudo, Costa Rica
Robinson-Neff, Valerie, 108 lb, Pinas Bay, Panama
Salomon, David, 94 lb 12 oz, Piha Passage, Nuku'alofa, Tonga
Venske, Sean, 81 lb 2 oz, Cape Vidal, Natal, Rep. of South Africa
Wain, Paul A., 116 lb, Cabo San Lucas, B.C.S., Mexico
Worsley, Philip, 101 lb 6 oz, South West Rocks, N.S.W., Australia

SALMON, ATLANTIC

Behrman, Darryl G., 38 lb 8 oz, Alta River, Norway

SALMON, CHINOOK

DiMartino, John M., 15 lb 1 oz, Lake Ontario, New York, USA
Gillam, Glenn F., 34 lb 8 oz, Kenai River, Alaska, USA
Goll, Kathy, 52 lb, Kenai River, Alaska, USA
Gougher, Ronald L., 33 lb 10 oz, Pulaski, New York, USA
Hillgardner, William J., 31 lb, Kodiak Island, Alaska, USA

Hoyez, E. Z., 62 lb, Kenai River, Alaska, USA
Miller, Kenneth L., 22 lb 9 oz, British Columbia, Canada
Werking, Raleigh, 37 lb 6 oz, Cook Inlet, Alaska, USA
Werking, Raleigh, 32 lb, Forks, Washington, USA
Werking, Raleigh, 35 lb 1 oz, Forks, Washington, USA
Werking, Raleigh, 35 lb 8 oz, Forks, Washington, USA
Yahiro, Jerry, 50 lb, Queen Charlotte Islands, B.C., Canada

SALMON, CHUM
Hudnall, Daniel J., 11 lb, Kobuk River, Alaska, USA
Hudnall, Lawrence E., 13 lb, Pah River, Alaska, USA

SALMON, COHO
Belanger, Craig S., 11 lb 8 oz, Kenai River, Kenai, Alaska, USA
Hower, Jr., Ken, 12 lb, Kauluk R., Kodiak Island, Alaska, USA
Leed, Burton R., 15 lb 4 oz, Karluk River, Alaska, USA
Middleton, Don A., 15 lb 2 oz, Kenai River, Alaska, USA
Prescott, III, John C., 13 lb 6 oz, British Columbia, Canada
Prescott, Jr., John C., 12 lb 5 oz, British Columbia, Canada

SALMON, SOCKEYE
Hudnall, Lawrence E., 11 lb 5 oz, Baranof Island, Alaska, USA

SEABASS, JAPANESE
Aihara, Motoji, 10 lb 5 oz, Tateyama Bay, Chiba, Japan

SEABASS, WHITE
Pfleger, Tom, 21 lb 2 oz, Catalina Island, California, USA
Pfleger, Tom, 16 lb 11 oz, Catalina Island, California, USA

SEATROUT, SPOTTED
Fairbanks, David Michael, 10 lb 1 oz, Daytona Beach, Florida, USA

SHARK, BLACKTIP
Cooper, C. Caldwell, 82 lb, Great Isaac Island, Bahamas
Spence, Gary, 80 lb 8 oz, Marathon, Florida, USA

SHARK, BLUE
Benson, Bob, 113 lb, Nantucket, Massachusetts, USA
Burr, Frank, 432 lb 1 oz, Matakawa Point, New Zealand
Curcione, Nick, 28 lb, Redondo Beach, California, USA
Smith, John R., 123 lb 7 oz, S. Miguel, Azores
Smith, John R., 105 lb 13 oz, S. Miguel, Azores
Zybura, Marion, 132 lb, Montauk Point, New York, USA

SHARK, BULL
Piazza, Robert F., 73 lb 12 oz, Islamorada, Florida, USA
Porter, William T., 64 lb, Bimini, Bahamas
Triwatana, Phanuphan, 771 lb 9 oz, Opal Reef, Cairns, Australia

SHARK, COPPER
Vandergoot, Marcel, 11 lb, Balgowan, S.A., Australia

SHARK, DUSKY
Gueral, Jean, 231 lb 7 oz, Nouadhibou, Mauritania
Lopuszanski, Daniel, 121 lb 4 oz, Nouadhibou, Mauritania

SHARK, HAMMERHEAD
Colling, Wayne, 88 lb 2 oz, Black Rocks, N.S.W., Australia
Falkland, James, 406 lb Pemba Channel, Shimoni, Kenya
Hennessy, Jr., George A., 148 lb 5 oz, St. Lucia, Natal, R.of S.Africa
Herald, Wesley D., 382 lb 15 oz, Cape Vidal, Natal, South Africa
Knight, Tom, 51 lb 12 oz, East London, Republic of South Africa
Norris, Peter C., 195 lb 1 oz, Groote Eylandt, N.T., Australia
Reinke, William J., 110 lb, Ft. Lauderdale, Florida, USA
Yates, Donald, 313 lb 14 oz, Cape Brett, New Zealand

SHARK, LEMON
Brockmeyer, James L., 280 lb, Ft. Myers Beach, Florida, USA
Porter, Austin, 135 lb, Key West, Florida, USA

SHARK, MAKO
Blattmachr, Jonathan G., 163 lb, Montauk, New York, USA
Guillanton, Patrick, 1,115 lb, Black River, Mauritius
Murray, C. D., 37 lb, Hawke Bay, New Zealand
Palumbo, John N., 104 lb, Montauk, Long Island, New York, USA
Stanford, Danita, 102 lb 11 oz, Richards Bay, Rep. of South Africa
Stotesbury, Cheryl, 13 lb 11 oz, Newport Beach, California, USA
Weaver, Robert, 450 lb, Montauk, Long Island, New York, USA
Wikowski, David Paul, 237 lb, Townsend Inlet, New Jersey, USA

SHARK, NARROWTOOTH
Anderson, Alan W.G., 149 lb 14 oz, (bronze whaler), Papua, N.Guinea
Avison, John, 441 lb 5 oz, (bronze whaler), Manukau Har., N.Zealand
Harding, Bernard, 176 lb 5 oz, Karavia Bay, Papua, New Guinea
Thomas, Paul L., 321 lb 13 oz, (bronze whaler), Australia
Tieste, Karl Lynton, 370 lb 5 oz, Cape Donnington, Australia

SHARK, PORBEAGLE
Richardson, Robert, 414 lb 7 oz, Pentland Firth, Scotland

SHARK, PORT JACKSON
Vandergoot, Marcel, 11 lb 3 oz, Port Broughton, Australia

SHARK, SANDBAR
Burrill, Ronald C., 118 lb, Assateague Island, Virginia, USA

SHARK, SIXGILLED
Hall, Clive, 771 lb 9 oz, Faial, Azores, Portugal
Reece, Capt. Jack, 1,069 lb 3 oz, Faial, Azores, Portugal

SHARK, THRESHER
Campi, Claudio, 283 lb 8 oz, Livorno, Italy
Casserley, Mike, 59 lb 3 oz, False Bay, South Africa
Derr, Lisa Zipser, 141 lb, Santa Monica Bay, California, USA
Everette, Jocelyn J., 302 lb, Kona Coast, Hawaii, USA
Levy, Robert I., 36 lb, Santa Monica Bay, California, USA
Savage, Skip, 180 lb, Ocean City, Maryland, USA
Schmidt, Wolfgang, 281 lb 9 oz, Isle of Wight, Great Britain
Willmott, Pamela, 317 lb 7 oz, Bermagui, N.S.W., Australia
Worsley, Philip, 171 lb 15 oz, Botany Bay, Sydney, Australia

SHARK, TIGER
De Dios, René, 629 lb, Bimini, Bahamas
Norton, Robert C., 179 lb 10 oz, Groote Eylandt, N.T., Australia
Pagan, Kevin R., 776 lb, Miami Beach, Florida, USA
Schatman, Jeffrey, 711 lb, Bimini, Bahamas

SHARK, WHITE
Czabayski, Ralph Jeffrey, 1,195 lb 15 oz, Port Lincoln, Australia
DeAngelis, Richard P., 686 lb, Key West, Florida, USA
Flourentzou, George, 1,058 lb 3 oz, Neptune Islands, Australia
Roccatti, Sergio, 1,037 lb, Port Lincoln, S.A., Australia

SHARK, WHITETIP
Hodges, Reid, 369 lb, San Salvador, Bahamas

SNAPPER, (SQUIREFISH)
Stone, Christopher G., 16 lb 12 oz, Pt. Lincoln, Australia

SNAPPER, CUBERA
Salmons, Matthew S., 69 lb, Sebastian Inlet, Florida, USA

SNOOK
Fairbanks, David Michael, 15 lb 4 oz, Clearwater, Florida, USA
Judge, Joseph P., 14 lb 8 oz, Barra del Colorado, Costa Rica
Miller, Deborah B., 20 lb 12 oz, Charlotte Harbor, Florida, USA
Nash, Allison H., 12 lb 3 oz, Bradenton, Florida, USA
Novak, Andy, 11 lb, Chokoloskee, Florida, USA
Novak, Andy, 11 lb, Chokoloskee, Florida, USA
Rehr, Joyce May, 10 lb 12 oz, Upper Captiva Island, Florida, USA
Rehr, Joyce May, 10 lb 2 oz, Upper Captiva Island, Florida, USA
Rehr, Joyce May, 10 lb 8 oz, Sanibel Island, Florida, USA
Rehr, Michael C., 20 lb 14 oz, Upper Captiva Island, Florida, USA
Young, Jay, 11 lb 6 oz, Loxahatchee River, Florida, USA

SPADEFISH, ATLANTIC
Robinson, III, Ellyson S., 11 lb 15 oz, Chesapeake Bay, Virginia, USA

SPEARFISH, SHORTBILL
Dunaway, Deborah Maddux, 26 lb 8 oz, Kona, Hawaii, USA
Frederiksen, Torben, 42 lb 8 oz, Keahole Point, Kona, Hawaii, USA
Handgis, Sharon, 28 lb, Kona Coast, Hawaii, USA
Meyer, Jeffery W., 42 lb, Kona, Hawaii, USA
Scott, M.D., Glenn L., 35 lb 6 oz, Keahole, Hawaii, USA
Vander Hoek, Capt. Gene, 35 lb 8 oz, Keauhou, Kona, Hawaii, USA
Vander Hoek, Capt. Gene, 27 lb, Kona, Hawaii, USA

STINGRAY, BLACK
Shearing, David, 126 lb 12 oz, Laurieton, N.S.W., Australia

STINGRAY, DIAMOND
Ehlers, Roger, 102 lb, Mission Bay, San Diego, California, USA

STINGRAY, SOUTHERN
Daniel, Jr., Patrick C., 204 lb, Galveston, Texas, USA
Wright, Davey, 239 lb, Padre Island Seashore, Texas, USA

STURGEON, WHITE
Anderson, Pete M., 322 lb 4 oz, Sacramento R., Pittsburg, CA, USA
Boelens, Gerald E., 20 lb 8 oz, Suisun Bay, California, USA
Bushnell, John, 21 lb 4 oz, Columbia River, Astoria, Oregon, USA
Kennelly, Steven B., 111 lb, Columbia River, Washington, USA
Mercer, Michael Edward, 80 lb 8 oz, San Pablo Bay, California, USA

STURGEON, BELUGA
Lehne, Mrs. Merete, 224 lb 13 oz, Guryev, Kasakstan

SWORDFISH
Booysen, Ivan L., 530 lb 3 oz, Cape Town, South Africa
Bursik, Erwin Viktor, 491 lb 6 oz, Cape Point, Rep. of S. Africa
Jurgens, Gerhard, 543 lb 6 oz, Cape Point, Rep. of South Africa
Phillips, Herbert R., 650 lb 5 oz, Algarrobo, Chile

Redfern, Jr., John R., 429 lb, Nantucket, Massachusetts, USA
Vogel, Barbara, 340 lb, Mazatlan, Sinaloa, Mexico

TAIMEN, SIBERIAN
Stoick, David L., 82 lb, Keta River, Russian Far East, Siberia

TANGUIGUE
Babarskas, Peter, 23 lb 11 oz, Onslow, W.A., Australia
Bastick, Lyn, 47 lb 2 oz, Exmouth, W.A., Australia
Benson, Stephen, 24 lb 4 oz, Groote Eylandt, N.T., Australia
Dalling, Kelly, 53 lb 9 oz, Edward Island, Queensland, Australia
Davies, Craig, 64 lb 13 oz, Townsville, Australia
Gibson, Jenny, 37 lb 4 oz, Groote Eylandt, N.T., Australia
Hardy, Stephen O., 24 lb 7 oz, Fraser Island, Queensland, Australia
Kenny, Stuart, 22 lb, Dampier, Archipelago, W.A., Australia
Laughton, Len, 23 lb, Port Hedland, W.A., Australia
Paterson, Michael, 33 lb 11 oz, Groote Eylandt, N.T., Australia

TARPON
Barkhurst, Jessica J., 221 lb 8 oz, West Delta, Venice, Louisiana, USA
Coupe, Jean-Francois, 151 lb 3 oz, Iles du Salut, Guyane, France
Coupe, Jean-Francois, 161 lb 13 oz, Iles du Salut, Guyane, France
Gibson, Jr., Thomas F., 262 lb, Port Michel, Gabon
Gondjout, Georges Desire, 198 lb, Ogooue River, Ozori, Gabon
Gorall, Warren L., 90 lb 12 oz, Indian River, Jensen Beach, FL, USA
Graf, Chris, 26 lb 4 oz, Islamorada, Florida, USA
Hanson, Garry D., 110 lb 6 oz, Balast Key, Key West, Florida, USA
Jarland, Frederique, 249 lb, Sherbro Island, Sierra Leone
Lewis N., Gabriel, 182 lb, Tortuguero River, Costa Rica
Miller, Deborah B., 176 lb 8 oz, Key West, Florida, USA
Morales Perales, Ricardo, 134 lb 7 oz, Tampico, Mexico
Morales Perales, Ricardo, 102 lb 15 oz, Tampico, Mexico
Perennes, Tanguy, 238 lb, Sherbro Island, Sierra Leone
Petronio, Jr., Everett, 146 lb, Islamorada, Florida, USA
Ratner, Jr., Herbert G., 91 lb, Key West, Florida, USA
Ray, Brenda J., 168 lb 8 oz, South Padre Island, Texas, USA
Renton, Donald O., 26 lb 7 oz, Sugarloaf, Florida, USA
Secrest, Ben P., 144 lb 6 oz, Miami, Florida, USA
Sheaf, Steven, 126 lb 8 oz, Sugarloaf, Florida, USA
Stephenson, Wade C., 110 lb, Boca Grande, Florida, USA
Thorn-Adam, Corinne, 225 lb, Sherbro Island, Sierra Leone
Torruella, Juan Carlos, 67 lb, San Jose Lagoon, Carolina, Puerto Rico
Wetlaufer, Johnny, 109 lb, Key West Harbor, Florida, USA

THREADFIN, KING
Boekhorst, Anthony, 10 lb 9 oz, Port Hedland, Australia

TIGERFISH
Houtmans, Raymond, 97 lb, Zaire River, Kinshasa, Zaire
Houtmans, Raymond, 92 lb 9 oz, Zaire River, Kinshasa, Zaire
Hunter, Don, 61 lb 11 oz, Kasaba Bay, Lake Tanganyika, Zambia
Plant, John, 10 lb 14 oz, Sanyati Gorge, Lake Kariba, Zimbabwe
Stubbs, Dr. John Michael, 12 lb 7 oz, Zambezi River, Zimbabwe

TOPE
Lange, Wilfried, 28 lb 3 oz, Tralee Bay, Ireland
Nuhn, Reinhard, 42 lb 1 oz, Helgoland, Germany

TREVALLY, GIANT
Handgis, Sharon, 38 lb 11 oz, Midway Island
Revill, Raymond Bruce, 31 lb 4 oz, Hervey Bay, Qld., Australia

TROUT, BROWN
Collins, Howard L. "Rip", 40 lb 4 oz, Heber Springs, Arkansas, USA
Reeder, Ralph T., 11 lb 15 oz, Oswego R., Oswego, New York, USA
Salamon, Tony, 30 lb 8 oz, North Fork River, Arkansas, USA
Salamon, Tony, 12 lb, White River, Arkansas, USA
Smith, M.D., James F., 16 lb, Bull Shoals, Arkansas, USA
Thompson, Tuhi Y., 10 lb 9 oz, Turangi, New Zealand

TROUT, CUTTHROAT
Hanes, Richard D., 12 lb 10 oz, Pyramid Lake, Nevada, USA

TROUT, LAKE
Coulombe, Marlin A., 46 lb, Great Bear Lake, N.W.T., Canada
Hudnall, Lawrence E., 11 lb, Selby River, Alaska, USA
Leed, Burton R., 13 lb, Walker Lake, Alaska, USA
Nelson, Arlin D., 10 lb 4 oz, Stark Lake, Snowdrift, N.W.T., Canada
Roschuk, Allan, 44 lb 2 oz, Manitoba, Canada
Roschuk, Allan, 32 lb 1 oz, Manitoba, Canada

TUNA, ATLANTIC BIGEYE
Burston, Rodger Thomas, 357 lb 2 oz, Puerto R., Gran Canaria, Spain
Deniz Cabrera, Roberto, 268 lb 15 oz, Puerto R., Gran Canaria, Spain
Hutchins, Mrs. Stephen R., 115 lb 4 oz, Oregon Inlet, N. Carolina, USA
Lehmkuhl, Herbert, 308 lb 10 oz, Puerto Rico, Gran Canaria, Spain
Milton, Denise Marguerite, 118 lb 6 oz, Cape Point, South Africa
Niebuhr, Berno, 315 lb 4 oz, Puerto Rico, Gran Canaria, Spain

Rogers, Shelby E., 214 lb, Madeira, Portugal

TUNA, BLACKFIN
Garisto, Joan M., 27 lb, Key West, Florida, USA
Murray, II, James R., 30 lb 12 oz, Boca Raton, Florida, USA

TUNA, BLUEFIN
Benn, Richard, 117 lb, Hatteras, North Carolina, USA
Caister, Derek Michael, 981 lb, North Lake, P.E.I., Canada
Cathcart, Jack, 850 lb, Auld's Cove, Nova Scotia, Canada
Collins, John Michael, 1,092 lb, North Lake, P.E.I., Canada
Cunningham, Jr., Colin M., 1,115 lb, North Lake, P.E.I., Canada
De Marpillero, Gianni, 186 lb 4 oz, Porto Ottiolu, Sardinia, Italy
DuVal, Mrs. William B., 41 lb 8 oz, Virginia Beach, Virginia, USA
Gilbreath, Karen, 45 lb, Ocean City, Maryland, USA
Glauco, Micheli, 230 lb 13 oz, Pescara, Adriatic Sea, Italy
Hutchins, Mrs. Stephen R., 209 lb, Hatteras, North Carolina, USA
Mannelli, Gianni, 210 lb 8 oz, Marina di Pisa, Italy
Mans, Andrew J., 915 lb, North Lake, Prince Edward Island, Canada
Mans, Andrew J., 931 lb, North Lake, Prince Edward Island, Canada
Mans, Andrew J., 1,100 lb, North Lake, P.E.I., Canada
Mans, Andrew J., 834 lb, North Lake, Prince Edward Island, Canada
Mans, Andrew J., 765 lb, North Lake, Prince Edward Island, Canada
Pfleger, Tom, 172 lb 8 oz, Guadalupe Island, Mexico
Sloan, Stephen, 72 lb, Montauk Island, New York, USA
Steffey, Dr. J. M., 1,230 lb, North Lake, P.E.I., Canada
Steyn, P., 852 lb, North Lake, Prince Edward Island, Canada

TUNA, DOGTOOTH
Villavicencio, Cristina Marina B., 30 lb, South China Sea
Villavicencio, Margarita Marina B., 49 lb 10 oz, South China Sea

TUNA, LONGTAIL
Hornhardt, Jason, 42 lb 15 oz, Port Hedland, Western Australia
Judges, Mal, 42 lb 7 oz, Little Halls, Noosa Heads, Qld., Australia
Maguire, Jim, 51 lb 10 oz, Moreton Isl., Brisbane, Qld., Australia
Maguire, Kathy, 46 lb 13 oz, Bribie Island, Brisbane, Qld., Australia
Revill, Raymond Bruce, 26 lb 1 oz, Hervey Bay, Qld., Australia
Steel, Darryl J., 20 lb 4 oz, Moreton Bay, Brisbane, Australia
Wortley, Eric, 49 lb, Dunk Island, Australia

TUNA, PACIFIC BIGEYE
Bracken, Marjorie J., 150 lb, San Diego, California, USA
Carlton, Lorraine, 157 lb, San Clemente Island, California, USA
Denholm, David M., 91 lb 8 oz, Catalina Island, California, USA
Denholm, Nicole L., 83 lb 8 oz, San Diego, California, USA
Freese, Roger L., 119 lb 8 oz, San Diego, California, USA
Hampton, Robert, 73 lb, San Diego, California, USA
Jurado E., Jorge F., 231 lb, Salinas, Ecuador
Schilling, Thomas G., 189 lb 3 oz, S. Coronado Island, CA, USA
Ware, Don, 214 lb, Coronado Islands, Mexico

TUNA, SKIPJACK
Flasch, Richard Franz, 13 lb 2 oz, Piton Pointe, Mauritius
McCabe, John R., 13 lb 4 oz, Miami Beach, Florida, USA
Rose, Colin, 21 lb 9 oz, Freeport, Bahamas

TUNA, SOUTHERN BLUEFIN
Flourentzou, George, 45 lb 3 oz, Ward Island, Australia
Hardy, Cecil J., 73 lb 13 oz, Port Lincoln, Australia

TUNA, YELLOWFIN
Basco, Pamela S., 157 lb, Kona, Hawaii, USA
Beukes, Santie, 113 lb 10 oz, Cape Point, Republic of South Africa
Brumby, Russell, 20 lb, Malindi, Kenya
Crozier, Capt. Bill, 264 lb 8 oz, Cabo San Lucas, B.C.S., Mexico
Du Plessis, Hennie, 128 lb 4 oz, Cape Town, R. of South Africa
Dunaway, Jerry, 24 lb 9 oz, Dakar, Senegal
Dunaway, Deborah Maddux, 14 lb, Pinas Bay, Panama
Dunn, David D., 68 lb 5 oz, White Island, New Zealand
Engelbrecht, John D., 43 lb 3 oz, East London, R. of South Africa
Everette, Jocelyn, 120 lb 8 oz, Kailua, Kona, Hawaii, USA
Frank, Nancy, 211 lb, Kailua, Kona, Hawaii, USA
Handgis, George, 167 lb, Keauhou, Kona, Hawaii, USA
Herzog, William A. "Al", 380 lb, San Benedicto Island, Mexico
Jericevich, Anthony, 101 lb 10 oz, Jeffrey's Bay, R. of South Africa
Lawson, Roy, 11 lb 7 oz, Catalina Island, California, USA
Lewandowski, Patti, 155 lb 8 oz, Kona, Hawaii, USA
McKay, Art, 153 lb 8 oz, Kona, Hawaii, USA
Pantry, Dylis Allison, 113 lb 5 oz, Challenger Bank, Bermuda
Pfleger, Thomas G., 258 lb 3 oz, Revillagigedo Island, Mexico
Rae, John McFadyen, 78 lb 7 oz, Whakatane, New Zealand
Reuter, A. C., 42 lb 5 oz, Maiquetia, Venezuela
Roper, Bobby, 150 lb 8 oz, South Pass, Louisiana, USA
Roper, Edward G., 179 lb, Mississippi River, Louisiana, USA

Row, Joelle Anne, 45 lb 13 oz, Hout Bay,Republic of South Africa
Schneider, Horst Martin, 110 lb,Hout Bay,Republic of South Africa
Sparg, Melvin, 68 lb 12 oz, Coffee Bay, Transkei
Thomson, David G., 105 lb 13 oz, Bermagui, N.S.W., Australia
Weber, Dr. Dieter, 12 lb 5 oz, Malindi, Kenya
Yergens, William P., 134 lb, Stuart, Florida, USA

WAHOO

Battistini, Sr., Luis A., 85 lb 12 oz, Mayaguez, Puerto Rico
Currie, Christine, 82 lb, Port Canaveral, Florida, USA
DuVal, Mrs. William B., 52 lb, Dry Tortugas, Florida, USA
Hicks, Taylor, 43 lb, Key West, Florida, USA
Mitchell, Melanie D., 21 lb 9 oz, Destin, Florida, USA
Pantry, Dylis Allison, 44 lb, Challenger Bank, Bermuda
Pantry, Dylis Allison, 46 lb 4 oz, Sally Tucker's, Bermuda

WALLEYE

Klick, Jimmy, 11 lb 3 oz, Nipawin, Saskatchewan, Canada
Sloyka, James J., 10 lb 14 oz, Bay of Quinte, Ontario, Canada

WEAKFISH

Robinson, III,Ellyson S.,11 lb 12 oz,Chesapeake Bay,Virginia,USA

YELLOWTAIL, CALIFORNIA

Prentice, Gordon C., 26 lb 6 oz, Loreto, B.C.S., Mexico

YELLOWTAIL, SOUTHERN

Behrens, Kev, 14 lb 5 oz, Bateman's Bay, N.S.W., Australia
Bolland, John, 68 lb 5 oz, Rocky Point, New Zealand
Coyle, Brian, 46 lb 4 oz, Waiheke, Auckland, New Zealand
Eady, Guy, 74 lb 1 oz, Cape Brett, New Zealand
Oates, Sharon, 64 lb 13 oz, Bay of Islands, Russell, New Zealand

23rd Annual IGFA Fishing Contest Winners

A total of 710 entries came in from around the world for the 23rd Annual Fishing Contest. Sixty-four per cent (456) were awarded first, second or third place. Certificates are given to the three heaviest catches of each species submitted that are caught in accordance with IGFA's International Angling Rules. The contest began with catches made between August 1, 1997 and July 31, 1998, and submitted to IGFA by October 31, 1998. The 24th Annual Fishing Contest is currently underway. All applications must conform to the world record rules.

FIRST PLACE

SPECIES	WEIGHT	PLACE	DATE	ANGLER
Albacore	15.50 kg (34 lb 2 oz)	St. Helens, Tasmania	Mar. 1, 1998	Sandra Kaye Harper
Amberjack, greater	29.14 kg (64 lb 4 oz)	Isla de Coiba, Panama	Mar. 4, 1998	Ray G. Hawkes
Barracuda, great	19.73 kg (43 lb 8 oz)	Ocracoke, North Carolina, USA	Aug. 31, 1997	Ellyson S. Robinson, III
Barracuda, Guinean	30.30 kg (66 lb 12 oz)	Mondia Branca, Luanda, Angola	Feb. 24, 1998	Nisa Ekberg
Barracuda, Pacific	5.62 kg (12 lb 6 oz)	Pt. Loma, San Diego, California, USA	July 30, 1998	Anthony Talavera
Barramundi	22.10 kg (48 lb 11 oz)	Port Hedland, Western Australia, Australia	Dec. 8, 1997	Gavin John Maher
Bass, European	3.00 kg (6 lb 9 oz)	Isle of Graciosa, Canary Islands, Spain	Oct. 10, 1997	Nicola Zingarelli
Bass, kelp (calico)	1.85 kg (4 lb 1 oz)	Palos Verdes, California, USA	June 23, 1998	Dr. John F. Whitaker
Bass, largemouth	7.82 kg (17 lb 4 oz)	Castaic Lake Lagoon, Castaic, California, USA	May 2, 1998	Bob Crupi
Bass, rock	1.36 kg (3 lb)	Lake Erie, Pennsylvania, USA	June 18, 1998	Herbert G. Ratner, Jr.
Bass, smallmouth	3.90 kg (8 lb 9 oz)	Pickwick Lake, Counce, Tennessee, USA	Mar. 11, 1998	E. Scott Yarbro, MD
Bass, striped	25.96 kg (57 lb 4 oz)	Watch Hill, Rhode Island, USA	Aug. 24, 1997	Janice Masciarelli
Bass, striped (landlocked)	28.91 kg (63 lb 12 oz)	Melton Hill Lake, Tennessee, USA	Feb. 2, 1998	Willis L. Marsh
Bass, white	1.72 kg (3 lb 12 oz)	Sabine River, Carthage, Texas, USA	Feb. 17, 1998	Keith Warren
Bass, whiterock	3.81 kg (8 lb 6 oz)	Beaver Lake, Rogers, Arkansas, USA	Dec. 3, 1997	Mark Powell
Bass, yellow	1.16 kg (2 lb 9 oz)	Duck River, Waverly, Tennessee, USA	Feb. 27, 1998	John T. Chappell
Bigeye	2.85 kg (6 lb 4 oz)	Baja da Guanabara, Rio de Janeiro, Brazil	Aug. 30, 1997	Jayme Garcia
Blackfish, smallscale	3.40 kg (7 lb 7 oz)	Hachijokojima, Hachijo Island, Japan	Jan. 8, 1998	Papa Otsuru
Bluefish	10.03 kg (22 lb 2 oz)	Hortons Point, Long Island, New York, USA	Nov. 12, 1997	Brian Cumings
Bluegill	0.68 kg (1 lb 8 oz)	Pace, Florida, USA	June 5, 1998	Lori Cooper
Bonefish	6.83 kg (15 lb 1 oz)	Islamorada, Florida, USA	Mar. 18, 1998	Gus Mujica
Bonito, Atlantic	4.74 kg (10 lb 7 oz)	Siracusa, Italy	Dec. 26, 1997	Giovanni Grimaldi
Bonito, Australian	4.80 kg (10 lb 9 oz)	Bass Island, Port Kembla, Australia	Feb. 22, 1998	Gregory Phillip Clarke
Bonito, Pacific	4.08 kg (9 lb)	San Diego, California, USA	Aug. 24, 1997	Don B. Walker
Bowfin	5.64 kg (12 lb 7 oz)	Rhodes Pond, North Carolina, USA	Dec. 26, 1997	Christopher Lee Rose
Bream, white	0.58 kg (1 lb 4 oz)	Nok, Germany	May 19, 1998	Holger Damerius
Brotula, bearded	7.98 kg (17 lb 9 oz)	Destin, Florida, USA	Aug. 16, 1997	William G. Siedow
Buffalo, bigmouth	4.98 kg (11 lb)	Oahe Tailwater, South Dakota, USA	May 2, 1998	Rick Hayden
Buffalo, smallmouth	26.76 kg (59 lb)	Town Lake, Austin, Texas, USA	Oct. 28, 1997	Gibbs Milliken
Bullhead, brown	2.74 kg (6 lb 1 oz)	Waterford, New York, USA	Apr. 26, 1998	Bobby Triplett
Burbot	2.49 kg (5 lb 8 oz)	Lake Erie, Pennsylvania, USA	Nov. 27, 1997	Richard E. Faler, Jr.
Buri (Japanese amberjack)	9.50 kg (20 lb 15 oz)	Miyazu, Kyoto, Japan	Apr. 29, 1998	Toshiyuki Fujioka
Captainfish	12.00 kg (26 lb 7 oz)	Archipelago of Bijago, Guinea-Bissau	May 17, 1998	Eric Legris
Carp, common	37.30 kg (82 lb 3 oz)	Lake Roduta, Romania	May 26, 1998	Christien Baldmair
Carp, grass	31.18 kg (68 lb 12 oz)	Somerland's Pond, North Carolina, USA	June 8, 1998	David Stowell
Catfish, blue	34.83 kg (76 lb 12 oz)	Lower Otay Lake, Chula Vista, California, USA	Feb. 21, 1998	Paul Daniel Zoch
Catfish, channel	5.66 kg (12 lb 8 oz)	Trailer Lake, Bucksville, Alabama, USA	July 5, 1998	Troy Beatty
Catfish, flathead	55.79 kg (123 lb 9 oz)	Elk City Reservoir, Independence, Kansas, USA	May 14, 1998	Ken Paulie
Catfish, gafftopsail	0.56 kg (1 lb 4 oz)	Gulf of Mexico, Florida, USA	June 11, 1998	Thomas Berg
Catfish, hardhead	0.59 kg (1 lb 5 oz)	Gulf of Mexico, Florida, USA	June 11, 1998	Thomas Berg
Catshark, smallspotted	0.90 kg (1 lb 15 oz)	Holmestrand, Norway	May 23, 1998	Bjoers Borgensen
Char, Arctic	7.26 kg (16 lb)	Tree River, Canada	Aug. 14, 1997	Ron Hickman
Chilipepper	1.13 kg (2 lb 8 oz)	San Clemente Island, California, USA	Feb. 14, 1998	Stephen D. Grossberg
Chub, gray sea	1.85 kg (4 lb 1 oz)	Midway Island	July 26, 1998	George Handgis
Cobia	8.16 kg (18 lb)	Key West, Florida, USA	Apr. 28, 1998	Mrs. William B. DuVal
Cod, Pacific	9.07 kg (20 lb)	Sequal Point, Kodiak Island, Alaska, USA	May 22, 1998	Sally Magnuson
Coralgrouper, blacksaddled	24.20 kg (53 lb 5 oz)	Hahajima, Ogasawara Island, Tokyo, Japan	Sept. 27, 1997	Hideo Morishita
Corvina, shortfin	3.15 kg (6 lb 15 oz)	Playa Hermosa, Mexico	Apr. 26, 1998	William E. Favor
Corvina, striped	0.90 kg (2 lb)	Playa Hermosa, Mexico	Apr. 5, 1998	William E. Favor
Crappie, black	1.64 kg (3 lb 10 oz)	Lake Logan Martin, Alabama, USA	Mar. 21, 1998	Mark E. Williamson
Croaker, long neck	15.02 kg (33 lb 2 oz)	Banjul, Gambia	Mar. 25, 1998	Alberto Madaria Hernandez
Croaker, silver	4.08 kg (9 lb)	Sao Benedito River, Brazil	Aug. 17, 1997	Larry Larsen
Cusk	16.30 kg (35 lb 14 oz)	Langesund, Norway	Apr. 26, 1998	Fredrik Amdal
Cutlassfish, Atlantic	3.68 kg (8 lb 1 oz)	Rio de Janeiro, Brazil	Sept. 6, 1997	Felipe Ricciulli Soares
Dentex	8.16 kg (17 lb 15 oz)	Palau, Sardinia, Italy	Aug. 8, 1997	Andrea Lia
Dogfish, smooth	12.15 kg (26 lb 12 oz)	Galveston, Texas, USA	Mar. 2, 1998	George A. Flores
Dolly Varden	6.12 kg (13 lb 8 oz)	Kivelino River, Alaska, USA	July 10, 1998	Phillip Wright
Dolphinfish	39.91 kg (88 lb)	Highbourne Cay, Exuma, Bahamas	May 5, 1998	Richard D. Evans
Dorado	3.14 kg (6 lb 15 oz)	Piquiri River, Mato Grosso, Brazil	Apr. 16, 1998	Sergio Rothier
Drum, black	41.05 kg (90 lb 8 oz)	New Smyrna Beach, Florida, USA	Mar. 29, 1998	Raleigh Werking
Drum, freshwater	5.13 kg (11 lb 5 oz)	Kentucky Lake, Kentucky, USA	Oct. 26, 1997	Steve Wendt
Drum, red	19.16 kg (42 lb 4 oz)	Oriental, North Carolina, USA	Aug. 27, 1997	Raleigh Werking
Escolar	27.50 kg (60 lb 10 oz)	El Hierro, Canary Islands, Spain	Nov. 24, 1997	Schneider Horst
Filefish, scrawled	2.15 kg (4 lb 11 oz)	Pompano Beach, Florida, USA	Jan. 20, 1998	Jonathan Mark Angel
Flounder, olive	4.02 kg (8 lb 13 oz)	Chiyoshi-city, Chiba, Japan	Dec. 10, 1997	Junzo Okada

SPECIES	WEIGHT	PLACE	DATE	ANGLER
Flounder, southern	1.13 kg (2 lb 8 oz)	Port Mansfield, Texas, USA	July 15, 1998	Terry R. Neal
Flounder, summer	2.35 kg (5 lb 3 oz)	Montauk, New York, USA	June 25, 1998	William Kuhle
Gar, longnose	4.94 kg (10 lb 14 oz)	Cape Fear River, North Carolina, USA	Aug. 30, 1997	Edward C. Davis
Gar, shortnose	1.36 kg (3 lb 4 oz)	Big Muddy River, Rend Lake, Illinois, USA	June 9, 1998	Rick Hayden
Gar, spotted	2.86 kg (6 lb 5 oz)	Buzz's Lake, Mount Vernon, Alabama, USA	July 19, 1998	Robert T. Cunningham, Jr.
Garfish	0.70 kg (1 lb 8 oz)	Detached Mole, Gibraltar	Aug. 31, 1997	R.H. Chichon
Grayling, Arctic	1.53 kg (3 lb 6 oz)	Great Bear Lake, Canada	July 30, 1998	Marlin A. Coulombe
Graysby	1.13 kg (2 lb 8 oz)	Stetson Rock, Texas, USA	Mar. 2, 1998	George A. Flores
Greenling, fat (ainame)	2.41 kg (5 lb 5 oz)	Todogasaki, Iwate, Japan	Dec. 29, 1997	Akira Tazawa
Grouper, convict	62.80 kg (138 lb 7 oz)	Amamioshima, Kagoshima, Japan	Sept. 24, 1997	Shinichi Tsurumi
Grouper, Hawaiian	10.65 kg (23 lb 8 oz)	Midway Island	July 27, 1998	George Handgis
Grouper, Hong Kong	1.05 kg (2 lb 5 oz)	Kyuroku Island, Aomori, Japan	Aug. 1, 1997	Shoji Sakuri
Grouper, longtooth	33.00 kg (72 lb 12 oz)	Hachijo Island, Tokyo, Japan	July 16, 1998	Yasuhiko Nagasaka
Grouper, moustache	55.00 kg (121 lb 3 oz)	Desroches Island, Seychelles	Jan. 1, 1998	Charles-Antoine Roucayrol
Grouper, speckled blue	16.30 kg (35 lb 14 oz)	Chichijima, Ogasawara, Tokyo, Japan	Apr. 10, 1998	Takeshi Uesugi
Grouper, yellowedge	18.64 kg (41 lb 1 oz)	Gulf of Mexico, Destin, Florida, USA	May 24, 1998	Christopher D. Allen
Grunt	1.02 kg (2 lb 4 oz)	Bimini, Bahamas	July 13, 1998	Jaclyn Hirsch
Guapote, jaguar	0.75 kg (1 lb 10 oz)	Barro Colorado, Costa Rica	Sept. 9, 1997	John C. Taylor
Guitarfish, blackchin	49.90 kg (110 lb)	Batanga, Gabon	June 11, 1998	Philippe Le Danff
Gurnard, grey	0.62 kg (1 lb 5 oz)	La Middleground, Kattegatt, Sweden	Apr. 20, 1998	Lars Kraemer
Haddock	6.80 kg (14 lb 15 oz)	Saltraumen, Germany	Aug. 15, 1997	Heike Neblinger
Halibut, Atlantic	161.20 kg (355 lb 6 oz)	Valevag, Norway	Oct. 20, 1997	Odd Arve Gunderstad
Halibut, California	19.45 kg (42 lb 14 oz)	Redondo Beach, California, USA	Jan. 28, 1998	Roberta Stotesbury
Halibut, Pacific	100.69 kg (222 lb)	Dutch Harbor, Alaska, USA	June 24, 1997	Fariba Zand
Happy, pink	2.20 kg (4 lb 13 oz)	Tiger Camp, Zambezi River, Zambia	Sept. 28, 1997	Toshimitsu Iwasaki
Houndfish	3.34 kg (7 lb 6 oz)	Victory Reef, Bahamas	June 22, 1998	Rick Lundell
Huchen, Japanese	3.35 kg (7 lb 6 oz)	Poronuma, Hokkaido, Japan	May 23, 1998	Takashi Yamada
Ide	2.88 kg (6 lb 5 oz)	Grangshammaran, Borlange, Sweden	June 27, 1998	Sonny Pettersson
Jack, crevalle	26.25 kg (57 lb 14 oz)	Southwest Pass, Louisiana, USA	Aug. 15, 1997	Leon D. Richard
Jack, horse-eye	11.68 kg (25 lb 12 oz)	Palm Beach, Florida, USA	Oct. 31, 1997	David Leavitt
Jack, Pacific crevalle	14.06 kg (31 lb)	Playa Zancudo, Costa Rica	Dec. 17, 1997	Roy Ventura Roig
Jau	25.00 kg (55 lb 1 oz)	Mato Grosso, Piquiri River, Brazil	Apr. 16, 1998	Romulo Coutinho
Jobfish, green	13.70 kg (30 lb 1 oz)	Amami Oshima, Kagoshima, Japan	July 12, 1998	Kei Hiramatsu
Jobfish, lavender	8.40 kg (18 lb 8 oz)	Chichijima, Ogasawara, Tokyo, Japan	Apr. 5, 1998	Yusuke Nakamura
Kahawai	6.20 kg (13 lb 10 oz)	Yallingup, Western Australia, Australia	Mar. 15, 1998	Dean Eggleston
Kawakawa	5.60 kg (12 lb 5 oz)	Dampier, Australia	Jan. 25, 1998	Tammy Yates
Kingfish, southern	0.85 kg (1 lb 14 oz)	Dauphin Island, Alabama, USA	Sept. 9, 1997	Marcus R. Kennedy
Kob	23.60 kg (52 lb)	Ardrossan, Australia	Feb. 22, 1998	Marcel Vandergoot
Kobudai	9.25 kg (20 lb 6 oz)	Kyuroku Island, Aomori, Japan	Aug. 1, 1997	Hitoshi Suzuki
Kokanee	2.35 kg (5 lb 3 oz)	South Platte River, Hartsel, Colorado, USA	Nov. 16, 1997	Jim W. Williams
Ladyfish	2.72 kg (6 lb)	Loxahatchee River, Jupiter, Floirda, USA	Dec. 20, 1997	Michael Baz
Leerfish (Garrick)	15.80 kg (34 lb 13 oz)	Catania, Italy	Oct. 19, 1997	Giovanni Barbagallo
Ling, European	2.09 kg (4 lb 10 oz)	Kraakvaag Fjord, Norway	July 25, 1998	Sandra Marquard
Lingcod	23.58 kg (52 lb)	East Chugach, Alaska, USA	July 17, 1998	Stephen P. Cushman
Mackerel, Atlantic	0.86 kg (1 lb 14 oz)	Kraakvaag Fjord, Norway	July 18, 1998	Sandra Marquard
Mackerel, broadbarred	6.80 kg (14 lb 15 oz)	Groote Eylandt, Australia	Nov. 2, 1997	Maryanne Thumwood
Mackerel, cero	5.62 kg (12 lb 6 oz)	Ocean Cay, Bahamas	June 14, 1998	Faith Black
Mackerel, frigate	1.72 kg (3 lb 12 oz)	Hat Head, New South Wales, Australia	Apr. 17, 1998	Glen Beers
Mackerel, king	24.49 kg (54 lb)	Andros Island, Bahamas	Mar. 7, 1998	Robert T. Harper, Jr.
Mackerel, Spanish	2.94 kg (6 lb 8 oz)	Marathon, Florida, USA	Feb. 19, 1998	Janet F. Farish
Madai	4.90 kg (10 lb 12 oz)	Oura, Kochi, Japan	Feb. 14, 1998	Yuichi Ueno
Marlin, black	474.91 kg (1047 lb)	Lizard Island, Australia	Oct. 10, 1997	Hugh Wily
Marlin, blue (Atlantic)	417.00 kg (919 lb 5 oz)	Abidjan, Ivory Coast	Feb. 22, 1998	Mary Pierre Fontaine
Marlin, blue (Pacific)	456.80 kg (1007 lb)	The Hook, New Zealand	Mar. 18, 1998	Tomy Harding
Marlin, striped	166.20 kg (366 lb 6 oz)	Mayor Island, New Zealand	Feb. 15, 1998	Barbara Woodill
Marlin, white	79.00 kg (174 lb 2 oz)	Rio de Janeiro, Brazil	Dec. 3, 1997	Paulo Fabiano Ferreira Filho
Matrincha	3.36 kg (7 lb 6 oz)	Rio Arinos, Brazil	Sept. 3, 1997	Marcio Mattos Borges de Oliveira
Mebaru	0.67 kg (1 lb 7 oz)	Koshigoe Port, Kanagawa, Japan	June 4, 1998	Yusuke Furuta
Medai	7.75 kg (17 lb 1 oz)	Ashizuri, Kochi, Japan	July 12, 1998	Akira Sato
Milkfish	10.75 kg (23 lb 11 oz)	St. Francis Island, Seychelles	Jan. 18, 1998	John M. Costello
Moray, blacktail	1.09 kg (2 lb 6 oz)	Gulf of Mexico, Texas, USA	Mar. 24, 1998	George A. Flores
Moray, purplemouth	0.75 kg (1 lb 10 oz)	Port Everglades Reef, Florida, USA	June 19, 1998	Rene G. de Dios
Moray, viper	1.32 kg (2 lb 14 oz)	Fowey Light, Florida, USA	May 25, 1998	Rene G. de Dios
Needlefish, flat	4.80 kg (10 lb 9 oz)	Zavora, Mozambique	Dec. 25, 1997	Leon Paul deBeer
Opah	59.78 kg (131 lb 12 oz)	Tanner Bank, California, USA	July 22, 1998	Christopher R. Isom
Oxeye	1.67 kg (3 lb 10 oz)	Amami Oshima, Kagoshima, Japan	July 19, 1998	Yuichiro Kawabata
Pacu, black	12.81 kg (28 lb 4 oz)	Pompano Beach, Florida, USA	Jan. 12, 1998	James L. Cohen, Sr.
Parrotperch, Japanese	4.40 kg (9 lb 11 oz)	Yokose, Hachijo Island, Tokyo, Japan	Apr. 11, 1998	Atsushi Fujioka
Payara	8.16 kg (18 lb 1 oz)	Uraima Falls, Venezuela	Feb. 9, 1998	Shoichiro Kawai
Peacock, blackstriped	1.70 kg (3 lb 12 oz)	Rio Cinaruco, Venezuela	Mar. 11, 1998	Dot Bean
Peacock, butterfly	4.64 kg (10 lb 4 oz)	Mataveni River, Orinoco, Colombia	Feb. 26, 1998	Steven Jensen
Peacock, speckled	9.29 kg (20 lb 8 oz)	Rio Pasamoni, Amazonas, Venezuela	Feb. 16, 1998	Steven "Zato" Yatomi
Pellona, Amazon	6.15 kg (13 lb 8 oz)	Cuara River Edo, Bolivar, Venezuela	Oct. 28, 1997	Carlos Aristeguieta L.
Perch, European	1.50 kg (3 lb 4 oz)	Eidsvoll, Norway	June 13, 1998	Johnny Hogli
Perch, Nile	96.61 kg (213 lb)	Lake Nasser, Egypt	Dec. 18, 1997	Adrian Brayshaw

SPECIES	WEIGHT	PLACE	DATE	ANGLER
Perch, white	1.24 kg (2 lb 12 oz)	Barnagat, New Jersey, USA	Apr. 15, 1998	Michael A. King
Permit	20.41 kg (45 lb)	Key Biscayne, Florida, USA	Apr. 29, 1998	Ken Pittman
Pickerel, chain	2.23 kg (4 lb 15 oz)	Lake Nockamixon, Pennsylvania, USA	Dec. 25, 1997	Martin J. Haring
Pickerel, redfin	0.90 kg (2 lb)	St. Paul's, North Carolina, USA	Feb. 7, 1998	Edward C. Davis
Pike, northern	12.72 kg (28 lb 1 oz)	Lac Lamartre, Canada	Aug. 25, 1997	T.O. McLean
Pinook	6.58 kg (14 lb 8 oz)	Garden River, Sault Ste Marie, Ontario, Canada	Sept. 22, 1997	Scott R. Smith
Piranha, Manualis	2.15 kg (4 lb 12 oz)	Rio Cinaruco, Venezuela	Jan. 12, 1998	Eric Ostmark
Piraputanga	0.62 kg (1 lb 6 oz)	Mato Grosso, Piguiri River, Brazil	Apr. 16, 1998	Helder Coutinho
Pollack, European	2.21 kg (4 lb 14 oz)	Kraakvaag Fjord, Norway	July 14, 1998	Sandra Marquard
Pollock	2.92 kg (6 lb 7 oz)	Perkins Cove, Ogunquit, Maine, USA	Nov. 3, 1997	Linda M. Paul
Pompano, Florida	0.79 kg (1 lb 12 oz)	Jupiter Beach, Florida, USA	Apr. 9, 1998	Daniel Allen Seybel
Puffer, smooth	2.99 kg (6 lb 9 oz)	Orange Beach, Alabama, USA	June 3, 1998	Randall H. Atherton
Queenfish	11.00 kg (24 lb 4 oz)	Dampier Creek, Broome, Australia	Nov. 8, 1997	Peter Dohnt
Redhorse, black	1.02 kg (2 lb 4 oz)	French Creek, Franklin, Pennsylvania, USA	Feb. 22, 1998	Richard E. Faler, Jr.
Redhorse, river	3.96 kg (8 lb 11 oz)	Trent River, Ontario, Canada	Aug. 6, 1997	Geoff J. Bernado
Rockfish, bank	1.98 kg (4 lb 6 oz)	San Clemente Island, California, USA	Feb. 14, 1998	Stephen D. Grossberg
Rockfish, dusky	1.81 kg (4 lb)	Kodiak, Alaska, USA	Sept. 27, 1997	Sally Magnuson
Rockfish, silvergray	0.82 kg (1 lb 13 oz)	Yakutat Bay, Alaska, USA	June 24, 1998	George Bogen
Roosterfish	41.40 kg (91 lb 4 oz)	Manzanillo, Mexico	June 28, 1998	Eduardo Vergara Camou
Rosefish, blackbelly	1.49 kg (3 lb 4 oz)	Hitra, Norway	Aug. 12, 1997	Fredrik Meyer
Sailfish, Atlantic	60.60 kg (133 lb 9 oz)	Luanda, Angola	Mar. 22, 1998	Eduardo Vale Moreira
Sailfish, Pacific	48.00 kg (105 lb 13 oz)	Mooloolaba, Queensland, Australia	Apr. 27, 1998	Ron Whiteside
Salmon, Atlantic	11.49 kg (25 lb 5 oz)	Namsen River Grong, Norway	June 7, 1998	Dr. John B. Baldwin
Salmon, chinook	19.33 kg (42 lb 10 oz)	Lake Marie Lodge, Lake Marie Creek, Alaska, USA	July 9, 1998	Bobby W. Wilson
Salmon, chum	11.77 kg (25 lb 15 oz)	Satsop River, Washington, USA	Oct. 19, 1997	Johnnie R. Wilson
Sandperch, namorado	20.20 kg (44 lb 8 oz)	Rio de Janeiro, Brazil	Mar. 7, 1998	Eduardo Baumeier
Sauger	1.81 kg (4 lb)	Pittsburgh, Pennsylvania, USA	Nov. 17, 1997	Herbert G. Ratner, Jr.
Seabass, blackfin	7.08 kg (15 lb 9 oz)	Chikura, Chiba, Japan	Apr. 18, 1998	Katsumi Shimada
Seabass, Japanese	6.35 kg (13 lb 15 oz)	Shionomisaki, Wakayama, Japan	Nov. 2, 1997	Masanori Kobayashi
Seabream, Okinawa	2.15 kg (4 lb 11 oz)	Amami-oshima, Kagoshima, Japan	Apr. 29, 1998	Hidehira Ike
Seabream, yellowfin	1.50 kg (3 lb 4 oz)	Nishinomiya Port, Hyogo, Japan	June 1, 1998	Tsunehisa Wake
Seatrout, spotted	3.81 kg (8 lb 6 oz)	Laguna Madre Beach, So. Padre Island, Texas, USA	Mar. 22, 1998	Kenny Brewer
Seerfish, Chinese	59.67 kg (131 lb 9 oz)	Lema Islands, Hong Kong	May 31, 1998	Peter Sprung
Shad, American	1.70 kg (3 lb 12 oz)	Chicopee River, Chicopee, Massachusetts, USA	Aug. 31, 1997	John J. Regan
Shark, blacktip	18.64 kg (41 lb 1 oz)	Garden City Beach, South Carolina, USA	Sept. 17, 1997	Rob Colwell
Shark, blue	73.93 kg (163 lb)	Chatham, Massachusetts, USA	Aug. 10, 1997	Mike Benson
Shark, great hammerhead	124.73 kg (275 lb)	Long Key Bridge, Florida, USA	Sept. 5, 1997	Rene G. de Dios
Shark, hammerhead	7.04 kg (15 lb 8 oz)	Hilton Head Island, South Carolina, USA	June 9, 1998	Tonya B. Jones
Shark, lemon	155.66 kg (255 lb)	Bimini, Bahamas	Oct. 5, 1997	Rene G. de Dios
Shark, mako	95.00 kg (209 lb 6 oz)	Kaikoura, New Zealand	Feb. 28, 1998	David W. Tattle
Shark, oceanic whitetip	167.37 kg (369 lb)	San Salvador, Bahamas	Jan. 24, 1998	Reid Hodges
Shark, porbeagle	62.90 kg (138 lb 10 oz)	Otago Heads, New Zealand	May 24, 1998	Dave Carr
Shark, shortfin mako	196.20 kg (432 lb 8 oz)	Cape Kari Kari, New Zealand	Jan. 8, 1998	John H. Griffiths
Shark, thresher	89.40 kg (197 lb 1 oz)	Kilcunda, Victoria, Australia	Dec. 4, 1997	Russell Taylor
Shark, tiger	285.31 kg (629 lb)	Bimini, Bahamas	Aug. 31, 1997	Rene G. de Dios
Snapper (squirefish)	16.35 kg (36 lb)	Slipper Island, New Zealand	Apr. 11, 1998	Dawn Irvine
Snapper, cubera	17.50 kg (38 lb 9 oz)	Ocean Reef, Florida, USA	Aug. 15, 1997	Diane Smolka
Snapper, emperor	16.00 kg (35 lb 4 oz)	Chichijima, Ogasawara, Tokyo, Japan	Apr. 10, 1998	Takeshi Uesugi
Snapper, gray	3.79 kg (8 lb 6 oz)	Marathon, Florida, USA	June 4, 1998	B.J. Meyers
Snapper, mullet	14.96 kg (33 lb)	Cano Island, Costa Rica	Sept. 23, 1997	Jose Francisco Reyes Astorga
Snapper, mutton	7.93 kg (17 lb 8 oz)	Islamorada, Florida, USA	May 25, 1998	Mary Katherine DeFoor
Snapper, Pacific cubera	17.69 kg (39 lb)	Playa Zancudo, Costa Rica	Mar. 5, 1998	Carol M. Emmert
Snapper, red	18.59 kg (41 lb)	28 Fathom Ledge, Florida, USA	July 24, 1998	Joshua S. Thompson
Snapper, yellow (amarillo)	4.98 kg (11 lb)	Playa Zancudo, Costa Rica	Dec. 17, 1997	Roy Ventura Roig
Snook	15.42 kg (34 lb)	Cabo San Lucas, Mexico	Sept. 27, 1997	Jeff Klassen
Snook, blackfin	3.15 kg (7 lb)	Playa Zancudo, Costa Rica	Mar. 31, 1998	Stuart A. Schleujener
Snook, fat	3.65 kg (8 lb 1 oz)	St. Lucie River, Stuart, Florida, USA	Nov. 15, 1997	Paul Strauss
Snook, Pacific blackfin	3.14 kg (6 lb 14 oz)	Rio Parrita, Costa Rica	Dec. 7, 1997	Victor Miranda Golfin
Sorubim, spotted	25.00 kg (55 lb 1 oz)	Mato Grosso, Piguiri River, Brazil	Apr. 18, 1998	Romulo Coutinho
Spadefish, Atlantic	5.41 kg (11 lb 15 oz)	Chesapeake Bay Bridge Tunnel, Virginia, USA	June 23, 1998	Ellyson S. Robinson, III
Spearfish	18.82 kg (41 lb 8 oz)	Keahole, Kona, Hawaii, USA	Mar. 12, 1998	Warren C. Keinath
Stargazer, northern	4.87 kg (10 lb 12 oz)	Cape May, New Jersey, USA	June 20, 1998	John E. Jacobsen
Stingray, southern	111.58 kg (246 lb)	Galveston Bay Complex, Texas, USA	June 30, 1998	Carissa Egger
Sturgeon, white	17.87 kg (39 lb 6 oz)	Santa Ana River Lakes, California, USA	Mar. 21, 1998	Robert Vandevelde
Sunfish, green (hybrid)	0.97 kg (2 lb 2 oz)	Patagonia Lake State Park, Arizona, USA	June 5, 1998	Mikey A. Porter
Sunfish, redear	2.40 kg (5 lb 4 oz)	Santee Cooper Cross, South Carolina, USA	June 18, 1998	Ray Lee
Swordfish	291.90 kg (643 lb)	Mercury Bay, New Zealand	Apr. 2, 1998	Ian O'Brien
Tarpon	91.62 kg (202 lb)	Banjul, Gambia	Mar. 18, 1998	Alberto Madaria Hernandez
Tautog	11.33 kg (25 lb)	Ocean City, New Jersey, USA	Jan. 20, 1998	Anthony R. Monica
Threadfin, king	11.40 kg (25 lb 2 oz)	Dampier, Australia	Dec. 13, 1997	Mark Cottrell
Tigerfish	8.90 kg (19 lb 9 oz)	Tiger Camp, Zambezi River, Zambia	Aug. 2, 1997	Ryuichi Takahashi
Tilapia, Mozambique	1.13 kg (2 lb 8 oz)	Delray Beach, Florida, USA	Nov. 10, 1997	Nick Cardella
Tilapia, threespot	4.30 kg (9 lb 7 oz)	Tiger Camp, Zambezi River, Zambia	Nov. 2, 1997	Michael Harris
Trevally, bigeye	7.80 kg (17 lb 3 oz)	Chichijima, Ogasawara, Tokyo, Japan	July 9, 1998	Hiroaki Shukunami
Trevally, bluefin	2.76 kg (6 lb 1 oz)	Christmas Island, Republic of Kiribati	Mar. 13, 1998	Bud Korteweg

SPECIES	WEIGHT	PLACE	DATE	ANGLER
Trevally, giant	54.10 kg (119 lb 4 oz)	Ile de la Reunion, France	Mar. 15, 1998	Hughes Savalli
Trevally, golden	14.15 kg (31 lb 3 oz)	Port Hedland, Australia	Aug. 16, 1997	Tammy Yates
Trevally, longnose	4.35 kg (9 lb 9 oz)	Midway Island	Aug. 9, 1997	Allan Durham
Trevally, white	15.25 kg (33 lb 9 oz)	Hahajima, Ogasawara, Tokyo, Japan	July 6, 1998	Kazuhiko Adachi
Trevally, yellowspotted	11.20 kg (24 lb 11 oz)	Inhaca Island, Maputo	Mar. 4, 1998	Peter Kidd
Tripletail	18.51 kg (40 lb 13 oz)	Ft. Pierce, Florida, USA	Mar. 4, 1998	Thomas D. Lewis
Trout, brook	3.28 kg (7 lb 4 oz)	Osprey Lake, Labrador, Canada	June 24, 1998	Robert A. King
Trout, brown	15.93 kg (35 lb 2 oz)	Rio Grande, Tierra del Fuego, Argentina	Mar. 1, 1998	Mark T. Gates, Jr.
Trout, cutthroat	4.98 kg (11 lb)	Pyramid Lake, Nevada, USA	Mar. 5, 1998	Fred Turner
Trout, golden	2.12 kg (4 lb 11 oz)	Thumb Lake, Wyoming, USA	Sept. 6, 1997	Chip Hane
Trout, lake	16.78 kg (37 lb)	Great Bear Lake, Canada	July 30, 1998	Marlin A. Coulombe
Trout, rainbow	5.33 kg (11 lb 12 oz)	Lake Michigan, Indiana, USA	Oct. 26, 1997	Thomas Berg
Trout, red-spotted masu	1.54 kg (3 lb 6 oz)	Yoshino River, Tokushima, Japan	May 17, 1998	Akihiko Masutani
Trout, tiger	1.02 kg (2 lb 4 oz)	Westfield River, Massachusetts, USA	May 9, 1998	John J. Regan
Tuna, bigeye (Atlantic)	120.00 kg (264 lb 8 oz)	Puerto de Mogan, Grand Canaria, Spain	July 11, 1998	Ulrich Dietze
Tuna, blackfin	19.95 kg (44 lb)	Cape May, New Jersey, USA	July 11, 1998	Ernie Henderson
Tuna, bluefin	158.75 kg (350 lb)	Hatteras, North Carolina, USA	Jan. 21, 1998	Elizabeth Hogan
Tuna, longtail	13.00 kg (28 lb 10 oz)	Mooloolaba, Queensland, Australia	Apr. 22, 1998	Bryan Peterson
Tuna, skipjack	10.50 kg (23 lb 2 oz)	Black River, Mauritius	Jan. 19, 1998	Michael Bartels
Tuna, yellowfin	86.00 kg (189 lb 9 oz)	Guarafori, Brazil	Dec. 27, 1997	Paulo Amorim
Tunny, little	6.40 kg (14 lb 2 oz)	Key West, Florida, USA	May 30, 1998	Linda Ann Luizza
Wahoo	22.60 kg (49 lb 13 oz)	Ponta Barra, Mozambique	Sept. 29, 1997	Hennie Geldennuys
Walleye	4.30 kg (9 lb 8 oz)	Pittsburgh, Pennsylvania, USA	Dec. 7, 1997	Herbert G. Ratner, Jr.
Weakfish	4.64 kg (10 lb 4 oz)	Cape May, New Jersey, USA	May 24, 1998	Robert Lummis, Jr.
Weakfish, acoupa	17.00 kg (37 lb 7 oz)	Canal do Boqueirao, Ilha do Governador, Brazil	Aug. 23, 1997	Gilberto Ferreira
Wels	36.28 kg (80 lb)	River Erbo, Aldover, Spain	July 7, 1998	Valerie Hall
Whitefish, lake	1.48 kg (3 lb 4 oz)	St. Mary's River, Ste Sault Mary, Ontario	Nov. 26, 1997	John Gausas, PhD.
Whiting, European	2.32 kg (5 lb 2 oz)	Devon, England	Mar. 21, 1998	Mick Oatham
Yellowtail, Asian	21.40 kg (47 lb 2 oz)	Chichijima, Ogasawara, Tokyo, Japan	July 4, 1998	Gakusei Ikeda
Yellowtail, California	33.22 kg (73 lb 4 oz)	Alijos Rocks, Baja California, Mexico	Dec. 3, 1997	Deena Nelson
Yellowtail, southern	43.80 kg (96 lb 8 oz)	White Island, New Zealand	Dec. 13, 1997	Anita Syben

SECOND PLACE

SPECIES	WEIGHT	PLACE	DATE	ANGLER
Albacore	4.71 kg (10 lb 6 oz)	San Diego, California, USA	June 23, 1998	Gary Brettnacher
Amberjack, greater	1.50 kg (3 lb 5 oz)	Boca Raton, Florida, USA	Dec. 19, 1997	Jim Ingalls
Barracuda, great	17.10 kg (37 lb 11 oz)	North East Island, Groote Eylandt, Australia	June 14, 1998	Lewis Fawcett
Barramundi	7.56 kg (16 lb 10 oz)	Dampier, Australia	Dec. 23, 1997	Nicole Livingstone
Bass, European	1.52 kg (3 lb 5 oz)	Alberese, Grosseto, Italy	Mar. 29, 1998	Marco Sammicheli
Bass, largemouth	7.51 kg (16 lb 9 oz)	Lake Isabella, California, USA	Mar. 18, 1998	Terry McAbee
Bass, rock	1.13 kg (2 lb 8 oz)	Lake Erie, Pennsylvania, USA	June 18, 1998	Herbert G. Ratner, Jr.
Bass, smallmouth	3.45 kg (7 lb 9 oz)	Pickwick Lake, Counce, Tennessee, USA	Jan. 23, 1998	E. Scott Yarbro, MD
Bass, striped	17.46 kg (38 lb 8 oz)	Chatham, Massachusetts, USA	Sept. 21, 1997	Stan Daggett
Bass, striped (landlocked)	14.51 kg (32 lb)	Norfork Lake, Mountain Home, Arkansas, USA	Jan. 24, 1998	Bill Fitzgerald
Bass, white	1.67 kg (3 lb 11 oz)	Sabine River, Louisiana, USA	Feb. 24, 1998	Gale Harvey Gleason
Bluefish	7.00 kg (15 lb 7 oz)	Virginia Beach, Virginia, USA	Nov. 11, 1997	Dennis Cline
Bluegill	0.66 kg (1 lb 7 oz)	Pace, Florida, USA	June 5, 1998	Zac Cooper
Bonefish	6.37 kg (14 lb 1 oz)	Islamorada, Florida, USA	Apr. 17, 1998	Richard L. Bowers
Bonito, Atlantic	3.74 kg (8 lb 4 oz)	Groton, Connecticut, USA	Oct. 15, 1997	Jack Balait
Bonito, Pacific	2.70 kg (5 lb 15 oz)	La Jolla, California, USA	July 23, 1998	Paul Victor Deibel, II
Bowfin	4.37 kg (9 lb 10 oz)	Chickahominy River, Virginia, USA	Feb. 21, 1998	Eddy Johnston
Buffalo, bigmouth	4.14 kg (9 lb 3 oz)	Rock River, Machoney Park, Illinois	Dec. 7, 1997	Dustin Genin
Bullhead, brown	0.92 kg (2 lb)	Whitney Point Reservoir, New York, USA	May 12, 1998	Sarah A. Basil
Carp, common	13.40 kg (29 lb 8 oz)	Town Lake, Austin, Texas, USA	May 5, 1998	Gibbs Milliken
Catfish, blue	34.01 kg (75 lb)	Lake Guntersville, Guntersville, Alabama, USA	Sept. 6, 1997	Jim Kitchens, Sr.
Catfish, channel	4.90 kg (10 lb 12 oz)	House Lake, Bucksville, Alabama, USA	Oct. 2, 1997	Troy Beatty
Catfish, flathead	28.57 kg (63 lb)	Cape Fear River, North Carolina, USA	Oct. 23, 1997	Edward C. Davis
Char, Arctic	4.08 kg (9 lb)	Coppermine River, Canada	Aug. 4, 1997	Marlin A. Coulombe
Cod, Pacific	9.07 kg (20 lb)	Kodiak, Alaska, USA	June 9, 1998	Eric Stirrup
Corvina, shortfin	1.51 kg (3 lb 5 oz)	Playa Hermosa, Mexico	Nov. 23, 1997	William E. Favor
Crappie, black	0.87 kg (1 lb 15 oz)	White Springs, Florida, USA	Jan. 18, 1998	Hamilton M. Franz
Cusk	5.75 kg (12 lb 10 oz)	Kraakvaag Fjord, Norway	July 29, 1998	Joerg Marquard
Dentex	7.17 kg (15 lb 12 oz)	Porto Cervo, Sardinia, Italy	July 7, 1998	Ottavio Bonfanti
Dolly Varden	5.37 kg (11 lb 13 oz)	Kelly River, Alaska, USA	July 13, 1998	Carl E. Brent
Dolphinfish	34.01 kg (75 lb)	Cabo San Lucas, Baja California Sur, Mexico	Nov. 30, 1997	Betty Ann Mehl
Drum, black	30.20 kg (66 lb 9 oz)	Chesapeake Bay Bridge Tunnel, Virginia, USA	June 24, 1998	Jon Holsenbeck
Drum, red	17.23 kg (38 lb)	Oriental, North Carolina, USA	Aug. 26, 1997	Raleigh Werking
Escolar	23.40 kg (51 lb 9 oz)	Imazawa, Shizuoka, Japan	Oct. 18, 1997	Hiromasa Kobayashi
Flounder, summer	1.13 kg (2 lb 8 oz)	Moriches Bay, East Moriches, New York, USA	July 13, 1998	Tom Cornicelli
Gar, longnose	2.94 kg (6 lb 8 oz)	South Fork, Miami River, Miami, Florida, USA	Feb. 19, 1998	Jay Wright, Jr.
Gar, shortnose	0.90 kg (1 lb 15 oz)	Red Rock Dam, Pella, Iowa, USA	July 26, 1998	Dan Lopez
Gar, spotted	2.38 kg (5 lb 4 oz)	Big Muddy River, Rend Lake, Illinois, USA	June 9, 1998	Rick Hayden
Grayling, Arctic	1.33 kg (2 lb 15 oz)	Great Bear Lake, Canada	Aug. 3, 1997	Marlin A. Coulombe

SPECIES	WEIGHT	PLACE	DATE	ANGLER
Grouper, yellowedge	11.39 kg (25 lb 2 oz)	Gulf of Mexico, Texas, USA	May 3, 1998	Alan L. Miller
Haddock	0.82 kg (1 lb 12 oz)	Kraakvaag Fjord, Norway	July 13, 1998	Sandra Marquard
Halibut, California	14.68 kg (32 lb 6 oz)	Marina Del Ray, California, USA	Nov. 22, 1997	Diane L. Greene
Halibut, Pacific	56.24 kg (124 lb)	Kodiak, Alaska, USA	Aug. 6, 1997	Paul Leader
Huchen, Japanese	2.80 kg (6 lb 2 oz)	Sarufutsu River, Hokkaido, Japan	May 15, 1998	Kaji Narita
Jack, crevalle	9.07 kg (20 lb)	Jupiter, Florida, USA	June 12, 1998	Jing Torn
Jack, horse-eye	8.84 kg (19 lb 8 oz)	Bimini, Bahamas	Aug. 14, 1997	Ray C. Stormont
Jack, Pacific crevalle	10.03 kg (22 lb 2 oz)	Cabo San Lucas, Baja California Sur, Mexico	Dec. 25, 1997	Stephen Jansen
Kahawai (Australian salmon)	3.15 kg (6 lb 15 oz)	Clare Bay, Australia	Sept. 24, 1997	John Marsh
Kawakawa	4.28 kg (9 lb 6 oz)	Wathumba Creek, Fraser Island, Australia	Dec. 16, 1997	Kim Bain
Kokanee	2.15 kg (4 lb 12 oz)	South Platte River, Hartsel, Colorado, USA	Nov. 16, 1997	Bill Perry
Leerfish (Garrick)	15.00 kg (33 lb 1 oz)	Isle of Graciosa, Canary Islands, Spain	Apr. 15, 1998	Nicola Zingarelli
Lingcod	21.77 kg (48 lb)	East Chugach, Alaska, USA	July 9, 1998	Marjorie L. Cushman
Mackerel, cero	2.49 kg (5 lb 8 oz)	Key West, Florida, USA	Jan. 22, 1998	Jerome C. Matthews
Mackerel, frigate	1.45 kg (3 lb 3 oz)	Botany Bay Heads, Sydney, Australia	Mar. 20, 1998	Douk Konstantaas
Mackerel, king	4.08 kg (9 lb)	Islamorada, Florida, USA	Jan. 13, 1998	Dianne Harbaugh
Mackerel, Spanish	2.94 kg (6 lb 8 oz)	Chassahowitzka River, Florida, USA	July 29, 1998	Marilyn Dietz
Marlin, black	101.00 kg (222 lb 10 oz)	Port Stephens, Australia	Mar. 26, 1998	Brian E. Kane
Marlin, blue (Atlantic)	406.19 kg (895 lb 5 oz)	San Juan, Puerto Rico	Aug. 17, 1997	Luis Viyella
Marlin, blue (Pacific)	409.60 kg (903 lb)	Salinas, Ecuador	May 30, 1998	Ernesto Jouvin
Marlin, striped	134.26 kg (296 lb)	Three Kings, New Zealand	May 17, 1998	Mike Levitt
Marlin, white	48.30 kg (106 lb 8 oz)	Algarve, Portugal	Aug. 30, 1997	Guido Fehr
Matrincha	2.80 kg (6 lb 2 oz)	Rio Arinos, Brazil	Sept. 1, 1997	Frederico Rodreigues Montefeltro
Mebaru	0.62 kg (1 lb 5 oz)	Nagaura, Chiba, Japan	Mar. 14, 1998	Michiaki Takahashi
Payara	7.99 kg (17 lb 10 oz)	Uraima Falls, Venezuela	Feb. 8, 1998	Shoichiro Kawai
Peacock, blackstriped	1.47 kg (3 lb 4 oz)	Cinaruco River, Venezuela	Feb. 25, 1998	Javier (Gordo) Garcia
Peacock, butterfly	2.72 kg (6 lb)	Miami, Florida, USA	Apr. 9, 1998	Herbert G. Ratner, Jr.
Peacock, speckled	9.07 kg (20 lb)	Rio Yatva, Amazonas, Venezuela	Feb. 17, 1998	Steven "Zato" Yatomi
Perch, Nile	95.25 kg (210 lb)	Lake Nasser, Egypt	June 24, 1998	Darren Robert Lord
Perch, white	0.85 kg (1 lb 14 oz)	Miacomet Pond, Nantucket, Massachusetts, USA	Mar. 10, 1998	Chad Whitlock
Permit	13.15 kg (29 lb)	Key West, Florida, USA	May 30, 1998	Susan Cocking
Pickerel, chain	1.41 kg (3 lb 2 oz)	Mingo Wildlife Refuge, Canada	Nov. 9, 1997	Bill Willmert
Pike, northern	12.02 kg (26 lb 8 oz)	Innoco River, Hill Lake, Alaska, USA	Aug. 11, 1997	Barry Reynolds
Pinook	6.57 kg (14 lb 8 oz)	Garden River, Sault Ste Marie, Canada	Sept. 23, 1997	Larry Cory
Pollock	1.44 kg (3 lb 2 oz)	Kraakvaag Fjord, Norway	July 18, 1998	Sandra Marquard
Queenfish	10.70 kg (23 lb 9 oz)	Magnetic Island, Townsville, Australia	Sept. 21, 1997	Terry Stevens
Roosterfish	18.82 kg (41 lb 8 oz)	Morro del Potosi, Zihuatanejo, Mexico	Apr. 19, 1998	Thomas B. Boyd
Sailfish, Atlantic	27.03 kg (59 lb 9 oz)	Isla Mujeres, Quintana Roo, Mexico	Apr. 28, 1998	Susan McCarthy
Sailfish, Pacific	38.10 kg (84 lb)	Quepos, Costa Rica	Jan. 20, 1998	Jodi Pate
Salmon, Atlantic	2.55 kg (5 lb 10 oz)	Lake Michigan, Indiana, USA	Jan. 28, 1998	Thomas Berg
Salmon, chinook	16.44 kg (36 lb 4 oz)	Lake Marie Lodge, Lake Marie Creek, Alaska, USA	July 10, 1998	David L. Wilson
Sauger	1.81 kg (4 lb)	Pittsburgh, Pennsylvania, USA	Dec. 7, 1997	Herbert G. Ratner, Jr.
Seabass, blackfin	6.90 kg (15 lb 3 oz)	Tateyama-shi, Chiba-ken, Japan	Jan. 14, 1998	Masaaki Ishikawa
Seabass, Japanese (suzuki)	5.76 kg (12 lb 11 oz)	Oita River, Oita, Japan	Nov. 1, 1997	Shigenori Kawanaka
Seatrout, spotted	3.62 kg (8 lb)	Sebastian Inlet, Florida, USA	Mar. 19, 1998	Richard A. Patton
Shark, blue	68.40 kg (150 lb 12 oz)	Tutukaka, Poor Knights, New Zealand	Dec. 7, 1997	Sam Mossman
Shark, hammerhead	4.88 kg (9 lb)	Key West, Florida, USA	Mar. 21, 1998	Bennett Stern
Shark, mako	93.50 kg (206 lb 2 oz)	Lebore Bay, Canturbury, New Zealand	Feb. 27, 1998	Grant Collings
Shark, oceanic whitetip	145.37 kg (320 lb 8 oz)	Rum Cay, Bahamas	Feb. 25, 1998	Richard Seaman
Shark, porbeagle	61.70 kg (136 lb)	Otago Heads, New Zealand	June 7, 1998	Dave Carr
Snapper (squirefish)	15.20 kg (33 lb 8 oz)	Outer Harbor, Australia	Sept. 22, 1997	Shaun Polley
Snapper, cubera	0.90 kg (2 lb)	Bobo's Lake, Andros Island, Bahamas	Feb. 24, 1998	Robert T. Cunningham, Jr.
Snapper, gray	2.60 kg (5 lb 12 oz)	Boca Paila, Quintana Roo, Yucatan, Mexico	July 17, 1998	Brian Katra
Snapper, mutton	3.79 kg (8 lb 6 oz)	Key West, Florida, USA	Apr. 27, 1998	Gerald K. Darkes
Snapper, Pacific cubera	2.26 kg (5 lb)	Tropic Star Lodge, Pinas Bay, Panama	Apr. 14, 1998	Scott Jacobson
Snook, common	14.51 kg (32 lb)	Indian River, Stuart, Florida, USA	May 28, 1998	Robert V. Krolak
Snook, fat	3.62 kg (8 lb)	Back Lagoon, Barra Colorado, Costa Rica	Jan. 11, 1998	Michael O'Harra
Stargazer, northern	2.29 kg (5 lb 1 oz)	Chesapeake Bay, Virginia, USA	Oct. 17, 1997	David A. Davis
Sunfish, redear	0.51 kg (1 lb 13 oz)	Western Branch, Richmond, Virginia, USA	June 3, 1998	Edward P. Decker
Swordfish	24.80 kg (54 lb 10 oz)	Watamu, Kenya	Apr. 5, 1998	Jeremy Block
Tarpon	41.78 kg (92 lb 2 oz)	Islamorada, Florida, USA	July 10, 1998	Jodi Pate
Tautog	4.53 kg (10 lb)	Tower Reef, Virginia Beach, Virginia, USA	Jan. 4, 1998	Ken Beach
Threadfin, king	6.88 kg (15 lb 2 oz)	Dampier, Australia	Dec. 30, 1997	Nicole Livingstone
Tigerfish	7.70 kg (16 lb 15 oz)	Tiger Camp, Zambezi River, Zambia	Aug. 26, 1997	Anderson Mazoka
Trevally, bigeye	4.90 kg (10 lb 12 oz)	Futami Bay, Chichijima, Ogasawara, Tokyo, Japan	Nov. 28, 1997	Masanori Miyagawa
Trevally, bluefin	1.85 kg (4 lb 1 oz)	Christmas Island, Republic of Kiribati	Mar. 11, 1998	Bud Korteweg
Trevally, giant	13.00 kg (28 lb 10 oz)	Groote Eylandt, Australia	Oct. 19, 1997	Robert Nichells
Trevally, golden	8.80 kg (19 lb 6 oz)	Exmouth, Australia	Aug. 17, 1997	John Ogg
Trevally, yellowspotted	11.00 kg (24 lb 4 oz)	Bazaruto Island, Mozambique	Nov. 29, 1997	Scott Saunders
Tripletail	8.05 kg (17 lb 12 oz)	Indian River, Ft. Pierce, Florida, USA	Aug. 27, 1997	Tony Ortega
Trout, brook	1.44 kg (3 lb 3 oz)	Pigg River, Virginia, USA	Mar. 25, 1998	Ricky Taylor
Trout, brown	12.70 kg (28 lb)	Rio Grande, Argentina	Mar. 13, 1998	William Van Dyke, III
Trout, lake	12.08 kg (26 lb 8 oz)	Lac La Martre, Canada	July 2, 1998	Gerald Chesin
Tuna, blackfin	14.51 kg (32 lb)	Miami, Florida, USA	June 7, 1998	Joseph G. Singer

SPECIES	WEIGHT	PLACE	DATE	ANGLER
Tuna, bluefin	20.41 kg (45 lb)	Jackspot, Ocean City, Maryland, USA	Aug. 18, 1997	Karen Gilbreath
Tuna, longtail	12.60 kg (27 lb 12 oz)	Moreton Bay, Queensland, Australia	Mar. 28, 1998	Steve Morgan
Tuna, skipjack	6.60 kg (14 lb 8 oz)	Puerto Rico, Gran Canaria, Spain	Aug. 23, 1997	Holger Damerius
Tuna, yellowfin	75.75 kg (167 lb)	Keauhou-Kona, Hawaii, USA	July 13, 1998	George Handgis
Tunny, little	5.89 kg (13 lb)	Key West, Florida, USA	July 13, 1998	Christine Perez
Wahoo	9.69 kg (21 lb 9 oz)	Destin, Florida, USA	Aug. 26, 1997	Melanie D. Mitchell
Walleye	4.30 kg (9 lb 8 oz)	Chatfield State Reservoir, Colorado, USA	June 4, 1998	Robert E. Hix
Weakfish	3.51 kg (7 lb 11 oz)	West Ocean City, Maryland, USA	May 25, 1998	Wanda S. Morgan
Whiting	1.95 kg (4 lb 5 oz)	Kraakvaag Fjord, Norway	July 24, 1998	Sandra Marquard
Yellowtail, Asian	21.20 kg (46 lb 11 oz)	Inanba, Tokyo, Japan	May 9, 1998	Hideki Urushibara
Yellowtail, California	5.95 kg (13 lb 1 oz)	San Clemente Island, California, USA	Aug. 17, 1997	Sandy Peck
Yellowtail, southern	25.20 kg (55 lb 8 oz)	Bay of Plenty, New Zealand	Jan. 21, 1998	Stephane Uzan

SPECIES	WEIGHT	PLACE	DATE	ANGLER
Amberjack, greater	0.90 kg (2 lb)	Midway Island	July 25, 1998	Sharon Handgis
Barracuda, great	14.62 kg (32 lb 4 oz)	Biscayne Bay, Miami Beach, Florida, USA	Dec. 28, 1997	Joey "Tomatoes" Posnick
Barramundi	2.54 kg (5 lb 9 oz)	Weipa, Australia	Nov. 21, 1997	Bruce Alderson
Bass, largemouth	6.86 kg (15 lb 1 oz)	Ikehara Reservoir, Nara, Japan	June 28, 1998	Kouichi Okano
Bass, rock	0.90 kg (2 lb)	Lake Erie, Pennsylvania, USA	June 18, 1998	Herbert G. Ratner, Jr.
Bass, smallmouth	3.27 kg (7 lb 3 oz)	Pickwick Lake, Florence, Alabama, USA	Jan. 17, 1998	E. Scott Yarbro, MD
Bass, striped	8.84 kg (19 lb 8 oz)	Misquamicit Beach, Rhode Island, USA	Aug. 6, 1997	Alan Caolo
Bass, white	1.62 kg (3 lb 9 oz)	Sabine River, Carthage, Texas, USA	Jan. 27, 1998	John Stephen Worthey
Bluefish	6.35 kg (14 lb)	Cape Cod Bay, Massachusetts, USA	July 19, 1998	Acha Lord
Bluegill	0.62 kg (1 lb 6 oz)	Steelwood Lake, Alabama, USA	Sept. 22, 1997	Robert T. Cunningham, Jr.
Bonefish	6.12 kg (13 lb 8 oz)	Chub Cay, Berry Islands, Bahamas	Aug. 24, 1997	Wayne M. Sandlin, Jr.
Bowfin	3.77 kg (8 lb 5 oz)	Buzz's Lake, Mount Vernon, Alabama, USA	July 12, 1998	Robert T. Cunningham, Jr.
Buffalo, bigmouth	4.08 kg (9 lb)	Rend Lake, Illinois, USA	Apr. 14, 1998	Rick Hayden
Bullhead, brown	0.63 kg (1 lb 6 oz)	Whitney Point Reservoir, New York, USA	Sept. 8, 1997	Sarah A. Basil
Carp, common	10.20 kg (22 lb 8 oz)	Lake Michigan, Indiana, USA	Oct. 12, 1997	Thomas Berg
Catfish, blue	31.07 kg (68 lb 5 oz)	Lake Texoma, Texas, USA	Jan. 15, 1998	Gene Kalnion
Catfish, flathead	23.58 kg (52 lb)	Rock Fish Creek, Fayetteville, North Carolina, USA	Mar. 27, 1998	Edward C. Davis
Cod, Pacific	8.61 kg (19 lb)	Dutch Harbor, Alaska, USA	June 23, 1998	Fariba Zand
Crappie, black	0.45 kg (1 lb)	Miacomet Pond, Nantucket, Massachusetts, USA	Mar. 11, 1998	Jenny Whitlock
Cusk	1.07 kg (2 lb 5 oz)	Kraakvaag Fjord, Norway	July 29, 1998	Sandra Marquard
Dentex	7.00 kg (15 lb 6 oz)	Isle of Lanzarote, Italy	Nov. 6, 1997	Nicola Vallani
Dolly Varden	5.10 kg (11 lb 4 oz)	Kelly River, Alaska, USA	July 11, 1998	Jim Seegraves
Dolphinfish	33.79 kg (74 lb 8 oz)	Port Canaveral, Florida, USA	Sept. 21, 1997	James Zaloga
Drum, black	29.93 kg (66 lb)	New Smyrna Beach, Florida, USA	Mar. 29, 1998	Raleigh Werking
Drum, red	14.74 kg (32 lb)	Grand Gosier Island, Louisiana, USA	Mar. 14, 1998	Rudolph A. Hall
Flounder, summer	1.08 kg (2 lb 6 oz)	Montauk, New York, USA	June 20, 1998	William Kuhle
Gar, longnose	0.85 kg (1 lb 14 oz)	St. Francis River, Missouri, USA	June 12, 1998	Bill Willmert
Gar, spotted	1.98 kg (4 lb 6 oz)	Mayfield Creek, Bardwell, Kentucky, USA	May 21, 1998	Bob Beard
Grouper, yellowedge	8.90 kg (19 lb 10 oz)	Galveston, Texas, USA	Mar. 3, 1998	Stanley W. Sweet
Halibut, California	6.25 kg (13 lb 12 oz)	Macklyn Cove, Brookings, Oregon, USA	July 3, 1998	Michael Cowley
Halibut, Pacific	33.56 kg (74 lb)	Kodiak, Alaska, USA	Aug. 1, 1997	Paul Leader
Jack, crevalle	7.71 kg (17 lb)	Islamorada, Florida, USA	May 13, 1998	Amy K. Knowles
Jack, horse-eye	6.61 kg (19 lb)	West End Grand Bahama, Bahamas	July 18, 1998	Steven A. Davis
Jack, Pacific crevalle	8.30 kg (18 lb 5 oz)	Puerto Vallarta, Jalisco, Mexico	Mar. 15, 1998	Irene McDonald Johnson
Kahawai	3.15 kg (6 lb 15 oz)	Ceduna, Australia	Sept. 25, 1997	John Marsh
Leerfish (Garrick)	13.00 kg (28 lb 10 oz)	Jeffrey's Bay, South Africa	May 1, 1998	Trevor Hansen
Lingcod	21.77 kg (48 lb)	East Chugach, Alaska, USA	July 13, 1998	Stephen P. Cushman
Mackerel, king	2.72 kg (6 lb)	Miami, Florida, USA	Jan. 1, 1998	Pamela W. Marmin
Mackerel, Spanish	1.81 kg (4 lb)	Marathon, Florida, USA	Feb. 12, 1998	Jamie Callion
Marlin, black	56.00 kg (123 lb 7 oz)	Port Stephens, Australia	Mar. 19, 1998	Fouad Sahiaoui
Marlin, blue (Atlantic)	375.12 kg (827 lb)	Ada Foah, Ghana, West Africa	July 5, 1998	Johan Zietsman
Marlin, blue (Pacific)	242.80 kg (535 lb 4 oz)	Tauranga, New Zealand	Feb. 7, 1998	Lindsay Stowe
Marlin, striped	110.62 kg (244 lb)	San Diego, California, USA	Aug. 23, 1997	Ray Lussa
Marlin, white	37.98 kg (83 lb 12 oz)	Mohmmabia, Morocco	Oct. 25, 1997	Fouad Sahiaoui
Matrincha	2.86 kg (6 lb 2 oz)	Rio Arinos, Brazil	Sept. 2, 1997	Frederico Rodreigues Montefeltro
Payara	4.70 kg (10 lb 4 oz)	Orinoco River, Puerto Ayacucho, Venezuela	Jan. 13, 1998	Eric R. Ostmark
Peacock, blackstriped	1.13 kg (2 lb 8 oz)	Rio Cinaruco, Venezuela	Mar. 11, 1998	Norman Earl Bean
Peacock, butterfly	2.49 kg (5 lb 8 oz)	Miami, Florida, USA	Mar. 4, 1998	Herbert G. Ratner, Jr.
Peacock, speckled	8.84 kg (19 lb 8 oz)	Rio Pasamoni, Amazonas, Venezuela	Feb. 17,1998	Steven "Zato" Yatomi
Perch, Nile	60.00 kg (132 lb 4 oz)	Nghode Island, Lake Victoria, Kenya	May 1, 1998	Dave Huckle
Perch, white	0.67 kg (1 lb 7 oz)	Pawcatuck River, Rhode Island, USA	May 6, 1998	Alan Caolo
Permit	11.79 kg (26 lb)	Islamorada, Florida, USA	May 13, 1998	Amy K. Knowles
Pickerel, chain	0.62 kg (1 lb 6 oz)	Miacomet Pond, Nantucket, Massachusetts, USA	Mar. 11, 1998	Jenny Whitlock
Queenfish	9.00 kg (19 lb 13 oz)	Salt Creek, Groote Eylandt, Australia	May 26, 1998	Michael Ward-Grodd
Sailfish, Atlantic	21.45 kg (47 lb 4 oz)	Puerto Aventuras, Mexico	May 11, 1998	Wendy Don
Sailfish, Pacific	37.81 kg (83 lb 8 oz)	Carrillo, Costa Rica	Jan. 10, 1998	Wendy Don
Salmon, chinook	12.24 kg (27 lb)	Nak Nek River, Bristol Bay, Alaska, USA	July 13, 1998	Felix Henrique Lairet

SPECIES	WEIGHT	PLACE	DATE	ANGLER
Sauger	1.36 kg (3 lb)	Pittsburgh, Pennsylvania, USA	Dec. 7, 1997	Herbert G. Ratner, Jr.
Seabass, blackfin	6.80 kg (14 lb 15 oz)	Shionomisaki, Kushimoto, Wakayama, Japan	Apr. 25, 1998	Shizuka Ueji
Seabass, Japanese	5.25 kg (11 lb 9 oz)	Oita River, Oita, Japan	Jan. 1, 1998	Tomoaki Kutsukake
Seatrout, spotted	3.02 kg (6 lb 10 oz)	Vero Beach, Florida, USA	Feb. 14, 1998	Marten Madsen Poppell
Shark, blue	31.20 kg (68 lb 12 oz)	North Reef, New Zealand	Feb. 8, 1998	Dianne Sands
Shark, hammerhead	3.74 kg (8 lb 4 oz)	Key West, Florida, USA	Jan. 18, 1998	Bennett Stern
Shark, mako	82.00 kg (180 lb 12 oz)	Whitianga, Mercury Bay, New Zealand	Feb. 22, 1998	Darcy John Stannard
Shark, oceanic whitetip	94.12 kg (207 lb 8 oz)	San Salvador, Bahamas	Jan. 10, 1998	Gary A. Carter
Snapper (squirefish)	15.00 kg (33 lb 1 oz)	Outer Harbour, Port Adelaide, Australia	Sept. 22, 1997	Roger John Harrison, N.F.C.
Snapper, mutton	3.51 kg (7 lb 12 oz)	Spanish Key, Abaco, Bahamas	Aug. 2, 1997	Robert Helmick
Snook, common	7.03 kg (15 lb 8 oz)	Chockoloskee, Florida, USA	July 1, 1998	Andy G. Novak
Sunfish, redear	0.53 kg (1 lb 2 oz)	Steelwood Lake, Alabama, USA	Sept. 14, 1997	Robert T. Cunningham, Jr.
Tarpon	37.64 kg (83 lb)	Islamorada, Florida, USA	June 15, 1998	Diana Owen Harris
Threadfin, king	6.00 kg (13 lb 3 oz)	Walker River, Australia	Mar. 25, 1998	Gregory Paul De Koning
Tigerfish	7.41 kg (16 lb 5 oz)	Charara, Kariba, Zimbabwe	Aug. 30, 1997	Stephen G. Mullett
Trevally, giant	4.71 kg (10 lb 6 oz)	Christmas Island, Republic of Kiribati	Mar. 17, 1998	Bud Korteweg
Trevally, golden	1.58 kg (3 lb 8 oz)	Playa Zancudo, Costa Rica	Dec. 14, 1997	Craig Whitehead, MD
Tripletail	5.75 kg (12 lb 10 oz)	Naples, Florida, USA	Sept. 15, 1997	Erik J. Madison, DVM
Trout, brown	8.84 kg (19 lb 8 oz)	Rio Grande, Tierra Del Fuego, Argentina	Feb. 10, 1998	Richard L. Vainer
Tuna, blackfin	13.78 kg (30 lb 6 oz)	Boca Raton, Florida, USA	Apr. 28, 1998	Lynne W. Mitchem
Tuna, bluefin	12.92 kg (28 lb 8 oz)	Indian River, Delaware, USA	Aug. 7, 1997	Rich Winnor
Tuna, longtail	10.00 kg (22 lb)	Mooloolaba, Queensland, Australia	Apr. 22, 1998	Camile Sigler, Jr.
Tuna, yellowfin	6.80 kg (15 lb)	Pinas Bay, Panama	May 11, 1998	Peter Woolley
Tunny, little	5.85 kg (12 lb 14 oz)	Key West, Florida, USA	Apr. 19, 1998	Bunny Eickelbeck
Weakfish	2.26 kg (5 lb)	Staten Island, New York, USA	May 17, 1998	Vincent L. Trapani
Yellowtail, Asian	20.40 kg (44 lb 15 oz)	Chichijima, Ogasawara, Tokyo, Japan	Jan. 31, 1998	Toshihiro Yokoshima
Yellowtail, southern	24.80 kg (54 lb 10 oz)	Cavalli Island, Bay of Islands, New Zealand	Aug. 6, 1998	Karene Cates-

IGFA's Member Discount Program

AUSTRALIA

Calypso Star Charter, Attn: Capt. Rolf Czabayski, (South Australia, Port Lincoln), Fully equipped custom 35-ft. Bertram *Calypso Star* specializing in fishing for great white shark and Southern bluefin tuna out of Lincoln Cove Resort Marina in Port Lincoln. Day, live aboard and fly fishing charters available. Tag and release practiced. If fish is a potential world record, capture allowed. (61) 08-8364-4428, mobile (61) 0418-817404, Fax (61) 08-8332-6360

The Cosmopolitan, (Surfers Paradise, Queensland), Comfortable Outrigger Hotel and Resort located in the heart of Surfers Paradise, a short stroll to the beach. Surrounded by shops, restaurants and nightlife. Two swimming pools, spas, sauna, business center and barbecue/picnic areas. Comfortable one bedroom suites with full kitchens. Please note reservations must be made in advance. 1-800-OUTRIGGER (688-7444) or (303) 369-7777, Website: www.outrigger.com

Fishing The Tropics, Attn: Les Marsh, owner, (Tropical North Queensland, Cairns), Guided calm water fishing on majestic world heritage listed rainforest rivers. Custom built sportfishing punts ideal for lure/fly fishing for Australia's premier light tackle sportfish including barramundi, trevally, mangrove jack, jungle perch. All top quality tackle, transfers to/from accommodation in late model 4WD, all inclusive. (61) 0740-342668, Fax: (61) 0740-578280 E-mail: fishtrop@ozemail.com.au Website: www.ozemail.com.au/~fishtrop/index.html

Hyperspace Sportfishing Tours, Attn: Capt. Steve or Michelle Jeston, (Townsville, Queensland), Sportfishing charters to tropical northern Australia with professional guide, Steve Jeston. Fly and conventional tackle fishing for barramundi and permit to marlin. Phone & fax (61) 747 25 5258

Jan Lee Charters, Attn: Capt. Chris Jones, (North Queensland -Cape Bowling Green/Cairns/Lizard Islands), Fully equipped custom 53-ft. sportfisher *Jan Lee* specializing in marlin fishing with heavy or light tackle. Day and live aboard charters available. Tag and release encouraged. (61) 77-735029, Fax (61) 77-735818

K.C.'s Custom Fishing Tackle, Attn: Kevin Carpenter, (Manly, Brisbane), Offering a large range of fishing equipment, baits, lures, hooks, custom rods, reel service, sport/game/fly tackle, fishing charters, etc. Located Shop 4 Manly Marine Centre, opposite public wharf Manly Harbour. (61)7-3348-6888, Fax (61)7-3348-6310

Paradise Centre, (Surfers Paradise, Queensland), Deluxe Outrigger Hotel and Resort offering a spectacular beachfront location with two acres of lawn and garden areas. Comfortable one, two and three bedroom suites with full kitchens. Two outdoor pools, spas, tennis courts, putting greens, business center and barbecue/picnic areas. Paradise Centre Shopping Complex offers more than 110 specialty shops, cafes and restaurants. Please note reservations must be made in advance. 1-800-OUTRIGGER (688-7444) or (303) 369-7777, Website: www.outrigger.com

Peninsula, (Surfers Paradise, Queensland), Deluxe Outrigger Hotel and Resort offering a beachfront location near shopping, dining and nightlife. Comfortable one, two and three bedroom suites with full kitchens featuring spectacular ocean and mountain views. Two outdoor pools, one indoor pool, spas, tennis and squash courts, restaurants, business center and barbecue/picnic areas. Please note reservations must be made in advance. 1-800-OUTRIGGER (688-7444) or (303) 369-7777, Website: www.outrigger.com

Sun City Resort, (Surfers Paradise, Queensland), Deluxe Outrigger Hotel and Resort centrally located featuring panoramic view of the Pacific Ocean and the Gold Coast. Seawater swimming lagoon, sheltered white sand beach, spa and heated pool, water slides, theme restaurants, exotic fish ponds, sauna and steam rooms, tennis courts, business center, fitness center, and a host of other guest amenities. Spacious one, two and three bedroom luxury suites with fully equipped kitchens. Please note reservations must be made in advance. 1-800-OUTRIGGER (688-7444) or (303) 369-7777, Website: www.outrigger.com

AUSTRIA

Hotel-Gasthof Braurup & Braurup Fishery, Attn: Matthias Gassner, (Mittersill, Salzburger Land), Comfortable 4-Star Hotel with bed & breakfast or half-board. Hotel amenities include sauna, steam bath, restaurant, pub, Bier-Garden, lift and the largest, private fishery in Austria consisting of 130 km of rivers and 8 lakes where you can fly fish or spin fish for brown, brook and rainbow trout amid breathtaking scenery. On the premises is also a full tackle shop for the purchase or rental of any or all tackle or equipment needed. (43) 6562-6216, Fax (43) 6562-6216-502, Webpage: http://www.hotelnet.co.uk/hotelnet/austria/braurup E-mail: braurup@ping.at

BAHAMAS

The ABC Boat Company Inc., Attn: Phil "Boot" LeBoutillier, (Abaco), *Bugs* a fully equipped 1995 23-ft. Parker Marine, deep vee, walk around sportfishing boat with 225 h.p. Johnson outboard located at Hope Town, Abaco, Bahamas. Available for bareboat charter. Office in Aspen, Colorado-Phone & Fax (970) 925-9236

The Bonefish School, Attn: Jake Jordan, (Exuma), Fly fishing instruction by renown flyfishing anglers held at Peace and Plenty Beach Inn in George Town, Exuma. Registration includes 7 nights lodging with meals, classroom instruction and 4 days guided fishing. Office in Marathon, Florida-(305) 743-0501, Fax (305) 743-5007

Emerald Palms By-The-Sea, Attn: Brenda A. Barry, (South Andros), Comfortable full-service mini-suite beachfront resort, amenities include swimming pool, tennis court and glass bottom sailboats. (242) 369-2661, Fax (242) 369-2667

Exuma Expeditions, c/o Micronesia Adventures, Attn: Steve Currey, (Exuma), Agency specializing in bonefishing and fly fishing trips to Exuma. Office in Utah-800-937-7238, Fax (801) 224-5715

Fortune Hills Golf & Country Club, Attn: Walter B. Kitchen, (Freeport), Discount on greens fees for 9-hole golf course. (242) 373-2222 or 373-4500, Fax (242) 373-5090

Great Abaco Beach Hotel, Attn: Terry Curry or Kevie Thomas, (Marsh Harbour, Abaco), Full-service beachfront resort with marina and tennis courts. (242) 367-2736 or 800-468-4799, Fax (242) 367-2819

Green Turtle Club and Marina, Attn: Reservations, (Green Turtle Cay, Abaco), Full-service beachfront resort. (242) 365-4271, Fax (242) 365-4272

Sea Spray Resort & Marina, Attn: Monty Albury, (Elbow Cay, Abaco), Comfortable, full service resort with 24-slip full service marina featuring air conditioned one and two bedroom villas, freshwater pool, restaurant, Calcutta baits, guides and 20-22 ft. boat rentals available for offshore, flats and reef fishing. (242) 366-0065, Fax (242) 366-0383

Treasure Cay Resort Hotel & Marina, Attn: Mike Sawyer, Marina Manager, (Treasure Cay, Abaco), Beautiful full service luxury resort located on white powdery beaches, discount also offered for dockage at full service marina. (242) 365-8250, Fax (242) 365-8847 or office in Ft. Lauderdale, Florida - (954) 525-7711 or 800-327-1584, Fax (954) 525-1699

VIP Charters Ltd, Attn: Walter B. Kitchen, (Freeport), Fully equipped custom 50-ft. sportfisher *Sandpiper* and 53-ft. Hatteras *Ono Chase* specializing in marlin and wahoo fishing. Can accommodate up to six. (242) 373-2222, Fax (242) 373-5090

Walker's Cay Hotel & Marina, Attn: Joanne Robinson, (Walker's Cay), Comfortable full-service hotel and marina. Office in Ft. Lauderdale, Florida-800-432-2092, Fax (954) 359-1414

BARBADOS, WEST INDIES

Blue Marlin Charters Inc., Attn: Lisa, (Christ Church), Fishing for blue marlin, sailfish, tuna, wahoo, dolphin and barracuda aboard either fully equipped 36-ft. custom built *Blue Marlin* or 42-ft. Post *Idyll Time*. Charters include transportation, all bait, tackle, rum punch, soft drinks, beer, sandwiches and hot lunch on full day charters. Coastal island tours and corporate cruises also available. (246) 436-4322, 435-6669, Fax (246) 435-6655, E-mail: bluemrln@caribsurf.com Website: http://www.world-traveler.com/barbados/bluemarl.html

BELIZE

Belize Travel Advisors USA, Attn: Norris Cravey, Discounts offered at Belize's Ramada Royal Reef Hotel plus fishing charters. Office in Texas-800-383-0819, Fax (281)422-5167

Captain Morgan's Retreat, Attn: Jack Chivers, (Ambergris Caye), Beachfront resort located on Ambergris Caye. Office in Minnesota- 800-447-2931, Fax (218) 847-0334

M/V Hot Dive Charters, Attn: Capt. Chris Berg, (Belize City), 60-ft. Ocean Yacht plus skiffs available for day or live-aboard deep sea sportfishing, light tackle flats fishing and cruising packages, destinations include Guatemala and offshore reefs. Phone & Fax (501) 2-34058

BERMUDA

Albatross Fisheries, Attn: Capt. James P. Olander or Virginia Olander, (St. Davids), Single and multiple day charters aboard fully equipped custom 38-ft. Striker Canyon Runner *Albatross IV* specializing in marlin fishing. (441) 297-0715, Fax (441) 297-2007

BRAZIL

Amazon Fishing Safaris, Attn: Gwendaline Bich, (Amazon), Live aboard *The Pearl of the Nhamunda*, a 90-ft. motoryacht accommodating 16 people in air conditioned cabins or suites with all meals and transfers from Manaus to the ship included for peacock bass fishing on the Rio Negro, Rio Solimones and Rio Branco. Anglers fish two per 15-ft. aluminum canoe with 15 h.p. outboard and guide which gives access to some waters otherwise inaccessible. Excursions available for non-fishing partners. Office in St Cyr au Mont D'Or France Phone & fax (33) 4-72-178950, E-mail: amazonfishingsafaris@wanadoo.fr

Marlin Charters, Attn: Flavio Mesquita, (Porto Seguro), Charter fleet of fully equipped sportfishermen out of Porto Seguro specializing in marlin fishing. Discount offered on accommodations as well as charters. Office in Rio de Janiero-Phone & Fax (55) 21-493-4784

Capt. Mauricio Paixao, (Rio de Janeiro), Fully equipped Rampage 28 accommodating up to 4 passengers, charters include fresh bait, lunch, snacks and beverages. Specializing in billfishing November to February. (55) 21-275-5420, Fax (55) 21-275-6958

Capt. Luiz Guilherme Queiroz, Dolphin Pesca, (Vitoria), Specializing in fishing for white and blue marlin peak season November through February. (55) 27-227-0128, E-mail: dolphin@gol.com.br

CANADA

Bear's Den Lodge, Attn: Brenda Barefoot, (Alban, Ontario), Comfortable lodging offering discounts on American Plan and Packages of 3 days or more plus boat/motor rentals. Internationally famous fishing camp conveniently located in the Delta with access to the French, Pickerel and Wanapitei Rivers and northeast Georgian Bay. Fishing for trophy walleye, pike, bass, and crappie with musky being their specialty. May-November (705) 857-2757, November-April (814) 839-2443

The Blackwater Company, Attn: Ron Thompson, (British Columbia), Specializing in wilderness dry fly fishing adventures. Discounts offered on available space only. (604) 392-5081, Fax (604) 392-1143

Bonnie Lee Charters, Attn: Capt. Gerry Freeman, (Granville Island, Vancouver), Fully equipped 22-ft. & 28-ft. boats specializing in salmon fishing in British Columbia. (250) 290-7447

Buck's Trophy Lodge, Attn: Shelly Lawrence, (Rivers Inlet, British Columbia), Complete fishing packages available at classic, comfortable, fly-in floating lodge accommodating up to 20 and featuring cabins with private bathrooms and showers. Excellent salmon fishing aboard fully equipped, 16-ft. fiberglass boats with 40 h.p. outboard motors and tackle provided. (604) 859-9779, Fax (604) 859-1661

Campbell River Lodge & Fishing Resort, Attn: Brian Clarkson, (Campbell River, British Columbia), Comfortable intimate fishing lodge with all-inclusive packages available specializing in salmon and steelhead fishing. (250) 287-7446 or 800-663-7212, Fax (250) 287-4063, E-Mail: crlodge@oberon.ark.com Website: http:www.vquest.com/crlodge

Campbell River Sportfishing Rentals, Inc., Attn: Jason Arbour, (Campbell River, British Columbia), Complete sportfishing packages available. (250) 287-7279, Fax (250) 287-4063

Cooper's Minipi Camps, Attn: Jack Cooper, (Happy Valley, Labrador), Lodges located at the headwaters of the Minipi River System and reached by helicopter or float plane from Goose Bay. (709) 896-2891, Fax (709) 896-9619

Eagle Pointe Lodge, Attn: Pete Ruaro, (Prince Rupert, British Columbia), Comfortable 12-guest lodge and cabin accommodations located on British Columbia's north coast bordering Alaska. Well equipped, fully guided 21-ft. cabin cruisers available for halibut and salmon fishing. Lodge is open June thru September and features gourmet dining. 800-726-5810 or May - September (604) 624-0825, October - April Phone & Fax (206) 241-6291 (office in Seattle, Washington)

Elk Island Lodge, Ltd., Attn: Kurt R. Krueger, (Gods Lake, Manitoba), Comfortable fly-in lodge located on Gods Lake, Manitoba featuring main lodge and modern guest cabins. Fly or spin fishing for northern pike, lake trout and walleye on Gods Lake and brook trout and whitefish on Gods River. Office in Wisconsin-(715) 445-3845, Fax (715) 445-4100

Enodah Wilderness Travel, Attn: Ragnar Wesstrom, (Yellowknife, Northwest Territories), Specializes in trophy pike fishing on Great Slave Lake. Also offers the "Great Slave Lake Grand Slam Fishing Jackpot" 8-day package. Two different lodges for lake trout, Arctic grayling and northern pike. Phone & Fax (867) 873-4334

Frank's Holiday Resort, Attn: Wanda O'Neill, (Chelmsford, New Brunswick), Located in eastern New Brunswick, directly on the Miramichi River, one of the best salmon fishing rivers in North America. The resort offers a comfortable, quiet setting, with year-round accommodations in well-outfitted log cabin style houses. Brochures available. (506) 622-7057, Fax (506) 622-0570

Haggard Cove Resort, Attn: Ron Clark, (Port Alberni-Barkley Sound, British Columbia), Comfortable lodge, all-inclusive plans and guided fishing in 24-ft. & 28-ft.

cabin cruisers specializing in salmon fishing. (604) 723-8457, Fax (604) 723-5657

High Arctic Adventures, Attn: Joe Stefanski, (Northern Arctic, Quebec), Fly-out fishing available in Quebec's Northern Arctic at Diana Lake Lodge or Lake Ternay Lodge specializing in salmon, trout and Arctic char. 1-800-662-6404 or office in New Hampshire-(603) 532-6607, Fax (603) 532-6404

Kluane Wilderness Lodge, Attn: Howard Miller, (Yukon Territory), Located 200 air miles northwest of Whitehorse on Wellesley Lake, this secluded mountain lodge is accessible only by float plane. Modern, spacious lodge accommodates 18 guests and offers all the comforts of home. Each cabin is equipped with beds, showers and bathroom facilities. Lake trout, northern pike and lake whitefish are abundant. For over 12 years they have operated on a catch and release policy to enhance the fish population. Fly fishing is popular as there are spawning shoals 4 to 5 miles in length where hip waders can be used or commercial boats are provided equipped with padded swivel seats, 15 h.p. motors and fish finders. Discount offered June 1 to September 1. Office in Kamloops, British Columbia (250) 828-1161, Fax (250) 828-1990

L'Auberge du Saumonier, Attn: Elie Elmaleh, (Gaspe, Quebec), Small intimate lodge located by the Bay of Gaspe where Dartmouth and York Rivers meet specializing in salmon fishing by wading. Classic Atlantic salmon flies & fish boxes available at lodge. (418) 368-2172

Liard Tours Ltd., Attn: Marianne or Urs Schildknecht, (Northern British Columbia), Fully-guided fishing packages at beautiful Highland Glen Lodge on Muncho Lake. (604) 776-3481 or 800-663-5269, Fax (604) 776-3482

Margaree River Fly Fishing Specialists, Attn: Edwin Taylor, (Nova Scotia), Daily guiding and complete packages available for fishing Margaree River, specializes in Atlantic salmon and trout fishing. (902) 248-2316

Minor Bay Camps, Attn: Gerald Howard, (Minton, Saskatchewan), Full American Plan Packages at full-service camp with comfortable log cabins on Minor Bay, available float plane based at camp. Winter-(306) 969-4711, Fax (306) 969-4712, Summer phone & fax (306) 633-4900

Rainbow Cottages Resort & Marina, Attn: Heather & Tony Kenny, (Bailieboro, Ontario), Family fishing resort with comfortable cottages on Otonabee River/Rice Lake, boats available, specializing in bass, walleye, bluegill, crappie, perch & musky fishing. Phone & Fax (705) 939-6995

Silver Water Wheel Lodge, Attn: James & Lynne Wood, (Ontario), Located on the center of Lac Seul, 500 sq. miles of Canadian wilderness fishing at your doorstep. Comfortable, full service, American plan fishing lodge with spacious guest cabins including full bathrooms, fireplaces and refreshment fridges. Fishing from 18-ft. Lund Pro V, 21-ft. Lund Baron or hand-made cedar boats. 1-800-567-8538 or winter-(807) 937-5315, summer-(807) 529-3373 or visit their at http://www.sww-lodge.com

The Water Boatman Ltd., Attn: Mike & Lyse Guinn, (Calgary, Alberta), Comfortable McKenzie drift boat specializing in flyfishing for rainbows and large brown trout on Bow and Crowsnest Rivers and other Alberta streams and lakes. (403) 271-0799, Fax (403) 278-5934

Wolverine Lodge, Attn: Fred or Renee Bettschen, (Manitoba), American Plan at comfortable fishing lodge located in northwest Lynn Lake, Manitoba, specializing in northern pike, walleye and trout fishing. Office in California-(760) 770-0810

CANARY ISLANDS

Golden Marlin S.L. - M/Y Dotsy Too, Attn: Guido L. Establet, (Tenerife), Fully equipped Bertram 46.6 SF *Dotsy Too* out of Puerto Colon featuring Penn International rods and reels from 30 to 130 lb test, including stand up fishing. Full and half-day trips include tackle, bait, lures, food, soft drinks, qualified crew, and fuel. Species available include blue & white marlin; bluefin, bigeye & yellowfin tuna; wahoo; dorado; and assorted sharks. Tag and release encouraged. Phone (34) 22-79-16-11 Ext. 410 or (34) 22-71-46-35, Fax (34) 22-79-66-35, Website: http://www.dotsytoo.com

CAYMAN ISLANDS

Bayside Watersports, Attn: Geri Ebanks, (Grand Cayman), Discounts on deep sea fishing, tarpon & bonefishing and bottom reef fishing aboard fully equipped sportfishermen. (345) 949-3200 or (345) 949-1750, Fax (345) 949-3700

CHILE

Salmo-Patagonia-Lodge, Attn: Luis Antunez, (Coyhaique), Comfortable lodge featuring large rooms with private baths, open bar, Chilean and international cuisine plus full service fly shop. Excellent fly fishing for trout and salmon with catch and release strictly enforced. Jet boats, drift boats, float tubes and cruiser boats available for stream and lake fishing with English-speaking guides. Central office in Madrid, Spain c/o El Solitario S.L.: 34-1-5930536 or 5930672, Fax: 34-1-5944168 or 5941109

COOK ISLANDS

The Rarotongan Resort Hotel, (Rarotonga), Deluxe Outrigger beachfront resort featuring swimming pool, restaurants, lounge, white sandy beaches and picturesque tropical gardens. Please note that reservations must be made in advance. 1-800-OUTRIGGER (688-7444) or (303) 369-7777, Website: www.outrigger.com

COSTA RICA

Angelo's Fishing Team, Attn: Angelo or Piero Zeffiro, (Playas del Coco, Guanacaste), Fully equipped sportfishing boats located on Pacific Coast. (Associated with Hotel La Flor de Itabo). (506) 6700011, Fax (506) 6700003

Blue Wing International, Attn: Dr. Alfredo Lopez, (East Coast River & Lake System), Luxurious 65-ft. mothership *Rain Goddess* accommodates from 6 to 12 fishermen offering fishing & nature tours in the jungles of Costa Rica's east coast. Amenities include sink & vanity in each of the 6 staterooms, 3 bathrooms with showers, fully carpeted, air-conditioned, gourmet meals, self-serve bar, cellular phone, and television with VHS video player. Fully equipped 16-ft. jon boats and powerful 20-ft. boats for fishing rivers, backwaters & river mouths, specializing in tarpon & snook. 5 & 7 day packages include arrival night at 1st class hotel in San Jose, ground transfers, round-trip flight into the area, gourmet meals, permits & licenses and open bar. (506) 231-4299, Fax (506) 231-3816 Internet: bluewing@sol.racsa.co.cr http://www.magi.com/crica/tours/bluewing.html

Costa Rican Dreams, Attn: Cathy Corry, (Quepos), Fully equipped charter fleet including 32-ft. Blackfin *Bobcat* specializing in light tackle and fly fishing for billfish. Tag and release encouraged. (506) 239-3387, Fax (506) 239-3383

El Ocotal Beach Resort, Attn: Rick Wallace, (Playa del Coco, Guanacaste), Comfortable full-service resort with fully equipped fishing fleet. Discount valid September 15 thru December 15. (506) 670-0321, Fax (506) 670-0083

Flamingo Bay Pacific Charters, Attn: Paul Hirschman, (Flamingo Bay & Quepos), Fully equipped sportfishing fleet providing the finest tackle, specializing in marlin, sailfish, wahoo, dorado and tuna fishing. Complete fishing packages available including comfortable accommodations. Office in Florida - Phone & Fax (954) 584-2184. Office in Costa Rica - 800-878-0728

Golfito Sportfishing, Attn: Bob Baker, (Golfito), Custom fully equipped 25-ft. & 23-ft. center consoles offering both offshore and inshore trips. Comfortable accommodations at Playa Zancudo in park-like setting available as well as complete fishing packages. Phone & Fax (506) 382-2716

HOOKER-ON-CALL Sportfishing Charters, Attn: Jens Klaus, (Golfito), Sportfishing aboard the fully equipped 38-ft Eclipse *Perfect Hooker*, a 1994 twin diesel sportfishing with air-conditioned salon. Top-of-the-line tackle for light to heavy and fly fishing include Shimano, Penn and Fin-Nor reels with custom-built rods, more than 200 rigged lures, 8 tuna tubes, 2 removable 50 gallon live bait wells and assorted gaffs. Strict tag & release policy for all billfish other than world records or 20-to-1 catches. Phone & fax: (506) 775 02 25, E-mail: landsea@sol.racsa.co.cr

Hotel La Flor de Itabo, Attn: Piero Zeffiro or Angelo, (Playas del Coco, Guanacaste), Comfortable hotel and vacation resort near the beach on Pacific Coast, (Associated with Angelo's Fishing Team). (506) 670-0011, Fax (506) 670-0003

Palmas Pacifica Sportfishing, Attn: Capt. Randy Rode, Fishing aboard fully equipped 25-ft. *Rode Runner* available January, February and March. Office in Marathon, Florida (305) 743-3424, Fax (305) 743-7186

Papagayo Excursions, Attn: Mary P. Ruth, (Guanacaste), Fleet of fully equipped 31-ft. sportfishing boats. Phone & fax (506) 654-4254

Rio Parismina Lodge, c/o Adventure Marketing, Inc.- Attn: Martha Fields, (Caribbean coast) Discount offered on total package which includes 2 nights in San Jose at first-class hotel; transfers; luxury accommodations, gourmet meals and all beverages at lodge as well as tarpon, snook and offshore fishing with English-speaking guides on fully equipped, state-of-the-art 21-ft modified V-hull ocean craft or 16-ft jon-boats for river fishing. First class resort lodge built on 50 private acres of lush jungle on the banks of the Parismina River with pool and jacuzzi. Office in Tampa, Florida - (800) 824-1255 or (813) 889-0662, Fax (813) 889-9189

Rio Sierpe Lodge, Attn: Michael Stiles, (Osa Peninsula-Pacific Coast), Comfortable full-service fishing lodge with fleet of fully-equipped sportfishing boats, including the 46-ft. *Michelle II.* Deep sea and river/estuary fishing available. (506) 284-5595, Fax (506) 786-6291

Roy's Zancudo Lodge, c/o Adventure Marketing, Inc. - Attn: Martha Fields, (Pacific Coast, Golfito), Discount offered on total package which includes a night's stay in San Jose at first-class hotel; transfers; lodging, meals and all beverages at lodge as well as guided fishing in new 24 & 25-ft center console boats for marlin, sailfish, roosterfish, snapper, snook and many other exotic species. Popular beachfront lodge recently opened to the public featuring four cabin suites with wet bar, refrigerator, and sitting room as well as private rooms. All have private baths. Office in Tampa, Florida -(800) 824-1255 or (813) 889-0662, Fax (813) 889-9189

Sportfishing Dominical S.A., Attn: Capt. Bill Aikens, Fully equipped custom 26-ft. sportfishing boats specializing in sailfish, marlin, tuna and wahoo at Quepos, Flamingo and Drake Bay/Cano Island. Complete fishing packages available. Office in Delaware - Phone & Fax (302) 684-0310

Tango Mar Beach Resort & Country Club, Attn: Tom R. Tucker and Jeannette Campos, (Golfo de Nicoyo), Full-service

beach resort with discounts also offered on fishing tours. (506) 443-2600, Fax (506) 443-2800

Tikal Tour Operators - Costa Rica, Attn: Renata Villers, Hotel accommodations and select fishing packages throughout Costa Rica. Office in Florida - (305) 599-8828, In Costa Rica - (506) 223-2811, Fax (506) 223-1916

FRENCH GUIANA

Society SOTHIS, Attn: Madam Madeleine Calcagni, (Ile Royale), Accommodations at The Inn on Royale Island, a comfortable bungalow hotel. Fishing aboard fully equipped fishing boats accommodating up to 4 anglers. Office in Kourou-(594) 32-11-00, Fax (594) 32-42-23

GRENADA

True Blue Inn, Attn: Gillian Potter, (St. George's), Full-service, comfortable beachfront resort. (473) 444-2000, Fax (473) 444-1247

INDONESIA

Manado Beach Hotel, Attn: Reservations, (North Sulawesi), Beautifully landscaped 4-star, full-service beachfront resort on Tasik Ria Beach. Features fitness center, 2 swimming pools, tennis courts and more. American breakfast included. (62) 0431-67001, Fax (62) 0431-67007

Moale Holidays-Medan (Sorake Beach Resort and Lantana Inn), Attn: Samsul Hadi, (Medan, North Sumatra). Complete fishing tours, water sports and charters available. 15-ft. & 12-ft. sportfishermen with 115 h.p. and 85 h.p. engines. Sorake Beach Resort on Nias Island is full service resort with tennis court, swimming pool and game center. (62) 61-811993, Fax (62) 61-811994

IRELAND

Ghillie Cottage & Blackwater Fly Fishing, Attn: Doug Lock, R.E.F.F.I.S. Salmon Fly Fishing Instructor Guide and Joy Arnold, ex England Ladies Fly Fishing Team, (County Cork) One of the Great Fishing Houses of Ireland, specializing in tuition in spey casting using 15 ft Aquarex double handed fly rods and fly fishing for Atlantic Salmon on Munster Blackwater River in Co. Cork. (353) 25-32720, Fax: (353) 25-33000, E-mail: flyfish@tinet.ie Website: http://homepage.tinet.ie/~flyfish

ITALY

Centro Pesca-Sardinia, Attn: Capt. Paolo Sala, (Porto Ottiolu/Budoni), Fully equipped 26-ft. sportfisherman *RHA* specializing in dentex, amberjack and bluefin tuna fishing. Associated with residence "Siabecco" and

Hotel "Due Lune" Puntaldia for accommodations if desired. Phone & Fax (39) 784-846188

JAMAICA

Turtle Resorts, Ltd., Attn: Dennis Latchman, (Ocho Rios), Oceanfront Turtle Beach Towers offers a care free vacation paradise from the beautiful white sand beach to furnished apartments with air conditioning, telephone, satellite television and fully equipped kitchens. (876) 974-2806, Fax (876) 974-5014

Villa Holidays, Attn: Inlen Johnson or Doreen Scott, (Montego Bay), Villas include maid service, cook, air conditioning, telephone & TV and pool. (876) 952-7844, Fax (876) 952-8236

KENYA

James Adcock Fishing Ltd., Attn: Capts. James & Ken Adcock, (Mombasa - Mtwapa Creek), Fully equipped sportfishing fleet specializing in sailfishing. (254) 11-485527, Fax (254) 11-316641

Maple Leaf Sportfishing, Attn: Stephen Davidson, (Mombasa), Fully equipped 30-ft. Burmese Teak sportfisher specializing in Pacific sailfish on the Kenya coast. Operating from Mombasa, Kilifi, Watamu or Malindi by arrangement. Can accommodate up to 4 anglers. Big Game Safaris also arranged on request. Phone & Fax (254) 11-490489

Takawiri Island Resort Ltd., Attn: R.S. Sandhu, (Lake Victoria), Full-service beachfront resort with charter fleet specializing in Nile perch fishing. Office in Kisumu - (254) 35-45088, Fax (254) 35-44644

MALAYSIA

Seaventures Sabah, Attn: Alan Maclachlan, Gamefishing charters in the Celebes and South China Seas off the Borneo coast. Fully equipped Performer 24 and accommodations provided in their own resorts. Office in Kota Kinabalu, Sabah - Phone (60) 88-261669 or 251669, Fax (60) 88-251667, E-mail: seavent@po.jaring.my

MALDIVES

Blue Horizon Pte. Ltd, (Maldives), Fishing safaris on a 45-ft to 60-ft live aboard motor yacht with English speaking local crew and chef. Trolling or cast fishing or both among the more than 1,000 islands where more than 95% is sea. Catch & release is strongly encouraged. (960) 321169, Fax (960) 328797

Blue Water Safaris Pty Ltd, Attn: Capt. William Morrall, (Bandos Island-Indian Ocean), Fully equipped 34-ft Sportfishers & brand new Bertram 28 specializing in blue, black and striped marlin fishing. Other species available include wahoo, sailfish and yellowfin tuna. Tag and release encouraged. (960) 440088, Fax (960) 443877

MARSHALL ISLANDS

Outrigger Marshall Islands Resort, (Majuro), Deluxe lagoon/ocean front resort located in Delap on Majuro Atoll featuring restaurant and cocktail lounge, tennis courts, saltwater swimming pool, and fitness center. Every room has a sitting area, lagoon view, and in-room refrigerator. Please note reservations must be made in advance. 1-800-OUTRIGGER (688-7444) or (303) 369-7777, Website: www.outrigger.com

MAURITIUS

La Pirogue Big Game Fishing & La Pirogue Hotel, Attn: Jean Pierre Henry and Maurice de Speville, (Wolmar, Flic en Flac), Full service beachfront hotel with casino and charter fleet of six fully equipped 42-ft. sportfishing boats. (230) 453 8441 or (230) 683 6579, Fax (230) 453 8449 or (230) 683 6162

Organisation de Peche du Nord - Corsaire Club, Attn: Roland de Speville Snr., (Trou aux Biches, Ile Maurice), Fleet of 10 fully equipped 40-ft. & 46-ft. cabin cruisers. (230) 261-6264, Fax (230) 261-6267

Striker Big Game Fishing, Attn: J. Maurice de Speville, (La Preneuse, Black River), Charter fleet of three fully equipped sportfishing boats. (230) 683-6387, Fax (230) 683-6386

MEXICO

Capt'n Mike's Tackle Towne and Fishing Adventures, Attn: Mike Barkhausen, (East Cape, Baja), Discounts offered to groups of four or more for deluxe custom condos in Cabo San Lucas which include use of full-size car during stay; comfortable rooms, villas and condos at beachfront resorts on Baja's East Cape, with 22-ft pangas, 23-ft super pangas and 28 to 33-ft cruisers ready to fish the Sea of Cortez. Complete fishing packages available. Office in Carlsbad, California: (760) 757-4220, Fax (760) 757-4040, Website: www.captnmikes.com

Casa Amigo, Attn: Judi Holder, (Cabo San Lucas), Private 4-bedroom villa in Cabo San Lucas. Office in Texas - (713) 681-3530, Fax (713) 520-6266

Club Exclusive & Big Bass Tours, Attn: Ramon Flores, (Lake Guerrero), Complete fishing packages at two full-service lakefront lodges specializing in bass fishing. Office in Texas - 800-531-7509, Fax (956) 687-8514

Cortez Yacht Charters, Attn: Larry Edwards, (Cabo San Lucas), Charter fleet consisting of fully equipped 22-ft. pangas to 60-ft. yacht sportfishers. All billfish must be released. Office in California - (619) 469-4255, Fax (619) 461-9303

CostaMar Sportfishing, Attn: Jeff or Roxana, Complete worldwide travel packages specializing in the Baja region. Office in California - (818) 224-3625, Fax (818) 224-3479

Cozumel Angler's Fleet & Cove - Club Nautico de Cozumel, Attn: Reservations, (Cozumel), Comfortable full-service waterfront resort with fleet of fully equipped charter boats. (52) 987-20118 or 21113, In USA - 800-253-2701, Fax (52) 987-21135

Fiesta Sportfishing, Attn: Linda or Dave Palmer, (Cabo San Lucas), Los Dorados Sportfishing Fleet, one of Cabo's most productive fleets, consists of fully equipped 28-ft. to 42-ft. sportcruisers plus 23-ft. super pangas out of marina at the Plaza Las Glorias Hotel. Fish for marlin, sailfish, yellowfin tuna, dorado, wahoo and roosterfish, can fish Sea of Cortez & Pacific in same day. Complete packages available. 800-839-2021, Office in Arizona, USA - (602) 814-0414, Fax (602) 813-0011

Hotel Central, Attn: Arturo de Cima Guerena, (Mazatlan), Full-service hotel. (69) 82-1888 or 82-1866, Fax (69) 82-7311

Hotel De Cima, Attn: Arturo de Cima Azcona, (Mazatlan), Full service hotel. (69) 82-7400 or 82-7300, Fax (69) 82-7311

Las Misiones San Felipe Hotel, Attn: Basilio Tzab Chale, (San Felipe, Baja), Full-service beach and tennis resort. (52) 657-71280 or 71284, Fax (52) 657-71283

Leilany Sportfishing, Attn: Capt. John Hanline, (Ixtapa/Zihuatanejo), Fully equipped 34-ft. custom sportfisher *Leilany* specializing in sailfish, marlin and yellowfin tuna fishing. (52) 755-4-2046, Fax (52) 755-4-4762

Mosquito Fleet, Attn: Paul Bechely, (Las Arenas & La Paz, Baja), Fully equipped charter fleet. Office in California - (310) 479-0234, Fax (310) 444-9846

The Original Rancho Buena Vista Hotel, Attn: Gary Graham, (South of La Paz, Baja), Full service beachfront family resort with tennis courts and fishing fleet of 24 fully equipped 24-ft. & 31-ft. cruisers. Office in California - (619) 225-1606 or 800-919-2252, Fax (619) 223-0221

Pisces Fleet, Attn: Marco or Tracy Ehrenberg, (Cabo San Lucas), Fully equipped charter fleet of 31-ft. Bertrams specializing in marlin fishing and offering certificates for released billfish. Tag and release strongly encouraged. (52) 114-31288, Fax (52) 114-30588, Website: http://www.mexon.line.com/pfleet1.htm E-mail: 104164.1105@compuserve.com

Ron Speed's Adventures, Attn: Ron Speed, Arranged travel packages specializing in bass fishing at Lake El Salto, Lake Comedero and Lake Oviachic. Office in Texas - (903) 489-1656, Fax (903) 489-2856

Quality Calinda Beach Cabo San Lucas, Attn: Ivan Garcia, (Cabo San Lucas), All around beachfront resort located in front of the Sea of Cortez. Rooms and junior suites with air conditioning, telephone & color satellite television. Resort has 3 completely remodeled swimming pools, jacuzzis and 2 tennis courts. (52) 114-30045, Fax (52) 114-30077

Solmar Hotel and Solmar Sportfishing Fleet, Attn: Jose Luis Sanchez, (Cabo San Lucas), Full-service beachfront resort with fully equipped charter fleet of boats ranging from 26-ft. to 60-ft. Office in California - (310) 459-9861 or 800-344-3349, Fax (310) 454-1686

Whitey's Casas, Attn: Clyde Squires, (Cabo San Lucas), Assorted condominiums and fishing charters. Office in California - (909) 681-6950, Fax (909) 360-1475

Yolaray Fishing Charters, Attn: Ray & Yolanda McPherson, (Puerto Vallarta), Fully equipped 34-ft. Sport Fishing Yacht *Yolaray* docked at Marina Vallarta, Slip B5. Charters include bait and tackle. Catch & release encouraged. Phone & Fax (52) 322-10037

MIDWAY ISLAND

Midway Sport Fishing, Inc., Attn: John R. Bone, Midway Atoll National Wildlife Refuge, Record breaking marlin, tuna, wahoo, mahi mahi, giant trevally and more are available at this historic, virgin and protected refuge in the Pacific. Fly fishing, light tackle and heavy tackle fishing from modern, well equipped boats with professional and courteous guides. Historic and nature tours provided. Clean and comfortable housing in renovated Officers Quarters, good food and the finest of tackle available. Discount on fishing only. Office in Georgia 1-888-BIG-ULUA or (770) 254-8326, Fax (770) 254-8329, Website: www.midwaysf.com

NEW CALEDONIA

Parkroyal Noumea, Attn: Fabrice Bohbote, (Noumea), Parkroyal Noumea is located in a tropical garden facing the white sand of the beautiful Anse Vata Beach. Accommodations range from 4 to 5 stars: the 4 stars building was totally refurbished in 1994 and the 5 stars wing is brand new. Amenities at this hotel include 3 restaurants, 2 bars, water sports, a superb lagoon pool, fitness room, boutique and a 1.200 sqm conference and banquet room. (687) 26 22 00, Fax: (687) 26 16 77 Website: http://www.parkroyal.com.au

Parkroyal Escapade Island Resort, Attn: Fabrice Bohbote, (Ilot Maitre), Tropical paradise just 20 minutes by boat from Noumea, a small intimate island resort featuring bungalow style accommodations, range of water sports, swimming pool, restaurant and pool bar. (687) 26-22-00, Fax: (687) 26-16-77 Website: http://www.parkroyal.com.au

NEW ZEALAND

Louie The Fish! Lite Tackle Tours, Attn: Louie or Sasa DeNolfo, (North Island-Turangi), Specializing in guided fly fishing trips in both fresh and salt water. (64) 7-386-7953, Fax (64) 7-386-0223
Poronui Ranch - Dry Fly Fishing, Attn: Simon C. Dickie, (North Island-Lake Taupo), Dry fly fishing for trophy brown and rainbow trout at ranch located among spring creeks and streams with helicopter flyouts available. (64) 7-378-9680, Fax (64) 7-378-8115
Southern Lakes Fishing Tours, Attn: Mrs. Annette King, (South Island-Christchurch), Organized and personalized camping tours of the South Island's rivers and lakes. Specializing in trout fishing in the North Otago, McKenzie Country and South Canterbury regions. All camping gear, fishing equipment, transfers and guides provided. (64) 3-025-352570, Fax (64)3-3844121

PAKISTAN

Capt. Aziz Agha, Agha's Sportfishing, (Karachi), Saltwater offshore fishing for mackerel, cobia, barrabuda, tuna, wahoo, queenfish, amberjack, trevally, snapper and grouper. Big game fishing also available for marlin, yellowfin tuna and mahi mahi. Up to 5 anglers accommodated on fully equipped 33-ft. Fly Bridge *Tiara* or wooden hull 48-ft. Sportfisher and 50-ft. boats. Advanced reservations required. (92) 21-4554835, Fax (92) 21-4528825

REPUBLIC OF PALAU

Palau Pacific Resort, Attn: Darin De Leon, (Koror), Full service resort nestled among 64 acres of verdant gardens and brilliant tropical flowers offering superb accommodations in spacious guest rooms and suites in the perfect environment for both relaxation and recreation. Located on a private white sand beach with beachfront pool. Discounts offered on deluxe garden view and ocean view rooms. (680) 488-2600, Fax (680) 488-1606 or 1601, E-mail: PPR@palaunet.com

PARAGUAY

Dorado Fishing, Attn: Jorge E. Xifra, (Asuncion), Guide service for freshwater dorado fishing on Parana River and fly fishing on the Apa River. (595) 21-492128, Fax (595) 21-211757, E-mail: XIFRA@INFONET.COM.PY

PORTUGAL

Tres Des Pesca Desportiva Lda., Attn: Capt. Paul Delsignore, (Monte Gordo, Algarve), Fully equipped 33-ft. Aqua Bell specializing in European all tackle and line class records. Discount also offered for accommodations at Atlantico Aparthotel. Phone & Fax (351) 081-512819

PUERTO RICO

Capt. Mike Benitez, Mike Benitez Marine Services, Inc., Attn: Erin Benitez, (San Juan), Fully equipped 45-ft. Hatteras sportfishermen out of Club Nautico de San Juan. (787) 723-2292 or 724-6265, Fax (787) 725-4344
Dorado Marine Center & "The Grand Illusion", Attn: Capt. Puchy Sanabria, (Dorado), Discount on fishing supplies and fishing from San Juan Bay Marina aboard fully equipped 32-ft. Topaz *The Grand Illusion*. (787) 796-4645, Fax (787) 796-7323
Puerto Rico Angling, Attn: Capt. Jose Campos, (San Juan), Fully equipped, custom sportfishermen specializing in billfishing. Phone & Fax (787) 724-2079
Capt. Juan Carlos Torruella - Tarpon Fishing, (San Juan), Fly fishing and light tackle specialist fishing the San Jose and Torrecilla Lagoons in San Juan. Fish aboard the fully equipped 18 ft Hewes *Tight Loop* with all bait and custom tackle provided. 100% release fishing for tarpon and snook. (787) 792-4524, Fax (787) 782-6655

SEYCHELLES

Allamanda Hotel, Attn: Tessie Ellinas, (Mahe), Full service, comfortable colonial-style beachfront hotel. Ten spacious rooms with sea views, continental bathroom facilities, fridge, telephone, hairdrier, coffee maker, fan and air conditioner. Restaurant and bar service on the beach and in the main building. (248) 366266, Fax (248) 366175
Game Fishing Enterprises Pty., Attn: Anna and Martin Lewis, (Mahe), *TAM TAM*, the Big Cat of the Indian Occan offers day charters or complete live-aboard fishing safaris around the islands of the Seychelles. Fully equipped with Shimano rods and reels, light tackle available, tag and release encouraged. 5 to 14 day packages available fishing on *TAM TAM* while staying on 72-ft, 8-berth luxury mothership *High Aspect*. Phone & Fax (248) 344266

SOUTH AFRICA

Bahari Charters, Attn: Capt. Andy Croucher, (Hout Bay) Deep sea fishing from Hout Bay on fully equipped 41-ft. Hatteras specializing in tuna fishing. (27) 21-7851583
Gamefish Charters, Attn: Capt. Ren Colyn or Maureen Colyn, (Hout Bay), Fully equipped 40-ft. catamaran *Cheetah* out of Hout Bay Harbour specializing in swordfish and tuna fishing with overnight trips available. All tackle provided. Days trips for up to 6. Overnight trips for 4 anglers. Phone & Fax (27) 21-790-4550

SOUTH PACIFIC

Horea Royal Fishing Club, c/o W.E.R.I. International USA, Attn: Becky Sovia or Jim Murphy, (Leeward Islands-Tahiti-Moorea, Tahaa-Raiatea, Huahine & Bora Bora) Fishing aboard fully equipped custom 47-ft. Davis *Horea Royal II*. Accommodations available at Marina Iti, a comfortable, waterfront polynesian-style guest house. Office in North Carolina - Phone & fax (919) 473-1732 or 800-775-2497
Louie The Fish! - Tropical Expeditions, Ltd., Attn: Robert Stone, (Pacific Harbor, Fiji Islands), Specializing in guided fly fishing trips. (679) 450-188, Fax (679) 450-426
Tea Nui Charters, Attn: Capt. Chris Lilley, (Moorea, French Polynesia), Sportfishing for marlin, tuna, wahoo and mahi-mahi out of Moorea aboard a 31-ft. Bertram Sportfisher professionally equipped with all Penn International reels and a captain with over 15 years experience in local waters. (689) 56-1508, Fax (689) 41-3297

SPAIN

Pesca Deportiva de Altura, S.L., (Marbella), Fish La Costa del Sol and surrounding areas aboard comfortable, fully equipped 43-ft. Egg Harbor *Arrantzale* with professional crew, berth in Puerto Banús. Big game fishing for bluefin tuna and shark or bottom fishing for grouper. Phone & fax (34)(95) 244-35-81, Boat 989-47-31-47

SWEDEN

Sportfishing in Sweden AB, Attn: Peter Prag, (Karlsborg), Modern harbor cabins in a full-service fishing lodge on Lake Vattern. (46) 505-610-33, Fax (46) 505-610-44
Lake Vattern Charters, Attn: Peter Prag, (Karlsborg), Fleet of fully equipped charter boats specializing in landlocked Atlantic salmon & Arctic char. (46) 505-610-33, Fax (46) 505-610-44

TANZANIA

Zanzibar Fishing Club, Attn: Carlo Vernocchi, Fully equipped 45-ft. custom sportfishing boat *Mshale* fishing the south of Pemba Channel and the northeast of Zanzibar and Leven Bank. (255) 54-32540, Fax (255) 54-33021

THAILAND

Phuket Island Resort, Attn: Mongkol Boonpron, (Phuket Island, Laemka Beach), Full-service beachfront resort with charter boats available. (76) 381010-7, Fax (76) 381018

ALASKA

Alaska North Adventures, Attn: Charles Eisenhower, (Kodiak Island & Bristol Bay area), Fresh and saltwater guided or unguided fishing for salmon, Dolly Varden, trout, halibut and cod out of Saltery Lake Lodge on Kodiak Island. The lodge features comfortable accommodations located on the shore of Saltery Lake. Guided and unguided float trips available in the Bristol Bay region with accommodations at tent camps on the rivers. (907) 376-8476, Fax (907) 376-8479, E-mail: akna@alaska.net

Alaska Wilderness Expeditions, Attn: Kevin Fitzgerald, (Talkeetna), Fully guided charters for fishing south central Alaska, all gear & bait provided, 2-week advance notice required. (907) 733-2704, Fax (907) 733-1067

Alaska's Fishing Unlimited Lodges, Attn: Brenda Bowles or Lorane Owsichek, (office in Anchorage), Full-service, fly-out lodge located in Bristol Bay. (907) 243-5899, Fax (907) 243-2473

Alaskan Fishing Adventures, Attn: Carol Berg, (office in Soldotna), Complete fishing packages. 1-800-548-3474 or (707) 262-9683

Aniak Air Guides, Attn: Rick Townsend, Unguided drop off fishing trips in Alaska's most remote areas with a Beaver float plane, 350 miles northwest of Anchorage. Rafts, canoes and camp gear available. (907) 675-4540

Bergie's Guide Service, Attn: Bruce Bergman, (Quinhagak), Comfortable base camp on the Kanektok River in southwest Alaska, guided drop-off fishing, cabin rentals, showers and tackle. Summer-(907) 556-8347, Winter-(907) 548-4148

Capt. Black Barts Charters, Attn: Capt. Bart Cowan, (Sitka), Fishing for King salmon, barn-door halibut, etc. aboard fast, fully equipped sportfisherman. Accommodations arranged if desired. (907) 747-7416

Big Mountain Lodge, Attn: Charles Hostetler, (office in Anchorage), Comfortable, modern lodge located on the Kvichak River in heart of Bristol Bay's sportfish area. Great fishing for trophy rainbow trout, Dolly Varden, lake trout, grayling, arctic char, northern pike and Pacific salmon. Guides, boats and flyout services available. Phone & Fax (907) 248-0601

Chilkat Valley Inn, Attn: Don or Lois Ouan, (Haines), Bed & Breakfast Inn situated on cliff overlooking Chilkat River. Port of Haines 8 miles - great fishing for salmon and halibut. (907) 766-3331

Chistochina Trading Post, Attn: Terry, (Gakona), Lodge specializing in salmon and lake trout fishing. (907) 822-3366

Classic Alaska Charters, Attn: Capt. Rob Scherer, (Ketchikan), Remote cruising to unspoiled fishing grounds aboard fully equipped 40-ft. motoryacht. Charters specializing in halibut and salmon fishing. Extended overnight capacity for groups of 3 to 6 persons. (907) 225-0608

Crackerjack Sportfishing Charters, Attn: Capt. Andy Mezirow, (Seward), Custom fishing adventures aboard fully equipped 28-ft. *Crackerjack* in waters of Resurrection Bay, Kenai Fjords National Park & Montague Island, specializing in halibut and salmon fishing. Can accommodate up to 6. Phone & Fax (907) 224-2606

Goodnews River Lodge, Attn: Frank Byerly, (Eagle River), The lodge is located 500 miles from the nearest road in the heart of the Togiak National Wildlife Refuge in an unspoiled, uncrowded and wildly beautiful setting. Some of the finest trout, char, salmon and grayling fishing Alaska has to offer. Over 23 years of experience is your guarantee of a very comfortable and successful trip. Discount limited to July or September bookings. (907) 694-5515, Fax (907) 694-5516

The Grand Aleutian Hotel, Attn: Jane Schroeder, (Dutch Harbor), Complete fishing packages available including luxury accommodations and gourmet cuisine at full service resort located in Alaska's breathtaking Aleutian Island Chain. Fully equipped sportfishing boats specialize in halibut fishing and fly-in salmon excursions to Volcano Bay available. (907) 581-3844 or 800-891-1194, Fax (907) 581-7150

Iliaska Lodge Inc., Attn: Mr. Ted Gerken, (Iliamna), Deluxe fly-fishing only lodge. (907) 571-1221

Island Point Lodge, Attn: Maggie Celli, (Petersburg), Comfortable lodge located in the Tongass National Forest on a saltwater channel with several buildings that can accommodate up to 16 fishermen. Self-guided fishing aboard 18-ft. Alaska Lund aluminum boats equipped with 48 h.p. outboard motors and 9 h.p. trolling motor for salmon, halibut, trout and Dolly Varden. Complete packages include meals, boat, motor, fuel, bait allotment, freezer space for catch and transfer to the lodge from Petersburg. (office in Massachusetts) (508) 366-4522, Fax (508) 366-5941

Ketchikan Sportfishing, Attn: Carol Dooley, (Ketchikan), Fleet of over 40 fully equipped boats ranging from 24-ft to 50-ft. for day charters. Lodge accommodations/fishing packages available. 1-800-488-8254 or (907) 225-7526, Fax (907) 225-7525

Kodiak Western Charters, Attn: Eric Stirrup, (Kodiak Island), Day or multi-day charters for halibut, salmon and bottomfish, from oceans to rivers, specializing in ultra light tackle with current IGFA records in both conventional and fly tackle categories. (907) 486-2200, Fax (907) 486-4084, E-mail: tenbears@ptialaska.net

Northern Comfort Charters, Inc., Attn: Edgar W. Pyle, (Valdez), Fully equipped boats specializing in salmon and halibut fishing. (907) 835-2331

Radar's Alaskan Bush Adventures, Inc., Attn: Capt. Robert "Radar" Orth, (Bethel), Custom fishing trips to remote locations accessible only by bush plane, your choice of custom float or base camp trips. Fly fishing is their specialty. Office in Winter Beach, Florida - (561) 388-2277, Fax (561) 388-2299

Royal Coachman Lodge, Attn: Bill Martin, (Bristol Bay area), Full-service lodge specializing in stream fishing. (907) 346-2595, Fax (907) 346-3733

Salmon Busters Fishing, Attn: Dan McQueen, (Ketchikan), Comfortable 21-ft. boats specializing in salmon and halibut fishing. (907) 225-2731

Stephan Lake Lodge, Attn: Jim Bailey, (Eagle River), Remote fly-in lodge on Stephan Lake specializing in spin & fly fishing for salmon, trout & Arctic grayling. Boats, motors, canoes and row boats available. (907) 696-2163, Fax (907) 694-4129

Tower Rock Lodge, Attn: Michael Tuhy, (office in Soldotna), Comfortable full service lodge located on the Kenai Peninsula. Fly-outs, halibut, salmon and fly fishing for rainbows is their specialty. Accommodating just 10 guests, staff is available to provide attention to every detail to ensure your Alaska Dream Vacation comes true. Video and newsletter available. 1-800-284-3474 or (904) 283-3662

Ultimate Rivers, Attn: Rene Limeres, (Anchorage), Fly fishing the Togiak, Kanektok & Nushagak Rivers for salmon, char & trout, and Russia for rainbow trout and taimen. (907) 346-2193

Yes Bay Lodge & Mink Bay Lodge, Attn: Shelly Dunn, (Ketchikan), Mink Bay Lodge is 50 miles south of Ketchikan in Misty Fjords National Monument and Yes Bay Lodge is 50 miles north in Tongass National Forest--both comfortable, full-service fishing lodges. (907) 225- 7906, Fax (907) 247-3875

CALIFORNIA

Ballyhood International Big Game Trolling Lures, Attn: Dave Stewart, (Santa Ana), Ballyhood, innovators in trolling natural baits, offers a free catalog and 25% discount to all IGFA members. These deep trolling lures reach depths of 30-ft. and offer the uniqueness of being trolled as is or add your bait (8"-20" baits). Specialists in big tuna, wahoo, blue marlin and shark. (714) 564-9468, Fax (714) 564-9513

Best Western-Golden Sails Hotel, Attn: Sonya Bergren, (Long Beach), Accommodations in comfortable hotel and includes one free breakfast buffet and two beverages per room, per day. 800-762-5333, Fax (310) 594-0623

Bongos Sportfishing Headquarters, Attn: Reservations, (Newport Beach), Sportfishing on fully equipped *Bongos* and *Bongos II*.

(714) 673-2810 or 8OO-64O-MAKO, In California l-8OO-2-BONGOS, Fax (714) 673-2819

Capt'n Mike's Tackle Towne and Fishing Adventures, Attn: Mike Barkhausen, (San Diego), Discounts offered to groups of four or more on long-range & short-range fishing trips out of San Diego on some of the top boats. Discounts also offered on merchandise. (760) 757-4220, Fax (760) 757-4040, Website: www.captnmikes.com

Holiday Inn Resort Monterey, Attn: Paul Apilado, (Monterey), Full service resort with tennis courts, swimming pool, saunas & putting green offering special price on complete fishing package for 2 including room, deep sea fishing with tackle provided. (408) 373-6141, Fax (408) 655-8608

The Longfin, Attn: Tom Ward, (Orange), Discount on terminal tackle. (714) 538-8010, Fax (714) 538-1368

Capt. John Pizza, Bear Ridge Guide Service,(Santa Rosa), Personalized, guided jet boat and drift boat fishing trips on the premier rivers of Northern California (Klamath, Smith, Eel and Sacramento). Specializing in salmon, steelhead and trout. Deluxe boats and the finest tackle provided. Accommodations available. (707) 539-9534

Westerner Motel, Attn: Adrian, (Monterey), Motel accommodations including complimentary continental breakfast, pets allowed. Discount offered Sunday thru Thursday excluding holidays & special events. 800-350-6685 or (408) 373-2911, Fax (408) 655-3450

COLORADO

Cross D Bar Trout Ranch, Attn: Dick Mandel, (Westcliffe), Fixed lodge in shadow of Sangre de Cristo Mountains with 4 lakes, basic & advanced fly fishing instruction available. (719) 783-2007

Fly Fishing Durango, Inc., Attn: Greg Weaver, (Durango), Year-round guides and outfitters for the San Juan River and southwestern Colorado, float & wade trips, float tube trips, discounts offered on full day trips only. (970) 382-0478

CONNECTICUT

Atlantic Fly Fishing Charters, Attn: Capt. Rich Ludemann, (Norwalk, CT/Fishers Island, NY), Fly and light tackle fishing for stripers, blues, bonita and albys for up to three anglers. Full and half day charters, instruction and executive packages available. (203) 834-9776 or on the net under Atlantic Fly Fishing Charters.

Capt. Jack Balint, Fish Connection Guide Service, (Manchester), Specializing in saltwater fly fishing and light tackle. Member of Team Hydra Sports operating a 1997 2250 Hydra Sports fishing the areas of Connecticut, New York and Rhode Island for striped bass, bluefish, bonito and little tunny. Large winter and spring fishery for striped

bass in Thames River. (860) 885-1739 or (860) 646-0851

Connecticut Island Charters, Attn: Capt. Roger K. Gendron, (Westport), Fleet of fully equipped late-model skiffs specializing in fly & light tackle fishing, maximum two anglers. Phone & Fax (203) 221-0763

Connecticut Woods & Water, Attn: Capt. Dan Wood, (Waterford), Fully equipped 26-ft. center console specializing in saltwater fly & light tackle fishing for striped bass, bluefish and bonito. (860) 442-6343

Helen B Charters, Attn: Capt. Bob Bociek, (Milford), Fully equipped sportfishing boats fishing Long Island Sound. Can accommodate 2 to 3 passengers and new 34-ft. sportfisher can accommodate 6 passengers. (203) 876-2910 or (203) 333-1912

Karen Ann Charters, Attn: Karen or Jeff Eckert, (Higganum), Fully equipped sportfishing boats offering discounts for shark, tuna & marlin fishing only. (203) 345-2570

FLORIDA HOTELS

AmeriSuites, Attn: Faith Engel, (Fort Lauderdale), All-suite hotel featuring complimentary deluxe continental breakfast, free local phone calls, refrigerator, microwave, wet bar, coffee maker with coffee, outdoor heated pool, free airport and local transportation, manager's reception, fitness center, business center and dataport telephones. Conveniently located near Ft. Lauderdale Convention Center on 17th Street Causeway. (954) 763-7670, Fax (954) 763-6269

Bass Haven Lodge & Restaurant, Attn: Jerry Hooten, (Welaka), Rooms and kitchenettes, boat house/marina, hot tub, great food. Located on St. Johns and Oklawaha Rivers with guides available. (904) 467-8812

Bayside Inn Resort, Attn: Reservations, (Key West), Waterfront resort. (305) 296-7593 or 800-888-3233, Fax (305) 294-5246

The Beach Resort, Attn: Barbara Nilson, (Daytona Beach), Full-service resort. (904) 672-3770, Fax (904) 673-7262

Biscayne Bay Marriott Hotel & Marina, Attn: Chris Bracken, (Miami), Full-service waterfront resort with marina. (305) 536-6377, Fax (305) 579-0108

Cheeca Lodge, Attn: Julie Olsen, (Islamorada), Comfortable full-service oceanfront resort with tennis courts, par 3 executive golf course, charter fishing and diving. (305) 664-4651, Fax (305) 664-2083

Clarion Hotel Hollywood Beach, (Hollywood Beach), Full service hotel featuring 309 spacious guest rooms with private balconies. Hotel amenities include fitness center, oversized outdoor swimming pool, tennis courts, tropical gardens, Tiki Bar, guest laundry, restaurant, lounge, food and beverage court and 18,000 square feet of meeting space. Located on the Intracoastal

Waterway just steps away from golden sand beach and just 9 miles from the IGFA World Fishing Center. (954) 458-1900 or 800-329-9019, Fax (954) 455-7222

Coconut Beach Resort, (Key West), Five star resort located on the Atlantic Ocean, hidden from the crowds but walking distance to shops and restaurants. Units are condo type and ocean front, one-bedroom suites, sleeping 4, two-bedroom suites, sleeping 6, both have complete kitchen facilities and living rooms with common balcony, studios sleeping 2, king bed and kitchenette, ocean and non-ocean front available. Pool and Jacuzzi facing the ocean, barbecue, grills. (305) 294-0057 or 800-835-0055, Fax (305) 294-5066, E-mail: cbrkw@bellsouth.net

The Continental Inn, Attn: Jeannette or Lawrence Listing, (Key Colony Beach), Tastefully appointed suites with private balconies, fully equipped kitchens, cable TV, telephones and daily maid service. Located on the Atlantic Ocean with a beautiful white sandy beach and heated pool. Golf, restaurants and dockage are within walking distance. (305) 289-0101 or 1-800-443-7352, Website: thefloridakeys.com/continentalinn

Crown Sterling Suites, Attn: Diane D'Amico, (Ft. Lauderdale), Full-service all-suite hotel with balconies, pool, whirlpool, sauna & free beach shuttle. (954) 527-2700, Fax (954) 760-7202

"Duval House", Attn: Reservations, (Key West), Historic inn in the heart of the old town, weekday discounts available May 1 - December 20. (305) 294-1666, Fax (305) 292-1701

Grove Isle Club & Resort, Attn: Haydee Leto, (Coconut Grove/Miami), Private island club resort located at Biscayne Bay, 85-slip marina, 12 tennis courts, pool & whirlpool, every room has balcony overlooking Biscayne Bay. (305) 858-8300, Fax (305) 858-5908

Hawk's Cay Resort and Marina, Attn: Cheryl Roll, (Marathon), Tropical West Indies-style full service resort on its own 60-acre private island with marina, Dolphin Habitat, tennis courts and nearby golf course. (305) 743-7000, Fax (305) 289-0651

Holiday Inn Beachside, Attn: Pat Share, (Key West), Comfortable full-service beachfront resort with private pier. (305) 294-2571, Fax (305) 292-7252

Holiday Inn Lauderdale-By-The-Sea, Attn: Phyllis Tess, (Lauderdale-By-The-Sea, just north of Ft. Lauderdale), Newly renovated hotel with pool located one block from private beach. (954) 776-1212, Fax (954) 776-1212 ext. 600

Lauderdale Beach Hotel, Attn: Lisa Palladino, (Fort Lauderdale), Full-service beachfront hotel offering luxury class, brand new rooms. Discount available May 15 to November 30. (954) 764-0088 or 800-327-7600, Fax (954) 463-9154

MacRae's of Homosassa, Attn: Gator MacRae, (Homosassa), Comfortable motel located on Homosassa River. (352) 628-2602, Fax (352) 628-1315

Park Shore Resort, Attn: Judie Wilkinson, (Naples), Beautiful full-service, all-suite resort featuring waterfalls, footbridges, pool, jacuzzi, and tennis courts. Golf courses and beaches less than 2 miles away. Discount valid May thru December 15th. (941) 263-2222, Fax (941) 263-0946

Pelican Cove Resort, Attn: Reservations, (Islamorada), Full-service waterfront resort with dock, tennis courts and private balconies. (305) 664-4435 or 800-445-4690, Fax (305) 664-5134

Placida Properties, Attn: Bernita Bulwan, (Southwest Florida-Boca Grande Area), Placida Beach, part of the Placida Harbour Club, offers stunning one and two bedroom condominiums with 7 miles of white sandy beaches and pool on this island get-away with scheduled ferry service. Boat slips on the island can accommodate boats up to 22-ft. 888-941-9444

Quality Inn Resort, Attn: Ron Scott, (Key West), Comfortable accommodations at AAA 3 Diamond Resort. (305) 294-6681, Fax (305) 294-5618

Radisson Suite Beach Resort, Attn: Reservations (Must ask for the IGFA rate), (Marco Island), Full-service resort featuring 214 one and two-bedroom suites and 55 guest rooms, all with private balcony and views of the beach. Suites come with fully equipped kitchen and large living room. Two full service restaurants and pizzeria. Recreational activities range from shelling to parasailing. Marco Island is the largest of the Ten Thousand Island chain, adjacent to the Everglades, and offers excellent backcountry fishing for snook, tarpon and redfish. 800-333-333 or (941) 394-4100, Fax (941) 394-0262

Rainbow Bend Fishing Resort, Attn: Barry or Jeannie, (Marathon), Comfortable oceanfront suites, two bedroom cottages and one-room and one bedroom patio efficiencies complete with well equipped kitchens. Full complimentary American breakfast served every morning in the Hideaway Cafe. Available charters located at their dock. (305) 289-1505, Fax (305) 743-0257

Ramada Plaza Beach Resort, Attn: Eileen Pearson, (Ft. Walton Beach), Comfortable full service beachfront resort. (850) 243-9161, Fax (850) 244-5763

Riverside Hotel, Attn: Mary Mathurin, (Fort Lauderdale), An intimate, sophisticated hotel with Old World hospitality located on Ft. Lauderdale's fashionable Las Olas Boulevard overlooking the New River. (954) 467-0671, Fax (954) 462-2148

Seabonay Beach Resort, Attn: Ruth Ann Mench, (Hillsboro Beach - between Ft. Lauderdale and Boca Raton), Beachfront resort with discounts offered on one-bedroom suite with oceanview. Not available during peak season and holiday weekends. (954) 427-2525 or 800-777-1961, Fax (954) 427-3228

Sheraton West Palm Beach Hotel, Attn: Judy Repash, (West Palm Beach), Comfortable full-service hotel, 1-800-833-3775 or (561) 833-1234, Fax (561) 833-1255

Sheraton Yankee Clipper Beach Resort, Attn: Kathy Buchanan, (Fort Lauderdale), Full-service beachfront resort. (954) 524-5551, Fax (954) 523-5376

Sheraton Yankee Trader Beach Resort, Attn: Kathy Buchanan, (Fort Lauderdale), Full-service beachfront resort. (954) 467-1111, Fax (954) 462-2342

Tarpon Bay Motel, Attn: Debra Markel, (Marathon), Tropical Keys atmosphere, quiet hideaway on the water with boat dockage. Motel rooms, efficiencies, and one-bedroom apartments available. Fishing charters and dive packages available on premises. 800-743-4922 or (305) 743-4922, Fax (305) 743-3917

FLORIDA GUIDES - EAST COAST

Capt. Gus Brugger, Pattern Setter Charters, (Sebastian), Year round light tackle and fly flats fishing on the Indian River Lagoon. Tarpon, kingfish, catch and release snook fishing and much more during the summer months, in and around Sebastian Inlet. Fall snook oversized redfish, flounder, etc. in winter/spring. Accommodation discounts available. Bait, tackle, license included. 18-ft Maverick flats skiff, Penn Reels. (561) 589-0008

Capt. Cliff Budd, A Seacret Spot, (Jupiter), Light tackle live bait sportfishing aboard 20-ft. tournament rigged openfisherman *Seacret Spot* in the Palm Beaches, specializing in sailfish and snook fishing. Bait, tackle and licenses included. Kids to seniors welcome. (561) 745-9178, Website: www.seacretspot.com

Capt. Charles A. Clyne, Salt & Fresh Water Fishing Charters, (Lake Worth/Palm Beach area), Specializing in light tackle and fly fishing in the (salt) Intracoastal Waterway aboard fully equipped 19-ft. Maverick Master; and (fresh) the lakes and canals in Palm Beach County aboard fully equipped 19-ft. Ranger 390V. (561) 588-1766 or 800-226-1766, Fax (561) 585-8191, E-mail: captain@flinet.com Website: http://www.netline.net/fl_captains/capclyne.html

Capt. Jon Cooper, (Ft. Lauderdale & Miami), Live bait and flyfishing for tarpon, permit and bonefish. (954) 267-9076 or (800) 224-9967, E-mail: bonefshman@aol.com.

Capt. Kevin Crown, (Miami area), Light tackle fishing aboard the fully equipped *Tail Bone*. (305) 232-3712

DAWN PATROL Fishing Charters, Attn: Capt. Doug Lillard, (Hollywood), Backcountry and flats fishing aboard 18-ft. Hewes Bonefisher or 16-ft. Lowes Tunnel Hull in Biscayne Bay, Flamingo (Everglades National Park) and Florida Keys. Spin, fly or plug fishing from expert to novice. (954) 424-9726

Capt. Robert Fisher, (Miami area), Offshore fishing out of Haulover Dock aboard fully equipped *Therapy*. (305) 945-1578, Fax (305) 757-3515

Capt. Frank Garisto, (Miami area), Specializing in bonefish, tarpon & permit fishing in Biscayne Bay. (305) 361-5040

Capt. Joe Gonzalez, Funny Bone Charters, (Miami area), Discount offered on full day charters only aboard fully equipped sportfisherman. (305) 642-6727

Capt. Mike Hakala, Floridays Fishing Excursions, (New Smyrna Beach), Fully equipped custom flats skiff specializing in fly and light tackle fishing on Indian River and Mosquito Lagoon for redfish, snook and sea trout. Located one hour from Orlando. All tackle provided. (904) 428-8530

Capt. Tom Horn, (Hillsboro Inlet-Pompano Beach), Half, 3/4 and full day charters, reef and offshore, trolling, wrecks and live bait fishing aboard fully equipped *Killin' Time*. Discount available anytime. (954) 946-2628

Capt. Joel Kalman, (Miami area), Specializing in flats fishing for bonefish, permit, tarpon & snook aboard fully equipped *Bad To The Bone*. (305) 361-5155

Capt. David King, Little Adam Charters, (Ft. Pierce), Fully equipped 27-ft. custom Bonaventure specializing in inshore & offshore fishing for snook, tarpon, redfish, dolphin, bait & tackle provided. (407) 468-9947

Capt. Mike Kirkpatrick, (Jacksonville & Northeast area), Light tackle and fly inshore fishing aboard the *LiL Debi*. (904) 388-5282

Capt. John Kumiski's Guide Service, Attn: Capt. John Kumiski, (Titusville area), Shallow water sightfishing for redfish, seatrout, tarpon, black drum, and other species as available in the Mosquito Lagoon, Indian River and Banana River, specializing in fly and light tackle. Canoe trips into the no motor zone of the Banana River a specialty. All licenses and tackle included. Discount offered on full day trips only. (407) 834-2954, E-mail: 73742.100@compuserve.com

Capt. Ed Kuvlesky, (Vero Beach), Light tackle, plug and fly fishing aboard 18-ft Maverick Master Angler in the Indian River Lagoon between the Sebastian and Ft. Pierce Inlets. Species targeted include snook, redfish, speckled trout and tarpon. Junior anglers more than welcome. All bait, tackle and licenses supplied. (561) 770-1376

Capt. Ron Mallet, (Fort Lauderdale area), Inshore or nearshore fishing out of Port Everglades on fully equipped Robalo 2140 *Just Add Water*. (954) 423-8700

Capt. George Mitchell, (Miami area), Fully equipped sportfishing boats for offshore and inshore fishing out of Black Point Marina. (305) 257-4665

Capt. Jerry Murphy, Tar-Bōn Charters, (Biscayne Bay & Upper Keys), Light tackle and fly fishing aboard flats skiff *Tar-Bōn* for tarpon, bonefish, permit, redfish. (954) 432-0197

Capt. John Myers, (Miami area), Discount offered on full day charters only. Fishing aboard fully equipped *The Blue Mistress II*. (305) 595-3560

Capt. Al Oakley, Sissy Baby Sportfish, Attn: Sissy Oakley, (Miami area), Fully equipped 45-ft. Hatteras available for fishing or cruising out of Miami Beach Marina. Discount weekdays only. (305) 531-4223

Capt. Darrick Parker, (Miami area), Specializing in light tackle & fly fishing on flats of Biscayne Bay, Keys & Flamingo aboard fully equipped *Bone Us*. (305) 669-8477

Capt. Frank Perez's Flats/Backcountry Fishing, (Miami area), Specializing in flats and backcountry fishing in Miami/Upper Keys area on fully equipped 18-ft. Hewes skiff with fly, spin and plug tackle provided. Miami-(305) 598-4448, Key Largo-(305) 852-4758, Fax (305) 262-9411

Capt. Paul Poirier, Gamefisher Sportfishing Adventures, (Fort Lauderdale), Fully equipped 40-ft. Gamefisherman *Gamefisher* offering discounts on full day charters, specializing in fishing for sailfish, dolphin and wahoo. (954) 725-3709, cellular phone (954) 415-7089

Capt. Greg Poland, Stake Out Charters, (Miami area), Specializing in flats light tackle and fly fishing for bonefish, snook, tarpon, permit and redfish in Biscayne Bay, Everglades National Park & Upper Keys. Casting instruction available. (305) 885-6646

Radar's Unlimited Adventures, Attn: Capt. Robert "Radar" Orth, (Winter Beach - Central east coast), Light tackle and fly fishing expert fishing the Indian River Lagoon System aboard 17-ft. Maverick Master Angler *Unlimited Access*. (561) 388-2277, Fax (561) 388-2299

Capt. John C. Royall d.b.a. The Grizzly Whistler Charters, (Merritt Island), Specializing in light tackle & fly fishing for trout, redfish & tarpon on Banana River of Indian River Lagoon system. 800-473-3474 or (561) 452-0863

Capt. Stan Saffan, (Miami area), Fully equipped *Therapy IV* out of Haulover Dock. (305) 945-1578, Fax (305) 757-3515

Sea Lover Sportfishing, (Ponce Inlet/Daytona Beach area), Discounts offered on full day charters only, located at Sea Love Marina. (904) 767-3406, Fax (904) 760-4210

Capt. Bouncer Smith, (Miami area), Specializing in tarpon and billfishing aboard fully equipped *Bouncer's Dusky*. Can accommodate up to three anglers. (305) 945-5114

Capt. Gerard Weber, Pars Fortune Fishing Charters, (Pompano Beach/Fort Lauderdale area), Fully equipped 28-ft. sportfisherman *Pars Fortune*, can accommodate up to four anglers. (954) 781-6893

Capt. William F. Wolfe, Jr., U and I Charters, (Fort Pierce), Offshore trolling on fully equipped 36-ft. Blackfin, can accommodate up to six people. (561) 466-5876

GUIDES - FLORIDA KEYS

Capt. Glenn Abend, Wild Bill Charters, (Key West), Fully equipped custom sportfisherman *Wild Bill* out of City Marina, Garrison Bight No. 13 Amberjack Pier, available for gulfstream, reef or wreck fishing, specializing in sailfish, bait & tackle provided. (305) 296-2533

Capt. Lee Baker, Bone Voyage Inc., (Islamorada & Upper Keys), Flats fishing specializing in casting & fly fishing for bonefish, tarpon & permit. (305) 664-2080, Fax (305) 664-2023

Capt. Michael Bednar, Bonefish Bednar, (Islamorada area), Specializing in fly fishing for bonefish, tarpon & permit. Catch & release only. (305) 664-8408

Capt. Dale Bittner, (Key West), Light tackle offshore, live bait, reef and wreck fishing aboard fully equipped *Bait Stealer* with experienced guide and world record holder. (305) 295-9109

Capt. Dave Bortscheller, Sea Dream Charters, (Marathon area). (305) 289-0626

Capt. Jamie Brody, Wishbone Charters, (Islamorada area), Specializing in backcountry fishing. Discount available July thru end of November. (305) 852-2983

Capt. Randy Brown, (Marathon area), Specializing in flats fishing. (305) 743-2648

Bulldog Marine LLC, Attn: Lee Arnett, M.D., (Islamorada), Fully equipped custom 30-ft. Gamefisherman *Bulldog* designed and equipped to specialize in fly and light tackle offshore fishing. Office in Spartansburg, South Carolina - (864) 585-8221, Fax (864) 542-9859

Capt. Jeff Burns, On The Fly Charters, (Key West), Fully equipped 32-ft. Intrepid *On The Fly* specializing in light tackle fishing. 800-946-6359, Fax (305) 745-4199

Captain Hook Sportfishing, Attn: Capts. Jan LeGraff & Chris Wettberg, (Florida Keys), Offshore fishing aboard fully equipped 54-ft. Rybovich out of Faro Marina in Marathon and backcountry fishing at Big Pine Key on 18-ft. Willy Roberts flats skiff. Phone & fax (305) 872-3696 E-mail: ComeFish@aol.com

Capt. Tony Catalfamo, Fantasy A.C. Charters, (Islamorada area), Offshore fishing aboard 38-ft. *Fantasy* for up to 6 out of Whale Harbor Marina specializing in light tackle & live bait fishing. Boat:(305) 342-0808, Dock: (305) 664-5176 or 800-428-4854, E-mail: capttony@icanect.ne Website: http//www.fishfla.com/captony.html

Capt. Larry Cohen, (Key West), Specializing in fly and light tackle fishing aboard fully equipped skiff out of Harborside Motel & Marina. (305) 294-7670

Capt. Rob Delph, (Key West), Fully equipped sportfisherman *Second Generation* accommodating up to 3 anglers. (305) 294-8314

Capt. Jerry Dixon, No Mercy Sportfishing, (Key West), Fishing aboard fully equipped 23-ft. *No Mercy* specializing in tarpon and reef fishing and live bait fishing for sailfish, tuna, wahoo, etc. (305) 294-6356 or 800-368-3029

Capt. Bob Dolan, Pole Position Charters, Attn: Kim Dolan, (Key Largo area), Charters available Monday thru Saturday aboard fully equipped sportfisherman *Release* (305) 245-5645

Capt. Bubba Gaston, Black Bean Inc., (Key West area), Specializes in light tackle and live bait fishing. (305) 294-6238

Capt. Ron Green, Daytripper Charters, (Islamorada area), Fully equipped 23-ft. & 32-ft. sportfishing boats specializing in yellowtail and dolphin in summer and live bait & fly fishing for sailfish in winter. (305) 852-9577 or 800-336-9093

Capt. Mark Henninger, (Key West), Specializing in flats & backcountry fishing aboard fully equipped *Erica*. Maximum 3 anglers. (305) 745-2665

Capt. J.A. (Joe) Johansen, (Islamorada area), Backcountry fishing specializing in light tackle & fly fishing for tarpon, bonefish & snook. (305) 852-3949

Capt. Jack Kelly, *Windy Day & Sea Dog II*, (Key West), Light tackle sportfishing available yearly, all tackle provided including fly. (305) 294-2189 or 800-831-6407

Capt. Rick Killgore, (Tavernier), Flats fishing for tarpon, bonefish, permit and redfish from Islamorada, Flamingo and Biscayne Bay. Fly fishing is a speciality. Phone & Fax (305) 852-1131 or phone (800) 484-3449 (Code 2068)

Capt. David G. Kreshpane, Black Ghost Outfitting & Guide Service, (Marathon), Discounts offered on full day charters aboard the fully equipped *Black Ghost* specializing in fly & light tackle fishing for bonefish, tarpon, snook & permit and Everglades Camping Trips - two-day pack in trips into the 'Glades' for largemouth bass, redfish, snook and tarpon with registered Everglades Parks guides. (305) 743-9666

Capt. Steven Lamp, Dream Catcher Charters, (Marathon-Marquesas), Specializing in backcountry, light tackle and fly fishing. Offshore trips available. Discount not valid for tournaments. (305) 745-2114, Cell phone 304-4494, Fax (305) 744-0159

Capt. Jeff Laning, Tunavision Charters, (Marathon), Varied fishing opportunities from tarpon to tuna, two boats, your choice of stand-up or strap-in fishing. (305) 289-9415

Capt. Bob Leisure, Key West Marine Recovery Services, (Key West), Fully equipped flats boat and custom offshore fishing boat, specializing in fly fishing. (305) 296-7563 or 295-9003

Capt. Roy Lindback, Tiki Charters, (Islamorada area), Discounts on full day offshore & backcountry fishing. (305) 664-2289

Lucky Fleet Inc., (Key West), Fully equipped fishing fleet including 34-ft. *Lucky*

Strike with Capt. Frank Kirwin, 34-ft. *Lucky Too* with Capt. Rees Hamner or 42-ft. *Lucky Charm* with Capt. Jay Weed. (305) 294-5395 or 294-7988.

Capt. Mitch Mathot, *Jersey Devil*, (Marathon area), Specializing in light tackle fishing. Discount available October and November and April. (305) 743-2764

Capt. Barry Meyer, Magic Charters, (Marathon area), Discounts available July thru March. (305) 743-3278

Capt. Chuck Nolan, *Good As Gold*, (Islamorada area), Specializing in backcountry fishing. (305) 852-7520

Capt. Sean O'Keefe, Backwater Fishing, (Key West area), Specializing in flats fly fishing. Discount available for full day charters only. (305) 294-4637

Capt. Frank Perez, (Upper Keys), Fully equipped 18-ft. Hewes skiff specializing in flats & backcountry fishing. Fly, spin and plug tackle provided. (305) 598-4448 or (305) 852-4758, Fax (305) 262-9411

Capt. James Perry, Keys Light-Tackle Sportfishing, (Lower Keys), Specializing in backcountry & oceanside flats fishing for tarpon, bonefish & permit. (305) 872-2323

Capt. Sy Phillips, Silver Bullet Charters, (Islamorada), Fully equipped sportfisherman. (305) 852-7262, Mobile Phone (305) 664-7526

Capt. Dan Purdy, White Cap Charters, (Sugarloaf Shores), Fully equipped sportfisherman fishing Key West/Lower Keys, specializing in flats fishing. (305) 745-2963, Fax (305) 745-9084

Capt. Randy Rode, Rode Runner Sportfishing, (Marathon-Florida Keys), Fully equipped 25-ft. *Rode Runner* specializing in tarpon fishing, available April, May and June. (305) 743-3424, Fax (305) 743-7186

Capt. Pete Ross, Winter Hawk Charters, (Islamorada), Discount on full day charters only. (305) 853-0761, Fax (305) 853-1098

Capt. John D. Sahagian, FUN YET Charters, (Lower Keys), Discount on full day charters only. Diving charters also available. (305) 872-3407 or 800-413-2048

Sea Boots Charters, Inc., Attn: Barbara, (Lower Keys). (305) 745-1530, Fax (305) 872-0780

Capt. Dexter Simmons, Fly Fishing Paradise, (Florida Keys), Fishing Lower Keys, Key West and Marquesas Keys aboard fully equipped *FlatsMaster* specializing in fly and light tackle fishing for tarpon, permit, bonefish, barracuda, cobia and sharks. Catch and release strongly encouraged. Accommodations can be arranged if desired. Phone & fax (305) 745-3304, E-mail: LCZZ92A@PRODIGY.COM, Website: http://pages.prodigy.com/captdexter

Capt. Bob Tiburzi, Off-Key Backcountry Fishing, (Islamorada), Specializing in backcountry fishing. (305) 664-2498

Capt. Don Van Esselstine, (Marathon area), Fully equipped 23-ft. center console *Missy Lynn* specializing in tarpon fishing, 2 angler maximum. (305) 289-0523

Capt. Ron Ward, Wayward Charters, (Key West area). (305) 872-0209

Capt. Frank Waters, Pursuit Fishing Charters, (Marathon, Florida Keys), Specializing in light tackle fishing aboard fully equipped 31-ft. *Pursuit*. (305) 664-7592

Capt. J.C. Wells, 2 Pisces Charters, Attn: Capt. J.C. or Sheri Wells, (Marathon), Fully equipped custom 31-ft. Morgan *2 Pisces* available for offshore and tarpon fishing, specializing in Gulf wreck fishing. (305) 743-0394

Capt. Mike Wilbur, Chaser Fishing Charters, (Key West), Specializing in flats fishing with fly & light tackle. (305) 296-7201, Fax (305) 294-5445

Capt. Dave Wyss, Guilt-Trip Charters, (Key Largo area), Specializing in flats fishing. Discount offered January thru May. (305) 367-2002

GUIDES - CENTRAL FLORIDA

Capt. John Inman, Trophy Bass Guide Service, (Welaka), Specializing in bass fishing. Package trips available. (904) 467-2016

Capt. Ray Maimone, Harvester Charter Fishing, (Buckhead Ridge-Lake Okeechobee), Specializes in live shiner fishing for bass, fly fishing for bluegill and trolling for crappie. Two passenger charters only aboard 19-ft Privateer center helm, equipped with fish finder, trolling motor, G.P.S., live well and cooler. Tackle provided. Local lodging available at discounted rate. Charters available January 1 to May 1. Catch and release of larger fish encouraged. (941) 467-8207 or (603) 926-0264 , E-mail: Gofish@nh.ultranet.com

Capt. Ron Rebeck, Florida Backcountry Charter Service, (DeBary), Fishing Mosquito Lagoon, Indian River, Banana River & St. Johns River. 800-932-7335

GUIDES - WEST COAST

Capt. Chris Asaro Backcountry Fishing, Attn: Capt. Chris Asaro, (Chokoloskee Island to Flamingo Outpost including Key Largo and Islamorada), Specializing in sightcasting for tarpon, snook, bonefish, redfish and permit. Fly fishing encouraged with appropriate flies provided. Ultra shallow water capabilities with a 16-ft roughneck skiff, 2 angler limit. (941) 695-2277, E-mail: CaptAsaro@aol.com Website: www.catalystdw.com/asaro

Capt. Henry Edwards, J.H. Edwards Charter Service, Inc., (Tampa), Fully equipped 23-ft. Dorado fishing Tampa Bay area specializing in snook, snapper, permit, pompano & tarpon, offshore trips also available. (813) 831-4207

Capt. Dave Eimers, (Naples), Flats Skiff *Flash* specializing in fly & light tackle fishing in the Naples/Ten Thousand Island area. (941) 353-4828

Capt. Gary Harris, Osprey Sportfishing, (Destin), Fully equipped, custom 35-ft. sportfisherman *Small Change* out of the Destin Fishing Fleet Marina. Specializes in live bait fishing. Comfortably accommodates up to six anglers. (904) 837-2884

Capt. Matthew Hoover, Night Flight Fishing Charters Inc., (Naples), Flats & backcountry fishing on fully equipped sportfisherman in the Naples/Ten Thousand Island area specializing in fly & light tackle fishing for snook. (941) 732-6550, Fax (941) 775-1210

Capt. Richard Hyland, (Boca Grande area), Saltwater fishing guide specializing in fly fishing, (941) 697-2190, Website: http://www.charterboats.com/rhyland.htm

Capt. G. Pierce Jones, RedFisher in Paradise Charters, (Apalachicola-St. Joseph Bay & Cape San Blas), Specializing in light tackle and fly fishing for trout, redfish and tarpon aboard 19-ft. Hewes RedFisher *Dead Solid Perfect*. Complete packages available including lodging in a three-bedroom beachfront home on Capt San Blas with gourmet meals. (904) 878-9846, Fax (904) 877-4167, Website: www.redfisher.com

Capt. Chris Klingel, (Boca Grande), Discount available August thru March for inshore fishing the Boca Grande area. (941) 764-7221

Capt. Dave Lear, (Big Bend Coast-Tallahassee), Light tackle spin and flycasting for tarpon, redfish, seatrout and mackerel for two anglers aboard fully-equipped 16-ft Silver King flats skiff along Florida's pristine Big Bend coast. Tagging available and release highly encouraged. (850) 216-1951, Fax (850) 216-1981

Light Tackle Fishing Expeditions, Attn: Kathy Ford, (Tampa), Fishing guide service specializing in fly & light tackle flats fishing for tarpon, snook, redfish & trout, offshore trips also available. (813) 963-1930 or 800-972-1930, Fax (813) 963-2823

Capt. Sandy Melvin, owner, Fishing Unlimited Outfitters and Fly Shop, Orvis authorized dealer, (Boca Grande), Specializing in fly and light tackle live bait fishing for snook, redfish and tarpon aboard 20-ft. Lake & Bay Flats Boat. (941) 964-0907 or (941) 964-0291, Fax (941) 964-1611

Capt. Jay Peeler, (Goodland), Fully equipped sportfisherman specializing in fly & light tackle fishing in the Ten Thousand Island area. (941) 642-1342

Capt. Butch Rickey, (Sarasota), Fully equipped 21-ft. Pro Cat *The BarHopp'R* specializing in backcountry fishing for redfish, snook & tarpon. 800-982-9776 or (941) 925-8890

Capt. Stephen Roy, Hyla Charters Backcountry Sportfishing, (St. Petersburg), Fully equipped Hewes flats skiff specializing in backcountry fishing in the St. Petersburg/Tampa Bay area. Phone & Fax (813) 866-0098

Capt. Zeke Sieglaff, (Boca Grande & Pine Island Sound), Fishing out of 17½-ft. Lake & Bay flats boat, specializing in fly fishing for tarpon, redfish and snook. Also fish Boca Grande Pass for tarpon out of 28-ft. custom Daniels. Days-(941) 964-2445, Evenings-(941) 964-2365; E-mail: tarpon@ewol.com; Website: www.flyfishing.florida.com

Capt. Dominic Ullom, Osprey Charters, (Destin), Charters a board fully equipped *Osprey*. Please note all record attempts must be made with anglers own tackle. (904) 654-1695, Cellular phone (904) 582-4662

Capt. Brian Vis, Amanda II Charters, Inc., (Gulf of Mexico/Boca Grande area), Fully equipped 34-ft. Hatteras specializing in tarpon & bottom fishing for grouper & snapper. (941) 964-2366 or 474-5904

Capt. Bill White Charter Services, (Bradenton), Backwater light tackle and fly fishing for snook, redfish, trout and tarpon for up to two anglers. Luxury offshore fishing for tarpon, kingfish, grouper, amberjack, tuna, snapper, barracuda and others for up to six passengers. All licenses, tackle and baits included. Trips must be scheduled in advance. (941) 756-9258, E-Mail: ProFishGyd@aol.com Website: http://www.concentric.com/~buteo/comefish.html

Capt. Henry I. Windes, Sea Catch Charters Inc., (Destin), Fully equipped, air conditioned charter boat *Super Sea Catch* Coast Guard approved for up to 30 passengers out of the Destin Fishing Fleet Marina. Overnights available. (904) 837-6631 Website: http://www.scruznet.com/~kwpsc/ssc.html

Capt. Lee C. Winton-Burnette, (Sarasota), Fully equipped Mako 181 Flats Boat specializing in fishing the flats of Sarasota Bay for snook, trout and redfish. Beach tarpon also available May - July (941) 350-8863

FLORIDA - OTHERS

Bimini Tackle, Attn: Steve, Greg or Jeff, (Pompano Beach), Pompano's newest 'Compleat' tackle shop specializing in inshore, offshore, fly and tournament fishing. Dedicated to having the best selection with experienced anglers to assist. Also features some of South Florida's finest rigged/unrigged frozen baits. (954) 781-6105, Fax (954) 781-4399

Lightning Rods, Attn: Justin Hudgens, (Fort Lauderdale), Custom Rod art and reel repair. Building any kind of custom rod for your fishing needs. All rods built to IGFA standards. (954) 731-4216

Patty Pavlik-Florida Artist, Attn: Patty Pavlik, (Palm Beach Gardens), Original hand-painted gamefish art featuring her signature "furniture art" director's chairs and personalized tournament awards. Custom orders/pieces available. (561) 626-9880

Pisces Portraits c/o Barramundi Corporation, Attn: George Liska, (Orlando), Unique fine art portraits of your released or trophy fish with or without your photo included in matting of the picture. 800-382-1817, Fax (352) 628-0203

T & R Tackle, Attn: George A. Copeland, (Ft. Lauderdale), Full service tackle and bait shop to meet all your needs. (954) 776-1055, Fax (954) 776-1590

World Famous Bait & Tackle, Attn: Jeffrey C. D'Amico, (Ft. Lauderdale), Discount on tackle & supplies specified by management. (954) 985-5661, Fax (954) 985-5767

GEORGIA

Capt. Al Klein, Bottom Line Charters, (Savannah), Voted "Best of Savannah" by *Savannah Morning News*, Fish aboard the comfortable, custom 36-ft. Sportfish, fully equipped with International fighting chair and Penn reels. Accommodates up to six passengers. Offshore fishing for grouper, snapper, kingfish and more. All licenses, bait and tackle included. Reservations required and discount available Monday thru Thursdays. (912) 897-6503

South Georgia Guide Service, Attn: Ben Baker, (Ashburn), Full and half-day guided fishing trips to private South Georgia ponds with emphasis on trophy bass on artificial lures. Catch and release except when bass is over 10 lbs. Catfish, bream and crappie trips also available. These waters are closed to the public or have limited public access. Mounting and tackle available if desired. Days: (912) 567-3655, Evenings: (912) 567-2222, Fax (912) 567-4402

Capt. Bob Morrissey, Saltwater Charters, (Savannah), Offshore fishing for red snapper, grouper and amberjacks. Light tackle fishing for smoker kings. Fish the Navy Towers off of the Georgia Coast for unparalleled excitement aboard the fully equipped 30-ft. *Saltshaker*. Advance reservations required. (912) 598-1814

HAWAII HOTELS

(ISLAND OF KAUAI)

Outrigger Kauai Beach, (Lihue), Deluxe beachfront hotel located on the Royal Coconut Coast featuring three swimming pools arranged around a dramatic rockscape and waterfalls, two restaurants, lobby bar and night club with nearby tennis courts and golf course. Please note reservations must be made in advance. 1-800-OUTRIGGER (688-7444) or (303) 369-7777, Website: www.outrigger.com

Kiahuna Plantation, (Koloa), Deluxe Outrigger beachfront resort condominium located at Poipu Beach featuring fully equipped one and two bedroom condos. Shopping and dining options are conveniently located across the street at the Poipu Shopping Village or nearby Koloa Town. Please note reservations must be made in advance. 1-800-OUTRIGGER (688-7444) or (303) 369-7777, Website: www.outrigger.com

Plantation Hale, (Kapaa), Superior Outrigger all-suite condominium property located on the Coconut Coast. All units are one-bedroom with fully equipped kitchens in garden setting. Property features pool, barbecue area and laundry facilities with nearby beaches and golf course. Please note reservations must be made in advance. 1-800-OUTRIGGER (688-7444) or (303) 369-7777, Website: www.outrigger.com

(ISLAND OF OAHU)

Outrigger Hobron, (Honolulu), An Outrigger Economy Hotel located 8 to 10 minutes walking distance to Waikiki Beach and Ala Moana Shopping Center. The hotel has a restaurant and cocktail lounge, swimming pool, sauna and laundry facilities. Many guest rooms have kitchenettes with ocean and mountain views. Please note reservations must be made in advance. 1-800-OUTRIGGER (688-7444) or (303) 369-7777, Website: www.outrigger.com

Outrigger Waikiki on the Beach, (Honolulu), Deluxe beachfront hotel located on Waikiki Beach featuring two full-service restaurants, indoor & outdoor lounges, Health Club, Business Center, concierge level, pool and whirlpool spa, in-room refrigerators, coffee makers and balconies. Please note reservations must be made in advance. 1-800-OUTRIGGER (688-7444) or (303) 369-7777, Website: www.outrigger.com

Outrigger Reef on the Beach, (Honolulu), Deluxe beachfront resort hotel located on Waikiki Beach featuring three restaurants, three cocktail lounges, extensive pool area with whirlpool spas, shopping mall, Business Center, concierge level, in-room refrigerators and coffee makers. Please note reservations must be made in advance. 1-800-OUTRIGGER (688-7444) or (303) 369-7777, Website: www.outrigger.com

Outrigger Prince Kuhio, (Honolulu), Deluxe hotel featuring beautiful ocean and mountain views, restaurant, lobby, bar, heated pool and whirlpool spa, pool bar, Business Center, concierge level, in-room refrigerators and coffee makers. Please note reservations must be made in advance. 1-800-OUTRIGGER (688-7444) or (303) 369-7777, Website: www.outrigger.com

Outrigger Reef Lanais, (Honolulu), Intimate, European-style, first class hotel located less than one block from the beach in Waikiki. Guest rooms feature park or ocean views with complimentary continental breakfast daily. Please note reservations must be made in advance. 1-800-OUTRIGGER (688-7444) or (303) 369-7777, Website: www.outrigger.com

Outrigger East, (Honolulu), Superior class hotel located one block from the beach in Waikiki featuring four restaurants, lobby bar, pool with pool bar and whirlpool spa,

Business Center, and in-room refrigerators. Please note reservations must be made in advance. 1-800-OUTRIGGER (688-7444) or (303) 369-7777, Website: www.outrigger.com

Outrigger West, (Honolulu), Superior class hotel located two blocks from Waikiki Beach and across from the International Market Place. Hotel features large pool with poolside bar, restaurant with lounge, in-room refrigerators and coffee makers. Please note reservations must be made in advance. 1-800-OUTRIGGER (688-7444) or (303) 369-7777, Website: www.outrigger.com

Outrigger Waikiki Tower, (Honolulu), Superior class hotel located one block from beach in Waikiki featuring restaurant with lounge, in-room refrigerators and coffee makers. Hotel shares pool with adjacent Outrigger Edgewater. Please note reservations must be made in advance. 1-800-OUTRIGGER (688-7444) or (303) 369-7777, Website: www.outrigger.com

Outrigger Reef Towers, (Honolulu), Superior class hotel located one block from Waikiki Beach featuring two restaurants, cocktail lounges, pool, in-room refrigerators, coffee makers and pool. Many rooms have kitchenettes. Please note reservations must be made in advance. 1-800-OUTRIGGER (688-7444) or (303) 369-7777, Website: www.outrigger.com

Outrigger Malia, (Honolulu), Superior class hotel located two blocks from the beach featuring restaurant with lounge, tennis court, whirlpool spa and laundry facilities. Please note reservations must be made in advance. 1-800-OUTRIGGER (688-7444) or (303) 369-7777, Website: www.outrigger.com

Outrigger Village, (Honolulu), Moderate class hotel located one block from Waikiki Beach and near Royal Hawaiian Shopping Center. Hotel features restaurant and bar, swimming pool, laundry facilities, and in-room refrigerators. Please note reservations must be made in advance. 1-800-OUTRIGGER (688-7444) or (303) 369-7777, Website: www.outrigger.com

Outrigger Islander Waikiki, (Honolulu), Centrally located, newly renovated hotel featuring in-room refrigerators, coffee makers and pool. Please note reservations must be made in advance. 1-800-OUTRIGGER (688-7444) or (303) 369-7777, Website: www.outrigger.com

Outrigger Ala Wai Towers, (Honolulu), Comfortable hotel located three blocks from Waikiki Beach, situated near the yacht harbor and Ala Moa Center. Hotel has no restaurant but does have pool and whirlpool spa, tennis court, laundry facilities, in-room refrigerators and coffee makers. Complimentary continental breakfast daily. Please note reservations must be made in advance. 1-800-OUTRIGGER (688-7444) or (303) 369-7777, Website: www.outrigger.com

Outrigger Surf, (Honolulu), Comfortable hotel centrally located two blocks from the beach, convenient to shopping and night life.

Hotel features restaurant with cocktail lounge, pool and kitchenettes. Please note reservations must be made in advance. 1-800-OUTRIGGER (688-7444) or (303) 369-7777, Website: www.outrigger.com

Outrigger Maile Sky Court, (Honolulu), Comfortable hotel located three blocks from the beach featuring restaurant, spacious pool deck with pool, jacuzzi and beverage bar, in-room refrigerators and some kitchenettes. Please note reservations must be made in advance. 1-800-OUTRIGGER (688-7444) or (303) 369-7777, Website: www.outrigger.com

Outrigger Hobron, (Honolulu), Comfortable hotel featuring cozy rooms with great city views near Ala Moana Center shopping mall, restaurant and cocktail lounge, swimming pool, sauna, laundry facilities, in-room refrigerators and coffee makers. Please note reservations must be made in advance. 1-800-OUTRIGGER (688-7444) or (303) 369-7777, Website: www.outrigger.com

Outrigger Royal Islander, (Honolulu), Comfortable, intimate boutique hotel located less than one block from the beach in Waikiki. Hotel has no pool but the facilities across the street at Outrigger Reef on the Beach are at your disposal. Please note reservations must be made in advance. 1-800-OUTRIGGER (688-7444) or (303) 369-7777, Website: www.outrigger.com

Outrigger Edgewater, (Honolulu), Comfortable, nostalgic Hawaiian hotel located one block from Waikiki Beach featuring four restaurants, laundry facilities and in-room refrigerators. Hotel shares a pool with the adjacent Outrigger Waikiki Tower. Please note reservations must be made in advance. 1-800-OUTRIGGER (688-7444) or (303) 369-7777, Website: www.outrigger.com

Outrigger Coral Seas, (Honolulu), Budget-class hotel located one block from the beach in Waikiki featuring two restaurants with cocktail lounges and in-room refrigerators. Guests are allowed to use the swimming pool at the adjacent Outrigger Village. Please note reservations must be made in advance. 1-800-OUTRIGGER (688-7444) or (303) 369-7777, Website: www.outrigger.com

Outrigger Waikiki Surf, (Honolulu), Budget-class hotel located three blocks from Waikiki Beach featuring in-room refrigerators, coffee makers, laundry facilities and small pool. Please note reservations must be made in advance. 1-800-OUTRIGGER (688-7444) or (303) 369-7777, Website: www.outrigger.com

Outrigger Waikiki Surf East, (Honolulu), Comfortable hotel located three blocks from the beach in a quiet section of Waikiki featuring swimming pool and laundry facilities but no food and beverage outlets. Kitchenettes are available in most rooms and suites. Please note reservations must be made in advance. 1-800-OUTRIGGER (688-7444) or (303) 369-7777, Website:

www.outrigger.com

Sheraton Moana Surfrider Hotel, Attn: Marla Kelly, (Honolulu), Full-service beachfront hotel--one of the distinguished Historic Hotels of America. (808) 923-2880, Fax (808) 922-5049

(ISLAND OF MAUI)

The Palms at Wailea, (Wailea), Deluxe Outrigger condominium resort located on a scenic bluff and just a short stroll to beautiful Wailea Beach. Resort features fully equipped one and two-bedroom condominium suites, pool with spa and lushly landscaped grounds with nearby championship golf courses and tennis club. Please note reservations must be made in advance. 1-800-OUTRIGGER (688-7444) or (303) 369-7777, Website: www.outrigger.com

Ka'anapali Royal, (Lahaina), Superior Outrigger condominium resort overlooking the 16th fairway of the North Ka'anapali Golf Course. The luxurious, fully equipped suites offer a complete kitchen, sunken living room, washer/dryer, and private lanai with wet bar. Amid the lushly landscaped grounds are a swimming pool, barbecue area, spa, sauna and tennis courts. Please note reservations must be made in advance. 1-800-OUTRIGGER (688-7444) or (303) 369-7777, Website: www.outrigger.com

Maui Eldorado Resort, (Ka'anapali), Superior Outrigger condominium resort conveniently located in the center of the Kaanapali resort area featuring fully equipped studio, one and two bedroom suites, three swimming pools and beachfront cabanas. Please note reservations must be made in advance. 1-800-OUTRIGGER (688-7444) or (303) 369-7777, Website: www.outrigger.com

Napili Shores Resort, (Lahaina), Superior Outrigger oceanfront condominium resort located on Napili Bay, overlooking the island of Molokai, featuring comfortable studio and one-bedroom suites with full kitchens, two pools, hot tub, barbecue/picnic areas, two restaurants and nearby golf courses and tennis courts. Please note reservations must be made in advance. 1-800-OUTRIGGER (688-7444) or (303) 369-7777, Website: www.outrigger.com

(THE BIG ISLAND OF HAWAII)

Kanaloa at Kona, (Kailua-Kona), Deluxe Outrigger resort condominium situated at the ocean's edge of Keauhou Bay and bordered by the championship golf course at Kona Country Club. Each spacious condo is fully equipped with kitchen, microwave oven, wet bar, washer/dryer and private lanai. Ocean suites feature in-room whirlpools. Resort amenities include three swimming pools and whirlpool spas, two lighted tennis courts, oceanfront restaurant and lounge. Please note reservations must be made in advance. 1-

800-OUTRIGGER (688-7444) or (303) 369-7777, Website: www.outrigger.com
Keauhou Beach Hotel, Attn: Reservations, (Kailua-Kona), Beautiful full-service oceanfront resort. 800-367-6025 or (808) 955-7600, Fax (808) 946-5846
Knutson & Associates, Attn: Marilyn, (Kailua-Kona), Selection of oceanfront condominiums. 800-800-6202 or (808) 326-2178
The Royal Waikoloan, (Kamuela), Deluxe Outrigger beachfront resort located at Anaeho'omalu Bay on the Kohala Coast featuring four restaurants, cocktail lounges, pool with whirlpool spa, pool bar, dance club, shops and tennis courts. Resort is adjacent to historic Hawaiian fishponds as well as the Waikoloa Golf Courses. Please note reservations must be made in advance. 1-800-OUTRIGGER (688-7444) or (303) 369-7777, Website: www.outrigger.com

HAWAII GUIDES

Capt. Allan Ayano, Lady Dee Sportfishing, (Kailua-Kona), Fully equipped custom 46-ft. Bertram specializing in light tackle fishing. (808) 322-8026 or (808) 322-0163, Fax (808) 326-1294
Capt. Dale Berning, Marlin Machine Charters Inc., (Kailua-Kona), Fully equipped custom 44-ft. sportfisherman. (808) 322-3474 or 326-2000 (Boat)
Capt. Chip Conklin, Enterprise Sportfishing, (Kailua-Kona), Fishing the Kona coast for marlin, tuna, wahoo, dolphin and others aboard the fully equipped twin-diesel 36-ft. sportfisher *Enterprise*. All bait, tackle and ice supplied. No fishing license required. USCG licensed and insured for up to six passengers. Phone & Fax (808) 329-3013, E-mail: chipkona@aol.com. Web page: http://www.charterboats.com/enterpris.htm
Capt. Del Dykes, Reel Action Light Tackle Sportfishing, (Kailua-Kona), Fully equipped 30-ft. Blackman *Reel Action* out of Honokohau Harbor specializing in both inshore and offshore light tackle fishing. Phone & Fax (808) 325-6811
Capt. Kelley Everette & Capt. Jocelyn Everette, Northern Lights Sportfishing, (Kailua-Kona), Fully equipped custom 37-ft. Merritt *Northern Lights* out of Honokahau Harbor specializing in light tackle fishing. (808) 325-6522, Fax (808) 329-8755
Capt. A.J. Friend, Hula Girl Sportfishing, (Kailua-Kona), Custom 31-ft. Innovator offering discounts for full day charters only. Tag & release strongly encouraged. (808) 326-7505 or (808) 936-1474
Capt. Gary Hicks, Golden Eagle Sportfishing Charters, (Honolulu), Big game sportfishing only minutes from Waikiki. Custom built sportfisher, fully equipped. All bait and tackle included. The *Golden Eagle* can accommodate up to a maximum of 8 anglers. Inter-island trips, share parties, full

day, 3/4 day and 1/2 day exclusive charters available. (808) 591-8911, Fax (808) 591-0268
Capt. Neal Isaacs, Anxious Fishing Charters, Inc., (Kailua-Kona), Fully equipped custom 33-ft. Bertram. (808) 326-1229
Capt. Butch LoSasso, Bill Buster Charters, (Kailua-Kona), Fully equipped custom 36-ft. Sportfisher specializing in big game fishing. Phone & Fax (808) 329-2657
Capt. Tom McNey, No Strings II Sportfishing, (Kailua-Kona), Fully equipped custom 35-ft. Contender specializing in fly fishing for billfish. 800-797-FISH or (808) 329-6267
Notorious Sportfishing, Attn: Capt. Jack or Kay Prettyman, (Kealakekua), Fully equipped 35-ft. Bertram specializing in marlin fishing. (808) 325-7558, Fax (808) 322-6507
Capt. Christopher Rose, Aerial Sportfishing Charters, (Lahaina, Maui), Fleet of fully equipped sportfishing boats including 36-ft. Chris Craft, 42-ft. Ditmar Donaldson & 44-ft. Pacemaker. (808) 667-9089, Fax (808) 661-3074
Capt. S. Kamal Salibi, True Blue Charters & Oceansports, (Island of Kauai), Fishing Hawaiian style aboard *Konane Star*, a fully equipped 55-ft. Delta Luxury vessel. Offshore big game, inshore bottom fishing and exclusive blue water expeditions available. Quality tackle and local experience with Aloha! (808) 245-9662 or (808) 639-0770
Capt. Gene Vander Hoek, Sea Genie Inc., (Kailua-Kona), Fully equipped custom 39-ft. Rybovich *Sea Genie II*, specializing in marlin fishing. Light, ultralight and fly fishermen welcome. (808) 325-5355, Fax (808) 325-5366

LOUISIANA

Big Red Guides & Outfitters, Attn: Capt. Bubby Rodriquez, (New Orleans), Fly fishing for redfish in shallow marsh in custom-built Go-Devil Mudboats (as seen on ESPN-TV), instruction available, complete fly shop. (504) 340-8887 or 800-966-4868
Painkiller Offshore Fishing Team, Attn: Capt. K.T. Cerullo, (office in Metairie), Fully equipped 28-ft. Tiara - Pursuit sportfishing boat *Painkiller* out of Cypress Cove Marina in Venice, Louisiana. Can accommodate up to four anglers. Offshore, inshore and fly fishing available with tag and release encouraged. Discount offered on offshore trips only with every fourth trip free. (504) 899-7949, Fax (504) 831-6945, Boat (504) 452-5959
Capt. Briant Smith, (Lake Charles), Orvis endorsed guide offering fly and light tackle saltwater fishing along the Southwest Louisiana Gulf Coast. Our primary species are redfish, sea trout and flounder (inshore) and cobia, mackerel, tripletail, bluefish, and others (offshore). Best time is May to December. Phone & Fax (318) 436-7800, E-

mail: CAPTBRIANT@aol.com Website: http://members.aol.com/captbriant/flyfish.html

MAINE

Casco Bay Sportfishing Company, Attn: Capt. Bill Bell, (North Windham), Fully equipped 32-ft. Brendan *Sea Quest* specializing in shark, tuna, bluefish & striped bass fishing, can accommodate up to six. (207) 893-1261
Capt. Doug Jowett, (Brunswick), Fly fishing for striped bass & blue fish on Kennebec River aboard fully equipped *Mainely* out of Bath, Maine and Cape Cod. All tackle & flies provided, no license required, catch & release encouraged, 2 person maximum. Season - May thru October. Fly fishing instruction available. (207) 725-4573

MARYLAND

Standard Bet Charters, Attn: Capt. Hank DeVito, (Glen Burnie), Fully equipped sportfisherman *Afternoon Delight* out of Breezy Point, specializing in striped bass fishing in Chesapeake Bay. (410) 760-8242

MASSACHUSETTS

Fishermen's Furs & Feathers, A Division of Castle Arms, Attn: Phil Castleman, (Springfield), Fishermen's Furs & Feathers offers IGFA members a 20% discount on any of their exotic feathers for fly tying. 800-525-4866, Fax (413) 731-1292
Capt. Walter Gibson, Rainbow Chaser Charters, (Gloucester), Fully equipped 30-ft. *Rainbow Chaser* specializing in cod, haddock, pollock, stripers, blues & shark fishing. (978) 957-5865
Capt. Steven James, Quality Time Charters, (Scituate), 32-ft Blackfin and 24-ft Grady White, IGFA all-tackle world record blue shark 454 lb, fully equipped for inshore and offshore fishing, specializing in cod, stripers, blues, sharks and tuna. Phone & Fax (781) 643-0012
Capt. Karen A. Kukolich, Tippet Charters, (Edgartown, Martha's Vineyard), Fly and light tackle fishing aboard 23-ft. Boston Whaler, rods supplied if needed. Walk around boat can accommodate two anglers. (508) 627-8556, Fax (508) 627-5066
Capt. Bob MacGregor, Hop-Tuit Charters, (West Falmouth), Fishing Cuttyhunk & Martha's Vineyard aboard fully equipped *Hop-Tuit* specializing in fly & light tackle fishing for striped bass, bluefish & bonito. (508) 540-7642
Capt. Todd MacGregor, MAC ATAC Sportfishing, (New Bedford), Specializing in Trophy Stripers, blues and tuna. Fishing Cuttyhunk, the Elizabeth Islands and Martha's Vineyard daily. Light tackle trips available. Accommodations arranged if desired. "Catching fish is absolutely guaranteed!!" (508) 992-9189, Fax (508)

992-8691, E-mail:
TODDMAC@JUNO.COM
Gamefisher Sportfishing Adventures, Attn: Capt. Paul Poirier, Fully equipped 40-ft. Gamefisherman *Gamefisher* offering discounts on giant bluefin tuna fishing. Office in Florida - (954) 725-3709, cellular phone (954) 415-7089

MICHIGAN

Capt. Dave Wyss, Guilt-Trip Charters, (Grayling), Discounts offered on trout fishing charters June thru September. (517) 348-3203, January - May (305) 367-2002

MINNESOTA

Pehrson Lodge Resort, Attn: Steve Raps, (Cook), Cabin lodge located on Lake Vermilion offering discounts on 3 or more nights lodging. (218) 666-5478, Fax (218) 666-2451

MONTANA

Bighorn River Country Lodge, Attn: Rob Warren, (Fort Smith), Comfortable, full service lodge located near the Bighorn River on the Native American lands of the Crow tribe offering excellent trout fishing. Amenities include satellite TV, hot tub, air-conditioned rooms and easy access for handicapped guests. Licensed guides and outfitters available for float trips. Discount offered on food and lodging only. (406) 666-2331

Montana River Outfitters, Attn: Craig Madsen or Mike Johnson, (Great Falls), Discounts offered on 2 or more days fishing Missouri River with lodging at Wolf Creek Cabins. (406) 761-1677, Fax (406) 452-3833

Osprey Expeditions, Attn: Gary Fritz, (office in Helena), Professional licensed guides & accommodations for flyfishing the Missouri, Blackfoot and Smith Rivers. Driftboat, wade and float tube trips available. 800-315-8502

NEW HAMPSHIRE

Lopstick Lodge & Cabins, Attn: Chuck Hopping, (Pittsburg), Housekeeping cabins with private trout pond on 1st Connecticut Lake. (603) 538-6659 or 800-538-6659

Capt. Ray Maimone, Harvester Ocean Charter Fishing, (Rye), Specializes in fishing for stripers, mackerel and bluefish aboard a fast 24.5-ft. Mako, comfortable for up to a four-person charter, fully equipped with Penn reels, fiberglass boat rods, ugly sticks, loran, VHF and fishfinder. Fly fishermen welcome. Charters available May 1 to November 1. (603) 926-0264 or (941) 926-0264, E-mail: Gofish@nh.ultranet.com

NEW JERSEY

Cape Rods, Attn: S.R. Murphy (Murf), (Cape May), Custom rods & repairs. Complimentary UPS (United Parcel Service) in the continental U.S. (609) 884-7206

Capt. Joe Galese, Current Affair Sportfishing Charters, (Cape May), Discounts offered on weekday trips aboard fully equipped 25-ft. Parker *Current Affair* rigged for inshore, offshore and canyon angling for all species found in mid-Atlantic waters including striped bass, tuna, sharks, marlin, bonito, blues, fluke, and weakfish. 800-491-9515 or (609) 884-1707

Capt. Dick Herb, Escapade Charters, Inc., (Avalon), Fully equipped 28-ft. Bertram out of Avalon specializing in bluefish, shark, tuna, bonito & mackerel fishing. (609) 861-5951, winter phone - (610) 647-4693

Capt. Bruce Miller, Mirage Sportfishing Charters, (Point Pleasant), Big game fishing out of the Manasquan Inlet aboard the fast, fully equipped, tournament rigged 43-ft. Egg Harbor sportfisherman *Mirage*. Up to six anglers for inshore or offshore fishing, with marlin, tuna and dolphin their speciality. All bait and full range of custom tackle, including 30 to 50-lb stand-up supplied. (732) 929-9103, E-mail: Captmarlin@aol.com Website: http://www.vitinc.com/nn/chart/mirage.html

Capt. Rich Newallis Jr., (Highlands), Fish the Sandy Hook and Raritan Bays aboard the *Just One More*, a 26-ft. Mako walkaround with twin 200 h.p. Yamahas, full electronics and safety equipment. Accommodates one to four anglers. Fluke, striped bass, weakfish and bluefish. All bait and tackle supplied. Striped bass trolling specialist. Tournament charters upon request. Leaves from Sandy Hook Bay Marina in Highlands. (908) 412-9147

Capt. Al Ristori, Capt. Al Ristori Charters, (Manasquan Park), Fully equipped 28-ft. center console *Sheri Berri II* specializing in tuna, sharks, stripers, blues and bottom fish. (732) 223-5729

SouthEast Sportfishing, Attn: Capt. Lindsay Fuller, (Beach Haven), Fully equipped 41-ft Ricky Scarborough Express Sportfisherman *June Bug* available for inshore, offshore, canyon and overnight trips out of Beach Haven, New Jersey, 2 hours south of New York City. Inshore trips target bluefish, bluefin tuna, bonita, fluke, stripers and wreck species. Offshore trips target white and blue marlin, yellowfin tuna, albacore and dolphin. All billfish are released. (609) 778-0200, Fax (609) 778-4961, E-mail: JuneBugO41@aol.com

Tackle Box Sportfishing, Attn: Capt. Phil Sciortino, Jr., (Sandy Hook area), Light tackle and fly fishing striped bass specialists practicing catch and release aboard fully equipped 23-ft. center console. Accommodates 1 to 3 anglers. (732) 264-7711

NEW MEXICO

Rizuto's Inc. - San Juan River Lodge, Attn: Chuck Rizuto, (Navajo Dam), Discount offered on lodging & guides. Specializes in fly fishing. (505) 632-1411, Fax (505) 632-8798

NEW YORK

Capt. Andy Becker, High Life II Sportfishing Charters, (Babylon, Long Island), Tournament rigged 31-ft. Rampage with tag & release encouraged. Accommodates 1 to 6 passengers. Bait, tackle, ice and soda included. (516) 361-7123, Fax (516) 366-4637

Capt. Scott Gaeckle, Aeolus, Inc., Alcyon Fly Fishing and Light Tackle Charters, (Southampton), Fully equipped custom 21 ft. Steiger Craft center console, fishing the eastern end of Long Island from Shinnecock to Montauk, most of which is nationally recognized as the Peconic Estuary System. Casting to striped bass, bluefish, weakfish, bonito, and little tunny from May to December. Full and half day trips available. Lodging information available upon request, 2 hours from New York City. (516) 287-3264, sgaeckle@peconic. net

Capt. Otto Haselman, Fishooker Charters, (Montauk, Long Island), Saltwater fishing inshore for striped bass, bluefish, fluke, cod. Offshore fishing for shark, including mako and thresher; bluefin, yellowfin, longfin and bigeye tunas; white and blue marlin; and mahi-mahi. Up to 6 anglers. Fast, comfortable custom built 35-ft. J-C Sportfisherman. Advance reservations required, brochure available. (516) 668-3821

Capt. Ron Miller, Sea-Ducer Saltwater Flyfishing Adventures, (Aquebogue, Long Island), Fully equipped custom ProLine 20-ft. Classic center console out of Lighthouse Marina, specializing in fly & light tackle fishing for striped bass, bluefish, dolphin & shark, group & private instruction at fly fishing school available. (516) 585-7883

Capt. Mike Pastore, RodMaster Sportfishing Charters, (Ontario), Fully equipped 26-ft. PennYan Flybridge Sportfisherman specializing in salmon, trout & bass fishing on Lake Ontario. (315) 524-4313

Patsy K II Charters, Attn: Capt. George P. Kazdin, (Hampton Bays), Sportfishing out of Shinnecock Inlet in Eastern Long Island aboard 32-ft. tournament equipped Albemarle sportfisherman. Inshore, offshore and canyon trips available. Specializing in marlin, tuna, shark and striped bass fishing. All bait and tackle included. 4 man limit offshore. (516) 283-4884 or 728-6595, Fax (516) 283-4893, E-mail: kazpool@pipeline.com

Capt. Michael Potts, Blue Fin IV, Inc., (Montauk), Fully equipped 41-ft. *Blue Fin IV* available for offshore, inshore or canyon-overnight charters out of Viking Dock in

Montauk Harbor. (516) 668-9323, Fax (516) 267-2078

Capt. Rob Robl, "Fly A-Salt" Saltwater Fly Fishing Charters, (Smithtown Bay), Fishing the diverse waters of Long Island's Smithtown Bay specializing in fly fishing for striped bass, bluefish, bonito and false albacore fishing. Special Long Island North Fork trips also available. (516) 243-4282

NORTH CAROLINA

Dolphin Realty Inc., Attn: Alice Dexter, (Hatteras), Large selection of weekly rentals available year round. (919) 986-2562 or 800-338-4775

Capt. Merv Finch, Redfish Charters, (Atlantic Beach), Gulfstream offshore fishing charters for tuna, wahoo, dolphin, sailfish and marlin aboard fully equipped 44-ft. Henriques sportfisherman *Redfish* out of Sea Water Marina. Release of marlin & sailfish encouraged. Phone & Fax (919) 247-3079

Capt. Chuck Harrill, Flapjack & Gung Ho Fishing Charters, (Carolina Beach), Fishing aboard fully equipped 49-ft. custom Carolina Sportfisherman and 46-ft. Hatteras. 800-288-3474

McLeod's Highland Fly Fishing, Attn: Mac Brown, (Bryson City), Discount offered on private instruction in fly fishing school & backcountry trips in the Great Smoky Mountains. (704) 488-8975 or 800-258-9840

Marlin Mania Charters, Attn: Capt. Jim Bowman, (Hatteras), Fully equipped 43-ft. custom *"Fast"* sportfisherman out of Teach's Lair Marina specializing in marlin fishing. (919) 995-4005

SouthEast Sportfishing, Attn: Capt. Lindsay Fuller, (Oregon Inlet), Fully equipped 41-ft Ricky Scarborough Express Sportfisherman *June Bug* available for charter from January through end of May for yellowfin tuna, bluefin tuna, white marlin, blue marlin, false albacore and dolphin. All billfish are released. Office in Moorestown, New Jersey - (609) 778-0200, Fax (609) 778-4961, E-mail: JuneBugO41@aol.com

OHIO

Capt. Pat Winke, Winke Guide Service, (Port Clinton), Discount offered for year-round weekday charters fishing Lake Erie and specializing in walleye & smallmouth bass fishing. (419) 798-4140 or 800-274-9255

PENNSYLVANIA

Barcaskey Outfitters, Attn: Michael Barcaskey, (Oakdale), Guided freshwater trips for all species. One day and over night. Specializing in the largest fish Pennsylvania has to offer. (412) 788-0728

Cape Rods, Attn: S.R. Murphy (Murf), (Philadelphia), Custom rods & repairs. Complimentary UPS (United Parcel Service) in the continental U.S. (215) 698-7987

RHODE ISLAND

Capt. Al Anderson, Rhode Island Charter Sportfishing Inc., (Narragansett), Fishing aboard the fully equipped 35-ft. *Prowler* out of Snug Harbor Marina specializing in tag & release of bluefin tuna, striped bass & sharks. (401) 783-8487, Fax (401) 783-4689

Capt. Dave Preble, Early Bird Charters, Inc., (Narragansett), Fishing aboard fully equipped 31-ft. *Early Bird* from Port Judith Marina. Specializing in striped bass, sharks, tuna & billfish. (401) 789-7596

Capt. Jim White, White Ghost Guide Service, (Narragansett Bay), Fly fishing and light tackle specialist. Action Craft Pro Saltwater Team Member, operating a 1997 ActionCraft 1810 Flatsmaster skiff in Narragansett Bay for striped bass, bluefish, weakfish, bonito and albacore. Springtime Grand Slam (bass, blues, weaks). Instruction and freshwater trips also available. Women and children welcome. (401) 828-9465, E-mail: WhiteGhos1@aol.com

SOUTH CAROLINA

Capt. John Cox, Curlew Charters, (Charleston), Fly & light tackle shallow water fishing on 16-ft. Hewes Tournament skiff, 2 angler limit, specializing in catch and release of redfish, crevalle jack, mackerel, bluefish & tarpon. (803) 884-1371, Fax (803) 744-2410

TENNESSEE

South Harpeth Outfitters, Inc., Attn: Ernie Paquette, (Nashville), One or two day guided fishing trips in remote streams & rivers specializing in trout & bass fishing with catch & release encouraged, flyfishing instruction available. (615) 298-2343

TEXAS

Bimini Custom Fishing Rods, Attn: Dave Mata, (San Antonio), Discounts offered on a full line of rods from fly to big game, brochures available. 800-596-7637 or phone & fax (210) 340-7637

Jeff Gunn's Lake Fork Guide Service, Attn: Jeff Gunn, (Lake Fork, Alba), Fish out of a Ranger 482V, specializing in catching trophy largemouth bass. Beautiful and legendary Lake Fork is home of "Ethel" and the Share-A-Lunker program (over 13 lbs). All quality tackle provided. Full time licensed professional guide. Group trips and accommodations can be arranged. (903) 765-2155

WYOMING

Squaw Creek Ranch & Outfitters, Attn: Rich Smith, (Cody), Comfortable ranch located in Clark's Fork River Valley, can accommodate up to 30, fly & light tackle fishing for trout in Clark's Fork, its tributaries and lakes. (307) 587-6178 or 800-532-7281, Fax (307) 587-5249

Wyoming Fly Fishing Connection, Attn: Gary or Robin Edwards, (Laramie), Fully equipped fishing on private ranches for native browns, cutthroats, rainbow and brookies. Accommodations in a turn-of-the-century log home. Supplies provided as needed. All top quality Loomis equipment. Trips have been featured in *Sports Afield* and on nationwide television shows. 800-347-4775 or Phone & fax (307) 742-3771, E-mail: information@flyfishing-connection.com Website: http://www:flyfishing-connection.com

U.S. VIRGIN ISLANDS

Capt. Red Bailey, Abigail III Sportfishing, (St. Thomas), Fully equipped custom 44-ft. *Abigail III* specializing in marlin fishing. Phone & Fax (340) 775-6147

Capt. Spike Herbert, Sapphire Fishing Charters, (St. Thomas), Fully equipped 46-ft. Rybovich *Phoenix* specializing in marlin fishing out of Sapphire Beach Resort and Marina. (340) 775-6465 or (340) 775-6100 or 800-524-2090, Fax (340) 775-4024

Capt. Bill McCauley, Prowler Sportfishing Charters, Attn: Capt. Bill or Rita McCauley, (St. Thomas), Discount offered on full day marlin fishing aboard fully equipped 40-ft. Jersey *Prowler* and state-of-the-art 45-ft. Hatteras *Prowler II*. Additional discount offered on multiple days booked. (340) 779-2515, Fax (340) 774-2766

Capt. Don Mertens, Bluefin II Sportfishing, Attn: Capt. Don or Carol Mertens, (St. Thomas), Fully equipped 44-ft. *Bluefin II* specializing in marlin fishing. (340) 775-6691

Ruffian Sportfishing, c/o St. Croix Marine, Attn: Reservations, (St. Croix), Fully equipped 41-ft. Hatteras Convertible *Ruffian* fishing Gallows Bay, Christiansted & St. Croix. (340) 773-7165 or 773-6011 or 733-0289, Fax (340) 778-8974

Sapphire Beach Resort & Marina, Attn: Reservations, (St. Thomas), Luxurious full-service beachfront resort & marina. (340) 775-6100, Fax (340) 775-2403

Shenanigans Sportfishing, c/o St. Croix Marine, Attn: Reservations, (St. Croix), Fully equipped 42-ft. Oceans Super Sport Convertible *Shenanigans* fishing Gallows Bay, Christiansted & St. Croix. (340) 773-7165 or 773-6011 or 733-0289, Fax (340) 778-8974

VENEZUELA

Grandpez Angling Adventures, Attn: Carlos Aristeguieta, Offering a discount on the fishing package to IGFA members at Caurama Lodge, located along the Caura River in southern Venezuela, specializing in conventional, light tackle and fly fishing for payara, sardinata, peacock bass, giant catfish and other exotics. Personalized attention by experienced world record holder. Office in Caracas - phone and fax (58-2) 941-2978, E-Mail: grandpez@cantv.net

Outdoor Adventures to Venezuela, c/o Don Bohannon, Exotic fishing & outdoor adventures arranged. Office in Georgia - (770) 496-0427, Fax (770) 496-1361

Pro Anglers International Service, Attn: Frank Ibarra, Fly fishing & light tackle specialists offering complete fishing programs for billfish, bonefish, tarpon, snook, peacock bass and payara at La Guaira, Guri Lake, Los Roques, Cinaruco River, Uraima, Ventuari River, Monserrate Lake & the Delta areas. Office in Caracas: Phone & Fax (58)-2-979-2796

ZAMBIA

Chiawa Camp c/o G & G Safaris Ltd., Attn: Grant Cumings, (Lusaka), Comfortable camp located along the Zambezi River specializing in tigerfish safaris and total African experience. (260) 1-261588, Fax (260) 1-262683

Tiger Fishing Tours Ltd., Attn: Bernard Esterhuyse, (Lusaka), Specializing in tigerfish safaris on Upper Zambezi River. Luxury lodge at Tiger Camp with meals, fuel, use of boats, tackle and daily laundry service included. Phone & Fax (260) 1-262810 E-mail: tiger@zamnet.zm

WORLDWIDE DESTINATIONS

Capt. Sandy Blum, Fishing consultant for worldwide fishing adventures. Office in Florida - (305) 937-0209, Fax (305) 937-0080

The Detail Company, Attn: Jeri Booth, Fishing trips organized to Alaska, Argentina, Colombia, Mexico, Uruguay, Africa & Scotland. Office in Texas - (713) 524-7235 or 800-292-2213, Fax (713) 524-7244

Five Star Expeditions, Inc., Attn: Ed Beattie, Worldwide fishing packages arranged. Office in Wyoming - (307) 332-3197, Fax (307) 332-3198

Select Sportfishing Packages, Inc., Attn: Beth Spearman, Worldwide sportfishing packages arranged. Office in Georgia - 800-654-7345

Worldwide Sportfishing Adventures, Attn: Kurt Strecker, Worldwide sportfishing packages arranged. Office in Arizona - Phone & Fax (602) 948-7707

MISCELLANEOUS SERVICES

Atlantic Cruising Club, Attn: Nancy Schilling Henry, Marina & Cruising Directory for east coast of the United States. Office in South Carolina - (803) 785-5587 or 800-825-5995

Ballyhood International Big Game Trolling Lures, Attn: Dave Stewart, (Santa Ana, California), Ballyhood, innovators in trolling natural baits, offers a free catalog and 25% discount to all IGFA members. These deep trolling lures reach depths of 30-ft. and offer the uniqueness of being trolled as is or add your bait (8"-20" baits). Specialists in big tuna, wahoo, blue marlin and shark. (714) 564-9468, Fax (714) 564-9513

The Bonefish School, Attn: Jake Jordan, (Exuma), Fly fishing instruction by renown flyfishing anglers held at Peace and Plenty Beach Inn in George Town, Exuma. Registration includes 7 nights lodging with meals, classroom instruction and 4 days guided fishing. Office in Marathon, Florida- (305) 743-0501, Fax (305) 743-5007

Cape Rods, Attn: S.R. Murphy (Murf), Discount on custom fishing rods and repairs. Complimentary UPS (United Parcel Service) in the continental U.S. (Philadelphia, Pennsylvania and Cape May, New Jersey). (215) 698-7987 or (609) 884-7206

Capt'n Mike's Tackle Towne and Fishing Adventures, Attn: Mike Barkhausen, (San Diego, California), Discounts offered on merchandise. (760) 757-4220, Fax (760) 757-4040, Website: www.captnmikes.com

Dorado Marine Center, Attn: Capt. Puchy Sanabria, (Dorado, Puerto Rico), Discounts offered on fishing supplies. (787) 796-4645, Fax (787) 796-7323

Fishermen's Furs & Feathers, A Division of Castle Arms, Attn: Phil Castleman, (Springfield, Massachusetts), Fishermen's Furs & Feathers offers IGFA members a 20% discount on any of their exotic feathers for fly tying. (800) 525-4866, Fax (413) 731-1292

Fortune Hills Golf & Country Club, Attn: Walter B. Kitchen, (Freeport, Bahamas), Discount on greens fees only. (242) 373-222 or 373-4500, Fax (242) 373-5090

Lightning Rods, Attn: Justin Hudgens, (Fort Lauderdale, Florida), Custom Rod art and reel repair. Building any kind of custom rod for your fishing needs. All rods built to IGFA standards. (954) 731-4216

The Longfin, Attn: Tom Ward, (Orange, California), Discount on terminal tackle. (714) 538-8010, Fax (714) 538-1368

Pisces Portraits c/o Barramundi Corporation, Attn: George Liska, (Orlando, Florida), Unique fine art portraits of your released or trophy fish with or without your photo included in matting of the picture. 800-382-1817, Fax (352) 628-0203

T & R Tackle, Attn: George A. Copeland, (Ft. Lauderdale, Florida), Full service tackle and bait shop to meet all your needs. (954) 776-1055, Fax (954) 776-1590

World Famous Bait & Tackle, Attn: Jeffrey C. D'Amico, (Ft. Lauderdale, Florida), Discount on tackle & supplies. (954) 985-5661, Fax (954) 985-5767

APPENDICES

APPENDIX I

WORLDWIDE RECORD-KEEPING ORGANIZATION   341

APPENDIX II

U.S.A. STATE RECORD-KEEPING AGENCIES & ORGANIZATION   343

APPENDIX III

A WORLDWIDE INVENTORY OF TAG AND RELEASE PROGRAMS FOR MARINE FISHES   346

Worldwide Record-keeping Organizations

Many sportfishing organizations throughout the world maintain freshwater and/or saltwater game fishing records for their continents, countries or territories. Each organization has its own criteria, rules and categories for maintaining records. Listed below are the addresses and brief descriptions of some of the major record-keeping organizations. IGFA welcomes information on other organizations or agencies not currently included on this list.

AFRICA

GAME FISH UNION OF AFRICA
P. O. Box 191, Harare, Zimbabwe

The Game Fish Union of Africa was founded in 1960 for the purposes of compiling a list of marine game fish records set in African waters, unifying game fishing rules, and encouraging game fishing both as a recreation and as a means of increasing the knowledge of the sea and marine fish. The Union's associate institutions include national game fishing organizations, scientific research organizations, universities and kindred bodies. Records are maintained for more than 40 species in several line class categories.

KENYA ASSOCIATION OF SEA ANGLING CLUBS
P. O. Box 84133, Mombasa, Kenya

The Kenya Association of Sea Angling Clubs acts as an overall governing body for sea angling, coordinates and furthers angling on the Kenya coast, maintains Kenya fishing records, and selects and appoints teams to represent Kenya in international competitions. The Association requires that Kenya records comply with the requirements of IGFA for world records. Records are maintained for approximately 20 species found off Kenya's coast in all-tackle and line class categories ranging from 1 kg to 60 kg.

NATAL PARKS BOARD
P. O. Box 662, Pietermaritzburg, Natal, South Africa

Freshwater records for fish taken in the rivers and dams of the province of Natal are maintained by this fishery agency. A list of the heaviest fish taken for species ranging from largemouth bass to tigerfish is compiled annually.

SOUTH AFRICAN FEDERATION OF SEA ANGLING
P.O. Box 35936, Menlo Park 0102 South Africa

The SAFSA is the parent body for all types of angling in the Republic of South Africa, including rock and surf, light tackle, boat angling, and more. Angling groups throughout the country are affiliated with the SAFSA and participate in competitions sponsored by the organization. Record-keeping is patterned after IGFA's with the same categories including all-tackle, line class, and fly rod for freshwater and saltwater. In addition records are kept for junior anglers under the age of 16.

ZIMBABWE ANGLING RECORDS
6, Divine Road, Milton Park
Harare, Zimbabwe
Attention: Howard Voss

Zimbabwe Angling Records maintains the freshwater angling records for the country. Begun in the 1950s, this organization now has over 80 records maintained for open age, junior, and line class categories. The regulations as stipulated by IGFA are adhered to whenever possible and 10 lb Bass Club applications are processed through the organization. Operating under the auspices of the National Anglers Union of Zimbabwe, the organization is in constant communication with other regional record-keeping organizations. Queries regarding fishing opportunities in Zimbabwe are welcomed from IGFA members.

AUSTRALIA

AUSTRALIAN NATIONAL SPORTFISHING ASSOCIATION
Secretary: John W. O'Sullivan, 9 Dennis St. AYR 4807

ANSA was conceived in 1967 as an association of State branches and clubs to promote sportfishing at the grassroots level. The parent body was officially established in 1969 at a meeting of delegates held at Nowra, New South Wales. At that meeting, approval was given by the clubs to form existing NSW and Queensland record charts the first official ANSA record chart. ANSA is now represented in New South Wales, Queensland, Victoria, South Australia, Western Australia, Northern Territory, Tasmania, Papua New Guinea and the Cocos-Keeling Islands and has an affiliated membership of 160 clubs. ANSA maintains records for Australian freshwater and saltwater species in a number of light line classes and several different fishing categories, including fly and game fishing.

GAME FISHING ASSOCIATION OF AUSTRALIA
P.O. Box 301, Nelson Bay, NSW 2315, Attn: Garry McDonald, secretary

Since its formation in 1938, the GFAA has been active in promotion and leadership of ethical offshore angling. Made up of delegates from over 50 member clubs in all Australian states, the GFAA coordinates and governs the sport of game fishing in the country's waters, keeps up-to-date lists of marine game fishing records for men and women in line class categories, and encourages and furthers recreational angling and conservation of related fish species and habitats. Working in close affiliation with the IGFA, the GFAA requests that all claims for world records be forwarded to the Secretary of GFAA through the state branch in whose waters the capture was made.

BERMUDA

BERMUDA GAME FISHING ASSOCIATION
P.O. Box 1306, Hamilton, Bermuda HMFX

Bermuda Game Fishing Association is an advisory body to the IGFA affiliated clubs in Bermuda and administered by a committee made up of members chosen from and by those clubs. The objectives of the Association shall be: a) to encourage the development of game fishing as a sport via competition and record keeping; b) to assist in conservation of marine resources via tag and release programs; c) to advise and assist clubs, organizations and government if required on (a) and (b).

EUROPE

AUSTRIAN RECORD FISH COMMITTEE (OSTERREICHISCHES REKORD-FISCH-KOMITEE), VOAFV

Lenaugasse 14, 1080 Wien, Osterreich (Austria)

The VOAFV is the official internationally registered fishing community of Austria, representing about 12,000 regular members and a large number of associated members. It runs 52 fishing clubs by direct administration in different parts of the country through officers elected by the club members. The Austrian Record Fish Committee was founded by the VOAFV in 1977 to register and give awards for record catches and best annual catches. The Committee keeps only all-tackle records and encourages catch and release fishing.

BRITISH LIGHT TACKLE CLUB

Nigel Baker, Hon. Fish Recorder, 5 Brigham Place, Felpham, Bognor Regis, Sussex, England, U.K.

The BLTC maintains a listing of British and European line class records in categories ranging from 4 kg to 60 kg, with limited line classes for certain species. Record claims for more than 50 different species from catfish to sharks are accepted from both members and nonmembers. In order to qualify, catches must be made in an area of waters defined by longitude 30° W to 60° E, latitude 23.5° N to 80° N and including Greenland.

BRITISH RECORD (ROD-CAUGHT) FISH COMMITTEE, NATIONAL FEDERATION OF SEA ANGLERS.

Chairman Jack Reece. Q.P.M. 51A Queen Street, Newton Abbot, Devon, TQ12 2QJ, England.

The Committee was formed to recognize and publish record weights of both fresh and saltwater fish caught on rod and line by fair angling methods in the waters of England, Wales, Scotland, Northern Ireland and the Channel Islands. Separate records are maintained for sea fishes caught from boat and from shore. Scottish and Welsh records which are also British records should be submitted to the Committed through its member organizations, the Scottish Federation of Sea Anglers and the Welsh Record (rod-caught) Fish Committee. Claims for fish caught in Eire should be made to the Irish Specimen Fish Committee.

EUROPEAN FEDERATION OF SEA ANGLERS

Hon. General Secretary: H.J. Holmes, Flat 15, Braal Castle, Halkirk, Caithness; KW12 6XE Scotland
For claims on European Line Class and All Tackle records: Hon. Fish Recorder: D. Wood, 78 Beech Road, Horsham, Sussex; RH12 4TX England

The EFSA is the governing body for the sport of sea angling with rod and line in European waters and the keeper of the European Record Fish List of Marine Species. Member Sections include Austria, Belgium, Denmark, England, France, Germany, Gibraltar, Ireland, Isle of Man, Italy, Netherlands, Norway, Scotland, Sweden, Switzerland and Wales. Affiliated member countries are South Africa, Egypt, Kenya, Namibia and Zimbabwe. The EFSA Maintains All-Tackle, line class and mini-fish records and encourages the keeping of national sea fish records on the same basis. Claims for European Records (not just by members of the European Federation) who have caught a potential record fish in the area defined by longitude 30º W to 65º E and latitude 23.5º N and including Greenland.

FINNISH SPORT FISHERMEN'S ASSOCIATION

P. O. Box 12, 00271 Helsinki, Finland.

Finnish Sport Fishermen's Association was established to promote the theme of fishing in a sporting manner in 1919. Finnish Sport Fishermen's Association started to register and give awards for record catches in 1980. The fishes must have been caught in the area of Finland. The Association registers the heaviest catches of each species, and those catches which surpass a minimum weight established by the Association.

IRISH SPECIMEN FISH COMMITTEE

Balnagowan, Mobhi Boreen, Glasnevin, Dublin 9, Ireland

The Committee was formed in 1955 to verify, record and publicize the capture of large fish on rod and line in Ireland's waters. Its members consist of representatives of the Irish Angling Federations, government departments, and official organizations interested in angling. The Committee records not only the heaviest catches of each species, but also those catches which surpass a minimum weight established by the Committee.

SCOTTISH FEDERATION OF SEA ANGLERS

The Hon. Secretary, 18 Ainslie Place, Edinburgh, Scotland EH3 6AU, U.K.

The SFSA is the governing body for the sport of sea angling in Scotland. It is accepted as the advisory body on sea angling by the Scottish Sports Council, the Scottish Tourist Board and the Highlands and Islands Development Board. The Federation consists of clubs or district associations in Scotland and individual members throughout the world. Scottish marine fish records are maintained for the heaviest catches made from boat and shore (rod and line caught).

WELSH RECORD (ROD-CAUGHT) FISH COMMITTEE, WELSH ANGLERS' COUNCIL

Attn: M. Browning, General Secretary, Lower Bastleford, Rosemarket, Milford Haven, Dyfed., Wales, U. K.

The Committee is a division of the Welsh Anglers' Council established by the Sports Council of Wales to "safeguard the interests of all Welsh anglers." The Committee exists to establish and maintain a list of rod-caught fish, marine and freshwater, taken from waters in Wales or from the waters around the coast of Wales. Record categories include fish caught from boat and from shore.

JAPAN

JAPAN GAME FISH ASSOCIATION

Asahi Bldg. 2F, 1-11-2, Ebisu, Shibuya-ku, Tokyo 150.

Starting in 1979, the Judging Committee of the JGFA has maintained records for 70 saltwater species. Records are updated at the end of every month. The JGFA publishes the following: JGFA News, JGFA Yearbook. Hidenori Onishi is chairman of the JGFA.

NEW ZEALAND

NEW ZEALAND BIG GAME FISHING COUNCIL

PO Box 93, Whangerei, Northland

Founded in 1957 to further the interests of ethical big game angling and to encourage the sport as a recreation and as a potential source of scientific data, the New Zealand Big Game Fishing Council presently has 37 affiliate clubs, each with equal representation and voting power. The council has promoted numerous international tournaments, including the now popular New Zealand Open, and has the responsibility for collating the national fishing records. Applications for world records can be made through the council to IGFA.

PAPUA NEW GUINEA

GAME FISHING ASSOCIATION OF PAPUA NEW GUINEA

Box 220, Kieta, Bougainville Island

Formed in 1975 to encourage and coordinate the sport of game fishing in Papua New Guinea and to formulate ethical angling regulations, the GFAPNG maintains national saltwater records for men and women in all-tackle and line class categories.

U.S.A. State Record-Keeping Agencies & Organizations

Almost every state in the U.S.A. maintains records, whether official or informal, for the largest fishes caught within their boundaries or off their coastlines.

Listed below are the addresses of state record programs with brief synopses of the nature of their record-keeping activities. Anglers desiring complete information, regulations and application forms should direct their inquiries to the agencies or organizations listed.

ALABAMA
Department of Conservation, Attn: Stan Cook, Game and Fish Division, 64 North Union St., Montgomery 36130

Freshwater records for the largest fish by species caught on rod and reel or cane pole; program begun in 1968; over 30 species listed.

ALASKA
Department of Fish & Game, Sport Fish Division. P.O. Box 25526, Juneau 99802-5526

Since 1968, freshwater and saltwater records for largest fish ever caught (State Champion); largest fish of a species caught each year (Annual Record); and fish exceeding a minimum weight annually (Trophy Fish).

ARIZONA
Fisheries Board, 2222 West Greenway Road, Phoenix 85023

Two record lists: one for species taken in inland waters and the other for fish caught in Colorado River waters. All species that are lawful to take are eligible.

ARKANSAS
Game & Fish Commission, Educational Services, No. 2 Natural Resources Drive, Little Rock, AR 72005

Since 1959, records for the largest fish caught. Over 35 species.

CALIFORNIA
Department of Fish and Game, 1416 Ninth St., Sacramento 95814

Saltwater angling records for largest fish of a species by weight. Inland water angling records for heaviest fish, both freshwater and anadromous species.

COLORADO
Division of Wildlife, 6060 Broadway, Denver 80216

1. Largest freshwater species by weight caught legally on hook and line. Over 30 fish categories. Program begun in 1965. 2. Longest freshwater species by length, released after caught legally by hook and line; 26 fish species. Program begun in 1995.

CONNECTICUT
Department of Environmental Protection, Bureau of Fisheries, 79 Elm Street, Hartford 06106

Freshwater and saltwater Trophy Fish program for largest fish taken of 40 different species plus all fish over a specified size.

DELAWARE
Department of Natural Resources and Environmental Control, 89 Kings Highway, Dover 19901

Freshwater and saltwater sportfishing records for 35 species. Program started in 1966.

FLORIDA
Game & Freshwater Fish Commission, Office of Information Services, Publications Section, 620 S. Meridian St., Tallahassee 32301

Freshwater records for the largest fish, approximately 25 species. Program begun in 1976.

Department of Environmental Protection, 3900 Commonwealth Blvd., Tallahassee 32303 or IGFA

A cooperative program for saltwater sportfishing records began in 1983. Record applications are screened by the International Game Fish Association. More than 70 species are currently listed in both conventional gear and fly fishing categories.

GEORGIA
Department of Natural Resources, Fisheries Management Section, Wildlife Resources Division, 2070 U.S. Highway 278, SE Social Circle, Georgia 30025

Freshwater largest fish records for 16 species.

Georgia Department of Natural Resources, Coastal Resources Division, One Conservation Way, Suite 300, Brunswick, GA 31520-8687

Saltwater game fish records in both men's and women's categories for the largest fish of a species listed.

Angling rules are patterned after IGFA's.

HAWAII
Freshwater Fishing Association, P.O. Box 964, Wahiawa 96786

State and annual records are awarded for the heaviest catches of 11 different freshwater species. The program is open to all licensed anglers in the state of Hawaii. The association is a private organization established by and for Hawaii's fishermen.

IDAHO
Department of Fish & Game, P.O. Box 25, Boise 83707

Heaviest fish records maintained for approximately 30 freshwater species since the mid-1950's.

ILLINOIS
Department of Conservation, Division of Fish and Wildlife, 524 South 2nd Street, Springfield 62706

Largest Fish records for specimens caught legally on pole and line; 40 "pure" species and three hybrids listed.

INDIANA
Department of Natural Resources, Division of Fish & Wildlife, 402 West Washington St., RM W273, Indianapolis 46204

Records for the heaviest catches. Over 40 species listed. Program begun in 1966.

IOWA
Department of Natural Resources, Wallace Office Bldg., Des Moines 50319

All-time records for the largest fish (by weight) for 30 different species. Large fish catches are recognized on an annual basis.

KANSAS
Department of Wildlife & Parks, 512 SE 25th Ave., Pratt Kansas 67124-8174

Records maintained since the 1940's for the heaviest catches. Over 30 species currently listed. Recognition is also given in a Master Angler

Award program for catches meeting minimum weight requirements.

KENTUCKY
Department of Fish & Wildlife, Division of Information & Education, #1 Game Farm Road, Frankfort 40601

Program begun circa 1950 to record the heaviest freshwater species caught on rod and reel. Approximately 40 species categories.

LOUISIANA
Department of Wildlife and Fisheries, Information & Education Division, P.O. Box 15570, Baton Rouge 70895

Records for the top ten catches are maintained for 15 freshwater and 36 saltwater species. Records are maintained by the Louisiana Outdoor Writers Association in cooperation with the Department of Wildlife and Fisheries.

MAINE
Department of Inland Fisheries & Wildlife, Station 41, Augusta 04333

Freshwater records only are maintained for the heaviest catches in state waters. Program begun in 1969.

Maine Department of Marine Resources, P.O. Box 8, West Boothbay Harbor, ME 04575

The department assumed the responsibility of maintaining saltwater game fish records in 1995. Contact Bruce J. Joule, recreational marine fisheries coordinator.

MARYLAND
Department of Natural Resources, Sport Fishing Information, 69 Prince George Street, Annapolis 21401

State records are awarded at the end of each year to the angler with the heaviest catch exceeding the current record for the species. In addition, awards are given for the largest of eight freshwater species caught during the state contest, April 1-Nov. 30.

MASSACHUSETTS
Division of Fisheries & Wildlife, Field Headquarters, Westboro 01581

Freshwater sportfishing records for 20 species taken by legal means in water open to the public. Also maintains Freshwater Sportfishing Awards Program for catches meeting specified weight requirements.

Division of Marine Fisheries, Recreational Fisheries Bureau, 100 Cambridge St., Boston 02202

A saltwater record program begun in 1983 for the heaviest catches in 19 species categories. Also sponsor a Saltwater Fishing Derby annually for catches meeting minimum weight requirements. Trophies are awarded for the largest catches submitted in men's, women's and junior divisions.

MICHIGAN
Department of Natural Resources, Fisheries Division, Box 30446, Lansing 48909

Since 1973, records for the heaviest catches taken by legal state sportfishing methods in public waters. Also a Master Angler Award program for catches meeting minimum weight requirements. The Master Angler Award program has a division for catch-and-release entries.

MINNESOTA
Department of Natural Resources, Section of Fisheries, Box 12, 500 LaFayette St., St. Paul 55155, or any of the six regional or 27 area fisheries offices in the state.

Angling records for the heaviest catches of more than 50 freshwater species.

MISSISSIPPI
Department of Wildlife, Fisheries and Parks, Fisheries Division, P.O. Box 451, Jackson 39205-0451.

Freshwater sportfishing records for the heaviest catches of 30 different species. Program begun in mid-1950's.

Department of Marine Resources, 152 Gateway Drive, Biloxi, MI 39531

An unofficial listing of saltwater records has been maintained since 1980 based on records of local fishing rodeos. However, as ordered by state statute 49-15-409, the department was directed to maintain saltwater recreational fishing records of marine fish species.

MISSOURI
Department of Conservation, Fisheries Division, P.O. Box 180, Jefferson City 65102-0180

Freshwater records for 53 species caught by pole, line and lure, and 38 species caught by other fishing methods.

MONTANA
Fish, Wildlife and Parks, Conservation Education Division, P.O. Box 200701, 1420 East Sixth Avenue, Helena, MT 59620-0701

Largest fish records by weight for freshwater species caught within the state. The fish must be legally harvested, weighed on an inspected scale and positively identified by department personnel.

NEBRASKA
Game and Parks Commission, P.O. Box 30370, Lincoln 68503

Hook and line records are maintained for more than 40 species. Also, a Master Angler Award program for catches meeting minimum weight requirements.

NEVADA
Division of Wildlife, P.O. Box 10678, Reno 89520-0022

Records for the heaviest catches as well as a Trophy Fish Program for catches meeting minimum weight requirements.

NEW HAMPSHIRE
Fish & Game Department, 2 Hazen Drive, Concord, NH 03301

Freshwater and saltwater records for the largest fish of over 40 different species. Also, a Trophy Fish Program for catches taken on sporting tackle which meet minimum weight requirements.

NEW JERSEY
Division of Fish, Game and Wildlife, Record Fish Program, P.O. Box 400, Trenton, NJ 08625

Thirty species of freshwater fish and 67 marine species are eligible for the record status. Only the heaviest of each species taken on sporting tackle, hooked and landed by the entrant are eligibie. A Skillful Anglers Award Program for catches meeting minimum weight requirements is available.

NEW MEXICO
Department of Game & Fish, P.O. Box 25112 Villagra Building, Santa Fe, NM 87504

State freshwater records for the largest catch of a species are recorded from entries in the Fishing Award program. Anglers receive a certificate for catches meeting specific length requirements.

NEW YORK
State Department of Environmental Conservation, Bureau of Fisheries, Room 518, 50 Wolf Road, Albany 12233

Freshwater records for the largest catches of 35 different species.

State Department of Environmental Conservation, Bureau of Fisheries, Region 1, Building 40, SUNY, Stony Brook, NY 11790-2356

Long Island Fisherman Publishing Corp., 14 Ramsey Road, Shirley, NY 11967, Attn: Tom Melton

Saltwater sportfishing records are maintained for the heaviest catches of 21 different species.

NORTH CAROLINA

Travel & Tourism Division, 430 N. Salisbury Street, Raleigh 27611

Freshwater and saltwater all-tackle records for the heaviest of 84 different species caught on hook and line in a sporting manner. Program started in the early 1970's.

OHIO

Department of Natural Resources, Division of Wildlife, 1840 Belcher Drive, Columbus 43224

Freshwater records for the largest catches (weight and length combined are compiled. Separate categories for hook and line and bowfishing records.

Outdoor Writers of Ohio

Record Fish Chairman Jeffrey Frischkorn, 7621 Dahlia Drive, Mentor-on-the-Lake, Ohio 44144

Outdoor writers keep freshwater records, consulting Department of Natural Resources for fish identification.

OKLAHOMA

Department of Wildlife Conservation, Information and Education Division, P.O. Box 53465, Oklahoma City 73152

Rod and line records for over 40 eligible freshwater species with an unrestricted division for other methods of catch.

OREGON

Bass and Panfish Club, Attn: Fish records chairman, P.O. Box 1-21, Portland 97207

Records for heaviest warm water game fish caught by legal sportfishing methods.

Department of Fish & Wildlife, P.O. Box 59, Portland 97207

Unofficial records are maintained for the largest freshwater game fish catches.

PENNSYLVANIA

Fish Commission, Anglers Award Program, P.O. Box 67000, Harrisburg, PA 17106-7000

Angler Award program in both senior and junior categories for freshwater catches meeting minimum weight requirements. Also recognition for the largest catch (state record), biggest fish of the year, and a special club for anglers catching muskellunge measuring 50 inches or more.

RHODE ISLAND

Division of Fish & Wildlife, Game Fish Award Program, Government Center, Wakefield RI 02879

Heaviest catch records for over 30 freshwater and saltwater species caught by angling methods. Program

started in 1976.

SOUTH CAROLINA

Department of Natural Resources, Freshwater Fish Records, P.O. Box 167, Columbia 29202

Freshwater records maintained since 1960 for heaviest catches on rod, reel and line or pole and line; 32 species listed.

Department of Natural Resources, Saltwater Fish Records, P.O. Box 12559, Charleston 29412

Since 1968, saltwater sportfishing records for the largest catches of 65 different species.

SOUTH DAKOTA

Department of Game, Fish and Parks, Information-Education Section, Foss Building, Pierre 57501

Freshwater records for the heaviest catches on hook and line for 60 species. Also an unrestricted category for other legal fishing methods.

TENNESSEE

Wildlife Resources Agency, P.O. Box 40747, Nashville 37204

Sportfishing records for the heaviest freshwater catches. Also a record listing for catches made by other fishing methods.

TEXAS

Parks & Wildlife Department, 4200 Smith School Road, Austin 78744

Rod and reel records for the largest catches in both freshwater and saltwater categories. Also an unrestricted listing for catches taken by other legal fishing methods which exceed the weight of the rod and reel records.

UTAH

Division of Wildlife Resources, Aquatic Section, 1594 West North Temple, Ste 2110, P.O. Box 146301, Salt Lake City, UT 84114-6301

Records for the largest catches made legally by angling methods are listed for over 20 freshwater species.

VERMONT

Fish & Wildlife Department, 103 South Main Street, Waterbury 05676

State and annual records are maintained for the largest fish caught by angling or ice fishing methods. Program begun in 1969.

VIRGIN ISLANDS (U.S.)

Division of Fish & Wildlife, 101 Estate Nazareth, St. Thomas 00802

VIRGINIA

Department of Game & Inland Fisheries, Fish Citation Program, Box 11104, Richmond 23230

Freshwater records for the heaviest catches of more than 20 different species. Program begun in 1963.

Virginia Saltwater Fishing Tournament, 968 S. Oriole Drive, Ste 102, Virginia Beach 23451

Marine game fish records maintained since 1960 for the largest fish of 29 species listed. Catches must conform to Virginia Saltwater Tournament regulations.

WASHINGTON

Department of Fish & Wildlife, 600 N. Capitol Way, Olympia 98501-1691

Freshwater and saltwater records dating back to 1943 for the largest catches of 51 freshwater and 47 saltwater species.

Department of Fisheries, Bldg. 4, Room 2129, 7600 Sand Pt. Way N.E., B in C-15700, Seattle 98115

Sportfishing Awards Program for catches meeting minimum qualifying weights, 35 saltwater species are eligible. Largest catches qualify for state records.

WEST VIRGINIA

Division of Natural Resources, Wildlife Resources Section, Capitol Complex, Building 3, 1900 Kanawha Blvd., E., Charleston, WV 25305

Freshwater records by length and weight maintained since 1956. Also a trophy fish citation program for catches meeting specified requirements.

WISCONSIN

Department of Natural Resources, Bureau of Fisheries Management and Habitat Protection. Box 7921, Madison 53707

Records for 50 species of fish caught in inland waters or the Great Lakes.

WYOMING

Game and Fish Department, Cheyenne 82006

Largest fish records for 20 freshwater species on rod, reel and line or pole and line.

APPENDIX III

A Worldwide Inventory of Tag and Release Programs for Marine Fishes

> **Key to information symbols**
> **A)** Species tagged
> **B)** Geographical area where fish are tagged
> **C)** Approximate number tagged & released from 1982 thru 1998
> **D)** Approximate number of tagged fish recaptured
> **E)** Type of tag(s) used
> **F)** Cooperators in the program
> **G)** Publication or Newsletter
> **H)** Chief scientist(s)

INTERNATIONAL PROGRAMS

Inter-American Tropical Tuna Commission, c/o Scripps Institution of Oceanography, 8604 La Jolla Shores Dr., La Jolla, CA 92037-1508 USA
A) Yellowfin tuna (*Thunnus albacares*), bigeye tuna (*T. obesus*), bluefin tuna (*T. thynnus*), skipjack tuna (*Katsuwonus pelamis*), black skipjack (*Euthynnus lineatus*), wahoo (*Acanthocybium solandri*); **B)** Pacific Ocean; **C)** 1982: 237 bluefin. 1985: 16 yellowfin, 5 skipjack, 1 black skipjack, 17 wahoo. 1986: 36 yellowfin. 1987: 5 yellowfin; 1988-98: none; **D)** 1982: 437 yellowfin, 97 bluefin, 8 skipjack, 25 black skipjack. 1985: 1 yellowfin, 1 skipjack, 1 wahoo. 1986: 6 yellowfin, 1987-98: none; **E)** Plastic dart, sonic; **F)** Scientists, sport and commercial fishermen, unloaders and cannery workers; **G)** Yes; **H)** Dr. William H. Bayliff

International Sablefish Tagging Program, Alaska Fisheries Science Center, 7600 Sandpoint Way NE, Bin C15700 Bldg.. 4, Seattle, WA 98115 USA
A) Sablefish (*Anoplopoma fimbria*); **B)** California to western Aleutian Islands and Bering Sea; **C)** 105,000 (U.S. and Japan); **D)** 7,100 (U.S. and Japan); **E)** Internal anchor; **F)** State fishery agencies (California, Oregon, Alaska, Wash.), Russia, CIS, Japan, Republic of Korea; **G)** Yes; **H)** Franklin R. Shaw

International Pacific Halibut Commission, P. O. Box 95009, University Station, Seattle, WA 98145-2009 USA
A) Pacific Halibut (*Hippoglossus stenolepis*); **B)** Oregon Coast to Bering Sea; **C)** 1982: 11,671, 1983: 12,124, 1984: 20,270, 1985: 18,902, 1986: 9,136, 1987: 3,198, 1988: 3,098, 1989: 2,372, 1990: 38, 1991: 38, 1992: 872, 1993: 4,389, 1994: 9,342, 1995: 4,904, 1996: 308; **D)** 14,569; **E)** Modified spaghetti, dart, lock-on; **F)** Scientists, sport and commercial fishermen; **G)** Yes; **H)** Don McCaughran, Director; Bob Trumble, Senior Biologist, Tracee Geernaert, Project Coordinator

International Commission for the Conservation of Atlantic Tunas (ICCAT), c/ Corazón de María, 8 - 6   28002 Madrid, SPAIN
A) Yellowfin tuna (*Thunnus albacares*), bluefin tuna (*T. thynnus*), bigeye tuna (*T. obesus*), albacore (*T. alalunga*), skipjack tuna (*Euthynnus pelamis*), swordfish (*Xiphias gladius*), white marlin (*Tetrapturus albidus*), blue marlin (*Makaira nigricans*), sailfish (*Istiophorus albicans*), black skipjack (*Euthynnus alletteratus*); **B)** Atlantic ocean and Mediterranean Sea; **C)** 1980: 20,317, 1981: 25,558, 1982: 14,509, 1983: 5,788, 1984: 6,321, 1985: 5,911, 1986: 9,673, 1987: 7,149, 1988: 690, 1989: 810, 1990: 1810, 1991: 3,500, 1992: 2,375, 1993: 3,410, 1994: 5,235, 1995: 9,800, 1996: 4,425 (Data for years 1987-1996 may be incomplete); **D)** 1980: 742, 1981: 1,913, 1982: 2,753, 1983: 217, 1984: 228, 1985: 166, 1986: 348, 1987: 163, 1988: 141, 1989: 176, 1990: 464; 1991: 440, 1992: 534, 1993: 205, 1994: 656, 1995: 270, 1996: 230; **E)** Steel dart, plastic dart; **F)** 25 Contracting Parties **G)** Yes, Newsletter, Biennial Report and other publications; **H)** Executive Sec. Dr. Adolfo Ribeiro Lima

Cooperative Marine Gamefish Tagging Program, NOAA/NMFS, Southwest Fisheries Science Center, P.O. Box 271, La Jolla Laboratory, La Jolla, CA 92038 USA E-mail: dholts@fantasia.ucsd.edu
A) Swordfish, striped marlin, blue marlin, black marlin and short-billed spearfish; **B)** Pacific and Indian Oceans; **C)** 19,050; **D)** 174; **E)** Nylon tip dart with yellow plastic tubing; **F)** Anglers, Billfish Clubs, Pacific Gamefish Research Foundation, Sec. de Pesca Mexico, Guam Dept. of Agriculture; **G)** Billfish Newsletter/ Scientific Pub.; **H)** David B. Holts

Fish Unlimited Fish Tagging Program, 1 Brander Parkway, P.O. Box 1073, Shelter Island, NY 11965 USA
A) Any fresh or salt water species; **B)** Worldwide; **C)** 12,000; **D)** 123; **E)** Nylon dart; **F)** Fish Unlimited, fishing clubs, anglers; **G)** Yes; **H)** Bill Smith

NATIONAL PROGRAMS

Africa

Kenya
African Billfish Foundation Tagging Program, P. O. Box 342, Watamu, Kenya, East Africa
A) Primarily billfish: Pacific sailfish, blue, black & striped marlin, broadbill swordfish; **B)** Indian Ocean, Kenya Coast - principal centers at Lamu, Watamu, Malindi and Shimoni; **C)** 1987-98: 219 black marlin; 101 blue marlin; 1,350 striped marlin; 291 broadbill swordfish; 12,509 sailfish; **D)** 1987-98: 6 black marlin; 10 striped marlin; 248 sailfish; 3 broadbill swordfish; **E)** Steel dart, plastic dart; **F)** Sport fishing club members; **G)** Yes; **H)** Capt. Charles Harris, Tina Harris and Gary Cullen

Republic of Namibia
Namibian Angling Fish Tagging Project (NAFTAP), Ministry of Fisheries and Marine Resources, P.O. Box 912, Swakopmund
A) Kob (*Argyrosomus inodorus*), westcoast steenbras (*Lithognathus aureti*), galjoen (*Dichistius capensis*), blacktail (*Diplodus sargus*) and various shark species; **B)** The entire Namibian coastline; **C)** Since 1991: 60,400 fishes comprising 25 different species were tagged and released; **D)** Approximately 1.5% recapture; **E)** Hallprint coded T-bar tags; **F)** Official tagging surveys, private anglers and angling clubs; **G)** No; **H)** Senior Fisheries Biologist, J.A. Holtzhausen

Zambia
Zambezi Tigerfish Tag and Release Program, P.O. Box 31730, Lusaka, Zambia
A) Tigerfish *(Hydrocynus vittatus)*; **B)** Western Zambia, Central Africa; **C)** 250; **D)** 13; **E)** Hallprint typetype PDA colour yellow; **F)** Tiger Fishing Tours Limited; **G)** Newsletter; **H)** Bernard Esterhuyse

Australia

Commonwealth Scientific & Industrial Research Organization (CSIRO), Division of Fisheries, GPO Box 1538, Hobart, TAS 7001
A) Tunas (almost entirely southern bluefin tuna); **B)** off the coasts of Western and Southern Australia and before 1980 New South Wales. Since 1992, 852 released from longline vessels off Southern and Eastern Australia; **C)** Before 1982: 52,750, 1982 and after: 79,554; **D)** Before 1982: 7,791, 1982 and after: 11,660; **E)** Plastic dart, 300 model archival tags in 1992/93, 437 archival tags in 1993/98; **F)** commercial and sport fishermen, scientists and fisheries agencies; **G)** Yes; **H)** Dr. Tom Polacheck

New South Wales Fisheries Research Institute, Gamefish Tagging Programme, New South Wales Fisheries Research Institute, P. O. Box 21, Cronulla, N.S.W. 2230
A) All marine gamefish species; **B)** Australia, Papua New Guinea; **C)** 94,000; **D)** 2,100; **E)** Steel, plastic dart; **F)** Scientists, sport and game fishermen; **G)** Yes; **H)** Mr. John Matthews

Suntag in Queensland, Queensland Department of Primary Industries and Australian National Sportfishing Association, 142 Venables Street, North Rockhampton, QLD 4701   E-mail: http//www.ansaqld.com.au
A) Barramundi (*Lates calcarifer*), narrow barred mackerel, (*Scomberomorus commerson*), school mackerel (*Scomberomorus queenslandicus*), spotted mackerel (*Scomberomorus munroi*), queenfish (*Scomberoides commersonianus*), giant trevally (*Caranx ignobilis*), bigeye trevally (*Caranx sexfasciatus*), black spot estuary cod (*Epinephelus malabaricus*), mangrove jack (*Lutjanus argentimaculatus*) and other species which are not gamefish. Tagging

is now being focused on regional projects with specific objectives and time frames; **B)** Queensland east coast and Gulf of Carpentaria; **C)** 193,000; **D)** 17, 000; **E)** Plastic dart and plastic anchor; **F)** Fisheries managers, scientists, ANSA members and recreational fishers; **G)** Yes, Austag Sportfish Tagging Report 97/98; **H)** Program Coordinator, Bill Sawynok, Chief Scientist Noel-Taylor Moore

Victag in Victoria, Australian National Sportfishing Association, 142 Venables Street, North Rockhampton, QLD 4701
A) Hammerhead shark (*Sphyrna spp*), gummy shark (*Mustelus anarcticus*), snapper (*Pagrus auratus*), yellowtail kingfish (*Seriola lalandi*), other species which are not gamefish; **B)** Victoria; **C)** 12,000; **D)** 365; **E)** Plastic dart and plastic anchor; **F)** Fisheries managers, scientists, ANSA members and recreational fishers; **G)** Sportfishing Tagging Report 96/97; **H)** Program Coordinator Tony Jones, Chief Scientist Patrick Coutin

Tastag in Tasmania, Australian National Sportfishing Association, 142 Venables Street, North Rockhampton, QLD 4701
A) New program established 1995, yellowfin tuna (*Thunnus albacares*), bluefin tuna (*Thunnus thynnus*), striped tuna (*Katsuwonus palamis*), albacore (*Thunnus alalunga*), blue shark (*Prionace glauca*0, mako shark (*Isurus oxyrinchus*), yellowtail kingfish (*Seriola lalandi*), other non-gamefish species; **B)** Tasmania; **C)** 1,500; **D)** 30; **E)** Plastic dart and plastic anchor; **F)** Fisheries managers, scientists, ANSA members and recreational fishers; **G)** Austag Sportfishing Tagging Program Report 96/97; **H)** Program Coordinator Nick Crawford, Chief Scientist Jeremy Lyle

Top Tag in the Northern Territory, Australian National Sportfishing Association, GPO Box 4604, Darwin, Northern Territory, 0801 Fax: 61 08 8983 3663
A) Broad bar mackerel (*Scomberomorus semifasciatus*), narrow bar mackerel (*Scomberomorus commerson*), school mackerel (*Scomberomorus queenslandicus*), spotted mackerel (*Scomberomorus munroi*), queenfish (*Scomberoides commersonianus*), giant trevally (*Caranx ignobilis*), cobia (*Rachycentron canadus*), giant threadfin (*Polynemus sheridani*), golden trevally (*Gnathanodon speciosus*), goldspot trevally (*Caranx fulvoguttatus*), longtail tuna (*Thunnus tonggol*), mackerel tuna (*Euthynnus affinis*); **B)** Northern Territory Coastline; **C)** Approximate number of fish tagged to 31/12/98: 2000; **D)** 60; **E)** Plastic dart; **F)** Dept Primary Industries and Fisheries, ANSA members and recreational fishermen; **G)** Austag Sportfish Tagging Report 97/98; **H)** Program Co-ordinator David Woodburn

Westag in Western Australia, Australian National Sportfishing Association, 142 Venables Street, North Rockhampton, QLD 4701
A) Established 1995, narrow barred mackerel, (*Scomberomorus commerson*) and other non-gamefish; **B)** Western Australia; **C)** 100; **D)** 6; **E)** Plastic dart and plastic anchor; **F)** Fisheries managers, scientists, ANSA members and recreational fishers; **G)** Austag Sportfish Tagging Report 96/97; **H)** Program Coordinator Susan Ayvazian

Canada

Department of Fisheries and Oceans, Pacific Biological Station, 3190 Hammond Bay Road, Nanaimo, B.C. V9R 5K6
A) Sablefish (*Anoplopoma fimbria*); **B)** West Coast of Canada; **C)** 228,274: **D)** 23,233; **E)** Anchor tags; **F)** D.F.O. scientists, Blackcod Fisherman's Association; **G)** Yes; **H)** G.A. McFarlane.

Department of Biology, Arcadia Univ., Wolfville, Nova Scotia B0P 1X0
A) American shad (*Alosa sapidissima*), Atlantic salmon (*Salmo salar*); **B)** Bay of Fundy, Miramichi River; **C)** 22,000; **D)** 1,000; **E)** Plastic dart; **F)** Scientists, sport and commercial fishermen; **G)** Yes; **H)** Dr. M. J. Dadswell

Department of Biology, Arcadia Univ., Wolfville, Nova Scotia B0P 1X0
A) Spiny dogfish, (*Squalus* acanthias) and striped bass (*Morone saxatilis*); **B)** Bay of Fundy, Minas Basin; **C)** 1996-1997: 2,000; **D)** 25; **E)** Plastic dart; **F)** Fishermen; **G)** No; **H)** Dr. M. J. Dadswell

Department of Fisheries and Oceans(Scotia-Fundy), Marine Fish Division, Bedford Institute of Oceanography, P.O. Box 1006, Dartmouth N.S. B2Y 4A2
A) Cod (*Gadus macrocephalus*), haddock (*Melanogrammus aeglefinus*), pollock (*Pollachius virens*), herring (*Clupea harengus*) and numerous other species; **B)** Nova Scotia Banks, Gulf of St. Lawrence; **C)** 49,215 cod, 31,580 haddock, 11,000 pollock, 68,790 herring, 3,225 misc. species; **D)** 7,632 groundfish, 913 herring, 4 misc. species; **E)** T-bar plastic anchor, Petersen disc; **F)** Scientists, sport and commercial fishermen; **G)** No; **H)** Mr. K. Zwanenburg, Dr. W. T. Stobo

England

Centre for Environmental Fisheries & Aquaculture Science (CEFAS), Lowestoft Laboratory, Pakefield Road, Lowestoft, Suffolk NR33 OHT UK
A) Plaice (*Pleuronectidae spp.*) sole (*Soleidae spp.*), cod (*Gadidae spp.*); **B)** North Sea and eastern English Channel; **C)** 6,705 plaice, 12,962 sole, 4,789 cod; **D)** 2,501 plaice, 3,947 sole, 1,528 cod; **E)** Petersen disc, Howitt flag, data storage tags; **F)** Scientists, commercial fishermen; **G)** No; **H)** Dr. R. Millner

Second Program:
A) European bass (*Dicentrarchus labrax*); **B)** Coast of England; **C)** 11,765; **D)** 752; **E)** Internal anchor, Howitt flag, & T-Bar; **F)** Scientists, sport & commer-cial fishermen; **G)** Journal of the Marine Biological Assoc., 67, PP183-217; **H)** G.D. Pickett

Third Program:
A) Plaice (*Pleuronectidae spp.*), cod (*Gadidae spp.*); **B)** Irish Sea and Western English Channel; **C)** 6,682 plaice, 8,599 sole, 724 cod, 28 spurdog, 116 lemon sole, 135 monk and 2,047 thornback ray; **D)** 821 plaice, 728 sole, 213 cod, 4 spurdog, 31 lemon sole, 2 monk and 242 thornback ray; **E)** Petersen Disc, Howitt flag and data storage tags; **F)** Scientists, commercial fishermen; **G)** No; **H)** Dr. M. Pawson

Ireland

Marine Sport Fish Tagging Programme, Central Fisheries Board, Mobhi Boreen, Glasnevin, Dublin 9
A) Blue shark (*Prionace glauca*), porbeagle shark (*Lamna nasus*), tope (*Galeohinus galeus*), monkfish (*Squatina squatina*), bass (*Morone labrax*), rays and skates (*Raja spp.*), flounder (*Platichthys flesus*); **B)** Irish Coast; **C)** 7,876 blue shark, 20 porbeagle shark, 1,818 tope, 651 monkfish, 434 bass, 4,233 rays and skates, 76 flounder; **D)** 242 blue shark, 4 porbeagle shark, 172 tope, 160 monkfish, 20 bass, 296 rays and skates, 15 flounder; **E)** Peterson-disc, Jumbo Rototags, Floy tag; **F)** Sport fishermen and charter skippers; **G)** Yes; **H)** Dr. P. Fitzmaurice

Japan

Skipjack Tagging Program, Tohoku National Fisheries Research Institute, 3-27-5 Shinhama, Shiogama, Miyagi 985; E-mail: beruka@myg.affrc.go.jp
A) Skipjack (*Katsuwonus pelamis*) and yellowfin tuna (*Thunnus albacares*); **B)** Northwest Pacific Ocean; **C)** 7,000 skipjack and 1,000 yellowfin each year; **D)** Approximately 320 skipjack and 80 yellowfin each year; **E)** Plastic dart; **F)** Commercial fishermen; **G)** Yes; **H)** Mio Takahashi

Japan Marine Fishery Resource Research Center (JAMARC), 6 Floor, Godo-Kaikan Building, 3-27 Kioi-Cho, Chiyoda-Ku, Tokyo 102-0094
A) Skipjack (*Katsuwonus pelamis*), yellowfin (*Thunnus albacares*), bigeye (*Thunnus obesus*), southern bluefin (*Thunnus maccoyii*) albacore (*Thunnus alalunga*), swordfish (*Xiphias gladius*), striped marlin (*Tetrapturus audax*), wahoo (*Acanthocybium solandri*), silky shark (*Carcharhinus falciformis*), whitetip shark (*Carcharhinus longimanus*), rockfish (*Sebastolobus macrochir)*; **B)** Pacific and Indian Ocean, Sea of Okhotsk, Tasman Sea; **C)** 3,548 skipjack; 5,480 yellowfin; 2,581 bigeye; 65,777 southern bluefin; 11 albacore; 5 swordfish; 2 striped marlin; 1 wahoo; 3 silky sharks; 2 whitetip sharks; 3,025 rockfish; **D)** 23 skipjack; 45 yellowfin; 28 bigeye; 4,865 southern bluefin; 305 rockfish; **E)** Plastic dart; **F)** Scientists belonging JAMARC; **G)** Yes; **H)** Dr. Masanori Takahashi

National Research Institute of Far Seas Fisheries, Fisheries Agency, The Government of Japan, 7-l, Orido 5 Chome, Shimizu-shi, 424
A) Bluefin tuna (*Thunnus thynnus*); **B)** Adjacent waters of Japan; **C)** 9,497; **D)** 937; **E)** Plastic dart, internal anchor; **F)** Prefectural fisheries experimental stations; **G)** Annual progress report of marine ranching prog; **H)** Tomoyuki Itoh

Japan Game Fish Association, Asahi Building 2F, 1-11-2 Ebisu, Shibuya-Ku, Tokyo, 150 E-mail: japan@jgfa.or.jp
A) Billfish, Japanese seabass, dolphin and other species; **B)** Coast of Japan; **C)** 66,801; **D)** 747; **E)** Plastic anchor, plastic dart; **F)** Sport fisherman; **G)** Yes, JGFA Yearbook, JGFA News, JGFA Tag & Release Handbook; **H)** Tsutomu Wakabayashi

Republic of Korea

National Fisheries Research and Development Agency, 65-3 Sirang-ri, Kijang-up, Yangsan-gun, Kyoungsangnam-do, 626-900
A) Yellowfin tuna (*Thunnus albacares*), albacore (*T. alalunga*), bigeye tuna (*T. obesus*), skipjack tuna (*Euthynnus pelamis*), sablefish

(*Anoplopoma fimbria*), filefish (*Novodon modestus*); **B)** Coastal area off Korea, Indian and Pacific Oceans; **C)** 6,355; **D)** 166; **E)** Plastic dart, internal anchor; **F)** Scientists and commercial fishermen; **G)** No; **H)** Gong Yeong

New Caledonia

Oceanic Fisheries Programme, South Pacific Commission, BP D5, Noumea
A) Skipjack tuna (*Euthynnus pelamis*), yellowfin tuna (*Thunnus albacares*), bigeye tuna (*Thunnus obesus*), longtail tuna (*Thunnus tonggol*), albacore (*Thunnus alalunga*), tanguigue (*Scomberomorus commerson*); **B)** Western tropical Pacific; **C)** 92,376 skipjack; 33,526 yellowfin; 6,796 bigeye; 82 longtail; 9,961 albacore; additional 14,000 fish tagged in the Philippines; **D)** 10,742 skipjack, 3,482 yellowfin, 599 bigeye, 3 longtail, 168 albacore, 7 tanguigue; **E)** Yellow plastic dart with caption SPC Noumea Reward; **F)** Scientists, commercial and artisanal fishermen, processors; **G)** Yes; **H)** Dr. Antony D. Lewis, Oceanic Fisheries Coordinator

New Zealand

Marine Gamefish Tagging Program, NIWA-Auckland, PO Box 1043, Whangarei
A) Striped marlin (*Tetrapterus audax*), yellowtail kingfish (*Seriola lalandi*), mako shark (*Isurus oxyrinchus*) and others; **B)** New Zealand; **C)** 23,444 for species mentioned in A: mostly yellowtail (*Seriola lalandi*), mako shark (*Isurus oxyrinchus*) and striped marlin (*Tetrapterus audax*): 4,608 for other species (ie: albacore, blue marlin, black marlin, blue shark and other sharks, broadbill swordfish and yellowfin): Total of 28,052 for all species; **D)** 1,064, for all species mentioned in A and 80 other species: Total of 1,144 for all species; **E)** Steel dart; **F)** Scientists, sport and commercial fishermen; **G)** Yes; **H)** B. Hartill, N. Davis, and R. Tasker

Tasman Bay and Golden Bay Snapper Tagging, MAF Fisheries, Ministry of Agriculture and Fisheries, Private Bag, Nelson
A) Snapper (*Pagrus auratus*); **B)** Nelson, New Zealand; **C)** 7,000; **D)** 1,800; **E)** **F)** **G)** **H)** Program has ceased

Pelorus Sounds Snapper Tagging, MAF Fisheries, Ministry of Agriculture and Fisheries, Private Bag, Nelson
A) Snapper (*Pagrus auratus*); **B)** Marlborough, New Zealand; **C)** 2,150; **D)** 400; **E)** **F)** **G)** **H)** Program has ceased

Senegal

Biologie Des Thonides Tropicau, Centre de Recherches Oceanographiques de Dakar, CRODT, B. P. 2241, Dakar
A) Yellowfin tuna (*Thunnus albacares*), bigeye tuna (*T. obesus*), skipjack tuna (*Euthynnus pelamis*), little tuna (*E. alletteratus*), Atlantic bonito (*Sarda sarda*), Atlantic sailfish (*Istiophorus albicans*); **B)** Northwest coast of Africa; **C)** 800 yellowfin, 650 bigeye, 4,400 skipjack, 900 little tuna, 400 Atlantic bonito, 210 Atlantic sailfish; **D)** 1,200 approximately; **E)** Steel dart, sonic; **F)** Scientists; **G)** Yes; **H)** H. T. Diouf

South Africa

Billfish Tagging Programme, Oceanographic Research Institute, P.O. Box 10712, Marine Parade, Durban, KwaZulu-Natal 4056
A) Black marlin (*Makaira indica*), blue Marlin (*M. nigricans*), striped marlin (*Tetrapturus audax*), sailfish (*Istiophorus playpterus*), shortbill spearfish (*Tetraptutus audax*), broadbill swordfish (*Xiphias gladius*); **B)** South Africa, Mozambique and Kenya; **C)** 1982-1998: 168 black marlin, 83 blue marlin, 152 striped marlin, 1909 sailfish, 4 shortbill speardish, 76 broadbill swordfish; **D)** 26; 1 black marlin, 24 sailfish, 1 broadbill swordfish; **E)** Hallprint steel dart tag; **F)** Scientists, sport fishermen; **G)** Yes; **H)** Rudy van der Elst, Elinor Bullen

National Tagging Programme, Oceanographic Research Institute, P.O. Box 10712, Marine Parade, Durban, Kwazulu-Natal, 4056
A) All marine angling fish including stingray: leerfish (*Lichia amia*), albacore (*Thunnus alalunga*), giant kingfish (*Caranx ignobilis*), king mackerel (*Scomberomorus commerson*), yellowfin tuna (*Thunnus albacares*) and others; **B)** Entire coastline of South Africa, Namibia and Mozambique; **C)** 1982-1998: total of 138,608: 4,270 leerfish, 1,000 albacore, 581 giant kingfish, 558 king mackerel, 499 yellowfin tuna and 131,700 others; **D)** 7,194 total: 314 leerfish, 30 albacore, 28 giant kingfish, 21 mackerel, 5 yellowfin tuna and 6,796 others; **E)** Hallprint steel dart, Hallprint plastic tip dart and locally made plastic sheep ear tags; **F)** Scientists, sport fishermen; **G)** Yes; **H)** Rudy van der Elst, Elinor Bullen

Spain

Marcado de Atunes en El Cantabrico, Instituto Espanol de Oceanografia, Laboratorio Oceanografico, Apdo. 240, Santander
A) Bluefin tuna (*Thunnus thynnus*), albacore tuna (*T. alalunga*), bigeye tuna (*T. obesus*), Skipjack tuna (*Katsuwonus pelamis*); **B)** Bay of Biscay; **C)** 5,774 bluefin tuna, 13,045 albacore tuna, 12 bigeye tuna, 2 skipjack tuna; **D)** 359 bluefin tuna, 324 albacore tuna; **E)** Steel dart; **F)** Scientists, commercial fishermen; **G)** Yes; **H)** Jose Luis Cort

Instituto Espanol de Oceanografia, Centro Oceanografico de Canarias, Apdo. 1373, 38080 Santa Cruz de Tenerife, Canary Islands, Spain **A)** Skipjack tuna (*Katsuwonus pelamis*), yellowfin tuna (*Thunnus albacares*); **B)** Canary Islands; **C)** Approximately 7,700 from 1982-94; **D)** 1,200; **E)** Plastic dart; **F)** Scientists, commercial fishermen; **G)** Yes; **H)** Alicia Delgado de Molina

United States
Alaska

Region II Commercial Resource Assessment, Alaska Department of Fish and Game, 3298 Douglas St., Homer 99603 E-mail: billb@fishgame.state.ak.us
A) Rockfish (*Sebastes spp.*), lingcod (*Ophiodon elongatus*), **B)** Inshore reef area of the outer Kenai Peninsula; **C)** 2,480 rockfish, 70 lingcod; **D)** 10 rockfish, 3 lingcod; **E)** internal anchor; **F)** Scientists, sport and commercial fishermen; **G)** No; **H)** William Bechtol

Marine Fish Program, Groundfish Stock Assessment, NOAA/NMFS, box 210155, Auke Bay 99821
A) Sablefish (*Anoplopoma fimbria*); **B)** Gulf of Alaska; **C)** 80,398; **D)** 3,706; **E)** Internal anchor; **F)** Scientists; **G)** No; **H)** Dr. G. Snyder

New Program;
Region II Commercial Resource Assessment, Alaska Department of Fish and Game, 3298 Douglas St., Homer 99603 E-mail: Billb@fishgame.state.ak.us
A) Pacific sleeper shark (*Somniosus pacificus*), spiny dogfish (*Squalus acanthias*); **B)** Prince William Sound; **C)** 350 sharks in September 1997 and 1998; **D)** 1 Pacific sleeper shark; **E)** Dart tags; **F)** Scientists, sport and commercial fishermen; **G)** No; **H)** William Bechtol

Tamgas Creek Hatchery, Metlakatla Indian Community, P. O. Box 410, Metlakatla 99926
A) Chum salmon (*Oncorhynchus keta*), coho salmonBay; fishermen; (*O. kisutch*) chinook (*O. tshawytscha*), steelhead (*Salmo gairdneri*); **B)** Southern southeast Alaska; **C)** 4,165,700; **D)** 13,300 (rack return to hatchery only, not in fisheries); **E)** Binary coded wire; **F)** Scientists; **G)** Yes; **H)** Steven Leask

Sablefish Tagging Studies, Alaska Department of Fish and Game, 304 Lake Street, Rm 103, Sitka, AK 99835
A) Sablefish (*Anoplopoma fimbria*); **B)** Southeastern Alaska; **C)** 27,100; **D)** 2,400; **E)** Internal anchor; **F)** Scientists, Commercial fishermen; **G)** Yes; **H)** Meg Cartwright

Lingcod Tagging Studies, Alaska Department of Fish and Game, 304 Lake Street, Rm 103, Sitka, AK 99835
A) Lingcod (*Ophiodon elongatus*); **B)** Southeastern Alaska; **C)** 2,297; **D)** 31; **E)** Internal anchor; **F)** Scientists, Commercial fishermen; **G)** Yes; **H)** Meg Cartwright

California

Brown Rockfish Biological Studies, NOAA/NMFS, Tiburon Laboratory, 3150 Paradise Drive, Tiburon 94920
Brown rockfish (*Sebastes auriculatus*); **B)** San Francisco Bay; **C)** 1,000; **D)** 400; **E)** Floy, T-bar; **F)** Scientists, sport; **G)** No; **H)** Dr. William H. Lenarz

California Pelagic Shark Tagging Program, California Department of Fish and Game, Marine Resources Division, Southern Operations, 330 Golden Shore, Suite 50, Long Beach 90802 E-mail: jugoretz@compuserve.com
A) Thresher shark (*Alopias vulpinus*), blue shark (*Prionace glauca*), shortfin mako shark (*Isurus oxyrinchus*), leopard shark (*Triakis semifasciata*); **B)** Pacific coastal waters - Monterey Bay to Cabo San Lucas, primarily Southern California Bight; **C)** 10,000 thru December 1998; **D)** 170 thru December 1998; **E)** Steel dart; **F)** Scientists, sport fishermen, commer-cial fishermen; **G)** Yes, annual newsletter "Shark Tagging News"; **H)** John Ugoretz

Central California Marine Sportfish Survey, California Department of Fish and Game, 20 Lower Ragsdale Drive, Monterey 93940

A) Rockfish (*Sebastes spp.*) 21 species, lingcod (*Ophiodon elongatus*), cabezon (*Scorpaenichthys marmoratus*), kelp greenling (*Hexagrammos decagrammus*) California halibut (*Paralichthys californicus*), starry flounder (*Platichthys stellatus*), spiny dogfish (*Squalus acanthias*); **B)** Central California; **C)** 7,500; **D)** 205; **E)** Floy spaghetti tag; **F)** Scientists, sport and commercial fishermen; **G)** Yes; **H)** Dr. Robert N. Lea

Cooperative Marine Gamefish Tagging Program, NMFS/NOAA, Southwest Fisheries Science Center, P. O. Box 271, La Jolla 92038 USA
A) Swordfish, striped marlin, blue marlin, black marlin, short-billed spearfish; **B)** Pacific and Indian Oceans; **C)** 19,050; **D)** 174 billfish recaptures since 1982; **E)** Nylon tip dart with yellow plastic tubing; **F)** Anglers, Billfish Clubs, Pacific Gamefish Research Foundation, Sec. de Pesca Mexico, Guam Dept. of Agriculture; **G)** Billfish Newsletter/Scientific Publications; **H)** David B. Holts

Cooperative National Marine Fisheries Service, American Fishermen's Research Foundation, Albacore Tuna Tagging Program, NOAA/NMFS, P. O. Box 271, La Jolla 92038
A) Albacore tuna (*Thunnus alalunga*); **B)** North and South Pacific Ocean; **C)** Since 1972: 29,000; **D)** Since 1972: 1,500; **E)** Plastic dart; **F)** Scientists, sport and commercial fishermen; **G)** No; **H)** Dr. Norm Bartoo

Florida

Earthwatch Lemon Shark Tagging Program, Bimini Biological Field Station, RSMAS, University of Miami, 4600 Rickenbacker Causeway, Miami 33149-1098
A) Lemon shark (*Negaprion brevirostris*); **B)** Bimini, Bahamas; **C)** 2,450; **D)** 720; **E)** PIT tag; intramuscular glass ampule encoding transponder; **F)** Scientists; **G)** 1994 Environ. Biology of Fishes **H)** Dr Samuel H Gruber

Cobia, Amberjack & Dolphin Tagging Program, Mote Marine Laboratory, 1600 Thompson Parkway, Sarasota 34236
A) Cobia (*Rachycentron canadum*), amberjack (*Seriola dumerili*), dolphin (*Coryphaena hippurus*); **B)** Off the southwest and southeast coast of Florida, Africa; **C)** 2,030; **D)** 224; **E)** Hallprint plastic dart tag; **F)** Scientists, recreational and commercial fishermen, and charter boat captains; **G)** No; **H)** Karen Burns, Carole Neidig

Cooperative Tagging Center, NMFS/NOAA, Southeast Fisheries Science Center, 75 Virginia Beach Drive, Miami 33149
A) Billfish (blue marlin, white marlin, sailfish, longbill spearfish, swordfish), tunas (bluefin, yellowfin, albacore, skipjack, bigeye, blackfin), sharks and other highly migratory species; **B)** Atlantic Ocean, Gulf of Mexico and the Caribbean Sea; **C)** Totals 1982-1998: total billfish: 82,582; total tunas: 23,580; Total sharks: 2781; total others: 45,705; **D)** Totals 1982-1998: Total billfish: 1,582; total tunas: 981; total sharks: 195; total others: 2,700; 1994-95 billfish: 271, 1994-95 tunas: 187, 1994-95 others: 1,488; **E)** Plastic double barb-dart; **F)** Recreational and commercial anglers, scientists and international fisheries organizations; **G)** Viannual Cooperative Tagging center Newsletter and Internet Web page: http://sefsc.noaa.gov/public/tag.html.; **H)** Dr. Eric Prince (Eric.Prince@noaa.gov), Dr. Mauricio Ortiz (Mauricio.Ortiz@noaa.gov)

Adult Fish Monitoring Program, Florida Department of Environmental Protection, Florida Marine Research Institute, 100 Eighth Avenue SE, St. Petersburg 33701-5905
A) Snook, red drum, sheephead, flounder, mullet, cobia, spotted seatrout, gag grouper, gray snapper; **B)** Pinellas, Martin, Brevard, St. Lucie, Satasota, Manatee, Lee, Charlotte, Dade, Collier, Palm Beach; **C)** 171,200 since 1982; **D)** 18,478; **H)** Ron Taylor, Jim Whittington, Brent Winner and Kim Amendola. **NOTE:** FMRI has ended all mark/recapture experiments, but continues to pay rewards for returns.

Reef Fish Tagging Program, Mote Marine Laboratory, 1600 Thompson Parkway, Sarasota 34236
A) American red snapper, red grouper, speckled hind, scamp, black grouper, gag, Nassau grouper, red hind, gray snapper, lane snapper, mangrove snapper, amberjack, vermillion snapper, mutton snapper; **B)** Naples to the Panhandle of Florida; **C)** 9,434; **D)** 975; **E)** Hallprint Plastic dart tags; **F)** Mote Marine Lab., commercial, charter and recreational fishermen, MML Scientists; **G)** No; **H)** Karen Burns

Snook Tagging Programs, Florida Department of Natural Resources, Bureau of Marine Research, 100 Eight Avenue, SE, St. Petersburg 33701 **A)** Snook (*Centropomus undecimalis*); **B)** Naples, Collier County; **C)** 10,000 since 1976; **D)** 1,550; **E)** Internal anchor; **F)** Scientists; **G)** No; **H)** Gerard E Bruger

Second Program:

B) Palm Beach, Brevard, and Martin Counties; **C)** 6,000 since 1984; **D)** 600; **E)** Internal anchor and dart; **F)** Scientists; **G)** No; **H)** Edwin W. Irby

Third Program:
B) Tampa Bay; **C)** 1,200 since 1985; **D)** not complete; **E)** Internal anchor; **F)** Scientists; **G)** No; **H)** Gerard E. Bruger

Georgia

Georgia Department of Natural Resources, Wildlife Resources Division, P.O. Box 2089, Waycross 31502
A) American shad (*Alosa sapidissima*); **B)** Georgia; **C)** 1982: 405, 1983: 368, 1984: 410, 1985: 619, 1986: 377, 1987: 565, 1988: 490, 1989: 302, 1990: 291, 1991: 272, 1992: 340, 1993: 259, 1994: 564, 1995: 549, 1996: 561, 1997: 500, 1998: 530; **D)** 1982: 211, 1983: 119, 1984: 145, 1985: 270, 1986: 195, 1987: 263, 1988: 209, 1989: 161, 1990: 132, 1991: 107, 1992: 129, 1993: 68, 1994: 146, 1995: 183, 1996: 148, 1997: 125, 1998: 155; **E)** Internal anchor; **F)** Sport and commercial fishermen; **G)** Yes; **H)** Bert Deener

Hawaii

Hawaii Institute of Marine Biology, Coconut Island, P.O. Box 1345, Kaneohe, HI 96744
A) Yellowfin tuna (*Thunnus albacares*) and bigeye tuna (*Thunnus obesus*); **B)** Cross Seamount & NOAA weather buoys 51002, 51003 and 51004;**C)** 1,347 yellowfins and 3, 097 bigeye tunas; **D)** 125 yellowfin and 193 bigeye tuna as of August 1997; **E) F) G) H)** K. Holland

Louisiana

Louisiana Dept. of Wildlife and Fisheries, P.O. Box 98000, Baton Rouge 70898-9000
A) Red drum (*Sciaenops ocellatus*); **B)** coastal Louisiana; **C)** 10,000; **D)** 700; **E)** Internal anchor; **F)** Scientists; **G)** No; **H)** Harry Blanchet

Marine Fish Cooperative Tagging Program, Coastal Conservation Assn. of Louisiana, 830 Union Street, 3rd Floor, New Orleans 70112
A) Red drum (*Sciaenops ocellatus*), spotted seatrout (*Cynoscion nebulosus*), black drum (*Pogonias cromis*), flounder (various), snapper (various), cobia (*Rachycentron canadum*), over 30 other marine species; **B)** Primarily coastal and estuary Louisiana; **C)** Sept. 1987- Sept. 1997: over 62,000; **D)** over 3,700; **E)** Plastic dart anchored yellow streamer; **F)** 1,340 participants: NMFS Cooperative Tagging System, Sea Grant, Aquarium of the Americas, New Orleans Personal Computer Club, numerous volunteers, recreational & commercial fishermen; **G)** Yes; **H)** Maumus F. Claverie, Jr.

Maine

Herring Tagging Studies, Maine Department of Marine Resources, McKown Pt., W. Boothbay Harbor 04575
A) Atlantic herring (*Clupea harengus*); **B)** Coast of Maine, New Brunswick, New Hampshire; **C)** 1980: 49,203, 1981: 47,360, 1982: 11,553, 1983: 14,209; **D)** 1980: 2,685; 1981: 1,641; 1982: 1,160, 1983: 1,213; **E)** Internal anchor, (T-bar spaghetti) **F)** Commerical stop seiners, purse seiners, weir fishermen; **G)** Yes; **H)** Edwin Creaser, David Libby

Maine Department of Marine Resources, McKown Point, West Boothbay Harbor 04575
A) Atlantic cod (*Gadus morhua*), haddock (*Melanogrammus aeglefinus*), American plaice (*Hippoglossoides platessoides*), yellowtail flounder (*Limanda ferruginea*); **B)** Sheepscot Bay; **C)** 6,200; **D)** 430; **E)** Internal anchor, spaghetti; **F)** Sports/ commercial fishermen; **G)** Perkins, H.C., S. B. Chenoweth and R. W. Langton. 1997. Gulf of Maine Atlantic cod complex, pattern of distribution and movement of the Sheepscot Bay substock. Bull. Natl. Res. Inst. Aquacultu., Suppl. 3: 101-107; **H)** Herbert Perkins (retired; present contact Linda Mercer)

Mississippi

Gulf Coast Research Laboratory, P.O. Box 7000, Ocean Springs 39566
A) Cobia, gulf killifish, red drum, spotted seatrout and striped bass; **B)** Northern Gulf of Mexico; **C)** 142,000; **D)** 3,000; **E)** Internal anchor, dart and elastomer; **F)** Scientists, sport fishermen; **G)** No; **H)** Robin M. Overstreet, James Warren, Jim Franks, Larry Nicholson and Read Hendon

Gulf Coast Research Laboratory, P.O. Box 7000, Ocean Springs 39566 E-mail: jfranks@seahorse.IMS.USM.edu
A) Cobia; **B)** Gulf of Mexico and south Atlantic; **C)** 11,000; **D)** 675; **E)** Dart tag; **F)** Sportfishers; **G)** Yes; **H)** Jim Franks

Gulf Coast Research Laboratory, P.O. Box 7000, Ocean Springs
39566; E-mail: jfranks@seahorse.IMS.USM.edu
A) Tripletail; **B)** Gulf of Mexico and south Atlantic; **C)** 250; **D)** 35;
E) Dart tag; **F)** Sportfishers; **G)** No; **H)** Jim Franks

New Jersey

American Littoral Society Fish Tagging Program, American
Littoral Society, Sandy Hook, Highlands 07732
A) All species, saltwater and anadromous; **B)** United States-Canada;
C) 212,236; **D)** 13,141; **E)** Plastic spaghetti tag; **F)** Sport fishermen;
G) Yes; **H)** Pam Carlsen

Delaware River Fisheries Research Project, F-48-R, New Jersey
Division of Fish, Game and Wildlife, New Jersey Freshwater
Fisheries Lab., P.O. Box 394, Lebanon 08833
A) American Shad (*Alosa sapidissima*); **B)** Delaware River; **C)**
3,450; **D)** 1,000; **E)** Plastic dart; **F)** Sport and commercial fishermen;
G) Yes; **H)**Mark Boriek

New York

Striped Bass Tagging Program, New York State Department of
Environmental Conservation, 205 Belle Meade Road, East Setauket
11733 and 21 S. Putt Corners Rd., New Paltz 12561
A) Striped bass (*Morone saxatilis*); **B)** Long Island Sound, New York
Harbor, Long Island South Shore Bays, Long Island East End
(Montauk to Southampton), Hudson River on spawning grounds and
nursery area; **C)** 26,000; **D)** 3,400; **E)** Internal anchor; **F)** Scientists,
sport, commercial fishermen; **G)** Yes; **H)** Byron H. Young, Victor J.
Vecchio, Kim A. McKown, Kathy Hattala, Andy Kahnle

Hudson River Foundation, Striped Bass Tag Recapture Program, 40
W 20th Street, Ninth Floor, New York, NY 10011
A) Striped bass; **B)** lower Hudson River; **C)** 200,000; **D)** 18,000; **E)**
Internal anchor tags; **F)** Scientists; **G)** No; **H)** John Waldman

North Carolina

University of North Carolina Institute of Marine Science, 3431
Arendell Street, Morehead City 28557
A) 201 species; **B)** North Carolina and the western Atlantic; **C)**
200,367; **D)** 6,078; **E)** Plastic dart, Australian dart tag, monel metal;
F) Scientists; **G)** No; **H)** Dr. Frank J. Schwartz

Inshore Paralichthid Flounder Tagging, North Carolina Division
of Marine Fisheries, P.O. Box 769, Morehead City 28557
A) Summer (*P. dentatus*), southern (*P. lethostigma*), gulf flounder
(*P.albigutta*); **B)** North Carolina coastal waters; **C)** 33,600; **D)** 1,900;
E) Laminated internal anchor; **F)** Fishermen, scientists; **G)** Yes; **H)**
Rick Monaghan

Striped Bass Stocking and Tagging, North Carolina Division of
Marine Fisheries, 1367 US Hwy. 17 South, Elizabeth City 27909
A) Striped bass (*Morone saxatilis*); **B)** North Carolina; **C)** 107,446;
D) 8,253; **E)** Carlin disc, cinch-up, internal anchor; **F)** Scientists; **G)**
Yes; **H)** Sara E. Winslow

Red Drum Tagging Program, North Carolina Division of Marine
Fisheries, Wanchese Field Office, PO Box 539, Wanchese NC 27891
A) Red drum (*Scienops ocellatus*); **B)** Inshore and coastal waters of
North Carolina; **C)** 26,650; **D)** 3,518; **E)** Internal anchor, steel dart
and plastic dart tags; **F)** Sport and commercial fishermen, scientists;
G) No; **H)** Lee M. Paramore

Oregon

Department of Fisheries and Wildlife, Oregon State University,
Corvallis 97331
A) Rockfish (*Sebastes spp.*), lingcod (*Ophiodon elongatus*), cabezon
(*Scorpaenichthys marmoratus*); **B)** Coastal, within 10 miles of Depoe
Bay, Oregon; **C)** 8,471; **D)** 550; **E)** Internal anchor; **F)** Sport and
commercial fishermen, state conservation agencies; **G)** No; **H)** Dr.
Howard F. Horton

Rhode Island

NMFS Cooperative Shark Tagging Program, NOAA/NMFS,
Narragansett Laboratory, 28 Tarzwell Dr., Narragansett 02882
A) All identifiable shark species except smooth dogfish (*Mustelus
canis*) and spiny dogfish (*Squalus acanthias*); **B)** Western and
Eastern Atlantic; **C)** 1980: 5,589, 1981: 5,432, 1982: 4,648, 1983:
6,215, 1984: 4,062, 1985: 7,203, 1986: 5,013, 1987: 5,760, 1988:
6,044, 1989: 5,263, 1990: 5,464, 1991: 6301, 1992: 8408; **D)** 1980:
160, 1981: 171, 1982: 144, 1983: 195, 1984: 175, 1985: 256, 1986:
242, 1987: 210, 1988: 304, 1989: 328, 1990: 385, 1991: 389, 1992:
507; **E)** Capsule dart; **F)** Scientists, sport and commercial fishermen,
U.S. observers on foreign vessels; **G)** Yes; **H)** John G. Casey, Nancy
E. Kohler

South Carolina

South Carolina Marine Game Fish Tagging Program, South
Carolina Department of Natural Resources, Marine Resources
Division, P.O. Box 12559, Charleston SC 29422 E-mail:
davyk@mrd.dnr.state.sc.us
A) Major game species; **B)** South Carolina; **C)** 95,000; **D)** 8,400; **E)**
Stainless steel harpoon and nylon dart; **F)** Scientists, sport and
commercial fishermen; **G)** Yes; **H)** Kay B. Davy

Texas Texas Parks and Wildlife Department, Coastal Fisheries
Division, 4200 Smith School Road, Austin 78744
A) Red drum (*Sciaenops ocellatus*), black drum (*Pogonias cromis*),
spotted seatrout (*Cynoscion nebulosus*), sheepshead (*Archosargus
probatocephalus*), Southern flounder (*Paralichthys lethostigma*), red
snapper(*Lutjanus campechanus*), misc. species; **B)** Texas coastal
waters; **C)** 111,600; **D)** 5,000; **E)** Internal abdominal anchor; **F)**
Scientists; **G)** Yes; **H)** Lawrence W. McEachron

Fish Trackers, Inc., P.O. Box 4746, Corpus Christi 78469
A) All marine species; **B)** Gulf of Mexico, Atlantic, Caribbean; **C)**
72,590 (started April 1985); **D)** 10,426; **E)** Steel dart, large and small
plastic dart; **F)** Scientists, sports and commercial fishermen, fishing
clubs, conservation organizations tournaments; **G)** Yes; **H)** Steve
Qualia

Washington

Black Rockfish Tagging, Marinefish Program, Washington
Department of Fish and Wildlife, 48 Devonshire Road, Montesano,
WA 98563
A) Black rockfish (*Sebastes melanops*); **B)** Washington and Oregon;
C) 1981: 4,739, 1982: 2,544, 1983: 2,033, 1984: 675, 1985: 4,687,
1986: 5,892, 1987: 5,360, 1988: 7,888, 1989: 92,089, 1990: 8,948; **D)**
1,819; **E)** Internal anchor; **F)** Scientists, sport fishermen; **G)** Yes; **H)**
Brian Culver, Farron Wallace

Lingcod Tagging, Marinefish Resources Program, Washington
Department of Fish and Wildlife, 48 Devonshire Road, Montesano,
WA 98563
A) Lingcod (*Ophiodon elongatus*); **B)** North Washington Coast; **C)**
1985: 1,000, 1986: 1,000, 1987: 1,000, 1988: 1,000, 1989: 1,000,
1990: 1,000, 1991: 4,000, 1992: 4,000, 1993: 3,500; **D)** 4,200; **E)**
Spaghetti tags; **F)** Scientists, sport fishermen; **G)** Yes; **H)** Brian
Culver, Farron Wallace

SALMON PROGRAMS

Canada

Canadian Department of Fisheries and Oceans, Suite 420 - 555
West Hastings St., Vancouver, B.C., V6B 5G3
A) Pacific Salmonids; **B)** British Columbia hatcheries, coastal
streams and Yukon Territory; **C)** 1980: 3.8 million, 1981: 4 million,
1982: 4.6 million, 1983: 6.5 million, 1984: 6.2 million, 1985: 10.7
million, 1986: 15 million, 1987: 13.8 million, 1988: 10 million, 1989:
9 million, 1990: 10.1 million, 1991: 10.2 million, 1992: 8.44 million,
8.17 million, 1993: 8,017,350, 1994: 6,172,240, 1995: 5.6 million,
1996: 7.0 million, 1997: 7.0 million, 1998: 6.5 million; **D)** 1986:
13,100, 1987: 13,860, 1988: 11,869, 1989: 8,552, 1990: 7,978, 1991:
5,397, 1992: 9,311, 1993: 7,998, 1994: 5,417, 1995: 46,000,
1996:35,000, 1997: 34,000, 1998: 25,000; **E)** Binary coded wire,
multiple fin clips, Peterson disc, Floy tag, spaghetti tag, sonic tag; **F)**
Fisheries management, enhancement and research biologists, fish
processors, sport fishermen and First Nations; **G)** No; **H)** Doug
Herriott

Salmonid Enhancement Program, British Columbia Environment
Lands & Parks, Fisheries Branch, Parliament Buildings, Victoria,
B.C., V8V 1X4
A) Steelhead trout (*Oncorhynchus mykiss*); **B)** British Columbia
Coast, Pacific and Yukon regions; **C)** 1980: 418,027, 1981: 449,115,
1982: 544,772, 1983: 678,170, 1984: 565,398, 1985: 897,122, 1986:
612,082, 1987: 706,828, 1988: 608,818, 1989: 149,245, 1990: 6,790,
1991: 10,493, 1992: 10,341, 1993: 0; **D)** Angling seasons: 1984/85:
7,621, 1985/86: 7,460, 1986/87: 6,219, 1987/88: 9,868, 1988/89:
6,733, 1989/90: 7,775, 1990/91: 6,697, 1991/92: 1,642, 1992/93:
751993/94: 115; **E)** Binary coded wire; **F)** Scientists, Government of
Canada and British Columbia; **G)** No; **H)** H.A. Andrusak

England

**The Centre for Environment, Fisheries and Aquaculture Science
(CEFAS),** Lowestoft Laboratory, Pakefield Road, Lowestoft, Suffolk
NR33 0HT UK

A) Atlantic salmon (*Salmo salar*), sea trout (*Salmo trutta*); **B)** North Atlantic; **C)** 830,000; **D)** 7,000; **E)** Binary coded wire, anchor, acoustic, and radio tags; **F)** Scientists, sport and commercial fishermen; **G)** No; **H)** E. C. E. Potter

Ireland

National Coded Wire Program, Fisheries Research Centre, Marine Institute, Abbotstown, Castleknock, Dublin 15
A) Atlantic salmon (*Salmon salar*); **B)** Irish coast; **C)** 2,112,417; **D)** 31,250; **E)** Binary coded nose tag; **F)** Scientists, sport and commercial fishermen; **G)** Yes; **H)** Niall O'Maoileidigh

Corrib Smolt Count, Fisheries Research Centre, Marine Institute, Abbotstown, Castleknock, Dublin 15
A) Atlantic salmon (*Salmon salar*); **B)** Western Irish coast, Corrib River; **C)** 12,799; **D)** 54; **E)** Floy; **F)** Scientists, sport and commercial fishermen; **G)** No; **H)** Niall O'Maoileidigh

Salmon Research Agency of Ireland, Newport, Co. Mayo
A) Atlantic Salmon (*Salmo salar*) and sea trout (*Salmo trutta*); **B)** N.E. Atlantic; **C)** 499,867 salmon smolts, 5,320 sea trout smolts, 2,536 salmon kelts; **D)** 10,965 salmon from smolts, 208 sea trout from smolts, 171 salmon from kelts; **E)** modified Carlin disc, binary coded wire, Lea hydrostatic and elastomer; **F)** Scientists, sport and commercial fishermen; **G)** Annual report; **H)** The Director, Ken Whelan

United States

Alaska

Alaska National Marine Fisheries Service, Auke Bay Laboratory, 11305 Glacier Highway 99801   E-mail: Adrian.Celewycz@NOAA.GOV
A) Chinook *Onchorhynchus tshawytscha*), coho (*O. kisutch*), chum (*O. keta*), sockeye (*O. nerka)* and pink salmon (*O. gorbuscha*); **B)** Southeastern Alaska; **C)** Chinook salmon: 3,189,976; pink salmon 469,417; sockeye salmon 291, 157; chum salmon: 110,775; **D)** Chinook salmon: 38,676; pink salmon 4,087; sockeye salmon 2,110; chum salmon: 2,696; **E)** Binary coded wire; **F)** Scientists; **G)** No; **H)** Adrian Celewycz

Metlakatla Indian Community, P. O. Box 416, Metlakatla 99926
A) Chum (*Oncorhynchus keta*), coho (*O. kisutch*), chinook salmon (*O. tshawytscha*) and steelhead (*Salmo gairdneri*); **B)** Southern SE Alaska; **C)** 4,165,700; **D)** 13,300 (rack return to hatchery only, not in fisheries); **E)** Binary coded wire; **F)** Scientists; **G)** Yes; **H)** Steven Leask

Idaho

Idaho Department of Fish and Game, Coded Wire Tag, Release and Recovery Program, 1540 Warner Avenue, Lewiston 83501
A) Chinook salmon (*Onchorhynchus tshawytscha*), steelhead trout (*Salmo gairdneri*); **B)** State of Idaho; **C)** 1982: 785,900, 1983: 556,750, 1984: 1,045,250, 1985: 689,125, 1986: 1,305,675, 1987: 1,934,093, 1988: 2,204,902, 1989: 1,807,273, 1990: 2,363,123, 1991: 1,449,606, 1992: 1,492,326, 1993: 4,099,822, 1994: 1,786,687, 1995: 2,937,686, 1996: 9,682,178, 1997: 8,157,326, 1998: 10,416,231; **D)** 1982: 2,198, 1983: 4,564, 1984: 3,712, 1985: 5,026, 1986: 3,362, 1987: 2,305, 1988: 1,675, 1989: 1,515, 1990: 1,939, 1991: 580, 1992: 1,124, 1993: 1,146, 1994: 1,300, 1995: 1,365, 1996: 1,415, 1997: 2,848, 1998: 1,542; **E)** Binary coded wire, sometimes with freeze brand, fluorescent grit, fin clips and always a left ventral on steelhead. All hatchery reared steelhead receive adipose clips to aid in preservation of wild stocks. Some wiretagged fish with PIT tags; **F)** Regional fishery biologists & managers, hatchery personnel & sport fishermen; **G)** Yes; **H)** Rodney C. Duke

Maryland

Striped Bass Tagging Program, U.S. Fish and Wildlife Service, MD Fisheries Resources Office, 177 Admiral Cochrane Drive, Annapolis, 21401
A) Striped bass; **B)** Atl. Coast - Cape Hatteras to Canadian border; **C)** ~300,000 released 1985 - 1997; **D)** 51,224 recaptures 1985 - 1997; **E)** Internal anchor tags; **F)** State and Federal Agencies; **G)** No; **H)** Jorge Skjeveland

Sturgeon Tagging Program, U.S. Fish and Wildlife Service, MD Fisheries Resources Office, 177 Admiral Cochrane Drive, Annapolis, 21401
A)   Atl.& short nose sturgeon; **B)** Atlantic Coast; **C)** Over 7,500 thru 1997; **D)** 110 returns thru 1997; **E)** T-bar anchor tags; **F)** Federal, State Agencies, Universities; **G)** No; **H)** Jorge Skjeveland

New Hampshire

New Hampshire Fish and Game Department, 2 Haven Drive, Concord 03301
A) Atlantic salmon (*Salmo salar*); **B)** Merrimack River Basin, and Nashua National Fish Hatchery; **C)** 1,982 (Broodfish); **D)** unknown until 1994; **E)** Petersen disk; **F)** U.S. Fish and Wildlife Service; **G)** Wildlife Journal, New Hampshire Fish & Game Dept.; **H)** Jonathan Greenwood

Oregon

Oregon Department of Fish and Wildlife, 17330 S.E. Evelyn Street, Clackamas 97015
A) Pacific salmon and steelhead; **B)** Oregon; **C)** 1982: 4.3 million, 1983: 4.1 million, 1984: 4.6 million, 1985: 5.0 million, 1986: 5.0 million, 1987: 5.9 million, 1988: 5.1 million, 1989: 5.2 million, 1990: 5.4 million, 1991: 8.6 million, 1992: 7.4 million, 1993: 9.0 million, 1994: 11.3 million, 1995: 9.7 million, 1996: 9.4 million; **D)** 1982: 24,000, 1983: 22,000, 1984: 31,000, 1985: 39,000, 1986: 69,000, 1987: 52,000, 1988: 61,000, 1989: 53,000, 1990: 32,000, 1991: 40,000, 1992: 25,000, 1993: 18,000, 1994: 25,000, 1995: 31,000, 1996: 34,000; **E)** Binary coded wire; **F)** Sport and commercial fishermen, NW Tribes, US Fish and Wildlife Service, NMFS, Bonneville Power Admin., Clatsop Economic Dev. Council, US Corps of Army Engineers and Pacific Salmon Commission; **G)** Yes; **H)** Christine Mallette and Bill Murray

Stock Assessment of Anadromous Salmonids, Oregon Department of Fish and Wildlife, 28655 Highway 34, Corvallis, OR 97333. E-mail: lewism@fsl.orst.edu
A) Coho salmon (*Oncorhynchus kisutch*), chinook salmon (*O. tshawytscha*); **B)** Oregon coastal hatcheries; **C)** 14.9 million chinook (1982-98), 65,000 in 1998; 16 million coho, (1982-98) 400,000 in 1998; **D)** 61,984 chinook (1983-94), 5,814 in 1997; 148,662 coho (1982-97), 9229 in 1997; **E)** Binary coded wire; **F)** National Marine Fisheries Service (NMFS), ODFW scientists, sport and commercial fishermen; **G)** Yes, Annual Report ODFW; **H)** Mark Lewis

Annual Stock Assessment of Salmonids, Oregon Department of Fish and Wildlife, 28655 Highway 34, Corvallis, OR 97333. E-mail: lewism@fsl.orst.edu
A) Coho salmon (*Oncorhynchus kisutch*), chinook salmon (*O. tshawytscha*); **B)** Oregon Columbia River Basin Hatcheries; **C)** Releases began in 1990. 5.1 million chinook (1990-98); 2.8 million coho, (1990-98); **D)** 3,638 chinook (1990-97), 978 1997: 11,552 coho (1990-97), 220 in 1997; **E)** Binary coded wire; **F)** Bonneville Power administration (BPA), ODFW, Yakima Indian Nation, Confederated Tribes of the Umchalla Indian Reservation, scientists, sport and commercial fishermen; **G)** Yes, Annual Report BPA; **H)** Mark Lewis

Virginia

BOAT/U.S. Clean Water Trust Fish Tag & Release Program, 880 South Picket Street, Alexandria, VA 22304
A) Saltwater and anadromous species including striped bass, bluefish, amberjack, cobia, king mackerel, Spanish mackerel, red drum, tautog, tarpon; **B)** East and Gulf coasts of the United States; **C)** Since July 1996: 3,046; **D)** 302; **E)** Plastic dart and steel dart; **F)** Sport fishermen; **G)** Biannual update; **H)** Jenny Pereira

Virginia Game Fish Tagging Program, Virginia Saltwater Fishing Tournament (VMRC) and Virginia Institute of Marine Science, College of William & Mary, P.O. Box 1346, Gloucester Point 23062;
E-mail: lucy@vims.edu or mrcswt@visi.net
A) Tautog (*Tautoga onitis*), spadefish(*Chaetodipterus faber*), cobia (*Rachycentron canadum*), black drum (*Pogonias cromis*), red drum (*Sciaenops ocellatus*), spotted seatrout (*Cynoscion nebulosus*), weakfish (*Cynoscion regalis*), black sea bass (*Centropristis striata*); **B)** Virginia Chesapeake Bay and offshore waters; **C)** Total (1995-98): 18,764; tautog: 2867, spadefish: 1346, cobia: 300, black drum: 539, red drum: 1147, spotted seatrout: 1911, weakfish: 7444, black sea bass: 3210; **D)** 1360; **E)** Hallprint T-bar and dart tags; **F)** Trained recreational fishermen, charter captains; **G)** Annual report; **H)** Jon A. Lucy (VIMS), Claude Bain (VSFT/VMRC)

Juvenile Summer Flounder Tagging Program, The College of William & Mary, Virginia Institute of Marine Science, P.O. Box 1346, Gloucester Point 23062
A) Summer flounder (*Paralichthys dentatus*); **B)** Eastern Shore of Virginia and the Virginia portion of the Chesapeake Bay; **C)** 1995-1998: 10,600; **D)** 12 recaptures to date; **E)** Floy FF-94 fine fabric T-bar anchor tags and Floy FD-94 T-bar anchor tags; **F)** VIMS biologists supported by the Virginia Marine Resource Commission saltwater license fund; **G)** No; **H)** Chief Scientists: John A. Musick and Richard T. Kraus

Chesapeake Bay Nursery Ground Delineation Study, The College of William & Mary, Virginia Institute of Marine Science, P.O. Box 1346, Gloucester Point 23062
A) Sandbar sharks (*Carcharhinus plumbeus*); **B)** Lower Chesapeake Bay, lagoons of the eastern shore of Virginia, inshore along southern Virginia coast; **C)** 1995-1998: 1,166 sharks tagged; **D)** 29 recaptures; **E)** Hallprint shrink-wrapped nylon double-return dart tags; **F)** VIMS biologists supported by the Virginia Marine Resource Commission saltwater license fund; **G)** No; **H)** Chief Scientists: John A. Musick and R. Dean Grubbs

Large Coastal Shark Tagging Program, The College of William & Mary, Virginia Institute of Marine Science, P.O. Box 1346, Gloucester Point 23062
A) All large coastal shark species: Primarily sandbar (*Carcharhinus plumbeus*), dusky (*Carcharhinus obscurus*), tiger (*Galeocerdo cuvieri*), sandtiger (*Carcharias taurus*), scalloped hammerhead (*Sphyrna lewini*), smooth Hammerhead (*Sphyrna zygaena*), blacktip (*Carcharhinus limbatus*), spinner (*Carcharhinus brevipinna*); **B)** Mid-Atl. Bight - Cape Hatteras, NC to Parramore Island, VA from 0 to 70 nautical miles from shore; **C)** See F; **D)** See F; **E)** NMFS M-style stainless dart tags; **F)** VIMS biologists with National Marine Fisheries Service (NMFS) Cooperative Shark Tagging Program; **G)** NMFS newsletter; **H)** John A. Musick

Washington

Muckleshoot Indian Tribe, 34900 212th Avenue, S.E., Auburn 98002
A) Chinook salmon (*Oncorhynchus tshawytscha*) coho salmon (*O. kitsutch*); **B)** Central Puget Sound, Washington; **C)Fall chinook salmon -** 400,000 each year, 1993-95 (project over); coho - 750,000; spring chinook - 750,000; **D)** N/A; **E)** CWT tagged (binary coded wire); **F)** Tribal fishermen and tribal fish enhancement staff; **G)** No; **H)** Dennis Moore and Richard Johnson

State of Washington Department of Fish and Wildlife, 600 Capitol Way N, Olympia 98501-1091
A) Chinook (*Oncorhynchus tshawytscha*), coho (*O. kitsutch*), chum (*O. keta*), & sockeye salmon (*O. nerka*); **B)** Northern Pacific; **C)** 1982: 5,400,000; 1983: 6,087,000; 1984: 6,640,000;1985: 9,250,000; 1986: 8,500,000; 1987: 8,200,000; 1988: 9,186,000; 1989: 7,415,000; 1990: 12,685,000; 1991: 10,673,000; 1992: 12,674,000; 1993: 10,281,608; 1994: 12,077,230; 1995: 13,584,000; 1996: 13,039,000; 1997: 14,602,000; 1998: 19,913,000; **D)** 1982: 55,000; 1983: 30,000; 1984: 37,000; 1985: 40,000; 1986: 47,000; 1987: 60,000; 1988: 72,000; 1989: 59,000; 1990: 53,000; 1991: 50,000; 1992: 60,000; 1993: 35,787; 1994: 29,190; 1995: 37,350; 1996: 41,170; 1997: 34,570; 1998: incomplete; **E)** Binary coded wire, visual implant; **F)** Scientists; **)** Yes; **H)**Lee Blankenship, Geraldine Vander Haegen

Coastal Zone and Estuarine Studies Division, Northwest and Alaska Fisheries Center, NOAA/NMFS, 2725 Montlake Blvd. E., Seattle 98112
A) Chinook salmon (*Oncorhynchus tshawytscha*) sockeye salmon (*O. nerka*) steelhead trout (*Salmo mykiss*); **B)** Columbia and Snake Rivers; **C)** 1,876,000 steelhead (McNary and Lower Granite Dams, Washington), 3,000,000 spring chinook (McNary and Lower Granite Dams, Washington), 10,280,000 fall chinook (McNary and Bonneville Dams, Washington), 607,000 sockeye salmon (Priest Rapids Dam, Washington); **D)** 37,475; **E)** binary coded wire and passive integrated transponder (PIT); **F)** Oregon, Washington, and Idaho State Fishery agencies, U. S. Fish & Wildlife Service, National Marine Fisheries Service, and U.S. Army Corps of Engineers; **G)** Yes; **H)** Gene Matthews

USFWS, Western Washington Office, Aquatic Resources Division, 510 Desmond Drive SE, Suite 102, Lacy WA 98503
A) Chinook salmon (*Oncorhynchus tshawytscha*), coho salmon (*O. kisutch*), chum salmon (*O. keta*), steelhead trout (*O. gairdneri*); **B)** Washington, Oregon, Idaho, California; **C)** 6 million per year; **D)** N/A; **E)** Binary coded wire; **F)** Scientists, sport fishermen, G. Yes; **H)** David P. Zajac

SPECIAL THANKS

This section on tag-and-release programs would not be possible without the cooperation of the various scientists and marine biologists worldwide who supply us with the information. IGFA thanks them, sincerely.

Index to Advertisers

Abel Reels 57
Aftco Mfg. Inc. 10
Alaska Trophy Fishing Safaris 111
Amazon Tours, Inc. 57
Ande Monofilament 76,77
Area Rule Engineering 19
Awning Depot 98
Beau Rivage 94
Berkley, Inc. 3
Bessemer Trust Company 83
Big Rock 71
Bimini Big Game Club & Hotel 33
Black Magic Tackle Ltd. 46,47
Blue Fin IV, Inc. 111
Boone Tackle Co., Inc. 38
Cabo Yachts, Inc. 11
Cairns Reef Charter Services 28
Calcutta Offshore Baits 117
Cal's 2-Speed Reel Conversions 40
Capt. Harry's Fishing Supply 8
Capt. Jeff Burns 113
Capt. Ray Rosher 113
Carpentaria Seafaris 111
Cheeca Lodge 113
Club Nautico de Cozumel 12,13
Cortez Yacht Charters 118
Costello Studios 86,87
Custom Rods by Dru 68,69
Don Ray, Artist 118
Eastaboga Tackle Mfg. 118
Econo Lodge Resort 113
European Fed. of Sea Anglers 88
Executive Expeditons 67
Federal Self Storage 115
Finest Kind Offshore Tackle 1
Fishooker 111
Florida Keys 85
Florida Sportsman Magazine 45
Fly Fishing in Salt Water Magazine 60

Free Spool Inc. 113
Frontiers International 110
Goldon Fishing Expeditions, Inc. 37
Harper, Capt. Lindsay 113
Hook Sportfishing Charters 75
Hook & Tackle Outfitters 103
Hotel Cabo San Lucas ....3rd cover
Hotel la Flor de Itabo 72
ITOC 59
Internet Waterway Inc. 79
JD's Big Game Fishing Tackle 118
J & M Tackle 104
Japan Game Fish Association 88
Jig Stop Tours 112
King Sailfish Mounts, Inc 90
Krieger Watch Corporation 73
Lee Palm Sportfishing 109
Lee's Tackle Inc 34
Maggie Proctor Marine Refinishing 93
Malin Company 14
MarkSport Studios Inc. 36
Marlin Club 14
Maxima America 114
Melton International 70
Mold Craft Products, Inc. 99
Murray Brothers 7
Normark Corporation 88
Northern Labrador Outdoors Ltd. 111
O. Mustad & Son 41
Offshore Angler 105
Oswego County Tourism 111
Outdoor World ....Back cover
Out Rover Inc. 57
Owner American Corp. 42
PODC Belau Tour 112
Pacific Trolling Gear 62
PanAngling Travel Services 113
Penn Fishing Tackle Mfg. Co. 23
Permit Sportfishing 99
Pesca Tours Fishing Charters 82,109

Prowler Sportfishing 112
Reid's Palace Hotel 64
Rio Parismina Lodge 112
Rio Products International, Inc. 97
River Palm Cottages & Fish Camp 97
Rolex Watch U.S.A., Inc. ....2nd cover
SCA Promotions 108
Salt Water Sportsman 27
Sampo 109
Scopinich Fighting Chairs Inc. 58
Seaguar 29
Sea of Cortez Sport Fishing 111
Shanghai & Double Header Charters 114
Smart Marine Products 94
Smith Galleries, Inc., Geoffrey C. 78
South Fishing Inc. 80
Sportfishing Adventures Inc. 112
Star Rods Inc. 6
Steve's Marine Design, Inc. 100
Stren Fishing Lines 50
Striker Big Game Fishing 113
T & A Tackle & Bait 91
The Fisherman's Center 20
Tibor Reel Corporation 95
Topline Manufacturing 91
Tournament Tackle Inc. 107
Treasure Cay Services 2
Treasure of Lost Galleons 48,49
Tropic Star Lodge 4
Ullberg Studios, Inc. 96
Ultra Com International 66
U.S. Seven Oceans, Inc. (Jinkai) 21
Vanmark, Inc. 115
VIP Charters Ltd. 112
Wayne Roman Yacht Sales 65
Weigh-In (Equalizer Sales) 106
West Weigh Scale Co. 84
William Lures 85
World Cup Blue Marlin Championship 63
Zuker's Inc. 102